District Su[
of the
Baltimore-Washington Conference

Rebecca Iannicelli
Annapolis
District

Wanda Duckett
Baltimore Metropolitan
District

Ann LaPrade
Baltimore Suburban
District

John Wunderlich, III
Cumberland-Hagerstown
District

JW Park
Central Maryland
District

Edgardo Rivera
Frederick
District

Gerard A. Green
Greater Washington
District

Johnsie Cogman
Washington East
District

Retiree Class of 2019

Ordination Class of 2019

Commissioned Class of 2019

TABLE OF CONTENTS

This edition of the Conference Journal conforms as far as possible with the report of the Committee on Examination of the Annual Conference Journals of the Northeastern Jurisdictional Conference.

I. Officers of the Annual Conference   8

II. Lists and Rolls
Alphabetical List of Churches   9
Alphabetical Roll and Directory - Clergy   57
Affiliate Members   186
Diaconal Ministers   186
Missionaries and Special Workers   187
Deaconesses   188
Chronological Roll of Clergy   189
  Bishops Emeriti living within the bounds of the BWC   189
  Elders in Full Connection   189
  Associate Members   209
  Deacons in Full Connection   210
Lay Members and Reserves   211
Conference Surviving Spouses' Directory   253

III. Daily Proceedings   266

IV. Business of Annual Conference   332

V. Appointments   380

VI. Reports   472
DISCIPLESHIP
Discipleship Council   472
  Leadership Development Board   474
  New Faith Expressions Board   475
  Young People's Ministry Board   476
  Advocacy & Action Board   477
  Wellness & Missions Board   478
  Connectional Table   479
Office of Leadership Development   481
Conference Board of Laity   482
New Faith Expressions   482
Young People's Ministry   483
Retreat & Camping Ministries   490
Wellness and Missions   491
Conference Secretary of Global Ministries   493
Advocacy and Action   493
Commission on Religion and Race   496
Deaf Ministries   497
Commission on Archives & History/UM Historical Society/Strawbridge
  Shrine Association   497
United Methodist Women   498
Committee on Hispanic-Latino Ministries   499
In Mission Together: Eurasia Committee   500

STEWARDSHIP
Council on Finance and Administration   502

Moving Committee   505
Conference Board of Pensions and Health Benefits   505
Board of Trustees   507

APPROVED STEWARDSHIP RECOMMENDATIONS
Recommendations from Council on Finance & Administration   508
2020 Budget   508
Recommendation from Commission on Equitable Compensation   522
Recommendation from the Conference Board of Pensions & Health Benefits   522

LEADERSHIP
Board of Ordained Ministry   524
Personnel Committee   524
Rules Committee   525
Commission on Communications   525

INSTITUTIONAL
Africa University   526
Board of Child Care   527
Boston University School of Theology   528
Candler School of Theology   529
United Theological Seminary   530
Wesley Theological Seminary   532

APPROVED RESOLUTIONS
Common Table   534
Purchase a New Episcopal Residence   534
Rotating Venue and Accommodation Stipends for Annual Conference   535
Unrestricted Bequest Received by Centre Street UMC   536
Amending the Rules: Duties of the Rules Committee   536
Provide Nursing and Pumping Accommodations within Bar   537
Requiring Consultations for Restructing Proposals   538

Keeping Our Sacred Trust: Sexual Ethics Policy for Minstry Leaders   540

CONFERENCE LEADERSHIP   543
Laity Serving on Conference Agencies   556

VII.   **Memoirs of Clergy and Clergy Spouses**   568

VIII.   **Roll of the Honored Dead**   601

IX.   **Historical**   602

X.   **Miscellaneous**
Extension Ministries   604
Joint Scholarship Coordinating Task Force   606

XI.   **Pastoral Record** (included in Alphabetical Clergy Directory on page 57)

XII.   **Audit**   608

XIII.   **Statistical Table**   638

XIV.   **Index**   736
Form for Journal Corrections   737
Conference Officials and Staff Telephone Directory   739

OFFICERS OF THE ANNUAL CONFERENCE

President
Bishop LaTrelle Easterling
11711 East Market Place
Fulton, MD 20759
410-309-3400
800-492-2525

Secretary
Kevin Silberzahn
923 Slash Pine Ct
Sykesville, MD 21784
410-309-3460

Treasurer
Paul Eichelberger
11711 East Market Place
Fulton, MD 20759
410-309-3400
800-492-2525

Conference Lay Leader
Delores Martin
16505 Magnolia Court
Silver Spring, MD 20905
301-421-9441

Chancellor
Thomas Starnes
1500 K Street, NW, Suite 1100
Washington, DC 20005
202-230-5192

ALPHABETICAL CHURCH LISTING

Adams #1375
937 Bayard Rd, Lothian, MD 20711-9609

AN | Adams || Lothian
C. (410) 741-1932
adamsumchurch@yahoo.com

Ager Road #7380
6301 Ager Rd, Hyattsville, MD 20782-1626

GW | Grace/Ager Road || Takoma Park
C. (301) 422-2132
thenehemiahcharge@gmail.com

Alberta Gary Memorial #7345
9405 Guilford Rd, Columbia, MD 21046-1911

CM | Alberta Gary || Columbia
C. (301) 498-7879
shawnvollmerhausen@gmail.com

Albright Memorial #7110
409 Rittenhouse St NW, Washington, DC 20011-1323

GW | Albright Memorial || DC
C. (202) 723-3525
albrightumc@verizon.net

Alexandria Chapel #8390
5605 Chicamuxen Rd, Indian Head, MD 20640-3691

WE | Alexandria Chapel || Indian Head
C. (301) 743-3939
Alexandria.chapel@gmail.com

Allegany #5290
PO Box 444, Frostburg, MD 21532-0444
(17305 Mount Savage Rd NW)

CH | Eckhart || Eckhart Mines
C. (301) 689-9585
harpold8736@comcast.net

Alpine #5510
1302 Valley Rd, Berkeley Springs, WV 25411-4801

CH | Alpine || Berkeley Springs
C. (304) 258-2847
alpine.charge@gmail.com

Ames #2335
112 Baltimore Pike, Bel Air, MD 21014-4118

BS | Ames || Bel Air
mintilghman@yahoo.com

Ames #4110
615 Baker St, Baltimore, MD 21217-2814

BM | Ames || Baltimore
C. (443) 438-6555
Ames.Memorial@hotmail.com

Araby #6110
4548 Araby Church Rd, Frederick, MD 21704-7706

CM | Araby || Frederick
C. (301) 694-8772
mount79@gmail.com

Arbutus #3110
1201 Maple Ave, Baltimore, MD 21227-2639

BM | Arbutus || Arbutus
C. (410) 204-8906
aumcmain@comcast.net

Arden #6510
4464 Arden Nollville Rd, Martinsburg, WV 25403-6109

FR | Arden || Arden
C. (304) 267-6165
mayblessyou@gmail.com

Arlington-Lewin #4115
5260 Reisterstown Rd, Baltimore, MD 21215-5019

BM | G.O.A.L. || Baltimore
C. (410) 542-3070
a-lumc@hotmail.com

Arnolia #3530
1776 E Joppa Rd, Baltimore, MD 21234-3621

BM | Arnolia || Baltimore
C. (410) 665-7005
arnoliaumc@arnolia.org

Asbury #1160
78 Church Rd, Arnold, MD 21012-2345

AN | Asbury || Arnold
C. (410) 349-2862
office@asburyumcarnold.org

Asbury #1110
87 West St, Annapolis, MD 21401-2426

AN | Asbury || Annapolis
C. (410) 268-9500
1asbury@verizon.net

Asbury #7115
926 11th St NW, Washington, DC 20001-4408

GW | Asbury || DC
C. (202) 628-0009
asburymail@asburyumcdc.org

Asbury #2565
11501 Philadelphia Rd, White Marsh, MD 21162-1308

BS | Asbury || White Marsh
C. (410) 256-2562
asburywm@aol.com

Asbury #1360
10420 Guilford Rd, Jessup, MD 20794-9118

AN | Asbury || Jessup
C. (301) 490-9295
asburyjessupchurch@verizon.net

Asbury #6530
110 W North St, Charles Town, WV 25414-1524

FR | Asbury || Charles Town
C. (304) 725-5513
churchoffice@myasburychurch.org

Asbury #6180
101 W All Saints St, Frederick, MD 21701-5519

FR | Asbury || Frederick
C. (301) 663-9380
asburyumcfmd1@verizon.net

Asbury #5315
PO Box 1009, Hagerstown, MD 21740-4811
(155 Jonathan St)

CH | Asbury || Hagerstown
C. (301) 791-0498
sharongibson_1@msn.com

Asbury #8130
4004 Accokeek Rd, Brandywine, MD 20613-6100

WE | Asbury/Zion Wesley || Waldorf
C. (301) 372-8891
asburyumcbrandywine@gmail.com

Asbury #9265
17540 Black Rock Rd, Germantown, MD 20874-2227

CM | Asbury || Germantown
C. (301) 540-2347
AsburyGermantown@gmail.com

Asbury #6700
4257 Kearneysville Pike, Shepherdstown, WV 25443

FR | Asbury || Shepherdstown
C. (304) 876-3112
info@4pillarchurch.org

Asbury Town Neck #1490
429 Asbury Dr, Severna Park, MD 21146-1373

AN | Asbury Town Neck || Severna Park
C. (410) 647-3461
asburytownneck@gmail.com

Asbury-Broadneck #1115
657 Broadneck Rd, Annapolis, MD 21409-5505

AN | Asbury-Broadneck || Annapolis
C. (410) 757-2995
asburybroadneck1@aol.com

Ashton #9110
17314 New Hampshire Ave, Ashton, MD 20861-9706

CM | Ashton || Ashton
C. (301) 774-7100
ashtonumchurch@gmail.com

Ayres Chapel #2520
3046 Ayres Chapel Rd, White Hall, MD 21161-9677

BS | Jarrettsville-Ayres || Jarrettsville
C. (410) 692-9222
pastornickbufano@gmail.com

Back River #2420
544 Back River Neck Rd, Essex, MD 21221-4604

BM | Back River || Essex
C. (410) 686-4195
office@backriverumc.com

Baldwin Memorial #1420
921A Generals Hwy, Millersville, MD 21108-2124

AN | Baldwin Memorial || Millersville
C. (410) 923-1166
bmumcoffice@yahoo.com

Barton #5110
18917 Legislative Road, Barton, MD 21521

CH | Barton/Westernport || Barton
C. (301) 463-2315
bartonUMC@gmail.com

Bedington #6520
580 Bedington Rd, Martinsburg, WV 25404-6509

FR | Bedington || Bedington
C. (304) 274-2011
Bedingtonumc@frontier.com

Beechfield #3150
541 S Beechfield Ave, Baltimore, MD 21229-4325

BM | Beechfield || Baltimore
C. (410) 644-7640
pastorholmes@comcast.net

Bel Air #2340
21 Linwood Ave, Bel Air, MD 21014-3914

BS | Bel Air || Bel Air
C. (410) 838-5181
ciampagliot@baumc.com

Bells #8145
6016 Allentown Rd, Camp Springs, MD 20746-4550

GW | Bells || Camp Springs
C. (301) 899-7521
deeministrator6016@gmail.com

Benevola #6115
19925 Benevola Church Rd, Boonsboro, MD 21713-1701

CH | Benevola || Boonsboro
C. (301) 791-3576
benevolachurch@myactv.net

Bentley Springs #3410
419 Bentley Rd, Parkton, MD 21120-9092

BS | Cedar Grove-Stablers-Bentley Sp || Parkton
C. (410) 357-5153
andfred@msn.com

Berkeley Place #6645
133 Spruce St, Martinsburg, WV 25401-4234

FR | Berkeley Pl.-Friendship || Martinsburg
C. (304) 754-7891
readsps27@gmail.com

12

Bethany #4235
2875 Bethany Ln, Ellicott City, MD 21042-2213

CM | Bethany || Ellicott City
C. (410) 465-2919
bettina@bethanyum.org

Bethany Korean #4236
8971 Chapel Ave, Ellicott City, MD 21043-1905

CM | Bethany Korean || Ellicott City
C. (410) 979-0691
dduru77@hotmail.com

Bethel #5135
21006 Twin Springs Dr, Smithsburg, MD 21783-1636

CH | Bethel || Chewsville
C. (301) 733-8387
bethel.church@myactv.net

Bethel #6345
PO Box B, Rohrersville, MD 21779-0080
(4300 Main Street)

CH | Bethel || Rohrersville
C. (301) 432-8885
dorisbonner@yahoo.com

Bethel #6515
PO Box 236, Bakerton, WV 25410-0236

FR | Bethel || Bakerton
C. (304) 876-3467
gvancamp@frontiernet.net

Bethel #8480
16101 Swanson Rd, Upper Marlboro, MD 20774-9066

WE | Bethel || Upper Marlboro
C. (301) 627-4515
bethelum@verizon.net

Bethesda #9185
11901 Bethesda Church Rd, Damascus, MD 20872-1540

CM | Bethesda || Damascus
C. (301) 253-3222
BethesdaBlessings@verizon.net

Bethesda #8515
PO Box 204, Valley Lee, MD 20692-0204

WE | Bethesda || Valley Lee
C. (301) 994-9416
(19309 Saint Georges Church Rd)

Bethesda #6720
3415 Kearneysville Pike, Shepherdstown, WV 25443

FR | Shenandoah || Shenandoah Junction
C. (304) 876-6272
sj-umc.org

Bethesda #4445
328 Klee Mill Rd, Sykesville, MD 21784-9242

FR | Bethesda || Sykesville
C. (410) 795-7677
drlpastor1@verizon.net

Bethesda #3145
6300 Harford Rd, Baltimore, MD 21214-1315

BM | Bethesda || Baltimore
C. (410) 426-3211
bethesdaumc@cavtel.net

Bethesda #9122
8300 Old Georgetown Rd, Bethesda, MD 20814-1416

GW | Bethesda || Bethesda
C. (301) 652-2990
bethesdaumc@washmorefeet.org

Bixlers #4530
3282 Charmil Dr, Manchester, MD 21102-1918

BS | Bixlers-Millers || Manchester
C. (410) 857-1121
pastorblakesmarr@gmail.com

Blairton #6650
71 Upper Road, Martinsburg, WV 25402

FR | Blairton || Martinsburg
C. (304) 264-3607
garyandbarbieg@frontier.com

Bolivar #6560
PO Box 205, Harpers Ferry, WV 25425-6322
(1215 W Washington St)

FR | Bolivar/Engle || Harpers Ferry
C. (304) 535-1375
srtryon@yahoo.com

Boring #4625
14819 Old Hanover Road, Upperco, MD 21155

BS | Boring-Piney Grove-Mt. Gilead || Boring
C. (410) 688-9992
ministryaccount23@yahoo.com

Bosley #3490
14800 Thornton Mill Rd, Sparks, MD 21152-9625

BS | Bosley-West Liberty || Sparks
C. (410) 771-4944
kathleencheyney@aol.com

Bowie #8120
13009 6th St, Bowie, MD 20720-3614

WE | Bowie || Bowie
C. (301) 464-8383
emmanuelinfo@gmail.com

Bradbury Heights #7120
4323 Bowen Rd SE, Washington, DC 20019-5613

GW | McKendree-Simms-Brookland || DC
C. (202) 583-1244
gaylehebron@hotmail.com

Brandenburg #4580
PO Box 1233, Sykesville, MD 21784-8626
(6050 Old Washington Rd)

FR | Brandenburg || Sykesville
C. (410) 549-7822
pastormark1umc@gmail.com

Brighter Day #7625
421 Alabama Ave SE, Washington, DC 20032-1517

GW | Brighter Day || DC
C. (202) 889-3660
churchoffice@bdmdc.org

Brightwood Park #7125
744 Jefferson St NW, Washington, DC 20011-7720

GW | Brightwood Park || DC
C. (202) 291-2763
Lawdad513@aol.com

Brook Hill #6185
8946 Indian Springs Rd, Frederick, MD 21702

FR | Brook Hill || Frederick
C. (301) 662-1727
brookhill@bhumc.org

Brookfield #8370
17400 Aquasco Rd, Brandywine, MD 20613-4212

WE | Brookfield Immanuel || Brandywine
C. (240) 681-3532
johncwarren@att.net

Brooklyn Community #2142
110 Townsend Ave, Baltimore, MD 21225-3052

BM | Brooklyn Area || Baltimore
C. (410) 789-3688
Brooklyncommumcbpmd@gmail.com

Brooks #8460
5550 Mackall Rd, Saint Leonard, MD 20685-2388

WE | Brooks || St Leonard
C. (410) 586-3972
brookschurch@comcast.net

Buckeystown Rt 85 #6150
PO Box 399, Buckeystown, MD 21717-0399
(3440 Buckeystown Pike)

FR | Buckeystown (Rt 85) || Buckeystown
C. (301) 874-2313
rice.charles@live.com

Buckeystown Rt.80 #6145
6923 Michael's Mills RD, Buckeystown, MD 21717

FR | Buckeystown (Rt 80) || Buckeystown
C. (301) 874-3930
shackque1911@yahoo.com

Bunker Hill #6525
PO Box 327, Bunker Hill, WV 25413-2589
(9863 Winchester Ave)

FR | Bunkerhill || Bunker Hill
C. (304) 229-8508
bhumchurch@gmail.com

Butlers Chapel #6590
29 Butlers Chapel Rd, Martinsburg, WV 25403-0983

FR | Butlers Chapel || Martinsburg
fcummings@frontier.com

Cabin John #9160
7703 MacArthur Blvd, Cabin John, MD 20818

GW | Cabin John || Cabin John
C. (301) 229-8233
ekhii2000@yahoo.com

Calvary #1120
301 Rowe Blvd, Annapolis, MD 21401-1602

AN | Calvary || Annapolis
C. (410) 268-1776
office@calumc.org

Calvary #4260
3939 Gamber Rd, Finksburg, MD 21048-2516

FR | Calvary || Gamber
C. (410) 795-9343
office@calvaryumcgamber.org

Calvary #6190
131 W 2nd St, Frederick, MD 21701-5328

FR | Calvary || Frederick
C. (301) 662-1464
office@calvaryumc.org

Calvary #6285
403 S Main St, Mount Airy, MD 21771-5346

CM | Calvary || Mt Airy
C. (301) 829-0358
church@calvary-mtairy.org

Calvary #6655
220 W Burke St, Martinsburg, WV 25401-3322

FR | Calvary || Martinsburg
C. (304) 267-4542
pastorlynnumc@comcast.net

Calvary #5580
PO Box 217, Great Cacapon, WV 25422-0217
(5137 Central Avenue)

CH | Calvary || Great Cacapon
C. (304) 258-3455
calvary5580@frontier.com

Calvary #5620
PO Box 354, Ridgeley, WV 26753-0354
(28 Knobley Street)

CH | Calvary || Ridgeley
C. (304) 738-8940
cumcridgeley@atlanticbbn.net

Calvary #8520
3235 Leonardtown Rd, Waldorf, MD 20601-3614

WE | Calvary || Waldorf
C. (301) 645-5247
office@calvumc.org

Camp Chapel #2530
5000 E Joppa Rd, Perry Hall, MD 21128-9314

BS | Camp Chapel || Perry Hall
C. (410) 256-5561
newsletter@campchapel.org

Camp Hill-Wesley #6565
PO Box 1, Harpers Ferry, WV 25425-0001
(645 W Washington Street)

FR | Camp Hill-Wesley || Harpers Ferry
C. (304) 535-6882
olvaughn@frontiernet.net

Cape St Claire #1125
855 Chestnut Tree Dr, Annapolis, MD 21409-5114

AN | Cape St Claire || Annapolis
C. (410) 757-4896
office@capeumc.org

Capitol Hill #7135
421 Seward Sq SE, Washington, DC 20003-1113

GW | Capitol Hill || DC
C. (202) 546-1000
office@chumc.net

Carlos #5130
PO Box 444, Frostburg, MD 21532-0444
(12401 Carlos Rd SW)

CH | Eckhart || Eckhart Mines
C. (301) 689-9585
harpold8736@comcast.net

Carroll-Western #8425
2325 Adelina Rd, Prince Frederick, MD 20678-3723

WE | Carroll-Western || Prince Frederick
C. (410) 535-2210
cwumc1@gmail.com

Carters #1270
6715 Old Solomons Island Road, Tracys Landing, MD 20779
'

AN | Chews Memorial/Carters || Owensville
C. (301) 855-2500
cartersumc@aol.com

Catalpa #5380
PO Box 165, Hancock, MD 21750-0165
(12314 Willow Rd)

CH | Sideling Hill || Little Orleans
C. (304) 443-5920
catalpapineyplainsumc@gmail.com

Catoctin #6355
7009 Kellys Store Rd, Thurmont, MD 21788-3025

FR | Catoctin || Thurmont
C. (301) 271-3885
kelkelbelle@hotmail.com

Catonsville #4180
6 Melvin Ave, Catonsville, MD 21228-4424

BM | Catonsville || Catonsville
C. (410) 747-1886
Cumc21228@verizon.net

Cecil Memorial #1130
15 Parole St, Annapolis, MD 21401-3916

AN | Cecil Memorial-Mt. Calvary || Annapolis
C. (410) 266-5651
cecilmemorialumc@yahoo.com

Cedar Grove #3415
2015 Mount Carmel Rd, Parkton, MD 21120-9792

BS | Cedar Grove-Stablers-Bentley Sp || Parkton
C. (410) 357-0252
andfred@msn.com

Cedar Grove-Oakland #1215
5965 Deale Churchton Rd, Deale, MD 20751-9730

AN | Cedar Grove-Oakland || Deale
C. (410) 867-7417
office@cgumc.org

Centenary #1515
6248 Shady Side Rd, Shady Side, MD 20764-9685

AN | Centenary || Shady Side
C. (410) 867-2048
marsha.purcell@comcast.net

Centenary #7615
PO Box FL 39, Flatts FL Bx, Bermuda

GW | Centenary || Bermuda
C. (441) 292-0742
dickstetler@dickstetler.com

Centenary #5185
14501 Bedford Rd NE, Cumberland, MD 21502-5201

CH | Wesley || Cumberland
C. (601) 310-9922
marjoriehurder@gmail.com

Centennial Memorial #6210
8 W 2nd St, Frederick, MD 21701-5327

FR | Centennial Memorial || Frederick
C. (301) 663-5273
lintondebra@gmail.com

Central #5150
15 S George St, Cumberland, MD 21502-3049

CH | Central || Cumberland
C. (301) 724-4080
centralumc@atlanticbbn.net

Centre #2445
313 Duffy Ct, Forest Hill, MD 21050-2554

BS | West Harford || Forest Hill
C. (443) 458-2092
centreumc@gmail.com

Chase #2362
6601 Ebenezer Rd, Baltimore, MD 21220-1217

BM | Chase || Middle River
C. (410) 335-2172
chaseumc6601@gmail.com

Cheltenham #8155
11111 Crain Hwy, Cheltenham, MD 20623-1100

WE | Cheltenham || Cheltenham
C. (301) 782-4260
cheltenhamumc@comcast.net

Cherry Hill #2155
PO Box 19811, Baltimore, MD 21225-0311
(3225 Round Road)

BM | Cherry Hill || Baltimore
C. (410) 355-0022
cherryhillumc@gmail.com

Cherry Run #5630
3165 Householder Rd, Hedgesville, WV 25427

CH | Sleepy Creek || Berkeley Springs
C. (304) 258-2108
sleepycrkchrgumc@gmail.com

Chesaco #2545
901 Chesaco Ave, Baltimore, MD 21237-2736

BS | Chesaco Charge || Rosedale
C. (410) 687-0250
georgeweitzel@gmail.com

Chestnut Hill #6570
1523 Hostler Rd, Harpers Ferry, WV 25425

FR | Chestnut Hill || Harpers Ferry
C. (703) 626-4978
bxrowley@gmail.com

Cheverly #7325
2801 Cheverly Ave, Cheverly, MD 20785-3125

GW | Cheverly || Cheverly
C. (301) 773-1314
cheverly@cheverlyumc.org

Chevy Chase #9165
7001 Connecticut Ave, Chevy Chase, MD 20815-4935

GW | Chevy Chase || Chevy Chase
C. (301) 652-8700
office@chevychaseumc.org

Chews Memorial #1438
492 Owensville Rd, Harwood, MD 20776-9487

AN | Chews Memorial/Carters || Owensville
C. (410) 798-1638
chewsumc@yahoo.com

Chicamuxen #8260
PO Box 2338, La Plata, MD 20646-2338
(6255 Chicamuxen Road)

WE | Chicamuxen || Chicamuxen
C. (301) 743-3926
jackie.bowie@comcast.net

Christ #8115
22919 Christ Church Rd, Aquasco, MD 20608-9784

WE | New Hope Fellowship || Upper Marlboro
C. (301) 888-1316
christumcaquasco@gmail.com

Christ #5160
336 Race St, Cumberland, MD 21502-4138

CH | Christ || Cumberland
C. (301) 777-1561
cumc@atlanticbbn.net

Christ #7140
900 4th St SW, Washington, DC 20024-4434

GW | Christ || DC
C. (202) 554-9117
christumcdc@gmail.com

Christ #2160
2005 E Chase St, Baltimore, MD 21213-3325

BM | Christ || Baltimore
C. (410) 732-5600
cumchurch@verizon.net

Christ #7350
7246 Cradlerock Way, Columbia, MD 21045-5054

CM | Christ || Columbia
C. (410) 381-6329
admin@cumcobic.org

Christ Church of Baltimore County #3285
2833 Florida Ave, Baltimore, MD 21227-3637

BM | Christ Church of Balt. Co. || Baltimore
C. (410) 789-9058
recycle815@aol.com

Christ Church of the Deaf #3115
1040 S Beechfield Ave, Baltimore, MD 21229-4938

BM | Christ Deaf / Magothy Deaf || Baltimore
C. (410) 242-6303
christdeafchurch@gmail.com

Church of The Redeemer #7475
1901 Iverson St, Temple Hills, MD 20748-5609

GW | Church of Redeemer || Temple Hills
C. (301) 894-8622
umcredeemer@verizon.net

Clarks Chapel #2365
2001 Kalmia Rd, Bel Air, MD 21015-1017

BS | Harford || Bel Air
C. (410) 838-5543
thea.becton@gmail.com

Clarksburg #9175
23425 Spire St, Clarksburg, MD 20871-9036

CM | Hyattstown-Clarksburg || Hyattstown
C. (301) 972-2203
revdwhodsdon@verizon.net

Clinton #8170
10700 Brandywine rd, Clinton, MD 20735

WE | Clinton || Clinton
C. (301) 868-1281
cumcmd@verizon.net

Clynmalira #3450
2920 Stockton Rd, Phoenix, MD 21131-1125

BS | Clynmalira || Phoenix
C. (410) 472-4107
Pastor@Clynmalira.org

Cokesbury #2125
PO Box 85, Abingdon, MD 21009-0085

BS | Cokesbury || Abington
C. (410) 676-6295
CokesburyAbingdon@gmail.com

Colesville #9450
52 Randolph Rd, Silver Spring, MD 20904-1200

GW | Colesville || Silver Spring
C. (301) 384-1941
churchoffice@cumc.org

College Park #7335
9601 Rhode Island Ave, College Park, MD 20740-1650

GW | College Park-Mowatt. || College Park
C. (301) 345-1010
cpumchurchlady@yahoo.com

College Park Hispanic Initiative #7396
9601 Rhode Island Ave, College Park, MD 20740-1650

GW | College Park-Mowatt. || College Park
C. (301) 345-1010

Community #7410
300 Brock Bridge Rd, Laurel, MD 20724-2414

AN | First/Community || Laurel
C. (301) 725-4918
communityumcpastor@gmail.com

Community #7145
1525 Levis St NE, Washington, DC 20002-2912

GW | Community || DC
C. (202) 399-7343
RVRobinson@co.pg.md.us

Community #1440
8680 Fort Smallwood Rd, Pasadena, MD 21122-2403

AN | Faith Community || Pasadena
C. (410) 255-1506
communityumc2@verizon.net

Community #1180
1690 Riedel Rd, Crofton, MD 21114-1631

AN | Community || Crofton
C. (410) 721-9129
scardwell@cumc.net

Community of Faith #9270
22420 Frederick Rd, Clarksburg, MD 20871-9452

CM | Community of Faith || Clarksburg
C. (301) 972-5520
church@cofumc.com

Community With A Cause #8295
PO Box 310, Lexington Park, MD 20653-0310

WE | Community with a Cause || Lexington Park
C. (240) 434-5358
pastor@community-umchurch.com

Concord-St. Andrews #9130
5910 Goldsboro Rd, Bethesda, MD 20817-6034

GW | Concord-Saint Andrews || Bethesda
C. (301) 229-3383
csaumc@gmail.com

Coopers #8175
PO Box 148, Dunkirk, MD 20754-0148
(9370 Southern Maryland Blvd)

WE | Cooper's || Dunkirk
C. (410) 257-2511
cooperschurch@yahoo.com

Corkran Memorial #7480
5200 Temple Hill Rd, Temple Hills, MD 20748-3524

WE | Corkran Memorial || Temple Hills
C. (301) 894-5577
corkranmemorialchurch@gmail.com

Covenant #9235
20301 Pleasant Ridge Dr, Montgomery Village, MD 20886-4015

CM | Covenant || Gaithersburg
C. (301) 926-8920
office@covenant-umc.org

Cowenton #2570
10838 Red Lion Rd, White Marsh, MD 21162-1702

BM | Cowenton-Piney Grove || Baltimore
C. (410) 335-3343
cpkumar222@gmail.com

Cranberry #2540
PO Box 78, Perryman, MD 21130-0078
(1632 Perryman Road)

BS | Presbury-Cranberry || Edgewood
C. (410) 273-6979
pastortiffanyp@gmail.com

Cresaptown #5140
PO Box 5206, Cresaptown, MD 21502-5611
(14805 McMullen Hwy SW)

CH | Cresaptown || Cresaptown
C. (301) 729-0052
youngsl@atlanticbb.net

Daisy #9490
PO Box 146, Lisbon, MD 21765-0146

CM | Daisy || Woodbine
C. (410) 489-2400
vchristian5242@gmail.com

Damascus #9190
9700 New Church St, Damascus, MD 20872-2014

CM | Damascus || Damascus
C. (301) 253-0022
office@damascusumc.org

Darkesville #6545
PO Box 746, Inwood, WV 25428-0746
(6705 Winchester Ave)

FR | Darkesville || Inwood
C. (304) 229-2406
darkesville@gmail.com

Darlington #2375
1524 Whiteford Rd, Street, MD 21154-1930

BS | Dublin-Darlington || Street
C. (240) 429-1376
lindayarrow.church@gmail.com

Davidsonville #1190
819 W Central Ave, Davidsonville, MD 21035-2318

AN | Davidsonville || Davidsonville
C. (410) 798-5511
dumcoffice@dumc.net

Davis Memorial #5165
14300 Uhl Hwy SE, Cumberland, MD 21502-8442

CH | Davis Memorial || Cumberland
C. (301) 724-3896
davismemorialumc@atlanticbb.net

Dawson #5440
22515 McMullen Hwy SW, Rawlings, MD 21557-2432

CH | Dawson || Rawlings
C. (301) 786-4652
dawsonchurch7@gmail.com

Deer Creek #2450
2729 Chestnut Hill Rd, Forest Hill, MD 21050-1712

BS | Deer Creek || Forest Hill
C. (410) 638-7856
deercreekcharge@gmail.com

Deer Park #4535
2205 Sykesville Rd, Westminster, MD 21157-7613

FR | Deer Park || Westminster
C. (410) 848-2313
csaylor@dpumc.net

Deer Park #4415
6107 Deer Park Rd, Reisterstown, MD 21136-5900

BS | Deer Park || Upperco
C. (410) 833-5123
umcdeerpark@comcast.net

Deerfield #6260
16405 Foxville Deerfield Rd, Sabillasville, MD 21780-9020

FR | Deerfield || Frederick
C. (301) 241-3036
rwfgd@comcast.net

Delmont #1475
1219 Delmont Rd, Severn, MD 21144-1904

AN | Delmont/Severn || Severn
C. (443) 278-6341
delmontspastor@gmail.com

Dickerson #9225
20341 Dickerson Church Road, Dickerson, MD 20842

CM | Dickerson-Forest Grove || Dickerson
C. (301) 349-5416
dickersonmdumc@gmail.com

Dorsey Emmanuel #1220
6951 Dorsey Rd, Elkridge, MD 21075-6210

AN | Northeast || Elkridge
C. (410) 796-8598
pastor@wesleychapelumcjessup.org

Doubs-Epworth #6160
5131 Doubs Rd, Adamstown, MD 21710-8920

FR | Greater Brunswick || Brunswick
C. (301) 810-5430
wcarpen14a@gmail.com

Douglas Memorial #7155
800 11th St NE, Washington, DC 20002-3740

GW | Douglas Memorial || DC
C. (202) 397-1562
douglasmemorial@gmail.com

Dublin #2550
1528 Whiteford Rd, Street, MD 21154-1930

BS | Dublin-Darlington || Street
C. (410) 457-8003
lindayarrow.church@gmail.com

Dumbarton #7160
3133 Dumbarton St NW, Washington, DC 20007-3309

GW | Dumbarton || DC
C. (202) 333-7212
dumbartonpastor@yahoo.com

Eastern #8330
PO Box 535, Lusby, MD 20657-0535
(975 Eastern Church Rd)

WE | Lusby || Lusby
C. (410) 326-2699
Lusbycharge@gmail.com

Eastern #2175
5315 Harford Rd, Baltimore, MD 21214-2255

BM | Eastern || Baltimore
C. (410) 752-8524
easternumchurch@verizon.net

Eastport #1135
926 Bay Ridge Ave, Annapolis, MD 21403-3033

AN | Eastport || Annapolis
C. (410) 263-5490
eastportumc@verizon.net

Ebenezer #4575
4901 Woodbine Rd, Sykesville, MD 21784-9348

CM | Ebenezer || Sykesville
C. (410) 795-6136
eumcwinfield@gmail.com

Ebenezer #2430
3345 Charles St, Fallston, MD 21047-1031

BS | West Harford || Forest Hill
C. (410) 692-2211
kfizer@minister.com

Ebenezer #7165
400 D St SE, Washington, DC 20003-2053

GW | Ebenezer || DC
C. (202) 544-1415
Ebenezerumc1@verizon.net

Ebenezer #6230
4010 Ijamsville Rd, Ijamsville, MD 21754-9516

CM | Ebenezer || Ijamsville
C. (301) 874-3007
churchebenezer38@gmail.com

Ebenezer #8285
4912 Whitfield Chapel Rd, Lanham, MD 20706-4220

WE | Ebenezer || Lanham
C. (301) 577-0770
church896@verizon.net

Eckhart #5255
PO Box 44, Frostburg, MD 21532-0044
(17031 Porter Road Southwest)

CH | Eckhart || Eckhart Mines
C. (301) 689-9585
harpold8736@comcast.net

Eden Korean #2180
56 Stevenson Ln, Baltimore, MD 21212-1206

BM | Eden Korean || Baltimore
C. (667) 206-4187
yshinpastor@gmail.com

Edgewater #1235
2764 Solomons Island Rd, Edgewater, MD 21037-1211

AN | Edgewater || Edgewater
C. (410) 974-4410
gerald@kurtsnyder.net

Edgewood #3365
1434 Bellona Ave, Lutherville, MD 21093-5451

BS | Lutherville || Lutherville
C. (410) 821-0850
deborah.givens@morgan.edu

Elderslie-St Andrews #4120
5601 Pimlico Rd, Baltimore, MD 21209-4313

BM | Pikesville Pimlico || Pikesville
C. (410) 664-3392
eldersliestandrews@verizon.net

Ellerslie #5265
PO Box 358, Ellerslie, MD 21529-0358
(14305 Temple Street)

CH | Creek Run || Ellerslie / Mt. Savage
C. (301) 724-4929
pboch10439@aol.com

Emanuel #4630
6517 Frederick Rd, Catonsville, MD 21228-3528

BM | Emanuel || Catonsville
C. (410) 747-0702
emanuelumc@verizon.net

22

Emmanuel #7440
10755 Scaggsville Rd, Laurel, MD 20723-1223

GW | Emmanuel || Scaggsville
C. (301) 725-5200
office@eumclaurel.org

Emmanuel #7310
11416 Cedar Ln, Beltsville, MD 20705-2609

WE | Emmanuel || Beltsville
C. (301) 937-7114
office@eumcbeltsville.com

Emmanuel #5320
802 Summit Ave, Hagerstown, MD 21740-6332

CH | Emmanuel || Hagerstown
C. (301) 733-4720
eumc.office@verizon.net

Emmanuel #8240
1250 Emmanuel Church Rd, Huntingtown, MD 20639-9214

WE | Emmanuel || Huntingtown
C. (410) 535-3177
emmanuelumc@comcast.net

Emmanuel #5177
24 Humbird St, Cumberland, MD 21502-4716

CH | Emmanuel || Cumberland
C. (301) 722-8101
Emmanuelumcumberland@gmail.com

Emmarts #4610
7100 Dogwood Rd, Baltimore, MD 21244-1801

BM | Mt. Zion-Emmarts || Baltimore
C. (410) 944-1131
emmartsumc@verizon.net

Emory #4420
1600 Emory Rd, Upperco, MD 21155-9774

BS | Emory || Upperco
C. (410) 429-6008
churchoffice@emoryunitedmethodist.org

Emory #4245
3799 Church Rd, Ellicott City, MD 21043-4501

CM | Emory || Ellicott City
C. (410) 465-6162
smoore4433@aol.com

Emory #2555
PO Box 94, Street, MD 21154-0094
(911 Cherry Hill Rd)

BS | Emory || Street
C. (410) 452-5220
pastor@emorychurch.org

Emory #7175
6100 Georgia Ave NW, Washington, DC 20011-5110

GW | Emory || DC
C. (202) 723-3130
admin@emoryfellowship.org

Emory Grove #9240
8200 Emory Grove Rd, Gaithersburg, MD 20877-3739

CM | Emory Grove || Gaithersburg
C. (301) 963-3434
Admin@emorygroveumc.com

Engle #6575
1563 Engle Switch Road, Harpers Ferry, WV 25425

FR | Bolivar/Engle || Harpers Ferry
C. (304) 535-6882
srtryon@yahoo.com

Epworth #9245
9008 Rosemont Dr, Gaithersburg, MD 20877-1519

CM | Epworth || Gaithersburg
C. (301) 926-0424
jennifer.fenner@eumc-md.org

Epworth #3290
600 Warren Rd, Cockeysville, MD 21030-1754

BS | Epworth || Cockeysville
C. (410) 667-6054
office@epworthalive.com

Epworth Chapel #4170
3317 Saint Lukes Ln, Baltimore, MD 21207-5703

BM | Epworth Chapel || Baltimore
C. (410) 944-1070
epworthchapel@aol.com

Essex #2425
524 Maryland Ave, Essex, MD 21221-6734

BM | Essex || Essex
C. (410) 686-2867
essexUMC@gmail.com

Fairhaven #9250
12801 Darnestown Rd, Gaithersburg, MD 20878

CM | Fairhaven || Gaithersburg
C. (301) 330-5433
fairhavenumc@gmail.com

Fairview #4345
3325 Old Liberty Road, New Windsor, MD 21776

CM | Fairview || New Windsor
C. (443) 671-6152
fieldcourt@yahoo.com

Fairview #3455
13916 Jarrettsville Pike, Phoenix, MD 21131-2040

BS | Timonium-Fairview || Timonium
C. (410) 666-8288
VRitenour@hotmail.com

Fairview Avenue #5180
640 Fairview Ave, Cumberland, MD 21502-1518

CH | Melvin-Fairview Ave || Cumberland
C. (301) 722-3300
momstaxi@atlanticbb.net

Faith #8110
15769 Livingston Rd, Accokeek, MD 20607-3315

WE | Faith || Accokeek
C. (301) 292-6104
treasurer@faithumc-accokeek.org

Faith #1445
905 Duvall Hwy, Pasadena, MD 21122-1808

AN | Faith Community || Pasadena
C. (410) 437-8515
FaithChurchUMC905@gmail.com

Faith #9410
6810 Montrose Rd, Rockville, MD 20852-4210

GW | Faith || Rockville
C. (301) 881-1881
jspencer@faithworkshere.com

Faith Community #2192
5315 Harford Rd, Baltimore, MD 21214-2255

BM | Faith Community || Baltimore
C. (410) 426-8177
faith_community@verizon.net

FaithPoint #6382
PO Box 133, Monrovia, MD 21770

CM | Faithpoint || Urbana
C. (301) 363-8165
office@faithpointum.org

Falls Road #3510
15335 Falls Rd, Sparks, MD 21152-9592

BS | Parkton || Parkton-Sparks
C. (410) 472-3158
jdzrcody@aol.com

Fallston #2435
1509 Fallston Rd, Fallston, MD 21047-1624

BS | Fallston Church || Fallston
C. (410) 877-7255
fallstonumc@fallstonumc.org

Ferndale #1268
117 Ferndale Rd, Glen Burnie, MD 21061-2626

AN | Ferndale || Ferndale
C. (410) 761-2880
ferndaleumcsecretary@gmail.com

First #7385
6201 Belcrest Rd, Hyattsville, MD 20782-2913

GW | First || Hyattsville
C. (301) 927-6133
church@fumchy.org

First #7415
424 Main St, Laurel, MD 20707-4116

AN | First/Community || Laurel
C. (301) 725-3093
office@fumcl.org

First #5515
49 S Green St, Berkeley Springs, WV 25411-1638

CH | First || Berkeley Springs
C. (304) 258-2766
firstumc3@frontier.com

First #5390
14 Church St, Lonaconing, MD 21539-1111

CH | George's Creek || Midland
C. (202) 304-9328
lonaconingumc@gmail.com

First Saints Community Church #8540
PO Box 95, Leonardtown, MD 20650-0095
(25550 Point Lookout Rd)

WE | First Saints Community || Leonardtown
C. (301) 475-7200
ingrid@firstsaints.org

Flint Hill #6380
2732 Park Mills Rd, Adamstown, MD 21710

CM | Ijamsville-Flint Hill || Ijamsville
C. (443) 994-9505
ijamsvilleflinthill@gmail.com

Flintstone #5270
PO Box 2, Flintstone, MD 21530-0002
(21690 National Pike NE)

CH | Flintstone || Flintstone
C. (301) 478-2369
flintstoneumcharge@verizon.net

Flohrville #4230
6620 Church St, Sykesville, MD 21784-8014

CM | Flohrville || Sykesville
C. (301) 917-7894
revkeystone@hotmail.com

Forest Grove #9230
6108 Dickerson Road, Dickerson, MD 20842

CM | Dickerson-Forest Grove || Dickerson
C. (301) 349-5416
forestgrovemdumc@gmail.com

Forest Memorial #8190
3111 Forestville Rd, Forestville, MD 20747-4405

GW | Forest Memorial || Forestville
C. (301) 736-4115
office@forestmemorialumc.org

Fork #3320
12800 Fork Rd, Fork, MD 21051-9728

BS | Fork - Waugh || Fork
C. (410) 592-8303
fork_waugh_secretary@forkumc.org

Foundry #7180
1500 16th St NW, Washington, DC 20036-1402

GW | Foundry || DC
C. (202) 332-4010
foundryumc@foundryumc.org

Fowler #1140
816 Bestgate Rd, Annapolis, MD 21401-3033

AN | Mt. Zion-Fowler || Annapolis
C. (410) 224-2149
Tbelt2047@msn.com

Frames Memorial #3460
303 Warren Rd, Cockeysville, MD 21030-2704

BS | Frames-Poplar || Cockeysville
C. (410) 667-8745
curtis.senft@yahoo.com

Francis Asbury National Korean #9427
2181 Baltimore Rd, Rockville, MD 20851-1230

GW | Francis Asbury Ntnl Korean || Rockville
C. (301) 309-6856
nationalkumc@hotmail.com

Franklin #1175
5345 Deale Churchton Rd, Churchton, MD 20733-9626

AN | Mt. Zion/Franklin || Lothian
C. (410) 867-3521
franklumc5345@gmail.com

Franklin P Nash #7185
2001 Lincoln Rd NE, Washington, DC 20002-1381

GW | McKendree-Simms-Brookland || DC
C. (202) 269-0572
fpnashum2@gmail.com

Friendship #9210
27701 Ridge Rd, Damascus, MD 20872-2423

CM | Friendship || Damascus
C. (301) 253-3411
tnewms5@gmail.com

Friendship #6660
166 Locust Grove Rd, Hedgesville, WV 25427-3072
Co John Brooks

FR | Berkeley Pl.-Friendship || Martinsburg
C. (304) 754-7891
readsps27@gmail.com

Friendship #1275
22 W Friendship Rd, Friendship, MD 20758-3203

AN | Friendship || Friendship
C. (410) 257-7133
bsuedean@friendshipmethodist.org

Frostburg #5310
48 W Main St, Frostburg, MD 21532-1642

CH | Frostburg || Frostburg
C. (301) 689-6626
office@frostburgumc.org

Gaither #4280
7701 Gaither Rd, Sykesville, MD 21784-7124

CM | Sykesville Parish || Sykesville
C. (410) 795-0714
admin@stpaulssykesville.org

Galesville #1280
4825 Church Ln, Galesville, MD 20765-3107

AN | Galesville || Galesville
C. (410) 867-3281
galesvilleumc@gmail.com

Ganotown #6550
1018 Winchester Ave, Martinsburg, WV 25401-1650

FR | Ganotown || Ganotown
C. (304) 267-4861
warnicar@comcast.net

Garfield #6425
13628 Stottlemyer Rd, Smithsburg, MD 21783-9220

CH | Garfield / St. Paul's || Smithsburg
C. (301) 582-8552
jdbear@comcast.net

Gary Memorial #4240
2029 Daniels Rd, Ellicott City, MD 21043-1971

CM | Gary Memorial || Ellicott City
C. (410) 465-7345
karenlillipax@gmail.com

Gerrardstown #6555
1781 Gerrardstown Road, Gerrardstown, WV 25420

FR | Gerrardstown || Gerrardstown
C. (304) 229-2351
parsonumc@gmail.com

Gethsemane #7320
910 Addison Rd S, Capitol Heights, MD 20743-4403

GW | Gethsemane || Capitol Heights
C. (301) 336-1219
info@gethsemaneumc.org

Glen Burnie #1320
5 2nd Ave SE, Glen Burnie, MD 21061-3626

AN | Glen Burnie || Glen Burnie
C. (410) 761-4381
office@gbumchurch.org

Glen Mar #7365
4701 New Cut Rd, Ellicott City, MD 21043-6603

CM | Glen Mar || Ellicott City
C. (410) 465-4995
barb.julian@glenmarumc.org

Glenelg #9285
13900 Burntwoods Rd, Glenelg, MD 21737-9721

CM | Glenelg || Glenelg
C. (410) 489-7260
admin@glenelgumc.org

Glenmont #9475
12901 Georgia Ave, Silver Spring, MD 20906-3743

GW | Glenmont || Wheaton
C. (301) 946-5577
glenmontumc@verizon.net

Glenn Dale #8225
8500 Springfield Rd, Glenn Dale, MD 20769-9603

WE | Glenn Dale || Glenn Dale
C. (301) 262-2299
glenndaleumc@gmail.com

Glyndon #4285
4713 Butler Rd, Glyndon, MD 21071-4210

BS | Glyndon || Glyndon
C. (410) 833-2033
glyndonumchurch@gmail.com

Good Hope Union #9455
14680 Good Hope Rd, Silver Spring, MD 20905-6018

GW | Good Hope Union || Silver Spring
C. (301) 879-8100
SecretaryGHU@goodhopeunion.org

Good Shepherd #8525
305 Smallwood Dr, Waldorf, MD 20602-2879

WE | Good Shepherd || Waldorf
C. (301) 843-6797
gsadmin@gsumc.com

Good Shepherd #7445
9701 New Hampshire Ave, Silver Spring, MD 20903-2334

GW | Good Shepherd || Silver Spring
C. (301) 434-3331
goodshepumc@verizon.net

Good Shepherd #3230
3800 Roland Ave, Baltimore, MD 21211-2003

BM | Good Shepherd || Baltimore
C. (410) 243-1129
HampdenPastor@gmail.com

Goshen #9255
19615 Goshen Rd, Gaithersburg, MD 20879-1819

CM | Goshen || Gaithersburg
C. (240) 683-5530
goshen_umc@comcast.net

Gough #3315
14200 Cuba Rd, Cockeysville, MD 21030-1214

BS | Hereford Combined || Hereford
C. (410) 771-6264

Govans-Boundary #3165
5210 York Rd, Baltimore, MD 21212-4257

BM | New Waverly-Govan Boundary || Baltimore
C. (410) 435-1550
govansboundryumc@gmail.com

Grace #3170
5407 N Charles St, Baltimore, MD 21210-2024

BM | Grace || Baltimore
C. (410) 433-6650
office@graceunitedmethodist.org

Grace #4310
4618 Black Rock Rd, Upperco, MD 21155-9545

BS | North Carroll || Hampstead
C. (410) 374-9400
nccpumc@gmail.com

Grace #2110
110 W Bel Air Ave, Aberdeen, MD 21001-3242

BS | Grace || Aberdeen
C. (410) 272-0909
gracemethodistchurch@yahoo.com

Grace #9260
119 N Frederick Ave, Gaithersburg, MD 20877-2441

CM | Grace || Gaithersburg
C. (301) 926-8688
dmlyon@graceumc.org

Grace #7465
7001 New Hampshire Ave, Takoma Park, MD 20912-5816

GW | Grace/Ager Road || Takoma Park
C. (301) 891-2100
thenehemiahcharge@gmail.com

Grace #8215
11700 Old Fort Rd, Fort Washington, MD 20744-2703

WE | Grace || Fort Washington
C. (301) 292-7828
r3slade3@gmail.com

Grace #5325
712 W Church St, Hagerstown, MD 21740-4560

CH | Grace || Hagerstown
C. (301) 739-1925
graceumchagerstown@gmail.com

Grace #5410
PO Box 15, Midland, MD 21532-0015
(19915 Church Street Sw)

CH | George's Creek || Midland
C. (202) 304-9328
kheerak@gmail.com

Graceland #2210
6714 Youngstown Ave, Baltimore, MD 21222-1025

BM | Graceland || Baltimore
C. (410) 633-8799
danielkutrick@comcast.net

Greenmount #4288
2001 Hanover Pike, Hampstead, MD 21074-1332

BS | North Carroll || Hampstead
C. (410) 239-9705
nccpumc@gmail.com

Greensburg #6665
2171 Greensburg Rd, Martinsburg, WV 25404-0364

FR | Mt Wesley-Greensburg || Martinsburg
C. (304) 261-2513
edhfhep@gmail.com

Greenspring #3390
2730 Spring Hill Rd, Owings Mills, MD 21117-4311

BS | Lutherville || Lutherville
C. (410) 821-0850
busterpete@comcast.net

Greenwood #5525
6752 Winchester Grade Rd, Berkeley Springs, WV 25411-6050

CH | Morgan || Berkeley Springs
C. (304) 258-2957
morganchargewv@gmail.com

Gwynn Oak #4130
5020 Gwynn Oak Ave, Baltimore, MD 21207-6803

BM | G.O.A.L. || Baltimore
C. (410) 542-1274
gwynnoakumc2@comcast.net

Halethorpe-Relay #3120
4513 Ridge Ave, Halethorpe, MD 21227-4440

BM | Halethorpe-Relay || Baltimore
C. (410) 242-5918
hrumc1@outlook.com

Hall #1325
7780 Solley Rd, Glen Burnie, MD 21060-8310

AN | Hall || Glen Burnie
C. (410) 360-1242
hallunitedmc@yahoo.com

Hampden #3175
3449 Falls Rd, Baltimore, MD 21211-2405

BM | Hampden || Baltimore
C. (410) 235-0679
hampdenumc@gmail.com

Hancock #5365
170 W Main St, Hancock, MD 21750-1432

CH | Hancock || Hancock
C. (301) 678-6440
HancockUMC@comcast.net

Harmony #6640
PO Box 1510, Falling Waters, WV 25419-1510
(9455 Williamsport Pike)

FR | Harmony || Marlowe
C. (304) 274-1719
jzalatoris1@gmail.com

Harwood Park #1225
6635 Highland Ave, Elkridge, MD 21075-5632

AN | Harwood Park/Mt. Zion || Elkridge
C. (410) 796-5565
RLDuncan1@aol.com

Havre De Grace #2455
101 S Union Ave, Havre de Grace, MD 21078-3111

BS | Havre De Grace || Havre De Grace
C. (410) 939-2464
hdgumc@verizon.net

Hedgesville #6610
201 S Mary St, Hedgesville, WV 25427-7459

FR | Hedgesville || Hedgesville
C. (304) 754-8793
humc.hedgesville@gmail.com

Hereford #3344
16931 York Rd, Monkton, MD 21111-1023

BS | Hereford || Hereford
C. (410) 343-0660
admin@herefordumc.org

Highland #5530
1302 Valley Rd, Berkeley Springs, WV 25411-4801

CH | Alpine || Berkeley Springs
C. (304) 258-2847
alpine.charge@gmail.com

Hiss #3440
8700 Harford Rd, Baltimore, MD 21234-4608

BM | Hiss || Baltimore
C. (410) 668-5665
office@hisschurch.org

Hollywood #8230
24422 Mervell Dean Rd, Hollywood, MD 20636-2709

WE | Hollywood || Hollywood
C. (301) 373-2500
office@hollywoodumcmd.org

Holy Cross #5625
3 Miller Lane, Ridgeley, WV 26753

CH | Holy Cross || Ridgeley
C. (304) 738-2206
Holycrossumc847@gmail.com

Hope Memorial St Mark #1240
3672 Muddy Creek Rd, Edgewater, MD 21037-3418

AN | Hope Memorial St Mark || Edgewater
C. (410) 798-6776
hopestmarkumc@comcast.net

Hopehill #6155
7647 Fingerboard Rd, Frederick, MD 21704-7634

FR | Hopehill || Frederick
C. (301) 874-1166
pastordavid@hopehillumc.org

Hopewell #2460
3600 Level Village Rd, Havre de Grace, MD 21078-1119

BS | Susquehanna || Havre De Grace
C. (410) 914-5276
Hopewellevel@gmail.com

Hopkins #9290
13250 Highland Rd, Highland, MD 20777-9721

CM | Hopkins || Highland
C. (301) 854-2150
hopkinsumc@gmail.com

Howard Chapel-Ridgeville #9355
1970 Long Corner Rd, Mount Airy, MD 21771-3738

CM | Howard Chapel-Ridgeville || Mt Airy
C. (301) 829-2391
payers001@comcast.net

Hughes #9480
10700 Georgia Ave, Wheaton, MD 20902

GW | Hughes || Wheaton
C. (301) 949-8383
Church_Office@hughesumc.org

Hughes Memorial #7190
25 53rd St NE, Washington, DC 20019-6602

GW | Hughes Memorial || DC
C. (202) 398-3411
adminasst@hughesmemorial.org

Huntingtown #8245
P O Box 550, Huntingtown, MD 20639-9114
4020 Hunting Creek Rd

WE | Huntingtown Church || Huntingtown
C. (410) 257-3020
office.humc@comcast.net

Hunt's Memorial #3487
1912 Old Court Rd, Towson, MD 21204-1849

BS | Hunt's Memorial || Riderwood
C. (410) 339-7770
office@huntsumc.org

Hyattstown #9315
26121 Frederick Rd, Clarksburg, MD 20871-9614

CM | Hyattstown-Clarksburg || Hyattstown
C. (301) 831-1194
revdwhodsdon@verizon.net

Idlewylde #3535
1000 Regester Ave, Idlewylde, MD 21239-1515

BS | St John-Idlewylde || Baltimore
C. (410) 377-9691
carol.pazdersky@gmail.com

Ijamsville #6235
4746 Mussetter Rd, Ijamsville, MD 21754-9627

CM | Ijamsville / Flint Hill || Ijamsville
C. (443) 994-9505
ijamsvilleflinthill@gmail.com

Immanuel #8235
17400 Aquasco Rd, Brandywine, MD 20613-4212

WE | Brookfield Immanuel || Brandywine
C. (240) 681-3532
johncwarren@att.net

Indian Head #8265
19 Mattingly Ave, Indian Head, MD 20640-1731

WE | Indianhead || Indianhead
C. (301) 743-2312
IndianHeadUMC@aol.com

Inwood #6615
62 True Apple Way, Inwood, WV 25428

FR | Inwood || Inwood
C. (304) 676-5202
talkmanjohn@gmail.com

Jackson Chapel #6330
5609 Ballenger Creek Pike, Frederick, MD 21703-7009

FR | Jackson Chapel || Frederick
C. (301) 694-7315
rexbowenssr@comcast.net

Jarrettsville #2475
1733 Jarrettsville Rd, Jarrettsville, MD 21084-1523

BS | Jarrettsville-Ayres || Jarrettsville
C. (410) 692-5847
jumc@zoominternet.net

Jefferson #6240
3882 Jefferson Pike, Jefferson, MD 21755-8121

FR | Greater Brunswick || Brunswick
C. (301) 810-5430
wcarpen14a@gmail.com

Jennings Chapel #9510
2601 Jennings Chapel Rd, Woodbine, MD 21797-7802

CM | Poplar Springs || Mt Airy
C. (410) 489-7185
poplarcharge@verizon.net

Jerusalem-Mt Pleasant #9420
11 Wood Ln, Rockville, MD 20850-2228

GW | Jerusalem-Mt Pleasant || Rockville
C. (301) 424-0464
Jmp1umc@aol.com

John Wesley #5330
129 N Potomac St, Hagerstown, MD 21740-4809

CH | John Wesley || Hagerstown
C. (301) 733-0391
jwumcmd@yahoo.com

John Wesley #2130
3817 Philadelphia Rd, Abingdon, MD 21009-1107

BS | John Wesley || Abingdon
C. (410) 676-0032
jwumcabingdon@gmail.com

John Wesley #1330
6922 Ritchie Hwy, Glen Burnie, MD 21061-2304

AN | John Wesley || Glen Burnie
C. (410) 766-6981
jwumcgb@yahoo.com

John Wesley #1145
2114 Bay Ridge Ave, Annapolis, MD 21403-2828

AN | John Wesley || Annapolis
C. (410) 263-4125
jwesley2114@yahoo.com

John Wesley #4135
3202 W North Ave, Baltimore, MD 21216-3014

BM | John Wesley || Baltimore
C. (410) 383-1525
baltjwumc@aol.com

John Wesley-Waterbury #1185
962 Generals Hwy, Crownsville, MD 21032-1424

AN | John Wesley-Waterbury || Crownsville
C. (410) 923-2248
johnwesleywaterbury@gmail.com

Johnsville #4450
1124 Johnsville Rd, Sykesville, MD 21784-8432

FR | Johnsville || Sykesville
C. (410) 581-3062
jumc1124@gmail.com

Johnsville #4523
11106 Green Valley Rd, Union Bridge, MD 21791-8408

FR | Johnsville || Union Bridge
C. (410) 775-7217
sharimccourt@aol.com

Jones Memorial #7210
4625 G St SE, Washington, DC 20019-7834

GW | Jones Memorial || DC
C. (202) 583-7116
lorettaewe1@verizon.net

Journey of Faith Church;The #8550
2900 Smallwood Dr W, Waldorf, MD 20603-4786

WE | The Journey of Faith || Waldorf
churchoffice@thejofc.org

La Plata #8275
3 Port Tobacco Rd, La Plata, MD 20646-4366

WE | La Plata || La Plata
C. (301) 934-2288
laplataumc@gmail.com

Lanham #8290
5512 Whitfield Chapel Rd, Lanham, MD 20706-2512

WE | Lanham || Lanham
C. (301) 577-1500
lanhamumc2@verizon.net

Lansdowne #3125
114 Lavern Ave, Baltimore, MD 21227-3022

BM | Lansdowne || Baltimore
C. (410) 247-4624
LansdowneUMC@gmail.com

LaVale #5370
565 National Hwy, LaVale, MD 21502-7047

CH | LaVale || LaVale
C. (301) 722-6800
churchoffice@umclavale.org

Leetown #6630
11133 Leetown Rd, Kearneysville, WV 25430-5521

FR | Leetown || Kearneysville
C. (304) 725-8304
leetownumc@frontiernet.net

Lewistown #6265
11032 Hessong Bridge Rd, Thurmont, MD 21788-2810

FR | Lewistown || Lewistown
C. (301) 898-7888
lumc21788@comcast.net

Lexington Park #8320
21760 Great Mills Rd, Lexington Park, MD 20653-3801

WE | Lexington Park || Lexington Park
C. (301) 863-8500
lpumc@md.metrocast.net

Liberty Central #6800
PO Box 337, Libertytown, MD 21762-0337
(12024 Main Street)

FR | Liberty || Libertytown
C. (301) 898-7305
jerrymarkc@comcast.net

Liberty Grove #9155
15225 Old Columbia Pike, Burtonsville, MD 20866-1615

GW | Liberty Grove || Burtonsville
C. (301) 421-9166
libertygrovemd@gmail.com

Lincoln Park #7215
1301 N Carolina Ave NE, Washington, DC 20002-6423

GW | Lincoln Park || DC
C. (202) 543-1318
LincolnPark@LPUMCDC.org

Linden Heights #3445
9914 Harford Rd, Parkville, MD 21234-1227

BS | Linden Heights || Carney
C. (410) 668-6181
lindenheightsumc@verizon.net

Linden-Linthicum #9180
12101 Linden Linthicum Ln, Clarksville, MD 21029

CM | Linden-Linthicum || Clarksville
C. (410) 531-5653
llumc@l-lumc.org

Linganore #6375
8921 Clemsonville Rd, Union Bridge, MD 21791-7413

FR | Linganore || Union Bridge
C. (301) 829-6937
LinganoreUMC@gmail.com

Linthicum Heights #1370
200 School Ln, Linthicum, MD 21090-2519

AN | Linthicum Heights || Linthicum Heights
C. (410) 859-0990
Office@lhumc.org

Lisbon #9350
PO Box 51, Lisbon, MD 21765-0051
(15875 Frederick Road)

CM | Lisbon || Lisbon
C. (410) 489-7245
lisbonumc@aol.com

Loch Raven #3540
6622 Loch Raven Blvd, Baltimore, MD 21239-1424

BM | Loch Raven || Baltimore
C. (410) 825-0900
office@lrumc.org

Locust #7355
6851 Martin Rd, Columbia, MD 21044-4017

CM | Locust || Columbia
C. (410) 531-5323
locustumc@yahoo.com

Lodge Forest #2410
2715 Lodge Forest Dr, Baltimore, MD 21219-1913

BM | Patapsco-Lodge Forest || Dundalk
C. (410) 477-0976
db.peters@comcast.net

Lovely Lane #3185
2200 Saint Paul St, Baltimore, MD 21218-5805

BM | Lovely Lane-Baltimore City || Baltimore
C. (410) 889-1512
LovelyLane.BCS@gmail.com

Macedonia #1425
1567 Sappington Station Rd, Gambrills, MD 21054-1051

AN | Macedonia || Odenton
C. (410) 674-9892
Ray.P.Talley@outlook.com

Magothy #1450
3703 Mountain Rd, Pasadena, MD 21122-2024

AN | Magothy || Pasadena
C. (410) 255-2420
secretary@magothy.org

Magothy Church of the Deaf #1455
3703 Mountain Rd, Pasadena, MD 21122-2024

BM | Christ Deaf / Magothy Deaf || Baltimore
C. Unlisted
ehart@bwcumc.org

Marley #1335
30 Marley Neck Rd, Glen Burnie, MD 21060-7508

AN | Marley || Glen Burnie
C. (410) 760-4720
marleyumc@yahoo.com

Marsden First #7610
151 South Shore Road, Smith's, HS01 BERMUDA

GW | Marsden First || Bermuda
C. (441) 293-7045
Marsden@link.bm

Martin Luther King Memorial #4145
5114 Windsor Mill Rd, Baltimore, MD 21207-6657

BM | Martin Luther King Meml || Baltimore
C. (410) 448-2312
mlkumc1@comcast.net

Marvin Chapel #6310
5101 Woodville Rd, Mount Airy, MD 21771-5845

CM | Prospect-Marvin Chapel || Mt Airy
C. (301) 829-9244
prospect.marvinchapel.umc@gmail.com

Marvin Chapel #6670
PO Box 1925, Inwood, WV 25428-1925

FR | Marvin Chapel || Martinsburg
C. (304) 229-2275
talkmanjohn@gmail.com

Maryland Line #3380
PO Box 60, Maryland Line, MD 21105-0060
(21500 York Road)

BS | Baltimore Co. || Maryland Line
C. (410) 343-0052
mdlnumc@verizon.net

Mayo #1148
1005 Old Turkey Point Rd, Edgewater, MD 21037-4028

AN | Mayo || Annapolis
C. (410) 798-6110
mayoumc@verizon.net

Mays Chapel #3522
11911 Jenifer Rd, Timonium, MD 21093-7473

BS | Mays Chapel || Timonium
C. (410) 560-3173
office@mayschapel.org

McKendree of Potomac Park #5242
13455 McMullen Hwy SW, Cumberland, MD 21502-5346

CH | McKendree of Potomac || Cresaptown
C. (301) 729-1993
mckendree5242@gmail.com

McKendree-Simms-Brookland #7620
2421 Lawrence St NE, Washington, DC 20018-2915

GW | McKendree-Simms-Brookland || DC
C. (202) 529-3075
churchoffice@msbumc.org

Melville Chapel #1265
5660 Furnace Ave, Elkridge, MD 21075-5110

AN | Northeast || Elkridge
C. (410) 796-0959
roursler22@hotmail.com

Melvin #5295
100 Reynolds St, Cumberland, MD 21502-2526

CH | Melvin-Fairview Ave || Cumberland
C. (301) 777-3997
rdmrlm@verizon.net

Memorial #9385
PO Box 358, Poolesville, MD 20837-2005
(17821 Elgin Rd)

CM | Memorial || Poolesville
C. (301) 349-2010
office@pmumc.org

Memorial #6755
PO Box 10, Summit Point, WV 25446-0010
(46 Steptoe Street)

FR | Memorial || Summit Point
C. (443) 841-2219
pastored@hopemtcarmel.org

Memorial First India #7462
9226 Colesville Rd, Silver Spring, MD 20910-1658

GW | Memorial First India || Silver Spring
C. (301) 585-8015
revhonnappa@hotmail.com

Messiah #4475
20 Middle St, Taneytown, MD 21787-2120

FR | Messiah || Taneytown
C. (410) 756-6085
rwb1.pastor@yahoo.com

Messiah #1340
7401 E Furnace Branch Rd, Glen Burnie, MD 21060-7243

AN | Messiah || Glen Burnie
C. (410) 761-1944
messiahumc4@verizon.net

Metropolitan #1480
548 Queenstown Rd, Severn, MD 21144-1310

AN | Metropolitan || Severn
C. (410) 768-3588
mumc21144@verizon.net

Metropolitan #2220
1121 W Lanvale St, Baltimore, MD 21217-2520

BM | Metropolitan || Baltimore
C. (410) 523-1366
metrosqr@verizon.net

Metropolitan #8420
3385 Metropolitan Church Rd, Indian Head, MD 20640-3213

WE | Metropolitan || Indian Head
C. (301) 375-9088
metroumc@verizon.net

Metropolitan Memorial DBA National UMC #7630
3401 Nebraska Ave NW, Washington, DC 20016-2759

GW | Metropolitan Memorial || DC
C. (202) 363-4900
hsimon@nationalchurch.org

Michaels #5540
PO Box 672, Hedgesville, WV 25427-0672
(884 Michaels Chapel Road)

CH | Berkeley Springs || Berkeley Springs
C. (301) 678-6394
michaelsumc.berk.springs@gmail.com

Middleburg #4490
3403 Uniontown Rd, Westminster, MD 21158-3577

FR | Middleburg-Uniontown || New Windsor
C. (410) 848-6940
dav1pat2@hotmail.com

Middletown #6280
7108 Fern Ct, Middletown, MD 21769-7440

FR | Middletown || Middletown
C. (301) 371-5550
admin@mtownumc.org

Middleway #6635
7435 Queen St, Kearneysville, WV 25430-0580

FR | Middleway || Middleway
C. (304) 728-4770
mumc@frontiernet.net

Milford Mill #4380
915 Milford Mill Rd, Pikesville, MD 21208-4614

BS | Milford Mill || Pikesville
C. (410) 486-5263
mmumc@aol.com

Mill Creek Parish #9425
7101 Horizon Ter, Derwood, MD 20855-1355

CM | Mill Creek Parish || Rockville
C. (301) 926-9024
mcpumchurch@gmail.com

Millers #4340
3435 Warehime Rd, Manchester, MD 21102-2017

BS | Bixlers-Millers || Manchester
C. (410) 374-4042
pastorblakesmarr@gmail.com

Millian Memorial #9430
13016 Parkland Dr, Rockville, MD 20853-3361

GW | Millian Memorial || Rockville
C. (301) 946-2500
millianumc@gmail.com

Mizo #7485
6810 Montrose Rd, Rockville, MD 20852-4210

GW | Mizo UMC || Rockville
C. (301) 222-3608
chhunga@yahoo.com

Monkton #3385
1930 Monkton Rd, Monkton, MD 21111-1632

BS | Monkton || Monkton
C. (410) 472-9116
abuss58981@aol.com

Montgomery #9215
28325 Kemptown Rd, Damascus, MD 20872-1326

CM | Montgomery || Damascus
C. (301) 253-4460
montumc@verizon.net

Morgan Chapel #4585
6750 Woodbine Rd, Woodbine, MD 21797-9402

CM | Morgan Chapel-Mt Olive || Woodbine
C. (443) 970-2485
revjim@morganchapel.church

Mount Bethel #5450
14110 Stottlemyer Rd, Smithsburg, MD 21783-9230

CH | Mt. Bethel/Mt. Lena || Boonsboro
C. (301) 416-0300
rk4home@aol.com

Mount Calvary #8150
37345 New Market Rd, Charlotte Hall, MD 20622-3086

WE | Mount Calvary/St. Matthews || Rt. 6
C. (301) 884-7320
pastor@route6charge.org

Mount Calvary #1165
1236 Jones Station Rd, Arnold, MD 21012-2301

AN | Cecil Memorial-Mt. Calvary || Annapolis
C. (410) 757-7140
mcumarnold@aol.com

Mount Carmel #1460
4760 Mountain Rd, Pasadena, MD 21122-5814

AN | Mount Carmel || Pasadena
C. (410) 255-8887
mtcarmel21122@gmail.com

Mount Carmel #3425
17036 Pretty Boy Dam Rd, Parkton, MD 21120-9690

BS | Parkton || Parkton-Sparks
C. (410) 357-5431
mtcarmelumc21120@comcast.net

Mount Carmel #9335
22222 Georgia Ave, Brookeville, MD 20833-0177

CM | Sunshine || Laytonsville
C. (301) 774-9330
stpaul208@aol.com

Mount Carmel #5115
11404 Tedrick Dr, Big Pool, MD 21711-1236

CH | Potomac || Big Pool
C. (240) 520-7708
bigpoolumc@gmail.com

Mount Carmel #6335
9411 Baltimore Rd, Frederick, MD 21704-6752

FR | Mt Carmel/New Market || Frederick
C. (301) 696-9735
donna.clawson@hopemtcarmel.org

Mount Gilead #4425
5302 Glen Falls Rd, Reisterstown, MD 21136-4503

BS | Boring-Piney Grove-Mt. Gilead || Boring
C. (410) 429-5255
ministryaccount23@yahoo.com

Mount Gregory #4455
PO Box 63, Glenwood, MD 21738-0063

CM | Growing Seed || Glenwood
C. (410) 489-5741
rev.rlbrown@gmail.com

Mount Harmony-Lower Marlboro #8365

155 E Mount Harmony Rd, Owings, MD 20736-3442

WE | Mt. Harmony-Lwr Marlboro || Mt. Harmony
C. (410) 257-2761
MtHarmonyLMUMC@comcast.net

Mount Hermon #5275
PO Box 2, Cumberland, MD 21501-0002
(13200 Williams Road)

CH | Flintstone || Flintstone
C. (301) 478-2369
flintstoneumcharge@verizon.net

Mount Hope #8475
PO Box 125, Sunderland, MD 20689-0125
(145 Dalrymple Road)

WE | Mount Hope || Sunderland
C. (410) 257-3206
mhumc145@verizon.net

Mount Lena #6125
21234 Mount Lena Rd, Boonsboro, MD 21713-1613

CH | Mt. Bethel/Mt. Lena || Boonsboro
C. (301) 733-8108
rk4home@aol.com

Mount Nebo #6130
134 S Main St, Boonsboro, MD 21713-1204

CH | Mount Nebo || Boonsboro
C. (301) 432-8741
mt.nebo@myactv.net

Mount Oak #8355
14110 Mount Oak Rd, Mitchellville, MD 20721-1208

WE | Mount Oak || Mitchellville
C. (301) 249-2230
MO@mtoak.org

Mount Olive #8430
10 Fairground Rd, Prince Frederick, MD 20678-4169

WE | Mount Olive || Prince Frederick
C. (410) 535-5756
officeadmin@mtoliveumchurch.com

Mount Olive #4390
5115 Old Court Rd, Randallstown, MD 21133-4701

BS | Mount Olive || Randallstown
C. (410) 922-2853
sallmond03@gmail.com

Mount Olive #4590
2927 Gillis Falls Rd, Mount Airy, MD 21771-8034

CM | Morgan Chapel-Mt Olive || Woodbine
C. (301) 854-2324
info@mountoliveumc.org

Mount Olivet #4190
823 Edmondson Ave, Catonsville, MD 21228-4448

BM | Mount Olivet || Catonsville
C. (410) 744-4451
olivet4190@gmail.com

Mount Olivet #5545
6752 Winchester Grade Rd, Berkeley Springs, WV 25411-6050

CH | Morgan || Berkeley Springs
C. (304) 258-2957
morganchargewv@gmail.com

Mount Pleasant #6390
9550 Liberty Rd, Frederick, MD 21701-3247

FR | Walkersville & Mt. Pleasant || Walkersville
C. (301) 898-5292
mypastorrich@aol.com

Mount Pleasant #5550
1302 Valley Rd, Berkeley Springs, WV 25411-4801

CH | Alpine || Berkeley Springs
C. (304) 258-2847
alpine.charge@gmail.com

Mount Savage #5425
PO Box 603, Mount Savage, MD 21545-0603
(12619 New Row Rd NW)

CH | Creek Run || Ellerslie / Mt. Savage
C. (301) 264-3535
mtsavageumc@yahoo.com

Mount Tabor #5460
18605 Oldtown RD SE, Oldtown, MD 21555

CH | Oldtown || Oldtown
C. (301) 478-5228
mttaborumc@yahoo.com

Mount Tabor #9340
24115 Laytonsville Rd, Laytonsville, MD 20882-3127

CM | South Damascus || Damascus
C. (301) 253-3871
Mttaboretchison@gmail.com

Mount Tabor #1285
1421 Saint Stephens Church Rd, Crownsville, MD 21032-2203

AN | Mount Tabor || Gambrills
C. (410) 721-3472
rubyhawk@verizon.net

Mount Tabor #2345
2350 Conowingo Rd, Bel Air, MD 21015-1404

BS | Deer Creek || Forest Hill
C. (410) 638-7856
deercreekcharge@gmail.com

Mount Vernon #2580
1510 Deep Run Rd, Whiteford, MD 21160-1302

BS | Mount Vernon || Whiteford
C. (410) 399-0288

Mount Vernon #7230
4147 Minnesota Ave NE, Washington, DC 20019-3575

GW | Mount Vernon || DC
C. (202) 398-7938
pastornelson1ac@gmail.com

Mount Vernon Place #3215
10 E Mount Vernon Pl, Baltimore, MD 21202-2309

BM | Mt Vernon Place || Baltimore
C. (410) 685-5290
mvpumcbaltimore@gmail.com

Mount Vernon Place #7235
900 Massachusetts Ave NW, Washington, DC 20001-4308

GW | Mount Vernon Place || DC
C. (202) 347-9620
churchoffice@mvpumc.org

Mount Washington-Aldersgate #3220
5800 Cottonworth Ave, Baltimore, MD 21209-3739

BM | Mt Washington-Aldersgate || Baltimore
C. (410) 323-4314
mwaumc@mwaumc.comcastbiz.net

Mount Wesley #6735
4622 Scrabble Rd, Shepherdstown, WV 25443-4083

FR | Mt Wesley-Greensburg || Martinsburg
C. (304) 261-2513
edhfhep@gmail.com

Mount Winans #2235
2501 Hollins Ferry Rd, Baltimore, MD 21230-3031

BM | Mount Winans || Baltimore
C. (410) 727-4211
mtwinansumc@gmail.com

Mount Zion #9310
12430 Scaggsville Rd, Highland, MD 20777-9727

CM | Mount Zion || Highland
C. (301) 854-2324
office@mtzionhighland.com

Mount Zion #4525
3800 Black Rock Rd, Upperco, MD 21155-9468

BS | Mount Zion Charge || Upperco
C. (410) 374-4231
johnmayden1@gmail.com

Mount Zion #3325
6212 Westover Dr, Mechanicsburg, Pa 17050-2340

BS | Baltimore Co. || Maryland Line
C. (443) 324-7861
dschulze6212@verizon.net

Mount Zion #4150
3050 Liberty Heights Ave, Baltimore, MD 21215-7448

BM | Mt. Zion-Emmarts || Baltimore
C. (410) 664-7490
mzumc@verizon.net

Mount Zion #2350
1643 E Churchville Rd, Bel Air, MD 21015-4803

BS | Mount Zion || Bel Air
C. (410) 836-7444
mtzionumc1@verizon.net

Mount Zion #1410
122 Bayard Rd, Lothian, MD 20711-9601

AN | Mount Zion || Lothian
C. (410) 867-4035
mz@mzumc.com

Mount Zion #1150
612 Second St, Annapolis, MD 21403-3332

AN | Mt. Zion-Fowler || Annapolis
C. (410) 268-5798
Shalom21230pj@AOL.com

Mount Zion #1465
8178 Artic Dr, Pasadena, MD 21122-4422

AN | Mount Zion || Pasadena
C. (410) 255-4602
mzmagothyumc@gmail.com

Mount Zion #6325
603 Main St, Myersville, MD 21773-8412

CH | Mount Zion || Myersville
C. (301) 293-1401
mtzionmyersville@gmail.com

Mount Zion #6350
PO Box 104, Sabillasville, MD 21780-0104
(13010 Mount Zion Road)

CH | Mt. Zion || Thurmont
C. (301) 824-6617
terplisajordan@gmail.com

Mount Zion #7240
1334 29th St NW, Washington, DC 20007-3351

GW | Mount Zion || DC
C. (202) 234-0148
mtzionumc.dc@gmail.com

Mount Zion #5555
5377 Martinsburg Rd, Berkeley Springs, WV 25411-5050

CH | Sleepy Creek || Berkeley Springs
C. (304) 258-2108
sleepycrkchrgumc@gmail.com

Mount Zion #6675
PO Box 3222 , Martinsburg, WV 25401-2720
(532 W Martin St)

FR | Mount Zion || Martinsburg
C. (304) 263-2667
pastoredhall@frontiernet.net

Mount Zion #9370
PO Box 324, Olney, MD 20830-0324
(5000 Brookville Road)

CM | Mount Zion || Olney
C. (240) 938-7190
pastorolivia.mtzion@gmail.com

Mount Zion #5585
PO Box 532, Great Cacapon, WV 25422-0532
(4581 Orleans Road)

CH | Mt. Zion Charge || Great Cacapon
C. (304) 258-2852
dickvoorhaar@hotmail.com

Mount Zion #7420
3592 Whiskey Bottom Rd, Laurel, MD 20724-1402

AN | Harwood Park/Mt. Zion || Elkridge
C. (301) 490-3707
mtzionumclmd@hotmail.com

Mount Zion #8450
PO Box 38, Saint Inigoes, MD 20684-0038
(17412 Mt. Zion Church Road)

WE | Mount Zion || St Inigoes
C. (301) 872-4006
delores.greene@navy.mil

Mount Zion #8350
27108 Mount Zion Church Rd, Mechanicsville, MD 20659-4889

WE | Mount Zion || Mechanicsville
C. (301) 884-4132
admin-mtzion@md.metrocast.net

Mount Zion-Ark Road #1415
41 Ark Rd, Lothian, MD 20711-2905

AN | Mt. Zion/Franklin || Lothian
C. (410) 867-0632
junedrake@verizon.net

Mount Zion-Finksburg #4265
PO Box 755, Finksburg, MD 21048-0755
(3006 Old Westminster Pike)

BS | Mount Zion || Finksburg
C. (410) 517-2300
julo1@verizon.net

Mountain View #9220
11501 Mountain View Rd, Damascus, MD 20872-1607

CM | Mtn. View-Pleasant Grove || Monrovia
C. (301) 253-2264
pastormhbaek@gmail.com

Mowatt Memorial #7375
40 Ridge Rd, Greenbelt, MD 20770-0724

GW | College Park-Mowatt. || College Park
C. (301) 474-9410
faylundin@yahoo.com

Murleys Branch #5280
PO Box 2 , Flintstone, MD 21530-2141
(18700 Williams Rd SE)

CH | Flintstone || Flintstone
C. (301) 478-2369
flintstoneumcharge@verizon.net

Murrill Hill #6580
16 Hilltop Rd, Harpers Ferry, WV 25425-5929

FR | Murrill Hill || Harpers Ferry
C. (304) 725-3959
des769@comcast.net

New Beginnings Fellowship #3500
4080 Federal Hill Rd, Jarrettsville, MD 21084-1217

BS | New Beginnings || Fallston
C. (410) 692-2600
eegayles@gmail.com

New Covenant #5210
1709 Frederick St, Cumberland, MD 21502-1037

CH | New Covenant || Cumberland
C. (301) 724-1150
revdonna@comcast.net

New Covenant Worship Center #3575
700 Wildwood Pkwy, Baltimore, MD 21229-1812

BM | New Covenant Worship || Baltimore
C. (410) 624-5330
ncwc.churchumc@gmail.com

New Hope Christian Fellowship #2412
2048 Watergate Ct, Edgewood, MD 21040-1824

BS | New Hope Christian || Edgewood
C. (410) 676-3531
newhope2048@yahoo.com

New Hope of Greater Brunswick #6137
7 S Maryland Ave, Brunswick, MD 21716-1110

FR | Greater Brunswick || Brunswick
C. (301) 834-7320
newhopebrunswick@gmail.com

New Hope of New Windsor #4640
3001 Hooper Rd, New Windsor, MD 21776-8121

FR | New Hope of New Windsor || New Windsor
C. (443) 465-5024
new_hope_pastor_mary@live.com

New Market #6340
PO Box 111, New Market, MD 21774-0111
(5501 Old New Market Rd)

FR | Mt Carmel/New Market || Frederick
C. (301) 865-3530
hometownchurch@comcast.net

New Street #6750
PO Box 188, Shepherdstown, WV 25443-0188
(202 West New Street)

FR | New Street || Shepherdstown
C. (304) 876-2362
nsumc@frontiernet.net

New Waverly #3217
644 E 33rd St, Baltimore, MD 21218-3504

BM | New Waverly-Govan Boundary || Baltimore
C. (410) 243-2481
newwave3217@gmail.com

Nichols-Bethel #1430
1239 Murray Rd, Odenton, MD 21113-1603

AN | Nichols-Bethel || Odenton
C. (410) 674-2272
office@nicholsbethel.org

Norrisville #2525
2434 Bradenbaugh Rd, White Hall, MD 21161-9661

BS | Norrisville || Norrisville
C. (410) 692-6179
thomasjsullivan@hotmail.com

North Bethesda #9140
10100 Old Georgetown Rd, Bethesda, MD 20814-1858

GW | North Bethesda || Bethesda
C. (301) 530-4342
macpastor@gmail.com

Northwood-Appold #3225
4499 Loch Raven Blvd, Baltimore, MD 21218-1500

BM | Northwood-Appold || Baltimore
C. (410) 323-6712
northwoodappoldumc@gmail.com

Nottingham-Myers #8485
15601 Brooks Church Rd, Upper Marlboro, MD 20772-8416

WE | New Hope Fellowship || Upper Marlboro
C. (301) 888-2171
nmumc@msn.com

Oak Chapel #9460
14500 Layhill Rd, Silver Spring, MD 20906-1913

GW | Oak Chapel || Silver Spring
C. (301) 598-0000
OakchapelUMC@verizon.net

Oakdale Emory #9375
3425 Emory Church Rd, Olney, MD 20832-2613

CM | Oakdale Emory || Olney
C. (301) 774-2030
info@oakdale.church

Oakland #4275
5901 Mineral Hill Rd, Sykesville, MD 21784-6824

FR | Oakland || Sykesville
C. (410) 795-5030
Office@oaklandumc.org

Oakland #6535
70 Oakland Ter, Charles Town, WV 25414-4869

FR | Oakland || Charles Town
C. (304) 725-3737
oaklandchurchumc@gmail.com

Old Otterbein #2240
112 W Conway St, Baltimore, MD 21201-2412

BM | Old Otterbein || Baltimore
C. (410) 685-4703
pastor@oldotterbeinumc.org

Oldtown #5430
18605 Oldtown Rd SE, Oldtown, MD 21555
(18811 Oldtown Rd SE)

CH | Oldtown || Oldtown
C. (301) 478-5869
oldtownumc@yahoo.com

Oliver's Grove #5435
18605 Oldtown Rd SE, Oldtown, MD 21555
(15500 Walnut Ridge Rd SE)

CH | Oldtown || Oldtown
C. (301) 478-5228
oliversgroveumc@yahoo.com

Olivet #8335
13575 Olivet Rd, Lusby, MD 20657-2633

WE | Olivet Charge || Lusby
C. (410) 326-8400
jbiggans@wmata.com

Orems #2515
1020 Orems Rd, Baltimore, MD 21220-4623

BM | Orems || Middle River
C. (410) 687-9483
oremsumc@verizon.net

Otterbein #5340
108 E Franklin St, Hagerstown, MD 21740-4906

CH | Otterbein || Hagerstown
C. (301) 739-9386
office@otterumc.org

Otterbein #6680
PO Box 2378, Martinsburg, WV 25402-2378
(549 North Queen Street)

FR | Otterbein || Martinsburg
C. (304) 263-0342
secretary@otterbeinumc.net

Oxon Hill #8380
6400 Livingston Rd, Oxon Hill, MD 20745-2909

WE | Oxon Hill || Oxon Hill
C. (301) 839-4748
OxonHillUMC@verizon.net

Park Place #5375
80 National Hwy, LaVale, MD 21502-7028

CH | Park Place || Cumberland
C. (301) 722-8145
vickitoad@hotmail.com

Parke Memorial #3430
18910 York Rd, Parkton, MD 21120-9201

BS | Baltimore Co. || Maryland Line
C. (410) 357-5587
dschulze6212@verizon.net

Parkhead #5120
11404 Tedrick Dr, Big Pool, MD 21711-1236
(9512 National Pike)

CH | Potomac || Big Pool
C. (301) 842-3212
bigpoolumc@gmail.com

Pasadena #1470
61 Ritchie Hwy, Pasadena, MD 21122-4356

AN | Pasadena || Pasadena
C. (443) 510-8846
pumc2@verizon.net

Patapsco #2385
7800 Wise Ave, Dundalk, MD 21222-3338

BM | Patapsco-Lodge Forest || Dundalk
C. (410) 288-5488
grover.katiej@gmail.com

Patapsco #4430
2930 Patapsco Rd, Finksburg, MD 21048-1106

BS | Shiloh-Patapsco || Hampstead
C. (410) 857-9210
ballenpsalm34@msn.com

Patuxent #8250
3500 Solomons Island Rd, Huntingtown, MD 20639-3810

WE | Huntingtown Combined || Huntingtown
C. (410) 535-9819
huntingtowncharge@gmail.com

Paw Paw #5610
PO Box 302, Paw Paw, WV 25434-0302
(57 Lee St)

CH | Paw Paw || Paw Paw
C. (304) 947-5289
darlenepowers@frontiernet.net

Paynes Chapel #6730
PO Box 354, Bunker Hill, WV 25413-0354
(631 Avanti Drive)

FR | Paynes Chapel || Bunker Hill
C. (304) 229-5220
payneschapel@frontier.com

Perry Hall #2535
9515 Belair Rd, Baltimore, MD 21236-1507

BS | Perry Hall || Perry Hall
C. (410) 256-6479
perryhallumc@verizon.net

Peters #8180
2785 Chaney Rd, Dunkirk, MD 20754-2303

WE | Peter's || Dunkirk
C. (410) 257-6620
petersumc@yahoo.com

Petworth #7245
32 Grant Cir NW, Washington, DC 20011-4601

GW | Petworth Charge || DC
C. (202) 723-5300
petworthumc1@verizon.net

Pikeside #6725
25 Paynes Ford Rd, Martinsburg, WV 25405-5854

FR | Pikeside || Martinsburg
C. (304) 263-4633
info@pikesideumc.org

Pine Grove #3570
20105 Kirkwood Shop Rd, White Hall, MD 21161-9175

BS | Hereford Combined || Hereford
C. (410) 357-4445
herefordcharge1@comcast.net

Pine Grove #3475
19401 Middletown Rd, Parkton, MD 21120-9662

BS | Pine Grove || Parkton
C. (410) 343-0729
pastorandrewbwc@gmail.com

Piney Grove #4175
4929 Piney Grove Rd, Reisterstown, MD 21136-4229

BS | Boring-Piney Grove-Mt. Gilead || Boring
C. (410) 688-9992
ministryaccount23@yahoo.com

Piney Grove #2355
201 Bowleys Quarters Rd, Middle River, MD 21220-2925

BM | Cowenton-Piney Grove || Baltimore
C. (410) 335-6927
cpkumar222@gmail.com

Piney Plains #5385
12708 Faith Cir NE, Little Orleans, MD 21766-1049

CH | Sideling Hill || Little Orleans
C. (304) 433-5920
catalpapineyplainsumc@gmail.com

Pisgah #8270
PO Box 168, Marbury, MD 20658-0168
(7020 Poorhouse Rd)

WE | Pisgah Church || Pisgah
C. (301) 743-3339
pisgahchurchumc@gmail.com

Pleasant Grove #9320
3425 Green Valley Rd, Ijamsville, MD 21754-9016

CM | Mtn. View-Pleasant Grove || Monrovia
C. (301) 865-5443
pastormhbaek@gmail.com

Pleasant Grove #4520
15300 Dover Rd, Reisterstown, MD 21136-3883

BS | Pleasant Grove || Reisterstown
C. (410) 429-5080
jwsterling1@gmail.com

Pleasant Hill #4370
10911 Reisterstown Rd, Owings Mills, MD 21117-2503

BS | Pleasant Hill || Owings Mills
C. (410) 356-4085
pleasanthillumc@msn.com

Pleasant View #6165
1865 Pleasant View Rd, Adamstown, MD 21710-9021

FR | Pleasant View || Adamstown
C. (410) 442-2761
mclark615@verizon.net

Pleasant Walk #6430
11240 Pleasant Walk Rd, Myersville, MD 21773-9218

CH | Pleasant Walk || Myersville
C. (301) 797-5433
pleasantwalkumc@gmail.com

Plum Point #8255
PO Box 971, Huntingtown, MD 20639-8769
(1800 Stinnett Rd)

WE | Huntingtown Combined || Huntingtown
C. (410) 535-5065
blackemera@gmail.com

Poplar Grove #3465
303 Warren Rd, Cockeysville, MD 21030-2704

BS | Frames-Poplar || Cockeysville
C. (410) 667-8745
curtis.senft@yahoo.com

Poplar Springs #9360
16661 Frederick Rd, Mount Airy, MD 21771-3311

CM | Poplar Springs || Mt Airy
C. (410) 489-7185
rev@hereintown.net

Potomac #9390
9908 S Glen Rd, Potomac, MD 20854-4128

GW | Potomac || Potomac
C. (301) 299-9383
jjacob@potomac-umc.org

Presbury #2415
806 Edgewood Rd, Edgewood, MD 21040-2436

BS | Presbury-Cranberry || Edgewood
C. (410) 676-3234
pastortiffanyp@gmail.com

Prospect #6315
5923 Woodville Rd, Mount Airy, MD 21771-7527

CM | Prospect-Marvin Chapel || Mt Airy
C. (301) 829-9244
prospect.marvinchapel.umc@gmail.com

Prosperity #5285
PO Box 2, Flintstone, MD 21530-0002
(13505 Pleasant Valley Road NE)

CH | Flintstone || Flintstone
C. (301) 478-2369
flintstoneumcharge@verizon.net

Providence #9325
3735 Kemptown Church Rd, Monrovia, MD 21770-8701

CM | Providence || Kemptown
C. (301) 253-1768
dwdadam@gmail.com

Providence #3370
1320 Providence Rd, Towson, MD 21286-1562

BS | Providence || Towson
C. (410) 823-5365
jackdayconnect@gmail.com

Providence-Fort Washington #8205
10610 Old Fort Rd, Ft Washington, MD 20744-2631

WE | Providence-Fort Wash || Fort Washington
C. (301) 292-2323
Provich@aol.com

Queens Chapel #7315
7410 Old Muirkirk Rd, Beltsville, MD 20705-1338

WE | Queens Chapel || Beltsville
C. (301) 210-9038
secretary@queenschapelumc.com

Randall Memorial #7250
1002 46th St NE, Washington, DC 20019-3810

GW | Randall Memorial || DC
C. (202) 396-0375
camerontwins@gmail.com

Rawlings #5445
PO Box 228, Rawlings, MD 21557-0228
(18910 McMullen Hwy Sw)

CH | Rawlings || Rawlings
C. (301) 729-0088
rawlingsumc@gmail.com

Rehoboth #5470
30 E Salisbury St, Williamsport, MD 21795-1112

CH | Rehoboth || Williamsport
C. (301) 223-9554
mirlinx51@gmail.com

Reisterstown #4435
246 Main St, Reisterstown, MD 21136-1214

BS | Reisterstown || Reisterstown
C. (410) 833-5440
rumcoffice1777@gmail.com

Rock Run #2378
4102 Rock Run Rd, Havre de Grace, MD 21078-1215

BS | Rock Run || Darlington
C. (410) 457-4145
plstenor@comcast.net

Rockville #9440
112 W Montgomery Ave, Rockville, MD 20850-4213

GW | Rockville || Rockville
C. (301) 762-2288
rockville_umc@rockvilleumc.org

Ryland-Epworth #7255
3200 S St SE, Washington, DC 20020-2410

GW | McKendree-Simms-Brookland || DC
C. (202) 582-4005
reumc7255@gmail.com

Salem #9275
23725 Ridge Rd, Germantown, MD 20876-4642

CM | South Damascus || Damascus
C. (301) 972-1804
salemumcgermantown@gmail.com

Salem #9150
12 High St, Brookeville, MD 20833

CM | Salem || Brookeville
C. (301) 774-7772
pastor@salemunitedmethodist.org

Salem #6250
25 S Main St, Keedysville, MD 21756-1348

CH | Salem Charge || Keedysville
C. (301) 432-4046
salemumc@salemcommunity.org

Salem #6435
12477 Wolfsville Rd, Myersville, MD 21773-9303

CH | Salem || Myersville
C. (301) 293-1616
revbsnyder@comcast.net

Salem #4335
7509 Windsor Mill Rd, Baltimore, MD 21244-2034

BM | Salem || Hebbville
C. (410) 655-4063
salemumcwm@gmail.com

Salem #2560
7901 Bradshaw Rd, Upper Falls, MD 21156-1804

BS | Salem || Upper Falls
C. (410) 592-2543
pastor@salemunited.org

Salem #3340
18221 Falls Rd, Hampstead, MD 21074-2818

BS | Salem || Hampstead
C. (410) 374-2421
jwicklein@verizon.net

Salem-Baltimore Hispanic #2310
3405 Gough St., Baltimore, MD 21224

BM | Salem-Baltimore Hispanic || Baltimore
C. (410) 276-8460
pastorsegovia.gs@gmail.com

Sandy Hook #6255
19018 Sandyhook Rd, Knoxville, MD 21758-1327

FR | Sandy Hook/Shenandoah Memorial || Knoxville
C. (304) 676-6774
pastorsharonlynn@gmail.com

Sandy Mount #4443
2101 Old Westminster Pike, Finksburg, MD 21048

FR | Sandy Mount || Sandy Mount
C. (410) 861-5788
sandymtumc@comcast.net

Savage #7435
9050 Baltimore St, Savage, MD 20763-9647

AN | Savage || Savage
C. (301) 725-7630
office@umcsavage.org

Severn #1485
1215 Old Camp Meade Rd, Severn, MD 21144-1138

AN | Delmont/Severn || Severn
C. (410) 551-7969
severnspastor@gmail.com

Severna Park #1510
731 Benfield Rd, Severna Park, MD 21146

AN | Severna Park || Severna Park
C. (410) 987-4700
spumc@severnaparkumc.org

Shaft #5415
19304 Shaft Rd SW, Frostburg, MD 21532-3743

CH | George's Creek || Midland
C. (301) 689-2158
kheerak@gmail.com

Sharp Street #9445
1310 Olney Sandy Spring Rd, Sandy Spring, MD 20860-1325

CM | Sharp Street || Sandy Spring
C. (301) 774-7047
sharppraise@verizon.net

Sharp Street Memorial #3250
1206 Etting St, Baltimore, MD 21217-3035

BM | Sharp St Memorial || Baltimore
C. (410) 523-7200
ssmumc@yahoo.com

Shenandoah Memorial #6715
436 Bloomery Road, Harpers Ferry, WV 25425

FR | Sandy Hook/Shenandoah Memorial || Knoxville
C. (304) 535-1375
pastorsharonlynn@gmail.com

Shiloh #5355
19731 Shiloh Church Rd, Hagerstown, MD 21742-4869

CH | Shiloh || Hagerstown
C. (301) 797-4083
shilohumc@myactv.net

Shiloh #8140
PO Box 182, Bryans Road, MD 20616-0182
(7305 Indian Head Highway)

WE | Shiloh || Bryan's Road
C. (301) 375-8816
shilohumc@verizon.net

Shiloh #4325
3100 Shiloh Rd, Hampstead, MD 21074-1625

BS | Shiloh-Patapsco || Hampstead
C. (410) 374-4231
ballenpsalm34@msn.com

Shiloh Community #8375
PO Box 267, Newburg, MD 20664-2517
(12760 Shiloh Church Rd)

WE | Shiloh Community || Newburg
C. (240) 441-8292
pastormae@msn.com

Silver Grove #6585
95 Church Hill Ln, Harpers Ferry, WV 25425-5149

FR | Silver Grove || Harpers Ferry
C. (304) 725-8608
silvergroveum@gmail.com

Silver Spring #9466
8900 Georgia Ave, Silver Spring, MD 20910-2757

GW | Silver Spring || Silver Spring
C. (301) 587-1215
akirkland@silverspringumcp.org

Simpson #9365
PO Box 522, Mount Airy, MD 21771-0522

CM | Growing Seed || Glenwood
C. (240) 550-9394
rev.rlbrown@gmail.com

Simpson-Hamline #7265
4501 16th St NW, Washington, DC 20011-4326

GW | Simpson-Hamline || DC
C. (202) 882-2122
shumcdc@yahoo.com

Smith Chapel #8415
PO Box 505, Marbury, MD 20658-0505
(7130 Poorhouse Rd)

WE | Smith Chapel Charge || Marbury
C. (301) 743-2227
smithchapel1901@aol.com

Smiths Chapel #2370
3109 Churchville Rd, Churchville, MD 21028-1805

BS | Smith's Chapel || Churchville
C. (410) 734-7113

Smithville #8185
3005 Ferry Landing Rd, Dunkirk, MD 20754-2941

WE | Smithville || Dunkirk
C. (410) 257-3160
smithvilleumcdunkirk@gmail.com

Sollers #1380
1219 Wrighton Rd, Lothian, MD 20711-9737

AN | South County || Shady Side/Lothian
C. (410) 741-1772
sollersumc673@gmail.com

Solley #1345
7600 Solley Rd, Glen Burnie, MD 21060-8308

AN | Solley || Glen Burnie
C. (410) 437-5641
pastor@solleyumc.org

Solomons #8470
14454 Solomons Island Road, Solomons, MD 20688-0403
WE | Solomons || Solomons
C. (410) 326-3278
solomonsumchurch@gmail.com

St Andrews #5345
1020 Maryland Ave, Hagerstown, MD 21740-7202
CH | St. Andrews || Hagerstown
C. (301) 739-7431
standrewsumchagerstown@gmail.com

St Andrews of Annapolis #1255
4 Wallace Manor Rd, Edgewater, MD 21037-1206
AN | St. Andrews of Ann || Annapolis
C. (410) 626-1610
standrewsum@gmail.com

St Edmonds #8160
3000 Darlymple Rd, Chesapeake Beach, MD 20732-0539
WE | St Edmond's || Chesapeake Beach
C. (410) 257-7311
stedmondsumc@verizon.net

St James #4565
12470 Old Frederick Rd, Marriottsville, MD 21104-1415
CM | West Ellicott City || West Friendship
C. (410) 442-2020
stjamessec@verizon.net

St James #4540
3000 Marston Rd, Westminster, MD 21157-7718
FR | St James || Westminster
C. (443) 536-7433
New_Hope_Pastor_Mary@live.com

St James Memorial #2265
1901 W Lexington St, Baltimore, MD 21223-1652
BM | St James || Baltimore
C. (410) 566-5058
STJAMEMUMC@yahoo.com

St John #8340
PO Box 535, Lusby, MD 20657-0535
(1475 Sollers Wharf Road)
WE | Lusby || Lusby
C. (410) 326-2987
lusbycharge@gmail.com

St John #1473
6019 Belle Grove Rd, Baltimore, MD 21225
BM | St John || Pumphrey
C. (410) 636-2578
tsjeinfo@gmail.com

St John United Church #7360
10431 Twin Rivers Rd, Columbia, MD 21044
CM | St John || Columbia
C. (410) 730-9137
SJUColumbia@gmail.com

St Johns #4320
1205 N Main St, Hampstead, MD 21074-2200
BS | North Carroll || Hampstead
C. (410) 239-8088
nccpumc@gmail.com

St Johns #3375
216 W SEMINARY AVE, LUTHERVILLE, MD 21093-5337
BS | St John-Idlewylde || Baltimore
C. (410) 825-3969
carol.pazdersky@gmail.com

St Johns #3240
2640 Saint Paul St, Baltimore, MD 21218-4531
BM | St Johns || Baltimore
C. (410) 366-7733
lolwtaj@gmail.com

St Luke #3345
16810 Hereford Rd, Monkton, MD 21111-1418

BS | Hereford Combined || Hereford
C. (410) 343-0968
herefordcharge1@comcast.net

St Luke #4440
60 Bond Ave, Reisterstown, MD 21136-1300

BS | St Lukes || Reisterstown
C. (410) 526-5044
stlukesumcreisterstown@gmail.com

St Luke #4460
350 River Rd, Sykesville, MD 21784-5513

CM | St Luke || Sykesville
C. (301) 977-6740
office_stlukeumcsykesville@aol.com

St Luke #4155
1100 N Gilmor St, Baltimore, MD 21217-2209

BM | St Luke || Baltimore
C. (410) 728-1183
dralw124@aol.com

St Luke #8445
12880 Point Lookout Road, Ridge, MD 20680-0072

WE | St Luke || Scotland
C. (301) 872-5142
pastorofstluke@gmail.com

St Lukes #6690
700 New York Ave, Martinsburg, WV 25401-2124

FR | St Lukes || Martinsburg
C. (304) 263-2788
stlukesumc700@comcast.net

St Lukes #4615
2119 Gwynn Oak Ave, Baltimore, MD 21207-6004

BM | St Lukes || Woodlawn
C. (410) 358-3874
ministermyers2013@gmail.com

St Mark #1350
1440 Dorsey RD, Hanover, MD 21076

AN | St Mark || Hanover
C. (410) 859-5352
tedmack@verizon.net

St Marks #9145
19620 White Ground Rd, Boyds, MD 20841-9412

CM | St Marks || Boyds
C. (443) 463-5851
Stmarksboydsumc@gmail.com

St Mark's #7425
601 8th St, Laurel, MD 20707-3920

AN | St Marks || Laurel
C. (919) 946-5062
stmarkslmd@gmail.com

St Matthews #8280
PO Box 1389, La Plata, MD 20646-1389
(10577 Charles Street)

WE | Mount Calvary/St. Matthews || Rt. 6
C. (301) 934-2203
pastor@route6charge.org

St Matthews #2390
101 Avon Beach Rd, Baltimore, MD 21222-6105

BM | St Matthews || Dundalk
C. (410) 285-4466
kayfran61@gmail.com

St Matthews #2280
627 N Bouldin St, Baltimore, MD 21205-2809

BM | St. Matthews-Orangeville || Baltimore
C. (443) 450-3831
cbtjr7@gmail.com

St Matthews #8125
14900 Annapolis Rd, Bowie, MD 20715-1802

WE | St Matthews || Bowie
C. (301) 262-1408
churchoffice@stmatthews-bowie.org

St Matthews #1520
6234 Shady Side Rd, Shady Side, MD 20764-9685

AN | South County || Shady Side/Lothian
C. (410) 867-7661
smumcss@gmail.com

St Matthews-New Life #3247
416 E 23rd St, Baltimore, MD 21218-5819

BM | St. Matthews-New Life || Baltimore
C. (410) 243-0378
st.matthewsnewlife@comcast.net

St Paul #8345
11000 Hg Trueman Rd, Lusby, MD 20657-2848

WE | St Paul || Lusby
C. (410) 326-4475
stpaulumcinfo@gmail.com

St Paul #2585
2434 Bradenbaugh Rd, White Hall, MD 21161-9661

BS | Norrisville || Norrisville
C. (410) 692-6179
thomasjsullivan@hotmail.com

St Paul #8385
6634 Saint Barnabas Rd, Oxon Hill, MD 20745-2905

WE | St. Paul || Oxon Hill
C. (301) 567-4433
admin@stpumcmd.org

St Paul #7330
2601 Colston Dr, Chevy Chase, MD 20815-3035

GW | St Paul || Chevy Chase
C. (301) 587-5370
stpaulumc-chevychase@verizon.net

St Paul #9345
21720 Laytonsville Rd, Laytonsville, MD 20882-1628

CM | Sunshine || Laytonsville
C. (301) 963-2185
stpaul208@aol.com

St Paul #4620
PO Box 250, New Windsor, MD 21776-0250

FR | St Paul || New Windsor
C. (410) 635-2442
stpaulnewwindsor@gmail.com

St Paul's #9330
10401 Armory Ave, Kensington, MD 20895-3994

GW | St Paul's || Kensington
C. (301) 933-7933
stpaulsunited@stpaulsk.org

St Paul's #5455
PO Box 205, Smithsburg, MD 21783-1950
(51 S. Main St)

CH | Garfield / St. Paul's || Smithsburg
C. (301) 824-3521
maryricketts622@gmail.com

St Paul's #4465
7538 Main St, Sykesville, MD 21784-7361

CM | Sykesville Parish || Sykesville
C. (410) 795-0714
admin@stpaulssykesville.org

St Paul Praise and Worship Center #2290
501 Reisterstown Rd, Pikesville, MD 21208

BM | Pikesville Pimlico || Pikesville
C. (410) 486-2028
sppwc501@verizon.net

Stablers #3435
PO Box 403, Parkton, MD 21120-0403
(1233 Stablers Church Road)

BS | Cedar Grove-Stablers-Bentley Sp || Parkton
C. (410) 343-1297
gladfec@yorkinternet.net

Stone Chapel #4545
1448 Stone Chapel Rd, New Windsor, MD 21776-8802

FR | Stone Chapel || New Windsor
C. (410) 635-2102
puri315@hotmail.com

Strawbridge #4365
PO Box 353, New Windsor, MD 21776-0353

FR | Strawbridge || New Windsor
C. (410) 635-6480
oneministry@strawbridgeumc.org

Sulphur Springs #5615
26600 Gorman Rd SE, Oldtown, MD 21555

CH | Sulphur Springs || Oldtown
C. (301) 478-5244
barneycathy@gmail.com

Taylorsville #4485
4356 Ridge Rd, Mount Airy, MD 21771-8932

FR | Taylorsville || Mt Airy
C. (410) 875-4101
taylorsvilleumc@comcast.net

Texas #3310
9635 Alda Dr, Parkville, MD 21234-1847

BS | Texas || Cockeysville
C. (410) 627-7698
sjfrog1@aol.com

The Everlasting Love #1310
251 SW Pershing Ave, Glen Burnie, MD 21061-3956

AN | The Everlasting Love || Glen Burnie
C. (443) 763-4566
churchp69@hotmail.com

Thurmont #6360
13880 Long Rd, Thurmont, MD 21788-2261

FR | Thurmont || Thurmont
C. (301) 271-4511
kfizer@minister.com

Timonium #3525
2300 Pot Spring Rd, Timonium, MD 21093-2726

BS | Timonium-Fairview || Timonium
C. (410) 252-5500
tumc@timoniumumc.org

Tom's Creek #6170
10926 Simmons Rd, Emmitsburg, MD 21727-8400

FR | Toms Creek || Emmitsburg
C. (301) 447-3171
tomscreekumc@gmail.com

Towson #3550
501 Hampton Ln, Towson, MD 21286-1311

BM | Towson || Towson
C. (410) 823-6511
towsonumc@towsonumc.org

Trinity #4210
2100 Westchester Ave, Catonsville, MD 21228-4757

BM | Trinity || Catonsville
C. (410) 747-5841
trinitycatonsvillepastor@gmail.com

Trinity #1155
1300 West St, Annapolis, MD 21401-3612

AN | Trinity || Annapolis
C. (410) 268-1620
office@trinityannapolis.org

Trinity #1435
952 Patuxent Rd, Odenton, MD 21113-2208

AN | Trinity || Odenton
C. (410) 672-5215
trinityumc_odenton@yahoo.com

Trinity #8435
90 Church Street, Prince Frederick, MD 20678-2142

WE | Trinity || Prince Frederick
C. (410) 535-1782
churchoffice@trinityumchurch.org

Trinity #6175
313 W Main St, Emmitsburg, MD 21727-9195

FR | Trinity || Emmitsburg
C. (301) 447-3740
rwb1.pastor@yahoo.com

Trinity #6225
703 W Patrick St, Frederick, MD 21701-4029

FR | Trinity || Frederick
C. (301) 662-2895
tumc@trinityfrederick.org

Trinity #6710
220 W Martin St, Martinsburg, WV 25401-3331

FR | Trinity || Martinsburg
C. (304) 263-9215
umctrinity@comcast.net

Trinity #5245
122 Grand Ave, Cumberland, MD 21502-3911

CH | Trinity || Cumberland
C. (301) 729-6828
TrinityCumberland5245@gmail.com

Trinity #9280
13700 Schaeffer Rd, Germantown, MD 20874-2225

CM | Trinity || Germantown
C. (301) 540-4300
office@trinity-germantown.org

Trinity-Asbury #5640
PO Box 672, Berkeley Springs, WV 25411-0672
(108 Wilkes St)

CH | Berkeley Springs || Berkeley Springs
C. (304) 258-1033
berkeleyspringsparish@frontier.com

Union #8490
14418 Old Marlboro Pike, Upper Marlboro, MD 20772-2838

WE | Union || Upper Marlboro
C. (301) 627-7389
unionumc1@gmail.com

Union #1385
PO Box 233, Lothian, MD 20711-0233
(274 W Bay Front Road)

AN | Union || Lothian
C. (410) 867-1661
Union.umc274@gmail.com

Union #2115
700 Post Rd, Aberdeen, MD 21001-2024

BS | Harford || Bel Air
C. (410) 939-3761
LJames109@comcast.net

Union #3135
5225 Sweet Air Rd, Baldwin, MD 21013-9723

BS | Union || Baldwin
C. (410) 592-7709
ems1391@aol.com

Union Chapel #3350
17341 Troyer Rd, Monkton, MD 21111-1322

BS | Hereford Combined || Hereford
C. (410) 472-1120
herefordcharge1@comcast.net

Union Chapel #2510
1012 Old Joppa Rd, Joppa, MD 21085-1510

BS | Union Chapel || Joppa
C. (410) 877-3246
ucjoppa@verizon.net

Union Chapel #5570
10123 Valley Rd, Berkeley Springs, WV 25411-3397

CH | Union Chapel || Berkeley Springs
C. (304) 258-2107
UCUMCWV@gmail.com

Union Memorial #1210
3328 Davidsonville Rd, Davidsonville, MD 21035-1946

AN | Union Memorial || Davidsonville
C. (410) 798-0526
unionmemorialumc424@gmail.com

Union Memorial #2320
2500 Harlem Ave, Baltimore, MD 21216-4838

BM | Union Memorial || Baltimore
C. (410) 945-2723
smithjpj@aol.com

Union Street #4550
22 Union St, Westminster, MD 21157-4508

FR | Union Street || Westminster
C. (410) 861-5822
Drlpastor1@verizon.net

Uniontown #4510
3403 Uniontown Rd, Westminster, MD 21158-3577

FR | Middleburg-Uniontown || New Windsor
C. (301) 639-9577
dav1pat2@hotmail.com

United #7275
1920 G St NW, Washington, DC 20006-4303

GW | United || DC
C. (202) 331-1495
info@theunitedchurch.org

Unity #2325
1433 Edmondson Ave, Baltimore, MD 21223-1243

BM | West Baltimore-Unity || Baltimore
C. (410) 728-4826
unityumc@gmail.com

University #7340
3621 Campus Dr, College Park, MD 20740

GW | University || College Park
C. (301) 422-1400
uumc.office@verizon.net

Uvilla #6760
3415 Kearneysville Pike, Shepherdstown, WV 25443

FR | Shenandoah || Shenandoah Junction
C. (304) 876-6272
pastor@sj-umc.org

Vale Summit #5463
PO Box 444, Frostburg, MD 21532-0444
(12630 Vale Summit Rd SW)

CH | Eckhart || Eckhart Mines
C. (301) 689-9585
harpold8736@comcast.net

Van Buren #7280
35 Van Buren St NW, Washington, DC 20012-2150

GW | Van Buren || DC
C. (202) 723-5454
vanburenunitedmethodistchurch@gmail.com

Vernon #3555
PO Box 188, White Hall, MD 21161-0188
(18600 Vernon Road)

BS | Baltimore Co. || Maryland Line
C. (410) 357-5049
vernonumc@yahoo.com

Violetville #3260
3648 Coolidge Ave, Baltimore, MD 21229-5140

BM | Violetville || Baltimore
C. (410) 525-3191
violetvilleumc@gmail.com

Walkersville #6420
22 Main St, Walkersville, MD 21793

FR | Walkersville & Mt. Pleasant || Walkersville
C. (301) 845-9860
revmikehenning@gmail.com

Wards Chapel #4410
11023 Liberty Rd, Randallstown, MD 21133-1012

BS | Wards Chapel || Randallstown
C. (410) 922-6556
wardschapel@verizon.net

Wards Memorial #8165
2265 Wards Chapel Rd, Owings, MD 20736-9353

WE | Wards Memorlal || Chesapeake Beach
C. (410) 257-7644
revtina03@verizon.net

Washington Grove #9470
303 Chestnut Ave, Washington Grove, MD 20880-2031

CM | Washington Grove || Washington Grove
C. (301) 869-3753
washingtongroveumc@gmail.com

Washington Square #5360
538 Washington Ave., Hagerstown, MD 21740-4662

CH | Washington Square || Hagerstown
C. (301) 739-2653
whagumparish@gmail.com

Water's Edge Partnership Initiative #3113
2400 Boston St Ste 102, Baltimore, MD 21224-4780

BM | Water's Edge Partnership || Baltimore
C. (301) 606-6687
sburke@watersedgepartnership.org

Waters Memorial #8465
5400 Mackall Rd, Saint Leonard, MD 20685-2307

WE | Waters Memorial || St Leonard
C. (410) 586-1716
watersumc@hotmail.com

Waugh #3335
11453 Long Green Pike, Glen Arm, MD 21057-9215

BS | Fork - Waugh || Fork
C. (410) 592-8303
fork_waugh_secretary@forkumc.org

Weller #6365
101 N Altamont Ave, Thurmont, MD 21788-1850

FR | Weller || Thurmont
C. (301) 271-2802
secretary@wellerumc.com

Wesley #4330
3239 Carrollton Rd, Hampstead, MD 21074-1912

BS | Wesley || Hampstead
C. (410) 374-4027
wesley@wesleychurch-hampstead.org

Wesley Chapel #1365
7745 Waterloo Rd, Jessup, MD 20794-9793

AN | Northeast || Elkridge
C. (410) 799-3494
pastor@wesleychapelumcjessup.org

Wesley Chapel #1390
1010 Wrighton Rd, Lothian, MD 20711-9735

AN | Wesley Chapel || Lothian
C. (410) 741-9258
marvene_young@hotmail.com

Wesley Chapel #6385
3519 Urbana Pike, Frederick, MD 21704

CM | Wesley Chapel || Urbana
C. (301) 663-4956
eph5v17@gmail.com

Wesley Chapel #5575
PO Box 513, Berkeley Springs, WV 25411-0513
(165 Pious Ridge Rd)

CH | Berkeley Springs || Berkeley Springs
C. (304) 258-1033
berkeleyspringsparish@frontier.com

Wesley Freedom #4225
961 Johnsville Rd, Eldersburg, MD 21784-4903

CM | Wesley Freedom || Eldersburg
C. (410) 795-2777
office@wesleyfreedom.org

Wesley Grove #1355
1320 Dorsey Rd, Hanover, MD 21076-1453

AN | Wesley Grove || Harmans
C. (410) 761-9119
cdamm@comcast.net

Wesley Grove #9515
23640 Woodfield Rd, Gaithersburg, MD 20882-2818

CM | South Damascus || Damascus
C. (301) 253-2894
WGUMC@wesleygroveumc.org

Wesleyan Chapel #2470
409 N Paradise Rd, Aberdeen, MD 21001-1629

BS | Susquehanna || Havre De Grace
C. (410) 914-5276
chapel.aberdeen@gmail.com

West Baltimore #4165
5130 Greenwich Ave, Baltimore, MD 21229-2314

BM | West Baltimore-Unity || Baltimore
C. (410) 945-8397
dr4man@verizon.net

West Liberty #4343
2000 Sand Hill Rd, Marriottsville, MD 21104-1649

CM | West Liberty || Marriottsville
C. (410) 442-2969
west.libertyumc.mail@gmail.com

West Liberty #3560
Robert E. Stevenson 20501 West Liberty Rd, White Hall, MD 21161

BS | Bosley-West Liberty || Sparks
C. (410) 343-0295
kathleencheyney@aol.com

West Montgomery #9580
21000 Beallsville Rd, Dickerson, MD 20842-9069

CM | West Montgomery || Barnesville
C. (443) 463-5851
westmontgomeryumc@gmail.com

Westernport #5465
434 Vine St, Westernport, MD 21562-1220

CH | Barton/Westernport || Barton
C. (301) 359-3515
westernportumc5465@gmail.com

Westminster #4555
165 E Main St, Westminster, MD 21157-5013

FR | Westminster || Westminster
C. (410) 848-8325
S.Haines@wumcmd.org

Westphalia #8510
9363 Darcy Rd, Upper Marlboro, MD 20774-2424

WE | Westphalia || Upper Marlboro
C. (301) 735-9373
swest@westphaliaum.org

William Watters Memorial #2485
1451 Jarrettsville Rd, Jarrettsville, MD 21084-1627

BS | West Harford || Forest Hill
C. (410) 692-5227
kfizer@minister.com

Williams Memorial #6740
3415 Kearneysville Pike, Shepherdstown, WV 25443

FR | Shenandoah || Shenandoah Junction
C. (304) 876-6272
pastor@sj-umc.org

Williamsport #5475
25 E Church St, Williamsport, MD 21795-1549

CH | Williamsport || Williamsport
C. (301) 223-7040
williamsportumc@gmail.com

Wilson Memorial #1290
PO Box 460, Gambrills, MD 21054-0460
(1113 Md Route 3 North)

AN | Wilson Memorial || Gambrills
C. (410) 721-1482
wilsonmem1113@gmail.com

Wiseburg #3565
810 Wiseburg Rd, White Hall, MD 21161-9466

BS | Parkton || Parkton-Sparks
C. (410) 357-4077
gbaer649061@comcast.net

Zion #4560
2716 Old Washington Rd, Westminster, MD 21157-7546

FR | Zion || Westminster
C. (410) 857-4444
puri315@hotmail.com

Zion #5250
12201 Bedford Rd NE, Cumberland, MD 21502-6811

CH | Wesley || Cumberland
C. (601) 310-9922
marjoriehurder@gmail.com

Zion #8325
21291 Three Notch Rd, Lexington Park, MD 20653-2428

WE | Zion || Lexington Park
C. (301) 863-5161

Zion Wesley #8535
11500 Berry Rd, Waldorf, MD 20603

WE | Asbury/Zion Wesley || Waldorf
C. (301) 645-7340
cindyholmes10@gmail.com

ALPHABETICAL ROLL AND DIRECTORY - CLERGY

Code Used (following Name):

CC = Charge Church
FE = Elder in full connection
AM = Associate Member of Conference
PM = Provisional (Probationary) Member of Conference
PD = Provisional (Probationary) Deacon
FD = Deacon in Full Connection
DM = Diaconal Minister (consecrated under provisions of 1992 Discipline or earlier)
OD = Deacon member of other annual conference
PE = Provisional (Probationary) Elder
OE = Elder member of other annual conference or other Methodist denomination
OF = Full member of other denomination
AF = Affiliate member
OA = Associate member of other Annual Conference
OP = Provisional (Probationary) member of other Annual Conference
FL = Full time Local Pastor
PL = Part time Local Pastor
RE = Retired Full Elder
RP = Retired Provisional Member
RA = Retired Associate Member
RD = Retired Deacon in Full Connection
RL = Retired Local Pastor
DR = Retired Diaconal Minister (consecrated under provisions of 1992 or earlier Discipline)
LP = Other Local Pastor
LM = Certified Lay Minister
PT = Part-Time Appointment
OR = Retired Serving other conference
SY = Lay Pastor

Appointments held in the Annual Conference are listed in the Pastoral Record according to the years of appointment and in conformity with the General Conference listings. Therefore, the yearly figure can be shown only once. Each date indicated in the record shows the first year of the particular appointment.

Appointments held before ADMISSION ON TRIAL are not located in the record.

KEY:

Name Clergy Status	Charge Conference/Appointment	Church/Office Phone
Address		Home Phone
Email		Cell Phone
Pastoral Record		

Abayomi, Kwame O.   RE   BM | Unity || Baltimore ||| 2325
3101 Waterview Ave, Baltimore, MD 21230-3511   H. (443) 253-9782
1983, St. Luke-Mt. Gregory Chg; 1986, Aquasco: Christ; 1989, Unity; 01-01-2007, Retired.

Abell, Patricia   FE   CM | St James || Marriottsville ||| 4565
12450 Old Frederick Rd, Marriottsville, MD 21104-1415   H. (410) 680-8426
pabell42@gmail.com
2011, Dickerson: Dickerson-Forest Grove.; 2016, West Friendship: West Ellicott City Chrg

Adams, Ann   RE CM | Ebenezer || Sykesville ||| 4575
1200 Pine Heights Ave , Baltimore, MD 21229-5128   H. (410) 646-0796
revannadams@msn.com
1999, Baltimore: Violetville & Baltimore: Fulton Siemers Mem./Christ Church of Deaf;
1-01-03, Attend school, 1-01-03, Baltimore: Violetville; 2004, Baltimore: Violetville/Christ
Baltimore Co; 1-01-05, Baltimore: Christ Church-Violetville Cooperative Parish, 2005, Christ
Church Baltimore County; 2007, Leave of Absence; 11-17-11, Retired; 2012, Middle River:
Orems.

Adams, Dauba D.   FL   CM | Providence || Monrovia ||| 9325
3735 Kemptown Church Rd, Monrovia, MD 21770-8701   H. (301) 253-1768
dwdadam@gmail.com
2011, Kemptown: Providence.

Aguilera, Teresa   SY   FR | Calvary || Martinsburg ||| 6655
349 Gantt Dr , Martinsburg, WV 25403-0278
salvation320@hotmail.com
1-1-16, Martinsburg: Calvary Charge

Aist, Clark   RE   WE | Cheltenham || Cheltenham ||| 8155
11701 Van Brady Rd , Upper Marlboro, MD 20772-7929   H. (301) 782-3302
clark.aist@gmail.com
1960, New Market; 1965, Attending school; 1969, Dir., Prot. Chap. Activities, St. Eliz. Hosp.
(Wash.); 1990, Dir. Chap. Ser. Br., Clinical Support Ser., Comm. Mental Health Ser., D.C;
2004, Retired.

Aist, George   RE WE | Cheltenham || Cheltenham ||| 8155
415 Russell Ave Apt 619, Gaithersburg, MD 20877-2838   H. (301) 216-5429
george.aist@gmail.com
1959, Oella-Bethany; 1963, Woodberry; 1966, New Windsor; 1968, St. Paul-Bethel, New
Windsor Parish; 1969, Intern, St. Eliz. Hosp. (Wash.); 1970, Residency, St. Eliz. Hosp. (Wash.);
1971, Friendship and Friendship: Carters; 1976, Fort Washington; 1980, Camp Springs:
Bells; 1988 Wash.: Wesley; 1992, Frostburg: Frostburg; 1999, Upper Marlboro: Bethel; 2004,
Retired; 2011, Accokeek: Faith; 2015, Retired

Albury, Kay F.   RE   BM | St Matthews || Baltimore ||| 2390   (410) 285-6644
5900 Loch Raven Blvd , Baltimore, MD 21239-2440   H. (443) 629-3211
kayfran61@gmail.com
1979, Attending school; 1980, Wash.: Asbury; 1982, Fairmont Hgts. Grace; 1985, Baltimore;
Ames; 2004, St Leonard: Brooks; 2009, Severna Park: Asbury Town Neck; 2011, Guide
Baltimore Region; 2013, Dundalk: St Matthews; 2019, Retired.

Aldridge, Jr., Chip D. FE GW | Dumbarton || Washington ||| 7160 (202) 885-8686
15508 Letcher Rd E, Brandywine, MD 20613-8521 H. (703) 836-1549
caldridge@wesleyseminary.edu
1983, W.N. Ca. Conference, 1989, Baltimore Conference, Assistant Director for Seminary
Relations, Wesley Theo. Seminary; 1992, Dir. of Seminary Relations, Wesley Theo. Seminary;
1995, Dir. of Recruitment, Wesley Theo. Seminary; 2000, Director of Admissions, Wesley Theo.
Seminary.

Alexander, Jo Anne RE FR | Oakland || Charles Town ||| 6535
104 Oakland Ter , Charles Town, WV 25414-4815 H. (304) 725-5233
rev.joanne@gmail.com
1977, Jefferson County Coop. Parish: Central Charge; 1980, Central Charge; 1984, Bethany-
Oakland ; 1987, Charles Town and Bethany; 9/19/93, Oakland; 2014, Retired.

Allen, Barbara PL BS | Shiloh || Hampstead ||| 4325 (410) 933-5301
3014 Brendan Ave, Baltimore, MD 21213 H. (443) 255-1802
ballenpsalm34@msn.com
2014, Hampstead: Shiloh -Patapsco Cooperative Parish.

Allen, Carletta FE AN | Asbury || Annapolis ||| 1110 (240) 938-1594
31 Lafayette Ave, Annapolis, MD 21401-2811 H. (240) 938-1954
asbury1pastor@gmail.com
1996, Wheaton: Hughes; 1999, Sykesville: St. Luke-Mt. Gregory Chg; 2005, Columbia:
Locust; 2011, Annapolis: Asbury.

Allen, Patricia FE WE | Oxon Hill || Oxon Hill ||| 8380 (410) 963-8942
6400 Livingston Rd, Oxon Hill, MD 20745-2909 H. (410) 963-8942
PastorP527@gmail.com
2007, Glen Burnie: Hall; 2015, Oxon Hill: Oxon Hill

Allmond, Sheridan B. FE BS | Mount Olive || Randallstown ||| 4390 (443) 386-1256
7410 Millwood Rd , Windsor Mill, MD 21244-2849 H. (443) 386-1256
sallmond03@gmail.com
2017, Randallstown: Mount Olive, 2010, Baltimore: Christ/Violetville; 2012, Highland:
Hopkins/Mt. Olivet.

Alsgaard, Erik FE GW | Metropolitan Memorial || Washington ||| 7630 (410) 309-3453
6821 Martin Rd, Columbia, MD 21044-4017
ealsgaard@bwcumc.org
2015, Extension Ministry.

Altman, Kathy L. FE FR | Sandy Mount || Finksburg ||| 4443
165 Winifred Dr, Hanover, PA 17331-7993 H. (240) 285-5800
RevKathyAltman@verizon.net
2008, Laytonsville: Mt Tabor; 2011, Westminster: Westminster; 2013, Annapolis: Mayo; 2018,
Sandy Mount: Sandy Mount.

Amos, Edison M. RE GW | Potomac || Potomac ||| 9390
561 NW Floresta Dr, Port St Lucie, FL 34983-8613 H. (772) 878-4634
1952, Attending school; 1953, St. James: St. James; 1957, Attending school; 1959, D.C.:
Dumbarton Ave; 1964, Baltimore: Epworth Chapel; 1972, Silver Spring: Good Shepherd;
1978, Rockville: Rockville; 1984, Potomac: Potomac; 1994, Retired.

Ampiah-Addison, John PL CM | Asbury || Germantown ||| 9265
8204 Coneflower Way, Gaithersburg, MD 20877-1037 H. (301) 987-2731
addisco5@yahoo.com
2014, Damascus: South Damascus; 2019, Germantown: Asbury.

Anderson, Cheryl B. FE CM | Grace || Gaithersburg ||| 9260
2121 Sheridan Rd , Evanston, IL 60201-2926 H. (847) 425-9382
cheryl.anderson@garrett.edu
1990, Gaithersburg: Grace; 1993, Attending school; 2000, Ext. Ministry, Garrett-Evangelical Theo. Sem.

Anderson, George W. RE WE | Mount Oak || Mitchellville ||| 8355
2912 Apple Green Ln , Bowie, MD 20716-3832 H. (301) 249-4281
georgeandcarol16@verizon.net
1954, Kansas Conference; 1962, Mont. Conference; 1967, Baltimore Conference, Mitchellville: Mt. Oak; 2001, Retired.

Ankeny, Edwin A. RE BM | Mount Vernon Place || Baltimore ||| 3215 (410) 309-3441
103 Kenilworth Park Dr Apt 3B, Towson, MD 21204-2265 H. (410) 296-5598
eaads@comcast.net
1959, Pittsbgh. Conference; 1961, Baltimore Conference, Parkton: Cedar Grove; 1965, Sandy Mount: Sandy Mount; 1968, Baltimore: Hillsdale-Chatsworth; 1974, Annpaolis: Eastport; 1983, Baltimore: Mount Vernon Place; 1996, Dist. Superintendent Balt. North; 2004, Retired.

Annis-Forder, Gayle E. FE CM | Linden-Linthicum || Clarksville ||| 9180
7604 Willow Bottom Rd, Sykesville, MD 21784-5651 H. (410) 552-8347
pastorgayle@l-lumc.org
1982, Attending school; 1983, Fred: Trinity; 1984, Wheaton: Glenmont; 1987, Reisterstown: Grace-Bosley Chg; 1992, Hebbville: Salem; 1996, Winfield: Ebenezer; 2006, Baltimore: Loch Raven; 2011, Clarksville: Linden-Linthicum.

Archibald, James P. RE CM | Damascus || Damascus ||| 9190
PO Box 1035 , Penney Farms, FL 32079-1035 H. (904) 529-8688
1950, No. Ill. Conf; 1955, Bolivar: Camp Hill; 1957, Baltimore: Calvary; 1960, Towson: Providence; 1964, Chevy Chase: St. Paul; 1969, D.C.: Capitol Hill; 1978, Silver Spring: Good Shepherd; 1987, Damascus: Damascus-Friendship Chg; 1996, Retired.

Argo, Archie D. (David) RE GW | Foundry || Washington ||| 7180
2877 Arizona Ter NW , Washington, DC 20016-2642
adavidargo@yahoo.com
1971, Western North Carolina Conference; 1975, Baltimore Conference, Indian Head: Indian Head Chg; 1980, D.C.: Eldbrooke; 1987, Glenelg: Glenelg; 1995, D.C.: Capitol Hill; 2000, Kensington: St. Paulís; 2003, District Superintendent, Greater Washington District; 2011, Director of Connectional Ministries; 01-01-2007, District Superintendent; 2011, Director of Connectional Ministries; 03-01-2012, Director of Connectional Ministries; 01-18-2013, Retired.

Armiger, Helen RE BM | Salem-Hebbville || Baltimore ||| 4335
910 70th Dr E, Sarasota, FL 34243-1213 H. 410-747-2396
helenarmiger@gmail.com
2001, Parkton: Cedar Grove-Parke Memorial Charge; 2006, New Windsor: St. Paul; 2007, New Windsor: St Paul; 2011, New Windsor: St. Paul/New Hope of New Windsor Coop. Parish; 2013, Hebbville: Salem.; 2016, Retired

Armstrong, Michael W. FE GW | Colesville || Silver Spring |||| 9450 (301) 384-1941
1917 Dana Dr , Adelphi, MD 20783-2120 H. (301) 434-0930
revmwarmstrong@gmail.com
American Baptist Conv; 2002, D.C.: Mckendree-Simms-Brookland; 2008, DC: McKendree-Simms-Brookland; 2011, Campus, Min. Howard University; 2014, Silver Spring: Colesville.

Armwood, Bernadette A. FE BM | St John || Baltimore |||| 1473 (410) 636-2578
7000 Rudisill Ct Apt 1B, Windsor Mill, MD 21244-5409 H. (410) 521-3551
armwoodb@aol.com
2006, Baltimore: Homestead; 2011, Barnesville: West Montgomery; 2018, Pumphrey: St John.

Arnicar, William L. SY FR | Ganotown || Martinsburg |||| 6550 (304) 839-6880
25 Crab Apple Ln, Ranson, WV 25438-1247 H. (304) 839-6880
warnicar@comcast.net
2018, Ganotown: Ganotown,

Arnold, Glen L. FE AN | Cedar Grove-Oakland || Deale |||| 1215 (410) 867-7417
10733 Castleton Turn, Upper Marlboro, MD 20774-1449 H. (301) 324-5610
pastor@cgumc.org
1989, St. Leonard: Waters Memorial; 1996, Glenn Dale: Glenn Dale; 2002, Sandy Mount: Sandy Mount; 2008, Jarrettsville: Jarrettsville; 2013, Deale: Cedar Grove-Oakland.

Arroyo, Giovanni FE FR | Trinity || Frederick |||| 6225
7612 Harmons Farm Ct, Hanover, MD 21076 H. (202) 495-2943
garroyog@aol.com
2004, Baltimore: Salem; 2007, Baltimore: Salem-Hispanic Charge; 2010, Ext. Ministry, GCORR: Team Leader for Program Ministries.

Atkins, Ann RE CH | Mc Kendree of Potomac Park || Cumberland |||| 5242
886 Sperry Ter, Cumberland, MD 21502-3405 H. (301) 268-6597
annvatkins@gmail.com
1991, Rawlings: Westernport; 01/1/93, Bethesda: North Bethesda; 1996, Hagerstown: Otterbein; 2000, Middle River: Orems; 2009, Cumberland: Centre Street; 2014, Leave of Absence; 2014, Retired.

Atkins, Harold P RE CH | Mc Kendree of Potomac Park || Cumberland |||| 5242
886 Sperry Ter, Cumberland, MD 21502-3405 H. (301) 268-6785
hpatkins@outlook.com
1993, Attending school; 1995, Mt. Rainier: Cedar Lane; 1996, Hagerstown: Washington Square; 2000, Baltimore: Bethesda; 2002, Baltimore: Overlea Chapel; 2009, Mount Savage: Mount Savage; 2011, Cresaptown: Cresaptown; 2018, Retired.

Atkinson, Donald RP BM | New Waverly || Baltimore |||| 3217 (410) 243-2481
2815 Mohawk Ave , Baltimore, MD 21207-7473 H. (410) 448-4662
2001, Lutherville: Lutherville Chg; 2004, Baltimore: New Waverly; 12/1/2005, Incapacity Leave; 2011, Retired.

Ayers, Jane SY BS | Ebenezer || Fallston |||| 2430
janeay@earthlink.net H. (410) 800-8672
2019, Forest Hill: West Harford

Ayers, Phillip R. FE   CM | Howard Chapel-Ridgeville || Mount Airy |||| 9355
13778 Blythedale Dr, Mount Airy, MD 21771-5852   H. (301) 751-3262
payers001@comcast.net
1986, Frederick: Trinity; 1992, Hyattstown; 1997, Mechanicsville: Mt. Zion; 2007,
Gaithersburg: Covenant; 2012, Baltimore: St. Johns-Idlewylde Coop Parish; 2014, Mt Airy:
Howard Chapel-Ridgeville.

Baek, Myungha FE   CM | Pleasant Grove || Ijamsville |||| 9320
7326 Springfield Ave, Sykesville, MD 21784-7549   H. (240) 477-2624
pastormhbaek@gmail.com
2012, Galesville: Galesville; 2013, Damascus: South Damascus; 2014, Monrovia: Mountain
View-Pleasant Grove.

Baker, John P. RE   GW | Foundry || Washington |||| 7180
3700 N Capitol St NW # 418, Washington, DC 20011-8400   H. (703) 360-2518
1986, D.C.: Foundry; 1991, Retired.

Baker, Kevin M. FE   CM | Oakdale Emory || Olney |||| 9375
3725 Route 97, Glenwood, MD 21738-9614   H. (410) 489-4406
kbaker@oakdale.church
1990, Prince Frederick: Trinity;1993, Deale: Cedar Grove (1/1/06, Cedar Grove-Oakland);
2006, Olney: Oakdale-Emory.

Baker, Richard FL   FR | Messiah || Taneytown |||| 4475   (410) 756-6085
3893 Sells Mill Rd , Taneytown, MD 21787-2547   H. (443) 375-9556
rwb1.pastor@yahoo.com
1999, Mount Pleasant: Mount Pleasant; 2012, Walkersville: Walkersville; 2014, Walkersville:
Walkersville/Mt. Pleasant/Mt. Zion Coop Parrish; 2018, Emmitsburg: Trinity, 2018,
Taneytown: Messiah.

Balderas, Miguel A. FE   GW | Liberty Grove || Burtonsville |||| 9155   (301) 946-2500
7980 Inverness Ridge Rd, Potomac, MD 20854-4009   H. (202) 841-0358
mbald20879@gmail.com
2004, Hyattsville: First; 2008, Oxon Hill: Oxon Hill; 2013, Rockville: Millian Memorial;
2019, Burtonsville: Liberty Grove,

Ball, William C. FL   FR | Pikeside || Martinsburg |||| 6725   (304) 263-4633
565 Tuscawilla Dr, Charles Town, WV 25414-5061   H. (304) 579-3233
billballwv@gmail.com
2017, Martinsburg: Pikeside,

Bandel, Lisa M. FE   BS | Wards Chapel || Randallstown |||| 4410
6252 Longleaf Pine Rd, Sykesville, MD 21784-4916   H. (443) 285-9616
pastorlisa@comcast.net
1997, Ellicott City: Bethany; 2002, Lisbon: Lisbon; 01-01-2011, Davidsonville:
Davidsonville.; 2016, Randallstown: Wards Chapel Charge

Bane, Harvey M. RL   FR | Marvin Chapel || Inwood |||| 6670
126 Cedar Ridge Dr, Lagrange, GA 30241-9436   H. (304) 754-8042
harbane22@aol.com
1994, Martinsburg: Berkeley Place; Martinsburg: Marvin Chapel/Bethel Bakerton.

Banks, Cindy   PL   WE | Shiloh || Bryans Road ||| 8140   (301) 503-6800
5660 Port Tobacco Rd, Indian Head, MD 20640-3511   H. (301) 503-6800
pastorcindyb@gmail.com
2007, Indian Head: Metropolitan-Indian Head Coop Parish; 03-01-2012, Bryanis Road:
Shiloh.

Banks, Jacques   PL   WE | Indian Head || Indian Head ||| 8265
5660 Port Tobacco Rd, Indian Head, MD 20640-3511   H. (301) 246-9078
pastorjtbanks@gmail.com
2007, Indian Head: Metropolitan-Indian Head Coop Parish; 10-01-2013, Indian Head: Indian
Head.

Barcelo, Maria A.   RE   (410) 263-5490
2028 1/2 Francisco St, Berkeley, CA 94709-2126   H. (410) 432-6159
revmaan.berkeleyca@gmail.com
2002, Baltimore: Grace, Associate; 2005, Annapolis: Eastport; 2014, Retired.

Barger, Rebecca K. (Kay)   RE   CH | Otterbein || Hagerstown ||| 5340
18710 Dover Dr, Hagerstown, MD 21742-2468   H. (240) 707-6516
rkbrkb@myactv.net
1970, Attending school; 1972, Baltimore: Brooklyn Associate; 1974, Baltimore: Roland Ave;
1979, Boonsboro: Mt. Nebo; 1984, Hagerstown: Emmanuel; 1990, Wheaton: Glenmont; 2000,
Rockville: Rockville; 2010, Retired; 09-01-13, Rockville:Mill Creek Parish.

Barnes, Jr., Robert   FE   WE | Mount Oak || Mitchellville ||| 8355   (301) 249-2230
225 New York Ave, Pasadena, md 21122   H. (410) 317-5177
pastorbob@mtoak.org
1986, Cumb.: First; 1990, Parkton; Cedar Grove-Parke Mem; 1994, Bedington: Bedington;
2011, Glen Burnie: Glen Burnie.; 2016, Mitchellville: Mount Oak Charge

---

Barnes, Roland   PL   WE | Carroll-Western || Prince Frederick ||| 8425   (301) 669-4933
27883 Ben Oaks Dr , Mechanicsville, MD 20659-3340   H. (301) 884-4466
rsbarnes@md.metrocast.net
2005, Prince Frederick: Carroll-Western.

Barnes, Valerie A.   FE   AN | Carters || Tracys Landing ||| 1270   (202) 903-3355
33 55th St SE , Washington, DC 20019-6565   H. (202) 903-3355
revvab@comcast.net
2017, Owensville: Chews Memorial/Carters, 1998, Germantown: Trinity, 1999, Chase: Chase
Chg; 1/1/02, Chase: Sharp Street; 2010, Leave of Absence; 2013, Baltimore: Beechfield.

Barr, Jr., Ira   FE   BM | Arbutus || Baltimore ||| 3110   (410) 204-8906
1227 Maple Ave, Halethorpe, MD 21227-2639   H. (410) 242-3466
irabarr2@verizon.net
1984, Attending school; 1986, Manchester: Manchester Chg; 1991, Manchester: Bixlers-
Millers Chg; 2004, Arbutus: Arbutus.

Barrick, Glenn   RL   BS | Cranberry || Perryman ||| 2540
412 Roundhouse Dr, Perryville, MD 21903-3041   H. (410) 642-2673
gbarrick54@gmail.com
2017, Retired, 2000, Perryman: Cranberry.

Barss, Reg   RE   AN | Magothy || Pasadena ||| 1450   410-255-2420
1227 River Bay Rd, Annapolis, MD 21409-4901   H. (410) 757-4709
rdbarss@verizon.net
06-30-18, Pasadena: Magothy, 1970, East Ohio Conference; 1972, Baltimore Conference,
Cumberland: Trinity; 1976, Baltimore: Andrew Chapel; 1979, Attending school; 1980, Chap.,
City of Memphis Women's Hospital; 1981, Savage: Savage; 1983, Linthicum Hgts: Linthicum
Hgts; 1990, Mayo: Mayo; 2001, Pasadena: Magothy.

Bateman, Juliana   SY   BM | Mount Washington-Aldersgate || Baltimore ||| 3220
302 Fourth Ave, Baltimore, MD 21227-3208   H.
juliana.bateman@gmail.com
09-01-16, Baltimore: Mt Washington-Aldersgate, 10-11-16, No Appointment,

---

Bauman, Jr., Edward W.   RE   GW | Foundry || Washington ||| 7180
7514 Cayuga Ave , Bethesda, MD 20817-4822   H. (301) 229-8923
papa7514@aol.com
1951, N.E. Ohio Conference; 1957, Baltimore Conference, Prof. Wesley Seminary; 1965, D.C.:
Foundry; 1992, Retired.

Baxter, Harry T   RE   GW | College Park || College Park ||| 7335
1203 Walker Rd Apt 116, Dover, DE 19904-6541   H. (302) 659-1251
Baxter1961@earthlink.net
1962, Philadelphia Conference; 1964, Baltimore Conference, Mt. Airy: Poplar Springs; 1968,
Arnold: Asbury; 1977, Hagerstown: Emmanuel; 10/83, Leave of Absence; 1986, Landover
Hills: Christ; 1991, Germantown: Morningstar; 1993, College Park: College Park; 2003,
Retired.

Beall, Kevin W.   PL   CM | Bethesda || Damascus ||| 9185
13220 Lewisdale Rd , Clarksburg, MD 20871-9665   H. (240) 994-7861
kwbeall7@gmail.com
12-20-17, Certified Candidate, 2018, Damascus: Bethesda,

Beaudwin, Walter   FE   WE | St Paul || Lusby ||| 8345   (410) 326-4475
10960 Hg Trueman Rd, Lusby, MD 20657-2847   H. (240) 925-6686
Walter.beaudwin@gmail.com
2005, Chicamuxen: Chicamuxen; 2008, Dunkirk: Smithville; 2015, Lusby: St Paul.

Becker, Janet   RE
314 Milton Ave, Glen Burnie, MD 21061-2238   H. (410) 766-4927
catonsville.trinity@verizon.net
1982, Attend school; 1983, Parkton: W. Liberty; 1989, Severn: Severn; 1995, Harmans: Wesley
Grove; 2006, Catonsville: Emanuel-Trinity; 2007, Catonsville: Emanuel-Trinity; 2015, Retired

---

Beehler, Susan R.   RE   GW | Metropolitan Memorial || Washington ||| 7630   (410) 635-2500
8103 LA Paloma Cir, El Paso, TX 79907-7412   H. (915) 858-5363
sraybeehler@gmail.com
1981, Attending school; 1982, Ecum. Campus Ministry; 1984, Wash: Metropolitan Memil;
1987, Jarrettsville: Jarrettsville; 1988 Leave of Absence; 1992, Staff Person, Hacienda Springs
Inc., Women Song & UTEP; 2003, Retired.

Beiber, Michael R.   FE   CH | Mount Zion || Myersville |||| 6325
601 Main StreetPO Box 299, Myersville, MD 21773-0299   H. (301) 293-1258
rev.mike.beiber@gmail.com
2008, Accokeek: Faith; 2011, Cheltenham: Cheltenham; 2014, Myersville: Mount Zion.

Bekhor, Stephanie   OE   AN | Marley || Glen Burnie |||| 1335
3708 Alton Pl NW, Washington, DC 20016-2206   H. (202) 870-1634
graisim@yahoo.com
3708 Alton Pl NW, Washington, DC 20016-2206   *R.*
Unlisted 2014, Glen Burnie: Marley.

Bell, Ruth   RD   CM | Glen Mar || Ellicott City |||| 7365
5400 Vantage Point Rd Apt 107, Columbia, MD 21044-2657   H. (410) 465-1183
jamesruthbell@verizon.net
1996, Glengary Parish; 1997, Ellicott City: Glen Mar; 1999, Deacon in Full Connecion;
08/01/01, D.C.: Metrpolitan Memorial; 11/1/03, Retired.

Belt, Cynthia   FE AN | Mount Zion || Laurel |||| 7420   (410) 276-3079
2647 Carver Rd , Gambrills, MD 21054-1716   H. (443) 336-7637
revcbelt@gmail.com
1997, Gambrills: Mt. Tabor; 1/1/2000, Severn: New Beginnings; 2006, Baltimore: Centennial
Caroline.; 3-1-16, Elkridge: Harwood Park/Mt. Zion Charge

Benjamin, Paul   RE   BS | Emory || Street |||| 2555
1501 Barrons Gate Ave, Woodbridge, NJ 07095-3851   H. (410) 638-7565
psrbenj03@aol.com
1993, Iowa Conference; 2000, Balti. Wash. Conference, Street: Emory; 2010, Retired.

Benjamin, Sherwyn   PE   CM | Damascus || Damascus |||| 9190   (202) 723-5300
13755 Lark Song Dr, Germantown, MD 20874-6214   H. (301) 972-4256
sabenjamin3@gmail.com
2013, DC: Petworth; 2018, Damascus: Damascus.

Bennett, Donna H.   RE
2361 Merrill Rd , York, PA 17403-5021   H. (717) 741-3749
1979, Joppa: Union Chapel; 1984, Harmans: Wesley Grove; 1988 Norrisville: Norrisville-
Ayers Chapel Chg; 1997, Disability Leave.

Bennett, John W.   RD   FR | Middletown || Middletown |||| 6280   (301) 371-5550
3 Sara Ln, Middletown, MD 21769-7885   H. (301) 371-6866
john_30201@msn.com
2004,Middletown: Middletown; 01-01-2011, Retired.

Bennett, Judith   SY   WE | Alexandria Chapel || Indian Head |||| 8390
5037 Preston Ln, Pomfret, MD 20675-3020   H. (301) 753-4335
pastor.alexandriachapel@gmail.com
2019, Indian Head: Alexandria Chapel.

Bennett, Michael W.   FE   CH | Rehoboth || Williamsport |||| 5470   (301) 223-9554
86 Aquifer Dr, Falling Waters, WV 25419-4303   H. (410) 980-5265
mirlinx51@gmail.com
2000, Berkeley Springs: Alpine Charge; 2004, Berkeley Springs: Union Chapel; 2006, Deale:
Cedar Grove; 2013, Williamsport: Rehoboth.

66

Bentzinger, Rebecca J.   FE   GW | Dumbarton || Washington |||| 7160   (202) 877-2045
435 M St NW , Washington, DC 20001-4607   H. (202) 783-3665
dczinger@aol.com
1979, Iowa Conference; 1984 Baltimore Conference, Staff Chap. CPE Superv. NIH; 01-15-93, Chap. Sup., Research Med. Ctr., Kansas City MO; 9-94, Chap./CPE, Childrenis Hospital; Pastoral Care; 9-15-97, Wash. Hospital Center; 2007, General Board of Higher Education.

Bergen, Charles D.   PL   CH | Trinity-Asbury || Berkeley Springs |||| 5640
214 Woodside Ln, Berkeley Springs, WV 25411-5886   H. (304) 671-8767
chuck.bergen@gmail.com
2013, Berkeley Springs: Berkeley Springs Parish; 2014, Berkeley Springs: Berkeley Springs Charge.

Berger, Brian A.   PL   WE | Waters Memorial || Saint Leonard |||| 8465   (443) 989-8711
PO Box 307, Arnold, MD 21012   H. (410) 507-5742
brianaberger@gmail.com
2018, St Leonard: Waters Memorial, 2015, Ferndale: Ferndale.

Berkowitz, Emily   FE   CM | Ashton || Ashton |||| 9110
18107 Rolling Meadow Way, Olney, MD 20832-1782   H. (301) 512-7311
revemilyb@gmail.com
2011, Buckeystown: Buckeystown (Rt 85); 2014, Ashton: Ashton.

Berry, Patricia   RL   WE | Mount Olive || Prince Frederick |||| 8430   (410) 535-5756
9104 Locksley Rd , Ft Washington, MD 20744-6853   H. (301) 839-0464
pberryo1@msn.com
2004, Waldorf: Zion Wesley; 2009, Prince Frederick: Mount Olive; 2017, Retired.

Beverly, Irvin E.   SY   WE | Bethesda || Valley Lee |||| 8515   (410) 326-3465
705 Coster Rd , Lusby, MD 20657-2955   H. (410) 326-3465
irvinbev@gmail.com
2000, Valley Lee: Bethesda.

Bice, William H.   RE   CH | Davis Memorial || Cumberland |||| 5165
14706 Uhl Hwy SE , Cumberland, MD 21502-8447   H. (301) 724-5726
whbsr@atlanticbb.net
1962, Asst. Baltimore Station: Broadway-E; 1964, So. Baltimore: Union Square; 1965, Solomons: Solomons; 1970, Silver Spring: Oak Chapel; 1973, Cumberland: Davis Mem; 1989, Smithsburg: St. Paul; 1997, Retired.

Birch, Bruce C.   RE   FR | Middletown || Middletown |||| 6280   (202) 885-8673
3030 Mill Island PkwyApt 313, Frederick, MD 21701-6819   H. (301) 846-0313
brucecbirch@mac.com
1963, Central Kansas Conference; 1969, Iowa Conference; 1972, Baltimore Conference, Prof. of O.T., Wesley Theo. Sem; 2009, Retired.

Birch, Judith B.   RD   GW | Dumbarton || Washington |||| 7160
8410 Donnybrook Dr , Chevy Chase, MD 20815-3880   H. (301) 589-5780
diaconal@aol.com
1995, Inter-Faith Chapel, Leisure World; 1999, Deacon in Full Connection; 01-01-2008, Extension Ministry; 01-01-2009, Retired.

Bishop, Christopher M.   FE   CM | FaithPoint || Monrovia ||| 6382   (301) 639-9583
30 8th Ave , Brunswick, MD 21716-1736 ·   H. (301) 639-9583
Chris@faithpointum.org
2007, Middletown: Middletown; 2012, Urbana: Faithpoint.

Bishop, Kathryn   FE   FR | New Hope of Greater Brunswick || Brunswick ||| 6137
30 8th Ave, Brunswick, MD 21716-1736   H. (240) 818-2828
pastorkatiebishop@yahoo.com
2006, Smithsburg: Garfield; 2010, Brunswick: New Hope of Greater Brunswick; 2017,
Brunswick: Greater Brunswick.

Bishop, Sr., James A.   FE   AN | Asbury Town Neck || Severna Park ||| 1490   (410) 647-4051
440 Asbury Dr, Severna Park, MD 21146-1372   H. (410) 544-1126
jamesbishop_atn1@verizon.net
1994, Central Pa. Conference; 2000, Balt. Wash. Conference, Baltimore: Sharp Street
Memorial; 2003, Gaithersburg: Goshen; 2011, Severna Park: Asbury Town Neck.

Bittner, Patricia L.   PL   CH | Flintstone || Flintstone ||| 5270   (301) 478-2369
21613 National PikePO Box 64, Flintstone, MD 21530-0064   H. (301) 697-7728
pastortrish13@gmail.com
2014, Cumberland: South Cumberland Ridgeley; 2015, Flintstone: Flintstone Charge.

Black, Richard   OE   GW | Lincoln Park || Washington ||| 7215
5459 Saint Rita Dr, Waldorf, MD 20602-3277   H. (301) 752-0516
rblack3190@gmail.com
2010, Charlotte Hall: Mt Calvary; 2011, Waldorf: Zion Wesley-Mt. Calvary; 2012, Waldorf:
Zion Wesley; 2013, Newburg: Shiloh Community; 2017, DC: Lincoln Park.

Blackwell, Tyrone   PL   GW | Millian Memorial || Rockville ||| 9430
5161 Atlantis Ln, White Plains, MD 20695-3180   H. (301) 645-6803
tyblackwell73@gmail.com
2010, Forestville: Forest Memorial; 2019, Rockville: Millian Memorial.

Blagmond, Winifred J.   RE   BM | St. Paul Praise and Worship Center || Pikesville ||| 2290
3711 Marmon Ave , Gwynn Oak, MD 21207-7169   H. (410) 375-8415
rev.wjblagmond@verizon.net
1998, New Windsor: Strawbridge; 2001, Rockville: Jerusalem-Mt. Pleasant; 2003, Bel Air:
Ames; 2010, Retired; 2014, Baltimore: Sharp Street, Hampden, Rodgers Forge.; 11-1-15,
Baltimore: Christ Deaf / Magothy Deaf

Blake, Thomas (Jay)   FE   BM | Eastern || Baltimore ||| 2175   (716) 310-6083
4202 Raab Ave, Nottingham, MD 21236-2415   H. (716) 310-6083
Priceless226@comcast.net
2011, Bel Air: Ames; 2014, Baltimore: Eastern.

Blanchard, Jr., John M.   RE
507 Jaeger Ct, Sicklerville, NJ 08081-1110   H. (856) 352-4358
john.blanchard80@yahoo.com
1998, Greater New Jersey Conf; 2005 Washington: Ebenezer; 2009, Glenn Dale: Glenn Dale;
2012, Lothian: Mount Zion (Ark Road).; 2016, Retired

Blanchard, Megan PD   CM | Mill Creek Parish || Rockville ||| 9425   (301) 926-9024
11601 Georgetowne Ct, Potomac, MD 20854-3720   H. (704) 787-3072
megan.b.blanchard@gmail.com
2018, Rockville: Mill Creek Parish,

Blauvelt, Laura D. FE   GW | Potomac || Potomac ||| 9390
14021 Loblolly Ter, Potomac, MD 20850-5472   H. (410) 833-6165
lblauvelt@potomac-umc.org
1984, Attending school; 1985, Marvin Chapel; 1986, Frederick: Calvary; 1988, Kemptown:
Providence; 1994, Milford Mill; 2001, College Park: University; 2004, Supt., Baltimore
North Dist; 01-01-2007, District Superintendent, Baltimore Suburban; 2007, Westminster:
Westminster; 2013, Baltimore Suburban District Superintendent; 2017, Potomac: Potomac.

Boehl, Susan E. FE   WE | La Plata || La Plata ||| 8275
14715 Wisteria Dr, Swan Point, MD 20645-2119   H. (240) 217-6369
sing4joy2hymn@gmail.com
2000, Lewistown: Lewistown; 2002, Mt. Airy: Prospect-Marvin Chapel Charge; 2008,
Williamsport: Williamsport; 2018, La Plata: La Plata.

Boldley, Leroy RL   WE | St Luke || Scotland ||| 8445   (301) 872-4006
PO Box 725 , Prince Frederick, MD 20678-0725   H. (410) 535-3724
1989, St Inigoes: Mt Zion; 2002, Scotland: St Luke.; 2016, Retired

Bolds, Stanley SY   AN | Mount Tabor || Crownsville ||| 1285
3400 Enfield Chase Court, Bowie, MD 20716   H. (412) 818-3654
bolds44@comcast.net
04-15-18, Gambrills: Mount Tabor,

Bond, Sr., Melvin T. PL   BM | Mount Olivet || Catonsville ||| 4190   (410) 608-1400
2434 W Lafayette Ave , Baltimore, MD 21216-4803   H. (410) 608-1400
tyronehhc46@comcast.net
2000, Baltimore: Cherry Hill; 2011, Baltimore: Unity; 2019, Catonsville: Mount Olivet.

Boone, Lisa M. PL   CH | Mc Kendree of Potomac Park || Cumberland ||| 5242
10213 Summers Ln, Hagerstown, MD 21740-1564   H. (516) 841-8973
lisaboone61@hotmail.com
2014, Cresaptown: McKendree of Potomac Park; 2018, Rawlings: Rawlings.

Boone, Sandra OE
525 S Chester St, Baltimore, MD 21231-3020   H. (443) 890-3430
sandy@watersedgepartnership.org
2012, Baltimore: Water's Edge Partnership.

Bortner, Ernest E. RE   CM | Ashton || Ashton ||| 9110
429 Saint Johns Dr , Satellite Beach, FL 32937-4023   H. (321) 777-0645
ebortner1@cfl.rr.com
1952, Attending school; 1955, Western Run; 1956, Cockeysville: Epworth; 1961, Temple Hills:
Corkran Memorial, 1969, Cumberland: Centre St; 1973, Bel Air: Bel Air; 1979, Colesville;
1983, Ferndale: Ferndale; 1986, Planid Giv. Off., Asbury Vil; 1989, Retired.

Bostic, Scott PE GW | Bethesda || Bethesda ||| 9122
4712 W Braddock Rd, Alexandria, VA 22311-4702   H. (404) 314-5291
scott@washmorefeet.org
2018, Bethesda: Bethesda,

Bourgeois, Sharon K. RE FR | Kabletown || Rippon ||| 6625
12411 Winchester Ave , Bunker Hill, WV 25413-2602   H. (304) 229-4702
bourgeois@springsips.com
1983, North Arkansas Conference; 1991, Baltimore Conference: Jefferson Chg; 1996,
Baltimore: Bethesda; 2000, Arden; 2008, Retired; 2009, Charles Town: Kabletown.

Bowen, Kenneth E. RE WE | Trinity || Prince Frederick ||| 8435   (301) 743-3339
4880 Hallowing Point Rd , Prince Frederick, MD 20678-3432   H. (410) 535-1369
1958 Attending school; 1959, Greenbelt; 1960, Wpper Co: Emory Circuit; 1963, Baltimore:
Roland Ave; 1966, Baltimore: Roland Ave.-Evergreen; 1969, Galesville: Galesville; 1972,
Sexton; 1978, Baltimore: Beechfield; 1984, Jessup: Wesley Chap; 1988, Fork: Fork-Waugh
Chg; 1994, Solomons: Solomons Chg; 1997, Retired.

Bowen, Sue PL FR | Westminster || Westminster ||| 4555
223 E Broadway St , Union Bridge, MD 21791-9106   H. (410) 775-2074
sue_bowen@comcast.net
2005, New Windsor: Bethel; 2013, Union Bridge: Union Bridge.; 5-17-16, Baltimore
Washington Conference

Bowens, Sr., Rex R. FL FR | Jackson Chapel || Frederick ||| 6330
817 Trail Ave , Frederick, MD 21701-4522   H. (240) 409-7313
rexbowenssr@comcast.net
1997, Bartonsville: Jackson Chapel.

Bowers, Walter F. RE FR | St Lukes || Martinsburg ||| 6690
403 Silver Ln, Martinsburg, WV 25401-3122   H. (304) 262-6512
bowerspep@aol.com
1967, Martinsburg; 1970, Attending school; 1973, Emmitsburg: Tomís Creek Charge; 1979,
Bunker Hill: Bunker Hill; 1988, Hagerstown: Washington Square; 1994, Arden: Arden; 2000,
Retired.

Boyd, Lillian L PE BS | Bel Air || Bel Air ||| 2340   (410) 688-9992
1829 Wye Mills Ln , Bel Air, MD 21015-8301   H. (410) 688-9992
tygjhs@verizon.net
2014, Boring: Boring-Piney Grove-Mt. Gilead Cooperative Parish.; 2016, Bel Air: Bel Air
Charge

Boyer, William R. RE FR | Sandy Mount || Finksburg ||| 4443
355 Grey Friars Rd , Westminster, MD 21158-3707   H. (410) 857-9003
w.m.boyer@comcast.net
1962, Attending school; 1964, Mt. Airy: Prospect-Marvin; 1968, Sandy Mount: Sandy Mount;
1978, Honorable Location; 1994, Silver Spring: Oak Chapel; 2005, Retired.

Braden, Robert M. RE CM | Damascus || Damascus ||| 9190
25605 Ridge Rd, Damascus, MD 20872-1841   H. (301) 253-6478
1963, Brunswick; N.Y. Hill; 1966, Thurmont: Thurmont; 1969, Damascus: Montgomery; 1976,
Washington Pastoral Counseling Service; 1977, American College of Radiology; 1979, Exec.
Asst., Am. Col. of Radiology; 1982, Sr. Prog. Staff Am. College Radiology; 1985, Retired.

Bradshaw, Joseph R.   RL   CH | Trinity || Cumberland ||| 5245
78 W Washington St, Apt 102, Chambersburg, PA 17201-2418   H. (717) 830-2664
georgiepie41@aol.com
1984, Buckeystown: Buckeystown; 1985, Martinsburg: Blairton; 1988, Salem: Keedysville; 1990, Berkeley Springs: Berkeley-Morgan Chg; 3/1/95, Retired.

Bragg, Sr., John   RL   FR | Westminster || Westminster ||| 4555
98 Greenvale Mews Dr, Westminster, MD 21157-6864   H. (410) 848-7479
jdbraggsr@comcast.net
2018, Retired, 2006, Woodbine: Brandenberg.

Brannan, Emora T.   RE   BM | Lovely Lane || Baltimore ||| 3185
6400 Blenheim Rd , Baltimore, MD 21212-1715   H. (410) 377-3390
emorabrannan@verizon.net
1965, Attending school; 1971, Cumberland: Grace; 1975, Baltimore: Lovely Lane, City Station; 1991, Baltimore: Grace; 2011, Retired.

Brantner, Konni M.   FD   GW | Millian Memorial || Rockville ||| 9430   (301) 598-4400
2804 Cairncross Ter , Silver Spring, MD 20906-1809   H. (301) 871-6275
stmattkmb@hotmail.com
1982, Chevy Chase: Chevy Chase; 1984, Bethesda: Concord-St. Andrews; 1986, Rockville: Millian Memorial; 1998, Silver Spring: Marvin Memorial; 2000, Deacon in Full Connection; No appointment; 4/1/2006, Min. of Edu., St. Matthew Presbyterian.

Breidenbaugh, Daniel   PE FR | Bunker Hill || Bunker Hill ||| 6525   (410) 592-6719
9887 Winchester Ave, Bunker Hill, WV 25413   H. (410) 487-2707
dbreidenbaugh@gmail.com
2017, Bunker Hill: Bunkerhill.

Brennan, Jr., Robert   FE   FR | Mount Wesley || Shepherdstown ||| 6735
173 Serpentine Way, Martinsburg, WV 25405-1108   H. (304) 901-4591
rbrennan001@gmail.com
1987, Cumberland: Wesley Chg; 1988, Hagerstown: Grace; 12-01-90, Hancock; 2000, Boonsboro: Mt. Nebo; 2011, Walkersville: Walkersville; 11-01-2011, Leave of Absence; 2013, Smithsburg: Garfield/Salem Cooperative Parish; 2014, Martinsburg: Calvary.; 2016, Medical Leave.

Brewer, Lee   FE   GW | Hughes || Wheaton ||| 9480   (301) 475-7200
22850 Bayside Rd, Leonardtown, MD 20650-5618   H. (301) 793-8364
drleebrew@aol.com
2017, Leonardtown: First Saints Community, 2006, Wheaton: Glenmont; 08-01-2014, Medical Leave.

Briddell, Adam   PE   GW | Mount Vernon Place || Washington ||| 7235
1100 Brotherton Avenue, Eugene, OR 97404   H. (202) 255-8369
adambriddell@gmail.com
2012, Bethesda: Bethesda; 2013, DC: Asbury; 2015, On loan to Oregon-Idaho Conference.

Brisbon, III, Herbert A.   FE   WE | Cheltenham || Cheltenham |||| 8155
7805 Mandan Rd Apt 101, Greenbelt, MD 20770-2135   H. (410) 900-0972
JmpPastorB@gmail.com
  2005, Baltimore: Wildwood Parkway; 2006, Christ Edmondson/Wildwood Pkwy Chg; 2007,
Baltimore: New Covenant Worship Center; 10-01-2009, Baltimore: West Balt Coop Parish;
2011, DC: Ebenezer Cooperative Circuit; 2014, Campus Ministry-Howard Univ.; 2016,
Rockville: Jerusalem-Mt Pleasant; 2019, Cheltenham: Cheltenham.

Briscoe, Jr., Andre R.   FE   BM | St. Matthews-New Life || Baltimore |||| 3247
5511 Pioneer Dr, Baltimore, MD 21214-1617   H. (443) 642-1015
andrebriscoejr@gmail.com
01-01-2015, Baltimore: St. Matthews-New Life.

Broadhurst, Allan R.   RE
8 Fresh Brook Rd , South Yarmouth, MA 02664-4016   H. (617) 362-2393
1956, Attending school; 1961, Prof. Univ. of Conn; 1973, Teacher, Cape Cod Community
College; 1987, Retired.

Broadwell, Chris M.   PL   AN | Cape St Claire || Annapolis |||| 1125   (410) 757-4896
A724 Rosedale St, Annapolis, MD 21401-2300   H. (318) 349-7110
office@capeumc.org
  2019, Annapolis: Eastport,

Brookman, Robert H.   RE
1101 Outlett Mills Ct , Catonsville, MD 21228-2642   H. (410) 788-2555
1973, Attending school; 1974, Baltimore: Trinity; 1976, Baltimore: Dorguth Memorial;
1981, Baltimore: Salem; 1985, Baltimore: Salem-Orangeville Chg; 1990, Baltimore: Salem/
Orangeville; 1993, Piney Grove: Piney Grove (Chase: Piney Grove); 1998, Jessup: Wesley
Chapel/ Harwood Park Chg; 2006, Leave of Absence; 08-04-2006, Retired.

Brooks, John   RLFR | Friendship || Hedgesville |||| 6660
166 Locust Grove Rd , Hedgesville, WV 25427-3072   H. (304) 754-7891
jjbrooks88@frontier.com
  2006, Inwood: Inwood; 2012, Martinsburg: Berkeley Place-Friendship; 2017, Retired.

Brooks, Kevin   PL   WE | Mount Calvary || Charlotte Hall |||| 8150
69 Harry S Truman Dr Apt 34, Upper Marlboro, MD 20774-1038   H. (301) 324-3102
pastor@route6charge.org
2013, La Plata: St. Matthewis.; 2016, Rt. 6: Mt. Calvary/St. Matthews Chg.

Brooks, Martin P.   FE   AN | Magothy || Pasadena |||| 1450   (410) 715-7380
2838 Leaf Shade Dr, Ellicott City, MD 21042-2559   H. (410) 739-1488
pastor@magothy.org
  2008, Upperco: Emory; 2010, Ellicott City: Ellicott City Cooperative Parish; 2015, Gamber:
Calvary; 2018, Pasadena: Magothy.

Bropleh, Laurence K.   FE   CM | Epworth || Gaithersburg |||| 9245
19738 Lindenfield Ct, Katy, TX 77449-8620   H. (281) 703-1591
lbropleh@aol.com
1993, Barnesville: Barnesville Chg; Barnesville: Mt. Zion-Warren; 1998, Reg. Exec. Sec., Sub-
Saharan African Region, Missional Personnel GBGM; 2001, D.C.: Jones Memorial; 9/1/03,
Ext. Min., World Council of Churches, UN Representative; 10-01-2006, Leave of Absence;
04-01-2013, Extension Ministry: University of Liberia of the UMC.

Bropleh, Rudy   FE   FR | Asbury || Shepherdstown ||| 6700   (304) 876-6543
262 Maddex Farm Dr, Shepherdstown, WV 25443-4344   H. (304) 707-2276
pastorb@4pillarchurch.org
2003, Baltimore: St. Matthews; 2004, Shepherdstown: Asbury.

Brosnan, David R.   RE   CH | Grace || Hagerstown ||| 5325
2003 Trent Blvd, New Bern, NC 28560-5323   H. (252) 288-6562
sbrosnan@gmail.com
2007, Hagerstown: Grace; 2008, Retired.

Brotemarkle, Charles L.   RL   CH | Central || Cumberland ||| 5150   (301) 724-4080
14215 Bedford Rd NE, Cumberland, MD 21502-6926   H. (301) 724-7614
leebrotemarkle@atlanticbb.net
1998, Cumberland: Park Place; 12-01-2006, Cumberland: Central; 2011, Retired.

Brought, Byron E.   FE   BS | Bel Air || Bel Air ||| 2340
1203 Brighton Ln, Bel Air, MD 21014-3308   H. (240) 418-3218
broughtb@baumc.com
1995, Frederick: Brook Hill; 1998, Silver Spring: Memorial; 1999, Olney: OakdaleEmory;
2005, Friendship: Friendship; 2015, Bel Air: Bel Air

Brought, Byron P.   RE   AN | Severna Park || Severna Park ||| 1510   (410) 987-4700
665 Dill Rd , Severna Park, MD 21146-4119   H. (410) 544-9188
bbrought@severnaparkumc.org
1966, Attending school; 1968, Baltimore: Hiss. Assoc; 1970, East Harford: Calvary; 1976,
Hebbville: Salem; 1981, Glenmont: Glenmont; 1986, Supt., Annap. Dist; 1992, Annapolis:
Calvary; 2010, Retired; 10-01-2012, Prince Frederick: Trinity.

Brown, Alexis F.   PE   GW | Asbury || Washington ||| 7115
7018 Knighthood Ln, Columbia, MD 21045-4817   H. (410) 905-8956
abrown@asburyumcdc.org
2013, DC: Van Buren.; 2016, Howard University

Brown, Arlester   RE   GW | Metropolitan Memorial || Washington ||| 7630
3001 Veazey Ter NW Apt 533, Washington, DC 20008-5402   H. (202) 244-2778
arlestero@aol.com
1966 CME, Louisiana Conference; 1969, Attending school; 1970, Baltimore Conference,
D.C.: Petworth Assoc; 1971, D.C.: Brookland; 1972, Sharp Street; 1975, CME New York-
Washington Conference; 1983, Transfer Baltimore Conference, Oxon Hill: St. Paul; 1986,
D.C., Hughes; 1988, D.C., Albright; 1991, Retired; 09-01-2008, Germantown: Asbury.

Brown, Caprice   PL   AN | Community || Laurel ||| 7410
16208 Angel Falls Ln , Bowie, MD 20716-3816   H. (301) 875-5515
brownbowie3@gmail.com
2016, Laurel: First/Community CP

Brown, Gregory S.   RE
19266 Coastal Hwy Unit 4, Rehoboth Beach, DE 19971-6117   H. (302) 684-2746
greg@gregbrownonline.com
1980, Attending school; 1982, D.C.: Calvary; 1988, Bethesda: Bethesda; 1992, Washington:
Wesley; 2001, Ext. Minister, Pastoral Counselor; 2007, Retired.

Brown, John R. RE   GW | Asbury || Washington |||| 7115
4675 Heritage Lakes Ct SW , Mableton, GA 30126-1254   H. (770) 732-6189
1981, Hillsdale-Chatsworth; 1983, Baltimore: Martin Luther King Memorial; 1984, D.C.:
Douglas Memorial; 1986, South Georgia Conference; 1988, Baltimore Conference, Balto: Mt.
Zion; 1993, Fort Washington: Grace; 1996, Silver Spring: Good Hope Union; 2000, Attending
School; 2006, On Loan to N. Ga; 2014, Leave of Absence.

Brown, Katherine E. FD   GW | Silver Spring || Silver Spring |||| 9466   (301) 585-5547
9104 Eton Rd , Silver Spring, MD 20901-4902   H. (301) 585-5547
katherinebrown2002@yahoo.com
2007, Rockville: Millian Memorial; 01-01-2011, Wesley Seminary, serving at Woodside.

Brown, Kenneth E. RE   (410) 349-2470
1400 Peregrine Path, Arnold, MD 21012   H. (410) 703-6619
keb2639@gmail.com
1973,Attending School; 1974, Martinsburg: Mt Olive-Mt Zion Chg; 1976, Westminster: Salem;
1981,Sabbatical; 1982, Ellicott City: Glen Mar & Conference Coordinator of Electric Media;
1987, Ellicott City: Glen Mar; 1991, Ellicott City: Glen Gary Greater Parish; 1995, Severna
Park: Severna Park. Assoc; 2003, Leave of Absence; 2004, Ext. Min.: Kent Island UMC;
5/1/2010, Ext. Min: Lutheran Church of the Redeemer, McLean, VA; 01-01-2012, Retired.

Brown, Marianne RE   WE | Solomons || Solomons |||| 8470   (410) 375-5276
17400 Aquasco Rd , Brandywine, MD 20613-4212   H. (410) 375-5276
revmarianne@comcast.net
2004, Norrisville: Norrisville; 2005, Araby: Araby; 09-01-2006, Rohrersville: Rohrersville;
2008, Baltimore: Arnolia; 2011, Brandywine: Brookfield Immanuel; 2018, Retired.

Brown, R. Lorraine PE   CM | Mount Gregory || Glenwood |||| 4455
121 Spring St, Gaithersburg, MD 20877-1921   H. (301) 990-1755
rev.rlbrown@gmail.com
2014, Glenwood: Growing Seed Cooperative Ministry.; 2016, Mt Airy: Prospect-Marvin
Chapel Charge; 2018, Glenwood: Growing Seed.

Brown, Susan M. RE   GW | St Pauls || Kensington |||| 9330   (301) 229-3383
8034 Lazy Trl, San Antonio, TX 78250-3058   H. (240) 595-3172
2013smhbrown@gmail.com
1998, Cumberland: First and New Start: Georges Creek; 1999, Hagerstown: Grace; 2001,
Walkersville: Rt. 26 Initiative; 08/03/01, Frederick: Cross Walk; 2/1/03, Leetown; 2003,
Severna Park Assoc; 2008, Annapolis: Cape St Claire; 2010, Rockville: Rockville; 2014,
Bethesda: Concord-St Andrews; 2018, Retired,.

Brown, William G. FE   CM | Glen Mar || Ellicott City |||| 7365   (410) 309-3427
6631 Monroe Ave, Sykesville, MD 21784-6345   H. (443) 854-6054
railroadrev@gmail.com
1994, Baltimore: Graceland; 1995, Baltimore: Christ of Balt. Co; 2000, Phoenix: New
Horizon; 02/15/01, No. Co. Initiative; 09-01-01, Cockeysville: Epworth; 2008, Eldersburg:
Wesley Freedom; 08-01-18, BWC Dir. New Faith Expressions.

Brown-Whale, Kimberly RE
1910 Knox Ave , Reisterstown, MD 21136-5612   H. (443) 275-1280
thebrownwhales@yahoo.com
1982, Westminster: St James; 1997, Hampstead: Salem; 1998, Hampstead: St Johns; 2007, Ext
Min.; GBMC; 2007, Essex: Essex; 2016, Baltimore: Brooklyn Area; 2019, Retired

74

Brown-Whale, Richard   RE   (410) 256-5561
1910 Knox Ave , Reisterstown, MD 21136-5612   H. (443) 275-1280
pastor@campchapel.org
1980, Attending School; 1981, Baltimore: Memorial; 1982, Westminster: St. James-Stone Chap-Salem Par. 1985, World Div.Gen Bd. of Global Min; 1997, Hampstead: Shiloh-Mt. Zion Chg; 01-01-2007, GBGM; 2007, Dundalk: Dundalk; 2008, Perry Hall: Camp Chapel; 2019, Aberdeen: Grace.

Brunkow, Thomas L.   RE GW | Silver Spring || Silver Spring ||| 9466
5201 Worthington Dr , Bethesda, MD 20816-1621   H. (301) 229-4296
tbrunkow@verizon.net
1962, Central Ill. Conference; 1965, Baltimore Conference, Asst. Rockville; 1967, Frederick: Trinity; 1975, D.C.: Dumbarton; 1987, College Park: University; 1993, Bethesda: Concord-St. Andrew`s; 2001, Silver Spring: Woodside; 2006, Retired.

Buckingham, Richard L.   RD   BM | Catonsville || Catonsville ||| 4180   (410) 747-1886
719 Maiden Choice Ln Apt HR432, Catonsville, MD 21228-6157   H. (410) 314-9449
ricklby@yahoo.com
1983, Reisterstown; 1985, Kensington: St. Paul`s; 2017, Retired.

Bufano, Nick M.   FE   BS | Idlewylde || Baltimore ||| 3535
214 W. Seminary Ave, Lutherville, MD 21093   H. (410) 692-4677
Pastornickbufano@gmail.com
2009, Norrisville: Norrisville; 2013, Jarrettsville: Jarrettsville-Ayers Chapel Cooperative Parish; 2019, Baltimore: St John-Idlewylde.

Burchell, Jr., Harry L.   RA CH | Mount Savage || Mount Savage ||| 5425
11504 Mountain Magic Ln NE, Cumberland, MD 21502-8101   H. (301) 777-3429
Nightwatch@atlanticbb.net
1987, Martinsburg: Berkeley Place-Friendship; 1989, Berkeley Springs: Alpine; 1994, Ridgeley: Holy Cross; 1995, AM, Ridgeley: Holy Cross; 2002 Midland Chg; 2014, Retired.

Burchell, Sandra H   PE   CH | Mount Savage || Mount Savage ||| 5425
11504 Mountain Magic Ln NE, Cumberland, MD 21502-8101   H. (301) 777-3429
Nightwatch@atlanticbb.net
12/1/2006, Cumberland: South Cumberland; 2009, Barton: Barton; 2011, Mount Savage: Mount Savage; 2014, Ellerslie/Mt. Savage: Creek Run Cooperative Parish.

Burgard, Donald L.   RE   CM | Glen Mar || Ellicott City ||| 7365
719 Maiden Choice Ln Apt HR302, Catonsville, MD 21228-6131
pastordonhawk@aol.com
1970, West Pa. Conference; 1971, Baltimore Conference, Harpers Ferry, W. Va.: Bolivar, 1973, Bedington: Bedington Chg; 1980, Williamsport: Williamsport; 1987, Cheverly: Cheverly; 1993, Catonsville: Trinity; 1996, Leave of Absence; 1998, Randallstown: Wardis Chapel; 2009, Retired; 2011, Baltimore: Old Otterbein.

Burgio, Deborah   PD   CM | Mount Zion || Highland ||| 9310   (410) 531-2271
14450 Triadelphia Mill Rd, Dayton, MD 21036-1220   H. (410) 531-2271
debbie.burgio@verizon.net
2019, ExtMin.

Burke, Steve   PL   BM | Waters Edge Partnership || Baltimore |||| 3113   (301) 606-6687
1806 Bank St, Baltimore, MD 21231-2506   H. (301) 606-6687
sburke@watersedgepartnership.org
2016, Baltimore: Water's Edge Partnership Initiative

Burkert, Cynthia   RE   BM | Old Otterbein || Baltimore |||| 2240   (410) 335-2172
3000 Dunmore Rd, Dundalk, MD 21222-5131   H. (410) 708-8632
cindyburkert216@gmail.com
2007, Chase: Ebenezer-Piney Grove Cooperative Parish; 2010, Chase: Bowleyís-Chase Cooperative Parish; 01-01-2014, Middle River:Chase; 2017, Retired.

Burtner, Roger E.   RE   CH | Salem || Keedysville |||| 6250   (301) 432-8885
35 Mount Hebron Rd , Keedysville, MD 21756-1357   H. (301) 432-5772
reb21756@msn.com
1951, Ortanna Chg; 1958, York: Second; 1962, Missionary to Nigeria; 1970, Director, CROP/ CWS; 1977, Withdrawn; 01/01/1983, Reinstated, Reisterstown: Grace-Bosley Chg; 1987, Rohrersville: Bethel; 1990, Retired; 1996, Great Cacapon: West Morgan Parish.

Butler, Jr., Henry G.   RE   CM | Bethesda || Damascus |||| 9185   (301) 253-3222
27912 Kemptown Church Rd , Damascus, MD 20872-1565   H. (301) 253-2721
sonwillcome@verizon.net
1980, Attending school; 1981, Boring: Pleasant Grove Chg. (1986 Pleasant Grove); 1988, Damascus: Bethesda.; 2016, Retired; 2016, Damascus: Bethesda

---

Butler, Sr., Darius K.   SY   BS | John Wesley || Abingdon |||| 2130   (410) 676-0032
2000 Brown St, Edgewood, MD 21040-3203   H. (443) 922-7979
dkbutler1.umc@gmail.com
2014, Abingdon: John Wesley.

Butler, Tori   OE   GW | Good Hope Union || Silver Spring |||| 9455
10101 Twin Rivers Rd Apt 237, Columbia, MD 21044-2672   H. (301) 879-8100
pastortcbutler@gmail.com
2016, Silver Spring: Good Hope Union

Butler, William E.   FE   WE | Queens Chapel || Beltsville |||| 7315   (410) 937-0873
16312 Marsham Dr , Upper Marlboro, MD 20772-3236   H. 301-627-0787
jbweb1@comcast.net
2001, Churchville: Churchville Chg; 9/9/04, Ext. Min., U.S. Military; 01/01/06, Churchville: Churchville Chg; 2007, Bowie: Living Spring-Wilson Cooperative Parish; 2010, Gambrills: Wilson; 08-31-2011; 10-08-2012, Lusby: Lusby; 2013, Baltimore: Union Memorial.; 2016, Beltsville: Queens Chapel Charge

---

Button, Gail L.   RE   BM | Orems || Baltimore |||| 2515
811 Sunnyfield Ln, Brooklyn Park, MD 21225-3367   H. (410) 636-1757
glbutton@gmail.com
2002, Reisterstown: Grace-Bosley Chg., 2003, Reisterstown: Grace; 2008, Glen Burnie: Messiah; 2011, Glen Burnie: Messiah-Solley; 2018, Retired, 2018, Middle River: Orems.

Buzby, Mary   PL   FR | New Hope of New Windsor || New Windsor |||| 4640
2126 Mayberry Rd, Westminster, MD 21158-2509   H. (443) 465-5024
bzbymry@aol.com
2012, New Windsor: New Hope of New Windsor.; 2016, Westminster: St James Charge

---

Bynum, Michael W.   FE   AN | Linthicum Heights || Linthicum ||| 1370
208 School Ln , Linthicum, MD 21090-2519   H. (240) 344-4532
pastorbynum@gmail.com
  2007, Jefferson: Jefferson-Doubs; 2009, New Windsor: Stone Chapel; 2012, Hancock:
  Hancock; 2018, Linthicum Heights: Linthicum Heights.

Byrne, Eugene D. (Dwight)   RE   CH | First || Lonaconing ||| 5390
2931 Bloom Rd , Finksburg, MD 21048-1802
pastorbyrne@yahoo.com
  1981, Rockville: Faith; 1982, Hagerstown: Otterbein; 1985, Cumberland: Trinity; 1988,
  Lewistown: Lewistown; 1990, Balt.: Sexton; 1995, Berkeley Springs: Francis Asbury-Wesley
  Chapel; 1997, Westminster: Deer Park; 2000, Brookeville: Salem; 2001, Silver Spring:
  Memorial; 2005, Lonaconing: First; 02-15-2007, Retired.

Cairns, Lynn D.   RE   CM | Mill Creek Parish || Rockville ||| 9425
457 Old Mill Rd , Gettysburg, PA 17325-8465   H. (717) 334-4193
ldcairns@embarqmail.com
  1975, Bethesda: N. Bethesda Assoc; 1980, Hyattstown: Hyattstown; 1990, Rockville: Mill
  Creek Parrish; 2005, Leave of Absence; 2006, Retired.

Caldwell, Cindy M.   FE   CH | Benevola || Boonsboro ||| 6115   (301) 791-3576
18122 Samuel Cir, Hagerstown, MD 21740-9599   H. (410) 937-0458
pastor.benevola@gmail.com
  2009, Street: Mt Vernon; 2011, Bel Air: Bel Air-Mt. Vernon Cooperative Parish; 2014,
  Buckeystown: Buckeystown (Rt 85); 2016, Boonsboro: Benevola Charge.

Cameron, Kevin   PL   CM | Dickerson || Dickerson ||| 9225
2907 Weller Rd , Silver Spring, MD 20906-3886   H. (301) 367-1433
kcameron1970@hotmail.com
  2019, Dickerson: Dickerson-Forest Grove,

Campbell, Bonnie   RA   AN | Davidsonville || Davidsonville ||| 1190   (410) 676-3234
38 Canvasback Cir, Bridgeville, DE 19933-2428   H. (443) 922-9904
revbonniecampbell@gmail.com
  1995, Baltimore: Violetville; 1996, Davidsonville: Davidsonville; 09-01-01, Ext. Min., Alaska
  Missionary Conference; 01-01-2008, Baltimore Washington Conference; 2010, Edgewood:
  Presbury; 2013, Retired.

Campbell, John   RE   AN | Davidsonville || Davidsonville ||| 1190
38 Canvasback Cir, Bridgeville, DE 19933-2428   H. (703) 855-9539
revjohncampbell@gmail.com
  1972, Attending school; 1974, Cheltenham; 1975, Foundry, Assoc; 1978, St. Johnis of
  Hamilton; 1984, Mt. Airy: Calvary; 1986, Alaska Miss. Conference, Bd. of Global Min;
  1992, Unalaska U.M. Min; 1995, Davidsonville Chg; 09-01-01, Ext. Min., Alaska Missionary
  Conference,; 2010, Fallston: Fallston Church; 03-01-2013, Retired.

Camper, Joycelyn   SY   CM | St Marks || Boyds ||| 9145
90 Waverley Dr Apt Q203, Frederick, MD 21702-3340   H. (301) 875-8855
because-he-lives@live.com
  2019, Boyds: St Marks.

Cannon, Jenny D.   FE   GW | Bethesda || Bethesda ||| 9122   (301) 652-2990
8300 Old Georgetown Rd , Bethesda, MD 20814-1416   H. (240) 205-5001
jenny.cannon@gmail.com
2006, Bethesda: Bethesda (Assoc.); 2012, Ashton: Ashton.

Cantley, Mike M.   FE   FR | St Lukes || Martinsburg ||| 6690   (410) 761-2880
215 Wren St N, Martinsburg, WV 25405-8895   H. (443) 501-6028
Revcantley@gmail.com
2010, Ferndale: Ferndale; 2015, Fork: Fork -Waugh; 2017, Martinsburg: St Lukes.

Capps, Kim K.   RE   GW | Emmanuel || Laurel ||| 7440   (301) 405-8451
11110 Nicholas Dr , Silver Spring, MD 20902-3533   H. (301) 649-2032
kim.capps@gmail.com
1983, Attending school; 1984, Shenandale Chg; 1986, Westminster; 11-88, Elderslie-St.
Andrews; 1991, College Park: University; 1996, Conference Youth Director; 1998, Chaplain,
University of Maryland; 01-01-2007, Extension Ministry; 2012, Retired.

Cardwell, Donnie J.   RL   FR | Murrill Hill || Harpers Ferry ||| 6580   (304) 596-7349
3036 Cherry Run Rd , Hedgesville, WV 25427-6099   H. (304) 596-7349
3036dc@comcast.net
1990, Baltimore-Washington Conf Off; 1996, Emmitsburg: Toms Creek; 2000, Harpers Ferry:
Chestnut Hill; 01-01-2010, Retired; 2013, Harpers Ferry: Murrill Hill.

Cardwell, Stan   FE   AN | Community || Crofton ||| 1180   (410) 721-9129
1690 Riedel Rd , Crofton, MD 21114-1631   H. (410) 721-9129
scardwell@cumc.net
1992, Cumberland: Christ; 1998, Attending School; 1999, Leonardtown: St. Paulís; 01-01-
2007, Leonardtown: First Saints Community; 2008, Bel Air: Bel Air; 2011, Bel Air: Bel Air-Mt.
Vernon Cooperative Parish; 2014, Berkeley Springs: First; 2015, Crofton: Community-Trinity
Coop Parish; 2015, Southern Region Resource person; 01-01-18, Crofton: Community.

Carlson, Roger J.   RE   GW | St Pauls || Kensington ||| 9330
5155 Osceola Ave, Saint Augustine, FL 32080-7191   H. (410) 349-2862
revrogerj@yahoo.com
1973, Attending school; 1976, Colesville; 1979, Germantown: Salem; 1988, Loch Raven;
1994, Olney: Oakdale-Emory; 2006, Annapolis: Cape St. Clare; 2008, Arnold: Asbury; 2013,
Retired.

Carney, Vernice S.   RE   GW | Brighter Day || Washington ||| 7625
14800 Pennfield Cir Apt 412, Silver Spring, MD 20906-1579   H. (301) 288-7990
vscarney@aol.com
1997, Germantown: Asbury; 2006, Retired.

Carns, Susan   RD   WE | La Plata || La Plata ||| 8275
3775 Foxhall Dr , White Plains, MD 20695-3404   H. (301) 645-4534
sbcarns@comcast.net
1998, Waldorf: Good Shepherd; 2001, Deacon in Full Connection; 2005, Mechanicsville: Mt.
Zion.

Carpenter, William   SY   FR | Jefferson || Jefferson ||| 6240
5551 Doubs Rd, Adamstown, MD 21710-8912   H. (904) 729-9484
wcarpen14a@gmail.com
11-29-15, Jefferson: Jefferson-Doubs Charge; 2017, Brunswick: Greater Brunswick.

Carr, Anthony T. FE
10121 Towhee Ave, Adelphi, MD 20783-1209   H. (805) 205-5100
anthony.carr@navy.mil
1994, Attending School; 1995, Hagerstown Chg; 1999, Bel Air: Mt. Zion; 2000, Glen Burnie;
2-01-04, Ext. Min., Naval Chaplain.

Carr, Arlene R. RE   FR | St Lukes || Martinsburg ||| 6690
2129 W New Haven Ave Apt 130, West Melbourne, FL 32904-3849   H. (321) 984-8089
1983, Jessup: Wesley Chapel; 1988, Catonsville: Catonsville; 1997, Martinsburg: St. Lukeís;
2002, Retired.

Carr, Clark D. FE   AN | Nichols-Bethel || Odenton ||| 1430   (410) 674-2272
1239 Murray Rd , Odenton, MD 21113-1603   H. (410) 451-1324
clarkdcarr@verizon.net
1980, Attending school; 1981, White Marsh: Ebenezer; 1982, Chase: Ebenezer; 11/1/87,
Chaplain, USA; 1-1-99, Brunswick Cooperative Parish; 2004, Hagerstown: Grace; 2013,
Odenton: Nichols-Bethel.

Carrington, Jr., Michael A. PL   BM | Martin Luther King Memorial || Baltimore ||| 4145
203 Staysail Dr, Joppa, MD 21085-4125   H. (443) 721-6183
michaelcarrington18@gmail.com
2018, Baltimore: Martin Luther King Meml,

Carrington, Shirley R. RE   AN | Chews Memorial || Edgewater ||| 1438
3708 Campfield Rd , Gwynn Oak, MD 21207-6350   H. (410) 484-2241
1992, Owensville: Chews Memorial; 2004, Retired.

Carter, Robert RE   WE | Trinity || Prince Frederick ||| 8435   (301) 645-5247
12646 Council Oak Dr, Waldorf, MD 20601-3585   H. (301) 885-2447
carterrob@calvumc.org
1976, Attending school; 1977, Galesville: Galesville; 1980, Dunkirk: Smithville; 1988,
Eastport; 11/01/92, Leave of Absence; 1994, Fork: Fork-Waugh Charge; 2005, Waldorf:
Calvary; 2008, Waldorf: Calvary-Shiloh; 03-01-2012, Waldorf: Calvary; 2018, Retired.

Carter-Rimbach, David RE   BM | Trinity || Catonsville ||| 4210
6316 Gentle Light Ln , Columbia, MD 21044-6035   H. (410) 245-2505
trinitycatonsvillepastor@gmail.com
1965, Attending school; 1966, Asst. Baltimore: Grace; 1969, Assoc. Westminster Parish;
1971, Elderslie; 1979, Elderslie-St. Andrews; 1989, Hampden; 1994, Clarksville: Linden-
Linthicum; 2007, Retired; 12-01-2012, Crofton: Community-Trinity Coop Parish; 2013,
Westminster: Zion; 2017, Catonsville: Trinity.

Carter-Rimbach, Joan FE BM | John Wesley || Baltimore ||| 4135   (410) 383-1525
6316 Gentle Light Ln , Columbia, MD 21044-6035   H. (240) 755-0190
srpastorjwbalto@gmail.com
1988, Westminster Chg;1991, Union St; 1994, Chap., Bd. of Child Care; 2000, Leave of
Absence; 2001, Pikesville: Milford Mill; 2005, Hyattsville: First; 2015, Highland: Mount
Zion; 2017, Baltimore: John Wesley,

Cassel, Jack H. RE AN | Severna Park || Severna Park ||| 1510
8129 Windy Field Ln , Millersville, MD 21108-1660 H. (410) 969-5301
jhcassel1935@gmail.com
1955, Attending school; 1960, Hellam Charge; 1964, Hanover: Grace-Green Springs; 1967, Baltimore: Immanuel; 1970, Ellicott City: Rockland; 1978, Walkersville; 1982, Fulton Siemers Memorial; 1987, Ferndale; 1991, Carrollis-Gills; 1992, Lutherville: Carrollis Gills/Stone Chapel Parish; 2000, Retired.

Chamberlain, Michael RE (202) 363-4900
1521 Eton Way, Crofton, MD 21114-1524 H. (410) 972-6707
mchamberlain@nationalchurch.org
01-01-18, DC: Metropolitan Memorial; Great Plains AC.

Chambers, Richard C. RE CH | Grace || Hagerstown ||| 5325
3385 Scar Hill Rd , Greencastle, PA 17225-9633 H. (717) 597-5602
1956, Va. Conference; 1961, Baltimore Conf., Ellerslie; 1966, Rawlings-Dawson; 1970, Hagerstown: St. Matthew's; 1974, Martinsburg: St. Lukeis; 1983, Waldorf: Calvary; 1989, Retired.

Chance, James E. (Ed) RE WE | La Plata || La Plata ||| 8275
1104 Cornwall Dr , La Plata, MD 20646-3544 H. (301) 392-0856
chancesrwe@gmail.com
1966, Central Illinois Conference; 1968, Baltimore Conference, Bethesda-Hyattstown; 1980, Aberdeen: Grace; 1989, Forestville: Forest Memorial; 1997, Waldorf: Calvary; 2005, Retired.

Chaney, Jr., William T. FE CM | Wesley Freedom || Eldersburg ||| 4225
25052 Owl Creek Dr, Aldie, VA 20105-5617 H. (240) 405-9808
pastorchaney@outlook.com
2006, West Baltimore; 2008, Guide Western Region; 2012, District Superintendent/Baltimore Metropolitan District; 2013, Baltimore: West Baltimore; 2014, Extension Ministry, GBOD

Chaney, Michelle FE CM | Wesley Freedom || Eldersburg ||| 4225
25052 Owl Creek Dr, Aldie, VA 20105-5617 H. (615) 346-9697
mhchaney@gmail.com
2007, Eldersburg: Wesley Freedom; 2011, Baltimore: Metropolitan; 10-1-2014, Transitional Leave; 2015, On Loan.

Chapman, Bruce W. RE FR | Hedgesville || Hedgesville ||| 6610
15247 Oak Spring St, San Antonio, TX 78232-4241
1981, Oak Chapel; 1982, Ager Road; 1984, Hedgesville Chg; 1/1/88, Chaplain USA; 2017, Retired.

Charters, Kathleen G. PD GW | Emmanuel || Laurel ||| 7440 (240) 463-7598
41 Mendel Dr, Sequim, WA 98382-8959 H. (360) 504-3150
kcharters@mac.com
2014, Ext Min: Defense Health Agency.

Chase, Jalene FE WE | Emmanuel || Beltsville ||| 7310 (301) 937-7114
6200 Heston Ter, Lanham, MD 20706-2398 H. (301) 325-6676
revjchase@gmail.com
2006, Washington: Community.; 2016, DC: Douglas Memorial Charge; 2018, Beltsville: Emmanuel,

---

Chattin, Terri R.   RE   BS | Reisterstown || Reisterstown ||| 4435   (410) 795-0714
37 Cedar Hill Rd, Randallstown, MD 21133-1510   H. (410) 322-6304
trchattin@gmail.com
   1979, S. In. Conference, 1980, Baltimore Conference, Charles Town: Asbury; 1983,
   Baltimore Conference staff; 1987, Clarksville: Linden-Linthicum; 1994, Arnold: Asbury;
   2002, Reisterstown: Reisterstown; 2005, Superintendent, Frederick District; 2013, Sykesville:
   Sykesville Parish; 2018, Retired.

Chesnutt, Lon B.   RE   CM | St John United Church || Columbia ||| 7360
713 Maiden Choice Ln Apt 2209, Catonsville, MD 21228-3953   H. (410) 737-8119
lchesnutt@aol.com
   1961, N. Georgia Conference; 1969, Baltimore Conference, Washington: Mt. Zion; 1975,
   Metropolitan Memorial, Assoc; 1978, Columbia: St. John; 1986, Glenmont; 1990, Baltimore:
   Hiss; 1994, Associate Council Director; 1997, Retired.

Cheyney, Kathleen   FD   BS | West Liberty || White Hall ||| 3560   (410) 627-7152
18603 York Rd , Parkton, MD 21120-9412   H. (410) 627-7152
kathleencheyney@aol.com
   1990, Attending school; 1993, Leave of Absence; 1994, Emergency Dept. Physician, Vencor
   Hos; 1997, Deacon in Full Connection; 2006, Veterinary Tech at VCA; 2009, Baltimore:
   St Johns; 2014, Maryland Line: Baltimore County Cooperative Parish; 01-01-17, Sparks:
   Bosley-West Liberty.

Chhunga, Biak   OE   GW | Mizo || Rockville ||| 7485   (301) 222-3608
5625 Kirkland Dr, Frederick, MD 21703-8653   H. (301) 222-3608
biakchhunga@gmail.com
   03-01-2008, Rockville: Mizo.

Childs, Zelda   PL   CM | Christ || Columbia ||| 7350
3516 Ellamont Rd, Baltimore, MD 21215   H. (410) 367-7336
zelcap@msn.com
   2011, Baltimore: Homestead; 01-31-18, Columbia: Christ.

Cho, Mi Ja   PE   FR | Arden || Martinsburg ||| 6510   (304) 267-6561
208 Daintree Dr, Martinsburg, WV 25403-1323   H. (703) 973-2004
mayblessyou@gmail.com
   2015, St Leonard: Waters Memorial; 2018, Arden: Arden.

Cho, Steven (Sunghwan)   OE   BS | Wards Chapel || Randallstown ||| 4410
1690 Linzee Dr, Westminster, MD 21157-7428   H. (202) 680-2394
peaceleader@hotmail.com
   09-01-2013, DC: Alpha Community Korean; 2015, New Windsor: Stone Chapel; 1-1-16,
   DC: Alpha Community Korean; 2-1-16, Westminster: Zion; 3-1-16, Baltimore Washington
   Conference; 01-01-17, DC: Alpha Community Korean Charge, 01-01-17, New Windsor: Stone
   Chapel, 01-01-17, Westminster: Zion, 2019, Randallstown: Wards Chapel.

Chung, Kiyul   RE   GW | Metropolitan Memorial || Washington ||| 7630
12-2-2103, Longke GanlanchengWangjing, Chaoyangqu , Beijing, 100101   H. 8.61E+12
kiyul2653@hotmail.com
   1984, N. Tex. Conference; 1987, Baltimore Conference Asian Campus Ministries, U of
   MD; 1994, Attending school; 1997, Timonium; 2000, Extension Min. 335.1, Korean Truth
   Commission; 2001, Leave of Absence; 2002, Washington: Mt. Vernon Place; 2004, Ext. Min.,
   Sec. Gen., World Culture Organ. Com; 2006, Prof. Methodist Theo. Sem.

Claiborne, Sr., Mark   PL   FR | Trinity || Frederick ||| 6225   (301) 524-6000
13816 Exeter Ct , Hagerstown, MD 21742-5313   H. (301) 524-6000
mclaib819@yahoo.com
10-01-17, Frederick: Centennial Memorial, 2019, Frederick: Trinity,

---

Clark, Eva L.   RE   GW | First || Hyattsville ||| 7385
723 Gleneagles Dr, Fort Washington, MD 20744-7006   H. (301) 292-1741
goodwater1@verizon.net
2006, Prof. Methodist Theological Sem.; 01-01-17, Pasadena: Faith Community.

Clark, Margaret   SY   FR | Pleasant View || Adamstown ||| 6165   (410) 442-2761
606 Souder Rd, Brunswick, MD 21716-1735   H. (301) 834-7519
mclark615@verizon.net
2019, Adamstown: Pleasant View.

Clawson, Scott   FL   FR | New Market || New Market ||| 6340   (301) 865-3530
9602 Baltimore Rd, Frederick, MD 21704-6756   H. (240) 409-8119
pastorscott62@gmail.com
2012, Frederick: Mt Carmel/New Market.

Claycomb Sokol, Donna   FE   GW | Mt Vernon Pl || Washington ||| 7235   (202) 347-9620
3566 Martha Custis Dr, Alexandria, VA 22302-2001   H. (202) 679-9310
donna@mvpumc.org
2000, Western No. Carolina Conf; 2005, D.C.: Mt. Vernon Place; 2008, Transferred into BWC Annual Conference.

Clements, Raymond E.   RE   AN | Linthicum Heights || Linthicum ||| 1370
6800 Louise Ct , Anchorage, AK 99507-6735   H. (907) 346-2064
ray@ak.net
1958, Rocky Mt. Conference; 1959, N. T. East; 1965, Baltimore Conference, Wesley Foundation, George Washington University; 1973, International Student Advisor, Geo. Wash. Univ; 1977, Assoc. Dean, Natil. Grad. Univ; 1981, Leave of Absence; 1987, Retired.

Clemons, Margaret E.   FE   CH | Grace || Hagerstown ||| 5325
19912 Fairmont Ct, Hagerstown, MD 21742-6717   H. (240) 513-6299
revmeclemons@gmail.com
1981, Attending school; 1982, University; 1986, Campus Min., Keene St. Col; 1993, Attending school; 10-11-95, Rockville: Faith; 1998, Mt. Airy: Poplar Springs Chg; 2002, Severn: Severn; 2011, Bowie: Bowie; 2018, Hagerstown: Grace.

Click, Peggy   RE   BS | Emory || Upperco ||| 4420   (410) 343-0729
3717 Sue Dan Dr, Hampstead, MD 21074-1835   H. (443) 253-0943
staretal@gmail.com
1988 Attending school; 1989, Rayville Chg; 1991, Parkton: Pine Grove; 2014, Retired; 2017, Upperco: Emory.

Cline, Jerry   FE   FR | Liberty Central || Libertytown ||| 6800   (301) 898-5888
PO Box 337 , Libertytown, MD 21762-0337   H. (301) 898-7505
jerrymarkc@comcast.net
1984, Attending school; 1985, Cumberland: Calvary; 1988, Cumberland: CalvaryBethel; 01-01-92, Ridgeley: Holy Cross; 1994, Libertytown: Liberty Charge.

Clipp, Robert T.   FE   BS | Grace || Aberdeen |||| 2110   (410) 272-0909
110 W Bel Air Ave , Aberdeen, MD 21001-3242   H. (410) 836-8486
pastorbobclipp@comcast.net
1978, Mt. Pleasant Chg; 1980, Shenandoah Junction Enlarged Chg; 1983, Linganore; 1989,
Brooklyn Heights; 1993, Perry Hall; 2005, Aberdeen: Grace.

Clipper-Thomas, Laverne   RA
PO Box 128 , Dickerson, MD 20842-0128   H. (301) 428-8680
pastorlaverne@aol.com
1988, Gaithersburg: Emory Grove; 1992, Sandy Spring: Sharp Street; 1996, Brandywine:
Gibbons; 1997, Washington: Bradbury Hgts./Mt. Vernon Chg; 2000, Baltimore: Howard
Park & Garrison Blvd; 01-16-01, Orchard Park Christian Jubilee; 2005, Franklin P. Nash;
01/02/06, Retired.

Close, John   RL   CH | Hancock || Hancock |||| 5365
17960 Garden Ln Apt 1, Hagerstown, MD 21740-8003   H. (301) 707-0976
johndclose@gmail.com
2009, Little Orleans: Piney Plains; 08-01-2011, Little Orleans: Sideling Hill; 2016, Retired.

Closson, Richard A.   RE   CM | Mountain View || Damascus |||| 9220
1415 Main St Lot 297, Dunedin, FL 34698-6228   H. (727) 736-6892
1953, WNY Conference; 1982, Honorable Location; 1986, Mountain View; 1988, Leave of
Absence; 1990, Retired.

Coakley, David   FE   BS | Union Chapel || Joppa |||| 2510   (301) 606-4779
1412 Stockton Rd, Joppa, MD 21085-1406   H. (301) 606-4779
davidcoakley6@gmail.com
2005, Lewistown; 01-01-2008, Union Bridge: Linganore.; 2016, Joppa: Union Chapel

Coates, Gregory A.   FE   (410) 235-3018
6501 N Charles St, Baltimore, MD 21204-6819   H. (410) 938-4896
gcoates@sheppardpratt.org
1986, Va. Conference; 1988, Peninsula Conference; 1990, Beechfield-Relay; 1995, HWR Mt.
Washington Parish; 1999, Baltimore: Good Shepherd; 2000, Baltimore: Rodgers Forge; 2004,
Ext. Min., Shephard Pratt Health System.

Cochran, Steven T.   FE   AN | Mount Zion || Lothian |||| 1410   (410) 867-4035
107 Monroe Manor Rd, Stevensville, MD 21666-2235   H. (443) 904-4011
revstc@gmail.com
1984, Parke Memorial-Wiseburg Chg; 1988, Parke Memorial-Cedar Grove Chg; 1990,
Hereford: Hereford; 2011, Reisterstown: Reisterstown; 2013, Director: Westminster Rescue
Mission; 2017, Lothian: Mount Zion, 06-30-19, Lothian: Mount Zion, 2019, Ferndale:
Ferndale.

Cockrell, Lysbeth B.   RE   AN | Solley || Glen Burnie |||| 1345   (410) 242-5918
516 Kinglets Roost Ln, Glen Burnie, MD 21060-8645   H. (667) 229-7506
lysbethcockrell@yahoo.com
2018, Retired, 2010, Annapolis: Cape St Claire.; 2016, Baltimore: Halethorpe-Relay Charge

Cofiell, Terri FE BS | Epworth || Cockeysville |||| 3290   (304) 274-1719
310 McGill Dr , Gerrardstown, WV 25420-4030   H. (304) 890-0348
terricofiell@comcast.net
2019, Cockeysville: Epworth, 1985, Attending school; 1986, Chap. Intern, Gallaudet;
1987, Magothy Church of the Deaf; 1992, Frederick: Trinity; 1995, Hyattsville: First; 1996,
Hedgesville; 2008, Marlowe: Harmony.

Cogman, Johnsie W. FE   (410) 309-3472
855 Chatsworth Dr , Accokeek, MD 20607-2032   H. (301) 437-1685
jcogman@bwcumc.org
2009, Waldorf: Zion Wesley; 2011, DC: Mount Zion; 08-01-2011, DC: Mt Zion/Bells Coop;
2-15-16, DC: Mount Zion Charge; 2019, Superintendent, Washington East District.

Colbert, Nona PL   WE | Mount Hope || Sunderland |||| 8475   (410) 257-3206
2456 Richmond Way, Waldorf, MD 20603   H. (240) 346-5301
Pastor1nona@outlook.com
12-01-17, Sunderland: Mount Hope,

Colbert, Samuel J. PL   AN | John Wesley || Annapolis |||| 1145   (410) 263-4125
1398 Primrose Rd, Annapolis, MD 21403-1401   H. (410) 280-5047
jwesley2114@yahoo.com
2006, Annapolis: John Wesley.

Cole Wilson, Stacey FE   (410) 309-3406
13300 Cormorant Pl, Bowie, MD 20720-4762   H. (443) 983-4112
scolewilson@bwcumc.org
2003, Linthicum Heights; 2007, Baltimore: Mount Winans; 2012, Silver Spring: Good Hope
Union.; 2016, Baltimore Washington Conference

Cole, Harry C. RE   CM | Damascus || Damascus |||| 9190
110 Homewood Ln, Frederick, MD 21702-3381   H. 301-304-9666
harryccole@msn.com
1996, Chap. Gaithersburg: Asbury Village; 1998, Damascus: Damascus/Friendship; 2001,
Retired.

Coleman, Mary J. RE   CM | Calvary || Mount Airy |||| 6285
69 Beaconhill Rd , Berlin, MD 21811-1613   H. (410) 641-7315
revmjsc@mchsi.com
1978, Attending school; 1979, Chevy Chase; 1981, Chase: Piney Grove; 1985, Poplar Springs
Chg; 1993, Randallstown: Wardis Chapel; 1998, Dist. Supt.: Washington East; 2005, Retired.

Collette, Carmen R. RE   CM | Community of Faith || Clarksburg |||| 9270
19512 Laguna Dr, Gaithersburg, MD 20879-1824   H. (240) 261-8327
craecollette@gmail.com
1983, Asbury-Mt. Zion Chg; 1984, D.C.: Asbury; 1987, Church of the Redeemer; 1991, Indian
Head: Metropolitan; 12-1-94, F. P. Nash; 1998, Gaithersburg: Emory Grove; 2001, Petworth/
Van Buren Charge; 2009, DC: Ebenezer; 2011, Leave of Absence; 2013, Retired; 2019,
Clarksburg: Community of Faith.

Collier, Ian PE   CM | Wesley Freedom || Eldersburg |||| 4225
9104 Thistledown Rd Apt 478, Owings Mills, MD 21117-8269   H. (518) 409-6614
icc228@georgetown.edu
2019, Eldersburg: Wesley Freedom.

84

Collier, Ronald L. RE
7254 Glen Albin Rd, La Plata, MD 20646-5907   H. (301) 932-3131
rlcollier214@comcast.net
1991, Fort Washington; 2003, Lusby: St. Paul; 2011, Retired.

Comer-Cox, Sherri PE   FR | Taylorsville || Mount Airy ||| 4485
2635 Old Taneytown Rd, Westminster, MD 21158-3531   H. (240) 925-6669
scomercox@msn.com
07-23-19, Leave of Absence - Personal, 2011, St Leonard: Waters Memorial; 2015, Mt Airy: Taylorsville

---

Compres, Fidel RA   GW | Randall Memorial || Washington ||| 7250
11660 Drumcastle Ter, Germantown, MD 20876-5635   H. (301) 972-5603
1998, Extension Ministry; 2003, Baltmore: Hispanic Initiative; 2006, Leave of Absence; 2007, Retired.

Conaway, Edward RL
4622 Debilen Cir Apt C, Pikesville, MD 21208-2425   H. (410) 466-5781
1991, Crownsville: John Wesley; 1994, Incapacity leave; 1996, Annapolis: Cecil Memorial; 1998, Retired; 2010, Woodlawn: St Lukes.

Condon, Glenda RP
2610 Fairfax St , Denver, CO 80207-3223   H. (303) 377-3580
ggcondon@gmail.com
1998, White Hall: West Liberty; 2003, Leave of Absence; 10/16/2005, Rocky Mountain Conference; 2006, Retired.

Connar, Thomas N. RE   CM | Mount Zion || Highland ||| 9310
33 Canvasback Cir, Bridgeville, DE 19933-2429   H. (302) 956-0318
tconnar@comcast.net
1970, West Ohio Conference; 1972, Baltimore Conference, Cedar Grove: Salem; 1974, Assoc. Loch Raven; 1976, Harmans: Wesley Grove; 1981, Brook Hill; 1992, Catonsville; 1998, Highland: Mt. Zion; 2007, Retired.

Connett, Reynold B. RE
9607 Vantage Terrace Ct SE , Olympia, WA 98513-6687   H. (360) 438-2139
1963, Virginia Conference; 1965, Baltimore Conference, Foundry Associate; 1966, Chaplain, U.S. Army; 1988, Retired.

Conte, Joseph A. RE   FR | Middletown || Middletown ||| 6280
6705 Lingane Rd, Chelsea, MI 48118-9435   H. 517-304-1210
jacfive1954@gmail.com
2002, Middletown; 2005, Camp Chapel; 01-01-2008, Wesley Theological Seminary; 2010, Baltimore: Old Otterbein ; 2013, Leave of Absence.

Conway, Robert L. RE
4001 Starlight CtP/O Box 158 , Huntingtown, MD 20639-3500   H. (410) 535-0739
rmconway2005@comcast.net
1993, Prince Frederick Chg; 2005, Prince Frederick: Mt. Olive; 2006, Retired.

Cook, Robert E. FE CM | Poplar Springs || Woodbine ||| 9360
16661 Frederick Rd , Mount Airy, MD 21771-3311 H. (301) 697-2712
rev@hereintown.net
1980, Baltimore Co.: Bentley-Freeland Chg; 1982, Shenandale Chg; 1984, Lewistown; 1985,
Flintstone Chg; 1991, Rawlings; 9-1-94, Ridgeley: Calvary, 1999, Cumberland: Wesley
Charge; 2008, Martinsburg: Pikeside; 2013, Mt Airy: Poplar Springs.

Cook, Thomas SY FR | Johnsville || Sykesville ||| 4450
11285 Old Frederick Rd, Marriottsville, MD 21104-1518 H. (410) 442-2761
pastorcook01@yahoo.com
2001, Gough; 2012, Sykesville: Johnsville.

Cooke, Vincent SY WE | Coopers || Dunkirk ||| 8175
15116 Lady Lauren Ln, Brandywine, MD 20613-7729 H. (240) 377-1400
vcooke1954@gmail.com
2019, Dunkirk: Cooper's.

Coolbaugh, Linda W. RD AN | Nichols-Bethel || Odenton ||| 1430 (410) 674-2272
301 Windfern Ct, Millersville, MD 21108-2419 H. (410) 987-5909
rev.linda@nicholsbethel.org
1992, Severna Park; 1999, Odenton: Nichols-Bethel; 01-01-2012, Retired.

Cooney, Andrew FE CM | Bethany || Ellicott City ||| 4235
1408 Quick Fox Ct, Eldersburg, MD 21784-6482 H. (443) 328-6382
acooney1968@gmail.com
1993, Hagerstown: St. Andrewís; 1999, Attending school; 2000, Berkeley Springs: First; 2014,
Ellicott City: Ellicott City Cooperative Parish.; 1-1-16, Ellicott City: Bethany Charge

---

Cooney, David S. RE FR | Calvary || Frederick ||| 6190
6620 Rockridge Rd, New Market, MD 21774-6618 H. (301) 882-4165
revcooney@gmail.com
1978, Cabin John; 1980, Frederick: Calvary; 1983, Ellicott City: Emory; 1987, Pasadena:
Mt. Carmel; 1992, Attending school; 1995, Cockeysville: Epworth; 09/01/01, Towson: Towson;
2011, Assistant to the Bishop; 2013, Damascus: Damascus; 2018, Retired,.

Cornelius, Janet M. RE CM | Damascus || Damascus ||| 9190
13820 Esworthy Rd , Germantown, MD 20874-3316 H. (301) 926-4925
janetmcornelius@comcast.net
1998, Reisterstown: Grace-Bosley; 2001, Laytonsville: Mt, Carmel-Mt. Tabor Chg; 2008,
Leave of Absence; 10-01-2008, Retired.

Cornwell, Rachel FE GW | Foundry || Washington ||| 7180
1304 Highland Dr, Silver Spring, MD 20910-1622 H. (301) 802-8234
rachelcornwell@me.com
2003, Bethesda: Bethesda Assoc; 2006, Silver Spring: Woodside; 2009, Silver Spring: Silver
Spring Cooperative Parish; 01-01-2014, Silver Spring: Silver Spring; 2017, Transitional
Leave, 2018, ExtMin.

Correll, Merle D. RE CH | Sulphur Springs || Oldtown ||| 5615
26501 Oldtown Rd SE, Oldtown, MD 21555-2026 H. (301) 478-5116
merlepat@gmail.com
1962,Wyoming Conf; 1968, Baltimore Conference, Frostburg;1970, Rawlings-Dawson; 1975,
Rawlings; 1980, Cumberland: Grace; 1982, Retired; 2006, Rawlings: Potomac Valley Parish.

Coveleskie, Linda J. RE   AN | Calvary || Annapolis ||| 1120
107 Gibson Cir , Chester, MD 21619-2184   H. 410-258-4679
ljcovs@gmail.com
1974, Attending school; 1976, Cumberland: Trinity; 1978,Bowie: St. Matthewís; 1983, Gamber: Calvary; 1988, St. Johnís of Hamilton; 1997, Leave of Absence; 2001, Ext. Ministry: St. Elizabethís School; 2008, Retired.

Cowan, Carl S. (Sandy) PL   CH | Barton || Barton ||| 5110
410 National Highway, LaVale, MD 21502   H. (301) 722-2419
bartonumc@gmail.com
2006, Rawlings: Potomac Valley Parish, Westernport; 2013, Barton: Barton/Westernport.

Craig, Richard RE   CH | Calvary || Great Cacapon ||| 5580
269 Keystone Ln, Berkeley Springs, WV 25411-3426   H. (304) 754-3393
RBCraig3@comcast.net
1981, Paw Paw; 1984, Darkesville-Paynes Chapel; 1986, Brentwood; 1989, Brentwood-Mt. Rainier Chg; 1992, Cheltenham; 1997, Forestville: Forest Memorial; 2004, Savage; 2009, Berkeley Springs: Berkeley Springs Parish; 2010, Berkeley Springs: Trinity-Asbury; 2012, Retired; 2019, Great Cacapon: Calvary.

Crane, Marian (Mernie) FE   AN | Pasadena || Pasadena ||| 1470   (410) 647-3090
1605 Old Mill Bottom Run, Annapolis, MD 21409-5556   H. (410) 725-5913
pastoratpumc@verizon.net
2004, U.S Naval Academy Chapel; 2006, Old Otterbein; 2014, Annapolis: Calvary; 2009, Shady Side: Centenary; 2014, Annapolis: Calvary.; 2016, Pasadena: Pasadena Charge

---

Craswell, Janet L. FD   GW | Metropolitan Mem || Washington ||| 7630   (202) 363-4900
702 Owens St , Rockville, MD 20850-2126   H. (240) 472-0763
jcraswell@nationalchurch.org
2005, Brookeville: Salem; 02-01-2014, DC: Metropolitan Memorial Parish.

Crider, Diane A. RE   BM | Towson || Towson ||| 3550
212 Gateswood Rd , Timonium, MD 21093-5245   H. (410) 308-1608
dfcrider@comcast.net
1981, Attending school; 1982, Baltimore: Memorial; 1987, Gaithersburg: Epworth; 1992, Dundalk: Patapsco; 1996, Riderwood: Huntís Memorial; 2002, Retired; 02-16-2009, Pikesville: Milford Mill; 2011, Upper Falls: Salem.

Crider, Robert F. (Frederick) RE   BM | Towson || Towson ||| 3550
212 Gateswood Rd , Timonium, MD 21093-5245   H. (410) 308-1608
dfcrider@comcast.net
1961, Mt. Olivet-Mt. Zion; 1963, Dayton OH: Epworth; Baltimore: Dorguth; Baltimore: Christ; 1964, Attending school; 1967, Baltimore: Christ; 1972, Simms; 1973, Lanham; Ebenezer, 1975, Martinsburg: Otterbein; 1983, Hagerstown: John Wesley; 1987, Supt., Cumberland-Hagerstown Dist; 1993, Linthicum Heights; 1996, Timonium; 2005, Retired; 2011, Upper Falls: Salem; 04-01-19, Upper Falls: Salem.

Crolley, Dennis PL   FR | Chestnut Hill || Harpers Ferry ||| 6570
41 Old Oak Ln, Harpers Ferry, WV 25425-4621
doc@gmsil.com
2010, Harpers Ferry: Chestnut Hill; 2015, Bakerton: Bethel; 1-1-16, Harpers Ferry: Chestnut Hill; 1-1-16, Bakerton: Bethel

---

Cubbage, Vicki   PL   CH | Park Place || LaVale ||| 5375   (301) 722-8145
433 National Hwy, Lavale, MD 21502-7141   H. (240) 522-0515
vickitoad@hotmail.com
2007, Cumberland: Park Place.

Cummings, Forrest   SY   FR | Butlers Chapel || Martinsburg ||| 6590
179 Alydar Rd, Hedgesville, WV 25427-7366   H. (304) 654-4714
fhc44@aol.com
2012, Martinsburg: Butlers Chapel; 01-01-2015, Ganotown: Ganotown.; 01-01-16,
Martinsburg: Butlers Chapel

Curry, Vicki   RE FR | Friendship || Hedgesville ||| 6660
211 Columbia Dr , Kearneysville, WV 25430-6406   H. (304) 262-9646
vcfrog@comcast.net
2001, Prince Frederick: Trinity; 2004, Darksville-Paynes Chapel Chg; 2007, Inwood:
Darkesville; 2008, Mt Airy: Prospect-Marvin Chapel; 2011, Retired.

Dailey, Frances   RE   BS | Timonium || Timonium ||| 3525   (443) 402-1145
2215 Nodleigh Ter, Jarrettsville, MD 21084-1115   H. (410) 252-5500
fdailey@timoniumumc.org
1986, Greater Cacapon: Calvary UMC; 1990, East Ohio Conf; 2007, Timonium: Timonium;
2014, Timonium: Timonium-Fairview Cooperative Parish; 2018, Retired.

Dailey, John   RE   BS | Clynmalira || Phoenix ||| 3450
2215 Nodleigh Ter, Jarrettsville, MD 21084-1115   H. (410) 692-4882
pastor@Clynmalira.org
1988, Martinsburg: Otterbein; 1989, Darkesville; 1990, East Ohio Conf; 2005, White Hall:
West Liberty; 2007, Havre De Grace: Susquehanna; 2010, Phoenix: Clynmalira.

Dameron, Glen W.   RE   CM | Oakdale Emory || Olney ||| 9375
531 Majorca Loop, Myrtle Beach, SC 29579-8004   H. (301) 467-5200
glen.dameron@verizon.net
1977, Attend School; 1978, Oak Chapel; 1980, Damascus-Friendship; 1985, Leave of
Absence; 1988, Street: Dublin-Emory; 1990, Street: Emory; 1993, La Vale: La Vale; 2007,
Monrovia: Mountain View-Pleasant Grove; 2010, Frederick: Trinity; 2013, Retired.

Daniels, Jr., Joseph W.   FE   GW | Emory || Washington ||| 7175   (202) 723-3130
14629 Stonewall Dr , Silver Spring, MD 20905-5857   H. (301) 879-3424
jdaniels@emoryfellowship.org
1993, D.C.: Emory; 2013, District Superintendent, Greater Washington.; 1-1-16, DC: Emory
Charge

Davies, Tunde O.   RE   WE | Huntingtown || Huntingtown ||| 8245   (410) 535-9819
PO Box 130, Barstow, MD 20610-0130   H. (410) 414-9791
tunde.davies4@gmail.com
1986, Cherry Hill; 1995, Huntingtown Chg; 2011, Retired.

Davis, Clarence   RE   BM | New Covenant Worship || Baltimore ||| 3575   (410) 624-5330
3502 Ellamont Rd , Baltimore, MD 21215-7423   H. (410) 367-2025
cdjuniorclergy@msn.com
1990 Brownis Chapel-West Liberty Chg; 1991, Pumphrey: St. John; 1996, Baltimore: Christ;
2006, Retired; 2012, Baltimore: New Covenant Worship Center.

Davis, Darrell I.   PL   FR | Middleburg || Westminster ||| 4490
4639 Bark Hill Rd, Union Bridge, MD 21791   H. (301) 639-9577
dav1pat2@hotmail.com
02/08/2015, New Windsor: Middleburg-Uniontown Charge.

Davis, Karen   FE   CM | Wesley Grove || Gaithersburg ||| 9515
23612 Woodfield Rd, Gaithersburg, MD 20882-2818   H. (410) 812-9437
PastorKaren24@msn.com
*1992, Cockeysville: Texas Chg; 1996, Edgemere: Lodge Forest; 01-01-00, Baltimore:
Grace; 2002, Ellicott City: Bethany; 2006, Carney: Linden Heights; 2012, Baltimore: Mount
Washington-Aldersgate-Overlea Coop Parish; 2015, Baltimore: Landsdown/St. Lukes; 2016,
Damascus: South Damascus Charge*

Davis, Richard S.   RE
133 Thorton Hall Rd, Kearneysville, WV 25430-2889
rdavis5000@aol.com
*1971, Attending school; 1973, Natl. Parks Ministry; 1974, Prospect-Marvin Chg; 1979,
Mt. Savage; 1983, Waters Memorial; 1987, Baltimore: St. Lukeís; 1991, Glenn Dale; 1996,
Beltsville: Emmanuel; 2006, Retired.*

Davis, Sr., Albert   LM   BM | Eastern || Baltimore ||| 2175
1300 E Cold Spring Ln , Baltimore, MD 21239-3911   H. (443) 201-6886
aldavis812@yahoo.com

Day, Jackson   RE   BS | Providence || Towson ||| 3370
719 Maiden Choice Ln , Catonsville, MD 21228-6138   H. (410) 303-8213
jackdayconnect@gmail.com
*1964, Little Orleans: Piney Plains Charge; 1967, Chaplain, U.S. Army; 1970, D.C.: Epworth;
1971, Honorable Location; 2001, Board of Church & Society; 2003, Hampstead: Grace; 2008,
Retired; 2010, Monkton: Monkton; 01-04-2012, Towson: Providence.*

Day, Sally J.   RE   CM | Calvary || Mount Airy ||| 6285
21 Dove Trl , Fairfield, PA 17320-8082   H. (717) 642-5905
1979, Attending school; 1989, Prot. Chap. MD Correctional Inst; 2005, Retired.

Deal, Albert   PL   CH | Salem || Keedysville ||| 6250
21824 Ringgold Pike, Hagerstown, MD 21742-1478   H. (301) 964-9993
aldeal1003@gmail.com
*05-05-2013, Thurmont: Mt. Zion; 2015, Keedysville: Salem.; 01-01-2016, Thurmont: Mt. Zion
Charge; 2019, Big Pool: Potomac.*

Dean, John H.   FL   FR | Deer Park || Westminster ||| 4535   (410) 848-2313
1531 S Rambling Way , Frederick, MD 21701-2515   H. (240) 575-9313
jdpreacher@outlook.com
2003, Urbana: Wesley Chapel; 2009, Boonsboro: Benevola.; 2016, Westminster: Deer Park.

Deans, David J.   FE   CM | Oakdale Emory || Olney ||| 9375
3415 Emory Church Road, Olney, MD 20832   H. (240) 389-0787
ddeans@oakdale.church
2003, Essex: Back River; 2010, Olney: Oakdale Emory.

DeFord, George RE WE | Smith Chapel || Marbury |||| 8415 (301) 743-2227
4452 Pleasant Hill Ct , Pomfret, MD 20675-3107 H. (301) 868-2382
secgensig@yahoo.com
1982, Laurel: St. Markis; 1993, Baltimore: Mt. Zion; 1996, D.C.: Ebenezer; 2000, Indian
Head: Metropolitan; 2008, Annapolis Southern Region guide; 2011, Pisgah: Smith Chapel-
Alexandria Chapel Cooperative Parish; 2011, Retired; 2013, Marbury: Smith Chapel.

DeGroote, Peter L. RE GW | Foundry || Washington |||| 7180
1490 7th St NW Apt 411, Washington, DC 20001-3391 H. (301) 328-0668
peterdeg@msn.com
1993, Shady Side: Centenary; 1996, Baltimore: Mt. Vernon; 1998, Essex: Back River; 2003,
College Park; 2004, D.C.: Foundry; 2006, D.C.: United; 2009, Retired.

DeHart, Wayne A. RE CM | Bethany || Ellicott City |||| 4235
3011 Auburn Vw, Ellicott City, MD 21042-7115 H. (410) 531-7839
waynedehart@verizon.net
1967, Attending school; 1969, North Harford; 1972, Bethesda: Bethesda Assoc; 1976,
West Baltimore; 1982, Ellicott City: Bethany; 1989, Bethesda: Bethesda; 1998, Dist. Supt.:
Frederick Dist; 2005, Baltimore-Washington Conf., Dir. of Human Res. and Connectional Life;
01-01-2007, Guide; 2010, Retired.

Deitiker, Janet FE BS | Cokesbury || Abingdon |||| 2125 (210) 743-3305
6636 Pembroke Rd, San Antonio, TX 78240-2719 H. (210) 725-6245
janet.deitiker@att.net
1998, Frederick: Brook Hill; 2001, Abingdon: Cokesbury; 2005, Leave of Absence; 04-01-
2009, Extension Minister.

DeLeo, Ali T. PE AN | Community || Pasadena |||| 1440 (410) 255-1506
1772 Woodtree Cir, Annapolis, MD 21409-5461 H. (410) 255-1506
alideleo@gmail.com
2017, Pasadena: Faith Community,

DeLong, Edwin C. RE GW | Emmanuel || Laurel |||| 7440
719 Maiden Choice Lane HR 135, Catonsville, Maryland 21228 H. (410) 608-1690
ecdelong1@gmail.com
1966, Attending school; 1968, Kensington: St. Paulis; 1969, Shady Side: Centenary; 1977,
Arnold: Asbury; 1985, Kensington: St. Paulis; 1991, Dist. Supt. Baltimore East; 1994, Dist.
Sup. Baltimore-Harford; 1999, Associate Council Director; 2005, Retired; 01-01-2007, Chase:
Ebenezer-Piney Grove Cooperative Parish; 2009, Baltimore: Old Otterbein; 08-01-16, BWC
Cabinet BM Dist. .

Dembeck, Chris PE BM | Halethorpe-Relay || Halethorpe |||| 3120
4513 Ridge Ave , Halethorpe, MD 21227-4440 H. (410) 952-3650
Chrisdembeck@gmail.com
2013, Baltimore: West Baltimore; 2014, Middle River: Orems; 2018, Baltimore: Halethorpe-
Relay.

Demby, Sandra E. RE BM | St. Matthews-New Life || Baltimore |||| 3247 (410) 531-6187
5113 Herring Run Dr , Baltimore, MD 21214-2143 H. (410) 254-3128
pastordemby@msn.com
1998, Hereford: Hereford; 1999, Gaithersburg: Epworth; 2000, Highland: Hopkins; 2012,
Retired.

Dennis, Lena Marie   FE   AN | John Wesley || Glen Burnie |||| 1330   (410) 766-6981
2701 E Strathmore Ave, Baltimore, MD 21214   H. (410) 685-0302
dhumbleone@aol.com
2005, Baltimore: Eastern; 2014, Glen Burnie: John Wesley.

Dennis, Mary E.   FD   CM | Glen Mar || Ellicott City |||| 7365   (818) 882-8005
7 North Stead Ct, Catonsville, MD 21228-2443   H. (410) 804-5147
MDen2154@gmail.com
2018, On Loan to California-Pacific Conference, 2000, Scaggsville: Emmanuel; 2003,
Ellicott City: Glen Mar; 2007, Western Region Guide; 03-01-2011, Director of Discipleship;
2012, Leave of Absence; 01-01-2013, Extension Ministry -Princeton University; 01-01-2014,
Transistional Leave; 8-16-15, Damascus: Montgomery Charge

Derby, Mark A.   RE   CM | Oakdale Emory || Olney |||| 9375
4900 Continental Dr, Olney, MD 20832-2972
revmaderby@gmail.com
1974, Attending school; 1976, Bowie-Kettering Charge; 1981, Montgomery; 1995, Rockville:
Faith; 2000, Supt., Baltimore-Harford Dist; 8/15/04 Supt, Washington West, 2006, Sup.
Washington West and Gaithersburg: Grace; 2014, Retired.

Dissmeyer, Timothy H.   RE   CM | Montgomery || Damascus |||| 9215
13465 Four Seasons Ct, Mount Airy, MD 21771-7501   H. (301) 829-1541
Tdissmeyer@aol.com
1981, D.C.: Mt. Vernon Place; 1984, Long Green Chg; 1989, Bowie: St. Matthewis; 1991,
Glen Burnie: Marley; 1992, Marley-Solley Chg; 1996, Linthicum Heights; 1999, Damascus:
Montgomery; 12-14-2006, Leave of Absence; 2007, Retired.

Ditto, James L.   RE   BS | Fallston || Fallston |||| 2435   (410) 879-1537
209 Cartland Way, Forest Hill, MD 21050-3107   H. (410) 893-5935
jimdit@comcast.net
1968, Attending school; 1969, Morgan, W. Va; 1971, Bel Air Assoc; 1974, Savage; 1978,
Brookville-Mt. Carmel; 1981, Hebbville: Salem; 1988, Fallston; 2010, Retired.

Dixon, Geri D. (Dee-Ann)   FE   FR | New Street || Shepherdstown |||| 6750   (304) 876-2362
655 Deer Mountain Dr , Harpers Ferry, WV 25425-5475   H. (304) 268-8521
dixon-gross@655dmd.com
1993, Charles Town: Asbury; 10-1-98, Charlestown: Asbury/Kabletown Coop. Parish; 2000,
Shepherdstown: New Street.

Dixon, Ruth   RL WE | Olivet || Lusby |||| 8335   (410) 610-1219
920 Ed Joy Rd, Lusby, MD 20657-2620   H. (410) 610-1219
pastor.ruth@hotmail.com
2008, St Leonard: Waters Memorial; 2015, Retired; 1-1-16, Leonardtown: First Saints
Community

Dixon-Proctor, Diane   RE CM | Sharp Street || Sandy Spring |||| 9445
127 Foxtrap Dr , Glen Burnie, MD 21061-6338   H. (410) 766-4890
ddpny@aol.com
1996, Churchton: Franklin; 1998, Glen Burnie: John Wesley; 2009, DC: Lincoln Park; 2017,
Retired, 01-01-18, Sandy Spring: Sharp Street.

Dize, Ellin M.   RL   FR | Stone Chapel || New Windsor ||| 4545
11733 Terry Town Dr , Reisterstown, MD 21136-3218   H. (410) 833-7440
edize@comcast.net
2001, Sykesville: Flohrville; 2005, New Windsor: Stone Chapel; 2009, Retired.

Dodson, Sr., Ronald   PL   BM | Faith Community || Baltimore ||| 2192   (410) 821-7502
9602 Wesland Cir, Randallstown, MD 21133-2042   H. (410) 922-0658
rondodson@verizon.net
2013, Baltimore: West Baltimore; 01-01-17, Baltimore: Metropolitan-W. Baltimore, 2017,
Baltimore: Faith Community.

Doggett, Carroll A.   RE   FR | Calvary || Frederick ||| 6190
7351 Willow RdCottage 12 , Frederick, MD 21702-2415   H. (240) 629-1961
carroll.doggett@gmail.com
1948, Stewartstown; 1953, Loch Raven; 1965, Rockville: Millian Memorial; 1970, Hyattsville:
First; 1974, Supt., Baltimore Southwest Dist; 1980, Frederick: Calvary; 1988, Retired.

Dominguez, Lemuel   FE   BS | Milford Mill || Pikesville ||| 4380   (410) 465-2919
813 Staffordshire Rd, Cockeysville, MD 21030-2926   H. (443) 240-2557
vessel187@gmail.com
2013, Baltimore: Bethesda; 2015, Ellicott City:Bethany; 2018, Pikesville: Milford Mill.

Dorrance, Sarah B.   FE   FR | Brook Hill || Frederick ||| 6185
202 Cone Branch Dr , Middletown, MD 21769-7843   H. (301) 471-9321
sarahdorrance@gmail.com
2008, Mt Airy: Taylorsville; 2015, Middletown: Middletown; 2019, Leave of Absence.

Dotterer, Vicki   RE   CM | Wesley Chapel || Frederick ||| 6385   (301) 972-0822
23013 Timber Creek Ln, Clarksburg, MD 20871-9440   H. (301) 956-0124
rev.vicki.d@gmail.com
1999, Urbana: Wesley Chapel; 2002, Bunker Hill; 2010, Woodfield: Wesley Grove; 2013,
Monrovia: Mountain View-Pleasant Grove; 2014, Retired.

Dowell, Timothy A.   FE   CM | Memorial || Poolesville ||| 9385   (410) 668-5665
210 East Rd, Mount Airy, MD 21771-2840   H. (443) 206-4949
pastortim@pmumc.org
2001, Susquehanna Charge; 2007, Urbana: Faithpoint; 2012, Baltimore: Hiss; 2018,
Poolesville: Memorial.

Duchesneau, Susan E.   RE AN | Ferndale || Glen Burnie ||| 1268   (410) 761-2880
790 Monaco Dr, Punta Gorda, FL 33950-8018   H. (410) 591-1830
sed228@verizon.net
1986, Attending school; 1988, Glen Burnie: Glen Burnie; 1991, Ferndale: Ferndale; 2010,
Retired.

Duckett, Wanda B.   FE   BM | Mount Zion || Baltimore ||| 4150   (410) 304-3435
5522 Sefton Ave , Baltimore, MD 21214-2341   H. (443) 629-9232
wduckett@bwcumc.org
2006, Baltimore: Monroe Street; 2010, Baltimore: Mount Zion; 2017, BWC Cabinet BM Dist.

Dudley, Ray   PL   FR | Deerfield || Sabillasville ||| 6260   (301) 241-3036
7316 Lakeview Rd, Frederick, MD 21701   H. (301) 898-5456
rwfgd@comcast.net
2008, Boonsboro: Mount Lena; 2011, Frederick: Deerfield.

Duke, Amy E.   FD   GW | Foundry || Washington ||| 7180   (202) 841-6881
244 Vanderbilt Ave Apt 1R, Brooklyn, NY 11205-4109   H. (347) 599-2000
AmyEllenDB@NationalSkillsCoalition.org
2006, Ext. Min., Center for Law and Social Policy.

Dunlop, Betty P.   RE   AN | Mayo || Edgewater ||| 1148   (410) 271-9383
4410 Forest Glen Ct , Annandale, VA 22003-4838   H. (703) 642-6490
betty.dunlop@verizon.net
*1997, DC: Foundry; 1998, Pikesville: Ames-Sudbrook; 2001, Hagerstown: St Andrews; 2004,
Mayo: Mayo; 2009, Retired.*

Dunmore, Marian   RE
702 16th St NE , Washington, DC 20002-4514
mariandunmore@aol.com
*1983, Churchville Chg; 1984, Glyndon Par; 1987, Wash. Urban Chg; 1989,Leave of Absence;
1992, Kenilworth-Parkside Sub. Abuse Prog; 1993, Leave of Absence; 1994, Dir. of Grief
Inst; 2000, Friendship: Carterís; 2004, Crownsville: John Wesley-Waterbury; 2006, Leave of
Absence; 04-28-2008, Retired.*

Dunnington, Kenneth   RE FR | Middletown || Middletown ||| 6280
620 Humberson Ln , Frederick, MD 21703-2223   H. (301) 631-5605
krdunnington@gmail.com
*1971, Attending school; 1973, Linthicum Heights Assoc; 1977, Immanuel-Curtis Bay; 1982,
Catonsville: Emanuel; 1987, Havre de Grace; 1994, Baltimore: Hiss; 2004, Frederick:
Calvary; 2013, Retired; 2013, Westminster: St James.; 2016, Lisbon: Lisbon Charge; 2019,
Middletown: Middletown.*

Durbin, Kyle   FE   CH | Frostburg || Frostburg ||| 5310
46 W Main St, Frostburg, MD 21532-1642   H. (443) 223-5717
ImKyleDurbin@gmail.com
2014; Shady Side: Centenary; 2016, Frostburg: Frostburg Charge.

Earle, Jr., George   RE   CH | Rehoboth || Williamsport |||| 5470   H. (301) 842-1130
14037 Barnhart Rd, Clear Spring, MD 21722-1140
pastrgeo@gmail.com
*1975, Maryland Line Charge; 1978, Scaggsville: Emmanuel; 1981, Attending school;
1982, New York Hill; 11-1-89, Brunswick Cooperative Parish; 1994, Frederick: Centennial
Memorial; 2011, Hedgesville: Hedgesville; 2014, Retired.*

Easterling, Jr., Marion   OE   CM | Locust || Columbia |||| 7355
6851 Martin Rd, Columbia, MD 21044-4017   H. (410) 531-5323
m7east@gmail.com
09-01-16, Harmans: Wesley Grove, 2019, Columbia: Locust,

Edmonds, Walter G.   RE   CM | Damascus || Damascus ||| 9190
3889 Maryland Manor Dr , Monrovia, MD 21770-8909   H. (301) 831-3472
WPEdmonds70@comcast.net
1968, So. NJ Conference; 1978, Wis. Conference; 1982, Baltimore Conference, Min. of
Music: St. Luke Lutheran; 1/1/88, Damascus: Damascus-Friendship Chg; 2011, Damascus:
Damascus; 2013, Retired.

Efodzi, Martina   PD   GW | Lincoln Park || Washington ||| 7215   (202) 797-4435
14440 W Side Blvd Apt 307, Laurel, MD 20707-6275   H. (202) 222-8861
arthealsdc@gmail.com
2016, Ext Min: Whitman-Walker Health.

Ehrgott, Curtis C.   FE   GW | Concord-St Andrews || Bethesda ||| 9130   (410) 207-4725
6308 Blackwood Rd, Bethesda, MD 20817-5904   H. (410) 207-4725
pastorcurtise@gmail.com
2005, Hampstead: Wesley; 2013, Hagerstown: Grace; 2018, Bethesda: Concord-Saint
Andrews.

Elliott, Sarah   PE   BS | Cokesbury || Abingdon ||| 2125   (410) 676-6295
2968 Dumbarton Dr, Abingdon, MD 21009   H. (703) 801-7355
pastorsarahelliott@gmail.com
2018, Abington: Cokesbury, 2016, Havre De Grace: Susquehanna Charge

---

Ellis, Howard R. (Ron)   RE   CH | Salem || Myersville ||| 6435
12404 Loy Wolfe Rd, Myersville, MD 21773-9507   H. (301) 293-8961
ellisron@comcast.net
1978, Buckeystown Route 85; 1979, Wolfsville Chg; 1989, Retired.

Elston, Sr., Gerald L.   PL   GW | Brightwood Park || Washington ||| 7125   (301) 899-7521
3136 Gershwin Ln , Silver Spring, MD 20904-6813   H. (301) 890-9559
Lawdad513@aol.com
2007, DC: Mount Zion -Bells Coop Parish; 03-01-2009, Camp Springs: Bells; 2011, DC:
Brightwood Park; 2015, DC: Albright Memorial.; 1-1-16, DC: Albright Memorial; 1-1-16,
DC: Brightwood Park

Emerick, Louis L.   RA   CH | Emmanuel || Hagerstown ||| 5320
8507 Mapleville Rd, Boonsboro, MD 21713-1818   H. (301) 791-6335
1950, Midland Chg; 1956, Union Grove; 1959, Cumberland: Trinity; 1969, Berkeley Springs
Chg; 1973, Hagerstown: Wash. Square; 1981, Glen Burnie; 1985, Fallston; 1988, Retired.

Emerson, Judith A.   FE   CM | Ebenezer || Sykesville ||| 4575
2091 Saint James Rd , Marriottsville, MD 21104-1436   H. (410) 442-2881
revjae@aol.com
1998, Odenton: Nichols Bethel; 1999, Towson; 2006, Winfield: Ebenezer.

Ennis, George W.   RE   (301) 475-1968
21754 Potomac View Dr , Leonardtown, MD 20650-2132   H.
georgeennis10545@msn.com
1968, Troy Conference; 1970, Baltimore Conference, Jessup-Guilford; 1974, Sykesville: St.
Paul; 1982, Leonardtown: St. Paulís; 1993, Hagerstown: Grace; 1997, Severna Park: Severna
Park; 1999, Wheaton: Hughes; 2008, Retired.

Eschliman, Jennifer   FE   CM | Glen Mar || Ellicott City ||| 7365   (410) 465-4995
4701 New Cut Rd , Ellicott City, MD 21043-6603   H. (410) 456-0656
jen.eschliman@glenmarumc.org
2010, Ellicott City: Glen Mar.

Eyler, Mark   PL   FR | Brandenburg || Sykesville ||| 4580
221 Apples Church Rd , Thurmont, MD 21788-1703   H. (301) 271-7939
pastormark1umc@gmail.com
2018, Sykesville: Brandenburg,

Farabee-Lewis, Iris   RE   BM | St Luke || Baltimore ||| 4155   (410) 566-5058
1503 Regester Ave , Loch Hill, MD 21239-1626   H. (443) 895-4563
st.jamesumc1@gmail.com
2017, Retired, 1991, Baltimore: Centennial-Caroline Street; 2006, Baltimore: St. James;
2012, Baltimore: St. James-Mt. Winans Cooperative Parish.

Farmer, James H.   RA   AN | Severna Park || Severna Park ||| 1510
37932 Bayview Cir E, Selbyville, DE 19975-2870
1988, Tom's Creek; 1993, Clinton: Clinton; 1999, Prince Frederick: Trinity; 2007, Annapolis
Southern Region guide; 01-01-2008, Assistant to Bishop; 2008, Severna Park: Severna Park;
2014, Retired.

Farrady, William C.   RE   GW | Rockville || Rockville ||| 9440
5607 Chincoteague Ct, Oceanside, CA 92057-5548   H. (760) 822-9253
godot7x@yahoo.com
1960, S. Carolina Conference; 1965, Baltimore Conference, Rockville: Francis Asbury; 1973,
Silver Spring: Marvin Memorial; 1979, Potomac; 1984, Rockville; 1991, Leave of Absence;
10-01-91, Retired.

Fauconnet, Michael   FE   AN | Mount Carmel || Pasadena ||| 1460   (410) 255-8887
4760 Mountain Rd , Pasadena, MD 21122-5814   H. (240) 405-2750
soujourner56@gmail.com
1982, Attending school; 1984, Marvin Memorial; 1986, Delmont; 12-88, Hampstead: Wesley;
1993, Street: Emory; 2000, Thurmont; 2006, New Market; 2011, Pasadena: Mount Carmel.

Fell, Kenneth R.   RE   CM | Covenant || Montgomery Village ||| 9235
20547 Summersong Ln, Germantown, MD 20874-1071   H. (301) 972-6381
kenfell@aol.com
1980, Southern NJ; 1983, Baltimore Conference, Union Bridge; 1985, Woodside; 1990,
Germantown: Trinity; 8-1-95, Sabbatical; 9-15-95, Monrovia Chg; 9-1-02, Poolesville:
Memorial; 2011, Glenelg: Glenelg; 2015, Retired; 09-01-18, Gaithersburg: Covenant.

Fenner, Jennifer L.   FE   CM | Epworth || Gaithersburg ||| 9245
16501 Alden Ave , Gaithersburg, MD 20877-1505   H. (443) 928-3771
jennifer.fenner@eumc-md.org
2007, Upper Marlboro: Bethel; 2010, Gaithersburg: Epworth.

Ferrell, Lee S.   FD   AN | Severna Park || Severna Park ||| 1510   (410) 987-4700
731 Benfield Rd, Severna Park, MD 21146   H. (410) 562-9811
lferrell@severnaparkumc.org
1976, Severna Park; 1980, Leave of Absence; 1982, Severna Park.

Fiedler, Claire L. RE AN | Linthicum Heights || Linthicum ||| 1370
725 Olive Wood Ln, Baltimore, MD 21225-3382 H. (410) 354-2871
clfiedler@juno.com
1980, Jessup: Wesley Chapel; 1984, Emmarts; 1996, Halethorpe-Relay.; 2016, Retired

---

Fisher, Robert SY CH | First || Berkeley Springs ||| 5515
146 Coite Ln, Statesville, NC 28625-1659 H. (704) 677-8826
rob.fisher1@gmail.com
01-01-2013, Berkeley Springs: Alpine; 2015, Retired.

Fizer, Jr., Ken J. FE FR | Thurmont || Thurmont ||| 6360
13880 Long Rd , Thurmont, MD 21788-2261 H. (301) 271-4511
kfizer@minister.com
1993, Keedysville: Salem; 2001, Martinsburg: Otterbein; 2010, Hagerstown: Shiloh; 2017, Fallston: Ebenezer-William Watters; 2019, Thurmont: Thurmont.

Flanagan, Angela FE GW | Silver Spring || Silver Spring ||| 9466
1010 Dale Dr, Silver Spring, MD 20910-4124 H. (443) 934-1078
aflanagan@silverspringumc.org
2013, Mt Airy: Calvary; 2017, Silver Spring: Silver Spring.

Fleet, Bryan K. FE WE | Patuxent || Huntingtown ||| 8250 (301) 868-6927
7806 Colonial Ln , Clinton, MD 20735-1825 H. (301) 868-6927
bryanf32@Verizon.net
2003, Barnesville: Mt. Zion-Warren; 06-01-2009, Barnsville: West Montgomery; 2011, Huntingtown: Huntingtown Combined.

Footen, John F. RA CH | Rawlings || Rawlings ||| 5445
341 Channing Dr, Chambersburg, PA 17201-3230 H. (301) 707-9585
johnfooten@hotmail.com
1986, Cumberland: Bethel-Mt. Fairview; 1988, Rawlings: Dawson; 01-01-93, Dawson-Westernport Charge; 1/1/04, Potomac Valley Parish; 2006 Ext. Min., Chaplain, Western Md. Health System; 11-01-2010, Retired.

Ford, Alice K. FE CM | Glenelg || Glenelg ||| 9285
7407 Leaf Shade Ct, Laurel, MD 20707 H. (410) 813-2709
pastoralice@gmail.com
2008, Rockville: Millian Memorial; 2013, Frederick: Calvary/Centennial Memorial Cooperative Parish; 2015, Glenelg: Glenelg.

Forman, Anthony PL BM | West Baltimore || Baltimore ||| 4165 (443) 690-9336
7420 Eldon Ct, Pikesville, MD 21208 H. (443) 944-2247
pastor4man@gmail.com
01-01-17, Baltimore: West Baltimore, 2019, Baltimore: West Baltimore-Unity,

---

Forman, Scheherazade PL BM | Violetville || Baltimore ||| 3260
7420 Eldon Ct, Pikesville, MD 21208 H. (443) 690-9336
dr4man31@gmail.com
01-01-17, Baltimore: West Baltimore, 2018, Baltimore: Violetville,

---

Fossett, David PL   FR | Hopehill || Frederick ||| 6155   (301) 670-9220
7647 Fingerboard Rd , Frederick, MD 21704-7634   H. (301) 874-1166
pastordavid@hopehillumc.org
2018, Frederick: Hopehill,

Foster, Daryl A. PL   BM | Cherry Hill || Baltimore ||| 2155   (410) 551-7969
18 N Belle Grove Rd , Catonsville, MD 21228-2049   H. (443) 278-6341
severnspastor@gmail.com
2004, Westminster: Union Street; 2016, Severn: Delmont/Severn; 2019, Baltimore: Cherry Hill.

Foster, Ronald K. FE   AN | Severna Park || Severna Park ||| 1510   (410) 987-4700
731 Benfield Rd, Severna Park, MD 21146   H. (240) 672-1321
ron@severnaparkumc.org
1985, E. Penna. Conference; 1986, Baltimore Conference, Benevola Chg; 1989, Reisterstown; 1998, Bethesda: Bethesda; 2014, Severna Park: Severna Park.

Fox, Douglas E. RE   CM | Christ || Columbia ||| 7350
6273 Cobbler Ct, Columbia, MD 21045-4503   H. (410) 294-2818
douglasefox@verizon.net
1974, West NY Conference; 1976, N. Car. Conference; 08-15-84, Baltimore Conference, Ecumenical Campus Min; 1988, Old Otterbein; 1992, Baltimore: Waverly-Wilson Parish; 1994, Columbia: Christ; 2000, D.C.: Capitol Hill; 2003, Pasadena: Community 2004, Faith Community Coop. Parish; 2006, Sabbatical Leave; 2009, Laurel: Community-Savage Cooperative Parish; 2011, Retired; 2011, Savage: Savage; 2013, Ellicott City: Gary Memorial.

Fraim, Marshall D. (Douglas) RL   FR | Sandy Hook || Knoxville ||| 6255
6426 Spring Forest Rd, Frederick, MD 21701-7634   H. (304) 535-1375
dougfraim@aol.com
1998, Harpers Ferry: Camp Hill-Wesley; 2002, Retired; 2013, Harpers Ferry: Harpers Ferry.

Frame, Bruce C. RL   BS | Monkton || Monkton ||| 3385
826 E Joppa Rd , Towson, MD 21286-5621   H. (410) 821-5927
pastorbruce@comcast.net
2019, Monkton: Monkton, 2003, Wiseburg; 03-01-2008, Parkton: Wiseburg-West Liberty Coop Parish; 2012, White Hall: West Liberty; 2014, Retired.

Franzen, Julia L. (Lisa) PL   FR | Berkeley Place || Martinsburg ||| 6645
PO Box 1925, Inwood, WV 25428-1925   H. (304) 229-2275
readsps27@gmail.com
2016, Harpers Ferry: Engle; 2016, Bolivar: Bolivar; 2017, Martinsburg: Berkeley Pl-Friendship.

Fraser, Daphne OE   CM | Fairview || Sykesville ||| 4345
17152 Moss Side Ln, Olney, MD 20832-2938   H. (301) 924-0647
fieldcourt@yahoo.com
2016, Taylorsville: Fairview.

Frazier, Malcolm FE   CM | Grace || Gaithersburg ||| 9260
15250 Siesta Key Way Apt 469, Rockville, MD 20850-5572   H. (240) 670-7680
frazier1950@verizon.net
2000, D.C.: Asbury/Howard Univ. (Wesley Foundation); 2002, Ext. Min., Howard Univ. (Wesley Foundation); 05-31-2011, General Board of Global Ministries; 2018, DC: Foundry, 02-18-19, Asbury Methodist Village.

Fringo, Robert J.   RE   BS | Camp Chapel || Perry Hall ||| 2530   (410) 256-5561
9513A Horn Ave , Nottingham, MD 21236-1523   H. (410) 256-5670
robjoe1927@aol.com
1956, Exeter Memorial: 1958, East Baltimore Station; 1960, Broadway-East Baltimore Parish;
1965, Fells Point; 1975, Ellicott City Parish; 1979, Ellicott City: Emory; 1983, Halethorpe;
3/1/96, Retired; 01-01-2008, Perry Hall: Camp Chapel.

Frum, Charles W. (Wayne)   RA   FR | Bunker Hill || Bunker Hill ||| 6525
1387 Trainer Road, Buckhannon, WV 26201   H. (301) 988-7654
pastorcwayne@gmail.com
2017, Retired, 1991, Indian Head Chg; 1995, Berkeley Springs: Berkeley-Morgan Charge;
2005, Hagerstown: Shiloh; 2010, Bunker Hill: Bunker Hill.

Fry, Rod C.   SY   CM | Ijamsville || Ijamsville ||| 6235
4240 Tabler Rd, Frederick, MD 21704-7779   H. (301) 633-5910
circuitrider.rodfry@gmail.com
2018, Ijamsville: Ijamsville.

Frye, Lawrence R.   RE   CH | Grace || Midland ||| 5410
874 Mount Jackson Rd , Mount Jackson, VA 22842-2864   H. (540) 477-4226
1963, Franklin Chg; 1967, Cumberland: Calvary; 1970, Wesley Circuit; 1974, Baltimore:
Salem; 1977, Susquehanna Chg; 1981, Indian Head; 1988, Pleasant Grove; 1992, Catonsville:
Emanuel; 1994, Midland Chg; 1999, Retired.

Funk, Robert E. (Eugene)   RE
143 Beech Hill Rd , Mount Desert, ME 04660-6202   H. (207) 244-9006
1957, Jessup-Harwood; 1960, Lansdowne: 1972, Reisterstown; 1984, Columbia: Christ; 1989,
Lutherville: St. Johnís; 1991, St. Johnís/Providence Parish.

Gaines, G. Sylvester   RE   AN | Wilson Memorial || Gambrills ||| 1290
6011 84th Ave , New Carrollton, MD 20784-2924   H. (301) 459-7310
gainesrev@yahoo.com
1973, Patapsco Park: St. John; 1976, Dundalk: St. Matthewís; 1984, Eastern; 1987,
McKendree; 1992, D.C.: Randall Memorial; 1995, Capitol Heights: Gethsemane.; 2016,
Retired

Gaines-Cirelli, Ginger E.   FE   GW | Foundry || Washington ||| 7180   (202) 332-4010
1500 16th St NW , Washington, DC 20036-1402
ggainescirelli@foundryumc.org
2001, Rockville: Francis Asbury; 2003, D.C.: Capitol Hill; 2008, Leave of Absence; 2010,
Bowie: St Matthews; 2014, DC: Foundry.

Galloway, Albert L.   RE   GW | Silver Spring || Silver Spring ||| 9466
5445 Kerns Ln, Indianapolis, IN 46268-4083   H. (317) 875-1081
allgalloway@aol.com
1958, Attending School; 1962, Silver Spring: Marvin Memorial; 1967, Indiana University:
Chaplain; 1988, Extension Ministry: Director of Pastoral Care IU; 1999, Director Lifeline
Foundation; 2003, Retired.

98

Garland, Lowell S. RE CH | Park Place || Lavale ||| 5375
3900 Camphor Pl, Cocoa, FL 32926-3163 H. (321) 633-0906
lowellruth@hotmail.com
*1957, New Market; 1958, Attending school;1959, Holston Conference; 1960, Brookeville-Mt.
Carmel; 1962, Asst. Marvin Memorial; 1964, Assoc., Chevy Chase; 1965, Attending school;
1967, Chap., Ind. Univ.-Purdue Univ; 1969, Cumberland: La Vale; 1977, Leave of Absence;
1978, Dir., Chap. Dept. IU Med Ctr; 1979, Westernport; 1980, Rawlings; 1988, LifeLink
Foundation of Fla; 1991, Retired.*

Gates-Ward, Laurie FE WE | Good Shepherd || Waldorf ||| 8525
5326 Flagfish Ct , Waldorf, MD 20603-4222 H. (301) 843-6797
revlaurie@aol.com
*1996, Lusby: St. Paul; 1998, Indian Head Chg; 1/1/2000, Edgemere: Lodge Forest; 2009,
Dundalk: Patapsco-Lodge Forest Cooperative Parish; 2012, Waldorf: Good Shepherd.*

Gautcher, III, Gerald P. PL BS | Deer Park || Reisterstown ||| 4415
6107 Deer Park Rd , Reisterstown, MD 21136-5900 H. (443) 520-2571
pjgautcher@gmail.com
2010, Baltimore: Salem-Baltimore Hispanic; 2012, Upperco: Deer Park.

Gayles, Ernest E. SY BS | Mount Vernon || Whiteford ||| 2580
3402 Bateman Ave, Baltimore, MD 21216 H. (410) 499-6656
eegayles@gmail.com
2019, Whiteford: Mount Vernon,

Geib, Lillian R. RE CM | Salem || Brookeville ||| 9150
18 Maple Leaf Rd , Spencer, VA 24165-3145 H.
2geiblp18@comcast.net
*1997, Solomons Chg., 1999, Lusby: Olivet; 9-01-01, Brookeville: Salem; 2008, Leave of
Absence; 08-01-2008, Retired.*

Geller, Jr., Donald G. PL WE | Community w. Cause || Lexington Park||| 8295
47306 Willow Wood Dr , Lexington Park, MD 20653-4413 H. (301) 789-1558
dgellerjr@md.metrocast.net
2015, Lexington Park: Community with a Cause.

George, Jack R. RE CH | New Covenant || Cumberland ||| 5210
15607 Winslow St SW , Cumberland, MD 21502-5850 H. (301) 729-3013
jackandelise65@aol.com
*1964, Attending school; 1966, Monroe Street; 1968, Leonardtown; 1973, Brandywine:
BrookfieldImmanuel Chg; 1983, LaVale; 1992, Lisbon; 2002, Retired; 2003, Cumberland:
Union Grove; 2011, Cumberland:Wesley.*

George, Mary SY CH | Trinity || Cumberland ||| 5245
15306 Greenleaf Dr SW , Cumberland, MD 21502-5714 H. (301) 729-6828
rmgeorge44@gmail.com
2015, Cumberland: S. Cumberland Ridgeley; 2016, Cumberland: Trinity.

Gibbs, Richard PL FR | Walkersville || Walkersville ||| 6420 (301) 600-1540
10645 Powell Rd, Thurmont, MD 21788-2832 H. (301) 898-7277
mypastorrich@aol.com
*01-01-17, Walkersville/Mt. Pleasant/Mt. Zion; 05-01-19, Walkersville: Walkersville & Mt.
Pleasant.*

Gibson, Sharon   PL   CH | Asbury || Hagerstown ||| 5315   (301) 791-0498
1620 Colonial Way, Frederick, MD 21702   H. (301) 663-0174
sharongibson_1@msn.com
2007, Hagerstown: Asbury UMC.

Gill, Darryl   RE   BS | St Johns || Lutherville ||| 3375
1907 Forest Ct , Timonium, MD 21093-4317   H. (410) 252-3120
0607DWG@gmail.com
1972, Sleepy Creek Circuit; 1974, Howard Chapel-Ridgely; 1981, Smithís Chapel; 1987,
Baltimore: St. Paul; 1991, Aldersgate; 1994, HWR-Mt. Washington Par.: Aldersgate/Otterbein;
1999, Frostburg; 2004, Upperco: Pleasant Grove; 2007, Retired; 05-01-2013, Sparks: Bosley.

Gillen, Joshua   PL   CH | Hancock || Hancock ||| 5365
168 W Main St , Hancock, MD 21750-1432   H. (443) 992-0466
pastorjgillen@gmail.com
2018, Hancock: Hancock,

Gim, Limja H.   RD   GW | Francis Asbury Ntl Korean || Rockville ||| 9427   (202) 895-2673
1830 Fountain Dr Unit 1503, Reston, VA 20190-4475   H. (703) 707-8207
lh.gim@verizon.net
2003, Ext. Min.; Chaplain, Washington Home & Community Hospice; 2014, Retired.

Gisselbeck, Loren L.   RE
5630 Grace Woods Dr Unit 203, Willoughby, OH 44094-8917   H. (440) 729-5076
1963, South Indiana Conference; 1970, Baltimore Conference, Frederick: Calvary Assoc;
1974, Burtonsville: Liberty Grove; 1980, Westminster Par. 1985 Westminster; 1986, Prince
Frederick: Trinity; 1997, Retired.

Gladding, Elsie M.   RE   AN | Baldwin Memorial || Millersville ||| 1420
1027 Mount Carmel Rd , Alton, VA 24520-3575   H. (434) 753-3035
elsiemaymckenney@hotmail.com
1979, Emmitsburg-Tomís Creek Chg; 1980, Harperís Ferry Enlarged Chg.: Camp Hill-Wesley;
1982, Chaplain, U.S. Navy; 1985, Bolivar-Harpers Larger Par; 1989, Leave of Absence; 1990,
Chap. Dept. Health and Mental Hygiene; 10-01-91, Deer Creek; 1993, Bunker Hill; 1-1-99,
New Market: Mt. Carmel-New Market Chg; 2001, New Market; 2003, Linganore; 12-01-2006,
Leave of Absence; 01-01-2009, Retired.

Glassbrook, Linda (Lynn)   RE   WE | Emmanuel || Huntingtown ||| 8240
2668 Highway 16 E, Sharpsburg, GA 30277-2516   H. (770) 253-1172
revlynng@outlook.com
1997, Clarksburg: Clarksburg; 2002, Huntingtown: Emmanuel; 2009, Middle River: Orems;
2012, Mount Pleasant: Mount Pleasant Parish; 2014, Retired.

Gleckler, Arthur D. (Dan)   RE   BM | Bethesda || Baltimore ||| 3145   (410) 426-3211
2726 Saint Paul St, Baltimore, MD 21218-4332   H. (410) 243-5313
adg2726stpaul@msn.com
1962, N. Tex. Conf; 1982, Batimore Conference, Mt Vernon Place; 1987, A. W. Wilson
Memorial; 1992, Govans-Boundary; 1996, Odenton: Trinity; 1997, Elkridge: Melville Chapel;
2000, Retired; 2001, Baltimore: Johnís; 2002, Baltimore: Union/Wilson; 2002, Baltimore:
Bethesda; 2014, Baltimore:Hampden; 11-01-16, Baltimore: Bethesda.

Glorioso, Mary Ellen   RE   BS | Linden Heights || Parkville ||| 3445   (410) 665-7005
8813 Spring Rd , Baltimore, MD 21234-2907   H. (410) 935-0378
pastormeg@yahoo.com
1998, Sykesville: Oakland; 2011, Baltimore: Arnolia; 2018, Retired.

Gobrecht, Chris S.   FE   BS | Timonium || Timonium ||| 3525   (443) 835-6590
2429 Chetwood Cir, Timonium, MD 21093-2533   H. (443) 835-6590
cgobrecht@timoniumumc.org
*1996, Hampstead: Grace; 2001, Mt. Airy: Taylorsville; 2006, Cumberland: New Covenant;
2018, Timonium: Timonium-Fairview.*

Gompf, Ronald   SY   BS | Wiseburg || White Hall ||| 3565
4113 Halifax Ct , Glen Arm, MD 21057-9117   H. (410) 882-4840
rgompf@comcast.net
2012, Parkton: Wiseburg; 2018, Retired.

Gorman, Mark   FE   BS | Centre || Forest Hill ||| 2445
313 Duffy Ct, Forest Hill, MD 21050-2554   H. (443) 458-2092
gorman.mark@gmail.com
2014, Forest Hill: Centre; 2019, Forest Hill: West Harford CP.

Gosnell, James   PE   AN | Metropolitan || Severn ||| 1480   (410) 521-9555
3 Adams Ridge Ct, Baltimore, MD 21244-3802   H. (410) 521-9555
pastorgosnell@gmail.com
*2007, Baltimore: St Matthews (Highlandtown); 2010, Baltimore: Martin Luther King
Memorial; 2018, Severn: Metropolitan.*

Gould, Karen N.   RE   AN | Trinity || Odenton ||| 1435
923 Boom Way, Annapolis, MD 21401   H. (410) 573-5313
kngould@verizon.net
*1987, Wheaton: Glenmont Charge; 1990, Baltimore: Christ; 1995, Gaithersburg: Grace;
1996, Friendship: Friendship; 1998, Disability Leave; 1999, Extension Ministry, Eastern
Pennsylvania Conference; 2002, Shady Side: Centenary; 2005, Retired.*

Gourley, Sr., Gary W.   LP   FR | Blairton || Martinsburg ||| 6650
295 Constitution Blvd , Martinsburg, WV 25405-8340   H. (304) 264-3607
garyandbarbieg@frontier.com
2007, Bunker Hill: Paynes Chapel; 2015, Martinsburg: Blairton

Grabowski, Marianne S.   RE   FR | Zion || Westminster ||| 4560
22 Eastwood Dr , Hanover, PA 17331-8155   H. (717) 633-5408
touchstonecc@comcast.net
*1981, Cent. Pa. Conference, Attending school; 1982, Sykesville: Bethesda-Zion Chg; 1987,
Leave of Absence; 10-17-87, Chaplain Mt. Vernon College; 1989, Wesley-Freedom; 1995,
Owings Mills: Pleasant Hill; 2002, Leave of Absence; 2006, Ext. Min., Pastoral Counselor;
2018, Retired .*

Grace, Gerald   RE   AN | Centenary || Shady Side ||| 1515
1500 Pernell Ct, Bowie, MD 20716-1606   H. 301-249-6013
geraldgrace150@gmail.com
*1984, Attending school; 1985, Mt. Gilead-Patapsco Chg; 1988, Berkeley Springs: Francis
Asbury-Wesley Chg; 1992, Monkton/Clynmalira Chg; 1996, Street: Dublin; 1999, Leave of
Absence; 2002, Hampstead: Greenmount; 2010, Mt Airy: Poplar Springs; 2013, Mitchellville:*

Mount Oak.; 2016, Retired; 2016, Shady Side: Centenary

Graves, David FE   WE | St Paul || Lusby ||| 8345   (410) 326-3043
211 Lake View Way NW, Leesburg, VA 20176   H. (240) 601-0218
davidgraves1982@gmail.com
2004, Burtonsville: Liberty Grove; 2006, Hyattstown; 2007, Bowie: Bowie; 2011, Lusby: St Paul.

Gray, Cecil C. FE   BM | Northwood-Appold || Baltimore ||| 3225   (410) 323-6712
4499 Loch Raven Blvd , Baltimore, MD 21218-1500   H. (443) 831-2527
o9h9y93oo@prodigy.net
Central Pa. Conference; 1997, Baltimore-Washington Conference, Faculty: Gettysburg College; 2002, Northwood-Appold.

Gray, Richard G. RE   AN | Calvary || Annapolis ||| 1120
967 Highpoint Dr , Annapolis, MD 21409-4752   H. (410) 757-3817
rggrayjr@gmail.com
1969, Attending school; 1972, Assoc. College Park; 1975, Cheltenham; 1981, Winfield: Ebenezer; 1990, Annapolis: Cape St. Claire; 2006, Pasadena: Faith Community Coop Parish; 2011, Retired; 03-01-2013, Mitchellville: Mount Oak.

Green, Jr., Gerard A. FE   CM | Fairhaven || Gaithersburg ||| 9250   (410) 309-3432
12410 Fellowship Ln , North Potomac, MD 20878-3409   H. (410) 309-3432
ggreen@bwcumc.org
1987, Attending school; 1988, Severn: Metropolitan; 1992, Gaithersburg: Epworth; 02/01/05, Attend School; 2011, Extension Ministry, Asbury Methodist Village.; 2016, Baltimore-Washington Conference: Greater Washington District Superintendent.

Green, Nancy L. RL   CH | Emmanuel || Hagerstown ||| 5320
1605 Mount Aetna Rd, Hagerstown, MD 21742-6735   H. (301) 797-5433
pastornancy@pipeline.com
1996, Wolfsville: Pleasant Walk.; 2016, Retired.

Green, Nathaniel J. PL   BM | Mount Winans || Baltimore ||| 2235   (443) 414-8128
3407 Cedardale Rd , Baltimore, MD 21215-7301   H. (443) 414-8128
revngreen@yahoo.com
2005, Dayton: Browns Chapel; 2006, Marriottsville: West Liberty; 2010, Baltimore: Monroe Street; 2012, Baltimore: Violetville; 2018, Baltimore: Mount Winans.

Green, William E. FE   GW | Foundry || Washington ||| 7180
1650 Harvard St NW, Washington, DC 20009-3740   H. (847) 644-9448
wgreen@foundryumc.org
2016, DC: Foundry.

Green, William T. FE   CM | Glen Mar || Ellicott City ||| 7365
6725 Summer Rambo Ct , Columbia, MD 21045-5405   H. (410) 381-1156
tiredtenor@comcast.net
1981, Oakdale-Emory; 1985, Baltimore: Mt. Vernon; 1987, Assoc. Council Dir; 1994, Glen Gary Greater Par.; 1997, Glen Mar; 1997, Disability Leave.

Green-Carden, Gay   PL   AN | Asbury || Jessup |||| 1360
8904 Chad Way, Clinton, MD 20735   H. (410) 693-0962
gaycarden@verizon.net
2009, Jessup: Asbury.

Greene, Gertrude M.   RD   BM | John Wesley || Baltimore |||| 4135   (410) 744-4451
309 Ritchie Hwy , Severna Park, MD 21146-1909   H. (410) 544-2395
sweetpeace@verizon.net
1997, Upperco: Boring-Dover Chg; 1998, Retired. 1999, Catonsville: Mount Olivet.

Greene, Sandra M.   RE   BM | New Waverly || Baltimore |||| 3217   (301) 277-8227
2712 Gresham Way Unit 103, Baltimore, MD 21244-3956   H. (443) 985-1511
sandragreene@comcast.net
1992, Attending school; 01-01-93, Congress Heights; 2001, D.C.: A.P. Shaw; 2004, Baltimore:
Mt. Zion; 2007, DC: McKendree-Simms-Brookland; 2008, Charlotte Hall: Mt Calvary; 2010,
Baltimore: New Waverly; 2014, Retired.

Greenfield, James M.   RE CH | Mount Savage || Mount Savage |||| 5425
11608 Bierman Dr SE, Cumberland, MD 21502-6407   H. (301) 338-2336
maxgreen77@atlanticbb.net
1994, Hampden: HWR-Mt. Wash. Par; 1998, Cumberland: Christ; 2004, Gaithersburg:
Epworth; 2006, Mt. Savage; 2009, Retired.

Greenwood, Andrew   FE   BS | Pine Grove || Parkton |||| 3475   (410) 343-0729
19308 Middletown Rd, Parkton, MD 21120-9691   H. (410) 487-4875
pastorandrewbwc@gmail.com
2011, Severn: Severn; 2012, Uppero: Emory; 2014, Parkton: Pine Grove.

Griffin, Winifred   SY   BS | Gough || Cockeysville |||| 3315
208 Bond Ave , Reisterstown, MD 21136-1315   H. (410) 526-2246
laity3trinity@aol.com
2015, Hereford: Hereford Combined.

Grimes, Kelly   FE   GW | Foundry || Washington |||| 7180   (410) 664-7490
12 Upman Ct, Baltimore, MD 21228-6400   H. (443) 467-4788
revklg@gmail.com
 2011, Baltimore: Epworth Chapel ; 2015, Catonsville: Emanuel-Trinity; 2017, Baltimore:
Mount Zion, 2019, DC: Foundry.

Groover, Mark A.   PE   FR | Asbury || Frederick |||| 6180
4012 Frankford Ave, Baltimore, MD 21206-3531   H. (443) 392-2075
newhope37@verizon.net
2006, Edgewood: New Hope Christian Fellowship; 02-01-2009, Bel Air: Clarkís-New Hope
Cooperative Parish.; 2016, Frederick: Asbury Charge

Gross, Olivia   PL   CM | Mount Zion || Olney |||| 9370   (410) 309-3443
6756 Greatnews Ln, Columbia, MD 21044-4110   H. (443) 745-8036
pastorolivia.mtzion@gmail.com
 2018, Olney: Mount Zion,

Grove, George E. RE   FR | Mount Wesley || Shepherdstown ||| 6735   (304) 263-9215
108 Forman Rd E, Shepherdstown, WV 25443-3578   H. (304) 267-6325
edhfhep@gmail.com
1962, Attending school; 1967, Mt. Horeb; 1968, Inwood; 1973, Assoc. Hagerstown: John Wesley; 1976, Hampstead: St. Johnis; 1986, Liberty Grove; 1991, Baldwin Memorial; 1995, Martinsburg: Trinity; 2009, Retired; 2009, Martinsburg: Mt Wesley-Greensburg.; 1-1-16, Martinsburg: Mt Wesley-Greensburg Charge

---

Grove, John W. RE   CM | Linden-Linthicum || Clarksville ||| 9180
9207 Butler Blvd Glen Lakes, Weeki Wachee, FL 34613-4034   H. (352) 597-1140
jwgandmag@aol.com
1963, Attending school; 1966, Linden-Linthicum; 1969, Chaplain U.S. Navy; 1996, Retired.

Grover, Katie FE   BM | Patapsco || Dundalk ||| 2385   (410) 477-0976
7611 Sparrows Point Blvd, Baltimore, MD 21219-1929
grover.katiej@gmail.com
2013, Dundalk: Patapsco-Lodge Forest Cooperative Parish.

Gunkel, Carroll R. RE   BM | Catonsville || Catonsville ||| 4180   (301) 972-1804
4110 Lotus Cir , Ellicott City, MD 21043-4873   H. (410) 465-5543
sumchurch@netzero.com
1959, Idlewylde; 1961, Asst. Northwood-Appold; 1963, Baltimore: Trinity; 1975, University; 1983, Bethesda: Bethesda; 1989, Dir. Dev. Asbury Village; 1992, D.C.: Mt. Vernon Place; 2002, Retired, 2003, Germantown: Salem.

Hainley, James D. RE   (410) 732-4288
863 Flintlock Dr , Bel Air, MD 21015-4879   H. (410) 399-9615
JHAINLEY@aol.com
1989, Chesaco: Chesaco Ave; 1999, Chesaco/Orangeville Charge; 2002, Retired.

Hall, Edward RL   FR | Mount Zion || Martinsburg ||| 6675   (304) 263-2667
271 Polk St, Harpers Ferry, WV 25425-6347   H. (304) 535-2765
pastoredhall@frontiernet.net
2002, Hyattstown; 2006, Martinsburg, Mt. Zion; 2017, Retired.

Hall, Kimberly FE   GW | Hughes Memorial || Washington ||| 7190
912 Vosler Loop, San Antonio, TX 78227-4901
kimberly.hall13.mil@mail.mil
2004, Highland: Mt. Zion (Assoc.); 2007, Prince Frederick: Trinity; 2008, Cockeysville: Epworth; 2012, US Army .

Hall, Richard D. FE   GW | McKendree-Simms-Brookland || Washington ||| 7620
1315 Q St NW , Washington, DC 20009-4316   H. (202) 462-6935
rdhall49@aol.com
2005, Laurel: Mt. Zion; 2011, DC: McKendree-Simms-Brookland Cooperative Ministry Parish.

Hallman, Carlee L. RE   CM | Araby || Frederick ||| 6110
415 Russell Ave Apt 719, Gaithersburg, MD 20877-2840   H. (301) 216-5331
carlee6508@yahoo.com
1985, Oldtown Chg; 1987, Bethesda-Zion Chg; 1992, Araby; 1996, Retired.

Halse, Susan   RE FR | Middletown || Middletown ||| 6280   (301) 371-5550
3030 Mill Island PkwyApt 313, Frederick, MD 21701-6819   H. (301) 846-0313
susanrhalse@gmail.com
1973, S.D. Conference; 1976, Westminster Par; 1981, Middletown; 2015, Retired

---

Halsey, Elizabeth L.   FE   (301) 422-5426
15509 Indianola Dr , Derwood, MD 20855-2706   H. (240) 462-7562
betsyhalsey@yahoo.com
1991, Lewistown; 1992, Baltimore: Mt. Vernon; 1994, HWR-Mt. Washington Par.: Mt. Vernon;
1996, Attending school; 2005, St. Luke Institute.

Hamilton, James   SY   BS | Clarks Chapel || Bel Air ||| 2365
28 Herbst Ln, Perryville, MD 21903-2221   H. (410) 378-2382
jchjrgolf@aol.com
2017, Bel Air: Harford,

Hammersla, Edgar W.   RE
3154 Gracefield Rd Apt 213, Silver Spring, MD 20904-0807
eeham1927@gmail.com
1951, Attending school; 1952, Central Cumberland; 1955, Lauraville; 1962, Bel Air; 1971,
Superintendent Baltimore, South East District; 1975, Superintendent, Annapolis District; 1977,
Rockville: Faith; 1982, Woodside; 1988, Retired.

Harden, William R.   RE   BS | Pleasant Grove || Reisterstown ||| 4520
828 Holliday Ln, Westminster, MD 21157   H. (410) 876-3871
revwrh@gmail.com
1995, Christ House;. 1997, Bowie: Bowie; 2000, Reisterstown; 07-13-2009, Reisterstown:
Reistertown-Pleasant Grove Coop Parish; 2011, Reisterstown: Pleasant Grove; 2011, Retired.

Harner, Victor   FE   BS | Perry Hall || Baltimore ||| 2535
8917 Yvonne Ave , Nottingham, MD 21236-2136   H. (410) 256-1028
rovervic@verizon.net
1986, Attending school; 1987, Oldtown Chg; 1990, Taneytown: Messiah; 1994, Jarrettsville;
2001, Lusby: St. Paul; 2003, Joppa: Union Chapel; 2011, Perry Hall: Perry Hall.

Harper, Lyle E.   RE   CM | Ashton || Ashton ||| 9110
PO Box 752 , Micaville, NC 28755-0752   H. (828) 284-4275
1955, Detroit Conference; 1958, Baltimore Conference, Solomons; 1961, Greenbelt; 1964,
Walkersville; 1969, Chevy Chase: St. Paul; 1976, Arnolia; 1981, Mill Creek Parish; 1984,
Superintendent, Washington Central Dist; 1990, Ashton; 1995, Retired.

Harpold, George   RL   CH | Eckhart || Frostburg ||| 5255
PO Box 444 , Frostburg, MD 21532-0444   H. (301) 689-9585
harpold8736@comcast.net
1978, Eckhart; 2001, Retired.

Harrell, Charles L.   RE   BS | Wesley || Hampstead ||| 4330   (410) 535-1782
1725 Forest Glen Dr , Prince Frederick, MD 20678-4514   H. (443) 975-5550
carolus101@gmail.com
1984, Attending school; 1990, Lusby: St. Paul; 2001, Rockville: Faith; 2007, Prince Frederick:
Trinity; 10-01-2012, Retired.

Harrell, Stanley G.   RE   BS | Wesley || Hampstead ||| 4330
2705 Aspen Dr , Hampstead, MD 21074-1712   H. (443) 291-6324
sharrell25@gmail.com
1957, Attending school; 1959, Hagerstown: St. Paulis; 1961, Cumberland: Central; 1966,
Hampstead: Wesley; 1974, D.C.: Mt. Vernon Place; 1980, Corkran Memorial; 1989, Waldorf:
Calvary; 1997, Retired; 2006, Bryans Road: Shiloh Charge.

Harris, Sr., Bernard M.   PL   GW | Bradbury Heights || Washington ||| 7120   (301) 254-5524
5002 Bass Pl SE , Washington, DC 20019-7613   H. (301) 254-5524
bharris73@comcast.net
2017, DC: McKendree-Simms-Brookland,

Harrod, Alfonso J.   RE   GW | McKendree-Simms-Brookland || Washington ||| 7620
4308 19th Pl NE , Washington, DC 20018-3308   H. (202) 529-6283
revalfonsoharrod@aol.com
1970, Lexington Park, Associate; 1972, D.C.: Brightwood; 1979, D.C.: Ebenezer; 1993,
Retired; 08-01-2010, Lanham: Lanham.

Harrod, JoeAnn T.   RA   BM | Beechfield || Baltimore ||| 3150   (410) 644-7640
5213 Fredcrest Rd , Baltimore, MD 21229-3215   H. (410) 525-2478
1997, Ellicott City: Mt. Zion; 1998, Baltimore: Beechfield; 2013, Retired.

Hart, Emily   PE   BM | Magothy Church of Deaf-Gallaudet || Pasadena ||| 1455
305 5th Ave, Brooklyn Park, MD 21225-4006   H. (443) 846-5110
ehart@bwcumc.org
2016, Pasadena: Magothy Church Deaf-Gallaudet.

Harvey, Charles E.   RE   (410) 437-8515
604 McKinsey Park Dr Apt 402, Severna Park, MD 21146-4567   H. (410) 647-1989
1954, Attending school; 1955, New Market; 1956, Epworth Chapel; 1964, Gaithersburg:
Epworth; 1976, Bowie: St. Matthewis; 1980, Bethesda: Bethesda; 1983, Pasadena:
Community; 1994, Retired.

Hawes, Kenneth B.   FE   CM | Fairhaven || Gaithersburg ||| 9250
3825 Oglethorpe St, Hyattsville, MD 20782-3018   H. (301) 699-2023
pastorken.fairhavenumc@gmail.com
1994, New York Conference; 2004, Baltimore-Washington Conf., Hagerstown: Emmanuel;
2008, Wheaton: Hughes; 2019, Gaithersburg: Fairhaven.

Hays, Douglas   FE   WE | Lexington Park || Lexington Park ||| 8320   (301) 863-8500
48050 Mayflower Dr, Lexington Park, MD 20653-2565   H. (443) 465-8128
dougjhays@hotmail.com
1983, Brentwood; 1986, Urbana Chg; 1988, Frederick: Christ Mission; 4-16-89, Christ-
Ballenger Creek; 2001, Leave of Absence; 9/1/03, Lutherville: Carrollis Gills/Stone Chapel
Parish; 2004, Timonium: Mays Chapel; 2010, Lexington Park: Lexington Park.

Hays, Lori H.   FE   WE | Lexington Park || Lexington Park ||| 8320   (301) 863-8500
48050 Mayflower Dr, Lexington Park, MD 20653-2565   H. (443) 465-7954
PastorLori7@gmail.com
2002, Doubs Charge; 2004, Lutherville: Carrollis Gills; 2006, Ext. Min., Holy Land Christian
Eumenical Foundation; 01-01-2007, Hampstead: Shiloh -Mount Zion; 2007, West Friendship:
St James; 2010, Lexington Park: Lexington Park.; 8-15-16, Baltimore Washington Conference

---

Healy, Linda W.   RP   FR | Buckeystown Rt 85 || Buckeystown |||| 6150
2124 Mitford Ct, Dacula, GA 30019-2487
revlhealy@aol.com
2003, Buckeystown (RT. 85); 12-01-2010, Retired.

Heath-Mason, Joseph P.   PE   GW | Metropolitan Memorial || Washington |||| 7630
5000 42nd Ave, Hyattsville, MD 20781-2011   H. (202) 885-3304
joeyh@american.edu
2012, New Windsor: Stone Chapel; 2013, Silver Spring: Silver Spring Cooperative Parish; 01-01-2014, Silver Spring: Silver Spring.; 2016, American University

Heflin, Katherine A.   FE   FR | Calvary || Frederick |||| 6190
1435 N Ford St, Lapel, IN 46051-9640
midorikate37@gmail.com
1997, Long Green Chg. 1-1-02, Cockeysville: Epworth; 2002, Leave of Absence; 2005, Camp Springs: Bells; 2007, Frederick: Calvary/Centennial Memorial Cooperative Parish; 04-01-2009, Leave of Absence.

Hemming, Alan   FL   WE | First Saints Community Church || Leonardtown |||| 8540
23134 Clover Ridge Ln , California, MD 20619-4117   H. (240) 538-4010
pastoralan@firstsaints.org
2012, Dunkirk: Smithville; 09-01-2014, Prince Frederick: Trinity; 2017, Leonardtown: First Saints Community.

Hendee, Charlotte A.   RE   AN | Galesville || Galesville |||| 1280
8 Charles Wesley CtWesley-By-The-Sea, Wells, ME 04090-5179   H. (443) 995-0613
umcnubble@gmail.com
1984, Attending school; 1986, Maryland Line: Maryland Line; 1993, Baltimore: Brooklyn Heights; 2000, Galesville: Galesville; 2012, Retired.

Henning, Charles M.   FE   FR | Walkersville || Walkersville |||| 6420   (301) 845-9860
7010 Keysville Rd, Keymar, MD 21757-9607   H. (443) 331-3295
revmikehenning@gmail.com
1999, Oldtown Chrg.; 2004, Hagerstown: St Andrew's 2018, Walkersville/Mt. Pleasant/Mt. Zion, 05-01-19, Walkersville: Walkersville & Mt. Pleasant.

Henry, Eddie L.   RE
169 Pine Trl , Delta, PA 17314-8686   H. (717) 456-5276
1962, Martinsburg Chg; 1964, Attending school; 1968, Cumberland: Christ; 1977, Havre de Grace; 1987, Essex; 4-17-98, Administrative Leave; 06-17-98, Essex; 2000, Annapolis: Trinity; 2007, Retired.

Herche, Jr., William A.   RE   AN | Mount Zion || Lothian |||| 1410
703C Wesley Dr, Waynesboro, PA 17268-7992   H. (717) 524-0354
baherche@gmail.com
1978, Assoc. Laurel: First, 1979, Baltimore Mt. Vernon; 1984, Mt. Nebo; 03-01-88, Leave of Absence; 1991, Parkton: Mt. Carmel; 1995, Baltimore: Lansdowne; 05-01-01, Ext. Ministry, Director/Manager Camp Manidokan; 01-01-2007, Camp Manidoken; 2007, Lothian: Mount Zion; 2017, Retired.

Herndon, Ray O. RE
250 Pantops Mountain Rd Apt 7404, Charlottesville, VA 22911-8720   H. (540) 672-2206
olinherndon@gmail.com
1960, N. Georgia Conference; 1963, Baltimore Conference, Bethany; 1968, Assoc. Marvin
Memorial; 1971, Martinsburg: St. Lukeís; 1974, Forest Hill Parish; 1979, Frostburg; 1983,
Wardís Chapel; 1988, Glen Burnie; 2000, Retired.

Hershberger, Robert RE   CH | New Covenant || Cumberland ||| 5210
35 Frost Ln, Cornwall, NY 12518-1305   H. (845) 534-9270
hershny@aol.com
1971, Attending school; 1972, Bunker Hill: Bunker Hill; 1979, Hampstead: Grace; 1981,
Chaplain, VA Med. Cen; 2012, Retired.

Hicks, Delonta SY   WE | St Luke || Scotland ||| 8445
12860 Shiloh Church Rd, Newburg, MD 20664-2515   H. (301) 259-2197
pastorofstluke@gmail.com
2016, Scotland: St Luke.

Hidey, Barry RE   BS | Fallston || Fallston ||| 2435
1775 Selvin Dr, Bel Air, MD 21015
bhidey@outlook.com
1979, Attending school; 1980, Reisterstown: Emory; 1986, Weller; 1989, Catoctin Mountain
Parish; 1993, Leonardtown: St. Paulís; 1999, Bel Air: Bel Air; 2011, Bel Air: Bel Air-Mt.
Vernon Cooperative Parish; 2014, Bel Air: Bel Air; 2015, Fallston: Ebenezer-William Watters
Cooperative Parrish; 2017, Retired.

Higby, Theodore D. RE
817 Jefferson Blvd, Hagerstown, MD 21740-5014   H. (240) 291-6194
Jarhead665@msn.com
1981, Parke-Wiseburg Chg; 1982, Andrew Chapel; 1985, Chaplain USA; 1989, Brandywine:
Brookfield Memorial-Immanuel; 1993, Martinsburg: St. Lukeís; 1997, Davis Memorial-
McKendree Chg; 2001, Lanham; 2002, Myersville: Mt. Zion; 2006, Jessup: Wesley Chapel/
Harwood Park Chg; 11-01-2007, Leave of Absence; 2013, Retired.

Highfield, David A. RE   FR | Westminster || Westminster ||| 4555
942 Litchfield Cir , Westminster, MD 21158-4407   H. (410) 596-2918
davidhighmd@gmail.com
1968, Peninsula Conference; 1969, Baltimore Conference, Attending school; 1970,
Cumberland: Central; 1974, Williamsport: Rehoboth; 1983, Huntís Memorial; 1992,
Westminster; 2007, Retired.

Hii, Ek C. FE   GW | Cabin John || Cabin John ||| 9160   (301) 229-8233
7703 MacArthur Blvd, Cabin John, MD 20818   H. (301) 229-8233
ekhii2000@yahoo.com
2001 Cabin John American-Chinese.

Hinson, Howard W. RE   BM | Metropolitan || Baltimore ||| 2220   (443) 253-7092
3701 Hillsdale Rd, Gwynn Oak, MD 21207-8075   H. (443) 253-7092
howard-hinson@verizon.net
1999, Westminster: Union Street; 2004, Retired; 2017, Baltimore: Metropolitan,

---

108

Hinton, Dellyne I.   FE   BM | Gwynn Oak || Baltimore ||| 4130   (410) 542-1274
5024 Gwynn Oak Ave, Baltimore, MD 21207-6803   H. (443) 803-5116
dell_hinton@comcast.net
1996, Bel Air; 2000, Catonsville (Assoc.); 2004, Baltimore: Sharp Street Memorial; 2012, Baltimore: Gwynn Oak.; 2016, Baltimore: Gwynn Oak/St Lukes Charge; 2019, Baltimore: G.O.A.L.

Hinzman, Parker   OR   FR | Bethesda || Shepherdstown ||| 6720
3415 Kearneysville Pike, Shepherdstown, WV 25443   H. (304) 876-6272
phinzman3415@comcast.net
2001, Shenandoah Junction: Shenandoah.

Hodges, Hosea L.   RE   (410) 867-0632
1041 Lake Claire Dr , Annapolis, MD 21409-4764   H. (410) 757-3580
hlhodges423@aol.com
2001, Annapolis: Fowler; 2003, Martinsburg: Mt. Zion; 01/01/06, Lothian: Mt. Zion (Ark Road); 01-01-2012, Retired; 12-20-2012, Friendship: Carterís.

Hodges, Margaret W.   FE   GW | Dumbarton || Washington ||| 7160
3706 Excalibur Ct Apt 202, Bowie, MD 20716-7333
1989, Washington Church of the Deaf; 1992, Magothy Church of the Deaf; 3-1-99, Disability Leave.

Hodsdon, David W.   OE   CM | Hyattstown || Clarksburg ||| 9315
4227 Headwaters Ln, Olney, MD 20832-1750   H. (301) 774-1846
revdwhodsdon@verizon.net
2009, Hyattstown: Hyattstown-Clarksburg; 2007, Hyattstown: Hyattstown; .

Hoffman, Douglas B.   FE   CH | First || Berkeley Springs ||| 5515
49 S Green St, Berkeley Springs, WV 25411-1638   H. (410) 303-8195
dhoffman@gofirst.org
1992, Baltimore: St. Paul; 1993, Baltimore: St. Matthews; 1994, EBUMC Con. Par.: St. Paul's/ St. Matthew's Chg. 10-15-94, Baltimore: St. Matthewís/St. Paulís Christian Center; 01-01- 98, Baltimore: St. Matthews; 1998, Reisterstown; 2000, Ellicott City: Rockland; 4/1/01, West Friendship: St. James; 2007, Gamber: Calvary; 2015, Berkeley Springs: First.

Hogue, Richard D.   RE   GW | Liberty Grove || Burtonsville ||| 9155
107 Guilford Dr , Summerville, SC 29483-5583   H. (843) 821-6230
revrichardhogue@gmail.com
1969, N. Ga. Conference; 1971, Baltimore Conference, Chesaco Avenue; 1974, Patapsco-Deer Park Chg; 1977, Linthicum Heights Assoc; 1979, Forest Hill Par; 1984, Wheaton: Hughes Assoc; 1994, Burtonsville: Liberty Grove; 2007, Retired.

Hohne, Donald J.   FD   CM | Wesley Freedom || Eldersburg ||| 4225   (443) 849-8396
6012 Crossway Ct , Sykesville, MD 21784-8419   H. (410) 549-3621
hohnefamily@msn.com
2011, Eldersburg: Wesley Freedom and Extension Ministry: Carroll County Hospice.

Holdbrook-Smith, Samuel FE   GW | Ryland-Epworth || Washington ||| 7255 (202) 582-4006
1207 Clovis Ave, Capitol Heights, MD 20743-5153   H. (301) 420-1628
revsamh@gmail.com
2000, Peninsula-Delaware Conference; 2013, Damascus: Friendship Community; 2018, DC: McKendree-Simms-Brookland.

Holimon, Esther M.   RE   GW | Forest Memorial || Forestville ||| 8190
10624 Seneca Spring Way, Montgomery Village, MD 20886-3925   H. (410) 241-2430
emholimon@aol.com
1983, Attending school; 1984, Ames; 1987, D.C.: Metropolitan Memorial; 1990, Chevy
Chase: St. Paul; 1992, D.C.: Christ; 2000, Baltimore: Union Memorial; 2013, Gaithersburg:
Fairhaven; 2019, Retired, 2019, Forestville: Forest Memorial.

Holley, Mary L. (Louise)   RL   BS | West Liberty || White Hall ||| 3560
3717 Ferndale Ave, Baltimore, MD 21207-7164   H. (410) 466-7972
marylouiseholley@gmail.com
1991, Brownis Chapel; 1996, Elderslie-St. Andrews; 2003 Retired, Baltimore: John Wesley
Assoc.

Holmes, Christopher T.   FE   AN | Community || Crofton ||| 1180
1535 Eton Way, Crofton, MD 21114   H. (410) 300-8847
chris@holmescoaching.com
1981, Attending school; 1982, Baltimore: Elderslie-St. Andrew; 11/01/88, Crofton:
Community; 2005, Superintendent, Annapolis District; 2012, Extension Ministry: Coach
Approach Trainer.

Holmes, Joel V.   PL   BM | Beechfield || Baltimore ||| 3150   (410) 354-9014
2431 Terra Firma Rd, Baltimore, MD 21225-1121   H. (443) 400-8443
joel_holmes@comcast.net
2017, Baltimore: Beechfield,

Holmes, William A.   RE   FR | Trinity || Frederick ||| 6225
Cottage #17351 Willow Rd, Frederick, MD 21702-2415   H. (301) 460-7773
bilnanh@msn.com
1953, N. Texas Conference; 1969, S.W. Texas Conference; 1974, Baltimore Conference, D.C.:
Metropolitan Memorial; 1998, Retired.

Honnappa, Samuel   FE   GW | Memorial First India || Silver Spring ||| 7462   (301) 585-8015
9221Watson Road, Silver Spring, MD 20910   H. (301) 589-1414
revhonnappa@hotmail.com
India Conference, Meth. Ch. of India; 1998, Baltimore-Washington Conference, 2001, Takoma
Park: Grove; 2002, Grace/First India Chg; 2006, Memorial. First India Coop. Parish; 01-01-
2007, Silver Spring: Memorial First India.

Hoover, Ashley B.   PE   GW | Jerusalem-Mt Pleasant || Rockville ||| 9420   (202) 433-5885
6012 North Dakota Ave NW, Washington, DC 20011   H. (301) 922-6200
hoovah06@gmail.com
2019, Rockville: Jerusalem-Mt Pleasant, 2011, Baltimore: Cherry Hill.

Hottinger, Gary R. (Bob)   RE   CM | Glenelg || Glenelg ||| 9285
2561 Glenkirk Dr, Burlington, NC 27215-9512   H. (336) 585-0881
pghottinger@twc.com
1970, Attending school; 1972, Union Grove Circuit; 1975, Hagerstown: Grace, Assoc; 1976,
Arden Chg; 1980, Millian Memorial; 1985, Poolesville: Memorial; 1991, Martinsburg:
Trinity; 1995, Glenelg; 2008, Retired.

110

Houston, Nicole FE   AN | Severna Park || Severna Park ||| 1510
1175 Rivershore Rd, Charleston, SC 29492-8243   H. 850-572-2065
NLchris1@gmail.com
2008, Severna Park: Severna Park.; 2016, Baltimore Washington Conference

---

Hudson, Rodney R. FE   BM | Ames || Baltimore ||| 4110   (410) 523-5556
9604 Grandhaven Ave, Upper Marlboro, MD 20772-5268   H. (240) 601-0872
Ames.Memorial@hotmail.com
2008, Baltimore: Ames.

Humbert, Kenneth M. RE FR | Westminster || Westminster ||| 4555   (443) 289-8446
198 Wyndtryst Dr, Westminster, MD 21158-4444
revkenh@starpower.net
1971, Attending school; 1974, Wheaton: Hughes; 1975, Gamber: Calvary; 1983, Frostburg;
1988, Randallstown: Mt. Olive; 1998, Odenton: Nichols-Bethel; 2013, Retired.

Humphrey, Stephen FE   WE | Mount Zion || Mechanicsville ||| 8350   (410) 676-1335
29025 Livingston Dr , Mechanicsville, MD 20659-3271   H. (240) 249-6156
preacher.steve.humphrey@gmail.com
1999, Baltimore: Graceland; 2000, Lutherville: Carrollís-Gills/Stone Chapel Parish; 9/1/03,
Walkersville: Walkersville; 2011, Joppa: Union Chapel.; 2016, Mechanicsville: Mount Zion
Charge

Humphries-Russ, Lynne PE   BS | Hopewell || Havre de Grace ||| 2460   (443) 920-3356
6206 Monroe Ave , Sykesville, MD 21784-6661   H. (410) 952-2792
pastorlynnehr@gmail.com
2010, Ellicott City: Alberta Gary Mem; 2012, Woodbine: Morgan Chapel-Mt Olive; 08-12-18,
Havre De Grace: Susquehanna.

Hunt, C. Anthony FE   BM | Epworth Chapel || Baltimore ||| 4170
1305 Cherokee Ln , Bel Air, MD 21015-4763   H. (410) 944-1070
cahunt@msn.com
1992, Bel Air: Ames; 01-01-98, Exec. Dir.: Multi Ethnic Center-Northeast Jurisdiction;
8/15/04 Superintendent, Baltimore-Harford Dist; 01-01-2007, District Superintendent
Baltimore Metro Region; 2012, Baltimore: Epworth Chapel .

Hunt, Darcy R. RE   BS | Jarrettsville || Jarrettsville ||| 2475   (704) 799-0105
120 Doyle Farm Ln, Mooresville, NC 28115-5794   H. (704) 799-7805
dhunt@wellhavencounseling.com
1978, Attending school; 1980, Fallston: Ebenezer; 1981, Leave of Absence; 1982, Fallston:
Ebenezer, 1997, Disability Leave.

Hunt, James M. RE   CM | Fairhaven || Gaithersburg ||| 9250
885 Nash Loop , The Villages, FL 32162-4541   H. (301) 888-2572
jmhsr1@msn.com
1968, Attending school; 1969, Morgan; 1971, Gaithersburg: Fairhaven Parish; 1978, D.C.:
Metropolitan Memorial; 1982, Columbia: Christ; 1984, D.C.: St. Lukeís; 1989, Upper
Marlboro: Bethel; 1996, Catonsville: Trinity; 1998, Brandywine: Brookfield-Immanuel; 2011,
Retired.

Hunter, III, Robert RE FR | Thurmont || Thurmont ||| 6360 (410) 838-4207
3539 Swan Lake Dr, Titusville, FL 32796-3781 H. (240) 288-8430
pastorbobhunter@gmail.com
1996, Jessup: Wesley Chapel/Harwood Park Chg; 1998, Sparks: Salem-Falls Road Chg.
(2000, Salem); 2006, Forest Hill: Centre; 2014, Thurmont: Thurmont; 2019, Retired.

Hurder Buhrman, Marjorie J. SY CH | Zion || Cumberland ||| 5250
14801 Bell St, Cresaptown, MD 21502-6589 H. (601) 310-9922
marjoriehurder@gmail.com
2017, Cumberland: Wesley.

Hurder Buhrman, Patrick M. PE CH | Cresaptown || Cresaptown ||| 5140
14801 Bell St, Cresaptown, MD 21502-6589 H. (301) 991-0639
pbuhrman@yahoo.com
2013, Rawlings: Rawlings/Dawson; 2018, Cresaptown: Cresaptown.

Hurley, Robert L. RE BM | Chase || Middle River ||| 2362 (410) 335-6927
800 Bollinger Dr Apt 206, Shrewsbury, PA 17361-1761 H. (410) 687-4709
1962, W. Va. Conference; 1964, Baltimore Conference, Maryland Line; 1970, Cockeysville:
Epworth; 1977, Essex; 1987, Retired.

Hurst, Elza RL FR | Toms Creek || Emmitsburg ||| 6170
17144 Bullfrog Rd , Taneytown, MD 21787-1013 H. (301) 898-7888
hurstcrow@comcast.net
1999, Boonsboro: Mt. Lena; 2000, Araby; 2005, Leave of Absence; 2007, Lewistown:
Lewistown; 2014, Retired.

Hutchison, G. W. (Whit) FE
102 Park Ave , Takoma Park, MD 20912-4311
whithutchison@hotmail.com
N. Georgia Conf; 1989, Baltimore Conference, Chaplain American Univ; 1991, Attending
school; 1994, Dir. of Dev. for Calvary-Casa del Pueblo Min; 1996, Greenbelt: Mowatt
Memorial; 9-1-97, Calvary-Casa del Pueblo; 1999, College Park: University; 2001, D.C.:
Wesley; 2009, Leave of Absence.

Hutton, Beth A. FE FR | Calvary || Finksburg ||| 4260
1800 Fallstaff Ct, Eldersburg, MD 21784-6274 H. (240) 388-6877
pastorbethhutton@gmail.com
2018, Gamber: Calvary, 06-14-2012, Middletown: Middletown.

Huzzard, Mary Ellen RE GW | Metropolitan Memorial || Washington ||| 7630
3705 Jones Bridge Rd , Chevy Chase, MD 20815-5726 H. (301) 657-8162
drhuzzard@aol.com
1977, Harperís Ferry Parish; 1978, Laurel: Md. City Community; 1984, Lutherville: St.
Johnís; 1989, Columbia: Christ; 1994, Chevy Chase; 1997, Cheverly: Cheverly; 1999, D.C.:
Eldbrooke; 2004, Ashton: Ashton; 2012, Retired.

Hwang, YuJung FE FR | Stone Chapel || New Windsor ||| 4545 (301) 349-5416
20331 Dickerson Church Rd, Dickerson, MD 20842-9526 H. (703) 303-2366
puri315@hotmail.com
2013, DC: Alpha Community Korean; 2014, Lisbon: Lisbon.; 2016, Dickerson: Dickerson-
Forest Grove; 2019, New Windsor: Stone Chapel, 2019, Westminster: Zion.

Hynson, Diana L.   RE   CM | Mount Zion || Highland ||| 9310
6104 Bradford Hills Dr, Nashville, TN 37211-7900   H. (615) 340-7053
dianalhynson@outlook.com
1974, Attending school; 1976, Southwest Christian Par; 1980, Arnolia; 1981, Loch Raven;
1985, Monkton Chg; 4/1/88, Nashville: General Board of Discipleship; 01-01-2012, Retired.

Ingalls-Howard, Sarah   SY   BS | Wesleyan Chapel || Aberdeen ||| 2470
406 Granville Ct, Havre de Grace, MD 21078   H. (352) 449-9388
sarahingallshoward@gmail.com
2019, Street: Dublin-Darlington.

Iannicelli, Rebecca K.   FE   (410) 309-3472
21 Austin Dr, Edgewater, MD 21037-2222
riannicelli@bwcumc.org
1998, Mechanicsville: Mt. Zion; 2005, Shady Side: Centenary; 2009, Crofton: Community-
Trinity Coop Parish; 12-01-2012, Leave of Absence; 01-01-2013, Annapolis Southern Region
Guide; 2013, District Superintendent, Washington East; 2019, Dist. Superintendent, Annapolis.

Ireland, Margaret   SY   WE | Calvary || Waldorf ||| 8520
2965 Edgewood Rd, Bryans Road, MD 20616-3304   H. (301) 306-4560
Pegatha@Outlook.com
2018, Accokeek: Faith

Iser, Frederick   RL   CH | Emmanuel || Cumberland ||| 5177
23 E Mary St, Cumberland, MD 21502-4721   H. (301) 777-0756
revfrediser@hotmail.com
1991, Flintstone Chg; 1974, Prosperity; 2011, Retired; 2011, Lonaconing: First.

Jackman, Dennis   FE   FR | Hedgesville || Hedgesville ||| 6610   (304) 754-8793
PO Box 2602 , Martinsburg, WV 25402-2602   H. (304) 267-2998
drdejackman@gmail.com
1984, Attending school; 1985, Dawson; 1988, Bunker Hill; 1993, Leave of Absence; 1998,
Martinsburg: Marvin Chapel; 2003, Marvin Chapel-Blairton Charge; 2006, Kabletown; 2011,
Berkeley Springs: Morgan; 2014, Hedgesville: Hedgesville.

Jackson, Brian W.   FE   GW | Randall Memorial || Washington ||| 7250   (240) 256-0739
2509 Testway Ave, Fort Washington, MD 20744-2447   H. (240) 256-0739
randallmemorial@verizon.net
1994, Attending school, 1/1/95, Sykesville: St. Luke-Mt. Gregory; 1999, Coordinator, Baltimore
Area Holy Boldness; 3/1/01, Baltimore: St. Markis; 2/1/04. Lexington Park: Zion; 2010, DC:
Randall Memorial.

Jackson, Elizabeth H.   FE CH | Otterbein || Hagerstown ||| 5340   (301) 739-9386
19002 Orchard Terrace Rd, Hagerstown, MD 21742-2730   H. (301) 373-4646
pastorelizabeth@otterumc.org
2012, Leonardtown: First Saints Comm.; 2014, Bel Air: Bel Air; 2016, Hagerstown: Otterbein.

Jackson, Hattie S.   RE   GW | Colesville || Silver Spring ||| 9450
1630 Portal Dr NW , Washington, DC 20012-1114   H. (202) 722-1640
bobhat777@aol.com
1992, Transferred from African Methodist Episcopal Zion Church; 1992, D.C.: Van Buren;
1994, Rockville: Jerusalem-Mt. Pleasant; 1997, Kensington: St. Paulis; 2000, Wheaton:
Glenmont; 2006, Retired.

Jackson, III, Walter D.   PE   BM | Chase || Middle River ||| 2362
7150 Daniel John Dr, Elkridge, MD 21075-5452   H. (443) 799-2868
walterjackson3@hotmail.com
  7-1-09, Baltimore: Orangeville Charge; 2017, Middle River: Chase.

Jackson, Kenneth L.   RA
7901 Laurel Lakes Ct Apt 301, Laurel, MD 20707-5053   H. (410) 908-4916
revrojack1@yahoo.com
  1979, Glyndon Parish; 1982, Leave of Absence; 1986, Retired.

Jacobson, David   PE   BM | Catonsville || Catonsville ||| 4180   (410) 247-4624
2105 Edmondson Ave, Catonsville, MD 21228-4209   H. (443) 840-9840
david@catonsvilleumc.org
  2016, Baltimore: Lansdowne Charge; 2019, Catonsville: Catonsville.

Jacobus, Linda A.   RE
530 Sassafras Dr, Lebanon, PA 17042-8718   H. (717) 454-0177
revlindaj64@yahoo.com
  1978, Attending school; 1980, Edgewater Chg; 1983, Severna Park; 1988 Hebbville: Salem;
  1992, Superintendent, Frederick Dist; 1998, Silver Spring: Colesville; 2005, Retired.

James, Jr., Cary   FE   BM | Sharp Street Memorial || Baltimore ||| 3250
7833 Crossbay Dr, Severn, MD 21144-1660   H. (410) 519-7343
revcjamesjr@yahoo.com
  2012, Baltimore: Sharp St Memorial; 2013, Baltimore: Sharp Street Memorial-Hampden
  Cooperative Parish; 2014, Baltimore: Sharp Street, Hampden, Rogers Forge; 2015, DC:
  Emory; 02-01-17, Baltimore: Sharp St Memorial.

Jang, Chi B.   RE   BM | Eden Korean || Baltimore ||| 2180
6840 Owings Overlook, Highland, MD 20777-9586   H. 443-838-2501
cbjumc1940@gmail.com
  Korean Methodist; 1988, Baltimore Conference, Baltimore: Eden Korean; 2010, Retired.

Jenkins, Bresean   SY   GW | Ebenezer || Washington ||| 7165   (202) 544-1415
10914 Hannes Ct, Silver Spring, MD 20901-1718   H. (352) 682-8348
breseanjenkins@gmail.com
  2016, DC: Ebenezer.

Jennings, John T.   RE   GW | Albright Memorial || Washington ||| 7110   (301) 776-8885
8015 14th St NW , Washington, DC 20012-1207   H. (202) 829-6558
je6798@verizon.net
  1994, Fairmont Heights: Grace; 1996, Petworth/Van Buren Chg; 2001, Laurel: St. Markis;
  2008, Retired; 07-17-2011, DC: Albright Memorial.

Jennings, Oliver   RA
327 Jennings Rd , Severna Park, MD 21146-1801   H. (410) 647-2459
  1997, Pasadena: Mt. Zion, 1999, Retired.

Jensen, Duane   FE   FR | Asbury || Charles Town ||| 6530
511 S Church St, Charles Town, WV 25414-1313   H. (301) 331-0432
pastorduane@comcast.net
  1997, Cockeysville: Texas Charge; 2000, Hancock: Hancock; 2012, Charles Town: Asbury.

114

Jessup, Barbara J. (Jodi)   RE
109 Hemlock Dr , Bracey, VA 23919-1958
bjodyj@me.com
2004, Dorsey Emmanuel; 2010, Retired.

Jewell, Alta G.   RE
5418 Old Middleton Rd Apt 304, Madison, WI 53705-2667   H. (608) 238-1004
1989, Chevy Chase; 1994, Disability Leave; 2005, Retired.

Jewell, Richard H.   RE   CH | Calvary || Ridgeley ||| 5620   (304) 738-8940
PO Box 85, Wiley Ford, WV 26767-0085   H. (304) 738-8734
revjewell@atlanticbb.net
*1991, Sleepy Creek; 1992, Cumberland: Kingsley; 1996, Kingsley-Grace Chg; 2000, New
Covenant; 2006, Hagerstown Parish; 2007, Hagerstown: John Wesley; 2012, Cumberland:
South Cumberland; 2014, Cumberland: South Cumberland Ridgeley; 2016, Retired; 2016,
Ridgeley: Calvary.*

Johnson, Anissa   SY   BS | Piney Grove || Reisterstown ||| 4175   (443) 627-7327
5609 Biddison Ave, Baltimore, MD 21206-3442   H. (443) 310-9864
ministryaccount23@yahoo.com
2016, Boring: Boring-Piney Grove-Mt Gilead.

Johnson, James K.   FE   CH | Bethel || Chewsville ||| 5135   (301) 733-8387
21002 Twin Springs Dr, Smithsburg, MD 21783-1636   H. (410) 688-4089
pastorjim@myactv.net
2002, Street: Dublin; 2014, Street: Dublin -Darlington.; 2016, Chewsville: Bethel Charge.

Johnson, Loretta E.   FE   GW | Jones Memorial || Washington ||| 7210   (202) 583-7116
6125 Teaberry Way, Clinton, MD 20735-3948   H. (301) 877-5162
lorettaewe1@verizon.net
*1999, Clinton: Clinton; 2000, Ext. Min., Dir., St. Paul Christian Center; 2001, Pikesville:
AmesSudbrook; 2003, Hagerstown: Asbury; 11/1/03, D.C.: Jones Memorial.*

Johnson, Mark W.   FE   BM | Towson || Towson ||| 3550   (410) 823-3640
3637 Sussex Rd, Pikesville, MD 21207-3818   H. (410) 653-4650
pastormark.johnson@gmail.com
08-01-2009, Randallstown: Mount Olive; 2017, Towson: Towson.

Johnson, Michael C.   FE   BM | Lansdowne || Baltimore ||| 3125
201 Walnut St, Mont Clare, PA 19453-5075   H. (610) 933-1775
Waataja@aol.com
*1978, SW Texas Conf; 1980, Baltimore Conference, Doubs; 1985, Lansdowne; 1993,
Baltimore: Wesley Memorial; 2001, Baltimore: Lansdowne; 09-01-08, Leave of Absence; 2012,
Attending School; 2014, Extension Ministry.*

Johnson, Patricia D.   FE   AN | Mount Zion || Annapolis ||| 1150
27 Deep Powder Ct # 1A, Woodstock, MD 21163-1110   H. 410-419-8483
shalom21230pj@aol.com
*1993, Baltimore: Mt. Winans; 2007, Baltimore: Unity; 2011, Mt. Zion; 2011, Annapolis: Mt.
Zion-Fowler Cooperative Parish.*

Johnson, Paul W.	FE	GW | Hughes Memorial || Washington ||| 7190	(202) 398-3411
12006 Hunterton St, Upper Marlboro, MD 20774-1614	H. (202) 398-3411
pwjohnson10@gmail.com
2006, Takoma Park: Grace; 2011, Takoma Park: Nehemiah; 2014, DC: Hughes Memorial.

Johnson, Roger W.	RE
1488 Tallowtree Dr, The Villages, FL 32162-2088	H. (201) 671-8561
1963, Wilson; 1967, Chaplain U.S. Army; 1987, Retired.

Johnson, Rollins R.	RL	FR | Bethesda || Sykesville ||| 4445
2214 Bluebird Dr , Westminster, MD 21157-7702	H. (410) 875-2469
dorisj@carr.org
2001, Sykesville: Bethesda; 2006, Retired.

Johnson, Sandi E.	FE	BM | Christ Church of Deaf || Baltimore ||| 3115	(410) 242-6303
3637 Sussex Rd, Pikesville, MD 21207-3818	H. (410) 653-4650
sjohnson@bwcumc.org
08-01-2009, Baltimore: Fulton Siemers ; 01-01-2014, Baltimore: Fulton Siemers Mem. Christ/ Magothy Church of Deaf.

Johnson, Selena M.	FE	GW | Mount Zion || Washington ||| 7240	(410) 428-7737
12006 Hunterton St, Upper Marlboro, MD 20774-1614	H. (410) 428-7737
oakchapelpastor@gmail.com
2012, DC: Mustard Seed Cooperative Parish; 2013, DC: McKendree-Simms-Brookland Cooperative Ministry Parish; 2014, Laurel: Community.; 2016, Silver Spring: Oak Chapel Charge; 2019, DC: Mount Zion.

Johnson, Victor O.	RE
4211 Canyonview Dr , Upper Marlboro, MD 20772-3417	H. (301) 574-4385
1976, St. Maryís Larger Parish; 1978, Chase Charge; 1982, Upper Marlboro: Union; 1995, Annapolis: Asbury; 2001, Upper Marlboro: Nottingham-Myers; 2006, Retired.

Johnson-Holmes, Hattie J.	RE BM | Sharp Street Mem. || Baltimore ||| 3250 (301) 928-3624
21 Victoria Sq, Frederick, MD 21702-1112	H. (301) 898-2905
havaholmes@yahoo.com
1994, Western NY Conference; 1996, Baltimore: B-H Mission Congregation; 02-01-1997, New Life Mission; 1999, Wheaton: Hughes; 2004, D.C.: Albright Memorial; 2009, DC:Albright-Petworth-Van Buren Cooperative Parish; 2010, DC: Brightwood Park/Albright; 2011, Rockville: Jerusalem-Mt Pleasant.; 2016, Retired

---

Jones, Bruce A.	RE	GW | Faith || Rockville ||| 9410
31262 Anchor Dr, Dagsboro, DE 19939-4363
bajones15@gmail.com
1978, Attending school; 1980, Trinity-Mt. View Charge; 1982, Trinity; 1990, Waldorf: Susanna Wesley; 11-18-90, Lakeside; 1993, Leave of Absence; 1994, Rockville: Francis Asbury; 1998, Rockville: Faith; 2001, Bethesda: Concord-St. Andrews; 2008, La Plata: La Plata; 2018, Retired.

Jones, Calvin D. (David) RE   BM | St Lukes || Baltimore ||| 4615
8207 Legacy Ln, Fort Wayne, IN 46835-1052   H. 260-485-7549
drcdavidjones@frontier.com
1971, Cent. Pa. Conference; 1977, Baltimore Conference; White Marsh Chg; 1978, Edwards Chapel/St. Andrewis of Annapolis; 1988, Dir. Pastoral Min. Charlestown Ecum. Parish; 1991, Woodlawn: St. Lukeis; 1994, Retired.

Jones, Dana PE WE | Mount Olive || Prince Frederick ||| 8430   (202) 238-4695
1o Fairground Road, Prince Frederick, MD 20689   H. (410) 474-1970
dmjones135@comcast.net
2012, Prince Frederick: Mount Olive.

Jones, Jeffrey FE   GW | North Bethesda || Bethesda ||| 9140   (301) 530-4342
24417 Welsh Rd, Gaithersburg, MD 20882-3933   H. (301) 253-6435
macpastor@gmail.com
1974, Attending school; 1976, Manchester Charge; 1979, Baltimore: Roland Avenue-Evergreen; 1985, Cockeysville: Epworth; 1995, Ashton; 2004, College Park: University; 2007, Burtonsville: Liberty Grove; 2014, Bethesda: North Bethesda.

Jones, Joan PL WE | St Edmonds || Chesapeake Beach ||| 8160   (410) 257-7311
PO Box 449, Owings, MD 20736   H. 410-257-7393
pastorjoan21350@live.com
1999, Chesapeake Beach: St. Edmondis.

Jones, Joye RE GW | North Bethesda || Bethesda ||| 9140
8311 20th Ave , Hyattsville, MD 20783-2104   H. (301) 434-2258
joyefulj@verizon.net
1995, Metropolitan Memorial; 1997, Baltimore: Idlewylde; 1/1/04, Silver Spring: Good Shepherd.; 2016, Retired

Jones, Jr., Granderson PL BS | New Hope Christian || Edgewood ||| 2412   (410) 272-2766
378 Oxford Ave , Aberdeen, MD 21001-3544   H. (410) 303-5158
nosrednarg@verizon.net
2008, Lutherville: Govans-Boundary; 2009, Aberdeen: Union; 2019, Edgewood: New Hope Christian Fllwshp,.

Jones, Jr., William C. FD BS | Epworth || Cockeysville ||| 3290   (410) 667-6054
1315 Rayville Rd , Parkton, MD 21120-9003   H. (410) 218-7714
revbjones@hypeyouthministry.org
2008, Cockeysville: Epworth.

Jones, Paulette V. PL   AN | Edgewater || Edgewater ||| 1235
8372 New Cut Rd, Severn, MD 21144-2810   H. (410) 209-0550
pastorpaulettevjones@gmail.com
01-01-18, Davidsonville: Union Memorial, 2018, Edgewater: Edgewater, 2008, Davidsonville: Union Memorial.

Jones, Sr., Jerome A. PL   AN | Wilson Memorial || Gambrills ||| 1290
1913 Rose Pl, Upper Marlboro, MD 20774-8559   H. (301) 821-6545
jeromejones35@gmail.com
2011, Waldorf: Zion Wesley-Mt. Calvary; 2012, Charlotte Hall: Mt. Calvary.; 2016, Temple Hills: Church of Redeemer Charge; 2018, Gambrills: Wilson Memorial.

Jones, Suzanne G. PL   CH | Salem || Keedysville ||| 6250
580 Morgana Dr, Shepherdstown, WV 25443-4751   H. (304) 876-8217
pastorsuzannejones@gmail.com
2016, Frederick: Trinity; 2019, Keedysville: Salem Charge.

Jones-Smith, Jacqueline   FE   GW | North Bethesda || Bethesda ||| 9140   (301) 879-8100
5801 Nicholson Ln Apt 902, North Bethesda, MD 20852-5724   H. (301) 881-8756
jonessmith5291@gmail.com
2004, D.C.: Asbury; 2005, Good Hope Union; 2012, Leave of Absence.

Joo, Eunjoung   FE   CM | St Pauls || Sykesville ||| 4465   (240) 461-4450
7326 Springfield Ave, Sykesville, MD 21784-7549   H. (240) 461-4450
revjoo@stpaulssykesville.org
*2018, Sykesville: Sykesville Parish, 2006, Glen Burnie, Assoc; 2010, Galesville: Galesville;
2014, Washington Grove: Washington Grove.*

Jordan-Griffin, Jason   FE   BM | Union Memorial || Baltimore ||| 2320   (410) 945-2723
7843 Foxfarm Ln, Glen Burnie, MD 21061-6324   H. (202) 277-8957
pastor@unionbaltimore.org
2010, Pumphrey: St John.; 2016, Baltimore: Union Memorial Charge

Jung, YouJung   SY   CM | Wesley Grove || Gaithersburg ||| 9515
4500 Massachusetts Ave NW, Box 264, Washington, DC 20016   H. (301) 788-4265
jyj2908@gmail.com
2019, Damascus: South Damascus,

Justice, Arthur   RL   BS | Mount Vernon || Whiteford ||| 2580
72 Kings Way Dr , North East, MD 21901-2706   H. (410) 652-2043
pstrart18@comcast.net
*1992, Big Pool: Potomac Chg; 1995, Edgewood: Presbury, 2010, Retired; 2014, Whiteford:
Mount Vernon.*

Kapfumvuti, Gladman R.   FE   WE | Asbury || Brandywine ||| 8130   (202) 306-2006
5011 Doctorfish Ct, Waldorf, MD 20603-4237   H. (202) 306-2006
gladmanw@verizon.net
*2003, D.C.: Ryland-Epworth; 2009, Reisterstown: St Lukes; 2013, Waldorf: Asbury/Zion
Wesley.*

Karpal, Richard S.   RE   WE | Emmanuel || Beltsville ||| 7310
13801 Belle Chasse BlvdUnit 413, Laurel, MD 20707-8425   H. (252) 756-4281
*1950, Kentucky Conf; 1956, Asst. Marvin Memorial; 1958, Hampstead: Grace-Grave Run;
1962, Hampden: Grace; 1966, Wardis Chapel; 1968, Attending school; 1972, Assoc. Rockville;
1978, Sandy Mount; 1980, Beltsville: Emmanuel; 1996, Retired.*

Karsner, Jennifer   FE   AN | Asbury || Arnold ||| 1160
78 Church Rd , Arnold, MD 21012-2345   H. (410) 349-2862
pastorjen@asburyumcarnold.org
2007, Mt Airy: Calvary; 2013, Arnold: Asbury.

118

Kaylor, Clarence A.   RE   CM | Damascus || Damascus ||| 9190
106 Homewood Ln, Frederick, MD 21702-3381   H. (301) 540-0667
tomkaylor@verizon.net
1960, Attending school; 1962, Glenelg; 1971, Frostburg; 1979, Waldorf: Good Shepherd;
1995, Gaithersburg: Covenant; 2000, Retired.

Keller, Richard   PL   BM | Christ Church of Balt Co || Baltimore ||| 3285   (410) 887-2791
2217 Smith Ave, Baltimore, MD 21227-1828   H. (410) 796-5697
recycle815@aol.com
01-01-2007, Phoenix: Fairview; 2012, Baltimore: Christ Church of Baltimore County.

Kells, Jr., Robert E.   FE   FR | Weller || Thurmont ||| 6365   (301) 271-2802
101 Dogwood Ave, Thurmont, MD 21788-1604   H. (301) 271-2838
rkellsjr@gmail.com
2013, Thurmont: Weller.

Kelly, Judith   RL   FR | Toms Creek || Emmitsburg ||| 6170   (410) 721-9129
1727 Tarleton Way , Crofton, MD 21114-2503   H. (443) 292-8474
callmejude@aol.com
2003, Crofton: Community; 2006, Emmitsburg: Toms Creek; 02-01-2012, Retired.

Kent, Arthur R.   RE   CM | St Pauls || Sykesville ||| 4465
609 Avon Square Ct, Silver Spring, MD 20905-5939   H. (410) 788-8567
kentbiz09@gmail.com
1970, Chase Circuit; 1972, Gaithersburg: Brookgrove-Stewarttown; 1978, Attending school;
1982, Union Square; 1984, Beechfield; 10-01-87, Otterbein Memorial; 1988, So. Baltimore
Parish; 1990, Baltimore: Dorguth/Good Shepherd; 1993, Woodbine: Morgan Charge; 1996,
Sykesville: Oakland-Flohrville Charge; 12-01-97, Sykesville: Oakland; 1998, Retired.

Kent, Lucinda   PL   GW | Van Buren || Washington ||| 7280   (301) 385-6630
4709 Ridgeline Ter, Bowie, MD 20720-3705   H. (301) 385-6630
pastorcindykent@gmail.com
2016, DC: Van Buren.

Kercheval, William C.   RL CH | Mount Bethel || Smithsburg ||| 5450
301 Chesapeake Dr Unit D, Waynesboro, PA 17268-7984   H. 717-655-5582
wckercheval@aol.com
1983, Smithsburg: Mount Bethel; 2003, Retired.

Kibbe, Orlando F.   RA   FR | Taylorsville || Mount Airy ||| 4485
13978 Penn Shop Rd , Mount Airy, MD 21771-4624   H. (410) 552-4727
ofbudki@msn.com
1981, Sparks: Salem-Falls Road Charge; 1993, Taylorsville: Taylorsville-Salem Charge; 1998,
Taylorsville; 2001, Retired; 01-01-2007, Monrovia: Mountain View-Pleasant Grove.

Kim, Hea S.   FE BS | Reisterstown || Reisterstown ||| 4435   (212) 870-3747
123 W 104th St Apt 10A, New York, NY 10025-9603   H. (821) 068-1635
1983, Concord-St. Andrews; 1984 D.C.: National Korean; 1985, Reisterstown; 1988, Attending
school; 1991, Leave of Absence; 01-01-92, General Board of Global Ministries.

Kim, Heerak PE   CH | Grace || Midland ||| 5410   (202) 304-9328
14706 Smith Hill Rd SW, Frostburg, MD 21532-4838   H. (202) 304-9328
kheerak@gmail.com
2017, Midland: George's Creek.

Kim, Narae PE   CH | Grace || Midland ||| 5410
14706 Smith Hill Rd SW, Frostburg, MD 21532-4838   H. (301) 655-2216
narae849.kim@gmail.com
10-01-2013, Sykesville: Flohrville; 2017, No Appointment, 2019, LaVale: LaVale.

Kim, Paul C. RE
2070 Harvest Ridge Cir, Buford, GA 30519-7359   H.
pkim122@hotmail.com
1968, Seoul Conference; 1978 Eastern Pa; 1989 Baltimore: Korean of Baltimore 09-01-93,
Glen Burnie: First Korean; 01-01-94, First Korean of Baltimore & Glen Burnie First Korean;
1998 HWR: Hampden/Mt. Vernon; 2004, D.C.: Mt. Vernon Place; 2005, Greenbelt: Mowatt
Memorial; 2008, Phoenix: Clynmalira; 05-16-2010, Retired.

King, Andrea M. FE   BM | New Waverly || Baltimore ||| 3217
PO Box 233, Fulton, MD 20759-0253   H. (843) 557-2455
revamking@yahoo.com
1997, Clarksburg: John Wesley, 2006, Germantown: Asbury/John Wesley Chg; 12-01-2006,
Leave of Absence; 02-01-2012, Ext. Min, Baltimore-Washington Conference, Associate
Director of Ministry with the Poor.; 2016, Abingdon: Abingdon Cooperative Parrish; 2017,
Highland: Hopkins/Mt. Olivet, 2019, Baltimore: New Waverly-Govan Boundary.

King, Curtis D. FE   BM | St James Memorial || Baltimore ||| 2265
PO Box 233, Fulton, MD 20759   H. (410) 622-4667
revcurtisking2@yahoo.com
2002, Gaithersburg: Emory Grove; 12-01-2006, Leave of Absence; 07-09-2014, Director
of Wesley Foundation, Grambling State U.; 3-1-16, Baltimore: Centennial-Caroline; 2017,
Baltimore: St James, 2017, ExtMin: Urban Behavior Associates, 01-01-19, Baltimore: St.
James-Mt. Winans.

King, Sonia L. FE   BM | Brooklyn Community || Baltimore ||| 2142   (301) 776-8885
643 Chapelgate Dr , Odenton, MD 21113-2138   H. (410) 320-3482
revslkzeta@gmail.com
2019, Baltimore: Brooklyn Area, 2005, Jessup: Asbury; 2009, DC: Brighter Day; 09-15-2009,
Pasadena: Mount Zion; 2014, Laurel: St Marks.

King, Sr., Eric W. FE   CM | Goshen || Gaithersburg ||| 9255
7820 Brink Rd, Gaithersburg, MD 20882-1616   H. (410) 935-1038
king1906@comcast.net
2017, Gaithersburg: Goshen, 1998, Bel Air: Ames; 2003, Leave of Absence; 2004, New Life;
2009, Baltimore: New Life-St. Matthews Cooperative Parish; 01-01-2012, Baltimore: St.
Matthews-New Life; 01-01-2015, Baltimore: Metropolitan-West Baltimore.

Kirkley, Robert G.. RE
PO Box 10 , Taylors Island, MD 21669-0010   H. (410) 397-3498
1951, Baltimore: Light Street; 1954, Baltimore: Mt. Washington; 1978, Lexington Park
Charge; 2000, Retired.

Kittrell, Angela M. PL   WE | Bowie || Bowie ||| 8120   (301) 464-8383
13011 6th St, Bowie, MD 20720-3614   H. (804) 313-7638
emmanuelinfo@gmail.com
2018, Bowie: Bowie,

Klauda, Jeanne W. RE   CM | Salem || Brookeville ||| 9150
840 Harbor View Ter , Annapolis, MD 21409-4641   H. (410) 349-0949
1976, Hyattsville: First; 1981, Brookeville-Salem; 1-1-86, N. Bethesda; 1999, Severna Park;
2003, Providence-Fort Washington; 2006, Retired.

Knepp, Sandra PL   AN | Trinity || Odenton ||| 1435   (410) 721-2461
1593 Forest Hill Ct, Crofton, MD 21114-1826   H. (443) 569-1867
pastorsandyk@gmail.com
2018, Odenton: Trinity,

Knoll, Travis FE BS | Hunts Memorial || Riderwood ||| 3487   (410) 339-7770
1703 Singer Rd, joppa, MD 21085   H. (410) 688-9613
pastortravisk@gmail.com
1996, Forest Hill: Deer Creek; 1999, Hagerstown: St. Andrews; 2001, Assoc., Eldersburg:
Wesley Freedom; 2004, Fallston: Ebenezer; 2009, Fallston: Ebenezer-William Watters
Cooperative Parish; 2015, Baltimore: Lovely Lane; 2017, Riderwood: Hunt's Memorial.

Kohl, Kathleen H. RE   GW | Colesville || Silver Spring ||| 9450   (301) 704-4547
1619 Catchworth Ct , Silver Spring, MD 20905-7006   H. (301) 236-4245
revkkohl@verizon.net
1986, Liberty Grove; 1989, Leave of Absence; 1991, Attending school; 6-9-95, Pastoral
Counseling & Consultation Centers of Greater Washington; 2017, Retired.

Kokoski, Jennifer L. PD BS | Union || Baldwin ||| 3135
3214 Black Rock Rd, Reisterstown, MD 21136-3819   H. (410) 596-1473
pastorjennk@gmail.com
2005, Westminster; 2009, Keedysville: South Mountain; 2011, Smithsburg: Garfield; 09-01-
2013, Baldwin: Union.

Kolda, David F. RE   CM | St James || Marriottsville ||| 4565
18388 Brussels Dr , South Bend, IN 46637-2335   H. (574) 273-4280
DJKOLDA@sbcglobal.net
1964, Attending school; 1966, Doubs; 1971, Union Bridge-Johnsville; 1977, Rockville: Faith;
1981, West Friendship.: St. James; 1994, Pasadena: Community; 2003, Retired.

Kopp, Lamar W. RE   CH | Otterbein || Hagerstown ||| 5340
6596 Orphanage Rd Parker House, Rm 307, Waynesboro, PA 17268   H. (717) 749-6596
lwkopp@gmail.com
1948, Baltimore: St. John's; 1954, Hebbville: Salem; 1976, Hagerstown: Otterbein; 1985,
D.C.: Metropolitan Memorial; 1989, Retired.

Kraus, Mary E. RE   GW | Dumbarton || Washington ||| 7160
510 W 6th St, Claremont, CA 91711-4254   H. (202) 986-6457
marykraus1943@gmail.com
1971, Minnesota Conference; 1974, Baltimore Conference, Columbia: Owen Brown Village;
1975, Columbia: Christ; 1978, Virginia Conference; 1982, D.C.: Metropolitan Memorial;
1984, Superintendent, Baltimore North Dist; 1990, D.C.: Dumbarton; 2009, Retired.

Krebs, Paul   SY   BS | Deer Creek || Forest Hill ||| 2450
13 Farwell Ct, Nottingham, MD 21236-2119   H. (410) 256-3129
pkrebs6214@gmail.com
2017, Forest Hill: Deer Creek,

Kriewald, Diedra H.   RE
400 Clocktower Ridge Dr Apt 207, Winchester, VA 22603-3882   H. (540) 667-0572
dkriewal@shentel.net
1978 Virginia Conference; Prof. Wesley Theo. Sem; 1995, Transfer to Baltimore-Washington Conference; 2007, Retired.

Kroll, Richard A.   RE   CH | Williamsport || Williamsport ||| 5475
10849 Donelson Dr , Williamsport, MD 21795-1421   H. (301) 223-9318
rkroll1089@gmail.com
1970, Attending school; 1971, Manchester Circuit; 1976, Benevola Chrg; 1979, Halethorpe; 1983, Martinsburg: Otterbein; 1994, Williamsport; 2003, Charles Town: Asbury; 2012, Retired.

Kuehnle, Norman B. (Bruce)   RE
419 Russell Ave Apt 309, Gaithersburg, MD 20877-2872   H. (410) 987-5085
1961, Attending school; 1963, Rogers Memorial; 1965, Shepherdstown: New Street; 1968, Bethesda: Bethesda Assoc; 1970, Chase: Cowenton-Ebenezer; 1977, Clarksville: Linden-Linthicum; 1985, Sabbatical Leave; 1986, Leave of Absence; 1987, Retired.

Kumar, Christine   PL   BM | Cowenton || White Marsh ||| 2570   (301) 526-3238
10830 Red Lion Rd, White Marsh, MD 21162-1702   H. (301) 526-3238
cpkumar222@gmail.com
2017, Baltimore: Cowenton-Piney Grove,

Kurtz, Ron R.   RE   CH | Mount Bethel || Smithsburg ||| 5450
20614 Pony Trl, Boonsboro, MD 21713-1805   H. (301) 393-4359
rk4home@aol.com
1977, Baltimore: Woodberry; 1980, Maryland Line; 1986, Attending school; 1988, Monkton-Clynmalira Charge; 1992, Boonsboro: Mt. Nebo; 1995, Attending school; 1997, Admin., Wesley Home; 9-15-99, Boonsboro: Mt. Nebo; 2000, Boonsboro: Mt. Lena; 2008, Special Assignment -Internal; 2009, Smithsburg: Mount Bethel; 2012, Boonsboro: Mt. Bethel/Mt. Lena Cooperative Parish; 2012, Retired.

Kutrick, Daniel   PL   BM | Dundalk || Baltimore ||| 2380   (410) 284-4818
442 Machias Pl, Middle River, MD 21220-2338   H. (410) 335-7154
danielkutrick@comcast.net
2011, Baltimore: Dundalk-Graceland Cooperative Parish; 2019, Baltimore: Graceland.

Lageman, August G.   RE   BM | Orangeville || Baltimore ||| 2250   (276) 466-7971
20449 Alvarado Rd , Abingdon, VA 24211-6369   H. (276) 475-5433
1972, Patapsco: Deer Park; 1974, West Baltimore, Assoc; 1976, Lutherville: St. Johnis; 1981, Balt. Past. Coun. Serv; 1991, Exec. Dir., Pastoral Counseling Services of Maryland; 1-1-97, U.S. Army Chaplain; 1-1-98, Leave of Absence; 2-1-99, Holston Conference; 2005, Retired.

Lambros, George   RL   BS | Smiths Chapel || Churchville ||| 2370   (410) 734-7113
1511 Cabin Rd , Aberdeen, MD 21001-1301
pglambros@comcast.net
2002, Chase: Piney Grove; 2009, Churchville: Smithis Chapel; 12-31-2010, Retired; 2011, Churchville: Smithis Chapel.

Lancaster, Mark A.   FE   FR | Westminster || Westminster ||| 4555   (765) 983-1805
4519 Sweet Potato Ridge Rd, Englewood, OH 45322-9770   H. (502) 222-5886
marklancaster116@juno.com
1981, Attending school; 1982, Assoc. Dir. for Campus Ministry; 1983, Aldersgate; 1984,
Westminster; 1986, Upperco: Emory; 1991, Maryland Food Committee; 5/1/99, Exec.
Director, Ministry of Money (Am. Friends Service Com.); 2/10/06, Presbyterian Church.

Langenstein, John S.   SY   FR | Bethesda || Shepherdstown ||| 6720   (304) 582-0206
3415 Kearneysville Pike, Shepherdstown, WV 25443   H. (202) 487-1418
jslangenstein@gmail.com
2019, Shenandoah Junction: Shenandoah,

Lankford, Ludwig L.   RE
8820 Walther Blvd.Apt. 2212, Baltimore, MD 21234-9045   H. (410) 321-6109
1962, Attending school; 1965, General Board Christian Social Concerns; 1970, Dir., Office
of Ed. and Trng. for Addic. Serv. Md. Dept. HMH; 1984, Stevenson; 1998, Leave of Absence,
1999, Retired.

Laprade, Ann   FE   (410) 309-3448
2547 Sutcliff Ter , Brookeville, MD 20833-3250   H. (301) 299-9383
alaprade@bwcumc.org
1983, Hagerstown: St. Andrewis; 1986, Rockville: Faith; 1990, Catonsville: West Baltimore;
2003, Carney: Linden Heights; 2006, Potomac: Potomac; 2017, ExtMin: Baltimore Suburban
District Superintendent.

Larsen, Ellis L.   RE   GW | Rockville || Rockville ||| 9440
415 Russell Ave Apt 1101, Gaithersburg, MD 20877-2844   H. (301) 216-5687
eleif@aol.com
1961, N. Ind. Conference; 1976, Baltimore Conference, Prof., Wesley Theological Sem; 1991,
Church Adm./Asst. Dean Wesley Theo. Sem; 2001, Retired.

Larsen, Stephen L.   FE   FR | Calvary || Frederick ||| 6190   (301) 662-1464
131 W 2nd St , Frederick, MD 21701-5328   H. (301) 848-8216
RevSteve@calvaryumc.org
01-01-18, Frederick: Calvary, 1987, Attending school; 1988 Frederick: Calvary; 1993,
Phoenix: Fairview, 1996, Carney: Linden Heights; 2003, Waldorf: Good Shepherd; 2012, Mt
Airy: Calvary.; 2016, Frederick: Calvary / Centennial Memorial

---

Lasater, Alisa L.   FE   GW | Capitol Hill || Washington ||| 7135
431 N West St, Alexandria, VA 22314-2122   H. 202-546-1000 x222
pastor@chumc.net
2008, DC: Capitol Hill; 2011, DC: Ebenezer Cooperative Circuit; 2014, DC: Capitol Hill.

Leatherwood, Neva H.   RE   CM | Bethany || Ellicott City ||| 4235
2613 Melba Rd , Ellicott City, MD 21042-1833   H. (410) 465-9483
1984, Alberta Gary Memorial; 1985, Lewistown; 1988, Pikesville: Ames; 1989, Ames-Stone
Chapel;1992, Wheaton: Hughes; 1994, Elkridge: Melville Chapel; 1997, D.C; HWR-MW Par.:
Mt. Washington; 11-1-98, Leave of Absence, 1999, Midland Chg; 2002, Leave of Absence;
08/01/02, Retired.

Lebo, John R. RE BS | Bel Air || Bel Air ||| 2340 (410) 879-2797
811 Tilghman Dr , Bel Air, MD 21015-3438 H. (410) 638-9750
1956, Attending school; 1961, Hagerstown: St. Pauls; 1964, Otterbein, Spry, Pa; 1970,
Hagerstown: Otterbein; 1982, Bel Air; 1996, Retired.

Lee, Dong Eun SY BS | Glyndon || Glyndon ||| 4285
pastorleegumc@gmail.com (202) 557-9568
2019, Glyndon: Glyndon.

Lee, Jean H. PE CM | Mount Carmel || Brookeville ||| 9335
21820 Laytonsville Rd , Laytonsville, MD 20882-1630 H. (301) 330-0539
jeanhlee5@gmail.com
2016, Laytonsville: Sunshine.

Lee, Keystone B. SY CM | Flohrville || Sykesville ||| 4230
13122 Dairymaid Dr, Germantown, MD 20874-2311 H. (301) 540-0980
revkeystone@hotmail.com
2017, Sykesville: Flohrville,

Lee, KyungLim S. FE GW | Francis Asbury Natl Korean || Rockville ||| 9427 (202) 885-8620
4500 Massachusetts Ave NW , Washington, DC 20016-5632 H. (301) 469-8537
kshinlee@wesleyseminary.edu
1988, Wis. Conference; 1992, Baltimore Conference, Prof. Wesley Theological Seminary.

Lee, Seung-Woo FE GW | Francis Asbury Natl Korean || Rockville ||| 9427 (301) 251-6636
9717 Corkran Ln, Bethesda, MD 20817-1531 H. (240) 601-3349
revlsw@hotmail.com
1976, Central Conference; 1982, Seoul Conference; 1986, Wisconsin Conference; 1991,
Baltimore Conference: Korean Mission of Washington; 11-19-95, Rockville: National Korean;
9/1/03, Rockville: Francis Asbury; 01-01-2011, Rockville: Francis Asbury National Korean.

Leedom, Michael J. FE CH | Union Chapel || Berkeley Springs ||| 5570
82 Chapel Ln , Berkeley Springs, WV 25411-6727 H. (304) 707-1250
pmikeunionchapel@gmail.com
2009, Cumberland: South Cumberland; 2012, Berkeley Springs: Union Chapel.

Leftwich, Michael E. RE CM | Mountain View || Damascus ||| 9220
11345 Windsor Rd, Ijamsville, MD 21754-8907 H. (301) 865-3321
1957, Cape St. Clair; 1959, Rogers Memorial; 1963, Withdrew; 1968, Readmitted, Linganore-
Keys Chapel Charge; 1980, Damascus: Bethesda; 1985, Arnold: Asbury; 1988, Mt. View-
Pleasant Grove; 07-18-95, Suspended; 09-15-95, Involuntary Leave of Absence; 1996,
Retirement (with conditions); 07-01-97, Conditions Satisfied.

Leith, Janice RE CH | New Covenant || Cumberland ||| 5210
10020 Christie Rd SE, Cumberland, MD 21502-8242 H. (410) 440-5179
janleith@juno.com
2005, Cockeysville: Texas Charge; 2014, Retired.

LeMaster, Elizabeth A. FE AN | Wesley Grove || Hanover ||| 1355 (410) 795-2777
6326 Barnett Ave, Eldersburg, MD 21784-6102 H. (304) 261-4763
ealemaster@gmail.com
2014, Keedysville: Salem; 2015, Eldersburg: Wesley Freedom; 2019, Harmans: Wesley Grove.

Lemon-Riley, Rebecca   RL BS | Piney Grove || Reisterstown ||| 4175   (410) 429-0997
2717 Silver Hill Ave, Baltimore, MD 21207-6776   H. (410) 448-4054
becky125@comcast.net
2001, Reisterstown: Piney Grove; 2008, Retired.

Leslie, Frank R. (Richard)   RE   CH | Melvin || Cumberland ||| 5295
317 Adam Rd, Frederick, MD 21701-6327   H. (908) 473-7768
jalrl@comcast.net
1968, W. Pa. Conference, 1982, Baltimore Conference, Wheaton: Hughes; 1984, Hyattsville: Ager Rd; 1990, Arbutus: Arbutus; 1996, Retired.

Lewis, Brenda L.   FE   CM | Bethany || Ellicott City ||| 4235   (410) 465-2919
9962 Sherwood Farm Rd, Owings Mills, MD 21117-5853   H. (410) 356-8453
brenda@bethanyum.org
2004, Fallston: Tabernacle; 2014, Abington: Cokesbury; 2018, Ellicott City: Bethany.

Lewis, David N.   RL   BM | Cherry Hill || Baltimore ||| 2155
1997, Baltimore: Cherry Hill Charge.

Lewis, G. D. (Doug)   RE   (202) 363-0232
5133 Warren Pl NW , Washington, DC 20016-4318   H. (202) 363-6027
g.dlewis@verizon.net
1964, Holston Conference; 1982, Baltimore Conference: President, Wesley Theological Seminary; 2002, Retired.

Lewis, John   RL FR | Marvin Chapel || Inwood ||| 6670   (304) 725-6137
PO Box 1925, Inwood, WV 25428-1925   H. (540) 931-3615
talkmanjohn@gmail.com
1999, Summit Point: Memorial; 2014, Harpers Ferry: Silver Grove; 2014, Retired; 2014, Harpers Ferry: Silver Grove Charge; 1-1-16, Harpers Ferry: Silver Grove; 2016, Kearneysville: Leetown/Marvin Chapel Coop; 04-01-19, Inwood: Inwood, 04-01-19, Martinsburg: Marvin Chapel.

Lewis, Marilyn   PL   AN | Adams || Lothian ||| 1375
PO Box 538, Arnold, MD 21012-0538   H. (410) 978-5262
merlewis@comcast.net
2017, Lothian: Adams.

Lewis, Weller R.   RE
PO Box 364 , Cambridge, MD 21613-0364   H. (703) 847-5000
wellerrlewis@gmail.com
1962, Attending school; 1966, Frederick: Brook Hill; 1967, DC.: Providence; 1974, Hagerstown: St. Matthewis; 1977, Poolesville: Memorial; 1982, Accokeek: Faith; 1984, Leave of Absence; 1987, Retired.

Lewis-Rill, Amy S.   FE   BS | Wesley || Hampstead ||| 4330   (410) 374-4027
3674 Stewartstown Rd, Stewartstown, PA 17363-8118   H. (443) 604-5245
revamys@aol.com
1991, Baltimore: Mt. Vernon, HWR Parish; 1992, Baltimore: Grace; 08-01-99, Catonsville: Emanuel; 2006, Baltimore: Good Shepherd; 2013, Hampstead: Wesley.

Ley, Diana L.   RE   CM | Epworth || Gaithersburg ||| 9245
9443 Fens Holw, Laurel, MD 20723-5734   H. (301) 725-2986
revley@verizon.net
1979, Gaithersburg: Epworth; 1987, DC.: Dumbarton; 1989, DC; United; 1997, Silver Spring: Marvin Memorial; 2008, Retired.

Lida, Michael   PL   FR | Silver Grove || Harpers Ferry ||| 6585   (301) 491-8357
40141 McKees Gap Road, Warfordsburg, PA 17267   H. (301) 491-8357
pastormikelida@gmail.com
2016, Harpers Ferry: Silver Grove.

Lievers, Ernest   PL   BS | Edgewood || Lutherville ||| 3365   (410) 706-7361
6221 Pilgrim Rd, Baltimore, MD 21214-1542   H. (410) 426-2781
busterpete@comcast.net
2004, Lutherville: Edgewood .

Lightner, Charles W.   RE   BS | Bel Air || Bel Air ||| 2340
12 Free St , Machias, ME 04654-1147   H. (207) 255-0514
1956, Upper Strasburg; 1958, Attending school; 1961, Benevola-Mt. Lena; 1969, Waldorf: Good Shepherd; 1979, Bel Air, 1999, Retired.

Lindsay, Richard D.   RL   FR | Union Street || Westminster ||| 4550   (443) 864-6727
5463 Gloucester Rd, Columbia, MD 21044-1911   H. (443) 864-6727
drlpastor1@verizon.net
1985, Greater New Jersey Conf; 1990, Catonsville: Mount Olivet; 10-01-2007, Arnold: Mount Calvary; 08-08-2011, Lothian: Sollers.; 2016, Retired; 2016, Westminster: Union Street; 2019, Sykesville: Bethesda.

Link, Conrad O.   FE   AN | Calvary || Annapolis ||| 1120
1910 Dulany Pl, Annapolis, MD 21409-6221   H. (301) 695-9468
COLink@calumc.org
1979, Gerrardstown-Ganotown Charge; 1984, Hagerstown: John Wesley; 1988, Mt. Nebo; 1992, Frederick: Brook Hill; 2010, Guide Western Region; 2012, District Superintendent, Cumberland-Hagerstown; 2019, Annapolis: Calvary.

Linton, Debra M.   FL   FR | Centennial Memorial || Frederick ||| 6210   (301) 694-8772
2045 Spring Run Cir, Frederick, MD 21702-6808   H. (301) 447-5955
lintondebra@gmail.com
08-17-2008, Araby: Araby; 2011, Adamstown: Adamstown.; 2016, Frederick: Calvary / Centennial Memorial; 10-01-17, Frederick: Centennial Memorial.

Llewellyn, Donald W.   RE   (410) 697-3272
Spring Arbor Assisted, 345 Ritchie Hwy, Severna Park, MD 21146   H. (410) 923-6572
paldl@comcast.net
1952, Attending school; 1953, Exeter Memorial; 1956, Violetville; 1960, Highland Avenue; 1965, Essex; 1970, Riviera Beach: Community; 1976, Parkside; 1981, Linthicum Heights; 1993, Retired.

Lloyd, Solomon O.   FE   CH | Mc Kendree of Potomac Park || Cumberland ||| 5242
6103 Chia Ave, Twentynine Palms, CA 92277-1951   H. (410) 504-4962
Solomon.lloyd@usmc.mil
11-01-07, Cresaptown: Mc Kendree UMC of Potomac Park; 2013, Extension Ministry: Navy Chaplain.

126

Long, Sr., Thomas   PL   WE | Bethel || Upper Marlboro ||| 8480
342 Whirlaway Dr, Prince Frederick, MD 20678-3287   H. (812) 207-6915
mintclong@comcast.net
2014, Lothian: Union; 2018, Upper Marlboro: Bethel.

Lossau, Kathleen S.   FE   AN | Severn || Severn ||| 1485
5501 45th Ave Apt 312, Hyattsville, MD 20781-1591   H. (217) 341-2181
rtrevdrk@gmail.com
*2019, Severn: Delmont/Severn, 1995, Bethesda Sykesville; 2000, Illinois Great Rivers Conf.;
2014, Street: Emory.; 2016, Silver Spring: Good Shepherd Charge*

Love, Antoine C.   FE   CM | Wesley Freedom || Eldersburg ||| 4225
5238 Kenstan Dr, Temple Hills, MD 20748-5446   H. (301) 449-5683
tlove@wesleyfreedom.org
*1998, Lexington Park: Zion; 1/1/04, Waldorf: Covenant Point; 2010, Waldorf: Covenant Point-
Lakeside Cooperative Parish; 01-01-2012, Waldorf: The Journey of Faith; 2014, Baltimore
Washington Conference, Director of Vibrant Communities.; 2-1-16, Cheverly: Cheverly
Charge; 2017, Baltimore-Washington Conference: Asst. to Bishop; 2019, Eldersburg: Wesley
Freedom.*

Lowans, Jerry J.   FE   CH | Washington Square || Hagerstown ||| 5360   (301) 739-2653
237 Collins Dr, Martinsburg, WV 25403   H. (304) 279-9051
jerrylowans1@gmail.com
1991, Hedgesville: Butlers Chapel; 2007, Hagerstown: West Hagerstown.

Lowans, Sharon L.   SY   FR | Sandy Hook || Knoxville ||| 6255
237 Collins Dr, Martinsburg, WV 25403   H. (304) 676-6774
pastorsharonlynn@gmail.com
2018, Knoxville: Sandy Hook, 2019, Knoxville: Sandy Hook/Shenandoah Memorial,

---

Lowe, Don B.   RE
3152 Gracefield Rd Apt 419, Silver Spring, MD 20904-0801   H. (703) 671-5831
*1961, Attending school; 1963, Assoc. Baltimore: Grace; 1966, Grace-Falls Road; 1968,
Baltimore: St. Johns; 1975, D.C.: Christ; 1984, Mill Creek Parish; 1990, Hyattsville: Ager
Road; 2000, Retired.*

Ludlum, Beth   FE   GW | Mount Vernon Place || Washington ||| 7235
6605 13th Pl NW, Washington, DC 20012-2309   H. (703) 314-1496
bethie_ksu@hotmail.com
*2013, GBHEM, Director of Student Faith and Leadership Formation; 2015, Ext. Min: Wesley
Seminary.*

Lundin, Fay B.   FE   GW | College Park || College Park-Mowatt Mem ||| 7335
1169 Claire Rd, Crownsville, MD 21032-1048   H. (202) 215-5209
Faylundin@yahoo.com
2007, College Park: College Park; 2008, College Park: College Park-Mowatt Memorial.

Lunt, Anders R. (Andy)   RE   CM | Glen Mar || Ellicott City ||| 7365
9000 Fathers Legacy Apt 100, Ellicott City, MD 21042-5149   H. (410) 418-4341
revdoclunt@gmail.com
*1967, Central Pa. Conference; 1970, Eastern Pa. Conference; 1973, Baltimore Conference,
Director of Communication; 1979, Ellicott City: Glen Mar; 1991, Glen Gary Greater Parish
1997, Glen Mar; 2010, Retired; 08-01-2010, Director of Grow Congregations.*

Lyles, Sr., Ernest   RE   GW | Metropolitan Memorial || Washington ||| 7630
PO Box 551, Shepherdstown, WV 25443-0551
pastorlyles@aol.com
*1984, Shepherdstown: Asbury-Mt. Zion; 1989, Shepherdstown: Asbury; 2004, D.C.: A. P. Shaw
2006, A.P. Shaw/Congress Heights Coop. Parish; 2009, DC: Brighter Day; 2017, Retired.*

Lyons, Jr., William K. (Ken)   RE   AN | Baldwin Memorial || Millersville ||| 1420
1329 Bluegrass Way , Gambrills, MD 21054-1052   H. (410) 674-6579
kedolyons@comcast.net
*1969, Etchison: Mt. Tabor; 1971, Millersville: Baldwin Memorial; 1991, Highland: Mt. Zion;
1998, Superintendent, Cumberland-Hagerstown Dist; 2003, Severna Park; 2008, Retired.*

Macaulay, Alhassan C.   FE AN | Franklin || Churchton ||| 1175   (301) 728-6885
7833 Metacomet Rd, Hanover, MD 21076-1246   H. (410) 551-3513
pastormacaulay@gmail.com
*2005, Sunderland: Mt. Hope; 2006, Baltimore: New Waverly; 2010, Brandywine: Asbury; 01-
01-2014, Churchton: Franklin.; 2016, Lothian: Mt. Zion/Franklin Charge*

Mack, Brenda J.   RE   AN | Chews Memorial || Edgewater ||| 1438
700 Freeman Dr Apt 415, Hampton, VA 23666-4375
magdalene_29@hotmail.com
*2006, Assoc., Hagerstown Parish; 2007, Ijamsville: Ebenezer; 2008, Owensville: Chews
Memorial; 2013, Owensville: Chews Memorial/Carteris; 2017, Retired.*

Mack, Burton L.   RE
700 Freeman Dr Apt 415, Hampton, VA 23666-4375   H. (410) 798-1638
burtonmack@msn.com
*1989, Lusby Chg; 1993, Silver Spring: Good Hope Union; 1996, Washington: Asbury;
8-15-97,Washington: Asbury/Wesley Foundation, Howard Univ; 1999, Washington: Asbury;
2000, Frederick: Asbury; 2008, Retired; 01-15-2011, Annapolis: Asbury-Broadneck; 01-01-
2012, Lothian: Mount Zion (Ark Road).*

Mackereth Fulton, Kathryn   PE   GW | St Pauls || Kensington ||| 9330   (301) 933-7933
7837 Thor Dr, Annandale, VA 22003-1437   H. (301) 524-5196
k.mackereth@gmail.com
2018, Kensington: St Paul's.

Maisch, William C.   FE   CM | Calvary || Mount Airy ||| 6285
24105 Preakness Dr , Damascus, MD 20872-2171   H. (301) 461-0301
pastorbillmaisch@comcast.net
*2002, Dickerson: Dickerson-Forest Grove Charge; 2005,Clarksburg; 2008, Sandy Mount:
Sandy Mount; 11-01-2012, Poolesville: Memorial; 2018, Mt Airy: Calvary.*

Manhart, George M.   RE
347 Laurel Dr , Lehighton, PA 18235-8990   H. (610) 377-8323
*1966, Idlewylde; 1969, Fallston; 1971, Baltimore: Wesley; 1978, Glen Burnie: Messiah; 1981,
Fulton Siemers Memorial; 1982, Bay Brook Chg; 1987, Retired.*

Manning, James D.   RE   AN | Nichols-Bethel || Odenton ||| 1430
3524 South River Ter, Edgewater, MD 21037-3245   H. (410) 798-4648
*1959, Dorguth Memorial; 1962, Christ Church of Baltimore Co; 1965, Odenton: Nichols-
Bethel; 1998, Retired.*

Manson, Evelyn H.   RE   WE | Ebenezer || Lanham ||| 8285   (202) 376-8931
16010 Excalibur RdApt C401, Bowie, MD 20716-3941   H. (301) 860-1578
revev4606@msn.com
1994, Chaplain, DC Detention Facility; 2001, La Plata: St Matthewis; 2005, Retired; 2010, La Plata: St Matthewis; 01-15-11, Pisgah: Smith Chapel-Alexandria Chapel Cooperative Parish.

Manthey, Robert E.   RE   FR | Calvary || Frederick ||| 6190
500 Pearson Cir Apt 4018, Frederick, MD 21702-3424   H. 240-629-8030
nanbob65@comcast.net
1964, Attending school; 1967, Friendship; 1969, Friendship and Carters; 1971, Mill Creek Parish; 1979, Lutherville: Timonium; 1988, Frederick: Calvary; 2004, Retired.

Marceron, Joanna   RL   AN | Galesville || Galesville ||| 1280   (410) 991-2253
327 S River Clubhouse Rd, Harwood, MD 20776-9534   H. (410) 991-2253
Jjmdiaconal@msn.com
2007, Hedgesville: Butlers Chapel-Jones Spring ; 2008, Kearneysville: Leetown/Butleris Chapel Cooperative Parish; 01-01-2012, Kearneysville: Leetown; 2013, Kearneysville: Leetown/Marvin Chapel Cooperative Parish; 2016, Retired; 01-13-17, Elkridge: Melville Chapel, 2017, Galesville: Galesville.

Marseilles, Susan C.   RE   BS | Idlewylde || Baltimore ||| 3535
20731 Ewing Rd , Preston, MD 21655-1470   H. (410) 673-1025
Revscm@aol.com
1990, Baltimore: Grace; 1992, Reisterstown: Grace-Bosley Chg; 1995, Woodfield: Wesley Grove; 1997, Fallston: Ebenezer; 2004, Idlewylde; 2005, Leave of Absence; 2006, Retired.

Marshall, Sherrin   RE   AN | Severna Park || Severna Park ||| 1510   (410) 647-3090
1333 Tall Timbers Dr, Crownsville, MD 21032-1531   H. (410) 923-4554
RevSDMarshall@aol.com
1999, Eastern Pennsylvania Conf; 2006, Marley; 2007, Pasadena: Pasadena.; 2016, Retired; 2017, Elkridge: Melville Chapel.

Martin, Donna J.   RE   (410) 719-8670
5623 Gardenville Ave , Baltimore, MD 21206-3706   H. (410) 483-1107
drdjmartin@aol.com
1967, W. Pa. Conference; 1992, Baltimore Conference, Berkeley Springs: Francis Asbury-Wesley Chg; 1995, Glen Gary Greater Parish 1997, Glen Mar; 2002, Leave of Absence; 2003, Ext. Min.: Heartland Hospice; 2009, Retired.

Martin, Mildred C.   RE   FR | Asbury || Charles Town ||| 6530
15 Canterbury Trl #21, Charles Town, WV 25414-9238   H. (181) 455-8692
mcmpurplelady@gmail.com
1975, Pac. NW Conference; 1977, Discontinued; 1985, Reinstated and Baltimore Conference, Washington: Wesley; 1988, Germantown: Salem; 1-1-90, Lanham: First; 1990, Rohrersville Chg; 1992, Galesvillle; 1994, Wyoming Conference; 1997, Cumberland: Emmanuel-Bethel; 2001, Sabbatical Leave; 2002, Union Grove Chg; 2003, Cheltenham; 06-30-2007, Retired; 2007, Gerrardstown: Gerrardstown UMC.

Martin, Wade   FE   FR | Asbury || Shepherdstown ||| 6700   (301) 447-3740
1805 Greenspring Pl Unit 202, Frederick, MD 21702-6017   H. (301) 606-8393
wmartin@bhumc.org
2005, Trinity-Catoctin Chg.2006, Trinity; 04-14-2008, Damascus: Montgomery; 05-01-2012, Damascus: North Damascus Coop Parish; 2014, Frederick: Brook Hill; 08-01-19, Disability.

Martin-Jones, Vivian L.   RA   CM | Ebenezer || Ijamsville ||| 6230
3920 Rosecrest Ave, Baltimore, MD 21215-3427   H. (301) 874-3007
masterpastor@comcast.net
2001, Ijamsville: Ebenezer; 2002, Baltimore: St. Luke; 2004, D.C.: Asbury; 2006, Retired; 10-1-15, Ijamsville: Ebenezer Charge

---

Marullo, Sam   FD   GW | Capitol Hill || Washington ||| 7135   (202) 489-4785
710 3rd St NE, Washington, DC 20002   H. (202) 489-4785
sam.marullo@gmail.com
2011, DC: Ebenezer Cooperative Circuit and Extension Ministry: Wesley Seminary.

Mason, Darryl K.   OF   WE | Metropolitan || Indian Head ||| 8420
3453 Linden Grove Dr, Waldorf, MD 20603-4039
councilonministries@westphaliaum.org
2019, Indian Head: Metropolitan,

Mason, Earl   RE   BS | Hunts Memorial || Riderwood ||| 3487
910 Rock Spring Rd, Bel Air, MD 21014-2320   H. (443) 386-6513
revearlmason@aol.com
1975, Curtis Bay; 1977, Monkton Charge; 1979, Darkesville-Paynes Chapel Chg;1980, Kingsley; 1992, Martinsburg: St. Lukes; 1993, Brandywine: Brookfield-Immanuel; 1998, Lutherville: St. John 2005, St. Johnis/Govans-Boundary Coop. Parish; 2008, Hampstead: Grace; 2011, Mt Airy: Prospect-Marvin Chapel.; 2016, Retired

---

Mason, James S.   RL   CM | Community of Faith || Clarksburg ||| 9270
7179 Browns Ln , Thurmont, MD 21788-2512   H. (301) 898-5397
1989, Charles Town: Mt Zion; 2001, Retired.

Mason, Kenneth J.   PL   CH | Alpine || Berkeley Springs ||| 5510
11 Cross Rd, Berkeley Springs, WV 25411-3658   H. (301) 399-5214
kmason169@yahoo.com
2013, Great Cacapon: Great Cacapon; 01-01-2015, Berkeley Springs: Alpine.

Matheny, Claire C.   FE   CM | Linden-Linthicum || Clarksville ||| 9180
5151 Darting Bird Ln, Columbia, MD 21044-1503   H. (202) 674-7805
scmatheny@gmail.com
2011, Kensington: St Paul's; 2018, ExtMin.

Matthews, Eugene   RE   AN | St Marks || Laurel ||| 7425
7448 Race Rd , Hanover, MD 21076-1114   H. (410) 379-0600
reveugene@comcast.net
1976, Central Summerfield; 1978, W. NY Conference; 1984, Baltimore Conference, Baltimore: Sharp. St. Memorial; 1988, Superintendent, Frederick Dist; 02-01-92, Washington: Asbury; 2004, Superintendent, Baltimore West District; 06-30-2008, Retired; 2008, Churchton: Franklin; 2013, Baltimore: Arlington-Lewin; 2019, Laurel: St Mark's.

Matthews, Roberta   RA   AN | St Matthews || Shady Side ||| 1520
1102 Cattail Commons Way, Denton, MD 21629-3015   H. (410) 479-4580
clergy4@comcast.net
01-01-92, D.C.: Community; 1995, Shady Side: St. Matthews; 2004, Davidsonville: Union Memorial; 01/01/05, Retired; 09-01-2011, Gambrills: Wilson; 2014; Shady Side: St Matthews, Interim.

Maves, Angela FD   GW | Dumbarton || Washington ||| 7160
2015 19th St NW , Washington, DC 20009-1307   H. (202) 234-5743
maves.angela@gmail.com
2005, ExtMin: George Washington University Hospital Chaplain.

Mawokomatanda, Isaac M. (Mapipi) RE   BM | Lovely Lane || Baltimore ||| 3185
85 Carrera Rd , Stockbridge, GA 30281-4390   H. (678) 284-9353
mapipi40@hotmail.com
Wyoming Conference; 2003, Baltimore-Wash. Conference, Mt. Washington; 09-01-04,
Baltimore: Christ Edmondson 1-01-05, Baltimore: Mt. Washington-Christ Edmondson Coop.
Parish; 2006, Mt. Washington-Aldersgate Chg; 2012, Retired.

Mayden, Jr., John SY   BS | Mount Zion || Upperco ||| 4525
5037 Westhills Rd, Baltimore, MD 21229-1218   H. 443-545-6643
johnmayden1@gmail.com
2014, Upperco: Mount Zion.

Mayes, Jesse E. RE
528 Catania Ln , Poinciana, FL 34759-4033   H. (863) 438-9643
jmayes331@aol.com
1982, Attending school; 1983, Poolesville Chg; 1984, Brandywine: Asbury; 1987, Van Buren;
1991, Attending school; 1994, Germantown: Asbury/John Wesley Chg; 1997, Upper Marlboro:
Union; 2003, D.C.: Ebenezer; 2005, Retired.

Mayor, Mary M. RE   FR | Arden || Martinsburg ||| 6510
1924 Westminster Cir Unit 6CIRLCE, Vero Beach, FL 32966-8078   H. 772-999-3281
marciamayor@msn.com
1994, Attending school; 1996, Havre de Grace: Susquehanna Chg; 2000, Baltimore: Good
Shepherd; 2002, Walkersville; 2003, Williamsport; 2008, Leave of Absence.

Maxham, Martha RD   CM | Grace || Gaithersburg ||| 4260
18039 Rocky Ridge Ln, Olney, MD 20832   H. (301) 570-4294
martha.maxham@gmail.com
1999, Rockville: Mill Creek Parish; 2019, Retired.

McCain, Terry PL   CM | Hopkins || Highland ||| 9290
8652 Concord Dr, Jessup, MD 20794   H. (301) 317-0074
TMc1024598@aol.com
2002, Marriottsville West Liberty; 2006, Elderslie-St Andrews; 2011, Baltimore: Elderslie-St.
Andrews/Govans Boundary; 2019, Highland: Hopkins.

McCanna, Lloyd B. RE   CH | Mount Olivet || Berkeley Springs ||| 5545
6752 Winchester Grade Rd , Berkeley Springs, WV 25411-6050   H. (304) 258-2957
lbmccanna@atlanticbb.net
1983, Charles Town: Asbury; 1986, Oakland; 1992, Oakland-Flohrville; 1994, Cumberland:
Centre Street; 2009, Martinsburg: Trinity; 2014, Berkeley Springs: Morgan; 2014, Retired.

McCarthy, Vivian C. FE   BS | Reisterstown || Reisterstown ||| 4435   (410) 833-5440
246 Main St , Reisterstown, MD 21136-1214   H. (410) 489-4344
pastorvivianmc@gmail.com
1986, Attending school; 1987, Rodgers Forge; 4-15-94, Baltimore-Washington Conference,
Assoc. Council Dir; 01-01-2007, Associate Council Director; 2007, District Superintendent/
Team Leader; 2013, Reisterstown: Reisterstown.

McCauley, John T. FE GW | St Paul || Chevy Chase ||| 7330 (301) 587-5370
12 Athey Ct , Burtonsville, MD 20866-1643 H. (301) 585-3311
Kebuki52QS@verizon.net
1999, Chevy Chase: St. Paul;.

McClay, Jr., Harold RE CH | Christ || Cumberland ||| 5160 (301) 777-1561
18608 McMullen Hwy SW , Rawlings, MD 21557-6614 H. (301) 729-0765
cumc@atlanticbbn.net
*1958, Attending school; 1960, Harpers Ferry: Bolivar; 1967, Cresaptown; 2005, Retired.
2006, Cumberland: Christ.*

McCorkle Garrett, Anne BS | Fairview || Phoenix ||| 3455
2758 Greene Ln, Baldwin, MD 21013-9523 H. (410) 692-9394
PastorAnne@comcast.net
2019, Timonium: Timonium-Fairview CP.

McCourt, Shari FE FR | Westminster || Westminster ||| 4555
S2120 Paddock Lane, Finksburg, MD 21048 H. (410) 596-4040
sharimccourt@aol.com
*8/1/2004, Assoc., New Windsor: Stone Chapel; 2005, Milford Mill; 02/16/2009, Leave of
Absence; 01/01/2011, Extension Ministry; 2011, Baldwin: Union; 2012, Phoenix: Union-
Fairview Charge; 2013, Westminster: Westminster; 2017, Westminster: Westminster/St. Paul,
03-15-18, New Windsor: St Paul, 2019, Union Bridge: Johnsville.*

McCubbin, Bonnie FE BM | Good Shepherd || Baltimore ||| 3230
813 Staffordshire Rd, Cockeysville, MD 21030-2926 H. (410) 868-1035
bonnie.mccubbin@gmail.com
*01-01-2010, Forest Hill: Deer Creek; 2012, Dundalk: Patapsco-Lodge Forest Cooperative
Parish; 2013, Baltimore: Good Shepherd.*

McCulloh, Ralph RE BM | Northwood-Appold || Baltimore ||| 3225 (254) 773-4600
1102 Skyline Dr, Medford, OR 97504-8558 H. (254) 899-1694
RALPHANDJEAN@gmail.com
*1960, Bristol: 1963, Upper Marlboro-Bethel; 1964, Assoc. Northwood-Appold; 1967,
Chaplain, USAF; 1994, Leave of Absence; 1999, Chaplain, Market Place Min., Dallas, TX;
1/1/2006, Spiritual Care Coord. Odyssey Healthcare; 2007, Retired.*

McCullough, Amy FE BM | Grace || Baltimore ||| 3170 (410) 433-6650
5405 N Charles St , Baltimore, MD 21210-2024 H. (410) 323-8286
amy@graceunitedmethodist.org
*11-01-16, Baltimore: Grace, 2017, Baltimore: Grace/Hampden, Florida Conference; 1999,
Baltimore-Washington Conference, Washington: Metropolitan Memorial, 2004, Greater
Metropolitan Charge; 2005, Attending School; 2008, Glenelg: Glenelg; 2011, Baltimore:
Grace; 2013, Baltimore: Grace-St Johns.*

McCullough, Richard K. RE CM | Glen Mar || Ellicott City ||| 7365
7322 Springfield Ave , Sykesville, MD 21784-7549 H. (410) 795-3684
rmcpastor7@aol.com
*1968, Mt. Pleasant-Mt. Zion Silver Hill; 1970, Assoc. Frostburg; 1973, Campus Minister,
Frostburg State College; 1979, Camp. Min., American Univ. 1986, Univ. Chap; 1988,
Frostburg; 1992, Eldersburg: Wesley-Freedom; 2008, Hampstead: St Johns; 2011, Retired.*

132

McCullough, Robert A. RE   FR | New Hope of Greater Brunswick || Brunswick |||| 6137
1 Breakwater Dr , Rehoboth Beach, DE 19971-9573
*1978, Penin. Conference; 1981, Baltimore Conference, Woodbine-Morgan Chg; 1985,
Taneytown: Messiah; 1990, D.C.: Metropolitan Memorial; 1995, Baltimore: Bethesda; 1996,
Brunswick Coop. Parish; 10-1-98, Disability Leave; 10-1-00, Retired.*

McCurdy, Mary S. (Sheila) RE   CM | St John United Church || Columbia |||| 7360
5565 Vantage Point Rd, Columbia, MD 21044-2610   H. (443) 739-9796
msmccurdy44@gmail.com
*1987, Attending school; 1988, Ellicott City: Bethany; 1993, Mt. Airy: Poplar Springs Chg;
1998, Randallstown: Mt. Olive; 2005, Gaithersburg: Epworth; 2010, Retired.*

McDade, Melissa FE   BS | Norrisville || White Hall |||| 2525
2434 Bradenbaugh Rd , White Hall, MD 21161-9661   H. (410) 692-6179
thomasjsullivan@hotmail.com
*1986, Parkton; Stablers:, 1991, Stableris-Vernon Chg; 1992, Whiteford: Whiteford Chg; 9-1-
97, Norrisville: Norrisville Charge.*

McDonald, II, Ramon FE AN | First || Laurel |||| 7415
4286 Warthen Dr , Harwood, MD 20776-9756   H. (410) 703-3092
RevRayMac@gmail.com
*1981, Severn: Delmont; 1983, Lothian: Mt. Zion; 2007, Mitchellville: Mount Oak; 03-20-2013,
Leave of Absence; 2013, Laurel: First.; 2016, Laurel: First/Community CP*

McDonald, Kenneth FE   AN | Glen Burnie || Glen Burnie |||| 1320
7 2nd Ave SE, Glen Burnie, MD 21061-3626   H. (410) 946-7487
kennethmcdo10888@gmail.com
*1986, Attending school; 1987, Hancock; 1991, Reisterstown: Emory; 1998, Catonsville:
Trinity; 2003, Waldorf: Lakeside; 2010, Lisbon: Lisbon; 2014, Damascus: Montgomery.; 2016,
Glen Burnie: Glen Burnie Charge*

McGowan, Michael SY   CH | Dawson || Rawlings |||| 5440
19506 McVeighs Aly SW, Frostburg, MD 21532-4820   H. (301) 697-0958
michael.mcgowan@acpsmd.org
 2018, Rawlings: Dawson.

Mcilwain, Brenda L. FE   WE | St John || Lusby |||| 8340   (410) 326-2987
3494 Old Crown Dr , Pasadena, MD 21122-6409   H. (410) 255-5355
brendapsdn@aol.com
2016, Lusby: Lusby Charge

McKinley, III, Robert RE AN | Community || Crofton |||| 1180
3776 Traemoor Rd, Southport, NC 28461-8219
*1972, Attending school; 1974, Curtis Bay; 1975, Severn: Severn; 1978, Leave of Absence;
1981, Honorable Location; 2012, Retired.*

McKinney, Michael A. RE
11205 Woodlawn Blvd , Upper Marlboro, MD 20774-2361   H. (202) 321-8465
revdoc33@hotmail.com
*1987, South Carolina Conf; 2004, Baltimore Washington Conference, Upper Marlboro: Union;
2009, Annapolis: Mt. Zion-Fowler Cooperative Parish; 2011, Retired.*

McLaughlin, Craig   FE   BS | Mount Zion || Bel Air ||| 2350   (410) 836-7444
625 Weatherby Rd, Bel Air, MD 21015   H. (410) 879-8840
lisa.craig4@verizon.net
1981, Attending school; 1982, Baltimore: St. Paul; 1987, Bel Air: Mt. Zion.

McLellan, Daniel C.   RE   BM | Faith Community || Baltimore ||| 2192
707 Maiden Choice Ln Apt 7G13, Catonsville, MD 21228-3980   H. (410) 314-9022
jlmclellan2510@gmail.com
*1964, Chase; 1966, Martinsburg Circuit; 1969, Garrison Blvd; 1970, Fells Point Par; 1971,
Baltimore: Eastern; 1976, Asst. Cong. Council Dir. for Youth and Young Adult Min; 1978,
Simpsonville: Atholton Chg; 1981, Baltimore: Central-Summerfield (Wildwood Parkway);
1995, Glen Burnie: Hall; 2007, Retired.*

McLellan, Jacquelyn L.   RE   BM | Faith Community || Baltimore ||| 2192   (410) 426-8177
707 Maiden Choice Ln Apt 7G13, Baltimore, MD 21228-3980   H. (410) 314-9022
jlmclellan2510@gmail.com
*1998, Baltimore: St. Matthewis; 2004 Temple Hills: Corkran Memorial; 2010, Baltimore:
Faith Community; 2017, Retired.*

McMurtrey, Amanda   FE   AN | Mayo || Edgewater ||| 1148   (410) 798-6110
1005 Old Turkey Point Rd , Edgewater, MD 21037-4028   H. (970) 231-5123
mayopastoramanda@gmail.com
2014, Damascus: Damascus; 2018, Annapolis: Mayo.

McNeil, Gregory J.   PL   AN | Union Memorial || Davidsonville ||| 1210 (410) 721-1482
105 Bagg Blvd, Odenton, Md 21113   H. (410) 674-5153
Preacher1006@gmail.com
*1998, Mt. Airy: Simpson; 2014, Gambrills: Wilson Memorial; 2018, Davidsonville: Union
Memorial.*

McSavaney, James D.   FE BM | Arnolia || Baltimore ||| 3530   (443) 540-1078
3420 Beech Ave, Baltimore, MD 21211-2643   H. (443) 540-1078
james@arnolia.org
*2014, Baltimore: Grace-St Johns; 11-01-16, Baltimore: Grace, 2017, Baltimore: Grace/
Hampden, 2018, Baltimore: Arnolia, .*

Medley, Ginger   FE   FR | Asbury || Shepherdstown ||| 6700
1169 Heron Ave, Miami Springs, FL 33166-3118   H. (540) 877-0680
g19751997@hotmail.com
2014, Shepherdstown: Asbury; 2017, On Loan - FL Conference.

Mejia, Daniel   FE WE | St Matthews || Bowie ||| 8125   (301) 262-1408
4106 Crosswick Turn, Bowie, MD 20715-1109   H. (301) 875-8988
danielmejia@stmatthews-bowie.org
2006, Beltsville: Emmanuel Charge; 2014, Bowie: St Matthews.

Mejia, Michelle   FE   GW | University || College Park ||| 7340
4106 Crosswick Turn, Bowie, MD 20715-1109   H. (301) 310-3204
eastportumcpastor@gmail.com
2011, Laurel: Community; 2014, Annapolis: Eastport; 2019, College Park: University.

134

Menne, Galen R. RE   WE | St Matthews || Bowie ||| 8125
6206 Gradys Walk , Bowie, MD 20715-4018   H. (301) 805-0891
galencarolyn@verizon.net
1964, Williamsport; 1966, New England Conference; 1969, Hagerstown: Otterbein; 1970,
Lothian: Mt. Zion; 1976, Damascus: Montgomery; 1981, Glenn Dale; 1991, Fort Washington:
Providence; 1996, Upper Marlboro: Bethel; 1999, Savage; 2004, Retired.

Mercer-Staten, Yvonne FE   GW | Simpson-Hamline || Washington ||| 7265 (202) 882-2122
12200 Quintette Ln, Bowie, MD 20720-4364   H. (443) 621-1891
rocka13@aol.com
1999, Hagerstown: Asbury; 2003, Aberdeen: Union; 2009, DC: Simpson-Hamline.

Meredith, Martha FE   GW | Rockville || Rockville ||| 9440   (301) 762-2288
509 Redland Blvd, Rockville, MD 20850   H. (410) 353-6846
pastor@rockvilleumc.org
2010, Severna Park: Severna Park; 2014, Rockville: Rockville.

Merki, Sheril D. RL   FR | Inwood || Inwood ||| 6615   (304) 229-8529
363 Universe Dr , Martinsburg, WV 25404-3496   H. (304) 264-0897
papmommurk@gmail.com
1997, Inwood: Inwood; 2003, Retired.

Meyer, Sharon   BS | Texas || Cockeysville ||| 3310
9635 Alda Dr, Parkville, MD 21234-1847   (410) 627-7698
sjfrog1@aol.com
2018, Cockeysville: Texas.

Middlebrooks, Walter   RE AN | Wesley Chapel || Lothian ||| 1390
5521 Thomas Sim Lee Ter , Upper Marlboro, MD 20772-7405   H. (240) 339-1789
walter_middlebrooks@comcast.net
1978, Peninsula Conference; 1980, Baltimore Conference, Anacostia Mission; 1981, Atholton
Larger Parish; 1982, Asbury-Hopkins Par; 1984, D.C.: Franklin P. Nash; 1988, Westphalia;
1995 Millian Memorial; 1999, Upper Marlboro: Nottingham-Myers; 2001, Annapolis: Asbury;
2011, Retired; 2013, Lothian: Wesley Chapel.

Miller, Jim FE   CM | Grace || Gaithersburg ||| 9260
11710 Barn Swallow Pl , New Market, MD 21774-7005   H. (301) 865-1276
jmiller@graceumc.org
1988, Peninsula-Delaware Conference; 1997, Hyattstown; 2000, Germantown: Trinity; 2014,
Gaithersburg: Grace.

Miller, Perry F. RE   CM | Wesley Freedom || Eldersburg ||| 4225
370 Grey Friars Rd, Westminster, MD 21158-3705   H. (410) 206-1746
eandpmiller@comcast.net
1963, Alabama-West Florida Conference; 1964, Baltimore Conference, Greenbelt; 1967,
Assoc. Mt. Vernon Place; 1968, Graceland Park; 1973, A.W. Wilson Memorial; 1976,
Eldersburg: Wesley Freedom; 1992, LaPlata; 2000, Pasadena: Mt. Carmel; 2003, Retired;
2003, Eldersburg: Wesley Freedom; 01-01-08, Jarrettsville: Jarrettsville; 01-01-10, Woodfield:
Wesley Grove; 11-01-12, Sandy Mount: Sandy Mount Charge.

Miller, Roderick   RE   BM | Mount Vernon Place || Baltimore ||| 3215   (410) 465-4995
3701 Saint Johns Ln , Ellicott City, MD 21042-5226   H. (410) 465-2335
miller.roderick.j@gmail.com
1983, Laurel: First; 1984, Joppa: Union Chapel; 1994, Ellicott City: Bethany; 2005,
Baltimore-Washington Conf., Director of Connectional Ministries; 01-01-2008, Guide; 2011,
Towson: Towson; 2017, Retired, 11-01-17, Ellicott City: Glen Mar, 02-01-19, Baltimore: Mt
Vernon Place.

Millett, Denise M.   RE   (410) 271-8696
1744 Tacoma Rd, Edgewater, MD 21037-2402   H. (410) 271-8696
dndmillett@msn.com
1999, Edgewater: Parkwood; 2009, Leave of Absence; 2010, Hampstead: Shiloh -Mount
Zion; 2014, Cheltenham: Cheltenham; 2019, Aberdeen: Grace.

Mills, Ianther M.   FE   GW | Asbury || Washington ||| 7115   (202) 628-0009
10406 Grandhaven Ave, Upper Marlboro, MD 20772-6603   H. (301) 574-9601
agapezoe@aol.com
1997, Catonsville; 2000, Good Hope Union; 2005, Washington East District Superintendent;
2013, DC: Asbury.

Mills, Sharon   RD
7369 Intersection Rd , Glen Rock, PA 17327-8850   H. (717) 825-1152
1993, Attending school; 1994, Essex: Back River; 1998, Mays Chapel; 2009, Retired.

Mitchell, Curtis L.   RE
4523 kinmount rd, lanham, md 20706-1957   H. (301) 577-7601
clamarmi@bellatlantic.net
1982, Atholton: Locust; 1988, Leave of Absence; 1990, D.C.: Emory; 1992, Retired.

Mitchell, Vera   RE   BM | Mt Washington-Aldersgate || Baltimore ||| 3220   (410) 323-4314
2 Kirkwyn Ct, Owings Mills, MD 21117-5556   H. (443) 288-3045
VMitchellMallett@gmail.com
1991, Homestead/Strawbridge Par; 1995, Attending School; 1996, Laurel: St. Markís;
2001, Temple Hills: Church of the Redeemer; 2007, Leave of Absence; 2011, Retired. 2012,
Baltimore: West Baltimore; 10-21-16, Baltimore: Mt Washington-Aldersgate.

Mitzel, Robert E.   RE   CM | Emory || Ellicott City ||| 4245
721 Maiden Choice Ln Apt CW204, Catonsville, MD 21228-6296   H. (410) 242-0018
dadmitz@aol.com
1949, Assoc., First Ch. City Station; 1950, Chesapeake; 1954, Maryland Line; 1961, Ellicott
City; 1968, Ellicott City: Emory-Mt. Zion Parish; 1972, Camp Springs: Bells; 1980, Cheverly;
1983, Prince Frederick: Trinity; 1986, Retired.

Montague, III, Daniel L.   FE   BS | Fork || Fork ||| 3320   (410) 592-8303
12828 Fork Rd , Fork, MD 21051-9728   H. (410) 592-5236
daniel.mont3@gmail.com
1992,Lewistown; 1996, Bolivar: Bolivar Chg; 1998, Martinsburg: Pikeside; 2-2-02, Waters
Memorial; 2008, Berkeley Springs: Sleepy Creek; 2014, Midland: Midland; 2017, Fork: Fork
-Waugh.

Moon, Margaret E. RL FR | Johnsville || Union Bridge ||| 4523
2044 Green Mill Rd , Finksburg, MD 21048-1931 H. (410) 236-2826
mmoon628@comcast.net
2000, Deer Park; 2006, Sykesville: Bethesda; 2008, Retired; 2008, Union Bridge: Union
Bridge; 11-01-2012, Union Bridge: Johnsville.

Mooney, Deborah PL FR | Leetown || Kearneysville ||| 6630
635 Bashore Dr , Martinsburg, WV 25404-7604 H. (304) 271-8936
debsark3@gmail.com
04-01-19, Kearneysville: Leetown,

Mooney, Mark C. FE BM | Hiss || Baltimore ||| 3440 (410) 668-5665
635 Bashore Dr , Martinsburg, WV 25404-7604 H. (304) 271-8936
pastormark@hisschurch.org
1983, Attending school; 1984, Greenmount; 1988, White Marsh: Ebenezer, Chase: Ebenezer;
8-15-99, Smithsburg: St. Paul; 2010, Martinsburg: Otterbein; 2018, Baltimore: Hiss.

Moore, Craig NL BS | Mount Vernon || Whiteford ||| 2580 (410) 685-5290
1101 Saint Paul St Apt 309, Baltimore, MD 21202-2623 H. (281) 732-3234
craigpmoore@gmail.com

Moore, Douglas E. RE
7114 Alaska Ave NW , Washington, DC 20012-1544
rfrin16ms@verizon.net
1950, N. C. Conference; 1966, Va. Conference; 1975, Baltimore Conference, Chaplain,
Federal City College; 1976, Chap. UDC, Lorton Prison Prog; 1993, Retired. 2001,
Poolesville: Elijah.

Moore, Howard E. (Ed) RE GW | Rockville || Rockville ||| 9440
4105 Lucy Long Dr, Rockingham, VA 22801-8390 H. (540) 208-7166
edmoore26@gmail.com
1976, Attending school; 1978, Clarksburg Charge; 1980, Bethesda; 1988, Sabbatical leave;
1989, Savage; 1993, College Park: University; 1999, Superintendent, Baltimore-Harford
Dist; 2000, Gaithersburg: Covenant; 2007, Leave of Absence; 2008, Director of Educational
Programs, Duke Divinity School.

Moore, III, E. M. (Maynard) RE GW | Metropolitan Memorial || Washington ||| 7630
6777 Surreywood Ln , Bethesda, MD 20817-1568 H. (301) 229-0828
emaynard8@yahoo.com
1960, Minn. Conference; 1981, Baltimore Conference: Director of Corporate and Foundation
Relations at American University; 1985, Retired.

Moore, Kathryn B. RE
1307 Peachwood Ln , Bowie, MD 20716-1818 H. (301) 218-6094
mnshereweare@comcast.net
1964, Ohio East Conference; 1966, Susquehanna Conference; 1968, Assoc. Foundry; 1970,
Supernumerary; 1972, Brookland; 1973, Douglas Memorial; 1984, D.C.: Christ; 1992, Camp
Springs: Bells; 1994, Unionville: Linganore; 1999, DC: Mt. Zion; 2000, Columbia: Christ;
2002, Arnold: Asbury; 1/1/03, Retired.

Moore, Kenneth P.   FE   WE | Zion || Lexington Park ||| 8325   (301) 247-5652
1204 Hollyoak Rd , Odenton, MD 21113-1917   H. (301) 247-5652
therevkenmoore@aol.com
1998, Randallstown: Mt. Olive; 1999, Odenton: Macedonia; 2002, Pasadena: Mt. Zion; 09-
01-2009, Lexington Park: Zion; 01-01-2015, Lexington Park: Lexington Park.

Moore, Kermit C.   PL   WE | Providence-Fort Washington || Ft Washington ||| 8205
9109 Bank St, Brandywine, MD 20613-7784   H. (301) 938-8971
kermitccmoore@gmail.com
2011, Pisgah: Smith Chapel-Alexandria Chapel Cooperative Parish; 2013, Indian Head:
Alexandria Chapel.; 2016, Fort Washington: Providence-Fort Washington.

Moore, L. Katherine   RE   BM | Arnolia || Baltimore ||| 3530
1 Buttick Court#101, Timonium, MD 21093   H. (410) 870-6738
rev.lkmoore@gmail.com
1978, Uniontown: Pipe Creek Chg; 1980, Abingdon Chg; 1990, Camp Chapel; 1996,
Disability Leave; 1997, Ellicott City: Emory; 2009, Annapolis: Mayo-Parkwood Cooperative
Parish; 2010, Annapolis: Mayo; 2013, Pasadena: Faith Community Cooperative Parish; 11-
01-16, Medical Leave (CPP), 05-01-17, Retired.

Moore, Sr., Sam   PL   CM | Emory || Ellicott City ||| 4245
7425 Brandenburg Cir, Sykesville, MD 21784-6682   H. (410) 549-5265
smoore4433@aol.com
2015, Ellicott City, Emory.

Moreland, Raymond T.   RE   FR | Calvary || Frederick ||| 6190
9731 Hall Rd , Frederick, MD 21701-6736   H. (301) 694-8405
agape12@comcast.net
1967, Attending school; 1969, Assist., Essex; 1970, Carrollis Gills-Stevenson; 1971, Attending
school; 1972, Assoc., Eastport; 1974, Frederick: Mt. Carmel/New Market; 1980, Graceland
Park; 1-1-83, Martinsburg: Trinity; 1991, Hagerstown: John Wesley; 1996, Assoc. Exec. Dir.,
Maryland Bible Society; 10-1-97, Exec. Dir. Maryland Bible Soc; 2010, Retired.

Moreno, Jorge   SY   BM | Salem-Baltimore Hispanic || Baltimore ||| 2310
9755 Bird River Rd, Baltimore, MD 21220-1701   H. (443) 898-2850
jorgeisel71@gmail.com
2017, Baltimore: Salem-Baltimore Hispanic.

Morgan, Laura C.   RE   FR | Westminster || Westminster ||| 4555
2 Stedtle Ave , Littlestown, PA 17340-1164   H. (717) 345-6455
revlauralee@comcast.net
1985, Flohrville-Gaither Chg; 1986, Shiloh-Dover Chg; 1991, Exec. Dir., Wesley Foundation,
Univ. of Delaware; 2005, Randallstown: Mt. Olive; 08-01-09, Retired.

Morganfield, Robbie   OF   WE | Journey of Faith || Waldorf ||| 8550   (301) 776-8885
7402 Baylor Ave, College Park, MD 20740-3004   H. (301) 312-9185
pastorrob@thejofc.org
2008, Laurel: St Marks; 2014, Waldorf: The Journey of Faith.

138

Morris, Calvin   RE   (312) 427-4830
6901 S Oglesby Ave Apt 7D, Chicago, IL 60649-1805   H. (773) 493-1737
1966, E. Pa. Conference; 1981, Baltimore Conference, Prof. Howard U; 1992, Inter-
denominational Theo. Ctr., Atlanta; 1998, Community Renewal Society, Chicago; 2007, Ext.
Min. -Chicago; 2012, Retired.

Mortimore, Richard J.   RE   BS | Fork || Fork ||| 3320   (410) 592-8303
128 Lently Farm Lane, Centrevillee, MD 21617   H. (410) 592-5236
underfrog@atlanticbb.net
1975, Timonium, Assoc; 1976, Parkton Parish; 1979, Mount Airy: Prospect-Marvin Chg;
1981, Bowie; 1983, Chesapeake Chg; 1987, Mt. Harmony-Lower Marlboro Chg; 1993,
Hedgesville; 1996, Lonaconing: First; 2005, Fork-Waugh Charge; 2015, Retired.

Mossburg, Caitlin   PL   FR | Lewistown || Thurmont ||| 6265
9308 Bethel Rd, Frederick, MD 21702-2010   H. (301) 662-4094
pastor.katym@gmail.com
2019, Lewistown: Lewistown,

Moser, Jr., Albert   RE   GW | Oak Chapel || Silver Spring ||| 9460   (410) 923-2248
2615 Telluride Pl, Silver Spring, MD 20906-6164   H. (240) 460-5461
amoser@asburyumcdc.org
1976, Attending school; 1977, Shepherdstown: Asbury-Mt. Zion; 1979, Oxon Hill: St. Paul;
1983, Rockville Chg; 1989, Gethsemane; 1995, DC.: Mt. Zion; 1999, Clinton; 2004, Wheaton:
Hughes Assoc; 2006, Macedonia/John Wesley/Waterbury Charge; 06-30-2012, Retired; 2012,
Odenton: Macedonia; 9-1-15, DC: Asbury Charge

Motter, Linda W.   FE   WE | Olivet || Lusby ||| 8335   (410) 326-8400
12814 Lake View Dr, Lusby, MD 20657-3246   H. (410) 570-4858
lindamotter@icloud.com
2011, Damascus: Damascus; 2014, Lusby: Olivet.

Mount, Timothy J.   PL   CM | Araby || Frederick ||| 6110
13226 Lake Geneva Way, Germantown, MD 20874   H. (301) 651-0718
mount79@gmail.com
2016, Araby: Araby.

Mulenga, Maidstone   FE   AN | St Mark || Hanover ||| 1350
2600 Maidens Ln, Edgewood, MD 21040   H. (202) 748-5172
maidstonem@gmail.com
2013, Ext. Min, Assistant to the Bishop/Director of Connectional Ministries; 04-01-17,
Council of Bishops.

Munoz-Rivera, Brindice   RE   (301) 907-4831
26 Billerica Rd , S Chelmsford, MA 01824-3011   H. (301) 469-5960
brindicemunoz@yahoo.com
1969, Puerto Rico Conf; 1979, Desert Southwest Conf; 1983, Cal-Pac Conf; 1988, Greater
N.J. Conf; 1995, Baltimore-Wash. Conference, Bethesda Hispanic; 2009, Retired.

Murray, Tommy   PE   GW | Brighter Day || Washington ||| 7625   (240) 357-5832
36 Welsh Ct, Charles Town, WV 25414-4406   H. (240) 357-5832
dvinejbz2@aol.com
2008, Charles Town: Mount Zion; 2012, Shepherdstown: Asbury; 2017, DC: Brighter Day.

Muteteke, Enger PD AN | Severna Park || Severna Park ||| 1510 (609) 561-4685
155 Barbara Rd, Severna Park, MD 21146-1303 H. (443) 962-5660
muteteke@gmail.com
2015, Glen Burnie: Glen Burnie.; 8-17-15, Extension Ministry; 03-15-17, Transitional Leave, 07-24-17, Elkridge: Melville Chapel, 09-01-17, No Appointment, 01-01-18, ExtMin.

Myers, David C. RE GW | Metropolitan Memorial || Washington ||| 7630 (301) 652-8700
6 Holly St, Gloucester, MA 01930-1740 H. (202) 652-8700
dam421@aol.com
1972, New England Conf; 2005, Baltimore-Washington Conf., D.C.: Saint Lukes; 2007, Chevy Chase: Chevy Chase; 2013, Retired.

Nedwell, Nancy RE BM | Lovely Lane || Baltimore ||| 3185
10 Sunny Meadow Ct Apt 102, Baltimore, MD 21209-5101 H. (443) 414-3551
nancynedwell@gmail.com
1975, N. Ind. Conference; 1983, Bowie: St. Matthewís; 1985, Hyattsville: First; 1995, Towson: Towson; 1999, Baltimore: Lovely Lane, Baltimore City Station; 2015, Retired.

Neighoff, Wilson E. RE BM | Hiss || Baltimore ||| 3440
131 N Somerset Ave , Crisfield, MD 21817-1525 H. (410) 968-0172
seabay131@aol.com
1959, Attending school; 1961, Baltimore: Hiss; 1966, Ext. Min.; 1975, Attending school; 1977, Honorable Location; 2012, Retired.

Nelson, Armon SY GW | Mount Vernon || Washington ||| 7230 (202) 706-6842
32 Grant Cir NW , Washington, DC 20011-4601 H. (615) 752-9555
armonchadellnelson@gmail.com
2013, Baltimore: West Baltimore; 2014, DC: Mount Vernon; 2018, DC: Petworth Charge.

Nelson, Donna FE BM | Back River || Essex ||| 2420 (410) 686-4195
544A Back River Neck Rd, Essex, MD 21221-4604 H. (410) 391-0879
donnaleenelson@gmail.com
2007, Cheltenham: Cheltenham; 2007, Cheltenham: Cheltenham; 2014, Essex: Back River.

Nelson, LaTaska SY GW | Community || Washington ||| 7145
32 Grant Cir NW , Washington, DC 20011-4601 H. (615) 977-9956
lataskam.nelson@gmail.com
2018, DC: Community, 2018, DC: Douglas Memorial,

Nenninger, James D. RE (540) 270-7873
14097 Rehobeth Church Rd , Lovettsville, VA 20180-3215 H. (540) 882-4165
james@nenningers.net
Central Pa. Conf; 10-14-95, Baltimore-Washington Conf., Dir. Pastoral Care, Sibley Mem. Hospital; 2008, Retired.

Neumark, Lawrence A. RE CH | Frostburg || Frostburg ||| 5310
307 Chieftan Ln , Boonsboro, MD 21713-2651 H. (301) 432-4747
neumark@myactv.net
1968, Attending school; 1970, E. Pa. Conference; 1979, Baltimore-Washington Conference, Prot. Chaplain, Frostburg State University; 01-01-2007, Chaplain, Frostburg; 2008, Retired.

Newhouse, Marilyn C. RE   CM | Christ || Columbia ||| 7350
3144 Gracefield Rd Apt 128, Silver Spring, MD 20904-5879   H. (301) 755-1686
mcnewhouse@aol.com
1999, Annapolis: Calvary; 2004, Columbia: Christ; 2012, Columbia: South Columbia.; 2016,
Baltimore Washington Conference; 01-01-17, Retired.

Newman, Eloise RP   WE | Wards Memorial || Owings ||| 8165 (410) 257-7644
13735 Carlene Dr, Upper Marlboro, MD 20772-6830   H. (301) 574-0757
revtina03@verizon.net
2003, Bradbury Heights; 2009, Chesapeake Beach: Wards Memorial; 2011, Retired.

Newman, Tyree SY   CM | Friendship || Damascus ||| 9210
14145 Flint Rock Rd, Rockville, MD 20853-2657   H. (301) 871-1723
tnewms5@gmail.com
2018, Damascus: Friendship.

Newman-Adams, Lesley PL WE | Corkran Memorial || Temple Hills ||| 7480 (301) 894-5577
1671 Tulip Ave, District Heights, MD 20747-2615   H. (301) 325-8715
lesleycnewman@gmail.com
2016, Temple Hills: Corkran Memorial.

Nickerson, Stacey FE   BS | Salem || Upper Falls ||| 2560   (410) 496-5610
7 Manor Brook Rd , Monkton, MD 21111-1606   H. (410) 472-4315
revstaceynickerson@gmail.com
1985, Attending school; 1987, Baltimore: Memorial; 1994, Baltimore: Idelwylde; 1997,
Baltimore: Arbutus; 2004, Monkton; 2010, Fallston: Fallston Church; 04-01-2013, Board of
Child Care; 2019, Upper Falls: Salem.

Nippard Kanahan, Mary Kathryn FE CM | St John || Columbia ||| 7360
9547 Michaels Way, Ellicott City, MD 21042-2463   H. (410) 428-8090
pastorkanahansju@gmail.com
2007, Upperco: Reisterstown Cooperative Parish; 2009, Ellicott City: Glen Mar; 2013,
Columbia: St John.

Norfleet-Walker, Denise H. FE   BM | St. Paul Praise & Worship || Pikesville ||| 2290
      (410) 486-2028
3201 Carlswood Cir, Windsor Mill, MD 21244-1380   H. (410) 496-8332
denise.norfleet@verizon.net
1993, Attending school; 1994, Leave of Absence, 10-16-94, Fallston Chg; 2004, Baltimore: St.
Paul; 2019, Pikesville: Pikesville Pimlico.

Nortey, Samson Y. FE   GW | Ager Road || Hyattsville ||| 7380   (301) 891-2100
45683 Edge Mill Ct , Great Mills, MD 20634-3312   H. (301) 866-0003
synortey@verizon.net
1993, Lusby: Lusby Charge; 10-05-12, Leave of Absence; 2014, Takoma Park: Nehemiah
Chrg.

Norvell, Laura FE   GW | Faith || Rockville ||| 9410   (240) 461-2340
15520 Santini Rd, Burtonsville, MD 20866   H. (240) 461-2340
norvelllm@gmail.com
2015, Ext. Min, Wesley Theological Seminary: Director of Development; 2018, Ferndale:
Ferndale, 2019, Rockville: Faith.

Nulton, Lynn P. RD CM | Glenelg || Glenelg ||| 9285
15255 Callaway Ct , Glenwood, MD 21738-9657 H. (410) 489-9918
lpnulton1@verizon.net
1994, Gaithersburg: Grace; 10-27-94, Chevy Chase; 2001, Rockville; 2011, Retired.

Nupp, John W. FE CM | Bethany || Ellicott City ||| 4235 (410) 309-3400
4654 Dower Dr , Ellicott City, MD 21043-6411 H. (410) 465-3639
jnupp@bwcumc.org
1994, Parkton: Cedar Grove-Parke Memorial; 2000, Germantown: Salem; 9/1/02, Glen Mar, Assoc; 2009, Randallstown: Wards Chapel.; 2016, Ext Min: Baltimore-Washington Conference

---

Obenshain, Norman J. FE BS | Havre De Grace || Havre De Grace ||| 2455 (410) 939-2464
101 S Union Ave , Havre de Grace, MD 21078-3111 H. (410) 939-1446
pastornormanobenshain@gmail.com
1987, Attending school; 1988 Hagerstown: St. Andrews; 1993, Maryland Line; 2001, Glyndon; 2011, Havre De Grace: Havre De Grace.

Odom, Jeffrey V. RE BM | Catonsville || Catonsville ||| 4180 (410) 356-3622
5 Williams Ct , Owings Mills, MD 21117-4889 H. (410) 356-3622
jvodom1@gmail.com
1981, Attending school; 1982, Carrollis-Gills Charge; 1988 Gamber: Calvary; 1993, Hampstead: Wesley; 2004, Bixlers-Millers Charge; 2008, Retired.

Offer, Ann P. RE
101 Melchior Rd, Millersville, MD 21108-1793
revannparkeroffer@verizon.net
1994, Crownsville: John Wesley; 2004, Shady Side: Saint Matthews; 2006, Retired.

O'Hern, Katie M. PE CH | John Wesley || Hagerstown ||| 5330
1408 Hamilton Blvd, Hagerstown, MD 21742 H. (585) 794-9663
pastorkohern@gmail.com
2017, Hagerstown: John Wesley.

Oliver, Roosevelt RL WE | Mount Hope || Sunderland ||| 8475
5889 Suitland Rd , Suitland, MD 20746-3307 H. (301) 735-0292
poppypreach@msn.com
1993, Glyndon; 1996, Reisterstown: St Lukes; 2008, Retired; 04-01-2011, Sunderland: Mount Hope.

Olson, Heather PE CM | Lisbon || Lisbon ||| 9350
1211 Cartley Ct, Woodbine, MD 21797-8624 H. (919) 247-5030
pastoraheather@gmail.com
2014, Baltimore:Cowenton-Piney Grove; 2017, Lisbon: Lisbon.

Orrence, Jr., Terry R. PL FR | Catoctin || Thurmont ||| 6355
6626 Gooseander Ct , Frederick, MD 21703-9535 H. (240) 344-0433
rtojr55@yahoo.com
2011, Thurmont: Catoctin; 11-01-2012, Thurmont: Mt. Zion.

Oskvig, Bryant M.   FE   GW | Chevy Chase || Chevy Chase ||| 9165   (202) 687-3568
8216 Buckspark Ln W, Potomac, MD 20854   H. (301) 365-3924
boskvig@gmail.com
1998, Western New York Conf; 2006, Metropolitan Memorial; 2007, Clarksville: Linden-
Linthicum; 2011, Georgetown University.

Osment, Luther   SY   FR | Camp Hill-Wesley || Harpers Ferry ||| 6565
PO Box 675 , Harpers Ferry, WV 25425-0675   H. (304) 535-3060
losment2@gmail.com
7-1-08, Harpers Ferry: Camphill Wesley/Engle Chg

Osuji Hall, Dionne   PL   CH | Shiloh || Hagerstown ||| 5355
516 Papa Ct, Hagerstown, MD 21740-4120   H. (301) 302-7509
deeosuji@hotmail.com
2017, Hagerstown: Shiloh.

Oursler, Richard C.   PL   AN | Dorsey Emmanuel || Elkridge ||| 1220   (410) 799-3494
7760 Waterloo Rd, Jessup, MD 20794   H. (410) 799-2128
roursler22@hotmail.com
2018, Elkridge: Northeast, 11-01-2007, Jessup: Wesley Chapel; 2010, Elkridge: Dorsey-
Emmanuel/Wesley Chapel.

Outlaw, Fritz   RE   BM | Mount Winans || Baltimore ||| 2235   (410) 947-1974
7505 Reserve Cir, Baltimore, MD 21244-1565   H. (410) 947-1974
mjhewlett@verizon.net
1985, Centerville-New Market Par; 1988, Attending school; 1989, Washington: Mt. Vernon;
1991, Attending school; 1995, Baltimore: Wildwood Parkway; 1998, Jessup: Asbury;
2000, Leave of Absence; 2001, Ext. Ministry, D.C. Govt; 2-1-04, Leave of Absence; 2004,
Macedonia; 2006, Hereford Combined ; 07-21-2009, Retired.; 4-16-16, Baltimore: Mount
Winans Charge

Owens, Christopher D.   FE WE | First Saints Comm. || Leonardtown ||| 8540 (301) 268-1620
1318 West St , Annapolis, MD 21401-3612   H. (410) 263-8043
pastorchris@firstsaints.org
2019, Leonardtown: First Saints Community, 2001, Hollywood; 2004, Upper Marlboro:
Bethel; 2007, Laurel: First; 2013, Annapolis Southern Region Guide; 2015, Annapolis: Trinity

---

Papp, Paul   FE   WE | Smithville || Dunkirk ||| 8185   (410) 627-6716
3983 Emrick Ln, Jarrettsville, MD 21084-1411   H. (410) 627-1335
pastorpapp@aol.com
05-01-18, Medical Leave, 2019, Dunkirk: Smithville, 1982, Pipe Creek Chg; 1983,
Whiteford Chg; 1987, Churchville: Smithis Chapel; 2009, Jefferson: Jefferson-Doubs; 2014,
Cockeysville: Texas.

Parham, Lovell   RE   BM | Metropolitan || Baltimore ||| 2220   (410) 944-4111
2704 Allendale Rd , Baltimore, MD 21216-2133   H. (410) 542-0744
lovell.parham@verizon.net
1962, Hamilton; 1963, Poolesville; 1964, Atholton; 1966, Eastern; 1968, Union Memorial;
1975, Ames Memorial; 1979, Homestead; 1981, Christ-Edmondson; 1983, Dir., Wesley
Found., Howard Univ; 1989, Union Memorial; 2000, Retired.

Park, Dae Sung FE CM | Bethany Korean || Ellicott City ||| 4236
20331 Dickerson Church Rd, Dickerson, MD 20842-9526 H. (410) 979-0691
dduru77@hotmail.com
2013, Ellicott City: Ellicott City Korean.

Park, DaeHwa FE GW | Good Shepherd || Silver Spring ||| 7445 (301) 725-7630
17506 Gallagher Way, Olney, MD 20832-2065 H. (301) 577-1500
daehwa@gmail.com
2000, Mowatt Memorial; 2005, Associate, Olney: Oakdale-Emory; 2010, West Friendship:
St James; 2013, Savage: Savage/Lanham; 2019, Savage: Savage; 2019, Silver Spring: Good
Shepherd.

Park, HiRho Y. FE CM | Fairhaven || Gaithersburg ||| 9250
7 Diamond Hill Ct, Germantown, MD 20874-5902 H. (615) 948-5702
hpark@gbhem.org
1992, Glen Burnie: Glen Burnie; 1996, Hebbville: Salem; 2001, Ext. Ministry, Wesley
Theological Sem; 05/01/03, Attending School; 08/01/05, Ext. Min., Gen. Bd. of Higher and
Ministry.

Park, Jong Hui FE AN | Everlasting Love || Glen Burnie ||| 1310 (443) 763-0732
251 SW Pershing Ave, Glen Burnie, MD 21061-3956 H. (443) 763-4566
churchp69@hotmail.com
2007, Glen Burnie: The Everlasting Love.

Park, JW FE CM | Fairhaven || Gaithersburg ||| 9250 (410) 309-3434
7 Diamond Hill Ct, Germantown, MD 20874-5902 H. (301) 972-9233
jpark@bwcumc.org
1992, Odenton: Trinity; 1996, Woodlawn: Emmarts; 2001, Gaithersburg: Fairhaven Parish;
2013, District Superintendent, Central Maryland.

Parker, Charles RE
7137 7th St NW , Washington, DC 20012-1801 H. (202) 363-4900
cparker@nationalchurch.org
1986, Attending school; 1987, Cape St. Claire; 1988, Leave of Absence; 1989, Exec. Dir.,
Bread for the City; 3-1-95, Emmaus Service for the Aging; 1-1-04, Co-Exec. Dir., Stewardship
Center and Foundation; 01-01-2007, Assistant to the Bishop; 2007, DC: Metropolitan
Memorial-St Lukes Coop Parish; 2009, DC: Metropolitan Memorial Parish; 01-01-18,
Retired.

Parker, Conrad D. RE (301) 292-7828
10676 Ashford Cir , Waldorf, MD 20603-3209 H. (301) 893-2760
cdparker2@verizon.net
1982, D.C.: Emory; 1983, Aquasco: Christ; 1986, Lanham: Ebenezer; 1990, Baltimore:
Northwood-Appold; 1996, Fort Washington: Grace; 2011, Retired.

Parker, II, Michael PE GW | Church of The Redeemer || Temple Hills ||| 7475
225 Harry S Truman Dr Apt 43, Largo, MD 20774-2035 H. (410) 900-3535
mparker.umc@gmail.com
10-01-2012, Fallston: Fallston Enlarged; 01-01-2014, Fallston: New Beginnings; 2014, Bel
Air: Ames.; 2016, Pumphrey: St John Charge; 08-01-17, ExtMin, 2018, Camp Springs: Bells,
2018, Temple Hills: Church of Redeemer.

144

Parker, Willie M.   RE   BM | Northwood-Appold || Baltimore ||| 3225   (410) 598-5401
P O Box 660931210 Winston Ave, Baltimore, MD 21239-3411   H. (410) 598-5401
williemaeparker@earthlink.net
1980, Lutherville Chg; 12/84, Newburg Chg; 1990, Solleris-Union Chg; 1993, Baltimore: Howard Park; 1994, Davidsonville Chg; 1998, Davidsonville: Union Memorial; 2004, Chews Memorial; 2008, Retired.

Parr, Jeanne   PL WE | Pisgah || Marbury ||| 8270
6091 Tapir Pl, Waldorf, MD 20603-4347   H. (301) 653-7570
jsngpraise@yahoo.com
2010, Chicamuxen: Chicamuxen; 2012, Pisgah: Pisgah Church.

Parrish, David   SY   FR | Brook Hill || Frederick ||| 6185   (301) 696-0740
750 Heather Ridge Dr Unit K, Frederick, MD 21702-8832   H. (240) 447-8360
david_parrish1027@yahoo.com
2014, Buckeystown: Buckeystown (Rt 80).

Patterson, Tiffany   FE   BS | Presbury || Edgewood ||| 2415   (770) 364-9403
1928 Bayberry Rd, Edgewood, MD 21040-2435   H. (770) 364-9304
pastortiffanyp@gmail.com
7-1-10, Smithsburg: Garfield Charge; 2017, Edgewood: Presbury-Cranberry.

Paul, Katie A.   OE   WE | Hollywood || Hollywood ||| 8230   (301) 373-2500
20860 Sandstone St, Lexington Park, MD 20653-2439   H. (580) 761-4169
kpaul@nccumc.org
2016, Hollywood: Hollywood Charge.

Paulen, Robert E.   RE
22 Read Ave, Dewey Beach, DE 19971-2311   H. (302) 226-2269
bobpaulen@netzero.net
1965, North Indiana Conf; 1968, Baltimore Conf., Exeter Memorial; 1970, Lauraville; 1973, Rognel Heights; 1978, Mt. Carmel; 1987, Bowie: St. Matthewis; 1995, Waldorf: Good Shepherd; 2003, Retired.

Paulson, Constance A.   RE   GW | St Pauls || Kensington ||| 9330
55 Cannon Dr, Ocean Pines, MD 21811-1730   H. (410) 641-5194
wesconnie55@gmail.com
1983, Attending school; 1984, Ager Road; 1987, Galesville; 1992, Washington: Eldbrooke; 1999, Rockville: Millian Memorial; 2008, Retired.

Paulson, Jeff A.   FE   BM | Catonsville || Catonsville ||| 4180   (301) 421-9166
10 Bloomingdale Ave , Catonsville, MD 21228-4606   H. (410) 788-3614
revjeff93@gmail.com
1993, Baltimore: Monroe Street; 1996, Baltimore: Mt. Clare Station Charge; 1999, Annapolis: Eastport; 2005, Perry Hall; 2011, Pasadena: Faith Community Cooperative Parish; 2013, Owings Mills: Pleasant Hill; 2017, Burtonsville: Liberty Grove; 2019, Retired.

Pax, Karen Lilli   PL   CM | Gary Memorial || Ellicott City ||| 4240
3011 Fall Staff Manor Ct Apt B, Baltimore, MD 21209-2829   H. (914) 309-8479
karenlillipax@gmail.com
2018, Ellicott City: Gary Memorial.

Payton, Kate   FE BS | Epworth || Cockeysville ||| 3290   (410) 667-6054
2406 Madison Ave Unit B, Baltimore, MD 21217-4038   H. (410) 667-6054
leadpastor@epworthalive.com
2006, Gaithersburg: Grace; 2009, DC: Metropolitan Memorial Parish.; 2016, Cockeysville:
Epworth Charge.

Pazdersky, Carol L.   FE   BS | Camp Chapel || Perry Hall ||| 2530   (410) 321-1808
730 Annatana Dr, Forest Hill, MD 21050   H. (410) 321-1808
carol.pazdersky@gmail.com
2019, Perry Hall: Camp Chapel, 2002, Norrisville; 2004, Assoc. Prince Frederick: Trinity;
2007, Bel Air: Bel Air; 2011, Bel Air: Bel Air-Mt. Vernon Cooperative Parish; 2014,
Baltimore: St. Johns-Idlewylde Coop Parish.

Peck, Davis W.   RE   AN | Davidsonville || Davidsonville ||| 1190
11740 Asbury Cir Apt 1105, Solomons, MD 20688-3067   H. (410) 394-3110
dumcoffice@dumc.net
1953, Erie Conf., 1956, Baltimore Conference, Gorsuch; 1957, Davidsonville; 1964, Petworth;
1966, Mt. Rainier; 1977, La Plata; 1992, Retired.

Peck-McClain, Andrew   FE   CM | Washington Grove || Washington Grove ||| 9470
5558 Burnside Dr, Rockville, MD 20853-2457   H. 862-204-9265
rev.apeckmcclain@gmail.com
2017, Emmitsburg: Trinity, 2018, Washington Grove: Washington Grove.

Penny, Sonja   PL   WE | Peters || Dunkirk ||| 8180
1613 Thomas Rd, Fort Washington, MD 20744-4130   H. (301) 292-1472
sjpenny1223@comcast.net
2019, Dunkirk: Peter's,

Perry, Anne   RE   BM | Christ || Baltimore ||| 2160
4802 Parkside Dr, Baltimore, MD 21206-6842   H. (410) 488-3339
1982, Lewin; 1985, Glen Burnie: John Wesley; 1992, Campus Min. Morgan State Univ; 1994,
Disability Leave; 9-15-97, Chaplain, Board of Child Care; 1998, Aberdeen: Union; 2003,
Retired.

Perry, Gene R.   RE   CH | Salem || Keedysville ||| 6250
45 Deer Ridge, PO Box 69, Norris, TN 37828-0069   H. (865) 494-6570
generayperry@bellsouth.net
1953, WV Conf; 1957, Assoc. Woodside; 1959, St. James; 1963, Pleasant Hill; 1965,
Baltimore: Bethesda; 1969, North Ave; 1973, Ellerslie: Christ-St. Mark's; 1976, Berkeley
Springs: First; 1979, Hagerstown: St. Andrews; 1983, Pikeside; 1984, St. George Island;
1987, Sexton; 1990, Keedysville: Salem; 1993, Retired.

Peterson, Kristina   RE   CH | First || Lonaconing ||| 5390
106 Sandalwood Dr , Gray, LA 70359-4611   H. (304) 266-2517
krajeskipeterson@msn.com
1973, Pac. NW Conference; 1984, Baltimore Conference, Cumberland: Emmanuel; 1985,
Cumberland Interfaith Consortium; 1989, Synod of the Trinity-Presbyterian; 1991, Leave of
Absence; 1996, Disaster Consultant for Church World Service; 2005, Attending School; 2011,
Retired.

146

Phillips, Arthe' V. (Taysie) PE AN | Centenary || Shady Side ||| 1515 (301) 639-4670
6538 Fish Hatchery Rd, Thurmont, MD 21788-2701 H. (301) 639-4670
taysie5@comcast.net
*2011, Sykesville: Bethesda; 2014, Lewistown: Lewistown; 2-15-15, Upperco: Emory; 2017,
Shady Side: Centenary, 2019, Aberdeen: Grace.*

Phillips, Sandi FL CM | Wesley Chapel || Frederick ||| 6385
3519 Urbana Pike, Frederick, MD 21704 H. (443) 956-5639
eph5v17@gmail.com
08-01-2009, Urbana: Wesley Chapel.

Phipps-Harmon, Janice PL GW | Emory || Washington ||| 7175 (301) 614-5924
1209 Tanley Rd , Silver Spring, MD 20904-2161
sunsistah@gmail.com
2016, DC: Emory.

Piel, William L. (Lou) RE BS | Mount Zion-Finksburg || Finksburg ||| 4265
1247 Weller Way, Westminster, MD 21158-4300 H. (410) 751-9049
julo1@verizon.net
*1962, Attending school; 1964, Mapleside-Melvin; 1969, Pleasant Hill; 1978, Arbutus;
1990, Gaithersburg: Grace; 2006, Retired; 01-01-2007, Hampstead: St Johns; 08-01-2007,
Finksburg: Mount Zion.*

Pierce, Irene C. RL GW | Asbury || Washington ||| 7115
109 Colton St , Largo, MD 20774-1501 H. (301) 336-0894
1993, Poolesville: Elijah; 1999, Retired.

Pierson, Robert FL CH | Davis Memorial || Cumberland ||| 5165
13200 Piney Flats Rd SE, Cumberland, MD 21502-7946 H. (240) 483-6865
bobapierson@yahoo.com
*2014, Timonium: Timonium-Fairview Cooperative Parish.; 2016, Cumberland: Davis
Memorial; 2016, Cumberland: Emmanuel.*

Piper, William G. LM CH | Sulphur Springs || Oldtown ||| 5615
20816 Oldtown Rd SE , Oldtown, MD 21555-1133 H. (301) 478-5244
barneycathy@gmail.com
2008, Great Cacapon: West Morgan Parish; 2009, Oldtown: Sulphur Springs.

Plymire, Larry M. RE BS | Milford Mill || Pikesville ||| 4380
630 Harmony Dr Apt 165, New Oxford, PA 17350-8224 H. (717) 624-5540
LJPLY@crosskeysvillage.net
*1965, Delbrook; 1968, Baltimore: Trinity; 1974, Bel Air: Bel Air; 1978, Owings Mills: Milford
Mill; 1978, Hagerstown, John Wesley; 1991, Silver Spring: Colesville; 1995, Middle River:
Orems; 2000, Retired; 2000, Westminster: St James-Stone Chapel; 2001, New Windsor: Stone
Chapel; 2002, Westminster: St James.*

Posey, Ralph D. RE CM | St Pauls || Sykesville ||| 4465
1001 Carpenters Way Apt M107, Lakeland, FL 33809-3907
poseypatch@gmail.com
*1954, Holston Conf; 1963, Woodfield: Wesley Grove; 1971, Parkside; 1976, Gaithersburg:
Epworth; 1986, Superintendent, Baltimore Northwest Dist; 1992, Assoc. Council Director;
1994, Retired.*

BALTIMORE-WASHINGTON CONFERENCE

Powe, Jr., Frederick D.   FEGW | University || College Park ||| 7340
12617 Falconbridge Dr, North Potomac, MD 20878-3412   H. (301) 963-1459
dpowe@wesleyseminary.edu
2015, Transfer into BWC and Extension Ministry, Wesley Theological Seminary: Professor of
Urban Ministry.

Powers, Darlene   LM   CH | Paw Paw || Paw Paw ||| 5610   (304) 947-7232
12 Mechem Way, Great Cacapon, WV 25422-3314   H. (304) 947-7232
darlenepowers@frontiernet.net
2011, Paw Paw: Paw Paw.

Price, Jr., Frederick   RL   AN | John Wesley-Waterbury || Crownsville ||| 1185
11404 Dundee Dr, Mitchellville, MD 20721-2422   H. (301) 464-0602
pricefa@verizon.net
7-1-14, Crownsville: John Wesley-Waterbury

Pride, Patricia A.   RE   BM | Christ || Baltimore ||| 2160   (410) 523-5556
3714 Eastman Rd , Randallstown, MD 21133-3412   H. (410) 496-2086
1986, Lutherville Charge; 1988, Baltimore: St. Markis; 1991, Temple Hills: Church of the
Redeemer; 1993, Laurel: St. Markis; 1994, Aquasco: Christ; 1998, Baltimore: Homestead/
Strawbridge; 1999, New Waverly/Homestead; 2002, New Waverly; 2004, Baltimore: Ames;
2008, Reisterstown: St Lukes; 2009, Retired; 01-17-2010, Churchville: Calvary.

Prieshoff, Trenton   SY   CM | Prospect || Mount Airy ||| 6315
24 N Wolfe St, Baltimore, MD 21231-1620   H. (317) 383-9429
trenton.prieshoff@inumc.org
 2018, Mt Airy: Prospect-Marvin Chapel,

Prioleau, Twanda E.   FE   BM | Christ || Baltimore ||| 2160
PO Box 522, Parkton, MD 21120-0522   H. (443) 271-9401
revtwandap@aol.com
2011, Baltimore: John Wesley.; 11-1-15, Baltimore: Christ.

Proctor, Charles A.   RE
8302 Maple St , Laurel, MD 20707-5093   H. (301) 498-4018
1984, Hopkins; 1996, Leave of Absence; 2003, Fowler; 2007, Retired.

Pugh, James   RL   CM | St Paul || Laytonsville ||| 9345
55B Queen Caroline Ct, Chester, MD 21619-2253
jgpugh46@msn.com
2008, Brookville: Mt Carmel; 2009, Laytonsville: Sunshine.; 2016, Retired

---

Pumphrey, Randy W.   FE   (202) 885-5794
2016 Perry St NE, Washington, DC 20018-3054   H. (202) 547-3423
spiritrp@aol.com
1983, Attending school; 1987, Chaplain: St. Elizabethis Hosp; 9-98, The Psychiatric Institute/
Whitman Walker Clinic.

Pupo-Ortiz, Yolanda E.   RE   CM | Epworth || Gaithersburg ||| 9245
18 Landsend Dr, Gaithersburg, MD 20878-1987   H. (301) 926-1387
yolanda@starpower.net
1983, S.N.E. Conf., Associate Gen. Sec., Gen. Com. on Rel. and Race; 1988, Bethesda
Hispanic Mission; 03-01-95, Gen. Sec. Comm. on Religion and Race; 2005, Retired; 12-01-

148

2009, Gaithersburg: Camino De Vida; 2010, Gaithersburg: Epworth.

Raines, Monica   PE   GW | Christ || Washington ||| 7140   (910) 580-6194
901 Wesley Pl SW , Washington, DC 20024-4211   H. (910) 580-6194
pastormcumcdc@gmail.com
2017, DC: Christ,

Rainey, Joe S.   RE
8350 Greensboro Dr Unit 531, McLean, VA 22102-3509   H. (703) 506-4639
jsrdlr@aol.com
*1963, North Georgia Conf; 1965, W. Va. Conf; 1967, Baltimore Conference, Director
Wesley Foundation, University of Maryland; 1968, Virginia Conference; 1970, Baltimore
Conference Chaplain, American University; 1978, Sabbatical leave; 1979, Attending school;
1981, NW Ctr. for Com. Mental Health; 1984, Tyson Cor., Psy. Ther. Assoc; 1993, Center for
Psychotherapy at Tysons Corner; 2006, Retired.*

Raker, William L.   RE   BM | Towson || Towson ||| 3550
8820 Walther Blvd Apt 4416, Baltimore, MD 21234-9035   H. (410) 665-7052
mjr8wlr@comcast.net
*1956, Attending school; 1960, Columbia Circuit; 1962, Bellefonte-Grace; 1965, Baltimore:
Olive Branch; 1970, Rodgers Forge; 1976, Fallston Charge; 1985, Oxon Hill; 1992,
Baltimore: Arnolia; 2000, Retired.*

Ranson, Jr., Leonard B.   RE   CH | Frostburg || Frostburg ||| 5310
908 Harvest Dr NW, Cedar Rapids, IA 52405-2808
*1954, Attending school; 1956, West Liberty; 1961, North Avenue; 1966, Frostburg; 1971,
Sabbatical leave; 1972, Attending school; 1976, Retired.*

Recinos, Harold J.   FE
PO Box 750133Perkins School of Theology, Dallas, TX 75275-0001   H. (214) 768-1773
hrecinos@smu.edu
*New York Conf; 1997, Baltimore-Washington Conference, Prof. of Theo., Culture & Urban
Ministry, Wesley Theological Seminary; 1-1-02, Perkins School of Theology.*

Rector, Saundra   FE   GW | Emmanuel || Laurel ||| 7440
8297 Hammond Branch Way , Laurel, MD 20723-1053   H. (301) 362-5996
sandyrector@verizon.net
*2005, Assoc., Greater Metropolitan; 2009, DC: Metropolitan Memorial Parish; 2010, Silver
Spring: Oak Chapel.; 2016, Johns Hopkins University Charge*

Reddinger, Faye   RL   BM | Arnolia || Baltimore ||| 3530
5533 Hutton Ave , Baltimore, MD 21207-5956   H. (410) 944-4073
1990, Perryman: Cranberry: 1992, Andrew Chapel; 2000, Retired.

Reddix-McCray, Irance'   PE   BM | St Johns || Baltimore ||| 3240
3317 Kenjac Rd, Windsor Mill, MD 21244-1323   H. (318) 348-5622
ievangel@aol.com
2014, Baltimore: Grace-St Johns; 11-01-16, Baltimore: St Johns.

Reese, Sheldon   FE   WE | Hollywood || Hollywood ||| 8230   (301) 373-2500
25 Edgewater St, Elizabethtown, NC 28337-6525   H. (301) 904-9489
brenreese@yahoo.com
1983, Attending school; 1984, Keedysville: Salem; 1988, Berkeley Springs: First; 1994,
Hollywood.; 2016, Baltimore Washington Conference

Reeves, Hallie L.   RE
9413 Sandy Creek Rd , Fort Washington, MD 20744-4872   H. (301) 839-1463
1985, St. Elizabeth Hosp; 8/1/03, Dunkirk Chg; 2006, Retired.

Reid, Randall   FE   CH | Emmanuel || Hagerstown ||| 5320   (301) 733-4720
812 Summit Ave, Hagerstown, MD 21740-6332   H. (301) 739-0442
eumc.pastor@verizon.net
2003, Wolfsville Charge; 2008, Hagerstown: Emmanuel.

Reidy, Dawn   PL FR | Paynes Chapel || Bunker Hill ||| 6730
1116 Hyslip Ford Rd , Bunker Hill, WV 25413-2976   H. (304) 671-0387
dreidy7@comcast.net
2015, Bunker Hill: Paynes Chapel.

Renn, Donna   FE   CH | New Covenant || Cumberland ||| 5210
1021 Kent Ave, Cumberland, MD 21502-3847   H. (301) 938-1450
revdonna@comcast.net
1996, Shenandoah Junction: Williams Memorial; 1999, Kemptown: Providence; 2011,
Sykesville: Oakland; 2018, Cumberland: New Covenant.

Revell, Frankie A.   FE   CH | La Vale || Lavale ||| 5370
26 Parkside Blvd, LaVale, Md 21502   H. (301) 338-3312
revellfa@gmail.com
2005, Berkeley Springs: Francis Asbury; 2009, Abington: Cokesbury; 2014, La Vale: La Vale.

Reynolds, Kirkland   FE   GW | Chevy Chase || Chevy Chase ||| 9165
10009 Dallas Ave, Silver Spring, MD 20901-2240   H. (240) 205-5001
kirklandreynolds@gmail.com
02-01-2007, Monrovia: Mountain View-Pleasant Grove; 2009, Silver Spring: Silver Spring
Cooperative Parish; 2013, Chevy Chase: Chevy Chase.

Rhodes, Clayton E.   RE   CH | Oldtown || Oldtown ||| 5430
184 Baker St, Rimersburg, PA 16248-4326   H. (814) 473-3844
1990, Oldtown Charge; 1996, Retired.

Rice, Charles   PL   FR | Buckeystown Rt 85 || Buckeystown ||| 6150
3441 Buckeystown Pike, PO Box 553, Buckeystown, MD 21717   H. (240) 608-5338
rice.charles@live.com
2016, Buckeystown: Buckeystown Rt 85.

Richards, Elizabeth J.   FE   FR | Calvary || Frederick ||| 6190
1006 Columbine Dr Apt 1A, Frederick, MD 21701-9200
sunfirebeth50@gmail.com
2003, Mountain View-Pleasant Grove Chg; 11-01-2006, Leave of Absence.

Ricker, Lawrence P. (Pat)   RE   CH | Shiloh || Hagerstown |||| 5355
18914 Rolling Rd, Hagerstown, MD 21742-2661   H. (301) 733-3520
revpatricker@gmail.com
1971, Attending school; 1972, Piney Plains; 1973, Crofton: Community; 1986, Ferndale;
1987, Washington County Hosp; 12-15-2010, Meritus Medical Center; 01-01-2014,
Hagerstown: John Wesley UMC; 2017, Retired.

Ricketts, Mary L.   OE   CH | Garfield || Smithsburg |||| 6425
35 E All Saints St Unit 118, Frederick, MD 21701-5951   H. (301) 582-8552
maryricketts622@gmail.com
01-01-2013, Smithsburg: St Paul's; 2014, Smithsburg: Garfield / St. Paul's Coop Parish; 2014,
Smithsburg: Garfield/Salem Coop Parish ; 1-1-2015, Smithsburg: Garfield / St. Paul's Coop
Parish.

Ricketts, Stephen   FE   FR | Linganore || Union Bridge |||| 6375   (301) 292-2323
8919 Clemsonville Rd , Union Bridge, MD 21791-7413   H. (240) 308-2148
srricketts@verizon.net
2001, Damascus; 2009, Fort Washington: Providence-Fort Washington.; 2016, Union Bridge:
Linganore.

Rider, Joshua D.   PL   CH | Piney Plains || Little Orleans |||| 5385
13203 Mann Rd NE , Little Orleans, MD 21766-1026   H. (304) 433-5920
jdrider@k12.wv.us
2016, Little Orleans: Sideling Hill Charge

Ridgely, Doris E.   RL   FR | Johnsville || Sykesville |||| 4450   (410) 795-1110
5701 Bartholow Rd , Sykesville, MD 21784-8812   H. (410) 795-0618
1996, Sykesville: Johnsville; 1999, Retired.

Rife, Carl B.   RE
624 Lafayette St, Lowell, MI 49331-1127   H. (717) 848-4807
carlrife@hotmail.com
1961, Lemoyne: Calvary, Associate; 1962, Youth Evangelist, General Board of Evangelism;
1963, Attending school; 1966 Silver Spring: Memorial; 1968, Lemoyne: Grace; 1970,
Attending school; 1971, Frederick: Brook Hill; 1981, Baltimore: Grace; 1984, Assoc. Dir.
Dev., United Theological Seminary; 1987, Pikesville: Milford Mill; 1994, Wheaton: Hughes;
1999, Retired.

Riggleman, Charles   FL   CH | Oldtown || Oldtown |||| 5430
18605 Oldtown RD SE, Oldtown, MD 21555   H. (301) 478-5228
umcpastorcr@gmail.com
1997, Cumberland: Mapleside; 2006, Oldtown.

Rigsby, Ben   PL   AN | Messiah || Glen Burnie |||| 1340
520 Shipley Rd, Linthicum, MD 21090-2829   H. (936) 615-5946
rev.ben.rigsby@gmail.com
2018, Glen Burnie: Messiah.

Rinker, Francis B. (Blaine) RA   FR | Westminster || Westminster ||| 4555
715 Norfield Ct, Westminster, MD 21158-9465   H. (443) 293-7007
gottaeat@comcast.net
1965, Bethel; 1967, Shenandale Chg; 1969, Midland; 1975, Cumberland: Assoc., Centre Street; 1978, Lonaconing: First; 1982, Jarrettsville; 1987, Bay Brook Charge; 1991, Overlea; 2002, Retired.

Rivera, Edgardo FE   (410) 309-3480
200 Shannonbrook Ln , Frederick, MD 21702-3637   H. (410) 660-7513
erivera@bwcumc.org
1998 Eastern Pennsylvania Conf.Reading:Iglesia Emanuel;2002 Central Pennsylvania Conf. Harrisburg:Stevens Emmanuel; 2007, Washington Region Guide; 02-01-2009, Military Chaplain, National Guard; 2013, District Superintendent, Frederick.

Rivera, Evelyn PE   FR | Middletown || Middletown ||| 6280   (301) 371-5550
200 Shannonbrook Ln , Frederick, MD 21702-3637   H. (301) 473-4645
pastorevelyn@mtownumc.org
2010, Wheaton: Hughes; 2018, Middletown: Middletown.

Ro, Sang K. RE
12307 Pomfret Ct , Midlothian, VA 23114-3229   H. (804) 378-5156
1971, Korean Presbyterian; 1975, North Dakota Conf; 1980, Iowa Conf; 1991, Baltimore Conference, Potomac Korean; 11-01-95, Retired.

Roark, Clarence L. (Pete) RE   BS | Glyndon || Glyndon ||| 4285   (717) 630-2274
1034 Bear Xing , Hanover, PA 17331-9426   H. (717) 630-2274
irishphud@gmail.com
1960, Stone Chapel; 1961, Union Bridge; 1965, Assoc. Towson; 1976, Glyndon Parish; 1990, Exec. Dir. Epworth Fed. Credit Union; 1996, Retired.

Roberson, Phillip R. FE   CH | Williamsport || Williamsport ||| 5475
17703 Daisy Dr, Hagerstown, MD 21740-9156   H. (240) 291-7260
rayroberson@icloud.com
1982, Louisville Conf; 1986, Baltimore Conference, Martinsburg: Trinity; 1987, Shiloh; 1991, Jarrettsville; 1994, Martinsburg: Otterbein; 1997, Marlowe: Harmony-Mt. Wesley Charge; 1999, Harmony-Mt. Wesley Coop. Parish; 2001, Harmony; 2008, Havre De Grace: Havre De Grace; 2011, Boonsboro: Mount Nebo; 2018, Williamsport: Williamsport.

Roberts, Ben OD   GW | Foundry || Washington ||| 7180   (202) 332-4010
150016th St. NW, Washington, DC 20036   H. (202) 332-4010
broberts@foundryumc.org
2015, DC: Foundry.

Roberts, David D. RE   BS | Smiths Chapel || Churchville ||| 2370
3111 Churchville Rd, Churchville, MD 21028-1805   H. (443) 412-5180
smchumchurch@gmail.com
1993, Cabin John; 1994, Clarksburg; 1997, Baltimore: Rodgers Forge; 2000, Forest Hill: Centre; 2006, Carrollis Gills; 2008, Maryland Line-Parkton: Maryland Line-Parke Memorial; 2014, Churchville: Smithis Chapel; 2014, Retired.

152

Roberts, Mary P. RE
8208 Lime Tree Way , Ellenton, FL 34222-4702   H. (941) 981-5089
revmproberts@gmail.com
1988, Cumberland: Trinity-Potomac Charge; 1993, Huntingtown: Emmanuel; 2002, Hunts
Memorial; 2008, Retired.

Roberts, Thomas P. RE   WE | Patuxent || Huntingtown ||| 8250   (609) 895-0806
10 Marilyn Ct , Lawrenceville, NJ 08648-2110   H. (202) 701-9622
troberts1800@gmail.com
1980, Calif.-Pacific Conf; 1988, Baltimore Conference, Cumberland: Grace; 1993,
Huntingtown: Huntingtown; 2000, Ext. Ministry, Melwood; 2008, Honorable Location; 2009,
Retired.

Roberts, W. McCarl RE   (410) 592-7709
665 Morning Glory Dr , Hanover, PA 17331-7827   H. (717) 632-4184
1955, Grace-Falls Road; 1962, Arnolia; 1974, Bowie: St. Matthewís; 1976, Maryland Bible
Society; 1995, Retired.

Robinson, Jason L. FE   WE | Brooks || Saint Leonard ||| 8460   (410) 586-3972
1065 Agricopia Dr, La Plata, MD 20646-3269   H. (301) 862-3138
jayrob1914@aol.com
2005, DC: Christ; 2009, St Leonard: Brooks.

Robinson, Mary E. PL   BM | Essex || Essex ||| 2425   (410) 686-2867
9722 Groffs Mill Dr, Owings Mills, MD 21117-6341   H. (443) 244-5907
drmarobi@gmail.com
2016, Essex: Essex.

Robinson, Theresa FE   BM | St. Paul Praise & Worship || Pikesville ||| 2290
                                                (410) 867-7661
7505 Reserve Cir Apt 303, Windsor Mill, MD 21244-1568   H. (410) 298-5951
Trob310@msn.com
1993, Mayo: St. Mark Hope Memorial; 1997, Baltimore: St. James; 2006, Shady Side: St.
Matthews. 2014; Medical Leave.

Robinson-Johnson, Douglas OE   GW | Metropolitan Memorial || Washington ||| 7630
3311 Nebraska Ave NW, Washington, DC 20016-2706   H. (781) 913-2799
Doug@NationalChurch.org
2019, DC: Metropolistan Memorial dba National Church.

Robison, Stephen RE   CH | Otterbein || Hagerstown ||| 5340
867 Dewey Ave, Hagerstown, MD 21742-3938   H. (301) 791-7148
s.robison@myactv.net
1973, Attending school; 1975, Union Grove; 1979, Boonsboro: Benevola Charge; 1986,
Hagerstown: Otterbein; 2016, Retired.

Rodeffer, Robert K. RE   WE | Emmanuel || Beltsville ||| 7310
621 Hobbs Dr , Silver Spring, MD 20904-6254   H. (301) 879-4304
rodeffer1@verizon.net
1955, Seat Pleasant; 1962, Prince Frederick: Trinity; 1967, Hamline; 1970, Lanham: First;
1976, Gaithersburg: Grace; 1990, Superintendent, Washington. East Dist; 1998, Retired.

Rodriguez, Leonardo   FE   BM | Salem-Baltimore Hispanic || Baltimore ||| 2310
eagle2258@yahoo.com
2013, Baltimore: Salem-Baltimore Hispanic and Ext. Ministry, Baltimore-Washington
Conference: Coordinator of Hispanic & Latino Ministries; 2015, Baltimore: Salem-Baltimore
Hispanic; 2016, Medical Leave.

Ross, Bernadette M.   RE   CH | La Vale || Lavale ||| 5370
1072 Braddock Rd, Cumberland, MD 21502-1924   H. (301) 724-2414
bross@atlanticbb.net
1988, Lonaconing: First; 1996, LaVale: LaVale; 2014, Retired.

Ross, Jr., Blango   PL   FR | Strawbridge || New Windsor ||| 4365   (410) 635-6480
317 Brushwood Dr , Owings Mills, MD 21117-1382   H. (443) 739-9591
ambrossjr@verizon.net
2005, New Windsor: Strawbridge.

Rothwell, Doris J.   PL   WE | Mount Zion || Saint Inigoes ||| 8450   (301) 866-6590
46534 Majestic Ct, Lexington Park, MD 20653-1863   H. (301) 997-8605
pastordorisrothwell@yahoo.com
2015, Dunkirk: Peters; 2019, St Inigoes: Mount Zion.

Rowley, William   PL   FR | Chestnut Hill || Harpers Ferry ||| 6570
2985 Kabletown Rd, Charles Town, WV 25414-4773   H. (703) 626-4978
bxrowley1952@yahoo.com
2017, Millville: Jefferson, 2019, Harpers Ferry: Chestnut Hill,

---

Rudisill, Jr., John   FE   CM | Montgomery || Damascus ||| 9215
28201 Kemptown Rd, Damascus, MD 20872-1324   H. (240) 520-5610
pastor.john.rudisill@verizon.net
1981, Attending school; 1982, Texas Chg; 1988, Dunkirk: Smithville; 1994, Joppa: Union
Chapel; 2003, Superintendent, Cumberland-Hagerstown Dist; 2011, Bedington: Bedington.;
2016, Damascus: Montgomery Charge

Rudolph, John B.   FE   BS | Greenmount || Hampstead ||| 4288
2009 Hanover Pike, Hampstead, MD 21074-1321   H. (410) 239-9705
revjrudolph@gmail.com
2006, Middleway; 2008, Emmitsburg: Trinity; 2011, Hampstead: North Carroll Cooperative
Parish.

Rudolph, Melissa   FE   BS | St Johns || Hampstead ||| 4320   (304) 279-8520
2009 Hanover Pike, Hampstead, MD 21074-1321   H. (304) 279-8520
Mchrudolph@yahoo.com
2004, Leetown; 2008, Frederick: Christ-Ballenger Creek; 2011, Hampstead: North Carroll
Cooperative Parish.

Ruggieri, Robert   PE   CH | Mount Nebo || Boonsboro ||| 6130
10856 Wolfsville Rd, Myersville, MD 21773-8820   H. (443) 994-9505
pastorbob2017@gmail.com
2013, Adamstown: Flint Hill; 2014, Ijamsville: Ijamsville-Flint Hill; 2018, Boonsboro:
Mount Nebo,.

Saari, Katharine FE   AN | Nichols-Bethel || Odenton |||| 1430
1241 Murray Rd, Odenton, MD 21113-1603   H. (443) 878-6997
2013, West Friendship: West Ellicott City; 2016, Leave of Absence; 2017, Odenton: Nichols-
Bethel.

Sands, Barbara J.   RE   CM | West Liberty || Marriottsville |||| 4343
696 West Watersville Road, PO Box 637, Mount Airy, MD 21771   H. (301) 829-2180
bjsands696@gmail.com
1985, Sykesville: Johnsville-White Rock Chg; 1986, Assoc. Conference Coun. Dir. for Ch. and
Com. Min; 1992, Annapolis: Asbury-Broadneck; 2004, D.C.: Simpson-Hamline; 01-01-2009,
Retired; 2009, Marriottsville: West Liberty.

Sangha, Moses   FE   WE | Glenn Dale || Glenn Dale |||| 8225   (301) 262-2299
2004 Sandstone Ct, Silver Spring, MD 20904-5329   H. (301) 758-3094
mosessangha@gmail.com
1990, Maryland City: Community; 1994, Sykesville: Oakland-Flohrville; 1996, Mt. Rainier:
Cedar Lane; 2000, Hyattsville: Ager Road; 2011, Leave of Absence; 2012, Glenn Dale: Glenn
Dale.

Sansom, William R.   RL   CH | Dawson || Rawlings |||| 5440
5 Fairfield Dr, Baltimore, MD 21228-5026
1971, Berkeley Springs, Circuit 11; 1973, Berkeley Springs: Alpine; 1975, Dawson-
Westernport; 1977, Westernport; 1979, Retired.

Sassaman, Scott   PL   FR | Middleway || Kearneysville |||| 6635
108 Kendig Ln, Martinsburg, WV 25404-7701   H. (304) 616-2810
pastorsassy16@gmail.com
 2013, Bakerton: Bethel; 2015, Summit Point: Memorial; 09-01-16, Middleway: Middleway,
01-01-19, Bakerton: Bethel.

Sawyerr, Victor E.   RE   GW | Colesville || Silver Spring |||| 9450   (301) 384-1941
9511 Rommel Dr , Columbia, MD 21046-1910   H. (410) 290-9612
pastorves@gmail.com
1983, Hagerstown: McKendree; 1985, Martin Luther King Memorial; 1987, Bel Air: Ames;
1990, Columbia Locust; 2005, Colesville; 12-01-2008, Leave of Absence; 2014, Retired.

Sayers, Mandy E.   FE   CM | Glen Mar || Ellicott City |||| 7365
2705 Thistledown Ter , Olney, MD 20832-1547   H. (443) 280-2885
pastormandy10@gmail.com
2010, Waldorf: Journey of Faith; 2012, Gaithersburg: Covenant; 09-08-18, Ellicott City: Glen
Mar.

Schaefer, Mark A.   FE   GW | Foundry || Washington |||| 7180   (202) 885-3336
5910 Osceola Rd, Bethesda, MD 20816-2031   H. (301) 320-3592
revschaef@gmail.com
2003, Ext. Min., Campus Ministry: American University.; 6-1-16, American University

---

Schammel, Margery L.   FD   BM | Towson || Towson |||| 3550   (410) 823-2485
4 Ansari Ct, Baldwin, MD 21013   H. (410) 592-3805
mlwschammel61@gmail.com
1994, Baltimore: Hiss; 1/01/04, Leave of Absence; 1/1/2006, Towson.

Schildt, John RE   CH | Bethel || Rohrersville ||| 6345
PO Box 145 , Sharpsburg, MD 21782-0145   H. (301) 432-0087
lyricww41@aol.com
1956, Big Pool-Wolfsville Chg; 1960, Wolfsville; 1961, St. Thomas; 1967, Chewsville: Bethel;
2004, Retired; 2007, Rohrersville: Rohrersville; 2019, Rohrersville: Bethel.

Schlieckert, Sarah FE   WE | Calvary || Waldorf ||| 8520   (240) 315-6965
9818 Golden Russet Dr Dunkirk, Dunkirk, MD 20754   H. (240) 315-6965
PastorSarahUMC@gmail.com
2005, Jefferson-Doubs Charge; 2009, Frederick: Calvary / Centennial Memorial Cooperative
Parish; 2014, Arden: Arden; 09-01-17, Elkridge: Melville Chapel, 2018, Waldorf: Calvary.

Schneider, Robert K. FE   GW | Oak Chapel || Silver Spring ||| 9460
2304 Kaywood Ln , Silver Spring, MD 20905-6407
2004, Oak Chapel; 2010, On Loan to New England Conference.

Schukraft, Keith RA   WE | First Saints Community Church || Leonardtown ||| 8540
43115 Gum Spring Dr , Leonardtown, MD 20650-4539   H. 301-475-8826
keith0811@verizon.net
2006, Leonardtown: St Pauls; 01-01-2008, Leonardtown: First Saints Community; 2012,
Huntingtown: Huntingtown.; 2016, Retired

Schultz, Laura RE   CM | Howard Chapel-Ridgeville || Mount Airy ||| 9355
401 Oak St, Windsor, CO 80550-5323   H. (301) 829-2391
revlauraschultz@gmail.com
1994, Taneytown: Messiah; 1999, Silver Spring: Memil; 2001, Camp Springs, Bells; 2005,
Cresaptown; 2007, Mt Airy: Howard Chapel-Ridgeville; 2014, Retired.

Schulze, Richard D. RE   BS | Maryland Line || Maryland Line ||| 3380   (443) 324-7861
6212 Westover Dr, Mechanicsburg, Pa 17050-2340   H. (443) 324-7861
dschulze6212@verizon.net
1965, East Harford; 1970, Attending school; 1971, Mayo Memorial; 1982, Forest Memorial;
1989, Wesley Memorial; 1993, Emmitsburg: Tomis Creek; 9-1-95, Lothian: Wesley Chapel;
1996, Monkton: Monkton-Clynmalira Chg. 01-03-04, Phoenix: Clynmalira; 2008, Freeland:
Bentley SpringsMt Zion; 2008, Retired; 2014, Maryland Line: Baltimore County Coop Parish.

Schwartz, Anna PE   CM | Glen Mar || Ellicott City ||| 7365
3657 Worthington Blvd, Frederick, MD 21704-7015   H. (316) 371-3679
anna.schwartz@glenmarumc.org
2018, Ellicott City: Glen Mar,

Schwarzmann, Henry F. RE
146 Kingston Rd , Greenwood, SC 29649-9569   H. (864) 229-2065
henryschwarzmann@hotmail.com
1971, Harwood Park; 1973, Baltimore: Otterbein Memorial; 1979, Otterbein-Aldersgate;
1980, Dundalk; 1984, Deer Park; 1997, Timonium: Mays Chapel; 1999, Millersville: Baldwin
Memorial; 2002, Leave of Absence; 12/01/02, Retired.

Scott, Bonnie FE   CM | Trinity || Germantown ||| 9280
28 Sebastiani Blvd, Gaithersburg, MD 20878-4120   H. (410) 303-2887
revbonniescott@gmail.com
2011, Eldersburg: Wesley Freedom; 01-01-2015, Germantown: Trinity.

156

Scott, Deb L. FE BM | Lovely Lane || Baltimore |||| 3185
17724 Caddy Dr, Derwood, MD 20855   H. (301) 641-4601
revdeb8@aol.com
*1980, Attending school; 1982, Colesville; 1985, Mt. Pleasant Chg; 1988, Cape St. Clair;
1990, Leave of Absence; 1994, Laytonsville Chg; 1999, Bethesda: North Bethesda; 2014,
Rockville: Mill Creek Parish.; 2016, Mt Airy: Calvary Charge; 2018, Baltimore: Lovely Lane-
Baltimore City.*

Scoville, Roberta J. RE
610 Chesapeake Dr, Havre de Grace, MD 21078-3623   H. (410) 939-7433
*1984, Cranberry; 1986, Baltimore: Grace; 1990, Street: Dublin; 1996, Perry Hall: Camp
Chapel; 2005, Timonium; 2007, Leave of Absence; 2008, Retired.*

Scroggins, Kara FE GW | Glenmont || Silver Spring |||| 9475   (202) 557-8396
10820 Torrance Dr, Kensington, MD 20895-2800   H. (202) 557-8396
Karascroggins@gmail.com
2013, Bethesda: Bethesda.; 1-1-16, Bethesda: Bethesda; 2018, Wheaton: Glenmont.

Sebring, Patricia L. FE FR | Otterbein || Martinsburg |||| 6680   (443) 510-3308
122 Metro Dr, Martinsburg, WV 25404-1419   H. (443) 510-3308
revdrpls@gmail.com
*2017, Baltimore: Lovely Lane-Baltimore City, 2018, Martinsburg: Otterbein, 2000,
Hagerstown: Otterbein; 2004, College Park; 2007, Huntingtown: Huntingtown; 2012, Carney:
Linden Heights; 2014, Galesville: Galesville.*

Segovia, Gustavo A. SY BM | Salem-Baltimore Hispanic || Baltimore |||| 2310
3403 Gough St, Baltimore, MD 21224   H. (540) 250-3503
pastorsegovia.gs@gmail.com
09-01-18, Baltimore: Salem-Baltimore Hispanic,

Senft, Curtis SY BS | Frames Memorial || Cockeysville |||| 3460
6308 Blackburn Ct, Baltimore, MD 21212-2220   H. (717) 818-3907
curtis.senft@yahoo.com
2013, Phoenix: Fairview; 2015, No Appointment; 2018, Cockeysville: Frames-Poplar.

Senyk, Joan I. RE BM | Govans-Boundary || Baltimore |||| 3165 (281) 507-0737
8808 C Ave Apt 120, Hesperia, CA 92345-5924   H. (281) 599-1310
1996, Govans-Boundary/St. Johnis Charge; 2000, Leave of Absence; 11-01-00, Retired.

Sergent, Joe D. RE
4 Kratz Rd , Shrewsbury, PA 17361-1335   H. (717) 235-3122
*1959, Shenandoah Junction; 1960, Bedington, W. Va; 1963, Jarrettsville; 1966, Lauraville;
1970, Upper Falls: Salem; 1977, Forestville: Forest Memorial; 1978, North Bethesda; 1981,
Millian Memorial; 1988, Timonium; 1996, Retired.*

Serufusa, Christopher N. FE CH | St Andrews || Hagerstown |||| 5345
1014 Maryland Ave , Hagerstown, MD 21740-7202   H. (240) 452-1918
cserufusa@gmail.com
*1996, Annapolis: Calvary; 1999, Mt. Pleasant Coop. Parish; 2002, Govans-Boundary;
2005, Sykesville: St Luke-Mt. Gregory Charge; 2014, Glenwood: Growing Seed Cooperative
Ministry; 2018, Hagerstown: St. Andrews.*

Shackelford, Derek T. SY FR | Buckeystown Rt 80 || Buckeystown ||| 6145
20 N Court St Unit 1, Frederick, MD 21701-5448 H. (240) 344-0491
shackque1911@yahoo.com
2018, Buckeystown: Buckeystown (Rt 80),

Shacochis, Jr., Charles J. RA CM | Ebenezer || Sykesville ||| 4575 (410) 795-0714
1614 Heather Hts, Eldersburg, MD 21784-6235 H. (410) 795-3871
chuckstg39@msn.com
2004, Sykesville: Sykesville Parish Charge; 10-01-2012, Retired.

Shamer, Richard RL FR | Zion || Westminster ||| 4560 (410) 857-4444
930 Pine Grove Rd , Hanover, PA 17331-8798 H. (410) 596-3876
1999, Upperco: Boring-Dover Charge; 2004, Westminster: Zion; 2012, Retired.

Shank, David A. RE AN | Linthicum Heights || Linthicum ||| 1370 (410) 859-0990
13301 Belle Chasse Blvd Unit 314, Laurel, MD 20707-8426 H. (410) 684-6776
dashank579@msn.com
1981, Hagerstown: Shiloh; 1987, Baltimore: Orems; 1995, Damascus: Montgomery; 1999,
Linthicum Heights.

Sharpe, Corey S. FE WE | Huntingtown || Huntingtown ||| 8245 (410) 257-3020
3980 Hunting Creek Rd , Huntingtown, MD 20639-9113 H. (443) 968-8149
coreysharpe19@gmail.com
2004, Assoc. Rockville: Faith; 2010, Havre De Grace: Susquehanna.; 2016, Huntingtown:
Huntingtown Church Charge

Shearer, Donald L. RE
1712 W Glendale Ave Apt 2020, Phoenix, AZ 85021-8816 H. (602) 544-8372
1957, W. Va. Conf; 1962, Baltimore Conference, Assoc., Hyattsville: First; 1967, Fort
Washington; 1974, Cumberland: First; 1979, Leave of Absence; 1981, Retired.

Shearer, Wilson A. RE CH | Otterbein || Hagerstown ||| 5340
163 Sunbrook Ln, Hagerstown, MD 21742-4197 H. (301) 739-1613
wilsonshearer@aol.com
1952 Attending school; 1954, Middleburg-Shiloh Chg; 1957, York: St. Lukeís; 1965, Youth
Ministry & Camping; 1970, Hagerstown: Otterbein; 1976, Superintendent, Frederick Dist;
1982, Asst. to Bishop; 1985, Hagerstown: Otterbein; 1996, Retired.

Sheffield-James, Gary FE CM | Mount Zion || Highland ||| 9310 (410) 963-8618
9601 Hickoryhurst Dr , Baltimore, MD 21236-4707 H. (410) 529-8102
pastorgary@mtzionhighland.com
1983, Shenandoah Juntion: Bethel-Bethesda Charge; 1985, Westminster: St. James-Stone
Chap-Salem Parish; 1989, Mt. Carmel-New Market Charge; 1998, Brookeville: Salem; 2000,
Baltimore: Arnolia; 2008, Riderwood: Huntís Memorial; 2017, Highland: Mount Zion.

Shields, Brenda FL FR | Messiah || Taneytown ||| 4475 (410) 756-6085
1010 Sunny Brook Dr, Glen Burnie, MD 21060-7023 H. (410) 756-6092
pastor_brenda@comcast.net
2010, Baldwin: Union; 2011, Taneytown: Messiah.

Shin, Yo-Seop   FE   BM | Eden Korean || Baltimore ||| 2180   (667) 206-4187
54 Stevenson Ln , Baltimore, MD 21212-1240   H. (443) 629-1752
yshinpastor@gmail.com
2010, Baltimore: Eden Korean .

Shirkey, John A.   RE
10216 Rockville Pike Apt 202, Rockville, MD 20852-3307   H. (301) 564-0572
1961, Attending school; 1963, Asst. Leonardtown; 1964, St. George Island; 1965, Assoc., Oxon
Hill; 1966, Oxon Hill Parish: St. Paul; 1969, Attending school; 1971, Exec. Dir., Center for
Comm. Dev; 1993, Retired.

Shockley, Louis   RE   AN | Macedonia || Odenton ||| 1425
8707 Royal Ridge Ln, Laurel, MD 20708-2457   H. (301) 617-9235
shockleylouis@gmail.com
1970, W. Ohio Conf; 1977, Baltimore Conference, Upper Marlboro Charge; 1979, Upper
Marlboro: Union; 1980, Seat Pleasant Large Parish; 1981, Gethsemane; 1989, Baltimore:
Metropolitan; 1994, Hyattsville: First; 1998, Supt., Baltimore West Dist; 2004, Washington:
Asbury; 2013, Crofton: Community-Trinity Coop Parish; 2015, Laurel: First; 2015, Retired.; ;
11-1-15, Odenton: Macedonia Charge

Shorb-Sterling, Sue E.   FE CM | Salem || Brookeville ||| 9150   (410) 474-7281
8 High St, Brookeville, MD 20833   H. (410) 474-7281
shorster@yahoo.com
2002, Olivet; 2008, Brookeville: Salem.

Showalter, Dave   FD   WE | St Paul || Lusby ||| 8345   (443) 624-1349
2060 Brians Way, Lusby, MD 20657-2477   H. (410) 326-2150
dave4godsteens.stpaul@comcast.net
2009, Lusby: St Paul.

Shrom-Rhoads, Kirstin   OD   (301) 834-7244
1620 Harpers Ferry Rd , Knoxville, MD 21758-1212   H. (717) 305-8410
director@manidokan.com
12-01-17, BWC Dir. Manidokan Camp & Retreats,

Shropshire, Andrew   SY   BM | Salem-Hebbville || Baltimore ||| 4335
3806 Yolando Rd , Baltimore, MD 21218-2043   H. (443) 320-3345
andrew.shropshire31@gmail.com
2018, Hebbville: Salem,

Shropshire, Jr., Walter   RE
300 Westminster Canterbury Dr Apt 426, Winchester, VA 22603-4279   H. (540) 665-5748
wshrop@erols.com
1977, Oakdale-Emory; 1980, Sunshine: Mt. Carmel; 1985, Leave of Absence; 1986, Cabin
John; 1990, Baltimore: Lovely Lane; 1991, D.C.: Foundry; 2003, Retired.

Shumaker, Scott D.   FE   BS | Mount Carmel || Parkton ||| 3425   (410) 357-5431
17036 Pretty Boy Dam Rd , Parkton, MD 21120-9690   H. (410) 357-5431
sshumaker2@comcast.net
2000, Cumberland: New Covenant; 2002, Big Pool: Potomac Chg; 2006, Parkton/Sparks: Mt.
Carmel/Falls Road Charge.

Shuman, II, Richard G. PL   FR | Oakland || Charles Town ||| 6535
104 Spyglass Hill Dr, Charles Town, WV 25414-3963   H. (304) 886-2106
shumanrick@comcast.net
09-01-17, Summit Point: Memorial, 2018, Charles Town: Oakland,

---

Sieglein, Gary RL   FR | Gerrardstown || Gerrardstown ||| 6555   (304) 229-2351
110 Dominion Rd, Gerrardstown, WV 25420-4378   H. (410) 286-1201
parsonumc@gmail.com
2001, Darlington; 2013, Gerrardstown: Gerrardstown; 2014, Retired.

Sigler, Bertha N. RL   FR | Bethel || Bakerton ||| 6515
3833 Burkittsville Rd , Knoxville, MD 21758-9724   H. (301) 834-9726
1999, Bakerton: Bethel; 2006, Retired.

Sigler, Thomas PL   FR | Darkesville || Inwood ||| 6545
Eastland Drive 226 Eastland Dr, Charles Town, WV 25414   H. (240) 446-9731
tesigler@gmail.com
2009, Inwood: Darkesville.

Silbaugh, Linda C. (Carole) RE
16569 Howard Millman Ln , Milton, DE 19968-3531   H. (302) 645-7225
carole.silbaugh@comcast.net
*1979, College Park; 1980, Mt. Harmony-Lower Marlboro Charge; 1985, Bowie; St.
Matthewís; 1989, Cheltenham; 1992, Pasadena: Mt. Carmel; 2000, Huntingtown; 2007,
Retired.*

Simms, Sr., Charles RE   (410) 721-3472
1421 Saint Stephens Church Rd, Crownsville, MD 21032-2203   H. (410) 216-9202
csimms70@aol.com
*1986, Sykesville: Johnsville-White Rock; 1987, Odenton: Macedonia; 1999, Leave of Absence;
9-1-99, Retired; 2002, Gambrills: Mount Tabor.; 2016, Retired*

Simpson, David W. RE   CM | Oakdale Emory || Olney ||| 9375
1129 Thornbury Dr, Parrish, FL 34219   H. (410) 596-5910
dsimpson670@comcast.net
*1988, Laytonsville: Mt. Carmel, Mt. Tabor Charge; 1989, Laytonsville: Mt. Tabor; 1990,
Olney: Oakdale-Emory; 1999, Baltimore-Washington Conference: Assistant to the Bishop;
2004, Director, Connectional Ministries; 2005, Ellciott City: Bethany; 2009, Ellicott City:
Ellicott City Cooperative Parish; 2014, Extension Ministry, Conference Global Initiatives
Coordinator; 2015, Frederick: Calvary/Centennial Memorial; 2016, Retired.*

Simpson, Richard W. RE FR | Jefferson || Jefferson ||| 6240
5 Maple Trl , Fairfield, PA 17320-8495   H. (717) 642-6236
richcar2@comcast.net
*1968, Eckhart; 1970, Harperís Ferry: Camp Hill; 1971, Hereford: Mt. Carmel; 1977,
Leonardtown: St. Paul; 1982, Catonsville: Wesley Memorial; 1989, Camp Chapel; 1990,
Sykesville: Ebenezer; 1996, Hagerstown: John Wesley; 2000, Charles Town: Asbury; 2003,
Retired.*

Sims, Mary Jo   RE   FR | Arden || Martinsburg |||| 6510
314 Surfwood Ct, Gerrardstown, WV 25420-4126   H. (443) 841-2219
stupot@comcast.net
1992, Dickerson: Dickerson/Forest Grove Charge; 1993, Chaplain, Shenandoah Univ; 1995, West Virginia Wesleyan College: Dean of the Chapel; 2001, Maryland Line; 2006, Assoc., Towson; 2011, Westminster: Deer Park; 09-01-2013, Retired; 2014, Summit Point: Memorial; 09-01-17, Arden: Arden,.

Sims, Troy   OD   GW | Capitol Hill || Washington |||| 7135   (202) 546-1000
421 Seward Sq SE , Washington, DC 20003-1113   H. (940) 867-2599
troy@chumc.net
2015, DC: Capitol Hill.

Sipes, Fred   PL   BS | Cedar Grove || Monkton |||| 3415
20106 Cameron Mill Rd , Parkton, MD 21120-9007   H. (410) 967-9134
andfred@msn.com
2013, Parkton: Cedar Grove.; 1-1-16, Parkton: Cedar Grove Charge; 2017, Parkton: Cedar Grove-Stablers-Bentley Sp.

Skillington, James E.   RE   CM | Morgan Chapel || Woodbine |||| 4585   (240) 565-0025
9238 Spring Valley Rd , Ellicott City, MD 21043-6432   H. (410) 740-1032
revjim@preachershop.com
1987, Oak Chapel; 09-01-90, Baltimore Conference Coordinator Communications & Public Relations; 3-28-92, Associate Council Director; 1994, Dir. of Communications; 6-16-96, Ext. Min., Kaleidoscope Min. Ltd. Village Life Ministries; 2018, Retired, 09-01-18, Woodbine: Morgan Chapel-Mt Olive.

Skorupinski, Emily E.   FL BM | Lansdowne || Baltimore |||| 3125
224 Pennsylvania Ave, Pasadena, MD 21122-5436   H. 410-937-9513
pastoremily@lansdowneumc.org
2019, Baltimore: Lansdowne,

Slade, Robert E.   FE   WE | Grace || Fort Washington |||| 8215   (301) 292-7828
16601 Tanyard Rd , Upper Marlboro, MD 20772-8102   H. (301) 888-1207
r3slade3@gmail.com
1994, Brandywine: Gibbons; 2-1-97, Leave of Absence; 1-1-2000, Valley Lee: Bethesda; 2000, D.C.: Mt. Zion; 03-01-2009, DC: Mount Zion; 2011, Fort Washington: Grace.

Slaugh, Charles   RL   FR | Middleburg || Westminster |||| 4490   (301) 960-9638
3152 Gracefield Rd Apt MS602, Silver Spring, MD 20904-5897   H. (301) 960-9638
charlesslaugh@gmail.com
2000, New Windsor: Pipe Creek-Brick; 01-01-2008, New Windsor: Middleburg-Uniontown; 2011, Retired.

Slayton, Kevin   PL   WE | Lanham || Lanham |||| 8290
644 E. 33rd Street, Baltimore, MD 21218, Baltimore, MD 21218   H. (410) 243-2481
revkevinslayton@gmail.com
2014, Baltimore: New Waverly.; 1-1-16, Baltimore: New Waverly Charge; 2019, Lanham: Lanham.

Sloan, Donald W. (Wayne) RL CH | Prosperity || Flintstone ||| 5285
1058 Beans Cove Rd, Clearville, PA 15535-8030 H. (814) 767-9418
janesloan28@yahoo.com
2011, Flintstone: Flintstone; 2015, Retired.

Smalls, Bejamin K. (Kevin) FE GW | Emory || Washington ||| 7175
26275 Northwestern Hwy, Southfield, MI 48076-3926 H. (248) 838-8089
kevinsmalls@aol.com
1997, Rockville: Jerusalem-Mt Pleasant; 2001, DC: Hughes Memorial; 2005, Ext Min; 2007, Beltsville: Queens Chapel; 2014, Beltsville: Queens Chapel / Ebenezer; 2016, On loan to Detroit Conference.

Smarr, William B. SY BS | Bixlers || Manchester ||| 4530
3282 Charmil Dr, Manchester, MD 21102-1918 H. (704) 860-7851
blakesmarr@gmail.com
2017, Manchester: Bixlers-Millers,

Smiley, Mark RE BM | Hiss || Baltimore ||| 3440
9600 Labrador Ln , Cockeysville, MD 21030-1715 H. (443) 286-6565
msmileyumc@gmail.com
1982, Eastern Pa. Conf; 1992, Baltimore Conf., Chief Fiscal Officer/Treasurer; 1993, Germantown: Salem; 1999, Timonium: Mays Chapel; 2004, Baltimore: Hiss; 2012, Discipleship Adventure Guide; 2013, Westminster; 1-1-2015, Retired

---

Smith, Constance C. FE WE | Nottingham-Myers || Upper Marlboro ||| 8485
18804 Aquasco Rd, Brandywine, MD 20613 H. (301) 888-1283
revconi53@yahoo.com
1987, Attending school; 1988, Centerville-New Market Parish; 1993, Baltimore: St. Markis; 1994, Baltimore: St. Markis-Howard Park; 1995, Baltimore: Eastern; 2005, D.C.: Hughes Memorial; 2014, Upper Marlboro: New Hope Fellowship.

Smith, Eddie FE AN | Hope Memorial St Mark || Edgewater ||| 1240 (410) 798-6776
100 Foxhorn Way, Glen Burnie, MD 21061 H. (410) 761-2249
hopestmarkumc@comcast.net
1985, Churchton Charge; 1989, Aquasco: Christ; 1991, Davidsonville Charge; 1994, Baltimore: St. Markis-Howard Park; 1995, Howard Park; 1997, Edgewater: Hope Memorial. 7/1/03, Hope Memorial St. Mark.

Smith, Errol G. RE CM | Mount Zion || Highland ||| 9310
422 Spalding Ct , Westminster, MD 21158-9411 H. (443) 293-7095
esmithconsult@aol.com
1960, Pittsburgh Conf; 1961, Baltimore Conference, Gamber: Calvary; 1964, Arlington; 1969, Assoc. Chevy Chase; 1973, Highland: Mt. Zion; 1982, Rockville: Faith; 1991, Lovely Lane: Baltimore City Station; 1999, Retired; 12-01-2012, Sykesville: Sykesville Parish.

Smith, Gaye S. RE FR | Calvary || Frederick ||| 6190
3800 Shamrock Dr, Charlotte, NC 28215-3220 H. (407) 249-3969
smith_ted_gaye@bellsouth.net
1980, North Bethesda; 1984, Scaggsville: Emmanuel; 1990, Hyattstown; 1992, Attending school; 1993, Frederick: Calvary; 1999, Retired.

Smith, Helen   RE   FR | Mount Carmel || Frederick ||| 6335   (301) 662-1303
4117 Mills Rd , Sharpsburg, MD 21782-1931   H. (301) 432-5644
sycamore@myactv.net
1974, North Carolina Conf; 1975, Dorsey: Emmanuel; 1981, Leave of Absence; 1986,
Woodfield: Wesley Grove; 1995, Boonsboro: Benevola; 2009, Leave of Absence; 2011,
Frederick: Calvary / Centennial Memorial Cooperative Parish.; 2016, Retired.

Smith, Jenny   FE   FR | Mount Carmel || Frederick ||| 6335   (301) 662-1303
6102 Dover St, Frederick, MD 21704-6694   H. (240) 409-4722
crazymethodists@comcast.net
2000, Walkersville: Walkersville; 2004, Frederick: Mt. Carmel.

Smith, Jr., Harry   FE   AN | Hall || Glen Burnie ||| 1325   (410) 360-1242
160 Barbara Rd, Severna Park, MD 21146-1359   H. (240) 246-4779
pastorhsmith@verizon.net
01-01-2007, Germantown: Asbury; 2008, Clarksburg: Community of Faith; 2013, Oxon Hill:
Oxon Hill.

Smith, Lillian C.   FE   GW | Cheverly || Cheverly ||| 7325   (301) 773-1314
506 Crain Hwy, Upper Marlboro, MD 20774   H. (301) 249-7669
pastor@cheverlyumc.org
2016, Cheverly: Cheverly Charge.

Smith, Mabel   RL   AN | Adams || Lothian ||| 1375   (410) 741-1932
7933 Mount Harmony Ln , Owings, MD 20736-3409   H. (443) 550-3259
mabelsmith9@comcast.net
2002, Charlotte Hall: Mt Calvary; 2008, Lothian: Adams; 2017, Retired.

Smith, Sandra E.   RL   WE | Grace || Fort Washington ||| 8215   (240) 304-8068
10375 Cassidy Ct, Waldorf, MD 20601-3761   H. (240) 304-8068
corwin77@aol.com
2006, Dunkirk: Cooperís; 2019, Retired.

Smith, Stephen   FL   BS | Emory || Street ||| 2555   (410) 452-5220
2011 Belton Ave, Bel Air, MD 21015   H. (443) 752-3111
pastorsmitty@verizon.net
2005, Bay Brook; 09-01-2008, Baltimore: Brooklyn-Bay Brook Cooperative Parish; 02-01-
2010, Baltimore: Brooklyn Area Cooperative Parish.; 2016, Street: Emory Charge.

Smith-Horn, LaReesa   FE BS | St Luke || Reisterstown ||| 4440
9020 Groffs Mill Dr, Owings Mills, MD 21117-6105   H. (410) 581-1612
revsmithorn@verizon.net
1987, Sykesville: St. Luke-Mt. Gregory-White Rock Charge; 1992, Severn: Metropolitan;
2006, Baltimore: Christ.; 10-15-15, Baltimore: John Wesley Charge; 2017, Retired, 2018,
Reisterstown: St Lukes.

Smothers, Rodney   FE   GW | Brighter Day || Washington ||| 7625   (410) 309-9958
3313 Dunwood Ridge Ter, Bowie, MD 20721-1259   H. (301) 218-4688
rsmothers@bwcumc.org
1981, N. Ga Conf; 06-15-01, Baltimore-Washington Conf., Gibbons-Resurrection; 2002,
Waldorf: Covenant Point; 1-1-04, Hyattsville: First; 2005, Ext. Min., Assoc. Council Dir.
Congregational Life; 2008, Oxon Hill: St Paul; 2010, Oxon Hill: St. Paul/Corkran Memorial
Cooperative Parish; 02-01-2013, Oxon Hill: St. Paul; 2014, Burtonsville: Liberty Grove;

2017, Baltimore-Washington Conf: Dir. of Lead. & Congreg. Development.

Snell, Adam   FE   GW | St Pauls || Kensington ||| 9330   (301) 933-7933
10100 Ashwood Dr, Kensington, MD 20895-4240   H. (410) 224-4750
absnell@stpaulsk.org
2004, Annapolis: Calvary; 2007, Kensington: St Pauls.

Snyder, Dean J.   RE   GW | Capitol Hill || Washington ||| 7135
11902 Kennedyville Rd, Kennedyville, MD 21645   H. (410) 708-9600
snyderdean@gmail.com
Central Pa. Conf; 8-1-97, Baltimore-Washington Conf., Assoc. Council Director; 03-01-99,
Dir. of Communications; 2002, DC: Foundry; 2014, Retired.

Snyder, Gerald   SY   AN | Edgewater || Edgewater ||| 1235   (410) 266-8198
1576 Chickasaw Rd, Arnold, MD 21012-2526   H. (410) 974-4410
gerald@kurtsnyder.net
2006, Edgewater: Edgewater.

Snyder, Robert E.   FE   CH | Salem || Myersville ||| 6435
517 Main St, Myersville, MD 21773-8436   H. (240) 385-6833
revbsnyder@comcast.net
2008, Myersville: Salem.

Sparks, Hayden L.   RE   CH | St Matthews || Hagerstown ||| 5350
107 Fairview Ave, Frederick, MD 21701-4017   H. (301) 682-6942
1956, Prospect-Marvin; 1958, Damascus: Montgomery; 1963, Poolesville; 1977, Hagerstown:
St. Matthews; 1978, Hagerstown: St. Matthews Cearfoss-Mt. Zion; 1979, Hagerstown: St.
Matthews-Mt. Zion Charge; 1985, St. Matthews; 1989, Wolfsville Charge; 1996, Retired.

Sparks, Kelly S.   RE
35 Coventry Cir E, Marlton, NJ 08053-2860
1972, West Virginia Conf; 1998, Baltimore-Washington Conf., Annapolis: Trinity; 2000, Glen
Burnie: Glen Burnie; 2011, Retired.

Spears, Susan A.   RE   BM | Union Memorial || Baltimore ||| 2320
3415 Dolfield Ave, Baltimore, MD 21215-7244   H. (410) 542-9207
holypraise@verizon.net
1991, White Marsh: Asbury; 1994, Chase: Sharp Street; 1996, Pumphrey: St John; 2010,
Lutherville: Govans-Boundary; 2010, Retired.

Spitzer, Kathy   RE   CH | Hancock || Hancock ||| 5365
340 Bennett Ln, Berkeley Springs, WV 25411-4706   H. (304) 261-2572
spitz49@frontier.com
2005, Berkley Springs: Sleepy Creek Charge; 2008, Arden: Arden; 2014, Retired.

Spong, Ian (Grant)   FL   CH | St Paul || Big Pool ||| 5125
11354 Tedrick Dr, Big Pool, MD 21711   H. (240)520-7708
grantspong@gmail.com
01-01-2011, Cumberland: Wesley; 2011, Berkeley Springs: Berkeley Springs; 2013, Big Pool:
Potomac.

Stang, Beverly C. RE   FR | Bolivar || Harpers Ferry ||| 6560
500 Pearson Cir Apt 4005, Frederick, MD 21702-3424   H. (240) 629-1957
bevo610@aol.com
1992, Boliver-Harperís Ferry Larger Parish; 1994, Urbana Charge; 1999, Germantown:
Salem; 2000, Ext. Ministry, Chaplain, Homewood at Crumland Farms; 2007, Retired.

Starkey, Robert B. PL   AN | Mount Zion || Pasadena ||| 1465   (410) 863-4888
8119 Elizabeth Rd , Pasadena, MD 21122-2208   H. (410) 903-1788
rstarkey1130@gmail.com
2010, DC: Petworth/Van Buren; 2011, DC: Mustard Seed Cooperative Parish; 2012, DC:
Randall Memorial.

Starnes, Luther W. RE   CM | Rockland || Ellicott City ||| 4255
5364 Smooth Meadow Way Unit 2, Columbia, MD 21044-1877   H. (410) 964-6410
lstartalk@aol.com
1960, Darlington; 1963, Camp Chapel; 1969, Landover Hills: Christ; 1971, Public Relations
Specialist, State of Maryland; 1974, Exec. Assist. to the Secretary, Md. Dept. of Human Res;
1978, Dir. of Pub. Info., Md. Dept. of Human Res; 1984, Retired. 2003, Ellicott City: Daniels
Gary Memorial.

Starnes, Thomas C. RE   GW | Chevy Chase || Chevy Chase ||| 9165
500 Pearson Cir Apt 2015, Frederick, MD 21702-3422   H. (302) 227-5577
starnesthomas@aol.com
1959, D.C.: Wilson, N. Car. Ave; 1960, Asst., D.C.: Capitol Hill Parish; 1961, North Harford;
1967, Bowie: St. Matthewís; 1974, Hyattsville: First; 1980, Superintendent, Washington West
Dist; 1986, D.C.: Capitol Hill; 11-1-88, Conference Council Director; 1991, Chevy Chase;
1994, Retired.

Starnes, Victoria J. FE   GW | Emmanuel || Laurel ||| 7440
37403 3rd St , Rehoboth Beach, DE 19971-3626   H. (302) 745-2278
revvicky@aol.com
1989, Boring; 1990, Scaggsville: Emmanuel; 2002, Leave of Absence; 2004, Brunswick
Charge; 01-01-2007, Brunswick: New Hope UMC of Greater Brunswick; 2010, Annapolis
Southern Region; 04-01-2013, on loan to Delaware Penisula Conference.

Statesman, Alfred E. RA
PO Box 293 , Valley Lee, MD 20692-0293   H. (301) 994-1040
statesmanalfred@yahoo.com
1969, Valley Lea: Bethesda; 1980, Lewin; 1982, Martinsburg: Mt. Zion; 2002, Retired.

Stearns, Jay E. RE
462 Cranes Roost Ct , Annapolis, MD 21409-5748   H. (410) 757-4483
1955, Attending school; 1955, PA Conference; 1961, Greenmount; 1965, PA Conference; 1969,
Brook Lane Psychiatric Center Chaplain; 1975, Pastoral Counseling Service/Consultant;
1983, Dir. P.C., Methodist Health Sys; 1987, Dir., ACPE and Past. Care; 1992, Dir. CPE-
Asbury Village; 2001, Retired.

Stetler, Richard E. RE   GW | Centenary || Flatts FL BX ||| 7615   443-951-8640
PO FL 39, Flatts, FL BX Bermuda   H. 301-576-0533
dickstetler@dickstetler.com
1966, Attending school; 1968, Cheverly; 1980, Arden; 12-1-88, D.C.: Capitol Hill; 1995,
Bowie: St. Matthewís; 2010, Retired; 01-15-2011, Bermuda: Centenary.

Stevenson, Charles RL (410) 542-3070
PO Box 1274, Owings Mills, MD 21117-1207 H. (410) 581-9382
1994, Catonsville: Mount Olivet; 1999, Lewin; 2003, Baltimore: Arlington-Lewin; 2013, Reisterstown: St Lukes.; 2016, Retired

---

Stewart, Anne R. RE AN | Friendship || Friendship ||| 1275 (410) 266-8596
6656 Highview Ter , Tracys Landing, MD 20779-2548 H. (443) 646-6643
revdranne@comcast.net
1974, Attending school; 1975, Intern Counselor and P.R. Rep. W.P.C.S; 1976, Sr. Coun., WPCS; 1989, Gaithersburg Pastoral Counseling Center, 10-3-94, Interfaith Counseling Services, Inc; 2009, Retired.

Stewart, Dawn L. FE CM | Covenant || Montgomery Village ||| 9235
12932 Sugarloaf Chapel Dr, Clarksburg, MD 20871-4397 H. (301) 848-2265
dawn.stewart@covenant-umc.org
2015, Glyndon: Glyndon; 2019, Gaithersburg: Covenant.

Stewart, Edward A. RE GW | Emory || Washington ||| 7175 (301) 567-4433
2501 Heatherwood Ct , Adelphi, MD 20783-1429 H. (301) 503-4926
esa2501@yahoo.com
1975, Va. Conf; 1977, Baltimore Conference, D.C.: Emory; 1978, D.C.: Franklin P. Nash; 1984, D.C.: Jones Memorial; 1988, Takoma Park: Grace; 1995, Superintendent, Annapolis Dist; 1998, Superintendent, Washington-Columbia Dist; 2003, Oxon Hill: St. Paul; 2008, Retired; 01-01-2014, Silver Spring: Colesville; 08-01-2014, Wheaton: Glenmont; 2-1-16, Frederick: Asbury; 2016, DC: Christ

---

Stewart, Frances W. RA GW | Metropolitan Mem || Washington ||| 7630 (202) 363-4900
2027 36th St SE , Washington, DC 20020-2419 H. (202) 803-2120
frankies2u@gmail.com
1992, Poolesville: Elijah; 2000, Damascus: DamascusFriendship; 2011, Severn: Metropolitan; 2018, DC: Metropolitan Memorial.

Stewart, Jr., Donald S. RE AN | Friendship || Friendship ||| 1275
6656 Highview Ter , Tracys Landing, MD 20779-2548 H. (443) 646-6643
annedon@comcast.net
1962, Attending school; 1964, Berkeley Springs; 1969, Attending school; 1970, Assoc. Hagerstown: John Wesley; 1971, Assoc. Damascus: Friendship; 1972, D.C.: Foundry; 1986, Gaithersburg: Epworth; 1992, Superintendent., Washington West Dist; 1999, Conference Council Director; 2004, Retired.

Stone, Gerald E. RE CM | Glen Mar || Ellicott City ||| 7365
115 Ford Dr, Westminster, MD 21157-4998 H. (410) 857-3544
GeraldStone48@gmail.com
1979, Doubs Charge; 1980, Kemptown Charge; 1982, Rockville: Faith; 1986, Hampstead: St. Johnis; 1990, Leave of Absence; 1993, Gamber: Calvary; 10/31/2005, Ext. Min., Military Leave; 01-01-2007, Military Leave; 02-01-2010, Retired.

Stone, Judith T. RL AN | Delmont || Severn ||| 1475
1279 Delmont Rd , Severn, MD 21144-1904 H. (410) 551-3535
job4215@clergy.net
1997, Severn: Delmont; 2012, Retired.

Stranathan, Malcolm   FE   FR | Westminster || Westminster |||| 4555
20 Ridge View Dr, Westminster, MD 21157-4460   H. (410) 660-6606
m.stranathan@wumcmd.org
1999, Waldorf: Lakeside; 2001, Keedysville: Salem; 2007, Highland: Mount Zion; 2015,
Westminster: Westminster; 2017, Westminster: Westminster/St. Paul.

Street, Wilhelmina   RL   CM | West Montgomery || Dickerson |||| 9580
3117 Ferndale Ave, Baltimore, MD 21207-6712   H. (443) 500-0672
kingshighway247@gmail.com
2019, Barnesville: West Montgomery; 01-01-19, Retired.

Strickler, Ann T.   RE   WE | Calvary || Waldorf |||| 8520
8524 Roundhill Rd, Charlotte Hall, MD 20622-3439   H. (301) 884-8473
pastorann1@verizon.net
2000, Bowie; 2007, Mechanicsville: Mount Zion.; 2016, Retired

---

Stroman, Dorothea B.   FE   WE | Clinton || Clinton |||| 8170   (301) 868-1281
6100 Parkview Ln, Clinton, MD 20735-3846   H. (240) 533-2744
beltstroman@gmail.com
1986, D.C.: Simpson-Hamline; 1988, Attending school; 1989, D.C.: Foundry; 1991, D.C.:
Albright Memorial; 2004, Clinton: Clinton.

Strong, Douglas M.   FE   CM | Oakdale Emory || Olney |||| 9375
3614 12th Ave W, Seattle, WA 98119   H. (206) 281-2473
dstrong@spu.edu
1979, S. N.J. Conf; 1992, Baltimore Conference, Prof. Wesley Theo. Seminary; 2007, Ext Min:
Seattle Pacific University College Ministries.

Stum, David E.   RE
2310 Lusaka Pl , Dulles, VA 20189-2310   H. (410) 997-6329
davestum44@gmail.com
1964, Attending school; 1969, Benevola Circuit; 1976, Bethesda: Bethesda; 1980, Covenant/
Washington Grove; 1985, Covenant; 1995, Gen. Bd. of Global Min; 1996, Silver Spring: Good
Shepherd. 1/1/04, Leave of Absence; 12/13/04, Ext. Min., U.S. Embassy, Nepal; 2006, Retired.

Stutler, Earl J. (Jim)   RE
1101 Pilgrim Ct , Crofton, MD 21114-1359   H. (410) 721-1817
jstutler@verizon.net
1968, West Va. Conf; 1970, Baltimore Conf. Assoc. Catonsville; 1972, Edgewater: Parkwood;
1977, Sykesville: Oakland; 1986, Sandy Mount; 2002, Davidsonville; 2010, Retired.

Suffecool, Barbara V.   FD   CH | Michaels || Berkeley Springs |||| 5540
2837 Western Pike, Hancock, MD 21750-1632   H. (301) 678-6394
SuffeBar@comcast.net
1996, Hancock: Minister of Music; 2017, Berkeley Springs: Michaels.

Sullivan, Shannon   FE   FR | Calvary || Frederick |||| 6190
6604 S Clifton Rd, Frederick, MD 21703-5838   H. (410) 937-8835
RevShannon@calvaryumc.org
2012, Forest Hill: Deer Creek; 2013, Edgewood: Presbury; 2017, Frederick: Calvary/
Centennial Mem., 01-01-18, Frederick: Calvary.

Summerhill, Diane E. RE FR | Bethesda || Sykesville |||| 4445
610 Klees Mill Rd, Westminster, MD 21157-8226   H. (410) 552-5547
Revmom34@msn.com
1984, Attending school; 1985, Emmanuel; 1987, Susquehanna Charge; 1993, Mt. Pleasant:
Mt. Pleasant Parish; 1999, Retired; 2002, Reisterstown: Mt Gilead-Patapsco; 12/01/2006,
Union Bridge: Linganore; 11/01/2012, Westminster: Zion Charge.

Summers, William S. (Scott) FL FR | Bedington || Martinsburg |||| 6520 (304) 274-2011
580 Bedington Rd, Martinsburg, WV 25404-6509   H. (240) 625-0858
revscooter65@gmail.com
1998, Little Orleans: Piney Plains; 2006, Big Pool: St Paul; 2013, Cumberland: Davis
Memorial; 12-01-2013, Cresaptown: McKendree of Potomac Park.; 2016, Bedington:
Bedington Charge

Sun, Peter K. RE CM | Bethany Korean Mission || Ellicott City |||| 4236
9417 Ashlyn Cir, Owings Mills, MD 21117-3281   H. (410) 654-2389
1967, New England Conf; 1970, N.Y. Conf; 1977, Baltimore Conference, Rockville: Korean;
1979, St. Lukeís and Korean; 1981, Bethesda: Korean Mission; 1990, Exec. Dir. National Fed.
of Asian American; 1996, Sabbatical leave; 1997, Retired.

Surber, Carissa G. PE AN | Severna Park || Severna Park |||| 1510 (410) 987-4700
925 Diggs Rd, Crownsville, MD 21032-1622   H. (443) 377-9918
csurber@severnaparkumc.org
09-01-2014, Crofton: Community-Trinity Coop Parish; 2016, Severna Park: Severna Park.

Sutton, Levon PL BM | Emanuel || Catonsville |||| 4630
3703 Buckingham Rd, Gwynn Oak, MD 21207-3814   H. (410) 299-3994
Levon_sutton@hotmail.con
2017, Catonsville: Emanuel,

Swain, Henry A. RE WE | Lanham || Lanham |||| 8290
2190 75th St N , Saint Petersburg, FL 33710-4641   H. (410) 480-1329
1964, Attending school; 1966, Accokeek: Faith; 1982, Lanham; 12-31-89, Retired.

Swecker, James FE WE | Trinity || Prince Frederick |||| 8435 (410) 535-1782
90 Church Street, Prince Frederick, MD 20678-2142   H. (410) 535-1782
jimswecker61@gmail.com
1986, So. Baltimore Parish; 1988, Williamsport: Rehoboth; 2013, Prince Frederick: Trinity.

Swift, Carolyn R. RE BS | Jarrettsville || Jarrettsville |||| 2475 (410) 692-5847
1205 McCleary Ter Apt 302, Bel Air, MD 21014-4544   H. (410) 937-6996
1977, Pennsylvania Conf; 1985, Baltimore Conference, Silver Spring: Colesville; 1989,
Washington Grove; 2001, Jarrettsville; 2004, Leave of Absence.

Synan, Carl A. RE BM | West Baltimore || Baltimore |||| 4165
505 Clinton Dr , Gastonia, NC 28054-5161   H. (704) 861-2074
1963, Wolfsville; 1965, Bd. of Evangelism; 1966, W. Ohio Conference; 1978, Pac. NW
Conference; 1982, Lonaconing; 1988, Chaplain & Dir. Ecu. Campus Min. Univ. So. Fl; 1991,
United Min. at Penn. State Univ; 2001, Wesley Memorial, 2003, Forty West Coop. Min; 2005,
West Baltimore; 2006, Retired.

Szpak, Michael P.   RE   GW | Foundry || Washington |||| 7180   (202) 637-5284
208 Franklin Ave , Silver Spring, MD 20901-4802   H. (301) 587-5949
mszpak@aflcio.org
1989, Extension Ministry, AFLCIO; 2014, Retired.

Tarpley, Reginald   FE   WE | Journey of Faith || Waldorf |||| 8550   (301) 523-9211
17010 Queen Anne Bridge Rd , Bowie, MD 20716-3437   H. (301) 249-5883
pastor.tarpley@gmail.com
*2009, DC:Albright-Petworth-Van Buren Coop Parish; 2010, Annapolis: Cecil Memorial; 2011,
Annapolis: Cecil Memorial-Mt. Calvary; 2017, Waldorf: The Journey of Faith.*

Tate, Deborah   RE   CM | Mount Zion || Olney |||| 9370   (202) 234-4128
14900 Emory Ln, Rockville, MD 20853-1650   H. (301) 460-0884
terrific03@aol.com
1984, Brookeville Charge; 2014, Extension Ministry.

Tate, Matthew P.   PE   WE | Emmanuel || Huntingtown |||| 8240
28750 Hancock Dr, Mechanicsville, MD 20659-3375
Matthewptate@gmail.com
5-1-16, Huntingtown: Emmanuel Charge.

Tavenner, Julian A.   RE   FR | Trinity || Emmitsburg |||| 6175
604 Marshview Dr Unit D, Waynesboro, PA 17268-7989   H. (717) 749-7730
jandmtav@comcast.net
*1955, Attending school; 1957, Mt. Zion-Emmanuel; 1960, Mt. Zion: Highland; 1962, Lay Hill;
1965, Havre de Grace; 1971, Westminster Parish; 1978, Coord. Rel. Act. Asbury Meth. Home,
Inc; 1986, Chaplain Adm., Asbury Village; 1992, Dir. of Dept. of Past. Care-Asbury Village;
1993, Retired.*

Tay, Stella S.   RD WE | Clinton || Clinton |||| 8170   (301) 412-7678
5303 Lorraine Dr , Temple Hills, MD 20748-2419   H. (301) 412-7678
stella.tay@hotmail.com
*6-11-94, Baltimore: Lewin; 9-30-95, Baltimore: St. Markís; 1998, Aquasco: Christ; 2001,
Oakland/ Union Coop. Parish; 1-1-06, Lothian: Union; 2014, Retired.*

Taylor, Barry L.   RL   FR | Walkersville || Walkersville |||| 6420
3075 Bayview Way , Pensacola, FL 32503-6915   H. (301) 639-4282
itisbarry@gmail.com
*1997, Union Bridge: Union Bridge; 2003, Thurmont: Catoctin Mountain Parish; 2009,
Retired; 2011, Thurmont: Mt Zion.*

Taylor, Daniel G.   RL   CH | Fairview Avenue || Cumberland |||| 5180
PO Box 688, Fort Ashby, WV 26719-0688   H. (304) 298-4876
dgtaylor@atlanticbb.net
1998, Cumberland: Melvin; 2004, Cumberland: Melvin-Fairview Ave; 2012, Retired.

Taylor, Marjorie E.   RP   GW | Faith || Rockville |||| 9410
26209 Rudale Dr , Clarksburg, MD 20871-9662   H. (301) 253-9672
mareltay@verizon.net
2003, Rockville: Faith, (Parish Nurse); 2006, Retired.

Taylor, Sandra S.   RE   WE | Good Shepherd || Waldorf ||| 8525   (202) 494-3330
4668 Duley Dr, White Plains, MD 20695-3113   H. (301) 870-7143
revsandy@comcast.net
1984, Attending school; 1985, Mt. Carmel-Mt. Tabor Charge; 1988, Severna Park; 1992, Oxon Hill: Oxon Hill; 2000, Waldorf: Lakeside; 2003, Catonsville: Trinity; 2006, Mount Harmony: Mt. Harmony/Lower Marlboro; 12-01-2013, Retired.

Taylor, Sr., John   SY   AN | Community || Pasadena ||| 1440   (410) 437-8515
1901 North Ave, Pasadena, MD 21122-3418   H. (410) 360-0934
revjet@verizon.net
2005, Assoc. Pasadena: Faith Community; 2018, Pasadena: Faith Community.

Teasdale, Mark R.   FE   CM | St James || Marriottsville ||| 4565
1004 Central Ave , Wilmette, IL 60091-2610   H. (847) 866-3954
mark.teasdale@garrett.edu
2000, Laurel: First; 2001, Rockland; 2005, Attending School; 2008, Ext Min: Garrett Theological Seminary: Assoc. Prof. of Evangelism.

Thames, Theresa S.   FE   GW | Foundry || Washington ||| 7180
172 Jonathon Dayton Ct, Princeton, NJ 08540-7693   H. (202) 746-0283
theresathames@gmail.com
2011, DC: Foundry; 2015, Cheverly: Cheverly; 3-1-16, Princeton University.

Thayer, David E.   FE   AN | St Andrews of Annapolis || Edgewater ||| 1255   (410) 266-0875
3187 Raven Ct, Annapolis, MD 21403-1626   H. 410-626-1610
revfam@aol.com
1978, Attending school; 1979, Flintstone: Union Grove Charge; 1981, Cheltenham: Cheltenham; 1989, Annapolis: St Andrews of Annapolis.

Thomas, Jr., Arthur   RE   FR | Messiah || Taneytown ||| 4475
1600 Westbrook Ave Apt 353, Richmond, VA 23227-3317   H. (240) 281-1523
1994, Reisterstown: Deer Park; 3-1-2000, Taneytown: Messiah; 2011, Bethesda: Concord-St Andrews; 2014, Manchester: Bixlers-Millers; 03-01-17, Retired.

Thomas, William G.   FE   BS | Hereford || Monkton ||| 3344   (410) 343-0660
PO Box 400 , Monkton, MD 21111-0400   H. (443) 340-7706
pastor@herefordumc.com
2011, Hereford: Hereford .

Thompson, Bruce C.   FE   AN | Pasadena || Pasadena ||| 1470
19 Berwick Ln, Bear, DE 19701-4767   H. (410) 562-2588
brucecthompson@gmail.com
1978, Attending school; 1980, Bristol: Wesley Chapel; 1984, Lauraville; 1986, Charles Town: Asbury; 1990, Lanham; 1997, Pasadena: Pasadena; 2007, Extension Ministry: Hospice of the Chesapeake; 2007, Leave of Absence.

Thompson, III, Henry C.   RE
5713 Second Ave, Baltimore, MD 21227-4308   H. (410) 242-4341
hctcbt@msn.com
1969, Fairview; 1972, North Harford; 1978, Timonium; 1980, Upper Marlboro: Bethel; 1989, Bethany; 1994, Loch Raven; 2006, Retired.

Thompson, Richard D. RE
206 Pintail Ct , Glen Burnie, MD 21060-7569   H. (410) 394-6239
dicktom@aol.com
1965, Attending school; 1967, Savage; 1970, Maryland City; 1974, Chaplain USA; 1993, Leave of Absence; 1994, Baltimore: Fulton-Siemers; 1995, Baltimore: Beechfield-Fulton Siemers Parish; 1998, Reisterstown: Emory; 09/26/01, Upperco: Emory; 2002, Aberdeen: Grace; 1/15/2005, Retired.

Thorpe, Jacqulyn B. RD   GW | Bethesda || Bethesda ||| 9122   (202) 806-0500
9303 Parkhill Ter , Bethesda, MD 20814-3962   H. (301) 530-1736
jacqulynt8@aol.com
1993, Prof. at Howard University; 2008, Retired.

Thrasher, Terrance RE   (410) 356-4085
7 Basswood Ct , Catonsville, MD 21228-5870   H. (410) 788-4674
pleasanthillumc@msn.com
1991, Melville Chapel; 1994, Catonsville: Emanuel; 8-15-99, Chase: Ebenezer; 2000, Laurel: First; 2002, Osings Mills: Pleasant Hill; 2013, Retired.

Tice, Harry K. (Kent) RE FR | Oakland || Charles Town ||| 6535   (304) 725-3737
104 Oakland Ter , Charles Town, WV 25414-4815   H. (304) 725-5233
kenttice@gmail.com
1973, Great Cacapon: Calvary-Otterbein; 1975, Assoc. College Park; 1978, Martinsburg: Friendship-Marvin Chapel, 1982, Marvin; 1985, Leave of Absence; 1986, Charles Town: Bethany-Oakland Charge; 09-19-93, Charles Town: Oakland; 01-01-18, Retired.

Tilghman, Marlon B. FE BS | Ames || Bel Air ||| 2335   (443) 629-7363
1118 Marksworth Rd , Baltimore, MD 21207-3962   H. (443) 629-7363
mintilghman@yahoo.com
2006, Glen Burnie: Solley; 2009, Pikesville: Milford Mill.; 2016, Bel Air: Ames Charge

Tillett , I, Stephen A. FE   AN | Asbury-Broadneck || Annapolis ||| 1115
1404 Saint Francis Cir, Severn, MD 21144-6821   H. (410) 320-8138
ABPASTOR@aol.com
1991, D.C.: Bradbury Heights; 1992, Bradbury Hgts./Petworth: First; 1996, Baltimore: Mt. Zion; 2004, Annapolis: Asbury-Broadneck.

Timity, Roland J. RE
1904 Sheffield Ct , Severn, MD 21144-1509   H. (410) 551-1334
1970, Oxon Hill: St. Paul; 1976, St. Paul-Westphalia Chg; 1979, Westphalia; 1983, Hanover: St. Mark; 1989, D.C.: Ryland-Epworth; 1992, Annapolis: Mt. Zion; 2005, Retired.

Tingley, Laurie FE   BS | Mays Chapel || Timonium ||| 3522
11911 Jenifer Rd , Timonium, MD 21093-7473   H. (443) 995-9215
lptingley@gmail.com
N. Carolina Conference; 2000, Arnold: Asbury; 11/08/02, Leave of Absence; 2005, Violetville; 01-01-2008, Bermuda: Centenary; 2010, Timonium: Mays Chapel.

Titcomb, Andrea RD   AN | St Andrews of Annapolis || Edgewater ||| 1255 (410) 266-0875
253 Lindenhall Ct, Riva, MD 21140-1518   H. (410) 956-6548
andytitcomb@hotmail.com
1992, Highland: Mt. Zion; 1994, Severna Park; 2006, Retired.

Tocknell, Philip FE   AN | Baldwin Memorial || Millersville ||| 1420   (410) 923-1166
929 Generals Hwy , Millersville, MD 21108-2124   H. (410) 923-2642
dltocknell@gmail.com
1988, Urbana Charge; 1992, Hampstead: Hampstead Parish; 1996, Hampstead: Greenmount;
2002, Millersville: Baldwin Memorial.

Torres, Braulio FE   AN | Calvary || Annapolis ||| 1120
1631 Elkwood Ct, Annapolis, MD 21409-5477   H. (202) 870-7656
artbyte1976@gmail.com
12-06-2009, Wheaton: Hughes; 2010, Rockville: Millian Memorial.; 2016, Annapolis: Calvary
Charge

Totten, Erin SY
729 Chestnut Hill Rd, Forest Hill, MD 21050-1716   H. (309) 221-9374
etotten0623@gmail.com
2014, Forest Hill: Deer Creek Charge

Totty, Mary Kay K. FE   GW | Dumbarton || Washington ||| 7160   (202) 333-7212
3130 O St NW, Washington, DC 20007   H. (202) 549-9897
revmktotty@yahoo.com
1989, Nebraska Conf; 1992, Baltimore Conf., Shenandoah Junction; 1996, Araby; 1998, New
Windsor: St. Paul; 2006, Providence-Fort Washington; 2009, DC: Dumbarton.

Trail, Gary W. RE   CH | Holy Cross || Ridgeley ||| 5625
PO Box 745, 46 Carpenter Ave., Ridgeley, WV 26753-0745   H. (304) 738-1054
1965, Cent. Pa. Conf; 1966, Penin. Conf; 1980, Baltimore Conf., Ridgeley: Holy Cross; 01-
01-92, Conference Approved Evangelist; 1994, Cumberland: Zion; 1996, Rawlings; 2001,
Retired; 2011, Frostburg: Frostburg.

Trail, Mary S. RE   CH | Union Chapel || Berkeley Springs ||| 5570
PO Box 745, 46 Carpenter Ave., Ridgeley, WV 26753-0745   H. (304) 738-1054
1994, Berkeley Springs: Alpine Charge; 12-01-99, Disability Leave, 2002, Holy Cross; 2004,
Retired.

Triplett, Ronald E. PE   GW | Gethsemane || Capitol Heights ||| 7320   (301) 336-1219
9900 Greenbelt Rd Ste E # 131, Lanham, MD 20706-2264   H. (410) 963-9536
pastorron@gethsemaneumc.org
2011, Oxon Hill: St. Paul/Corkran Memorial Cooperative Parish; 02-01-2013, Temple Hills:
Corkran Memorial; 01-01-2014, Temple Hills: Church of Redeemer; 2014, Temple Hills:
Temple Hills.; 2016, Capitol Heights: Gethsemane Charge

Tryon, Sam PL   FR | Bolivar || Harpers Ferry ||| 6560
300 Cormorant Pl Apt 2004, Frederick, MD 21701-1929   H. (740) 513-5582
srtryon@yahoo.com
2017, Harpers Ferry: Bolivar/Engle,

Tso, Man-King RE   GW | Dumbarton || Washington ||| 7160
mankingtso@yahoo.com
1973, Cal-Nev Conf; 1979, Baltimore Conf., Chinese Community Church; 1989, D.C.:
Dumbarton; 1990, Gen. Sec., Hong Kong Christian Council; 2001, Dir., Hong Kong
Counseling & Mediation Service; 2005, Retired.

Turnage, Patricia SY AN | Mount Calvary || Arnold |||| 1165
732 Queenstown Rd , Severn, MD 21144-1220   H. (410) 292-1823
cottonfieldcricket@gmail.com
2017, Annapolis: Cecil Memorial-Mt. Calvary,

Tzan, Douglas D. FE CM | St Pauls || Sykesville |||| 4465
6415 Tamarack Cir, Sykesville, MD 21784-7968   H. (410) 795-0940
dtzan@stpaulssykesville.org
1995, Middletown; 1998, Friendship: Friendship; 2005, Attending School; 2013, Sykesville:
Sykesville Parish.

Unger, John OF FR | Camp Hill-Wesley || Harpers Ferry |||| 6565   (304) 389-1866
1022 Williamsport Pike, Martinsburg, WV 25404-4274   H. (304) 389-1866
PastorUnger@gmail.com
2013, Bolivar: Bolivar.; 2016, Harpers Ferry: Camphill Wesley-Engle Cha

---

Upton, Dennis L. RE CH | Otterbein || Hagerstown |||| 5340
16505 Virginia Ave, Unit 1001, Williamsport, MD 21795-1426   H. (301) 223-7918
dupton94@myactv.net
1966, Attending school; 1970, Cumberland: Mapleside Melvin; 1972, Hagerstown: St.
Andrewís; 1976, Aldersgate; 1978, Bel Air; 1981, Hampstead: Grace; 1984, Brunswick: First;
11-01-89, Linganore; 1994, Hagerstown: Emmanuel; 2003, New Market; 2006, Hagerstown:
Washington Square-St. Matthewís Charge; 2007, Retired.

Upton, Wayne H. RE BM | Chase || Middle River |||| 2362   (717) 993-8074
63 Enola Dr , Stewartstown, PA 17363-8776   H. (717) 683-4523
wayneeumc@yahoo.com
1968, Keedysville: Salem; 1973, Idlewylde; 1977, Long Green Charge; 1984, Forest Hill
Parish; 1988, William Watters Memorial; 1994, Galesville; 2000, Chase: Ebenezer; 01-01-07,
Retired.

Vader, Stephanie FE GW | Emmanuel || Laurel |||| 7440   (301) 725-5200
5340 Sunny Field Ct, Ellicott City, MD 21043-8208   H. (301) 802-2582
revvader@comcast.net
1995, Attending school; 1996, Shady Side: Centenary; 2002, Scaggsville: Emmanuel.

Valentin-Castanon, Eliezer FE FR | Trinity || Frederick |||| 6225 (301) 662-2895
5108 McLauren Ln, Frederick, MD 21703-6816   H. (301) 620-8885
seniorpastor@trinityfrederick.org
1989, NY Conf; 2002, Baltimore-Washington Conf., Gen.Bd. Church & Society; 10/1/2005,
Assoc. Gen. Sect., Gen. Com. on Religion and Race; 01-01-2010, Monrovia: Mountain View-
Pleasant Grove; 2013, Frederick: Trinity.

Valentine, Kenneth RE AN | Wesley Grove || Hanover |||| 1355   (301) 401-2775
809 Chesapeake Dr, Stevensville, MD 21666-2711   H. (301) 401-2775
revksv@yahoo.com
2000, Hagerstown: John Wesley; 2006, Harmans: Wesley Grove; 2013, Upper Marlboro:
Bethel; 2018, Retired.

Van Gilder, Kirk FE GW | Foundry || Washington ||| 7180
1223 Maryland Ave NE, Washington, DC 20002-5335 H. (202) 250-2602
kirker@mac.com
1997, Christ Church of the Deaf; 1998, D.C.: Gallaudet/Deaf Spirit Mission; 2001, Pasadena: Magothy Church of the Deaf; 01/01/03, Attending School; 09-01-2011, Ext. Ministry, Gallaudet University.

---

van Vliet, Wendy R. FE AN | Davidsonville || Davidsonville ||| 1190 (410) 707-5530
152 Duval Ln , Edgewater, MD 21037-1613 H. (410) 707-5530
pastorWendyvv@gmail.com
2011, Severn: Delmont; 2012, Severn: Delmont/Severn.; 2016, Davidsonville: Davidsonville Charge

---

Vanisko, Alicia FE BS | Linden Heights || Parkville ||| 3445 (410) 668-6181
8774 Autumn Hill Dr, Ellicott City, MD 21043-5440 H. (410) 480-4717
alicialhumc@verizon.net
2008, Ellicott City: Alberta Gary Mem; 2010, Annapolis: Calvary; 2014, Carney: Linden Heights.

Vardiman, Rebecca J. RE CH | Frostburg || Frostburg ||| 5310
437 Independence St , Cumberland, MD 21502-1611 H. (301) 777-9046
rebeccavardiman@gmail.com
1992, Attending school; 1993, Ellerslie: Ellerslie; 2004, Frostburg: Frostburg; 12-01-2010, Ext. Ministry, Chaplain; 10-20-2012, Leave of Absence; 2013, Cumberland: Wesley/Mt Zion; 7.1.2017, Retired.

Venson, Mark FE WE | Ebenezer || Lanham ||| 8285 (301) 577-1926
1011 Saint Michaels Dr , Mitchellville, MD 20721-1976 H. (301) 390-7932
mdvmrk@aol.com
1987, Attending school; 1988, Columbia: Locust; 1990, Lanham: Ebenezer.

Vieth, Richard F. RE (717) 393-0654
821 Willow Valley Lakes Dr , Willow Street, PA 17584-9037 H. (717) 569-5908
RJVIETH@gmail.com
1953, Baltimore: Milton Ave; 1957, Minister to Wesley Foundation, U. of Md; 1960, Attending school; 1961, Wesley Foundation, U. of Md; 1967, Attending school; 1973, Lancaster Theological Seminary; 1993, Retired.

Vineyard, Maurice E. RE BM | Bethesda || Baltimore ||| 3145
217 Booth St Apt 111, Gaithersburg, MD 20878-5480 H. (304) 754-6077
jkvineyard@comcast.net
1962, Holston Conf; 1964, Baltimore Conf., Scaggsville: Emmanuel; 1969, Baltimore: Bethesda; 1976, Randallstown: Mt. Olive; 1988, Silver Spring: Woodside; 2000, Retired.

Vitek, Cathy PL CM | Bethany || Ellicott City ||| 4235
824 Riverside Dr, Pasadena, MD 21122-1730 H. (443) 794-8188
cathy@bethanyum.org
05-16-17, Ellicott City: Bethany,

Vollmerhausen, Shawn PL CM | Alberta Gary Memorial || Columbia ||| 7345
8820 Birchwood Way, Jessup, MD 20794-9583 H. (410) 790-5214
shawnvollmerhausen@gmail.com
2016, Columbia: Alberta Gary.

174

Voorhaar, Edward RE   WE | Chicamuxen || La Plata ||| 8260   (301) 934-2288
1006 East Patuxent Drive, La Plata, MD 20646   H. (301) 934-2485
epvoorhaar@verizon.net
1970, Cheltenham; 1972, Assoc. Annapolis: Trinity; 1974, Brookville: Mt. Carmel; 1976,
Friendship: Friendship Charge; 1990, Hagerstown: Emmanuel; 1994, West Friendship:
St. James; 9-1-2000, La Plata; 2008, Retired; 2009, Huntingtown: Emmanuel; 2012,
Chicamuxen: Chicamuxen.

Voorhaar, Richard LM   CH | Mount Zion || Great Cacapon ||| 5585
PO Box 543, Great Cacapon, WV 25422-0543   H. (304) 258-6263
dickvoorhaar@hotmail.com
2008, Great Cacapon: West Morgan Parish; 2009, Great Cacapon: Calvary; 2011, Great
Cacapon: Great Cacapon; 2016, Great Cacapon: Mt. Zion Charge.

Walker, Jr., Robert E. FE AN | Mount Zion || Pasadena ||| 1465   (410) 255-4602
3201 Carlswood Cir, Windsor Mill, MD 21244-1380   H. (410) 496-8332
rewalkerjr@gmail.com
1994, Laurel: St. Marks; 1996, Westminster: Union Street; 1999, Randallstown: Mt. Olive;
2000, Baltimore: Elderslie-St. Andrews; 9/1/04, Aquasco: Christ; 2011, Baltimore: Western
Baltimore Cooperative Parish; 01-01-2012, Baltimore: New Covenant-Emmarts; 2012,
Gambrills: Wilson/ John Wesley-Waterbury; 2014, Pasadena: Mount Zion.

Walker, Karin FE   BS | Fallston || Fallston ||| 2435   (410) 877-7255
2919 Placid Dr , Baldwin, MD 21013-9514   H. (410) 303-9200
Karin.Walker@fallstonumc.org
1987, Attending school; 1988, Cockeysville: Texas Charge; 1992, Upper Falls: Salem; 2003,
Kensington: St. Paul; 2007, District Superintendent, Baltimore; 2013, Fallston: Fallston.

Walker, Kenneth W. FE   FR | Trinity || Martinsburg ||| 6710   (304) 263-9215
600 Artisan Way, Martinsburg, WV 25401-2999   H. (304) 850-8696
pastorkenw@comcast.net
1993, Attending school; 1994, Forest Hill: Centre; 2000, Lexington Park; 2010, Frederick:
Brook Hill; 2014, Martinsburg: Trinity.

Wallace-Penn, Yvonne FE GW | First || Hyattsville ||| 7385   (301) 927-6133
PO Box 1725, Hyattsville, MD 20788-0725   H. 410-221-8893
pastorp@fumchy.org
2015, Hyattsville: First.

Walton, Derrick K. PL   WE | Mount Zion || Saint Inigoes ||| 8450
20565 Pershing Dr, Lexington Park, MD 20653-5253   H. (240) 538-3709
pastordmtzion@gmail.com
2013, St Inigoes: Mt Zion.

Wamble, Marvin R. FE   AN | St Matthews || Shady Side ||| 1520   (410) 867-7661
12005 Ishtar St , Fort Washington, MD 20744-6058   H. (202) 439-3226
marvelousworks1@gmail.com
2007, Newburg: Shiloh Community; 2010, Newburg: Shiloh Community-St. Matthewis; 2013,
Lusby: Lusby.; 2016, Shady Side/Lothian: South County Chg.

Ward, Ronald L. RE
103 Mystic Woods Ln , Severna Park, MD 21146-1232   H. (410) 647-5990
rlwgoodshepherd@aol.com
1981, DC: Petworth; 1987, Severna Park: Asbury-Town Neck; 2009, Retired; 01-01-2011, Bel
Air: Ames.

Ward, Ruth A. RE   FR | Weller || Thurmont ||| 6365
26 Lantern Ln , Shippensburg, PA 17257-8769   H. (717) 377-6444
1980, Louisville Conf; 1982, Baltimore Conf., D.C.: Foundry; 1984, Norrisville: Norrisville-
Ayres Chapel; 4/1/88, Westlake Mission: Susanna Wesley; 1990, Pikesville: Sudbrook; 1992,
Pikesville Parish; 1994, Pikesville: Ames-Sudbrook; 1998, Thurmont: Weller; 2006, Retired.

Warehime, Jr., William H. RE   FR | Calvary || Frederick ||| 6190   (410) 259-3301
1020 Eastbourne Ter, Frederick, MD 21702-5115   H. (410) 259-3301
apastorbill@gmail.com
1997, New Windsor: Pipe Creek Charge; 2000, Emmitsburg: Tomís Creek; 2006, Chewsville:
Bethel; 2012, Hagerstown: John Wesley; 01-01-2014, Retired; 01-01-2015, New Windsor:
Middleburg-Uniontown; 2015, Western Region Resource Person.

Warehime, Linda A. RE   FR | Brook Hill || Frederick ||| 6185
1020 Eastbourne Ter, Frederick, MD 21702-5115   H. (301) 639-4966
lindawarehime@myactv.net
2006, Frederick: Brook Hill,; 2012, Chewsville: Bethel.; 2016, Retired

---

Warner, James M. RE
161 E Beach Rd # A, Charlestown, RI 02813-1602   H. (401) 322-7675
1960, South Iowa Conf; 1967, Baltimore Conf., Rockville; 1972, Woodfield: Wesley Grove;
1976, Towson; 1995, Millersville: Baldwin Memorial; 1999, Retired.

Warner, Timothy B. FE   CM | Emory Grove || Gaithersburg ||| 9240   (301) 926-9024
17105 Laburnum Ct, Rockville, MD 20855-2504   H. (301) 216-0982
warner.tb@gmail.com
2005, Boyds: St. Marks; 2008, Montgomery County Executive Office Community Partnerships;
08-01-2013, Gaithersburg: Emory Grove .; 2016, Rockville: Mill Creek Parish

---

Warrell, Doris E. FD   GW | Dumbarton || Washington ||| 7160   (202) 722-2280
743 Hamilton St NW , Washington, DC 20011-4031   H. (000) 000-0000
dew818@rcn.com
2004, D.C. Campaign to Prevent Teen Pregnancy; 11-09-2009, PT-Field Dir Middle East
Peace, PT-Bright Stars Bethlehem.

Warren, John FE   WE | Brookfield || Brandywine ||| 8370   (240) 681-3532
621 Connaught Ct., Upper Marlboro, MD 20772   H. (301) 627-4834
johncwarren@att.net
1980, Martinsburg: Mt. Zion, 1982, Baltimore: Mt. Zion; 08-01-88, D.C.: Simpson-Hamline;
1998, Columbia: St. Johnís; 2000, Oxon Hill; 2008, Bethesda: Concord-St Andrews; 2011,
DC: Mustard Seed Cooperative Parish; 2013, DC: McKendree-Simms-Brookland Cooperative
Ministry Parish; 01-01-17, DC: McKendree-Simms-Brookland, 2018, Brandywine: Brookfield
Immanuel.

Watson, Harold W.   RE
3236 Pope St SE , Washington, DC 20020-2318   H. (202) 584-1813
bighwwatson@aol.com
1976, Huntingtown Charge; 1980, Silver Spring: Woodside; 1982, DC: Congress Heights;
1988, D.C.: Franklin P. Nash; 12-1-94, Indian Head: Metropolitan; 2000, Retired.

Watson, Jr., Herbert   FE   AN | St Mark || Hanover ||| 1350   (410) 859-5352
138 Wesley Ave, Catonsville, MD 21228-3142   H. (410) 747-5835
pastorstmarkumc@gmail.com
1978, Attending school; 1979, Baltimore: Caroline Street; 1982, DC: Asbury; 1984, Dundalk:
St. Matthewís; 1990, Baltimore: Christ; 1996, Hanover: St. Mark.

Watson, Patricia S.   FE   WE | First Saints Community Church || Leonardtown ||| 8540
44945 Voyage Path Apt 2, California, MD 20619-2476   H. (240) 808-4207
pastortrish@firstsaints.org
2007, Indiana Conference; 2007, Keedysville: South Mountain; 2009, Berkeley Springs: Union
Chapel; 2012, Cockeysville: Epworth.; 2016, Leonardtown: First Saints Community Char

---

Watts, Warren W.   RE   FR | Calvary || Martinsburg ||| 6655   (304) 263-6205
220 W Burke St , Martinsburg, WV 25401-3322   H. (304) 754-8557
watts2341@comcast.net
1963, Piney Plains; 1964, Harperís Ferry: Camp Hill; 1966, Arden; 1969, Cumberland:
Trinity; 1972, Baltimore: Messiah; 1973, Keedysville: Salem; 1977, Ext. Ministry, WPCS;
1983, Ext. Ministry, Tri-County Pastoral Counseling Service; 2008, Retired.

Ways, Franklin L.   RE
12300 Surrey Circle Dr , Ft Washington, MD 20744-6244   H. (301) 292-4063
Highlandtown: Wesley; 1988, Jarrettsville; 1991, Accokeek: Faith; 1994, Camp Springs: Bells;
2001, Leave of Absence; 2002, Pikeside; 2004, Retired.

Weaver, Kendrick   FE   WE | Union || Upper Marlboro ||| 8490   (301) 627-7389
14324 Colonel Clagett Ct, Upper Marlboro, MD 20772-2900   H. (301) 627-1461
pastorkdweaver@gmail.com
2004, Bowie: Saint Matthews; 2007, Glenn Dale: Glenn Dale; 2009, Upper Marlboro: Union.

Webb, Nancy   RE   BM | Grace || Baltimore ||| 3170   (410) 433-6650
5203 Catalpha Rd , Baltimore, MD 21214-2102   H. (410) 444-7222
revnjwebb@gmail.com
1977, Jefferson County Coop. Par; 1980, Baltimore: Remington-Woodberry Parish; 1987,
Woodberry; 1988, Sabbatical leave; 1989, New Windsor: St. Paul; 1992, Baltimore: Elderslie-
St. Andrews; 1998, D.C.: Foundry; 2005, Baltimore: Grace; 2012, Retired.

Webner, Clifford   RE   BS | Perry Hall || Baltimore ||| 2535   H. (410) 788-3362
CLIFFWEBNER@gmail.com
1989, Mt. Airy: Taylorsville Charge; 1993, Savage; 1999, Rt. 32, Howard Co. New Church
Start; 11-1-00, Extension Ministry; 2001, Dundalk: Patapsco; 2003, Upper Falls: Salem;
2011, Baltimore: Loch Raven; 2017, Retired.

Weitzel, George H.   RE   BS | Chesaco || Baltimore ||| 2545   (410) 668-5665
11938 White Heather Rd, Cockeysville, MD 21030-1991   H. (410) 790-2828
georgeweitzel@gmail.com
1997, Glen Burnie: Messiah; 2008, Retired.; 5-1-16, Rosedale: Chesaco Charge

---

Welch, Edwin H. RE   CH | Centre Street || Cumberland ||| 5155
1910 Kanawha Ave SE, Charleston, WV 25304-1020   H. (304) 343-3946
edwinwelch@ucwv.edu
1966, Attending school; 1971, Assoc. Prof. West Va. Wesleyan; 1976, Prof. of Sociology,
Lebanon Valley College, 1981, Dean, Lakeland College; 1982, VP Acad. Aff. & Dean,
Wartburg College; 1989, President, Univ. of Charleston, W.Va; 2015, Retired.

Weller, Jean J. RP   CM | Glen Mar || Ellicott City ||| 7365
10869 Hilltop Ln, Columbia, MD 21044-3722   H. (410) 964-5681
jweller123@comcast.net
2003, Baltimore Southwest Charge; 2006, Olive Branch-Good Shepherd; 04-16-2007, Leave of
Absence; 2012, Retired.

Welliver, Kenneth B. RE
3112 Gracefield Rd Apt 422, Silver Spring, MD 20904-1870   H. (304) 472-1624
1952, Attending school; 1959, Prof. Natl. College; 1964, Prof. W.Va. Wesleyan College; Dean,
W. Va. Wesleyan College; 1997, Retired.

Wellman, Robert RE   FR | Oakland || Sykesville ||| 4275   (410) 861-5788
1932 Carrollton Rd, Finksburg, MD 21048-1133   H. (410) 622-5558
bobwellman@comcast.net
1976, W. Pa. Conf; 1992, Baltimore Conf., Mt. Pleasant Parish; 04-23-93, Leave of Absence;
1994, Martinsburg: St. Lukeis; 1997, Woodfield: Wesley Grove; 12-09-00, Leave of Absence;
2006, Cumberland: Davis Memorial; 2013, Sandy Mount: Sandy Mount; 2018, Retired, 2018,
Sykesville: Oakland.

Wentz, David RE   AN | Trinity || Annapolis ||| 1155
1240 County Road K A, Hartshorn, MO 65479-9600
davidnwentz@gmail.com
1983, Mt. Airy: Prospect-Marvin Charge; 9-11-84, Accokeek: Faith; 1991, Pasadena:
Magothy; 2001, Mitcheville: Mt. Oak; 2007, Annapolis: Trinity; 2015, Retired

---

Werner, Jr., Leslie E. RE
1604 Farnborn St , Crofton, MD 21114-1518   H. (410) 793-0756
1957, Idlewylde; 1958, Attending school; 1961, Director, Protestant Chaplain Eastern Shore
State Hosp; 1965, Staff Chaplain, St. Elizabethis Hosp; 1969, Dir., Chaplaincy Services,
Baltimore City Hosp; 1974, Exec. Dir. Pas. Counseling Ctrs. of Greater Baltimore; 1990,
Good Shepherd Past. Counseling Ctr; 1995, Baldwin Memorial Pastoral Counseling Ctr;
1996, Glen Burnie: Marley-Solley Charge; 2004, Retired.

Werts, Dana L. FE   FR | Brook Hill || Frederick ||| 6185   (301) 662-1727
PO Box 2938, Westminster, MD 21158-7938   H. (240) 651-5178
dwerts@bhumc.org
2012, Frederick: Brook Hill.

West, Timothy FE   WE | Westphalia || Upper Marlboro ||| 8510   (301) 735-9373
14860 Augusta Classic Pl, Hughesville, MD 20637-2422   H. (301) 274-9165
tweststeps@aol.com
1992, Glen Burnie: John Wesley; 1998, Upper Marlboro: Westphalia.

Whalen, Jr., Joseph   FE   GW | Marsden First || Smith ||| 7610
1 South Breakers Road, Smiths, HS01   H. 441-293-7045
jfwhalen73@link.bm
9/1/01, Baltimore-Washington Conf., Gen. Bd. of Global Min.: Bermuda: Marsden Memorial;
2003, Bermuda: Marsden First.

White, Ed   SY   FR | Memorial || Summit Point ||| 6755
1628 Greenfield Rd, Adamstown, MD 21710-8707   H. (610) 427-3883
pastored@hopemtcarmel.org
2019, Summit Point: Memorial.

White, Stephen R.   RL   CM | Wesley Freedom || Eldersburg ||| 4225
131 Saddletop Dr, Taneytown, MD 21787-1547   H. (410) 795-4366
1998, Mt. Airy: Howard Chapel-Pridgeville; 2002, Monrovia: Mountain View; 2006, Mt Airy:
Taylorsville; 2008, Retired.

Whiting, Robert G.   RL
10635 Breezewood Dr , Woodstock, MD 21163-1312   H. (410) 465-5467
rgwhiting@verizon.net
2002, Finksburg: Mt Zion; 2006, Retired; 2008, Upperco: Boring.

Wicklein, Jarrett   RE   BS | Salem || Hampstead ||| 3340   (410) 374-2421
316 Kimrick Pl , Timonium, MD 21093-2945   H. (410) 561-7555
jwicklein@verizon.net
1966, Morgan; 1969, Assoc. Millian Memorial; 1972, Middletown; 1981, Arnolia; 1992,
Riderwood: Huntis Memorial; 1996, Baltimore: Mt. Vernon Place; 2006, Retired.

Wiggins, Alfreda   RE   BM | St Luke || Baltimore ||| 4155
27 Deep Powder Ct , Woodstock, MD 21163-1110   H. (410) 922-4408
dralw124@aol.com
1981, Attending school; 1982, Hereford Charge; 1983, Baltimore: Christ Edmondson, 01-01-
95, Baltimore: John Wesley; 2011, Retired; 2012, Baltimore: St Luke.

Wiles, T. B. (Brent)   SY   CH | Holy Cross || Ridgeley ||| 5625
126 Wempe Dr, Cumberland, MD 21502-4224   H. (240) 920-8805
brent@tomwiles.com
2018, Ridgeley: Holy Cross.

Wilkerson, Faith   FE   WE | Mt Harmony-Lower Marlboro || Owings ||| 8365
                                                                  (410) 326-8400
155 E Mount Harmony Rd, Owings, MD 20736-3442   H. (410) 257-2761
revfaithlewis@yahoo.com
2004, D.C.: Metropolitan Memorial; 2006, Washington: Greater Metropolitan Charge, Assoc;
2008, Lusby: Olivet; 2014, Mount Harmony: Mt Harmony-Lower Marlboro.

Wilkins-Arnold, Meredith A.   FE   AN | Trinity || Annapolis ||| 1155   (410) 268-1776
1910 Dulany Pl, Annapolis, MD 21409-6221   H. (240) 298-7068
gracetrumpsworks@gmail.com
2010, Solomons: Solomons; 2016, Annapolis: Calvary Charge; 2019, Annapolis: Trinity.

Williams, Daryl FE   WE | St Paul || Oxon Hill ||| 8385
12621 Spriggs Request Ct, Bowie, MD 20721-2512   H. (301) 445-2091
Revdlw@gmail.com
2005, Baltimore-Washington Conf., Dir. Investments and Planned Giving; 01-01-2007,
Director, UM Foundation; 01-01-2008, Executive Director, UM Foundation; 01-01-2009,
Upper Marlboro: Nottingham-Myers; 2011, Upper Marlboro: New Hope Fellowship; 2014,
Oxon Hill: St. Paul.

Williams, Gertie T. RP   CM | Daisy || Woodbine ||| 9490
8490 Thomas Williams Way, Columbia, MD 21045-2482   H. (410) 461-1155
ladirev4@gmail.com
1998, Takoma Park: Grace; 07-15-01, New Windsor: Strawbridge; 2004, Retired; 2017,
Woodbine: Daisy.

Williams, Jeremiah G.   RE BM | Metropolitan || Baltimore ||| 2220
2106 Cedar Circle Dr , Baltimore, MD 21228-3747   H. (410) 455-6079
jwill34007@verizon.net
1984, Strawbridge; 1987, Garrison Blvd; 1994, Baltimore: Metropolitan; 2011, Retired.

Williams, John H. RE
561 Pinnacle Dr, Haines City, FL 33844-6318   H. (410) 610-9097
williams_johnh@yahoo.com
1969, Bristol: Wesley Chapel; 1974, Solomons Charge; 1980, Cumberland: Centre St; 1987,
McKendree; 1988, Centre St.; 1989, Laurel: First; 1993, Superintendent, Cumberland-
Hagerstown Dist; 1998, Retired.

Williams, Maceo M. RE   BM | Union Memorial || Baltimore ||| 2320   (410) 448-2312
3511 Lynchester Rd , Baltimore, MD 21215-7414   H. (410) 367-5365
Peninsula-Delaware Conf; 1995, Baltimore: M. L. King, Jr. Memorial; 2010, Retired.

Williams, Mamie A. RE   GW | Lincoln Park || Washington ||| 7215
3703 Stoneybrook Rd, Randallstown, MD 21133-4134   H. (410) 655-2769
MAW813@aol.com
1976, Attending school; 1977, D.C.: Calvary; 1982, Baltimore: Centennial; 1985, Centennial
Caroline St. Charge; 1988, DC: Hughes Memorial; 1998, Superintendent, Annapolis Dist;
2005, Exec. Dir. NEJ Multi-Ethnic Center; 2007, Annapolis: Fowler; 2009, Glen Burnie: John
Wesley; 2014, Germantown: Trinity; 1-1-2015, Medical Leave; 2019, Retired.

Williams, Perry RE   GW | University || College Park ||| 7340   (301) 422-1400
St. Paul's Umc, Shawnee, OK 74801   H. (301) 422-1400
p.l.w.342@gmail.com
2003, Baltimore-Washington Conf., Lusby: St. Paul; 2004, Eldersburg: Wesley Freedom; 2007,
College Park: University; 06-01-2013, On loan to Oklahoma Annual Conference.

Williams, Terri SY   BM | Epworth Chapel || Baltimore ||| 4170   (443) 850-1659
4019 Offutt Rd, Randallstown, MD 21133-3300   H. (443) 850-1659
terrikw1@aol.com
2019, Baltimore: Epworth Chapel.

180

Wilson, Heath FE   FR | Toms Creek || Emmitsburg ||| 6170   (410) 758-7707
16252 Toms Creek Church Rd, Emmitsburg, MD 21727-8437   H. (410) 758-7707
HWilsonVT@gmail.com
08-01-2008, Prince Frederick: Trinity; 2014, Emmitsburg: Toms Creek Charge

Wilson, Julie FD   FR | Mt Airy || Taylorsville ||| 4485   (301) 662-1464
16252 Toms Creek Church Rd, Emmitsburg, MD 21727-8437   H. (410) 758-7705
JMW1976@gmail.com
2011, Ext. Ministry: Board of Church and Society; 2013, Prince Frederick: Trinity; 2014,
Frederick: Calvary/Centennial Memorial Cooperative Parish; 01-01-18, Frederick: Calvary,
01-01-18, Frederick: Centennial Memorial; 2019, Mt Airy: Taylorsville.

Wilson, Lynn L. FL   FR | Calvary || Martinsburg ||| 6655   (304) 267-4542
53 Adelade Cir , Harpers Ferry, WV 25425-6949   H. (304) 728-7530
pastorlynnumc@comcast.net
2003, Urbana: Flint Hill; 2005, Frederick: Trinity; 2016, Martinsburg: Calvary Charge

Wilson, Shawn M. FE   BS | Pleasant Hill || Owings Mills ||| 4370 (240) 683-5530
10816 Gulfstream Ct, Damascus, MD 20872-2163   H. (413) 237-6331
swivwi@aol.com
2011, Gaithersburg: Goshen; 2017, Owings Mills: Pleasant Hill.

Wingeier-Rayo, Diana OE GW | Hughes || Wheaton ||| 9480   (512) 806-4667
9714 Admiralty Dr, Silver Spring, MD 20910-1401   H. (512) 806-4667
djuliawingeier50@gmail.com
2018, Wheaton: Hughes,

Winkfield, George FE   BM | Loch Raven || Baltimore ||| 3540
835 Braeside Rd , Baltimore, MD 21229-2116   H. (410) 788-3362
pastorwinkfield@gmail.com
2010, Abingdon: John Wesley; 2012, Woodlawn: Emmarts; 2017, Baltimore: Loch Raven.

Wirkus, Lisa A. FE   CH | Pleasant Walk || Hagerstown ||| 6430
982 Kasinof Ave, Hagerstown, MD 21742-4606   H. (240) 329-4232
deafumcpastor@gmail.com
2008, Smithsburg: Mount Bethel; 2009, Pasadena: Magothy Church Deaf-Gallaudet; 2013,
Extension Ministry; 09-01-2013, Peninsula-Delaware Conference.; 2016, Myersville: Pleasant
Walk; 2016, Thurmont: Mt. Zion

Wogaman, John P. RE   GW | Foundry || Washington ||| 7180
3126 Gracefield Rd Apt 213, Silver Spring, MD 20904-5825   H. (202) 363-1242
jpwogaman@aol.com
1955, Pac. and SW Conf; 1962, Cal.-Nev. Conf; 1969 E. Pa. Conf; 1977, Baltimore Conf.,
Dean, Professor of Christian Ethics, Wesley Theological Seminary; 1992, D.C.: Foundry;
2002, Retired.

Wolfe, Charles E. RE   BM | Mount Washington-Aldersgate || Baltimore ||| 3220
5151 Buffalo Speedway Apt 4333, Houston, TX 77005-4300   H. (410) 857-1011
1978, Shiloh-Dover Charge; 1986, Baltimore: Mt. Washington; 1991, Libertytown: Liberty
Charge; 1994, Retired.

Womack, Owen B. RE FR | Middleway || Kearneysville ||| 6635
6 Gibson Road, Inwood, WV 25428   H. (304) 229-6214
owenwomack@frontier.com
1956, Glen Burnie: Solley; 1958, Baltimore: Exeter Memorial; 1961, Maryland Line; 1964, Bel Air: Mt. Zion; 1970, Charles Town: Asbury; 1973, Martinsburg: Calvary; 1988, West Baltimore; 1990, Hampstead: St. Johns; 1994, Berkeley Springs: First; 2000, Retired; 10-01-2014, Middleway: Middleway.

Wood, Chris A. FE WE | The Journey of Faith Church || Waldorf ||| 8550
120 N State St , Dover, DE 19901-3835   H. (302) 736-2316
1988, West Va. Conf; 1989, Baltimore Conf; Westminster; 1992, LaVale; 1993, Waldorf: Lakeside; 2000, Ext. Ministry, Mission West Virginia, Inc.; 01-01-2008, Wesley College: Vice President for Institutional Advancement.

Wood, Jr., Daniel FL BM | Grace || Baltimore ||| 3170   (410) 433-6650
413 Lyman Ave, Baltimore, MD 21212-3512   H. (803) 295-8445
dcwood.jr@gmail.com
2018, Baltimore: Grace,

Wood, Jane RE GW | Rockville || Rockville ||| 9440
23 Martins Ln, Rockville, MD 20850-1853   H. (240) 393-0991
revjanewood@verizon.net
1996, Boyds: St Marks; 1998, Lusby: St Paul; 2003, Rockville: Jerusalem-Mt Pleasant; 2011, Columbia: Locust; 2019, Retired.

Wood-Powe, Sherri E. FE GW | Oak Chapel || Silver Spring ||| 9460 (301) 598-0000
12617 Falconbridge Dr, North Potomac, MD 20878-3412   H. (301) 123-4567
pastorsewp@gmail.com
2013, College Park: University; 2019, Silver Spring: Oak Chapel.

Woodrow, Kathryn T. FE CM | Damascus || Damascus ||| 9190   (301) 253-0022
441 Bostwick Ln, Gaithersburg, MD 20878-1933   H. (301) 330-2161
kathryn.woodrow@damascusumc.org
1987, Attending school; 1989, Colesville; 1991, Baltimore: Mt. Washington; 1994, Baltimore: HWR-Mt. Washington Parish; 1996, Leave of Absence; 1999, Frederick: Calvary; 2007, Rockville: Faith; 2018, Damascus: Damascus.

Worrel, Mary K. RE BM | Hampden || Baltimore ||| 3175
1080 E 33rd St Apt 211, Baltimore, MD 21218-3785   H. (410) 889-1537
revworrel@msn.com
1999, Baltimore: Aldersgate/Strawbridge; 2006, Myersville: Mt. Zion; 2014, Retired.

Wray, Edwin M. RE
2600 Croasdaile Farm Pkwy Apt A360, Durham, NC 27705-1302   H. (919) 384-2812
edwinwray50@gmail.com
1960, Greater NJ Conference; 1963, Attending school; 1966, Assoc. Milford Mill; 1972, Cumberland: Emmanuel; 1983, Martinsburg: St. Lukeís; 2-01-92, Glyndon Parish; 2001, Retired.

Wright, Arthuree R. RD GW | Gethsemane || Capitol Heights ||| 7320 (202) 345-6269
2203 Durbin Ct , Bowie, MD 20721-2817   H. (301) 925-7886
arthureewright@gmail.com
1996, Associate Director for Information, Howard University Libraries; 2018, Retired.

Wright, Daniel   RE   FR | St Lukes || Martinsburg ||| 6690
695 Aqueduct Avenue, Martinsburg, WV 25404   H. (304) 671-3575
danwright1949@gmail.com
1995, Baltimore: Grace; 1996, Berkeley Springs: Cherry Run; 2001, Cumberland: Davis Memorial; 2004, Cumberland: Christ; 2005, Berkeley Springs: Francis Asbury; 06-01-2009, Leave of Absence; 2014, Retired; 2014, Ganotown: Ganotown.

Wright, II, Harold (Chip)   RE
408 Halsey Rd, Annapolis, MD 21401-3221   H. (301) 639-6199
revhbw2@aol.com
1976, Attending school; 1977, Upperco: Emory Charge; 1980, Mt. Carmel-New Market Charge; 1985, Washington Grove: Washington Grove; 1989, Frederick: Trinity; 2010, Annapolis: Calvary.; 2016 Retired

---

Wright, Jr., Obie   RE   GW | Gethsemane || Capitol Heights ||| 7320
2203 Durbin Ct , Bowie, MD 20721-2817   H. (301) 925-7886
obiewright@verizon.net
1986, D.C.: Community-Mt. Vernon; 1987, D.C.: Mt. Vernon; 1989, Rockville Charge; 1990, Rockville: Jerusalem-Mt. Pleasant; 1994, D.C.: Ryland-Epworth; 2003, Incapacity Leave; 2009, Retired.

Wright, Kevin   FE   GW | Foundry || Washington ||| 7180
490 Riverside Dr, New York, NY 10027-5706   H. (980) 322-6389
kevinwright@gmail.com
10-01-2013, DC: Converge Charge; 3-9-15, Ext. Ministry, Riverside Church, New York.

Wright, Marion M. (Monroe)   RE   GW | United || Washington ||| 7275
1331 C St NE, Washington, DC 20002-6466
lanhamumc@msn.com
1980, Manchester Charge; 1982, Millers; 1983, Attending school; 1987, So. N.E. Conf.; 1993, Cumberland: Grace; 1994, Cumberland: E. Cumberland Mult. Chg. Parish: First/Grace; 1995, Cumberland: Grace; 1996, Laytonsville: St. Paul; 2000, Myersville: Mt. Zion; 2002, Lanham; 2009, DC: United; 2012, Retired.

Wright, Rebecca A.   FE   BS | Wesley || Hampstead ||| 4330   (615) 598-1414
PO Box 821 , Sewanee, TN 37375-0821   H. (615) 598-5134
rwright@sewanee.edu
1974, Attending school; 1976, Sleepy Creek Charge; 1978, Hampstead: Wesley; 1981, Attending school; 1988, So. N. E. Conf.; 1990, Ext. Ministry, Asst. Prof. of Old Testament, Univ. of the South.

Wunderlich, III, John M.   FE   (410) 309-3444
616 Hunting Ridge Dr, Frederick, MD 21703-2218   H. (301) 997-5810
jwunderlich@bwcumc.org
1992, Westminster: St. James/Stone Chapel; 1995, Eldersburg: Wesley Freedom; 2001, Frederick: Christ-Ballenger Creek; 2008, Leonardtown: First Saints Community; 2019, BWC: Cumberland-Hagerstown District Superintendent.

Yarbrough, Catharine A. (Anne)   RE
PO Box 1544 , Shelburne, NS   H. (902) 874-0346
anne.yarbrough@gmail.com
1987, Deale: Chesapeake Charge; 1988, Kensington: St. Paulis; 1995, Germantown: Trinity; 2000, D.C.: St. Lukeis; 2005 Leave of Absence; 12-31-2008, Retired.

Yarrow, Linda S. PE BS | Jarrettsville || Jarrettsville ||| 2475
1727 W. Jarrettsville Rd, Jarrettsville, MD 21084 H. (240) 429-1376
lindayarrow.church@gmail.com
 05-01-2012, Laytonsville: Mt Tabor; 2012, Damascus: North Damascus Cooperative Parish; 2013, Damascus: South Damascus.; 2016, Street: Dublin-Darlington Charge; 2019, Jarrettsville: Jarrettsville-Ayres.

Yates, Jr., Leo A. FD GW | Emmanuel || Laurel ||| 7440 (443) 991-3795
7612 Harmons Farm Ct, Hanover, MD 21076 H. (443) 991-3795
leoyjr@aol.com
2013, Frederick: Calvary/Centennial Memorial Cooperative Parish.; 1-1-16, Frederick: Calvary / Centennial Memorial

---

Yocum, Carol C. RE CM | Damascus || Damascus ||| 9190
109 Troon Cir , Mount Airy, MD 21771-5002 H. (301) 829-4822
carolyocum@msn.com
1973, Detroit Conference; Baltimore Conf; 1975, Harperís Ferry Parish; 1977, Thurmont: Weller-Deerfield Charge; 1986, Mt. Airy: Calvary; 2005, Reisterstown: Reisterstown; 07-13-2009, Reisterstown: Reistertown-Pleasant Grove Coop Parish; 2011, Retired.

Yocum, Dennis E. RE CM | Damascus || Damascus ||| 9190
109 Troon Cir , Mount Airy, MD 21771-5002 H. (301) 829-4822
dyocum9236@aol.com
1973, Cent. Pa. Conf; 1976, Lewistown: Lewistown Charge; 1984, Thurmont: Weller-Deerfield Charge; 1986, Mt. Airy: Calvary; 2012, Retired.

Yost, John R. RE FR | St Lukes || Martinsburg ||| 6690 (304) 263-2788
812 Honeysuckle Dr, Martinsburg, WV 25401-9223 H. (304) 267-6234
pastorjohnyost@comcast.net
 1982, Martinsburg: Sleepy Creek Charge; 1985, Shenandoah Junction: Shenandoah Junction Charge; 1988, Hagerstown: John Wesley; 1991, Martinsburg Enlarged Charge; 2002, Martinsburg: St. Lukes; 2017, Retired.

Young, David J. FD GW | Foundry || Washington ||| 7180 (703) 786-0352
2507 N Jefferson St , Arlington, VA 22207-1447 H. (703) 786-0352
dndweiszyoung@yahoo.com
1997, Specialty, Church and Society; 1998, Ext. Ministry, Foreign Service: Hanoi; 2003, U.S. State Dept.

Young, Jacob FE WE | Emmanuel || Beltsville ||| 7310
11421 Emack Rd, Beltsville, MD 20705-2625 H. (410) 903-0085
hajunlove@gmail.com
 1999, Washington Korean Mission; 2001, Christ Church of Baltimore Co; 2004, Catonsville; 2009, Manchester: Bixlers-Millers; 2014, Beltsville: Emmanuel; 05-01-18.

Young, Jean S. RE CM | Epworth || Gaithersburg ||| 9245
518 School Ln, Rehoboth Beach, DE 19971-1802 H. (302) 227-4097
revjsy@aol.com
1978, Attending school; 1980, Brentwood; 1983, Laytonsville: St. Paul; 1986, Superintendent, Washington West Dist; 1992, Gaithersburg: Epworth; 1996, Disability Leave; 2002, Retired.

Young, Jr., Thomas E.   FE AN | Friendship || Friendship ||| 1275
6754 Old Solomons Island Rd , Friendship, MD 20758-9704   H. (240) 522-2038
youngtrumpet5@gmail.com
1980, Berkeley Springs: Morgan Charge; 1981, Cumberland: Calvary; 1985, Rohrersville Charge; 1987, Mount Savage; 1991, Hagerstown: Grace; 1994, Brunswick Coop. Parish; 1996, Dundalk: Patapsco; 2001, Mayo; 2004, Martinsburg: Pikeside; 2008, Ridgeley: Ridgeley; 2014, Cumberland: Blue Bridge Coop Parish; 2018, Friendship: Friendship.

Young, Judy S.   RE   CM | Covenant || Montgomery Village ||| 9235
196 Longstreet Dr, Gettysburg, PA 17325-8920   H. (717) 398-2195
jsmithyoung@gmail.com
2004, Mill Creek Parish associate; 2006, Washington Grove; 2014, Leave of Absence; 12-01-17, Retired.

Young, Mark C.   FE   BS | Fallston || Fallston ||| 2435   (704) 799-0105
155 Queens Cove Rd , Mooresville, NC 28117-9609   H. (704) 799-7805
myoung@wellhavencounseling.com
1978, Attending school; 1981, Fallston: Ebenezer; 1989, Attending school; 1991, Pastoral Coun. Sub. Past. Coun. Clinic; 8-1-94, Homestead Pastoral Counseling Service; 3/20/2006, Leave of Absence.

Young, Ronald   PL   CM | St Luke || Sykesville ||| 4460   (240) 361-4007
9341 Chadburn Pl, Montgomery Village, MD 20886-4033   H. (301) 977-6740
pastorrony44@gmail.com
2016, Glenwood: Growing Seed Coop Min.; 2018, Sykesville: St Luke.

Yunger, Dottie   FE   WE | Solomons || Solomons ||| 8470   (410) 326-3278
14454 Solomons Island RdPO Box 403, Solomons, MD 20688-0403   H. (202) 674-7788
patuxentpastor@gmail.com
2013, DC: Metropolitan Memorial Parish.; 2016, Solomons: Solomons Charge

Zalatoris, Jeff   FE   FR | Harmony || Falling Waters ||| 6640
606 S Raleigh St, Martinsburg, WV 25401-2144   H. (681) 260-2772
jzalatoris1@gmail.com
2018, Lewistown: Lewistown, 2019, Marlowe: Harmony,

Zirlott, Cynthia I.   OD   CH | Frostburg || Frostburg ||| 5310   (301) 687-7490
100 Braddock St, Unit 308, Frostburg, MD 21532-2479   H. (540) 303-2309
c.zirlott@frostburg.edu
2008, Ext Min: Frostburg Campus Ministry.

Zoller, Darryl   RE
869 Blossom Dr , Hanover, PA 17331-2074   H. (410) 474-4913
darrylzoller331@gmail.com
1973, Attending school; 1974, Little Orleans: Piney Plains Charge; 1976, Lutherville: Carrollis Gills Charge; 1980, Hampstead: Greenmount; 1983, Fork-Waugh Charge; 1988, Darlington Charge; 1994, Hagerstown: Grace; 1999, Unionville: Linganore; 2003, Smithville; 2008, Manchester: Bixlers-Millers; 2009, Parkton: Stablers Vernon; 2009, Retired; 2014, Parkton: Stablers Bentley Springs Cooperative Parish

Zook, Galen   SY BM | Hampden || Baltimore ||| 3175
3449 Falls Rd , Baltimore, MD 21211-2405   H. (443) 857-9835
galenzook@gmail.com
2018, Baltimore: Hampden,

Zsittnik, John W.   RE
15941 Spruell St , Huntersville, NC 28078-4239   H. (704) 947-6370
1970, Attending school; 1971, Central Circuit; 1972, Assoc. Wheaton: Glenmont; 1975,
Laurel: Md. City Community; 1978, Waldorf: Calvary-Zion Wesley Charge; 1980 Upper Falls:
Salem; 1985, Rehoboth; 1988, Harmans: Wesley Grove; 1995, Boonsboro: Mt. Nebo; 07-15-
99, Suspension; 09-15-99, Leave of Absence; 2002, New Covenant Assoc; 2004, Marley-Solley
Charge; 2006, Leave of Absence; 2008, Baltimore: Hiss; 08-05-2008, Retired.

AFFILIATE/DIACONAL MEMBERS, MISSIONARIES AND DEACONESSES

Affiliate Members (Para. 344.3, 344.4)

Suerdieck, Christina K. (Keith)   (301) 447-3817
1427 Ramblewood Dr, Emmitsburg, MD 21727-8933   revchris.suerdieck@gmail.com

Zirlott, Cynthia I.   (540) 303-2309
141 Center St, Frostburg, MD 21532-1814   c.zirlott@frostburg.edu

Diaconal Ministers (Retired)

Doggett, Nan Austin   (240) 629-1961
7351 Willow Rd, Cottage 12, Frederick, MD 21702-2415   nanmariedoggett@gmail.com

Jones, Lois Arlene   (301) 441-3769
6100 Westchester Park Dr, Apt 409, College Park, MD 20740-2845

Moore, Cora   (301) 430-0686
13600 Missoula Ct, Upper Marlboro, MD 20774-8606

Myers, Lillian   (301) 223-6759
16505 Virginia Ave, Cottage 223, Williamsport, MD 217951309

Otto, Vivian W.   (301) 216-5299
415 Russell Ave, Apt 404, Gaithersburg, MD 20877-2848   vivianwotto@comcast.net

Sanderson, Donnalee Judd   (301) 277-7869
3918 Longfellow St, Hyattsville, MD 20781-1742   aesdjs@comcast.net

Taylor, Thelma L.   (301) 645-5783
12300 Channel Ct, Newburg, MD 20664-2220

Winget, Katherine B.

Missionaries

These are missionaries who have gone out from the BWC or who have four or more local churches supporting them.

Jae Hyoung Choi, #13973Z – serving as a missionary in residence at the headquarters of Global Ministries in Atlanta.
https://advance.umcmission.org/p-1516-jae-hyoung-choi.aspx

Belinda Forbes, #12109Z – serving in Managua, Nicaragua with Acción Médica Cristiana (Christian Medical Action or AMC).
https://advance.umcmission.org/p-1489-belinda-forbes.aspx
Read more about her ministry on her blog: www.belindagbgm.blogspot.com

Miguel Mairena, #12877Z – serving in Puebla, Mexico with Give Ye Them to Eat
https://advance.umcmission.org/p-1494-miguel-mairena.aspx

Nan McCurdy, #1081Z – serving in Puebla, Mexico with Give Ye Them to Eat
https://advance.umcmission.org/p-1475-nan-mccurdy.aspx
Email her at nanmigl@yahoo.com

Jennifer Moore, #3022165 – serving as a Christian educator in the Republic of Macedonia
https://advance.umcmission.org/p-1639-jennifer-moore.aspx

Albert Willicor, #15151Z – serving as Chief Medical Officer at Ganta United Methodist Hospital in Ganta, Liberia
https://advance.umcmission.org/p-1541-albert-willicor.aspx

Alina Saucedo, #15151Z--- service completed

Note: Twenty-four additional missionaries are supported by at least one local church in the Baltimore-Washington Conference.

Secretary of Global Ministries for the Baltimore-Washington Conference
Jane Grays
7118 Piney Wood Place
Laurel, Maryland 20707
Email: ladyjanegra@aol.com

Retired Missionaries from the Baltimore Washington Conference
Ellen Hoover (Democratic Republic of the Congo)
Jeffery Hoover (Democratic Republic of the Congo)
Rev. Roger and Sylvia Burtner (Nigeria)
Dorothy Warner (Japan)
Gayle Lesure

2017-2018 Appointment Requests
of Deaconesses, Home Missioners and Home Missionaries

	Relationship	Appointment/Address
Logan K. Alley Foundry UMC Greater Washington	Deaconess	**Intake and Data Quality Coordinator** Bridges to Independence 5805 Goucher Dr, Berwyn Heights, MD 20740 Logan_17@emoryfellowship.org
Carolyn Anderson Emory UMC Greater Washington	Deaconess	**Director of Membership Connections** Emory United Methodist Church PO Box 2365, Waldorf, MD 20604 canderson@emoryfellowship.org
Gertrude Dailey Metropolitan UMC Annapolis	Deaconess	**Director of Food Pantry/Clothes Closet** Metropolitan UMC 508 Jones Rd, Severn, MD 21144 rgdailey@comcast.net
Jane O. Grays Emmanuel UMC Washington East	Deaconess	**Volunteer Assistant, Recreation Services** Patuxent River Health and Rehabilitation Ctr 7118 Piney Woods Pl, Laurel, MD 20707 LadyJaneGra@aol.com
Patricia N. Marks Epworth UMC Greater Washington	Deaconess	**Criminal Justice Liaison** Patmos Ministries PO Box 8732, Gaithersburg, MD 20898 pnmarks@hotmail.som
Jefferey B Murrell Silver Spring UMC Greater Washington	Home Missioner	**Environmental Project Manager** US Dept of Energy 1400 East West Hwy, #1409, Silver Spring, MD 20910 jeffbm1@hotmail.com

Office of Deaconess and Home Missioner
deaconess@unitedmethodistwomen.org

CHRONOLOGICAL ROLL OF CLERGY

£ = *Elders Orders Recognized*   # = *Deacons Orders Recognized*

Bishops Emeriti living within the bounds of the Baltimore-Washington Annual Conference

	Received On Probation	Ordained Deacon	
Elder			
Forrest Christopher Stith	1958	1958	1960

Elders in Full Connection

	Received On Probation	Ordained Deacon	
Elder			
Carroll Arthur Doggett, Jr.	1948	1948	1950
Lamar Warner Kopp	1948	—	1952
Robert Earle Mitzel	1949	1949	1951
Douglas E. Moore	1950	1950	1953
Louis Lee Emerick	1950	1957	1959
Edward Walter Bauman, Jr.	1951	1951	1953
Roger Ellsworth Burtner	1951	—	1956
Edgar Ward Hammersla	1951	1951	1953
Robert Bruce Poynter	1951	1951	1953
Wilson Augustus Shearer	1951	—	1954
Edison McKinley Amos	1952	1953	1954
Ernest Edward Bortner, Jr.	1952	1953	1957
Robert Glasgow Kirkley	1952	1952	1954
Donald Wayne Llewellyn	1952	1952	1955
Kenneth Bruce Welliver	1952	1954	1955
Richard A. Closson	1953	1953	1955
William Arthur Holmes	1953	1953	1955
Davis William Peck	1953	1955	1956
Gene Ray Perry	1953	1954	1959
Richard Frederick Vieth	1953	1953	1955
George Wiley Anderson	1954	1956	1966
Charles Edgar Harvey	1954	1954	1957
Ralph Daniel Posey	1954	1954	1958
Leonard Buckland Ranson, Jr.	1954	1954	1956
George Roland Allen	1955	1960	1962
Jack Hilner Cassel	1995	—	1960
Lyle Edward Harper	1955	1956	1960
Walter McCarl Roberts, Jr.	1955	1956	1957
Robert Kenneth Rodeffer	1955	1955	1957
Jack Edwin Stearns	1955	—	1961
(1993 Journal, page 155, changed to J. Edwin Stearns as preferred usage)			
Julian Alpheus Tavenner	1955	1955	1957
John Philip Wogaman	1955	1955	1957
Allan Roscoe Broadhurst	1956	1958	1959
Richard Carlton Chambers	1956	1956	1958

	Received On Probation	Ordained Deacon	Elder
Robert Joseph Fringo	1956	1956	1958
Richard Samuel Karpal	1956	1956	1958
John Robert Lebo	1956	—	1961
Charles Weicht Lightner	1956	—	1961
William Larue Raker	1956	—	1960
John William Schildt	1956	—	1962
Hayden Luther Sparks	1956	1958	1959
Owen Byrd Womack	1956	1956	1958
James Parker Archibald	1957	1957	1959
Robert Eugene Funk	1957	1957	1962
Lowell Sanford Garland	1957	1957	1959
Stanley Graham Harrell	1957	1957	1961
Michael Leftwich	1957	1957	1959
Donald Lloyd Shearer	1957	1959	1962
Leslie Ewald Werner, Jr.	1957	1957	1959
Kenneth Elwood Bowen	1958	1958	1961
Raymond Earl Clements, Jr.	1958	1959	1960
Albert Lewellyn Galloway	1958	1958	1961
Harold Robinson McClay, Jr.	1958	1960	1961
George Albert Aist	1959	1959	1962
Edwin Alonzo Ankeny	1959	1959	1961
Carroll Reese Gunkel	1959	1959	1961
Ellis L. Larsen	1959	1959	1961
James Davis Manning	1959	1959	1961
Joe David Sergent	1959	1959	1961
Thomas Cowan Starnes	1959	1959	1961
Clark Sunderland Aist	1960	1960	1962
William Casper Farrady	1960	1960	1964
Ray Olin Herndon	1960	1960	1962
Clarence Albert Kaylor	1960	1960	1963
Ralph Emory McCulloh	1960	1960	1962
Ernest Maynard Moore, III	1960	—	1964
Larry Martin Plymire	1960	—	1965
Carl Bruce Rife	1960	—	1966
Clarence Lendon Roark, III	1960	1960	1963
Errol Gene Smith	1960	1960	1962
Luther Williams Starnes	1960	1960	1962
James Maylon Warner	1960	1962	1964
Edwin Michael Wray	1960	—	1963
Lon Benton Chesnutt	1961	1961	1963
Robert Frederick Crider, Jr.	1961	—	1967
Norman Bruce Kuehnle	1961	1961	1964
Don Bruce Lowe	1961	1961	1964
William Dennis Nelson	1961	1961	1963
John Adams Shirkey	1961	1961	1965
Harry Topping Baxter, Jr.	1962	1962	1964
William Humphries Bice	1962	1962	1965
William R. Boyer	1962	1962	1964

	Received On Probation	Ordained Deacon	Elder
Thomas Brunkow	1962	1962	1967
Merle Duane Correll	1962	1962	1965
George Edward Grove	1962	—	1967
Eddie Lynn Henry	1962	—	1968
Robert Lee Hurley	1962	1962	1964
Ludwig Lindeman Lankford	1962	1962	1965
Weller Ross Lewis, Jr.	1962	1962	1970
Lovell Parham	1962	1962	1964
William Louis Piel	1962	1962	1966
Donald Stanley Stewart, Jr.	1962	1962	1964
Maurice Edward Vineyard	1962	1962	1964
Bruce Charles Birch	1963	1963	1965
Robert Manning Braden, Sr.	1963	1963	1966
Reynold Block Connett	1963	1963	1965
Lawrence Ray Frye	1963	—	1967
Loren Louis Gisselbeck	1963	1963	1966
John Wesley Grove	1963	1963	1967
Roger Ward Johnson	1963	1963	1965
Perry Frank Miller	1963	1963	1966
Joe Sharp Rainey	1963	1963	1965
Carl Alfred Synan	1963	1963	1969
(2005 Journal, page 361, changed to Carl Anthony Synan)			
Warren Wayne Watts	1963	1963	1966
Jackson Harvey Day	1964	1964	1967
Jack Ronald George	1964	1964	1969
Don Edwin Howard	1964	1964	1967
David Frank Kolda	1964	1964	1967
Granville Douglass Lewis	1964	1964	1966
Robert Edward Manthey	1964	1964	1968
Daniel Christopher McLellan, Jr.	1964	1964	1968
Galen Russell Menne	1964	—	1969
Kathryn Louise Bailey Moore	1964	—	1967
David Edward Stum	1964	—	1969
Henry Archibald Swain	1964	1964	1967
Emora Thomas Brannan	1965	1965	1968
Curtis Fletcher Campaigne	1965	1965	1968
David Walter Carter-Rimbach	1965	1965	1968
Robert Eugene Paulen	1965	1965	1967
Richard Dennis Schulze	1965	1965	1967
Richard Douglas Thompson	1965	1965	1969
Gary Wayne Trail	1965	1965	1967
Byron Paul Brought	1966	1966	1970
James Eddie Chance	1966	1966	1968
Edwin Clifton DeLong	1966	1966	1969
Calvin S. Morris	1966	1966	1968
Richard Edwin Stetler	1966	—	1968
Dennis Lee Upton	1966	—	1970
Edwin Hugh Welch	1966	1966	1972

	Received On Probation	Ordained Deacon	Elder
Jarrett Torbit Wicklein	1966	1966	1969
Wayne Allen DeHart	1967	1967	1970
Anders Robert Lunt	1967	1967	1969
Raymond Theodore Moreland, Jr.	1967	1967	1971
Walter Franklin Bowers, Sr.	1968	1971	1974
James Lee Ditto	1968	1968	1973
Walter George Edmonds	1968	1968	1970
George Warren Ennis	1968	1968	1970
David Allan Highfield	1968	1968	1971
James Morgan Hunt	1968	1968	1971
Frank Richard Leslie	1968	1968	1974
Richard Kenneth McCullough	1968	1968	1970
Lawrence A. Neumark	1968	1968	1971
Richard Wayne Simpson	1968	1968	1971
Earl James Stutler	1968	1968	1971
Richard Gordon Gray, Jr.	1969	1969	1973
Richard Denver Hogue	1969	1969	1972
William Kenneth Lyons, Jr.	1969	1969	1973
Henry Clay Thompson, III	1969	1969	1973
John H. Williams	1969	1969	1973
Rebecca Kay Barger	1970	1970	1973
Reg Donn Barss	1970	1970	1973
Donald Lee Burgard	1970	1970	1974
Thomas Norman Connar	1970	1970	1973
Alfonso John Harrod	1970	—	1976
Daniel Charles Henderson	1970	1970	1974
Gary Robert Hottinger	1970	1970	1973
Arthur Russell Kent	1970	1970	1972
Richard Arthur Kroll	1970	1970	1974
Peter Yoon Kyung Sun	1970	1970	1972
Louis Shockley, Jr.	1970	1970	1973
Roland Jeremy Randolph Timity	1970	1970	1972
Edward Martin Voorhaar	1970	1970	1974
John William Zsittnik	1970	1970	1973
Archie David Argo	1971	1971	1973
Richard Sewell Davis	1971	1971	1974
Kenneth Ray Dunnington	1971	1971	1974
Robert Delton Hershberger	1971	1971	1973
Kenneth Michael Humbert	1971	1971	1975
Mary Emaline Kraus	1971	1971	1974
Lawrence Patrick Ricker	1971	1971	1974
Henry Franklin Schwarzmann	1971	1971	1974
Franklin Lyle Ways	1971	1971	1973
John Howard Campbell	1972	1972	1975
Darryl Lee Gill	1972	1972	1975
August Gerard Lageman	1972	1972	1974
Alva Daniel Tice	1972	1970	1979
Robert Henry Brookman	1973	1973	1975

	Received On Probation	Ordained Deacon	Elder
Kenneth Earl Brown	1973	1973	1975
Roger John Carlson	1973	1973	1977
Goldsboro Sylvester Gaines	1973	1973	1979
Susan Raye Halse	1973	1973	1976
Stephen Daryl Robison	1973	1973	1976
Harry Kent Tice	1973	1973	1978
Man-King Tso	1973	—	1974
Wayne Hamilton Upton	1973	1973	1976
Darryl Claude Zoller	1973	1973	1977
Rebecca Abts	1974	1974	1977
(1982 Journal, page 171, changed to Rebecca Abts Wright)			
Linda Jane Coveleskie	1974	1974	1977
Mark Alan Derby	1974	1974	1977
Douglas Earl Fox	1974	1974	1978
Diana Leigh Hynson	1974	1974	1978
Jeffrey Wendover Jones	1974	1974	1977
Helen Steiner Smith	1974	1974	1976
Anne Ross Stewart	1974	1974	1976
Lynn Dean Cairns	1975	1975	1977
George Glover Earle, Jr.	1975	1975	1977
Pamela J. Holliman	1975	1975	1984
Earl Edward Mason	1975	1975	1978
Richard Jack Mortimore	1975	1975	1978
Edward Allen Stewart	1975	1975	1978
Carol Sue Cosens Yocum	Transfer 1975	1973	1976
Nancy Susan W. Nedwell	1975	1975	1978
Roland Myers Brown, III	1976	1976	1978
Robert Dennis Carter	1976	1976	1978
Victor Olatunde Johnson	1976	1976	1978
Jeanne Williamson Klauda	1976	1976	1980
Eugene William Matthews	1976	1976	1979
Howard Edgar Moore	1976	1976	1979
Albert Moser, Jr.	1976	1976	1978
Harold William Watson	1976	—	1976
Mamie Alethia Williams	1976	1976	1979
(1988 Journal, page 192, changed to Mamie Alethia Williams-Munjoma)			
(1992 Journal, page 46, changed to Mamie Alethia Williams)			
Harold Bell Wright, II	1976	1976	1978
Dennis Edward Yocum	Transfer 1976	1973	1977
JoAnne Alexander	1977	1977	1981
Mary Ellen Huzzard	1977	1977	1979
Calvin David Jones	Transfer 1977		1969
Ronald Ray Kurtz	1977	1977	1980
Walter Shropshire, Jr.	1977	1977	1992
Carolyn Ruth Swift	1977	1977	1980
Nancy Jarrell Webb	1977	1977	1979
Dong Yeok Cho	1978	—	1978
(1983 Journal, page 179, changed to David Dong Cho)			

	Received On Probation		Ordained Deacon	Elder
Robert Thomas Clipp		1978	1978	1980
Mary Jane Coleman		1978	1978	1981
David Scott Cooney		1978	1978	1981
Howard Ronald Ellis		1978	1978	1981
William Allan Herche, Jr.		1978	1978	1982
Darcy Ruth Hunt		1978	1978	1981
Linda Ann Jacobus		1978	1978	1981
Michael Clifford	1978		1978	1981
Bruce Appelgate Jones		1978	1978	1981
Robert Albert McCullough, Jr.		1978	1978	1985
(1983 Journal, page 179, changed to Robert Albert Dixon McCullough)				
Walter Edward Middlebrooks		1978	1978	1981
Linda Katherine Moore		1978	1978	1981
David Eugene Thayer		1978	1978	1980
Bruce Carl Thompson		1978	1978	1981
Herbert Wesley Watson, Jr.		1978	1978	1980
Charles Edward Wolfe		1978	—	1978
Jean Sutliff Young		1978	1978	1981
Mark Condron Young		1978	1978	1982
Kay Francis Albury		1979	1979	1981
(1981 Journal, page 170, changed to Kay Francis Albury-Smith)				
(1994 Journal, page 204, changed to Kay Albury)				
(2003 Journal, page 357, changed to Kay F. Albury-Pierce)				
(2007 Journal, page 360 changed to Kay F. Albury)				
Rebecca Jane Bentzinger		1979	1979	1987
Terri Rae Chattin		1979	1979	1981
Sally Jo Day		1979	1979	1993
Donna Marie Hennessey		1979	1979	1981
(1996 Journal, changed to Donna M. Hennessey Bennett)				
Barry Ellsworth Hidey		1979	1979	1981
Diana Louise Ley		1979	1979	1981
Conrad Oscar Link		1979	1979	1981
Elsie May McKenney		1979	1979	1981
(2007 Journal, page 360 changed to Elsie May McKenney Gladding)				
Linda Carole Silbaugh		1979	1979	1981
Gerald Edgar Stone		1979	1979	1981
Mark Robert Waddell		1979	1979	1981
Gregory Stephen Brown		1980	1980	1983
Henry Granville Butler, Jr.		1980	1980	1982
Clark Duncan Carr		1980	1980	1982
Robert Edward Cook		1980	1980	1983
Claire Lynn Fiedler		1980	1980	1982
Miriam Hope Jackson		1980	1980	1983
Ruth Ann Miller		1980	1980	1985
(2004 Journal, page 354, changed to Ruth Ann Ward)				
Willie Mae Parker		1980	1980	1982
Deborah Lynn Scott		1980	1980	1987
Gaye Shires Smith		1980	1980	1982
John Chester Warren		1980	1980	1982

	Received On Probation	Ordained Deacon	Elder
Richard Edward Whale	1980	1980	1982
(1982 Journal, page 171, changed to Richard Edward Brown-Whale)			
Marion Monroe Wright, Jr.	1980	—	1981
Thomas Edward Young, Jr.	1980	1980	1983
Susan Ray Beehler	1981	1981	1984
Eugene Dwight Byrne	1981	1981	1983
Bruce William Chapman	1981	1981	1983
Margaret Eleanor Clemons	1981	1981	1984
Richard Barkley Craig	1981	1981	1984
Timothy Dissmeyer	1981	1981	1983
William Thomas Green	1981	1981	1985
Theodore Daniel Higby	1981	1981	1984
Christopher Todd Holmes	1981	1981	1984
Mark Alan Lancaster	1981	1981	1985
Ramon Ernest McDonald, II	1981	1981	1984
Craig Alan McLaughlin	1981	1981	1984
Jeffrey Vaughn Odom	1981	1981	1984
John William Rudisill, Jr.	1981	1981	1986
David Alvin Shank	1981	1981	1983
Marianne Kay Sickles	1981	1981	1985
(2001 Journal, page 348, changed to Marianne Sickles Seabrease)			
(2005 Journal, page 361, changed to Marianne Sickles Grabowski)			
Diane Arthur Wagner	1981	1981	1984
(1993 Journal, page 155, changed to Diane A. W. Crider)			
Ronald Lee Ward	1981	1981	1983
Alfreda Lynette Wiggins	1981	1981	1985
Gayle Elizabeth Annis	1982	1982	1985
(1997 Journal, page 336, changed to Gayle E. Annis-Forder)			
Kimberly Ann Brown-Whale	1982	—	1984£
George Franklin DeFord	1982	1982	1988
Michael Pierre Fauconnet	1982	1982	1986
Arthur Dan Gleckler	1982	1962	1984
Jesse Ephraim Mayes	1982	1982	1987
Curtis Lamar Mitchell	1982	1982	1985
Paul Alexander Papp	1982	1982	1986
Conrad DeLante Parker	1982	1982	1985
Annie Vee Perry-Daniel	1982	1982	1985
(1999 Journal, page 349, changed to Anne Perry)			
Philip Ray Roberson	1982	1982	1988
Janet Lee Todd	1982	1982	1986
(1984 Journal, page 176, changed to Janet Lee Todd Becker)			
Arlester Brown	Transfer 1982	—	1983
Carmen Rae Collette	1983	1983	1986
Marian Elizabeth Dunmore	1983	1983	1986
Constance Alwine Fitzkee	1983	1983	1986
(1995 Journal, page 242, changed to Constance A. Paulson)			
Norman Anthony Handy, Sr.	1983	1983	1987
(2002 Journal, page 350, changed to Kwame Osayaba Abayomi)			
Douglas James Hays	1983	1983	1985

	Received On Probation	Ordained Deacon	Ordained Elder
Esther Marie Holimon	1983	1983	1986
Gary Lee James	1983	1983	1986
(1985 Journal, page 182, changed to Gary Lee Sheffield-James)			
Hea Sun Kim	1983	1983	1985
Ann Russell Laprade	1983	1983	1985
Lloyd Baxter McCanna	1983	1983	1986
Roderick Joseph Miller	1983	1983	1985
Mark Carroll Mooney	1983	1983	1986
Randy Wayne Pumphrey	1983	1983	1989
Sheldon Monroe Reese	1983	1983	1986
Victor Emmanuel Sawyer	1983	1983	1987
Kim Kathleen Capps Sickels	1983	1983	1986
(1984 Journal, page 176, changed to Kim Kathleen Capps)			
Gladys Clare Sloane	1983	1983	1986
John William Taugher	1983	1983	1990
David Northrop Wentz	1983	1983	1988
John Richard Yost	1983	1983	1990
Ira Bruce Barr, Jr.	1984	1984	1989
Laura Suzanne Blauvelt	1984	1984	1987
(1987 Journal, page 183, changed to Laura Suzanne Blauvelt Easto)			
(2018 Journal, changed to Laura Blauvelt)			
Kiyul Chung	1984	1984	1989
Jerry Mark Cline	1984	1984	1988
Steven Ted Cochran	1984	1984	1988
Gerald Owens Grace	1984	1984	1988
Charles LaBre Harrell	1984	1984	1992
Charlotte Ann Hendee	1984	1984	1988
Dennis Edward Jackman	1984	1984	1989
Neva Hartman Leatherwood	1984	1984	1987
Ernest Derwin Lyles	1984	1984	1987
Kristina Peterson-Synan	1984	1973	1987
(1986 Journal, page 175, changed to Kristina Peterson)			
Charles Albert Proctor	1984	1984	1992
Roberta Anne Jacksteit Scoville	1984	1984	1988
Diane Elinor Summerhill	1984	1984	1989
Deborah Tate	1984	1984	1992
Sandra Sue Whitt Taylor	1984	1984	1988
Jeremiah Galloway Williams	1984	1984	1988
Robert Scott Barton	1985	1985	1989
Gregory A. Coates	1985	1985	1989
Terri Susan Cofiell	1985	1985	1988
Ronald Foster	1985	1985	1988
Carlee Louise Hallman	1985	1985	1987
Mildred Constance Costello Martin	1985	1975	1987
Stacey Eileen Fischer Nickerson	1985	1985	1989
Fritz Outlaw	1985	1985	1990
Hallie Lawson Reeves	1985	—	1989
Barbara Jean Corpening Sands	1985	1985	1989

	Received On Probation	Ordained Deacon	Elder
Eddie Smith	1985	1985	1988
Laura Lee Cock Wilson	1985	1985	1989
(2008 Journal, page 399, changed to Laura Lee Morgan)			
Phillip Ray Ayers	1986	1986	1994
John Patrick Baker	1986	1986	1990
Robert William Barnes, Jr.	1986	1986	1988
Arlene Rose Carr	1986	1986	1988
Tunde Ekundayo Othniel Davies	1986	1986	1988
Susan Elizabeth Fachet Duchesneau	1986	1986	1990
Victor Emmanuel Harner	1986	1986	1989
Kathleen Harriet Kohl	1986	1986	1988
Vivian Margaret Crouse McCarthy	1986	1986	1989
Kenneth Allen McDonald	1986	1986	1989
Charles Arthur Parker	1986	1986	1991
Charles Alvin Simms	1986	1986	1991
Dorothea Joanne Belt Stroman	1986	1986	1988
James Edward Swecker	1986	1986	1988
Patricia Ann Pride	1986	—	1990
Obie Wright, Jr.	1986	—	1988£
Robert Garrahan Brennan, Jr.	1987	1987	1989
Karen Nordlof Gould	1987	1987	1989
Gerard Americus Green, Jr.	1987	1987	1990
Karin Christine Wagner Hammond	1987	1987	1990
(1992 Journal, page 64, changed to Karin Christine Wagner Walker)			
Stephen Lee Larsen	1987	1987	1990
Mary Sheila McCurdy-Dunbar	1987	1987	1990
(1988 Journal, page 192, changed to Mary Sheila McCurdy)			
Norman James Obenshain	1987	1987	1990
James Edgar Skillington, III	1987	1987	1994
Constance Clarice Smith	1987	1987	1992
LaReesa Celestine Smith	1987	1987	1989
(2008 Journal, page 399, changed to LaReesa Smith-Horn)			
Mark Dwayne Venson	1987	1987	1990
Kathryn Lynn Tarwater	1987	1987	1991
(2001 Journal, page 348, changed to Kathryn T. Woodrow)			
Catherine Anne Yarbrough	1987	1987	1989
John Roger Brown	Transfer 1988	1981	1985
Joan Eileen Carter	1988	1988	1992
(1992 Journal, changed to Joan Eileen Carter-Rimbach)			
Margaret Hundley Click	1988	1988	1991
Chi Bon Jang	Transfer 1988		
Mary Roberts	Transfer 1988	—	1990
Philip Douglas Tocknell	1988	1988	1991
Chris Andrew Wood	1988	1988	1991
William D. Aldridge, Jr.	Transfer 1989	1983	1991
Glen Lyle Arnold	1989	1989	1991
Ann Elizabeth Gordon	1989	1989	1991
(2007 Journal, page 360, changed to Drew Phoenix)			

	Received On Probation	Ordained Deacon	Elder
James David Hainley	1989	1989	1991
Margaret Wood Hodges	1989	1989	1991
Alta Groves Jewell	1989	1989	1991
Burton L. Mack	1989	1989	1991
Yolanda Pupo-Ortiz	Transfer 1989	1983	1985
Victoria Jane Starnes	1989	1989	1992
Michael Patrick Szpak	1989	1989	1992
Clifford Carlson Webner	1989	1989	1991
Cheryl Barbara Anderson	1990	1990	1992
Kevin Michael Baker	1990	1990	1993
Kathleen Frances Cheyney	1990	1990	
Clarence Davis	1990	1990	1993
Leon Kess	Transfer 1990	—	1993£
Susan C. Marseilles	1990	1990	1992
Clayton Eugene Rhodes	1990	1990	1992
Moses Sangha	Transfer 1990	—	1992£
(2001 Journal, page 348, changed to Moses S. Sangha)			
Evan DeZelle Young	1990	1990	1992
Ann Roxine Vincent	1991	1991	1994
(1993 Journal, page 155, changed to Ann Vincent Atkins)			
Sharon Bourgeois	Transfer 1991	1983	1987
Eva Lee Clark	1991	1991	1993
Ronald Lee Collier, Sr.	1991	1991	1993
Iris Waveleen Farabee	1991	1991	1993
(1997 Journal, page 336, changed to Iris Farabee-Lewis)			
Elizabeth Lou Halsey	1991	1991	1994
Mae Etta Harrison	1991	1991	1993
Richard Harold Jewell	1991	1991	1994
Paul Kim	Transfer 1991	1968	1973£
Seung Woo Lee	Transfer 1991	—	1978£
Melissa Ann McDade	1991	1991	1994
Sang Kook Ro	Transfer 1991	—	1975£
Susan Alston Spears	Transfer 1991	—	1993£
Stephen Andrew Tillett, I	1991	1991	1994
Terrance Lee Thrasher	Transfer 1991	—	1993£
Vera Mitchell Traore	1991	1991	1993
(1993 Journal, page 155, changed to Vera Mitchell Baskerville)			
(2003 Journal, page 357, changed to Vera Mitchell)			
William Wan	Transfer 1991		1991£
(1994 Journal, page 204, changed to William K. Wan)			
Amy Sarah Yurgealitis	1991	1991	1993
(1996 Journal, page 243, changed to Amy Sarah Lewis)			
(2014 Journal, changed to Amy Sarah Lewis-Rill)			
Joseph F. Whalen, Jr.	Transfer 1991		1979
Stan Glenn Cardwell	1992	1992	1996
Shirley Rice Carrington	1992	1992	1994
Karen Michelle Davis	1992	1992	1995
Sandra Marie Sullivan Greene	1992	1992	1999

	Received On Probation	Ordained Deacon	Elder
(2008 Journal, page 399 changed to Sandra Marie Greene)			
Charles Anthony Hunt	1992	1992	1995
Hattie Sanders Jackson	Transfer 1992		1994
Kyung-Lim Shin Lee	Transfer 1992	1988	1990
(1999 Journal, page 349, changed to KyungLim Shin Lee)			
Donna Martin	Transfer 1992	1967	1986
Lewis Newton McDonald	Transfer 1992		1994£
Daniel L. Montague	Transfer 1992	1991#	1997
HiRho Yoon Park	Transfer 1992	1992	1993
JungWoo Park	Transfer 1992	1992	1995
Mary Jo Sims-Baden	1992	1992	1995
(2001 Journal, page 348, changed to Mary Jo Sims)			
Mark Louis Smiley	Transfer 1992	1982	1986
Beverly Craig Stang	1992	1992	1995
Douglas M. Strong	Transfer 1992	1979	1986
Mary Kay Totty-Kublawi	Transfer 1992	1989	1991
(2003 Journal, page 357, changed to Mary Kay Totty)			
Rebecca Jane Vardiman	1992	1992	1995
Robert T. Wellman	Transfer 1992	1976	1980
Timothy West	1992	1992	1994
John Mengel Wunderlich, III	1992	1992	1994
Harold Preston Atkins	1993	1993	1998
Laurence Konmla Bropleh	1993	1993	1996
Robert Lee Conway	1993	1993	1995
Andrew James Cooney	1993	1993	1995
Joseph Wayne Daniels	Transfer 1993	1993#	1995
Peter Leland DeGroote	1993	1993	1996
Geri Dee-Ann Dixon	1993	1993	1997
Kenneth Joseph Fizer	1993	1993	1996
Lauren Heather Lay	1993	1993	1997
Denise Henrietta Norfleet	1993	1993	1998
(2007, changed to Denise Norfleet-Walker)			
Samson Yebuah Nortey	1993	1993	1995
John David Roberts	1993	1993	1996
Theresa Annette Robinson	1993	1993	1996
Saroj Sabitha Sangha	1993	1993	1996
Kenneth William Walker	1993	1993	1996
William Garrett Brown	1994	1994	1998
Anthony Theodore Carr	1994	1994	1998
James Maxwell Greenfield	1994	1994	1999
Douglas Bruce Hoffman	1994	1994	1998
Brian Wade Jackson	1994	1994	2000
John Thomas Jennings, Jr.	1994	1994	1998
Hattie Jean Johnson-Holmes	1994	1994	2001
Evelyn Hill Manson	1994	1994	1997
Mary Marcia Mayor	1994	1994	1998
John William Nupp	1994	1994	1997
Ann Miller Parker	1994	1994	2000

	Received On Probation	Ordained Deacon	Elder
(2008, changed to Ann Parker Offer)			
Laura Lynn Schultz	1994	1994	1997
Robert Earl Slade	1994	1994	2003
Mary Gebe Stevens	1994	1994	1997
Robert Early Walker	1994	1994	2000
Byron Edward Brought	1995	1995	1998
William Richard Harden	1995	1995	1998
Joye Faith Jones	1995	1995	1998
Diedra Hanner Kriewald	Transfer 1995	1978	1980
James Martin Lucas, Jr.	1995	1995	1998
James David Nenninger	Transfer 1995	1968	1970
Bernadette Marie Ross (former AM)	1995	1995	2005
David Wayne Simpson	1995	1993	1997
Douglas Dean Tzan	1995	1995	1998
Stephanie Elizabeth Vader	1995	1995	1999
Maceo Merton Williams	Transfer 1995	1986	1990
Carletta Davoria Allen	1996	1996	2002
Harry Collier Cole	1996	1996	1999
Diane Dixon-Proctor	Transfer 1996		1986£
Laurie Elizabeth Gates	1996	1996	1999
(2003 Journal, page 357, changed to Laurie Gates-Ward)			
Christopher Scott Gobrecht	1996	1996	1999
Donna Lynn Filbey Herritt	1996	1996	1999
(2010 Journal, page 336, changed to Donna Renn)			
Robert Henry Hunter, III	1996	1996	1999
Dellyne Ivy Russell	1996	1996	1999
(1998 Journal, page 348, changed to Dellyne I. Hinton)			
Joan Ilene Senyk	Transfer 1996	1994#	1999
Christopher Nassamba Serufusa	1996	1996	1999
Arthur Dicken Thomas, Jr.	Transfer 1996	1979#	1999
Lisa Marie Bandel	1997	1997	2000
(1999 Journal, page 349, changed to Lisa Marie Bandel-Sparks)			
Cynthia Bonita Belt	1997	1997	2000
Vernice Slade Carney	1997	1997	2002
Betty Preston Dunlop	1997	1997	2000
Lillian Hughes Rodgers Geib	1997	1997	2000
Linda Jean Glassbrook	1997	1997	2000
(2012 Journal, change to Linda J. Burnette)			
(2014 Journal, change to Linda J. Glassbrook)			
Cecil Conteen Gray	Transfer 1997		
Gertrude Madora Greene	1997	1997	
Katherine Ann Heflin	1997	1997	2000
Duane LeRoy Jensen	1997	1997	2000
Andrea Lynn Middleton	1997	1997	2000
(2001 Journal, page 348, changed to Andrea M. King)			
(2002 Journal, page 350, Andrea Middleton King preferred)			
James Martin Miller	Transfer 1997	1990	1994
Ianther Marie Mills	1997	1997	2000

	Received On Probation	Ordained Deacon	Ordained Elder
Brindice Muñoz	Transfer 1997	1969	1971
Harold Joseph Recinos	Transfer 1997	1982	1984
Benjamin Kevin Smalls	1997	1997	2000
Dean Joel Snyder	Transfer 1997	1970	1972
Kirk Alan VanGilder	1997	1997	2000
William Henry Warehime, Jr.	1997	1997	2000
George Henry Weitzel, Jr.	1997	1997	2000
Jane Elizabeth Wood	1997	1997	2009
Valerie Ann Barnes	1998	1998	2004
Winifred Johnson Blagmond	1998	1998	2002
Glenda Gay Beach Condon	1998	1998	
Janet Terry Michalski Cornelius	1998	1998	2001
Janet Deitiker	1998	1998	2002
(2007 Journal, page 360 changed to Janet Deitiker Wilson)			
(2011 Journal, changed to Janet Deitiker)			
(2016 Journal, changed to Janet Deitiker Tracy)			
Judith Ann Emerson	1998	1998	2001
Mary Ellen Glorioso	1998	1998	2001
Susan Margaret Hallager	1998	1998	2001
(2014 Journal, change to Susan Margaret Brown)			
Carolyn Althea Hipkins	1998	1998	2001
Eric Wellington King, Sr.	1998	1998	2001
Harold DeSantis Lewis	Transfer 1998	1994	1996
Antoine Carlton Love	1998	1998	2001
Jacquelyn Ray Lowery McLellan	1998	1998	2001
Kenneth Percell Moore	1998	1998	2002
Kelly Steven Sparks	Transfer 1998	1972	1976
Gertie Thomas Williams	1998	1998	
Ann Parsons Adams	1999	1999	2002
Sandra Elizabeth Demby	1999	1999	2003
Charles Michael Henning	1999	1999	2002
Stephen Walter Humphrey, Jr.	1999	1999	2002
Elza May Hoffman Hurst	1999		1999
Travis Dean Knoll	1999	1999	2003
Yvonne Mercer-Staten	1999	1999	2002
Denise Marie Yepsen Millett	1999	1999	2002
Marilyn Cheryl Newhouse	1999	1999	2002
Amy Elizabeth Peed	Transfer 1999	1996	2000
(2004 Journal, page 354, changed to Amy Peed McCullough)			
Jeffrey Allen Paulson	1999	1999	2002
Malcolm Ronald Stranathan	1999	1999	2002
Mary Katherine Worrel	1999	1999	2002
Yong-Seok Yang	1999	1999	2006
(2003 Journal, page 357, changed to Jacob Yongseok Yang)			
(2004 Journal, page 354, changed to Jacob Yongseok Young)			
Paul Benjamin	Transfer 2000		1998
James A. Bishop	Transfer 2000		1994
Susan Elizabeth Boehl	2000	2000	2003

	Received On Probation	Ordained Deacon	Elder
Malcolm Larry Frazier	2000	2000	2003
Samuel Holdbrook-Smith	2000	2000	2003
Loretta Ewell Johnson	2000	2000	2003
Patricia Louise Sebring	2000	2000	2003
Ann Travis Strickler	2000	2000	2003
Wendy Shenk-Evans	Transfer 2000	1997	1999
Scott Dale Shumaker	2000	2000	2003
Mark Robert Teasdale	2000	2000	2003
Laurie Pierce Tingley	Transfer 2000	2000	2006
Kenneth Steven Valentine	Transfer 2000	1975	1978
Helen Stark Armiger	2001		2004
Donald Atkinson	2001		
Michael Wilson Bennett	2001		2004
William Edward Butler	2001	2001	2004
Vicki Lane Setzer Curry	2001	2001	2004
Patricia Craig Dols	2001	2001	2004
Timothy Andrew Dowell	2001		2004
Ginger Elise Gaines-Cirelli	2001	2001	2004
Hosea Lee Hodges	2001	2001	2005
Patricia Delores Johnson	2001	2001	2007
Christopher David Owens	2001		2004
Stephen Ralph Ricketts	2001		2004
Rodney Thomas Smothers	Transfer 2001	1981	1984
Joseph Whalen	Transfer 2001		1979
Daniel Lewis Wright	2001		2004
Wendy Susan Young	2001		2004
(2003 Journal, page 357, changed to Wendy Susan Cordova)			
Maria Andita H. Barcelo	2002	2002	2005
Gail Lynn Button	2002	2002	2005
Joseph Anthony Conte	2002	2002	2005
Kara Suzanna Cooper	2002		
Vicki Michael Dotterer	2002	2002	2008
Lori Marie Hoffman	2002	2002	2005
(2004 Journal, page 354, changed to Lori Hoffman Hays)			
Byung-June Hwang	2002		
Curtis Dean King	2002	2002	2006
Pamela Jean Marsh	2002	2002	2005
Sue Ellen Shorb-Sterling	2002	2002	2005
Eliezer Valentin-Castanon	Transfer 2002	1989	1993
Rudolph Monsio Bropleh	2003	2003	2006
Rachel Anne Cornwell	2003	2003	2006
David John Deans	2003	2003	2006
Bryan Keith Fleet	2003	2003	2009
Linda Williams Healy	2003		
Isaac Mapipi Mawokomatanda	Transfer 2003		
Eloise Montgomery Newman	2003	2003	
DaeHwa Park	2003	2003	2006
Randall Scott Reid	2003	2003	2006

	Received On Probation	Ordained Deacon	Elder
Elizabeth Jane Richards	2003	2003	2006
(2003 Journal, page 357, changed to Elizabeth Richards Leger)			
(2010 Journal, page 336, changed to Elizabeth Jane Richards)			
Mark Andrew Schaefer	2003	2003	2006
Jean Ellyn Jewett Weller	2003		
Perry Lynn Williams	Transfer 2003		2005
Stacey Cole Wilson	2003	2003	2006
Miguel Angel Balderas	2004		2007
Kimberly Hall	2004		2008
Barbara JoAnne Jessup	2004		2007
Shari Michelle McCourt	2004		2013
Carol Leydig Pazdersky	2004		2007
Melissa Corrine Hamill Rudolph	2004		2007
Robert Kenneth Schneider	2004		2008
Corey Scott Sharpe	2004		2007
Jennifer Kay Smith	2004		2007
Judy Smith Young	2004		2012
Kenneth Blake Hawes	Transfer 2004	1994	1997
Michael A. H. McKinney	Transfer 2004	1987	1991
Sarah Marie Andrews	2005		2008
John McKinley Blanchard, Jr.	2005		2008
Jennifer Lynn Brown	2005	Discontinued	
(2009 Journal, page 400, changed to Jennifer Brown Kokoski)			
David Alan Coakley	2005		2009
Curtis Christian Ehrgott	2005		2012
Richard David Hall	2005		2008
Rebecca Kathleen Iannicelli	2005		2008
Jacqueline Jones-Smith	2005		2008
Olexiy Karakcheyev	2005		2008
Viktoriya Karakcheyeva	2005		2008
Sonia Lynette King	2005		2008
Janice Elizabeth Leith	2005		2012
William Clifford Maisch	2005		2008
Wade Alexander Martin	2005		2008
Saundra Elizabeth Rector	2005		2009
Adam Benedict Snell	2005		2008
Kathy Jean Spitzer	2005		2008
Timothy Brian Warner	2005		2008
Kendrick Demond Weaver	2005		2008
Michael Walter Armstrong (transfer American Baptist)	2005		2006
Lena Marie Dennis (transfer Natl. Baptist Church)	2005		2002
Jason Lawrence Robinson	Transfer 2005	2000	2002£
Herbert Alexander Brisbon III	2006		2009
Marian Sams Crane	2006		2009
EunJoung Joo	2006		2009
Faith Fairchild Lewis	2006		2009
(2019 Journal, changed to Faith Wilkerson)			
Alhassan Kayinde Caliph Macaulay	2006		2009

	Received On Probation	Ordained Deacon	Elder
Brenda Joyce Mack	2006		2010
Glen Travis Strickler	2006		2010
Ingrid Yee-Ying Wang	2006		2009
Linda Allport Warehime	2006		2009
Patricia Allen	2007		2011
Christopher Michael Bishop	2007		2010
Kathryn Jane Posey Bishop	2007		2010
Jennifer Dawn Cannon	2007		2010
Glenn Anthony Capacchione	2007		
Jerry Leslie Lowans	2007		2010
Cynthia Michelle Moore-Valentine	2007		2010
(2010 Journal, page 336, change to Cynthia Michelle Moore)			
James Winchester Ridout	2007		Discontinued
Walter Lee Beaudwin	2008		2012
Marianne Theresa Brown	2008		2013
(2014 Journal, change to Marianne T. Christofferson)			
Lory Adele Cantin	2008		Discontinued
Jalene Cynthia Chase	2008		2012
(2010 Journal, page 336, change to Jalene Cynthia Chase-Sands)			
(2018 Journal, changed to Jalene Cynthia Chase)			
John Hayward Dean	2008		Discontinued
Sarah Babylon Dorrance	2008		2011
Jennifer Lynn Fenner	2008		2011
David Paul Graves	2008		2011
Ek Ching Hii	2008		2012
Jennifer Ann Karsner	2008		2011
John Bentley Rudolph	2008		2011
Robert Eric Snyder	2008		2011
Donna Claycomb-Sokol	Transfer 2008		2003
Sherrin Marshall	Transfer 2008		2002
Kate Suttle Murphey	Transfer 2008		2009
David Myers	Transfer 2008		1974
Bryant Melvin Oskvig	Transfer 2008		2004
Lee Brewer	Transfer 2009		
Cynthia Burkert	Transfer 2009		2003
Mary Kathryn Kanahan	2009		2013
Daniel Mejia	Transfer 2009		2004
Frankie Allen Revell	2009		2012
Kirkland Reynolds	2009		2012
Marlon Brooks Tilghman	2009		2012
Paul Wesley Johnson	2010		2014
Jason Jordon-Griffin	2010		2014
Martha Pruett Meredith	2010		2013
Edgardo Rivera	Transfer 2010		2005
Elizabeth Amanda Sayers	2010		2013
Harry E. Smith, Jr.	2010		2013
Jennifer Lyn Stallings	2010		2013
(2014 Journal, change to Jennifer L. Eschliman)			

	Received On Probation	Ordained Deacon	Elder
Alicia Loar Vanisko	2010		2013
William Thomas Chaney, Jr.	Transfer 2010		2010£
Kathy Lynn Altman	2011		2015
Bernadette Althea Armwood	2011		2016
Michael Ryan Beiber	2011		2014
Emily Claire Berkowitz	2011		2014
Cynthia Marie Caldwell	2011		2015
Kecia Ford	2011		Discontinued
Kelly Linette Grimes	2011		2014
Lisa Ann Jordan	2011		2016
(2017 Journal, change to Lisa Jordan Werkis)			
Linda Ann Walkins Motter	2011		2014
Bonnie Elisabeth Scott	2011		2014
David Christopher Shank	2011		Discontinued
Jason Nathaniel Shank	2011		Discontinued
Theresa Thames	2011		2016
Sheridan Barclift Allmond	2012		2015
Adam Briddell	2012		2016
Alice Ford	Transfer 2012		2007
Andrew Scott Greenwood	2012		2015
Nicole Leigh Christopher	Transfer 2012		2011
(2013 Journal, changed to Nicole Leigh Christopher Houston)			
Elizabeth H. Jackson	2012		2015
James Kevin Johnson	2012		2016
Tiffany Renee Kromer	2012		2016
(2016 Journal, changed to Tiffany Renee Patterson)			
Bonnie J. McCubbin	2012		2016
Sandra Lee Phillips	2012		Discontinued
Twanda E. Prioleau	2012		2016
Wendy Ruth van Vliet	2012		2016
Dana L. Werts	2012		2015
Heath E. Wilson	2012		2018
George L. Winkfield	2012		2015
J.T. Blake	Transfer 2013		2010
Martin Brooks	Transfer 2013		2010
Nicholas Bufano	2013		2018
Michael Bynum	2013		2016
Michelle H. Chaney (transfer African Methodist Episcopal)	2013		2000
Frances Dailey	Transfer 2013		1993
Wanda B. Duckett (transfer African Methodist Episcopal)	2013		2010
Angela Flanagan	2013		2016
Katie Grover	2013		2016
Joseph P. Heath	2013		2019
(2017 Journal, changed to Joseph P. Heath-Mason)			
YuJung Hwang	2013		2017
Mark Johnson	Transfer 2013		1995
Sandra Johnson	Transfer 2013		2002
Robert Edward Kells, Jr.	2013		2017

	Received As Provisional	Ordained Deacon	Elder
Timothy Kromer	2013	Discontinued	
Michael Leedom	Transfer 2013		
Beth Ludlum	2013		2016
Fay Lundin	Transfer 2013		1996
Maidstone Mulenga	Transfer 2013		
Dae Sung Park	2013		2016
Katharine Schechter Saari	2013		2018
Yo-Seop Shin (transfer Korean Methodist)	2013		1993
Shannon Sullivan	2013		2016
Braulio Torres	2013		2016
Marvin Wamble	2013		2016
Daryl Lamar Williams (transfer African Methodist Epis.)	2013		2001
Linda Yarrow	2013		
Doratha Yunger	2013		2016
Myung-Ha Baek	2014		2017
Laura Markle Downton	2014		
Mark Christopher Gorman	2014		2017
Cary James, Jr. (transfer African Methodist Epis.)	2014		
Selena Marie Johnson	2014		2017
Dana Maurice Jones	2014		
Gladman Kapfumvuti	Transfer 2014		
Alisa Lasater	Transfer 2014		
Brenda Lee Lewis	2014		2018
Solomon Lloyd	Transfer 2014		
Claire Matheny	Transfer 2014		
John McCauley	Transfer 2014		
James David McSavaney	2014		2018
Ginger Ray Medley	2014		2017
Kara June Scroggins	2014		2017
Reginald Tarpley	2014		2018
Ronald Fleming-Triplett	2014		2019
Kevin Wright (transfer Wesleyan)	2014		2015
Erik Alsgaard	Transfer 2015	1986	1988
Giovanni Arroyo	2015		2018
Andre' Briscoe, Jr.	2015		2019
LaDelle Brooks			2015
Michael Cantley	2015		2019
Johnsie Cogman	Transfer		2015
Sherri Comer-Cox	2015		
Lemuel Dominguez	2015		2019
Kyle Durbin	2015		2019
Elizabeth LeMaster	2015		2018
Laura Norvell	2015		2018
Michael Parker II	2015		
Yvonne Penn	Transfer 2015		
F. Douglas Powe	Transfer 2015		2013
Leonardo Rodriguez			2015£
Jessica Statesman	2015		2019

	Received As Provisional	Ordained Deacon	Elder
(2017 Journal, changed to Jessica Statesman Hayden)			
Dawn Stewart	2015		2018
Carissa Surber	2015		2019
Beth Anne Williams	2015		2018
(2016 Journal, change to Beth Anne Hutton)			
Meredith Wilkins-Arnold	Transfer		2015
Sherri E. Wood-Powe			2015£
Patricia Abell	2016		2019
Lillian Boyd	2016		2019
Alexis Brown	2016		2019
R. Lorraine Brown	2016		
Sandra Hetz Burchell	2016		
Lysbeth Cockrell		Transfer 2016	
Mark Groover	2016		
Kathleen Lossau		Transfer 2016	
Brenda McIlwain	2016		2019
Michelle Renee Mejia		Transfer 2016	
Taysie Phillps	2016	Discontinued	
Irance Reddix	2016		2019
Lillian C. Smith		Transfer 2016	
Daniel James Breidenbaugh	2017		
Alison Thomas DeLeo	2017		
Rodney Rydell Hudson		Transfer 2017	
Walter Daniel Jackson, III	2017		
Heerak Kim	2017		
Tommy Maurice Murray	2017		
Kathleen O'Hern	2017		
Heather Jean Olson	2017		
Monica Elizabeth Raines	2017		
Evelyn Rivera	2017		
William Glenn Thomas		readmitted 2017	
Donna Lee Nelson	Transfer 2018		
Sherwyn Benjamin	2018		
Scott Bostic	2018		
Patrick Michael Hurder Buhrman	2018		
Mi Ja Cho	2018		
Christopher Dembeck	2018		
Sarah Elliott	2018		
James Gosnell	2018		
Lynne Humphries-Russ	2018		
David Jacobson	2018		
Kathryn Mackereth	2018		
Robert Ruggieri	2018		
Anna Schwartz	2018		
Emily Smiley Hart	2018		
Matthew Tate	2018		
Ian Collier	2019		
Gerald Elston	2019		

	Received As Provisional	Ordained Deacon	Elder
Ashley Hoover	2019		
Narae Kim	2019		
Raphael Koikoi	2019		
Dong Eun (Vivian) Lee	2019		
Jean Lee	2019		
Isaiah Redd	2019		
Jeffrey Zalatoris	2019		
Sung Hwan Cho	Transfer 2019		

Chronological Roll of Associate Members

	Received On Probation/ As Provisional	Ordained Deacon
Elder		
Ernest Francis Johnson	1969	1948
1950		
Lloyd Charles McClarren	1969	1968
William Henry Peters	1969	1961
1964		
Milton Walter Benny, Jr.	1971	1969
Francis Blaine Rinker	1973	1970
Harold W. Malone	1977	1972
Kenneth L. Jackson	1979	
Orlando F. Kibbe	1981	
James Houston Farmer	1988	1988
Laverne Maxine Clipper Thomas	1988	1988
(2002 Journal, page 350, changed to Laverne Maxine Clipper-Thomas)		
Guy H. Johnson	1989	1989
Alfred E. Statesman	1990	
Dennis E. Dorsch	1990	1990
Lewis Keene	1991	1991
Harry Lewis Burchell, Jr.	1995	1995
John Francis Paul Footen	1995	1995
Roberta Carter Matthews	1995	1995
JoeAnn Turner Harrod	1997	1997
Oliver Jennings, Sr.	1997	1997
Jane Elizabeth Wood	1997	1997
James W. Diggs	1999	1999
Bonnie Bell MacCallum Campbell	2000	2000
Vivian Louise Jones	2001	2001
Charles Wayne Frum	2002	2002
George Edward Hackey, Jr.	2007	2007
Francess Waldren Stewart	2010	
Charles Joseph Shacochis, Jr.	2011	
Keith B. Schukraft	2012	

Chronological Roll of Deacons in Full Connection

	Received On Probation/As Provisional	Ordained
Richard Lee Buckingham	From Diaconal	1997
Kathleen Frances Cheyney	From PM	1997
Dorothy Davis Clark	From Diaconal	1997
Linda Lavon Wassam Coolbaugh	From Diaconal	1997
Lee Steer Ferrell	From Diaconal	1997
Lynn Janet Porter Nulton	From Diaconal	1997
Chiew Len Teo Pang	From Diaconal	1997
(1999 Journal, page 349, changed to Chiewlen Teo)		
Margery Lynn Schammel	From Diaconal	1997
Patti Marye Smith	From Diaconal	1997
(2003 Journal, page 357, changed to Patti Smith Fenske)		
Andrea Titcomb	From Diaconal	1997
Sharon Leinert Mills	From PM	1998
Stella Sofia Austin Tay	From Diaconal	1998
Ruth Wilder Bell	From Diaconal	1999
Judith LeeAnn Brown Birch	From Diaconal	1999
Martha Jane Knobel Maxham	From Diaconal	1999
Barbara Vivian Suffecool	From Diaconal	1999
Jacqulyn Brown Thorpe	From Diaconal	1999
Arthuree Rosemille McLaughlin Wright	From Diaconal	1999
Konni Marquart Brantner	From Diaconal	2000
Mary Elizabeth Edmond Dennis	2000	2003
Susan Beth Carns	From Diaconal	2001
Limja Huh Gim	2003	2006
Marjorie Ellen Taylor	2003	
John William Bennett	2004	2007
Doris Elaine Warrell	2004	2007
Janet Louise Craswell	2005	2008
Karen Renee Weaver	2005	Discontinued
Amy Ellen Barron Duke	2006	2009
(2009 Journal, page 400, changed to Amy Ellen Duke-Benfield)		
Katherine Elizabeth Brown	2007	2012
Donald Joseph Hohne	2007	2011
William Creighton Jones, Jr.	2008	2011
David Showalter	2009	2012
Angela Maves	2009	2015
Joseph Andrew Love	2011	Discontinued
Samuel William Marullo	2011	2014
Julie Marie Wilson	2011	2016
Kathleen Grace Charters	2014	
Enger Muteteke	2015	
Leo Yates, Jr.	2015	2018
Kathy Barna	2016	
Martina Martin Efodzi	2016	2019
(2019 Journal, changed to Martina Efodzi)		
Jennifer Lynn Kokoski	2017	
Megan B. Blanchard	2018	
Deborah Burgio	2019	
T.C. Morrow	2019	

LAY MEMBERS AND RESERVES

ANNAPOLIS DISTRICT

Brown, Nelsa   *Adams || Lothian |||| 1375*   (410) 263-6446
1805 Whiton Ct, Annapolis, MD 21401-4420   Whiton1805@yahoo.com

Spriggs, Tarell   *Adams || Lothian |||| 1375*   (410) 741-1441
799 Bayard Rd, Lothian, MD 20711-9607   msspriggs23@yahoo.com

Beers, Nancy   *Asbury || Arnold |||| 1160*   (410) 757-6174
1424 Gilbert Rd, Arnold, MD 21012-2545   jbeers1424@comcast.net

Miller, Vera   *Asbury || Jessup |||| 1360*   (410) 300-8443
802 Cooks Ln, Baltimore, MD 21229-1368   vahall17@hotmail.com

Glenn, Althea   *Asbury Town Neck || Severna Park |||| 1490*   (410) 647-7279
230 ritchie hwy, severna park, MD 21146-1908   althea.glenn1@verizon.net

Wilburn, Louella   *Asbury Town Neck || Severna Park |||| 1490*   (443) 261-9864
105 Simmons Rd, Severna Park, MD 21146-1905   DrLouWilburn@gmail.com

Cromwell, Sandra *Asbury-Broadneck || Annapolis |||| 1115*   (410) 757-2995
741 Crucible Ct, Millersville, MD 21108-1546   sandrac38@gmail.com

Turner, Michele   *Asbury-Broadneck || Annapolis |||| 1115*   (410) 349-1095
314 Light Bright Ct., Edgewater, MD 21037   shellys_space@msn.com

Tocknell, Deborah *Baldwin Memorial || Millersville |||| 1420*   (410) 923-2642
929 Generals Hwy, Millersville, MD 21108-2124   dltocknell@gmail.com

Mills, Nancy   *Calvary || Annapolis |||| 1120*   (443) 254-5848
1395 Patuxent Ridge Rd, Odenton, MD 21113-6002   education@calumc.org

Wintrode, Brenda *Calvary || Annapolis |||| 1120*   (410) 757-2368
1140 Neptune Pl, Annapolis, MD 21409-4700   brenda_wintrode@yahoo.com

Howard, Bertiner   *Carters || Tracys Landing |||| 1270*   (703) 971-8048
5391 Harbor Court Dr, Alexandria, VA 22315-3945   bvhoward@hotmail.com

Vauls, Donna   *Cecil Memorial || Annapolis |||| 1130*   (410) 263-5001
3433 Rockway Ave, Annapolis, MD 21403-4854   dlvauls@yahoo.com

Haas, Jeanne   *Cedar Grove-Oakland || Deale |||| 1215*   (443) 646-2925
9071 Mary Ann Dr, Owings, MD 20736-9584   jhaas72@comcast.net

Haas, Mike   *Cedar Grove-Oakland || Deale |||| 1215*   (443) 646-2925
9071 Mary Ann Dr, Owings, MD 20736-9584   mhaas72@comcast.net

Witte, Greg   *Cedar Grove-Oakland || Deale |||| 1215*   (240) 764-4795
1239 Ellicott Ave, Churchton, MD 20733-9785   greg@GWNC.com

Christian, Brian   *Centenary || Shady Side |||| 1515*   (410) 867-2432
6324 Shady Side Rd, Shady Side, MD 20764-9703   lonewolf74@verizon.net

Purcell, Marsha   *Centenary || Shady Side ||| 1515*   (410) 867-4019
5159 S Creek View Way, Churchton, MD 20733   marsha.purcell@comcast.net

Salisbury, Glendola   *Chews Memorial || Edgewater ||| 1438*   (410) 867-7714
1183 Grove Ave, Shady Side, MD 20764-9532   gsalisbury80@gmail.com

Deehring, Bryan   *Community || Crofton ||| 1180*   (323) 883-1959
1752 Castleford Sq Apt 17, Crofton, MD 21114-1927   bryandeehring@mac.com

Harvey, Lisa   *Community || Pasadena ||| 1440*   (410) 437-8406
8597 Bay Rd, Pasadena, MD 21122-3164   harveymart@yahoo.com

Stevens, Gene   *Community || Pasadena ||| 1440*   (410) 360-0673
6917 Galesbury Ct, Glen Burnie, MD 21060-8689   geneds1@comcast.net

Durbin, Pam   *Davidsonville || Davidsonville ||| 1190*   (410) 721-2291
1703 Dryden Way, Crofton, MD 21114-1412   pdurbin1@gmail.com

Matousek, Lee   *Davidsonville || Davidsonville ||| 1190*   (410) 798-1346
3610 Solomons Island Rd, Edgewater, MD 21037-3620   leem21@verizon.net

Shriner, Brian   *Delmont || Severn ||| 1475*   (410) 969-7252
819 Danza Rd, Severn, MD 21144-2106   bethannshriner@yahoo.com

Phillips, Craig   *Dorsey Emmanuel || Elkridge ||| 1220*   (443) 472-3962
   cphil624@yahoo.com

Keller, Michael   *Eastport || Annapolis ||| 1135*   (410) 263-7409
310 Riverview Ave, Annapolis, MD 21403-3328   mjkeller@att.net

Keller, Mike   *Eastport || Annapolis ||| 1135*   mjkeller@att.net

Purdy, Dudley   *Edgewater || Edgewater ||| 1235*   (410) 224-2146
105 Wallace Manor Rd, Edgewater, MD 21037-1205   bvanbrackle@yahoo.com

Ludwig, Chuck   *Faith || Pasadena ||| 1445*   (410) 439-4128
758 224th St, Pasadena, MD 21122   chuckandjean50@verizon.net

Stepp, Shawna   *Ferndale || Glen Burnie ||| 1268*   (443) 603-8103
306 Ferndale Rd, Glen Burnie, MD 21061-2440   SarabiDS9@gmail.com

Miller, Trevor   *First || Laurel ||| 7415*   (301) 776-4989
9321 Madison Ave, Laurel, MD 20723-1988   trevstermillhouse@yahoo.com

Mullins, Theresa   *Fowler || Annapolis ||| 1140*   (410) 867-1781
918 Franklin Manor Rd, Churchton, MD 20733-9701   peepah2@hotmail.com

Thompson, Kathleen   *Franklin || Churchton ||| 1175*   (410) 867-0803
717B Tyler Point Rd, Deale, MD 20751-9733   kthompson@host.sdc.edu

Kernan, Greg   *Friendship || Friendship ||| 1275*   (301) 855-7455
7324 Woodshire Ave, Chesapeake Beach, MD 20732-3124   gregory410@comcast.net

Walls, Ginger   *Friendship || Friendship ||| 1275*   (443) 964-8575
722 Fairhaven Rd, Tracys Landing, MD 20779-2511   walls.ginger@gmail.com

Fredericks, Stanley   *Galesville || Galesville ||| 1280*   (301) 627-0755
929 Fiorenza Dr, Lothian, MD 20711-9530   swfredericks@comcast.net

Harris, Kathleen   *Glen Burnie || Glen Burnie ||| 1320*   (410) 761-4478
905 Family Cir, Glen Burnie, MD 21060   office@gbumchurch.org

Mand, Valerie   *Glen Burnie || Glen Burnie ||| 1320*   (443) 261-6088
24 Chesapeake Mobile Ct, Hanover, MD 21076-1559   VJMand28@gmail.com

Falls, Gerry   *Harwood Park || Elkridge ||| 1225*   (410) 799-0138
7967 Max Blobs Park Rd, Jessup, MD 20794-9204   gerryandedfalls@juno.com

Boysaw, Shirlette *Hope Memorial St Mark || Edgewater ||| 1240*   (410) 672-6074
1000 Ice Castle Ct, Gambrills, MD 21054-1564   tsojdirector@aol.com

Boston, Gereald   *John Wesley || Annapolis ||| 1145*   (410) 799-7410
28 New Jersey Ave NW, Glen Burnie, MD 21061-3029   epatriciab@aol.com

Moon, Colleen   *John Wesley || Annapolis ||| 1145*   (410) 295-0403
2 Garden Gate Ct, Annapolis, MD 21403-1404   cmoon129@verizon.net

Krouser, Emma   *John Wesley || Glen Burnie ||| 1330*   (410) 672-6085
2414 Pineville Crest Ct, Odenton, MD 21113-2521   e5m7krou2@gmail.com

Liles, Addie   *John Wesley || Glen Burnie ||| 1330*   (443) 618-8844
7824 Foxfarm Ln, Glen Burnie, MD 21061-6321   aliles@cadca.org

Robinson, Catherine   *John Wesley-Waterbury || Crownsville ||| 1185*   (410) 768-7935
310 Shannon Forest Ct, Glen Burnie, MD 21060-8322   brrbnsns4@aol.com

Brown, Bruce   *Linthicum Heights || Linthicum ||| 1370*   (410) 971-7937
502 Hawthorne Rd, Linthicum, MD 21090-2310   bigtime66@verizon.net

Talley, Raymond *Macedonia || Odenton ||| 1425*   (410) 551-2110
8005 Ponderosa Dr, Severn, MD 21144-1751   ray.p.talley@outlook.com

Hawley, Betty   *Marley || Glen Burnie ||| 1335*   bettyhawley1@gmail.com

Hurley, Carol   *Mayo || Edgewater ||| 1148*   (410) 295-7743
110 Thomas Gantt Rd, Huntingtown, MD 20639-8544   c.hurley@comcast.net

Burke, Mary   *Melville Chapel || Elkridge ||| 1265*   (410) 796-0863
6250 Old Washington Rd, Elkridge, MD 21075-5303   mehburke@aol.com

Grable, Brad   *Melville Chapel || Elkridge ||| 1265*   (301) 404-0402
5734 Elkridge Heights Rd, Elkridge, MD 21075-5325   bgrable43@yahoo.com

Deel, David   *Messiah || Glen Burnie ||| 1340*   rippledeep@gmail.com

Shanks, Kathy   *Messiah || Glen Burnie |||| 1340*
7903 Colchester Ct, Pasadena, MD 21122-2000

(443) 702-7609
WCShanks@comcast.net

Dailey, Gertrude   *Metropolitan || Severn |||| 1480*
508 Jones Rd, Severn, MD 21144-1301

(410) 761-5816
rgdailey@comcast.net

Jenkins, Jason   *Metropolitan || Severn |||| 1480*
2554 Blue Water Blvd, Odenton, MD 21113-3305

(410) 305-0063
jvjenkins42@gmail.com

Clarke, Juanita   *Mount Calvary || Arnold |||| 1165*
1821 Fox Hollow Run, Pasadena, MD 21122-3332

(410) 279-2381
grandstar24@verizon.net

Ettinger, Bob   *Mount Carmel || Pasadena |||| 1460*
1909 Main Ave, Pasadena, MD 21122-3416

(410) 360-6774
bobesue80@yahoo.com

Ettinger, Susan   *Mount Carmel || Pasadena |||| 1460*
1909 Main Ave, Pasadena, MD 21122-3416

(410) 360-6774
bobesue80@yahoo.com

Fauconnet, Leslie   *Mount Carmel || Pasadena |||| 1460*
4760 Mountain Rd, Pasadena, MD 21122-5814

(240) 405-2750
soujourner56@gmail.com

Darden, Alverta   *Mount Tabor || Crownsville |||| 1285*
904 Country Ter, Severna Park, MD 21146-4713

(410) 647-7046
Bettyboop9mmcal@aol.com

Hawkins, Betty   *Mount Tabor || Crownsville |||| 1285*
1421 Saint Stephens Church Rd, Crownsville, MD 21032

(410) 721-3472
ghaw425549@gmail.com

Bryant, Valerie   *Mount Zion || Annapolis |||| 1150*
13307 Hillrod Ln, Upper Marlboro, MD 20774-1966

(336) 202-6249
vbryant624@verizon.net

Gibson, Mary   *Mount Zion || Laurel |||| 7420*
9346 Canterbury Riding, Laurel, MD 20723

(301) 498-9431
mdgibson50@aol.com

Talley, DelLisa   *Mount Zion || Laurel |||| 7420*
3830 6th St, Baltimore, MD 21225-2104

(447) 369-4726
dellisa.talley@yahoo.com

Harrison, Joe   *Mount Zion || Lothian |||| 1410*
3613 Birdsville Rd, Davidsonville, MD 21035-2513

(410) 798-6195
joswharr@comcast.net

Hines, John   *Mount Zion || Lothian |||| 1410*
411 Osbourne Rd, Tracys Landing, MD 20779-2525

(410) 257-0753
jchinesjr@comcast.net

Demby, Ernest   *Mount Zion || Pasadena |||| 1465*
1406 Wigeon Way Unit 203, Gambrills, MD 21054-1354

(410) 721-9205
ERNSR1@gmail.com

Adams, Alfreda   *Mount Zion-Ark Road || Lothian |||| 1415*
5045 Solomons Island Rd, Lothian, MD 20711-9786

(410) 867-2329
apadreams@live.com

Stanton, Juanita   *Mount Zion-Ark Road || Lothian |||| 1415*
4601 Sutherland Cir, Upper Marlboro, MD 20772-6104

(301) 627-8176
stanton4601@comcast.net

Foster, Phyllis   *Nichols-Bethel || Odenton |||| 1430*
527 Rita Dr, Odenton, MD 21113-1703

(410) 674-8174
azfoste@comcast.net

Lewis, Dorothy *Nichols-Bethel || Odenton |||| 1430*
908 Winterhaven Cir, Gambrills, MD 21054-1210

(410) 672-7266
danl0131@msn.com

Mabry, Donna *Nichols-Bethel || Odenton |||| 1430*
8603 Wintergreen Ct, Odenton, MD 21113-3859

(410) 672-5978
mabryeasy@verizon.net

Oren, Barry *Nichols-Bethel || Odenton |||| 1430*
736 Cecil Ave N, Millersville, MD 21108-1947

(443) 326-3208
barryoren35@gmail.com

Wallace, Doug *Nichols-Bethel || Odenton |||| 1430*
7623 Ayrshire Ct, Severn, MD 21144-1242

(410) 969-8640
dougwall12@verizon.net

Whalen-White, Denice *Nichols-Bethel || Odenton |||| 1430*
7422 Quixote Ct, Bowie, MD 20720-4354

(301) 395-7617
swhalen05@yahoo.com

Jester, Deborah *Pasadena || Pasadena |||| 1470*
506 Kent Ave, Pasadena, MD 21122

(410) 647-5452
DJest@aol.com

Seibert, Michael *Pasadena || Pasadena |||| 1470*
632 Westmoreland Pl, Severna Park, MD 21146-3544

(443) 909-6641
rescue1396@ymail.com

Woodworth, Laurence *Savage || Savage |||| 7435*
9095 Thamesmeade Rd, Laurel, MD 20723-5811

(301) 717-0021
lswoodworth4@gmail.com

Woorworth, Larry *Savage || Savage |||| 7435*

Lswoodworth4@gmail.com

Benjamin, Erica *Severna Park || Severna Park |||| 1510*
7922 Severn Hills Way, Severn, MD 21144

(410) 987-4700
ebenjamin@severnaparkumc.org

Kraus, Heather *Severna Park || Severna Park |||| 1510*
583 Highbank Rd, Severna Park, MD 21146-2307

(410) 544-6451
hkraus@semmes.com

Smith, Beth *Severna Park || Severna Park |||| 1510*
527 Corbin Pkwy, Annapolis, MD 21401-6549

Miller, Gloria *Sollers || Lothian |||| 1380*
7709 Wingate Dr, Glenn Dale, MD 20769-2010

(301) 805-0132
gloria7709@comcast.net

Randall, Marvel *Sollers || Lothian |||| 1380*
631 Birchleaf Ave, Seat Pleasant, MD 20743-1802

(301) 336-2489
marvelsr@comcast.net

Deel, David *Solley || Glen Burnie |||| 1345*
8102 Glen Hollow Dr, Glen Burnie, MD 21061-6133

(410) 863-7395
rippledeep@gmail.com

Denny, Lisa *St Andrews of Annapolis || Edgewater |||| 1255*

(443) 924-6463
bdenny1207@gmail.com

Smith, Martin *St Andrews of Annapolis || Edgewater |||| 1255*
938 Tidewater Grove Ct, Annapolis, MD 21401-6834

(410) 571-1682
jcsmithmsw@aol.com

Walsh, Karen *St Andrews of Annapolis || Edgewater |||| 1255*
1651 Lee Drive Edgewater, MD 21037

(410) 798-5732
kwalsh5241@verizon.net

Gordon, Erika   *St Mark || Hanover |||| 1350*   (410) 298-4476
3240 Kelox Rd, Gwynn Oak, MD 21207-6280   eritopaz@aol.com

Dunscomb, Tyra   *St Matthews || Shady Side |||| 1520*   (410) 867-4633
5540 Franklin Blvd, Churchton, MD 20733-9742   tdun1223@yahoo.com

Johnson, Jean   *St Matthews || Shady Side |||| 1520*   (410) 867-9483
5876 Shady Side Road, Churchton, MD 20733-0231   evieevie2@hotmail.com

Wallace, Joshua   *Trinity || Annapolis |||| 1155*
849 Meadow Heights Ln, Arnold, MD 21012-1213   wallacejm86@yahoo.com

Swain, Kathleen   *Trinity || Odenton |||| 1435*   (410) 451-8220
2303 Weymouth Ln, Crofton, MD 21114-1212   kdssrs98@gmail.com

Swain, Scott   *Trinity || Odenton |||| 1435*   (410) 533-5551
2303 Weymouth Ln, Crofton, MD 21114-1212   srskds98@gmail.com

Swann, Frances   *Union || Lothian |||| 1385*   (410) 263-3037
3854 Queen Anne Bridge Rd, Davidsonville, MD 21035-2403   sswann9173@aol.com

Anderson, Carolyn   *Union Memorial || Davidsonville |||| 1210*   (410) 956-4598
3443 Riva Rd, Davidsonville, MD 21035-2019   cmanderson71@hotmail.com

Edmonds, Carlos   *Union Memorial || Davidsonville |||| 1210*   (410) 798-4785
1568 Governor Bridge Rd, Davidsonville, MD 21035-1513   carlosedmunds@aol.com

Oursler, Janet   *Wesley Chapel || Jessup |||| 1365*   (410) 799-2128
7760 Waterloo Rd, Jessup, MD 20794   janetoursler@comcast.net

Manifold, Donald   *Wesley Chapel || Lothian |||| 1390*   (410) 741-1756
827 Marlboro Rd, Lothian, MD 20711-9621   SueandMuff@verizon.net

Smoot-Wood, Patricia   *Wesley Grove || Hanover |||| 1355*   (410) 519-5474
207 Raccoon Run Ct, Hanover, MD 21076-1263   smoot-wood@verizon.net

Thompson, Betty   *Wilson Memorial || Gambrills |||| 1290*   (410) 721-1482
1735 Remington Dr, Crofton, MD 21114-1845   Butterfly_1@verizon.net

Young, Myra   *Wilson Memorial || Gambrills |||| 1290*   (301) 805-5885
16406 Elysian Ln, Bowie, MD 20716-3258   vanpelt2@verizon.net

BALTIMORE METROPOLITAN DISTRICT
Anderson, Cynthia   *Ames || Baltimore |||| 4110*   (410) 725-2629
4702 Wrenwood Ave, Baltimore, MD 21212-4639   cvalleyhigh@aol.com

Anderson, Cynthia Marlene*Ames || Baltimore |||| 4110*   (410) 725-2629
615 Baker St, Baltimore, MD 21217-2814   cvalleyhigh@aol.com

Button, Liela *Arbutus || Baltimore ||| 3110* (410) 644-9184
3913 Wilkens Ave, Baltimore, MD 21229-5037

Frank, Adalyn *Arbutus || Baltimore ||| 3110*
6053 Florey Rd, Hanover, MD 21076-1018 gailfrank@verizon.net

Frank, Gail *Arbutus || Baltimore ||| 3110* (410) 796-1512
6053 Florey Rd, Hanover, MD 21076-1018

Smith, Lida *Arbutus || Baltimore ||| 3110* (410) 242-5541
2520 Kensington Gdns Unit 104, Ellicott City, MD 21043-3611

McNeill, Brenda *Arlington-Lewin || Baltimore ||| 4115* (410) 466-4582
6300 Laurelton Ave, Baltimore, MD 21214-1131 brendamcneill41@gmail.com

Nickerson, Craig *Arnolia || Baltimore ||| 3530* (410) 561-5310
318 Presway Rd, Timonium, MD 21093-2927 craig_n@icloud.com

Darden, John *Back River || Essex ||| 2420* (410) 967-5661
1600 Evergreen Way Apt 101, Essex, MD 21221-2606 jdarden244@gmail.com

Freyer, Mary *Back River || Essex ||| 2420* (410) 686-8982
2018 Middleborough Rd, Essex, MD 21221-1516 office@backriverumc.com

Clemons, Myra *Beechfield || Baltimore ||| 3150* beechfieldumc@yahoo.com

Siegel, Laura *Bethesda || Baltimore ||| 3145* (410) 561-7484
2305 Wuthering Rd, Timonium, MD 21093-2652 BLJSiegel@msn.com

Pyle, Linda *Catonsville || Catonsville ||| 4180* (410) 788-1642
6122 Moorefield Rd, Catonsville, MD 21228-2756 cumclinda@verizon.net

Solloway, Emma *Catonsville || Catonsville ||| 4180* (410) 788-6293
205 Worthmont Rd, Catonsville, MD 21228-5452 essolloway@verizon.net

Belt, Keya *Centennial-Caroline || Baltimore ||| 2150* (410) 695-3146
1502 King Philip Cir, Severn, MD 21144-3419 keyabelt@yahoo.com

Long, Alvin *Centennial-Caroline || Baltimore ||| 2150* (443) 418-6376
4508 Arizona Ave, Baltimore, MD 21206-3629 ministeralsr@comcast.net

Kehr, Marcella *Chase || Middle River ||| 2362* (410) 335-5650
6723 Mallard Rd, Baltimore, MD 21220-1214 kehrm@hotmail.com

Cherisier, Rashida *Cherry Hill || Baltimore ||| 2155* (410) 833-0405
41 Brookshire Dr, Reisterstown, MD 21136-3623 rcherisier@yahoo.com

Jones, Doris *Cherry Hill || Baltimore ||| 2155* (410) 265-5731
3619 Forest Garden Ave, Baltimore, MD 21207-6308 latricejohnson85@gmail.com

Keene, Frances *Christ || Baltimore ||| 2160* (410) 444-7745
1904 Northbourne Rd, Baltimore, MD 21239-3725 saintpeterchick@gmail.com

218

Smith, Alice   *Christ || Baltimore ||| 2160*   (410) 532-2732
1145 E Northern Pkwy, Baltimore, MD 21239-1932   alsmithenator@gmail.com

Rodriguez, Moses   *Christ Church of Balt. Co. || Baltimore ||| 3285*   (410) 789-5810
2834 Alabama Ave, Baltimore, MD 21227-2204   mrodrigue7@rollins.com

Shearer, Charlotte *Christ Church of the Deaf || Baltimore ||| 3115*   (443) 844-5480
5320 Dorsey Hall Dr, Ellicott City, MD 21042-7863   charlotte_shearer@comcast.net

Young, Veronica   *Christ Church of the Deaf || Baltimore ||| 3115*   (443) 762-2338
                                                                    vglovesgod@yahoo.com

Burns, Edith   *Cowenton || White Marsh ||| 2570*   (410) 404-5610
7017 Graces Quarters Rd, Baltimore, MD 21220-1600   edithburns81050@gmail.com

Dean, Joyce   *Eastern || Baltimore ||| 2175*   (410) 366-4263
618 E 36th St, Baltimore, MD 21218-2527   joycepearl1@verizon.net

Sanders, Cathy   *Eden Korean || Baltimore ||| 2180*   (410) 561-7591
8 Bailiffs Ct, Timonium, MD 21093-1969   adairbrady@verizon.net

Yoon, John   *Eden Korean || Baltimore ||| 2180*   yshinpastor@gmail.com

Collins, Chenris   *Emanuel || Catonsville ||| 4630*   emanuelumc@verizon.net

Schlenker, Beverly   *Emanuel || Catonsville ||| 4630*   (410) 744-2448
2137 Rockwell Ave, Baltimore, MD 21228-4718   emanuelumc@verizon.net

Cooke, Ralph   *Epworth Chapel || Baltimore ||| 4170*   (410) 833-8668
                                                                   ralphc_cooke@comcast.net

Morgan, Pamela   *Epworth Chapel || Baltimore ||| 4170*   (410) 581-3811
6 Belladonna Ct, Owings Mills, MD 21117-1331   pmorganrun@aol.com

Houghtaling, Charles   *Essex || Essex ||| 2425*   (410) 499-4719
922 Foxcroft Ln, Baltimore, MD 21221-5924   chashoughtaling@hotmail.com

Martin, Hattie   *Faith Community || Baltimore ||| 2192*   (410) 665-1925
119 Morgan Elis Way, Baltimore, MD 21206-1444   hattie45_99@msn.com

Mitchell, Wanda   *Faith Community || Baltimore ||| 2192*   (410) 206-9325
6311 Marietta Ave, Baltimore, MD 21214-2255   wandalmitchell@gmail.com

Keith, Randy   *Good Shepherd || Baltimore ||| 3230*   (443) 827-5158
1000 W 38th St, Baltimore, MD 21211-1817   keithfam@gmail.com

White, Lenetta   *Govans-Boundary || Baltimore ||| 3165*   (443) 629-7478
2602 Roselawn Ave, Baltimore, MD 21214-1701   blackdogdog11@gmail.com

Kahl, George   *Grace || Baltimore ||| 3170*   (410) 337-0089
7903 Springway Rd, Baltimore, MD 21204-3517   gkahl533740@comcast.net

Schmidt, Douglas *Grace || Baltimore ||| 3170* (410) 494-2789
7911 Sherwood Ave, Towson, MD 21204-3658 dnschm@aol.com

Conjar, Chuck *Graceland || Baltimore ||| 2210* (410) 866-8218
6176 Radecke Ave, Baltimore, MD 21206-2932 cconjar@gmail.com

Weaver, Elizabeth *Graceland || Baltimore ||| 2210* (410) 284-0993
1757 Melbourne Rd, Baltimore, MD 21222-4823 Cyberliz@verizon.net

Flowers, Saundra *Gwynn Oak || Baltimore ||| 4130* (410) 281-0974
7404 Shirley Rd, Baltimore, MD 21207-4569 sgflow@comcast.net

DeHaven, William *Hampden || Baltimore ||| 3175* (410) 833-1574
139 W Chestnut Hill Ln, Reisterstown, MD 21136-3206 aeroplanebill@gmail.com

Pembamoto, Lutebula *Hiss || Baltimore ||| 3440* (410) 444-2479
5917 Walther Ave, Baltimore, MD 21206-2335 ldannypembamoto@gmail.com

Whiteley, Norman *Hiss || Baltimore ||| 3440* (443) 635-4208
7836 Birmingham Ave, Baltimore, MD 21234-5406 workingnorm@gmail.com

Bond, Gertrude *Homestead || Baltimore ||| 3180* (410) 825-6885
2856 Lake Ave, Baltimore, MD 21213-1218 gebond2004@msn.com

Clark Jr., Ernest *John Wesley || Baltimore ||| 4135* (443) 631-6172
5513 Belleville Ave, Baltimore, MD 21207-6945 ernest5513@gmail.com

Lee, Sarah *John Wesley || Baltimore ||| 4135* (443) 204-6042
3411 Henry Harford Dr, Abingdon, MD 21009 sarahlee451@verizon.net

Brown, Greg *Lansdowne || Baltimore ||| 3125* (410) 796-5240
6314 Troy Ct, Elkridge, MD 21075-6183 gelzabrown@verizon.net

Miller, Carl *Loch Raven || Baltimore ||| 3540* (410) 529-7534
9532 Oakbranch Way, Baltimore, MD 21236 CBMiller212361948@yahoo.com

Hodge, Duncan *Lovely Lane || Baltimore ||| 3185* (410) 467-3060
69 Penny Ln, Baltimore, MD 21209-2726

Strawbridge, John *Lovely Lane || Baltimore ||| 3185* (410) 243-5344
1435 Union Ave, Baltimore, MD 21211-1906 johnstrawbridge@hotmail.com

Andrews, Alma *Magothy of Deaf-Gallaudet || Pasadena ||| 1455* (410) 255-4530
3703 Mountain Rd, Pasadena, MD 21122-2024 almandrews4@gmail.com

Moreland, Lionel S *Magothy of Deaf-Gallaudet || Pasadena ||| 1455*
smoreland44@gmail.com

Moore, Donnell *Metropolitan || Baltimore ||| 2220* (410) 690-2673
3929 Annellen Rd, Baltimore, MD 21215 donnelljmoore@hotmail.com

Pettaway, Stephanie *Metropolitan || Baltimore ||| 2220* (410) 323-7834
1514 Northgate Rd, Baltimore, Md 21218 steppettaway@aol.com

Pierce, Jack   *Metropolitan || Baltimore ||| 2220*
5211 Norwood Ave, Baltimore, MD 21207-6761

Hart, Geoffrey   *Mount Vernon Place || Baltimore ||| 3215*   (443) 681-9474
533 S Sharp St, Baltimore, MD 21201-2413   Geoffrey.Hart@outlook.com

Adair, Verdell   *Mount Zion || Baltimore ||| 4150*   (410) 367-5187
3508 Callaway Ave, Baltimore, MD 21215-7125

Cunningham, Fronie   *Mount Zion || Baltimore ||| 4150*   (410) 664-3946
4008 Grantley Rd, Baltimore, MD 21215-7234   fcunn802@aol.com

Callum, Rose   *New Covenant Worship || Baltimore ||| 3575*   (410) 243-2999
3601 Loch Raven Blvd, Baltimore, MD 21218   Rose_Callum3601@comcast.net

Mincy-White, La-Venna   *New Waverly || Baltimore ||| 3217*   (443) 680-4221
10305 Society Park Dr Apt D, Cockeysville, MD 21030   lmincywhite@yahoo.com

Smith, Robert   *New Waverly || Baltimore ||| 3217*   (410) 209-7231
2701 N Rosedale St, Baltimore, MD 21216-1938   bobsmith1946@netzero.net

Lee, Veris   *Northwood-Appold || Baltimore ||| 3225*   (410) 484-4014
2800 Stone Cliff Dr Unit 308, Baltimore, MD 21209-3843   Verislee@aol.com

Fisher, Daniel   *Old Otterbein || Baltimore ||| 2240*   (410) 255-7198
713 214th St, Pasadena, MD 21122-1301   danielbfisher@icloud.com

Greene, Leigh   *Orangeville || Baltimore ||| 2250*   (443) 488-1728
1008 Iris Ave, Baltimore, MD 21205-3027   greeneleigh2@gmail.com

Hart, Nikki   *Orems || Baltimore ||| 2515*   (410) 687-3191
921 Homberg Ave, Essex, MD 21221   nikkishart@comcast.net

Calvert, Sheila   *Patapsco || Dundalk ||| 2385*   (410) 285-6420
1246 Willow Rd, Dundalk, MD 21222-1428   smcslc326@msn.com

Stowell, Lawrence *Piney Grove || Middle River ||| 2355*   (410) 679-0557
910 Averill Rd, Joppa, MD 21085-3803   larrystowell@comcast.net

Busky, Lauren   *Salem-Baltimore Hispanic || Baltimore ||| 2310*   (410) 661-3709
8704 Fowler Ave, Baltimore, MD 21234-4231   labusky@comcast.net

Moore, Samuel   *Sharp Street Memorial || Baltimore ||| 3250*   (410) 205-7825
4122 W Rogers Ave, Baltimore, MD 21215-4329   samuelwmoore@hotmail.com

Stemley, Elizabeth *Sharp Street Memorial || Baltimore ||| 3250*   (443) 850-8544
1190 West Northern PWKY 610, Baltimore, MD 21210   estemley1190@comcast.net

Booker, Jennifer   *St James Memorial || Baltimore ||| 2265*   (443) 676-5131
319 N Payson St, Baltimore, MD 21223-1501   jenylyte813@gmail.com

Foy, Vernette   *St John || Baltimore ||| 1473*   (410) 789-9573
5501 Park Rd, Baltimore, MD 21225-3435   vnetta710@aol.com

Hammack, Kevin *St John || Baltimore ||| 1473*
221 Midland Ave, Baltimore, MD 21225-3242

(410) 789-3903
KRHSR231@aol.com

Stevenson, Janie *St Johns || Baltimore ||| 3240*
610 E Lake Ave, Baltimore, MD 21212-3134

(410) 464-2850
janievons@yahoo.com

Terry, Roxanne *St Johns || Baltimore ||| 3240*
44 Dunkirk Rd, Baltimore, MD 21212-1705

(443) 895-4223
rocketrn@hotmail.com

Gray, Lillie *St Luke || Baltimore ||| 4155*
4011 Bowers Ave, Baltimore, MD 21207-7009

(410) 466-4849
lgray3760@gmail.com

Scott, Zelda *St Luke || Baltimore ||| 4155*
8501 Coltrane Ct Unit 408, Ellicott City, MD 21043-5128

(410) 281-9546
zeldas2@verizon.net

Gadsden, Larry *St Matthews || Baltimore ||| 2390*
909 Foxwood Ln, Essex, MD 21221-5929

(410) 844-0759
larry.gadsden@va.gov

Williamson, Beulah *St Matthews || Baltimore ||| 2390*
6429 Washington Ave, Glen Burnie, MD 21060-6362

(410) 789-3037
melmel6@verizon.net

Parran, Yvonne *St. Matthews-New Life || Baltimore ||| 3247*
8505greenlane, baltimore, MD 21244

(410) 655-8918
yvonneparran@verizon.net

Swann, Derrick *St. Paul Praise and Worship || Pikesville ||| 2290*
6807 Real Princess Ln, Gwynn Oak, MD 21207-4493

(410) 736-8542
swann.derrick@ymail.com

Gralley, Kevin *Towson || Towson ||| 3550*

kevin.gralley@gmail.com

Livingston, Rachel *Towson || Towson |||| 3550*
4421 Marble Hall Rd Apt 279, Baltimore, MD 21218-1544

(302) 230-6141
yandya@towsonumc.org

Bien, Barbara *Trinity || Catonsville ||| 4210*
2011 Windys Run Rd, Catonsville, MD 21228-5884

(410) 978-7091
bbien@comcast.net

Johns, Ellen *Union Memorial || Baltimore ||| 2320*
2312 W Mosher St, Baltimore, MD 21216-4508

(410) 945-6807
administrator@unionbaltimore.org

Carey, Kathalene *Unity || Baltimore ||| 2325*
2418 Lauretta Ave, Baltimore, MD 21223-1020

(410) 362-9085
kathalene.carey@gmail.com

Hayden, Jan *West Baltimore || Baltimore ||| 4165*
142 Pleasant Valley Drive, Baltimore, MD 21228

(410) 747-7733
jhayden@cbmove.com

BALTIMORE SUBURBAN DISTRICT

Presberry, Christina   *Ames || Bel Air ||| 2335*   (410) 245-2421
61 Allendale Street, Bel Air, MD 21014   christinapresberry69@gmail.com

Harford, Thomas   *Bixlers || Manchester ||| 4530*   (410) 346-7022
2747 Blacks School House Rd, Taneytown, MD 21787-1450   tharford755@gmail.com

Duckworth, Brittain   *Bosley || Sparks ||| 3490*

Smith, Mary   *Camp Chapel || Perry Hall ||| 2530*   (410) 882-0976
8369 Tapu Ct, Baltimore, MD 21236-3017   msmith9862@aol.com

Smith, William   *Camp Chapel || Perry Hall ||| 2530*   (410) 551-5055
773 Pine Drift Dr, Odenton, MD 21113-2505   wjs32246@verizon.net

Brady, Rose   *Cedar Grove || Monkton ||| 3415*   mulehollerfarm@comcast.net

Mainolfi, Hope   *Centre || Forest Hill ||| 2445*
325 Martindale Ln, Forest Hill, MD 21050   hope0715@aol.com

Smart, Jeffery   *Centre || Forest Hill ||| 2445*   (410) 638-1478
1210 Glastonbury Way, Bel Air, MD 21014-3333   jshist@comcast.net

Wilmer, Lynne   *Chesaco || Baltimore ||| 2545*   (302) 927-0429
28379 Dagsboro Woods Dr, Dagsboro, DE 19939-4558   lfwilmer123@gmail.com

Becton, Thea   *Clarks Chapel || Bel Air ||| 2365*   (443) 866-7481
1230 Carroll St, Baltimore, MD 21230-1809   ryansmom0512@hotmail.com

Davis, Valerie   *Clynmalira || Phoenix ||| 3450*   (410) 207-9729
7 W Main Blvd, Timonium, MD 21093-2203   ValPriceDavis@gmail.com

Potter, Marianne   *Cokesbury || Abingdon ||| 2125*   (410) 671-4126
1234 Bush Rd, Abingdon, MD 21009-1209   potterm18@gmail.com

Riley, Bruce   *Cokesbury || Abingdon ||| 2125*   (410) 459-1254
602 Portsmouth Ct, Bel Air, MD 21014-2769   beefybobcat@comcast.net

Harter, Gary   *Cranberry || Perryman ||| 2540*   (443) 307-5732
227 Forest Green Rd, Aberdeen, MD 21001-4315   gary.harter1990@gmail.com

Hanna, James   *Darlington || Darlington ||| 2375*   (410) 457-4547
2106 Shuresville Rd, Darlington, MD 21034   Susquehannaelf@aol.com

Ryan, M.   *Deer Park || Reisterstown ||| 4415*   (410) 833-1238
5834 Deer Park Rd, Reisterstown, MD 21136-6026   kathyryan626@hotmail.com

Waddell, Pat   *Dublin || Street ||| 2550*
1817 Kalmia Rd, Bel Air, MD 21015-1014   DublinUMC@gmail.com

Ballard, Jack   *Ebenezer || Fallston ||| 2430*   (410) 557-7246
2911 Nelson Ln, Fallston, MD 21047-1328   ballardica@gmail.com

Givens, Calvin   *Edgewood || Lutherville ||| 3365*   (410) 532-8832
717 Radnor Ave, Baltimore, MD 21212-4506   cegivens@live.com

Bostic, Mary   *Emory || Street ||| 2555*
738 Cherry Hill Rd, Street, MD 21154-1628   marybostic738@gmail.com

Bostic, Robert   *Emory || Street ||| 2555*
738 Cherry Hill Rd, Street, MD 21154-1628   bobbostic46@gmail.com

Bowen, Jack   *Emory || Street ||| 2555*   (410) 836-0423
1332 Macton Rd, Street, MD, Street, MD 21154   bowtrem@gmail.com

Lastner, Rick   *Emory || Street ||| 2555*   (410) 638-8244
310 Colgate Dr, Forest Hill, MD 21050-1355   rnlastner@gmail.com

Schaller, Sandy   *Emory || Upperco ||| 4420*   (443) 838-5851
1721 Antler Ln, Finksburg, MD 21048-2026   slschaller@yahoo.com

Roscoe, Susan   *Epworth || Cockeysville ||| 3290*   (410) 667-0024
10400 Cranbrook Hills Pl, Cockeysville, MD 21030-2748   simunyiri@yahoo.com

Waltrup, Beth   *Epworth || Cockeysville ||| 3290*   (410) 828-9205
606 Debaugh Ave, Towson, MD 21204-3808   bwaltrup@gmail.com

Megill, Betty   *Fallston || Fallston ||| 2435*   (410) 877-7255
1509 Fallston Rd, Fallston, MD 21047-1624   fallstonumc@fallstonumc.org

Megill, Glenn   *Fallston || Fallston ||| 2435*   (410) 642-2510
15 Owens Landing Ct Apt B, Perryville, MD 21903-3058   revbmegill@aol.com

Humphreys, James   *Fork || Fork ||| 3320*   (410) 592-2131
12533 Merritt Ave, Fork, MD 21051-9719   cjfork44@comcast.net

Bennighof, Jane   *Frames Memorial || Cockeysville ||| 3460*   (410) 252-5150
1704 Ridgely Garth, Lutherville, MD 21093-5240   janleith@juno.com

Rittler, Robert   *Glyndon || Glyndon ||| 4285*   (410) 239-8147
3413 Buttonwood Ct, Reisterstown, MD 21136-4401   rrittler@aol.com

Laughton, Ann   *Grace || Aberdeen ||| 2110*   (410) 838-0220
2503 Fairway Dr, Bel Air, MD 21015-6327   ann.laughton@yahoo.com

Cavey, Christian   *Grace || Upperco ||| 4310*   (443) 465-1002
4705 Black Rock Rd, Hampstead, MD 21074-3014   chris@cavey.com

Rada, Renee   *Greenmount || Hampstead ||| 4288*   (410) 239-2233
4050 Wheatland Ct, Hampstead, MD 21074-1559   radaranch@verizon.net

Moore, Thomas   *Greenspring || Owings Mills ||| 3390*   (410) 363-1586
405 Greenspring Valley Rd, Owings Mills, MD 21117-4324

Ashby, Dee   *Havre De Grace || Havre De Grace ||| 2455*   (443) 502-5018
110 S Lodge Ln, Havre de Grace, MD 21078-3108   jdsashby11@comcast.net

Rusin, Dan   *Havre De Grace || Havre De Grace ||| 2455*   (410) 272-4020
302 Kendrick Dr, Aberdeen, MD 21001-2344   kimdanrusin@verizon.net

Trimboli, Peg   *Havre De Grace || Havre De Grace ||| 2455*   (443) 243-1238
205 Bald Eagle Way, Belcamp, MD 21017-1711   Ptrimboli54@comcast.net

Woodford, Kat   *Havre De Grace || Havre De Grace ||| 2455*
katherinewoodford1977@gmail.com

Gardner, Mark   *Hereford || Monkton ||| 3344*   (410) 343-1184
1400 Mount Carmel Rd, Parkton, MD 21120-9768   admin@herefordumc.org

Thomas, Linda   *Hereford || Monkton ||| 3344*   admin@herefordumc.org

Tibbs, Robert   *Hopewell || Havre de Grace ||| 2460*   (410) 734-6873
3545 Old Level Rd, Havre de Grace, MD 21078-1021   shadowspringsfarm@comcast.net

Cochnar, Kenneth *Idlewylde || Baltimore ||| 3535*   (410) 321-7263
1413 Shefford Rd, Baltimore, MD 21239-1435   Ken.Cochnar@gmail.com

Grap, Charles   *Idlewylde || Baltimore ||| 3535*   (410) 830-9517
1319 Heather Hill Rd, Baltimore, MD 21239-1416   cgrap@verizon.net

Wernz, Julie   *Idlewylde || Baltimore ||| 3535*   (410) 321-9493
1302 Heather Hill Rd, Baltimore, MD 21239-1414   jwernz@gmail.com

Glinsky, Annette   *Jarrettsville || Jarrettsville ||| 2475*   (410) 557-7335
3129 Troyer Rd, White Hall, MD 21161-9302   aglinsky@peoplepc.com

Gauhar, Saleem   *Linden Heights || Parkville ||| 3445*   (410) 661-4187
Www Mannahouseinc Org, Parkville, MD 21234-1906   Saleem.gauhar.manna@gmail.com

Boykin, Alauna   *Maryland Line || Maryland Line ||| 3380*   (443) 605-3157
20991 Gunpowder Rd, Millers, MD 21102-2537   boykinalauna@gmail.com

Gorman, Katherine   *Mays Chapel || Timonium ||| 3522* katherine.gorman@duke.edu

Spicer, Norma   *Milford Mill || Pikesville ||| 4380*   (410) 730-6969
9590 Old Route 108, Ellicott City, MD 21042-6356   gratzpa@aol.com

Spicer, William   *Milford Mill || Pikesville ||| 4380*   (410) 730-6969
9590 Old Route 108, Ellicott City, MD 21042-6356   gratzpa@aol.com

Bowling, James   *Mount Carmel || Parkton ||| 3425*   (410) 343-2119
17300 Bushland Rd, Parkton, MD 21120-9476   jtbowling@comcast.net

Newton, Richard   *Mount Gilead || Reisterstown ||| 4425*   (410) 429-3945
14201 Hanover Pike, Reisterstown, MD 21136-4106   Richard.a.newton.civ@mail.mil

Diggs, Adrienne   *Mount Olive || Randallstown ||| 4390*
4 Egypt Farms Rd, Owings Mills, MD 21117-5047   adiggs5@comcast.net

Knop, Gerard   *Mount Zion-Finksburg || Finksburg |||| 4265*   (410) 517-0042
209 Greenview Ave, Reisterstown, MD 21136-2404   jknop@verizon.net

Gayles, Ernest   *New Beginnings Fellowship || Fallston |||| 3500*   (410) 499-6656
3402 Bateman Ave, Baltimore, MD 21216   eegayles@gmail.com

Miller, George   *Parke Memorial || Parkton |||| 3430*   (410) 357-4807
18672 Middletown Rd, Parkton, MD 21120-9090   george_miller1983@verizon.net

Taylor, Marie   *Patapsco || Finksburg |||| 4430*   (410) 356-7213
233 Embleton Rd, Owings Mills, MD 21117-1729   memetaylor233@gmail.com

Knuth, Robert   *Pine Grove || Parkton |||| 3475*   (410) 357-4588
20027 Cameron Mill Rd, Parkton, MD 21120-9006   rwk2845@aol.com

Rice, Catherine   *Pine Grove || White Hall |||| 3570*   (410) 452-5202
2809A Whiteford Rd, Whiteford, MD 21160-1137   crice51@verizon.net

Johnson, Rosita   *Piney Grove || Reisterstown |||| 4175*   (410) 833-0138
53 Bond Ave, Reisterstown, MD 21136-1327   bearde1@verizon.net

Freeman, Audrey   *Pleasant Hill || Owings Mills |||| 4370*   (410) 521-3069
8301 Streamwood Dr, Pikesville, MD 21208-2139   freemanpik@aol.com

Covert Moyer, Mary   *Presbury || Edgewood |||| 2415*   (410) 671-7450
221 Kennard Ave, Edgewood, MD 21040-3711   poohbear559@comcast.net

Muffoletto, Brian   *Providence || Towson |||| 3370*   (410) 661-6608
43304 Belrock Circle #101, Nottingham, MD 21236   bmuffoletto@bcps.org

Harry, Susan   *Reisterstown || Reisterstown |||| 4435*   (410) 876-2476
1505 Carriage Hill Dr, Westminster, MD 21157-6501   gwtwsue2@comcast.net

Henry, Susan   *Reisterstown || Reisterstown |||| 4435*   (410) 833-0963
122 Glyndon Trace Drive, Owings Mills, MD 21117   susanhenry434@yahoo.com

Sell, Mary   *Shiloh || Hampstead |||| 4325*   (410) 259-5634
2109 Walsh Dr, Westminster, MD 21157-3442   avonlady0803@netscape.net

Hamilton, Juli   *Smiths Chapel || Churchville |||| 2370*   (410) 879-5558
3430 Churchville Rd, Aberdeen, MD 21001-1029   pjpc@comcast.net

Keen, Connie   *Smiths Chapel || Churchville |||| 2370*   (443) 327-6988
837 Dilbert, Churchville, MD 21001   keenc@vmcmail.com

Perry, Nancy   *St Johns || Hampstead |||| 4320*   (410) 239-4255
4299 Hermitage Ct, Manchester, MD 21102-3100   NPerry@carrollcc.edu

Dumas, Ronald   *St Johns || Lutherville |||| 3375*   (410) 668-2984
8445 Water Oak Rd, Baltimore, MD 21234-3743   ronalddumas2@gmail.com

McKoy, Sharon   *St Luke || Reisterstown |||| 4440*   (410) 833-3105
143 Glyndon Trace Dr, Reisterstown, MD 21136-1948

Smith, Joseph   *St Luke || Reisterstown ||| 4440*
1917 Crestview Rd, Baltimore, MD 21239-3208   Josephjs.slowriver@gmail.com

Cassell, Judy   *Texas || Cockeysville ||| 3310*   (410) 628-6974
PO Box 243, Phoenix, MD 21131-0243   loladdy2.jc@gmail.com

Thomas, Anita   *Union || Baldwin ||| 3135*   (410) 877-2872
2315 Pleasantville Rd, Fallston, MD 21047-1434   EMS1391@AOL.COM

Byrne, Betty   *Union Chapel || Joppa ||| 2510*   (410) 676-1244
705 Oak Rd, Joppa, MD 21085-3935   bettyboop0666@aol.com

Smith, Katie   *Union Chapel || Joppa ||| 2510*   (410) 569-8992
312 Plumtree Rd, Bel Air, MD 21015-6013   katiesmith312@verizon.net

Ellis, Bill *Wards Chapel || Randallstown ||| 4410*   (410) 549-1530
6012 Snowdens Run Rd, Eldersburg, MD 21784-6737   billellis@ellislist.com

Winand, CJ   *Wards Chapel || Randallstown ||| 4410*   (410) 922-3950
10907 Steffeny Rd, Randallstown, MD 21133-1022

Sichel, Matthew   *Wesley || Hampstead ||| 4330*   (443) 507-0686
2578 Mindi Dr, Manchester, MD 21102-1828   popsichel@hotmail.com

Yost, Linda   *Wesley || Hampstead ||| 4330*   (410) 239-0429
1910 Upper Forde Ln, Hampstead, MD 21074-1500   ljyost@verizon.net

Bushie, Richard   *West Liberty || White Hall ||| 3560*   (410) 357-5645
20500 Kirkwood Shop Rd, White Hall, MD 21161-8600   rbushie1@comcast.net

Figinski, Mary   *William Watters Memorial || Jarrettsville ||| 2485*   (443) 371-6852
102 Marshall Dr, Forest Hill, MD 21050-3019   mary-jane.fig@hotmail.com

Millwe, Glen   *Wiseburg || White Hall ||| 3565*   mfmkatz@aol.com

CUMBERLAND-HAGERSTOWN DISTRICT
Gandy, Troy   *Asbury || Hagerstown ||| 5315*   (240) 468-6883
1202 Carroll Heights Blvd, Hagerstown, MD 21742-3017   exquisite13@hotmail.com

Wright, Susie   *Asbury || Hagerstown ||| 5315*   (240) 527-1978
15 Manor Dr Apt 101, Hagerstown, MD 21740-8858   susiewright319@yahoo.com

Lauder, Dave   *Barton || Barton ||| 5110*   (301) 463-3654
18914 Legislative Rd SW, Barton, MD 21521-2016   dlauder@eglenursing.com

Lauder, David   *Barton || Barton ||| 5110*   (301) 463-3654
18914 Legislative Rd SW, Barton, MD 21521-2016   dlauder@eglenursing.com

Hein, Becky   *Benevola || Boonsboro ||| 6115*   (301) 432-5780
72 N Main St, Keedysville, MD 21756-1340   becky4lit@msn.com

Sprecher, Brandon *Bethel || Chewsville |||| 5135* (301) 733-0999
20777 Trovinger Mill Rd, Hagerstown, MD 21742-5214 brandonsprecher@aol.com

Sprecher, Brett *Bethel || Chewsville |||| 5135* (301) 733-0999
20777 Trovinger Mill Rd, Hagerstown, MD 21742-5214 sprecherbret@aol.com

Jones, Keith *Calvary || Great Cacapon |||| 5580* (304) 258-7790
80 Sunrise Ln, Great Cacapon, WV 25422-3395 cobiakeith@gmail.com

King, Jo *Calvary || Great Cacapon |||| 5580* (304) 963-0644
298 Linwood Dr, Hedgesville, WV 25427-4371 joannking77@yahoo.com

Smith, Billie *Calvary || Ridgeley |||| 5620* (304) 738-3810
77 Knobley, Ridgeley, WV 26753-0786 bin1959@yahoo.com

Hardinger, Deborah *Centenary || Cumberland |||| 5185* (301) 777-1482
1825 Frederick St, Cumberland, MD 21502-1039 mybabyshy@hotmail.com

Brotemarkle, Alma *Central || Cumberland |||| 5150* (301) 724-7614
14215 Bedford Rd NE, Cumberland, MD 21502-6926 Centralumc@atlanticbbn.net

Moore, Vivian *Cresaptown || Cresaptown |||| 5140* (301) 759-5810
820 Greene St, Cumberland, MD 21502-2744 vcmoore@atlanticbb.net

Robinson, Richard *Cresaptown || Cresaptown |||| 5140* (301) 729-0819
14917 Lone Oak Rd, Cresaptown, MD 21502-5580 shirleyanddick@atlanticbb.net

Leffler, Mary Jo *Davis Memorial || Cumberland |||| 5165* (724) 388-4573
mjlefer@aol.com

Ward, Jason *Dawson || Rawlings |||| 5440* (301) 786-4562
23665 McMullen Hwy SW, Rawlings, MD 21557-2440 rwillson14@myactv.net

Nelson, Ralph *Eckhart || Frostburg |||| 5255* (301) 689-6552
11811 Kemp Dr NW, Frostburg, MD 21532-3120

Reith, Shirley *Ellerslie || Ellerslie |||| 5265* (240) 522-0286
PO Box 173, Ellerslie, MD 21529-0173 rmpark3@gmail.com

Whitworth, Alan *Ellerslie || Ellerslie |||| 5265* (410) 365-6590
12690 Clarksville Pike, Clarksville, Maryland 21029

Whitworth, Donna *Ellerslie || Ellerslie |||| 5265* (410) 365-6590
12690 Clarksville Pik, Clarksville, MD 21029 wdowhit@aol.com

Marlin, Ben *Emmanuel || Hagerstown |||| 5320* (304) 258-4665
9227 Helmsdale Pl, Hagerstown, MD 21740-9629 hbmarlin@hotmail.com

Marlin, Rosalie *Emmanuel || Hagerstown |||| 5320* (561) 866-4614
9227 Helmsdale Pl, Hagerstown, MD 21740-9629 ramarlin@hotmail.com

Widmyer, Fred *First || Berkeley Springs |||| 5515* (304) 258-0181
26 Garden Ct, Berkeley Springs, WV 25411 fwidmyer@gmail.com

Clarke, Mary   *First || Lonaconing ||| 5390*   (301) 463-2860
15714 Rockville St SW, Lonaconing, MD 21539-1255   mjtjc@verizon.net

Morgan, N.   *Frostburg || Frostburg ||| 5310*   (301) 689-9532
127 Frost Ave, Frostburg, MD 21532-1621   skmorgan20@gmail.com

Bear, J   *Garfield || Smithsburg ||| 6425*   (301) 639-2393
12933 Wolfsville Rd, Smithsburg, MD 21783-9312   jdbear@comcast.net

Davison, Linn   *Grace || Hagerstown ||| 5325*   (301) 665-9297
640 Trafalgar Dr, Hagerstown, MD 21742-1230   ldavisonjr@msn.com

Houk, Shirley   *Greenwood || Berkeley Springs ||| 5525*   (304) 258-6621
48 Lois Ln, Berkeley Springs, WV 25411-5786   shouk38@gmail.com

Close, Julie   *Hancock || Hancock ||| 5365*   (301) 707-0976
C/O Lori Close, Hagerstown, MD 21740-8003   julierclose@gmail.com

Shaw, Pamela   *Hancock || Hancock ||| 5365*   (717) 294-6279
PO Box 8, Hancock, MD 21750-0008   shaws@frontiernet.net

Riggleman, Todd   *Holy Cross || Ridgeley ||| 5625*   (301) 707-5101
109 S Pennsylvania St, Ridgeley, WV 26753-9767   toddriggleman64@gmail.com

Weakley, Karen   *Holy Cross || Ridgeley ||| 5625*   (304) 303-3000
70 S West Virginia St, Ridgeley, WV 26753-9584   karen_w4@hotmail.com

Bell, Robert   *John Wesley || Hagerstown ||| 5330*   (301) 797-1755
1402 Oak Hill Ave, Hagerstown, MD 21742-3222   robertmbell@verizon.net

White, Carol   *John Wesley || Hagerstown ||| 5330*   (301) 797-0659
18827 Preston Rd, Hagerstown, MD 21742-2715   clwwcpa@myactv.net

Golden, Shawn   *La Vale || Lavale ||| 5370*   (301) 876-1181
605 N Second St, Cumberland, MD 21502-7234   shawnmgold@hotmail.com

Weimer, Alice   *Mc Kendree of Potomac Park || Cumberland ||| 5242*   (301) 729-
                                                                           1760
12029 Iris Ave, Cumberland, MD 21502-5427   gippymom@atlanticbb.net

O'Neal, Barbara   *Melvin || Cumberland ||| 5295*   (301) 722-0448
110 Reynolds St, Cumberland, MD 21502-2526   barbandjr21@aol.com

Stotler, Jack   *Michaels || Berkeley Springs ||| 5540*   (304) 676-6265
290 Budding Dogwood Ln, Hedgesville, WV 25427   berkeleyspringsparish@frontier.com

Crilly, Wanda   *Mount Lena || Boonsboro ||| 6125*   (301) 791-3446
10901 Gaywood Dr, Hagerstown, MD 21740-7724   Crill4@myactv.net

Basile, Dianna   *Mount Nebo || Boonsboro ||| 6130*   (301) 791-2079
11841 Greenhill Dr, Hagerstown, MD 21742-4416   dkaybasile@aol.com

Frye, John   *Mount Olivet || Berkeley Springs |||| 5545*   (202) 365-8206
5061 Winchester Grade Rd, Berkeley Springs, WV 25411-1053   john.2012@gmail.com

Hoover, Cheryl   *Mount Olivet || Berkeley Springs |||| 5545*   (304) 258-7773
5327 Winchester Grade Rd, Berkeley Spgs, WV 25411-6049   choovie@aol.com

Boch, P. *Mount Savage || Mount Savage |||| 5425*   (301) 264-3243
12419 Snyder Dr NW, Lavale, MD 21502-6031   pboch0@gmail.com

Burchell, Harry   *Mount Savage || Mount Savage |||| 5425*   (301) 777-3429
11504 Mountain Magic Ln NE, Cumberland, MD 21502   Nightwatch@atlanticbb.net

Deal, Tim   *Mount Tabor || Oldtown |||| 5460*

Riggleman, Jane   *Mount Tabor || Oldtown |||| 5460*   (301) 478-5228
18605 Oldtown RD SE, Oldtown, MD 21555   jriggleman1956@gmail.com

Kesecker, Sandy   *Mount Zion || Berkeley Springs |||| 5555*   (304) 258-4016
269 Cain Ln, Berkeley Springs, WV 25411-5146   cek1@peoplepc.com

McBee, Mary   *Mount Zion || Berkeley Springs |||| 5555*   (304) 258-2108
1626 Potomac Rd, Berkeley Springs, WV 25411-4378   mcbeland@localnet.com

Buhrman, Dorothy   *Mount Zion || Sabillasville |||| 6350*   (301) 241-3628
6509 Browns Quarry Rd, Sabillasville, MD 21780-9412   dotm16509@gmail.com

Shumaker, Wanda *New Covenant || Cumberland |||| 5210*   (301) 338-2959
707 E Oldtown Rd, Cumberland, MD 21502-3750   gobrec@yahoo.com

Steckman, Kevin   *Oldtown || Oldtown |||| 5430*   (240) 362-7486
829 E First St, Cumberland, MD 21502-4372   steckman6@atlanticbb.net

Brown, Cindy   *Otterbein || Hagerstown |||| 5340*   (301) 491-0401
759 Morningside Ave, Hagerstown, MD 21740-5072   Cindy.brown@otterumc.org

Brown, Tom   *Otterbein || Hagerstown |||| 5340*   (301) 491-0401
759 Morningside Ave, Hagerstown, MD 21740-5072   fm1brown@outlook.com

Bucy, Russell   *Park Place || Lavale |||| 5375*   (301) 729-2662
16 Harold St, Lavale, MD 21502-7448   rbucy16@webtv.net

Hull, Dale   *Parkhead || Big Pool |||| 5120*   (301) 842-3202
12061 Cove Rd, Clear Spring, MD 21722-1617   hulld@myactv.net

Dalton, Thomas   *Pleasant Walk || Hagerstown |||| 6430*   (301) 293-1041
11821 Pleasant Walk Rd, Myersville, MD 21773-9435   tkdalton@comcast.net

Abernathy, Eltra   *Rawlings || Rawlings |||| 5445*   (304) 813-8606
12278 Knobley Road, Keyser, WV 26726-0524   wifehusband65@aol.com

Morrison, Dawn   *Rehoboth || Williamsport |||| 5470*   (301) 797-5870
18219 Woodside Dr, Hagerstown, MD 21740-9548   djonesmorrison@msn.com

Morrison, Harry *Rehoboth || Williamsport |||| 5470*
18219 Woodside Dr, Hagerstown, MD 21740-9548

(301) 797-5870
bm92384@msn.com

Stottlemyer, Sue *Salem || Myersville |||| 6435*
12405 Loy Wolfe Rd, Myersville, MD 21773-9506

(301) 293-1470
ses1313@comcast.net

Clise, Elaine *Shaft || Frostburg |||| 5415*
12304 Upper Georges Creek Rd SW, Frostburg, MD 21532-3706

(301) 689-2434
elaine@tcracecars.com

Brown, Bonnie *Shiloh || Hagerstown |||| 5355*
19731 Shiloh Church Rd, Hagerstown, MD 21742-4869

(301) 991-7839
shilohumc@myactv.net

McRae, John *St Andrews || Hagerstown |||| 5345*
243 N Broad St, Waynesboro, PA 17268-1305

(717) 749-5899
jmcrae00@comcast.net

Donaldson, John *Trinity || Cumberland |||| 5245*
204 Grand Ave, Cumberland, MD 21502-3913

(301) 729-8809
revjewell@atlanticbb.net

George, Robert *Trinity || Cumberland |||| 5245*
15306 Greenleaf Dr SW, Cumberland, MD 21502-5714

(301) 729-6828
rmgeorge44@gmail.com

Leedom, Jill *Union Chapel || Berkeley Springs |||| 5570*
82 Chapel Ln, Berkeley Springs, WV 25411-6727

(540) 247-8679
luv123128@gmail.com

Weiss, Debbie *Union Chapel || Berkeley Springs |||| 5570*
317 Prado Way, Berkeley Springs, WV 25411-3108

(304) 258-8831
hardeb831@aol.com

Tagg, Lee *Washington Square || Hagerstown |||| 5360*
17920 Constitution Cir, Hagerstown, MD 21740-2464

(301) 739-6068
lee.tagg@gmail.com

Litten, Rick *Wesley Chapel || Berkeley Springs |||| 5575*
89 Briarwood Cir, Berkeley Springs, WV 25411-4214

(304) 258-4038
ricklitten@frontier.com

Cavin, Janet *Westernport || Westernport |||| 5465*
306 Baughman St, Westernport, MD 21562-1804

(301) 359-3885

Daniels, John *Westernport || Westernport |||| 5465*
207 Central Ave, Westernport, MD 21562-1722

(301) 359-9366

Baker, Carol *Williamsport || Williamsport |||| 5475*
13954 Patriot Way, Hagerstown, MD 21740

(301) 799-9089
cgranb@gmail.com

Manuel, Nancy *Williamsport || Williamsport |||| 5475*
20100 Clay Rd, Hagerstown, MD 21742-4303

(301) 739-4967
wvharpersferry@yahoo.com

CENTRAL MARYLAND DISTRICT

Keller, Jan *Alberta Gary Memorial || Columbia ||| 7345* (410) 964-5635
6813 Allview Dr, Columbia, MD 21046-1103 Kellerjanice@gmail.com

Miller, Barry *Alberta Gary Memorial || Columbia ||| 7345* (301) 490-8079
9412 Guilford Rd, Columbia, MD 21046-1912 barrymiller09@gmail.com

Miller, Marissa *Alberta Gary Memorial || Columbia ||| 7345* (301) 490-8079
9412 Guilford Rd, Columbia, MD 21046-1912 barrymiller09@gmail.com

Greger, Don *Araby || Frederick ||| 6110* don.greger@gmail.com

Barnhill, Leander *Asbury || Germantown ||| 9265* (301) 869-7921
17540 Black Rock Rd, Germantown, MD 20874-2227 asburygermantown@gmail.com

Greene, Kenneth *Asbury || Germantown ||| 9265* (301) 540-1813
17546 Black Rock Rd, Germantown, MD 20874-2227

Henderson, Constance *Asbury || Germantown ||| 9265* (301) 449-3117
5104 Lansing Dr, Temple Hills, MD 20748-5444 cashend496@yahoo.com

Jackson, Hasel *Asbury || Germantown ||| 9265* (301) 780-3274
15706 Saint Thomas Church Rd, Upper Marlboro, MD 20772-8137 None

Ralston, Debbie *Ashton || Ashton ||| 9110* (301) 774-7863
101 Brinkwood Rd, Brookeville, MD 20833-2304 geneva_deb@comcast.net

Sledge, Jeffrey *Bethesda || Damascus ||| 9185* (240) 315-5957
6102 Twain Dr, New Market, MD 21774-6262 jeffreyasledge@gmail.com

Stanley, Roy *Bethesda || Damascus ||| 9185* (301) 865-1162
11424 Meadowlark Dr, Ijamsville, MD 21754-8918 rojostanley@hotmail.com

Simpson, John *Calvary || Mount Airy ||| 6285* (301) 829-2557
208 E Church St, Mount Airy, MD 21771-5460 john.simpson2@comcast.net

Simpson, Leslie *Calvary || Mount Airy ||| 6285* (301) 829-2557
208 E Church St, Mount Airy, MD 21771-5460 lajsimpson@hotmail.com

Fitzgerald, Kevin *Christ || Columbia ||| 7350* (410) 309-0856
6438 Oaken Door, Columbia, MD 21045-4513 qespios@icloud.com

Balentine, Cindy *Covenant || Montgomery Village ||| 9235* (301) 916-1197
13100 Millhaven Pl Apt L, Germantown, MD 20874 cynthia.balentine@montgomery-countymd.org

Balentine, Cynthia *Covenant || Montgomery Village ||| 9235* (301) 916-1179
13100 Millhaven Pl Apt L, Germantown, MD 20874-6317 balentine7@verizon.net

Maisch, Jill *Covenant || Montgomery Village ||| 9235* (301) 461-0015
24105 Preakness Dr, Damascus, MD 20872-2171 jillmaisch@comcast.net

Dorsey, Beverly   *Daisy || Woodbine |||| 9490*   dorsey874629@bellsouth.net

Fisher, Kay   *Daisy || Woodbine |||| 9490*   (443) 418-6698
simplykay1@gmail.com

Barr, Richard   *Damascus || Damascus |||| 9190*
24500 Fossen Rd, Damascus, MD 20872-2195   vikingtoo@aol.com

Custer, Bonnie   *Damascus || Damascus |||| 9190*   BonCuster@aol.com

Wilkinson, Eleanor   *Dickerson || Dickerson |||| 9225*   (301) 972-8709
ewilkinson@erac.com

Young, Mary   *Dickerson || Dickerson |||| 9225*   (301) 253-4351
25130 Tralee Ct, Damascus, MD 20872-2716   mertyoung@aol.com

Brown, Susan   *Ebenezer || Sykesville |||| 4575*   (410) 442-2884
2091 Saint James Rd, Marriottsville, MD 21104-1436   stmpnsusan@aol.com

Rapids, Lori   *Ebenezer || Sykesville |||| 4575*   (443) 671-6295
2205 Skylark Dr, Westminster, MD 21157-7856   blrapids@comcast.net

Whitehead, Ron   *Emory || Ellicott City |||| 4245*   (410) 461-6165
4502 Rolling Mdws, Ellicott City, MD 21043-6551   ronwhitehead172@verizon.net

Washington, Kia   *Emory Grove || Gaithersburg |||| 9240*   (301) 515-5744
19620 Waters Rd # 3510, Germantown, MD 20874-2610   kia778@hotmail.com

Arze, Beatriz   *Epworth || Gaithersburg |||| 9245*   (301) 972-6267
19047 Staleybridge Rd, Germantown, MD 20876-1724

Conteh, Francis   *Epworth || Gaithersburg |||| 9245*   (301) 365-8076
7312 Bradley Blvd, Bethesda, MD 20817-2130   contehfrank2017@yahoo.com

Gallegos, Miguel   *Epworth || Gaithersburg |||| 9245*   (202) 288-8137
1120 Sandy Hollow Ct, Silver Spring, MD 20905-6050   migallegos@gmail.com

Sirleaf, Lasana   *Epworth || Gaithersburg |||| 9245*   (240) 551-7681
9008 Rosemont Dr, Gaithersburg, MD 20877-1519   sirleaf.lasana@yahoo.com

Bernard, Sharie   *Fairhaven || Gaithersburg |||| 9250*   (301) 948-1430
420 Phelps St, Gaithersburg, MD 20878-2193   shariemb@gmail.com

Hallman, Thompkins   *Fairhaven || Gaithersburg |||| 9250*
1801 Clydesdale Pl NW Apt 320, Washington, DC 20009   fairhavenumc@gmail.com

Dotson, Carman   *Fairview || Sykesville |||| 4345*   (443) 536-1106
173 Grand Dr, Taneytown, MD 21787-2401   Cheeco319@aol.com

Dochter, Linda   *FaithPoint || Monrovia |||| 6382*
500 Patton Cir Apt B, Frederick, MD 21703-8464   dochter30@gmail.com

Hanes, Libby   *Forest Grove || Tuscarora ||| 9230*   (301) 668-5422
3763 Urbana Pike, Frederick, MD 21704-7737   ehanes257@gmail.com

Stansbury, Jacqueline   *Friendship || Damascus ||| 9210*   (301) 212-9894
119 Bates Ave, Gaithersburg, MD 20877-1272   mamadukes214@gmail.com

Teal, Mike   *Gaither || Sykesville ||| 4280*   (410) 861-6362
1603 Crestleigh Ct, Finksburg, MD 21048-1935   miketeal@hotmail.com

Kaidy, James   *Gary Memorial || Ellicott City ||| 4240*   (410) 382-9829
4269 Bright Bay Way, Ellicott City, MD 21042-5939   jtkaidy1@att.net

Barnes, John   *Glen Mar || Ellicott City ||| 7365*   (410) 570-4136
7124 Millbury Ct, Elkridge, MD 21075-5567   jparkerbar@aol.com

Barnes, Ruella   *Glen Mar || Ellicott City ||| 7365*
7124 Millbury Ct, Elkridge, MD 21075-5567   ruebarn1@gmail.com

Bucks, Betsy   *Glen Mar || Ellicott City ||| 7365*   (410) 379-2686
7200 Third Ave Apt C025, Sykesville, MD 21784-5236   betsybucks@comcast.net

Bucks, Dale   *Glen Mar || Ellicott City ||| 7365*   (413) 812-4230
7200 Third Ave Apt C025, Sykesville, MD 21784-5236   dalebucks@comcast.net

Eschliman, Dan   *Glen Mar || Ellicott City ||| 7365*   (410) 456-0656
1615 Brimfield Cir, Sykesville, MD 21784-5940   eschliman@gmail.com

Bennett-Floyd, Anita   *Goshen || Gaithersburg ||| 9255*   (301) 528-9574
11709 Virginia Pine Dr, Germantown, MD 20876-4302   nanigraphics@aol.com

Spriggs, Joanne   *Goshen || Gaithersburg ||| 9255*   (443) 708-8663
914 N Augusta Ave, Baltimore, MD 21229-1824   joannespriggs914@comcast.net

Nichols, Melissa   *Grace || Gaithersburg ||| 9260*   (301) 869-0543
16529 Sioux Ln, Gaithersburg, MD 20878-2048   manichols59@gmail.com

Murray, Judith   *Hopkins || Highland ||| 9290*   (410) 381-7209
6318 Early Red Ct, Columbia, MD 21045-4490   jm.murray@verizon.net

Day, Ruth   *Howard Chapel-Ridgeville || Mount Airy ||| 9355*   (301) 829-6045
13819 Penn Shop Rd, Mount Airy, MD 21771-4625   payers001@comcast.net

Haller, George   *Howard Chapel-Ridgeville || Mount Airy ||| 9355*   (301) 829-0991
18707 Penn Shop Rd, Mount Airy, MD 21771-3933

Spear, Marilyn   *Ijamsville || Ijamsville ||| 6235*   (301) 831-3116
10264 Champions Ct, Ijamsville, MD 21754-9611   marilynspear@comcast.net

Brunson, Dave   *Jennings Chapel || Woodbine ||| 9510*
3120 Florence Rd, Woodbine, MD 21797   dbrunsonrenewal@hotmail.com

Annis-Forder, Richard   *Linden-Linthicum || Clarksville ||| 9180*   (410) 552-8347
7604 Willow Bottom Rd, Sykesville, MD 21784-5651   annis.forder@gmail.com

Stankewich, Mary *Linden-Linthicum || Clarksville ||| 9180* (410) 465-6118
5151 Bonnie Branch Rd, Ellicott City, MD 21043-7043 srstankewich@cs.com

Higgins, Dan *Lisbon || Lisbon |||| 9350* (410) 489-9519
1779 Gillis Falls Rd, Woodbine, MD 21797-9318 danfhiggins@hotmail.com

King, Conchita *Locust || Columbia |||| 7355* (410) 992-7741
6575 Freetown Rd, COLUMBIA, MD 21044 cmking9@verizon.net

Hitchens, Ralph *Memorial || Poolesville |||| 9385* (240) 687-5246
17 Selby Ct, Poolesville, MD 20837-2410 rmhitchens45@gmail.com

Culbertson, Linda *Mill Creek Parish || Rockville ||| 9425* (301) 774-7049
3913 Springarden St, Olney, MD 20832-1265 joliculb@gmail.com

Mattis, Carole *Mill Creek Parish || Rockville ||| 9425* (301) 990-7411
16 Silver Kettle Ct, Gaithersburg, MD 20878-2718 cmattis@verizon.net

Robier, Kelly *Mill Creek Parish || Rockville ||| 9425* (301) 460-4885
5137 Clavel Ter, Rockville, MD 20853-1548 kelly.robier@gmail.com

Harmon, Sandra *Montgomery || Damascus ||| 9215* (301) 309-1699
215 Hutton St, Gaithersburg, MD 20877-2055 jsharmon2@verizon.net

Hamilton, Kathie *Mount Gregory || Glenwood |||| 4455* (410) 489-5628
3311 Saddle Horse Ct, Glenwood, MD 21738-9526 kreginahamilton@yahoo.com

Sevier, Ken *Mount Olive || Mount Airy |||| 4590* (410) 795-8053
2847 Sommersby Rd, Mount Airy, MD 21771-8049 kensevier@mindspring.com

Gardner, Carol *Mount Tabor || Damascus |||| 9340* (410) 549-7351
727 Central Ave, Sykesville, MD 21784-7511 cgardnccs@aol.com

Ames, Bettye *Mount Zion || Highland |||| 9310* (410) 531-6251
15150 Sapling Ridge Dr, Dayton, MD 21036-1259 bettyeames101@gmail.com

Dennis, Steve *Mount Zion || Highland |||| 9310* (301) 854-2325
office@mtzionhighland.com

Hall, Shirley *Mount Zion || Olney |||| 9370* (301) 703-1185
201 Watersville Rd Apt 33, Mount Airy, MD 21771-5517 hallshirley1223@yahoo.com

Shelton, Joyce *Mount Zion || Olney |||| 9370* (301) 774-4312
4521 Mount Olney Ln, Olney, MD 20832-1011 j_i_shelton@hotmail.com

Baker, Michelle *Oakdale Emory || Olney |||| 9375* (410) 489-4406
3725 Route 97, Glenwood, MD 21738-9614 mbaker@oakdale.church

Cooper, Cristin *Oakdale Emory || Olney |||| 9375* (240) 432-2607
4815 Tothill Dr, Olney, MD 20832-1889 ccooper@oakdale.church

Myers, Leslie *Oakdale Emory || Olney |||| 9375* (301) 774-1126
18908 Abbey Manor Dr, Brookeville, MD 20833-3241 lmyers@oakdale.church

Browning, Charles   *Poplar Springs || Woodbine ||| 9360*   (410) 489-4126
1874 Woodbine Rd, Woodbine, MD 21797-8504   chb735ph@aol.com

Newcomer, David   *Providence || Monrovia ||| 9325*   (301) 748-5814
3716 Basford Rd, Frederick, MD 21703-7828   nuke3716@gmail.com

Shiflett, Marge   *Providence || Monrovia ||| 9325*   (301) 865-7080
3321 Sue Mac Ct, Monrovia, MD 21770-8725   mshiflett@comcast.net

Ambrose, Debbie   *Salem || Brookeville ||| 9150*   (301) 774-4135
3700 Roseneath St, Olney, MD 20832-1345   DJCAmbrose@gmail.com

Bartley, Robert   *Salem || Brookeville ||| 9150*   (301) 570-3518
5 Church St, Brookeville, MD 20833-2507   buck@bartleycorp.com

Savage, Brandon   *Salem || Brookeville ||| 9150*   (202) 246-4963
18413 Bowie Mill Rd, Olney, MD 20832-1807   brandon@brandonsavage.net

Staub, Jerry   *Salem || Germantown ||| 9275*   (301) 253-4746
24715 Ridge Rd, Damascus, MD 20872-2133   Staubjerry55@aol.com

Stull, Joseph   *Sharp Street || Sandy Spring ||| 9445*   (301) 774-6455
4517 Mount Olney Ln, Olney, MD 20832-1011   stullj@comcast.net

Groomes, Deborah   *Simpson || Mount Airy ||| 9365*   (301) 932-4398
93 Brookside Pl, Waldorf, MD 20601-8989   deborahgroomes5456@gmail.com

Benson, Donna   *St James || Marriottsville ||| 4565*   (410) 795-3275
7202 Orchid Ln, Eldersburg, MD 21784-5927   knitterdmb@comcast.net

Bostron, Debra   *St James || Marriottsville ||| 4565*   (410) 489-4059
1164 Day Rd, Sykesville, MD 21784-5607   debra.bostron@gmail.com

Thompson, Alvin *St John United Church || Columbia ||| 7360*   (301) 596-6230
6324 Frostwork Row, Columbia, MD 21044   actnet@comcast.net

Cook, Thomas J.   *St Luke || Sykesville ||| 4460*   (410) 795-3568
7405 Village Rd, Sykesville, MD 21784-7435   cookthomas39@gmail.com

Cartledge, Alyssa *St Marks || Boyds ||| 9145*   (301) 801-0258
10304 Deakins Hall Dr, Adelphi, MD 20783-1219   a3cartledge@gmail.com

Turner, Beverly   *St Marks || Boyds ||| 9145*   (301) 931-3495
7901 Laurel Lakes Ct Apt 228, Laurel, MD 20707-5049   beverly.skins@verizon.net

Robert, Frank   *St Pauls || Sykesville ||| 4465*   (410) 552-5433
7135 Wimmer Ln, Sykesville, MD 21784-6626   frobert@BWCUMC.org

Mulholland, Nancy   *Trinity || Germantown ||| 9280*   (301) 330-1029
882 Diamond Dr, Gaithersburg, MD 20878-1803   nmulhollandflute@gmail.com

Cookus, Bart   *Wesley Freedom || Eldersburg ||| 4225*   (304) 676-3263
6326 Barnett Ave, Eldersburg, MD 21784-6102   btcookus@hotmail.com

Feldman, Sharon *Wesley Freedom || Eldersburg ||| 4225*
7492 Windswept Ct, Sykesville, MD 21784-7150

(410) 552-1197
sfeldman@wesleyfreedom.org

Perrine, Sherry *Wesley Freedom || Eldersburg ||| 4225*
6155 Deanna Dr, Sykesville, MD 21784-8653

(410) 781-4981
sherryperrine@hotmail.com

Silberzahn, F. *Wesley Freedom || Eldersburg ||| 4225*
923 Slash Pine Ct, Sykesville, MD 21784-7948

(410) 549-7592
fkdennis@comcast.net

Sherwood, Mike *Wesley Grove || Gaithersburg ||| 9515*
2905 Greenhill Ct, Ijamsville, MD 21754-9047

(301) 253-2894
midas7310@aol.com

Dorsey, Nelson *West Liberty || Marriottsville ||| 4343*
21 Fannies Meadow Ct, Westminster, MD 21158-4406

(410) 751-2562
nbdorseysr@comcast.net

Johnson, Pamela *West Montgomery || Dickerson ||| 9580*
40 Prairie Rose Ct, Gaithersburg, MD 20878-2821

(301) 512-8224
johnsonpamela291@gmail.com

Morgan, Jeffrey *West Montgomery || Dickerson ||| 9580*
510 Rock Lodge Rd, Gaithersburg, MD 20877-3404

(240) 246-7020
last_one_78@yahoo.com

FREDERICK DISTRICT

Deardorff, Anne *Arden || Martinsburg ||| 6510*
3687 Golf Course Rd, Martinsburg, WV 25405-5644

(304) 886-9372
abdeardorff@qg.com

Stilwell, Leslie *Arden || Martinsburg ||| 6510*
153 Ye Olde McDonald Orchard Ln, Inwood, WV 25428-5314

(304) 229-3391
lams35@msn.com

Straley, Erin *Arden || Martinsburg ||| 6510*
106 Bunting Ave, Martinsburg, WV 25405-2493

ees96@yahoo.com

Ambush, Delores *Asbury || Frederick ||| 6180*
303 Heather Ridge Dr, Frederick, MD 21702-1403

(301) 694-9515
dambush@verizon.net

Cranford, Charles *Asbury || Shepherdstown ||| 6700*
91 Prides Xing, Shenandoah Junction, WV 25442-4576

(304) 876-7162
ccranford@4pillarchurch.org

Hosby, Patricia *Asbury || Shepherdstown ||| 6700*
PO Box 1432, Martinsburg, WV 25402-1432

(304) 901-4434
tricia1950@comcast.net

Deeds, Nancy *Bedington || Martinsburg ||| 6520*
1480 Mouth of Opequon Rd, Martinsburg, WV 25404-7220

(304) 274-1518
njdeeds@frontier.com

Schoppert, Michelle *Berkeley Place || Martinsburg ||| 6645*
202 Spruce St, Martinsburg, WV 25401-4236

(304) 839-5246
mrschoppert@hotmail.com

Smith, Maurice *Bethel || Bakerton ||| 6515*
33 Mason Dr, Harpers Ferry, WV 25425-4079

(304) 876-2354
mandgsmith@comcast.net

Spring, Sheila *Bolivar || Harpers Ferry ||| 6560*
34 Boxwood Ln, Charles Town, WV 25414-5848

(304) 279-6586
slspring314@gmail.com

Snody, Larry   *Brook Hill || Frederick ||| 6185*   (301) 624-0002
1920 Belford Dr, Frederick, MD 21702-3282   ldsnody@yahoo.com

Staley, Nancy   *Brook Hill || Frederick ||| 6185*   (301) 898-5092
2501 Catoctin Ct Unit 1B, Frederick, MD 21702-5935   nancy.kae@comcast.net

Filkins, Elizabeth *Buckeystown Rt 85 || Buckeystown ||| 6150*
4955 Pintail Ct, Frederick, MD 21703-9505   elizabethfilkins79@comcast.net

Isherwood, R.   *Bunker Hill || Bunker Hill |||| 6525*   (304) 229-8198
664 Goldmiller Rd, Gerrardstown, WV 25420-4268   nisherwood@frontier.com

Sadler, William   *Calvary || Finksburg ||| 4260*   (410) 795-4028
3722 Sykesville Rd, Sykesville, MD 21784-9543   william.sadler@nyu.edu

Jacobs, Robert   *Calvary || Frederick ||| 6190*   (301) 371-8987
2214 Quebec School Rd, Middletown, MD 21769-7103   bobjacobs@calvaryumc.org

Sheppard, Bruce *Calvary || Frederick ||| 6190*   (301) 898-3464
8613 Discovery Blvd, Walkersville, MD 21793-7842   brucehelenshep@msn.com

Sheppard, Helen *Calvary || Frederick ||| 6190*   (301) 898-3464
8613 Discovery Blvd, Walkersville, MD 21793-7842   brucehelenshep@msn.com

Frye, Doug   *Calvary || Martinsburg |||| 6655*   (304) 263-4998
608 Foxcroft Ave, Martinsburg, WV 25401-5310   Fryed1@msn.com

Holland, Jim   *Calvary || Martinsburg |||| 6655*   (304) 268-3137
325 Alpine Dr, Bunker Hill, WV 25413-3205   jholland@k12.wv.us

Frye, Eddie   *Catoctin || Thurmont ||| 6355*   (301) 271-4795
6715 Kellys Store Rd, Thurmont, MD 21788-3020   CatoctinUMC@gmail.com

Swope, Karen   *Catoctin || Thurmont ||| 6355*   (301) 271-2748
7536 Franklinville Rd, Thurmont, MD 21788-1104   Swopes6@verizon.net

Jacobs, Christine *Centennial Memorial || Frederick ||| 6210*   (301) 639-0812
7220 Edgemont Rd, Frederick, MD 21702-3500   fireball0711@hotmail.com

Summers, Arthur *Centennial Memorial || Frederick ||| 6210*   (301) 662-4092
7910 Edgewood Farm Rd, Frederick, MD 21702-2910   a.f.s.7910@aol.com

Weister, Kay   *Chestnut Hill || Harpers Ferry ||| 6570*   (304) 725-4467
15 Baltusrol Dr, Charles Town, WV 25414-3884   kay.grove@lcps.org

Shultz, David   *Darkesville || Inwood |||| 6545*   (304) 279-3573
83 Goshen Ln, Martinsburg, WV 25404-1327   david.shultz9@frontier.com

Masser, Connie   *Deerfield || Sabillasville |||| 6260*   (301) 241-3218
16321 Foxville Deerfield Rd, Sabillasville, MD 21780-9022

Matlock, Barbara *Engle || Harpers Ferry |||| 6575*
344 Jefferson Ave, Charles Town, WV 25414-1126

(304) 839-7285
Barbara.Matlock@fcps.org

Brooks, John *Friendship || Hedgesville |||| 6660*
166 Locust Grove Rd, Hedgesville, WV 25427-3072

(304) 754-7891
jjbrooks88@frontier.com

Boone, Richard *Gerrardstown || Gerrardstown |||| 6555*
77 Solarwood Ct, Gerrardstown, WV 25420-4120

(304) 268-9657
noemailgumc@gmail.com

McWilliams, Genevive *Harmony || Falling Waters |||| 6640*
24 Chesley Dr, Falling Waters, WV 25419-7004

(304) 274-1999
gemquilter@frontier.com

Erskine, Judith *Hedgesville || Hedgesville |||| 6610*
1820 Tomahawk Run Rd, Hedgesville, WV 25427-3147

(304) 754-8425
judyrooney.erskine@gmail.com

Hill, Kendra *Hopehill || Frederick |||| 6155*
5508 Duke Ct, Frederick, MD 21703

(301) 471-6072
k.hill6072@gmail.com

Kern, Ruby *Inwood || Inwood |||| 6615*
113 Tudor Dr, Inwood, WV 25428-5357

(304) 229-3244
pastorcharlie38@comcast.net

Brown-Jenkins, Sonja *Jackson Chapel || Frederick |||| 6330*
207 Shannonbrook Ln, Frederick, MD 21702-3636

(301) 676-0076
jenks@xecu.net

Thompson, Jacqueline *Jackson Chapel || Frederick |||| 6330*
191 Greenway Dr, Frederick, MD 21702-3902

(240) 674-2033
jthom829@comcast.net

Dinsmore, Charlotte *Jefferson || Jefferson |||| 6240*
5842 Broad Run Rd, Jefferson, MD 21755-9115

(301) 371-4483
Cod-cnh@fred.net

Read, Kathleen *Jefferson || Jefferson |||| 6240*
3897 Gibbons Rd, Point of Rocks, MD 21777-2023

(301) 874-2859
kdmr447@aol.com

Butler, Jerome *Johnsville || Sykesville |||| 4450*
1124 Johnsville Rd, Sykesville, MD 21784-8432

(410) 795-9896
johnsville1124@gmail.com

Collins, Ronald *Johnsville || Sykesville |||| 4450*
4255 Star Cir, Randallstown, MD 21133-5326

(410) 581-3062
ronc952@gmail.com

Bennett, Charlotte *Leetown || Kearneysville |||| 6630*
288 Jefferson Ave, Charles Town, WV 25414-1124

(304) 725-1102
PALAGR@frontiernet.net

Carroll, Celeste *Lewistown || Thurmont |||| 6265*
25 Cody Drive #31, Thurmont, MD 21788

(240) 415-3707

Gray, James *Lewistown || Thurmont |||| 6265*
21201 Reno Monument Rd, Boonsboro, MD 21713-2832

(240) 315-7894
jgray7714@gmail.com

Cline, Judith *Liberty Central || Libertytown |||| 6800*
PO Box 337, Libertytown, MD 21762-0337

(303) 898-7305
judimc1@comcast.net

Devilbiss, Donna *Linganore || Union Bridge |||| 6375*
1650 Linzee Dr, Westminster, MD 21157-7428

(410) 635-2926
donna.corky@yahoo.com

Ramsburg, Nola   *Linganore || Union Bridge ||| 6375*   (240) 446-4544
9310 Stauffer Rd, Walkersville, MD 21793-7603   nbramsburg@gmail.com

Ramsburg, Robert   *Linganore || Union Bridge ||| 6375*   (240) 446-4163
9310 Stauffer Rd, Walkersville, MD 21793-7603   nbramsburg@gmail.com

Aughenbaugh, Millie   *Messiah || Taneytown ||| 4475*
7145 Keysville Rd, Keymar, MD 21757-9604   ma9737@gmail.com

Fritz, Maxine   *Middleburg || Westminster ||| 4490*   (410) 775-7068
                                                                dav1pat2@hotmail.com

Agostini, Heidi   *Middletown || Middletown ||| 6280*   (240) 818-8607
10308 Church Hill Rd, Myersville, MD 21773-9028   heidiagostini@hotmail.com

Frederick, Dave   *Middletown || Middletown ||| 6280*   (301) 662-0713
2406 Ellsworth Way Apt 3A, Frederick, MD 21702-3165   dave3471@gmail.com

Koob, Michael   *Middletown || Middletown ||| 6280*   (301) 834-9332
1400 Baker Pl W Apt 21, Frederick, MD 21702-3241   mikekoob@hotmail.com

Koob, Sherie   *Middletown || Middletown ||| 6280*   (202) 329-7113
1400 Baker Pl W Apt 21, Frederick, MD 21702-3241   sheriekoob@hotmail.com

Brown, John   *Middleway || Kearneysville ||| 6635*   (304) 725-5164
21 Friendship Ct, Charles Town, WV 25414-5058   putter2121@gmail.com

Humphrey, Todd   *Mount Carmel || Frederick ||| 6335*   (301) 682-4947
6416 View Point Ct, Frederick, MD 21703-8629   wtoddhumphrey@icloud.com

Smith, John   *Mount Pleasant || Frederick ||| 6390*   (703) 845-0459
5616 Gary Ave, Alexandria, VA 22311-1504   sproctorsmith@comcast.net

Tabler, Debbie   *Mount Wesley || Shepherdstown ||| 6735*   (304) 267-6929
2953 Scrabble Rd, Martinsburg, WV 25404-0126   dbasketlady@frontier.com

Shaw, Mae   *Mount Zion || Martinsburg ||| 6675*   (304) 839-8460
PO Box 2412, Martinsburg, WV 25402-2412   bunbas629@aol.com

Cox, Sandy   *New Hope of Greater Brunswick || Brunswick ||| 6137*   (301) 834-8802
3532 Chick Ln, Knoxville, MD 21758-9133   sandycox44@gmail.com

Shew, Larry   *New Hope of Greater Brunswick || Brunswick ||| 6137*   (301) 834-9734
18 Concord Dr, Brunswick, MD 21716-1446   MrUmp13@aol.com

Gross, David   *New Street || Shepherdstown ||| 6750*   (304) 267-9797
655 Deer Mountain Dr, Harpers Ferry, WV 25425-5475   dixon-gross@655dmd.com

Magaha, Dennis   *Oakland || Charles Town ||| 6535*   (304) 876-1730
PO Box 625, Kearneysville, WV 25430-0625   gmagaha@citilink.net

Zaleski, John   *Oakland || Charles Town ||| 6535*   (304) 728-0743
70 Oakland Ter, Charles Town, WV 25414-4869

Frye, Linda   *Oakland || Sykesville |||| 4275*   office@oaklandumc.org

Corwin-Roach, Stan   *Otterbein || Martinsburg |||| 6680*   (301) 263-6316
217 Dancing Leaf Dr, Martinsburg, WV 25403-1113   stancorwinroach@hotmail.com

Reidy, Dawn   *Paynes Chapel || Bunker Hill |||| 6730*   (304) 671-0387
1116 Hyslip Ford Rd, Bunker Hill, WV 25413-2976   dreidy7@comcast.net

Roth, Susan   *Pikeside || Martinsburg |||| 6725*   (304) 678-9464
227 Tather Dr, Martinsburg, WV 25405-7204   susanroth125@gmail.com

Clark, Margaret   *Pleasant View || Adamstown |||| 6165*   (301) 834-7519
606 Souder Rd, Brunswick, MD 21716-1735   mclark615@verizon.net

Pittinger, George   *Sandy Mount || Finksburg |||| 4443*   (410) 857-2853
1855 Monarch Meadow Ct, Finksburg, MD 21048-1342   gpittinger@yahoo.com

Grey, James   *Silver Grove || Harpers Ferry |||| 6585*   (304) 725-4372
177 Shenanwood Dr, Harpers Ferry, WV 25425-4438   jgrey@restonlim.com

Bevard, Laura   *St James at Dennings || Westminster |||| 4540*   (443) 536-7433
3242 Ridge Rd, Westminster, MD 21157-7441   lbevard@comcast.net

Layne, Kim   *St Lukes || Martinsburg |||| 6690*   (304) 283-6956

Truax, Steven   *St Lukes || Martinsburg |||| 6690*   (304) 263-5749
419 S Georgia Ave, Martinsburg, WV 25401-1919   stevetruax@me.com

Blizzard, Tim   *Stone Chapel || New Windsor |||| 4545*   tim_blizzard@hotmail.com

Frye, Liza   *Stone Chapel || New Windsor |||| 4545*   (410) 430-1670
191 Leppo Rd, Westminster, MD 21158-1332   lfrye@cc-md.org

Brown, Charlotte   *Strawbridge || New Windsor |||| 4365*   charlotte51brown@gmail.com

Cordell, Clarence   *Thurmont || Thurmont |||| 6360*   (301) 271-4971
4 Linda Ct, Thurmont, MD 21788-1613   cj@cordellcustomhomes.com

Ohler, Donna   *Toms Creek || Emmitsburg |||| 6170*   (443) 244-3788
161 Gettysburg Rd, Littlestown, PA 17340-9772   dmohler45@gmail.com

Sebold, Tracy   *Trinity || Emmitsburg |||| 6175*   (717) 794-5397
116 Thunder Trl, Fairfield, PA 17320-9703   tsebold116@comcast.net

Wivell, William   *Trinity || Emmitsburg |||| 6175*   (301) 447-3766
16636 Toms Creek Church Rd, Emmitsburg, MD 21727-8429   wdwrpw@gmail.com

Pickens, Michele   *Trinity || Frederick |||| 6225*   (301) 695-8596
119 Deerfield Pl, Frederick, MD 21702-3727   spic192459@aol.com

Welker, Kevin   *Trinity || Frederick |||| 6225*   (301) 606-3019
Trinity Umc 703 W Patrick St, Frederick, MD 21701   wyclef5525@aol.com

Welker, Laura *Trinity || Frederick ||| 6225* (301) 678-8703
1903 Whetstone Ct, Frederick, MD 21702-3087 yardwelk@aol.com

Walker, Diane *Trinity || Martinsburg ||| 6710* (304) 350-8696
600 Artisan Way, Martinsburg, WV 25401-2999 dianeowalker@comcast.net

Brown, Mildred *Union Street || Westminster ||| 4550*

Thompson, Mildred *Union Street || Westminster ||| 4550*
401 Russell Ave Apt 202, Gaithersburg, MD 20877-2806 mildredt@gmail.com

Fritz, E. *Uniontown || Westminster ||| 4510* (410) 775-7068
PO Box 11, Keymar, MD 21757-0011 dav1pat2@hotmail.com

Sipes, Sherry *Uniontown || Westminster ||| 4510* (410) 848-3305

Alexander, Henry *Weller || Thurmont ||| 6365* (301) 271-7164
15006 Mud College Rd, Thurmont, MD 21788-1331 mount-terp@prodigy.net

Pitt, Catherine *Weller || Thurmont ||| 6365* (717) 642-8576
85 Jacks Mountain Rd, Fairfield, PA 17320-8277 catherinep23@comcast.net

Gentile, Scott *Westminster || Westminster ||| 4555* (410) 848-1479
573 Marshall Dr, Westminster, MD 21157-4614 scottgentile@comcast.net

Henderson, Ronald *Williams Memorial || Shepherdstown ||| 6740* (304) 930-1351
94 Bitner Ln, Kearneysville, WV 25430-5059

Wandel, Linda *Zion || Westminster ||| 4560* (410) 795-6935
725 Fannie Dorsey Rd, Sykesville, MD 21784-8206

Zepp, Ronald *Zion || Westminster ||| 4560* (410) 848-0712
2743 Old Washington Rd, Westminster, MD 21157-7545 morganrun@verizon.net

GREATER WASHINGTON DISTRICT

Ross, Andrea *Ager Road || Hyattsville ||| 7380* (301) 559-7334
6006 37th Ave, Hyattsville, MD 20782-2930 andreaandsparky1@verizon.net

White, Gertrude *Albright Memorial || Washington ||| 7110* (202) 427-8501
PO Box 70574, Bethesda, MD 20813-0574 trudytil@aol.com

Adams, Sandy *Asbury || Washington ||| 7115* (240) 355-1348
629 Girard St NE, Washington, DC 20017-1321 sporto25@hotmail.com

McEachron, Jeanarta *Asbury || Washington ||| 7115* (202) 584-0840
3520 Texas Ave SE, Washington, DC 20020-2364 jeanarta.mceachron@gmail.com

Travis, Carol *Asbury || Washington ||| 7115* (301) 459-6303
6501 Hillwood Dr, Riverdale, MD 20737-3030 carol6303@aol.com

Wyles, Darryl   *Asbury || Washington |||| 7115*   dwyles@hotmail.com

Davis, Greta   *Bells || Camp Springs |||| 8145*   (301) 449-6316
5300 Fadden Ct, Camp Springs, MD 20748-4120   gdavis2011@comcast.net

Gillette, Bob   *Bethesda || Bethesda |||| 9122*
7 Eastmoor Dr, Silver Spring, MD 20901-1937   gillette.robert@gmail.com

Stephens, Rosalyn   *Bradbury Heights || Washington |||| 7120*   (301) 952-1864
11401 Southglen St, Upper Marlboro, MD 20772-2753   vernsgirl@aol.com

Howard, Nate   *Brighter Day || Washington |||| 7625*   (202) 561-6675
3004 9th St SE, Washington, DC 20032-4227   howard810@verizon.net

Criddell, Hortense   *Brightwood Park || Washington |||| 7125*   (202) 882-6129
6427 6th St NW, Washington, DC 20012-2613   robertsonvanessa@verizon.net

Du, Bingchen   *Cabin John || Cabin John |||| 9160*   christhillcount@gmail.com

Hii, Esther   *Cabin John || Cabin John |||| 9160*   (301) 229-8233
7703 MacArthur Blvd, Cabin John, MD 20818   cjumc@hotmail.com

Lu, Nelson   *Cabin John || Cabin John |||| 9160*   mkyhawk@yahoo.com

Wang, Helen   *Cabin John || Cabin John |||| 9160*   chihying2wang@yahoo.com

Smith, Sandra   *Capitol Hill || Washington |||| 7135*   (301) 218-1261
3850 Enfield Chase Ct Apt 119, Bowie, MD 20716-2222   rlrenshaw@aol.com

Pethen, Valerie   *Centenary || Flatts FL BX |||| 7615*   (441) 236-3270
Coral Chimneys, Paget, PA DV 04   valeries@ibl.bm

Watkins, Candice *Cheverly || Cheverly |||| 7325*   (301) 773-2253
5801 Dewey St, Cheverly, MD 20785-2937   CLW747@comcast.net

Martin, Marvin   *Christ || Washington |||| 7140*   (202) 488-8916
907 6th St SW Apt 309C, Washington, DC 20024-3827   mmjjde@aol.com

Critchlow, Desmond   *Church of The Redeemer || Temple Hills |||| 7475* (301) 899-2534
2609 Boones Ln, District Heights, MD 20747-3374   desocritch05@yahoo.com

McCrae, Daniel   *Church of The Redeemer || Temple Hills |||| 7475*   Mccraedm@verizon.net

Jenkins, Maxine   *Colesville || Silver Spring |||| 9450*   (301) 622-1240
712 Downs Dr, Silver Spring, MD 20904   mjenk83601@aol.com

Hough, Vernie   *Community || Washington |||| 7145*   (240) 455-7430
1915 Arcadia Ave, Capitol Heights, MD 20743-5706   vhough49@yahoo.com

Parker, Lynda   *Community || Washington |||| 7145*
1426 Kearny St NE, Washington, DC 20017-2956   bandl010108@gmail.com

Wise, William *Concord-St Andrews || Bethesda ||| 9130* (301) 299-9473
8229 W Gainsborough Ct, Potomac, MD 20854-4273 wiseharvey@aol.com

Lacy, Linda *Dumbarton || Washington ||| 7160* (703) 578-3017
2405 S Dinwiddie St, Arlington, VA 22206-1000 linda.lacy@gmail.com

Milewski, Jennifer *Dumbarton || Washington ||| 7160* jennifer.milewski@gmail.com

Quinn, Mittie *Dumbarton || Washington ||| 7160* (703) 734-0724
1722 Linwood Pl, McLean, VA 22101-5119 umcmittie@gmail.com

Gibson, Gloria *Ebenezer || Washington ||| 7165* (202) 544-1415
400 and D St. S.E., Washington, DC 20003 gjarey@hotmail.com

Davies, Judy *Emmanuel || Laurel ||| 7440* (301) 497-6445
11017 Chelsea Way, Laurel, MD 20723 cathyjd18@verizon.net

Schwartz, Chris *Emory || Washington ||| 7175* (301) 536-1818
18305 Queen Elizabeth Dr, Olney, MD 20832-1719 wchrisschwartz@hotmail.com

Keller, Marjorie *Faith || Rockville ||| 9410* (301) 984-6137
7303 Old Stage Rd, Rockville, MD 20852-4440 m.susan.keller@verizon.net

Prillaman, Hunter *Faith || Rockville ||| 9410* (301) 299-2692
8509 Fox Run, Potomac, MD 20854-2505 hprill@aol.com

Miller, Pamella *First || Hyattsville ||| 7385* (410) 695-6627
5416 Kenilworth Ter Apt 2, Riverdale, MD 20737-3132 pamela_miller@hotmail.com

King, Marshall *Forest Memorial || Forestville ||| 8190* (301) 736-6091
2903 Sydney Ave, District Heights, MD 20747-2849 kb3mcm@gmail.com

Winfield, Arleen *Forest Memorial || Forestville ||| 8190* (301) 773-7508
3512 Jeff Rd, Glenarden, MD 20774-2610 arleendw@comcast.net

Beadle, Nicholas *Foundry || Washington ||| 7180*
3221 Connecticut Ave NW Apt 308, Washington, DC 20008-2562 nick.beadle@gmail.com

Brown, Ann *Foundry || Washington ||| 7180*
3514 Macomb St NW, Washington, DC 20016-3162 ann.brown@troutman.com

Cecil, Guy *Foundry || Washington ||| 7180*
1319 T St NW, Washington, DC 20009-4438 ghcecil@gmail.com

Gilliam, Jay *Foundry || Washington ||| 7180*
2576 Sherman Ave NW, Washington, DC 20001-2235 jayrgilliam@gmail.com

Johnson, Andrea *Foundry || Washington ||| 7180* (612) 414-2150
218 S Alfred St, Alexandria, VA 22314-3639 andrealynn.johnson@gmail.com

Kidwell-Slak, Kerry *Foundry || Washington ||| 7180* (301) 403-8989
4704 College Ave, College Park, MD 20740-3507 kmkidwell@yahoo.com

Kramer, Allison   *Foundry || Washington |||| 7180*
1441 Newton St NE, Washington, DC 20017-3010   allisongraham77@gmail.com

Lawrence, Janet   *Foundry || Washington |||| 7180*   (321) 543-3355
1216 Maryland Ave NE, Washington, DC 20002-5336   jml0309@gmail.com

Morrow, Tara   *Foundry || Washington |||| 7180*   (202) 689-5884
5805 Goucher Dr, Berwyn Heights, MD 20740-2624   tcmorrow8@gmail.com

Tatum, Fredia   *Franklin P Nash || Washington |||| 7185*   (202) 374-2089
4202 58th Ave, Bladensburg, MD 20710-1950   queenebony30@yahoo.com

Williams, Joseph   *Gethsemane || Capitol Heights |||| 7320*   (301) 249-6226
12514 Woodsong Ln, Mitchellville, MD 20721-4224   maewill5@aol.com

Myers, Caroleann   *Glenmont || Silver Spring |||| 9475*   (301) 871-1746
302 Topside Dr, Stevensville, MD 21666-2870   caroleannshalom@comcast.net

Alleyne, Audrey   *Good Hope Union || Silver Spring |||| 9455*   (301) 490-1575
9532 Chaton Rd, Laurel, MD 20723-1481   aealleyne@comcast.net

Boston, Arletta   *Good Hope Union || Silver Spring |||| 9455*   (301) 421-9638
16430 Batson Rd, Spencerville, MD 20868-9705   arlejohn_9@msn.com

Boston, Marie   *Good Hope Union || Silver Spring |||| 9455*   (301) 421-9638
16430 Batson Rd, Spencerville, MD 20868-9705   arlejohn@verizon.net

Michell, Priscilla   *Good Shepherd || Silver Spring |||| 7445*   (301) 919-6080
9737 Mount Pisgah Rd Apt 1610, Silver Spring, MD 20903   pmichell2015@gmail.com

Pimentel, Mayuris   *Hughes || Wheaton |||| 9480*   (856) 577-7411
2208 Colston Dr Apt 201, Silver Spring, MD 20910-2507   mayuris.pimentel@gmail.com

Woods, Eloise   *Hughes || Wheaton |||| 9480*   (301) 649-1887
1305 Wheaton Ln, Silver Spring, MD 20902-3659   woodem02@aol.com

Bain, Carol   *Hughes Memorial || Washington |||| 7190*   (301) 336-1341
1206 Addison Road S, Capitol Heights, MD 20743   cabain1231@aol.com

Blake, Peggy   *Jerusalem-Mt Pleasant || Rockville |||| 9420*   (301) 580-4354
482 Winding Rose Dr, Rockville, MD 20850-2864   peggyjblake@verizon.net

Greene, Louann   *Jones Memorial || Washington |||| 7210*   (202) 583-7523
2501 Branch Ave SE, Washington, DC 20020-1417   lgreene6@comcast.net

Adebesin, Bisi   *Liberty Grove || Burtonsville |||| 9155*   (301) 879-0075
3508 Tagore Ct, Burtonsville, MD 20866-1697   badebesin@gmail.com

Long, James   *Lincoln Park || Washington |||| 7215*   (410) 338-1968
3307 Crossland Ave, Baltimore, MD 21213-1002   jklpumc@gmail.com

Maynard, Janet   *Marsden First || Smith |||| 7610*   (441) 292-4847
6 Gospel Lane, Bermuda, HM 14 BERMU   janetrev@logic.bm

Jones, Judy   *McKendree-Simms-Brookland || Washington ||| 7620*   (301) 773-0525
8621 Irvin Ave, Glenarden, MD 20706-1523   Jones8621@verizon.net

Lyons, Otelia   *McKendree-Simms-Brookland || Washington ||| 7620*   (301) 386-4896
5300 Newton St Unit 404, Bladensburg, MD 20710-2361   jones8621@verizon.net

Bachman, Ellen   *Metropolitan Memorial || Washington ||| 7630*   (703) 212-9045
611 N Pegram St, Alexandria, VA 22304-2727   ellenbachman@comcast.net

Rousset, Tim   *Metropolitan Memorial || Washington ||| 7630*   Tim.rousset@gmail.com

Kelley, Dawn   *Millian Memorial || Rockville ||| 9430*   (301) 869-8010
16545 S Westland Dr, Gaithersburg, MD 20877-1226   djkelley5@verizon.net

Weigel, Dwayne   *Millian Memorial || Rockville ||| 9430*   (301) 946-2500
13217 Vandalia Dr, Rockville, MD 20853-3352   dwayne4748@earthlink.net

Dika, Lal Biak   *Mizo || Rockville ||| 7485*   (301) 972-1723
20011 Wyman Way, Germantown, MD 20874   fdika@hotmail.com

Smith, Carolyn   *Mount Vernon || Washington ||| 7230*   (301) 735-1962
3717 Dianna Rd, Suitland, MD 20746-2227   grateful2122@gmail.com

Conner, James   *Mount Vernon Place || Washington ||| 7235*   (202) 740-1269
430 M St SW Apt N800, Washington, DC 20024-2639   jcconner87@gmail.com

Carter-Coleman, Pamela   *Mount Zion || Washington ||| 7240*   (202) 882-6298
1816 Taylor St NW, Washington, DC 20011-5348   pamaka76@gmail.com

Haynes, Edmund *Mount Zion || Washington ||| 7240*   (240) 271-9828
223 Castleton Pl, Largo, MD 20774-1445   edmundhaynes@hotmail.com

Walsh-Barberesi, Diane   *Mount Zion || Washington ||| 7240*   (301) 807-7214
4612 Creek Shore Dr, Rockville, MD 20852-2406   DWalshB@verizon.net

Ow, Ken   *North Bethesda || Bethesda ||| 9140*   (301) 520-9990
13415 Rippling Brook Dr, Silver Spring, MD 20906   kenow999@gmail.com

Nieves, Domingo *Oak Chapel || Silver Spring ||| 9460*   (301) 946-7951
1607 Ingram Ter, Silver Spring, MD 20906-5932   Domingo98@earthlink.net

Stevens, Valerie *Petworth || Washington ||| 7245*   (240) 354-3606
4201 Rainier Ave, Mount Rainier, MD 20712-1742   VSanBS@aol.com

Doggett, Bill   *Potomac || Potomac ||| 9390*   (301) 986-1955
8011 Glenbrook Rd, Bethesda, MD 20814-2603   wdoggett@doggettarchitects.com

Garte, Sy   *Rockville || Rockville ||| 9440*   (917) 526-3980
516 Calvin Ln, Rockville, MD 20851-1137   sygarte@gmail.com

Brown, Sheila   *Ryland-Epworth || Washington ||| 7255*   (202) 575-1896
2015 Branch Ave SE, Washington, DC 20020-3335   shb3@verizon.net

246

Browning, Bob   *Silver Spring || Silver Spring ||| 9466*   (301) 774-0305
18909 Clover Hill Ln, Olney, MD 20832-1211   suznbob@verizon.net

Browning, Suzanne   *Silver Spring || Silver Spring ||| 9466*   (301) 774-0305
18909 Clover Hill Ln, Olney, MD 20832-1211   suznbob@verizon.net

McGinnia, Rebecca   *Silver Spring || Silver Spring ||| 9466*   (301) 681-5565
10204 Haywood Dr, Silver Spring, MD 20902-4929   rmcginni@umd.edu

Newman, Dianna *Simpson-Hamline || Washington ||| 7265*   (202) 726-1570
519 Crittenden St NW, Washington, DC 20011-4742   dnewman10@live.com

Atolagbe, Desiree T.   *St Paul || Chevy Chase ||| 7330*   (301) 275-1962
2100 Porter Rd, Silver Spring, MD 20910-5011   lilft@aol.com

Greene, Tina   *St Paul || Chevy Chase ||| 7330*

Munthali, Elisa   *St Paul || Chevy Chase ||| 7330*   (301) 949-8420
4100 Dana Ct, Kensington, MD 20895-3651   elisa.munthali@gmail.com

Raulin, Kenzie   *St Pauls || Kensington ||| 9330*   kenzier@rcn.com

Schinski, Vern   *St Pauls || Kensington ||| 9330*   (301) 774-4391
19400 Dubarry Dr, Brookeville, MD 20833-2617   vschinski5@verizon.net

Lozier, Elaine   *United || Washington ||| 7275*   (202) 686-1229
5230 Sherier Pl NW, Washington, DC 20016-3324   danlozier@cs.com

Madill, George   *United || Washington ||| 7275*   (703) 354-4083
6322 Fenton Ct, Alexandria, VA 22312-6321   g.madill@att.net

Sanford, Jonathan*United || Washington ||| 7275*   (202) 546-6257
637 11th St NE, Washington, DC 20002-5317   jonathan.e.sanford@gmail.com

Prather, Ray   *University || College Park ||| 7340*   (301) 422-1400
3621 Campus Dr, College Park, MD 20740-3116   laurelduo@msn.com

Harris, Alma   *Van Buren || Washington ||| 7280*   (301) 261-3989
1726 Denton Ct, Crofton, MD 21114-1914   almaaka1954@aol.com

Williams, Evelyn   *Van Buren || Washington ||| 7280*
4809 3rd St NW, Washington, DC 20011-4720

WASHINGTON EAST DISTRICT

Bennett, Judith *Alexandria Chapel || Indian Head ||| 8390* (301) 753-4335
5037 Preston Ln, Pomfret, MD 20675-3020 pastor.alexandriachapel@gmail.com

Simmons, Rita *Alexandria Chapel || Indian Head ||| 8390* (240) 286-5792
1911 Michael Rd, Waldorf, MD 20601-3304 rita.v.simmons@gmail.com

Taylor, Rhonda *Alexandria Chapel || Indian Head ||| 8390* (301) 743-3907
Attn Asst. Treasure Alex Chapel, Indian Head, MD 20640 rlbond2@gmail.com

Brooks, Taylor *Asbury || Brandywine ||| 8130* (301) 843-9135
2507 Legation Pl, Waldorf, MD 20601-2666 sbrooks909@aol.com

Chase, Peggy *Asbury || Brandywine ||| 8130* (202) 384-6739
14310 S Springfield Rd, Brandywine, MD 20613-9257 jccpec74@yahoo.com

Piscacek, Gordon *Bethel || Upper Marlboro ||| 8480* (301) 336-4481
10905 Joyceton Dr, Largo, MD 20774-1454 gp18@verizon.net

Beverly, Eilene *Bethesda || Valley Lee ||| 8515* (410) 326-3465
705 Coster Rd, Lusby, MD 20657-2955 eilenebev@comcast.net

Coale, Karen *Bowie || Bowie ||| 8120* (301) 352-3888
11926 Frost Dr, Bowie, MD 20720-4429 kpcoale@aol.com

Reynolds, Linwood *Brooks || Saint Leonard ||| 8460* (410) 535-3422
1730 Joe Harris Rd, Prince Frederick, MD 20678-3667 linwoodreynolds46@gmail.com

Akins, Keith *Calvary || Waldorf ||| 8520* (301) 789-1036
1121 Clark Ave, Waldorf, MD 20602-2969 finance-ch@calvumc.org

Williams, Susie *Chicamuxen || La Plata ||| 8260* (301) 743-3638
5475 Port Tobacco Rd, Indian Head, MD 20640-3570 jackie.bowie@comcast.net

Brown, Henrietta *Christ || Aquasco ||| 8115* (301) 203-2767
15812 Menk Rd, Accokeek, MD 20607-9528 henribrown@aol.com

Barron, Cameron *Clinton || Clinton ||| 8170* (202) 583-5105
3609 Suitland Rd SE, Washington, DC 20020-1249 brb822@aol.com

Fauber, June *Clinton || Clinton ||| 8170* (301) 466-7357
14510 April St, Accokeek, MD 20607-9770 junefauber@gmail.com

Waltrip, Dwaine *Community w. Cause || Lexington Park||| 8295* (240) 317-5184
20881 Three Notch Rd Unit B, Lexington Park, MD 20653 masterchief@md.metrocast.net

Cleveland, Bertina *Coopers || Dunkirk ||| 8175* (310) 855-4943
4090 Ferry Landing Rd, Dunkirk, MD 20754-8907 tinacleve55@comcast.net

Stovall, Diana *Corkran Memorial || Temple Hills ||| 7480* (301) 630-4144
3600 Farness Ct, Temple Hills, MD 20748-4810 dianastovall39@hotmail.com

Clark, Sr, Ronald *Eastern || Lusby |||| 8330*   (410) 326-0064
540 Hutchins Road, #39, Dowell, MD 20629   clarky1520@gmail.com

Jackson, Alice *Ebenezer || Lanham |||| 8285*   (301) 336-7595
1609 Pebble Beach Dr, Bowie, MD 20721-2375   ajac956@aol.com

Ladd, Theodore *Emmanuel || Beltsville |||| 7310*   (301) 937-6796
11722 Emack Rd, Beltsville, MD 20705-1546   tedladd02@aol.com

White, Roy *Emmanuel || Beltsville |||| 7310*   (301) 236-9685
14300 Twig Rd, Silver Spring, MD 20905-7012   rwhite8088@aol.com

Ireland, Jeff *Emmanuel || Huntingtown |||| 8240*   (410) 535-4743
2165 Wilson Rd, Huntingtown, MD 20639   stoakleyfarm@comcast.net

Russell, Rowena *Emmanuel || Huntingtown |||| 8240*   (301) 855-1769
    emmanuelumc@comcast.net

Jacobs, John *Faith || Accokeek |||| 8110*   (301) 375-9448
6422 Hard Bargain Cir, Indian Head, MD 20640-3045   yeti1963aa@gmail.com

Perry, Darrell *Faith || Accokeek |||| 8110*   (301) 934-2416
6011 Exchange Dr, La Plata, MD 20646-5682   pkperry2@verizon.net

Cullison, David *First Saints Community || Leonardtown |||| 8540*   (301) 863-1298
23387 Hosta Ln, California, MD 20619-6168   davashcat@yahoo.com

Lanzi, Sarah *First Saints Community || Leonardtown |||| 8540*   (240) 298-8206
Campus Box #147, Washington, DC 20016-5632   smlanzi3@gmail.com

Priest, Edgar *First Saints Community || Leonardtown |||| 8540*   (301) 475-2077
42303 Riverwinds Dr, Leonardtown, MD 20650-5726   priest1@md.metrocast.net

Jackson, Elizabeth *Glenn Dale || Glenn Dale |||| 8225*   (301) 249-4430
1910 Arbor Hill Ln, Bowie, MD 20716-1520   Elizabeth.jackson@ars.usda.gov

Kindred, Elliott *Glenn Dale || Glenn Dale |||| 8225*   (301) 860-1199
10605 Forestgate Pl, Glenn Dale, MD 20769-2037   kspirits1@verizon.net

Flanagan, Linda *Good Shepherd || Waldorf |||| 8525*   (301) 645-1375
236 Barksdale Ave, Waldorf, MD 20602-2860   waldorfangel@gmail.com

Lavoie, Cathy *Good Shepherd || Waldorf |||| 8525*   (301) 645-2717
2803 Lomax Ct, Waldorf, MD 20602-1753   lavoie20602@aol.com

Hutchins-Robinson, Tina *Grace || Fort Washington |||| 8215*   (301) 249-4038
12509 Cambleton Dr, Upper Marlboro, MD 20774-1727   tina.robinson@navy.mil

Robinson, Frances *Grace || Fort Washington |||| 8215*   (301) 839-5223
9107 Friar Rd, Fort Washington, MD 20744-6802   robinsonf@aol.com

King, Steven *Hollywood || Hollywood |||| 8230*   (301) 373-5980
43495 Sunny Ridge Ln, Hollywood, MD 20636-2548   Slkbking@hotmail.com

Knight, Michael *Hollywood || Hollywood ||| 8230* (301) 373-5421
44749 Emma Ln, Hollywood, MD 20636-4847 mike2knight@md.metrocast.net

Barney, Rich *Huntingtown || Huntingtown ||| 8245* (410) 257-1994
6620 Michele Ct, Huntingtown, MD 20639-9055 rich.barney@outlook.com

Gerber, Deb *Huntingtown || Huntingtown ||| 8245* (301) 855-3178
3145 Kenni Ln, Dunkirk, MD 207540000 topontour@comcast.net

Cross, Sandra *Immanuel || Brandywine ||| 8235* (301) 888-2280
13801 Martin Rd, Brandywine, MD 20613-8774 sandygrama@comcast.net

Johnson, Wayne *Indian Head || Indian Head ||| 8265*
131 Quailwood Court, LaPlata, MD 20646

Miller, Danny *Indian Head || Indian Head ||| 8265* (301) 743-2490
5680 W Mount Aventine Rd, Indian Head, MD 20640-1131 millerdannyl@aol.com

Risley, James *La Plata || La Plata ||| 8275* (301) 392-6011
706 Clarks Run Rd, La Plata, MD 20646-9563 jfrisley@mac.com

White, Doris *La Plata || La Plata ||| 8275* (301) 934-0999
409 Butternut Ct, La Plata, MD 20646-9507 doris409@verizon.net

White, Ken *La Plata || La Plata ||| 8275* (301) 934-0999
409 Butternut Ct, La Plata, MD 20646-9507 kenwhite409@verizon.net

Nagbe, Kili *Lanham || Lanham ||| 8290* (240) 491-2854
5620 Whitfield Chapel Rd Apt 301, Lanham, MD 20706-2548 kateabela@gmail.com

Nagbe, Kili Moses *Lanham || Lanham ||| 8290*
5620 Whitfield Chapel Rd Apt 301, Lanham, MD 20706-2548 kateabela@gmail.com

Reed, Scott *Lexington Park || Lexington Park ||| 8320* (402) 690-1190
20839 Sunlight Ct, Lexington Park, MD 20653-2454 scott.reedspeed@gmail.com

Farmer, Patricia *Metropolitan || Indian Head ||| 8420* (301) 743-3161
22 Rivers Edge Ter, Indian Head, MD 20640-1562 farmer2@comcast.net

Parks, Lillian *Metropolitan || Indian Head ||| 8420* (301) 283-6336
PO Box 1315, Bryans Road, MD 20616 lvparks@verizon.net

Bates, Bonnie *Mount Harmony-Lower Marlboro || Owings ||| 8365* (410) 257-0542
7201 Briscoe Turn Rd, Owings, MD 20736-9033 bonniesbates@gmail.com

Leavitt, Jon *Mount Harmony-Lower Marlboro || Owings ||| 8365* (301) 801-3358
2905 Chaneyville Rd, Owings, MD 20736-9666 jondleavitt@hotmail.com

Uunila, Kirsti *Mount Harmony-Lower Marlboro || Owings ||| 8365* (410) 286-7131
PO Box 1222, North Beach, MD 20714-1222 blueheron77@comcast.net

Mackall, Nevelin *Mount Hope || Sunderland |||| 8475*   (443) 964-5892
7365 Clyde Jones Rd, Owings, MD 20736-3047   nevelinmackall@comcast.net

Offord, Sallie *Mount Hope || Sunderland |||| 8475*   (301) 855-8081
PO Box 54, Sunderland, MD 20689-0054   Esweetie808@aol.com

Johnson, Jennifer *Mount Oak || Mitchellville |||| 8355*   (301) 218-3788
16613 Peach St, Bowie, MD 20716-3525   jmartjohn@aol.com

Holland, Dean *Mount Olive || Prince Frederick |||| 8430*   (410) 535-9392
245 Hope Ln, Huntingtown, MD 20639-3504   holland4family@comcast.net

Cullison, JoAnn *Mount Zion || Mechanicsville |||| 8350*   (240) 997-5828
37719 Asher Rd, Mechanicsville, MD 20659   cullisonj123@gmail.com

Greene, Delores *Mount Zion || Saint Inigoes |||| 8450*   (301) 994-0634
46178 Drayden Rd, Drayden, MD 20630-3015   delores.greene.ctr@navy.mil

Contee, Wanda *Nottingham-Myers || Upper Marlboro |||| 8485*   (301) 404-6513
N/A, Brandywine, MD 20613-8671   wandacontee201338@gmail.com

Stelloh Garner, Chris *Olivet || Lusby |||| 8335*   (301) 855-4876
5941 Cherry Hill Rd, Huntingtown, MD 20639-9682   stelgar@comcast.net

Anders, Earlene *Oxon Hill || Oxon Hill |||| 8380*   (301) 630-0650
4250 Southwinds Pl, White Plains, MD 20695-4236   earleneteresa@verizon.net

Stephens, Anna *Oxon Hill || Oxon Hill |||| 8380*   (301) 423-0350
7510 Lenham Dr, Ft Washington, MD 20744-2153   cleatusgirl16@gmail.com

Long, Mona *Patuxent || Huntingtown |||| 8250*   (410) 535-0316
monadlong@yahoo.com

Norman, Darlene *Patuxent || Huntingtown |||| 8250*   (301) 868-4423
3500 Solomons Island Rd, Huntingtown, MD 20639-3810   ednorman@verizon.net

Smith, Erica *Peters || Dunkirk |||| 8180*   (240) 286-4582
590 Grovers Turn Rd, Owings, MD 20736-3206   ericahsmith.es@gmail.com

Elliott, Jane *Pisgah || Marbury |||| 8270*   (301) 934-2786
7030 Perfect Pl, Port Tobacco, MD 20677-3033   kcandjanetoo@gmail.com

Willett, Chester *Pisgah || Marbury |||| 8270*   cwillett@khov.com

Freeland, Joyce *Plum Point || Huntingtown |||| 8255*   joycefreeland11@msn.com

Hutchins, Mary *Plum Point || Huntingtown |||| 8255*   (410) 535-2656
1725 Stinnett Rd, Huntingtown, MD 20639-8768   reid1996@yahoo.com

Russell, Sandra *Providence-Ft Washington || Ft Washington |||| 8205*   (301) 516-2222
4900 Melwood Rd, Upper Marlboro, MD 20772-9527   dcandsandy@verizon.net

Houston, Dothlyn *Queens Chapel || Beltsville ||| 7315*
14750 4th St Apt 319, Laurel, MD 20707-3874
(301) 490-6591
dhou893693@aol.com

Macan, Christine *Shiloh || Bryans Road ||| 8140*
Indian Head, MD 20640-3221
(301) 502-6585
mara4391@yahoo.com

Littlejohn, Vera *Smith Chapel || Marbury ||| 8415*
4545 Kinmount Rd, Lanham, MD 20706-1957
(301) 577-0816
veralpepsi@aol.com

Mason, Gail *Smith Chapel || Marbury ||| 8415*
9844 Ushers Pl, Waldorf, MD 20601-3723
(301) 257-9049
gmason1966@yahoo.com

Jackson, James *Smithville || Dunkirk ||| 8185*
3882 Yellow Bank Rd, Dunkirk, MD 20754-9350
(443) 964-6344
jackson.30west@verizon.net

Wessinger, Rebecca *Smithville || Dunkirk ||| 8185*
9919 Jonathan Dr, Dunkirk, MD 20754
(410) 257-3160
rebecca_wessinger@yahoo.com

Yunger, Phil *Solomons || Solomons ||| 8470*
PO Box 733, Solomons, MD 20688-0733
(202) 674-7788
dottieyunger@gmail.com

Estep, Corlise *St Edmonds || Chesapeake Beach ||| 8160*
PO Box 539, Chesapeake Beach, MD 20732-0539
(410) 257-9013
Corlisea@hotmail.com

Gross, Doris *St Edmonds || Chesapeake Beach ||| 8160*
5673 Old Ridge Path Ln, Lothian, MD 20711-2103
(410) 867-2518
stedmondsumc@verizon.net

Beverly, Julius *St John || Lusby ||| 8340*
7920 Main Falls Cir, Baltimore, MD 21228-2420
(410) 788-1244
hlbev745@verizon.net

Clark, Sr., Ronald *St John || Lusby ||| 8340*
540 Hutchins Road, Lusby, MD 20629
(410) 326-0064
lusbycharge@gmail.com

Goins, Cheryl *St Luke || Scotland ||| 8445*
PO Box 116, Prince Frederick, MD 20678-0116
(410) 535-8646
candjg@verizon.net

Goins, Jeffrey *St Luke || Scotland ||| 8445*
PO Box 116, Prince Frederick, MD 20678-0116
(410) 535-8646
candjg@verizon.net

Eisinger, Marian *St Matthews || Bowie ||| 8125*
3704 Idolstone Ln, Bowie, MD 20715-1414
(301) 805-8625
teisinger@comcast.net

Lesche, Robert *St Matthews || Bowie ||| 8125*
4307 Taunton Dr, Beltsville, MD 20705
(301) 937-8714
bdlesche@msn.com

Beaudwin, Lauren *St Paul || Lusby ||| 8345*
10960 Hg Trueman Rd, Lusby, MD 20657-2847
(410) 257-3160
LSB210@aol.com

Mulvey, Dennis *St Paul || Lusby ||| 8345*
thejoeman2001@yahoo.com

Showalter, Debra *St Paul || Lusby ||| 8345*
2060 Brians Way, Lusby, MD 20657-2477
(410) 326-2150
debandbo@comcast.net

Johnson, Deborah   *St Paul || Oxon Hill |||| 8385*   (202) 309-0640
1800 Palmer Rd Apt 233, Fort Washington, MD 20744   deborahj8888@gmail.com

Marshall, Cora   *St Paul || Oxon Hill |||| 8385*   (301) 248-1484
2605 Kingsway Rd, Ft Washington, MD 20744-3326   cpmarshall25@gmail.com

Johnson, Faye   *The Journey of Faith Church || Waldorf |||| 8550*   (301) 351-4253
15701 Alhambra Ct, Accokeek, MD 20607   fayej@aol.com

Cox, Richard   *Trinity || Prince Frederick |||| 8435*   (410) 535-1385
5420 Sixes Rd, Prince Frederick, MD 20678-5720   racox55@verizon.net

Woodford, Sandra   *Trinity || Prince Frederick |||| 8435*   (410) 535-5547
1735 German Chapel Rd, Prince Frederick, MD 20678   thewoodfords@hotmail.com

Walker Hodges, Wanda   *Union || Upper Marlboro |||| 8490*   (301) 218-2195
1304 Wigeon Ct, Upper Marlboro, MD 20774   wandawalker3832@att.net

Jones, Ellis   *Wards Memorial || Owings |||| 8165*   (443) 964-4684
1833 Horace Ward Rd, Owings, MD 20736-9326   eljones6@comcast.net

Wallace, Barbara   *Wards Memorial || Owings |||| 8165*   (443) 891-6898
PO Box 626, Owings, MD 20736-0626   barbiedollwallace56@gmail.com

Diehl, Marlene   *Waters Memorial || Saint Leonard |||| 8465*   (410) 586-0503
3997 Sharmrock Court, Port Republic, MD 20676   natediehl@comcast.net

Willey, Levi   *Waters Memorial || Saint Leonard |||| 8465*   (410) 251-8552
2410 Parkers Creek Road, Pt. Republic, MD 20678   lwj007@aol.com

Willy, Levi   *Waters Memorial || Saint Leonard |||| 8465*   (410) 251-8552
2410 Parkers Creek Rd, Port Republic, MD 20676-2234   lwj007@aol.com

Gaskin, Robert   *Westphalia || Upper Marlboro |||| 8510*   (301) 249-7417
2914 Spriggs Request Way, Mitchellville, MD 20721-2582   rbf3@verizon.net

Kent, Gwendolyn   *Westphalia || Upper Marlboro |||| 8510*   (301) 868-9245
6103 Wigan Ct, Clinton, MD 20735-3757   gbkent@gmail.com

West, Stephanie   *Westphalia || Upper Marlboro |||| 8510*   (301) 274-9165
14860 Augusta Classic Pl, Hughesville, MD 20637-2422   swest@westphaliaum.org

White, Delores   *Westphalia || Upper Marlboro |||| 8510*   (301) 735-8333
2609 Brooks Dr, Suitland, MD 20746-1106   Ford2White@verizon.net

Jordan, Andrian   *Zion || Lexington Park |||| 8325*   (240) 587-9310
23622 Fairmeade Way, California, MD 20619-3306   andrianjordan@gmail.com

Fletcher, Charlie   *Zion Wesley || Waldorf |||| 8535*   (202) 500-5321
9800 Fox Run Dr, Clinton, MD 20735-3070   fletchtec@aol.com

CONFERENCE SURVIVING SPOUSES' DIRECTORY

Abernethy, Agnes (Rev. Rufus)   (410) 267-6640
3316 Arundel On The Bay Rd, Annapolis, MD 21403-4757

Adams, Wyoming (Rev. Donald C.)   (301) 645-7352
2504 Porter Ave, Suitland, MD 20746-1130

Allen, Shirley (Rev. George)   (410) 747-8208
5906 Leewood Ave, Catonsville, MD 21228-3101

Ammons, Betty Jane (Rev. Harold A.)   (410) 247-3249
1125 Gloria Ave, Arbutus, MD 21227-2332

Anderson, Iona Josephine (Rev. William)   (301) 724-0210
10 N Liberty St, Apt 206, Cumberland, MD 21502-2341

Andrews, Grace M. (Rev. David Hafer)   (301) 416-0650
5110 Foxville Rd, Smithsburg, MD 21783

Andrews, Susan (Rev. Richard W.)   (410) 967-6789
401 Russell Ave, Apt 712, Gaithersburg, MD 20877-2818

Austin, Ethel C (Rev. Thomas N., III)   (301) 782-2873
12803 Lusbys Ln, Brandywine, MD 20613-7878

Ball, Virginia (Rev. Richard L.)
1 Bunche St, Annapolis, MD 21401-3807

Bartlett, Frances (Rev. Walter Raymond)   (410) 848-7536
228 Saint Mark Way, Westminster, MD 21158-4164

Bangs, Mildred (Rev. Edwin)

Basil, Jane (Rev. Irving)   (410) 486-7451
4014 Raleigh Rd, Baltimore, MD 21208-5717

Belk, Ruby Shearin Knock (Rev. Stanley F.)   (936) 634-1861
1302 Tom Temple Dr, Apt 228, Lufkin, TX 75904-5552

Bennett, Marian E (Rev. Harry L.)   (717) 245-0618
212 Todd Cir, Carlisle, PA 17013-3596

Benny, Barbara (Rev. Milton)   (717) 498-0343
2 East Grandview Avenue, Mercersburg, PA 17236

Bice, Churalene (Rev. Stanley R.)   (301) 572-0078
3152 Gracefield Rd, Apt 308, Silver Spring, MD 20904

Bishop, Ruth H (Rev. Leighton) (541) 488-3415
280 Normal Ave, Ashland, OR 97520-1328

Boehl, Joyce A. (Rev. Allan) (304) 274-1719
PO Box 115, Falling Waters, WV 25419-0115

Boling, Francette (Rev. Mark) (410) 628-7448
6516 Sherwood Rd, Baltimore, MD 21239-1349

Bosman, Brenda (Rev. Walter) (410) 861-5158
1806 Bloom Rd, Westminster, MD 21157

Bratton, Nettie (Rev. Morris H.) (512) 240-5700
139 Estrella Crossing Apt 127, Georgetown, TX 78628

Breeden, Alice G. (Rev. Elmer Ray) (205) 339-6367
11575 Courtney Ln, Northport, AL 35475-4954

Broome, Mary Beth (Rev. Richard) (304) 263-0103
22 Paynes Ford Rd, Martinsburg, WV 25405

Brown, Carolyn (Rev. Roland "Bud") (410) 409-6707
225 Greenvale Mews Dr, Westminster, MD 21157

Brown, Joyce Lea (Rev. Barclay)
8264 Academy Rd, Ellicott City, MD 21043

Brown, Rev. Marianne T. (Rev. Lynn A.) (240) 681-3612
17400 Aquasco Rd, Brandywine, MD 20613-4212

Bunce, Nargis (Rev. N. Ellsworth) (904) 529-4648
PO Box 1058, Penney Farms, FL 32079-1058

Bussard, Annamarie (Rev. William J.) (410) 371-0562
9563 Devonwood Court, Rosedale, MD 21237

Carr, Rev. Arlene (Rev. Ronald)
2129 W. New Haven Ave., Apt 130, West Melbourne, FL 32904

Cartwright, Sarah (Rev. Robert C.) (410) 561-0428
226 Brackenwood Ct, Timonium, MD 21093-2616

Cater, Rose (Rev. Joseph E.) (202) 337-1771
4530 Q Pl NW, Washington, DC 20007-2571

Cathcart, June Rochelle (Rev. Charles) (304) 728-2282
PO Box 152, Shenandoah Junction, WV 25442-0152

Chambly, Mary Ann (Rev. James) (304) 263-6837
118 Kimberly Dr, Martinsburg, WV 25404-0675

Cho, Myong (Rev. David)   (201) 421-6167
7253 Flushing Wood Grove, East Stroudsburg, PA 18360

Chung, Esther (Rev. Wayne)   (240) 722-6088
18048 Wagonwheel Court, Olney, MD 20832

Clark, Dorothy Davis (Rev. James R.)   (410) 552-4092
656 Ocean Pkwy, Ocean Pines, MD 21811-9402

Clipp, Jane Ruth (Rev. Albert)   (304) 263-5774
304 South Alabama Avenue, Martinsburg, WV 25401

Collignon, David (Rev. Margaret)   (410) 472-2085
3 Manor Brook Rd, Monkton, MD 21111-1606

Collins, Lorraine B. (Pastor Charles)
445 Collins Rd, Edgewater, MD 21037

Conley, Alma Jane (Rev. Harold I)   (352) 368-6777
6514 NW 37th Ter, Gainesville, FL 32653-0879

Cooney, Doris (Rev. C. Douglas)   (410) 737-1556
715 Maiden Choice Ln, Apt Cr203, Catonsville, MD 21228-5747

Corbett, Sarah Anne (Rev. Jack E.)   (301) 229-6229
415 Russell Ave, Apt 415, Gaithersburg, MD 20877-2848

Creek, Jean A. (Rev. Charles)   (410) 544-1249
107 Magothy Bridge Rd, Severna Park, MD 21146-1203

Cross, Virginia I. (Rev. Michael A.)
15732 Leib School Rd, Stewartstown, PA 17363

Crossland, Doris (Rev. Elton M.)   (410) 882-2780
2621 Proctor Ln, Baltimore, MD 21234-1733

Custis, Levurn (Rev. Harvey)   (301) 893-2710
6202 Panther Ct, Waldorf, MD 20603-4409

Davis, Virginia H. (Rev. William H.)   (410) 266-8561
4906 Lindsay Rd, Baltimore, MD 21229-1235

Dawson, Patricia (Rev. David C.)   (301) 644-5800
7401 Willow Rd, Apt 116, Frederick, MD 21702-2500

Day, Cindy Thomas (Rev. Basil Boyer)
684 Brandy Ln, Westminster, MD 21157-7652

Day, Verna L. (Rev. John M.)   (443) 874-7530
4502 Kathland Ave, Baltimore, MD 21207

DeMent, Mabel "Chris" (Rev. James L.)   (410) 790-8935
2908 Chenoak Avenue, Parkville, MD 21234

Diggs, Frances A. (Rev. James W.)   (240) 925-5593
21328 Windsor Drive, Lexington Park, MD 20653

Donick, Janet (Rev. Andrew J.)   (301) 872-5882
PO Box 43, Scotland, MD 20687-0043

Doggett, Florence (Rev. Herbert L.D.)   (301) 293-2195
10463 Churchill Road, Myersville, MD 21773

Downs, Helen (Rev. S. Eugene)
719 Monkton Rd, Monkton, MD 21111-1115

Dubchak, Lidiya (Rev. Emmanuel M. Gitlin)

Duncan, Tracy (Pastor Richard)   (443) 618-6808
PO Box 129, Jessup, MD 20749

Ebinger, Mary R. (Rev. Warren)   (301) 987-6555
407 Russell Ave, Apt 405, Gaithersburg, MD 20877-2854

Elgert, Laura (Rev. C. Roger)   (410) 747-6308
528 Northridge St, Denton, TX 76201-0827

Embrey, Mary Jo (Rev. James R.)
270 McMillan Court, Martinsburg, WV 25404

Emmerling, Joyce C. (Rev. Kenneth)

Ernst, Doris (Rev. Henry E.)   (667) 367-2923
505 High Acre Drive, Apt. 123, Westminster, MD 21157

Evansmore, Jean D. (Rev. Steward Frazier)   (410) 531-7855
4028 Jumper Hill Ln, Ellicott City, MD 21042

Ewald, Barbara (Rev. John "Jack" E.)   (301) 299-6355
325 Woods Road, Hedgesville, WV 25427

Farris, Elizabeth R. (Rev. John W.)   (304) 258-2852
178 Dads Ln, Great Cacapon, WV 25422

Fisher, Amy E. (Rev. Henry L.)
10525 Greenwich Dr, Williamsport, MD 21795

Fisher, Betsy P. (Rev. James L.)   (410) 242-4323
715 Maiden Choice Ln, Catonsville, MD 21228-5999

Fisher, Frances (Rev. R. Edwin)   (803) 256-8490
900 Gregg St, Apt 2B, Columbia, SC 29201-3913

Fisher, Mary (Rev. James L.)   (301) 271-7875
7912 Rocky Ridge Rd, Thurmont, MD 21788-1348

Fisk, Betty (Pastor Francis J.)
30 Jacqueline Dr, New Oxford, PA17350

Ford, Alice Beverly (Rev. John Linwood)   (301) 845-6943
8618 Discovery Blvd, Walkersville, MD 21793

Forkkio, Esther (Rev. John A.)   (301) 330-8771
10408 Capehart Ct, Gaithersburg, MD 20886-3931

Gabler, Alverta Leslie (Rev. Elmer David Slater)   (410) 840-2086
2728 Leppo Ln, Finksburg, MD 21048-1104

Garrison, Sylvia G (Rev. J. Lloyd)   (410) 766-6470
416 Queenstown Rd, Severn, MD 21144-1307

Gassman, Audrey (Rev. E. Theodore)
586 6th St, Pasadena, MD 21122-5009

Giles, Lillie (Rev. Albert)   (301) 431-3181
2012 Edgewater Pkwy, Silver Spring, MD 20903-1208

Goodman, Nina Harpold (Rev. Edward)   (410) 256-9075
10104 Fontaine Dr, Baltimore, MD 21234-1204

Graham, Norma Lee (Rev. Bruce)   (301) 598-1265
14702 Bigby Ct, Silver Spring, MD 20906-1836

Graham, Patricia (Rev. Leroy S.)   (270) 781-8096
2108 Gotts Hydro Rd S, Bowling Green, KY 42103-9542

Gray, Carole B (Rev. Elliott G.)

Gray, Edward (Rev. Lillie)   (410) 741-9290
995 Marlboro Road, Lothian MD, 20711

Grayson, Edna (Rev. Julian)   (202) 396-7839
4041 Clay Place NE, Washington, DC 20019-3340

Greynolds, Earline (Rev. William)   (410) 252-2294
11811 Greenspring Ave, Owings Mills, MD 21117-1603

Groseclose, William "Bill" (Rev. Marguerite)   (724) 452-2351
101 Burgess Drive, Zelienople, PA 16063

Hall, Marjorie (Rev. Charles W.)   (863) 453-6706
2001 S. Lee Street, Americus, GA 31709-4715

Harris, Lucy (Rev. Carlton)   (410) 788-8947
27 Montrose Manor Ct, Apt D, Baltimore, MD 21228-5014

Harris, Victoria (Rev. James L.)
2501 W Cold Spring Ln, Baltimore, MD 21215-6916

Harrison, Dorothy (Rev. Clifford)
7407 Willow Road, Frederick, MD 21702

(301) 644-5754

Haskins, Deborah (Rev. Bruce)
4400 Wentworth Place, Baltimore, MD 21207

(301) 502-6527

Hastings, Jeannette M. (Rev. Charles H.)
1739 Presidio Dr, Clermont, Fl 34711-6533

(813) 822-1241

Hathorne, Debra (Rev. Bruce A.)
34 Sierra Ln, Arnold, MD 21012-2450

(410) 757-0906

Henderson, Harriette (Rev. Hal T.)
229 St. Marys Lane, Stafford, VA 22556

(703) 447-9758

Henry, Shirley M. (Rev. Charles W.)
P.O. Box 263, Charles Town, WV 25414

(304) 725-8631

Heslop, Julia Ann Terrell (Rev. William H.)
9 Hidden Lake Ct, Berlin, MD 21811-1257

(410) 208-6911

Heydt, Deborah Sue (Rev. Edward)
1503 Barrett Street, Havre De Grace, MD 21078

(410) 939-4428

Hoffman, Madelyn (Rev. John O.)
23 Well St, Huntingtown, MD 20639-9410

(410) 535-0128

Hogle, Teddy (Rev. C. Alan)
54 Indian Springs Lane, East Haven, CT 06512

Houck, Ruth Rill (Rev. Chester Wilson)
226 Houch Rd, Westminster, MD 21157-6620

(301) 340-7210

Howard, Bessie (Rev. Don)
10001 Windstream Drive, Unit 608, Columbia, MD 21044

Hutchins, Gloria (Rev. Joshua)
13002 Cannon Pl, Upper Marlboro, MD 20774-8679

(301) 249-0285

Iley, Elizabeth (Rev. Charles H.)
413 Navarre Way, Altamonte Street, FL 32714

Johnson, Alma W. (Rev. P. Paul)
24 Lincoln Ct, Annapolis, MD 21401-4113

(410) 266-6125

Johnson, Hattie (Rev. Guy H.)
741 Decatur St, NE, Washington, DC 20017

(202) 635-4961

Johnson, Sonora (Rev. Andrew)   (410) 947-5979
136 N Culver St, Baltimore, MD 21229-3007

Johnson, William (Rev. Karen A. Jones-Johnson)   (443) 801-7247
9441 Farewell Road, Columbia, MD 21045

Johnson-Holmes, Rev. Hattie Jean (Rev. Val Morrow Holmes)
21 Victoria Square, Frederick, MD 21702

Jones, Janice (Rev. James)   (410) 647-7035
105 Leslie Ct, Severna Park, MD 21146-1205

Keene, Frances L. (Rev. Lewis I.)   (410) 444-7745
1904 Northbourne Road, Baltimore, MD 21239

Keidel, Gladys (Rev. Keith W.)
700 Hollinshead Spring Rd, Apt B-105, Skillman, NJ 08558

Kemp, Phyllis B. (Rev. T. Ward)   (717) 632-7116
425 Westminster Ave, Hanover, PA 17331-9141

Kess, Letitia (Rev. Leon C.)   (404) 556-0591
6211 Pimlico Road, FL 1, Baltimore, MD 21209

Kemmerer, Barbara (Rev. Norman)   (443) 507-5142
4466-632 Woodsman Drive, Hampstead, MD 21074

Kent, Gwendolyn (Rev. Otto)   (410) 768-3588
554 Queenstown Rd, Severn, MD 21144-1310

Kiely, Arlene (Rev. Harry C.)   (301) 755-6575
3142 Gracefield Rd, Apt 214, Silver Spring, MD 20904

Kirk, Edith (Rev. Chester W.)   (301) 260-1157
17428 Cherokee Ln, Olney, MD 20832-2163

Lane, Grace W. (Rev. Albert K.)   (410) 861-9939
2525 Baltimore Blvd, Trlr 24, Finksburg, MD 21048-1826

Lansing, Phyllis (Rev. John William)
715 Maiden Choice Ln, #CR403, Baltimore, MD 21228

Lee, Sarah M. (Rev. Won Uk)   (240) 354-1727
2 Drumcastle Ct, Germantown, MD 20876-5633

Leisher-Goode, Dorothy K. (Rev. Richard Goode)   (443) 204-3149
6415 Danville Ave, Baltimore, MD 21224

Letto, Dennis Lee (Rev. Kathryn)   (301) 372-8704
296 Creek Blvd, Pasadena, MD 21122-5024

Lewis, Jacqueline (Rev. Donald) (501) 767-2134
286 Country View Trl, Pearcy, AR 71964-9750

Lichtenwalter, Jan (Rev. Marvin A. Boyles) (321) 383-2523
2890 Saint Marks Dr, Titusville, FL 32780-6741

Link, Jane (Rev. J. Howard) (410) 398-7291
7 Glen Creek Cir, Apt C, Elkton, MD 21921-8927

Lockman, Joan (Rev. Irvin) (410) 636-7437
6573 Hall Ave, Glen Burnie, MD 21060-6334

Logan, Andrea (Rev. Douglas M.) (301) 559-5428
1207 Valley Drive, Hyattsville, MD 20782

Long, Janet A. (Rev. Girard Francis)
1012 Samantha Lane, #302, Odenton, MD 21113

Luckett, Pauline G. (Rev. Albert)
5161 Blanton Dr, Las Vegas, NV 89122

Lyles, Catherine (Rev. William T.)

Lytle, Julia (Rev. Raymond) (334) 271-5815
128 Natchez Dr, Montgomery, AL 36117-4013

Mack, Jeanette (Rev. Joseph D.)
3803 Bonner Rd, Baltimore, MD 21216-1202

Malone, Dona (Rev. Harold W.) (239) 471-7935
1120 SW 52nd St, Cape Coral, FL 33914

Marsh, Cathy E. (Rev. Theodore D.) (240) 522-0906
165 Northwoods Drive, Hedgesville, WV 25427

Marsh, Mary Ann (Rev. Michael G.) (304) 258-5975
210 Bucky's Lane, Berkeley Springs, WV 25411

Mason, Ella (Rev. J. Sherman) (301) 874-5843
3546 Hopeland Rd, Frederick, MD 21704-7670

Matthews, Robert (Rev. Callie M.) (410) 757-3593
202 Brownswood Rd, Annapolis, MD 21409

Mayers, Patricia Hulsey (Rev. Judson D.) (814) 238-4014
648 Wiltshire Dr, State College, PA 16803

Mayne, Mehrle F. (Rev. Charlotte J.) (301) 662-4320
6820 Buckingham Lane, Buckeystown, MD 21717

McCants, Bernice (Rev. James Keywal)
417 Dentwood Dr, Fort Washington, MD 20744

McClarren, Evelyn (Rev. Lloyd Charles) (814) 553-8316
1268 Salem Road, West Decatur, PA 16878

McCarthy, Dan (Rev. Elaine Emeth) (301) 681-5677
931 Loxford Ter, Silver Spring, MD 20901-1126

McClatchey, Ramona (Rev. Russell B.) (304) 754-5533
84 Kreglow Ct, Hedgesville, WV 25427

McFarland-Honan, Clare M. (Rev. Richard F. McFarland)
6370 Winona Ave, San Diego, CA 92120

McKenney, Nampeo D. (Rev. Martin L.) (301) 390-5317
405 Jones Falls Court, Bowie, MD 20721

McNally, Laura Mae (Rev. J. William)
20903 Runnymeade Ter, Apt 401W, Ashburn, VA 20147

Meland-Donophan, Paula (Rev. Charles Donophan)
171 Shamrock Dr, Salisbury, MD 21804

Merki, Sheril (Rev. William) (304) 264-0897
363 Universe Dr, Martinsburg, WV 25404-3496

Metcalf, Katherine (Leslie G.) (410) 788-6832
48 Holmehurst Avenue, Catonsville, MD 21228

Miller, Christine (Rev. Ray E.)
4992 Autumn Trl, Grovetown, GA 30813-4408

Miller, Marguerite (William C.)
3015 Northwind Road, Baltimore, MD 21234

Miller, Mary Estelle (Rev. Everett G.) (410) 235-8067
301 W Cold Spring Ln, Baltimore, MD 21210-2803

Minners-Nelson, Rev. Elizabeth Ann (Rev. William Nelson) (843) 421-2346
209 Collins Glenn Drive, Murrell S Inlet, SC 29576

Moales, Norma Jean (Rev. Robert E.) (301) 733-7242
1534 Kensington Dr, Hagerstown, MD 21742

Morgan, Gladys M. (Rev. Garland P.) (240) 674-8331
108 Easy Street, Thurmont, MD 21788

Moore, Joan S. (Rev. Maurice S.) (410) 998-8624
4730 Atrium Court, Apt. 530, Owings Mills, MD 21117

Nair, Arettia (Rev. Robert L.) (301) 722-2542
1009 Virginia Ave, Cumberland, MD 21502-4638

Nicol, Francis S. (Rev. Leonora)   (301) 879-1911
229 Amberleigh Dr, Silver Spring, MD 20905-5992

Niner, Madeline R. (Rev. Charles E.)   (410) 882-6270
300 International Cir, # 331, Cockeysville, MD 21030-1300

O'Connell, Sandra E. (Rev. Ralph L. Minker)   (703) 724-1537
44412 Sunset Maple Dr, Ashburn, VA 20147-3888

Owens, Nellie (Rev. Vincent E.)

Patrick, June (Rev. Hubert L.)   (410) 838-9017
2101 Fairlane Rd, Bel Air, MD 21015-1109

Park, Mary (Rev. John S.)   (301) 387-2037
95 Sky Valley Rd, Swanton, MD 21561

Peacher, Bernice (Rev. Eric)   (410) 252-3534
12300 Rosslare Ridge Rd, Unit 402, Timonium, MD 21093-8207

Peters, Marcella (Rev. William)   (410) 314-9042
719 Maiden Choice Ln, HR 704, Baltimore, MD 21228

Petzold, Roxine (Rev. Milton H.)

Phillips, Deborah (Rev. Colin A.)   (443) 834-5540
2004 Academy Court, Emmitsburg, MD 21727

Pinkney, Helen (Pastor John)
1406 Brooke Rd, Capitol Heights, MD 20743

Polk, Carol (Rev. William E.)
615 Chestnut Ave., Apt 1415, Towson, MD 21204

Price, Ruby (Rev. John O.)   (301) 628-8358
305 S Winding Brooke Dr, Seaford, DE 19973-4813

Price, Teaette (Rev. Bruce)   (410) 732-1188
2335 Boston St, Unit 6, Baltimore, MD 21224-3682

Rainey, Rev. Joe S. (Rev. Diane L.)   (703) 343-0368
8350 Greensboro Drive, #805, McLean, VA 22102

Ransom-Knecht, Sally (Rev. Lewis Frank Ransom)   (410) 252-6776
Edenwald, 800 Southerly Rd #702, Towson, MD 21286-8145

Reno, Louise (Rev. Ramon F.)   (575) 202-8014
2882 North Roadrunner Parkway, Apt. 226, Las Cruces, NM 88011

Rettenmayer, Rev. Linda (Rev. Stephen)   (540) 221-0861
50 Regiment Drive, Gettysburg, PA 17325

Richmond, Mary Ella (Rev. Clifford H.)   (301) 216-5531
401 Russell Ave, Apt 603, Gaithersburg, MD 20877-2824

Schauer, Carole Jean (Rev. LeRoy E.)   (410) 208-3635
22 Gatehouse Trl, Ocean Pines, MD 21811-2023

Scheel, Emma Lou (Pastor Thomas)   (301) 969-6138
415 West Potomac, Brunswick, MD 21716

Scouten, JoRetha (Rev. Wesley G.)   (717) 352-3160
3893 Alfalfa Ln, Fayetteville, PA 17222-9466

Seymour, Mildred (Rev. Charles E.)   (301) 216-5132
3002 Scenic View Dr, Forest Hill, MD 21050-1400

Shenefelt, Alberta (Rev. Tedford)   (410) 751-9114
201 Saint Mark Way, Apt 202, Westminster, MD 21158-6138

Slaugh, Charles (Pastor Holly Elaine)
3114 Gracefield Rd, Apt. 503, Silver Spring, MD 20904-7855

Sloan, David (Rev. Carole M.)   (301) 577-7240
6619 Greenland St, Riverdale, MD 20737-3062

Smith, Laura P. (Rev. John T.)   (410) 382-5926
1038 Bear Crossing, Hanover, PA 17331

Smith, Louise B. (Rev. James H.)   (410) 922-7656
4730 Duncannon Rd, Pikesville, MD 21208-2045

Snodgrass, Hubert (Rev. Donna)   (410) 452-5785
3516 Prospect Road, Street, MD 21154

Snowden, Cecelia (Rev. John D.)   (301) 577-7476
5428 Whitfield Chapel Rd, Lanham, MD 20706

Stansbury, Evelyn (Rev. George A.)   (410) 757-6423
161 Brown's Woods Rd, Annapolis, MD 21401

Stewart, Alma R. (Rev. Charles W.)   (301) 216-4582
333 Russell Avenue, #121, Gaithersburg, MD 20877

Strait, Isabelle (Rev. Roger)   (570) 827-0438
43 Buffards Riverside East, Lawrenceville, PA 169299765

Sulmonetti, Juanita (Rev. Earl W.)
7213 Timber Lane, Falls Church, VA 22046 (daughter)

Talbot, Joanne (Rev. J. William)
220 NW 7th St, Delray Beach, FL 33444

Talley, Kimberly (Rev. James F.W.)   (410) 781-6262
PO Box 33, New Windsor, MD 21776

Tay, Rev. Stella Sofia Austin (Rev. Manuel)   (301) 423-1497
5303 Lorraine Dr, Temple Hills, MD 20748-2419

Taylor, Alta (Rev. Walter L.)   (410) 242-8698
713 Maiden Choice Ln, Apt 2204, Baltimore, MD 21228-3616

Thomas, Therese (Rev. John R.)   (410) 381-7123
7261 Eden Brook Dr, Columbia, MD 21046

Thompson, Geraldine (Rev. Vernon L.)   (321) 258-2672
1461 Cape Sable Drive, Melbourne, FL 32940

Tice, Rebecca (Rev. Alva D.)   (540) 830-5650
125 Alleghany Drive, McGaheysville, VA 22840

Trail, Rev. Mary Stevens (Rev. Glenn F.)   (252) 221-4188
209 Cherokee Trail, Edenton, NC 27932

Toles-Felton, Lisa (Rev. Leonard Ray)   (410) 480-0496
3731 Bonnybridge Place, Ellicott City, MD 21043-4127

Tyson, Lois Fry (Rev. Kenneth Aubrey)   (301) 644-5882
7407 Willow Rd. Apt 361, Frederick, MD 21702

Van Metre, Sandra K. (Rev. Edward R.)   (304) 264-0480
108 York Rd, Martinsburg, WV 25403-2371

Vaughn, Martha (Rev. Alfred A.)   (410) 325-1355
5465 Bucknell Rd, Baltimore, MD 21206-3823

Wallace, Carolyn (Rev. Horace Lee)   (410) 461-2325
8321 Governor Grayson Way, Ellicott City, MD 21043-3450

Walsh, Doris (Rev. Samuel W.)

Walther, Rosemary (Rev. John H.)   (301) 330-5508
403 Russell Ave, Apt 306, Gaithersburg, MD 20877-2825

Walz, Prudence (Rev. Arthur F.)   (410) 284-0590
1700 Church Rd, Dundalk, MD 21222

Wanek, Betty June (Rev. Frank G.)   (443) 567-6113
1003 Running Creek Way, Unit G, Bel Air, MD 21014-2346

Washington, Darlene (Rev. Johnnie)   (410) 867-7574
5308 Sweetwater Dr, West River, MD 20778-2107

Weatherholtz, Joanne K. (Rev. William Rogers Wells)   (410) 875-2129
3155 Cardinal Dr, Westminster, MD 21157-7703

Weiss, Stephanie P. (Rev. Gerald W.) (410) 242-2286
717 Maiden Choice Ln, St 325, Catonsville, MD 21228

White, Evelyn Greene (Rev. Leon H.) (410) 360-0983
5800 16th St NW, Washington, DC 20011-2804

Whye, Ruth Carmichael (Rev. De Priest Wolford) (410) 947-2715
5765 Whistling Winds Walk, Clarksville, MD 21029-1662

Williams, Dorothy (Rev. Edwin W.) (334) 877-1171
3250 Lincoln Dr, Selma, AL 36701

Wright, Fay (Rev. John Evans)
P.O. Box 357, Bunker Hill, WV 25413-0357

Wyatt, Linda Wright (Rev. William P.) (303) 364-3326
166 S Eagle Circle, Aurora, CO 800121-536

Yingling, Phyllis (Rev. L. Carroll)
717 Maiden Choice Lane, Apt. T19, Baltimore, MD 21228-6153

Zimmerman, Shirley Ann (Rev. William F.) (540) 635-4853
2199 Mountain View Rd, Apt. 115, Stafford, VA 22556-6475

Zinn, Carolyn J. (Rev. William Carl) (301) 964-0161
1257 Crescent Road, Hagerstown, MD 21742

DAILY PROCEEDINGS

Clergy Executive Session
Marriott Waterfront, Baltimore
Wednesday, May 29, 2019

As clergy assembled, Bishop LaTrelle Easterling declared, "God is good!" to which the assembled chanted "All the time!" The bishop continued, "And all the time" and after the reply, "God is good," she said, "Amen. This is the day that the Lord has made, we shall rejoice and be glad in it!" Marshals were instructed to secure the doorways to enable the commencement of the Clergy Executive Session of the Baltimore-Washington Conference at 1:37 p.m. She asked the Chair of the Board of Ordained Ministry (BOOM), the Rev. Dr. C. Anthony Hunt, to read the Clergy Session Organizing Motion. The motion passed.

Bishop Easterling invited everyone to experience a time of worship, "to center ourselves to begin our work in prayer and receive the feel of the movement of the Holy Spirit." She beckoned Marcia McFee, the worship leader, to begin the worship. McFee invited everyone to take a deep breath. The music "Stay with Me" began playing and was played during the Scripture reading. She asked everyone to continue singing as a Communion chalice was brought up the aisle to the front table. The song "Stay with me" was a prayer in the gathering "to remain with Jesus as his Spirit seeks to work in and through us, to discern God's will for each of us." The time of worship ended with the song, "God is Love and Love is God."

Next, Dave Schoeller, the BWC's Business Data Analyst, provided instructions for the use of the electronic voting units, provide by Padget Electronics. He provided an overview of the voting technology and processes.

Rev. Maidstone Mulenga, the Director of Communications for the Council of Bishops, made a motion to "suspend the use of the voting device… for this 2019 legislation, and that all subsequent votes during the session be taken by raising of our hands or standing up or as you [the bishop] deem appropriate." After receiving a second, Mulenga explained that he made the motion "because it is time we become open" and "say who we really are." He went on to say that eliminating the voting machines would provide a means to "celebrate our brothers and sisters in an open manner" by not hiding "behind the voting devices." Secondly, he explained that voting openly will dispel ideas that "certain groups vote for certain candidates in certain ways." He called for voting to be open, letting each person, whether voting for or against candidates, be open in their vote.

Rev. Rudy Bropleh spoke against the motion, saying that with the "volume of persons" in attendance, raising hands or cards had the "propensity for confusion" and possible inaccuracy.

Rev. Laura Blauvelt, Potomac UMC, spoke in favor of the motion, saying that "this is the annual conference where we are called to stand and say who we are as the Baltimore-Washington Conference." She concluded that this "begins with us in this session as we vote on the candidates in the BOOM report."

Rev. Smiley continued his speech against the motion, recommending that people be welcomed to stand if they wanted to stand. This would allow the use of the voting devices.

Bishop Easterling recognized Rev. Alisa Lasater Wailoo of Capitol Hill UMC, who was speaking for the motion. She explained that, "we expect transparency in our congregation" and that "it is in place where we allow things to hide, it's in silence" and "those places where we hide, that things are not of God come out." She continued, "And if we claim that God is the light, then let's let the light shine. My hope is that we could stand for these things." She believes this approach would allow unity in spite of differences and it meant "that we be real about who we care." However, in cases of close votes, she favored using the machines to finalize the vote.

Rev. Lori Hays of Lexington Park UMC, was recognized by the chair and requested information. She asked if someone could tell them the logistical challenges of voting by hand instead of using the equipment.

Schoeller returned and explained that a backup plan included the option of paper ballots estimated to take 45 minutes to an hour turn-around time from the time the vote was taken.

Rev. Mary Kay Totty, of Dumbarton UMC, asked for clarification that the motion did not require a paper ballot and only applied to the clergy session. "So, it's going to be basic votes affirming or non-affirming — yes or no — votes."

The bishop asked Mulenga to clarify. Mulenga responded that his motion was specific only to voting for candidates recommended by the Board of Ordained Ministry (BOOM).

Rev. Kathy Lesko, who identified as "lesbian clergy" of Good Shepherd UMC, rose in her "heart" to speak in favor of the motion. She said, "Too many of us have had to live in the shadows too long" and many were "greatly... hurt by that." She said some may have known that she is gay, and some may not, but "the most important thing to me is that you are my brother and sister in Christ." She also requested that the clergy not be limited to standing because some, like she, herself, who uses a wheelchair, cannot stand.

Cathy Vitek, a licensed local pastor at Bethany UMC, rose to speak against the motion because of concerns that those not permitted to vote during the session might be seen as making a judgment, rather than just not voting because they would not be standing or using cards.

Rev. Michael Leedom, Union Chapel in Berkeley Springs, rose to offer an amendment to the original motion. He suggested the voting devices be used and those who wished to stand be given the opportunity after the vote. The bishop ruled the motion out of order.

Rev. Mark Gorman, Rules Chair, questioned how the body was going to proceed with voting on the motion. He explained that the rules indicate that "certain kinds of votes require a one-third majority," but he was not sure the rule applied to the vote. He asked if the body was "seeking a full majority for this?" Also, he asked, "what would happen if someone were to request a secret ballot" and "would that override this motion or be subsequent to it."

Bishop Easterling stated that the motion required a simple majority to change the way the body votes. If, during the proceedings, a secret ballot became necessary, she would deal with that when it happened. She called for the vote. The motion did not pass. The bishop called for the BOOM Report.

Rev. C. Anthony Hunt presented the report on behalf of the Board of Ordained Ministry of the Baltimore-Washington Conference. (This report is included in the Ministry Reports.) Hunt explained that BOOM represents "the diversity of the BWC geographically, racially, theologically, and in many other ways." He asked all members of the BOOM to stand and then invited everyone to celebrate them. He thanked Bishop Easterling for her ongoing prayers and the Rev. John Nupp, Executive Minister of Call and Clergy Care, for his "outstanding leadership in managing and facilitating the perfecting of our practices for supporting clergy and those preparing for ordained and licensed ministry." He thanked Nupp and asked that he be recognized. The bishop acknowledged that Nupp lost his father the preceding week and celebrated his home-going over the weekend. She praised and thanked him for his faithfulness and said that he and his family will continue to be prayed for.

Hunt then continued with the detailed report and called on the Dean of the Cabinet, Rev. Conrad O. Link. Bishop Easterling asked the gathering to take a moment to thank Hunt for "his exemplary leadership of the Board of Ordained Ministry."

Link gave the response to Question 17, beginning with thanks to Bishop Easterling for the "privilege of serving" as the Dean of the Cabinet for the past two years and expressing his appreciation for his DS colleagues. The bishop thanked him for the report and thanked him for his tenure as a Cabinet member and Dean of the Cabinet.

Hunt continued with Question 18, which was voted on as a whole and approved. Question 19 was informational. Question 20, which was about people who have completed studies for the license as a local pastor, who are approved but not now appointed, passed. Questions 21.a., full-time local pastors, and 21.b., part-time local pastors, who are approved and under appointment were handled together and were affirmed.

Rev. Bruce Jones, retired, asked if the voting time could be reduced to 30 seconds for the remainder of votes. A point of order was raised by Rev. Heath Wilson, Tom's Creek UMC, who asked if a third choice was needed for those abstaining when using electronic voting.

Mulenga offered that not voting when using electronic voting devices was equivalent to abstaining. The bishop said that her response would have been the same but wanted Schoeller to comment. He confirmed that not voting is abstaining and is not reflected on the device or included in the vote tally.

Rev. Kara Scroggins, Glenmont UMC, stated that part B of the last vote had the name of a part-time licensed local pastor, Kevin Cameron, who was appointed at the Dickerson charge. Rev. J. W. Park, Central Maryland District Superintendent, responded that Kevin Cameron was not yet appointed and thus his name was not on the list and the matter was confidential.

Rev. Stephen Ricketts, Linganore UMC, asked if the body had dealt with Jones's question about reducing the voting time to 30 seconds. The bishop replied "yes" and agreed that when people were comfortable with using the device, the voting time would be reduced to 30 seconds.

Hunt continued with the report, 21.b., with two persons from other annual conferences licensed in other annual conferences, and students serving within the bounds of the BWC. The bishop called for the vote and a 30-second voting window. It passed.

Question 23, reinstated as a local pastor, was approved with a show of voting cards. Question 24 was informational. Question 25 listed those from other Christian denominations approved to serve within the bounds of the BWC. It was approved. The affiliate members without vote, of which there were two listed in Question 26.b., were approved by over two-thirds vote. Rev. Tori Butler rose with a correction to the spelling of her name in Question 24.a. The correction was noted.

As Question 28 was announced, Rev. Katie Bishop, New Hope of Greater Brunswick, offered a motion "that the entire class of persons being considered for Deacon and Elder provisional status be considered and voted upon as a class and that the entire class of persons being considered for full membership as Deacons and Elders in the annual conference be considered and voted upon as a class." The motion was seconded.

Rev. Bishop explained that after years of going through the process —including local churches affirming their call, district boards, psych evaluations, theological education, etc. — she concluded that "By taking them as a class we affirm the hard work of these many hands that has brought all of these candidates forward so that that they might serve and do the work of our church and our community." Bishop Easterling checked on her understanding of the motion and Rev. Bishop explained the voting would be in one block for provisional Deacons and Elders and one block for full-membership Deacons and Elders.

Rev. Kathy Cole, a retired Elder, spoke in support of the motion by lifting up the "very hard work" of the Board of Ordained Ministry and reiterating much of what Rev. Bishop said. She said that if the process was flawed for one candidate, it could be assumed that it was flawed for all the candidates.

Rev. Charles Harrell, retired, spoke against the motion for two reasons. First, he spoke from his years of attending Executive Session, noting that with "the exception of one session" the session had always "voted for each of the candidates individually."

Bishop Easterling intervened to ask that attendees refrain from interrupting those who had the floor as thus far the session had been conducted with "great courtesy and grace."

With regard to a person being elected into full connection, Harrell explained that each person being elected into full connection had "each had the opportunity to come before the body and be voted on individually," and that the two classes should have the same privilege. Referring to statements made by a previous speaker, Harrell recalled that last year "some questions were raised around the process" of BOOM and the district committees that resulted in a request for a ruling of law. He concluded that there should be "appropriate scrutiny of the two classes coming through" and, therefore, he was speaking against the motion.

Rev. Ianther Mills, Asbury UMC in Washington, spoke for the motion because all of the candidates had been "individually examined by the Board of Ordained Ministry and found to have met the requirements of the Book of Discipline, delineated in the paragraphs 324 for Provisional, 334 for Deacons, 335 for Elders, and recommended by this executive session by three quarter majority vote of the board." She said that the motion "simply affirms the work of the board by specifying that we receive the candidate recommendations as a whole," and stated that any other action would be a "redundant process."

Rev. Daniel Montague, Fork and Wall UMCs, rose to speak against the motion. He stated that the maker of the motion pointed out that a lot of hours and process had gone into developing the candidates and he felt that "it's important enough for us to deal with them individually" and not as a block.

Katie Weston, a lay member of BOOM and a member of Emmanuel UMC in Laurel, spoke for the motion. Weston suggested that "to not be able to vote for one of the candidates in the class would suggest that one has knowledge of one of the candidates" outside of the process. This would be tantamount to making a decision based upon "rumor and bias." She urged a commitment to an open process.

Rev. Robert Barnes, Mount Oak Fellowship, spoke against the motion. While the work of BOOM should be respected, Barnes said it is the "governing voting body that decides." The system is that the body votes and he urged the body to be serious about that responsibility.

Rev. Rudy Bropleh, Asbury UMC in Shepherdstown, raised a point of order citing the Book of Discipline and reading ¶3001 of the Rules of the Session. He said that a "couple of candidates do not meet the test" and he wanted to make a motion to "redact the report to bring it in compliance with our rules" and with the Book of Discipline.

Bishop Easterling said that Bropleh had asked for a point of order and was trying to make a motion. Bropleh said that the point of order is that the report as presented does not comply with paragraphs 305.2, 306, 310 and Judicial Council decisions 1343 and 1344. Bishop Easterling ruled the point of order out of order.

Rev. Loretta Johnson, Jones Memorial UMC, raised a question regarding approving the motion in light of "what was just passed recently by the special General Conference under the Traditional Plan."

"My question," she said, "is in view and in light of the Traditional Plan that was approved by the special General Conference in February, and also by the Judicial Council upholding the majority of the tenants of that plan, how would approving these candidates go against the Traditional Plan that was approved at the special General Conference?"

Bishop Easterling explained that "the Traditional Plan as a whole did not pass the special session of General Conference; portions of it did. Some portions of it were upheld by the Judicial Council, and other portions of it were not. The portions that were upheld do not take effect until January 1, 2020." For the current BOOM Report, the body would use the 2016 Book of Discipline "as printed."

The bishop announced that there had been a call for the question. The maker of the motion asked to have the final word and again reiterated the work of BOOM and that her motion affirmed the board's work, and "the broader commitment of this annual conference to support the candidates as they serve God and build up the Kingdom of God in the world."

The bishop called it an important vote and asked Nupp to offer a prayer following a moment of silence, after which the vote would be taken. Rev. Paul Papp, of Frames Memorial UMC who is currently on medical disability leave, asked how much of the current Discipline of the denomination should be followed this year. Bishop Easterling stated that his question was out of order. The motion passed 66.76 percent for and 33.24 percent against.

Hunt returned to the report, Question 28, and invited Rev. Scott Shumaker, Registrar for Provisional Members, to come forward. He presented the two provisional candidates, Deborah Burgio and T.C. Morrow. He then introduced the candidates for provisional Elder: Ian Collier, Gerald Elston, Ashley Hoover, Narae Kim, Raphael Koikoi, Dong Eun (Vivian) Lee, Jean Lee, Isaiah Redd, and Jeffrey Zalatoris.

Rev. Mark Gorman, Center UMC, asked if the "information that the board provided on candidates last year who are returning this year in any way altered or changed"? He wanted to know if the information given at last year's Executive Session was still on the table regarding those candidates. Hunt replied, "as I stated in our report, we have handled and addressed all information we have received."

Bishop Easterling again reminded those present of the importance of the vote and asked Rev. Antoine Love to offer prayer. The provisional candidates were approved, and Shumaker offered a prayer for them when they returned to the session and were invited to sit with the body. Bishop Easterling explained that in the next day's plenary, they would be allowed to vote on some matters.

As Hunt invited attention back to the report, Bishop Easterling reminded everyone that the clergy session is a closed session and that no one should be posting on social media. Question 29.a., persons continuing as Provisional Members, were approved. Questions 29.b. and c. had no one listed. Question 29.d. Provisional Member transferred from other conferences was approved. Hunt noted that Steven Cho was being transferred this year.

Hunt proposed that Question 30, Ronald Fleming-Triplett, ordained clergy received from other Christian denominations, be handled with full members because the person is transferring his orders. The bishop concurred. He was removed from Question 31.a.

Hunt invited Rev. Al Hammer, the Full Member Registrar, to come forward. He introduced those deemed to qualify for full membership. In Question 32. a., Martina March Efodzi was the sole Deacon. In Question 32.b, Full member Elders were Patricia Lynn Abell, Lillian Lynn Boyd, Andre Robert Briscoe, Jr, Alexis Faith Brown, Henry Michael Cantley, Lemuel Dominguez, Kyle Durbin, Jessica Statesman Hayden, Joseph Heath-Mason, Brenda Mcilwain, Carissa Gabrielle Moore Surber, and recognition of orders for Ronald Fleming Triplett.

The bishop once again reminded everyone of that this was a "sacred and important part of the work" of the session as persons were invited into full membership. She asked Rev. Stacey Cole Wilson to pray before the vote. A question was raised asking if it was possible to reduce voting time to 15 seconds. The voting time was not changed. All were approved by two-thirds vote and welcomed to the session. The bishop then asked the historic questions to the group as a class. At the conclusion, Bishop Easterling presented the class to the session as candidates for the ordination service on Friday.

Rev. Amy McCulloh, BOOM Vice Chair, continued the report. Question 41 was informational and McCulloh asked for a moment of privilege to thank Hammer, who is transferring to Western Pennsylvania Conference, but who has served as registrar and in many other capacities in the conference.

Question 42, who are discontinued as provisional members, contained two names. McCulloh explained that the names will appear in other places in the report. It carried. Question 43.a. and b. were skipped. A correction was made to 43.c., who has been placed on administrative location, because Jacob Young should be moved to 43.c.3. The change was noted.

Questions 44 to 47 had no one listed. Question 48 reported the names of those who have died in the last few months and who will be remembered during the Service of Remembrance. Bishop Easterling asked McCulloh to offer a prayer for the deceased.

Question 49 was informational. Question 50, are there provisional, ordained, or associate members on leave of absence. Questions 50.a.1. and 3. were handled together and were approved. Question 52, those granted medical leave, was approved. Question 53 are there Deacons and Elders in full connection retiring this year and Question 54 are associate members also retiring. Those retiring were invited to stand as their names were said.

Martha J. Maxham was a retiring Deacon. The Elders retiring included: Kay Albury, Kimberly A. Brown-Whale, Richard E. Brown-Whale, Steven T. Cochran, Esther Holimon, Robert H. Hunter, III, Gay W. Hutchinson, Pamela J. Marsh, Denise M. Yepsen Millett, Jeffrey A. Paulson, Bruce C. Thompson, Mark R. Waddell, Mamie Williams, and Jane E. Wood. The Associate member retiring was George E. Hackey, Jr. Both questions passed. Question 56.a. was informational and listed retiring local pastors. McCulloh offered prayers for those retiring.

Questions 58 through 71 were either informational or had no names listed. Associate members, Elders (and Provisionals) and Deacons in full connection listed in Question 72.a. were approved for less than full-time service. Question 76 lists Provisional and Full Elders who are appointed to Extension Ministries. Question 76.c. those appointed to other valid ministries required a vote.

Rev. Hunt said,"I present the report as amended and move its adoption." The Board of Ordained Ministry report was approved.

Rev. Bill Brown, Wesley Freedom UMC, stated that his name should be listed in Question 76 because he is moving into Extension Ministry July 1, 2019. The correction was noted. Question 76.c. was voted upon and passed.

Rev. Chip Aldridge, of Wesley Seminary who holds his charge conference membership with Dumbarton UMC, requested a moment of personal privilege. He recounted attending the wedding of Joey and Matthew Heath Mason and the blessing of TC Morrow and Logan Alley after their legal marriage in the District of Columbia. He did not perform the weddings but stated that he and many others in the room had "pledged that we have readiness for doing weddings for same gender couples." He continued that he had blessed the relationship of same gender couples since the 1980's and "after appropriate consideration and preparation," had "celebrated the marriage of a number of couples," refusing to "abide by the pastoral limitations imposed on marriage created by the UMC discipline." He pledged to continue to resist "this prejudiced law which identifies one group for discrimination by our church."

Aldridge said that in the last 35 years, there was one marriage he had not celebrated — his own. He and his partner met in 1983 and have lived together since 1986. He mentioned there was not option to marry, their home was blessed by their pastor and while marriage equality became the law of the United States, it was not so in the UMC. He also spoke of the disappointment experienced with the 2019 Special General Conference results and the UMC telling many that "they or their loved ones are considered less than human." Acknowledging that the conversation continues knowing there are lesbians, gay, bisexual, transgender and others in the room, he concluded his remarks saying, "One of our core values is to do no harm" and that a good step was being made in that direction. He also noted that the date and place had not been set, but that he and his partner will be married.

Bishop Easterling thanked him from sharing from his heart and out of his pain. McCulloh concluded the report; the remaining questions were informational. Hunt moved that report be approved by the body and it was approved. The bishop thanked Hunt and the Board of Ordained Ministry for their "phenomenal work."

Laity Session
Marriott Waterfront, Baltimore
Wednesday, May 29, 2019

There are no official minutes of the Laity Session. Marcia McFee, of Worship Design Studio, was the guest speaker.

Opening Worship
Wednesday, May 29, 2019

As worshippers entered the dimly lit ballroom, images were projected onto the ceiling depicting a moving, changing cosmos of planets, stars, shooting stars, streaming lights and other bodies. Professor and consultant, Marcia McFee, designed this opening and served as worship leader during the entire Annual Conference Session.

McFee invited "friends to take a deep breath" as she audibly inhaled and exhaled. And then took another deep breath saying, "As close as breath, God is with us." Soft music played as she continued to have the assembled join her in taking deep breaths. "Oh, the wonder of it all," she said, as she called the people of the Baltimore-Washington Conference to worship. The song instrumental, "So Will I (100 Billion X)" played. She acknowledged that many were present "with a mixed bag of emotions — joyful, sorrowful, ambivalent, hopeful," she said. "Here we are."

In the darkened ballroom, with the galaxies illuminating the ceiling, McFee marveled at the conference's theme, "We are One," in a church that lately feels divided. She reminded the congregation that all things are created by God with the essence of love at their center.

"Art, religion, science, all agree we are one. We are all made of the stuff of the universe… all made of the same matter. We believe that God is the maker, the potter, the artisan, the architect, the Holy One and Creator of All. This is the reality, whether we perceive it or not," McFee said.

A vocal ensemble sang the verses of "So Will I," about the creation of the galaxies, the planets, the stars and seeing the heart of God in everything God made and singing God's praises as McFee spoke and prayed. At the song's end, McFee said, "We have no choice but to be united even if we don't look or act united. What affects me affects you. What affects you affects me."

The vocal ensemble sang "Your Love Divine." At the song's end, McFee asked everyone to stand and turn and face the center of the room where there was an elevated Communion Table and illuminated blue baptismal bowl — symbols of our faith in Jesus Christ and the center of the assembled body.

Four people standing around the table on the elevated platform lead the litany, "Call of the Road." The response was the song, "We are on the Road to Love." This was followed by the opening song of praise, "How Great Thou Art."

Bishop LaTrelle Easterling began speaking about "the road to love." She said we are all "saints and sinners" who have the "capacity to love without bounds." She continued, "At times we are ruled by fear… that fear often resides within our own perceptions of ourselves. Hatred of the other is rooted in the inability to accept the love of God for us."

A soloist sang the anthem, "You Say." As the music continued to play softly, Bishop Easterling asked the congregation to believe that "each of us is made in image of God," and instructed us to "believe God" when we hear we are "loved." All we need to do to get back to the love is to know that "God assures us that we also can accept forgiveness and come back to love." She proclaimed that, "It is always and already right. Here. Now." And that in the name of Jesus Christ, we are forgiven.

The congregation was invited to join in singing the last verse of "You Say." The Scripture, Ephesians 4:4-6, was read in unison.

Bishop Easterling came forward to begin her sermon fervently singing "Come Ye Disconsolate." She spoke of the times in life when there is an experience of "excruciating, heart-piercing pain" that will not lose its grip and appears "surreal."

She spoke of pain some United Methodists felt during the 2019 Special Session of the General Conference. Such moments "disturb our metaphorical and literal equilibrium and the foundation under our feet feels like it will just give way." The oft-quoted statement "God will never give us more than we can bear," was described by the bishop as "one of the most theologically bankrupt and incorrect statements ever offered in Christendom." She spoke of the times in life that will "almost crush us" and instructed those who did not know what she was talking about "to just keep on living."

The Good News is that "our spiritual ancestors understood that we did not have to bear this pain alone. They understood that God is an ever-present help in time of trouble." In times of trouble and pain, "Jesus Christ becomes our strength." She urged, "Beloved don't try to shoulder it all by yourself. Christ's rod and Christ's staff will comfort us."

She told of Dr. Edith Eva Eger, a Holocaust survivor who, at the age of 16, was taken along with most of her family to Auschwitz. After her parents were killed in a gas chamber, Edith, a trained dancer, was forced to dance for Dr. Josef Mengele. In 1945 after enduring "unspeakable suffering and brutality that almost killed her," Eger was rescued from beneath a pile of corpses by liberating American troops. Eger's "life's work became how to escape the clutches of death every day and how to find joy, how to choose life, how to choose hope, how to choose love."

"Love is not an emotion. Love is an act of the will," the bishop stressed.

Returning to the story of Eger, Bishop Easterling said the question for Eger was "could she survive life" after liberation. Eger, the bishop continued, "had to choose to live. She had to choose love." Bishop Easterling explained that "we can't choose to banish the dark, but we can choose to kindle the light." In 1966 Eger read the words of another survivor, Viktor Frankl, "who taught her that everything can be taken from you but one thing… to choose one's attitude in any given set of circumstances." Eger learned from Frankel that "each moment is a choice" no matter what the experience. "We have a choice."

The bishop said the question becomes, "What will we do with our pain?" After offering several options, she said, "or will we offer it to Jesus who can take this tangible agony and turn it into a cruciform offering of salvific transformation where we allow it to break us open so that our tears might be poured into alabaster jars to become anointing and healing and comfort and love for those we meet along the way."

She explained that as we heal, we can "choose to be drawn closer to one another or we can choose to become more distant from one another. As we heal, we can allow this experience to help us understand one another's pain… or wallow in our own."

Bishop Easterling acknowledged the pain of the LGBTQIA brothers and sisters quickened by the Special Session of General Conference. While we all experience pain, Dr. Eger has taught those whom come to her for help and healing that "there is no hierarchy of suffering."

As believers, we are bound together because we are "baptized into Jesus the Christ." The bishop decried the divisions that abound today and called for a time of standing together, saying, "I believe that we wrestle not against flesh and blood, but against the rulers and principalities." She called upon all to rebuke it in the name of Jesus. She spoke about the erosion of rights afforded LBGTQIA persons, the attacks on black men and women in their homes and schools and communities. She urged those assembled to "walk down this road together." Bishop Easterling lamented the young people turning to opioids to "self-medicate" in the face of despair, isolation and loneliness.

"We are living in a time when oppression and supremacy and patriarchy as being espoused as Christian values coupled with nationalism and touted as a new awakening," she exclaimed. "Wake up, beloved." She said this is time of hate crimes on the rise and people joining organization "to hate other people because of the color of their skin, or their faith, or their native tongue." When hate groups came into the Baltimore-Washington Conference, the United to Love Rally was held to "show them love is greater than hate and loves casts out all fear. Love stands together and is united. Love welcomes everybody."

As a part of the worship, Janay Parker, a member of the West River program staff, shared with the congregation how the BWC's West River Camp became a place of refuge and hope for her when she struggled with a mother who was addicted to drugs. Her father, a state trooper, passed away which left the family without a source of income. Her mother's addiction led to many different treatment facilities and homelessness. At one facility things changed, her mother seems to get better and Janay danced, played lacrosse and was accepted into a School for the Arts. A dance major, she graduated with a 3.5 average and was accepted in to the University of Maryland, Eastern Shore, majoring in criminal justice. In November 2016, her mother died from a drug overdose.

West River became Janay's "home away from home." Her first camp experience was at Camp Hope, a camp for children whose parents are dealing with addiction or who are incarcerated. She was introduced to a new world and kept coming back.

In the summer of 2018, she was suffering from depression and built up anger. An email from Chris Schlieckert (West River director) asked if she wanted to apply and interview for West River. She said the first summer on the program staff was just what she needed. "God placed me with such amazing humans in my life during such a dark moment," she said. "To me it is where I found myself again." She said it was crucial to make sure others had the opportunity to experience the "life changing moments that I have had the pleasure of experiencing at West River." She asked those present to "dig deep and help us continue this kingdom building ministry." The offering raised $9, 858 for camperships.

Marcia McFee told the congregation that they were going to take a journey on the road to love. Together, the worship took people on a symbolic and physical journey on the Road to Love, past three basins of water (a basin of tears, the baptismal basin, the servant's basin) and Communion — from wonder to praise to lament to strength to joy.

Bible Study
Thursday, May 30, 2019 | 8:30 a.m.

Musicians provided gathering music, including a rousing rendition of "I Saw the Light" with guitar accompanists, and then "How Great Is Our God" and "How Great Thou Art."

Rev. Kyle Durbin gave the opening prayer. He welcomed and introduced the Rev. Dr. Marvin McMickle, who he described as one of the most respected preachers in the nation. McMickle served as pastor of Antioch Baptist Church in Cleveland, Ohio, for nearly 25 years before becoming president of Colgate Rochester Crozer Divinity School in Rochester, NY. He is also a professor and a prolific author of 17 books, including "Be My Witness: The Great

Commission for Preachers," and other resources on preaching, ministry and African-American History.

During the Bible study, McMickle spoke from Luke 16: 19-22. He acknowledged the presence of the bishop and thanked her for the invitation to come and speak with the Baltimore-Washington Conference. He shared that United Methodist students are a significant part of their student body and that the school is certified by the University Senate to offer instruction to United Methodist students. He brought greetings from Crozer's resident Methodist historian and theologian, Dr. John Tyson, whose books include major scholarly work on both John and Charles Wesley.

McMickle expertly exegeted the phrases in the Scripture, explaining that the garments of the man dressed in purple and fine linen were dyed with the most expensive dye worn by royalty and the wealthy. He is rich. And he ate sumptuously everyday, eating the finest food, everyday. Lazarus, the beggar covered in sores, was at the rich man's gate. The rich man could not come and go without seeing him and did not help him. McMickle said to think "gated community, guard booth, secured property."

McMickle said he wanted the listeners to see the contrast and the coexistence. One man was rich and "everything he did was exorbitant — what he wore, what he ate, where he lived." And at his gate, people laid the beggar named Lazarus who could not walk, was crippled, paralyzed, immobile. Lazarus was covered in sores. Dogs licked the open sores on his body. He may have been laid there to beg for alms. Lazarus would have eaten crumbs from the rich man's table. The crumbs were not offered.

They both die. Lazarus wakes up in the bosom of Abraham in heaven. The rich man wakes up in hell. McMickle said the hermeneutical question is, "Why does the rich man go to hell?" It was not because he was rich; Abraham was rich. It was because he did not pay attention to the poor man just outside his gate. His eyes and his heart were not open to the poor man.

"Here's my caution for the Baltimore-Washington Conference," he warned. "Do not let your church, because either of your ministry, vision, or your preaching — don't let your whole church wake up in hell."

The church's response may be, "we are good Methodists" who know the Wesley hymns and theology, always attend service, and are on the choir or other committees. McMickle explained that the problem with those rituals is that "we make them a substitute for righteousness." All the rituals from praying, to what we wear, to the order of the service, the culture might be considered empty. "The prophets say God does not care if all you are offering to God is ritual, if you are not paying attention to... those just outside the door of your church, you may wake up in hell."

He showed a slide and asked the audience to read a quote from Peruvian liberation theologian, Gustavo Gutteriez, to see whether or not there is any excuse for us not to notice Lazarus.

"All theological inquiry is contextual. Our context today is characterized by a glaring disparity between the rich and the poor. No serious Christian can quietly ignore this situation. It is no longer possible for someone to say 'Well, I did not know' about the suffering of the poor. Poverty has a visibility today that it did not have in the past. The faces of the poor must now be confronted."

McMickle said that not only do we know about and see poverty today, we also know people who are struggling.

"Having seen economic injustice, having seen wealth disparity, we have made a conscious decision to go to church," he said. "On the way to church, we drive through places of poverty, driving expensive cars and dressed in 'purple and fine linen,' and then we go to brunch for $50 plus a tip. And when the mission plate comes, we "write the Lord a $10 check" as our sacrificial gift to the poor. You didn't even give the poor the crumbs that fell from your table."

He then shared a quote from Martin Luther King Jr.'s "I Have a Dream" speech, a part, he said, nobody wants to quote: "African Americans live on islands of poverty in a sea of great prosperity." McMickle "flipped" that quote and changed it to: "Many churches and their congregants are an island of prosperity surrounded by a great sea of poverty." Many congregants have moved out of the neighborhood and some churches have moved so far away, people couldn't get Lazarus to the front gate.

He again quoted Gutierrez: "All Christians must take the Gospel message of justice and equality seriously. Christians cannot forgo their responsibility to say a prophetic word about unjust economic conditions. Poverty poses a major challenge to every Christian conscience." McMickle asked, "Does it? Does it pose a problem for your conscience?" Or, he asked, "Are we a rich man dressed in purple and fine linen, who ate sumptuously every day; and, at our gate, they laid a beggar named Lazarus?"

McMickle, a graduate of Union Seminary and Columbus University with his first Doctorate earned from Princeton Seminary, told the story of how difficult it could be to escape poverty without help and with the "poverty of low expectations." He was born in poverty and when he was 10-years-old, his father left the family. An older brother enlisted and went to Vietnam because it felt safer there. As a high school senior, his guidance counselor told him that he didn't have what it took to "make it in college." But his mother told him, "the guidance counselor gets no vote." His mother, God and he voted yes — yes to college and yes to the future.

McMickle said his point was that "people who are born in poverty, people who are born with deprivation, people who are born into circumstances from which it may appear there is no way out, can, with someone's intervention, with someone whispering a word of encouragement to them, and not giving up on them because of the environment in which they were born, they might grow up one day to give a talk in front of the Baltimore-Washington Conference of The United Methodist Church.

"Luke 16 is a challenge to you to go home to your home church and look outside your window and see who or what is there."

He urged those present to not blame people for what they do to survive. "Blame the conditions in the richest county in the history of the world that allow this. The United States ranks second out of 35 developed countries on a scale of what economist call 'relative child poverty,' with 23.1 percent of children living in poverty. Only Romania ranks higher." Economist Sheldon Danzinger explains it this way, he said, "Among rich countries, the U.S. is exceptional. We are exceptional in our tolerance of poverty."

McMickle said that he lives in Rochester, NY, where 50 percent of children live in poverty. He spoke of the difficulty faced by these children in trying to succeed in school. He gave examples of what poverty looks like in the United States. It's an individual living on $12,000 a year, or $1,000 a month, or $33 a day; or, a family of four living in "regular poverty" living on $23,450 a year. In extreme poverty, 1.65 million Americans live on $12,000 a year or $1.97 a day.

As he reached the end of his Bible study, McMickle focused on one of the "major factors in our economic system… the continuing income wealth gap between the rich and the poor." He cited how "the CEO's of Starbucks, or CVS, or McDonalds earn in one hour what their workers earn in six months: $13 million vs. $40,000 per year." The extreme case was a Wal-Mart employee earning $19,177 per year in 2017, while the CEO earned $22.2 million.

He said that poverty is the church's challenge. As the church grapples with issues of human sexuality, the issue of poverty will still be with us. He repeated Luke 16: 19-22 and concluded: "They both died. Poor man goes to heaven; the rich man goes to hell. Please do not let you or your church wake up in hell."

Bishop Easterling thanked him for his presentation.

First Plenary Session
Thursday, May 30, 2019 | 9:30 a.m.

Bishop Easterling opened the first Plenary Session by introducing herself: "I am Bishop LaTrelle Miller Easterling. My pronouns are she, her and hers." She called the 235th session of the Baltimore-Washington Conference to order and introduced those on the dais — Cynthia Taylor, Conference Secretary; Rev. Ken Humbert, Parliamentarian; Delores Martin, conference Lay Leader; Kevin Silberzahn, the Conference Secretary in-training who has been nominated to be the new Conference Secretary; Rev. Antoine Love, Assistant to the Bishop; Conference Chancellor, Thomas Starnes; and Rev. Mark Gorman, chair of the Rules Committee.

She thanked Zina Johnson, Minister of Music at First UMC Hyattsville, for gracing the assemblage with her music ministry at the Annual Conference Session.

The conference secretary, Cynthia Taylor, made the Organizational Motion and it was approved. Taylor announced that a curtained-off area had been set up in the back-right corner of the ballroom to accommodate nursing mothers. The special section was part of the bar and included electricity for a pumping machine, a changing table, and a monitor to watch the proceedings. Bishop Easterling stated that those using the special area would be allowed to vote because the area was within the bar of the conference.

For those times during holy conferencing when people are moved by something that is said or just need someone to be a "holy presence," prayer partners are available, the bishop explained.

Next, Rules Committee Chair, Rev. Mark Gorman provided a review of the Rules of the Session using the General Rules as a framework. The bishop called for a vote on the Rules of the Session. They were adopted.

The 2019 General Conference Special Session in February, which upheld and strengthened the denomination's stance on homosexuality, "caused the foundation under our United Methodist churches to shake in a way it has not in 150 years," said Bishop Easterling, as she shared with the Annual Conference the reason that this year's session would start differently.

As she traveled and attended meetings and met with groups, individuals and congregations, she heard over and over the request to "not start our session of holy conferencing with business as usual, because things are not usual." After praying about how to begin the session, she was introduced to the Samoan Circle process. She described that as a process in which people "come and sit together in a circle to take up matters that are highly controversial matters where they are unlikely to meet consensus in any short period of time and matters where the body that is convening is too large for everyone to be able to engage in a meaningful way." The people respond to questions and "speak out of their experience from their hearts," not talking to one another and not talking to the audience. They share their truth for it to be heard and received as a gift.

She reminded the gathering that at the Pre-Conference Briefing, they were told about the conference developing a curriculum with a working title, "Who Are We? – An Introspective Analysis of Head and Heart." It will include segments on "Who are we as the People of God?" "Who are we as the People of the Wesleyan Movement?" and "Who are We as the Baltimore-Washington Conference?" It will invite the people of the conference into a time of study, discernment, and listening to one another.

The Samoan Circle Process was the beginning of this, she said. "I beg of you, listen with open minds. Listen with open hearts. Listen with an open spirit." She assured everyone that this was about listening and not about changing minds or positions or trying to convince anyone of anything. She described the participants as "voices from across our conference, voices from across the theological perspective, across races, and gender and proclivity." Take a breath, she said, as she explained each step of the process that included a "talking piece" and the timeframe.

Each of the circle participants was asked to introduce themselves and tell how long they have been United Methodist. They included:
Rev. Rebecca Iannicelli, superintendent of the Washington East District, a part of the United Methodist Church since 1996;
Rev. Jessica Hayden, chair of the Discipleship Council, a United Methodist her entire life;
Rev. Michele Johns, Deacon at Silver Spring UMC, United Methodist heritage since 1834;
Tom Price, United Methodist for over 30 years;
Rev. Joe Daniels, United Methodist 40 of his 59 years confirmed, left and came back;
Delores Martin, Conference Lay Leader, United Methodist since 1990;
Rev. Kevin Baker, Wesleyan Covenant Association, United Methodist since birth, left and came back.

Next, they were asked, "From your perspective, what is the core tenet of our faith? Responses included: "our faith is Jesus is Lord and his Word is true;" "to love as Jesus loved and to love each other without judgment;" "Jesus is our Lord and savior;" "we worship a triune God and the gift of the Son;" "grace and liberation;" "God's universal grace that is available to all people;" and "to spread scriptural holiness over the land."

The Circle Process focuses on a series of questions and answers. They included:
- "What has been your greatest source of pain since the special session of General Conference?" Several got emotional as they spoke about the pain they experienced from the actions of General Conference.
- From your perspective, what is at stake within The United Methodist Church right now? The group did unite about what is at stake for the church. "Everything, absolutely everything," they said.
- Where do you see God at work? And where do you find hope?

Bishop Easterling said that the members of the Samoan Circle made themselves "vulnerable." She asked people not to approach any of them and attempt to engage them in debate but to receive their sharing as a gift. She asked for prayers for one another, for this Conference Session, and expressed the hope that it may inspire those gathered to carry the process back into their churches, congregations and other places. She thanked each of them for being "courageous enough to come and share so beautifully and so openly."

As Rev. Conrad Link came forward to pray, the bishop led the singing of "Alleluia" and the circle participants linked arms and joined in singing. After the prayer, Bishop Easterling asked the assembled to take a few moments to hug a person near them, look them in the eye and say, "God loves you, I love you, and there's nothing you can do about it."

After a brief break, the bishop called the session back to order. She welcomed home "the daughter of this conference," Bishop Cynthia Moore-Koikoi of the Western Pennsylvania Conference. Bishop Moore-Koikoi called the name of Rev. Dr. Helen Fleming, who she said prayed for her election as a bishop and who died earlier this year. She thanked the Baltimore-Washington Conference and praised God "for all that you have poured into my life and continue to pour into my life." She said it was good to be home and that she needed to say that she was home to celebrate the man in her life, her husband, Raphael Koikoi, who was going to be commissioned on Friday. She thanked all "who had a hand in getting him to the place where he will be tomorrow."

Bishop Easterling welcomed to the dais the chair of the Episcopacy Committee, Rev. James Miller, who invited members of the Episcopacy Committee to join him on the stage. He thanked them for being supportive of the bishop and the first family. He works with the residence committee and referenced legislation about a new episcopal residence. He thanked John Strawbridge and the work of the trustees and conference staff for their assistance. He gave thanks for the opportunity to celebrate the ministry of Bishop Easterling and to celebrate the ministry of the Rev. Marion Easterling, Jr., the bishop's husband.

Miller said he recently learned that Rev. Marion Easterling was an avid golfer and helped create the Seeds of Security Golf Tournament. Miller announced that a gift had been given in Rev. Easterling's honor to Seeds of Security. Rev. Easterling thanked the committee and everyone for their prayers, support and good wishes.

The Rev. Gary Henderson of United Methodist Communication was invited to come forward to make a presentation. He said that he came to present an award that recognizes and celebrates excellence in communications ministry. The award was described as "a sort of communications Oscar or Emmy, rooted in the faithful call to share the good news of the Gospel of Jesus Christ." He explained that the Epi Award is short for the Greek work, *epikoinonia*, which is the language of the New Testament and means communication. It was being presented to Melissa Lauber. As a very surprised Lauber came forward, Henderson said that she "embodies with excellence, the spirit of Christian communication." (Editor's note: yes, she does.) He thanked God for the communication ministry of the Baltimore-Washington Conference and all those who work tirelessly to tell the church's story. He then thanked the entire communications team, Lauber, Rev. Erik Alsgaard, Alison Burdett, Myca Jones, and Linda Worthington. "Without communication, there is no community," he said. "On behalf of our General Secretary, Dan Kraus, and the more than one hundred fans that you have in Nashville, Tennessee, I am pleased to present you with the Epikoinonia, the Oscar, the Emmy, for communication ministry."

Bishop Easterling expressed the conference's gratefulness for the shared Communication Ministry of the annual conference. Bishop shared that Lauber is a deeply spiritual woman and it was wonderful to "employ persons who have excellent acumen in the discipline in which they lead. It's even better when they are at the top of their game in that discipline and are rooted and committed disciples of Jesus Christ. And that is who Melissa Lauber is." She thanked Henderson for recognizing her.

As David Schoeller came forward to provide instruction on using the voting devices, Bishop Easterling read a note she was handed during the break from Stephen Ricketts, Linganore

United Methodist Church, asking if the voting devices could be used for all votes so that those in the mother's nursing room may also participate. The bishop agreed.

Schoeller started with thanking Padgett Communications and the team that was going to work with the annual conference. He gave an overview of the company and its record with the BWC, other conferences and several Fortune 500 companies. He checked to ensure everyone had the right unit. Schoeller then led everyone in practicing the different kinds of voting they would be doing.

Bishop Easterling thanked Schoeller and announced that it was time for the lunch. She asked Chris Schlieckert, Director of Retreat and Camping Ministries, to offer a prayer for the noontime meal. She also asked that there be a moment of silence, which had been requested for our fallen soldiers as we had just observed Memorial Day.

Second Plenary Session
Thursday, May 30, 2019 | 2:00 p.m.

Bishop Easterling opened the second plenary session and asked the presenters of resolutions to proceed to the Green Room in order to be prepared to present their resolutions. After reestablishing the bars of the annual conference, the Bishop invited Rev. Julie Wilson to present the first resolution — "Resolution for a Common Table."

Wilson, a Deacon at Calvary UMC in Frederick, said that she, like millions of Americans, suffers from food allergies. The resolution asks that the Baltimore-Washington Conference, require that annual conference, regional and district events offer only a gluten-free common loaf for Communion.

Rev. Cindy Burkett, Old Otterbein UMC, raised a point of order, informing the bishop that the back of the room was very noisy and that it was difficult to hear. Bishop Easterling asked the Marshals to help keep order and asked everyone to be mindful so that all would be able to hear.

Pastor Bill Ball, Pikeside UMC in Martinsburg, offered an amendment that the presiding clergy at communion be given discretion to determine the needs of those participating. Rev. Terry Cofiell, Harmony UMC in Falling Waters, W.Va., spoke against the amendment stating that clergy do not always know which people need gluten-free bread.

Deborah Burgio, Mount Simon UMC, Highland, spoke against the amendment, saying that when she and her daughter attended their church for the first time, the fact they had celiac disease and could take Communion made it their church home. There were no speeches for the amendment. It did not pass.

Rev. Katie Bishop, Greater Brunswick Charge, spoke for the resolution. She has celiac disease and an allergy to dairy and eggs. She described the difficulty she had participating "in the fullness of the service" the previous night because of worrying about getting the right Communion and about cross-contamination.

Steven Art, lay member, had a question on the intent or implication of the wording of the motion. He asked if the resolution passed, would there be gluten-free bread only at the Annual Conference Sessions going forward, to which the bishop responded yes.

Rev. Sherri Wood-Powe, University UMC, College Park, and co-chair of the annual conference worship team, rose to offer an amendment that every station for Communion have both allergen-free bread and a dedicated chalice and regular bread and a dedicated chalice.

Rev. David J. Deans, Oakdale UMC, requested a point of information, asking for clarification regarding when the original resolution would apply. Wilson clarified that it would apply at every Baltimore-Washington Conference, regional, and district event that offers Communion.

Rev. Laurie Gates-Ward, Good Shepherd UMC, Waldorf, spoke against the amendment, citing just a crumb of gluten would put her and others with celiac disease in bed for days. The bishop, seeing no other speakers, called for the vote. The amendment did not pass. Rev. Bruce Jones asked that the voting time be changed to 30 seconds and the bishop and plenary accepted the suggestion.

The maker declined to speak on the resolution and felt those who spoke made the case for the importance of passing this resolution. She reiterated that it did not apply to local churches. The resolution passed.

As the makers of Resolution 2, "Supporting Deliberations for New Expressions of Methodism," came forward, the bishop introduced and welcomed to the dais Kim Carr, Lay Leader of the Annapolis District. John Hine presented the resolution.

Matt Sichel, lay member, Wesley Hampstead UMC, offered an amendment by substitution, which he read.

The amendment, titled "Vision of Ministry with All People Consistent with the Book of Discipline," was a response to the 2019 General Conference. That special session "discerned, through Holy Conferencing, a way forward, reaffirming our 47-year stated position with regard to same-sex practice, which considers 'the practice of homosexuality incompatible with Christian teaching,' while affirming 'that all persons are individuals of sacred worth, created in the image of God.'"

The amendment resolved that "the Baltimore-Washington Conference of The United Methodist Church calls on its General Superintendent, Cabinet, Conference Leadership and other responsible parties to develop ministries with the LGBTQ community consistent with the Discipline, that affirm the sacred worth, gifts and graces of that community, while also conforming to the standards of sexual holiness delineated in the Discipline."

It further proposed the following, that "the Baltimore-Washington Conference seeks to be:
- A church which is welcoming of all, while also maintaining for all the high standards of accountable discipleship in every aspect of life that was characteristic of early Methodism;
- A renewed commitment to the high standards of faithful discipleship, and with this, a review of every aspect of our ethics, sexual and otherwise, including the ways in which sinful heterosexual behaviors and practices around sexuality, marriage, and family have been winked at while an undue and hypocritical onus has been inflicted on our LGBTQ+ sisters and brothers;
- A zeal refreshed for ministry with and for the poor; with prisoners and the addicted; in support of healthy lives, families, neighborhoods, and communities; in confronting racism, sexism, and all other dehumanizing and life-destroying expressions of transpersonal evil;
- Prayer for a fresh outpouring of the Holy Spirit upon every congregation and each believer; and with this a recalling to self-examination and true repentance, to renewed emphasis on prayer and spiritual disciplines, and fresh manna in sacramental life, praise

and liturgy, and effective evangelism and church body-life;

- An understanding of "love" which goes beyond subjective feelings and external, sensory experiences, and focuses instead on the great objective work of Jesus Christ on the cross, His atoning work for our salvation, and the reclaiming and renewal of the created order;
- A vision for reaching our entire conference region for Jesus Christ and his saving Gospel, and for partnering with United Methodists and other Christians nationally and globally, invoking Wesley's own vision that 'The world is our parish.'"

The amendment was seconded.

Rev. Mark Gorman, Rules Chair and pastor of Center UMC, rose with a point of order regarding parliamentary procedure. Rule 22 requires the original matter, Resolution 2, be completed and then the body can return to Sichel's substitute. The bishop agreed. She reminded the plenary to keep its tone of voice and volume appropriate.

Rev. Bryant Oskvig, Extension Ministry, Georgetown University, asked questions to clarify how Rule 22 would work. Rev. Debbie Scott, Lovely Lane UMC, asked if the maker of the "original motion" was aware the substitution was coming. The maker responded that he knew something was coming but that did not change anything.

Daniel Colbert, lay member, Silver Spring UMC, opposed the resolution because he disagreed "with its premise that our differences are irreconcilable" and that "our disagreement make it impossible to be in connection." He said he loved all aspects of the diversity in the room. He made a choice to be with people who don't "always see things the way" he does. He said that "we can learn from each other and we can be better followers of Jesus" as a result. He opposed the resolution because he rejects "the idea that our differences in thought mean that we cannot be united in love" and that we "cannot surround each other with a community of love and forgiveness." He said unity is not thinking alike, it is "walking this road together" and he wants to walk this road with "all of you."

Rev. Kevin Baker, Oakdale Emory UMC, spoke in favor of the resolution. He stated his belief that "God is trying to birth some new things." He said the church is doing harm and that God is "bigger than one institution" and can do anything. He supports a "very loving and "gracious way" in the midst of differences to love and bless one another and "continue to serve the world and share the love of Christ."

Rev. Ernest Maynard Moore, retired, Greater Washington District, asked if the title of the resolution is part of the resolution. Bishop Easterling replied that the resolutions speak for themselves and that the "Be it resolved" section is the part that is binding for the body if they support the resolution. Moore said the title was misleading and that there were other defects in the resolution; for example, it says that there "are two factions within The United Methodist Church" when in fact there are many more. He mentioned a number of areas that were missing and/or debatable. Bishop Easterling counted his comments as a speech against. The maker of the resolution said that he believed that the speaker was using an earlier version of the resolution that did not reflect several changes that had been made.

Rev. Robert Barnes, Mount Oak UMC, rose to speak for the motion. He noted that the Commission on the Way Forward said, "We do have irreconcilable differences." While he did not want to see division, Barnes believes in the long term it needed to be considered. He also thinks that for young people, division would be the "healthiest thing for all concerned. And it might be the best thing of our relationship."

Rev. Andrew Cooney, Bethany UMC, Ellicott City, asked, "are we officially sanctioning a body that represents the Speaker of the motion" or "is [this] guidance for our delegates" or are "we creating a group of people who will speak for us…?" Hines said the resolution was not intended as formal guidance for the delegates. He said that the resolution could be a "referendum of the body" of whether it is "for continued fighting" or "for a negotiated settlement."

Rev. Debbie Scott, Lovely Lane, UMC rose to offer an amendment to the main motion. After the word "Methodism" on line 24 put a period and strike the rest of the resolution.

Bishop Easterling requested speeches for and against the amendment.

George Prochaska, Cowenton UMC, White Marsh, spoke against the amendment. He felt the resolution was moot because it did not resolve the issues of either those for inclusion or those for exclusion.

Rev. Kevin Bacon, Oakdale UMC, spoke for the amendment. He thought the amendment spoke to the spirit of the resolution because "we are at a place where it may be better to love each other in new expressions."

There was a call to move the question. The bishop was told that voting members were sitting outside the bar and asked if it was because there were not enough seats within the bar. She asked for a vote on calling the question by voice. The vote passed. Bishop Easterling then asked everyone to move in so that people outside the bar would not have to crawl, clamber, sneak or wriggle over people to get a seat.

Tim Rousset, National UMC, Washington, raised a point of order regarding the voting devices. He asked if it would make sense to enlarge the voting area to the whole room. Bishop said she appreciated his statement and wanted to see if there was enough room within the bar for everyone. She also informed everyone that when doing a voice vote, it should include voting by hand for the hearing impaired. The amendment to delete the text after the word "Methodism" passed. The bishop returned to the resolution.

Rev. Laura Blauvelt, Potomac UMC, rose to call the question on all that was before the plenary. The motion was seconded. The bishop said the motion was non-debatable. Rules Chair, Rev. Mark Gorman, asked what question was being called. He believed the only thing that could be voted on was the amendment and any other amendments that might be offered. After that, the substitute needed to be addressed before voting on the main motion. Blauvelt explained that she was calling the question on all that was before the body, meaning the amendment, Matt Sichel's substitution, and vote the main question and "cut off debate." Gorman explained that the rules of the session provide that time be allowed to perfect Matt's motion and allow for debate before the question can be called on that part unless someone had another amendment to the main motion.

Bishop Easterling agreed that debate could be closed on the main motion but could not bypass the amendment by substitution. Rev. Paul Johnson, Hughes Memorial UMC, Washington, moved to table the main motion. Rev. Katie Bishop asked whether the substitution would be tabled along with the main motion. The bishop responded that both would be tabled. The vote passed to table the motion.

While the bishop had Padgett check on the voting, she explained that the next resolution was regarding purchase of a new Episcopal residence. She asked Bishop Moore Koikoi to preside while the resolution was being debated out of her integrity and desire for open debate and consideration of the motion without concern.

Padgett suggested that the body return to one minute for regular votes and to consider two minutes when time comes to begin voting on delegates. Bishop Easterling invited Bishop Cynthia Koikoi to come to the dais to preside and asked that she be welcomed.

Bishop Cynthia asked for a moment of personal privilege. She spoke of being baptized into the Washington Conference a few decades ago and that "only God knew that I would be sitting here today presiding over the Baltimore-Washington Conference. Rev. Maurice S. W. Moore [her father] is beaming down from heaven today."

John Strawbridge, lay leader at Lovely Lane UMC and chair of the conference Trustees, presented the "Resolution to Purchase a New Episcopal Residence." Strawbridge spoke about the problem with "black mold intrusion in the Episcopal residence." The Episcopal family had to be moved out of the residence while remediation of the mold took place. Funds were expended for the mold remediation process that involved cleaning the residence and removing walls and flooring. The Trustees took this opportunity to look at the property and in consultation with the Committee on the Episcopacy, the Episcopal residence committee, and the Committee on Finance and Administration, the decision was reached to "get the house in good order" and put the house, purchased in 1986, on the market for sale. A new Episcopal residence that meets "current standards for an Episcopal residence," including ground floor entry, bathrooms and bedrooms, would be purchased. This would be "good stewardship" for our [current] Episcopal family and any future family that would live in the residence. Several other problems in the current residence drove the decision that it was best not to continue to put more money into the residence to update it but "to make the property in legally and morally good condition." The residence would then be sold, and a new Episcopal residence purchased.

Bishop Moore Koikoi opened the floor for comments. Rev. Mary Kay Totty, Dumbarton UMC, Washington, preferred pronouns she, her, hers, spoke for the resolution. She said she had heard "murmurs" that given the state of The United Methodist Church, why would we be making such a big purchase? She related the purchase of the new Episcopal residence to Jeremiah 32, in which, in the midst of Jeremiah's own dire prophecy of the country's impending destruction, a jailed Jeremiah still buys property from his relative and has the deed recorded and sealed and "put away as a sign of hope as a sign of commitment that yes there will be God's faithful people left in Jerusalem in years to come." Like us today, even in bad times, there will be people doing ministry and living out their faith, Totty concluded. "Whatever happens, buying a new Episcopal residence is a sign of hope that there will still be a Methodist presence in Baltimore and Washington in the future ahead."

Heidi Agostini, who identified herself as "lay member from Middletown United Methodist Church," rose to ask a question. The Bishop recognized Sheri Koob, lay member, Middletown UMC, who raised a point of order. She said that Middletown has three lay members and Agostini, a reserve, should not have voice, per rule 3009.7. Koob explained that the alternate is not allowed in the bar of the conference when all the regular lay members of their congregation are seated. Bishop sustained the point of order.

Stan Fredericks, Galesville UMC, asked "what the new residence might cost" and the net cost between the sale of the old residence and the purchase of the new. Strawbridge replied that because they could not put the existing residence on the market, they could not get an idea of the cost of a residence in a "comparable" location to the Conference Center and comparable in size. It is possible the new residence may cost more.

Rev. Chris Bishop, FaithPoint UMC, rose to ask a question. He said he understood that mold had been on ongoing issue for the conference and pointed out that the Manidokan Camping Director and her family has been out of their house for months in an AirBnB. He said there seems to be a trend of not caring for conference properties and asked what the plans are going forward.

Strawbridge said that they were trying to care for conference properties, and they are addressing the camp director's house at Manidokan. Their aim is "good stewardship" of those properties and to make the best decision they can regarding the properties.

Jim Hannah, Darlington UMC, raised concerns about the mold issue and selling the house for the safety of the Episcopal family. In selling the property, morally, what does that mean as far as the conference's responsibility to whoever might purchase the property and live there?

Strawbridge responded that at both the Connectional Table and the committee working on this have discussed this issue. The residence has been tested by environmental agencies and certified as safe. Moral and legal obligations have been met to make the house saleable. "Under no circumstance" would the conference wish to "unknowingly pass a health risk on to another family."

Rev. Jen Karsner, Asbury UMC in Arnold, asked about a cap on the cost of the new residency. She asked what the estimate of the cost to buy a new residence would be. Strawbridge replied that he could not answer that question at the moment. They cannot proceed until they have the motion and, thus, have not been able to start looking at the market. He said that, as Trustees, their duty is to be the best financial stewards they possibly can and that the resolution states that the Council on Finance and Administration has responsibility for approving the funding plan.

Rev. Stephen Ricketts, Linganore UMC, asked if the motion failed, would the bishop be returning to the current Episcopal residence and with the mold gone, does it meet modern accessibility standards (ADA) and issues that the next bishop may need resolved?

"It does not meet the current guidelines for Episcopal residences now," Strawbridge replied.

Katie Davis, Chevy Chase UMC, asked about the comparable size and area for the next episcopal residence. Strawbridge responded that he did not have the square footage or number of bathrooms but said they were looking at a 10- to 15-mile radius of the Conference Center and sizable enough to fit a family with children.

Rev. Alisa Lasater Wailoo, Capitol Hill UMC, shared that she lived in a home with mold and was diagnosed with both memory and processing issues. She healed significantly once she was removed from the home but still lives with some of the consequences. She spoke of the importance of removing a family from a home that has already suffered from that exposure. She was concerned that being exposed again makes a family more susceptible and worried about the Episcopal family returning to the home. She spoke for the resolution.

Rev. Stan Fredericks, Galesville UMC, spoke against the resolution even though he appreciated the need for it, but he does not think it is "appropriate to give you all a blank check."

Rev. Stephen Tillett, Asbury-Broadneck UMC, asked the "approximate price" they were trying to sell the house for. He explained that information would inform everyone of how much is needed. Strawbridge explained he could not put the property on the market without the motion and he did not have an offer price for the house yet.

Bishop announced that she was going to go to the next person, but that a tornado warning had been issued and she was going to push the plenary to take a vote as soon as possible.

Blake Statler, Emory UMC, spoke against the resolution because the black mold issue put lives at-risk and it was possible it could appear again. There was a call for the question and the vote passed.

Rev. Katie Bishop, Greater Brunswick Charge, reading from the conference rules, said that all proposals requiring funding have to go to CFA and "shall carry a reasonable cost estimate of the total cost of the project plus a statement of the of the source of funds in addition to the proposed benefits." She asked if this applied to the current resolution. Strawbridge explained that what she read applies to everything including the rental of the hotel for the annual conference. What the resolution applies to is ¶2515, which applies to the purchase of conference property that requires the action of the annual conference.

Bishop Moore Koikoi said there was a request to have someone from CFA to come and comment on the resolution. Phil Potter, Chair of CFA, said that they had been working with the Trustees and the staff as they have gone through the mold issue and looked at the issue of buying a replacement property. He said that there is not enough data or information gathered to determine the value of the existing property, nor has a replacement property been located or priced. CFA has nothing to specifically rule on regarding price. Under the Discipline, CFA must authorize the Trustees to proceed to look at this proposition, locate another property, and conduct the exchange. CFA would participate in the final financing if that is required. At this point CFA has no data, information or prices to rule on. Bishop thanked Potter for the information and called for the vote. The resolution passed.

Bishop Moore Koikoi requested that the marshals keep the body informed regarding the weather. She also asked people to stay away from the windows. She shared that the hotel staff was tracking the storm and that the ballroom was a shelter-in-place area.

Bishop Easterling returned to the ballroom, saying that she learned about the shelter in place and announced to the body, "I just want to say we already know that one of the safest places we could be is on holy ground."

John Strawbridge presented Resolution 5, "Resolution for Unrestricted Bequest Received by Centre Street United Methodist Church in the Cumberland-Hagerstown District." Centre Street closed June 30, 2018, and in December received an unrestricted bequest. Strawbridge explained that the published resolution had been changed after consultation with the Connectional Table and the district superintendent and could be found on the conference website or the annual conference app. The resolution designated the bequest for "non-urban ministry in Cumberland-Hagerstown District," the district in which the bequest was made.

Michael Llewelyn, LaVale UMC, offered an amendment that the funds be given for capital improvements at LaVale UMC. It was seconded. The church is three- to five-miles away from Centre Street. More than 30 members from Centre Street have joined LaVale. LaVale has a building committee and Llewelyn is co-chair. LaVale has infrastructure needs including handicap accessibility; most of their building is not accessible. Many of those who came Centre Street are elderly and have accessibility issues and can only get two of the three floors in the building. Funds have been designated by LaVale to have a feasibility study for improvements that need to be done. He thinks that the Rice Estate would have liked the money to "follow their brothers and sisters from Centre Street."

William Sadler, Calvary Gambler UMC, Frederick District, spoke against the motion. Sadler, a former Board of Trustee member, knows the work that goes into being a trustee. He explained that they have "the big picture in mind" and are best suited to determine how the funds are designated.

Angela Pearson, Emmanuel UMC, in Cumberland, rose to speak against the amendment. Bishop Easterling asked her to stop, as a speech "for" was needed first.

Rev. Lloyd McKenna, Morgan Charge, retired and former pastor at Centre Street, was not sure if he was speaking for or against the amendment. He agreed with the trustees' decision to keep the funds in Cumberland-Hagerstown District. Humpty Dumpty Learning Center, housed in Centre Street for decades, will need a new location. The elevator at the church is not working and if the bequest was used to fix it, the property would sell better. Those proceeds could provide funding for all kinds of ministry in Cumberland-Hagerstown District.

Bishop said it was a speech against. Strawbridge asked for a point of order and said the amendment would be qualified as a substitute amendment because it would call for the trustees "to bypass" the process of working with the district superintendent to administer the funds. Bishop Easterling asked Llewelyn, the maker of the amendment, to come to the microphone. Easterling asked if he intended to present an amendment by substitution, because the maker of the resolution feels the amendment proposes changes to the entire process of how the Board of Trustees handles these kinds of issues. Llewelyn agreed his proposed amendment is a substitution. Bishop Easterling agreed that it was an amendment by substitution and would be returned to after the main motion was perfected.

There had been no speeches for or against the resolution, so the floor was invited to make comments.

Angela Pearson, Emmanuel UMC, in Cumberland, spoke in favor of the resolution. She also participates in Davis Memorial Church. She said the members of Centre Street scattered throughout the community and intend to join Vale, Emmanuel Davis and other churches. She spoke to the importance of an "impoverished" community investing in its own community and keeping funds there to help support youth, children and provide experiences they wouldn't otherwise have. She added that it was very important to invest in people and their spiritual development and not just in facilities.

Rev. Maidstone Mulenga, Council of Bishops, asked for a definition of the term "non-urban" ministry. Rev. Conrad Link, Cumberland-Hagerstown District Superintendent, explained that the district is designated Appalachia Land and all of it is non-urban. The towns do not meet the United States geographic information for urban setting; they are too small. The entire district is not urban, and the money could be used anywhere in Allegheny County.

Billy Smith spoke against the resolution, sharing that the children in Allegheny are in impoverished schools. She requested that the district superintendent look at all churches in need, not just one because many need repairs and handicap accessibility.

Michael Llewelyn rose with a point of order asking to withdraw his amendment in view of the actual language of the resolution. It was allowed. He stated that he supported the resolution as presented.

Rev. Patrick Herberman, Christian Church, spoke for the resolution speaking to the "spirit of how the money was given" and using the funds "in the environment where it was originally given." The money was being designated to ministries as opposed to a capital improvement of a building or organization.

Mary Jo Leffler, Davis Memorial UMC and former lay leader of Centre Street, spoke for the amendment and her thought that the Rice family would appreciate their legacy going to children and churches in Allegheny County. Bishop Easterling confirmed it was a speech for. Strawbridge commented that regarding the original draft supporting camping ministries, they are continuing to find ways to support that ministry. The bishop called for the vote and the resolution carried.

Rev. Rudy Bropleh, Asbury UMC, Shepherdstown, presented Resolution 4, "Rotating Venue and Accommodation Stipends for Annual Conference." The resolution addresses the difficulty some pastors and laypersons have in getting to the Annual Conference Session and/ or remaining for the duration of the Annual Conference Session. One example was those traveling from the Western Region, a third of the annual conference, who commute and by the second day they are so weary, some do not attend the third day. The resolution's goals are "accessibility, affordability, inclusivity and as a result, productivity." The resolution calls for researching other locations for the Annual Conference Session and presenting the research at the next Annual Conference Session. There is no cost associated with the research; this was confirmed in conversations with the conference treasurer and data from Phil Potter, CFA Chair. The resolution also included a stipend to help churches that are financially unable to send their lay and clergy person to the Annual Conference Session. Criteria will be developed and presented at next year's Annual Conference Session.

Bishop Easterling asked if the body was amenable to going to two minutes for speeches for and against, and it passed. Matthew Sichel, Wesley Hampstead UMC, stated that he lived two to three miles from the Pennsylvania line in northern Carroll County and that the resolution isn't just for the Western Region. He said that when the Annual Conference Session is in Washington, D.C., it takes him "an inordinate amount of time to get down and back." This resolution applies to those coming from all over the conference into Baltimore or Washington, D.C. He pointed out that historically there had been rotating spaces to the West. He spoke for the resolution.

Julie Wilson, Calvary UMC in Frederick, offered an amendment to strike line 26 (item 2) through line 28 of the resolution. She pointed out those living in Baltimore and DC and Frederick "know that measuring distance in time doesn't work well."

Rev. Michael Parker, clergy, Greater Washington, asked if it had been considered that the island of Bermuda is within the bounds of the annual conference.

A speaker rose to speak for the resolution. It was ruled out of order. The next speaker asked why only Baltimore was mentioned on line 25 and not Washington. Bropleh explained that was an example and that Baltimore is probably the furthest to get to "given the extremes of the annual conference." Rev. Steve Tillett asked if the maker of the original motion accepted the amendment as a friendly amendment. Stating that there is no such thing as a friendly amendment, Bishop Easterling asked Bropleh if he would accept editing the resolution to end at location. He said no.

Rev. Daniel Montague, Fork and Wall UMCs, spoke against the amendment by striking number two because "it's difficult to measure" that way (by time). He spoke against removing number two all together.

A speaker asked if an amendment to the amendment was allowable. The bishop allowed her to proceed. The amendment would read: "The cost and administrative requirements to provide free accommodations to the clergy and lay delegates who represent local churches that can demonstrate need" and strike "that fall outside of a 1.5-hour travel band." She explained that in light of the discussion about economic conditions in Allegheny and all of the region, "economic conditions are not equal" and to stay in DC and similar places is expensive." She believes her amendment allows more help to people to be able to afford to attend the Annual Conference Session.

Bropleh said that an edit had been done but it was submitted after the deadline. It read, "a formula to be determined by the annual conference based on need." If we are unable to move to different places, they could at least provide some kind of subsidy for those with established need as determined by the treasurer and CFA, he said. It will be reported on at the next annual conference report. Bropleh accepted the amendment. The bishop returned to the original amendment.

Rev. John Nupp, Executive Minister for Call and Clergy Care, spoke against the amendment having had lunch with the fellowship of local pastors and associate members, many of who do not have vote, and many of whom are most affected by the decisions of the body in the location of the Annual Conference Session. He asked that consideration be given not only to location, but also providing for those in attendance who were traveling at their own cost.

Rev. Carol Yocum, retired, asked if those who arranged accommodations could speak to other places the Annual Conference Session could meet as in the past they met at universities and stayed in dorms. However, accessibility issues led to going to hotels. The bishop said that that would be part of the research for the location.

Ken Ow, North Bethesda UMC, who said he was also wearing a CFA and GCFA hat, and said changing the location to a central location, could mean more expenses than the conference can accommodate. He spoke in favor of the amendment.

Rev. Bruce Jones, retired and former Arrangements chair for the conference, said that they had done the research and found only Baltimore and Washington hotels were large enough to provide a ballroom to seat 1,600 people as well as space for exhibits, meals and the number of rooms needed. He said there was nothing in Western Maryland, including Rocky Gap. Bishop Easterling agreed with the accuracy of his statement and added that there are venues being built continuously that might be able to accommodate the Annual Conference Session and that would be a part of the research.

Rev. Eliezer Valentin-Castanon, Trinity UMC in Frederick, asked for clarification on what was being worked on because the amendment to the amendment was accepted. Bishop Easterling clarified that the original amendment needed to be voted upon. The amendment did not pass.

Bill Rally, a local pastor at Chestnut Hill UMC in Harpers Ferry, spoke for the resolution saying that it was a hardship for his colleagues in rural locations to attend because of the expense to the church and to them.

Bropleh said that the motion was asking for permission to do research. The RFP is about to go out and the Annual Conference Sessions will be in Baltimore through 2024. The resolution as amended was adopted.

Bishop Easterling announced the start of balloting for the delegates to General Conference. Before the start of the balloting for lay delegates, a video by Bishop Sandra Steiner Ball was played as the plenary went into prayer.

There was no lay delegate election on the first ballot. Rev. Joan Carter-Rimbach, John Wesley

UMC, asked the bishop to remind people that only laity were voting. The bishop commented that voting devices would allow only the laity to vote.

Dawn Ragnar, New Chapel UMC, reported that the issue she was having was that due to the delay, the device said that it "sent," but her remaining number did not go down and the device was saying she had one vote left but it was blocking her and she was not sure which vote did not get in.

Gemma from Padgett directed everyone to look at their voting device while they were voting, to make sure their first selection was sent and to not enter another choice until the device showed the remaining number of votes go down. Because a lot of data was being sent at the same time, the process could be slower. Bishop Easterling suggested writing down voting choices on a piece of paper and marking through the votes already sent.

Rev. Tillett suggested voting be three minutes. The plenary said five minutes. Bishop Easterling took a vote and the plenary remained at three minutes for voting. The body asked to redo the vote and take three minute and the vote was redone. Easterling suggested clergy prepare for their vote.

Amy Nisonger, Damascus UMC, shared that the people she was sitting with experienced a 30-second delay after each vote and could the time be extended to four minutes. The bishop replied that the voting was at about five minutes and she wanted to keep going a little longer because it looked like the voting was almost complete. There was no election on Laity Ballot 1.

Bishop Easterling called for the approval of the Consent Calendar. Conference Secretary, Cynthia Taylor, reported that she had received a request to have an item removed from the Consent Calendar that was submitted in a timely manner and contained the 10 signatures required. The request was to remove the Discipleship Council Restructure Proposal. All other matters remain on the consent calendar. The consent calendar, as amended, passed. Bishop Easterling announced the first clergy ballot would be given four minutes. There was no election on Clergy Ballot 1.

The bishop thanked the plenary for being patient, nimble and flexible. She asked Rev. Deb Scott to offer the prayer for the evening meal.

Service of the Saints
Thursday, May 30, 2019 | 7:00 p.m.

Families and friends of pastors, pastors' spouses and conference lay people filled the Grand Ballroom as they came to remember their loved ones who had died since the 2018 Annual Conference Session.

As people gathered, a pianist and violinist played. Worship Leader, Marsha McFee, stood next to a round table on an elevated platform in the center of the room where lighted devotional candles, festooned with ribbons of the names of those being remembered, encircled the baptismal basin. She invited all to take a deep breath. The circle, she explained, was "a circle of hope, love and life."

A hauntingly beautiful song, "I'm with You/Be Still" was sung by a duet as one of them played the guitar. Bishop LaTrelle Easterling offered the greeting. The opening hymn of praise was, "Break Not the Circle of Praise." The Rev. Ann Laprade, superintendent of the Baltimore

Suburban District, gave the Opening Prayer.

McFee then sang, "Circle of life, Jesus our light, journey from death to new life" and asked the congregation to join her in singing those words. Sharon Milton, Emory Fellowship, delivered a poetic reading. At the conclusion of the reading, the congregation repeated the "Circle of life" refrain.

The Rev. Gerard Green, superintendent of the Greater Washington District, read Ephesians 4:3. After which, the refrain was sung. The Rev. Conrad Link, Dean of the Cabinet, read Matthew 6: 6-13, followed by the refrain.

The Rev. Ianther Mills, pastor of Asbury UMC in Washington, began her sermon repeating the words of Ephesians 4:3 from The Message. She told a story about Gracie Allen, the wife and comedic partner of comedian George Burns.

Allen left a message in her papers to be discovered by her husband after her death: "Never place a period where God has placed a comma." He was 68 when Gracie died and "rather than place a period after his career, George Burns on went on to star in a number of movies, including playing God twice. He died at age 100 having lived the life of a comma." It became the theme for the evening.

"Gracie Allen's message to George Burns reminds us that there is no period after the names of clergy, clergy spouses and lay members who we honor today," Mills said. "Each of them has lived lives poured out for others and, because of that their influence and impact, lives on in us."

Mills also illustrated the place of the loved ones in the hearts of the survivors with a story about Nicaraguans calling "presente" at a memorial service. A group of Christians from the United States visited Nicaragua during war-torn days and a young man in the group was killed. On the next Sunday, a memorial service was held. During the Communion service, there was a pause and the congregation was silent. Then someone called out a name and in one voice the people shouted, "presente." Another name was called out and once again, the response was "presente." During the service, at least 20 names were called out and each time the response was "presente." The pastor leading the U.S. group did not understand what was happening until he heard the name Oscar Romero. And then, he realized that all the names were those of people who died. "Although those people named had all died, their presence and their influence was still found — it was present," Mills explained.

Using the parable of the seed, she helped the congregation understand that just as a seed dies and produces new life, so did those being remembered. Mills shared a few stories of how some of them poured out love. They included a founder of a women's Veterans Resource Center who received recognition from First Lady Michele Obama for her work; a pastor and chaplain who provided pastoral counseling during the growth of HIV/AIDS epidemic during the 1980's; another pastor who founded Operation Outreach at Seattle Pacific College for short-term summer mission trips for students; a clergy spouse who was a local licensed preacher for more than 55 years and worked alongside her husband teaching Sunday School, chairing church committees, and serving on a mission trip to Cuba in 1956; and a lay member who served as Annapolis District United Methodist Men president and supported the conference prayer center and the UMM potato project.

"Gracie Allen's note reminds us that there is no period after the name of those who labored so that we would continue to be in ministry at this point in time," Mills said. "God has placed a comma there and the story is not over."

As Mills concluded her sermon, she asked, "What will you do with all that has been entrusted to you?" She then asked the congregation to raise their hand and shout "*presente*" in response to several questions she asked that related to how they had served the church and the community. She then said, "By God's grace, if you have ever just helped somebody, stand on your feet, as you are able, and shout, "*presente!*"

She said, "You are the fruit of someone's love. Love poured out, extravagant love, all-out love. God is still speaking, people. And so, as we remember and recall the names of all who have gone before us, can you hear them saying, 'never put a period where God has placed a comma.'"

The response was the hymn, "Give Me Jesus." Bishop Easterling introduced the Act of Remembrance with brief remarks about remembering and recalling those who have gone before us. She explained that bringing forth the light to symbolize and memorialize the loved ones "we will see in life everlasting, is to say that they are *presente* here with us today." Bishop Easterling requested: "As we bring forth this light may we call their name and remember them in this place."

Cynthia Taylor, Conference Secretary, said, "We gather here today to celebrate and remember those who faithfully served God and now rest in the light of God's eternal love. Their witness and work remain forever with us and in the countless lives that were touched by them. As their names are read, you are invited to stand if you are one who received the gift of their life and ministry."

In the candlelight service, as each name was called, the pictures of those being remembered were shown on the on the screen, a lighted candle was processed from the table in the center of the room to the altar at the front of the room, a bell was rung, and those who knew and remembered them stood and shouted "*presente*."

Verse 1 of "For All the Saints" was sung.

The Rev. Edgardo Rivera, superintendent of the Frederick District, read the names of the bishops and bishops' spouses being remembered. Bishops: Benjamin Roy Chamness; William B. Oden; C. Dale White. Bishops Spouses: Mary Ann Hunt; Mary Jean Russell; and Melvena Maway Morris Nagbe

Verse 2 of "For All the Saints" was sung.

The Rev. Rebecca Iannicelli, superintendent of the Washington East District, read the names of the clergy: Pastor Walter M. Bosman, Rev. William J. Bussard, Rev. Wayne Chung, Rev. Mary W. Conaway, Rev. James "Jay" L. DeMent, Rev. Herbert Levi David Doggett, Rev. William W. Ehlers, Rev. James R. Embrey, Pastor Helen C. Fleming, Pastor Charles W. Henry, Rev. Bernard F. Hillenbrand, Pastor Lewis I. Keene, Rev. Raymond M. Kingsborough, Rev. Edwin H. Langrall, Rev. Lloyd Marcus, Rev. Ted D. Marsh, Rev. Maurice S. Moore, Rev. Zan Lee Perry, Rev. John T. Smith, Rev. Charles W. Stewart, Rev. Ernest W. P. Thayil, Rev. Vernon L. Thompson, Rev. John Charles Walker, Rev. Pauline V. Wilkins, and Rev. William Carl Zinn.

Verse 3 of "For All the Saints" was sung.

The Rev. Wanda Duckett, superintendent of the Baltimore Metropolitan District, read the names of clergy spouses: Ethel L. Ankeny, Ozeal Beatrice Shyne Brown, Fred D. Carney, Sr., Eleanor Emerick, Lillian Frazier, Du Shun Gim, Eleanor Hall, Lucy Bell Haynes Harrell,

Ann C. Johnson, Phyllis B. Kemp, Gurney L. Leatherwood, Margaret E. Lovejoy, LaRue E. Manhart, Loretta J. Miller, Ruby Price, Marilyn Joyce Raker, Janice Sheesley, Margaret M. Thayil, Adelheid Weber, Ruth C. Williams, Anne Feimster Wise, and Aliceann Wohlbruck.

Verse 4 of "For All the Saints" was sung.

The Rev. J. W. Park, superintendent of the Central Maryland District, read the laity names: Loretta Anita Lassiter, William Duval "Dewey" Parrish, Sandra King Shaw, Darvin James Hebron, David George Vader, and David John Werner, Sr.

Marcia McFee invited everyone to lift up all the beloved names of all who they wished to remember. Bishop Easterling led the congregation in prayer.

McFee lead the congregants in the act of anointing each other's hands with oil. During the anointing, the music, "Anointing Fall on Me," was played. As people anointed those next to them, they said "The healing power of Christ be with you."

Bishop Easterling offered the Benediction. The closing hymn was, "Soon and Very Soon."

Bible Study
Friday, May 31, 2019 | 8:00 a.m.

A trio, two playing guitars, sang, "Bless the Lord Oh My Soul," "Trading My Sorrows," and "This is the Air I Breathe" as the congregation gathered for morning Bible Study.

Rev. Kyle Durbin invited the congregation to a time of contemplative prayer, sometimes called breath prayer. On the in-breath, he said, think of any name of God that comes to us and breathe the name in. On the out breath, lay before God whatever need that is on your mind. He guided them in starting the prayer and then was silent while he and the congregation practiced their breath prayers. He ended this time with a prayer.

Durbin introduced the Bible Study leader, Rev. Marvin McMickle. McMickle thanked all who returned for Part 2 of his discussion on poverty and economic justice. He said he wanted to "challenge" listeners individually, as clergy, as lay leaders, and as congregations "to think about the issue of poverty and prosperity in such close proximity. That one could travel less than a mile from your church location and could run into living conditions, levels of income, realities of concentrated poverty, extreme poverty, that are in some instances, like third-world countries." He compared this to being downtown at the Inner Harbor and seeing yachts and boats, "lined up manifestations of prosperity and wealth and comfort and excess." Then, he said, go less than a mile from there and see "Luke 16" and the rich man dressed in purple with a beggar named Lazarus at his gate.

McMickle reviewed the entirety of the previous day's text and the Martin Luther King, Jr. quote that was part of his 1963 "I Have a Dream" speech, in which he said that African Americans live on a island of poverty in the midst of a great sea of material prosperity. McMickle flipped the quote over, saying that "many churches in most urban areas are an island of prosperity surrounded by a great sea of poverty." He instructed that we need to find a way to engage with what is going on outside the doors of the church.

He explained that, "It was not the individual issues of poverty versus the individual issues of prosperity, it is their proximity to one another." He said, "whether or not we end up in hell depends on the degree to which we have engaged on the issue of poverty that impacts us." It is not the following of rituals that concerns God; it is the "degree to which we have paid attention."

He then spoke about the ways in which poverty and economic deprivation have been used historically "as tools of prolonged oppression." He referred to a book by Aldon Morris, "The Origins of the Civil Rights Movement." In the book, Morris introduces a concept he called "the tripartite forms of oppression." According to McMickle, "these were the ways in which historical oppression, based upon race, was both practiced and prolonged."

Morris said there were three forms of oppression used primarily against African Americans by those who wanted to keep them in check: 1) keep people in poverty (keep them "hopelessly poor"); 2) political powerlessness (keep them from voting via voter suppression and intimidation.); and 3) intimidation and violence to maintain that status quo (if 1 and 2 don't work, use terror, violence, and lynching). McMickle suggested that those unaware of American history should study the history of lynching in the United States of America. He said there were 3,000 known lynchings in this country — acts of terrorism. Terrorism, McMickle said, continues in this country today.

The other tripartite system is captured in the the Womanist Theology movement. McMickle spoke of the limited places women can go when they are seeking careers in ministry and he thanked The United Methodist Church "for being the joyful recipient of so many African-American women who were Baptist." In Womanist Theology, the tripartite formula is three pronged: those "who suffer from racism, gender discrimination, and poverty or class distinction." The church needs to address all these things if they are to be at "the business of the work of God."

Addressing the popular phrase, "Make America Great Again," McMickle said that he wants America "to be as great as it can be." His objection is to the word "again." He said he does not know "when this again was." He asked, "when might that have been and who was left out?" He recounted American history going from the first African Americans brought to this county as indentured servants in the 17th century, the 18th century trafficking of as many as 12 million people from Africa to enslavement in America, the 19th century's Indian Removal Act and the Trail of Tears where thousands of Cherokee Indians died under forced removal, and the 20th century before child labor laws and before women had the right to vote and when lynch mobs ruled the land. McMickle said he thought the "again" was when whites were simply in charge.

McMickle suggested four things that can be done to address issue of poverty:

Have a biblical vision for the future; imagine a future different from the ruling elite. Allow your values to inform your behavior. Draw from Micah 6:8, "He has shown us what is good: do justice, love kindness and humble obedience to God's moral laws; especially regarding widows, orphans and strangers."
Use your voice to speak up and advocate for policies and practices on behalf of economic justice; be a voice for the voiceless.
Vote to elect people at the local, county, state and national level who will legislate for JUSTICE and not for JUST US.

McMickle reflected on the previous day's discussion on the roles of the LGBTQIA people in The United Methodist Church. He said, "Let's keep the Bible out of this because if you put the Bible in here, you're going to have more stuff against you than you do for you." He said that there are 26 chapters in Leviticus and one verse on homosexuality, and reasoned that, "you cannot pick out your one favorite verse and ignore all the rest that's in the same book." He said that, "At the expense of an entire book of the Bible, you have only one option: embrace the book of Leviticus and live by a 10th century B.C. holiness code with dietary restrictions, clothing restrictions and sexual restrictions, or conclude that we do not live as a culture in a secular democracy by 10th century holiness code." He provided similar examples in Romans 1.

"No selective exegesis," McMickle exhorted. "No one-verse theology." He said that, "we tend, you and I, to demonize the one thing that we do not do and call that God's will." He asked the assembly what they do about all the other things that they do that are the in Scriptures he referred to. For example, he said, "If you're not going to ordain folk of a particular sexual practice, then don't ordain adulterers."

McMickle called attention to Mathew 10:3-4, in which we are introduced to the Lord's 12 disciples. Jesus began his ministry calling every-day, amiable fishermen, a "Galilean mafia, "McMickle said. But then Jesus tossed in Matthew the tax collector, and Simon the Zealot. Zealots, he explained hated tax collectors. The pair were natural enemies, but both followed Jesus and were able to co-exist in the same circle. "I can't think of any two more unlikely people to be near Jesus," he said. "Some of you may be Matthew the tax collector. Some of you might be Simon the Zealot." He concluded his Bible Study with the words: "Do not break up. Get in line behind Jesus and let Jesus lead you all the way."

Third Plenary Session
Friday, May 31, 2019 | 9:00 a.m.

Bishop Easterling opened the session and shared that she had left the ballroom because she received word that Kyle Durbin's father was making his transition. She said that Kyle was a candidate for ordination that evening and asked the plenary to pause for a prayer for him and his family. His district superintendent, Rev. Conrad Link, was asked to pray.

The bishop asked the plenary to welcome the Washington East District Lay Leader, Rosalind Pinkney, who came to the dais.

Rev. Ianther Mills, Asbury UMC in Washington, D.C., informed the bishop that the captioning cut off at least two lines on the screen display and asked if it could be turned off during voting. The captioning cut off four names, resulting in an unfair advantage. Bishop Easterling thanked her and confirmed that, during voting, the closed captioning would not be shown on the screen.

Bishop Easterling invited the lay delegate candidates to come forward and briefly introduce themselves. Twenty-one did so. The bishop thanked them.

Deacon Megan Blanchard, Provisional, Mill Creek Parish, asked to pray over the session. Bishop thanked her for the prayer.

A gentleman observed that he counted 21 people introducing themselves as candidates for lay delegate and only 20 names were in the pre-con booklet, so someone was left out. Bishop Easterling explained that a page was missing from the pre-con book and an insert had been available at the pages' table and copies were being distributed as she spoke.

Bishop Easterling called for a Laity ballot and asked Bishop Cynthia Moore Koikoi to pray before it commenced. There was no election on Laity Ballot 2. As the clergy prepared to vote, the bishop reminded them that only those persons eligible to vote would be able to do so. Other devices would not be activated during the process. Rev. Ianther Mills was elected on Clergy Ballot 2 as the first clergy delegate. She will serve as head of the delegation.

Bishop Easterling recognized a group of young people at the microphone. Nathan Jones, Epworth UMC in Cockeysville, requested a moment of privilege for the Young People's Ministry. Nathan said that the young people of the Baltimore-Washington Conference were excited to be celebrated during holy conferencing this Annual Conference and were "extremely thankful for the opportunity you have given us to come forward and talk about the amazing thing we have been doing in the church on Saturday." Considering how long the conference session had taken thus far, the young people asked that the conference do no harm to young people and remember Saturday was a day to celebrate young people and all that they have done. They understood that there was important business and decisions that will affect the conference for decades, especially young people, as they are the future of the church. They asked that the conference be "mindful and respectful of others and do no harm and make sure that we're using our time to the best of its ability."

Bishop Easterling said the chair happily received the moment of privilege with one correction, "you are not the church of the future, you are the church of right now."

The bishop said that she prayed that when she was "able to gavel us out of session today, that you will not take you leave." She asked that the plenary would remain on Saturday to continue to celebrate "our young people."

Rev. Sarah Dorrance, Middletown UMC, made a motion to suspend the rules and reduce speeches for and against from three to two minutes. The motion carried.

Rev. Mark Gorman, Rules Chair, presented two resolutions on behalf of the Rules Committee to be voted upon separately. Resolution 6, "Amending the Rules: Duties of the Rules Committee," asked the Annual Conference to vote to define the role narrowly and to put in writing that the Rules Committee will provide advice to the annual conference "about how to proceed with any proposed changes to the structure of the annual conference." The annual conference will act; the Rules Committee is acting in an advisory role, he said. Approval required two-thirds majority because the Rules Committee works under the "Rules of the Session." Resolution 8, "Requiring Consultation for Restructuring Proposals," would provide for the involvement of the Discipleship Council and Nominations Committee to give "concurrence or non-concurrence on any proposed restructuring." Resolution 8 required a simple majority because it has to do with Policies and Procedures.

Lon Chestnut, Retired Elder, spoke against Resolution 6, finding it a "dangerous proposal" akin to "our own Judicial Council," which he said we did not need. Rev. Sandy Johnson, Deaf Ministries, spoke for the resolution, saying that the Rules Committee and other committees work "very hard make sure that we are in compliance with those things that we have established in this conference." She asked that the body "continue to honor their work and the work that we all do."

Dawn Brooks, lay member from Jackson Chapel UMC and Rules Committee member, rose to offer a point of clarification and a speech for. She clarified that the entire Rules Committee put the resolution forth and "all were in agreement that any proposal for restructuring of the Annual Conference should be reviewed by the Rules Committee to ensure it falls within the guidelines and to offer any suggestions for revision if needed and to be a second set of eyes." She said the resolution was "put forth to help and not to hinder." There was no additional voice against and Rev. Gorman gave remarks before the vote, reiterating that the intent was to help and not to hinder.

John Hines, Annapolis District, rose to ask a clarifying question on Resolution 8. Bishop Easterling advised that the plenary was voting on Resolution 6 and would get back to 8. Resolution 6 carried.

Resolution 8 was the same adding the Nominations Committee and the Discipleship Council. Mittie Quinn, Dumbarton UMC in Greater Washington, spoke in favor of the resolution. She was one of the individuals who asked for the structure to be pulled from the Consent Calendar because she felt the body needed time and opportunity to discuss it. Since the two groups represent the Annual Conference when not in session, she felt it was appropriate for them to have a voice in the restructuring.

Rev. Phil Wogaman, Retired Clergy, Foundry UMC, asked if this would preclude anything developing at the time of Annual Conference. He said that any small changes would have to be developed prior to Annual Conference when the committees meet. Gorman replied that things brought to the floor at Annual Conference could be decided then or referred to the groups during Annual Conference. Wogaman asked if deciding at the time would require a suspension of the rules. Gorman replied that for it to not go before the Rules Committee, it would require a suspension of the rules but not for the groups in the resolution.

Rev. Daryl Williams, St. Paul UMC in Oxon Hill, spoke against the resolution because group are empowered to do their work and are "adding multiple layers of bureaucracy that will slow down the work and the ability to make disciples in the most effective ways." He compared this to the way BOOM has been empowered to do its work. He believed that flattening the conference structures would help things more forward a little bit more quickly.

Rev. Gorman stated the belief that the resolutions are empowering people. Resolution 8 was approved.

Rev. Bonnie McCubbin, Good Shepherd UMC in Baltimore, and Rev. Lemuel Dominquez, Milford Mill UMC, came forward to present Resolution 7, "Resolution to Provide Nursing and Pumping Accommodations Within the Bar at Annual Conference." McCubbin shared her experience last year when, during opening worship, her son was baptized during the Annual Conference Session by Bishop Easterling. On the final day of the session, she recounted her many difficulties attempting to breastfeed her son. She hoped that the resolution would ensure that others did not go through this and "no child has to go hungry." She wanted to ensure that all people have the access they deserve.

Rev. John Rudolf, North Carroll Cooperative Parish in Hampstead, spoke in favor of the resolution. He said that for the last 14 years, every other year, he brought a baby. They have seven children. He said sometimes "you just have to bring a child" and he was "in support of all that we can do for mothers and fathers and those bringing kids." He concluded, "Let's just be hospitable. Thanks be to God."

There was a motion for unanimous consent and the resolution passed unanimously.

A prayer video from Bishop Bickerton, New York Annual Conference, was shown after which there was another vote for the lay delegation. As the system was processing, Bishop Easterling asked the clergy to prepare themselves to vote for five persons next.

Rev. Scott Shumaker, Parkton Cooperative Parish in Baltimore County, asked if all of the count totals could be shown. Rev. HiRho Park requested a moment of personal privilege. She serves the General Board of Higher Education and Ministry. She stated that, at GBHEM, she "supports all racial ethnic clergy ministries." She reminded the plenary "to be conscientious of electing an inclusive delegation." She spoke of the "diverse constituencies" including "Asians, Asian-Pacific Islanders, Hispanic, Latino, Latina, and Native Americans." She hoped that the BWC would be "mindful of a minority among minorities to give them a voice representing this body."

The first lay delegate was Cynthia Taylor, elected on Lay Ballot 3.

Rev. Bryant Oskvig voiced concern that his voting device was set for six instead of five and those around him were saying their devices had four remaining when they should only have three. Padgett replied that the system was set to five.

Another clergyperson said the same thing was happening to him, adding that when he voted, he had to reenter his vote for the counter to go down and to have the correct count for the remainder of the vote. Oskvig said that people all around him had the same issue and requested the vote be reset and started over, to which the bishop agreed.

Bishop Easterling announced Clergy Ballot 3 and Rev. Joseph Daniels was elected on that ballot.

Rev. Melissa Rudolph presented Resolution 9, "Pertaining to Attendance at Meetings for General and Jurisdictional Conference Delegates" on behalf of the 2016 delegation. She said the resolution was the work of the entire delegation; it involved 2014 rules required attendance at the delegation meetings. At the delegation's meeting in January 2019, the delegation voted 20 for the resolution and two against the resolution. The resolution put "parameters around what it means to be in attendance and what qualifies as an excused absence." She said it was up to the body to determine what the accountability measures should be for someone not in attendance.

Rev. Mark Gorman, speaking as Rule Chair, offered a Point of Information, that the Rules Committee voted concurrence with the resolution. And, he wanted to speak in favor of the resolution personally. He spoke in favor of the resolution because he believes the Conference needs to support the delegation when they say they need this resolution. He pointed out that there is a possibility of a constitutional issue. Despite that, he supported the resolution.

Rev. Marlon Tilghman, Ames UMC in Bel Air, offered an amendment at line 30 and 31 to delete the publishing of the attendance of the 2020 delegation attendance record prior to the election of the 2024 delegation. He saw the statement as a form of shaming those unable to attend the meeting.

Rev. Mary Kay Totty, Dumbarton UMC, rose to speak against the amendment, stating her belief that the purpose of the resolution is to help the conference "be aware when people run for delegations two quadrennium or more running, to have a fair sense of the reliability and dependability of people participating in the process." While she agreed that there are "valid" reasons for people being unable to attend a meeting, there is also a "need to have a sense of where people prioritize their commitment to the delegation and therefore to this conference."

Rev. Lynn Glassbrook, Retired Clergy, asked for more information from Gorman regarding the constitutional problems. Gorman said the amendment on the floor raised the question of whether of not reporting back attendance records is "functionally the same thing as reporting back voting record, which the Judicial Council has said cannot be required." The second issue is that the attendance policy may not be enforceable. He plans to request a declaratory decision on the resolution, if passed.

Rev. Sandi Johnson, Deaf Ministries, rose to speak for the amendment in light of there being excused absences and after a certain number of absences one is dropped from the group. Therefore, the last sentence is not necessary. Dawn Ragnar, lay member of Union Chapel in Joppa, asked if "a delegate who has two unexcused absences is removed from the delegation, is that delegate eligible to be voted on in the next session?" Rev. Rudolf said yes.

An unnamed person rose to offer an amendment to the amendment beginning at line 17 and Gorman raised a point of order that the amendment under consideration was lines 30 to 31. The amendment to the amendment was out of order.

Mittie Quinn offered a "friendly amendment" to change "will be published" to "will be made available prior to elections." Rev. Sarah Schlieckert, Calvary UMC in Waldorf, raised a point of order, Conference Rule 22, because the amendment was a substitution, because Rev. Tilghman's amendment was a motion to delete. Bishop Easterling was not sure Rule 22 was applicable and asked Tilghman if he would accept the friendly amendment and he said "no."

Rev. Mary Jo Sims rose to submit a question to or request a clarification from Rev. Gorman. Her understanding was that the conference was allowed "to add additional requirements, but that it must at least meet the requirements of the discipline." Gorman replied that he was not suggesting that the Conference was not so allowed; he said it was a question that the Judicial Council "had not taken up."

Rev. Joan Carter-Rimbach, John Wesley UMC in Baltimore, spoke against the amendment. She said that in Tampa (General Conference 2012), there was a member of the delegation who never attended any of the delegation meetings and "when the delegate came to General Conference, people saw her for the very first time." She spoke against it because "we want to expect our delegates be there to show and to be accountable."

Will Gouty, lay member, Silver Spring UMC, spoke for the amendment because he believed "it should not be anyone's business how many excused" absences one has and it should not be published as long as they are getting the work done.

Jan Hayden, lay member, West Baltimore UMC, asked why the person who missed all the meetings was not dropped. Rudolph said the resolution was the reason the rule came into being in 2014. Tilghman spoke on his amendment again, reiterating his earlier statements that publishing the amendment was not necessary. A voice vote was taken and because it sounded so close, the voting devices were used and the amendment did not pass.

Bishop Easterling recognized someone with a point of order but because there was an order of the day, she asked if the question was brief. Dan Rusin, Havre De Grace UMC, asked why conference calls or Skype or some other means was not used. Bishop Easterling said it was not brief and moved to the order of the day – the Board of Ordained Ministry Report.

Rev. Robert Barnes, Mount Oak Fellowship in Mitchellville, was recognized for a point of order. He requested three ruling of laws related to the work about to come before the body. He had a written copy to submit but asked if he could read a shorter version covering the point in fewer words. Bishop Easterling agreed as long as the substance of the request was present in what he was going to read.

The ruling of law was regarding the actions of the Clergy Executive Session of the 2019 Annual Conference. He stated that, "On Wednesday afternoon, we voted to receive two candidates, one for commissioning and one for ordination, who are according to what we know, in same sex relationships within same sex marriages and therefore ineligible for ordination and commissioning."

"The Executive (clergy) Session was denied an opportunity to individually question the Board of Ordained Ministry and the two candidates" in question, Barnes said. The Book of Discipline requires a 75 percent approval vote.

Barnes first request asked if the "process of block voting to approve a group of candidates for ordination or commissioning violated the Disciplinary requirement for a 75 percent affirmative vote for each candidate, and prevented the clergy session from questioning the two candidates about whom Judicial Council Ruling 1368 was made."

His second request asked if the "vote to affirm the candidates was consistent with church law, in that only two-thirds of the clergy session voted to affirm the process of voting for all candidates as a block."

His final request asked whether "the two candidates in question" – Morrow and Heath-Mason – "are properly candidates for commissioning and ordination."

Easterling agreed that there was a ruling last year by the Judicial Council, Ruling 1368, which gave direction concerning a bishop's ability to involve themselves in the work of the Executive Session of the annual conference and "made it clear that it would be premature for a bishop to involve themselves in that aspect of the work."

Bishop Easterling said that the Book of Discipline gives her 30 days to respond to such requests, and that she would respond within that time.

Rev. C. Anthony Hunt, chair of the Board of Ordained Ministry, presented the BOOM report. The report is in the Journal under Reports in the Leadership section. In his report, he shared that the Board is comprised of 60 lay and clergy persons who serve on behalf of more than 1,200 persons under their care as either candidates for ministry, actively commissioned provisional members, Deacons and Elders in full connection, and retired members.

"As a board," Hunt said, "we are pleased to share that we have performed a full inquiry and examination as to discern the qualifications, the fitness and the readiness for ministry in The United Methodist Church of each of the persons being presented today or who will be ordained tonight and have been presented to our executive session as candidates for commissioning whom there are 11 and ordination and full membership, of which there are 13." Hunt took a moment of personal privilege on behalf of the Board of Ordained Ministry to thank Bishop Latrelle Easterling for her "ongoing prayers and support," as well as her guidance of their work. He also thanked Rev. John Nupp, Executive Minister for Call and Clergy Care, for his "outstanding staff leadership in managing, guiding and facilitating the perfecting of our practices for supporting clergy and those preparing for ordain and licensed ministry." Hunt asked for the plenary to acknowledge Nupp.

Rev. Scott Dale Shumaker, Provisional Registrar, introduced the provisional candidates, of which there were two, and the provisional Elders, of which there were nine. Rev. Al Hammer, Full Member Registrar, introduced those to join in full connection, of which there was one Deacon and 11 to be ordained as Elders, and one who was joining by recognition of orders.

Rev. Amy McCullough, Vice Chair of the Board of Ordained Ministry, joined at the podium by Nupp, Rev. Rebecca Iannicelli, and Delores Martin, Conference Lay Leader, presented the conference's "Sexual Ethics Policy," which she said was a "joint work." McCullough, Nupp,

Iannicelli and Rev. Tony Love began the process of meeting together to craft the policy over an 18-month period. They wanted to create a policy to meeting the needs of the congregations and the people of the Baltimore-Washington Conference. Working collaboratively, the group reviewed existing policies of other Annual Conferences and then drafted a policy that was revised several times by the BOOM, the Cabinet and the Bishop's Office. The policy was shared with the Conference Chancellor and they collaborated with the General Commission on the Status and Role of Women (COSROW). During the process, they also began implementing it. In January 2019, Becky Posey Williams trained more than 600 clergy on sexual ethics "to understand and adhere to the standards of the policy." McCullough explained that pieces of the policy were also covered in the Book of Discipline and the policy did not replicate what was already there but "to work in tandem with that."

Nupp added that if the plenary chose to enact the policy at the session, there would be a special link on the BWC website dedicated to the policy that included a fillable form to report an incident and a flyer with a toll-free number for reporting an incident or discussing an incident with the COSROW contact in Chicago. He said their hope is that the form and flyer be displayed in "every single faith community and church" because this is a serious problem for members and anyone visiting a church or faith community.

Bishop recognized Rev. Tiffany Patterson, Presbury UMC in Edgewood, who rose to offer an amendment to the policy. The amendment was to the first sentence of section VII, as follows: "Bishops or their designees shall establish and offer to all parties a Response Team that stands ready to be deployed and available whenever an individual and congregation experiences a trauma." She spoke as a victim of clergy sexual misconduct, an abuse of power that changed the course of her and her family's life, her ministry and the congregation. She said that she was not speaking out of her pain, but "out of the strength that comes from God's healing and a call to advocate for victims of sexual misconduct." She said she was "incredibly grateful" for the policy and believed her amendment will "allow and ensure for every victim and congregation to have the opportunity to receive necessary support and resources for healing, along with effective assessment, intervention, training and accountability as needed."

Rev. Jessica Hayden, Old Otterbein UMC in Baltimore, spoke for the amendment as someone who worked with survivors of sexual trauma and recognized the need for support to be available not just to the survivor but for "all of the individuals that are adversely affected when ever sexual misconduct occurs." There was no speech against and the bishop called for the vote. The amendment carried. There was no further action on the policy. The bishop called for the vote by voice and hand. The policy was approved.

Bishop Easterling asked for a moment to respond to what appeared to be unanimous support of the policy. She emphasized the importance of the policy for the conference. She shared that a new response team had been established and was being trained and would be ready to be deployed soon. The bishop expressed her pride in the conference and its willingness to support the sexual ethics policy and to understand "it is a necessary and unfortunate, but necessary part of our work together." This concluded report of the Board of Ordained Ministry. The bishop thanked Hunt and asked the plenary to join her in thanking the Board of Ordained Ministry for "their incredible work."

Bishop Easterling returned to Resolution 9. Rev. Stephen Ricketts, Linganore UMC, asked what happens when a person who has to many absences is removed? Rev. Rudolph replied that an alternate would move into that slot. Brandon Savage, Salem UMC in Brookville, moved that the resolution be tabled, submitted to the Judicial Council for review, and reviewed at next year's Annual Conference Session. Rev. Bill Brown, Wesley Freedom, raised a point of order that an unpassed resolution could not go to Judicial Council and the bishop agreed. She said that because it was hypothetical and the body had not acted on it, the Judicial Council would not give an opinion on it. However, the resolution could be tabled. Savage asked how his request was different from General Conference 2019 when the Judicial Council was asked to review items going before that General Conference and issued rulings. Bishop Easterling explained that in 2016 the work was referred to the Commission on a Way Forward and the process was different. She explained that the resolution required some action by the body and if they supported it, it could then be referred as the Rules Chair mentioned earlier the he was going to request a Declaratory Decision if the resolution was passed. The motion was withdrawn.

Rev. Maidstone Mulenga spoke against the resolution based on Judicial Council Decision 592, which said, "all requirements for qualification, election, and service of the delegates are contained in the Discipline are powers reserved for the General Conference." He believed the Judicial Council would rule that we don't have the authority to make the rule and it will have been a waste of time. Gorman, Rules Chair, raised a Point of Information, that if Mulenga's interpretation was correct that would mean that the Conference's current policy is also out of order.

Rev. Sarah Dorrance, Middletown UMC, spoke in favor of the resolution because it holds "fellow clergy in accountability and our fellow delegates." While acknowledging the time demands of everyone, she said, "Let's have people who are representing us be present, so they understand the full things that are in front of us." She also called for the vote on the resolution. Seeing no other speakers against the amendment, the bishop invited Rudolph to make a final statement. The resolution passed.

Rev. Mark Gorman moved that under paragraph 2610.2 of the 2016 Book of Discipline, the annual conference request the following Declaratory Decision from the Judicial Council "in light of the Book of Discipline, paragraphs 13.1 and 2 and paragraph 34, as well as judicial Council decision 592." The question is, "can an annual conference adopt attendance policies for delegates to the General and Jurisdictional conferences? And, can those policies include consequences such as removal or reporting attendance records to the annual conference?" Bishop Easterling called for a vote and the referral passed.

Ballot 4 for Lay and Clergy Delegates was held after a prayer video from Bishop Peggy Johnson. Megan Blizzard was elected as the second lay delegate and Rev. Ginger Gaines-Cirelli was elected as the third clergy delegate.

Bishop Easterling invited Carlene Vollmer, Resource Consultant for Cokesbury, to make a presentation. In her introduction, Vollmer said that she is a member of the staff of the United Methodist Publishing House, which includes the work of Cokesbury, Abingdon Press and the Common English Bible. She invited people to come by the Ministry Resource Center in the Harborside Ballroom.

Bishop Eastering introduced the Black College Fund Ambassador, James Cognan, a candidate for ordination in the Baltimore-Washington Conference, a scholar-athlete, and Magna Cum Laude graduate of Claflin University in Orangeburg, South Carolina. In August 2016, he enrolled at Yale University where he received a full scholarship to pursue his Master of Divinity degree. He is a former seminary intern of Hope United Methodist Church in Southfield, Mich., and the UMC of the Resurrection in Leawood, Kansas.

Cogman, gave a rousing, inspiring, passionate presentation beginning with the declaration, "I am somebody" – poor, destitute, always standing tall, making mistakes, walking differently, dressing differently, a different face, maybe a different language, a different race but must be respected and always protected, never rejected – "because I am a child of God."

He greeted the gathering on behalf of Dr. Cynthia Bond Hopson, Assistant General Secretary for the Black College Fund and Ethnic Programs. Claflin, founded in 1869 by two Methodist missionaries, Governor William Claflin and his son Lee, is the oldest historically Black college or University in South Carolina. He was drawn to the school because it "epitomizes the maintenance of tradition while embracing constant evolution." The diverse school taught him to think out of the box and to "realize there is no limit to what one can accomplish." He said that was what the school did for him – he arrived "a student and left a scholar, a narrow perspective but left an open-minded world traveler, confused but left with a sense of call, a baseball player but left out a preacher… I can say that I would not be the man or minister I am today without God, my family, Yale, but most importantly Claflin University."

Cogman, a representative of The Black College Fund, said it represents 11 historically Black colleges and universities affiliated with the UMC. Support of the fund allows students like him and the other 15,999 students attending the institutions opportunities to be successful. He was proud to announce that his home conference, the Baltimore-Washington Annual Conference, paid 100.4 percent of its apportionment. He thanked the annual conference for its support and asked for the continued support of the fund. He then ended, repeating, "I am somebody, you are somebody. We are united to love." Cheers and resounding applause erupted. His proud mother, Rev. Johnsie Cogman, new District Superintendent of the Washington East District, came to the stage for a photograph with him and the Bishop.

The conference secretary read several announcements including instructions for the Ordination Session. The Bishop thanked Rosalind Pinkney, Washington District Lay Leader, for joining the dais. Rev. Rudy Bropleh was asked to offer the prayer for lunch.

Fourth Plenary Session
Friday, May 31, 2019 | 2:00 p.m.

As people gathered, two guitar-playing singers, accompanied by piano and drums, led the singing of "Stand by Me," "Every Praise is to Our God," and "Open the Eyes of My Heart, Lord."

Bishop LaTrelle Easterling called the plenary session to order and announced that the delegation voting would continue. Christopher Broadwell, Lay Pastor at Cape St. Claire in Annapolis, asked the bishop to explain why she introduced herself with the pronouns "her, hers, she," and had heard several people introduce themselves using that language. The bishop invited a member of BWARM to come and offer an explanation. Rev. Julie Wilson explained, "When you see a person, we assume their gender" based on appearance and assume it is the "gender that they were assigned at birth." Everyone is not the gender identity they appear to be. She said that people who are "cisgendered of the gender assigned at birth" are clear about their pronouns," it helps those who are not cisgendered or are gender queer or transgender feel more comfortable "being open and honest about their pronouns."

Bishop Easterling welcomed Richard Willson, Lay Leader of the Cumberland-Hagerstown District, to the dais. The bishop asked the new district superintendents to come forward. Rev. Johnsie Cogman, the new district superintendent of the Washington East District, and Rev. John Wonderlich, new superintendent of the Cumberland-Hagerstown District, were introduced and celebrated.

As she announced the fifth ballot, Bishop Easterling asked that the prayer video by Bishop Sudarshana Devadhar, Bishop of the New England Annual Conference, be shown. Melissa Lauber, BWC Director of Communications, was elected by the laity and the clergy elected Rev. C. Anthony Hunt.

Bishop Easterling welcomed Dr. Scott L. Johnson from the Upper New York Annual Conference to the dais for the Laity Address.

Dr. Johnson's roles in The United Methodist Church have been numerous and significant. He was elected Lay Leader of former Western New York Annual Conference in 2004 and 2008 and served as first conference lay leader of the Upper New York Annual Conference 2010–2016. In 2008, he was elected President of the Association of Annual Conference Lay Leaders and served two terms. Elected twice as a delegate to General Conference, he led the Upper New York delegation in 2012. He was part of the Council of Bishop's Call to Action Team and the Commission on a Way Forward. Johnson currently serves as pastor of First UMC of Buffalo.

Johnson thanked BWC Lay Leader, Delores Martin, for being a truth teller and said that everything they did as an association and as a Jurisdictional Table of Conference Lay Leaders, was better because of her. He also thanked Bishop Easterling for her hospitality and her leadership across the United Methodist connection.

He said that he had been asked to share thoughts about the "current moment in the church," from his perspective as a member on the Commission on the Way Forward.
This gave him pause because his thought was that the work of the commission was done, and they had "ceased to meet." He explained that the commission knew that not everyone would be pleased with what they did.

"The Church has turned the proverbial page," he said, "and our shared story is still being written." Citing the recent HBO Games of Thrones finale, he asked the BWC members to think about what it means to be part of an ongoing story that moves in directions they weren't anticipating. But he also assured them that God, who is the author of our story, is indeed engaged with, in, through and around you. "Make sure," Johnson stressed, "that you are playing your part in the unfolding story of The United Methodist Church."

The bishop called for a sixth ballot. Greg Witte, Cedar Grove UMC in Deale, moved that Resolution 2 be "untabled" before moving to another resolution. The motion was seconded. The motion did not pass. And the bishop again called for the sixth ballot.

Angela Pearson, Emmanuel UMC in Berlin, who said she had planned to make the same motion, requested a moment of privilege. Bishop Easterling said that the chair was "trying to be very respectful of moments of privilege" and that there was much business to complete. She reminded all that the young people had asked that the annual conference "try to move through our business in as graceful and expeditious manner as we could." The bishop asked the nature of the personal privilege.

The response was that the personal privilege was to "talk about all and all voices being respectfully heard." The bishop honored the request and asked that the speaker be succinct. Pearson said that she was from a "tradition of Eastern Europe suppression and oppression of being able to speak your truth." She spoke about the difficulty of the current times and the challenge for people to hear each other and said that it was important for all voices, "whether they are the majority or not" to be listened to. She expressed concern that the previous day, the "minority vote" was not given the "grace of the discussion on Resolution 2 in the same way in which we've looked at other topics." She was disturbed and concerned that "there's an element to this body that feel they cannot speak up because perhaps they are in the minority." She thanked Bishop Easterling for her time.

Matt Sichel, lay member, Wesley UMC in Hampstead, asked for a division of the house on the last question or to use the voting devices. Bishop Easterling asked if this was in terms of the tabling and it was. She said she believed it was clearly a decision to let that remain tabled. Sichel asked if he could ask for a division of the house. Bishop Easterling replied that the division could only occur before the question had been moved and that once the question had been moved and voted upon, the division of the house is out of order.

After listening to the video from Bishop Jeremiah J. Park, resident bishop of the Harrisburg Area, laity ballot 6 was completed and there was no election. Rev. Mary Jo Sims, retired clergy, asked for a brief moment of privilege. She reminded the clergy of being the most the diverse conference in the connectional system and asked that the clergy consider age, ethnicity, and order (Deacon and Elder). There was no election on clergy ballot 6.

Someone asked for an explanation of the 51 invalid votes on clergy ballot 6. Bishop Easterling asked for Pagett or Dave Schoeller to provide an explanation. Gemma, from Pagett, explained that the invalid votes meant that the individuals did not make the maximum number of selections on the ballot. Bishop Easterling reminded the voters that their ballots would be invalid if they did not vote for the number of persons needing to be selected. Gemma also reminded the voters to note the names of individuals already elected because if they were voted on again that would invalidate their ballot because too few choices would be made.

Rev. Jeff Jones, North Bethesda UMC, made a motion to stop the list of clergy at those names that received 10 votes so the last three or four pages won't scroll up. The motion was seconded. The motion passed.

Rev. Kevin Baker, Oakdale UMC, asked if it would be possible to table the rest of the amendments until the work was completed. The bishop replied that while he was allowed to make the motion, the people bringing the resolutions had given thought to not wanting to cause the session to either go late or "interfere with our promise to prioritize our young people tomorrow." She said that if the makers of the resolutions were given the opportunity, she thought they would move the work along. Baker asked if the bishop was asking him not to make the motion to which she replied that he asked a question and she gave an answer.

Baker decided to make the motion; it was seconded. The motion did not pass. Rev. Sandi Johnson, Deaf Ministries, asked if they could see the clergy names again now that there was a limit of 10 to the number would be able to see. Bishop agreed to show the names again on the next ballot.

Dan Ruben, Havre De Grace UMC, made a motion to do Resolution 18 next and the bishop ruled it out of order.

Rev. Debbie Scott, Lovely Lane, presented Resolution 10, "A Resolution to Call Us Back to Our Methodist Roots," to be sent to General Conference 2020. She requested the resolution be moved forward to General Conference and let them perfect it. Matthew Monk, St. John's in Baltimore, asked for a moment of personal privilege. He affirmed the resolution and invited everyone to St. John's after the "Easter conference happens" at Lovely Lane. The bishop said it was a speech for.

An unidentified person made a speech against the resolution. He agreed with the "ideals" of the resolution. His concern was that if one went back to 1784, there would be no gender inclusion and no equality for African Americans. He would be for it if it was rewritten and did not romanticize the history of Methodism.

Rev. Daniel Montague, Fork, offered an amendment to the resolution, striking everything after the word "roots" on line 36 to the end of line 37. The motion was seconded. Scott accepted the amendment.

Joshua Hamlet, Hall UMC in Glen Burnie, asked for a clarification of the meaning of lines 27 to 31 of the resolution. Scott responded that she was trying to include some of the church's history regarding slavery.

Rev. Douglas Tzan, St. Paul's UMC in Sykesville, offered an amendment to line 9 to delete "a decaying institutionalized" and insert "the" to read, "to renew the church." Strike the of beginning on line 10 at "in response to those 18th century Anglicans" and all of line 11. Strike line 13 after "freedom," the words "and created a vision of justice and liberation." Strike line 14 and 15, and line 22 through 31.

A point of order was raised that the proposed amendment was a substitution. Bishop Easterling asked Tzan how many more strikes he had, and he had one with two additions. Bishop Easterling ruled that it was an amendment by substitution. He agreed to submit it as such.

Rev. Scott withdrew the resolution in light of the time. She said they were willing to withdraw and perfect it and send it to General Conference on their own.

Resolution 11, "A Resolution Calling for an Adjoined/Special Session of Annual Conference," was brought forward in consultation with the bishop by Scott, who was standing with Phil Potter, CFA chair, and John Strawbridge, Trustee Chair. Scott asked that it be referred to Bishop Easterling. The bishop received it.

Resolution 12, "A Resolution for Representation of LGBTQIA+ Persons on Conference Commissions, Committees and Agencies," was presented by Scott and Rev. Angela Flanagan, co-chairs of the Advocacy Committee of BWARM. They were joined on this stage by members of the committee that worked on writing the resolution for BWARM. Rev. Kirkland Reynolds, Chevy Chase UMC, introduced the resolution that intentionally includes LGBTQIA+ people in conference ministries.

Scott advised that the resolution involved a rules change and left it to the bishop's discretion to determine whether a vote was required. Rev. Mark Gorman, Rules Committee Chair, explained that it does not require a rules change because this was a policy issue. The resolution was referred to the Connectional Table for action.

Resolution 13, "Resolution on Conservation of Conference Ministry Funding," was presented by Mittie Quinn, lay member to annual conference. The resolution was to put the Baltimore-Washington Conference on record, "speaking into what we value and where we want to see our funds directed to fulfill our mission and resource local church ministry and not to fund church trials." Scott stated that the resolution had received concurrence by the Connectional Table and recognizing it as aspirational, requested it be referred to the Conference Council on Finance and Administration. Bishop Easterling concurred.

Daniel Colbert, Silver Spring UMC, presented Resolution 14, "Resolution on Doing No Harm through the Ordination Prohibition." Colbert explained that the "whereas clauses" for the next three resolutions were quite long and that they had a number of footnotes. He stressed that they are grounded in our Wesleyan heritage. They start with the first General Rule, "Do no harm" and then apply each element of the Wesleyan Quadrilateral (Scripture, tradition, reason and experience). The resolutions "share a simple truth" that "the punitive polices of the Traditional Plan passed by the Special General Conference do great harm to our LGBTQIA+ siblings in Christ." The resolution aspires that the Book of Discipline ban on LGBTQIA+ clergy and candidates for ordination not be binding on our conference.

Scott explained that the Connectional Table did not concur with the resolution and that it is aspirational. She asked that it be referred to the Board of Ordained Ministry. Bishop Easterling referred it.

Megan Blizzard introduced Resolution 15, "Resolution to Do No Harm Through Marriage Prohibition." She shared recent research that shows "consistently higher rates of suicide, suicide attempts and suicidal ideation among LGBTQIA youth and young adults." She continued, "while religious identity lowers the risk of suicide in the heterosexual young people, the opposite is true for LBGTQIA+ young people. Affiliating with the faith tradition actually increases the risk of suicide for us [young people]." The resolution aspires to "understand the pertinent paragraphs of the Book of Disciple as nonbinding because it is in direct contradiction to the very first rule, Do No Harm."

Scott said that the aspirational resolution had concurrence with the Connectional Table and requested it be referred to the Discipleship Council. The bishop referred it.

Bishop Easterling recognized Rev. Amanda McMurtrey, Mayo UMC in Edgewater. She said that she "greatly appreciated" what BWARM and Scott were doing. However, the discussions around her indicated that some of the body did not "fully comprehend" what was happening relating to the "aspirational nature" of the resolutions and what "referring to these different groups" was doing. It appeared some people felt their voices were not being heard nor their votes. She asked that someone explain to the body the process that was being used.

Bishop Easterling explained, "When a resolution is presented to the body as aspirational, it does not force the annual conference to act in a particular way nor constrict it from acting in a particular way." While the hope is that some action will be taken, the resolutions being referred do not change any of the ways the conference is conducting itself or the business it is currently doing. The makers of the resolutions are simply "depositing them with the board and agencies they feel are most impacted by the work or would try to carry out the work within the annual conference." She reiterated that the resolutions were aspirational and not binding on this conference and would not change the way conference was conducting business currently.

Rev. Leo Yates, Jr., Deacon, presented Resolution 16, "Resolution to Do No Harm Across the Northeast Jurisdiction." He explained that the resolution builds on the previous two resolutions and asked that the resolution be shared with conference secretaries and the bishops and each annual conference of our jurisdiction. The resolution urges the Northeast Jurisdiction bishops to work together to develop nondiscriminatory LGBTQIA+ ministries, policies, and procedures governing our annual conferences. He concluded that the resolution "seeks to strengthen our connection." The resolution was referred to the bishop and the conference secretary.

Rev. Julie Wilson, Deacon, presented Resolution 17, "Resolution to Use Conference Funds to Support LGBTQIA+ Faithful and Their Allies." The resolution addressed the difficulty in supporting a vision and mission with our LGBTQIA+ siblings without any financial support. With a focus on the next generation, the resolution asked the conference to make a commitment to use conference funds in the support of ministry with the LGBTQIA+ community, which includes young people struggling with issues of self-identity, suicide ideation, etc. She concluded, "This resolution will help expand our resources to be fully inclusive as a church the way that God calls us to be." Scott said that the resolution received concurrence by the Connectional Table and was aspirational. The resolution was referred to the Conference Council on Finance and Administration with the bishop's agreement.

Resolution 18, "Resolution to Affiliate with the Western Jurisdiction," was presented by Rev. Angela Flanagan, Silver Spring UMC. She explained that as a conference we have continually voted for resolutions calling for an inclusive church. The Western Jurisdiction has been operating as an inclusive church and invited others to join them. The resolution accepts the offer and Flanagan moved its adoption. Bishop Easterling responded that her understanding was that the resolution was not aspirational in nature.

Rev. Bryant Oskvig made the following motion to amend by substitution:
"WHEREAS, the 2016 Discipline precludes full ministry to LGBTQIA+ persons and restricts the ministry by LGBTQIA+ persons; and

"WHEREAS, the General Conference of 2019 created public perceptions that have disinclined LGBTQIA+ persons and their allies from involvement and membership in The United Methodist Church; and

"WHEREAS, the General Conference of 2019 enacted more prescribed punitive enforcement measures for the restrictions and curtailments of ministry as legislated in the 2016 Discipline; and

"WHEREAS, the Baltimore-Washington Conference has a long history of meaningfully deep ministry for and with LGBTQIA+ persons; and

"WHEREAS, ¶590 of the 2016 Book of Discipline allows for the creation of a mission to "provide and develop ministry with a particular group or region whose potential and needs cannot be met within the existing structures and resources of annual or district conference(s)."

"WHEREAS, the establishment of mission for the development and continuation of current full ministry with and for LGBTQIA+ persons is a local congregational endeavor and not require any expenditure of Annual Conference funds for support;

"THEREFORE BE IT RESOLVED that the Baltimore-Washington Conference establish a mission for LGBTQIA+ persons within the conference in consultation with the General Board of Global Ministry as stipulated in the Book of Discipline, ¶591.2.

"THEREFORE BE IT FURTHER RESOLVED that as stated in the Book of Discipline, ¶591.4, the Bishop of the Baltimore-Washington Conference shall preside over the mission.

"THEREFORE BE IT FURTHER RESOLVED that the Discipleship Council in consultation with the Steering Committee of BWARM shall develop a leadership structure and secure leadership for the mission by December 31, 2019.

"THEREFORE BE IT FURTHER RESOLVED the Discipleship Council in consultation with the Steering Committee of BWARM shall develop a process by which congregations may designate themselves as part of the mission, and the Annual Conference will publicize the process prior to November 15, 2019.

"THEREFORE BE IT FURTHER RESOLVED that the Mission is to officially begin prior to January 1, 2020."

Bishop Easterling recognized Rev. Katie Bishop, Greater Brunswick Charge, who raised a point of order regarding the financial implications of the resolution and the need for CFA to rule before the body could consider the resolution. Bishop Easterling agreed that creating a Mission Conference within the Baltimore-Washington Conference area would have financial implications. Oskvig said it was a Mission and not a Mission Conference. The bishop asked for a moment to confer with the chancellor and for a copy of the proposed amendment by substitution.

She reported back that, in consultation with the chancellor and the parliamentarian, there appeared to be a way for the matter to be resolved that honors what the session was trying to do in terms of being judicious with the time, the maker of the original motion agreed to accept this as a substitute motion that would then be referred to the Discipleship Council.

Rev. Bishop reminded Bishop Easterling that she had raised a point of order and that should have superseded everything, and the session would not yet be on the substitution. She said the "piece of legislation goes against our constitution and therefore, is out of order" and that the body could not take it up. The bishop agreed that she was correct on the original piece of legislation and that it was voted non-concurrence by the Connectional Table. She explained that the substitution had been accepted and was to be referred to the Discipleship Council for "discernment and analysis." That action would not bind the annual conference to anything at that time.

Rev. Bishop replied that "as a pastor trying hard to walk in the middle right now, and I know there's not a middle. I know that. I've seen that." She felt that the point of order motion would make it so that nothing could be referred.

Bishop Easterling explained that a point of order does not require a second; there is no debate and no amendment. It interrupts everything. It does not allow for any of the normal parliamentary procedures. Bishop Easterling apologized that Rev. Bishop was not recognized in the proper order. She ruled the pastor's point of order out of order. She added that "in the spirit of what's trying to be accomplished here, something was offered, and a way forward that does not bind the conference, does not require action on the conference right now, but would refer it to a committee within the conference to offer further discernment gives us a path forward."

Rev. Bishop asked if the resolutions going to committee would come back to the body if anything were changed. Bishop Easterling assured her that no action could be taken until it was brought back to the Annual Conference Session. The resolutions that were aspirational, if voted on, would not have led the conference "to act in anyway at all." The substitute motion does not violate the Book of Discipline and would be referred to committee. It would come back to the Annual Conference Session before any action could be taken on it.

Rev. Bishop said that as somebody in the annual conference, "who is longing to find a way to hold us together," she went to UMC Next on behalf of the annual conference. Her hope was that the conference "could make sure there are many voices who are hearing and experiencing and talking about this particular piece of legislation so that everyone might be able to share their hopes and dreams for the future of the church."

Bishop Easterling reflected on the Samoan Circle Process from the previous morning as way to model "how we can engage" in "very contentious and emotion-laden topics." She said that the Connectional Table and Discipleship Ministries have been trying to find ways to include the voices of more people. She emphasized the importance of pastors and lay leaders and other persons that receive information from the conference office, sharing it with other people. And, when there are meetings or Samoan Circle processes on a district or in a cluster, let people know about it and perhaps they might come.

She asked those voting to prepare for the Ballot 7. Nathan Jones, Epworth UMC in Cockeysville, asked about the dates indicated in the substitution amendment needing to be changed. The bishop explained that no action was required on the dates.

Mittie Quinn, lay member, offered a motion that on the next ballot, the top three laity and the top two clergy round out the General Conference delegation. Bishop Easterling received the motion on behalf of the laity. Clergy made the motion on its behalf. The laity motion passed.

Bishop Easterling then asked the clergy to vote on the motion that the top two vote getters round out the clergy delegation. The motion passed.

Rev. Stephen Tillett, Asbury-Broadneck UMC, requested a division on the vote that the bishop clarified was an up and down vote, and that he was really asking for a recount using the voting devices. It was clarified that the vote was just for clergy.

Rev. Charles Harrell, retired clergy, made a point of order. It appeared to him that laity might have voted when it should have been only clergy. Bishop Easterling said that he was correct and that the voting devices would only allow clergy to vote.

A point of order was raised regarding an earlier vote to un-table Resolution 2 and the bishop did not allow the voting devices because the vote had already been taken. He said in the present situation, the vote had been taken, but the bishop said they were going to use the devices to vote again.

Bishop Easterling said she recalled that a vote had been taken prior to the parliamentary procedure that was asked to be used. Matt Sichel said he asked for "exactly what was just asked for on the vote to lift Resolution 2 off the table." He recounted that a hand vote and voice was taken that he said did not look as close as it was called. He requested to do the vote again with the voting device and the bishop rules against that because the vote had already been taken.

Bishop Easterling explained that Sichel asked for a division of the house on un-tabling a motion that had already been voted on. Because the language he used left her uncertain, she went with the way it was asked. She asked if what he wanted was in fact a recount. The response was, "I guess so." He said that he requested the voting devices be used at the time. He said that was what he was trying to say. The bishop again confirmed with him that he did ask for a division of the house. And he replied that he did and confused the words. She returned to the matter at hand and then, if necessary, come back to Sichel's issue.

A clergy ballot was held to decide if on the next ballot, the top two vote getters would complete the clergy delegation to General Conference. The motion carried.

Rev. C. Anthony Hunt, Epworth Chapel UMC, asked if there was anything in the rules that required delegates elected to receive 50% of the vote because that was not in the motion. Bishop Easterling responded that the rules do say that. Hunt asked if there was a need to suspend the rules to move forward. A vote by laity and clergy to suspend the rules was taken using the devices. The vote passed.

Rev. Stephen Tillett, Asbury-Broadneck UMC, was recognized and said, "I truly, truly hope that the New England Patriots go 0 and 16." This was met with laughter, applause and cheers. The bishop said she will simply say, "You hate us, cause you ain't us." Also met with laughter.

A motion was made for a recount of Resolution 2. Bishop Easterling explained that balloting would occur first.

Marcella Kehr, Chase UMC in Middle River, laity, asked if there was intent to redo the laity vote, to which the bishop responded, "Yes."

Mark Gorman raised a point of order. He said one option was for the bishop to declare a "final ballot" and take the list in order. The other option would be to come back after Ordination Service. He believed it was best to do the Discipleship Ministry report before ordination. Bishop said the rule was that an hour before the final ballot, she could call for a final ballot and "fill in the slots using that final ballot." Gorman responded that was correct and cited section 3009 of the rules.

Rev. Bryant Oskvig, Georgetown Extension Ministries, moved that the plenary suspend the rules and take three ballots. The first would be for General Conference delegates, the second for Jurisdictional Conference, and the third for two alternates. Bishop responded that with only 40 minutes remaining, she had to receive the Stewardship Report as well as the Connectional Ministry Report. Easterling concluded that to finish the business of Annual Conference Session, the plenary would return to the ballroom after the Service of Ordination.

A vote was taken to do a recount to untable Resolution 2, which required one-third majority. The vote did not pass.

Rev. Cary James, Board of Pensions, presented a report of their recommendations. The complete report is in the Reports section of the Journal. He reported that the rate changes from Wespath were minimal for the coming year and the local church and participant rates for HealthFlex were kept the same for 2020.

He then discussed the constitutionality of disaffiliation agreements. The Judicial Council established a three-part test to determine if a disaffiliation petition is constitutional. (See Judicial Council Decision No. 1329.)

He then explained the "Unfunded Pension Obligations." The Book of Discipline amended ¶1504 which specifies that Wespath will determine the aggregate funding obligations of the annual conference using market factors. The annual conference will determine the local church share. Disaffiliating churches will pay a "Withdrawal Liability" in an amount equal to its pro rata share of the aggregate funding obligation. The BWC Procedure will be issued on October 15, 2019, and it will include the sharing formula.

He concluded with a discussion of the conference unfunded obligations that were BWC Pension Liabilities of $54.3 million, and Retiree Medical Liabilities of $6.1 million. The committee will receive updated figures from Wespath in September 2019. The report and its recommendations were approved.

Phil Potter, chair of the Council on Finance and Administration, presented their report. He said that it was an important budget for 2020. He directed everyone to the conference website for all of the slides he was presenting. The 2020 benevolence factor, each church's mission share, remained at 17.6%, the same as 2019. The collection rate was reduced from 92% in 2019 to 91% for 2020 to be consistent with actual performance. The overall budget was reduced by $88,000. The budget assumption for 2020 was $14.0 million apportionment income. Apportionment income decreased by $247,000. There were slight increases for the districts and ministry teams "as stewardship areas absorb the overall reduction".

Being aware of the challenges facing the annual conference, a Budget Risk Management Plan (a 4-year contingency plan) has been put in place should the need arise. The same proposal was presented last year. The CFA Recommendations were presented.

Rev. Charles Harrell rose with two questions. Regarding the Risk Management plan, he asked if the items that made up the $29 million were in priority order or simply options on the table. Potter said they were options on the table; however, they would likely first use the money from the reserves CFA established. Harrell's second question was related to the pension report and to disaffiliation agreements. He was concerned about future liability for medical expenses. Rev. Carey James explained that part of Wespath's analysis that they're going to use to determine that market rate "will be in this point in time." When the numbers from Wespath come out in September, the BWC Board of Pensions, will come up with a formula for each of its churches. Harrell suggested the board include some actuarial figure.

Rev. Maidstone Mulenga, Director of Communications for the Council of Bishops, asked if the BWC is "dedicated to paying 100% of apportionment to all seven funds of the General Church." Rev. Daryl Williams, CFA vice-chair, responded that the BWC "will be paying its global share in full as we have for the last decade."

Deborah Haskins, Christ UMC, noted that the Abundant Health budget was among the lowest budgeted items and had been reduced. She was concerned that there are such great needs in our communities. She asked if moving forward there was going to be an increase in that budget. Williams said he could not answer that question directly but assumed that as ministries were created and fulfilling needs, CFA will look at funding that need as necessary.

Bishop Easterling called for a vote on the report and it was approved. Paul Eichelberger, Conference Treasurer, came to the podium to give a more detailed answer to Haskins' question. He said that the Abundant Health budget would go up next year. What made it go down was that there was no Zimbabwe partnership school in the 2020 budget and it would return to the budget in 2021.

Kim Ayres, Chair of the Commission on Equitable Compensation, presented her Committee's recommendation for the minimum salary for 2020 be increased by 2 percent, or $880, to $44,492. No change was recommended to the housing allowance. This follows a trend of the last three years to increase minimum salary by 2 percent. The recommendations were approved.

Charlie Moore came forward to celebrate and bring greetings in the name of Jesus Christ from the Board of Directors of Africa University along with Vice Chancellor Munahse Furusa, the faculty, administration and most of all the students of Africa University. He was joined by Rev. Lloyd Rollins and Karen Conroy, development staff members of Africa University, who presented Bishop Easterling and CFA President Phil Potter, a "recognition of a continuation of our conferences payment of over 100% in conference apportionment to Africa University." Moore who is Chair of the Finance Committee of the Africa University Board of Directors, reported that the university is strong and thriving in developing leaders for the continent of Africa. Since Vice Chancellor Furusa took over leadership of the university four years ago, enrollment has increased 40% from 1,800 students to over 2,500. The school would be celebrating its 25th graduating class, bringing the total that have graduated to over 8,000. In the midst of dire economic and political situations, the university continues to thrive financially. A current financial campaign to raise $50 million for endowment purposes and infrastructure improvement is at 98.3% of that goal. Lastly, he showed a picture of the swimming pool on the Africa University Campus for which the conference raised a love offering in honor of the retirement of Bishop and Mrs. Matthews. It was dedicated in February 2019.

Bishop Easterling asked for a hand for the Stewardship Team for their work.

The bishop announced that she received a note from Rev. Jackson Day that he was withdrawing Resolution 19. Rev. Scott Shumaker asked everyone to clean out the area as quickly as possible by taking everything they had in the room and straightening the chairs in the row because there was not going to be enough time if the session went past 5 o'clock.

Bishop Easterling reminded the plenary that it suspended the rules of the session and she explained the voting process for the remaining members of the delegation. The process was approved in separate votes by laity and clergy.

Rev. Stephen Tillett asked for a point of information on the church properties. He asked if there was going to be any opportunity to hear the report and discuss it. The bishop responded that one of the items that had to be voted on was moving to allow the closure of those churches.

Laity voted to round out the three remaining slots for General Conference delegates. Elected on this 7th ballot were Ken Ow with 54.79%, Sarah Ford with 41.32% and Daniel Colbert with 40.41%.

Bishop Easterling was reminded that she agreed to show the clergy list before the vote. The clergy elected Giovanni Arroyo with 53.12% and Sarah Schlieckert with 40.72%. The bishop asked that laity prepare to vote for six jurisdictional lay delegates. Vivian Moore, laity, Creasaptown, requested a moment of personal privilege. She said she thought it was really important for the delegation to represent the diversity of the BWC and said that the six delegates to General Conference were "all from the metropolitan area." She encouraged the laity to "consider the rest of the conference in electing our delegates to jurisdiction. Megan Blizzard, who said she was the second laity delegate elected, said she is from the Western Region at Westminster UMC.

Becky Hine from, Benevola UMC, asked the bishop to clarify who they can vote for and how many people they were voting for. Bishop explained the next voting would be a laity ballot for Jurisdictional Conference. The six people being voted on were reserves to those elected for General Conference, so if a delegate to General Conference was unable to participate, a reserve would move up to replace them on the General Conference delegation. The General and Jurisdictional delegates attend the Jurisdictional Conference, which will be held in Baltimore-Washington Conference in 2020. Rev. Gorman was asked to pray as the plenary prepared to vote.

Rev. Stephen Ricketts, Linganore, asked if there was room in the schedule to move the ordination service back 15 minutes. Bishop Easterling said no because there were people traveling from long distances to attend and who knew ordination started at 7 p.m. She said that it was apparent that the session would continue after the service. During the voting, someone asked if they could see the last clergy voting before voting again.

The six NEJ Laity delegates elected on Ballot 1 in order of votes received were: Chris Schlieckert (52.20%), Christie Latona (49.65%), Tracy Collins (47.10%), Sharon Milton, (46.17%), Nathan Jones (42.92%) and Chet Jechura (39.68%).

The bishop explained what would happen in terms of the dinner schedule if ordination were pushed back to 7:30 p.m. Then the clergy vote began. The NEJ Clergy delegates elected on Ballot 1 in order of votes received were: Stacey Cole-Wilson (62.41%), JW Park (47.52%), Leo Yates (43.97%), Conrad Link (40.07%), Kirkland Reynolds (35.46%) and Bryant Oskvig (33.33%).

Bishop Easterling pushed the Ordination Service back to 7:30 p.m. and asked the members to come back after the service and immediately commence voting on the Nominations Report. Rev. Bonnie McCubbin asked for a moment of personal privilege and shared that pushing the Ordination Service back to 7:30 p.m. puts an "undue hardship on small children trying to be there to see their parent ordained." The children generally go to bed before the service begins and that her son would probably not be able to attend. She said, "We need to work together to make things happen in the future." Bishop Easterling apologized. The conference secretary made announcements prior to dismissal.

Rev. Debbie Scott asked for an approximate time to return after ordination and the bishop said about 20 minutes. She hoped the body would be succinct and was really trying to not impose on the youth's time on Saturday as they had been planning for some time to come and celebrate their confirmations. Bishop introduced Linda Yost, the new United Methodist Women president, and asked her to offer the prayer as the assembly broke for dinner.

Ordination and Commissioning Worship Service
Friday, May 31, 2019 | 7:30 p.m.

Music played softly as family, friends, and annual conference members gathered. Marcia McFee opened the service exclaiming, "God is good!"

She welcomed everyone to an "exciting night," where "we affirm God's call on these people's lives and give thanks to God for this call to ministry through our baptism, which we all have." Speaking of the diverse gifts everyone brings to ministry, she declared the night a "celebration of the necessity of diversity." She continued, "This exciting ritual of commissioning and ordination embodies this very truth – we are never more fully alive than when we are in love with each other." Quoting Mikey Hart, Grateful Dead Drummer, who said, "Falling in love is falling in rhythm," McFee said that the night's services would be called "Rhythms of Love."

The assemblage would be "bringing our different rhythms together as we celebrate the love brought into the world tonight by those being commissioned and ordained for ministry within The United Methodist Church." She explained that the congregation would "encircle them as community, witnesses to their rite of passage, and call them to offer ministries of hope and justice for all people."

As McFee played a drum and the choir sang "Come Let Us Worship God," the procession began with bearers of symbols of faith and ordination (light, cross, baptismal bowl, Bible, Deacon's bowl and towel, chalice, paten, Elder's stole and Deacon's stole) coming forward and placing each item on the altar. With the choir singing a West African song, "Hallelujah," the commissionees and ordinands gathered around the elevated central table followed by sponsors who encircled them from the floor. The choir changed to a slow piece as the candidates on the elevated platform dipped their hands into the baptismal bowl and sent water out over the heads of those in the circle. After which, as the pianist played "God of Grace and God of Glory," they descended the elevated area and proceeded to their seats.

As the choir led the congregation in singing "God of Grace and God of Glory," and "Hallelujah," the clergy, Board of Ordained Ministry leaders, and Bishops Moore Koikoi and Easterling processed in.

Bishop Easterling greeted the congregation and led them in prayer. Bishop Moore Koikoi offered the "Recognition of Our Common Ministry." Bishop Easterling scooped up water in the baptismal vessel, let it flow from her hand and asked the congregation to say: "Remember your baptism and be thankful." The bishops descended from the platform and processed to the stage.

A soloist sang "O Love That Will Not Let Me Go" as young people walked about dipping palm leaves in bowls of water and sprinkling the congregation with water to help them remember their baptism. At the conclusion, Bishop Moore Koikoi spoke the words of the Gospel of John:1 and then said, "And in the beginning, God ordained that this day would come to fruition... So, I welcome you to God's ongoing revelation of God's plan for the church and for the world. Amen"

Conference Lay Leader Delores Martin, on behalf of local church congregations who first examined and approved the candidates, and Board of Ordained Ministry Chair, Rev. Anthony Hunt, on behalf of the Board of Ordained Ministry, which recommended the candidates, joined in presenting the candidates.

Rev. Scott Shumaker, Registrar for the Provisional Membership, announced the names of the persons to be commissioned as Deacons and the names of persons being commissioned for the work of an Elder. Each stood as his or her name was read. Rev. Al Hammer, Registrar for Full Members, read the names of persons to be ordained as each person stood.

Bishop Easterling presented the candidates to the congregation and asked that they declare their assent to the commissioning, ordination, or recognition. The bishop then proceeded with the General Examination of the candidates for commissioning, ordination and recognition stood facing her.

At the completion of the questions, the candidates turned and faced the congregation as the first verse of "How Shall I Come Before the Lord" was sung. As the congregation continued singing, those to be commissioned came forward.

Rev. Twanda Prioleau read "The Lesson For Commissioning," Acts 13:1-3. Bishop Easterling performed "The Examination of Persons Being Commissioned." The candidates knelt, facing the congregation. The bishop stood behind each candidate and laid hands upon the shoulders of each as she prayed for them. When Bishop Easterling came to Raphael Koikoi, she stepped back as a spirit-filled Bishop Cynthia Moore Koikoi came forward to the applause of the congregation, placed her hands upon her husband's shoulders, and commissioned him. Bishop Easterling continued with the remaining candidates. She then presented the newly commissioned ministers to the applause of the congregation.

Commissioned as Provisional Deacons were Deborah Burgio and T.C. Morrow.

Commissioned as Provisional Elders were Ian Collier, Gerald Elston, Ashley Hoover, Narae Kim, Raphael Koikoi, Dong Eun (Vivian) Lee, Jean Lee, Isaiah Redd, and Jeffrey Zalatoris.

The choir led the congregation in singing "Let the Glory of the Lord, Rise Upon Us" as the newly commissioned ministers returns to their seats.

McFee led the procession of the Christ candle and Bible to the elevated center platform, singing "Jesus, We Are Here" and beating her drum. Rev. Prioleau read Joel 2:28-29 and Ephesians 4:7-13. As the Christ candle and the Bible were returned to the altar, the congregation again sung, "Jesus We Are Here."

In her sermon, Bishop Easterling reminded the newly commissioned and those about to be ordained that they were not volunteers but servants. Volunteers, she said, decide when they'll show up. "You are servants of the living God," she said. "Lose yourself in the service of others."

She spoke about the various reasons people enter ministry and added that, whatever the reason, "every day they will be asked to put themselves on the line. And every moment God is asking the ultimate question. Oh, listen now. Are you ready to die to self and live for me?

"Living for Christ requires humility," she instructed. She talked about the dearth of humility in today's society. "Living for Christ means that you have and you are and you will continue to resist your egoist self." She reminded the class, "ego is not self-esteem." She quoted CS Lewis, who said, "Humility isn't thinking less of yourself; it's thinking of yourself less."

"Christ is the ultimate alchemist," the bishop said. "Christ is ultimately the one who brings us to transformation. But I also know, transformed lives transform, lives. When they see us walk different, they take notice. When they see us talk different, they take notice. When they see people abuse us and we smile and bless them anyway, they take notice. When they threaten to files charges on you, but you follow God anyway, they take notice."

She told those present, "We can't serve in fear. Fear and love cannot inhabit the same dwelling. And perfect love casts out all fear."

Bishop Easterling commended the class for continuing to follow their call, even after the Special Session of General Conference earlier this year. "You felt the tectonic shift and you have continued to say yes, anyhow," she said. "You are entering the ministry in a time in the church not seen in 150 years."

The bishop ended her sermon with the same benediction she offered to the class of 2018 at Wesley Theological Seminary saying, "Today marks the end of a season in your journey and yet, it is actually a new beginning. Your time of formation is not over. As a matter of fact, some of your greatest learning lies ahead."

"Empty yourself," she encouraged, "that you may be filled with the nondiscriminatory grace of God." Knowing that some of the new ministers may be sent to places where they may not be welcomed because of their race, orientation, language, ethnicity or gender, she urged them to "love the people, love the people and they will love you."

Rick Oursler then offered information on Seeds of Security, a program started by Bishop Easterling, which provides immediate temporary housing for people in need of protection from intimate partner violence. Seeds of Security collaborates with community organizations and has a network of contacts throughout all the districts. The organization began 2019. It now has more than $36,000 available to assist victims of domestic violence. Pastors were told that if they learn of someone in need of help, there is an e-mail hotline, sos@bwcumc.org, that is monitored. A challenge was made to churches and clusters and different United Methodist church groups to become monthly hotel room sponsors. An offering was taken to benefit Seeds of Security.

Delores Martin introduced the "Examination of Deacons and Elders" by reading the "unique qualities of a Deacon in the life of the church." Bishop Easterling then conducted the examination of the Deacon to be ordained. Martin then read the qualities of an Elder and the bishop conducted their examination. After prayer, the choir sang, "Veni Sancte Spiritus (Come Holy Spirit)." Bishop Cynthia Moore Koikoi prayed.

The candidate for deacon, Martina Martin Efodzi, knelt as she was ordained and the bishop,

Conference Lay Leader, district superintendent and her sponsors laid hands upon her. Bishop Easterling ordained each candidate as their sponsors, a district superintendent and the conference Lay Leader laid hands upon them. Each was also draped with a stole. Those ordained Elders were: Patricia Lynn Abell, Lillian Lynn Boyd, Andre Robert Briscoe Jr., Alexis Faith Brown, Henry Michael Cantley, Lemuel Dominquez, Kyle Durbin, Joseph Heath-Mason, Brenda Mcilwain, Jessica Statesmen Hayden, and Carissa Surber. Ronald E. Fleming Triplett's orders were recognized, and he was welcomed as an Elder in The United Methodist Church. The choir sang "Let the Glory of Our Lord Rise Among Us" as the newly ordained were celebrated.

The bishop gave an invitation for those who were experiencing a call to come forward where members of the Cabinet, BOOM and others were there to welcome them. Bishop Easterling prayed and gave thanks to God for "the anointing that has fallen on this place, for those commissioned and ordained to serve in Christ holy church," and for the young people who came forward to offer their lives to God in service. She concluded by praying, "May the power, the grace, the love and the anointing of God follow you every day of your life and may your cup overflow with love and may that love pour out into all creation."

Setting the Appointments
Marcia McFee invited the district superintendents to stand around the Bible at the center of the stage. All pastors and their lay leaders were asked to stand where they were. Bishop Easterling said that the Cabinet had met, "heard the needs of the community," and "heard the hearts of the community." They prayed and listened to the Holy Spirit. They made the appointments they felt God was calling them to make and the bishop asked that they be received in love. Bishop Easterling declared the appointments for the 2019-2020 Baltimore-Washington Conference to be set.

Bishop Easterling gave the dismissal with blessing. She announced that the annual conference was to reconvene by no later than10:30 p.m. to continue its work. The recessional hymn was "Draw the Circle Wide."

Fifth Plenary Session
Friday, May 31, 2019 | 10:30 p.m.

Bishop Easterling thanked the plenary for returning. She said that information had been brought to her attention and asked Rules Chair, Rev. Mark Gorman, to explain.

He rose for a point of order and also for a moment of personal privilege. The point of order was that ¶34 of The Book of Discipline was revised at the 2016 General Conference by constitutional amendment, which was voted upon by the annual conferences of The United Methodist Church. A key sentence was that "delegates shall be elected by a minimum of a simple majority of the ballots cast." Some of the delegates voted on earlier in the day, near the end of the slate, were not elected by a majority and those would need to be redone.

His moment of privilege was to explain that, as Rules Chair, according to paragraph 3002.5.b., he was to review and update all references to the Book of Discipline to reflect the most recent version of the Book of Discipline. He offered his sincere apologies to the bishop and the entire Annual Conference Session for failing to lead in that duty. The bishop accepted his apology and also apologized to the body for not catching the change.

While Pagett prepared for the voting, Bishop Easterling welcomed Sarah Ford, chair of

Nominations, to present the Leadership Report. Ford said that last year the committee instituted "Interest Forms" to better discern the gifts and talents needed and where they were needed. She asked everyone, from middle school to high school to young adults and retirees, to complete the Interest Form because they want to hear from all voices. The committee focused on diversity and inclusion. She announced the selection of Franklin Kevin Silberzahn as the new conference secretary and an assistant secretary to be selected soon. The slate was approved.

Deborah Johnson, Chair of the New Faith Expressions Board, and Rev. Bill Brown, Director of New Faith Expressions at the Baltimore-Washington Conference beginning July 1, came forward to present the Henry Denman Award for Evangelism. The award was given in each annual conference for evangelism expressed in word, sign and deed, and brings people into "a life transforming relationship with Jesus Christ." The clergy recipient was Rev. Alexis Peña Vasquez, Brook Hill UMC in Frederick, and the lay recipient was Linda Worthington, Chevy Chase UMC. Pastor Alexis was not present and he was recognized for his "tireless efforts" to grow weekly worship to an average of 45 people, expanding Bible Study to two nights per week, starting men's and women's groups, and leading people to Christ and a deeper relationship with Jesus." Linda Worthington was recognized as an "unrivaled advocate for the work of God found in the UMConnection newspaper." In addition to serving on BWC Communications for several years as a staff writer, she continues to volunteer as a writer and her stories "expands the number of people who are encouraged and equipped by new strategies for reaching people."

Rev. Jessica S. Hayden, chair, presented the Discipleship Council report and said they had accomplished a lot during the year. She began with the clarified vision they developed, that "Transformed Lives Transform Lives," and reintroduced the BWC's mission that "The Baltimore-Washington Conference inspires and equips local faith communities to develop disciples of Jesus Christ for the transformation of the world." (See "Reports" section in the Journal for the complete presentation.)

Highlights of the report included:
Approved Project Transformation DC through the Ministry Relationship Oversight Committee. The mission of the project is to engage young adults in purposeful leadership and ministry to support children in holistic development and to connect churches with communities.
Involved more than 630 people in providing feedback and engaging in conversations regarding one or more aspects of the realignment in the Discipleship Agency areas.
Awarded $40,000 in Mission Innovation Grants in Fall 2018.
Annual conference leaders are now at the center of decision-making.

Hayden advised that the Rules Committee chair and the conference secretary recommended that the realignment be presented as a report to allow it to be clearly presented as opposed to a series of resolutions. This provided annual conference members an opportunity to amend the report and vote it up or down. Connectional Table and Nominations also voted concurrence with the recommendations.

Rev. Gorman, Rules Chair, spoke saying that last year the Rules Committee requested inclusion to give concurrence or non-concurrence with the restructuring. The committee did vote concurrence. He read a brief statement that the Rules Committee believes the plan is "in line with our conference rules and the 2016 Book of Discipline" and commended Discipleship Ministries for "seeking many voices in the process."

Mittie Quinn, lay member, requested that the Discipleship Council add an eighth social action team, the LGBTQIA Justice Team. Bishop Easterling asked how the team would fit into the report because BWARM and WCA had been added. Rev. Hayden confirmed that had happened, in addition to MSFA. Quinn responded that she was requesting an eighth Action Team for the Advocacy and Action Board. Hayden asked if the chair of the Action and Advocacy Team was present. Gorman said that the purpose of presenting the report was so that it could be amended, and that Quinn's request needed to be offered as an amendment to the report. Quinn offered it as an amendment.

Rev. Debbie Scott, Lovely Lane UMC, asked for a moment of privilege and commended Hayden, who had just been ordained, for being with the session and thanked her for her dedication. She also spoke in favor of the amendment in light of some of the things referred to the Council; she thought it would be most appropriate. The amendment passed.

Bishop Easterling returned to the balloting. Based on the updated Book of Discipline, printed in the errata, there were two laity slots to fill and one clergy for General Conference. After those slots were filled, the jurisdictional delegates would be voted upon.

Rev. Sam Marullo, Capitol Hill UMC, proposed a process to expedite the voting, suggesting that the slate in rank order (those with the highest percentage of the vote) be used and that there be one vote for the top vote getters on the clergy and then the laity side to complete the General Conference delegation and do the same with the jurisdictional ballot. Bishop Easterling asked Gorman for his input. She wanted to make sure the voting was done properly.

After confirming his understanding of the amendment with the maker, Gorman, going to the Discipline, said that it doesn't say the vote has to be on each individual. However, the clergy ballot, per the Discipline, includes every clergy person on every ballot. So the amendment would not work for clergy. Marullo said that clergy had been eligible through every round of voting and that people could vote "no" on the slate if there were clergy from the "extended" list people wanted to vote for.

Bishop Easterling explained that because the change to the Book of Discipline was new, there were no Judicial Council rulings to help interpret and understand this change. Rev. Scott, Lovely Lane UMC, asked if it was possible to get an opinion from the chancellor. The bishop proceeded with the laity vote while the chancellor considered the proposed amendment.

The seventh laity balloting list was shown in preparation for voting. Bishop Easterling asked that the prayer video from Bishop Schol, Greater New Jersey Area, be shown before the vote. Judy Pimental, Lay Member, Hughes UMC in Wheaton, asked for clarification of who was eligible to be voted upon. Bishop Easterling explained that those elected for Jurisdictional were available to be elected as a General Conference delegate because they remained on the slate. She stated that the last person elected was Ken Ow.

Bishop Easterling asked Marullo to explain his amendment. Bishop Easterling affirmed that Kenneth Ow was elected for General Conference and the two others elected, Sarah Ford and Daniel Colbert, did not reach the majority vote. Marullo said he was proposing that Ford and Colbert be treated as a slate with a "yes" vote and only laity voting.

Mittie Quinn, Lay Member, voiced objection over Marullo making recommendations on how the laity should vote since she was not allowed to do so for clergy. She did concur with his amendment.

Bishop Easterling checked in with the chancellor. She said she would rather continue the voting process without the proposed amendment. Rev. Kate Mackereth, St. Paul's UMC in Kensington, asked if it would be in order to vote on Marullo's proposal.

Bishop Easterling said it would not because "to take an up or down vote on something that may or may not be in keeping with what's now in the Book of Discipline doesn't necessarily get us into safe territory." Mackareth expressed concern that the longer the vote took, the more people would end up leaving and it was less likely votes will be representative of the conference. Rev. Daryl Williams, St. Paul UMC in Oxon Hill, said that the time being spent on the amendment could be spent on the "normative process" for voting.

Bishop Easterling proceeded with the laity ballot 8 for General Conference. Daniel Colbert was elected with 70.28% of the vote and Sarah Ford was elected with 69.58% of the vote. This completed the General Conference delegates. The bishop asked that the last clergy ballot be shown and said that the last person elected by a simple majority was Rev. Giovanni Arroyo. Bishop advised that the Conference Secretary suggested that laity prepare to vote for the NEJ delegates during this time. Clergy ballot 8 had no election.

Bishop announced a laity ballot for jurisdictional delegates and asked clergy to be prepared for their next vote. Nathan Jones, Epworth UMC in Cockeysville, asked to see the six delegates who were "incorrectly voted into the NEJ delegation." Bishop said that Padgett would show Ballot 8.

Rev. Bill Brown, Wesley Freedom UMC, asked Rev. Gorman if the constitutional amendment also applies to jurisdictional delegates. He responded it did.

Bishop Easterling announced that Chris Schlieckert was duly elected by a simple majority of 52% and laity needed to elect five more jurisdictional lay delegates.

Bill Sandler, Calvary UMC in Finksburg, asked if Chris Schlieckert, who was elected to Jurisdictional Conference with a majority, before the updated Discipline was explained, only the "first six" for the laity had been resolved. Bishop Easterling replied that the question had been asked and answered. Schlieckert would have been eligible for the General Conference vote.

Five laity were elected as NEJ delegates on Ballot 2, all with a simple majority: Christie Latona, Tracy Collins, Sharon Milton, Nathan Jones and Chet Jechura (in the order listed). "The laity are showing us how to get this done," declared Bishop Easterling. Bishop then announced the ninth clergy ballot and Rev. Sarah Schlieckert was elected with 63.43% of the vote.

Laity were instructed to prepare to elect their alternates for Jurisdictional Conference. As Padgett prepared the ballot, Bishop Easterling asked the district superintendents to come forward for the closed church reports. The bishop asked to have the closed church reports done by district and, if the body allowed, voting on them as an entire district instead of one by one.

She started with Rev. Conrad Link, Dean of the Cabinet and superintendent of the Cumberland-Hagerstown District, who gave introductory remarks and spoke about the life cycle of the church. Half of his colleagues on the Cabinet worked with the "Legacy Churches" book. He presented three church closings from the Cumberland-Hagerstown District. Grace United Methodist Church in Berkeley Springs closed as of Aug 19, 2018. The Board of Trustees of Mount Zion United Methodist Church also in Berkeley Springs, were authorized to take possession of the real and personal tangible and intangible property of Grace United Methodist Church, and to make a determination of how that property may best be used for the Kingdom of God. Mount Zion sold the property and has received the funds. St. Paul United Methodist Church was closed as of September 30, 2018. Mount Carmel United Methodist Church in Boonsboro closed as of June 30, 2019. The Conference Board of Trustees was authorized to take possession of real and personal tangible and intangible property of St. Paul United Methodist Church in Big Pool, Maryland, and Mount Carmel United Methodist Church, Boonsboro, Maryland, and to make a determination of how the property may best be used for the Kingdom of God.

Bishop Easterling asked that at the end of the entire district presentations of closed churches, a prayer for the "life and ministry and faithfulness of the saints who have been a part of these churches for their history." The report was voted upon and received.

Rev. Gerard Green, Greater Washington District Superintendent, presented Grace United Methodist Church in Fairmount Heights, which closed September 1, 2018. The Conference Board of Trustees are authorized to take possession of the real and personal tangible and intangible property of Grace United Methodist Church and to make a determination of how the property may best be used for the Kingdom of God. The effective date was June 3, 2019.

Rev. Stephen Tillett rose to offer a motion. He said, "The closing of black congregations and the sale leave a unique ancestral void in the history and soul of a community." He moved that the proceeds from any sale of African-American churches be held for repurposing until after the 2020 General Conference. After the motion was seconded, Tillett said that the church he served, Asbury-Broadneck, was established in 1838 and had just celebrated 180 years last year. After the Civil War, the formerly enslaved men and women purchased land for their families, descendants, the church and the cemetery. He said that in 1968, when the denomination came together, they had to relinquish that. He said that African- American Methodist denominations are still together and did not schism over "this." His motion proposes that any historically African-American congregation being closed should have its resources be held until after General Conference 2020. At that time, a determination will be made regarding what needs to be done. His idea was that the resources should go with the people who brought them in the first place.

John Strawbridge, Lovely Lane UMC and chair of the Conference Trustees, spoke against the amendment. He explained, "Disciplinary policy restricts how funds for closed churches are used." Closed churches in urban areas are designated for those urban areas, and money from closed churches in non-urban areas go to non-urban areas. The trustees work with the district superintendents to ensure the best stewardship of the funds and that they go where they are needed. Holding funds until after General Conference means buildings sit accumulating expenses and the buildings have to continue to be maintained, i.e., lawns mowed, insurance paid, security, etc. This drains the funds. In the past five to six years, over 54% of money from all closed churches have gone to predominately African-American ministries. He urged that the amendment not be adopted.

Rev. Tim Warner, Emory Grove UMC in Gaithersburg, rose to speak in support of the amendment. He said that it wasn't just about urban churches; it is about black churches, some of which are suburban, and some are rural. He pastors a church in the upper part of Montgomery County and said that there were several small African-American churches that are more than 100 years old "whose assets are viewed as community assets" by the church and the community. He continued, "Black communities have been losing assets in this denomination almost since its inception." And with the potential division of the denomination he would hate to see "further loss to these communities, not just the churches."

Rev. Marlon Tilghman, Ames UMC, offered a speech for the amendment. He said that the Trust Clause, "like red-lining, re-gentrification, and systematic policies, have hurt black churches. Thus, any decisions and proceeds from those churches would best serve those communities and honor the legacy givers of that community." He referred to Resolution 5, which approved an unrestricted bequest staying in a non-urban community, and said it sets the precedent for the motion. He said that closing a black church without a plan to repurpose the funds in that community tells them that the UMC has "abandoned them once again."

District Superintendent Green spoke against the amendment. While has said that he understood the desire of the maker of the motion to have those funds allocated to African-American congregations, his plan was to have those funds "designated specifically for the renovation of African-American congregations within the Greater Washington District."

The maker of the amendment, Tillett, was given an opportunity to speak again. He explained that his amendment sought to have funds from the sale held until after General Conference 2020. He said that what the superintendent proposed might not be "completely pertinent to the future for African-American churches if there is a schism." He said that discussions were being held at the BMCR national level suggests any schism might be a three-way schism. If so, the African-American church may choose to "do our own thing" and would want their assets to go with them "as they should." That is the reason to wait a year to see what happens.

Rev. Joe Daniels, Emory Fellowship in D.C., raised a point of order. He said that whatever decision is made, it needs to be made regardless of who the district superintendent is, because the decisions "go beyond perhaps… one person serving in a particular position" and that needs to be taken into consideration.

Rev. Debbie Scott, Lovely Lane UMC, raised a point of information. She said that it had been said consistently, "we cannot vote on hypotheticals" and the current amendment was "in the ground of hypothetical." The bishop said that the amendment before the body was appropriate and not hypothetical and repeated her understanding of the amendment. Specifically, that "any proceeds from that sale be held and not used until after General Conference 2020 determination about what the denomination may decide," remain in the hands of the trustees until after that time.

Tillett affirmed the bishop's explanation. He said that, according to ¶2549.7, the funds or a portion of the funds would be spent in similar communities. He said that Rev. Warner noted that it is not only urban communities. Broadneck UMC was rural and is now suburban. The amendment was about black churches, urban, suburban or rural.

Alisa Lasater Wailoo, Capitol Hill UMC, asked for a point of clarification. She said there were four historically black churches in her neighborhood in need of repairs (heaters, furnaces, etc.). She expressed concerns that it would difficult for those churches to wait a year and a half for the funds. She recognized that it was a much bigger issue but wanted to be clear. Tillett affirmed she was correct.

Rev. Lynn Glassbrook, a retired elder, asked if the amendment related to the Greater Washington church being closed, which was correct.

The vote for the amendment was by device and it passed. The vote was then taken for the church closure and it passed to close Grace United Methodist Church in Fairmount Heights with an effective date of June 3, 2019.

Rev. JW Park, Superintendent of the Central Maryland District presented two resolutions for church closings. The first resolution was for the closing of Rockland UMC in Ellicott City, which was closed on June 30, 2018. The church has been working with the Trustees over the past 12 months. Once the vote to close Rockland was approved by the Annual Conference Session, the final steps would be taken to make the building the home of a new, growing congregation called Bethany Korean UMC. The legacy of Rockland lives on in Bethany Korean Methodist Church. The second resolution was for the closing of Mount Zion UMC, also in Ellicott City, which was closed on December 31, 2018. The determination on the use of the property was to be made by the Conference Board of Trustees.

Rev. Tillett rose to offer the "same motion" for Mount Zion in Ellicott City. Bishop asked that the vote be taken for Rockland before addressing the amendment. The resolution to close Rockland UMC effective June 3, 2019 passed. The Mount Zion amendment was seconded.

John Strawbridge, Lovely Lane UMC and Chair of Conference Trustees, urged that the amendment not be passed because the money was designated for use in the community and referred to the amendment as doubly restricting the funds. He again mentioned the current spending distributions, of which 54% goes to predominately African-American communities. The amendment would delay funds and withhold them from communities and various congregations the amendment was hoping to benefit. It hampers the work of the conference and the work with the district superintendent.

Rev. Joseph Daniels, Emory Fellowship in D.C., rose to give support to the amendment. He wanted to say to the trustee chair that he hoped "every consideration was being given to the changing economic and real estate climate, particularly in the Washington D.C. area." He explained that "every piece of property that is sold in what used to be a predominantly black community, because of gentrification, is becoming predominantly white." As the black church finds itself in the midst of decisions being made and debated over LGBT issues, "the issues being debated are over who's going to control money, assets, property." He continued, "If we are not taking into consideration the justice questions, then many people in the margins will be left out."

George Prochaska, Cowenton UMC, spoke against the resolution. His concern was that it was not an African-American issue; it was an LGBT issue. He said, "You're trying to hold the money so that you can cut and run and won't lose money." Bishop Easterling asked that the assemblage "refrain from using language that can be inflammatory and that is pejorative." Prochaska apologized. He felt that the issue affected all on both sides and some of what was said, "belittles people who are trying to fight for inclusion in LGBT issues."

Rev. Tim Warner, Emory Grove UMC, rose to support the amendment and renew his comments that this "was about kinship communities that have existed since slavery who understand these churches as community assets." He explained that, "should the church split for whatever reason, communities will still remain but without their assets again, in United Methodist and American history." Saying that he pastors a black church and a white church, he said the white church called him the day after the decision at General Conference. In his black church, it was not an issue. He said the issue was about property and proceeds and "we ought to be very clear to make sure that these assets are protected."

Tillett was given the opportunity for a final statement and said he knew this was frustrating to the Chair of Trustees and for everyone. He was sure people would much rather be making disciples for Jesus Christ for the transformation of the world instead of having the same debate over and over again. His hope was that the church would not schism, but should that happen, "the ancestral properties… should run down to the ancestors, or descendants of those ancestors, to do with as we see fit going forward." The amendment carried, as did the resolution to close Mount Zion United Methodist Church effective June 3, 2019.

Rev. Edgardo Rivera, Frederick District Superintendent, presented two churches for closure. Salem United Methodist Church in Martinsburg closed as of April 12, 2019, and Mount Zion

UMC in Frederick closed as of April 30, 2019. For both properties the Conference Board of Trustees was authorized to take possession of the real and personal, tangible and intangible property. The closings were approved with a June 3, 2019, effective date.

Bishop Easterling called for the clergy jurisdictional slate to be voted upon. Rev. Stacey Cole-Wilson had 62.4% on NEJ Ballot 1, so there were five to elect on Ballot 2. The following were elected in order of votes received: Revs. JW Park, Conrad Link, Leo Yates, Kirkland Reynolds, and Bryant Oskvig.

Rev. Wanda Bynum-Duckett, Baltimore Metropolitan District Superintendent, presented three resolutions for closure. She began with the African-American congregation. Homestead United Methodist Church closed on May 15, 2019. Rev. Tillett reiterated the motion he previously made and it was seconded.

Guy Cecil, Foundry in Washington, D.C., rose to speak in favor of the amendment, particularly "in this time of transition" for everyone. He wanted "to acknowledge some lament in the conversation" that had happened. Cecil wanted "to assure everyone that the LGBT community is the last community that wants to be at the center of this type of attention." He continued, "Our marriages are not sins to be confessed, or to be liberated from. Our marriages are part of God's liberation for our life." He said that LGBTQIA+ persons are "part of all our churches" and in all of our communities are murdered and commit suicide. He concluded, "I support this amendment because I want us to be one church, not just at the expense of my own oppression."

Rev. Sheridan Allmond, Vice Chair, Conference Board of Trustees, rose to speak against the amendment. She said that it was with a heavy heart but that she also understood the work of the conference trustees and "a fourth of every dollar that we are responsible for is debated in every meeting to make sure that every part of our population, no matter what race, ethnicity, gender... is cared for." She acknowledged that there "were voices at the table" that "question if we are doing the right thing." Her concern was the number of times between the present and General Conference 2020, "that there are going to be churches, who are going to be told no, because we won't have the funding available."

Justice Randolph, Lay Delegate at Large, spoke in favor of the amendment because of his day job. He works for Bread for the World, an advocacy organization that seeks to end hunger by changing policies and programs in the U.S. The organization's research shows that "food insecurity and hunger are significantly more prevalent in communities of African descent" because of "less access to wealth and fewer resources." He said, "this is the direct result of laws and policies of organizations like The United Methodist Church." He thought the amendment was an "extremely reasonable request" and "would go a very short way to beginning to remedy that problem."

An unidentified pastor spoke against the amendment. He said that while a precedent had been set, he was disturbed that "we are beginning the process of setting aside or moving assets to protect them for future use." He said it was like the Civil War, "when generals started moving the munitions south," so that, after the war started, they would "have their stuff." His concern was "once we start doing this, other people are going to start dong this."

Duckett, as the maker of the resolution, said that although Homestead was closing, the community was "very much attached to that location, which is strategic in terms of mission." She said that while a detailed plan was not yet determined, the funds "would best be used in that community to help with the very real needs that are on the ground in that community. Some of those people simply cannot wait." The amendment did not carry. The resolution to close Homestead passed and is effective June 3, 2019.

The two remaining churches were presented together. Orangeville United Methodist Church closed as of April 15, 2019, and Dundalk United Methodist Church closed April 30 2019. For both churches, the Conference Board of Trustees would make a determination as to how the properties would best be used for the Kingdom of God. The resolutions passed and Bynum-Duckett prayed for all the churches that had closed.

Bishop Easterling called for the laity ballot for four jurisdictional alternates and said the clergy should prepare for their ballot, electing four. She expressed how grateful she was for the assembly's "patience and steadfastness so that we might preserve our time tomorrow with our young people."

Rev. Joan Carter Rimbach, John Wesley UMC in Baltimore, rose to remind clergy that they had been voting as an inclusive slate and the last ballot for jurisdictional conference were all male. She asked the clergy to be mindful of their inclusiveness.

Carol White, John Wesley in Hagerstown, asked to see an alphabetical listing of those remaining candidates for laity. Bishop Easterling asked for a list of the lay delegates eligible for election and also reminded everyone to turn in their voting devices at the conclusion of the evening so they could be shipped to the next conference.

Sam Tryon, Harpers Ferry Charge, asked for a moment of personal privilege to affirm the "servant ministry of the staff people who had served so diligently so that we could holy conference together." Those present stood and applauded. The bishop thanked Tryon for bringing it to the attention of the plenary.

On Ballot 1 for jurisdictional laity alternates, Mittie Quinn and Charlie Moore were elected.

Megan Blizzard, young adult representative at large, took a brief moment of personal privilege to address the body on behalf of the young people; many of whom she said had gone to bed because they had to be back in the ballroom at 8 a.m. She thanked the body for all the work done that night to allow the young people to be present the next day, a day they put a lot of work into. She again thanked the body and reminded everyone that the program started at 9 a.m. and hoped to see everyone there.

On Ballot 1 for clergy alternates, there was no election. Lutebula Danny Pembamoto was elected on Ballot 2 for laity alternates. Rev. Tony Love, Assistant to the Bishop, took the chair to allow the bishop to leave for a few minutes. Love announced the clergy ballot for four alternates. He suggested that a word of prayer might help and asked someone to pray. Bill Sadler, Calvary-Gambler UMC, prayed. Clergy voted and finished as Love welcomed Bishop Easterling back. She thanked Love for covering the chair. The four jurisdictional alternates selected on Clergy Ballot 4 were the Revs. Edgardo Rivera, Malcolm Frazier, Laura Norvell, and Melissa Rudolph.

As Bishop Easterling called for the laity vote for the last alternate, someone asked, "Can we let Tony preside?" and the bishop laughingly replied, "Maybe he's got the magic touch." Heather H. Kraus was elected as the final lay alternate for jurisdictional on Laity Ballot 3.

Bishop Easterling thanked everyone and announced it was 1:02 a.m. and said, "God bless you." She asked the conference secretary to read the closing motion. Cynthia Taylor, conference secretary, asked for a moment of personal privilege and said, "Thank you for the privilege of serving as your conference secretary," to which the bishop replied, "She has been absolutely phenomenal. I'm so grateful for all the work she has done." Taylor then read the closing motion and Bishop Easterling brought the 235th session of the Baltimore-Washington Conference to a close.

Young People's Ministry Day
Saturday, June 1, 2019

Saturday, June 1, was a special day in the life of the Annual Conference Session. An extra day was added to the agenda and, for the first time in memory, the whole day was set apart to celebrate young people and their ministry. "We thought that something was missing in Young People's Ministry in the BaltimoreWashington Conference," said Christie Latona, Director of Connectional Ministries. "We need to be more effectively reaching the next generation." For example, Latona said that 437 churches in the BWC have at least one youth, ages 12-18, participating in a Christian formation group, such as Sunday school or other small group ministries; 37 churches in the conference have 50 or more youth participating in groups. However, 179 churches have zero youth in such groups. Those numbers are about to change. In a strategic plan adopted by the conference, the BWC agreed to make the choice to "disproportionately invest in young people; to focus less on the structure of programs and more on the structure of connections; and to seek to focus the next three years on building the essential infrastructure for a thrilling, integrated, deep-impact ministry to young people in the conference."

The day began as a youth-led revival broke out in the Grand Ballroom. Shouts of "hallelujah!" echoed through the room. Bishop LaTrelle Easterling was invited to the stage, where young people laid hands on her in prayer. Tears streamed down the bishop's face and she ended up dancing on the way back to her seat.

Megan Blizzard, chair of the Young People's Board, spoke passionately about the urgency of reaching young people today. "One of the core values of Young People's Ministry is respectful urgency," she said. "It means engaging in Christ's work while being humble, faithful and intentional about doing no harm." Blizzard – who was elected as a lay delegate to General Conference – said that the Bible is full of young people in ministry. Jesus, she said, was 33; Samuel was 11; David became king at 30. "God has called us, your young people, and commanded us to speak. Are you listening?" she asked. "If Jesus were one of the young people in your pews, would you follow him or ask him to follow you? Would you listen to his gospel, or tell him his ideas are too outside the norm and 'when he's older,' he can be in leadership?"

Mark DeVries, one of the consultants who helped formalize the strategic plan, said that hundreds of people offered input on this new direction. He shared the "why" behind the process. DeVries used the image of planting oak trees for young people's ministry. Oak trees, he said, take a long time to grow, and some of them can live for 500 years or longer. The best time to plant an oak tree, if you need a long log with which to create a center beam, is 500 years ago. "The second-best time," he said, "is right now."

What we're doing in young people's ministry, he said, is investing in young people "that you'll never meet, that will bear fruit 400, 500 years from now. Whose job is it to plant these trees? All of us."

However, he said, there's only one substance oak trees grow in: dirt. "It's going to get messy," he said, speaking of young people's ministry. "But all of the good stuff is on the other side of the mess." He encouraged people to be "crazy about the kids" and to "love them irrationally," because that's how relationships are formed, and people's lives are transformed.

Photos from YPM Saturday by Tony Richards Photography

General Conference Delegates

Clergy:
Ianther Mills
Joe Daniels
Ginger Gaines-Cirelli
C. Anthony Hunt
Giovanni Arroyo
Sarah Schlieckert

Laity:
Cythnia Taylor
Megan Blizzard
Melissa Lauber
Ken Ow
Daniel Colbert
Sarah Ford

Jurisdictional Conference Delegates

Clergy:
Stacey Cole-Wilson
JW Park
Conrad Link
Leo Yates
Kirkland Reynolds
Bryant Oskvig

Alternates:
Edgardo Rivera
Malcolm Frazier
Laura Norvell
Melissa Rudolph

Laity:
Chris Schlieckert
Christie Latona
Tracy Collins
Sharon Milton
Nathan Jones
Chet Jechura

Alternates:
Mittie Quinn
Charlie Moore
Lutebula Danny Pembamoto
Heather Kraus

Bishop Latrelle Easterling

Cynthia Taylor, Conference Secretary

BUSINESS OF ANNUAL CONFERENCE

The Minutes of the Baltimore-Washington Annual Conference held in Baltimore, Maryland from May 29, 2019, through June 1, 2019, Bishop LaTrelle Easterling, Presiding.

Date When Organized: 1784   Number of This Session: 235th

PART I ORGANIZATION AND GENERAL BUSINESS
1.   Who are elected for the quadrennium (¶¶603.7, 619)?
     Secretary?   Kevin Silberzahn
     Mailing Address: 11711 East Market Place, Fulton, MD 20759-2594
     Telephone: (410) 499-5304
     Email: bwcsecretary@bwcumc.org
     Statistician? Rev. Daryl L. Williams
     Mailing Address: 12621 Spriggs Request Court, Bowie, MD 20721
     Telephone: (240) 715-2204
     Email: Revlw@gmail.com
     Treasurer? Paul Eichelberger
     Mailing Address: 11711 East Market Place, Fulton, MD 20759-2594
     Telephone: (410) 309-3424 or (800) 492-2525 X424
     Email: peichelberger@bwcumc.org

2.   Is the Annual Conference incorporated (¶603.1)? Yes

3.   Bonding and auditing:
     What officers handling funds of the conference have been bonded, and in what amounts (¶¶618, 2511)?
     There is a blanket bond from GCFA for all persons who handle conference funds.
     Have the books of said officers or persons been audited (¶¶617, 2511)?
     Yes. (See report of Auditor.)

4.   What agencies have been appointed or elected?
     a) Who have been elected chairpersons for the mandated structures listed?

Structure	Chairperson	Phone	Email
Council on Finance and Administration (¶611)	Phil Potter	(202) 363-4900	phil.potter@verizon.net
Board of Ordained Ministry (¶635)	Rev. Tony Hunt	(410) 944-1070	cahunt@msn.com
Board of Pensions (¶639)	Rev. Cary James	(443) 575-6375	revcjamesjr@yahoo.com
Board of Trustees (¶2512)	John Strawbridge	(410) 243-5344	johnstrawbridge@hot-mail.com
Committee on Episcopacy (¶637)	Rev. Jim Miller	(301) 926-8688	jmiller@graceumc.org
Administrative Review Committee (¶636)	None listed		

     b) Indicate the name of the agency (or agencies) and the chairperson(s) in your annual conference that is (are) responsible for the functions related to each of the following general church agencies (¶610.1):

General Agency	Conference Agency	Chair	Phone	Email
General Board of Church and Society	Advocacy and Action	Tom Contee	(301) 412-1451	tomcontee13@gmail.com
General Board of Discipleship	Leadership Development Board	Nona Colbert	(240) 346-5301	pastor1nona@outlookc.om
General Board of Global Ministries	Wellness & Missions	Rev. Heath Wilson	(410) 758-7707	HWilsonVT@gmail.com
General Board of Ordained Ministry	Board of Ordained Ministry	Rev. C. Anthony Hunt	(410) 758-7707	HWilsonVT@gmail.com
GBHEM	Young People's Ministry Board	Shemaiah Strickland	(404) 771-7437	shemaiahstrickland@gmail.com
General Commission on Archives & History	Commission on Archives & History	Rev. Emora Brannan	(410) 377-3390	emorabrannan@verizon.net
GCCUIC	Christian Unity and Interfaith Concerns Forum	Rev. Dell Hinton	(443) 803-5116	dell_hinton@comcast.net
GCORR	Advocacy & Action Board's Racial Justice Team (CCORR)	Moorosi Mokuena	(240) 683-6480	moorsi_mokuena@msn.com
GCOSROW	Advocacy & Action Board's Gender Equity Team (COSROW)	Andrea Johnson	(612) 414-2150	andrealynn.johnson@gmail.com
UM Communicatons	Commission on Communications	Rev. Terri Cofiell	(304) 229-3050	terricofiell@comcast.net

c) Indicate the conference agencies which have responsibilities for the following functions:

General Agency	Conference Agency	Chair	Phone	Email
Criminal Justice and Mercy Ministries (¶657)	Advocacy & Action Board's Restorative Justice Team (RJAMM)	Rev. Sonia King	(410) 320-3482	revslkzeta@gmail.com
Disability Concerns (¶653)	Commission on Disability Concerns	Dixie Catlett	(202) 270-7632	dixiecatdc@gmail.com

General Agency	Conference Agency	Chair	Phone	Email
Equitable Compensation (¶625)	Commission on Equitable Compensation	Rev. Kathy Altman	(240) 285-5800	revkathy-altman@verizon.net
Laity	Board of Laity	Delores Martin	(301) 421-9441	litte_martin@verizon.net
Native American Ministry (¶654)	Native American Ministry	Thomas Crawford	(240) 217-3708	tscottscrawford.new@gmail.com
Small Membership Church (¶645)	Small Membership Church Forum	Rick Oursler	(410) 799-2128	roursler22@hotmail.com

d) Indicate the president or equivalent for the following organizations.

Organization	Agency	Chair	Phone	Email
Conference United Methodist Women (¶647)	United Methodist Women	Linda Yost	(410) 239-0429	ljyost@verizon.net
Conference United Methodist Men (¶648)	United Methodist Men	Hampton Conway	(301) 210-5091	ummhamp@yahoo.com
Conference Council on Youth Ministry (¶649)	Council on Youth Ministry	TBD		
Conference Council on Young Adult Ministry (¶650)	Council on Young Adult Ministries	Megan Blizzard	(410) 596-0696	megblizz@yahoo.com

e) Have persons been elected for the following district boards and committees? Yes or no.
  (1) District Boards of Church Location & Building (¶2518.2)? Yes.
  (2) Committees on District Superintendency (¶669)? Yes.
  (3) District Committees on Ordained Ministry (¶666)? Yes.

f) What other councils, boards, commissions, or committees have been appointed or elected in the annual conference?

Structure	Chair	Phone	Email
Discipleship Council	Rev. Jessica Hayden	(410) 241-5543	
Connectional Table	Delores Martin	(301)421-9441	little_martin@verizon.net
Nominations Committee	Sarah Ford	(410) 466-7605	svford@verizon.net
Rules Committee	Rev. Mark Gorman	(443) 458-2092	gorman.mark@gmail.com

Structure	Chair	Phone	Email
Conference Sessions Committee	Bishop LaTrelle Easterling	(410) 309-3400 x300	bishopeasterlingoffice@bwcumc.org
Conference Moving Committee	Rev. Jeff Paulson	(410) 641-5194	revjeff93@gmail.com
Conference Committee on Hispanic-Latino Minstries	Rev. Giovanni Arroyo	(202) 495-2943	garroyog@aol.com

5.   Have the secretaries, treasurers and statisticians kept their respective records according to the prescribed forms (¶606.8)? Yes

6.   What is the report of the statistician? See the Statistical Tables.

7.   What is the report of the treasurer? See the Council of Finance & Administration report.

8.   What are the reports of the district superintendents as to the status of the work within their districts? (See Question 17, Section V. Appointments)

9.   What is the schedule of minimum base compensation for pastors for the ensuing year (¶¶342,625.3)?
The equitable compensation base for our Annual Conference is indexed to the average Cash Salary.
For 2015, the amount is $40,760   For 2016, the amount is $41,760
For 2017, the amount is $42,303   For 2018, the amount is $43,148.82
For 2019, the amount is $44,012   For 2020, the amount is $44,892

10. What amount has been apportioned to the pastoral charges within the conference to be raised for the support of the district superintendents for the ensuing year (¶614.1a)?
The amount for 2015: $1,566,062   The amount for 2016: $1,538,878
The amount for 2017: $1,646,599   The amount for 2018: $1,679,531
The amount for 2019: $1,545,169   The amount for 2020: $1,552,895

11. What amount has been apportioned to the pastoral charges within the conference to be raised for the support of the pension and benefit programs of the conference for the ensuing year (¶¶614.1d, 1507)?
a)The amount apportioned (direct billed) for pension and health benefits for:
2018: $9,841,767.20   2019: $10,003,426.00   2020: $

b)What are the apportionments to this conference for the ensuing year:
1) World Service Fund: 2018: $1,892,600   2019: $1,844,272
2) Ministerial Education Fund: 2018: $639,232   2019: $622,910
3) Black College Fund: 2018: $254,984   2019: $248,473
4) Africa University Fund: 2018: $57,064   2019: $55,607
5) Episcopal Fund: 2018: $560,476   2019: $546,164
6) General Administrative Fund: 2018: $224,731   2019: $218,992
7) Interdenominational Coop Fund: 2018: $49,993   2019: $48,716

12. What are the findings of the annual audit of the conference treasuries? See Audit report.

13. Conference and district lay leaders (¶¶603.9, 660):
    a) Conference lay leader: Delores Martin

    b) Associate Conference lay leader: vacant

    c) District and associate district lay leaders:
    Annapolis: Kim Carr; Washington East: Rosalind Pinkney;
    Baltimore-Metro: Ophelia Brown-Carter; Baltimore Suburban: Thea Becton
    Central Maryland: Rod Fry ; Greater Washington: Mary McCurty
    Cumberland-Hagerstown: Richard Willson; Frederick: Barbara Shew

14. List local churches which have been:
    a) Organized or continued as New Church Starts (¶259,1-4, continue to list until moved to
    14c, d, e, or f)

GCFA#	Church	District	Address	Phone	Date Founded
164032	Community with a Cause	WE	Lexington Park, MD	(240) 434-5358	

    b) Organized or continues as Mission Congregation (¶259,1-4, continue to list until
    moved to 14c, d, e, or f) - NONE
    c) Organized or continued Satellite congregations (¶247.22, continue to list here until
    listed in questions 14.a, d, e or f) - NONE
    d) Organized as Chartered (¶259.5-10) - NONE
    e) Merged (¶¶2545, 2546)?
    (1) United Methodist with United Methodist:

District	GCFA#	Church #1	GCFA#	Church #2	GCFA#	Merged	Date

    (2) Other mergers? - NONE

    f) Discontinued or abandoned (¶¶229, 341.2, 2549) (State which for each church listed.)
    (1) New Church Start (¶259.2,3)
    (2) Mission Congregation (¶259.1a)
    (3) Satellite Congregation
    (4) Chartered Local Church (¶259.5)
    Discontinued - (CH District) Grace UMC, Berkeley Springs, WV; Mount Carmel
    UMC, Boonsboro, MD; St Paul UMC, Big Pool, MD
    Discontinued (CM District) - Rockland UMC, Ellicott City, MD; Mount Zion UMC,
    Ellicott City, MD
    Discontinued (FR District) - Salem UMC, Martinsburg, WV; Mount Zion UMC,
    Frederick , MD
    Discontinued (BM District) - Homestead UMC, Baltimore, MD; Dundalk UMC,
    Baltimore, MD; Grace UMC, Fairmont Heights, MD

    g) Relocated and to what address? - NONE

    h) Changed name of church? (Example: "First" to "Trinity") - Ellicott City: Bethany
    Korean Mission CG to Ellicott City: Bethany Korean CG

    i) Transferred this year into this conference from other United Methodist conference(s)
    and with what membership (¶¶41, 260)? - NONE

    j) What cooperative parishes in structured forms have been established? (¶206)

    k) What other changes have taken place in the list of churches? - NONE

15. Are there Ecumenical Shared Ministries in the conference? (¶207, 208). - No.
    a) Federated church? - NONE
    b) Union Church? - NONE
    c) Merged Church? - NONE
    d) Yoked Parish? - NONE

16. What changes have been made in district and charge lines? (List GCFA number) CG = Charge; CP = Cooperative Parish

BM: Baltimore: Dundalk-Graceland CP (Dundalk/Graceland) broke out to create: Baltimore: Graceland CG (164167)

Woodlawn: Emmarts CG (166031) and Baltimore: Mt. Zion CG (969526) charges become Baltimore: Mt. Zion-Emmarts CG

Baltimore: West Baltimore CG (165663) and Baltimore: Unity CG (164475) charges become Baltimore: West Baltimore-Unity Charge
Baltimore: Gwynn Oak/St Lukes CG (165537/166463) and Baltimore: Arlington-Lewin CG (165366) charges become Woodlawn: St. Lukes and Baltimore: G.O.A.L. CG

Baltimore: Elderslie-St. Andrews/Govan CG (Elderslie-St. Andrews – 165402 & Govans-Boundary – 162328) & Baltimore: New Waverly CG (162705) & Pikesville: St. Paul Praise and Worship CG (969971) becomes Baltimore: New Waverly-Govans Boundary CG and Pikesville: Pikesville Pimlico CG

BS: Cockeysville: Texas CG (Frames Memorial /Poplar Grove/Texas) becomes Cockeysville: Texas CG (163380) and Cockeysville: Frames-Poplar CP (Frames Memorial – 163287 & Poplar Grove – 163391)

CM: Highland: Hopkins/Mt. Olivet CG becomes Catonsville: Mount Olivet CG (971531 and moving to BM District from the CM District) and Highland: Hopkins CG (971724)

Damascus: South Damascus CG (Wesley Grove/ Mt. Tabor/Salem/Asbury) becomes Germantown: Asbury (971757) and Damascus: South Damascus (Wesley Grove – 170432, Mt. Tabor – 169810, & Salem – 169502)

CH: Big Pool: Potomac CG – (Mt. Carmel – 162625, Parkhead – 162658, & St. Paul – 162740) becomes Big Pool: Big Pool CGS – (Mt. Carmel – 162625, & Parkhead – 162658)

FR: Walkersville: Walkersville/Mt. Pleasant/Mt. Zion Charge becomes Walkersville: Walkersville (170168)/Mt. Pleasant (170272) Charge
Rohrersville Charge – (Mt. Carmel/Bethel) has become Rohersville: Bethel CG – (Bethel – 162842)

Kearneysville: Leetown/Marvin Chapel CG (167707/166543) becomes Kearneysville: Leetown CG and Martinsburg: Marvin Chapel CG

Millville: Jefferson CG (Chestnut Hill/Shenandoah Memorial) and Knoxville: Sandy Hook charges become Harpers Ferry: Chestnut Hill (166884) and Knoxville: Sandy Hook/ Shenandoah Memorial CG (166782 & 166565)

GW: Savage: Savage/Lanham (Savage – 165047 & Lanham – 168085) becomes Lanham: Lanham

WE: Indian Head: Indian Head CG (Indian Head – 168063) & Bryan's Road: Shiloh CG (Shiloh – 168586) charges become Indian Head: Indian Head-Shiloh CG

Board of Ordained Ministry Report to the Executive Session of the Baltimore-Washington Conference

PART II PERTAINING TO ORDAINED AND
LICENSED CLERGY

(Note: A (v) notation following a question in this section signifies that the action or election requires a majority vote of the clergy session of the Annual Conference. If an action requires more than a simple majority, the notation (v 2/3) or (v 3/4) signifies that a two-thirds or three-fourths majority vote is required. Indicate credential of persons in Part II: FD, FE, PD, PE, and AM when requested.)

17. Are all the clergy members of the conference blameless in their life and official administration (¶¶604.4, 605.7)?

Response from the Dean and the Cabinet.　　Conrad O. Link

Once again, the historical question of conference clergy behavior, integrity, morality, professionalism and personal conduct is before us. Are most clergy striving to live a life faithful to the Gospel and their call? My fellow Superintendents and I believe the answer is yes. Thanks be to God: pastors are keeping and still living up to their call of being a Servant-Leader.

Being a pastor in this second decade of the new millennium is incredibly difficult. Responding to a congregation that issues demands from 40-50 year members who remember when the church was packed; 25 year members going through family life crises; persons of all ages discovering and living out their sexual identity in an ever changing world and relating to others who are doing the same; teenagers who are weekly losing classmates to opioid overdose, gun violence, and suicide; and children who do not yet know who Jesus is and why they should learn of him are just a few examples of the population stresses on a pastor seeking to be tuned into his/her congregation and community. And, let us not forget, these same pastors are called upon to preach a message that speaks to the needs of each of these populations in corporate worship. In the midst of this ministry landscape, there has been a significant increase in the number of colleagues who struggle with what it means to follow a life that serves as an example for others while seeking to be their own person and live a private life.

These stresses will not go away. How each of us as elders, deacons, local pastors, extension ministers, and others deal with the stresses makes all the difference. We need one another. We need each other for collegial support, conversation, safe spaces, care and friendship. Some of our colleagues do not seek collegial support and are in danger of acting out their stress or coping with stress in some very unhealthy ways. Some of these unhealthy behaviors will lead to the loss of vocation, the breakup of families, and the abandonment of faith. We need each other. These stresses, and the need for support, were explained to us during the Sexual Boundary Training that over 600 pastors participated in this recent January 2019.

Let me be direct with a challenge and observation: if you listen to these words and believe they do not apply to you, then perhaps you are a person who is either already in distress or on the edge of doing something that is detrimental to yourself or your call to be in ministry with others.

The Bishop and cabinet fields at least one or two significant complaints every month as well as a variety of letters from laity complaining about both pastors and other laity. Sadly, a few times each year a presenting issue moves beyond a supervisory action and requires severe disciplinary action.

Sadly, we, the Bishop and District Superintendents, believe a number of these issues did not have to rise to the level of discipline. Pastors need to take a serious look at the professional and personal manner with which they conduct their ministry. Collegial conversation, honest reflection, talking with a mental health professional, seeking spiritual guidance, having a mentor, are just a few tools needed to help clergy avoid boundary violations and damage to career. You do not need to function alone.

This past appointment year has been extra stressful on the church, church members, pastors and pastoral families. The special session of General Conference held in St. Louis in February 2019 left many in the UMC feeling victorious and vindicated over long held beliefs; it left many in the UMC feeling hurt and abandoned; it left many in the UMC confused, frustrated and unsettled. In the meantime, clergy are called to minister to all. These feelings continue and will continue. Future issues will arise as we experience new realities in our culture and contexts for ministry. For example, it is expected that the future will allow for pastors to declare themselves for limited itineracy, whereby a variety of professional, personal, geographical, economic, housing, and other dimensions of life will require less than full commitment to the current itinerant system.

Clergy are called to remember that we meet Christ in the hungry, thirsty, homeless, naked, sick and imprisoned (Matthew 25); that we reach out to the least, the last and the lost (Luke 15) and that our guide is Jesus who gave both the Great Commandment and the Great Commission.

There is no easy answer. The call of God on our lives is not an easy path; it is a heavy burden and a great privilege to carry the cross with Christ. It is not for the faint of heart, for the trivial-minded nor for those not willing to engage in hard work. This work requires serious-minded persons who keep their eyes fixed upon Jesus, the pioneer and perfecter of our faith (Hebrews 12). Do not grow weary or lose heart. Help one another. Seek out one another. Do not do ministry alone. We need one another.

May God bless you as you continue your faith journey to become the person God knows and intends for you to be.
Rev. Conrad O. Link

18. Who constitute:
   a) The Administrative Review Committee (¶636)? (v) requires three clergy in full connection and two alternates.

   | **Clergy in Full Connection** | **Alternate Clergy in** |

   Full Connection

   | Rev. Marlon Tilghman | Rev. Clark Carr |
   | Rev. Steve Larsen | Rev. Loretta |

Johnson

   Rev. Mary Kay Totty

   b) The Conference Relations Committee of the Board of Ordained Ministry (¶ 635.1d)

Rev. Jen Karsner	Rev. Paul Johnson
Rev. Norman Obenshain	Rev. Laurie Tingley
Rev. Susan Boehl	Rev. Mary Jo Sims
Rev. Jason Jordan-Griffin	Rev. Lena Marie Dennis
Rev. Bob Wellman	Rev. Lee Ferrell
Rev. Patricia Watson	

   c) The Committee on Investigation (¶ 2703.2) requires "four clergy members in full connection, three professing members, three alternate clergy members in full connection and six alternative lay members, three of whom shall be diaconal ministers if available...nominated by the presiding bishop in consultation with the Board of Ordained Ministry (for clergy members) and the conference board of laity(for professing members)"

   Clergy Members:
   1. Rev. LaReesa Smith-Horn (BA)   2. Rev. Teri Cofiell (BA)
   3. Rev. David Cooney (WA)   4. Rev. Braulio Torres (SO)

   Professing members:
   1. Maxine Jenkins (WA)   2. Norwood Bentley (WS)   3. open

   Alternate clergy:
   1. Rev. Conrad Link (SO)   2. Rev. Alfreda Wiggins (BA)   3. Rev. Michael Bennett (WS)

   Alternate professing members:
   Griff Hall (SO)   Kirsten Gullickson (WA)   Brian
   Gould (BA)

19. Who are the certified candidates? (¶¶310, 313, 314) (NOTE: Everyone who wants to become an LP, PE, or PD must first become a certified candidate.)
   a. Who are currently certified as candidates for ordained or licensed ministry?
      INFORMATIONAL

NAME	DISTRICT	CHARGE CONFERENCE	DATE CERTIFIED
Alicia Brooks O'Brien	A	St. Andrew of Annapolis	2014

John Taylor	A	Pasadena: Faith-Community Coop Parish	2017
Terri Williams	BM	Epworth Chapel	2019
Katherine Gorman	BS	Mays Chapel	2018
Anissa Johnson	BS	Milford Mill	2015
John Mayden	BS	Upperco:Mt. Zion	2019
Matthew Sichel	BS	Hampstead: Wesley	2016
Deborah House	CH	Bethel:Rohrersville	2019
Joshua Gillen	CH	Hancock: Hancock	2017
Helen Ballew	CM	Trinity	2016
Cristin Cooper	CM	Olney: Oakdale	2017
Miguel Gallegos	CM	Gaithersburg: Epworth	2017
David Norton	CM	Highland: Mt. Zion	2018
Melaina Trice	CM	Ashton	2015
William Carpenter	F	Greater Brunswick Charge	2011
Caitlin Mossburg	F	Brookhill	2017 (not previously listed)
Kristin Weschler	F	Frederick: Trinity	2018
Kevin Cameron	GW	Glenmont	2019
Deryl Davis	GW	DC: Foundry	2012
Chet Jechura	GW	DC: Foundry	2018
Kevin Highfield	GW	Mt. Vernon Place	2018
Bernardo Lourenco	GW	Simpson Hamlin	2017
Sharon Milton	GW	Emory Fellowship	2018
Admire Russell	GW	Good Shepherd	2012
Denise Ryles-McKoy	GW	McKendree Simms Brookland	2018
Bo Hwan Wang	GW	National Korean	2017
Melanie Weldon-Soiset	GW	Van Buren	2017
Roberta White	GW	DC: Hughes Memorial	2012
Bruce Jackson	WE	Lexington Park: Zion	2016
Judith Bennett	WE	LaPlata: St Matthews	2019
Jacob Cogman	WE	Oxon Hill: St Paul	2018
James Cogman	WE	Oxon Hill: St Paul	2018
Vernona Colbert	WE	Ft Washington: Grace	2019
Angela Kittrell	WE	Bowie: Bowie	2018
Shemaiah Strickland	WE	Queen's Chapel	2019
Dale Thomas	WE	Leonardtown: First Saints	2019
Rebecca Wessinger	WE	Dunkirk: Smithville	2015

b. Who have had their candidacy for ordained or licensed ministry accepted by a District Committee on Ordained Ministry in another annual conference? (Include name of accepting conference.)

NAME	RECEIVING CONFERENCE	ORIGINALLY CERTIFIED	ACCEPTED BY DISTRICT

| Tai Courtemanche | GW | Oak Chapel | 2014: Transfer W. PA |
| Dahlia Leigh | GW | Takoma Park: Grace | 2017: Transfer to VA |

of study or the M.Div. (¶319.4)? PLEASE NOTE: Persons on this list must receive an episcopal appointment. (3/4 **v**)

a) Full-time local pastors (¶318.1) (3/4 **v**). Listed by district

NAME (year certified)	DIST	APPOINTMENT	YEARS COMPLETED WITH COURSE OF STUDY
*Christopher Broadwell [16]	A	Annapolis: Eastport	MDIV
*Emily Skorupinski [18]	BM	Lansdowne: Lansdowne	MDIV
Stephen E. Smith [05]	BS	Street: Emory	LLPS 05 (4.0)
*Joshua Gillen [17]	CH	Hancock: Hancock	MDIV
Robert Pierson [16]	CH	Cumberland: Davis/Emmanuel	LLPS16 (1.0)
*Charles Riggleman [97]	CH	Oldtown: Oldtown Charge	MDIV LLPS 07
*Dauba Denise Adams [10]	CM	Kemptown: Providence	MDIV
*Sandra Phillips [09]	CM	Frederick: Wesley Chapel	MDIV
*Richard Wilson Baker [10]	F	Emmitsburg: Trinity/Taneytown: Messiah	LLPS 99
William Ball [16]	F	Martinsburg: Pikeside	LLPS 15 (.25)
*Rex Bowens [99]	F	Frederick: Jackson Chapel	LLPS 99
*Scott Clawson [12]	F	New Market: Mt. Carmel/New Market	LLPS 12
*John Dean [03]	F	Westminster: Deer Park	MDIV
*Debra Marie Linton [08]	F	Frederick: Centennial Memorial	MDIV
Scott Summer [10]	F	Bedington: Bedington	LLPS 10 (4.25)
*Rebecca Lynn Wilson [02]	F	Martinsburg: Calvary	LLPS 03
*Alan Hemming [11]	WE	First Saints Community	MDIV

b).Part-time local pastors (¶318.2) (fraction of full-time in one-quarter increments). (3/4 **v**)

NAME	DIST	APPOINTMENT	YEARS COMPLETED

			WITH COURSE OF STUDY
*Caprice Brown [10]	A	25% - Laurel: Community First Coop. Parish	MDIV
*S. Jerry Colbert [06]	A	50% - Annapolis: John Wesley	LLPS 06
Gay Green-Cardin [11]	A	50% - Jessup: Asbury	LLPS 10 (3.75)
Jerome Jones [11]	A	50% - Crofton: Wilson Memorial	LLPS 12
*Sandra Knepp [16]	A	25% - Odenton: Trinity	MDIV
Marilyn Lewis [17]	A	25% - Lothian: Adams	LLPS 17
*Gregory J. McNeil [97]	A	25% Union Memorial	LLPS 97
Richard Oursler [11]	A	50% - Dorsey Emmanuel/Wesley Chapel	LLPS 10 (4.0)
*Michael Rigsby [08]	A	50% - Glen Burnie: Messiah	MDIV
*Dale Thomas [19]	A	50% - Cape St. Claire	MDIV
*Patricia Turnage [17]	A	50% - Cecil Memorial/Mt. Calvary Charge	MDIV
Melvin Bond [11]	BM	50% - Unity	LLPS 11
Steve Burke [12]	BM	25% - Water's Edge	LLPS 16 (0.75)
*Michael Carrington, Jr. [17]	BM	50% Martin Luther King Jr Memorial	MDIV
Ronald S. Dodson, Sr. [16]	BM	25% - Faith Community	LLPS 16
Scheherazade Forman [16]	BM	25% - West Baltimore	LLPS 16
Anthony Forman [14]	BM	25% - West Baltimore	LLPS 14
Daryl A. Foster [00]	BM	50% - Cherry Hill	LLPS 04
Nathaniel Green [05]	BM	25% - Violetville	LLPS 05 (1.25)
Joel Holmes [18]	BM	25% - Beechfield	LLPS 17
Richard Keller [12]	BM	50% - Christ	LLPS 11 (4.25)
Christine Kumar [17]	BM	75% - Cowenton-Piney Grove	LLPS 17 (Wesley)
Daniel Kutrick [10]	BM	25% -Graceland	LLPS 11 (4.25)
Jorge Moreno [17]	BM	25% - Salem Hispanic	LLPS (4.0)
Mary Robinson [11]	BM	75% - Essex	Wesley)
*Levon Sutton [17]	BM	25% - Catonsville Emmanuel	MDIV

Charlie Taylor [18]	BM	25% - St Matthews	MDIV
*Daniel Wood, Jr. [12]	BM	75% - Baltimore: Grace	MDIV
Barbara Allen [12]	BS	50% - Hampstead: Shiloh-Patapsco Coop. Parish	LLPS 15 (1.5)
Gerald Paul Gautcher [10]	BS	50% - Reisterstown: Deer Park	LLPS 10 (3.5)
Granderson Jones [00]	BS	25% - New Hope Christian Fellowship	LLPS 15 (1.5)
*Ernest Lievers [04]	BS	25% - Edgewood/Greenspring	LLPS 04
*John Mayden [19]	BS	25%Upperco: Mt Zion	MDIV (Candler)
*Alfred Sipes [15]	BS	50% - Cedar Grove-Bentley Springs-Stablers	MDIV
*Charles Bergen [14]	CH	50% - Berkeley Springs: Berkeley Springs Charge	LLPS 14 (MDIV)
Patricia Bittner [14]	CH	50% - Flintstone: Flintstone Charge	LLPS 13 (2.0)
Lisa Boone [16]	CH	25% - Cumberland: McKendree of Potomac Park & Rawlings	LLPS 16
Vicki Cubbage [16]	CH	25% - LaVale: Park Place	LLPS 12
Albert Deal [11]	CH	50% Big Pool Charge	LLPS 12 (3.75)
*Sharon Gibson [98]	CH	25% - Hagerstown: Asbury	LLPS 98
Suzanne Jones [16]	CH	25% Keedysville: Salem	LLPS 16 (Wesley)
Kenny Mason [13]	CH	25% - Berkeley Springs: Alpine Charge	LLPS 13 (3.25)
Dionne Hall [15]	CH	50% - Hagerstown: Shiloh	MDiv (Wesley)
Joshua Rider [16]	CH	25% - Little Orleans: Sideling Hill	LLPS 16 (.50)
John Ampiah-Addison [12]	CM	50% - Asbury	LLPS 14 (1.5)
Kevin Beall [17]	CM	75% - Bethesda (Damascus)	LLPS 18 (0.25)
Zelda Childs [10]	CM	50% - Christ Columbia	LLPS 11 (3.5)
*Terry L. McCain [01]	CM	50% - Highland: Hopkins	LLPS 01
T.J. Mount [15]	CM	50% - Araby: Araby CG	MDIV
Samuel Moore [15]	CM	50% - Ellicott City: Emory	LLPS 16 (.75)
Olivia Gross [18]	CM	25% - Brookville: Mt. Zion	LLPS 19

*Cathryn Vitek [09]	CM	75% - Bethany	LLPS 14
Shawn Vollmerhausen [17]	CM	25% - Alberta Gary	LLPS 17
Ronald Young [16]	CM	25% - St Luke's	LLPS 16 (.75)
Mary Buzby [13]	F	50% - New Windsor: New Hope/Westminster: St. James	LLPS 13 (4.75)
Mark Claiborne, Sr. [17]	F	25% - Frederick: Centennial Memorial	LLPS 16 (Wesley)
Darrell Davis [17]	F	25% - New Windsor: Middleburg – Uniontown	LLPS 17
Ray Dudley [08]	F	25% - Frederick: Deerfield	LLPS 08 (3.0)
Mark Eyler [18]	F	25% - Sykesville: Brandenburg	LLPS 18
David Fossett [17]	F	25% - Frederick: Hopehill	LLPS 17
Lisa Franzen [16]	F	25% - Martinsburg: Berkeley Place/Friendship	LLPS 16 (1.25)
Richard Gibbs [16]	F	25% - Frederick: Walkersville/Mt. Pleasant	LLPS 16 (1.75)
Michael Lida [16]	F	25% - Chestnut Hill: Silver Grove	LLPS 16 (.25)
Debbie Mooney [18]	F	50% - Kearneysville: Leetown	LLPS 18
*Caitlin Mossburg [17]	F	50% - Lewistown: Lewistown	MDIV
Robert Orrence [09]	F	25% - Thurmont: Catoctin	LLPS 11 (2.5)
Dawn Reidy [16]	F	25% - Bunker Hill: Payne's Chapel	LLPS 16
Charles Rice [16]	F	50% - Frederick: Buckeystown 85	LLPS 16 (3.0)
Blango E. Ross, Jr. [01]	F	50% - New Windsor: Strawbridge	LLPS 05 (3.5)
William Rowley [17]	F	75% - Chestnut Hill	LLPS 17
Scott Sassaman [13]	F	25% - Middleway: Middleway	LLPS 14 (2.25)
Richard Shuman, II [17]	F	50% - Charles Town: Oakland/Summit Point: Memorial	LLPS 17

346

Thomas Sigler, Jr. [17]	F	75% - Inwood: Darkesville	LLPS 17
Samuel Tryon [17]	F	25% - Harpers Ferry: Bolivar/Engle	MDIV in progress (Wesley)
Tyrone Blackwell [18]	GW	50% - Millian Memorial	MDIV (Howard)
Janice Phipps-Harmon [14]	GW	25% - Emory	LLPS14 (1.5)
Bernard Harris [15]	GW	25% - McKendree- Simms- Brookland CP	LLPS 06 (1.75)
Lucinda Kent [16]	GW	25% - Van Buren	LLPS 18
Cindy L. Banks [12]	WE	25% - Shiloh	LLPS 12 (.5)
Jacques T. Banks [09]	WE	50% - Indian Head	LLPS 09 (4.25)
*Roland Matthew Barnes [97]	WE	50% - Carroll Western	LLPS 99
*Brian Berger [15]	WE	25% St Leonard: Waters Memorial	MDIV
Kevin Brooks [13]	WE	50% -Charlotte Hall: Mt. Calvary – St. Matthews	LLPS 13 (.25)
Vernona Colbert [19]	WE	25% Sunderland: Mt Hope	LTPS 2018
*Donald Gene Geller, Jr. [12]	WE	25% - Lexington Park: Community with a Cause	MDIV
Angela Kittrell [18]	WE	50% Bowie:Bowie	MDIV
*Joan Ann Jones [04]	WE	50% - St. Edmonds	MDIV
Thomas Christopher Long [13]	WE	50% - Upper Marlboro: Bethel	LLPS 02 (Asbury)
*Kermit C.C. Moore [11]	WE	50% - Ft. Washington: Providence-Ft. Washington	LLPS 11
*Lesley Newman-Adams [15]	WE	50% - Temple Hills: Corkran Memorial	MDIV
*Jeanne A. Parr [10]	WE	50% - Pisgah	MDIV
Sonja Penny [15]	WE	25% - Dunkirk: Peters	LLPS 16
Doris Rothwell [15]	WE	25% - St. Inigoes: Mt. Zion	LLPS 15 (.25)

b) Students from other annual conferences or denominations serving as local pastors and enrolled in a school of theology listed by the University Senate (¶318.3,4)? (3/4 **v**)

NAME	DISTRICT	APPOINTMENT	SEMINARY	HOME CONFERENCE
Jeffrey Postell	A	Solley	Wesley	West Florida/Alabama
Blake Smarr	BS	Bixlers-Millers	Wesley	Western North Carolina

c) Students who have been certified as candidates in your annual conference and are serving as local pastors in another annual conference while enrolled in a school of theology listed by the University Senate (¶318.3) (3/4 **v**)

NAME	FIRST YEAR LICENSE AWARDED	YEARS COMPLETED IN COURSE OF STUDY
None		

d) Persons serving as local pastors while seeking readmission to conference membership (¶¶365.4, 367, 368.3)? (If not in this conference indicate name of conference where serving.) (3/4 **v**)

NAME	DISTRICT	YEARS COMPLETED IN COURSE OF STUDY
None		

22. Who have been discontinued as local pastors (¶320.1)? INFORMATIONAL

NAME	DISTRICT	DATE DISCONTINUED
None		

23. Who have been reinstated as local pastors (¶320.4)(v)?

NAME	DISTRICT	YEARS COMPLETED IN COURSE OF STUDY
*Sandra Phillips	CM	MDIV

24. What ordained ministers or provisional members from other Annual Conferences or Methodist denominations are approved for appointment in the Annual Conference while retaining their conference or denominational membership (¶¶331.8, 346.1)? (List alphabetically; indicate Annual Conference or denomination where membership is held. Indicate credential.) INFORMATIONAL

a. Annual Conferences

NAME	CLERGY STATUS	DIST	APPOINTMENT	HOME CONFERENCE
Jane Ayers	RE	BS	West Harford Coop Parish (25%)	Peninsula-Delaware

Stephanie Bekhor	FE	A	Marley (50%)	Desert Southwest Conference
Tori Chane' Butler	FE	GW	Good Hope Union	Texas Conference
Marion Easterling	FE	CM	Locust	New England Conference
William Edward Green	FE	GW	DC: Foundry	Northern Illinois Conference
David Hodsdon	FE	CM	Hyattstown: Clarksburg Charge (75%)	Yellowstone Conference
Katherine Ann Paul	FE	WE	Hollywood	North Carolina Conference
Andrew Peck-McClain	FE	CM	Washington Grove (75%)	New York Conference
Mary Ricketts	FE	CH	Smithsburg Charge (75%)	Upper New York Conference
Benjamin Brodie Roberts	FD	GW	Foundry UMC	North Carolina Conference
Douglas Robinson-Johnson	FE	GW	National	The New England Conference
Kirstin Shrom-Rhoads	FD on 6/5/19	CH	Manidokan Camp	West Ohio Conference
Troy Sims	FD	GW	Capitol Hill	North Texas Conference
Diana Wingeier-Rayo	FE	GW	Silver Spring: Hughes	Western North Carolina

a)   Other Methodist Denominations

NAME	CLERGY STATUS	District	APPOINTMENT	DENOMINATION
Richard Black	Elder	GW	Lincoln Park	African Methodist Episcopal
Biak Chhunga	Elder	GW	Rockville: Mizo Fellowship	Upper Myanmar Methodist Church
Daphne Fraser	Elder	CM	Fairview	African Methodist Episcopal

25. What clergy in good standing in other Christian denominations have been approved to serve appointments or ecumenical ministries within the bounds of the Annual Conference while retaining their denominational affiliation (¶¶331.8, 346.2)? (v) (Designate with an asterisk those who have been accorded voting rights within the annual conference. Indicate credentials.)

NAME	STATUS	DIST	APPT	DENOMINATION
Sharon Lowans	Ordained	F	Sandy Hook & Shenandoah Memorial	Wesleyan
John Unger	Ordained	F	Camp Hill-Wesley	Lutheran

26. Who are affiliate members: (List alphabetically; indicate annual conference or denomination where membership is held.)

    a) With vote (¶586.4b [v])?   None

    b) Without vote (¶¶334.5, 344.4)? **(2/3 v)**

NAME	MEMBER CONFERENCE/DENOMINATION	DISTRICT	FIRST YEAR OF AFFILIATION
Christina K. Suerdieck	Virginia Conference	F	2010
Cynthia Zirlott	Virginia Conference	CH	2008

NOTE: If your conference has admitted or ordained persons as a courtesy to another conference, list these persons in Question 40 only. If persons have been admitted or ordained by another annual conference as a courtesy to your conference, list these persons in Questions 27-39 whichever are appropriate, giving the date and name of the accommodating conference.

27. Who are elected as associate members? ¶322 (3/4 **v**) (List alphabetically—see note preceding Question 27):

NAME
None

28. Who are elected as Provisional Members and what seminary are they attending, if in school? (under ¶¶322.4, 324, 325) (3/4 v)

    a. Provisional Deacons:

        • Under the provisions of ¶324.4a, c? (3/4 v)   (NOTE: All have completed seminary)

NAME	SEMINARY
Deborah Burgio	Wesley Theological Seminary
T.C. Morrow	Wesley Theological Seminary

        • Under the provisions of ¶324.5? (3/4 v)

NAME	SEMINARY
None	

    b. Provisional Elders:

        1. Under the provisions of ¶324.4a, b? (3/4 v)   (NOTE: All have completed seminary)

NAME	SEMINARY
Ian Collier	Duke Divinity School
Gerald Elston	Wesley Theological Seminary
Ashley Hoover	Wesley Theological Seminary
Narae Kim	Wesley Theological Seminary
Raphael Koikoi	Wesley Theological Seminary
Dong Eun (Vivian) Lee	Wesley Theological Seminary
Jean Lee	Wesley Theological Seminary
Isaiah Redd	Wesley Theological Seminary
Jeffrey Zalatoris	Wesley Theological Seminary

2. Under the provisions of ¶324.6? (3/4 **v**)

NAME		SEMINARY
None		

3. Under the provisions of ¶322.4? (**3/4 v**)

NAME	SEMINARY
None	

29. Who are continued as provisional members, in what year were they admitted to provisional membership, and what seminary are they attending, if in school (¶326, ¶327 (v)?

a. In preparation for ordination as a deacon? (PD) (¶326.1 (v) (Note: All have completed seminary)

NAME	ORIGINAL YEAR OF MEMBERSHIP	SPECIALITY
Kathleen Grace Charters	2014	Medical Ministry to Veterans
Enger Muteteke	2015	
Jennifer Kokoski	2017	Hospice
Megan B. Blanchard	2018	

In preparation for ordination as an elder? (PE) (¶326.2) (v)

NAME	ORIGINAL YEAR OF MEMBERSHIP
Linda Yarrow	2013
Laura Markle Downton	2014
Dana Maurice Jones	2014
Sherri Comer-Cox	2015
Michael Parker, II	2015
R. Lorraine Brown	2016
Sandra Hetz Burchell	2016
Mark Groover	2016

Irance Reddix	2016
Daniel Breidenbaugh	2017
Alison DeLeo	2017
Walter D. Jackson, III	2017
Heerak Kim	2017
Tommy M. Murray	2017
Kathleen M. O'Hern	2017
Heather Olson	2017
Monica E. Raines	2017
Evelyn Rivera	2017
Sherwyn Benjamin	2018
Scott Bostic	2018
Patrick Hurder Buhrman	2018
Mi Ja Cho	2018
Christopher Dembeck	2018
Sarah Elliott	2018
James Gosnell	2018
Lynne Humphries-Russ	2018
David Jacobson	2018
Kathryn Mackereth	2018
Robert Ruggieri	2018
Emily Smiley Hart	2018
Matthew Tate	2018
Anna Schwartz	2018

b.   Provisional deacons who became provisional elders? (v)

NAME	ORIGINAL YEAR OF MEMBERSHIP
None	

c. Provisional elders who became provisional deacons? (v)

NAME	ORIGINAL YEAR OF MEMBERSHIP
None	

d. Provisional members who transferred from other conferences or denominations? (¶347.1&2) (v)

NAME	CLERGY STATUS (PD or PE)	ORIGINAL YEAR OF MEMBERSHIP	PREVIOUS CONFERENCE OR DENOMINATION
SungHwan (Steven) Cho	PE	2019	Korean Methodist

30.   What ordained clergy, coming from other Christian denominations, have had their orders recognized (¶347.6): (v) **A person's orders may be recognized when they are transferring their membership into your annual conference from another Christian denomination. A person who is listed in Q.30 must also be listed in either Q. 31 a or b, depending on the transfer status.**

Name	Clergy Status	Previous Denomination
Ronald Fleming-Triplett	FE	Penecostal/Apostolic

31. What ordained clergy have been received from other Christian denominations (¶347.3): (List alphabetically—see note preceding Question 27):

a. As provisional members (¶347.3c? (v)

NAME	CLERGY STATUS (PD or PE)	DATE RECEIVED	FORMER DENOMINATION
Ronald Fleming-Triplett	PE	2014	Penecostal/Apostolic

b. As local pastors (¶347.3)? (v)

NAME	CLERGY STATUS (FL or PL)	DATE RECEIVED	FORMER DENOMINATION
None			

32. Who are elected as members in full connection? (List alphabetically—see note preceding Question 27. **Anyone appearing on this question must also be listed somewhere in questions 33-34 or 36, unless the clergy's orders from another denomination were recognized on question 30 in a previous year.) (3/4 v):**

a. Deacons

NAME	SEMINARY
Martina Martin Efodzi	Howard University School of Divinity

b. Elders

NAME	SEMINARY
Patricia Abell	Wesley Theological Seminary
Lillian Boyd	Wesley Theological Seminary
Andre Briscoe	Wesley Theological Seminary
Alexis Brown	Wesley Theological Seminary
Michael Cantley	Wesley Theological Seminary
Lemuel Dominguez	Wesley Theological Seminary
Kyle Durbin	Wesley Theological Seminary
Joseph Heath-Mason	Wesley Theological Seminary
Brenda Mcilwain	Wesley Theological Seminary
Jessica S. Hayden	Wesley Theological Seminary
Carissa Surber	Wesley Theological Seminary

33. Who are ordained as deacons and what seminary awarded their degree? Or, if their master's degree is not from a seminary, at what seminary did they complete the basic graduate theological studies?: (List alphabetically-see note preceding Question 27)

a. After provisional membership (¶330)? (**3/4 v**)

NAME	SEMINARY
Martina Martin Efodzi	Howard University School of Divinity

b. Transfer from elders? (¶309) (**3/4 v**)

None.

34. Who are ordained as elders and what seminary awarded their degree?

a. After provisional membership? (¶335) (3/4 v)

NAME	SEMINARY
Patricia Abell	Wesley Theological Seminary
Lillian Boyd	Wesley Theological Seminary
Andre Briscoe	Wesley Theological Seminary
Alexis Brown	Wesley Theological Seminary
Michael Cantley	Wesley Theological Seminary
Lemuel Dominguez	Wesley Theological Seminary
Kyle Durbin	Wesley Theological Seminary
Joseph Heath-Mason	Wesley Theological Seminary
Brenda Mcilwain	Wesley Theological Seminary
Jessica S. Hayden	Wesley Theological Seminary
Carissa Surber	Wesley Theological Seminary

Transfer from deacon? (¶309) (3/4 v)
None.

35. What Provisional Members, previously discontinued, are readmitted (¶364)? (**v**) None.

36. Who are readmitted (¶¶365–367 [**v**], ¶368 [2/3 v]):

NAME	CLERGY STATUS	PREVIOUS STATUS
None		

37. Who are returned to the effective relationship after voluntary retirement (¶357.7): (**v**)

NAME	CLERGY STATUS	YEAR RETIRED
None		

38. Who have been received by transfer from other annual conferences of The United Methodist Church (¶¶347.1, 416.5, 635.2n)? (List alphabetically. Indicate credential. See note preceding Question 27.) (v)
None.

39. Who are transferred in from other Methodist denominations (¶347.2)? (List alphabetically. Indicate credential.) INFORMATIONAL

None.

40. Who have been ordained as a courtesy to other conferences, after election by the other conference? (See note preceding Question 27. Such courtesy elections or ordinations do not require transfer of conference membership.) INFORMATIONAL

    a. Deacons in full connection. None.

    b. Elders in full connection. None.

41. Who have been transferred out to other annual conferences of The United Methodist Church (¶416.5)? (List alphabetically. Indicate credential. See note preceding Question 27.) INFORMATIONAL

NAME	CLERGY STATUS	NEW CONFERENCE	DATE OF TRANSFER
Neville "Al" Hammer III	FD	Western Pennsylvania	07-01-2019
Robin Johnson	FD	Western North Carolina	06-19-2019

42. Who are discontinued as provisional members (¶327)? (Indicate credential)

    a) By expiration of eight-year time limit (¶327)

NAME	CLERGY STATUS	DATE

    b) By voluntary discontinuance (¶327.6) (v)

NAME	CLERGY STATUS	DATE
Arthe (Taysie) Phillips	PE	07-01-2019
Sandra Phillips	PE	07-01-2019

    c) By involuntary discontinuance (¶327.6) (v)
       None.

    d) By reaching Mandatory Retirement Age (¶327.7)
       None.

43. Who are on location?

    a. Who has been granted honorable location (¶358.1)? (Give date when this action became effective. Record Charge Conference where membership is held):

        (1) This year? (v) None.

        (2) Previously?

NAME	Year originally granted	CHARGE CONFERENCE MEMBERSHIP	District	Year of Most Recent Report
Robert C. Warren, Jr.	1967			
William Dorsey Young, III	1970	Columbia: Christ	CM	
Lewis M. Buckler	1971	La Plata: La Plata	WE	
Douglas Dewhirst	1971			
Paul W. Galvin	1972			
Douglas E. Harton	1972			
James H. Fields, Sr.	1973			
R. Allen Streett	1974			
Alexander M. Tickner	1974			
G. Paul Carr	1975			
Aubrey Linville Leomer	1975			
James Davis Palmer	1976	Washington: Dumbarton	GW	
Howard K. Congdon	1978			
S. Edward Ferrell, Jr.	1978			
Edwin Graham	1978			
Luther H. Martin	1978			
Allen Powell	1979			
William E. Ravenscroft	1979	Hagerstown: Otterbein	CH	
Richard Ernest Hagenston	1982			
Richard Earl Schwinger	1983	Glenelg	CM	
Franklin Earl Smith	1985			
Lyle Edward Wilson	1987	Friendship: Damascus	CM	
Steven Lee Bowman	1987	Bel Air: Bel Air	BS	
James Michael Easterday	1987	Hagerstown: Otterbein	CH	
Eleanor White Jones Hawse	1988	Clarksburg: Clarksburg	CM	
Nelson McGill Pittinger	1988	Frederick: Calvary	F	

Ronald Ralph Runkles	1988	Mechanicsville: Mt. Zion	WE	
Ralph Erskine Wilson, III	1988	Parkville: Arnolia	BM	
Melvin James Fair, Jr.	1991	Owings Mills: Pleasant Hill	BS	
Kristen Johnson Aiken	1994	Westminster:Westminster	F	
Miriam Hope Jackson	1996	Gaithersburg: Epworth	CM	
Richard L. Blucher	1997	Washington: Foundry	GW	
Richard Perry Bowman	1997	Washington: Dumbarton	GW	
Wendy Starr Flegal	1999	Washington: Dumbarton	GW	
Carolyn Sue Bray	2002	Friendship: Friendship	A	
Carol Armstrong-Moore	2003	Washington: Chevy Chase	GW	
Kathryn L. Preston	2005	Baltimore: Mt. Vernon Place	BM	
Vincent R. Liburd	2005	Rockville: Rockville	GW	
Suzanne Weber	2007	Washington: foundry	GW	
Wendy Shenk-Evans	2008	Washington: Christ	GW	
James Lucas	2010	Crofton: Community	A	
William Wan	2011	Rockville: Faith	GW	
Robert Barton	2014	Mechanicsville: Mt. Zion	WE	
Drew Phoenix	2014	DC: Dumbarton	GW	
Lauren Heather Lay	2015	Hughes: Wheaton	GW	

b. Who on honorable location are appointed ad interim as local pastors? (¶358.2) (Indicate date and appointment):
None.

c. Who has been placed on administrative location (¶359)? (Give date when this action became effective. Record Charge Conference where membership is held. Indicate credential.):

(1) This year? (**v**) None.

(2) Ad Interim Administrative Location? (v) None.

(3) Previously?

NAME	YEAR ORIGINALLY PLACED	CHARGE CONFERENCE MEMBERSHIP	YEAR OF MOST RECENT REPORT
Jacob Young	07-01-2018		

44. Who have been granted the status of honorable location–retired (¶358.3)? (Record Charge Conference where membership is held.)

   a. This year? **(v)**   None.

   b.. Previously?

NAME	STATUS	YEAR HONORABLE LOCATION ORIGINALLY GRANTED	CC MEMBERSHIP	DISTRICT
Robert McKinley, III			Crofton: Community	A
Wilson Edward Neighoff			Baltimore: Hiss	BM
Thomas P. Roberts	RE 07/01/08		Huntingtown: Patuxent	WE

45. Who have had their status as honorably located and their orders terminated (¶358.2)? **(v)** (Give date when this action became effective. Indicate credential.) None.

46. Who have had their conference membership terminated? (Give date when this action became effective. Indicate credential.)

   a. By withdrawal to unite with another denomination (¶360.1, .4)? (v)
       None

   b. By withdrawal from the ordained ministerial office (¶360.2, .4)? (v)
       None

   c. By withdrawal under complaints or charges (¶¶360.3, .4; 2719.2)? (v)
       None.

   d. By termination of orders under recommendation of the Board of Ordained Ministry (¶358.2, 359.3)? **(v)** None.

   e. By trial (¶2713)? **(v)**
       None.

47. Who have been suspended under the provisions of ¶362.1d, 2704.2c or ¶2711.3? (Give effective dates. Indicate credential.) INFORMATIONAL

None.

48. Deceased (List alphabetically in the spaces provided): INFORMATIONAL
    a) What associate members have died during the year?
       Active:

NAME	DATE OF BIRTH	DATE OF DEATH
Theodore D. Marsh	11-22-1953	09-07-2018

   Retired:

NAME	DATE OF BIRTH	DATE OF DEATH
William J Bussard	05-01-1943	11-20-2018
Lewis I. Keene	07-05-1933	02-13-2019
Lloyd E. Marcus	04-27-1928	06-01-2018
Maurice S. Moore	09-03-1939	11-19-2018

    b) What provisional members have died during the year? (Indicate credentials.)
       Active: None

   Retired: None

    c) What elders have died during the year?
       Active:

NAME	DATE OF BIRTH	DATE OF DEATH
Wayne Chung	04-21-1956	01-13-2019
James L. DeMent	06-13-1958	03-19-2019

   Retired:

NAME	DATE OF BIRTH	DATE OF DEATH
Mary W. Conaway	01-26-1943	08-30-2018
Herbert L. D. Doggett	06-25-1926	09-03-2018
William W. Ehlers	02-23-1924	02-29-2019
Henry E. Ernst	11-10-1929	05-02-2019
Hal T. Henderson, Sr.	02-13-1933	04-08-2019
Bernard F. Hillenbrand	05-11-1925	10-05-2018
Raymond M. Kingsborough	10-05-1922	11-25-2018
Edwin H. Langrall	11-30-1926	11-12-2018
John T. Smith	10-24-1937	04-01-2019

Earl W. Sulmonetti	03-10-1931	05-05-2019
Charles W. Stewart	10-26-1921	01-01-2019
Ernest W.P. Thayil	11-17-1931	01-04-2019
Vernon L. Thompson	07-14-1927	06-01-2018
John C. Walker	05-06-1927	11-21-2018
Pauline V. Wilkins	04-13-1932	10-11-2018
William Carl Zinn	08-24-1937	01-02-2019

   d)   What deacons have died during this year?

   Active: None.

   Retired: None.

   e)   What local pastors have died during the year?

   Active: None

   Retired:

NAME	DATE OF BIRTH	DATE OF DEATH
Walter M. Bosman	02-09-1951	08-02-2018
Helen C. Fleming	08-13-1939	12-13-2018
Charles W. Henry	09-11-1938	02-03-2019

   f)   What Certified Lay Ministers have died during the year? None.

49. What provisional or ordained members (elders and deacons) have received appointments in other Annual Conferences of The United Methodist Church while retaining their membership in this Annual Conference (¶¶331.8, 346.1)? (List alphabetically; indicate annual conference where appointed. Indicate credential.) INFORMATIONAL

NAME	CLERGY STATUS	CONFERENCE WHERE APPOINTED	APPOINTMENT	DATE
Adam Briddell	FE	Oregon-Idaho Conference	First UMC of Eugene	07-01-2015
Michelle Chaney	FE	Virginia Conference	Centreville UMC	08-01-2016
Mary Dennis	FD	California-Pacific	North District Change Manager	07-01-2018 11-01-2018

			East District Change Manager	
Ginger Ray Medley	FE	Florida Conference	Poinciana UMC	07-01-2017
Enger Muteteke	PD	Greater New Jersey	Good Shepherd & Lifegate (effective 7/1/2019)	07-01-2018
Kate Payton	FE	Minnesota		07-01-2019
Robert Schneider	FE	New England Conference	First UMC of Littleton	07-01-2010
Kevin Smalls	FE	Detroit Conference	Hope	06-01-2016
Jacqueline Jones-Smith	FE	Florida Conference	Christ UMC	07-01-2016
Vicky Starnes	FE	Peninsula Delaware Conference	Epworth	04-01-2013
Perry Williams	FE	Oklahoma Conference	St. Paul's	06-01-2014

50. Who are the provisional, ordained members or associate members on leave of absence and for what number of years consecutively has each held this relation (¶353)? (Indicate credential. Record Charge Conference where membership is held.)

    a.   Voluntary **(v)**

        (1) Personal, 5 years or less (¶353.2a3 (v)

NAME	CLERGY STATUS	DATE EFFECTIVE	CHARGE CONFERENCE	DISTRICT
Sarah Dorrance	FE	07-01-2019 (0)	Brook Hill	F
Laura Markle Downton	PE	01-19-2017 (2)	Foundry	GW
Nicole Houston	FE	07-01-2016 (3)	Severna Park	A

        (2) Personal, more than 5 years (¶353.2a3 (2/3 v) None.

        (3) Family, 5 years or less (¶353.2b3 (v)

NAME	CLERGY STATUS	DATE EFFECTIVE	CHARGE CONFERENCE	DISTRICT
Chiew Len Teo	FD	05-01-2016 (3)	Good Shepherd: Silver Spring	GW

        (4) Family, more than 5 years (¶353.2b3 (2/3 v) None.

(5) Transitional (¶353.2c) (leave granted for up to 12 months) (v) None.

    b. Involuntary?
        (1)   Involuntary Leave (¶354)? **(2/3 v)**
        None.
        (2)   Ad Interim Involuntary Leave (JCD 1355) (v)
        None.

51. Who are granted sabbatical leave (¶351)? **(v)** (Give date when this relation became effective; indicate credential.)
None.

52. Who have been granted medical leave due to medical or disabling conditions (¶356)? (v) (Give effective dates:

NAME	CLERGY STATUS	DATE EFFECTIVE	CHARGE CONFERENCE	DISTRICT
Robert Brennan	FE	07-01-2016 (3)	Martinsburg: Calvary	F
Lee Brewer	FE	11-01-2017 (1)	Hughes	GW
William Green	FE	07-01-1997 (22)	Ellicott City: Glen Mar	CM
Katherine Heflin	FE	04-01-2009 (11)	Frederick: Calvary	F
Margaret Wood Hodges	FE	03-01-1999 (20)	DC: Dumbarton	GW
Elizabeth Jane Richards	FE	11-01-2006 (12)	Damascus: Damascus	CM
Theresa Robinson	FE	04-01-2014 (5)	St. Paul's Praise & Worship Center	BM
Sheldon M. Reese	FE	04-01-2016 (3)	Perry Hall	BS
Leo Rodriguez	FE	06-30-2016 (3)	Salem-Baltimore Hispanic	BM
Ingrid Wang	FE	09-01-2016 (3)	Pasadena: Pasadena	A

53. What Members in full connection have been retired (¶357): (List alphabetically giving full name—first, middle, last—in that order. If retiring in the interim between conference sessions (¶357.2d), indicate the effective date of retirement.) **(Under ¶357.1, no vote required; under ¶357.2, (v); under ¶357.3, (2/3 v)**

Deacons **READ NAMES ALOUD FOR RECOGNITION**

a.   This year?

NAME	DATE EFFECTIVE
Martha J. Maxham	07-01-2019

b.   Previously?

NAME	DATE EFFECTIVE
Ruth Bell	11-01-2003
John William Bennett	01-01-2011
Judith Lee Ann Brown Birch	12-31-2008
Richard Lee Buckingham	06-30-2017
Susan Carns	07-01-2015
Linda Coolbaugh	01-01-2012
Limja Huh Gim	07-01-2014
Gertrude Greene	07-01-1998
Sharon Leinert Mills	07-01-2009
Lynn Nulton	07-01-2012
Stella S. Tay	07-01-2014
Jacqulyn Thorpe	07-01-2008
Andrea Titcomb	07-01-2006
Arthuree Wright	06-30-2018

Elders READ NAMES ALOUD FOR RECOGNITION

a.   This year?

NAME	DATE EFFECTIVE
Kay Albury	07-01-2019
Kimberly A. Brown-Whale	07-01-2019
Richard E. Brown-Whale	07-01-2019
Steven T. Cochran	07-01-2019
Esther Holimon	07-01-2019
Robert H. Hunter, III	07-01-2019

Gay W. Hutchinson	02-01-2019
Pamela J. Marsh	07-01-2019
Denise M. Yepsen Millett	07-01-2019
Jeffrey A. Paulson	07-01-2019
Bruce C. Thompson	07-01-2019
Mark R. Waddell	07-01-2019
Mamie Williams	07-01-2019
Jane E. Wood	07-01-2019

b. Previously?

NAME	DATE EFFECTIVE
Kwame Abayomi	12-31-2006
Ann Adams	11-16-2011
Clark Aist	07-01-2004
George Aist	07-01-2004
JoAnne Alexander	07-01-2014
Edison Amos	07-01-1994
George Anderson	07-01-2001
Edwin Ankeny	07-01-2004
James Archibald, Jr.	07-01-1996
A. David Argo	01-18-2013
Helen Armiger	07-01-2016
Ann V. Atkins	07-01-2015
Harold P. Atkins	07-01-2018
John Baker	07-01-1991
Maria Andita H. Barcelo	07-01-2014
Reg D. Barss	07-01-2018
R. Kay Barger	07-01-2010
Edward Bauman, Jr.	07-01-1992
Harry Baxter, Jr.	07-01-2003
Janet Lee T. Becker	07-01-2015
Susan Beehler	07-01-2003
Paul Benjamin	07-01-2010
Donna Hennessey Bennett	07-01-2012
William Bice	07-01-1997
Bruce Birch	07-01-2009
Winifred J. Blagmond	12-30-2009
John M. Blanchard, Jr.	07-01-2016
Ernest Bortner, Jr.	07-01-1989
Sharon Bourgeois	07-01-2008
Kenneth Bowen	07-01-1997
Walter Bowers, Sr.	07-01-2000
William Boyer	07-01-2005
Robert Braden, Sr.	06-07-1985
Emora T. Brannan	07-01-2011
Allan Broadhurst	06-12-1987
Robert Brookman	08-04-2006
Byron P. Brought	07-01-2010
Arlester Brown	07-01-1991
Gregory Brown	07-01-2007
John Roger Brown	05-27-2015
Kenneth Earl Brown	12-31-2011
Marianne Brown	07-01-2018
Susan Brown	07-01-2018

Thomas Brunkow	07-01-2006
Donald L. Burgard	07-01-2009
Cynthia H. Burkert	07-01-2017
Roger Burtner	07-01-1990
Henry G. Butler, Jr.	07-01-2016
Gail Button	07-01-2018
Eugene Byrne	02-15-2007
Lynn Cairns	07-01-2006
Curtis Campaigne	07-01-1988
John Howard Campbell	03-01-2013
Kim K. Capps	07-01-2012
Roger John Carlson	07-01-2013
Vernice Carney	07-01-2006
Arlene Carr	07-01-2002
Shirley Carrington	07-01-2004
Robert D. Carter	07-01-2018
David Carter-Rimbach	07-01-2007
Jack Cassel	07-01-2000
Richard Chambers	07-01-1989
James Chance	07-01-2005
Bruce Chapman	07-01-2017
Terri R. Chattin	07-01-2018
Lon Chesnutt	07-01-1997
Kiyul Chung	02-02-2015
Eva L. Clark	09-04-2012
Raymond Clements, Jr.	06-12-1987
Margaret H. Click	07-01-2014
Richard Closson	01-01-1990
Lysbeth Cockrell	07-01-2018
Harry Cole	07-01-2001
Mary Jane Coleman	07-01-2005
Carmen Collette	06-01-2013
Ronald L. Collier, Sr.	07-01-2011
Thomas Connar	07-01-2007
Reynold Connett	07-01-1988
Joseph A. Conte	07-01-2016
Robert Conway	07-01-2006
David S. Cooney	07-01-2018
Janet Cornelius	09-15-2008
Merle Correll	06-16-1982
Linda Coveleskie	07-01-2008
Richard Craig	07-01-2012
Diane A. Crider	07-01-2002

obert Crider, Jr.	07-01-2005
icki S. Curry	07-01-2011
rances C. Dailey	07-01-2018
ilen W. Dameron	07-01-2013
unde Davies	07-01-2011
larence Davis	07-01-2006
larold Davis	06-20-1979
ichard Davis	07-01-2006
ackson Day	07-01-2008
ally Day	07-01-2005
ieorge F. DeFord	07-01-2011
eter L. DeGroote	07-01-2009
Vayne A. DeHart	07-01-2010
dwin DeLong	07-01-2005
andra E. Demby	07-01-2012
lark A. Derby	07-01-2014
imothy Dissmeyer	07-01-2007
ames L. Ditto	07-01-2010
iane Dixon-Proctor	07-01-2018
arroll Doggett, Jr.	07-01-1988
atricia C. Dols	10-08-2012
icki M. Dotterer	07-01-2014
usan Duchesneau	07-01-2010
etty Preston Dunlop	07-01-2009
larian Dunmore	07-01-2008
enneth R. Dunnington	07-01-2013
ieorge G. Earle, Jr.	07-01-2014
Valter G. Edmonds	01-01-2013
loward Ellis	07-01-1989
ieorge Ennis	07-01-2008
is Farabee-Lewis	07-01-2017
Villiam Casper Farrady	10-01-1991
enneth R. Fell	07-01-2015
laire L. Fiedler	07-01-2016
ouglas Fox	07-01-2011
obert Fringo	03-01-1996
awrence Frye	07-01-1999
obert Funk	07-01-1998
i. Sylvester Gaines, Sr.	07-01-2016
lbert Galloway, Jr.	01-01-2003
owell Garland	07-01-1991
illian Geib	07-26-2008
ack George	07-01-2002
arryl Gill	07-01-2007
oren Gisselbeck	07-01-1997
lsie May Gladding	01-01-2009
inda J. Glassbrook	07-01-2014
rthur Gleckler	07-01-2000
lary Ellen Glorioso	07-01-2018
aren Gould	07-01-2005
ierald Grace	07-01-2016
larianne S. Grabowski	07-01-2018
ichard Gordon Gray, Jr.	07-01-2011
andra M. Greene	07-01-2014

James M. Greenfield	07-01-2009
G. Edward Grove	09-01-2009
John Grove	07-01-1996
Carroll Gunkel	07-01-2002
James Hainley	07-01-2002
Carlee Hallman	07-01-1996
Susan Halse	07-01-2015
Edgar Hammersla	07-01-1988
William Richard Harden	07-01-2011
Lyle Harper	07-01-1995
Charles L. Harrell	10-01-2012
Stanley Harrell	07-01-1997
Mae Etta Harrison	12-01-2013
Alfonso Harrod	07-01-1993
Charles Harvey	07-01-1994
Charlotte A. Hendee	07-01-2012
Eddie Henry	07-01-2007
William Herche	07-01-2017
R. Olin Herndon	07-01-2000
Robert D. Hershberger	07-01-2012
Barry E. Hidey	07-01-2017
Theodore D. Higby	07-01-2013
David black	07-01-2007
Hosea L. Hodges	01-01-2012
Richard Hogue	07-01-2007
William Holmes	07-01-1998
G. Robert Hottinger	07-01-2008
Kenneth M. Humbert	07-01-2013
Darcy R. Hunt	07-01-2016
James M. Hunt	07-01-2011
Robert Hurley	06-12-1987
Mary Ellen Huzzard	07-01-2012
Diana L. Hynson	12-31-2011
Hattie Jackson	07-01-2006
Linda Jacobus	07-01-2005
Chi Bon Jang	07-01-2010
John Jennings, Jr.	07-01-2008
B. Jody Jessup	07-01-2010
Alta Jewell	07-01-2005
Richard Jewell	07-01-2016
Roger Johnson	06-12-1987
Victor Johnson	07-01-2006
Hattie Johnson-Holmes	07-01-2016
Bruce A. Jones	07-01-2018
Calvin Jones	07-01-1994
Joye Jones	07-01-2016
Richard Karpal	07-01-1996
Clarence Kaylor	07-01-2000
Arthur Kent	07-01-1985
Paul Choonam Kim	05-16-2010
Robert Kirkley	07-01-2000
Jeanne Klauda	07-01-2006
Kathleen H. Kohl	07-01-2017
David Kolda	07-01-2003

Lamar Kopp	07-01-1989
Mary E. Kraus	07-01-2009
Diedra Kriewald	07-01-2007
Richard A. Kroll	07-01-2012
Norman Kuehnle	06-12-1987
Ronald R. Kurtz	07-01-2012
August Lageman	07-01-2005
Ludwig Lankford	07-01-1999
Ellis Larsen	07-01-2001
Neva Leatherwood	08-01-2002
John Lebo	07-01-1996
Michael Leftwich	07-01-1996
Janice E. Leith	07-01-2014
Frank Leslie	07-01-1996
G. Douglass Lewis	07-01-2002
Weller Lewis, Jr.	06-12-1987
Diana Ley	07-01-2008
Charles Lightner	07-01-1999
Donald Llewellyn	07-01-1993
Don Lowe	07-01-2000
Anders R. Lunt	07-01-2010
Ernest D. Lyles, Sr.	07-01-2017
William Kenneth Lyons, Jr.	07-01-2008
Brenda Mack	07-01-2017
Burton Mack	07-01-2008
Vera L. Mitchell Mallett	09-29-2011
James Manning	07-01-1998
Evelyn H. Manson	07-01-2005
Robert Manthey	07-01-2004
Susan Marseilles	07-01-2006
Sherrin Marshall	07-01-2016
Donna J. Martin	07-01-2009
Mildred Martin	07-01-2007
Earl Mason	07-01-2016
Eugene Matthews	07-01-2008
Mapipi Isaac Mawokomatanda	07-01-2012
Jesse Mayes	07-01-2005
Mary Marcia Mayor	07-01-2016
Lloyd B. McCanna	07-01-2014
Harold McClay, Jr.	07-01-2005
Ralph McCulloh	07-01-2007
Richard K. McCullough	07-02-2011
Robert McCullough	10-01-2000
Mary Sheila McCurdy	07-01-2010
Michael A.H. McKinney	07-01-2011
Daniel McLellan, Jr.	07-01-2007
Jacquelyn L. McLellan	07-01-2017
Galen Menne	07-01-2004
Walter E. Middlebrooks	07-01-2011
Perry Miller	07-01-2003
Roderick J. Miller	07-01-2017
Curtis Mitchell	07-01-1992
Robert Mitzel	06-20-1986
Douglas Moore	07-01-1993

Ernest Maynard Moore	07-01-1985
Howard E. Moore	07-01-2015
L. Katherine Moore	07-01-2017
Kathryn B. Moore	01-01-2003
Raymond T. Moreland, Jr.	07-01-2010
Laura Lee C. Morgan	08-01-2009
Calvin S. Morris	07-01-2012
Richard J. Mortimore	07-01-2015
Albert Moser, Jr.	07-01-2012
Brindice Munoz-Rivera	07-01-2009
David C. Myers	07-01-2013
Nancy S. Nedwell	07-01-2015
James Nenninger	07-01-2008
Lawrence Neumark	07-01-2008
Marilyn Cheryl Newhouse	07-01-2017
Jeffrey Odom	07-01-2008
Fritz Outlaw	07-01-2009
Lovell Parham	07-01-2000
Charles Parker	01-01-2018
Conrad D. Parker	07-01-2011
Willie Parker	07-01-2008
Ann Parker-Offer	07-01-2006
Robert Eugene Paulen	07-01-2003
Constance Paulson	07-01-2008
Davis Peck	07-01-1992
Anne Perry	07-01-2003
Gene Perry	07-01-1993
Kristina J. Peterson	07-01-2011
W. Louis Piel	07-01-2006
Larry Plymire	07-01-2000
Ralph Posey	07-01-1994
Robert Poynter	06-12-1987
Patricia Pride	07-01-2009
Charles Proctor	07-01-2007
Yolanda Pupo-Ortiz	07-01-2005
Joe Rainey	07-01-2006
William Raker	07-01-2000
Leonard Ranson, Jr.	05-29-1975
Hallie Reeves	07-01-2006
Clayton Rhodes	07-01-1996
L. Patrick Ricker	07-01-2017
Carl Rife	07-01-1999
Sang Ro	11-01-1995
Clarence Roark, III	07-01-1996
J. David Roberts	07-01-2014
W. McCarl Roberts	07-01-1995
Mary Roberts	07-01-2008
Stephen D. Robison	07-01-2016
Robert Rodeffer	07-01-1998
Bernadette M. Ross	07-01-2014
Barbara Sands	12-31-2008
Saroj S. Sangha	07-01-2018
Victor E. Sawyer	07-01-2014
John Schildt	07-01-2004

Laura L. Schultz	07-01-2014
Richard Schulze	07-01-2008
Henry Schwarzmann	12-01-2002
Roberta Scoville	07-01-2008
Joan Senyk	11-01-2000
Joe Sergent	07-01-1996
David Shank	07-01-2018
Donald Shearer	07-01-1981
Wilson Shearer	07-01-1996
John Shirkey	07-01-1993
Louis Shockley	07-01-2015
Walter Shropshire, Jr.	07-01-2003
Linda Silbaugh	07-01-2007
Charles Simms	09-01-1999
David W. Simpson	07-01-2016
Richard Simpson	07-01-2003
Mary Jo Sims	09-01-2013
James Skillington	07-01-2018
Mark L. Smiley	12-31-2014
Errol Smith	07-01-1999
Gaye Smith	07-01-1999
Helen Smith	07-01-2016
LaRessa C. Smith-Horn	07-01-2017
Dean J. Snyder	07-01-2014
Hayden Sparks	07-01-1996
Kelly S. Sparks	07-01-2011
Susan A. Spears	07-01-2010
Kathy J. Spitzer	07-01-2014
Beverly Stang	07-01-2007
Luther Starnes	06-15-1984
Thomas Starnes	07-01-1994
Jay Stearns	07-01-2001
Richard E. Stetler	07-01-2010
Anne Ross Stewart	07-01-2009
Edward Stewart	07-01-2008
Donald Stewart, Jr.	07-01-2004
Gerald E. Stone	07-01-2010
Ann Strickler	07-01-2016
David Stum	07-01-2006
E. James Stutler	07-01-2010
Diane Summerhill	07-01-1999
Peter Yoon Sun	07-01-1997
Henry Swain	01-01-1990
Carolyn R. Swift	07-01-2009
Carl Synan	07-01-2006
Michael P. Szpak	07-01-2014
Deborah Tate	07-01-2016
Julian Tavenner	07-01-1993
Sandra Taylor	12-01-2013
Arthur D. Thomas, Jr.	03-01-2017
Henry Thompson, III	07-01-2006
Richard Douglas Thompson	01-15-2005

Terrence Thrasher	07-01-2013
Kent Tice	01-01-2018
Roland J. Timity	07-01-2005
Gary Trail	07-01-2001
Mary Trail	07-01-2004
Man Tso	07-01-2005
Dennis Upton	07-01-2007
Wayne Upton	01-01-2007
Kenneth S. Valentine	07-01-2018
Rebecca Vardiman	07-01-2017
Richard Vieth	07-01-1993
Maurice Vineyard	07-01-2000
Edward Voorhaar	07-01-2008
Ronald L. Ward	07-01-2009
Ruth Ward	07-01-2006
Linda Warehime	07-01-2016
William H. Warehime, Jr.	01-01-2014
James Warner	07-01-1999
Harold Watson	07-01-2000
Warren Watts	07-01-2008
Franklin Ways	07-01-2004
Nancy Webb	07-01-2012
Clifford C. Webner	07-01-2017
George Weitzel, Jr.	07-01-2008
Edwin H. Welch, Sr.	07-01-2015
Kenneth Welliver	07-01-1997
Robert Wellman	07-01-2018
David M. Wentz	07-01-2015
Leslie Werner, Jr.	07-01-2004
Jarrett Wicklein	07-01-2006
Alfreda L. Wiggins	07-01-2011
Jeremiah G. Williams	07-01-2011
John Williams	07-01-1998
Marceo M. Williams	07-01-2010
John Wogaman	07-01-2002
Charles Wolfe	07-01-1994
Owen Womack	07-01-2000
Mary K. Worrel	07-01-2014
Edwin Wray	07-01-2001
Daniel L. Wright	07-01-2014
Harold B. Wright, II	07-01-2016
Marion Monroe Wright	07-01-2012
Obie Wright, Jr.	07-01-2009
Catharine Anne Yarbrough	12-31-2008
Carol C. Yocum	07-01-2011
Dennis E. Yocum	07-01-2012
John R. Yost	07-01-2017
Jean Young	07-01-2002
Judy Young	12-01-2017
Darryl C. Zoller	07-01-2009
John Zsittnik	08-05-2008

54. What associate members have been retired (¶357): (List alphabetically giving full name—first, middle, last—in that order. If retiring in the interim between conference sessions (¶357.2d), indicate the effective date of retirement.) **(Under ¶357.1, no vote required; under ¶357.2, (v); under ¶357.3, (2/3 v)**

a. This year?

NAME	DATE EFFECTIVE
George E. Hackey, Jr.	07-01-2019

b. Previously?

NAME	DATE EFFECTIVE	NAME	DATE EFFECTIVE
Harry L. Burchell, Jr.	07-01-2014	JoeAnn Turner Harrod	07-01-2013
Bonnie Campbell	07-01-2013	Kenneth Jackson	06-20-1986
Laverne Clipper-Thomas	02-01-2006	Oliver Jennings, Sr.	07-01-1999
Fidel Compres	02-01-2013	Vivian Martin Jones	07-01-2006
Louis Emerick	07-01-1988	Orlando Kibbe	07-01-2001
James H. Farmer	07-01-2014	Roberta Matthews	01-01-2005
John Francis Footen	10-29-2010	Francis Rinker	07-01-2002
Charles Wayne Frum	07-01-2017	Keith Schukraft	07-01-2016
		Charles Joseph Shacochis	10-01-2012
		Alfred Statesman	07-01-2002

55. What Provisional Members have been previously retired (¶358, 2008 *Book of Discipline*): (Indicate credentials)

NAME	DATE EFFECTIVE
Donald Atkinson	07-01-2001
Glenda Condon	07-01-2006
Linda W. Healy	12-01-2010
Eloise Newman	07-01-2011
Marjorie Ellen Taylor	07-01-2006
Jean Weller	07-01-2012
Gertie Williams	07-01-2004

56. Who have been recognized as retired local pastors (¶320.5):

a. This year? INFORMATIONAL

NAME	Status	DATE EFFECTIVE
Arthe' (Taysie) Phillips	FTLP	07-01-2019
Sandra E. Smith	PTLP	07-01-2019
*Ian Grant Spong	FTLP	07-01-2019
Wilhelmina Street	PTLP	12-31-2018

b. Previously?
FULL TIME LOCAL PASTORS RETIRED

NAME	DATE EFFECTIVE
Joseph Bradshaw	03-01-1995
Donnie Jane Cardwell	01-01-2010

Frederick N. Iser	07-01-2011
Arthur F. Justice	07-01-2010
Judith Kelly	07-01-2012
Roosevelt Oliver	07-01-2008
Maria Rivera	07-01-2016
Charles Slaugh	07-01-2011
Stephen White	07-01-2008

PART TIME LOCAL PASTORS RETIRED

NAME	DATE EFFECTIVE
Harvey Bane	07-01-2007
Glenn O. Barrick	07-01-2017
Patricia Berry	07-01-2017
Leroy W. Boldley	07-01-2016
John Drury Bragg, Sr.	07-01-2018
John M. Brooks	07-01-2017
C. Lee Brotemarkle	07-01-2011
John Close	07-01-2016
Edward Conaway	07-01-1998
Ruth G. Dixon	07-01-2015
Ellin M. Dize	10-01-2008
M. Douglas Fraim	07-01-2002
Bruce C. Frame	07-01-2014
Nancy L. Green	07-01-2016
Edward L. Hall	07-01-2017
George Harpold	07-01-2001
Mary Louise Holley	07-01-1999
Elza M. Hurst	07-01-2014
Bertha Johnson	07-01-1989
Rollins Johnson	07-01-2006
Paulette Jones	07-01-2018
William Kercheval	07-01-2003
George Lambros	09-19-2002

David Lewis	07-01-2002
John E. Lewis	07-01-2014
Richard D. Lindsay	07-01-2016
Joanna Marceron	07-01-2016
James S. Mason, Jr.	07-01-2001
Robert McDonald-Walker	07-01-2010
Sheril Merki	07-01-2004
Margaret Moon	07-01-2008
Irene Pierce	07-01-1999
John Potts, Jr.	01-01-1984
Frederick Price	07-01-2015
James Pugh	07-01-2016
Faye Reddinger	07-01-2000
Doris Ridgely	07-01-1999
Rebecca Riley	07-01-2008
Richard Shamer	07-01-2012
Gary Sieglein	07-01-2014
Bertha Sigler	07-01-2006
Donald Wayne Sloan	06-30-2015
Mabel E. Smith	07-01-2017
Charles H. Stevenson	07-01-2016
Judith Stone	09-12-2011
Barry Lynn Taylor	07-01-2009
Daniel Taylor	07-01-2012
Robert Whiting	07-01-2006

57. What is the number of clergy members of the Annual Conference:
   a) By appointment category and conference relationship?
      (NOTES:
         (1) Where applicable, the question numbers on this report form corresponding to each category have been placed in parenthesis following the category title. Where these question numbers appear, the number reported in that category should agree with the number of names listed in the corresponding questions.
         (2) For the three categories of Appointments to Extension Ministries, report as follows:
            ¶344.1a,c): the number of clergy members appointed within United Methodist connectional structures, including district superintendents, or to an ecumenical agency.
            ¶344.1b): the number of clergy members appointed to extension ministries, under endorsement by the Division of Chaplains and Related Ministries of the General Board of Higher Education and Ministry.
            ¶344.1d): the number of clergy members appointed to other valid ministries, confirmed by a two-thirds vote of the Annual Conference.
   Note: Report those in extension ministry in one category only.
   See the Discipline paragraphs indicated for more detailed description of these appointment categories.
   (Note: Those approved to serve as a local pastor, but not currently under appointment, are not counted as clergy members of the conference.)

Categories	Deacons in Full Connection	Elders in Full Connection	Provisional Deacons	Provisional Elders	Associate Members & Affiliate Members With Vote	Full–time Local Pastors	Part–time Local Pastors
Pastors and deacons whose primary appointment is to a Local Church (¶¶331.1c, 339) (76, 77b)	10	239	1	45	2	17	91
Deacons (in full connection and provisional) serving Beyond the Local Church (¶331.1a, b) (77a)	8	xxxxx xxxxx xxxxx	5	xxxxx xxxxx xxxxx	xxxx xxxxx xxxxx	Xxxxx xxxxx xxxxx	xxxxx xxxxx xxxxx
Appointments to Extension Ministries (¶316.1; 344.1a, c) (76a)	xxxxx xxxxx xxxxx	32	xxxxx xxxxx xxxxx	1	0	0	0
Appointments to Extension Ministries (¶316.1; 344.1b, c) (76b)	xxxxx xxxxx xxxxx	5	xxxxx xxxxx xxxxx	0	0	0	0
Appointments to Extension Ministries (¶316.1; 344.1d) (76c)	xxxxx xxxxx xxxxx	21	xxxxx xxxxx xxxxx	1	0	0	0
appointments to Attend School (¶331.3) (78)	0	2	0	0	0	Xxxxx Xxxxx	xxxxx xxxxx
Appointed to Other Annual Conferences (49)	2	9	1	0	0	Xxxxx Xxxxx	xxxxx xxxxx
On Leave of Absence (50a1, a2)	0	1	0	1	0	Xxxxx Xxxxx	xxxxx xxxxx
On Family Leave (50a3, a4)	1	0	0	0	0	xxxxx xxxxx	xxxxx xxxxx
On Sabbatical Leave (51)	0	0	0	0	0	xxxxx xxxxx	xxxxx xxxxx
On Incapacity Leave (52)	0	10	0	0	0	xxxxx xxxxx	xxxxx xxxxx
On Transitional Leave (50a5)	0	0	0	xxxxx xxxxx	xxxx xxxx	xxxxx xxxxx	xxxxx xxxxx
Retired (53, 54, 55)	15	419	1	6	19	11	50
Total Number, Clergy Members	36	738	7	54	21	28	141
Grand Total, All Conference Clergy Members	1025						

b) By gender and racial/ethnic identification? (NOTE: See the instruction for item 57 for guidelines to assist in the racial/ethnic identification count.)

	Clergy Demographics													
Categories	Deacons in Full Connection		Elders in Full Connection		Provisional Deacons		Provisional Elders		Associate Members & Affiliate Members with Vote		Full time Local Pastors		Part time Local Pastors	
	Male	Female	Male	Female	Male	Female	Male	Female	Male	Female	Male	Female	Male	Female
Asian	0	2	22	9	0	0	1	2	0	0	0	0	0	2
Black	0	3	92	66	0	2	13	8	5	5	2	1	35	26
Hispanic	0	0	9	1	0	0	1	1	0	0	1	1	1	0
Native American	0	0	1	1	0	0	0	0	0	0	0	0	0	0
Pacific Islander	0	0	0	0	0	0	0	0	0	0	0	0	0	0
White	9	21	354	178	0	5	10	18	10	1	16	7	55	22
Multi-Racial	0	1	1	4	0	0	0	0	0	0	0	0	0	0
Grand Total, All Conference Clergy Members*	9	27	479	259	0	7	25	29	15	6	19	9	91	50
Total	1025													

PART III CERTIFICATION IN SPECIALIZED MINISTRY
(¶635.2u, *The Book of Discipline*)
Note: Indicate credential of persons in Part III: FD, FE, PD, PE, AM, FL, PL, and LM.

Note: CE – Christian Education; YM – Youth Ministry; EV – Evangelism; SF – Spiritual Formation; OAM – Older Adult Ministry; CRM – Camping and Retreat Ministry; MM – Music Ministry; PC – Pastoral Counseling.

58. Who are the candidates in process for certification in specialized ministry? INFORMATIONAL

NAME	CLERGY/LAY STATUS	District	SPECIALIZED MINISTRY
John Ampiah-Addison	LP	CM	OAM
Matthew H. Aldrich	Laity	BS	EV
Richard M. Barr	Laity	CM	CE
Carol Bowen	Laity	CM	YM
Andre Briscoe, Jr.	PE	BM	MM
Debbie Burgio	Laity	CM	OAM
Don Hauprich	Laity	GW	CE
Sonseeahray Hopkins	Laity	CM	CE
Shelia Isaacson	Laity	WE	SF & YM
Robert D. Jacoby	Laity	CM	YM
Faye Johnson	Laity	WE	EV
David W. Lanzer	Laity	A	YM
Katherine Martin	Laity	BS	SF
Marie A. Matthews	Laity	GW	CE
Leslie A. Myers	Laity	CM	CE
Shirl Ollie	Laity	F	CE
Dorothy Presberry	Laity	BS	SF
DaMali Goings Rector	Laity	WE	EV, YM & CE
Bonnie Ruff	Laity	BM	YM
Barry Shortt	Laity	BS	CE, YM
Janet Swecker	Laity	WE	CE
Melanie J. Whelan	Laity	F	SF

59. Who is certified in specialized ministry? (List the areas of specialized ministry. Indicate by an asterisk those certified this year.) INFORMATIONAL

This year:

NAME	CLERGY/LAY STATUS	SPECIALIZED MINISTRY
None		

Previously:

Christian Education (CE)

Konni M. Brantner	FD	GW	CE, YM
Kenneth E. Brown	RE	A	EV, Church Business Administrator
Richard Lee Buckingham	RD	GW	CE, YM
Mary Dennis	FD	CM	CE
Lee Steer Ferrell	FD	A	CE, YM
W. Kenneth Lyons, Jr.	RE	A	MM
Martha Maxham	FD	CM	CE
Stella S. Tay	RD	A	CE
Andrea Titcomb	RD	A	EV

60. Who are transferred in as a certified person in specialized ministry? None.

61. Who are transferred out as a certified person in specialized ministry? None.

62. Who have been removed as a certified person in specialized ministry? None.

PART IV CERTIFIED LAY MINISTRY
(¶¶268, AND 666.11 *The Book of Discipline*)

63. Who are certified as lay ministers (¶ 268, and 666.11)? (List alphabetically giving full name—first, middle, last—in that order, by district) INFORMATIONAL

NAME	DISTRICT	YEAR CERTIFIED or RECERTIFIED
Patsy Baker Blackshear	A	2017
Shirlette Boysaw	A	2017
Sue Bradshaw-Shelton	A	2017
Nelsa Brown	A	2017
Celia Carr	A	2016
Ronnette Cook	A	2018
Romesca Estep	A	2017
Anita Diane Green	A	2016
Rhonda Green	A	2017
Charlotte Green	A	2017
Barry Oren	A	2017
Phylis Parker	A	2017
Yolanda Perry	A	2017
Verna Prehn	A	2017
June Richardson	A	2017
Michael Simms, Sr.	A	2017
Raymond Talley	A	2017
Desiree Vanloo	A	2017
Kim Walker	A	2018
Anita Wamble	A	2016
Ronald Waters	A	2017
Marvene Young	A	2017
Ruby Bond	BM	2019
Patrick M. Burke	BM	2017
John G. Danz, Jr.	BM	2019
Larry Gadsden	BM	2018
Irene Gillis	BM	2017
Ettadean Denise Hyman	BM	2017
Hazel B. Jackson	BM	2019
Wendy Johnson	BM	2017
Sheryl C. Morsell	BM	2017
Millie F. Rice	BM	2017
Colleen Shaneybrook	BM	2017
Elizabeth Mitchell Stemley	BM	2017
Jan Taylor	BM	2017
Eileen Cecelia Washington	BM	2019
Norman Whiteley, Jr.	BM	2017
Gwendiville Young	BM	2019
Edie Beard	BS	2017
Riccardo Jefferson, Sr.	BS	2017
Sarah Lee	BS	2018
Kathy Ryan	BS	2019
Carl Cowan	CH	2019
Thomas Dalton	CH	2019
Rebecca Hein	CH	2019
William Piper	CH	2019
Darlene G. Powers	CH	2019
Billie Jean Johnson Smith	CH	2019
Richard Voorhaar	CH	2019
Susie Wright	CH	2019
Joycelyn Yvonne Camper	CM	2019
Wendy Feaga	CM	2018
Rodney Fry	CM	2018
Margie Matthews	CM	2018

Shirley Jean Myers	CM	2018
Ronald S. Collins, Sr.	F	2018
Sherry Crockett	F	2018
Toni Dufficy	F	2018
Kathy Duppins-Smallwood	F	2017
Sherie Koob	F	2017
Mary Newcomb	F	2018
Merri Sayler	F	2019
Audrey Arthur	GW	2017
Carol Bergman	GW	2017
Barbara Brooks	GW	2017
Sukumar Christopher	GW	2017
Olubanke Daka	GW	2017
Latitia Felus	GW	2017
Joyce Harris	GW	2017
Sherene Harris	GW	2017
Gayle Hebron	GW	2018
Vijaya G. Henry	GW	2017
Kenneth Hover	GW	2018
Tawana Jackson	GW	2018
Wesley Jackson	GW	2017
George Jones	GW	2017
Tiffany Jones	GW	2017
Annie London	GW	2017
Hilda Macauley	GW	2017
Lynda Parker	GW	2017
Karen Robinson	GW	2017
Qawi Robinson	GW	2017
Fredia Tatum	GW	2017
Milton Washington, III	GW	2017
Vickie West	GW	2017
Sharee Wharton	GW	2017
Romain Young	GW	2017
Carol A. Bell	WE	2018
Yvonne Caughman	WE	2018
Pearl Chase	WE	2018
Joshua Chinagorom	WE	2018
Vincent Cooke	WE	2018
Sherry Spriggs Emerson	WE	2018
June M. Fauber	WE	2018
Linda Flanagan	WE	2017
Lillian Forbes	WE	2018
ViNita Gibson-Gross	WE	2018
Alice Adams Gray	WE	2017
Delores Green	WE	2018
Delonta Hicks	WE	2017
Nurbert Hughes	WE	2018
Peggy Ireland	WE	2018
Deborah L. Johnson	WE	2018
Faye Johnson	WE	2017
Ellis Jones	WE	2018
Mellie Landon	WE	2019
Cary Montgomery	WE	2018
Delila Parham	WE	2018
Gregory L. Parham	WE	2018
Patricia Queen	WE	2017
Johnnie Randolph	WE	2018
DaMali Rector-Goings	WE	2017
Jocelyn Richardson	WE	2019
Deborah Sellman	WE	2017
Clairmonte Simon	WE	2018
Nicole Smith	WE	2017

Perry Taylor	WE	2019
Larry Titus	WE	2017
Gloria Turner-Simpkins	WE	2017
Jack Woodford	WE	2018
Margaret Young	WE	2018

PART V DIACONAL MINISTERS
(Paragraph numbers in questions 64-71 refer to The 1992 *Book of Discipline*)

64. Who are transferred in as diaconal ministers (¶312)? None.

65. Who are transferred out as diaconal ministers (¶ 312)? None.

66. Who have had their conference relationship as diaconal ministers terminated by Annual Conference action (¶313.3)? (**Under ¶313.3a, no vote; under ¶313.3b, v 2/3**)
None.

67. What diaconal ministers have died during the year?

    a. Active: None.

    b. Retired: None

68. What diaconal ministers have been granted leaves of absence under ¶313.1a, c, d) (disability, study/sabbatical, or personal leave): (**v**) None.

69. What diaconal ministers have been granted an extended leave (¶313.1e): None.

70. Who have returned to active status from extended leave (¶313.1e)? (v) None.

71. Who have taken the retired relationship to the Annual Conference as diaconal ministers (¶313.2): (**Under ¶313.2b, v 2/3**)

    a. . This year? None.

    b. Previously?

NAME	DISTRICT	DATE EFFECTIVE
Lillian G. Myers	CH	
Nan Austin Doggett	F	
Donnalee Sanderson	GW	
Lois Arlene Jones	GW	
Vivian W. Otto	GW	
Cora Elizabeth Moore	WE	
Thelma Theresa Lyles Taylor	WE	
Katherine Winget		

PART VI APPOINTMENTS AND CONCLUDING BUSINESS

72. Who are approved for less than full-time service?

    a. What associate members and elders (and provisionals) are approved for appointment to less than full-time service, what is the total number of years for which such approval has been granted to each, and for what fraction of full-time service (in one–quarter increments) is approval granted (for purposes of equitable compensation claim and pension credit) (¶¶ 338.2, 342.2, 1506)? (**v 2/3, after 8 years v 3/4**):

NAME	APPOINTMENT	FRACTION OF FT SERVICE	YEARS LESS THAN FT	DISTRICT
Cynthia B. Belt FE	Mt. Zion/Harwood Park	75%	(9)	A

Gerald Elston PE	BrightwoodPark/ Albright Memorial	50%	(0)	GW
Lori Hoffman Hays FE	Lexington Park: Lexington Park	50%	(8)	WE
Ashley Hoover PE	Jerusalem/Mt. Pleasant	50%	(0)	GW
Dana M. Jones PE	Prince Frederick: Mt. Olive	50%	(6)	WE
Gladman Kapfumvuti FE	Asbury-Zion Wesley	50%	(1)	WE
Narae Kim PE	LaVale: LaVale Associate	50%	(0)	CH
Jong Hui Park FE	The Everlasting Love	50%	(2)	A
Lisa Jordan Wirkus FE	Sabillasville: Mt. Zion & Wolfsville: Pleasant Walk	25%	(6)	CH

b. What deacons in full connection and provisional deacons are approved for less than full-time service (¶331.7)?

NAME	APPOINTMENT	FRACTION OF FT SERVICE	YEARS AT LESS THAN FULL-TIME	DISTRICT
Konni M. Brantner FD	Rockville: Millian Memorial	50%	2006-2019	GW
Kathleen Cheyney FD	Bosley: West Liberty	50%	1-1-2017 to 2019	BS
Angela Maves FD	DC: Dumbarton	50%	2009-2019	GW
Enger Muteteke PD	Grace Union, Winslow & Elm	50%	07-01-2019	Greater New Jersey
Barbara Suffecool FD	Hancock UMC	25%	1996-2019	CH
Julie Wilson FD	Calvary	50%	2014-2019	F

73. Who have been appointed as Interim Pastors under the provisions of ¶338.3 since the last session of the annual conference, and for what period of time?

NAME	DISTRICT	APPOINTMENT	EFFECTIVE DATES
Fred Crider	BS	Salem: Upper Falls	04-1-2019 to 06-30-2019
Kenneth Dunnington	F	Middletown UMC	07-01-2019 to 06-30-2020
Ken Fell	CM	Covenant	10-2018 to 06-30-2019
Bruce Frame	BS	Monkton	12-9-2018 to 06-30-2019
Joye Jones	GW	Faith: Rockville	01-01-2019 to 06-02-2019
Art Justice	BS	Whiteford: Mt Vernon	12-16-2018 to 06-30-2019
Antoine Love	CM	Wesley Freedom	07-01-2019 to 06-30-2020
Roderick Miller	CM	Glen Mar UMC	11-01-2017 to 08-01-2018
Roderick Miller	BM	Mt Vernon Place	12-2018 to present
Michael Chamberlain	GW	National Church	01-01-2018 to 06-30-2019

74. What changes have been made in appointments since the last annual conference session? (Attach list. Include and identify Appointments Beyond the Local Church (Deacons) and Appointments to Extension Ministries (Elders.) Give effective dates of all changes.)

NAME	APPOINTMENT	EFFECTIVE DATE
Amanda Sayers	Glen Mar UMC	09-08-2018
Evan Young	Discipleship Ministries	04-22-2019

75. What elders (full connection and provisional), associate members, and local pastors are appointed to ministry to the local church and where are they appointed for the ensuring year? (Attach a list.)

76. What elders (full connection and provisional), associate members, and local pastors are appointed to extension ministries for the ensuring year?

a. Within the connectional structures of United Methodism (¶344.1a, c)? INFORMATIONAL

NAME	CLERGY STATUS	DATE EFFECTIVE	EXTENSION MINISTRY ASSIGNMENT	DIST	CHARGE MEMBER CONFERENCE

Erik Alsgaard	FE	07-01-2013	BWC Communications	GW	National UMC
William D. Aldridge, Jr.	FE	07-01-1989	Wesley Theological Seminary	GW	Dumbarton
Cheryl B. Anderson	FE	07-01-2000	Garrett Theological Seminary	CM	Gaithersburg: Grace
Giovanni Arroyo	FE	07-01-2015	Commission on Religion & Race	F	Frederick: Trinity
Rebecca Bentzinger	FE	07-01-2007	General Board of Higher Education & Ministry	GW	Dumbarton
Laurence K. Bropleh	FE	04-01-2013	University of Liberia	CM	Epworth
Alexis F. Brown	FE	07-01-2016	Howard University	GW	DC: Asbury
Bill Brown	FE	07-01-2019	Director of New Faith Expressions	CM	Glen Mar
William T Chaney, Jr.	FE	07-01-2014	General Board of Discipleship	CM	Wesley Freedom
Johnsie Cogman	FE	07-01-2019	District Superintendent	WE	
Wanda Duckett	FE	07-01-2017	District Superintendent	BM	
Gerard A. Green, Jr.	FE	07-01-2016	District Superintendent	CM	Gaithersburg: Fairhav
Joseph P. Heath-Mason	FE	07-01-2016	American University	GW	National UMC
Rebecca Iannicelli	FE	07-01-2013	District Superintendent	A	
HeaSun Kim	FE	01-01-1992	General Board of Global Ministries	BS	Reisterstown
Raphael Koikoi	PE	02-01-2017	Upper Allegheny Valley Director of Ministry and Community Development	BM	John Wesley
Ann Laprade	FE	07-01-2017	District Superintendent	BS	
Kyung-Lim Shin Lee	FE	07-01-1992	Wesley Theological Seminary	GW	National Korean
Beth Ludlum	FE	07-01-2015	Wesley Theological Seminary	GW	Mt. Vernon Place
Maidstone Mulenga	FE	05-01-2017	Council of Bishops	A	St. Marks: Hanover
Laura Norvell	FE	07-01-2015	Wesley Theological Seminary	GW	Emmanuel
John Nupp	FE	07-01-2016	Director of the Center for Clergy Excellence	CM,	Bethany
HiRho Yoon Park	FE	08-01-2005	General Board of Higher Education & Ministry	CM	Fairhaven
J.W. Park	FE	07-01-2013	District Superintendent	CM	Fairhaven
F. Douglas Powe	FE	07-01-2015	Wesley Theological Seminary	GW	University
Harold J. Recinos	FE	01-01-2002	Perkins School of Theology		
Edgardo Rivera	FE	03-01-2013	District Superintendent	F	
Mark Schaefer	FE	07-02-2002	American University	GW	Foundry
Rodney Smothers	FE	07-01-2017	Congregational Development Resource Specialist	GW	Brighter Day
Mark Teasdale	FE	07-01-2008	Garrett Theological Seminary	GW	Rockville
Stacey Cole Wilson	FE	07-01-2016	Director of Congregational Excellence	BM	New Waverly
John Wunderlich	FE	07-01-2019	District Superintendent	CH	
Evan D. Young	FE	04-22-2019	Discipleship Ministries	WE	Oxon Hill: St. Paul

b. To ministries endorsed by the Board of Higher Education and Ministry (¶344.1b)?

INFORMATIONAL

NAME	CLERGY STATUS	DATE EFFECTIVE	EXTENSION MINISTRY ASSIGNMENT	DIST	CHARGE MEMBER CONFERENCE
Kimberly Hall	FE	07-01-2012	United States Army	GW	Hughes Memorial
Christopher T. Holmes	FE	07-01-2012	Call to Action Coaching	A	Community/Trinity
Solomon Lloyd	FE	12-01-2013	United States Navy	CH	Cumberland: McKendree of Potomac Park
Saundra White Rector	FE	07-01-2016	Greater Baltimore Medical Center	GW	Scaggsville: Emmanuel
Mark C. Young	FE	07-01-1991	Pastoral Counseling	BS	Ebenezer Fallston

c. To other valid ministries under the provisions of ¶344.1d? (2/3 v)

NAME	CLERGY STATUS	DATE EFFECTIVE	EXTENSION MINISTRY ASSIGNMENT	DIST	CHARGE MEMBER CONFERENCE
Gregory Coates	FE	07-01-2004	Shepherd Pratt Health Systems	BM	Lovely Lane
Rachel Cornwell	FE	07-01-2018	The James Company	GW	Foundry
Malcolm Frazier	FE	02-18-2019	Director of Pastoral Care and Counseling Asbury Methodist Village	CM	Gaithersburg
David Graves	FE	07-01-2015	Institute of Grace	WE	St. Paul's - Lusby
Elizabeth L. Halsey	FE	07-01-2005	St. Luke Institution	A	Community/Trinity
Jessica Statesman Hayden	FE	07-01-2017	Inspirit Counseling Center	BM	Old Otterbein
Whit Hutchinson	FE	07-01-2009	National Interfaith Sanctuary	GW	National UMC
Michael C. Johnson	FE	07-01-2014	Spiritual Director	BM	Lansdowne
Curtis King	FE	07-01-2016	Urban Behavioral Associates	BM	Baltimore: St. James
Mark A. Lancaster	FE	01-01-2015	E Health Records International		Epworth
Claire Matheny	FE	07-01-2018	Kittamaqundi Community Church	GW	Linden-Linthicum
Randy Wayne Pumphrey	FE	07-01-1998	Whitman Walker Clinic	GW	Bradbury Heights
Bryant Oskvig	FE	07-01-2011	Georgetown University	GW	Chevy Chase
Irance Reddix	PE	07-01-2017	Addulum Health Care	BM	Baltimore: St. Johns
Douglas M. Strong	FE	07-01-2007	Seattle Pacific University	CM	Olney: Oakdale Emory
Theresa Thames	FE	03-01-2016	Princeton University	GW	Foundry
Janet Deitiker Tracy	FE	07-01-2012	University Health Systems	BS	Abington/Cokesbury
Kirk VanGilder	FE	09-01-2011	Gallaudet University	GW	Foundry
Chris A. Wood	FE	08-01-2016	Davis & Elkin College	F	Westminster
Kevin Wright	FE	01-15-2019	Urban Arts Partnership	GW	Foundry
Rebecca A. Wright	FE	01-01-1996	School of Theology, University of the South	BS	Hampstead: Wesley
Doratha Yunger	FE	07-01-2019	Calvert Marine Museum	WE	Solomons: Solomons

77. Who are appointed as deacons (full connection and provisional) for the ensuing year?

a) Through non-United Methodist agencies and settings beyond the local church (¶331.1a)?

NAME	CLERGY STATUS	DATE EFFECTIVE	EXTENSION MINISTRY ASSIGNMENT	DIST	CHARGE MEMBER CONFERENCE
Konni M. Brantner	FD	04-01-2006	St. Matthews Presbyterian Church, Director of Youth, Education & Outreach	GW	Rockville: Millian Memorial
Katherine Elizabeth Brown	FD		Wesley Theological Seminary, Loyola University	GW	Silver Spring UMC
Deborah Burgio	PD	07-01-2019	Winter Grace	CM	Fulton: Mt Zion
Kathleen Charters	PD	10-01-2016	Uniform Services - University of the Health Sciences	GW	Emmanuel
Amy Ellen Duke-Benfield	FD	07-01-2006	Center for Law & Social Policy	GW	Foundry
Donald Hohne	FD	07-01-2011	Gilchrist Hospice Care	CM	Wesley Freedom
Jennifer Kokoski	PD	07-01-2017	Gilchrist Hospice Care	BS	Baldwin: Union
Martina Martin Efodzi	PD	01-01-2016	Whitman-Walker Health	GW	Lincoln Park
Angela Maves	FD	07-01-2009	George Washington University Hosp.	GW	Dumbarton
T.C. Morrow	PD	07-01-2019	National Religious Campaign Against Torture & Foundry	GW	Foundry
Doris Warrell	FD	11-09-2009	Churches for Middle East Peace and Washington Seminar Center	GW	Dumbarton
Leo Yates, Jr.	FD	02-01-2018	Maryland Division of Rehabilitation Services	A	Magothy
David Young	FD	07-01-2003	U.S. State Department	GW	Foundry

b) Through United Methodist Church-related agencies, schools, within a local congregation, charge or cooperative parish within the connectional structures of The United Methodist Church (¶331.1b, c)?

NAME	CLERGY STATUS	DATE EFFECTIVE	EXTENSION MINISTRY ASSIGNMENT	DIST	CHARGE MEMBER CONFERENCE
Megan Blanchard	PD	07-01-2018	Mill Creek Parish	CM	Mill Creek Parish
Kathleen Cheyney	FD	01-01-2017	Bosley: Sparks-West Liberty Charge	BS	West Liberty
Janet Craswell	FD	02-01-2014	National UMC	GW	National UMC
Lee Ferrell	FD	07-01-1997	Severna Park	A	Severna Park
William Jones, Jr.	FD	07-01-2008	Cockeysville: Epworth	BS	Cockeysville: Epworth
Samuel Marullo	FD	07-01-2011	Wesley Theological Seminary	GW	Capitol Hill
Margery Schammel	FD	01-01-2006	Towson Charge	BM	Towson Charge
David Showalter	FD	07-01-2009	Lusby: St. Paul Charge	WE	Lusby: St. Paul Charge
Barbara Suffecool	FD	07-01-1996	Hancock: Hancock	CH	Hancock: Hancock
Julie Wilson	FD	07-01-2014	Calvary	F	Calvary

78. Who are appointed to attend school (¶416.6)? (List alphabetically all those whose primary appointment is to attend school.)
INFORMATIONAL

NAME	CLERGY STATUS	DIST	CHARGE CONFERENCE	SCHOOL
Lisa Bandel	FE	BS	Reisterstown	07-01-2019
Anthony Carr	FE	GW	Silver Spring: Good Shepherd	07-01-2014

79. Where are the diaconal ministers appointed for the ensuing year (¶310) [1992 Discipline]?
INFORMATIONAL

80. What other personal notations should be made? (Include such matters as changes in pension credit (¶1506.5), corrections or additions to matters reported in the "Business of the Annual Conference" form in previous years, and legal name changes of clergy members and diaconal ministers.)

Dionne Osuji (PL) name change due to divorce. New name is Dionne Hall.

Leslie Newman-Sewell, name change due to marriage. New name is Leslie Newman-Adams.

Faith Lewis. Name change due to marriage is Faith Wilkerson.

81. Where and when shall the next Conference Session be held (¶603.2, 3)? The 235th Session of the Baltimore-Washington Conference of The United Methodist Church will be convened on May 27-29, 2020. Marriott Waterfront Hotel, 700 Aliceanna Street, Baltimore, MD 21202.

82. Corrections

Laura Norvell should have been listed as appointed to Ferndale: Ferndale UMC (A) as 25% July 1, 2018 – June 30, 2019

Caitlin Mossburg should have been listed in 19a as certified in 2017.

Granderson Jones should have been removed from 21b and listed in 20 as he did not have an appointment from July 1, 2016 until July 1, 2019. He is now properly listed in 21b.

ANNAPOLIS DISTRICT

Superintendent
Rebecca K. Iannicelli. FE   (410) 309-3445
21 Austin Dr, Edgewater, MD 21037-2222
riannicelli@bwcumc.org

Adams #1375   C. (410) 741-1932
937 Bayard Rd, Lothian, MD 20711-9609   adamsumchurch@yahoo.com
  Marilyn Lewis PL   R. (410) 978-5262
  PO Box 538, Arnold, MD 21012-0538   merlewis@comcast.net

Asbury #1110   C. (410) 268-9500
87 West St, Annapolis, MD 21401-2426   1asbury@verizon.net
  Carletta Allen FE   R. (240) 938-1954
  31 Lafayette Ave, Annapolis, MD 21401-2811   asbury1pastor@gmail.com

Asbury #1360   C. (301) 490-9295
10420 Guilford Rd, Jessup, MD 20794-9118   asburyjessupchurch@verizon.net
  Gay Green-Carden PL   R. (410) 693-0962
  8904 Chad Way, Clinton, MD 20735   gaycarden@verizon.net

Asbury #1160   C. (410) 349-2862
78 Church Rd, Arnold, MD 21012-2345   office@asburyumcarnold.org
  Jennifer Karsner FE   R. (410) 349-2862
  78 Church Rd, Arnold, MD 21012-2345   pastorjen@asburyumcarnold.org

Asbury Town Neck #1490   C. (410) 647-3461
429 Asbury Dr, Severna Park, MD 21146-1373   asburytownneck@gmail.com
  James A. Bishop, Sr. FE   R. (410) 544-1126
  440 Asbury Dr, Severna Park, MD 21146-1372   jamesbishop_atn1@verizon.net

Asbury-Broadneck #1115   C. (410) 757-2995
657 Broadneck Rd, Annapolis, MD 21409-5505   asburybroadneck1@aol.com
  Stephen A. Tillett , I FE   R. (410) 320-8138
  1404 Saint Francis Cir, Severn, MD 21144-6821   ABPASTOR@AOL.COM

Baldwin Memorial #1420   C. (410) 923-1166
921A Generals Hwy, Millersville, MD 21108-2124   bmumcoffice@yahoo.com
  Philip Tocknell FE   R. (410) 923-2642
  929 Generals Hwy, Millersville, MD 21108-2124   dltocknell@gmail.com

Calvary #1120   C. (410) 268-1776
301 Rowe Blvd, Annapolis, MD 21401-1602   office@calumc.org
  Conrad O. Link FE   R. (301) 695-9468
  1910 Dulany Pl, Annapolis, MD 21409-6221   COLink@calumc.org

  Braulio Torres FE   R. (202) 870-7656
  1631 Elkwood Ct, Annapolis, MD 21409-5477   artbyte1976@gmail.com

Cape St. Claire #1125
855 Chestnut Tree Dr, Annapolis, MD 21409-5114
   Dale Thomas PL
   6256 Shady Side Rd, Shady Side, MD 20764-3100

C. (410) 757-4896
office@capeumc.org
R. (240) 682-6395
dale@capeumc.org

Cecil Memorial-Mt. Calvary
Cecil Memorial #1130
15 Parole St, Annapolis, MD 21401-3916
Mount Calvary #1165
1236 Jones Station Rd, Arnold, MD 21012-2301
   Patricia Turnage SY
   732 Queenstown Rd, Severn, MD 21144-1220

C. (410) 266-5651
cecilmemorialumc@yahoo.com
C. (410) 757-7140
mcumarnold@aol.com
R. (410) 292-1823
cottonfieldcricket@gmail.com

Cedar Grove-Oakland #1215
5965 Deale Churchton Rd, Deale, MD 20751-9730
   Glen L. Arnold FE
   10733 Castleton Turn, Upper Marlboro, MD 20774-1449

C. (410) 867-7417
office@cgumc.org
R. (301) 324-5610
pastor@cgumc.org

Centenary #1515
6248 Shady Side Rd, Shady Side, MD 20764-9685
   Faith Wilkerson FE
   155 E. Mount Harmony Rd, Owings, MD 20736-3442

   Jackie Waymire SY

C. (410) 867-2048
marsha.purcell@comcast.net
R. (410) 474-4156
revfaithlewis@yahoo.com

jwaymirecentenary@gmail.com

Chews Memorial/Carters
Carters #1270
6715 Old Solomons Island Road, Tracys Landing, MD 20779
Chews Memorial #1438
492 Owensville Rd, Harwood, MD 20776-9487
   Valerie A. Barnes FE
   33 55th St SE, Washington, DC 20019-6565

C. (301) 855-2500
cartersumc@aol.com
C. (410) 798-1638
chewsumc@yahoo.com
R. (202) 903-3355
revvab@comcast.net

Community #1180
1690 Riedel Rd, Crofton, MD 21114-1631
   Stan Cardwell FE
   1690 Riedel Rd, Crofton, MD 21114-1631

C. (410) 721-9129
scardwell@cumc.net
R. (410) 721-9129
scardwell@cumc.net

Davidsonville #1190
819 W Central Ave, Davidsonville, MD 21035-2318
   Wendy R. van Vliet FE
   152 Duval Ln, Edgewater, MD 21037-1613

C. (410) 798-5511
dumcoffice@dumc.net
R. (410) 707-5530
pastorWendyvv@gmail.com

Delmont/Severn
Delmont #1475
1219 Delmont Rd, Severn, MD 21144-1904
Severn #1485
1215 Old Camp Meade Rd, Severn, MD 21144-1138
   Kathleen S. Lossau FE
   5501 45th Ave Apt 312, Hyattsville, MD 20781-1591

C. (443) 278-6341
delmontspastor@gmail.com
C. (410) 551-7969
severnspastor@gmail.com
R. (217) 341-2181
rtrevdrk@gmail.com

Eastport #1135
926 Bay Ridge Ave, Annapolis, MD 21403-3033
Chris M. Broadwell PL
Annapolis, MD 21401-2300

C. (410) 263-5490
eastportumc@verizon.net
R. (318) 349-7110
office@capeumc.org

Edgewater #1235
2764 Solomons Island Rd, Edgewater, MD 21037-1211
Paulette V. Jones PL
8372 New Cut Rd, Severn, MD 21144-2810

C. (410) 974-4410
gerald@kurtsnyder.net
R. (410) 209-0550
pastorpaulettevjones@gmail.com

Gerald Snyder SY
1576 Chickasaw Rd, Arnold, MD 21012-2526

R. (410) 974-4410
gerald@kurtsnyder.net

Faith Community
Community #1440
8680 Fort Smallwood Rd, Pasadena, MD 21122-2403
Ali T. DeLeo PE

C. (410) 255-1506
communityumc2@verizon.net
R. (410) 255-1506

Faith #1445
905 Duvall Hwy, Pasadena, MD 21122-1808
Ali T. DeLeo PE
1772 Woodtree Cir, Annapolis, MD 21409-5461

C. (410) 437-8515
FaithChurchUMC905@gmail.com
R. (410) 255-1506
alideleo@gmail.com

John Taylor, Sr. SY
1901 North Ave, Pasadena, MD 21122-3418

R. (410) 360-0934
revjet@verizon.net

Ferndale #1268
117 Ferndale Rd, Glen Burnie, MD 21061-2626
Steven T. Cochran FE
107 Monroe Manor Rd, Stevensville, MD 21666-2235

C. (410) 761-2880
ferndaleumcsecretary@gmail.com
R. (443) 904-4011
revstc@gmail.com

First/Community
Community #7410
300 Brock Bridge Rd, Laurel, MD 20724-2414

C. (301) 725-4918
communityumcpastor@gmail.com

First #7415
424 Main St, Laurel, MD 20707-4116
Caprice Brown PL
16208 Angel Falls Ln, Bowie, MD 20716-3816

C. (301) 725-3093
office@fumcl.org
R. (301) 875-5515
brownbowie3@gmail.com

Ramon (Ray) McDonald, II FE
4286 Warthen Dr, Harwood, MD 20776-9756

R. (410) 703-3092
RevRayMac@gmail.com

Friendship #1275
22 W Friendship Rd, Friendship, MD 20758-3203
Thomas E. Young, Jr. FE
6754 Old Solomons Island Rd, Friendship, MD 20758

C. (410) 257-7133
bsuedean@friendshipmethodist.org
R. (240) 522-2038
youngtrumpet5@gmail.com

Galesville #1280
4825 Church Ln, Galesville, MD 20765-3107
Joanna Marceron RL
327 S River Clubhouse Rd, Harwood, MD 20776-9534

C. (410) 867-3281
galesvilleumc@gmail.com
R. (410) 991-2253
Jjmdiaconal@msn.com

Glen Burnie #1320
5 2nd Ave SE, Glen Burnie, MD 21061-3626
Kenneth McDonald FE
7 2nd Ave SE, Glen Burnie, MD 21061-3626

C. (410) 761-4381
office@gbumchurch.org
R. (410) 946-7487
kennethmcdo10888@gmail.com

Hall #1325
7780 Solley Rd, Glen Burnie, MD 21060-8310
Harry Smith, Jr. FE
160 Barbara Rd, Severna Park, MD 21146-1359

C. (410) 360-1242
hallunitedmc@yahoo.com
R. (240) 246-4779
pastorhsmith@verizon.net

Harwood Park/Mt. Zion
Harwood Park #1225
6635 Highland Ave, Elkridge, MD 21075-5632
Mount Zion #7420
3592 Whiskey Bottom Rd, Laurel, MD 20724-1402
Cynthia Belt FE
2647 Carver Rd, Gambrills, MD 21054-1716

C. (410) 796-5565
RLDuncan1@aol.com
C. (301) 490-3707
mtzionumclmd@hotmail.com
R. (443) 336-7637
revcbelt@gmail.com

Hope Memorial St Mark #1240
3672 Muddy Creek Rd, Edgewater, MD 21037-3418
Eddie Smith FE
100 Foxhorn Way, Glen Burnie, MD 21061

C. (410) 798-6776
hopestmarkumc@comcast.net
R. (410) 761-2249
hopestmarkumc@comcast.net

John Wesley #1145
2114 Bay Ridge Ave, Annapolis, MD 21403-2828
Samuel J. (Jerry) Colbert PL
1398 Primrose Rd, Annapolis, MD 21403-1401

C. (410) 263-4125
jwesley2114@yahoo.com
R. (410) 280-5047
jwesley2114@yahoo.com

John Wesley #1330
6922 Ritchie Hwy, Glen Burnie, MD 21061-2304
Lena Marie Dennis FE
7501 Trafalgar Cir Apt 127, Hanover, MD 21076-5012

C. (410) 766-6981
jwumcgb@yahoo.com
R. (443) 845-3591
dhumbleone@aol.com

John Wesley-Waterbury #1185
962 Generals Hwy, Crownsville, MD 21032-1424
Frederick Price, Jr. RL
11404 Dundee Dr, Mitchellville, MD 20721-2422

C. (410) 923-2248
johnwesleywaterbury@gmail.com
R. (301) 464-0602
pricefa@verizon.net

Linthicum Heights #1370
200 School Ln, Linthicum, MD 21090-2519
Michael W. Bynum FE
208 School Ln, Linthicum, MD 21090-2519

C. (410) 859-0990
Office@lhumc.org
R. (240) 344-4532
pastorbynum@gmail.com

Macedonia #1425
1567 Sappington Station Rd, Gambrills, MD 21054-1051
Louis Shockley RE
8707 Royal Ridge Ln, Laurel, MD 20708-2457

C. (410) 674-9892
Ray.P.Talley@outlook.com
R. (301) 617-9235
shockleylouis@gmail.com

Magothy #1450
3703 Mountain Rd, Pasadena, MD 21122-2024
Martin P. Brooks FE
2838 Leaf Shade Dr, Ellicott City, MD 21042-2559

C. (410) 255-2420
secretary@magothy.org
R. (410) 739-1488
pastor@magothy.org

Marley #1335
30 Marley Neck Rd, Glen Burnie, MD 21060-7508
Stephanie Bekhor OE
3708 Alton Pl NW, Washington, DC 20016-2206

C. (410) 760-4720
marleyumc@yahoo.com
R. (202) 870-1634
graisim@yahoo.com

Mayo #1148
1005 Old Turkey Point Rd, Edgewater, MD 21037-4028
Amanda McMurtrey FE
1005 Old Turkey Point Rd, Edgewater, MD 21037
C. (410) 798-6110
mayoumc@verizon.net
R. (970) 231-5123
mayopastoramanda@gmail.com

Messiah #1340
7401 E Furnace Branch Rd, Glen Burnie, MD 21060-7243
Ben Rigsby PL
520 Shipley Rd, Linthicum, MD 21090-2829
C. (410) 761-1944
messiahumc4@verizon.net
R. (936) 615-5946
rev.ben.rigsby@gmail.com

Metropolitan #1480
548 Queenstown Rd, Severn, MD 21144-1310
James Gosnell PE
3 Adams Ridge Ct, Baltimore, MD 21244-3802
C. (410) 768-3588
mumc21144@verizon.net
R. (410) 521-9555
pastorgosnell@gmail.com

Mount Carmel #1460
4760 Mountain Rd, Pasadena, MD 21122-5814
Michael Fauconnet FE
4760 Mountain Rd, Pasadena, MD 21122-5814
C. (410) 255-8887
mtcarmel21122@gmail.com
R. (240) 405-2750
soujourner56@gmail.com

Mount Tabor #1285
1421 Saint Stephens Church Rd, Crownsville, MD 21032-2203
Stanley Bolds SY
3400 Enfield Chase Court, Bowie, MD 20716
C. (410) 721-3472
rubyhawk@verizon.net
R. (412) 818-3654
bolds44@comcast.net

Mount Zion #1410
122 Bayard Rd, Lothian, MD 20711-9601
Vaughan Hayden
122 Bayard Rd, Lothian, MD 20711-9601
C. (410) 867-4035
mz@mzumc.com
R. (443) 553-5541
pastorhayden@mzumc.com

Mount Zion #1465
8178 Artic Dr, Pasadena, MD 21122-4422
Robert E. Walker, Jr. FE
3201 Carlswood Cir, Windsor Mill, MD 21244-1380
C. (410) 255-4602
mzmagothyumc@gmail.com
R. (410) 496-8332
rewalkerjr@gmail.com

Mt. Zion/Franklin
Franklin #1175
5345 Deale Churchton Rd, Churchton, MD 20733-9626
Mount Zion-Ark Road #1415
41 Ark Rd, Lothian, MD 20711-2905
Alhassan C. Macaulay FE
7833 Metacomet Rd, Hanover, MD 21076-1246
C. (410) 867-3521
franklumc5345@gmail.com
C. (410) 867-0632
junedrake@verizon.net
R. (410) 551-3513
pastormacaulay@gmail.com

Mt. Zion-Fowler
Fowler #1140
816 Bestgate Rd, Annapolis, MD 21401-3033
Mount Zion #1150
612 Second St, Annapolis, MD 21403-3332
Patricia D. Johnson FE
27 Deep Powder Ct # 1A, Woodstock, MD 21163-1110
C. (410) 224-2149
Tbelt2047@msn.com
C. (410) 268-5798
Shalom21230pj@AOL.com
R. 410-419-8483
shalom21230pj@aol.com

Nichols-Bethel #1430
C. (410) 674-2272
1239 Murray Rd, Odenton, MD 21113-1603
office@nicholsbethel.org
Clark D. Carr FE
R. (410) 451-1324
1239 Murray Rd, Odenton, MD 21113-1603
clarkdcarr@verizon.net

Katharine Saari FE
R. (443) 878-6997
1241 Murray Rd, Odenton, MD 21113-1603
pastorkatie1@gmail.com

Northeast
Dorsey Emmanuel #1220
C. (410) 796-8598
6951 Dorsey Rd, Elkridge, MD 21075-6210
pastor@wesleychapelumcjessup.org
Melville Chapel #1265
C. (410) 796-0959
5660 Furnace Ave, Elkridge, MD 21075-5110
roursler22@hotmail.com
Jennifer Osterfeld
R. (410) 867-4035
114 Bayard Rd, Lothian, MD 20711
jenn@mzumc.com
Wesley Chapel #1365
C. (410) 799-3494
7745 Waterloo Rd, Jessup, MD 20794-9793
pastor@wesleychapelumcjessup.org
Richard C. Oursler PL
R. (410) 799-2128
7760 Waterloo Rd, Jessup, MD 20794
roursler22@hotmail.com

Pasadena #1470
C. (443) 510-8846
61 Ritchie Hwy, Pasadena, MD 21122-4356
pumc2@verizon.net
Marian (Mernie) Crane FE
R. (410) 725-5913
1605 Old Mill Bottom Run, Annapolis, MD 21409
pastoratpumc@verizon.net

Savage #7435
C. (301) 725-7630
9050 Baltimore St, Savage, MD 20763-9647
office@umcsavage.org
DaeHwa Park FE
R. (202)277-8553
17506 Gallagher Way, Olney, MD 20832-2065
daehwa@gmail.com

Severna Park #1510
C. (410) 987-4700
731 Benfield Rd, Severna Park, MD 21146
spumc@severnaparkumc.org
Lee S. Ferrell FD
R. (410) 562-9811
731 Benfield Rd, Severna Park, MD 21146
lferrell@severnaparkumc.org

Ronald K. Foster FE
R. (240) 672-1321
731 Benfield Rd, Severna Park, MD 21146
ron@severnaparkumc.org

Carissa G. Surber FE
R. (443) 377-9918
925 Diggs Rd, Crownsville, MD 21032-1622
csurber@severnaparkumc.org

South County
Sollers #1380
C. (410) 741-1772
1219 Wrighton Rd, Lothian, MD 20711-9737
sollersumc673@gmail.com
St Matthews #1520
C. (410) 867-7661
6234 Shady Side Rd, Shady Side, MD 20764-9685
smumcss@gmail.com
Marvin R. Wamble FE
R. (202) 439-3226
12005 Ishtar St, Fort Washington, MD 20744-6058
marvelousworks1@gmail.com

Solley #1345
C. (410) 437-5641
7600 Solley Rd, Glen Burnie, MD 21060-8308
pastor@solleyumc.org
Jeffrey Postell
R. (334) 207-2274
7070 Ducketts Ln, Apt 304, Elkridge, MD 21075-7002
preachjdp@gmail.com

St Mark #1350
1440 Dorsey Rd, Hanover, MD 21076
Herbert Watson, Jr. FE
138 Wesley Ave, Catonsville, MD 21228-3142

C. (410) 859-5352
tedmack@verizon.net
R. (410) 747-5835
pastorstmarkumc@gmail.com

St Mark's #7425
601 8th St, Laurel, MD 20707-3920
Eugene Matthews RE
7448 Race Rd, Hanover, MD 21076-1114

C. (301) 776-8885
stmarkslmd@gmail.com
R. (410) 379-0600
reveugene@comcast.net

St Andrews of Annapolis #1255
4 Wallace Manor Rd, Edgewater, MD 21037-1206
David E. Thayer FE
3187 Raven Ct, Annapolis, MD 21403-1626

C. (410) 626-1610
standrewsum@gmail.com
R. 410-626-1610
revfam@aol.com

The Everlasting Love #1310
251 SW Pershing Ave, Glen Burnie, MD 21061-3956
Jong Hui Park FE
251 SW Pershing Ave, Glen Burnie, MD 21061-3956

C. (443) 763-4566
churchp69@hotmail.com
R. (443) 763-4566
churchp69@hotmail.com

Trinity #1435
952 Patuxent Rd, Odenton, MD 21113-2208
Sandra Knepp PL
1593 Forest Hill Ct, Crofton, MD 21114-1826

C. (410) 672-5215
trinityumc_odenton@yahoo.com
R. (443) 569-1867
pastorsandyk@gmail.com

Trinity #1155
1300 West St, Annapolis, MD 21401-3612
Meredith A. Wilkins-Arnold FE
1910 Dulany Pl, Annapolis, MD 21409-6221

C. (410) 268-1620
office@trinityannapolis.org
R. (240) 298-7068
gracetrumpsworks@gmail.com

Union #1385
274 W Bay Front Rd, PO Box 233, Lothian, MD 20711
Randy Truesdale
8841 Heathermore Blvd #101, Upper Marlboro, MD 20772

C. (410) 867-1661
union.umc274@gmail.com
R. (301) 793-0378
randytruesdale30@gmail.com

Union Memorial #1210
3328 Davidsonville Rd, Davidsonville, MD 21035
Gregory J. McNeil PL
105 Bagg Blvd, Odenton, Md 21113

C. (410) 798-0526
unionmemorialumc424@gmail.com
R. (410) 674-5153
Preacher1006@gmail.com

Wesley Chapel #1390
1010 Wrighton Rd, Lothian, MD 20711-9735
Marvene Young
7201 Burning Timber Ln, Owings, MD 20736-3036

C. (410) 741-9258
marvene_young@hotmail.com
R. (301) 873-2711
marvene_young@hotmail.com

Wesley Grove #1355
1320 Dorsey Rd, Hanover, MD 21076-1453
Elizabeth A. LeMaster FE
6326 Barnett Ave, Eldersburg, MD 21784-6102

C. (410) 761-9119
cdamm@comcast.net
R. (304) 261-4763
ealemaster@gmail.com

Wilson Memorial #1290
PO Box 460, Gambrills, MD 21054-0460
(1113 Md Route 3 North)

C. (410) 721-1482
wilsonmem1113@gmail.com

Jerome A. Jones, Sr. PL
1913 Rose Pl, Upper Marlboro, MD 20774-8559

R. (301) 821-6545
jeromejones35@gmail.com

Certified Candidate
Alicia B. O'Brien CC
1002 Jackson St, Annapolis, MD 21403-2115

R. (410) 507-6264
aliciabrooksobrien@gmail.com

Certified Lay Minister
Frank Lanzer LM
1709 Basil Way, Gambrills, MD 21054-1817

R. (410) 721-6010
flanzer@verizon.net

Paula Madden LM
2491 Deerfield Ln, Chesapeake Beach, MD 20732-4612

R. (443) 262-2635
pajaty@comcast.net

Extension Ministry
Anthony T. Carr FE
10121 Towhee Ave, Adelphi, MD 20783-1209

R. (805) 205-5100
anthony.carr@navy.mil

Elizabeth L. (Betsy) Halsey FE
15509 Indianola Dr, Derwood, MD 20855-2706

R. (240) 462-7562
betsyhalsey@yahoo.com

Christopher T. Holmes FE
1535 Eton Way, Crofton, MD 21114

R. (410) 300-8847
chris@holmescoaching.com

Maidstone Mulenga FE
2600 Maidens Ln, Edgewood, MD 21040

R. (202) 748-5172
maidstonem@gmail.com

Enger Muteteke PD
155 Barbara Rd, Severna Park, MD 21146-1303

R. (443) 962-5660
muteteke@gmail.com

Bruce C. Thompson FE
19 Berwick Ln, Bear, DE 19701-4767

R. (410) 562-2588
brucecthompson@gmail.com

Honorable Location
Robert McKinley, III RE
3776 Traemoor Rd, Southport, NC 28461-8219

Leave of Absence
Nicole Houston FE
1175 Rivershore Rd, Charleston, SC 29492-8243

R. 850-572-2065
NLchris1@gmail.com

Medical Leave
Ingrid Wang FE
2345 Dartmouth Ln, Crofton, MD 21114-1208

R. 410-451-4331
pastor.ingrid1@gmail.com

Retired
Maria A. (MaAn) Barcelo RE
2028 1/2 Francisco St, Berkeley, CA 94709-2126

R. (410) 432-6159
revmaan.berkeleyca@gmail.com

Robert H. Brookman RE
1101 Outlett Mills Ct, Catonsville, MD 21228-2642

R. (410) 788-2555

Byron P. Brought RE
665 Dill Rd, Severna Park, MD 21146-4119

R. (410) 544-9188
bbrought@severnaparkumc.org

Kenneth E. Brown RE
1400 Peregrine Path, Arnold, MD 21012
R. (410) 703-6619
keb2639@gmail.com

Bonnie Campbell RA
38 Canvasback Cir, Bridgeville, DE 19933-2428
R. (443) 922-9904
revbonniecampbell@gmail.com

John Campbell RE
38 Canvasback Cir, Bridgeville, DE 19933-2428
R. (703) 855-9539
revjohncampbell@gmail.com

Shirley R. Carrington RE
3708 Campfield Rd, Gwynn Oak, MD 21207-6350
R. (410) 484-2241

Jack H. Cassel RE
8129 Windy Field Ln, Millersville, MD 21108-1660
R. (410) 969-5301
jhcassel1935@gmail.com

Raymond E. Clements RE
6800 Louise Ct, Anchorage, AK 99507-6735
R. (907) 346-2064
ray@ak.net

Lysbeth B. (Lys) Cockrell RE
516 Kinglets Roost Ln, Glen Burnie, MD 21060-8645
R. (667) 229-7506
lysbethcockrell@yahoo.com

Linda W. Coolbaugh RD
301 Windfern Ct, Millersville, MD 21108-2419
R. (410) 987-5909
rev.linda@nicholsbethel.org

Linda J. Coveleskie RE
107 Gibson Cir, Chester, MD 21619-2184
R. 410-258-4679
ljcovs@gmail.com

Susan E. Duchesneau RE
790 Monaco Dr, Punta Gorda, FL 33950-8018
R. (410) 591-1830
sed228@verizon.net

Betty P. Dunlop RE
4410 Forest Glen Ct, Annandale, VA 22003-4838
R. (703) 642-6490
betty.dunlop@verizon.net

Marian Dunmore RE
702 16th St NE, Washington, DC 20002-4514
mariandunmore@aol.com

James H. (Jim) Farmer RA
37932 Bayview Cir E, Selbyville, DE 19975-2870

Claire L. Fiedler RE
725 Olive Wood Ln, Baltimore, MD 21225-3382
R. (410) 354-2871
clfiedler@juno.com

G. S. (Sylvester) Gaines RE
6011 84th Ave, New Carrollton, MD 20784-2924
R. (301) 459-7310
gainesrev@yahoo.com

Elsie M. Gladding RE
1027 Mount Carmel Rd, Alton, VA 24520-3575
R. (434) 753-3035
elsiemaymckenney@hotmail.com

Karen N. Gould RE
8512 Festival Way, Charlotte, NC 28215-3276
R. (410) 573-5313
kngould@verizon.net

Gerald Grace RE
1500 Pernell Ct, Bowie, MD 20716-1606
R. 301-249-6013
geraldgrace150@gmail.com

Richard G. Gray RE
967 Highpoint Dr, Annapolis, MD 21409-4752
R. (410) 757-3817
rggrayjr@gmail.com

Edgar W. Hammersla RE
3154 Gracefield Rd Apt 213, Silver Spring, MD 20904-0807
eeham1927@gmail.com

Charlotte A. Hendee RE
8 Charles Wesley Ct, Wells, ME 04090-5179
R. (443) 995-0613
umcnubble@gmail.com

Eddie L. Henry RE
169 Pine Trl, Delta, PA 17314-8686
R. (717) 456-5276

William A. Herche, Jr. RE
703C Wesley Dr, Waynesboro, PA 17268-7992

R. (717) 524-0354
baherche@gmail.com

Hosea L. Hodges RE
1041 Lake Claire Dr, Annapolis, MD 21409-4764

R. (410) 757-3580
hlhodges423@aol.com

Oliver Jennings RA
327 Jennings Rd, Severna Park, MD 21146-1801

R. (410) 647-2459

Barbara J. (Jodi) Jessup RE
109 Hemlock Dr, Bracey, VA 23919-1958

bjodyj@me.com

Norman B. (Bruce) Kuehnle RE
419 Russell Ave Apt 309, Gaithersburg, MD 20877-2872

R. (410) 987-5085

William K. (Ken) Lyons, Jr. RE
1329 Bluegrass Way, Gambrills, MD 21054-1052

R. (410) 674-6579
kedolyons@comcast.net

Brenda J. Mack RE
700 Freeman Dr Apt 415, Hampton, VA 23666-4375

magdalene_29@hotmail.com

James D. Manning RE
3524 South River Ter, Edgewater, MD 21037-3245

R. (410) 798-4648

Joanna Marceron RL
327 S River Clubhouse Rd, Harwood, MD 20776-9534

R. (410) 991-2253
Jjmdiaconal@msn.com

Sherrin Marshall RE
1333 Tall Timbers Dr, Crownsville, MD 21032-1531

R. (410) 923-4554
RevSDMarshall@aol.com

Roberta Matthews RA
1102 Cattail Commons Way, Denton, MD 21629-3015

R. (410) 479-4580
clergy4@comcast.net

Michael A. McKinney RE
11205 Woodlawn Blvd, Upper Marlboro, MD 20774-2361

R. (202) 321-8465
revdoc33@hotmail.com

Walter Middlebrooks RE
5521 Thomas Sim Lee Ter, Upper Marlboro, MD 20772

R. (240) 339-1789
walter_middlebrooks@comcast.net

Ann P. Offer RE
101 Melchior Rd, Millersville, MD 21108-1793

revannparkeroffer@verizon.net

Davis W. Peck RE
11740 Asbury Cir Apt 1105, Solomons, MD 20688-3067

R. (410) 394-3110
dumcoffice@dumc.net

Arthe' V. (Taysie) Phillips PE
6538 Fish Hatchery Rd, Thurmont, MD 21788-2701

R. (301) 639-4670
taysie5@comcast.net

Charles A. Proctor RE
8302 Maple St, Laurel, MD 20707-5093

R. (301) 498-4018

Henry F. Schwarzmann RE
146 Kingston Rd, Greenwood, SC 29649-9569

R. (864) 229-2065
henryschwarzmann@hotmail.com

Linda C. (Carole) Silbaugh RE
16569 Howard Millman Ln, Milton, DE 19968-3531

R. (302) 645-7225
carole.silbaugh@comcast.net

Charles Simms, Sr. RE
1421 Saint Stephens Church Rd, Crownsville, MD 21032-2203

R. (410) 216-9202
csimms70@aol.com

Mabel Smith PL
7933 Mount Harmony Ln, Owings, MD 20736-3409

R. (443) 550-3259
mabelsmith9@comcast.net

Kelly S. Sparks RE
35 Coventry Cir E, Marlton, NJ 08053-2860

Jay E. (Jack) Stearns RE   R. (410) 757-4483
462 Cranes Roost Ct, Annapolis, MD 21409-5748

Anne R. Stewart RE   R. (443) 646-6643
6656 Highview Ter, Tracys Landing, MD 20779-2548   revdranne@comcast.net

Donald S. Stewart, Jr. RE   R. (443) 646-6643
6656 Highview Ter, Tracys Landing, MD 20779-2548   annedon@comcast.net

Judith T. Stone RL   R. (410) 551-3535
1279 Delmont Rd, Severn, MD 21144-1904   job4215@clergy.net

Earl J. (Jim) Stutler RE   R. (410) 721-1817
1101 Pilgrim Ct, Crofton, MD 21114-1359   jstutler@verizon.net

Roland J. Timity RE   R. (410) 551-1334
1904 Sheffield Ct, Severn, MD 21144-1509

Andrea Titcomb RD   R. (410) 956-6548
253 Lindenhall Ct, Riva, MD 21140-1518   andytitcomb@hotmail.com

Kenneth (Ken) Valentine RE   R. (301) 401-2775
809 Chesapeake Dr, Stevensville, MD 21666-2711   revksv@yahoo.com

James M. Warner RE   R. (401) 322-7675
161 E Beach Rd # A, Charlestown, RI 02813-1602

David Wentz RE
1240 County Road K A, Hartshorn, MO 65479-9600   davidnwentz@gmail.com

Leslie E. Werner, Jr. RE   R. (410) 793-0756
1604 Farnborn St, Crofton, MD 21114-1518

John W. Zsittnik RE   R. (704) 947-6370
15941 Spruell St, Huntersville, NC 28078-4239

BALTIMORE METROPOLITAN DISTRICT

Superintendent
Wanda B. Duckett FE
5522 Sefton Ave, Baltimore, MD 21214-2341
wduckett@bwcumc.org

(410) 309-3435
R. (443) 629-9232

Ames #4110
615 Baker St, Baltimore, MD 21217-2814
Rodney R. Hudson FE
9604 Grandhaven Ave, Upper Marlboro, MD 20772

C. (443) 438-6555
Ames.Memorial@hotmail.com
R. (240) 601-0872
Ames.Memorial@hotmail.com

Arbutus #3110
1201 Maple Ave, Baltimore, MD 21227-2639
Ira Barr, Jr. FE
1227 Maple Ave, Halethorpe, MD 21227-2639

C. (410) 204-8906
aumcmain@comcast.net
R. (410) 242-3466
irabarr2@verizon.net

Arnolia #3530
1776 E Joppa Rd, Baltimore, MD 21234-3621
James D. McSavaney FE
3420 Beech Ave, Baltimore, MD 21211-2643

C. (410) 665-7005
arnoliaumc@arnolia.org
R. (443) 540-1078
james@arnolia.org

Back River #2420
544 Back River Neck Rd, Essex, MD 21221-4604
Donna Nelson FE
544A Back River Neck Rd, Essex, MD 21221-4604

C. (410) 686-4195
office@backriverumc.com
R. (410) 391-0879
donnaleenelson@gmail.com

Beechfield #3150
541 S Beechfield Ave, Baltimore, MD 21229-4325
Joel V. Holmes PL
2431 Terra Firma Rd, Baltimore, MD 21225-1121

C. (410) 644-7640
pastorholmes@comcast.net
R. (443) 400-8443
joel_holmes@comcast.net

Bethesda #3145
6300 Harford Rd, Baltimore, MD 21214-1315
Arthur D. (Dan) Gleckler RE
2726 Saint Paul St, Baltimore, MD 21218-4332

C. (410) 426-3211
bethesdaumc@cavtel.net
R. (410) 243-5313
adg2726stpaul@msn.com

Brooklyn Community #2142
110 Townsend Ave, Baltimore, MD 21225-3052
Sonia L. King FE
643 Chapelgate Dr, Odenton, MD 21113-2138

C. (410) 789-3688
Brooklyncommumcbpmd@gmail.com
R. (410) 320-3482
revslkzeta@gmail.com

Catonsville #4180
6 Melvin Ave, Catonsville, MD 21228-4424
David Jacobson PE
2105 Edmondson Ave, Catonsville, MD 21228-4209

C. (410) 747-1886
Cumc21228@verizon.net
R. (443) 840-9840
david@catonsvilleumc.org

Chase #2362
6601 Ebenezer Rd, Baltimore, MD 21220-1217
Walter D. Jackson, III PE
7150 Daniel John Dr, Elkridge, MD 21075-5452

C. (410) 335-2172
chaseumc6601@gmail.com
R. (443) 799-2868
walterjackson3@hotmail.com

Cherry Hill #2155
PO Box 19811, Baltimore, MD 21225-0311
(3225 Round Road)
Daryl A. Foster PL
18 N Belle Grove Rd, Catonsville, MD 21228-2049

C. (410) 355-0022
cherryhillumc@gmail.com

R. (443) 278-6341
severnspastor@gmail.com

Christ #2160
2005 E Chase St, Baltimore, MD 21213-3325
Twanda E. Prioleau FE
PO Box 522, Parkton, MD 21120-0522

C. (410) 732-5600
cumchurch@verizon.net
R. (443) 271-9401
revtwandap@aol.com

Christ Church of Baltimore County #3285
2833 Florida Ave, Baltimore, MD 21227-3637
Richard Keller PL
2217 Smith Ave, Baltimore, MD 21227-1828

C. (410) 789-9058
recycle815@aol.com
R. (410) 796-5697
recycle815@aol.com

Christ Deaf / Magothy Deaf
Christ Church of the Deaf #3115
1040 S Beechfield Ave, Baltimore, MD 21229-4938
Magothy Church of the Deaf #1455
3703 Mountain Rd, Pasadena, MD 21122-2024
Sandi E. Johnson FE
3637 Sussex Rd, Pikesville, MD 21207-3818

C. (410) 242-6303
christdeafchurch@gmail.com

ehart@bwcumc.org
R. (410) 653-4650
sjohnson@bwcumc.org

Emily Hart PE
305 5th Ave, Brooklyn Park, MD 21225-4006

R. (443) 846-5110
ehart@bwcumc.org

Cowenton-Piney Grove
Cowenton #2570
10838 Red Lion Rd, White Marsh, MD 21162-1702
Piney Grove #2355
201 Bowleys Quarters Rd, Middle River, MD 21220-2925
Christine Kumar PL
10830 Red Lion Rd, White Marsh, MD 21162-1702

C. (410) 335-3343
cpkumar222@gmail.com
C. (410) 335-6927
cpkumar222@gmail.com
R. (301) 526-3238
cpkumar222@gmail.com

Eastern #2175
5315 Harford Rd, Baltimore, MD 21214-2255
Thomas (Jay) Blake FE
4202 Raab Ave, Nottingham, MD 21236-2415

C. (410) 752-8524
easternumchurch@verizon.net
R. (716) 310-6083
Priceless226@comcast.net

Eden Korean #2180
56 Stevenson Ln, Baltimore, MD 21212-1206
Yo-Seop Shin FE
54 Stevenson Ln, Baltimore, MD 21212-1240

C. (667) 206-4187
yshinpastor@gmail.com
R. (443) 629-1752
yshinpastor@gmail.com

Emanuel #4630
6517 Frederick Rd, Catonsville, MD 21228-3528
Levon Sutton PL
3703 Buckingham Rd, Gwynn Oak, MD 21207-3814

C. (410) 747-0702
emanuelumc@verizon.net
R. (410) 299-3994
Levon_sutton@hotmail.con

Epworth Chapel #4170
3317 Saint Lukes Ln, Baltimore, MD 21207-5703
Charles A. (Tony) Hunt FE
1305 Cherokee Ln, Bel Air, MD 21015-4763

C. (410) 944-1070
epworthchapel@aol.com
R. (410) 944-1070
cahunt@msn.com

Terri Williams SY
4019 Offutt Rd, Randallstown, MD 21133-3300

R. (443) 850-1659
terrikw1@aol.com

Essex #2425
524 Maryland Ave, Essex, MD 21221-6734
Mary E. Robinson PL
9722 Groffs Mill Dr, Owings Mills, MD 21117-6341

C. (410) 686-2867
essexUMC@gmail.com
R. (443) 244-5907
drmarobi@gmail.com

Faith Community #2192
5315 Harford Rd, Baltimore, MD 21214-2255
Ronald Dodson, Sr. PL
9602 Wesland Cir, Randallstown, MD 21133-2042

C. (410) 426-8177
faith_community@verizon.net
R. (410) 922-0658
rondodson@verizon.net

G.O.A.L.
Arlington-Lewin #4115
5260 Reisterstown Rd, Baltimore, MD 21215-5019
Gwynn Oak #4130
5020 Gwynn Oak Ave, Baltimore, MD 21207-6803
Dellyne I. Hinton FE
5020 Gwynn Oak Ave, Baltimore, MD 21207-6803

C. (410) 542-3070
a-lumc@hotmail.com
C. (410) 542-1274
gwynnoakumc2@comcast.net
R. (410) 542-1274
dell_hinton@comcast.net

Good Shepherd #3230
3800 Roland Ave, Baltimore, MD 21211-2003
Bonnie McCubbin FE
813 Staffordshire Rd, Cockeysville, MD 21030-2926

C. (410) 243-1129
HampdenPastor@gmail.com
R. (410) 868-1035
bonnie.mccubbin@gmail.com

Grace #3170
5407 N Charles St, Baltimore, MD 21210-2024
Amy McCullough FE
5405 N Charles St, Baltimore, MD 21210-2024

C. (410) 433-6650
office@graceunitedmethodist.org
R. (410) 323-8286
amy@graceunitedmethodist.org

Daniel (Dane) Wood, Jr. FL
413 Lyman Ave, Baltimore, MD 21212-3512

R. (803) 295-8445
dcwood.jr@gmail.com

Graceland #2210
6714 Youngstown Ave, Baltimore, MD 21222-1025
Daniel Kutrick PL
442 Machias Pl, Middle River, MD 21220-2338

C. (410) 633-8799
danielkutrick@comcast.net
R. (410) 335-7154
danielkutrick@comcast.net

Halethorpe-Relay #3120
4513 Ridge Ave, Halethorpe, MD 21227-4440
Chris Dembeck PE
4513 Ridge Ave, Halethorpe, MD 21227-4440

C. (410) 242-5918
hrumc1@outlook.com
R. (410) 952-3650
Chrisdembeck@gmail.com

Hiss #3440
8700 Harford Rd, Baltimore, MD 21234-4608
Mark C. Mooney FE
635 Bashore Dr, Martinsburg, WV 25404-7604

C. (410) 668-5665
office@hisschurch.org
R. (304) 271-8936
pastormark@hisschurch.org

John Wesley #4135
3202 W North Ave, Baltimore, MD 21216-3014
Joan Carter-Rimbach FE
6316 Gentle Light Ln, Columbia, MD 21044-6035

C. (410) 383-1525
baltjwumc@aol.com
R. (240) 755-0190
srpastorjwbalto@gmail.com

Lansdowne #3125
114 Lavern Ave, Baltimore, MD 21227-3022
Emily E. Skorupinski FL
224 Pennsylvania Ave, Pasadena, MD 21122-5436

C. (410) 247-4624
LansdowneUMC@gmail.com
R. 410-937-9513
pastoremily@lansdowneumc.org

Loch Raven #3540
6622 Loch Raven Blvd, Baltimore, MD 21239-1424
George Winkfield FE
835 Braeside Rd, Baltimore, MD 21229-2116

C. (410) 825-0900
office@lrumc.org
R. (410) 788-3362
pastorwinkfield@gmail.com

Lovely Lane #3185
2200 Saint Paul St, Baltimore, MD 21218-5805
Deb L. Scott FE
17724 Caddy Dr, Derwood, MD 20855

C. (410) 889-1512
LovelyLane.BCS@gmail.com
R. (301) 641-4601
revdeb8@aol.com

Martin Luther King Memorial #4145
5114 Windsor Mill Rd, Baltimore, MD 21207-6657
Michael A. Carrington, Jr. PL
203 Staysail Dr, Joppa, MD 21085-4125

C. (410) 448-2312
mlkumc1@comcast.net
R. (443) 721-6183
michaelcarrington18@gmail.com

Metropolitan #2220
1121 W Lanvale St, Baltimore, MD 21217-2520
Howard W. Hinson RE
3701 Hillsdale Rd, Gwynn Oak, MD 21207-8075

C. (410) 523-1366
metrosqr@verizon.net
R. (443) 253-7092
howard-hinson@verizon.net

Mount Olivet #4190
823 Edmondson Ave, Catonsville, MD 21228-4448
Melvin T. Bond, Sr. PL
2434 W Lafayette Ave, Baltimore, MD 21216-4803

C. (410) 744-4451
olivet4190@gmail.com
R. (410) 608-1400
tyronehhc46@comcast.net

Mount Winans #2235
2501 Hollins Ferry Rd, Baltimore, MD 21230-3031
Nathaniel J. Green PL
3407 Cedardale Rd, Baltimore, MD 21215-7301

C. (410) 727-4211
mtwinansumc@gmail.com
R. (443) 414-8128
revngreen@yahoo.com

Mount Vernon Place #3215
10 E Mount Vernon Pl, Baltimore, MD 21202-2309
Rod Miller RE
3701 Saint Johns Ln, Ellicott City, MD 21042-5226

C. (410) 685-5290
mvpumcbaltimore@gmail.com
R. (410) 465-2335
miller.roderick.j@gmail.com

Mount Washington-Aldersgate #3220
5800 Cottonworth Ave, Baltimore, MD 21209
   Vera Mitchell RE
   2 Kirkwyn Ct, Owings Mills, MD 21117-5556

C. (410) 323-4314
mwaumc@mwaumc.comcastbiz.net
R. (443) 288-3045
VMitchellMallett@gmail.com

New Covenant Worship Center #3575
700 Wildwood Pkwy, Baltimore, MD 21229-1812
   Clarence Davis RE
   3502 Ellamont Rd, Baltimore, MD 21215-7423

C. (410) 624-5330
ncwc.churchumc@gmail.com
R. (410) 367-2025
cdjuniorclergy@msn.com

New Waverly-Govan Boundary
Govans-Boundary #3165
5210 York Rd, Baltimore, MD 21212-4257
New Waverly #3217
644 E 33rd St, Baltimore, MD 21218-3504
   Andrea M. King FE
   PO Box 233, Fulton, MD 20759-0253

C. (410) 435-1550
govansboundryumc@gmail.com
C. (410) 243-2481
newwave3217@gmail.com
R. (843) 557-2455
revamking@yahoo.com

Northwood-Appold #3225
4499 Loch Raven Blvd, Baltimore, MD 21218-1500
   Cecil C. Gray FE
   4499 Loch Raven Blvd, Baltimore, MD 21218-1500

C. (410) 323-6712
northwoodappoldumc@gmail.com
R. (443) 831-2527
o9h9y93oo@prodigy.net

Orems #2515
1020 Orems Rd, Baltimore, MD 21220-4623
   Gail L. Button RE
   811 Sunnyfield Ln, Brooklyn Park, MD 21225-3367

C. (410) 687-9483
oremsumc@verizon.net
R. (410) 636-1757
glbutton@gmail.com

Patapsco-Lodge Forest
Lodge Forest #2410
2715 Lodge Forest Dr, Baltimore, MD 21219-1913
Patapsco #2385
7800 Wise Ave, Dundalk, MD 21222-3338
   Katie Grover FE
   7611 Sparrows Point Blvd, Baltimore, MD 21219-1929

C. (410) 477-0976
db.peters@comcast.net
C. (410) 288-5488
grover.katiej@gmail.com

grover.katiej@gmail.com

Pikesville Pimlico
Elderslie-St Andrews #4120
5601 Pimlico Rd, Baltimore, MD 21209-4313
St. Paul Praise and Worship Center #2290
501 Reisterstown Rd, Pikesville, MD 21208
   Denise H. Norfleet-Walker FE
   3201 Carlswood Cir, Windsor Mill, MD 21244-1380

C. (410) 664-3392
eldersliestandrews@verizon.net
C. (410) 486-2028
sppwc501@verizon.net
R. (410) 496-8332
denise.norfleet@verizon.net

Salem-Baltimore Hispanic #2310
3405 Gough St., Baltimore, MD 21224
   Jorge Moreno SY
   9755 Bird River Rd, Baltimore, MD 21220-1701

C. (410) 276-8460
pastorsegovia.gs@gmail.com
R. (443) 898-2850
jorgeisel71@gmail.com

   Gustavo A. Segovia SY
   3403 Gough St, Baltimore, MD 21224

R. (540) 250-3503
pastorsegovia.gs@gmail.com

Sharp Street Memorial #3250
1206 Etting St, Baltimore, MD 21217-3035
 Cary James, Jr. FE
 7833 Crossbay Dr, Severn, MD 21144-1660

C. (410) 523-7200
ssmumc@yahoo.com
R. (410) 519-7343
revcjamesjr@yahoo.com

St John #1473
6019 Belle Grove Rd, Baltimore, MD 21225
 Bernadette A. Armwood FE
 7000 Rudisill Ct Apt 1B, Windsor Mill, MD 21244-5409

C. (410) 636-2578
tsjeinfo@gmail.com
R. (410) 521-3551
armwoodb@aol.com

St Johns #3240
2640 Saint Paul St, Baltimore, MD 21218-4531
 Irance' Reddix-McCray PE
 3317 Kenjac Rd, Windsor Mill, MD 21244-1323

C. (410) 366-7733
lolwtaj@gmail.com
R. (318) 348-5622
ievangel@aol.com

St Luke #4155
1100 N Gilmor St, Baltimore, MD 21217-2209
 Alfreda Wiggins RE
 27 Deep Powder Ct, Woodstock, MD 21163-1110

C. (410) 728-1183
dralw124@aol.com
R. (410) 922-4408
dralw124@aol.com

St Matthews #2390
101 Avon Beach Rd, Baltimore, MD 21222-6105
 Kay F. Albury RE
 5900 Loch Raven Blvd, Baltimore, MD 21239-2440

C. (410) 285-4466
kayfran61@gmail.com
R. (443) 629-3211
kayfran61@gmail.com

St. Matthews-New Life #3247
416 E 23rd St, Baltimore, MD 21218-5819
 Andre R. Briscoe, Jr. FE
 5511 Pioneer Dr, Baltimore, MD 21214-1617

C. (410) 243-0378
st.matthewsnewlife@comcast.net
R. (443) 642-1015
andrebriscoejr@gmail.com

Towson #3550
501 Hampton Ln, Towson, MD 21286-1311
 Mark W. Johnson FE
 3637 Sussex Rd, Pikesville, MD 21207-3818

C. (410) 823-6511
towsonumc@towsonumc.org
R. (410) 653-4650
pastormark.johnson@gmail.com

 Margery L. Schammel FD
 4 Ansari Ct, Baldwin, MD 21013

R. (410) 592-3805
mlwschammel61@gmail.com

Trinity #4210
2100 Westchester Ave, Catonsville, MD 21228
 David Carter-Rimbach RE
 6316 Gentle Light Ln, Columbia, MD 21044

C. (410) 747-5841
trinitycatonsvillepastor@gmail.com
R. (410) 245-2505
trinitycatonsvillepastor@gmail.com

Union Memorial #2320
2500 Harlem Ave, Baltimore, MD 21216-4838
 Jason Jordan-Griffin FE
 7843 Foxfarm Ln, Glen Burnie, MD 21061-6324

C. (410) 945-2723
smithjpj@aol.com
R. (202) 277-8957
pastor@unionbaltimore.org

Violetville #3260
3648 Coolidge Ave, Baltimore, MD 21229-5140
 Scheherazade Forman PL
 7420 Eldon Ct, Pikesville, MD 21208

C. (410) 525-3191
violetvilleumc@gmail.com
R. (443) 690-9336
dr4man31@gmail.com

Water's Edge Partnership Initiative #3113
2400 Boston St Ste 102, Baltimore, MD 21224-4780
Steve Burke PL
1806 Bank St, Baltimore, MD 21231-2506

C. (301) 606-6687
sburke@watersedgepartnership.org
R. (301) 606-6687
sburke@watersedgepartnership.org

West Baltimore-Unity
Unity #2325
1433 Edmondson Ave, Baltimore, MD 21223-1243
West Baltimore #4165
5130 Greenwich Ave, Baltimore, MD 21229-2314
Anthony Forman PL
7420 Eldon Ct, Pikesville, MD 21208

C. (410) 728-4826
unityumc@gmail.com
C. (410) 945-8397
dr4man@verizon.net
R. (443) 944-2247
pastor4man@gmail.com

Certified Candidate
Christopher B. Allen CC
3014 Brendan Ave, Baltimore, MD 21213

R. (410) 485-9230
christopherballen89@gmail.com

Certified Lay Minister
Albert Davis, Sr. LM
1300 E Cold Spring Ln, Baltimore, MD 21239-3911

R. (443) 201-6886
aldavis812@yahoo.com

Hazel Jackson LM
3331 Ripple Rd, Baltimore, MD 21244-2859

R. (410) 496-4811
hazel.jackson@comcast.net

Sheryl C. Morsell LM
623 Charraway Rd, Baltimore, MD 21229-4404

R. (410) 646-4926
SheryL4906@verizon.net

Extension Ministry
Gregory A. Coates FE
6501 N Charles St, Baltimore, MD 21204-6819

R. (410) 938-4896
gcoates@sheppardpratt.org

Michael C. Johnson FE
201 Walnut St, Mont Clare, PA 19453-5075

R. (610) 933-1775
Waataja@aol.com

Curtis D. King FE
PO Box 233, Fulton, MD 20759

R. (410) 622-4667
revcurtisking2@yahoo.com

Medical Leave
Theresa Robinson FE
7505 Reserve Cir Apt 303, Windsor Mill, MD 21244-1568

R. (410) 298-5951
Trob310@msn.com

Leonardo Rodriguez FE

eagle2258@yahoo.com

Retired
Kwame O. Abayomi RE
3101 Waterview Ave, Baltimore, MD 21230-3511

R. (443) 253-9782

Kay F. Albury RE
5900 Loch Raven Blvd, Baltimore, MD 21239-2440

R. (443) 629-3211
kayfran61@gmail.com

Edwin A. Ankeny RE
103 Kenilworth Park Dr Apt 3B, Towson, MD 21204-2265

R. (410) 296-5598
eaads@comcast.net

Helen Armiger RE
910 70th Dr E, Sarasota, FL 34243-1213

R. 410-747-2396
helenarmiger@gmail.com

Donald Atkinson RP
2815 Mohawk Ave, Baltimore, MD 21207-7473
R. (410) 448-4662

Winifred J. Blagmond RE
3711 Marmon Ave, Gwynn Oak, MD 21207-7169
R. (410) 375-8415
rev.wjblagmond@verizon.net

Emora T. Brannan RE
6400 Blenheim Rd, Baltimore, MD 21212-1715
R. (410) 377-3390
emorabrannan@verizon.net

Richard L. (Rick) Buckingham RD
719 Maiden Choice Ln Apt HR432, Catonsville, MD 21228-6157
R. (410) 314-9449
ricklby@yahoo.com

Cynthia Burkert RE
3000 Dunmore Rd, Dundalk, MD 21222-5131
R. (410) 708-8632
cindyburkert216@gmail.com

Gail L. Button RE
811 Sunnyfield Ln, Brooklyn Park, MD 21225-3367
R. (410) 636-1757
glbutton@gmail.com

David Carter-Rimbach RE
6316 Gentle Light Ln, Columbia, MD 21044
R. (410) 245-2505
trinitycatonsvillepastor@gmail.com

Diane A. Crider RE
212 Gateswood Rd, Timonium, MD 21093-5245
R. (410) 308-1608
dfcrider@comcast.net

Robert F. (Frederick) Crider RE
212 Gateswood Rd, Timonium, MD 21093-5245
R. (410) 308-1608
dfcrider@comcast.net

Sandra E. Demby RE
5113 Herring Run Dr, Baltimore, MD 21214-2143
R. (410) 254-3128
pastordemby@msn.com

Iris Farabee-Lewis RE
1503 Regester Ave, Loch Hill, MD 21239-1626
R. (443) 895-4563
st.jamesumc1@gmail.com

Gertrude M. Greene RD
309 Ritchie Hwy, Severna Park, MD 21146-1909
R. (410) 544-2395
sweetpeace@verizon.net

Sandra M. Greene RE
2712 Gresham Way Unit 103, Baltimore, MD 21244
R. (443) 985-1511
sandragreene@comcast.net

Carroll R. Gunkel RE
4110 Lotus Cir, Ellicott City, MD 21043-4873
R. (410) 465-5543
sumchurch@netzero.com

JoeAnn T. Harrod RA
5213 Fredcrest Rd, Baltimore, MD 21229-3215
R. (410) 525-2478

Howard W. Hinson RE
3701 Hillsdale Rd, Gwynn Oak, MD 21207-8075
R. (443) 253-7092
howard-hinson@verizon.net

Robert L. Hurley RE
800 Bollinger Dr Apt 206, Shrewsbury, PA 17361-1761
R. (410) 687-4709

Chi B. Jang RE
6840 Owings Overlook, Highland, MD 20777-9586
R. 443-838-2501
cbjumc1940@gmail.com

Hattie J. Johnson-Holmes RE
21 Victoria Sq, Frederick, MD 21702-1112
R. (301) 898-2905
havaholmes@yahoo.com

Calvin D. (David) Jones RE
8207 Legacy Ln, Fort Wayne, IN 46835-1052
R. 260-485-7549
drcdavidjones@frontier.com

August G. Lageman RE
20449 Alvarado Rd, Abingdon, VA 24211-6369
R. (276) 475-5433

David N. Lewis RL

Isaac M. (Mapipi) Mawokomatanda RE
85 Carrera Rd, Stockbridge, GA 30281-4390
R. (678) 284-9353
mapipi40@hotmail.com

Ralph McCulloh RE
1102 Skyline Dr, Medford, OR 97504-8558
R. (254) 899-1694
RALPHANDJEAN@gmail.com

Daniel C. McLellan RE
707 Maiden Choice Ln #7G13, Catonsville, MD 21228
R. (410) 314-9022
jlmclellan2510@gmail.com

Jacquelyn L. McLellan RE
707 Maiden Choice Ln #7G13, Baltimore, MD 21228
R. (410) 314-9022
jlmclellan2510@gmail.com

Rod Miller RE
3701 Saint Johns Ln, Ellicott City, MD 21042-5226
R. (410) 465-2335
miller.roderick.j@gmail.com

L. Katherine Moore RE
1 Buttick Court, Timonium, MD 21093
R. (410) 870-6738
rev.lkmoore@gmail.com

Nancy Nedwell RE
10 Sunny Meadow Ct Apt 102, Baltimore, MD 21209
R. (443) 414-3551
nancynedwell@gmail.com

Wilson E. Neighoff RE
131 N Somerset Ave, Crisfield, MD 21817-1525
R. (410) 968-0172
seabay131@aol.com

Jeffrey V. (Jeff) Odom RE
5 Williams Ct, Owings Mills, MD 21117-4889
R. (410) 356-3622
jvodom1@gmail.com

Fritz Outlaw RE
7505 Reserve Cir, Baltimore, MD 21244-1565
R. (410) 947-1974
mjhewlett@verizon.net

Lovell Parham RE
2704 Allendale Rd, Baltimore, MD 21216-2133
R. (410) 542-0744
lovell.parham@verizon.net

Willie M. Parker RE
P O Box 66093, Baltimore, MD 21239-3411
R. (410) 598-5401
williemaeparker@earthlink.net

Anne Perry RE
4802 Parkside Dr, Baltimore, MD 21206-6842
R. (410) 488-3339

Patricia A. Pride RE
3714 Eastman Rd, Randallstown, MD 21133-3412
R. (410) 496-2086

William L. Raker RE
8820 Walther Blvd Apt 4416, Baltimore, MD 21234-9035
R. (410) 665-7052
mjr8wlr@comcast.net

Faye Reddinger RL
5533 Hutton Ave, Baltimore, MD 21207-5956
R. (410) 944-4073

Joan I. Senyk RE
8808 C Ave Apt 120, Hesperia, CA 92345-5924
R. (281) 599-1310

Mark Smiley RE
9600 Labrador Ln, Cockeysville, MD 21030-1715
R. (443) 286-6565
msmileyumc@gmail.com

Susan A. Spears RE
3415 Dolfield Ave, Baltimore, MD 21215-7244
R. (410) 542-9207
holypraise@verizon.net

Carl A. Synan RE
505 Clinton Dr, Gastonia, NC 28054-5161
R. (704) 861-2074

Wayne H. Upton RE
63 Enola Dr, Stewartstown, PA 17363-8776
R. (717) 683-4523
wayneeumc@yahoo.com

Richard F. Vieth RE
821 Willow Valley Lakes Dr, Willow Street, PA 17584
R. (717) 569-5908
RJVIETH@gmail.com

Maurice E. Vineyard   RE
217 Booth St Apt 111, Gaithersburg, MD 20878-5480

R. (304) 754-6077
jkvineyard@comcast.net

Nancy Webb   RE
5203 Catalpha Rd, Baltimore, MD 21214-2102

R. (410) 444-7222
revnjwebb@gmail.com

Jeremiah G. Williams   RE
2106 Cedar Circle Dr, Baltimore, MD 21228-3747

R. (410) 455-6079
jwill34007@verizon.net

Maceo M. Williams   RE
3511 Lynchester Rd, Baltimore, MD 21215-7414

R. (410) 367-5365

Charles E. Wolfe   RE
5151 Buffalo Speedway Apt 4333, Houston, TX 77005-4300

R. (410) 857-1011

Mary K. Worrel   RE
1080 E 33rd St Apt 211, Baltimore, MD 21218-3785

R. (410) 889-1537
revworrel@msn.com

BALTIMORE SUBURBAN DISTRICT

Superintendent
Ann LaPrade FE
2547 Sutcliff Ter, Brookeville, MD 20833-3250
alaprade@bwcumc.org

(410) 309-34448
R. (301) 299-9383

Ames #2335
112 Baltimore Pike, Bel Air, MD 21014-4118
Marlon B. Tilghman FE
1118 Marksworth Rd, Baltimore, MD 21207-3962

mintilghman@yahoo.com
R. (443) 629-7363
mintilghman@yahoo.com

Asbury #2565
11501 Philadelphia Rd, White Marsh, MD 21162-1308
Herman E. Randall SY
4 Banyan Wood Ct Apt 204, Baltimore, MD 21221

C. (410) 256-2562
asburywm@aol.com
R. (410) 391-5556
chefhermancooks@verizon.net

Baltimore Co.
Maryland Line #3380
PO Box 60, Maryland Line, MD 21105-0060
(21500 York Road)

C. (410) 343-0052
mdlnumc@verizon.net

Mount Zion #3325
6212 Westover Dr, Mechanicsburg, Pa 17050-2340

C. (443) 324-7861
dschulze6212@verizon.net

Parke Memorial #3430
18910 York Rd, Parkton, MD 21120-9201

C. (410) 357-5587
dschulze6212@verizon.net

Vernon #3555
PO Box 188, White Hall, MD 21161-0188
(18600 Vernon Road)
Richard D. (Dennis) Schulze RE
6212 Westover Dr, Mechanicsburg, Pa 17050-2340

C. (410) 357-5049
vernonumc@yahoo.com

R. (443) 324-7861
dschulze6212@verizon.net

Bel Air #2340
21 Linwood Ave, Bel Air, MD 21014-3914
Lillian L. (Lynn) Boyd PE
1829 Wye Mills Ln, Bel Air, MD 21015-8301

Byron E. Brought FE
1203 Brighton Ln, Bel Air, MD 21014-3308

C. (410) 838-5181
ciampagliot@baumc.com
R. (410) 688-9992
tygjhs@verizon.net

R. (240) 418-3218
broughtb@baumc.com

Bixlers-Millers
Bixlers #4530
3282 Charmil Dr, Manchester, MD 21102-1918

C. (410) 857-1121
pastorblakesmarr@gmail.com

Millers #4340
3435 Warehime Rd, Manchester, MD 21102-2017
William B. (Blake) Smarr SY
3282 Charmil Dr, Manchester, MD 21102-1918

C. (410) 374-4042
pastorblakesmarr@gmail.com
R. (704) 860-7851
blakesmarr@gmail.com

Boring-Piney Grove-Mt. Gilead
Boring #4625
14819 Old Hanover Road, Upperco, MD 21155

C. (410) 688-9992
ministryaccount23@yahoo.com

Mount Gilead #4425　　　　　　　　C. (410) 429-5255
5302 Glen Falls Rd, Reisterstown, MD 21136-4503　　ministryaccount23@yahoo.com
Piney Grove #4175　　　　　　　　C. (410) 688-9992
4929 Piney Grove Rd, Reisterstown, MD 21136-4229　　ministryaccount23@yahoo.com
　Anissa Johnson　SY　　　　　　　R. (443) 310-9864
　5609 Biddison Ave, Baltimore, MD 21206-3442　　ministryaccount23@yahoo.com

Bosley-West Liberty
Bosley #3490　　　　　　　　C. (410) 771-4944
14800 Thornton Mill Rd, Sparks, MD 21152-9625　　kathleencheyney@aol.com
West Liberty #3560　　　　　　　C. (410) 343-0295
20501 West Liberty Rd, White Hall, MD 21161　　kathleencheyney@aol.com
　Kathleen Cheyney　FD　　　　　R. (410) 627-7152
　18603 York Rd, Parkton, MD 21120-9412　　kathleencheyney@aol.com

Camp Chapel #2530　　　　　　　C. (410) 256-5561
5000 E Joppa Rd, Perry Hall, MD 21128-9314　　newsletter@campchapel.org
　Carol L. Pazdersky　FE　　　　　R. (410) 321-1808
　730 Annatana Dr, Forest Hill, MD 21050　　carol.pazdersky@gmail.com

Cedar Grove-Stablers-Bentley Sp
Bentley Springs #3410　　　　　　C. (410) 357-5153
419 Bentley Rd, Parkton, MD 21120-9092　　andfred@msn.com
Cedar Grove #3415　　　　　　　C. (410) 357-0252
2015 Mount Carmel Rd, Parkton, MD 21120-9792　　andfred@msn.com
Stablers #3435　　　　　　　　C. (410) 343-1297
PO Box 403, Parkton, MD 21120-0403　　gladfec@yorkinternet.net
(1233 Stablers Church Road)
　Fred Sipes　PL　　　　　　　R. (410) 967-9134
　20106 Cameron Mill Rd, Parkton, MD 21120-9007　　andfred@msn.com

Chesaco #2545　　　　　　　　C. (410) 687-0250
901 Chesaco Ave, Baltimore, MD 21237-2736　　georgeweitzel@gmail.com
　George H. Weitzel　RE　　　　　R. (410) 790-2828
　11938 White Heather Rd, Cockeysville, MD 21030　　georgeweitzel@gmail.com

Clynmalira #3450　　　　　　　C. (410) 472-4107
2920 Stockton Rd, Phoenix, MD 21131-1125　　Pastor@Clynmalira.org
　John Dailey　RE　　　　　　R. (410) 692-4882
　2215 Nodleigh Ter, Jarrettsville, MD 21084-1115　　pastor@Clynmalira.org

Cokesbury #2125　　　　　　　C. (410) 676-6295
PO Box 85, Abingdon, MD 21009-0085　　CokesburyAbingdon@gmail.com
　Sarah Elliott　PE　　　　　　R. (703) 801-7355
　2968 Dumbarton Dr, Abingdon, MD 21009　　pastorsarahelliott@gmail.com

Deer Creek
Deer Creek #2450　　　　　　　C. (410) 638-7856
2729 Chestnut Hill Rd, Forest Hill, MD 21050-1712　　deercreekcharge@gmail.com
Mount Tabor #2345　　　　　　　C. (410) 638-7856
2350 Conowingo Rd, Bel Air, MD 21015-1404　　deercreekcharge@gmail.com
　Paul Krebs　SY　　　　　　　R. (410) 256-3129
　13 Farwell Ct, Nottingham, MD 21236-2119　　pkrebs6214@gmail.com

Deer Park #4415
6107 Deer Park Rd, Reisterstown, MD 21136-5900
   Gerald P. (Jerry) Gautcher, III PL
   6107 Deer Park Rd, Reisterstown, MD 21136-5900

C. (410) 833-5123
umcdeerpark@comcast.net
R. (443) 520-2571
pjgautcher@gmail.com

Emory #4420
1600 Emory Rd, Upperco, MD 21155-9774
   Peggy Click RE
   3717 Sue Dan Dr, Hampstead, MD 21074-1835

C. (410) 429-6008
churchoffice@emoryunitedmethodist.org
R. (443) 253-0943
staretal@gmail.com

Emory #2555
PO Box 94, Street, MD 21154-0094
(911 Cherry Hill Rd)
   Stephen Smith FL
   2011 Belton Ave, Bel Air, MD 21015

C. (410) 452-5220
pastor@emorychurch.org
R. (443) 752-3111
pastorsmitty@verizon.net

Epworth #3290
600 Warren Rd, Cockeysville, MD 21030-1754
   Terri Cofiell FE
   310 McGill Dr, Gerrardstown, WV 25420-4030

C. (410) 667-6054
office@epworthalive.com
R. (304) 890-0348
terricofiell@comcast.net

   William C. Jones, Jr. FD
   1315 Rayville Rd, Parkton, MD 21120-9003

R. (410) 218-7714
revbjones@hypeyouthministry.org

Fallston #2435
1509 Fallston Rd, Fallston, MD 21047-1624
   Karin Walker FE
   2919 Placid Dr, Baldwin, MD 21013-9514

C. (410) 877-7255
fallstonumc@fallstonumc.org
R. (410) 303-9200
Karin.Walker@fallstonumc.org

Fork - Waugh
Fork #3320
12800 Fork Rd, Fork, MD 21051-9728
Waugh #3335
11453 Long Green Pike, Glen Arm, MD 21057
   Daniel L. Montague, III FE
   12828 Fork Rd, Fork, MD 21051-9728

C. (410) 592-8303
fork_waugh_secretary@forkumc.org
C. (410) 592-8303
fork_waugh_secretary@forkumc.org
R. (410) 592-5236
daniel.mont3@gmail.com

Frames - Poplar
Frames Memorial #3460
3030 Warren Rd, Cockeysville, MD 21030-2704
Poplar Grove #3465
13600 Poplar Hill Rd, Phoenix, MD 21131
   Curtis Senft SY
   6308 Blackburn Ct, Baltimore, MD 21212-2220

C. (410) 667-8745

curtis.senft@yahoo.com
R. (410) 592-5236
curtis.senft@yahoo.com

Grace #2110
110 W Bel Air Ave, Aberdeen, MD 21001-3242
   Robert T. Clipp FE
   110 W Bel Air Ave, Aberdeen, MD 21001-3242

C. (410) 272-0909
gracemethodistchurch@yahoo.com
R. (410) 836-8486
pastorbobclipp@comcast.net

Harford
Clarks Chapel #2365
2001 Kalmia Rd, Bel Air, MD 21015-1017

C. (410) 838-5543
thea.becton@gmail.com

Union #2115
700 Post Rd, Aberdeen, MD 21001-2024
James Hamilton SY
28 Herbst Ln, Perryville, MD 21903-2221

C. (410) 939-3761
LJames109@comcast.net
R. (410) 378-2382
jchjrgolf@aol.com

Havre De Grace #2455
101 S Union Ave, Havre de Grace, MD 21078-3111
Norman J. Obenshain FE
101 S Union Ave, Havre de Grace, MD 21078

C. (410) 939-2464
hdgumc@verizon.net
R. (410) 939-1446
pastornormanobenshain@gmail.com

Hereford #3344
16931 York Rd, Monkton, MD 21111-1023
William G. (Bill) Thomas FE
PO Box 400, Monkton, MD 21111-0400

C. (410) 343-0660
admin@herefordumc.org
R. (443) 340-7706
pastor@herefordumc.com

Hereford Combined
Gough #3315
14200 Cuba Rd, Cockeysville, MD 21030-1214

C. (410) 771-6264

Pine Grove #3570
20105 Kirkwood Shop Rd, White Hall, MD 21161-9175

C. (410) 357-4445
herefordcharge1@comcast.net

St Luke #3345
16810 Hereford Rd, Monkton, MD 21111-1418

C. (410) 343-0968
herefordcharge1@comcast.net

Union Chapel #3350
17341 Troyer Rd, Monkton, MD 21111-1322
Winifred (Winnie) Griffin SY
208 Bond Ave, Reisterstown, MD 21136-1315

C. (410) 472-1120
herefordcharge1@comcast.net
R. (410) 526-2246
laity3trinity@aol.com

Hunt's Memorial #3487
1912 Old Court Rd, Towson, MD 21204-1849
Travis Knoll FE
1703 Singer Rd, joppa, MD 21085

C. (410) 339-7770
office@huntsumc.org
R. (410) 688-9613
pastortravisk@gmail.com

Jarrettsville-Ayres
Ayres Chapel #2520
3046 Ayres Chapel Rd, White Hall, MD 21161-9677

C. (410) 692-9222
lindayarrow.church@gmail.com

Jarrettsville #2475
1733 Jarrettsville Rd, Jarrettsville, MD 21084-1523
Linda S. Yarrow PE
1727 W Jarrettsville Rd, Jarrettsville, MD 21084

C. (410) 692-5847
jumc@zoominternet.net
R. (240) 429-1376
lindayarrow.church@gmail.com

John Wesley #2130
3817 Philadelphia Rd, Abingdon, MD 21009-1107
Darius K. Butler, Sr. SY
2000 Brown St, Edgewood, MD 21040-3203

C. (410) 676-0032
jwumcabingdon@gmail.com
R. (443) 922-7979
dkbutler1.umc@gmail.com

Linden Heights #3445
9914 Harford Rd, Parkville, MD 21234-1227
Alicia Vanisko FE
8774 Autumn Hill Dr, Ellicott City, MD 21043-5440

C. (410) 668-6181
lindenheightsumc@verizon.net
R. (410) 480-4717
alicialhumc@verizon.net

Lutherville
Edgewood #3365
1434 Bellona Ave, Lutherville, MD 21093-5451
Greenspring #3390
2730 Spring Hill Rd, Owings Mills, MD 21117-4311
   Ernest (Buster) Lievers   PL
   6221 Pilgrim Rd, Baltimore, MD 21214-1542

C. (410) 821-0850
deborah.givens@morgan.edu
C. (410) 821-0850
busterpete@comcast.net
R. (410) 426-2781
busterpete@comcast.net

Mays Chapel #3522
11911 Jenifer Rd, Timonium, MD 21093-7473
   Laurie Tingley   FE
   11911 Jenifer Rd, Timonium, MD 21093-7473

C. (410) 560-3173
office@mayschapel.org
R. (443) 995-9215
lptingley@gmail.com

Milford Mill #4380
915 Milford Mill Rd, Pikesville, MD 21208-4614
   Lemuel Dominguez   FE
   813 Staffordshire Rd, Cockeysville, MD 21030-2926

C. (410) 486-5263
mmumc@aol.com
R. (443) 240-2557
vessel187@gmail.com

Monkton #3385
1930 Monkton Rd, Monkton, MD 21111-1632
   Bruce C. Frame   RL
   826 E Joppa Rd, Towson, MD 21286-5621

C. (410) 472-9116
abuss58981@aol.com
R. (410) 821-5927
pastorbruce@comcast.net

Mount Olive #4390
5115 Old Court Rd, Randallstown, MD 21133-4701
   Sheridan B. Allmond   FE
   7410 Millwood Rd, Windsor Mill, MD 21244-2849

C. (410) 922-2853
sallmond03@gmail.com
R. (443) 386-1256
sallmond03@gmail.com

Mount Vernon #2580
1510 Deep Run Rd, Whiteford, MD 21160-1302
   Ernest E. Gayles   SY
   3402 Bateman Ave, Baltimore, MD 21216

C. (410) 399-0288

R. (410) 499-6656
eegayles@gmail.com

Mount Zion #2350
1643 E Churchville Rd, Bel Air, MD 21015-4803
   Craig McLaughlin   FE
   625 Weatherby Rd, Bel Air, MD 21015

C. (410) 836-7444
mtzionumc1@verizon.net
R. (410) 879-8840
lisa.craig4@verizon.net

Mount Zion-Finksburg #4265
PO Box 755, Finksburg, MD 21048-0755
(3006 Old Westminster Pike)
   William L. (Lou) Piel   RE
   1247 Weller Way, Westminster, MD 21158-4300

C. (410) 517-2300
julo1@verizon.net

R. (410) 751-9049
julo1@verizon.net

Mount Zion #4525
3800 Black Rock Rd, Upperco, MD 21155-9468
   John Mayden, Jr.   SY
   5037 Westhills Rd, Baltimore, MD 21229-1218

C. (410) 374-4231
johnmayden1@gmail.com
R. 443-545-6643
johnmayden1@gmail.com

New Beginnings Fellowship #3500
4080 Federal Hill Rd, Jarrettsville, MD 21084-1217
   Ernest E. Gayles   SY
   3402 Bateman Ave, Baltimore, MD 21216

C. (410) 692-2600
eegayles@gmail.com
R. (410) 499-6656
eegayles@gmail.com

New Hope Christian Fellowship #2412   C. (410) 676-3531
2048 Watergate Ct, Edgewood, MD 21040-1824   newhope2048@yahoo.com
Granderson Jones, Jr. PL   R. (410) 303-5158
378 Oxford Ave, Aberdeen, MD 21001-3544   nosrednarg@verizon.net

Norrisville
Norrisville #2525   C. (410) 692-6179
2434 Bradenbaugh Rd, White Hall, MD 21161-9661   thomasjsullivan@hotmail.com
St Paul #2585   C. (410) 692-6179
2434 Bradenbaugh Rd, White Hall, MD 21161-9661   thomasjsullivan@hotmail.com
Melissa McDade FE   R. (410) 692-6179
2434 Bradenbaugh Rd, White Hall, MD 21161-9661   thomasjsullivan@hotmail.com

North Carroll
Grace #4310   C. (410) 374-9400
4618 Black Rock Rd, Upperco, MD 21155-9545   nccpumc@gmail.com
Greenmount #4288   C. (410) 239-9705
2001 Hanover Pike, Hampstead, MD 21074-1332   nccpumc@gmail.com
St Johns #4320   C. (410) 239-8088
1205 N Main St, Hampstead, MD 21074-2200   nccpumc@gmail.com
John B. Rudolph FE   R. (410) 239-9705
2009 Hanover Pike, Hampstead, MD 21074-1321   revjrudolph@gmail.com

Melissa Rudolph FE   R. (304) 279-8520
2009 Hanover Pike, Hampstead, MD 21074-1321   Mchrudolph@yahoo.com

Parkton
Falls Road #3510   C. (410) 472-3158
15335 Falls Rd, Sparks, MD 21152-9592   jdzrcody@aol.com
Mount Carmel #3425   C. (410) 357-5431
17036 Pretty Boy Dam Rd, Parkton, MD 21120-9690   mtcarmelumc21120@comcast.net
Wiseburg #3565   C. (410) 357-4077
810 Wiseburg Rd, White Hall, MD 21161-9466   gbaer649061@comcast.net
Scott D. Shumaker FE   R. (410) 357-5431
17036 Pretty Boy Dam Rd, Parkton, MD 21120-9690   sshumaker2@comcast.net

Perry Hall #2535   C. (410) 256-6479
9515 Belair Rd, Baltimore, MD 21236-1507   perryhallumc@verizon.net
Victor Harner FE   R. (410) 256-1028
8917 Yvonne Ave, Nottingham, MD 21236-2136   rovervic@verizon.net

Pine Grove #3475   C. (410) 343-0729
19401 Middletown Rd, Parkton, MD 21120-9662   pastorandrewbwc@gmail.com
Andrew Greenwood FE   R. (410) 487-4875
19308 Middletown Rd, Parkton, MD 21120-9691   pastorandrewbwc@gmail.com

Pleasant Grove #4520   C. (410) 429-5080
15300 Dover Rd, Reisterstown, MD 21136-3883   jwsterling1@gmail.com
William R. (Dick) Harden RE   R. (410) 876-3871
828 Holliday Ln, Westminster, MD 21157   revwrh@gmail.com

Pleasant Hill #4370
10911 Reisterstown Rd, Owings Mills, MD 21117-2503
Shawn M. Wilson FE
10816 Gulfstream Ct, Damascus, MD 20872-2163

C. (410) 356-4085
pleasanthillumc@msn.com
R. (413) 237-6331
swivwi@aol.com

Presbury-Cranberry
Cranberry #2540
PO Box 78, Perryman, MD 21130-0078
(1632 Perryman Road)
Presbury #2415
806 Edgewood Rd, Edgewood, MD 21040-2436
Tiffany Patterson FE
1928 Bayberry Rd, Edgewood, MD 21040-2435

C. (410) 273-6979
pastortiffanyp@gmail.com

C. (410) 676-3234
pastortiffanyp@gmail.com
R. (770) 364-9304
pastortiffanyp@gmail.com

Providence #3370
1320 Providence Rd, Towson, MD 21286-1562
Jackson Day RE
719 Maiden Choice Ln, Catonsville, MD 21228-6138

C. (410) 823-5365
jackdayconnect@gmail.com
R. (410) 303-8213
jackdayconnect@gmail.com

Reisterstown #4435
246 Main St, Reisterstown, MD 21136-1214
Vivian C. McCarthy FE
246 Main St, Reisterstown, MD 21136-1214

C. (410) 833-5440
rumcoffice1777@gmail.com
R. (410) 489-4344
pastorvivianmc@gmail.com

Rock Run #2378
4102 Rock Run Rd, Havre de Grace, MD 21078-1215

C. (410) 457-4145
plstenor@comcast.net

Salem #2560
7901 Bradshaw Rd, Upper Falls, MD 21156-1804
Stacey Nickerson FE
7 Manor Brook Rd, Monkton, MD 21111-1606

C. (410) 592-2543
pastor@salemunited.org
R. (410) 472-4315
pastor@salemunited.org

Salem #3340
18221 Falls Rd, Hampstead, MD 21074-2818
Jarrett Wicklein RE
316 Kimrick Pl, Timonium, MD 21093-2945

C. (410) 374-2421
jwicklein@verizon.net
R. (410) 561-7555
jwicklein@verizon.net

Shiloh-Patapsco
Patapsco #4430
2930 Patapsco Rd, Finksburg, MD 21048-1106
Shiloh #4325
3100 Shiloh Rd, Hampstead, MD 21074-1625
Barbara Allen PL
3014 Brendan Ave, Baltimore, MD 21213

C. (410) 857-9210
ballenpsalm34@msn.com
C. (410) 374-4231
ballenpsalm34@msn.com
R. (443) 255-1802
ballenpsalm34@msn.com

Smiths Chapel #2370
3109 Churchville Rd, Churchville, MD 21028-1805
David D. Roberts RE
3111 Churchville Rd, Churchville, MD 21028-1805

C. (410) 734-7113

R. (443) 412-5180
smchumchurch@gmail.com

St John-Idlewylde
Idlewylde #3535
1000 Regester Ave, Idlewylde, MD 21239-1515

C. (410) 377-9691
carol.pazdersky@gmail.com

St Johns #3375   C. (410) 825-3969
216 W Seminary Ave, Lutherville, MD 21093-5337   carol.pazdersky@gmail.com
Nick M. Bufano FE   R. (410) 692-4677
214 W Seminary Ave, Lutherville, MD 21093   Pastornickbufano@gmail.com

St Luke #4440   C. (410) 526-5044
60 Bond Ave, Reisterstown, MD 21136-1300   stlukesumcreisterstown@gmail.com
LaReesa Smith-Horn FE   R. (410) 581-1612
9020 Groffs Mill Dr, Owings Mills, MD 21117-6105   revsmithorn@verizon.net

---

Susquehanna
Hopewell #2460   C. (410) 914-5276
3600 Level Village Rd, Havre de Grace, MD 21078-1119   Hopewelllevel@gmail.com
Wesleyan Chapel #2470   C. (410) 914-5276
409 N Paradise Rd, Aberdeen, MD 21001-1629   chapel.aberdeen@gmail.com
Lynne Humphries-Russ PE   R. (410) 952-2792
6206 Monroe Ave, Sykesville, MD 21784-6661   pastorlynnehr@gmail.com

Texas #3310   C. (410) 627-7698
9 Galloway Ave, Cockeysville, MD 21030-4905   sjfrog1@aol.com
Sharon Meyer FE   R. (410) 952-2792
6206 Monroe Ave, Sykesville, MD 21784-6661   pastorlynnehr@gmail.com

Timonium-Fairview
Fairview #3455   C. (410) 666-8288
13916 Jarrettsville Pike, Phoenix, MD 21131-2040   VRitenour@hotmail.com
Timonium #3525   C. (410) 252-5500
2300 Pot Spring Rd, Timonium, MD 21093-2726   tumc@timoniumumc.org
Chris S. Gobrecht FE   R. (443) 835-6590
2429 Chetwood Cir, Timonium, MD 21093-2533   cgobrecht@timoniumumc.org

Anne McCorkle Garrett SY   R. (410) 692-9394
2758 Greene Ln, Baldwin, MD 21013   PastorAnne@comcast.net

Union #3135   C. (410) 592-7709
5225 Sweet Air Rd, Baldwin, MD 21013-9723   ems1391@aol.com
Jennifer L. Kokoski PD   R. (410) 596-1473
3214 Black Rock Rd, Reisterstown, MD 21136-3819   pastorjennk@gmail.com

Union Chapel #2510   C. (410) 877-3246
1012 Old Joppa Rd, Joppa, MD 21085-1510   ucjoppa@verizon.net
David Coakley FE   R. (301) 606-4779
1412 Stockton Rd, Joppa, MD 21085-1406   davidcoakley6@gmail.com

Wards Chapel #4410   C. (410) 922-6556
11023 Liberty Rd, Randallstown, MD 21133-1012   wardschapel@verizon.net
Steven (Sunghwan) Cho OE   R. (202) 680-2394
1690 Linzee Dr, Westminster, MD 21157-7428   peaceleader@hotmail.com

Wesley #4330   C. (410) 374-4027
3239 Carrollton Rd, Hampstead, MD 21074-1912   wesley@wesleychurch-hampstead.org
Amy S. Lewis-Rill FE   R. (443) 604-5245
3674 Stewartstown Rd, Stewartstown, PA 17363-8118   revamys@aol.com

West Harford
Centre #2445   C. (410) 667-8745
313 Duffy Ct, Forest Hill, MD 21050-2554   centreumc@gmail.com
Ebenzer #2430   C. (410) 692-2211
3345 Charles St, Fallston, MD 21047-1031   gorman.mark@gmail.com
William Watters Memorial #2485   C. (410) 692-5227
1451 Jarrettsville Rd, Jarrettsville, MD 21084-1627   gorman.mark@gmail.com
   Mark Gorman FE   R. (443) 458-2092
   313 Duffy Ct, Forest Hill, MD 21050-2554   gorman.mark@gmail.com

   Jane Ayers RE   (410) 800-8672
    janeay@earthlink.net

Certified Candidate
   Alfred E. Anipes CC

   James Bolyard CC   R. (410) 980-8381
   148 E Orange Ct, Parkville, MD 21234-8016   PartOfHisPlan@GMail.com

Certified Lay Minister
   M. K. (Kathy) Ryan LM   R. (410) 833-1238
   5834 Deer Park Rd, Reisterstown, MD 21136-6026   kathyryan626@hotmail.com

Extension Ministry
   Janet Deitiker FE   R. (210) 725-6245
   6636 Pembroke Rd, San Antonio, TX 78240-2719   janet.deitiker@att.net

   Hea S. Kim FE   R. (821) 068-1635
   123 W 104th St Apt 10A, New York, NY 10025-9603

   Rebecca A. Wright FE   R. (615) 598-5134
   PO Box 821, Sewanee, TN 37375-0821   rwright@sewanee.edu

   Mark C. Young FE   R. (704) 799-7805
   155 Queens Cove Rd, Mooresville, NC 28117   myoung@wellhavencounseling.com

Leave of Absence
   Carolyn R. Swift RE   R. (410) 937-6996
   1205 McCleary Ter Apt 302, Bel Air, MD 21014-4544

Retired
   Glenn Barrick RL   R. (410) 642-2673
   412 Roundhouse Dr, Perryville, MD 21903-3041   gbarrick54@gmail.com

   Paul Benjamin RE   R. (410) 638-7565
   1501 Barrons Gate Ave, Woodbridge, NJ 07095-3851   psrbenj03@aol.com

   Donna H. Bennett RE   R. (717) 741-3749
   2361 Merrill Rd, York, PA 17403-5021

   Richard Brown-Whale FE   R. (443) 275-1280
   1910 Knox Ave, Reisterstown, MD 21136-5612   pastor@campchapel.org

   Terri R. Chattin RE   R. (410) 322-6304
   37 Cedar Hill Rd, Randallstown, MD 21133-1510   trchattin@gmail.com

   Peggy Click RE   R. (443) 253-0943
   3717 Sue Dan Dr, Hampstead, MD 21074-1835   staretal@gmail.com

Glenda Condon RP
2610 Fairfax St, Denver, CO 80207-3223
R. (303) 377-3580
ggcondon@gmail.com

Frances Dailey FE
2215 Nodleigh Ter, Jarrettsville, MD 21084-1115
R. (410) 252-5500
fdailey@timoniumumc.org

James L. Ditto RE
209 Cartland Way, Forest Hill, MD 21050-3107
R. (410) 893-5935
jimdit@comcast.net

Robert J. Fringo RE
9513A Horn Ave, Nottingham, MD 21236-1523
R. (410) 256-5670
robjoe1927@aol.com

Robert E. (Eugene) Funk RE
143 Beech Hill Rd, Mount Desert, ME 04660-6202
R. (207) 244-9006

Darryl Gill RE
1907 Forest Ct, Timonium, MD 21093-4317
R. (410) 252-3120
0607DWG@gmail.com

Mary Ellen Glorioso RE
8813 Spring Rd, Baltimore, MD 21234-2907
R. (410) 935-0378
pastormeg@yahoo.com

Ronald Gompf SY
4113 Halifax Ct, Glen Arm, MD 21057-9117
R. (410) 882-4840
rgompf@comcast.net

James D. Hainley RE
863 Flintlock Dr, Bel Air, MD 21015-4879
R. (410) 399-9615
JHAINLEY@aol.com

Charles L. Harrell RE
1725 Forest Glen Dr, Prince Frederick, MD 20678-4514
R. (443) 975-5550
carolus101@gmail.com

Stanley G. Harrell RE
2705 Aspen Dr, Hampstead, MD 21074-1712
R. (443) 291-6324
sharrell25@gmail.com

Barry Hidey RE
1775 Selvin Dr, Bel Air, MD 21015
bhidey@outlook.com

Mary L. (Louise) Holley RL
3717 Ferndale Ave, Baltimore, MD 21207-7164
R. (410) 466-7972
marylouiseholley@gmail.com

Darcy R. Hunt RE
120 Doyle Farm Ln, Mooresville, NC 28115-5794
R. (704) 799-7805
dhunt@wellhavencounseling.com

Arthur Justice RL
72 Kings Way Dr, North East, MD 21901-2706
R. (410) 652-2043
pstrart18@comcast.net

George Lambros RL
1511 Cabin Rd, Aberdeen, MD 21001-1301
pglambros@comcast.net

John R. Lebo RE
811 Tilghman Dr, Bel Air, MD 21015-3438
R. (410) 638-9750

Rebecca Lemon-Riley RL
2717 Silver Hill Ave, Baltimore, MD 21207-6776
R. (410) 448-4054
becky125@comcast.net

Charles W. Lightner RE
12 Free St, Machias, ME 04654-1147
R. (207) 255-0514

George M. Manhart RE
347 Laurel Dr, Lehighton, PA 18235-8990
R. (610) 377-8323

Susan C. Marseilles RE
20731 Ewing Rd, Preston, MD 21655-1470
R. (410) 673-1025
Revscm@aol.com

Donna J. Martin RE
5623 Gardenville Ave, Baltimore, MD 21206-3706
R. (410) 483-1107
drdjmartin@aol.com

Earl Mason RE
910 Rock Spring Rd, Bel Air, MD 21014-2320

R. (443) 386-6513
revearlmason@aol.com

Sharon Mills RD
7369 Intersection Rd, Glen Rock, PA 17327-8850

R. (717) 825-1152

Richard J. Mortimore RE
128 Lently Farm Lane, Centrevillee, MD 21617

R. (410) 592-5236
underfrog@atlanticbb.net

Larry M. Plymire RE
630 Harmony Dr Apt 165, New Oxford, PA 17350

R. (717) 624-5540
LJPLY@crosskeysvillage.net

Clarence L. (Pete) Roark RE
1034 Bear Xing, Hanover, PA 17331-9426

R. (717) 630-2274
irishphud@gmail.com

Mary P. Roberts RE
8208 Lime Tree Way, Ellenton, FL 34222-4702

R. (941) 981-5089
revmproberts@gmail.com

W. M. (McCarl) Roberts RE
665 Morning Glory Dr, Hanover, PA 17331-7827

R. (717) 632-4184

Roberta J. Scoville RE
610 Chesapeake Dr, Havre de Grace, MD 21078-3623

R. (410) 939-7433

Joe D. Sergent RE
4 Kratz Rd, Shrewsbury, PA 17361-1335

R. (717) 235-3122

LaReesa Smith-Horn FE
9020 Groffs Mill Dr, Owings Mills, MD 21117-6105

R. (410) 581-1612
revsmithorn@verizon.net

Charles Stevenson RL
PO Box 1274, Owings Mills, MD 21117-1207

R. (410) 581-9382

Henry C. Thompson, III RE
5713 Second Ave, Baltimore, MD 21227-4308

R. (410) 242-4341
hctcbt@msn.com

Clifford Webner RE

R. (410) 788-3362
CLIFFWEBNER@gmail.com

Robert G. (Bob) Whiting RL
10635 Breezewood Dr, Woodstock, MD 21163-1312

R. (410) 465-5467
rgwhiting@verizon.net

CENTRAL MARYLAND DISTRICT

Superintendent
JW Park FE   (410) 309-3493
7 Diamond Hill Ct, Germantown, MD 20874-5902   R. (301) 972-9233
jpark@bwcumc.org

Alberta Gary Memorial #7345   C. (301) 498-7879
9405 Guilford Rd, Columbia, MD 21046-1911   shawnvollmerhausen@gmail.com
Shawn Vollmerhausen PL   R. (410) 790-5214
8820 Birchwood Way, Jessup, MD 20794-9583   shawnvollmerhausen@gmail.com

Araby #6110   C. (301) 694-8772
4548 Araby Church Rd, Frederick, MD 21704-7706   mount79@gmail.com
Timothy J. (TJ) Mount PL   R. (301) 651-0718
13226 Lake Geneva Way, Germantown, MD 20874   mount79@gmail.com

Asbury #9265   C. (301) 540-2347
17540 Black Rock Rd, Germantown, MD 20874-2227   AsburyGermantown@gmail.com
John Ampiah-Addison PL   R. (301) 987-2731
8204 Coneflower Way, Gaithersburg, MD 20877-1037   addisco5@yahoo.com

Ashton #9110   C. (301) 774-7100
17314 New Hampshire Ave, Ashton, MD 20861-9706   ashtonumchurch@gmail.com
Emily Berkowitz FE   R. (301) 512-7311
18107 Rolling Meadow Way, Olney, MD 20832-1782   revemilyb@gmail.com

Bethany #4235   C. (410) 465-2919
2875 Bethany Ln, Ellicott City, MD 21042-2213   bettina@bethanyum.org
Andrew Cooney FE   R. (443) 328-6382
1408 Quick Fox Ct, Eldersburg, MD 21784-6482   acooney1968@gmail.com

Brenda L. Lewis FE   R. (410) 356-8453
9962 Sherwood Farm Rd, Owings Mills, MD 21117-5853   brenda@bethanyum.org

Cathy Vitek PL   R. (443) 794-8188
824 Riverside Dr, Pasadena, MD 21122-1730   cathy@bethanyum.org

Bethany Korean #4236   C. (410) 979-0691
8971 Chapel Ave, Ellicott City, MD 21043-1905   dduru77@hotmail.com
Dae Sung Park FE   R. (410) 979-0691
20331 Dickerson Church Rd, Dickerson, MD 20842-9526   dduru77@hotmail.com

Bethesda #9185   C. (301) 253-3222
11901 Bethesda Church Rd, Damascus, MD 20872-1540   BethesdaBlessings@verizon.net
Kevin W. Beall PL   R. (240) 994-7861
13220 Lewisdale Rd, Clarksburg, MD 20871-9665   kwbeall7@gmail.com

Henry G. Butler, Jr. RE   R. (301) 253-2721
27912 Kemptown Church Rd, Damascus, MD 20872   sonwillcome@verizon.net

Calvary #6285
403 S Main St, Mount Airy, MD 21771-5346
William C. (Bill) Maisch FE
24105 Preakness Dr, Damascus, MD 20872-2171

C. (301) 829-0358
church@calvary-mtairy.org
R. (301) 461-0301
pastorbillmaisch@comcast.net

Christ #7350
7246 Cradlerock Way, Columbia, MD 21045-5054
Zelda Childs PL
3516 Ellamont Rd, Baltimore, MD 21215

C. (410) 381-6329
admin@cumcobic.org
R. (410) 367-7336
zelcap@msn.com

Community of Faith #9270
22420 Frederick Rd, Clarksburg, MD 20871-9452
Carmen R. Collette RE
19512 Laguna Dr, Gaithersburg, MD 20879-1824

C. (301) 972-5520
church@cofumc.com
R. (240) 261-8327
craecollette@gmail.com

Covenant #9235
20301 Pleasant Ridge Dr, Montgomery Village, MD 20886
Dawn L. Stewart FE
12932 Sugarloaf Chapel Dr, Clarksburg, MD 20871

C. (301) 926-8920
office@covenant-umc.org
R. (301) 848-2265
dawn.stewart@covenant-umc.org

Daisy #9490
PO Box 146, Lisbon, MD 21765-0146
Gertie T. Williams RP
8490 Thomas Williams Way, Columbia, MD 21045-2482

C. (410) 489-2400
VCHRISTIAN5242@gmail.com
R. (410) 461-1155
ladirev4@gmail.com

Damascus #9190
9700 New Church St, Damascus, MD 20872-2014
Sherwyn Benjamin PE
13755 Lark Song Dr, Germantown, MD 20874-6214

C. (301) 253-0022
office@damascusumc.org
R. (301) 972-4256
sabenjamin3@gmail.com

Kathryn T. Woodrow FE
441 Bostwick Ln, Gaithersburg, MD 20878

R. (301) 330-2161
kathryn.woodrow@damascusumc.org

Dickerson-Forest Grove
Dickerson #9225
20341 Dickerson Church Road, Dickerson, MD 20842
Forest Grove #9230
6108 Dickerson Road, Dickerson, MD 20842
Kevin Cameron PL
2907 Weller Rd, Silver Spring, MD 20906-3886

C. (301) 349-5416
dickersonmdumc@gmail.com
C. (301) 349-5416
forestgrovemdumc@gmail.com
R. (301) 367-1433
kcameron1970@hotmail.com

Ebenezer #4575
4901 Woodbine Rd, Sykesville, MD 21784-9348
Judith A. Emerson FE
2091 Saint James Rd, Marriottsville, MD 21104-1436

C. (410) 795-6136
eumcwinfield@gmail.com
R. (410) 442-2881
revjae@aol.com

Ebenezer #6230
4010 Ijamsville Rd, Ijamsville, MD 21754-9516
Vivian L. Martin-Jones RA
3920 Rosecrest Ave, Baltimore, MD 21215-3427

C. (301) 874-3007
churchebenezer38@gmail.com
R. (301) 874-3007
masterpastor@comcast.net

Emory #4245
3799 Church Rd, Ellicott City, MD 21043-4501

C. (410) 465-6162
smoore4433@aol.com

Sam Moore, Sr. PL
7425 Brandenburg Cir, Sykesville, MD 21784-6682

R. (410) 549-5265
smoore4433@aol.com

Emory Grove #9240
8200 Emory Grove Rd, Gaithersburg, MD 20877-3739
Timothy B. Warner FE
17105 Laburnum Ct, Rockville, MD 20855-2504

C. (301) 963-3434
Admin@emorygroveumc.com
R. (301) 216-0982
warner.tb@gmail.com

Epworth #9245
9008 Rosemont Dr, Gaithersburg, MD 20877-1519
Jennifer L. Fenner FE
16501 Alden Ave, Gaithersburg, MD 20877-1505

C. (301) 926-0424
jennifer.fenner@eumc-md.org
R. (443) 928-3771
jennifer.fenner@eumc-md.org

Fairhaven #9250
12801 Darnestown Rd, Gaithersburg, MD 20878
Kenneth B. Hawes FE
3825 Oglethorpe St, Hyattsville, MD 20782

C. (301) 330-5433
fairhavenumc@gmail.com
R. (301) 699-2023
pastorken.fairhavenumc@gmail.com

Fairview #4345
3325 Old Liberty Road, New Windsor, MD 21776
Daphne Fraser OE
17152 Moss Side Ln, Olney, MD 20832-2938

C. (443) 671-6152
fieldcourt@yahoo.com
R. (301) 924-0647
fieldcourt@yahoo.com

FaithPoint #6382
PO Box 133, Monrovia, MD 21770
Christopher M. Bishop FE
30 8th Ave, Brunswick, MD 21716-1736

C. (301) 363-8165
office@faithpointum.org
R. (301) 639-9583
Chris@faithpointum.org

Flohrville #4230
6620 Church St, Sykesville, MD 21784-8014
Keystone B. Lee SY
13122 Dairymaid Dr, Germantown, MD 20874-2311

C. (301) 917-7894
revkeystone@hotmail.com
R. (301) 540-0980
revkeystone@hotmail.com

Friendship #9210
27701 Ridge Rd, Damascus, MD 20872-2423
Tyree Newman SY
14145 Flint Rock Rd, Rockville, MD 20853-2657

C. (301) 253-3411
tnewms5@gmail.com
R. (301) 871-1723
tnewms5@gmail.com

Gary Memorial #4240
2029 Daniels Rd, Ellicott City, MD 21043
Karen Lillipax PL
3011 Fallstaff Manor Ct, Apt B, Baltimore, MD 21209-2829

C. (410) 465-7345
karenlillipax@gmail.com
R. (914) 309-8479
katenlilipax@gmail.com

Glen Mar #7365
4701 New Cut Rd, Ellicott City, MD 21043-6603
Mandy E. Sayers FE
2705 Thistledown Ter, Olney, MD 20832-1547

C. (410) 465-4995
barb.julian@glenmarumc.org
R. (443) 280-2885
pastormandy10@gmail.com

Jennifer (Jen) Eschliman FE
4701 New Cut Rd, Ellicott City, MD 21043-6603

R. (410) 456-0656
jen.eschliman@glenmarumc.org

Anna Schwartz PE
3657 Worthington Blvd, Frederick, MD 21704-7015

R. (316) 371-3679
anna.schwartz@glenmarumc.org

Glenelg #9285
13900 Burntwoods Rd, Glenelg, MD 21737-9721
  Alice K. Ford FE
  7407 Leaf Shade Ct, Laurel, MD 20707

C. (410) 489-7260
admin@glenelgumc.org
R. (410) 813-2709
pastoralice@gmail.com

Goshen #9255
19615 Goshen Rd, Gaithersburg, MD 20879-1819
  Eric W. King, Sr. FE
  7820 Brink Rd, Gaithersburg, MD 20882-1616

C. (240) 683-5530
goshen_umc@comcast.net
R. (410) 935-10338
king1906@comcast.net

Grace #9260
119 N Frederick Ave, Gaithersburg, MD 20877-2441
  Jim Miller FE
  11710 Barn Swallow Pl, New Market, MD 21774-7005

C. (301) 926-8688
dmlyon@graceumc.org
R. (301) 865-1276
jmiller@graceumc.org

Growing Seed
Mount Gregory #4455
PO Box 63, Glenwood, MD 21738-0063
Simpson #9365
PO Box 522, Mount Airy, MD 21771-0522
  R. Lorraine Brown PE
  121 Spring St, Gaithersburg, MD 20877-1921

C. (410) 489-5741
rev.rlbrown@gmail.com
C. (240) 550-9394
rev.rlbrown@gmail.com
R. (301) 990-1755
rev.rlbrown@gmail.com

Hopkins #9290
13250 Highland Rd, Highland, MD 20777-9721
  Terry McCain PL
  8652 Concord Dr, Jessup, MD 20794

C. (301) 854-2150
hopkinsumc@gmail.com
R. (301) 536-8424
TMc1024598@aol.com

Howard Chapel-Ridgeville #9355
1970 Long Corner Rd, Mount Airy, MD 21771-3738
  Phillip R. (Phil) Ayers FE
  13778 Blythedale Dr, Mount Airy, MD 21771-5852

C. (301) 829-2391
payers001@comcast.net
R. (301) 751-3262
payers001@comcast.net

Hyattstown-Clarksburg
Clarksburg #9175
23425 Spire St, Clarksburg, MD 20871-9036
Hyattstown #9315
26121 Frederick Rd, Clarksburg, MD 20871-9614
  David W. Hodsdon OE
  4227 Headwaters Ln, Olney, MD 20832-1750

C. (301) 972-2203
revdwhodsdon@verizon.net
C. (301) 831-1194
revdwhodsdon@verizon.net
R. (301) 774-1846
revdwhodsdon@verizon.net

Ijamsville
Flint Hill #6380
2732 Park Mills Rd, Adamstown, MD 21710
Ijamsville #6235
4765 Mussetter Rd, Ijamsville, MD 21754-9627
  Rod Fry SY
  4240 Tabler Rd, Frederick, MD 21704-7779

C. (443) 994-9505
ijamsvilleflinthill@gmail.com
C. (443) 994-9505
ijamsvilleflinthill@gmail.com
R. (301) 633-5910
circuitriderrodfry@gmail.com

Linden-Linthicum #9180
12101 Linden Linthicum Ln, Clarksville, MD 21029
  Gayle E. Annis-Forder FE
  7604 Willow Bottom Rd, Sykesville, MD 21784-5651

C. (410) 531-5653
llumc@l-lumc.org
R. (410) 552-8347
pastorgayle@l-lumc.org

Lisbon #9350
PO Box 51, Lisbon, MD 21765-0051
(15875 Frederick Road)
   Heather Olson PE
   1211 Cartley Ct, Woodbine, MD 21797-8624

C. (410) 489-7245
lisbonumc@aol.com

R. (919) 247-5030
pastoraheather@gmail.com

Locust #7355
6851 Martin Rd, Columbia, MD 21044-4017
   Marion Easterling, Jr. OE
   6851 Martin Rd, Columbia, MD 21044-4017

C. (410) 531-5323
locustumc@yahoo.com
R. (410) 531-5323
m7east@gmail.com

Memorial #9385
PO Box 358, Poolesville, MD 20837-2005
(17821 Elgin Rd)
   Timothy A. Dowell FE
   210 East Rd, Mount Airy, MD 21771-2840

C. (301) 349-2010
office@pmumc.org

R. (443) 206-4949
pastortim@pmumc.org

Mill Creek Parish #9425
7101 Horizon Ter, Derwood, MD 20855-1355
   Timothy B. Warner FE
   17105 Laburnum Ct, Rockville, MD 20855-2504

C. (301) 926-9024
mcpumchurch@gmail.com
R. (301) 216-0982
warner.tb@gmail.com

   Megan Blanchard PD
   11601 Georgetowne Ct, Potomac, MD 20854-3720

R. (704) 787-3072
megan.b.blanchard@gmail.com

Montgomery #9215
28325 Kemptown Rd, Damascus, MD 20872-1326
   John Rudisill, Jr. FE
   28201 Kemptown Rd, Damascus, MD 20872-1324

C. (301) 253-4460
montumc@verizon.net
R. (240) 520-5610
pastor.john.rudisill@verizon.net

Morgan Chapel-Mt Olive
Morgan Chapel #4585
6750 Woodbine Rd, Woodbine, MD 21797-9402
Mount Olive #4590
2927 Gillis Falls Rd, Mount Airy, MD 21771-8034
   James E. Skillington RE
   9238 Spring Valley Road, Ellicott City, MD 21043

C. (443) 970-2485
revjim@morganchapel.church
C. (301) 703-9755
info@mountoliveumc.org
R. (410) 740-1032
revjim@preachershop.com

Mount Zion #9370
PO Box 324, Olney, MD 20830-0324
(5000 Brookville Road)
   Olivia Gross PL
   6756 Greatnews Ln, Columbia, MD 21044-4110

C. (240) 938-7190
pastorolivia.mtzion@gmail.com

R. (443) 745-8036
pastorolivia.mtzion@gmail.com

Mount Zion #9310
12430 Scaggsville Rd, Highland, MD 20777-9727
   Gary Sheffield-James FE
   9601 Hickoryhurst Dr, Baltimore, MD 21236-4707

C. (301) 854-2324
office@mtzionhighland.com
R. (410) 529-8102
pastorgary@mtzionhighland.com

Mtn. View-Pleasant Grove
Mountain View #9220
11501 Mountain View Rd, Damascus, MD 20872-1607

C. (301) 253-2264
pastormhbaek@gmail.com

Pleasant Grove #9320
3425 Green Valley Rd, Ijamsville, MD 21754-9016
Myungha (Myung-Ha) Baek FE
7326 Springfield Ave, Sykesville, MD 21784-7549

C. (301) 865-5443
pastormhbaek@gmail.com
R. (240) 477-2624
pastormhbaek@gmail.com

Oakdale Emory #9375
3425 Emory Church Rd, Olney, MD 20832-2613
Kevin M. Baker FE
3725 Route 97, Glenwood, MD 21738-9614

C. (301) 774-2030
info@oakdale.church
R. (410) 489-4406
kbaker@oakdale.church

David J. Deans FE
3415 Emory Church Road, Olney, MD 20832

R. (240) 389-0787
ddeans@oakdale.church

Poplar Springs
Jennings Chapel #9510
2601 Jennings Chapel Rd, Woodbine, MD 21797-7802
Poplar Springs #9360
16661 Frederick Rd, Mount Airy, MD 21771-3311
Robert E. Cook FE
16661 Frederick Rd, Mount Airy, MD 21771-3311

C. (410) 489-7185
poplarcharge@verizon.net
C. (410) 489-7185
rev@hereintown.net
R. (301) 697-2712
rev@hereintown.net

Prospect-Marvin Chapel
Marvin Chapel #6310
5101 Woodville Rd, Mount Airy, MD 21771
Prospect #6315
5923 Woodville Rd, Mount Airy, MD 21771
Trenton Prieshoff SY
24 N Wolfe St, Baltimore, MD 21231-1620

C. (301) 829-9244
prospect.marvinchapel.umc@gmail.com
C. (301) 829-9244
prospect.marvinchapel.umc@gmail.com
R. (317) 383-9429
trenton.prieshoff@inumc.org

Providence #9325
3735 Kemptown Church Rd, Monrovia, MD 21770-8701
Dauba D. Adams FL
3735 Kemptown Church Rd, Monrovia, MD 21770-8701

C. (301) 253-1768
dwdadam@gmail.com
R. (301) 253-1768
dwdadam@gmail.com

Salem #9150
12 High St, Brookeville, MD 20833
Sue E. Shorb-Sterling FE
8 High St, Brookeville, MD 20833

C. (301) 774-7772
pastor@salemunitedmethodist.org
R. (410) 474-7281
shorster@yahoo.com

Sharp Street #9445
1310 Olney Sandy Spring Rd, Sandy Spring, MD 20860-1325
Diane Dixon-Proctor RE
127 Foxtrap Dr, Glen Burnie, MD 21061-6338

C. (301) 774-7047
sharppraise@verizon.net
R. (410) 766-4890
ddpny@aol.com

South Damascus
Mount Tabor #9340
24115 Laytonsville Rd, Laytonsville, MD 20882-3127
Salem #9275
23725 Ridge Rd, Germantown, MD 20876-4642
Wesley Grove #9515
23640 Woodfield Rd, Gaithersburg, MD 20882-2818
Karen Davis FE
23612 Woodfield Rd, Gaithersburg, MD 20882

C. (301) 253-3871
Mttaboretchison@gmail.com
C. (301) 972-1804
salemumcgermantown@gmail.com
C. (301) 253-2894
WGUMC@wesleygroveumc.org
R. (410) 812-9437
PastorKaren24@msn.com

YouJung Jung SY
Campus Box 264, Washington, DC 20016-5632

R. (301) 788-4265
jyj2908@gmail.com

St James #4565
12470 Old Frederick Rd, Marriottsville, MD 21104-1415
Patricia Abell FE
12450 Old Frederick Rd, Marriottsville, MD 21104-1415

C. (410) 442-2020
stjamessec@verizon.net
R. (410) 680-8426
pabell42@gmail.com

St John United Church #7360
10431 Twin Rivers Rd, Columbia, MD 21044
Mary Kathryn (Mary Ka) Nippard Kanahan FE
9547 Michaels Way, Ellicott City, MD 21042-2463

C. (410) 730-9137
SJUColumbia@gmail.com
R. (410) 428-8090
pastorkanahansju@gmail.com

St Luke #4460
350 River Rd, Sykesville, MD 21784-5513
Ronald Young PL
9341 Chadburn Pl, Montgomery Village, MD 20886

C. (301) 977-6740
pastorrony44@gmail.com
R. (240) 550-9394
pastorrony44@gmail.com

St Marks #9145
19620 White Ground Rd, Boyds, MD 20841-9412
Joycelyn Camper SY
90 Waverley Dr Apt Q203, Frederick, MD 21702-3340

C. (443) 463-5851
stmarksboydumc@gmail.com
R. (301) 875-8855
because-he-lives@live.com

Sunshine
Mount Carmel #9335
22222 Georgia Ave, Brookeville, MD 20833-0177
St Paul #9345
21720 Laytonsville Rd, Laytonsville, MD 20882-1628
Jean H. Lee PE
21820 Laytonsville Rd, Laytonsville, MD 20882-1630

C. (301) 774-9330
stpaul208@aol.com
C. (301) 963-2185
stpaul208@aol.com
R. (301) 330-0539
jeanhlee5@gmail.com

Sykesville Parish
Gaither #4280
7701 Gaither Rd, Sykesville, MD 21784-7124
St Paul's #4465
7538 Main St, Sykesville, MD 21784-7361
Eunjoung Joo FE
7326 Springfield Ave, Sykesville, MD 21784-7549

C. (410) 795-0714
admin@stpaulssykesville.org
C. (410) 795-0714
admin@stpaulssykesville.org
R. (240) 461-4450
revjoo@stpaulssykesville.org

Douglas D. Tzan FE
6415 Tamarack Cir, Sykesville, MD 21784-7968

R. (410) 795-0940
dtzan@stpaulssykesville.org

Trinity #9280
13700 Schaeffer Rd, Germantown, MD 20874-2225
Bonnie Scott FE
28 Sebastiani Blvd, Gaithersburg, MD 20878-4120

C. (301) 540-4300
office@trinity-germantown.org
R. (410) 303-2887
revbonniescott@gmail.com

Washington Grove #9470
303 Chestnut Ave, Washington Grove, MD 20880-2031
Andrew Peck-McClain FE
5558 Burnside Dr, Rockville, MD 20853-2457

C. (301) 869-3753
washingtongroveumc@gmail.com
R. 862-204-9265
rev.apeckmcclain@gmail.com

Wesley Chapel #6385
3519 Urbana Pike, Frederick, MD 21704
Sandi Phillips FL
3519 Urbana Pike, Frederick, MD 21704

C. (301) 663-4956
eph5v17@gmail.com
R. (443) 956-5639
eph5v17@gmail.com

Wesley Freedom #4225
961 Johnsville Rd, Eldersburg, MD 21784-4903
Antoine C. (Tony) Love FE
5238 Kenstan Dr, Temple Hills, MD 20748-5446

Ian Collier PE
9104 Thistledown Rd #478, Owings Mills, MD 21117

C. (410) 795-2777
office@wesleyfreedom.org
R. (301) 449-5683
tlove@wesleyfreedom.org

R. (518) 409-6614
icollier@wesleyfreedom.org

West Liberty #4343
2000 Sand Hill Rd, Marriottsville, MD 21104-1649
Barbara J. Sands RE
696 West Watersville Rd, PO Box 637, Mount Airy, MD 21771

C. (410) 442-2969
west.libertyumc.mail@gmail.com
R. (301) 829-2180
bjsands696@gmail.com

West Montgomery #9580
21000 Beallsville Rd, Dickerson, MD 20842-9069
Wilhelmina Street RL
3117 Ferndale Ave, Baltimore, MD 21207-6712

C. (443) 463-5851
westmontgomeryumc@gmail.com
R. (443) 500-0672
kingshighway247@gmail.com

Certified Candidate
Helen Ballew CC
19109 Munger Farm Rd, Poolesville, MD 20837-2175

R. (301) 661-1149
helenballew@yahoo.com

Cristin Cooper CC
4815 Tothill Dr, Olney, MD 20832-1889

R. (240) 432-2607
ccooper@oakdale.church

Miguel A. Gallegos CC
1120 Sandy Hollow Ct, Silver Spring, MD 20905-6050

R. (202) 288-8137
migallegos@gmail.com

David Norton CC
6229 Sebring Dr, Columbia, MD 21044-3925

R. (410) 336-4042
iotanu330@gmail.com

Melaina Trice CC
17400 New Hampshire Ave, Ashton, MD 20861-9777

R. (301) 774-7100
aumcyouthleadablaze@gmail.com

Disability
William T. (Thomas) Green FE
6725 Summer Rambo Ct, Columbia, MD 21045-5405

R. (410) 381-1156
tiredtenor@comcast.net

Extension Ministry
Cheryl B. Anderson FE
2121 Sheridan Rd, Evanston, IL 60201-2926

R. (847) 425-9382
cheryl.anderson@garrett.edu

Laurence K. Bropleh FE
19738 Lindenfield Ct, Katy, TX 77449-8620

R. (281) 703-1591
lbropleh@aol.com

William G. Brown FE
6631 Monroe Ave, Sykesville, MD 21784-6345

R. (443) 854-6054
railroadrev@gmail.com

Debbie (Deborah) Burgio PD
14450 Triadelphia Mill Rd, Dayton, MD 21036-1220

R. (410) 531-2271
debbie.burgio@verizon.net

William T. Chaney, Jr. FE
25052 Owl Creek Dr, Aldie, VA 20105-5617
R. (240) 405-9808
pastorchaney@outlook.com

Malcolm Frazier FE
1802 Mount Pisgah Ln Apt 33, Silver Spring, MD 20903-2142
R. (240) 670-7680
frazier1950@verizon.net

Donald J. (Don) Hohne FD
6012 Crossway Ct, Sykesville, MD 21784-8419
R. (410) 549-3621
hohnefamily@msn.com

Claire C. Matheny FE
5151 Darting Bird Ln, Columbia, MD 21044-1503
R. (202) 674-7805
scmatheny@gmail.com

John W. Nupp FE
4654 Dower Dr, Ellicott City, MD 21043-6411
R. (410) 465-3639
jnupp@bwcumc.org

HiRho Y. Park FE
7 Diamond Hill Ct, Germantown, MD 20874-5902
R. (615) 948-5702
hpark@gbhem.org

Douglas M. Strong FE
3614 12th Ave W, Seattle, WA 98119
R. (206) 281-2473
dstrong@spu.edu

Mark R. Teasdale FE
1004 Central Ave, Wilmette, IL 60091-2610
R. (847) 866-3954
mark.teasdale@garrett.edu

On Loan

Michelle Chaney FE
25052 Owl Creek Dr, Aldie, VA 20105-5617
R. (615) 346-9697
mhchaney@gmail.com

Mary E. Dennis FD
7 North Stead Ct, Catonsville, MD 21228-2443
R. (410) 804-5147
MDen2154@gmail.com

Retired

Ann Adams RE
1200 Pine Heights Ave, Baltimore, MD 21229-5128
R. (410) 646-0796
revannadams@msn.com

James P. Archibald RE
PO Box 1035, Penney Farms, FL 32079-1035
R. (904) 529-8688

Ruth Bell RD
5400 Vantage Point Rd Apt 107, Columbia, MD 21044
R. (410) 465-1183
jamesruthbell@verizon.net

Ernest E. Bortner RE
429 Saint Johns Dr, Satellite Beach, FL 32937-4023
R. (321) 777-0645
ebortner1@cfl.rr.com

Robert M. Braden RE
25605 Ridge Rd, Damascus, MD 20872-1841
R. (301) 253-6478

Donald L. Burgard RE
719 Maiden Choice Ln #HR302, Catonsville, MD 21228
pastordonhawk@aol.com

Lynn D. Cairns RE
457 Old Mill Rd, Gettysburg, PA 17325-8465
R. (717) 334-4193
ldcairns@embarqmail.com

Lon B. Chesnutt RE
713 Maiden Choice Ln Apt 2209, Catonsville, MD 21228-3953
R. (410) 737-8119
lchesnutt@aol.com

Richard A. Closson RE
1415 Main St Lot 297, Dunedin, FL 34698-6228
R. (727) 736-6892

Harry C. Cole RE
110 Homewood Ln, Frederick, MD 21702-3381
R. 301-304-9666
harryccole@msn.com

Mary Jane Coleman RE
69 Beaconhill Rd, Berlin, MD 21811-1613

R. (410) 641-7315
revmjsc@mchsi.com

Thomas N. Connar RE
33 Canvasback Cir, Bridgeville, DE 19933-2429

R. (302) 956-0318
tconnar@comcast.net

Janet M. Cornelius RE
13820 Esworthy Rd, Germantown, MD 20874-3316

R. (301) 926-4925
janetmcornelius@comcast.net

Glen W. Dameron RE
531 Majorca Loop, Myrtle Beach, SC 29579-8004

R. (301) 467-5200
glen.dameron@verizon.net

Sally Jo Day RE
21 Dove Trl, Fairfield, PA 17320-8082

R. (717) 642-5905

Wayne A. DeHart RE
3011 Auburn Vw, Ellicott City, MD 21042-7115

R. (410) 531-7839
waynedehart@verizon.net

Mark A. Derby RE
4900 Continental Dr, Olney, MD 20832-2972

revmaderby@gmail.com

Timothy H. Dissmeyer RE
13465 Four Seasons Ct, Mount Airy, MD 21771-7501

R. (301) 829-1541
Tdissmeyer@aol.com

Diane Dixon-Proctor RE
127 Foxtrap Dr, Glen Burnie, MD 21061-6338

R. (410) 766-4890
ddpny@aol.com

Vicki Dotterer RE
23013 Timber Creek Ln, Clarksburg, MD 20871-9440

R. (301) 956-0124
rev.vicki.d@gmail.com

Walter G. Edmonds RE
3889 Maryland Manor Dr, Monrovia, MD 21770-8909

R. (301) 831-3472
WPEdmonds70@comcast.net

Kenneth R. Fell RE
20547 Summersong Ln, Germantown, MD 20874-1071

R. (301) 972-6381
kenfell@aol.com

Douglas E. Fox RE
6273 Cobbler Ct, Columbia, MD 21045-4503

R. (410) 294-2818
douglasefox@verizon.net

Lillian R. Geib RE
18 Maple Leaf Rd, Spencer, VA 24165-3145

2geiblp18@comcast.net

John W. Grove RE
9207 Butler Blvd, Weeki Wachee, FL 34613-4034

R. (352) 597-1140
jwgandmag@aol.com

Carlee L. Hallman RE
415 Russell Ave Apt 719, Gaithersburg, MD 20877-2840

R. (301) 216-5331
carlee6508@yahoo.com

Lyle E. Harper RE
PO Box 752, Micaville, NC 28755-0752

R. (828) 284-4275

Gary R. (Bob) Hottinger RE
2561 Glenkirk Dr, Burlington, NC 27215-9512

R. (336) 585-0881
pghottinger@twc.com

James M. (Jim) Hunt RE
885 Nash Loop, The Villages, FL 32162-4541

R. (301) 888-2572
jmhsr1@msn.com

Diana L. Hynson RE
6104 Bradford Hills Dr, Nashville, TN 37211-7900

R. (615) 340-7053
dianalhynson@outlook.com

Clarence A. Kaylor RE
106 Homewood Ln, Frederick, MD 21702-3381

R. (301) 540-0667
tomkaylor@verizon.net

Arthur R. Kent RE
609 Avon Square Ct, Silver Spring, MD 20905-5939

R. (410) 788-8567
kentbiz09@gmail.com

Jeanne W. Klauda RE
840 Harbor View Ter, Annapolis, MD 21409-4641

R. (410) 349-0949

David F. Kolda RE
18388 Brussels Dr, South Bend, IN 46637-2335

R. (574) 273-4280
DJKOLDA@sbcglobal.net

Neva H. Leatherwood RE
2613 Melba Rd, Ellicott City, MD 21042-1833

R. (410) 465-9483

Michael E. Leftwich RE
11345 Windsor Rd, Ijamsville, MD 21754-8907

R. (301) 865-3321

Diana L. Ley RE
9443 Fens Holw, Laurel, MD 20723-5734

R. (301) 725-2986
revley@verizon.net

Anders R. (Andy) Lunt RE
9000 Fathers Legacy Apt 100, Ellicott City, MD 21042-5149

R. (410) 418-4341
revdoclunt@gmail.com

James S. Mason RL
7179 Browns Ln, Thurmont, MD 21788-2512

R. (301) 898-5397

Martha J. Maxham RD
18039 Rocky Ridge Ln, Olney, MD 20832-1778

R. (301) 570-4294
martha.maxham@gmail.com

Richard K. McCullough RE
7322 Springfield Ave, Sykesville, MD 21784-7549

R. (410) 795-3684
rmcpastor7@aol.com

Mary S. (Sheila) McCurdy RE
5565 Vantage Point Rd, Columbia, MD 21044-2610

R. (443) 739-9796
msmccurdy44@gmail.com

Perry F. Miller RE
370 Grey Friars Rd, Westminster, MD 21158-3705

R. (410) 206-1746
eandpmiller@comcast.net

Robert E. Mitzel RE
721 Maiden Choice Ln Apt CW204, Catonsville, MD 21228

R. (410) 242-0018
dadmitz@aol.com

Marilyn C. Newhouse RE
3144 Gracefield Rd Apt 128, Silver Spring, MD 20904-5879

R. (301) 755-1686
mcnewhouse@aol.com

Lynn P. Nulton RD
15255 Callaway Ct, Glenwood, MD 21738-9657

R. (410) 489-9918
lpnulton1@verizon.net

Ralph D. Posey RE
1001 Carpenters Way Apt M107, Lakeland, FL 33809-3907

poseypatch@gmail.com

James (Jim) Pugh RL
55B Queen Caroline Ct, Chester, MD 21619-2253

R.
jgpugh46@msn.com

Yolanda E. Pupo-Ortiz RE
18 Landsend Dr, Gaithersburg, MD 20878-1987

R. (301) 926-1387
yolanda@starpower.net

Laura Schultz RE
401 Oak St, Windsor, CO 80550-5323

R. (301) 829-2391
revlauraschultz@gmail.com

Charles J. Shacochis, Jr. RA
1614 Heather Hts, Eldersburg, MD 21784-6235

R. (410) 795-3871
chuckstg39@msn.com

David W. Simpson RE

dsimpson670@comcast.net

Errol G. Smith RE
422 Spalding Ct, Westminster, MD 21158-9411

R. (443) 293-7095
esmithconsult@aol.com

Luther W. Starnes RE
5364 Smooth Meadow Way Unit 2, Columbia, MD 21044-1877

R. (410) 964-6410
lstartalk@aol.com

Gerald E. Stone RE
115 Ford Dr, Westminster, MD 21157-4998

R. (410) 857-3544
GeraldStone48@gmail.com

Peter K. Sun RE
9417 Ashlyn Cir, Owings Mills, MD 21117-3281

R. (410) 654-2389

Deborah Tate RE
14900 Emory Ln, Rockville, MD 20853-1650

R. (301) 460-0884
terrific03@aol.com

Jean J. (JJ) Weller RP
10869 Hilltop Ln, Columbia, MD 21044-3722

R. (410) 964-5681
jweller123@comcast.net

Stephen R. White RL
131 Saddletop Dr, Taneytown, MD 21787-1547

R. (410) 795-4366

Gertie T. Williams RP
8490 Thomas Williams Way, Columbia, MD 21045-2482

(410) 461-1155
ladirev4@gmail.com

Carol C. Yocum RE
109 Troon Cir, Mount Airy, MD 21771-5002

R. (301) 829-4822
carolyocum@msn.com

Dennis E. Yocum RE
109 Troon Cir, Mount Airy, MD 21771-5002

R. (301) 829-4822
dyocum9236@aol.com

Jean S. Young RE
518 School Ln, Rehoboth Beach, DE 19971-1802

R. (302) 227-4097
revjsy@aol.com

Judy S. Young RE
196 Longstreet Dr, Gettysburg, PA 17325-8920

R. (717) 398-2195
jsmithyoung@gmail.com

Transitional Leave

Neville (Al) Hammer, III FD
9906 Evergreen Ave, Columbia, MD 21046-1026

R. (410) 428-7466
alhammeriii@gmail.com

CUMBERLAND-HAGERSTOWN DISTRICT

Superintendent
John Wunderlich FE   (410) 309-3444
616 Hunting Ridge Dr, Frederick, MD 21703-2218
jwunderlich@bwcumc.org

Alpine
Alpine #5510   C. (304) 258-2847
1302 Valley Rd, Berkeley Springs, WV 25411-4801   alpine.charge@gmail.com
(5181 Pious Ridge Rd)
Highland #5530   C. (304) 258-2847
1302 Valley Rd, Berkeley Springs, WV 25411-4801   alpine.charge@gmail.com
(4360 Highland Ridge Rd)
Mount Pleasant #5550   C. (304) 258-2847
1302 Valley Rd, Berkeley Springs, WV 25411-4801   alpine.charge@gmail.com
(3360 Johnson Mill Rd)
   Kenneth J. Mason PL   R. (301) 399-5214
   11 Cross Rd, Berkeley Springs, WV 25411-3658   kmason169@yahoo.com

Asbury #5315   C. (301) 791-0498
PO Box 1009, Hagerstown, MD 21740-4811   sharongibson_1@msn.com
(155 Jonathan St)
   Sharon Gibson PL   R. (301) 663-0174
   1620 Colonial Way, Frederick, MD 21702 sharongibson_1@msn.com

Barton/Westernport
Barton #5110   C. (301) 463-2315
18917 Legistlative Rd, Barton, MD 21521   bartonumc@gmail.com
Westernport #5465   C. (301) 359-3515
434 Vine St, Westernport, MD 21562-1220   westernportumc5465@gmail.com
   Carl S. (Sandy) Cowan PL   R. (301) 722-2419
   410 National Highway, LaVale, MD 21502 bartonumc@gmail.com

Benevola #6115   C. (301) 791-3576
19925 Benevola Church Rd, Boonsboro, MD 21713-1701   benevolachurch@myactv.net
   Cindy M. Caldwell FE   R. (410) 937-0458
   18122 Samuel Cir, Hagerstown, MD 21740-9599   pastor.benevola@gmail.com

Berkeley Springs
Michaels #5540   C. (301) 678-6394
PO Box 672, Hedgesville, WV 25427-0672   michaelsumc.berk.springs@gmail.com
(884 Michaels Chapel Road)
Trinity-Asbury #5640   C. (304) 258-1033
PO Box 672, Berkeley Springs, WV 25411-0672   berkeleyspringsparish@frontier.com
(108 Wilkes St)
Wesley Chapel #5575   C. (304) 258-1033
PO Box 513, Berkeley Springs, WV 25411-0513   berkeleyspringsparish@frontier.com
(165 Pious Ridge Rd)
   Charles D. Bergen PL   R. (304) 671-8767

214 Woodside Ln, Berkeley Springs, WV 25411-5886

chuck.bergen@gmail.com

Barbara V. Suffecool FD
2837 Western Pike, Hancock, MD 21750-1632

R. (301) 678-6394
SuffeBar@comcast.net

Bethel #6345
PO Box B, 4300 Main St, Rohrersville, MD 21779-0080
John Schildt RE
PO Box 145, Sharpsburg, MD 21782-0145

C. (301) 432-8885
dorisbonner@yahoo.com
R. (301) 432-0087
lyricww41@aol.com

Bethel #5135
21006 Twin Springs Dr, Smithsburg, MD 21783-1636
James K. Johnson FE
21002 Twin Springs Dr, Smithsburg, MD 21783-1636

C. (301) 733-8387
bethel.church@myactv.net
R. (410) 688-4089
pastorjim@myactv.net

Big Pool
Mount Carmel #5115
11404 Tedrick Dr, Big Pool, MD 21711-1236
Parkhead #5120
11404 Tedrick Dr, Big Pool, MD 21711-1236
Albert (Al) Deal PL
21824 Ringgold Pike, Hagerstown, MD 21742-1478

C. (240) 520-7708
bigpoolumc@gmail.com
C. (301) 842-3212
bigpoolumc@gmail.com
R. (301) 964-9993
aldeal1003@gmail.com

Calvary #5580
PO Box 217, Great Cacapon, WV 25422-0217
(5137 Central Avenue)
Richard Craig RE
269 Keystone Ln, Berkeley Springs, WV 25411-3426

C. (304) 258-3455
calvary5580@frontier.com

R. (304) 754-3393
RBCraig3@comcast.net

Calvary #5620
PO Box 354, Ridgeley, WV 26753-0354
(28 Knobley Street)
Richard H. Jewell RE
PO Box 85, Wiley Ford, WV 26767-0085

C. (304) 738-8940
cumcridgeley@atlanticbbn.net

R. (304) 738-8734
revjewell@atlanticbb.net

Central #5150
15 S George St, Cumberland, MD 21502-3049
Charles L. (Lee) Brotemarkle RL
14215 Bedford Rd NE, Cumberland, MD 21502-6926

C. (301) 724-4080
centralumc@atlanticbbn.net
R. (301) 724-7614
leebrotemarkle@atlanticbb.net

Christ #5160
336 Race St, Cumberland, MD 21502-4138
Harold McClay, Jr. RE
18608 McMullen Hwy SW, Rawlings, MD 21557-6614

C. (301) 777-1561
cumc@atlanticbbn.net
R. (301) 729-0765
cumc@atlanticbbn.net

Creek Run
Ellerslie #5265
PO Box 358, Ellerslie, MD 21529-0358
(14305 Temple Street)
Mount Savage #5425
PO Box 603, Mount Savage, MD 21545-0603
(12619 New Row Rd NW)

C. (301) 724-4929
pboch10439@aol.com

C. (301) 264-3535
mtsavageumc@yahoo.com

Sandra H. Burchell PE
11504 Mountain Magic Ln NE, Cumberland, MD 21502

R. (301) 777-3429
Nightwatch@atlanticbb.net

Cresaptown #5140
PO Box 5206, Cresaptown, MD 21502-5611
(14805 McMullen Hwy SW)

C. (301) 729-0052
youngsl@atlanticbb.net

   Patrick M. Hurder Buhrman PE
   14801 Bell St, Cresaptown, MD 21502-6589

R. (301) 991-0639
pbuhrman@yahoo.com

Davis Memorial #5165
14300 Uhl Hwy SE, Cumberland, MD 21502-8442
   Robert Pierson FL
   13200 Piney Flats Rd SE, Cumberland, MD 21502

C. (301) 724-3896
davismemorialumc@atlanticbb.net
R. (240) 483-6865
bobapierson@yahoo.com

Dawson #5440
22515 McMullen Hwy SW, Rawlings, MD 21557-2432
   Michael McGowan SY
   19506 McVeighs Aly SW, Frostburg, MD 21532-4820

C. (301) 786-4652
dawsonchurch7@gmail.com
R. (301) 697-0958
michael.mcgowan@acpsmd.org

Eckhart
Allegany #5290
PO Box 444, Frostburg, MD 21532-0444
(17305 Mount Savage Rd NW)

C. (301) 689-9585
harpold8736@comcast.net

Carlos #5130
PO Box 444, Frostburg, MD 21532-0444
(12401 Carlos Rd SW)

C. (301) 689-9585
harpold8736@comcast.net

Eckhart #5255
PO Box 44, Frostburg, MD 21532-0044
(17031 Porter Road SW)

C. (301) 689-9585
harpold8736@comcast.net

Vale Summit #5463
PO Box 444, Frostburg, MD 21532-0444
(12630 Vale Summit Rd SW)

C. (301) 689-9585
harpold8736@comcast.net

   George Harpold RL
   PO Box 444, Frostburg, MD 21532-0444

R. (301) 689-9585
harpold8736@comcast.net

Emmanuel #5177
24 Humbird St, Cumberland, MD 21502-4716
   Robert Pierson FL
   13200 Piney Flats Rd SE, Cumberland, MD 21502

C. (301) 722-8101
Emmanuelumcumberland@gmail.com
R. (240) 483-6865
bobapierson@yahoo.com

Emmanuel #5320
802 Summit Ave, Hagerstown, MD 21740-6332
   Randall Reid FE
   812 Summit Ave, Hagerstown, MD 21740-6332

C. (301) 733-4720
eumc.office@verizon.net
R. (301) 739-0442
eumc.pastor@verizon.net

First #5515
49 S Green St, Berkeley Springs, WV 25411-1638
   Douglas B. Hoffman FE
   175 Congress St, Berkeley Springs, WV 25411

C. (304) 258-2766
firstumc3@frontier.com
R. (410) 303-8195
dhoffman@gofirst.org

Flintstone
Flintstone #5270
C. (301) 478-2369
PO Box 2, Flintstone, MD 21530-0002
flintstoneumcharge@verizon.net
(21690 National Pike NE)
Mount Hermon #5275
C. (301) 478-2369
PO Box 2, Cumberland, MD 21501-0002
flintstoneumcharge@verizon.net
(13200 Williams Road)
Murleys Branch #5280
C. (301) 478-2369
PO Box 2 , Flintstone, MD 21530-2141
flintstoneumcharge@verizon.net
(18700 Williams Rd SE)
Prosperity #5285
C. (301) 478-2369
PO Box 2, Flintstone, MD 21530-0002
flintstoneumcharge@verizon.net
(13505 Pleasant Valley Road NE)
 Patricia L. (Trish) Bittner PL
R. (301) 697-7728
 21613 National Pike, Flintstone, MD 21530-0064
pastortrish13@gmail.com

Frostburg #5310
C. (301) 689-6626
48 W Main St, Frostburg, MD 21532-1642
office@frostburgumc.org
 Kyle Durbin FE
R. (443) 223-5717
 46 W Main St, Frostburg, MD 21532-1642
ImKyleDurbin@gmail.com

Garfield / St. Paul's
Garfield #6425
13628 Stottlemyer Rd, Smithsburg, MD 21783-9220
jdbear@comcast.net
St Paul's #5455
PO Box 205, Smithsburg, MD 21783-1950
maryricketts622@gmail.com
 Mary L. Ricketts OE
R. (301) 582-8552
 35 E All Saints St Unit 118, Frederick, MD 21701-5951
maryricketts622@gmail.com

George's Creek
First #5390
C. (202) 304-9328
14 Church St, Lonaconing, MD 21539-1111
lonaconingumc@gmail.com
Grace #5410
C. (202) 304-9328
PO Box 15, Midland, MD 21532-0015
kheerak@gmail.com
(19915 Church Street SW)
Shaft #5415
C. (301) 689-2158
19304 Shaft Rd SW, Frostburg, MD 21532-3743
kheerak@gmail.com
 Heerak Kim PE
R. (202) 304-9328
 14706 Smith Hill Rd SW, Frostburg, MD 21532-4838
kheerak@gmail.com

Grace #5325
C. (301) 739-1925
712 W Church St, Hagerstown, MD 21740-4560
graceumchagerstown@gmail.com
 Margaret E. Clemons FE
R. (240) 513-6299
 19912 Fairmont Ct, Hagerstown, MD 21742-6717
revmeclemons@gmail.com

Hancock #5365
C. (301) 678-6440
170 W Main St, Hancock, MD 21750-1432
HancockUMC@comcast.net
 Joshua Gillen PL
R. (443) 992-0466
 168 W Main St, Hancock, MD 21750-1432
pastorjgillen@gmail.com

Holy Cross #5625
3 Miller Lane, Ridgeley, WV 26753
T. Brent Wiles SY
126 Wempe Dr, Cumberland, MD 21502-4224

C. (304) 738-2206
Holycrossumc847@gmail.com
R. (240) 920-8805
brent@tomwiles.com

John Wesley #5330
129 N Potomac St, Hagerstown, MD 21740-4809
Katie M. O'Hern PE
1408 Hamilton Blvd, Hagerstown, MD 21742

C. (301) 733-0391
jwumcmd@yahoo.com
R. (585) 794-9663
pastorkohern@gmail.com

LaVale #5370
565 National Hwy, Lavale, MD 21502-7047
Frankie A. Revell FE
26 Parkside Blvd, LaVale, Md 21502

C. (301) 722-6800
churchoffice@umclavale.org
R. (301) 338-3312
revellfa@gmail.com

Narae Kim PE
14706 Smith Hill Rd SW, Frostburg, MD 21532-4838

R. (301) 655-2216
narae849.kim@gmail.com

McKendree of Potomac Park #5242
13455 McMullen Hwy SW, Cumberland, MD 21502-5346
Lisa M. Boone PL
10213 Summers Ln, Hagerstown, MD 21740-1564

C. (301) 729-1993
mckendree5242@gmail.com
R. (516) 841-8973
lisaboone61@hotmail.com

Melvin-Fairview Ave
Fairview Avenue #5180
640 Fairview Ave, Cumberland, MD 21502-1518
Melvin #5295
100 Reynolds St, Cumberland, MD 21502-2526
Daniel G. (Dan) Taylor RL
PO Box 688, Fort Ashby, WV 26719-0688

C. (301) 722-3300
momstaxi@atlanticbb.net
C. (301) 777-3997
rdmrlm@verizon.net
R. (304) 298-4876
dgtaylor@atlanticbb.net

Morgan
Greenwood #5525
6752 Winchester Grade Rd, Berkeley Springs, WV 25411
Mount Olivet #5545
6752 Winchester Grade Rd, Berkeley Springs, WV 25411
Lloyd B. McCanna RE
6752 Winchester Grade Rd, Berkeley Springs, WV 25411

C. (304) 258-2957
morganchargewv@gmail.com
C. (304) 258-2957
morganchargewv@gmail.com
R. (304) 258-2957
lbmccanna@atlanticbb.net

Mt. Bethel/Mt. Lena
Mount Bethel #5450
14110 Stottlemyer Rd, Smithsburg, MD 21783-9230
Mount Lena #6125
21234 Mount Lena Rd, Boonsboro, MD 21713-1613
Ron R. Kurtz RE
20614 Pony Trl, Boonsboro, MD 21713-1805

C. (301) 416-0300
rk4home@aol.com
C. (301) 733-8108
rk4home@aol.com
R. (301) 393-4359
rk4home@aol.com

Mount Nebo #6130
134 S Main St, Boonsboro, MD 21713-1204
Robert Ruggieri PE
10856 Wolfsville Rd, Myersville, MD 21773-8820

C. (301) 432-8741
mt.nebo@myactv.net
R. (443) 994-9505
pastorbob2017@gmail.com

Mount Zion #6325
603 Main St, Myersville, MD 21773-8412
   Michael R. Beiber FE
   601 Main Street, Myersville, MD 21773-0299

C. (301) 293-1401
mtzionmyersville@gmail.com
R. (301) 293-1258
rev.mike.beiber@gmail.com

Mount Zion #6350
PO Box 104, Sabillasville, MD 21780-0104
(13010 Mount Zion Road)
   Lisa A. Wirkus FE
   982 Kasinof Ave, Hagerstown, MD 21742-4606

C. (301) 824-6617
terplisajordan@gmail.com

R. (240) 752-6710
deafumcpastor@gmail.com

Mount Zion #5585
PO Box 532, Great Cacapon, WV 25422-0532
(4581 Orleans Road)
   Richard Voorhaar LM
   PO Box 543, Great Cacapon, WV 25422-0543

C. (304) 258-2852
dickvoorhaar@hotmail.com

R. (304) 258-6263
dickvoorhaar@hotmail.com

New Covenant #5210
1709 Frederick St, Cumberland, MD 21502-1037
   Donna Renn FE
   1021 Kent Ave, Cumberland, MD 21502-3847

C. (301) 724-1150
revdonna@comcast.net
R. (301) 938-1450
revdonna@comcast.net

Oldtown
Mount Tabor #5460
18605 Oldtown Rd SE, Oldtown, MD 21555
(13801 Oldtown Rd)

C. (301) 478-5228
mttaborumc@yahoo.com

Oldtown #5430
18605 Oldtown Rd SE, Oldtown, MD 21555
(18811 Oldtown Rd)

C. (301) 478-5869
oldtownumc@yahoo.com

Oliver's Grove #5435
18605 Oldtown Rd SE, Oldtown, MD 21555
(15500 Walnut Ridge Rd SE)
   Charles Riggleman FL
   18605 Oldtown RD SE, Oldtown, MD 21555

C. (301) 478-5228
oliversgroveumc@yahoo.com

R. (301) 478-5228
umcpastorcr@gmail.com

Otterbein #5340
108 E Franklin St, Hagerstown, MD 21740-4906
   Elizabeth H. Jackson FE
   19002 Orchard Terrace Rd, Hagerstown, MD 21742

C. (301) 739-9386
office@otterumc.org
R. (301) 373-4646
pastorelizabeth@otterumc.org

Park Place #5375
80 National Hwy, LaVale, MD 21502-7028
   Vicki Cubbage PL
   433 National Hwy, LaVale, MD 21502-7141

C. (301) 722-8145
vickitoad@hotmail.com
R. (240) 522-0515
vickitoad@hotmail.com

Paw Paw #5610
PO Box 302, Paw Paw, WV 25434-0302
   Darlene Powers LM
   12 Mechem Way, Great Cacapon, WV 25422-3314

C. (304) 947-5289
darlenepowers@frontiernet.net
R. (304) 947-7232
darlenepowers@frontiernet.net

Pleasant Walk #6430   C. (301) 797-5433
11240 Pleasant Walk Rd, Myersville, MD 21773-9218   pleasantwalkumc@gmail.com
  Lisa A. Wirkus FE   R. (240) 752-6710
  982 Kasinof Ave, Hagerstown, MD 21742-4606   deafumcpastor@gmail.com

Rawlings #5445   C. (301) 729-0088
PO Box 228, Rawlings, MD 21557-0228   rawlingsumc@gmail.com
(18910 McMullen Hwy SW)
  Lisa M. Boone PL   R. (516) 841-8973
  10213 Summers Ln, Hagerstown, MD 21740-1564   lisaboone61@hotmail.com

Rehoboth #5470   C. (301) 223-9554
30 E Salisbury St, Williamsport, MD 21795-1112   mirlinx51@gmail.com
  Michael W. Bennett FE   R. (410) 980-5265
  86 Aquifer Dr, Falling Waters, WV 25419-4303   mirlinx51@gmail.com

Salem #6435   C. (301) 293-1616
12477 Wolfsville Rd, Myersville, MD 21773-9303   revbsnyder@comcast.net
  Robert E. (Bob) Snyder FE   R. (240) 385-6833
  517 Main St, Myersville, MD 21773-8436   revbsnyder@comcast.net

Salem #6250   C. (301) 432-4046
25 S Main St, Keedysville, MD 21756-1348   salemumc@salemcommunity.org
  Suzanne G. Jones PL   R. (304) 876-8217
  580 Morgana Dr, Shepherdstown, WV 25443-4751   pastorsuzannejones@gmail.com

Shiloh #5355   C. (301) 797-4083
19731 Shiloh Church Rd, Hagerstown, MD 21742-4869   shilohumc@myactv.net
  Dionne (Dee) Osuji Hall PL   R. (301) 302-7509
  516 Papa Ct, Hagerstown, MD 21740-4120   deeosuji@hotmail.com

Sleepy Creek
Cherry Run #5630   C. (304) 258-2108
3165 Householder Rd, Hedgesville, WV 25427   sleepycrkchrgumc@gmail.com
Mount Zion #5555   C. (304) 258-2108
5377 Martinsburg Rd, Berkeley Springs, WV 25411   sleepycrkchrgumc@gmail.com
  Anthony Pirrone SY   R. (304) 754-5054
  291 Steamboat Run Rd, Shepherdstown, WV 25443   tpirrone4given@comcast.net

Sideling Hill
Catalpa #5380   C. (304) 443-5920
PO Box 165, Hancock, MD 21750-0165   catalpapineyplainsumc@gmail.com
(12314 Willow Rd)
Piney Plains #5385   C. (304) 433-5920
12708 Faith Cir NE, Little Orleans, MD 21766   catalpapineyplainsumc@gmail.com
  Joshua D. Rider PL   R. (304) 433-5920
  13203 Mann Rd NE, Little Orleans, MD 21766-1026   jdrider@k12.wv.us

St Andrews #5345   C. (301) 739-7431
1020 Maryland Ave, Hagerstown, MD 21740   standrewsumchagerstown@gmail.com
  Christopher N. Serufusa FE   R. (240) 452-1918
  1014 Maryland Ave, Hagerstown, MD 21740-7202   cserufusa@gmail.com

Sulphur Springs #5615
26600 Gorman Rd SE, Oldtown, MD 21555
   William G. (Barney) Piper LM
   20816 Oldtown Rd SE, Oldtown, MD 21555-1133

C. (301) 478-5244
barneycathy@gmail.com
R. (301) 478-5244
barneycathy@gmail.com

Trinity #5245
122 Grand Ave, Cumberland, MD 21502-3911
   Mary George SY
   15306 Greenleaf Dr SW, Cumberland, MD 21502-5714

C. (301) 729-6828
TrinityCumberland5245@gmail.com
R. (301) 729-6828
rmgeorge44@gmail.com

Union Chapel #5570
10123 Valley Rd, Berkeley Springs, WV 25411-3397
   Michael J. Leedom FE
   82 Chapel Ln, Berkeley Springs, WV 25411-6727

C. (304) 258-2107
UCUMCWV@gmail.com
R. (304) 707-1250
pmikeunionchapel@gmail.com

Washington Square #5360
538 Washington Ave., Hagerstown, MD 21740-4662
   Jerry J. Lowans FE
   237 Collins Dr, Martinsburg, WV 25403

C. (301) 739-2653
whagumparish@gmail.com
R. (304) 279-9051
jerrylowans1@gmail.com

Wesley
Centenary #5185
12916 N Cresap St Apt 19, Cumberland, MD 21502-5201
Zion #5250
12916 N Cresap St Apt 19, Cumberland, MD 21502-5201
   Marjorie J. Hurder Buhrman SY
   14801 Bell St, Cresaptown, MD 21502-6589

C. (601) 310-9922
marjoriehurder@gmail.com
C. (601) 310-9922
marjoriehurder@gmail.com
R. (601) 310-9922
marjoriehurder@gmail.com

Williamsport #5475
25 E Church St, Williamsport, MD 21795-1549
   Phillip R. (Ray) Roberson FE
   17703 Daisy Dr, Hagerstown, MD 21740-9156

C. (301) 223-7040
williamsportumc@gmail.com
R. (240) 291-7260
rayroberson@icloud.com

Extension Ministry
   Solomon O. Lloyd FE
   6103 Chia Ave, Twentynine Palms, CA 92277-1951

R. (410) 504-4962
Solomon.lloyd@usmc.mil

   Cynthia I. Zirlott OD
   100 Braddock St Unit 308, Frostburg, MD 21532-2479

R. (540) 303-2309
c.zirlott@frostburg.edu

Retired
   Ann Atkins RE
   886 Sperry Ter, Cumberland, MD 21502-3405

R. (301) 268-6597
annvatkins@gmail.com

   Harold P. (Hal) Atkins RE
   886 Sperry Ter, Cumberland, MD 21502-3405

R. (301) 268-6785
hpatkins@outlook.com

   Rebecca K. (Kay) Barger RE
   18710 Dover Dr, Hagerstown, MD 21742-2468

R. (240) 707-6516
rkbrkb@myactv.net

   William H. (Bill) Bice RE
   14706 Uhl Hwy SE, Cumberland, MD 21502-8447

R. (301) 724-5726
whbsr@atlanticbb.net

   Joseph R. Bradshaw RL
   78 W Washington St Apt 102, Chambersburg, PA 17201-2418

R. (717) 830-2664
georgiepie41@aol.com

David R. Brosnan RE
2003 Trent Blvd, New Bern, NC 28560-5323

R. (252) 288-6562
sbrosnan@gmail.com

Harry L. Burchell, Jr. RA
11504 Mountain Magic Ln, Cumberland, MD 21502

R. (301) 777-3429
Nightwatch@atlanticbb.net

Roger E. Burtner RE
35 Mount Hebron Rd, Keedysville, MD 21756-1357

R. (301) 432-5772
reb21756@msn.com

Eugene D. (Dwight) Byrne RE
2931 Bloom Rd, Finksburg, MD 21048-1802

pastorbyrne@yahoo.com

Richard C. Chambers RE
3385 Scar Hill Rd, Greencastle, PA 17225-9633

R. (717) 597-5602

John Close RL
17960 Garden Ln Apt 1, Hagerstown, MD 21740-8003

R. (301) 707-0976
johndclose@gmail.com

Merle D. Correll RE
26501 Oldtown Rd SE, Oldtown, MD 21555-2026

R. (301) 478-5116
merlepat@gmail.com

Richard Craig RE
269 Keystone Ln, Berkeley Springs, WV 25411-3426

R. (304) 754-3393
RBCraig3@comcast.net

George Earle, Jr. RE
14037 Barnhart Rd, Clear Spring, MD 21722-1140

R. (301) 842-1130
pastrgeo@gmail.com

Howard R. (Ron) Ellis RE
12404 Loy Wolfe Rd, Myersville, MD 21773-9507

R. (301) 293-8961
ellisron@comcast.net

Louis L. Emerick RA
8507 Mapleville Rd, Boonsboro, MD 21713-1818

R. (301) 791-6335

Robert (Rob) Fisher SY
146 Coite Ln, Statesville, NC 28625-1659

R. (704) 677-8826
rob.fisher1@gmail.com

John Footen RA
341 Channing Dr, Chambersburg, PA 17201-3230

R. (301) 707-9585
johnfooten@hotmail.com

Lawrence R. Frye RE
874 Mount Jackson Rd, Mount Jackson, VA 22842-2864

R. (540) 477-4226

Lowell S. Garland RE
3900 Camphor Pl, Cocoa, FL 32926-3163

R. (321) 633-0906
lowellruth@hotmail.com

Jack R. George RE
15607 Winslow St SW, Cumberland, MD 21502-5850

R. (301) 729-3013
jackandelise65@aol.com

Nancy L. Green RL
1605 Mount Aetna Rd, Hagerstown, MD 21742-6735

R. (301) 797-5433
pastornancy@pipeline.com

James M. (Max) Greenfield RE
11608 Bierman Dr SE, Cumberland, MD 21502-6407

R. (301) 338-2336
maxgreen77@atlanticbb.net

Robert Hershberger RE
35 Frost Ln, Cornwall, NY 12518-1305

R. (845) 534-9270
hershny@aol.com

Frederick Iser RL
23 E Mary St, Cumberland, MD 21502-4721

R. (301) 777-0756
revfrediser@hotmail.com

William C. Kercheval RL
301 Chesapeake Dr Unit D, Waynesboro, PA 17268-7984

R. 717-655-5582
wckercheval@aol.com

Lamar W. Kopp RE
Quincy Village, 6596 Orphanage Rd, Waynesboro, PA 17268

R. (717) 749-6596
lwkopp@gmail.com

Richard A. Kroll RE
10849 Donelson Dr, Williamsport, MD 21795-1421

R. (301) 223-9318
rkroll1089@gmail.com

Janice Leith RE
10020 Christie Rd SE, Cumberland, MD 21502-8242

R. (410) 440-5179
janleith@juno.com

Frank R. (Richard) Leslie RE
317 Adam Rd, Frederick, MD 21701-6327

R. (908) 473-7768
jalrl@comcast.net

Lillian Myers DR
Cottage 1223, Williamsport, MD 21795-1321

R. (301) 223-6759
lillbud@msn.com

Lawrence A. Neumark RE
307 Chieftan Ln, Boonsboro, MD 21713-2651

R. (301) 432-4747
neumark@myactv.net

Gene R. Perry RE
45 Deer Ridge, Norris, TN 37828-0069

R. (865) 494-6570
generayperry@bellsouth.net

Kristina Peterson RE
106 Sandalwood Dr, Gray, LA 70359-4611

R. (304) 266-2517
krajeskipeterson@msn.com

Leonard B. Ranson, Jr. RE
908 Harvest Dr NW, Cedar Rapids, IA 52405-2808

Clayton E. Rhodes RE
184 Baker St, Rimersburg, PA 16248-4326

R. (814) 473-3844

Lawrence P. (Pat) Ricker RE
18914 Rolling Rd, Hagerstown, MD 21742-2661

R. (301) 733-3520
revpatricker@gmail.com

Stephen Robison RE
867 Dewey Ave, Hagerstown, MD 21742-3938

R. (301) 791-7148
s.robison@myactv.net

Bernadette M. Ross RE
1072 Braddock Rd, Cumberland, MD 21502-1924

R. (301) 724-2414
bross@atlanticbb.net

William R. Sansom RL
5 Fairfield Dr, Baltimore, MD 21228-5026

Wilson A. Shearer RE
163 Sunbrook Ln, Hagerstown, MD 21742-4197

R. (301) 739-1613
wilsonshearer@aol.com

Donald W. (Wayne) Sloan RL
1058 Beans Cove Rd, Clearville, PA 15535-8030

R. (814) 767-9418
janesloan28@yahoo.com

Hayden L. Sparks RE
107 Fairview Ave, Frederick, MD 21701-4017

R. (301) 682-6942

Kathy Spitzer RE
340 Bennett Ln, Berkeley Springs, WV 25411-4706

R. (304) 261-2572
spitz49@frontier.com

Gary W. Trail RE
PO Box 745, Ridgeley, WV 26753-0745

R. (304) 738-1054

Mary S. Trail RE
PO Box 745, Ridgeley, WV 26753-0745

R. (304) 738-1054

Dennis L. Upton RE
16505 Virginia Ave Unit 1001, Williamsport, MD 21795-1426

R. (301) 223-7918
dupton94@myactv.net

Rebecca J. Vardiman RE
437 Independence St, Cumberland, MD 21502-1611

R. (301) 777-9046
rebeccavardiman@gmail.com

Edwin H. Welch RE
1910 Kanawha Ave SE, Charleston, WV 25304-1020

R. (304) 343-3946
edwinwelch@ucwv.edu

FREDERICK DISTRICT

Superintendent
Edgardo Rivera FE
200 Shannonbrook Ln, Frederick, MD 21702-3637
erivera@bwcumc.org

(410) 309-3480
R. (301) 660-7513

Arden #6510
4464 Arden Nollville Rd, Martinsburg, WV 25403-6109
Mi Ja (Mi) Cho PE
208 Daintree Dr, Martinsburg, WV 25403-1323

C. (304) 267-6165
mayblessyou@gmail.com
R. (703) 973-2004
mayblessyou@gmail.com

Asbury #6700
4257 Kearneysville Pike, Shepherdstown, WV 25443
Rudy Bropleh FE
262 Maddex Farm Dr, Shepherdstown, WV 25443

C. (304) 876-3112
info@4pillarchurch.org
R. (304) 707-2276
pastorb@4pillarchurch.org

Asbury #6180
101 W All Saints St, Frederick, MD 21701-5519
Mark A. Groover PE
4012 Frankford Ave, Baltimore, MD 21206-3531

C. (301) 663-9380
asburyumcfmd1@verizon.net
R. (443) 392-2075
newhope37@verizon.net

Asbury #6530
110 W North St, Charles Town, WV 25414-1524
Duane Jensen FE
511 S Church St, Charles Town, WV 25414-1313

C. (304) 725-5513
churchoffice@myasburychurch.org
R. (301) 331-0432
pastorduane@comcast.net

Bedington #6520
580 Bedington Rd, Martinsburg, WV 25404-6509
William S. (Scott) Summers FL
580 Bedington Rd, Martinsburg, WV 25404-6509

C. (304) 274-2011
Bedingtonumc@frontier.com
R. (240) 625-0858
revscooter65@gmail.com

Berkeley Pl.-Friendship
Berkeley Place #6645
133 Spruce St, Martinsburg, WV 25401-4234
Friendship #6660
166 Locust Grove Rd, Hedgesville, WV 25427-3072
Julia L. (Lisa) Franzen PL
PO Box 1925, Inwood, WV 25428-1925

C. (304) 754-7891
readsps27@gmail.com
C. (304) 754-7891
readsps27@gmail.com
R. (304) 229-2275
readsps27@gmail.com

Bethel #6515
PO Box 236, Bakerton, WV 25410-0236
Scott Sassaman PL
108 Kendig Ln, Martinsburg, WV 25404-7701

C. (304) 876-3467
gvancamp@frontiernet.net
R. (304) 616-2810
pastorsassy16@gmail.com

Bethesda #4445
328 Klee Mill Rd, Sykesville, MD 21784-9242
Richard D. Lindsay RL
5463 Gloucester Rd, Columbia, MD 21044-1911

C. (410) 795-7677
drlpastor1@verizon.net
R. (443) 864-6727
drlpastor1@verizon.net

Blairton #6650
71 Upper Road, Martinsburg, WV 25402
   Gary W. Gourley, Sr. SY
   295 Constitution Blvd, Martinsburg, WV 25405-8340

C. (304) 264-3607
garyandbarbieg@frontier.com
R. (304) 264-3607
garyandbarbieg@frontier.com

Bolivar/Engle
Bolivar #6560
PO Box 205, Harpers Ferry, WV 25425-6322
(1215 W Washington St)

C. (304) 535-1375
srtryon@yahoo.com

Engle #6575
1563 Engle Switch Road, Harpers Ferry, WV 25425
   Sam Tryon PL
   300 Cormorant Pl Apt 2004, Frederick, MD 21701-1929

C. (304) 535-6882
srtryon@yahoo.com
R. (740) 513-5582
srtryon@yahoo.com

Brandenburg #4580
PO Box 1233, Sykesville, MD 21784-8626
(6050 Old Washington Rd)
   Mark Eyler PL
   221 Apples Church Rd, Thurmont, MD 21788-1703

C. (410) 549-7822
pastormark1umc@gmail.com
R. (301) 271-7939
pastormark1umc@gmail.com

Brook Hill #6185
8946 Indian Springs Rd, Frederick, MD 21702
   Dana L. Werts FE
   PO Box 2938, Westminster, MD 21158-7938

C. (301) 662-1727
brookhill@bhumc.org
R. (240) 651-5178
dwerts@bhumc.org

Buckeystown Rt.80 #6145
6923 Michael's Mills RD, Buckeystown, MD 21717
   Derek T. Shackelford SY
   20 N Court St Unit 1, Frederick, MD 21701-5448

C. (301) 874-3930
shackque1911@yahoo.com
R. (240) 344-0491
shackque1911@yahoo.com

Buckeystown Rt 85 #6150
PO Box 399, Buckeystown, MD 21717-0399
(3440 Buckeystown Pike)
   Charles Rice PL
   3441 Buckeystown Pike, Buckeystown, MD 21717-0553

C. (301) 874-2313
rice.charles@live.com
R. (240) 608-5338
rice.charles@live.com

Bunker Hill #6525
PO Box 327, Bunker Hill, WV 25413-2589
(9863 Winchester Ave)
   Daniel Breidenbaugh PE
   9887 Winchester Ave, Bunker Hill, WV 25413

C. (304) 229-8508
bhumchurch@gmail.com
R. (410) 487-2707
dbreidenbaugh@gmail.com

Butlers Chapel #6590
29 Butlers Chapel Rd, Martinsburg, WV 25403-0983
   Forrest Cummings SY
   179 Alydar Rd, Hedgesville, WV 25427-7366

fcummings@frontier.com
R. (304) 654-4714
fhc44@aol.com

Calvary #6655
220 W Burke St, Martinsburg, WV 25401-3322
   Teresa Aguilera SY
   349 Gantt Dr, Martinsburg, WV 25403-0278

   Lynn L. Wilson FL
   53 Adelade Cir, Harpers Ferry, WV 25425-6949

C. (304) 267-4542
pastorlynnumc@comcast.net

salvation320@hotmail.com

R. (304) 728-7530
pastorlynnumc@comcast.net

Calvary #4260
3939 Gamber Rd, Finksburg, MD 21048-2516
Beth A. (Beth Anne) Hutton FE
1800 Fallstaff Ct, Eldersburg, MD 21784-6274

C. (410) 795-9343
office@calvaryumcgamber.org
R. (240) 388-6877
pastorbethhutton@gmail.com

Calvary #6190
131 W 2nd St, Frederick, MD 21701-5328
Stephen L. Larsen FE
131 W 2nd St, Frederick, MD 21701-5328

C. (301) 662-1464
office@calvaryumc.org
R. (301) 848-8216
RevSteve@calvaryumc.org

Shannon Sullivan FE
6604 S Clifton Rd, Frederick, MD 21703-5838

R. (410) 937-8835
RevShannon@calvaryumc.org

Julie Wilson FD
16252 Toms Creek Church Rd, Emmitsburg, MD 21727-8437

R. (410) 758-7705
JMW1976@gmail.com

Camp Hill-Wesley #6565
PO Box 1, Harpers Ferry, WV 25425-0001
(645 W Washington Street)
John Unger OF
1022 Williamsport Pike, Martinsburg, WV 25404-4274

C. (304) 535-6882
olvaughn@frontiernet.net

R. (304) 389-1866
PastorUnger@gmail.com

Catoctin #6355
7009 Kellys Store Rd, Thurmont, MD 21788-3025
Terry R. Orrence, Jr. PL
6626 Gooseander Ct, Frederick, MD 21703-9535

C. (301) 271-3885
kelkelbelle@hotmail.com
R. (240) 344-0433
rtojr55@yahoo.com

Centennial Memorial #6210
8 W 2nd St, Frederick, MD 21701-5327
Debra M. Linton FL
2045 Spring Run Cir, Frederick, MD 21702-6808

C. (301) 663-5273
lintondebra@gmail.com
R. (301) 447-5955
lintondebra@gmail.com

Chestnut Hill #6570
1523 Hostler Rd, Harpers Ferry, WV 25425
William (Bill) Rowley PL
2985 Kabletown Rd, Charles Town, WV 25414-4773

C. (703) 626-4978
bxrowley@gmail.com
R. (703) 626-4978
bxrowley1952@yahoo.com

Darkesville #6545
PO Box 746, Inwood, WV 25428-0746
(6705 Winchester Ave)
Thomas Sigler PL
Eastland Drive 226 Eastland Dr, Charles Town, WV 25414

C. (304) 229-2406
darkesville@gmail.com

R. (240) 446-9731
tesigler@gmail.com

Deer Park #4535
2205 Sykesville Rd, Westminster, MD 21157-7613
John H. Dean FL
1531 S Rambling Way, Frederick, MD 21701-2515

C. (410) 848-2313
csaylor@dpumc.net
R. (240) 575-9313
jdpreacher@outlook.com

Deerfield #6260
16405 Foxville Deerfield Rd, Sabillasville, MD 21780-9020
Ray Dudley PL
7316 Lakeview Rd, Frederick, MD 21701

C. (301) 241-3036
rwfgd@comcast.net
R. (301) 898-5456
rwfgd@comcast.net

Ganotown #6550
1018 Winchester Ave, Martinsburg, WV 25401-1650
William L. Arnicar SY
25 Crab Apple Ln, Ranson, WV 25438-1247

C. (304) 267-4861
warnicar@comcast.net
R. (304) 839-6880
warnicar@comcast.net

Gerrardstown #6555
1781 Gerrardstown Road, Gerrardstown, WV 25420
Gary Sieglein RL
110 Dominion Rd, Gerrardstown, WV 25420-4378

C. (304) 229-2351
parsonumc@gmail.com
R. (410) 286-1201
parsonumc@gmail.com

Greater Brunswick
Doubs-Epworth #6160
5131 Doubs Rd, Adamstown, MD 21710-8920
Jefferson #6240
3882 Jefferson Pike, Jefferson, MD 21755-8121
New Hope of Greater Brunswick #6137
7 S Maryland Ave, Brunswick, MD 21716-1110
Kathryn Bishop FE
30 8th Ave, Brunswick, MD 21716-1736

C. (301) 810-5430
wcarpen14a@gmail.com
C. (301) 810-5430
wcarpen14a@gmail.com
C. (301) 834-7320
newhopebrunswick@gmail.com
R. (240) 818-2828
pastorkatiebishop@yahoo.com

William Carpenter SY
5551 Doubs Rd, Adamstown, MD 21710-8912

R. (904) 729-9484
wcarpen14a@gmail.com

Harmony #6640
PO Box 1510, Falling Waters, WV 25419-1510
(9455 Williamsport Pike)
Jeff Zalatoris FE
606 S Raleigh St, Martinsburg, WV 25401-2144

C. (304) 274-1719
jzalatoris1@gmail.com

R. (681) 260-2772
jzalatoris1@gmail.com

Hedgesville #6610
201 S Mary St, Hedgesville, WV 25427-7459
Dennis Jackman FE
PO Box 2602, Martinsburg, WV 25402-2602

C. (304) 754-8793
humc.hedgesville@gmail.com
R. (304) 267-2998
drdejackman@gmail.com

Hopehill #6155
7647 Fingerboard Rd, Frederick, MD 21704-7634
David Fossett PL
7647 Fingerboard Rd, Frederick, MD 21704-7634

C. (301) 874-1166
pastordavid@hopehillumc.org
R. (301) 874-1166
pastordavid@hopehillumc.org

Inwood #6615
62 True Apple Way, Inwood, WV 25428
John Lewis RL
PO Box 1925, Inwood, WV 25428-1925

C. (304) 676-5202
talkmanjohn@gmail.com
R. (540) 931-3615
talkmanjohn@gmail.com

Jackson Chapel #6330
5609 Ballenger Creek Pike, Frederick, MD 21703-7009
Rex R. Bowens, Sr. FL
817 Trail Ave, Frederick, MD 21701-4522

C. (301) 694-7315
rexbowenssr@comcast.net
R. (240) 409-7313
rexbowenssr@comcast.net

Johnsville #4450
1124 Johnsville Rd, Sykesville, MD 21784-8432
Thomas Cook SY
11285 Old Frederick Rd, Marriottsville, MD 21104

C. (410) 581-3062
jumc1124@gmail.com
R. (410) 442-2761
pastorcook01@yahoo.com

Johnsville #4523
11106 Green Valley Rd, Union Bridge, MD 21791-8408
   Shari McCourt FE
   S2120 Paddock Lane, Finksburg, MD 21048

C. (410) 775-7217
sharimccourt@aol.com
R. (410) 596-4040
sharimccourt@aol.com

Leetown #6630
11133 Leetown Rd, Kearneysville, WV 25430-5521
   Deborah Mooney PL
   635 Bashore Dr, Martinsburg, WV 25404-7604

C. (304) 725-8304
leetownumc@frontiernet.net
R. (304) 271-8936
debsark3@gmail.com

Lewistown #6265
11032 Hessong Bridge Rd, Thurmont, MD 21788-2810
   Caitlin Mossburg PL
   9308 Bethel Rd, Frederick, MD 21702-2010

C. (301) 898-7888
lumc21788@comcast.net
R. (301) 662-4094
pastor.katym@gmail.com

Liberty Central #6800
PO Box 337, 12024 Main St, Libertytown, MD 21762-0337
   Jerry Cline FE
   PO Box 337, Libertytown, MD 21762-0337

C. (301) 898-7305
jerrymarkc@comcast.net
R. (301) 898-7505
jerrymarkc@comcast.net

Linganore #6375
8921 Clemsonville Rd, Union Bridge, MD 21791-7413
   Stephen Ricketts FE
   8919 Clemsonville Rd, Union Bridge, MD 21791-7413

C. (301) 829-6937
LinganoreUMC@gmail.com
R. (240) 308-2148
srricketts@verizon.net

Marvin Chapel #6670
PO Box 1925, Inwood, WV 25428-1925
   John Lewis RL
   PO Box 1925, Inwood, WV 25428-1925

C. (304) 229-2275
talkmanjohn@gmail.com
R. (540) 931-3615
talkmanjohn@gmail.com

Memorial #6755
46 Steptoe St, PO Box 10, Summit Point, WV 25446-0010

C. (443) 841-2219
pastored@hopemtcarmel.org

Messiah #4475
20 Middle St, Taneytown, MD 21787-2120
   Richard Baker FL
   3893 Sells Mill Rd, Taneytown, MD 21787-2547

C. (410) 756-6085
rwb1.pastor@yahoo.com
R. (443) 375-9556
rwb1.pastor@yahoo.com

Middleburg-Uniontown
Middleburg #4490
3403 Uniontown Rd, Westminster, MD 21158-3577
Uniontown #4510
3403 Uniontown Rd, Westminster, MD 21158-3577
   Darrell I. Davis PL
   4639 Bark Hill Rd, Union Bridge, MD 21791

C. (410) 848-6940
dav1pat2@hotmail.com
C. (301) 639-9577
dav1pat2@hotmail.com
R. (301) 639-9577
dav1pat2@hotmail.com

Middletown #6280
7108 Fern Ct, Middletown, MD 21769-7440
   Kenneth Dunnington RE
   620 Humberson Ln, Frederick, MD 21703-2223

C. (301) 371-5550
admin@mtownumc.org
R. (301) 631-5605
krdunnington@gmail.com

   Evelyn Rivera PE
   200 Shannonbrook Ln, Frederick, MD 21702-3637

R. (301) 473-4645
pastorevelyn@mtownumc.org

Middleway #6635
7435 Queen St, Kearneysville, WV 25430-0580
   Scott Sassaman PL
   108 Kendig Ln, Martinsburg, WV 25404-7701

    C. (304) 728-4770
    mumc@frontiernet.net
    R. (304) 616-2810
    pastorsassy16@gmail.com

Mount Zion #6675
PO Box 3222 , Martinsburg, WV 25401-2720
(532 W Martin St)
   Edward Hall RL
   271 Polk St, Harpers Ferry, WV 25425-6347

    C. (304) 263-2667
    pastoredhall@frontiernet.net
    R. (304) 535-2765
    pastoredhall@frontiernet.net

Mt Carmel/New Market
Mount Carmel #6335
9411 Baltimore Rd, Frederick, MD 21704-6752
New Market #6340
PO Box 111, New Market, MD 21774-0111
(5501 Old New Market Rd)
   Scott Clawson FL
   9602 Baltimore Rd, Frederick, MD 21704-6756

   Jenny Smith FE
   6102 Dover St, Frederick, MD 21704-6694

    C. (301) 696-9735
    donna.clawson@hopemtcarmel.org
    C. (301) 865-3530
    hometownchurch@comcast.net

    R. (240) 409-8119
    pastorscott62@gmail.com

    R. (240) 409-4722
    crazymethodists@comcast.net

Mt Wesley-Greensburg
Greensburg #6665
2171 Greensburg Rd, Martinsburg, WV 25404-0364
Mount Wesley #6735
4622 Scrabble Rd, Shepherdstown, WV 25443-4083
   George E. (Ed) Grove RE
   108 Forman Rd E, Shepherdstown, WV 25443-3578

    C. (304) 261-2513
    edhfhep@gmail.com
    C. (304) 261-2513
    edhfhep@gmail.com
    R. (304) 267-6325
    edhfhep@gmail.com

Murrill Hill #6580
16 Hilltop Rd, Harpers Ferry, WV 25425-5929
   Donnie J. Cardwell RL
   3036 Cherry Run Rd, Hedgesville, WV 25427-6099

    C. (304) 725-3959
    des769@comcast.net
    R. (304) 596-7349
    3036dc@comcast.net

New Hope of New Windsor #4640
3001 Hooper Rd, New Windsor, MD 21776-8121
   Mary Buzby PL
   2126 Mayberry Rd, Westminster, MD 21158-2509

    C. (443) 465-5024
    new_hope_pastor_mary@live.com
    R. (443) 465-5024
    bzbymry@aol.com

New Street #6750
PO Box 188, Shepherdstown, WV 25443-0188
(202 West New Street)
   Geri D. (Dee-Ann) Dixon FE
   655 Deer Mountain Dr, Harpers Ferry, WV 25425-5475

    C. (304) 876-2362
    nsumc@frontiernet.net

    R. (304) 268-8521
    dixon-gross@655dmd.com

Oakland #6535
70 Oakland Ter, Charles Town, WV 25414-4869
   Richard G. Shuman, II PL
   104 Spyglass Hill Dr, Charles Town, WV 25414-3963

    C. (304) 725-3737
    oaklandchurchumc@gmail.com
    R. (304) 886-2106
    shumanrick@comcast.net

Oakland #4275
5901 Mineral Hill Rd, Sykesville, MD 21784-6824
Robert Wellman RE
1932 Carrollton Rd, Finksburg, MD 21048-1133

C. (410) 795-5030
Office@oaklandumc.org
R. (410) 622-5558
bobwellman@comcast.net

Otterbein #6680
PO Box 2378, Martinsburg, WV 25402-2378

Patricia L. Sebring FE
122 Metro Dr, Martinsburg, WV 25404-1419

C. (304) 263-0342
secretary@otterbeinumc.net
(549 North Queen Street)
R. (443) 510-3308
revdrpls@gmail.com

Paynes Chapel #6730
PO Box 354, Bunker Hill, WV 25413-0354

Dawn Reidy PL
1116 Hyslip Ford Rd, Bunker Hill, WV 25413-2976

C. (304) 229-5220
payneschapel@frontier.com
(631 Avanti Drive)
R. (304) 671-0387
dreidy7@comcast.net

Pikeside #6725
25 Paynes Ford Rd, Martinsburg, WV 25405-5854
William C. (Bill) Ball FL
565 Tuscawilla Dr, Charles Town, WV 25414-5061

C. (304) 263-4633
info@pikesideumc.org
R. (304) 579-3233
billballwv@gmail.com

Pleasant View #6165
1865 Pleasant View Rd, Adamstown, MD 21710-9021
Margaret Clark SY
606 Souder Rd, Brunswick, MD 21716-1735

C. (410) 442-2761
mclark615@verizon.net
R. (301) 834-7519
mclark615@verizon.net

Sandy Hook/Shenandoah Memorial
Sandy Hook #6255
19018 Sandyhook Rd, Knoxville, MD 21758-1327
Shenandoah Memorial #6715
436 Bloomery Road, Harpers Ferry, WV 25425
Sharon L. Lowans SY
237 Collins Dr, Martinsburg, WV 25403

C. (304) 676-6774
pastorsharonlynn@gmail.com
C. (304) 535-1375
pastorsharonlynn@gmail.com
R. (304) 676-6774
pastorsharonlynn@gmail.com

Sandy Mount #4443
2101 Old Westminster Pike, Finksburg, MD 21048
Kathy L. Altman FE
165 Winifred Dr, Hanover, PA 17331-7993

C. (410) 861-5788
sandymtumc@comcast.net
R. (240) 285-5800
RevKathyAltman@verizon.net

Shenandoah
Bethesda #6720
3415 Kearneysville Pike, Shepherdstown, WV 25443
Uvilla #6760
3415 Kearneysville Pike, Shepherdstown, WV 25443
Williams Memorial #6740
3415 Kearneysville Pike, Shepherdstown, WV 25443
John S. Langenstein CC
3415 Kearneysville Pike, Shepherdstown, WV 25443

C. (304) 876-6272
pastor@sj-umc.org
C. (304) 876-6272
pastor@sj-umc.org
C. (304) 876-6272
pastor@sj-umc.org
R. (202) 487-1418
jslangenstein@gmail.com

Silver Grove #6585
95 Church Hill Ln, Harpers Ferry, WV 25425-5149
Michael Lida PL
40141 McKees Gap Road, Warfordsburg, PA 17267

C. (304) 725-8608
silvergroveum@gmail.com
R. (301) 491-8357
pastormikelida@gmail.com

St. James #4540
3000 Marston Rd, Westminster, MD 21157-7718
Mary Buzby PL
2126 Mayberry Rd, Westminster, MD 21158-2509

C. (443) 536-7433
New_Hope_Pastor_Mary@live.com
R. (443) 465-5024
bzbymry@aol.com

St Lukes #6690
700 New York Ave, Martinsburg, WV 25401-2124
Mike M. Cantley FE
215 Wren St N, Martinsburg, WV 25405-8895

C. (304) 263-2788
stlukesumc700@comcast.net
R. (443) 501-6028
Revcantley@gmail.com

St Paul #4620
PO Box 250, New Windsor, MD 21776-0250
Shari McCourt FE
S2120 Paddock Lane, Finksburg, MD 21048

C. (410) 635-2442
stpaulnewwindsor@gmail.com
R. (410) 596-4040
sharimccourt@aol.com

Stone Chapel #4545
1448 Stone Chapel Rd, New Windsor, MD 21776-8802
YuJung Hwang FE
20331 Dickerson Church Rd, Dickerson, MD 20842-9526

C. (410) 635-2102
puri315@hotmail.com
R. (703) 303-2366
puri315@hotmail.com

Strawbridge #4365
PO Box 353, New Windsor, MD 21776-0353
Blango Ross, Jr. PL
317 Brushwood Dr, Owings Mills, MD 21117-1382

C. (410) 635-6480
oneministry@strawbridgeumc.org
R. (443) 739-9591
ambrossjr@verizon.net

Taylorsville #4485
4356 Ridge Rd, Mount Airy, MD 21771-8932
Julie Wilson FD
16252 Toms Creek Church Rd, Emmitsburg, MD 21727-8437

C. (410) 875-4101
taylorsvilleumc@comcast.net
R. (410) 758-7705
JMW1976@gmail.com

Thurmont #6360
13880 Long Rd, Thurmont, MD 21788-2261
Ken J. Fizer, Jr. FE
13880 Long Rd, Thurmont, MD 21788-2261

C. (301) 271-4511
kfizer@minister.com
R. (301) 271-4511
kfizer@minister.com

Tom's Creek #6170
10926 Simmons Rd, Emmitsburg, MD 21727-8400
Heath Wilson FE
16252 Toms Creek Church Rd, Emmitsburg, MD 21727-8437

C. (301) 447-3171
tomscreekumc@gmail.com
R. (410) 758-7707
HWilsonVT@gmail.com

Trinity #6175
313 W Main St, Emmitsburg, MD 21727-9195
Richard Baker FL
3893 Sells Mill Rd, Taneytown, MD 21787-2547

C. (301) 447-3740
rwb1.pastor@yahoo.com
R. (443) 375-9556
rwb1.pastor@yahoo.com

Trinity #6225
703 W Patrick St, Frederick, MD 21701-4029
  Eliezer Valentin-Castanon   FE
  703 W Patrick St, Frederick, MD 21701-4029

  Mark Claiborne, Sr.   PL
  13816 Exeter Ct, Hagerstown, MD 21742-5313

C. (301) 662-2895
tumc@trinityfrederick.org
R. (301) 620-8885
seniorpastor@trinityfrederick.org

R. (301) 524-6000
mclaib819@yahoo.com

Trinity #6710
220 W Martin St, Martinsburg, WV 25401-3331
  Kenneth W. (Ken) Walker   FE
  600 Artisan Way, Martinsburg, WV 25401-2999

C. (304) 263-9215
umctrinity@comcast.net
R. (304) 850-8696
pastorkenw@comcast.net

Union Street #4550
22 Union St, Westminster, MD 21157-4508
  Richard D. Lindsay   RL
  5463 Gloucester Rd, Columbia, MD 21044-1911

C. (410) 861-5822
Drlpastor1@verizon.net
R. (443) 864-6727
drlpastor1@verizon.net

Walkersville & Mt. Pleasant
Mount Pleasant #6390
9550 Liberty Rd, Frederick, MD 21701-3247
Walkersville #6420
22 Main St, Walkersville, MD 21793
  Richard Gibbs   PL
  10645 Powell Rd, Thurmont, MD 21788-2832

  Charles M. (Mike) Henning   FE
  7010 Keysville Rd, Keymar, MD 21757-9607

C. (301) 898-5292
mypastorrich@aol.com
C. (301) 845-9860
revmikehenning@gmail.com
R. (301) 898-7277
mypastorrich@aol.com

R. (443) 331-3295
revmikehenning@gmail.com

Weller #6365
101 N Altamont Ave, Thurmont, MD 21788-1850
  Robert E. (Bob) Kells, Jr.   FE
  101 Dogwood Ave, Thurmont, MD 21788-1604

C. (301) 271-2802
secretary@wellerumc.com
R. (301) 271-2838
rkellsjr@gmail.com

Westminster #4555
165 E Main St, Westminster, MD 21157-5013
  Malcolm Stranathan   FE
  20 Ridge View Dr, Westminster, MD 21157-4460

C. (410) 848-8325
S.Haines@wumcmd.org
R. (410) 660-6606
m.stranathan@wumcmd.org

Zion #4560
2716 Old Washington Rd, Westminster, MD 21157-7546
  YuJung Hwang   FE
  20331 Dickerson Church Rd, Dickerson, MD 20842-9526

C. (410) 857-4444
puri315@hotmail.com
R. (703) 303-2366
puri315@hotmail.com

Certified Lay Minister
  Jack Charlton   LM
  28 Shoal Creek Ct, Martinsburg, WV 25405-5745

  Bertram Edmonston, III   LM
  13410 Tower Rd, Thurmont, MD 21788-1411

  Sherie L. Koob   LM
  3819 S Mountain Rd, Knoxville, MD 21758-9606

R. (304) 260-0108
charltons5@msn.com

R. (240) 367-6139
gtjc460@aol.com

R. (202) 329-7113
sheriekoob@hotmail.com

Extension Ministry

Giovanni Arroyo FE
7612 Harmons Farm Ct, Hanover, MD 21076

R. (202) 495-2943
garroyog@aol.com

Mark A. Lancaster FE
4519 Sweet Potato Ridge Rd, Englewood, OH 45322

R. (502) 222-5886
marklancaster116@juno.com

Incapacity Leave

Elizabeth J. Richards FE
1006 Columbine Dr Apt 1A, Frederick, MD 21701

sunfirebeth50@gmail.com

Leave of Absence

Sherri Comer-Cox PE
2635 Old Taneytown Rd, Westminster, MD 21158-3531

R. (240) 925-6669
scomercox@msn.com

Sarah B. Dorrance FE
202 Cone Branch Dr, Middletown, MD 21769-7843

R. (301) 471-9321
sarahdorrance@gmail.com

Medical Leave

Robert Brennan, Jr. FE
173 Serpentine Way, Martinsburg, WV 25405-1108

R. (304) 901-4591
rbrennan001@gmail.com

Katherine A. Heflin FE
1435 N Ford St, Lapel, IN 46051-9640

midorikate37@gmail.com

On Loan

Ginger Medley FE
1169 Heron Ave, Miami Springs, FL 33166-3118

R. (540) 877-0680
g19751997@hotmail.com

Retired

Jo Anne Alexander RE
104 Oakland Ter, Charles Town, WV 25414-4815

R. (304) 725-5233
rev.joanne@gmail.com

John W. (William) Bennett RD
3 Sara Ln, Middletown, MD 21769-7885

R. (301) 371-6866
john_30201@msn.com

Bruce C. Birch RE
3030 Mill Island Pkwy, Frederick, MD 21701-6819

R. (301) 846-0313
brucecbirch@mac.com

Sharon K. Bourgeois RE
12411 Winchester Ave, Bunker Hill, WV 25413-2602

R. (304) 229-4702
bourgeois@springsips.com

Walter F. Bowers RE
403 Silver Ln, Martinsburg, WV 25401-3122

R. (304) 262-6512
bowerspep@aol.com

William R. Boyer RE
355 Grey Friars Rd, Westminster, MD 21158-3707

R. (410) 857-9003
w.m.boyer@comcast.net

John Brooks RL
166 Locust Grove Rd, Hedgesville, WV 25427-3072

R. (304) 754-7891
jjbrooks88@frontier.com

Donnie J. Cardwell RL
3036 Cherry Run Rd, Hedgesville, WV 25427-6099

R. (304) 596-7349
3036dc@comcast.net

Arlene R. Carr RE
2129 W New Haven Ave Apt 130, West Melbourne, FL 32904-3849

R. (321) 984-8089

Bruce W. Chapman RE
15247 Oak Spring St, San Antonio, TX 78232-4241

Joseph A. Conte RE
6705 Lingane Rd, Chelsea, MI 48118-9435

R. 517-304-1210
jacfive1954@gmail.com

David S. Cooney RE
6620 Rockridge Rd, New Market, MD 21774-6618

R. (301) 882-4165
revcooney@gmail.com

Vicki Curry RE
211 Columbia Dr, Kearneysville, WV 25430-6406

R. (304) 262-9646
vcfrog@comcast.net

Ellin M. Dize RL
11733 Terry Town Dr, Reisterstown, MD 21136-3218

R. (410) 833-7440
edize@comcast.net

Carroll A. Doggett RE
7351 Willow Rd, Frederick, MD 21702-2415

R. (240) 629-1961
carroll.doggett@gmail.com

Marshall D. (Douglas) Fraim RL
6426 Spring Forest Rd, Frederick, MD 21701-7634

R. (304) 535-1375
dougfraim@aol.com

Charles W. (Wayne) Frum RA
1387 Trainer Road, Buckhannon, WV 26201

R. (301) 988-7654
pastorcwayne@gmail.com

Marianne S. Grabowski RE
22 Eastwood Dr, Hanover, PA 17331-8155

R. (717) 633-5408
touchstonecc@comcast.net

Susan Halse RE
3030 Mill Island Pkwy, Frederick, MD 21701-6819

R. (301) 846-0313
susanrhalse@gmail.com

Linda W. Healy RP
2124 Mitford Ct, Dacula, GA 30019-2487

revlhealy@aol.com

David A. Highfield RE
942 Litchfield Cir, Westminster, MD 21158-4407

R. (410) 596-2918
davidhighmd@gmail.com

William A. Holmes RE
Cottage #1, Frederick, MD 21702-2415

R. (301) 460-7773
bilnanh@msn.com

Kenneth M. Humbert RE
198 Wyndtryst Dr, Westminster, MD 21158-4444

revkenh@starpower.net

Robert (Bob) Hunter, III RE
3539 Swan Lake Dr, Titusville, FL 32796-3781

R. (240) 288-8430
pastorbobhunter@gmail.com

Elza Hurst RL
17144 Bullfrog Rd, Taneytown, MD 21787-1013

R. (301) 898-7888
hurstcrow@comcast.net

Rollins R. Johnson RL
2214 Bluebird Dr, Westminster, MD 21157-7702

R. (410) 875-2469
dorisj@carr.org

Judith (Judy) Kelly RL
1727 Tarleton Way, Crofton, MD 21114-2503

R. (443) 292-8474
callmejude@aol.com

Orlando F. Kibbe RA
13978 Penn Shop Rd, Mount Airy, MD 21771-4624

R. (410) 552-4727
ofbudki@msn.com

Robert E. Manthey RE
500 Pearson Cir Apt 4018, Frederick, MD 21702-3424

R. 240-629-8030
nanbob65@comcast.net

Mildred C. Martin RE
15 Canterbury Trl # 21, Charles Town, WV 25414-9238

R. (181) 455-8692
mcmpurplelady@gmail.com

Mary M. Mayor RE
1924 Westminster Cir Unit 6CIRLCE, Vero Beach, FL 32966

R. 772-999-3281
marciamayor@msn.com

Robert A. McCullough RE
1 Breakwater Dr, Rehoboth Beach, DE 19971-9573

Sheril D. Merki RL
363 Universe Dr, Martinsburg, WV 25404-3496
R. (304) 264-0897
papmommurk@gmail.com

Margaret E. Moon RL
2044 Green Mill Rd, Finksburg, MD 21048-1931
R. (410) 236-2826
mmoon628@comcast.net

Raymond T. Moreland RE
9731 Hall Rd, Frederick, MD 21701-6736
R. (301) 694-8405
agape12@comcast.net

Laura C. Morgan RE
2 Stedtle Ave, Littlestown, PA 17340-1164
R. (717) 345-6455
revlauralee@comcast.net

Robert B. (Bruce) Poynter RE
7351 Willow Rd Unit 7, Frederick, MD 21702-2415
R. (240) 629-1956
rbp1927@gmail.com

Doris E. Ridgely RL
5701 Bartholow Rd, Sykesville, MD 21784-8812
R. (410) 795-0618

Francis B. (Blaine) Rinker RA
715 Norfield Ct, Westminster, MD 21158-9465
R. (443) 293-7007
gottaeat@comcast.net

Richard Shamer RL
930 Pine Grove Rd, Hanover, PA 17331-8798
R. (410) 596-3876

Bertha N. Sigler RL
3833 Burkittsville Rd, Knoxville, MD 21758-9724
R. (301) 834-9726

Richard W. Simpson RE
5 Maple Trl, Fairfield, PA 17320-8495
R. (717) 642-6236
richcar2@comcast.net

Mary J. (Mary Jo) Sims RE
314 Surfwood Ct, Gerrardstown, WV 25420-4126
R. (443) 841-2219
stupot@comcast.net

Charles Slaugh RL
3152 Gracefield Rd #MS602, Silver Spring, MD 20904
R. (301) 960-9638
charlesslaugh@gmail.com

Gaye S. Smith RE
3800 Shamrock Dr, Charlotte, NC 28215-3220
R. (407) 249-3969
smith_ted_gaye@bellsouth.net

Helen Smith RE
4117 Mills Rd, Sharpsburg, MD 21782-1931
R. (301) 432-5644
sycamore@myactv.net

Beverly C. Stang RE
500 Pearson Cir Apt 4005, Frederick, MD 21702-3424
R. (240) 629-1957
bevo610@aol.com

Diane E. Summerhill RE
610 Klees Mill Rd, Westminster, MD 21157-8226
R. (410) 552-5547
Revmom34@msn.com

Julian A. Tavenner RE
604 Marshview Dr Unit D, Waynesboro, PA 17268-7989
R. (717) 749-7730
jandmtav@comcast.net

Barry L. Taylor RL
3075 Bayview Way, Pensacola, FL 32503-6915
R. (301) 639-4282
itisbarry@gmail.com

Arthur Thomas, Jr. RE
1600 Westbrook Ave Apt 353, Richmond, VA 23227
R. (240) 281-1523
arthurdthomas333@gmail.com

Harry K. (Kent) Tice RE
104 Oakland Ter, Charles Town, WV 25414-4815
R. (304) 725-5233
kenttice@gmail.com

Ruth A. Ward RE
26 Lantern Ln, Shippensburg, PA 17257-8769
R. (717) 377-6444

Linda A. Warehime RE
1020 Eastbourne Ter, Frederick, MD 21702-5115
R. (301) 639-4966
lindawarehime@myactv.net

William H. (Bill) Warehime, Jr. RE
1020 Eastbourne Ter, Frederick, MD 21702-5115

R. (410) 259-3301
apastorbill@gmail.com

Warren W. Watts RE
220 W Burke St, Martinsburg, WV 25401-3322

R. (304) 754-8557
watts2341@comcast.net

Kenneth B. Welliver RE
3112 Gracefield Rd Apt 422, Silver Spring, MD 20904-1870

R. (304) 472-1624

Robert (Bob) Wellman RE
1932 Carrollton Rd, Finksburg, MD 21048-1133

R. (410) 622-5558
bobwellman@comcast.net

Owen B. Womack RE
6 Gibson Road, Inwood, WV 25428

R. (304) 229-6214
owenwomack@frontier.com

Daniel Wright RE
695 Aqueduct Avenue, Martinsburg, WV 25404

R. (304) 671-3575
danwright1949@gmail.com

John R. Yost RE
812 Honeysuckle Dr, Martinsburg, WV 25401-9223

R. (304) 267-6234
pastorjohnyost@comcast.net

GREATER WASHINGTON DISTRICT

Superintendent
Gerard A. (Gerry) Green, Jr. FE (410) 309-3432
12410 Fellowship Ln, North Potomac, MD 20878-3409 R. (410) 309-3432
ggreen@bwcumc.org

Albright Memorial #7110 C. (202) 723-3525
409 Rittenhouse St NW, Washington, DC 20011-1323 albrightumc@verizon.net
Gerald L. Elston, Sr. PE R. (301) 890-9559
3136 Gershwin Ln, Silver Spring, MD 20904-6813 Lawdad513@aol.com

Asbury #7115 C. (202) 628-0009
926 11th St NW, Washington, DC 20001-4408 asburymail@asburyumcdc.org
Ianther M. Mills FE R. (301) 574-9601
10406 Grandhaven Ave, Upper Marlboro, MD 20772-6603 agapezoe@aol.com

Bells #8145 C. (301) 899-7521
6016 Allentown Rd, Camp Springs, MD 20746-4550 deeministrator6016@gmail.com
Michael Parker, II PE R. (410) 900-3535
188 Ethel Dr Apt 4, Laurel, MD 20724-2112 mparker.umc@gmail.com

Bethesda #9122 C. (301) 652-2990
8300 Old Georgetown Rd, Bethesda, MD 20814-1416 bethesdaumc@washmorefeet.org
Jenny D. Cannon FE R. (240) 205-5001
8300 Old Georgetown Rd, Bethesda, MD 20814-1416 jenny.cannon@gmail.com

Scott Bostic PE R. (404) 314-5291
4712 W Braddock Rd, Alexandria, VA 22311-4702 scott@washmorefeet.org

Brighter Day #7625 C. (202) 889-3660
421 Alabama Ave SE, Washington, DC 20032-1517 churchoffice@bdmdc.org
Tommy Murray PE R. (240) 357-5832
36 Welsh Ct, Charles Town, WV 25414-4406 dvinejbz2@aol.com

Brightwood Park #7125 C. (202) 291-2763
744 Jefferson St NW, Washington, DC 20011-7720 Lawdad513@aol.com
Gerald L. Elston, Sr. PE R. (301) 890-9559
3136 Gershwin Ln, Silver Spring, MD 20904-6813 Lawdad513@aol.com

Cabin John #9160 C. (301) 229-8233
7703 MacArthur Blvd, Cabin John, MD 20818 ekhii2000@yahoo.com
Ek C. Hii FE R. (301) 229-8233
7703 MacArthur Blvd, Cabin John, MD 20818 ekhii2000@yahoo.com

Capitol Hill #7135 C. (202) 546-1000
421 Seward Sq SE, Washington, DC 20003-1113 office@chumc.net
Alisa L. Lasater FE R. 202-546-1000 x222
431 N West St, Alexandria, VA 22314-2122 pastor@chumc.net

Troy Sims   OD   R. (940) 867-2599
421 Seward Sq SE, Washington, DC 20003-1113   troy@chumc.net

Centenary #7615   C. (441) 292-0742
PO Box FL 39, Flatts FL Bx, BERMUDA   dickstetler@dickstetler.com
Richard E. (Dick) Stetler   RE   R. 301-576-0533
PO FL 39, Flatts, FL BX BERMUDA   dickstetler@dickstetler.com

Cheverly #7325   C. (301) 773-1314
2801 Cheverly Ave, Cheverly, MD 20785-3125   cheverly@cheverlyumc.org
Lillian C. Smith   FE   R. (301) 249-7669
506 Crain Hwy, Upper Marlboro, MD 20774   pastor@cheverlyumc.org

Chevy Chase #9165   C. (301) 652-8700
7001 Connecticut Ave, Chevy Chase, MD 20815-4935   office@chevychaseumc.org
Kirkland Reynolds   FE   R. (240) 205-5001
10009 Dallas Ave, Silver Spring, MD 20901-2240   kirklandreynolds@gmail.com

Christ #7140   C. (202) 554-9117
900 4th St SW, Washington, DC 20024-4434   christumcdc@gmail.com
Monica Raines   PE   R. (910) 580-6194
901 Wesley Pl SW, Washington, DC 20024-4211   pastormcumcdc@gmail.com

Church of The Redeemer #7475   C. (301) 894-8622
1901 Iverson St, Temple Hills, MD 20748-5609   umcredeemer@verizon.net
Michael Parker, II   PE   R. (410) 900-3535
188 Ethel Dr Apt 4, Laurel, MD 20724-2112   mparker.umc@gmail.com

Colesville #9450   C. (301) 384-1941
52 Randolph Rd, Silver Spring, MD 20904-1200   churchoffice@cumc.org
Michael W. Armstrong   FE   R. (301) 434-0930
1917 Dana Dr, Adelphi, MD 20783-2120   revmwarmstrong@gmail.com

College Park-Mowatt.
College Park #7335   C. (301) 345-1010
9601 Rhode Island Ave, College Park, MD 20740-1650   cpumchurchlady@yahoo.com
Mowatt Memorial #7375   C. (301) 474-9410
40 Ridge Rd, Greenbelt, MD 20770-0724   faylundin@yahoo.com
Fay B. Lundin   FE   R. (202) 215-5209
1169 Claire Rd, Crownsville, MD 21032-1048   Faylundin@yahoo.com

College Park Hispanic Initiative #7396   C. (301) 345-1010
9601 Rhode Island Ave, College Park, MD 20740-1650   misionnuevavida365@gmail.com

Community #7145   C. (202) 399-7343
1525 Levis St NE, Washington, DC 20002-2912   RVRobinson@co.pg.md.us
LaTaska Nelson   SY   R. (615) 977-9956
32 Grant Cir NW, Washington, DC 20011-4601   lataskam.nelson@gmail.com

Concord-St. Andrews #9130   C. (301) 229-3383
5910 Goldsboro Rd, Bethesda, MD 20817-6034   csaumc@gmail.com
Curtis C. Ehrgott   FE   R. (410) 207-4725
6308 Blackwood Rd, Bethesda, MD 20817-5904   pastorcurtise@gmail.com

Douglas Memorial #7155
800 11th St NE, Washington, DC 20002-3740
LaTaska Nelson SY
32 Grant Cir NW, Washington, DC 20011-4601

C. (202) 397-1562
douglasmemorial@gmail.com
R. (615) 977-9956
lataskam.nelson@gmail.com

Dumbarton #7160
3133 Dumbarton St NW, Washington, DC 20007-3309
Mary Kay K. Totty FE
3130 O St NW, Washington, DC 20007

C. (202) 333-7212
dumbartonpastor@yahoo.com
R. (202) 549-9897
revmktotty@yahoo.com

Ebenezer #7165
400 D St SE, Washington, DC 20003-2053
Bresean Jenkins SY
10914 Hannes Ct, Silver Spring, MD 20901-1718

C. (202) 544-1415
Ebenezerumc1@verizon.net
R. (352) 682-8348
breseanjenkins@gmail.com

Emmanuel #7440
10755 Scaggsville Rd, Laurel, MD 20723-1223
Stephanie Vader FE
5340 Sunny Field Ct, Ellicott City, MD 21043-8208

C. (301) 725-5200
office@eumclaurel.org
R. (301) 802-2582
revvader@comcast.net

Emory #7175
6100 Georgia Ave NW, Washington, DC 20011-5110
Joseph W. Daniels, Jr. FE
14629 Stonewall Dr, Silver Spring, MD 20905-5857

Janice Phipps-Harmon PL
1209 Tanley Rd, Silver Spring, MD 20904-2161

C. (202) 723-3130
admin@emoryfellowship.org
R. (301) 879-3424
jdaniels@emoryfellowship.org

sunsistah@gmail.com

Faith #9410
6810 Montrose Rd, Rockville, MD 20852-4210
Laura Norvell FE
15520 Santini Rd, Burtonsville, MD 20866

C. (301) 881-1881
jspencer@faithworkshere.com
R. (240) 461-2340
revlaura@faithworkshere.com

First #7385
6201 Belcrest Rd, Hyattsville, MD 20782-2913
Yvonne Wallace-Penn FE
PO Box 1725, Hyattsville, MD 20788-0725

C. (301) 927-6133
church@fumchy.org
R. 410-221-8893
pastorp@fumchy.org

Forest Memorial #8190
3111 Forestville Rd, Forestville, MD 20747-4405
Esther M. Holimon RE
10624 Seneca Spring Way, Montgomery Village, MD 20886

C. (301) 736-4115
office@forestmemorialumc.org
R. (410) 241-2430
emholimon@aol.com

Foundry #7180
1500 16th St NW, Washington, DC 20036-1402
Ginger E. Gaines-Cirelli FE
1500 16th St NW, Washington, DC 20036-1402

William E. Green FE
1650 Harvard St NW, Washington, DC 20009-3740

Kelly Grimes FE
12 Upman Ct, Baltimore, MD 21228-6400

C. (202) 332-4010
foundryumc@foundryumc.org
R.
ggainescirelli@foundryumc.org

R. (847) 644-9448
wgreen@foundryumc.org

R. (443) 467-4788
revklg@gmail.com

Ben Roberts OD
1500, Washington, DC 20036

R. (202) 332-4010
broberts@foundryumc.org

Francis Asbury National Korean #9427
2181 Baltimore Rd, Rockville, MD 20851-1230
Seung-Woo Lee FE
9717 Corkran Ln, Bethesda, MD 20817-1531

C. (301) 309-6856
nationalkumc@hotmail.com
R. (240) 601-3349
revlsw@hotmail.com

Gethsemane #7320
910 Addison Rd S, Capitol Heights, MD 20743-4403
Ronald E. Triplett PE
9900 Greenbelt Rd Ste E # 131, Lanham, MD 20706

C. (301) 336-1219
info@gethsemaneumc.org
R. (410) 963-9536
pastorron@gethsemaneumc.org

Glenmont #9475
12901 Georgia Ave, Silver Spring, MD 20906-3743
Kara Scroggins FE
10820 Torrance Dr, Kensington, MD 20895-2800

C. (301) 946-5577
glenmontumc@verizon.net
R. (202) 557-8396
Karascroggins@gmail.com

Good Hope Union #9455
14680 Good Hope Rd, Silver Spring, MD 20905
Tori Butler OE
10101 Twin Rivers Rd Apt 237, Columbia, MD 21044

C. (301) 879-8100
SecretaryGHU@goodhopeunion.org
R. (301) 879-8100
pastortcbutler@gmail.com

Good Shepherd #7445
9701 New Hampshire Ave, Silver Spring, MD 20903-2334
DaeHwa Park FE
17506 Gallagher Way, Olney, MD 20832-2065

C. (301) 434-3331
goodshepumc@verizon.net
R. (301) 577-1500
daehwa@gmail.com

Grace/Ager Road
Ager Road #7380
6301 Ager Rd, Hyattsville, MD 20782-1626
Grace #7465
7001 New Hampshire Ave, Takoma Park, MD 20912-5816
Samson Y. Nortey FE
45683 Edge Mill Ct, Great Mills, MD 20634-3312

C. (301) 422-2132
thenehemiahcharge@gmail.com
C. (301) 891-2100
thenehemiahcharge@gmail.com
R. (301) 866-0003
synortey@verizon.net

Hughes #9480
10700 Georgia Ave, Wheaton, MD 20902
Diana Wingeier-Rayo OE
9714 Admiralty Dr, Silver Spring, MD 20910-1401

C. (301) 949-8383
Church_Office@hughesumc.org
R. (512) 806-4667
djuliawingeier50@gmail.com

Hughes Memorial #7190
25 53rd St NE, Washington, DC 20019-6602
Paul W. Johnson FE
12006 Hunterton St, Upper Marlboro, MD 20774-1614

C. (202) 398-3411
adminasst@hughesmemorial.org
R. (202) 398-3411
pwjohnson10@gmail.com

Jerusalem-Mt Pleasant #9420
11 Wood Ln, Rockville, MD 20850-2228
Ashley B. Hoover PE
6012 North Dakota Ave NW, Washington, DC 20011

C. (301) 424-0464
Jmp1umc@aol.com
R. (301) 922-6200
hoovah06@gmail.com

Jones Memorial #7210
4625 G St SE, Washington, DC 20019-7834
Loretta E. Johnson FE
6125 Teaberry Way, Clinton, MD 20735-3948

C. (202) 583-7116
lorettaewe1@verizon.net
R. (301) 877-5162
lorettaewe1@verizon.net

Liberty Grove #9155
15225 Old Columbia Pike, Burtonsville, MD 20866-1615
Miguel A. Balderas FE
7980 Inverness Ridge Rd, Potomac, MD 20854-4009

C. (301) 421-9166
libertygrovemd@gmail.com
R. (202) 841-0358
mbald20879@gmail.com

Lincoln Park #7215
1301 N Carolina Ave NE, Washington, DC 20002-6423
Richard Black OE
5459 Saint Rita Dr, Waldorf, MD 20602-3277

C. (202) 543-1318
LincolnPark@LPUMCDC.org
R. (301) 752-0516
rblack3190@gmail.com

Marsden First #7610
151 South Shore Road, Smith's, HS01 Bermuda
Joseph Whalen, Jr. FE
1 South Breakers Road, Smiths, HS01

C. (441) 293-7045
Marsden@link.bm
R. 441-293-7045
jfwhalen73@link.bm

McKendree-Simms-Brookland
Bradbury Heights #7120
4323 Bowen Rd SE, Washington, DC 20019-5613
Franklin P Nash #7185
2001 Lincoln Rd NE, Washington, DC 20002-1381
McKendree-Simms-Brookland #7620
2421 Lawrence St NE, Washington, DC 20018-2915
Ryland-Epworth #7255
3200 S St SE, Washington, DC 20020-2410
Richard D. (R. David) Hall FE
1315 Q St NW, Washington, DC 20009-4316

C. (202) 583-1244
gaylehebron@hotmail.com
C. (202) 269-0572
fpnashum2@gmail.com
C. (202) 529-3075
churchoffice@msbumc.org
C. (202) 582-4005
reumc7255@gmail.com
R. (202) 462-6935
rdhall49@aol.com

Bernard M. Harris, Sr. PL
5002 Bass Pl SE, Washington, DC 20019-7613

R. (301) 254-5524
bharris73@comcast.net

Samuel Holdbrook-Smith FE
1207 Clovis Ave, Capitol Heights, MD 20743-5153

R. (301) 420-1628
revsamh@gmail.com

Memorial First India #7462
9226 Colesville Rd, Silver Spring, MD 20910-1658
Samuel Honnappa FE
9221 Watson Road, Silver Spring, MD 20910

C. (301) 585-8015
revhonnappa@hotmail.com
R. (301) 589-1414
revhonnappa@hotmail.com

Metropolitan Memorial #7630 (DBA National UMC)
3401 Nebraska Ave NW, Washington, DC 20016-2759
Douglas Robinson-Johnson RE
3311 Nebraska Ave NW, Washington, DC 20016-2706

C. (202) 363-4900
hsimon@nationalchurch.org
R. (781) 913-2799
eatlightly@gmail.com

Janet L. Craswell FD
702 Owens St, Rockville, MD 20850-2126

R. (240) 472-0763
jcraswell@nationalchurch.org

Millian Memorial #9430
13016 Parkland Dr, Rockville, MD 20853-3361
Tyrone (Ty) Blackwell PL
5161 Atlantis Ln, White Plains, MD 20695-3180

C. (301) 946-2500
millianumc@gmail.com
R. (301) 645-6803
tyblackwell73@gmail.com

Mizo #7485
6810 Montrose Rd, Rockville, MD 20852-4210
   Biak Chhunga   OE
   5625 Kirkland Dr, Frederick, MD 21703-8653
C. (301) 222-3608
chhunga@yahoo.com
R. (301) 222-3608
biakchhunga@gmail.com

Mount Vernon #7230
4147 Minnesota Ave NE, Washington, DC 20019-3575
   Armon Nelson   SY
   32 Grant Cir NW, Washington, DC 20011-4601
C. (202) 398-7938
pastornelson1ac@gmail.com
R. (615) 752-9555
armonchadellnelson@gmail.com

Mount Vernon Place #7235
900 Massachusetts Ave NW, Washington, DC 20001-4308
   Donna Claycomb Sokol   FE
   3566 Martha Custis Dr, Alexandria, VA 22302-2001
C. (202) 347-9620
churchoffice@mvpumc.org
R. (202) 679-9310
donna@mvpumc.org

Mount Zion #7240
1334 29th St NW, Washington, DC 20007-3351
   Selena M. Johnson   FE
   12006 Hunterton St, Upper Marlboro, MD 20774-1614
C. (202) 234-0148
mtzionumc.dc@gmail.com
R. (410) 428-7737
oakchapelpastor@gmail.com

North Bethesda #9140
10100 Old Georgetown Rd, Bethesda, MD 20814-1858
   Jeffrey (Jeff) Jones   FE
   24417 Welsh Rd, Gaithersburg, MD 20882-3933
C. (301) 530-4342
macpastor@gmail.com
R. (301) 253-6435
macpastor@gmail.com

Oak Chapel #9460
14500 Layhill Rd, Silver Spring, MD 20906-1913
   Sherri E. Wood-Powe   FE
   12617 Falconbridge Dr, North Potomac, MD 20878-3412
C. (301) 598-0000
OakchapelUMC@verizon.net
R. (301) 123-4567
pastorsewp@gmail.com

   Albert Moser, Jr.   RE
   2615 Telluride Pl, Silver Spring, MD 20906-6164
R. (240) 460-5461
amoser@asburyumcdc.org

Petworth #7245
32 Grant Cir NW, Washington, DC 20011-4601
   Armon Nelson   SY
   32 Grant Cir NW, Washington, DC 20011-4601
C. (202) 723-5300
petworthumc1@verizon.net
R. (615) 752-9555
armonchadellnelson@gmail.com

Potomac #9390
9908 S Glen Rd, Potomac, MD 20854-4128
   Laura D. Blauvelt   FE
   14021 Loblolly Ter, Potomac, MD 20850-5472
C. (301) 299-9383
jjacob@potomac-umc.org
R. (410) 833-6165
lblauvelt@potomac-umc.org

Randall Memorial #7250
1002 46th St NE, Washington, DC 20019-3810
   Brian W. Jackson   FE
   2509 Testway Ave, Fort Washington, MD 20744-2447
C. (202) 396-0375
camerontwins@gmail.com
R. (240) 256-0739
randallmemorial@verizon.net

Rockville #9440
112 W Montgomery Ave, Rockville, MD 20850-4213
   Martha Meredith   FE
   509 Redland Blvd, Rockville, MD 20850
C. (301) 762-2288
rockville_umc@rockvilleumc.org
R. (410) 353-6846
pastor@rockvilleumc.org

Silver Spring #9466
8900 Georgia Ave, Silver Spring, MD 20910-2757
Angela Flanagan FE
1010 Dale Dr, Silver Spring, MD 20910-4124

C. (301) 587-1215
akirkland@silverspringumcp.org
R. (443) 934-1078
aflanagan@silverspringumc.org

Simpson-Hamline #7265
4501 16th St NW, Washington, DC 20011-4326
Yvonne Mercer-Staten FE
12200 Quintette Ln, Bowie, MD 20720-4364

C. (202) 882-2122
shumcdc@yahoo.com
R. (443) 621-1891
rocka13@aol.com

St Paul #7330
2601 Colston Dr, Chevy Chase, MD 20815-3035
John T. McCauley FE
12 Athey Ct, Burtonsville, MD 20866-1643

C. (301) 587-5370
stpaulumc-chevychase@verizon.net
R. (301) 585-3311
Kebuki52QS@verizon.net

St Paul's #9330
10401 Armory Ave, Kensington, MD 20895-3994
Kathryn Mackereth Fulton PE
7837 Thor Dr, Annandale, VA 22003-1437

C. (301) 933-7933
stpaulsunited@stpaulsk.org
R. (301) 524-5196
k.mackereth@gmail.com

Adam Snell FE
10100 Ashwood Dr, Kensington, MD 20895-4240

R. (410) 224-4750
absnell@stpaulsk.org

United #7275
1920 G St NW, Washington, DC 20006-4303
William Federici
1920 G St NW, Washington, DC 20006-4303

C. (202) 331-1495
info@theunitedchurch.org
R. (202) 331-1495
revfederici.tuc@gmail.com

University #7340
3621 Campus Dr, College Park, MD 20740
Michelle Mejia FE
4106 Crosswick Turn, Bowie, MD 20715-1109

C. (301) 422-1400
uumc.office@verizon.net
R. (301) 310-3204
eastportumcpastor@gmail.com

Van Buren #7280
35 Van Buren St NW, Washington, DC 20012
Lucinda Kent PL
4709 Ridgeline Ter, Bowie, MD 20720-3705

C. (202) 723-5454
vanburenunitedmethodistchurch@gmail.com
R. (301) 385-6630
pastorcindykent@gmail.com

Attending School
Katherine E. Brown FD
9104 Eton Rd, Silver Spring, MD 20901-4902

R. (301) 585-5547
katherinebrown2002@yahoo.com

Certified Candidate
Deryl Davis CC
2606 Myrtle Ave NE, Washington, DC 20018-2630

Admire Russell CC
5310 Cedar Ln Apt 203, Columbia, MD 21044-1676

R. (301) 828-5875
admire_russell@yahoo.com

Roberta S. White CC
208 49th St NE, Washington, DC 20019-4601

R. (202) 583-3099
MsRSWhite@aol.com

Transitional Leave
    Mark A. Schaefer FE   R. (301) 320-3592
    5910 Osceola Rd, Bethesda, MD 20816-2031   revschaef@gmail.com

Disability
    Margaret W. Hodges FE
    3706 Excalibur Ct Apt 202, Bowie, MD 20716-7333

Extension Ministry
    Chip D. Aldridge, Jr. FE   R. (703) 836-1549
    15508 Letcher Rd E, Brandywine, MD 20613-8521   caldridge@wesleyseminary.edu

    Erik Alsgaard FE
    6821 Martin Rd, Columbia, MD 21044-4017   ealsgaard@bwcumc.org

    Rebecca J. Bentzinger FE   R. (202) 783-3665
    435 M St NW, Washington, DC 20001-4607   dczinger@aol.com

    Alexis F. Brown PE   R. (410) 905-8956
    7018 Knighthood Ln, Columbia, MD 21045-4817   abrown@asburyumcdc.org

    Kathleen G. Charters PD   R. (360) 504-3150
    41 Mendel Dr, Sequim, WA 98382-8959   kcharters@mac.com

    Rachel Cornwell FE   R. (301) 802-8234
    1304 Highland Dr, Silver Spring, MD 20910-1622   rachelcornwell@me.com

    Amy E. Duke FD   R. (347) 599-2000
    244 Vanderbilt Ave,1R, Brooklyn, NY 11205   AmyEllenDB@NationalSkillsCoalition.org

    Martina Efodzi PD   R. (202) 222-8861
    14440 W Side Blvd Apt 307, Laurel, MD 20707-6275   arthealsdc@gmail.com

    Kirk Van Gilder FE   R. (202) 250-2602
    1223 Maryland Ave NE, Washington, DC 20002-5335   kirker@mac.com

    Kimberly Hall FE
    912 Vosler Loop, San Antonio, TX 78227-4901   kimberly.hall13.mil@mail.mil

    Joey P. Heath-Mason PE   R. (202) 885-3304
    5000 42nd Ave, Hyattsville, MD 20781-2011   joeyh@american.edu

    KyungLim S. Lee FE   R. (301) 469-8537
    Wesley Theological Seminary, Washington, DC 20016   kshinlee@wesleyseminary.edu

    Beth Ludlum FE   R. (703) 314-1496
    6605 13th Pl NW, Washington, DC 20012-2309   bethie_ksu@hotmail.com

    Sam Marullo FD   R. (202) 489-4785
    710 3rd St NE, Washington, DC 20002   sam.marullo@gmail.com

    Angela Maves FD   R. (202) 234-5743
    2015 19th St NW, Washington, DC 20009-1307   maves.angela@gmail.com

    Laura Norvell FE   R. (240) 461-2340
    15520 Santini Rd, Burtonsville, MD 20866   revlaura@faithworkshere.com

    Bryant M. Oskvig FE   R. (301) 365-3924
    8216 Buckspark Ln W, Potomac, MD 20854   boskvig@gmail.com

    Frederick D. Powe, Jr. FE   R. (301) 963-1459
    12617 Falconbridge Dr, North Potomac, MD 20878   dpowe@wesleyseminary.edu

Randy W. Pumphrey FE
2016 Perry St NE, Washington, DC 20018-3054
R. (202) 547-3423
spiritrp@aol.com

Harold J. Recinos FE
PO Box 750133, Dallas, TX 75275-0001
R. (214) 768-1773
hrecinos@smu.edu

Saundra (Sandy) Rector FE
8297 Hammond Branch Way, Laurel, MD 20723-1053
R. (301) 362-5996
sandyrector@verizon.net

Robert K. Schneider FE
2304 Kaywood Ln, Silver Spring, MD 20905-6407

Rodney Smothers FE
3313 Dunwood Ridge Ter, Bowie, MD 20721-1259
R. (301) 218-4688
rsmothers@bwcumc.org

Theresa S. Thames FE
172 Jonathon Dayton Ct, Princeton, NJ 08540-7693
R. (202) 746-0283
theresathames@gmail.com

Doris E. Warrell FD
743 Hamilton St NW, Washington, DC 20011-4031
dew818@rcn.com

Kevin Wright FE
490 Riverside Dr, New York, NY 10027-5706
R. (980) 322-6389
kevinwright@gmail.com

Leo A. Yates, Jr. FD
7612 Harmons Farm Ct, Hanover, MD 21076
R. (443) 991-3795
leoyjr@aol.com

David J. Young FD
2507 N Jefferson St, Arlington, VA 22207-1447
R. (703) 786-0352
dndweiszyoung@yahoo.com

Leave of Absence

G. W. (Whit) Hutchison FE
102 Park Ave, Takoma Park, MD 20912-4311
whithutchison@hotmail.com

On Loan

Jacqueline Jones-Smith FE
5801 Nicholson Ln #902, North Bethesda, MD 20852
R. (301) 881-8756
jonessmith5291@gmail.com

Bejamin K. (Kevin) Smalls FE
26275 Northwestern Hwy, Southfield, MI 48076-3926
R. (248) 838-8089
kevinsmalls@aol.com

Retired

Edison M. Amos RE
561 NW Floresta Dr, Port St Lucie, FL 34983-8613
R. (772) 878-4634

Archie D. (David) Argo RE
2877 Arizona Ter NW, Washington, DC 20016-2642
adavidargo@yahoo.com

John P. Baker RE
3700 N Capitol St NW # 418, Washington, DC 20011-8400
R. (703) 360-2518

Edward W. Bauman, Jr. RE
7514 Cayuga Ave, Bethesda, MD 20817-4822
R. (301) 229-8923
papa7514@aol.com

Harry T. Baxter RE
1203 Walker Rd Apt 116, Dover, DE 19904-6541
R. (302) 659-1251
Baxter1961@earthlink.net

Susan R. Beehler RE
8103 LA Paloma Cir, El Paso, TX 79907-7412
R. (915) 858-5363
sraybeehler@gmail.com

Judith B. Birch RD
8410 Donnybrook Dr, Chevy Chase, MD 20815-3880
R. (301) 589-5780
diaconal@aol.com

Allan R. Broadhurst RE
8 Fresh Brook Rd, South Yarmouth, MA 02664-4016

R. (617) 362-2393

Arlester Brown RE
3001 Veazey Ter NW Apt 533, Washington, DC 20008-5402

R. (202) 244-2778
arlestero@aol.com

Gregory S. Brown RE
19266 Coastal Hwy Unit 4, Rehoboth Beach, DE 19971

R. (302) 684-2746
greg@gregbrownonline.com

John R. Brown RE
4675 Heritage Lakes Ct SW, Mableton, GA 30126-1254

R. (770) 732-6189

Susan M. (Sue) Brown RE
8034 Lazy Trl, San Antonio, TX 78250-3058

R. (240) 595-3172
2013smhbrown@gmail.com

Thomas L. Brunkow RE
5201 Worthington Dr, Bethesda, MD 20816-1621

R. (301) 229-4296
tbrunkow@verizon.net

Kim K. Capps RE
11110 Nicholas Dr, Silver Spring, MD 20902-3533

R. (301) 649-2032
kim.capps@gmail.com

Roger J. Carlson RE
5155 Osceola Ave, Saint Augustine, FL 32080-7191

R. (410) 349-2862
revrogerj@yahoo.com

Vernice S. Carney RE
14800 Pennfield Cir Apt 412, Silver Spring, MD 20906-1579

R. (301) 288-7990
vscarney@aol.com

Michael Chamberlain RE
1521 Eton Way, Crofton, MD 21114-1524

R. (410) 973-6707

Kiyul Chung RE
12-2-2103, Longke Ganlancheng, Beijing, 100101

R. 8613521708686
kiyul2653@hotmail.com

Eva L. Clark RE
723 Gleneagles Dr, Fort Washington, MD 20744-7006

R. (301) 292-1741
goodwater1@verizon.net

Laverne Clipper-Thomas RA
PO Box 128, Dickerson, MD 20842-0128

R. (301) 428-8680
pastorlaverne@aol.com

Fidel Compres RA
11660 Drumcastle Ter, Germantown, MD 20876-5635

R. (301) 972-5603

Reynold B. Connett RE
9607 Vantage Terrace Ct SE, Olympia, WA 98513-6687

R. (360) 438-2139

Richard S. Davis RE
133 Thorton Hall Rd, Kearneysville, WV 25430-2889

rdavis5000@aol.com

Peter L. DeGroote RE
1490 7th St NW Apt 411, Washington, DC 20001-3391

R. (301) 328-0668
peterdeg@msn.com

Edwin C. DeLong RE
719 Maiden Choice Lane HR 135, Catonsville, Maryland 21228

R. (410) 608-1690
ecdelong1@gmail.com

William C. Farrady RE
5607 Chincoteague Ct, Oceanside, CA 92057-5548

R. (760) 822-9253
godot7x@yahoo.com

Albert L. Galloway RE
5445 Kerns Ln, Indianapolis, IN 46268-4083

R. (317) 875-1081
allgalloway@aol.com

Limja H. Gim RD
1830 Fountain Dr Unit 1503, Reston, VA 20190-4475

R. (703) 707-8207
lh.gim@verizon.net

Alfonso J. Harrod RE
4308 19th Pl NE, Washington, DC 20018-3308

R. (202) 529-6283
revalfonsoharrod@aol.com

Richard D. Hogue RE
107 Guilford Dr, Summerville, SC 29483-5583
R. (843) 821-6230
revrichardhogue@gmail.com

Esther M. Holimon RE
10624 Seneca Spring Way, Montgomery Village, MD 20886
R. (410) 241-2430
emholimon@aol.com

Mary Ellen Huzzard RE
3705 Jones Bridge Rd, Chevy Chase, MD 20815-5726
R. (301) 657-8162
drhuzzard@aol.com

Hattie S. Jackson RE
1630 Portal Dr NW, Washington, DC 20012-1114
R. (202) 722-1640
bobhat777@aol.com

John T. Jennings RE
8015 14th St NW, Washington, DC 20012-1207
R. (202) 829-6558
je6798@verizon.net

Alta G. Jewell RE
5418 Old Middleton Rd Apt 304, Madison, WI 53705-2667
R. (608) 238-1004

Bruce A. Jones RE
31262 Anchor Dr, Dagsboro, DE 19939-4363
R.
bajones15@gmail.com

Joye Jones RE
8311 20th Ave, Hyattsville, MD 20783-2104
R. (301) 434-2258
joyefulj@verizon.net

Lois A. Jones DR
6100 Westchester Park Dr Apt 409, College Park, MD 20740-2845
R. (301) 441-3769

Kathleen H. (Kathy) Kohl RE
1619 Catchworth Ct, Silver Spring, MD 20905-7006
R. (301) 236-4245
revkkohl@verizon.net

Mary E. Kraus RE
510 W 6th St, Claremont, CA 91711-4254
R. (202) 986-6457
marykraus1943@gmail.com

Ellis L. Larsen RE
415 Russell Ave Apt 1101, Gaithersburg, MD 20877-2844
R. (301) 216-5687
eleif@aol.com

G. D. (Doug) Lewis RE
5133 Warren Pl NW, Washington, DC 20016-4318
R. (202) 363-6027
g.dlewis@verizon.net

Ernest Lyles, Sr. RE
PO Box 551, Shepherdstown, WV 25443-0551
pastorlyles@aol.com

Jesse E. Mayes RE
528 Catania Ln, Poinciana, FL 34759-4033
R. (863) 438-9643
jmayes331@aol.com

Douglas E. Moore RE
7114 Alaska Ave NW, Washington, DC 20012-1544
rfrin16ms@verizon.net

E. M. (Maynard) Moore, III RE
6777 Surreywood Ln, Bethesda, MD 20817-1568
R. (301) 229-0828
emaynard8@yahoo.com

Howard E. (Ed) Moore RE
4105 Lucy Long Dr, Rockingham, VA 22801-8390
R. (540) 208-7166
edmoore26@gmail.com

Brindice Munoz-Rivera RE
26 Billerica Rd, S Chelmsford, MA 01824-3011
R. (301) 469-5960
brindicemunoz@yahoo.com

David C. Myers RE
6 Holly St, Gloucester, MA 01930-1740
R. (202) 652-8700
dam421@aol.com

James D. Nenninger RE
14097 Rehobeth Church Rd, Lovettsville, VA 20180-3215
R. (540) 882-4165
james@nenningers.net

Charles Parker RE
7137 7th St NW, Washington, DC 20012-1801
R. (202) 363-4900
cparker@nationalchurch.org

Constance A. Paulson RE
55 Cannon Dr, Ocean Pines, MD 21811-1730
R. (410) 641-5194
wesconnie55@gmail.com

Jeff A. Paulson FE
10 Bloomingdale Ave, Catonsville, MD 21228-4606
R. (410) 788-3614
revjeff93@gmail.com

Irene C. Pierce RL
109 Colton St, Largo, MD 20774-1501
R. (301) 336-0894

Carl B. Rife RE
624 Lafayette St, Lowell, MI 49331-1127
R. (717) 848-4807
carlrife@hotmail.com

Sang K. Ro RE
12307 Pomfret Ct, Midlothian, VA 23114-3229
R. (804) 378-5156

Donnalee J. Sanderson DR
3918 Longfellow St, Hyattsville, MD 20781-1742
R. (301) 927-6133
aesdjs@comcast.net

Victor E. Sawyerr RE
9511 Rommel Dr, Columbia, MD 21046-1910
R. (410) 290-9612
pastorves@gmail.com

John A. Shirkey RE
10216 Rockville Pike Apt 202, Rockville, MD 20852-3307
R. (301) 564-0572

Walter Shropshire, Jr. RE
300 Westminster Canterbury Dr Apt 426, Winchester, VA 22603
R. (540) 665-5748
wshrop@erols.com

Dean J. Snyder RE
11902 Kennedyville Road, Kennedyville, MD 21645
R. (410) 708-9600
snyderdean@gmail.com

Thomas C. Starnes RE
500 Pearson Cir Apt 2015, Frederick, MD 21702-3422
R. (302) 227-5577
starnesthomas@aol.com

Victoria J. Starnes RE
37403 3rd St, Rehoboth Beach, DE 19971-3626
R. (302) 745-2278
revvicky@aol.com

Edward A. (Allen) Stewart RE
2501 Heatherwood Ct, Adelphi, MD 20783-1429
R. (301) 503-4926
esa2501@yahoo.com

Frances W. Stewart RA
314 E Locust St, Covington, VA 24426
R. (202) 803-2120
frankies2u@gmail.com

David E. Stum RE
2310 Lusaka Pl, Dulles, VA 20189-2310
R. (410) 997-6329
davestum44@gmail.com

Michael P. Szpak RE
208 Franklin Ave, Silver Spring, MD 20901-4802
R. (301) 587-5949
mszpak@aflcio.org

Marjorie E. Taylor RP
26209 Rudale Dr, Clarksburg, MD 20871-9662
R. (301) 253-9672
mareltay@verizon.net

Jacqulyn B. Thorpe RD
9303 Parkhill Ter, Bethesda, MD 20814-3962
R. (301) 530-1736
jacqulynt8@aol.com

Man-King Tso RE
mankingtso@yahoo.com

Ronald L. Ward RE
103 Mystic Woods Ln, Severna Park, MD 21146-1232
R. (410) 647-5990
rlwgoodshepherd@aol.com

Mamie A. Williams RE
3703 Stoneybrook Rd, Randallstown, MD 21133-4134
R. (410) 655-2769
MAW813@aol.com

Perry Williams RE
Shawnee, OK 74801
R. (301) 422-1400
p.l.w.342@gmail.com

John P. Wogaman RE
3126 Gracefield Rd Apt 213, Silver Spring, MD 20904-5825

R. (202) 363-1242
jpwogaman@aol.com

Jane Wood RE
23 Martins Ln, Rockville, MD 20850-1853

R. (240) 393-0991
revjanewood@verizon.net

Arthuree R. Wright RD
2203 Durbin Ct, Bowie, MD 20721-2817

R. (301) 925-7886
arthureewright@gmail.com

Marion M. (Monroe) Wright RE
1331 C St NE, Washington, DC 20002-6466

lanhamumc@msn.com

Obie Wright, Jr. RE
2203 Durbin Ct, Bowie, MD 20721-2817

R. (301) 925-7886
obiewright@verizon.net

Catharine A. (Anne) Yarbrough RE
PO Box 1544, Shelburne, NS

R. (902) 874-0346
anne.yarbrough@gmail.com

WASHINGTON EAST DISTRICT

Superintendent
Johnsie Cogman. FE   (410) 309-3472
855 Chatsworth Dr, Accokeek, MD 20607-2032
jcogman@bwcumc.org

Alexandria Chapel #8390   C. (301) 743-3939
5605 Chicamuxen Rd, Indian Head, MD 20640-3691   Alexandria.chapel@gmail.com
  Judith Bennett SY   R. (301) 753-4335
  5037 Preston Ln, Pomfret, MD 20675-3020   pastor.alexandriachapel@gmail.com

Asbury/Zion Wesley
Asbury #8130   C. (301) 372-8891
4004 Accokeek Rd, Brandywine, MD 20613   asburyumcbrandywine@gmail.com
Zion Wesley #8535   C. (301) 645-7340
11500 Berry Rd, Waldorf, MD 20603   cindyholmes10@gmail.com
  Gladman R. Kapfumvuti FE   R. (202) 306-2006
  5011 Doctorfish Ct, Waldorf, MD 20603-4237   gladmanw@verizon.net

Bethel #8480   C. (301) 627-4515
16101 Swanson Rd, Upper Marlboro, MD 20774-9066   bethelum@verizon.net
  Thomas Long, Sr. PL   R. (812) 207-6915
  342 Whirlaway Dr, Prince Frederick, MD 20678-3287   mintclong@comcast.net

Bethesda #8515   C. (301) 994-9416
PO Box 204, Valley Lee, MD 20692-0204
(19309 Saint Georges Church Rd)
  Irvin E. Beverly SY   R. (410) 326-3465
  705 Coster Rd, Lusby, MD 20657-2955   irvinbev@gmail.com

Bowie #8120   C. (301) 464-8383
13009 6th St, Bowie, MD 20720-3614   emmanuelinfo@gmail.com
  Angela M. Kittrell PL   R. (804) 313-7638
  13011 6th St, Bowie, MD 20720-3614   emmanuelinfo@gmail.com

Brookfield Immanuel
Brookfield #8370   C. (240) 681-3532
17400 Aquasco Rd, Brandywine, MD 20613-4212   johncwarren@att.net
Immanuel #8235   C. (240) 681-3532
17400 Aquasco Rd, Brandywine, MD 20613-4212   johncwarren@att.net
  John Warren FE   R. (301) 627-4834
  621 Connaught Ct., Upper Marlboro, MD 20772   johncwarren@att.net

Brooks #8460   C. (410) 586-3972
5550 Mackall Rd, Saint Leonard, MD 20685-2388   brookschurch@comcast.net
  Jason L. Robinson FE   R. (301) 862-3138
  1065 Agricopia Dr, La Plata, MD 20646-3269   jayrob1914@aol.com

Calvary #8520
3235 Leonardtown Rd, Waldorf, MD 20601-3614
Sarah Schlieckert FE
9818 Golden Russet Dr Dunkirk, Dunkirk, MD 20754

C. (301) 645-5247
office@calvumc.org
R. (240) 315-6965
PastorSarahUMC@gmail.com

Carroll-Western #8425
2325 Adelina Rd, Prince Frederick, MD 20678-3723
Roland Barnes PL
27883 Ben Oaks Dr, Mechanicsville, MD 20659-3340

C. (410) 535-2210
cwumc1@gmail.com
R. (301) 884-4466
rsbarnes@md.metrocast.net

Cheltenham #8155
11111 Crain Hwy, Cheltenham, MD 20623-1100
Herbert A. Brisbon, III FE
7805 Mandan Rd Apt 101, Greenbelt, MD 20770-2135

C. (301) 782-4260
cheltenhamumc@comcast.net
R. (410) 900-0972
JmpPastorB@gmail.com

Chicamuxen #8260
PO Box 2338, La Plata, MD 20646-2338
(6255 Chicamuxen Road)
Edward Voorhaar RE
1006 East Patuxent Drive, La Plata, MD 20646

C. (301) 743-3926
jackie.bowie@comcast.net

R. (301) 934-2485
epvoorhaar@verizon.net

Clinton #8170
10700 Brandywine rd, Clinton, MD 20735
Dorothea B. Stroman FE
6100 Parkview Ln, Clinton, MD 20735-3846

C. (301) 868-1281
cumcmd@verizon.net
R. (240) 533-2744
beltstroman@gmail.com

Community With A Cause #8295
PO Box 310, Lexington Park, MD 20653-0310
Donald G. Geller, Jr. PL
47306 Willow Wood Dr, Lexington Park, MD 20653

C. (240) 434-5358
pastor@community-umchurch.com
R. (301) 789-1558
dgellerjr@md.metrocast.net

Coopers #8175
PO Box 148, Dunkirk, MD 20754-0148
(9370 Southern Maryland Blvd)
Vincent Cooke SY
15116 Lady Lauren Ln, Brandywine, MD 20613-7729

C. (410) 257-2511
cooperschurch@yahoo.com

R. (240) 377-1400
vcooke1954@gmail.com

Corkran Memorial #7480
5200 Temple Hill Rd, Temple Hills, MD 20748
Lesley Newman-Adams PL
1671 Tulip Ave, District Heights, MD 20747-2615

C. (301) 894-5577
corkranmemorialchurch@gmail.com
R. (301) 325-8715
lesleycnewman@gmail.com

Ebenezer #8285
4912 Whitfield Chapel Rd, Lanham, MD 20706-4220
Mark Venson FE
1011 Saint Michaels Dr, Mitchellville, MD 20721-1976

C. (301) 577-0770
church896@verizon.net
R. (301) 390-7932
mdvmrk@aol.com

Emmanuel #7310
11416 Cedar Ln, Beltsville, MD 20705-2609
Jalene Chase FE
6200 Heston Ter, Lanham, MD 20706-2398

C. (301) 937-7114
office@eumcbeltsville.com
R. (301) 325-6676
revjchase@gmail.com

Emmanuel #8240
1250 Emmanuel Church Rd, Huntingtown, MD 20639
    Matthew P. Tate   PE
    28750 Hancock Dr, Mechanicsville, MD 20659-3375

C. (410) 535-3177
emmanuelumc@comcast.net

Matthewptate@gmail.com

Faith #8110
15769 Livingston Rd, Accokeek, MD 20607-3315
    Margaret (Peggy) Ireland   SY
    2965 Edgewood Rd, Bryans Road, MD 20616-3304

C. (301) 292-6104
treasurer@faithumc-accokeek.org
R. (301) 375-9678
Pegatha@Outlook.com

First Saints Community Church #8540
PO Box 95, Leonardtown, MD 20650-0095
(25550 Point Lookout Rd)
    Christopher D. Owens   FE
    1318 West St, Annapolis, MD 21401-3612

C. (301) 475-7200
ingrid@firstsaints.org

R. (410) 263-8043
pastorchris@firstsaints.org

    Patricia S. Watson   FE
    44945 Voyage Path Apt 2, California, MD 20619-2476

R. (240) 808-4207
pastortrish@firstsaints.org

    Alan Hemming   FL
    23134 Clover Ridge Ln, California, MD 20619-4117

R. (240) 538-4010
pastoralan@firstsaints.org

Glenn Dale #8225
8500 Springfield Rd, Glenn Dale, MD 20769-9603
    Moses Sangha   FE
    2004 Sandstone Ct, Silver Spring, MD 20904-5329

C. (301) 262-2299
glenndaleumc@gmail.com
R. (301) 758-3094
mosessangha@gmail.com

Good Shepherd #8525
305 Smallwood Dr, Waldorf, MD 20602-2879
    Laurie Gates-Ward   FE
    5326 Flagfish Ct, Waldorf, MD 20603-4222

C. (301) 843-6797
gsadmin@gsumc.com
R. (301) 843-6797
revlaurie@aol.com

Grace #8215
11700 Old Fort Rd, Fort Washington, MD 20744-2703
    Robert E. Slade   FE
    16601 Tanyard Rd, Upper Marlboro, MD 20772-8102

C. (301) 292-7828
r3slade3@gmail.com
R. (301) 888-1207
r3slade3@gmail.com

Hollywood #8230
24422 Mervell Dean Rd, Hollywood, MD 20636-2709
    Katie A. Paul   OE
    20860 Sandstone St, Lexington Park, MD 20653-2439

C. (301) 373-2500
office@hollywoodumcmd.org
R. (580) 761-4169
kpaul@nccumc.org

Huntingtown #8245
P O Box 550, Huntingtown, MD 20639-9114
(4020 Hunting Creek Rd)
    Corey S. Sharpe   FE
    3980 Hunting Creek Rd, Huntingtown, MD 20639

C. (410) 257-3020
office.humc@comcast.net

R. (443) 968-8149
coreysharpe19@gmail.com

Huntingtown Combined
Patuxent #8250
3500 Solomons Island Rd, Huntingtown, MD 20639-3810
Plum Point #8255
PO Box 971, Huntingtown, MD 20639-8769
(1800 Stinnett Rd)

C. (410) 535-9819
huntingtowncharge@gmail.com
C. (410) 535-5065
blackemera@gmail.com

Bryan K. (BK) Fleet   FE
7806 Colonial Ln, Clinton, MD 20735-1825

R. (301) 868-6927
bryanf32@Verizon.net

Indian Head #8265
19 Mattingly Ave, Indian Head, MD 20640-1731
Jacques Banks   PL
5660 Port Tobacco Rd, Indian Head, MD 20640-3511

C. (301) 743-2312
IndianHeadUMC@aol.com
R. (301) 246-9078
pastorjtbanks@gmail.com

Journey of Faith Church;The #8550
2900 Smallwood Dr W, Waldorf, MD 20603-4786
Reginald Tarpley   FE
17010 Queen Anne Bridge Rd, Bowie, MD 20716-3437

churchoffice@thejofc.org
R. (301) 249-5883
pastor.tarpley@gmail.com

La Plata #8275
3 Port Tobacco Rd, La Plata, MD 20646-4366
Susan E. Boehl   FE
14715 Wisteria Dr, Swan Point, MD 20645-2119

C. (301) 934-2288
laplataumc@gmail.com
R. (240) 217-6369
sing4joy2hymn@gmail.com

Lanham #8290
5512 Whitfield Chapel Rd, Lanham, MD 20706-2512
Kevin Slayton   PL
644 E. 33rd Street, Baltimore, MD 21218

C. (301) 577-1500
lanhamumc2@verizon.net
R. (410) 243-2481
revkevinslayton@gmail.com

Lexington Park #8320
21760 Great Mills Rd, Lexington Park, MD 20653-3801
Douglas Hays   FE
48050 Mayflower Dr, Lexington Park, MD 20653-2565

C. (301) 863-8500
lpumc@md.metrocast.net
R. (443) 465-8128
dougjhays@hotmail.com

Lexington Park #8320
21760 Great Mills Rd, Lexington Park, MD 20653-3801
Lori H. Hays   FE
48050 Mayflower Dr, Lexington Park, MD 20653-2565

C. (301) 863-8500
lpumc@md.metrocast.net
R. (443) 465-7954
PastorLori7@gmail.com

Lusby
Eastern #8330
PO Box 535, Lusby, MD 20657-0535
(975 Eastern Church Rd)
St John #8340
PO Box 535, Lusby, MD 20657-0535
(1475 Sollers Wharf Road)
Brenda L. Mcilwain   FE
3494 Old Crown Dr, Pasadena, MD 21122-6409

C. (410) 326-2699
Lusbycharge@gmail.com

C. (410) 326-2987
lusbycharge@gmail.com

R. (410) 255-5355
brendapsdn@aol.com

Metropolitan #8420
3385 Metropolitan Church Rd, Indian Head, MD 20640-3213
Darryl K. Mason   OF
3453 Linden Grove Dr, Waldorf, MD 20603-4039

C. (301) 375-9088
metroumc@verizon.net

darrylkmason@gmail.com

Mount Calvary/St. Matthews
Mount Calvary #8150
37345 New Market Rd, Charlotte Hall, MD 20622-3086
St Matthews #8280
PO Box 1389, La Plata, MD 20646-1389
(10577 Charles Street)
   Kevin Brooks PL
   69 Harry S Truman Dr Apt 34, Upper Marlboro, MD 20774

C. (301) 884-7320
pastor@route6charge.org
C. (301) 934-2203
pastor@route6charge.org

R. (301) 324-3102
pastor@route6charge.org

Mount Hope #8475
PO Box 125, Sunderland, MD 20689-0125
(145 Dalrymple Road)
   Nona Colbert PL
   2456 Richmond Way, Waldorf, MD 20603

C. (410) 257-3206
mhumc145@verizon.net

R. (240) 346-5301
Pastor1nona@outlook.com

Mount Oak #8355
14110 Mount Oak Rd, Mitchellville, MD 20721-1208
Robert (Bob) Barnes, Jr. FE
225 New York Ave, Pasadena, md 21122

C. (301) 249-2230
MO@mtoak.org
R. (410) 317-5177
pastorbob@mtoak.org

Mount Olive #8430
10 Fairground Rd, Prince Frederick, MD 20678
Dana Jones PE
1o Fairground Road, Prince Frederick, MD 20689

C. (410) 535-5756
officeadmin@mtoliveumchurch.com
R. (410) 474-1970
dmjones135@comcast.net

Mount Zion #8350
27108 Mount Zion Church Rd, Mechanicsville, MD 20659
Stephen Humphrey FE
  29025 Livingston Dr, Mechanicsville, MD 20659

C. (301) 884-4132
admin-mtzion@md.metrocast.net
R. (240) 249-6156
preacher.steve.humphrey@gmail.com

Mount Zion #8450
PO Box 38, Saint Inigoes, MD 20684-0038
(17412 Mt. Zion Church Road)
   Doris J. Rothwell PL
   46534 Majestic Ct, Lexington Park, MD 20653-1863

C. (301) 872-4006
delores.greene@navy.mil

R. (301) 997-8605
pastordorisrothwell@yahoo.com

Mount Harmony-Lower Marlboro #8365
155 E Mount Harmony Rd, Owings, MD 20736
Faith Wilkerson FE
155 E Mount Harmony Rd, Owings, MD 20736-3442

C. (410) 257-2761
MtHarmonyLMUMC@comcast.net
R. (410) 257-2761
revfaithlewis@yahoo.com

New Hope Fellowship
Christ #8115
22919 Christ Church Rd, Aquasco, MD 20608-9784
Nottingham-Myers #8485
15601 Brooks Church Rd, Upper Marlboro, MD 20772-8416
Constance C. Smith FE
18804 Aquasco Rd, Brandywine, MD 20613

C. (301) 888-1316
christumcaquasco@gmail.com
C. (301) 888-2171
nmumc@msn.com
R. (301) 888-1283
revconi53@yahoo.com

Olivet #8335
13575 Olivet Rd, Lusby, MD 20657-2633
Linda W. Motter FE
12814 Lake View Dr, Lusby, MD 20657-3246

C. (410) 326-8400
jbiggans@wmata.com
R. (410) 570-4858
lindamotter@icloud.com

Oxon Hill #8380
6400 Livingston Rd, Oxon Hill, MD 20745-2909
Patricia Allen FE
6400 Livingston Rd, Oxon Hill, MD 20745-2909

C. (301) 839-4748
OxonHillUMC@verizon.net
R. (410) 963-8942
PastorP527@gmail.com

Peters #8180
2785 Chaney Rd, Dunkirk, MD 20754-2303
Sonja Penny PL
1613 Thomas Rd, Fort Washington, MD 20744-4130

C. (410) 257-6620
petersumc@yahoo.com
R. (301) 292-1472
sjpenny1223@comcast.net

Pisgah #8270
PO Box 168, Marbury, MD 20658-0168
(7020 Poorhouse Rd)
Jeanne Parr PL
6091 Tapir Pl, Waldorf, MD 20603-4347

C. (301) 743-3339
pisgahchurchumc@gmail.com

R. (301) 653-7570
jsngpraise@yahoo.com

Providence-Fort Washington #8205
10610 Old Fort Rd, Ft Washington, MD 20744-2631
Kermit C. Moore PL
9109 Bank St, Brandywine, MD 20613-7784

C. (301) 292-2323
Provich@aol.com
R. (301) 938-8971
kermitccmoore@gmail.com

Queens Chapel #7315
7410 Old Muirkirk Rd, Beltsville, MD 20705-1338
William E. Butler FE
16312 Marsham Dr, Upper Marlboro, MD 20772-3236

C. (301) 210-9038
secretary@queenschapelumc.com
R. 301-627-0787
jbweb1@comcast.net

Shiloh #8140
PO Box 182, Bryans Road, MD 20616-0182
(7305 Indian Head Highway)
Cindy Banks PL
5660 Port Tobacco Rd, Indian Head, MD 20640-3511

C. (301) 375-8816
shilohumc@verizon.net

R. (301) 503-6800
pastorcindyb@gmail.com

Shiloh Community #8375
PO Box 267, Newburg, MD 20664-2517
(12760 Shiloh Church Rd)

C. (240) 441-8292

Smith Chapel #8415
PO Box 505, Marbury, MD 20658-0505
(7130 Poorhouse Rd)
George DeFord RE
4452 Pleasant Hill Ct, Pomfret, MD 20675-3107

C. (301) 743-2227
smithchapel1901@aol.com

R. (301) 868-2382
secgensig@yahoo.com

Smithville #8185
3005 Ferry Landing Rd, Dunkirk, MD 20754-2941
Paul Papp FE
3001 Ferry Landing Rd, Dunkirk, MD 20754-2941

C. (410) 257-3160
smithvilleumcdunkirk@gmail.com
R. (410) 627-1335
pastorpapp@aol.com

Solomons #8470
14454 Solomons Island Road, Solomons, MD 20688-0403
Dottie Yunger FE
14454 Solomons Island Rd, Solomons, MD 20688

C. (410) 326-3278
solomonsumchurch@gmail.com
R. (202) 674-7788
patuxentpastor@gmail.com

St. Edmonds #8160
3000 Darlymple Rd, Chesapeake Beach, MD 20732-0539
Joan Jones PL
PO Box 449, Owings, MD 20736

C. (410) 257-7311
stedmondsumc@verizon.net
R. 410-257-7393
pastorjoan21350@live.com

St Luke #8445
12880 Point Lookout Road, Ridge, MD 20680-0072
Delonta Hicks SY
12860 Shiloh Church Rd, Newburg, MD 20664-2515

C. (301) 872-5142
pastorofstluke@gmail.com
R. (301) 259-2197
pastorofstluke@gmail.com

St Matthews #8125
14900 Annapolis Rd, Bowie, MD 20715-1802
Daniel Mejia FE
4106 Crosswick Turn, Bowie, MD 20715

C. (301) 262-1408
churchoffice@stmatthews-bowie.org
R. (301) 875-8988
danielmejia@stmatthews-bowie.org

St Paul #8345
11000 Hg Trueman Rd, Lusby, MD 20657-2848
Walter Beaudwin FE
10960 Hg Trueman Rd, Lusby, MD 20657-2847

C. (410) 326-4475
stpaulumcinfo@gmail.com
R. (240) 925-6686
Walter.beaudwin@gmail.com

Dave Showalter FD
2060 Brians Way, Lusby, MD 20657-2477

R. (410) 326-2150
dave4godsteens.stpaul@comcast.net

St Paul #8385
6634 Saint Barnabas Rd, Oxon Hill, MD 20745-2905
Daryl Williams FE
12621 Spriggs Request Ct, Bowie, MD 20721-2512

C. (301) 567-4433
admin@stpumcmd.org
R. (301) 445-2091
Revdlw@gmail.com

Trinity #8435
90 Church Street, Prince Frederick, MD 20678-2142
James (Jim) Swecker FE
90 Church Street, Prince Frederick, MD 20678-2142

C. (410) 535-1782
churchoffice@trinityumchurch.org
R. (410) 535-1782
jimswecker61@gmail.com

Union #8490
14418 Old Marlboro Pike, Upper Marlboro, MD 20772-2838
Kendrick Weaver FE
14324 Colonel Clagett Ct, Upper Marlboro, MD 20772

C. (301) 627-7389
unionumc1@gmail.com
R. (301) 627-1461
pastorkdweaver@gmail.com

Wards Memorial #8165
2265 Wards Chapel Rd, Owings, MD 20736-9353
Eloise Newman RP
13735 Carlene Dr, Upper Marlboro, MD 20772-6830

C. (410) 257-7644
revtina03@verizon.net
R. (301) 574-0757
revtina03@verizon.net

Waters Memorial #8465
5400 Mackall Rd, Saint Leonard, MD 20685-2307
Brian A. Berger PL
PO Box 307, Arnold, MD 21012

C. (410) 586-1716
watersumc@hotmail.com
R. (410) 507-5742
brianaberger@gmail.com

Westphalia #8510
9363 Darcy Rd, Upper Marlboro, MD 20774-2424
Timothy (Tim) West FE
14860 Augusta Classic Pl, Hughesville, MD 20637-2422

C. (301) 735-9373
swest@westphaliaum.org
R. (301) 274-9165
tweststeps@aol.com

Zion #8325   C. (301) 863-5161
21291 Three Notch Rd, Lexington Park, MD 20653-2428
    Kenneth P. Moore FE   R. (301) 247-5652
    1204 Hollyoak Rd, Odenton, MD 21113-1917   therevkenmoore@aol.com

---

Certified Candidate
    Rashida Walker CC   R. (240) 601-6987
    2509 Bellefield Ct, Ft Washington, MD 20744-3368   rchukiw@yahoo.com

Medical Leave
    Sheldon Reese FE   R. (301) 904-9489
    25 Edgewater St, Elizabethtown, NC 28337-6525   brenreese@yahoo.com

Retired
    Clark Aist RE   R. (301) 782-3302
    11701 Van Brady Rd, Upper Marlboro, MD 20772-7929   clark.aist@gmail.com

    George Aist RE   R. (301) 216-5429
    415 Russell Ave Apt 619, Gaithersburg, MD 20877-2838 george.aist@gmail.com

    George W. Anderson RE   R. (301) 249-4281
    2912 Apple Green Ln, Bowie, MD 20716-3832   georgeandcarol16@verizon.net

    Patricia (Pat) Berry RL   R. (301) 839-0464
    9104 Locksley Rd, Ft Washington, MD 20744-6853   pberryo1@msn.com

    Leroy Boldley RL   R. (410) 535-3724
    PO Box 725, Prince Frederick, MD 20678-0725

    Kenneth E. Bowen RE   R. (410) 535-1369
    4880 Hallowing Point Rd, Prince Frederick, MD 20678-3432

    Marianne Brown RE   R. (410) 375-5276
    17400 Aquasco Rd, Brandywine, MD 20613-4212   revmarianne@comcast.net

    Susan Carns RD   R. (301) 645-4534
    3775 Foxhall Dr, White Plains, MD 20695-3404   sbcarns@comcast.net

    Robert Carter RE   R. (301) 885-2447
    12646 Council Oak Dr, Waldorf, MD 20601-3585   carterrob@calvumc.org

    James E. (Ed) Chance RE   R. (301) 392-0856
    1104 Cornwall Dr, La Plata, MD 20646-3544   chancesrwe@gmail.com

    Ronald L. Collier RE   R. (301) 932-3131
    7254 Glen Albin Rd, La Plata, MD 20646-5907   rlcollier214@comcast.net

    Robert Lee Conway RE   R. (410) 535-0739
    4001 Starlight Ct, Huntingtown, MD 20639-3500   rmconway2005@comcast.net

    Tunde O. Davies RE   R. (410) 414-9791
    PO Box 130, Barstow, MD 20610-0130   tunde.davies4@gmail.com

    Ruth Dixon RL   R. (410) 610-1219
    920 Ed Joy Rd, Lusby, MD 20657-2620   pastor.ruth@hotmail.com

    George W. Ennis RE
    21754 Potomac View Dr, Leonardtown, MD 20650   georgeennis10545@msn.com

    Loren L. Gisselbeck RE   R. (440) 729-5076
    5630 Grace Woods Dr Unit 203, Willoughby, OH 44094-8917

Linda (Lynn) Glassbrook RE
2668 Highway 16 E, Sharpsburg, GA 30277-2516

R. (770) 253-1172
revlynng@outlook.com

Kenneth L. Jackson RA
7901 Laurel Lakes Ct Apt 301, Laurel, MD 20707-5053

R. (410) 908-4916
revrojack1@yahoo.com

Victor O. Johnson RE
4211 Canyonview Dr, Upper Marlboro, MD 20772-3417

R. (301) 574-4385

Richard S. Karpal RE
13801 Belle Chasse Blvd, Laurel, MD 20707-8425

R. (252) 756-4281

Robert G. Kirkley RE
PO Box 10, Taylors Island, MD 21669-0010

R. (410) 397-3498

Weller R. Lewis RE
PO Box 364, Cambridge, MD 21613-0364

R. (703) 847-5000
wellerrlewis@gmail.com

Evelyn H. Manson RE
16010 Excalibur Rd, Bowie, MD 20716-3941

R. (301) 860-1578
revev4606@msn.com

Galen R. Menne RE
6206 Gradys Walk, Bowie, MD 20715-4018

R. (301) 805-0891
galencarolyn@verizon.net

Curtis L. Mitchell RE
4523 kinmount rd, lanham, md 20706-1957

R. (301) 577-7601
clamarmi@bellatlantic.net

Kathryn B. Moore RE
1307 Peachwood Ln, Bowie, MD 20716-1818

R. (301) 218-6094
mnshereweare@comcast.net

Calvin Morris RE
6901 S Oglesby Ave Apt 7D, Chicago, IL 60649-1805

R. (773) 493-1737

Roosevelt Oliver RL
5889 Suitland Rd, Suitland, MD 20746-3307

R. (301) 735-0292
poppypreach@msn.com

Conrad D. Parker RE
10676 Ashford Cir, Waldorf, MD 20603-3209

R. (301) 893-2760
cdparker2@verizon.net

Robert E. (Bob) Paulen RE
22 Read Ave, Dewey Beach, DE 19971-2311

R. (302) 226-2269
bobpaulen@netzero.net

Hallie L. Reeves RE
9413 Sandy Creek Rd, Fort Washington, MD 20744-4872

R. (301) 839-1463

Thomas P. Roberts RE
10 Marilyn Ct, Lawrenceville, NJ 08648-2110

R. (202) 701-9622
troberts1800@gmail.com

Robert K. Rodeffer RE
621 Hobbs Dr, Silver Spring, MD 20904-6254

R. (301) 879-4304
rodeffer1@verizon.net

Keith Schukraft RA
43115 Gum Spring Dr, Leonardtown, MD 20650-4539

R. 301-475-8826
keith0811@verizon.net

Sandra E. Smith RL
10375 Cassidy Ct, Waldorf, MD 20601-3761

R. (240) 304-8068
corwin77@aol.com

Alfred E. Statesman RA
PO Box 293, Valley Lee, MD 20692-0293

R. (301) 994-1040
statesmanalfred@yahoo.com

Ann T. Strickler RE
8524 Roundhill Rd, Charlotte Hall, MD 20622-3439

R. (301) 884-8473
pastorann1@verizon.net

Henry A. Swain RE
2190 75th St N, Saint Petersburg, FL 33710-4641

R. (410) 480-1329

Stella S. Tay RD
5303 Lorraine Dr, Temple Hills, MD 20748-2419

R. (301) 412-7678
stella.tay@hotmail.com

Sandra S. (Sandy) Taylor RE
4668 Duley Dr, White Plains, MD 20695-3113

R. (301) 870-7143
revsandy@comcast.net

Richard D. Thompson RE
206 Pintail Ct, Glen Burnie, MD 21060-7569

R. (410) 394-6239
dicktom@aol.com

Harold W. Watson RE
3236 Pope St SE, Washington, DC 20020-2318

R. (202) 584-1813
bighwwatson@aol.com

Franklin L. Ways RE
12300 Surrey Circle Dr, Ft Washington, MD 20744-6244

R. (301) 292-4063

John H. Williams RE
561 Pinnacle Dr, Haines City, FL 33844-6318

R. (410) 610-9097
williams_johnh@yahoo.com

NO DISTRICT

Certified Candidate
Tracey Perry CC   R. (443) 314-6264
11920 Thurloe Dr, Timonium, MD 21093-7419   queenieqp500@gmail.com

Extension Ministry
Kirstin Shrom-Rhoads OD   R. (717) 305-8410
1620 Harpers Ferry Rd, Knoxville, MD 21758-1212   director@manidokan.com

Chris A. Wood FE   R. (302) 736-2316
120 N State St, Dover, DE 19901-3835

Stacey Cole Wilson FE   R. (443) 983-4112
13300 Cormorant Pl, Bowie, MD 20720-4762   scolewilson@bwcumc.org

Retired
Janet Becker RE   R. (410) 766-4927
314 Milton Ave, Glen Burnie, MD 21061-2238   catonsville.trinity@verizon.net

John M. Blanchard, Jr. RE   R. (856) 352-4358
507 Jaeger Ct, Sicklerville, NJ 08081-1110   john.blanchard80@yahoo.com

Edward Conaway RL   R. (410) 466-5781
4622 Debilen Cir Apt C, Pikesville, MD 21208-2425

Charles E. Harvey RE   R. (410) 647-1989
604 McKinsey Park Dr Apt 402, Severna Park, MD 21146-4567

Ray O. Herndon RE   R. (540) 672-2206
250 Pantops Mountain Rd Apt 7404, Charlottesville, VA 22911   olinherndon@gmail.com

Theodore D. Higby RE   R. (240) 291-6194
817 Jefferson Blvd, Hagerstown, MD 21740-5014   Jarhead665@msn.com

Linda A. Jacobus RE   R. (717) 454-0177
530 Sassafras Dr, Lebanon, PA 17042-8718   revlindaj64@yahoo.com

Roger W. Johnson RE   R. (201) 671-8561
1488 Tallowtree Dr, The Villages, FL 32162-2088

Paul C. Kim RE
2070 Harvest Ridge Cir, Buford, GA 30519-7359   pkim122@hotmail.com

Diedra H. Kriewald RE   R. (540) 667-0572
400 Clocktower Ridge Dr Apt 207, Winchester, VA 22603-3882   dkriewal@shentel.net

Ludwig L. Lankford RE   R. (410) 321-6109
8820 Walther Blvd., Baltimore, MD 21234-9045

Donald W. Llewellyn RE
Spring Arbor Assisted Living, Severna Park, MD 21146-1923

R. (410) 923-6572
paldl@comcast.net

Don B. Lowe RE
3152 Gracefield Rd Apt 419, Silver Spring, MD 20904-0801

R. (703) 671-5831

Burton L. Mack RE
700 Freeman Dr Apt 415, Hampton, VA 23666-4375

R. (410) 798-1638
burtonmack@msn.com

Denise M. Millett RE
1744 Tacoma Rd, Edgewater, MD 21037-2402

R. (410) 271-8696
dndmillett@msn.com

Joe S. Rainey RE
8350 Greensboro Dr Unit 531, McLean, VA 22102-3509

R. (703) 506-4639
jsrdlr@aol.com

Donald L. Shearer RE
1712 W Glendale Ave Apt 2020, Phoenix, AZ 85021-8816

R. (602) 544-8372

Terrance Thrasher RE
7 Basswood Ct, Catonsville, MD 21228-5870

R. (410) 788-4674
pleasanthillumc@msn.com

Edwin M. Wray RE
2600 Croasdaile Farm Pkwy #A360, Durham, NC 27705

R. (919) 384-2812
edwinwray50@gmail.com

Harold (Chip) Wright, II RE
408 Halsey Rd, Annapolis, MD 21401-3221

R. (301) 639-6199
revhbw2@aol.com

REPORTS

Discipleship Council

The Discipleship Council: (a) functions, as necessary, on behalf of the Annual Conference in between sessions; (b) ensures that Conference resources align to our vision, mission, and critical issues; and (c) discerns, develops, reviews, and evaluates the strategic direction of the Conference toward its vision and goals. It coordinates and consults with the Conference Council on Finance and Administration regarding the annual budget.

In the midst of leadership transitions, we have had a very productive year. In the Summer of 2018, our chairperson, Jen Ihlo, resigned due to unexpected work, General Conference, and family demands. In the Fall of 2018, the Rev. Jenny Cannon switched from being Secretary to serving as Interim Chair, and Carol Travis assumed the role of Secretary. In the Spring of 2019, the Rev. Jessica Hayden was named as Chair. In this year of experimentation, the chairs from the five interim boards participated with voice and no vote.

We accomplished the following:

1. Clarified our vision. The Baltimore-Washington Conference inspires and equips local faith communities to develop disciples of Jesus Christ for the transformation of the world. Our vision includes that our discipleship agencies will provide the structure, support and opportunity for more engagement within and beyond the local church so that more transformed lives transform lives.
2. Approved Project Transformation (PT) DC as a BWC partnered ministry. This decision has zero budgetary implications and allows them to submit an institutional report each year as their ministry within our annual conference grows. PT DC's mission is to engage young adults in purposeful leadership and ministry, support children in holistic development, and connect churches with communities. Their first summer was 2018, where 98 children participated in summer programming at Hughes Memorial United Methodist in Ward 7, and Brighter Day Ministries in Ward 8. Ninety percent of them felt that they would do well in reading at school this year. The Agreement between Project Transformation DC and the BWC is online at bwcumc.org/ptdcagreement.
3. Created a simpler process for the Ministry Relationship Oversight Committee to enable it to do its work. (https://www.bwcumc.org/administration/ministry-relationships/)
4. Clarified the BWC organizational structure and developed recommendations for realignment in collaboration with the Interim Discipleship Agency Boards, Connectional Table, and the Rules Committee.

At the 2018 Annual Conference Session, more than 80 percent of members affirmed experimenting with refocusing and realigning our collective ministry for greater impact.

Since the 2018 Annual Conference Session, BWC leaders and staff continued having conversations with a wide variety of stakeholders to discern what our next steps should be. As of April 1, 2019, more than 630 people have been involved in providing feedback and engaging in conversations regarding one or more aspects of the realignment in the Discipleship Agency areas. The Discipleship Council affirms the following:

- The realignment and refocusing has enabled the BWC to invest more in local faith community efforts through the first round of Missional Innovation Grants for Young People's Ministry, Advocacy & Action and Abundant Health. (bwcumc.org/news-and-views/missional-innovation-grants-support-creative-discipleship/)
- The realignment and refocusing has resulted in stronger collaborative staff-agency relationships which means that Annual Conference leaders are at the center, not the periphery, of decision making.
- The realignment and refocusing has allowed the BWC to have more flexibility, nimbleness and visibility with regards to urgent advocacy needs.

- There are more functional boards and more people engaged in ministry that is focused on grassroots efforts.

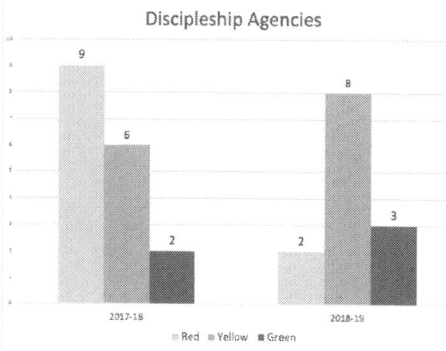

Discipleship Agencies

Red = Not functional due to not meeting or meeting to write the journal report.

Yellow = Meeting regularly, understand their why and not yet making desired impact. More than half of those in the yellow category this year believe they will be able to be green next year if given the opportunity to continue their work.

Green = Fully functional and making progress toward their purpose.

2006-2017 Baltimore-Washington Conference Agency Structure

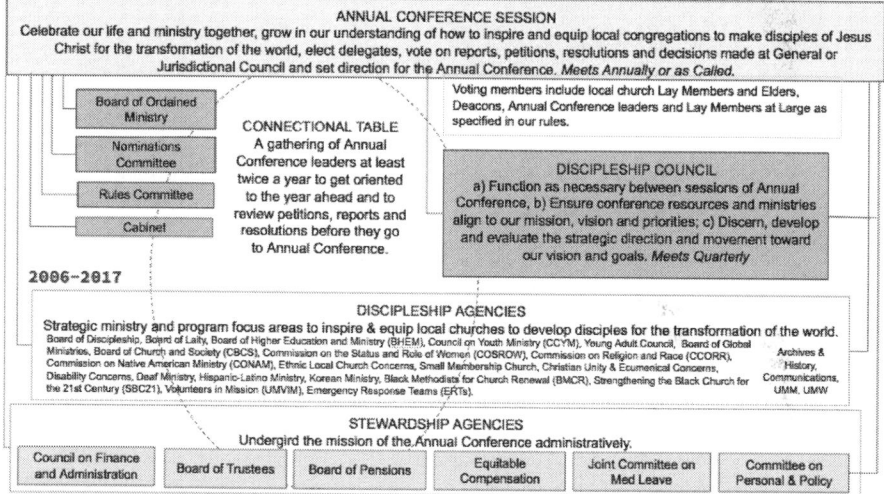

Recommended 2019 Baltimore-Washington Conference Agency Structure

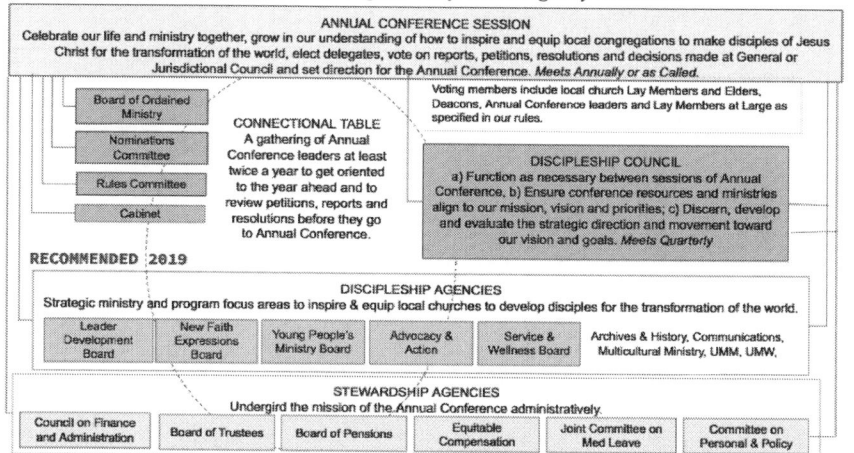

The structural simplification of Discipleship agencies provides for more clarity of purpose, cohesion, and clearer connection to the mission and ministry of local faith communities. All requirements contained within the Book of Discipline are maintained.

Strategic Focus and Streamlining of Discipleship Agencies

Notes on above:

- CBCS = Conference Board of Church and Society (now referred to as Advocacy and Action)
- COSROW = Commission on the Status and Role of Women (now referred to as Gender Equality).
- CCORR = Conference Commission on Religion and Race (now the executive team of Racial Justice).
- *Multicultural Ministry falls within the Advocacy and Action budget but impacts all five strategic areas. It includes: African American Ministry (Strengthening the Black Church for the 21st Century, and Black Methodists for Church Renewal), Deaf Ministry, Hispanic/Latino Ministry, Native American Ministry (formerly known as CONAM).
- **We seek to refrain from creating a committee when calling a meeting of leaders is sufficient. For example, an annual forum for leaders (lay and clergy) who are interested in learning and addressing ethnic local concerns/opportunities with follow-up action items taken by people who can implement them is more impactful than seven people on a committee. Annual forum notes and action items will be shared with all Discipleship board chairs and other leadership as deemed appropriate.

Leadership Development Board

Purpose:
We seek to equip and mature leaders who develop disciples of Jesus Christ who know their purpose and use their gifts to build up the body of Christ for the transformation of the world. We nurture a culture in and through the Leadership Development Board of call, competency, and spiritual maturity through teams working together to equip vibrant lay and clergy leadership throughout the conference. The Leadership Development Board coordinates, supports and contributes to all leadership efforts within the conference.

Responsibilities:
- Coordinate and communicate a master Board calendar for all leadership training within the conference.
- Meet at least quarterly and additionally as necessary, with agendas distributed one week

before each meeting, with a focused approach to each meeting.
- Ensure that new initiatives are aligned with the vision and strategic plan for leadership development in the conference.
- Engage others outside the Leadership Development Board through task forces, chaired by Board members, in the following areas:
  - Develop a coaching network to equip coaches that will walk alongside leaders implementing discipleship systems.
  - Develop a partnership with the Leadership Academy Team to provide resources and opportunities for training.
  - Develop a partnership with the Call and Clergy Care office to work with clergy and laity who feel the call to ministry in the local church.
  - Partner with our local seminaries to cultivate a pipeline of mature spiritual leaders.
  - Comply with all requirements of the Book of Discipline related to leadership development which aren't owned by other agencies and boards within the conference (¶629.Board of Discipleship functions, ¶631 Conference Board of Laity).

Team Composition: Eleven voting members including: BOOM Chair (or designee), Conference Lay Leader, Director of Lay Servant Ministries, up to six people with skills and demonstrated fruitfulness in discipleship and leadership development (three lay, three clergy), one Youth, and one Young Adult.

Ex Officio (voice, no vote): Director of Leadership and Congregational Development, Executive Minister of Call and Clergy Care, Wesley Seminary rep.

Time Commitment: Quarterly meetings (3-4 hours) either in person or via Zoom. Taskforce and subcommittee meetings as needed (depending upon the task).

New Faith Expressions Board
Purpose:
We encourage the development of New Faith Expressions, which are communities of faith in-tune with our changing culture. These communities of faith are developed with those who are not yet a part of a church in mind. We believe it will take all kinds of faith communities to reach all kinds of people. New faith expressions are not tied to a physical building (or even to keeping a church alive) but to a building of community for a purpose: to engage people in a life-giving relationship with Jesus.

Responsibilities:
Constantly cast a vision for a planting culture, where everyone feels freed up to plant a new place for new people in their community.
- By the grace of God, be able to lead people to do what they might think is impossible.
- Encourage evangelism in order to create new places and spaces for new people within and beyond the bounds of existing congregations.
- Develop and oversee systems for identifying, training, and supporting pastors and/or laity to create new faith expressions.
- Develop a strong cadre of clergy and laity who have the gifts and graces to lead new faith expressions.
- Identify and train potential partner churches to reach new people by creating new faith communities.
- Create an overarching strategic plan to accomplish the mission including vision, values, goals, priorities, and strategies.
- Assist the District Superintendents, in their role as chief mission strategists of the district, in their work of starting new faith communities and transforming existing congregations

to reach new people.
- Coordinate the use of Conference resources, in strategic ways, to help us live out our mission of inspiring and equipping local faith communities to develop disciples of Jesus Christ for the transformation of the world.

Team Composition: Ten voting members (at least one from each district) selected by the Committee on Nominations using interest forms.

Ex Officio (voice, no vote): Director of New Faith Expressions and Coordinator of Hispanic Ministries

Young People's Ministry Board
Purpose:
We nurture a culture, in and through the Young People's Ministry (YPM) Board, of loving, joyful, and hard-working teams working together to create and sustain a vibrant young people's ministry throughout the conference. The YPM Board coordinates, oversees, supports and contributes to the crafting of the vision of all young people's ministry within the conference (including, but not limited to, ROCK, campus ministry, the work of Conference Council for Youth Ministry, the work of Young Adult Council, the work of the Board of Higher Education and Ministry, and camping and retreat ministry).

Responsibilities:
- Speak into, endorse, support, and share a three-year strategic design and execution process for young people's ministry in the conference.
- Ensure that clear communication takes place between the various areas of young people's ministry in the conference.
- Coordinate and communicate a master calendar for all board-related young people's ministry programming in the conference.
- Meet at least quarterly and additionally as necessary, with agendas distributed one week before each meeting, with a calm, confident, and focused approach to each meeting.
- Ensure that new initiatives are aligned with the vision and strategic plan for young people's ministry in the conference.
- Engage others outside the Interim Young People's Ministry Board through task forces, chaired by Board members in the following areas:
  - Database
  - Training
  - Grants and Scholarships
  - Campus Ministry (many functions of BHEM)
  - Young Adult Ministry (formerly Young Adult Council)
  - Student Leader Cohort (many functions of CCYM)
  - ROCK
- Comply with all requirements of the Book of Discipline related to young people's ministry.
- Assess strategic ministry needs and troubleshoot key pressure points efficiently and effectively.

Team Composition: Ten voting members (at least four of which are youth) selected by the Committee on Nominations using interest forms completed by youth and young adults and ensuring there is balanced representation from all areas (Student Leadership Cohort, campus ministry, Retreat and Camping ministry, and Young Adult Ministry).

Ex Officio (voice, no vote): ROCK event coordinator, Retreat & Camping Ministry rep, Campus Ministry rep, two advocate advisers who hold leadership roles in the local church and have extensive experience with young people, and a staff rep.

Advocacy & Action Board

Purpose:

We inspire and equip faith communities to develop disciples of Jesus Christ for the transformation of the world by collaborating with others to transform systems that disenfranchise, marginalize, and oppress. The Advocacy and Action Board is tasked with establishing a clear, consistent and impact-driven BWC presence on urgent policy matters at local, state, and national levels, and helps set Conference-wide justice priorities rooted in our Social Principles.

Responsibilities:

- Develop, share, and implement a strategic plan for justice ministry throughout the conference that includes vision, values, goals, priorities, and execution strategies that is revised and re-evaluated annually.
- Coordinates, oversees, supports, and contributes to the implementation of its vision through the work of social action teams, specialized committees, and forums:
  - Seven Social Action Teams: Climate/Environmental Justice, Gender Equality (COSROW ¶644), Gun Violence Prevention, Immigration Reform, Racial Justice (CCORR ¶643), Restorative Justice (R/CJAMM), Wealth Equity
  - Representation from the following: Commission on Disability Concerns (¶653), Committee on Hispanic/Latino ministries (¶655), Deaf Ministries, Grow Church through Ministries for Asian Americans, Native American Ministry (CONAM ¶654), Strengthening the Black Church for the 21st Century
  - Three Annual Forums: Small Membership Church, Ethnic Local Church Concerns, Christian Unity and Interreligious Relationships
- Comply with all requirements of the Book of Discipline related to Advocacy & Action (e.g. ¶629, ¶642, ¶643, and ¶644 and relevant parts of ¶632, ¶645, ¶653, ¶654, ¶655).
- Ensure that new initiatives are aligned with the vision and strategic plan for BWC's justice ministry.
- Organize needed training for local churches and leaders on community organizing, intercultural proficiency, and justice as a spiritual discipline to grow and multiply disciples.
- Coordinate with the Office of Leadership and Congregational Development/Leader Development Board to hold Annual Forums (see above).
- Assess strategic ministry needs and troubleshoot key pressure points efficiently and effectively.
- Create and/or identify systems to track progress and maintain connection with Advocacy & Action servant leaders and other engaged persons.
- Ensure clear communication between all aspects of the Advocacy & Action network.
- Coordinate and communicate an external master calendar for all Advocacy & Action board-related programming throughout the conference.
- Meet at least quarterly and additionally as necessary, with meaningful and productive agendas that foster a calm, confident, and focused approach to each meeting.
- Establish and maintain work groups, task forces, and/or subcommittees, chaired by Board members or designees, to ensure effective implementation of the strategic plan.

Team Composition: Fifteen voting members with passion and commitment to justice and service to include: 7 chairs of each A&A Social Action Team; 3 annual forum leaders (see above), and 4 others whose collective gifts span grant administration, project management, legislative advocacy, and data analysis and evaluation, selected by the Committee on Nominations using interest forms as well as ensuring at least three board members are young adults.

Ex Officio (voice, no vote): Representatives from: Deaf Ministries, Committee on Disability Concerns, Justice for Our Neighbors (JFON), UMW, UMM, Native American Ministries (CONAM), Committee on Hispanic/Latino Ministries, and a staff representative.

Wellness & Missions Board

Purpose:

We nurture a culture, in and through the Wellness & Missions (WM) Board, of loving, passionate, and committed teams, working together to create and sustain programs and ministries that develop disciples of Jesus Christ through alleviating human suffering, meeting human needs, and proactively creating abundant health for individuals and communities.

Responsibilities:

- Speak into, endorse, support, and share a long-range strategic design and execution process for wellness and service ministry throughout the conference (revise and re-evaluate annually).
- The WM Board is responsible for crafting the vision of all health ministry and mission outreach work within the conference. It coordinates, oversees, supports, and contributes to living out that vision through specialized programs, ministry offerings, and organizational efforts including, but not limited to:
  - Volunteers in Mission (VIM)
  - Early Response Teams (ERT) / Disaster Response
  - HIV-AIDS Ministry / Quality of Life Retreats
  - Global and national missionary itineration
  - Holistic health ministry training and events
  - Health advocacy and linking individuals to health services
  - Collaborating on Mission u
  - The work of Seeds of Security / Domestic Violence/Intimate Partner Violence Prevention (DV/IPV)
  - Wellness & Preventive Health Care
- Comply with all requirements of the Book of Discipline related to Board of Global Ministries ¶633.
- Ensure that new initiatives are aligned with the vision and strategic plan for BWC Wellness and Missions.
- Assess strategic ministry needs and troubleshoot key pressure points efficiently and effectively.
- Ensure that clear communication takes place between all areas of Wellness and Mission Service.
- Coordinate and communicate an external master calendar for all Wellness and Mission Service programming throughout the conference.
- Meet at least quarterly and additionally as necessary, with meaningful and productive agendas that foster a calm, confident, and focused approach to each meeting.
- Establish and maintain work groups, task forces, and/or subcommittees, chaired by Board members or designees, to ensure effective implementation of the strategic plan.

Team Composition: Thirteen voting members with passion and commitment to health and mission ministry including the Conf. Secretary of Global Ministries, VIM Coordinator, and Disaster Response Coordinator, one youth or young adult, and nine others who have gifts in grant administration, project management, training and instruction, and/or data analysis and evaluation, selected by the Committee on Nominations using interest forms.

Ex Officio (voice, no vote): UMW representative, UMM representative, and a staff representative

Connectional Table

Some conference leaders believe that instead of the Connectional Table we should simply call meetings of Annual Conference leaders as necessary: once in the fall for orientation and any generative work needed to the coming year and then again to review petitions, reports and resolutions before they go to Annual Conference. Furthermore, voting concurrence/non-concurrence doesn't hold the weight that many attribute to it as often the issues are complex and members have admitted not really understanding what they are voting on.

There was discussion at the Connectional Table and Discipleship Council about the purpose and, ultimately need for the 8 members who have no Annual Conference leadership position. The original logic for was so that the votes of Connectional Table on resolutions represents something of the Annual Conference as a whole and not just Conference leadership. However, 8 votes out of 89 isn't significant and the need for those persons given the current function of the table isn't clear.

In the event that the Connectional Table is continued, we are recommending a slight decrease in the number of voting members from 89 to 84 as follows:

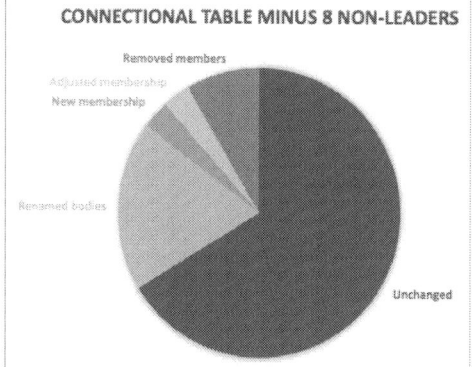

CONNECTIONAL TABLE MINUS 8 NON-LEADERS

- Rename 9 member bodies (2 members each) to reflect the new Discipleship Agency structure;
- Remove 8 members with no other Annual Conference position;
- Adjust the numbers of members from three bodies; and
- Add 6 new members (VIM Coordinator; one member from each caucus without current representation (B-WARM, MFSA, and WCA); and chair plus one from New Faith Expressions Board.

Membership of the Connectional Table is as follows with recommended changes in bold.

2014-2017 Membership[1]	2019 Membership Changes
1-Conference Lay Leader	same
1-Conference Secretary	same
1-Resident Bishop	same
16-District Superintendents and District Lay Leaders	same
8-District Reps With No Other Leadership Experience	**0-District Reps with No Other Leadership Experience**
1-Nominations	same
1-Conference Secretary of Global Ministries	same
Reps from chapters of local caucuses	
1-Black Methodists for Church Renewal	same
1-Korean Caucus	same
	1-VIM Coordinator
2-Discipleship Council	same
2-Retreat and Camping Ministries (RCM)[2]	**Young People's Ministry Board's RCM Reps**
2-Committee on Hispanic/Latino Ministries ~~and Korean Caucus~~[3]	*Committee on Hispanic/Latino Ministries*
2-Commission on Religion & Race	same
2-Commission on Disability Concerns	same
2-Youth Ministries	**Young People's Ministry Board's High School Youth Reps (or equivalent)**
2-Young Adult Ministries	**Young People's Ministry Board's Young Adult Reps from Young Adult Ministries (or equivalent)**
2-United Methodist Women	same
2-United Methodist Men	same
2-Council on Finance and Administration	same
2-Board of Ordained Ministry	same
2-Rules Committee	same
2-Board of Trustees	same
2-Board of Pensions	same

2-Commission on Equitable Compensation	same
2-Commission on Archives/History	same
2-Communications	same
2-Personnel & Policy	same
2-Episcopacy	same
2-Deaf Ministries	same
2-Board of Church & Society	Advocacy & Action Board (or equivalent)
2-Board of Discipleship[4]	Leader Development Board (or equivalent)
2-Board of Global Ministries	Wellness & Service Board (or equivalent)
2-Board of Higher Education and Ministry	YPM Board's Campus Ministry Task Force (or equivalent)
2-Commission on the Status and Role of Women (COSROW)	Advocacy & Action Board's Gender Equity (COSROW) or equivalent
2-Commission on Native American Ministry (CONAM)	Advocacy & Action Board's Native American Ministry Team (CONAM) or equivalent
2-Commission on Small Member Church (SMC)	1-Convener of SMC Forum
2-Commission on Ethnic Local Church Concerns (ELCC)	1-Convener of ELC Forum
2-Commission on Christian Unity & Interreligious Concerns (CUIC)	1-Convener of CUI Forum
	2-New Faith Expressions Board (or equivalent)
Non-Voting Membership	
Assistant to the Bishop	
Director of Connectional Ministry	
Director of Communications	
Conference Treasurer	

In the coming year, we seek to identify shared metrics that are meaningful for all and keep us aligned and focused on our mission.

- Progress on Discipleship Agency board goals (see ministry report for details) which are essential to the BWC's mission of inspiring and equipping local faith communities to develop disciples of Jesus Christ for the transformation of the world so that more transformed lives transform
- Number of people:
  - Engaged and
  - Maturing in Wesleyan discipleship
- Impact being made in communities in which our churches and ministries reside.

Discipleship Council Recommendations:

1. The adoption of a BWC vision statement that includes the tagline: transformed lives transform lives.
2. The approval of a ministry partnership with Project Transformation DC, a ministry that seeks to bring together young adult interns, local United Methodist congregations, and children/youth of underserved neighborhoods for academic and personal enrichment during the summer months. The agreement between the Project Transformation and the BWC, which was approved by the Ministry Relations Oversight Committee, Discipleship Council and reviewed by the Chancellor, is at www.bwcumc.org/ptdcagreement.
3. The realignment of Discipleship Agencies to allow for more effective, focused and nimble ministry by re-forming Discipleship Agencies into these five boards:
   a. Leadership Development
   b. New Faith Expressions
   c. Young People's Ministry

[1] Per 2006 Journal. The number indicates the number of people represented
[2] The BWC hasn't had a Retreat and Camping Ministry Board since 2005
[3] Per 2006 structure author's annotation, the Korean Caucus should show up under the local caucuses and not be listed as a part of Hispanic/Latino Ministries
[4] BWC has been operating without a Board of Discipleship for many years

    d. Advocacy and Action

    e. Wellness and Missions

    This includes allowing Discipleship Agencies to modify task forces as needed to address ministry needs while maintaining Book of Discipline requirements.

4. The modifications as noted to the Connectional Table which allow for appropriate interfacing with new Discipleship Agency structure and remove eight members who have no Annual Conference Leadership Role.

5. Update language within BWC's Policies and Procedures manual as needed to reflect the name changes contained within this report.

Submitted by Rev. Jessica Hayden, Discipleship Council Chair, and Christie Latona, Director of Connectional Ministries.

Office of Leadership Development

The Office of Leadership Development's primary role is to provide resources to equip laity, pastors and congregations in learning and leadership development.

Our goals for 2018:
- Promote local and national training events provided resources, strategies and tools for new and revitalized congregations;
- Increase annual conference resources to equip congregations to enhance both internal and external mission and evangelistic opportunities to fulfill our call to make disciples of Jesus Christ for the transformation of the world.

Our mission impact for 2018:
- Leader training was offered through Tending the Fire, The Laity Fix, and Five Things Your Visitors Are Thinking, But Won't Ask;
- Local church workshops on leadership development, conflict management, community engagement, planning tools, and stewardship;
- Congregations were resourced through MissionInsite, Lifeway, Readiness 360 and DISC Assessments;
- Coaching resources were provided toward certification;
- Scholarships were provided for pastors and laity to attend the Mid-Atlantic Stewardship Academy;
- Scholarships were awarded for pastors and laity to attend Exponential New Church Training and the Leadership Institute;
- The new Leadership Development Board has been developed;
- Additional resources added this year are LeaderPod UMC, a new podcast series;
- Two new publications this year; Resurgence: Navigating the Changing Ministry Landscape, and Blank Slate: Write Your Own Rules for a 22nd-Century Church Movement;
- This office has also managed grants for leader development, new ministry, and new and renewed congregation development request.

Our objectives for 2019:
- Expand our collaborative work with New Faith Expression through strategic implementation of vital ministry places birthed out of new and existing vital congregations;
- Equip a network of Resurgence Coaches to turn around congregations;
- Enlarge our strategic focus on discipleship systems;
- Launch a BWC Leadership Academy.

Rev. Rodney T. Smothers, Director of Leadership and Congregation Development

Conference Board of Laity
The Ministry of the Laity is responsible for making disciples of Jesus Christ to support the mission of the Baltimore-Washington Conference. The Board continues its efforts to encourage the participation of all laypersons in broader areas and understanding life of the various ministries of the Conference.

The District Lay Leaders are actively engaged in and carrying out their missions. Richard Willson, Cumberland-Hagerstown, represented the group by attending the NEJ Association of Conference Lay Leaders in Springfield, Mass.

The Conference Committee on Lay Servant Ministry has done exceedingly well under the leadership of Linda Flanagan. The Committee cares for the training of Lay Servants and Certified Lay Servant Ministers.

The main goal for this year was to train laity across the Conference. The eight districts hosted many classes that included various topics. There were four regional Leadership Days training sessions across the Conference. This goal was exceeded far above expectations. It is also exciting to encourage young disciples to participate in the Lay Servant classes.

It was a blessing to celebrate the appointment of one the District Lay Leaders (also a CLM), Rod Fry, as pastor of two small churches: Ijamsville and Flint Hill UMC. He also has a thriving Motorcycle Ministry, reaching out to the secular community. The goal is to continue this ministry.

The Lay Leaders serve on many Local, District and Conference Boards and Committees, and often chair them.

The major project that is planned is to have a one or two-day retreat with all laity in the Conference, to share how they can get involved. This will especially be focused on interest in Lay Servant training, CLM training, Lay Members to Annual Conference, etc. Another focus area will be discussions regarding General Conference decisions proceedings and how we look to the future.

Another goal is to focus on encouraging youth and young adults to become more active and involved in the life of the church.

Delores Martin, Conference Lay Leader

New Faith Expressions
Our purpose is to create new places and spaces for new people in order to reach more new people, more young people, and more diverse people who become more like Christ in the world.

Every church was once a new church. Every church began as a dream of a person or group of people who desired that a new group of people know Christ and be a part of the community that we know of as the church.

As United Methodists within the Baltimore Washington Conference, we have inherited this church-planting ethic. We are also in the unique position of being the birth place of the Methodist Movement within the United States, and so we stand on the shoulders of giants who planted the churches in which we find ourselves.

My assignment since August was to "survey" the lay of the land and get an understanding of why what we have tried has not worked and to establish a base line for what New Faith Expressions can look like for our Annual Conference. A New Faith Expression is a community of faith in-tune with our changing culture. These communities of faith are developed with those in mind who are not yet a part of a church. We believe it will take all kinds of churches to reach all kinds of people.

Many of our communities have church buildings on every corner, but we must realize approximately 80 percent of the American population is not participating in a church gathering on any given Sunday.

New faith expressions are not tied to a physical building (or even to keeping a church alive) but to a building of community for a purpose: to engage people in a life-giving relationship with Jesus. While we have had some successes in this area, we have struggled due to the following:
- Significant push back of other United Methodist churches in areas where new churches were being launched;
- A lack of initial and ongoing training for new church planters;
- The transition from the founding pastor to the second or third clergy leader.

As we move forward, we will be focusing on:
- Developing a process and system for identifying and training Clergy and Laity who could start New Faith Expressions;
- Work with the District Superintendents, in their role as chief missional strategist, in their work of starting new faith communities and transforming existing congregations to reach new people;
- Develop a comprehensive plan for launching New Faith Expressions throughout our Annual Conference.

Rev. Bill Brown, Interim Director of New Faith Expressions

Young People's Ministry
Overview
The executive summary of the strategic plan for Young People's Ministry includes the following components:
- The Strategic Planning Process and Summary
- Specific Recommendations for Annual Conference 2019 for Young People's Ministry
- Progress Report
- Retreat & Camping Ministries (RCM) Strategic Plan
- The Young People's Ministry Visioning Documents
- The Young People's Ministry Board Job Description
- The Strategic Planning Process and Summary

Over the past 14 months, the Young People's Ministry of the Baltimore-Washington Conference of The United Methodist Church (BWC) has engaged in a process of developing a comprehensive strategic plan for Young People's Ministry in the conference. A significant number of stakeholders throughout the conference have given input to this plan.
In January 2018, Ministry Architects facilitated an initial listening session with 45 people engaged in a wide variety of ways in ministry to young people throughout the conference. Soon after this gathering, in May 2018, a Young People's Ministry survey was sent to all conference churches, with 157 people responding.

In September 2018, Mark DeVries and Aqueelah Ligonde from Ministry Architects met with approximately 110 stakeholders in young people's ministry in six focus groups, collaboratively developing the contours of the strategic plan.

Mark DeVries also met with groups of 35 stakeholders in October 2018 and January 2019 to invite much needed input on the various expressions of the values and goals for the Young People's Ministry.

The strategic assessment report, originally crafted in September 2018, has been revised several times as additional groups of stakeholders have spoken into the plan. The final version of the report includes these elements:
- Background on the Conference and each ministry within YPM
- A dashboard representing pertinent data from the GCFA statistical report
- Current assets within YPM
- Current challenges facing YPM
- Key principles of the strategic plan for YPM
- Visioning documents, including core values, 3-year goals, benchmarks, and strategies
- Recommendations for developing the structure of YPM
- Specific recommendations for youth ministry, young adult ministry, and campus ministry
- Recommendations for Annual Conference 2019
- A timeline for sequencing the execution of all recommendations

In addition to the conference vision and mission, the strategic plan has been informed by the following overarching, foundational priorities:
- We have made the choice to disproportionately invest in young people (aligned with the research of Sticky Faith and Growing Young) and in developing leadership.
- We will focus on building healthy connective tissue between expressions of Young People's Ministry as much or more than we focus on creating new programs. As a result, we will focus first on building the structures of connection between current expressions of Young People's Ministry in the conference. This includes:
- Building the essential infrastructure for a vibrant, integrated, deep-impact ministry for young people in the conference.
- Improving our database and strategies for communication.
- We will support innovation that enables the church to continue co-creating with God, aligning with Wesleyan discipleship and remaining relevant. This includes:
- Cultivating an innovative ethos around student ministry, camping ministry, campus ministry, and young adult ministry in the conference, providing latitude for the development of communication channels and innovative programs that may not naturally fit into the conference's current structure (the books, Orbiting the Giant Hairball and Innovator's Dilemma can serve as a reference point).
- Holding fast to the combination of healthy systems and a willingness to embrace disruptive innovation.
- We will advocate the shift from seeing young people as recipients of mission to seeing them as partners and agents of mission and ministry themselves.

Anticipated Changes After Annual Conference 2019
The strategic plan recommends the following approvals related to the work of Young People's Ministry in the BWC and hopes the Annual Conference affirms that as a part of the Discipleship Council Report:
- Transition the Interim Young People's Ministry Board to an official permanent board with a clearly defined composition of members including youth, young members and ex officio members representing campus ministry, RCM, ROCK (see job description).
- Transition aspects of the Conference Council on Youth Ministry to a Student Leadership Cohort that includes district youth coordinators and up to 30 youth from across the

conference and their mentors.

Additionally:
Pilot campus ministry training hub at UMD as an innovation for campus ministry.
Create Task Forces to develop infrastructure and innovation in the following areas:
Training
Database
Young adult ministry
Youth ministry
Campus ministry
Grants and scholarships
Site-based retreat and camping ministry
Student Leader Cohort
Affirm RCM to raise money for camperships each year to a maximum of $500,000/year so that every child can afford to go to a BWC camp.

Progress Report
In the months in which the strategic plan has been drafted, some implementation has already begun to take place, including:
- Significant steps have been taken to update Arena with Young People's Ministry stakeholders.
- A timeline and game plan for introducing a campus ministry hub at UMD have been developed and implementation has begun.
- Job descriptions for Young People's ministry task forces have been created and recruiting of task force members has begun.

Submitted by: Shemaiah Strickland, Chair, Jack Arnold, Vice Chair, and Cheryl Cook, Coordinator of Young People's Ministry and Special Projects

Retreat & Camping Ministries Strategic Plan
Parallel to the Young People's Ministry strategic planning process with Ministry Architects, Retreat and Camping Ministries (RCM) engaged Kaleidoscope Inc., a camp and retreat center consultant, to evaluate the ministry's current operations and provide strategic plans for increased ministry effectiveness and sustainability. Kaleidoscope met with site stakeholders, RCM staff, and a working team of RCM staff and conference leaders to gather feedback on the sites, process site usage data, and explore potential areas for growth over the course of several months in the Fall of 2018. To view our ministry report and the comprehensive strategic plan go to bwcumc.org/RCMnext. Here are the highlights.

Long-Term Growth Drivers
Focus summer camp program model to provide excellent, vital ministry, maximizing the unique setting of each property.
Expand the model for retreats to better serve adult and family groups.
Develop intercultural proficiency in each location to connect people, history, program, property, and faith development.

RCM Strategic Analysis
Camp Harmison – Berkeley Springs, WV
While thousands of people have experienced Christ in the beautiful and rustic setting of Harmison since it began operation in 1959, through analysis and prayerful discernment, we discovered there is not a viable model for sustainable ministry and will cease operations in Fall of 2019.

We are helping Camp Joy and others find a new home so they can continue their ministry in the Berkeley Springs area or at Manidokan.

We are in conversation with the relevant parties to ensure the Harmison legacy is honored as we reallocate and focus resources to other sites.

A celebration of Camp Harmison will be scheduled for the Fall.

Manidokan Camp & Retreat Center – Knoxville, MD

While usage of Manidokan has nearly doubled over the past 10 years, it is considered a small sized operation and is thus on the edge of viability.

One of the major limiting factors is capacity. Overnight capacity should be increased to 200 (150 youth beds, 50 adult beds) from the current 112 year-round accommodations.

The programming at Manidokan should focus on adventure and utilizing the 400+ acre property.

Both retreat and summer camp groups should take better advantage of local attractions including Harpers Ferry, West Virginia, the C&O Canal, and Antietam Battlefield.

The site must differentiate youth, intergenerational, and adult spaces to better meet the unique needs of those groups.

West River

West River is the most used property in the BWC RCM and considered a medium sized and sustainable operation. However, the site has not maximized its potential.

The sleeping capacity of West River is sufficient, but the quality of the accommodations must be improved and differentiated between adult and youth spaces to better meet the needs of those populations.

The day camp program started in 2012 has sold out in recent years and should be aggressively expanded to two or three times the current size.

The waterfront is a big draw for campers and guests, so the programming at the site should take better advantage of that resource. Every camper and guest should have an opportunity to interact with the water, not just observe it.

Next Steps

Beginning in 2019 RCM will take steps to implement these recommendations including:

Cease operation at Camp Harmison and reallocate resources to Manidokan and West River.

Focus Manidokan adventure programming with two new rustic programs and visit several camps with successful adventure programs in our connection to glean best practices.

Expand West River day camp by 50% in 2019 and develop plans for continued expansion of the program over the next several years.

Create a development program for RCM.

Align staff to free up time needed to focus on identified growth areas.

Complete the long-range planning process with site master plans for Manidokan and West River.

Submitted by: Chris Schlieckert, Director of Retreat and Camping Ministries

Young People's Ministry Visioning Documents
YOUNG PEOPLE'S MINISTRY VALUES

DO NO HARM. DO GOOD. STAY IN LOVE WITH GOD.

Courageous Love: We have been called by Christ into an inclusive love that welcomes all, celebrates differences, and anchors difficult conversations in respect and kindness.

Humble Urgency: We have been invited to a work of incomparable importance, and we remain equally committed to doing no harm in our efforts to achieve this mission.

Bold Innovation: We are purposeful about creativity, invention, and experimentation in order to maximize the reach and effectiveness of each initiative designed to express the love of God.

Faithful Openness: We are rooted in God's love through Jesus Christ, who calls us beloved, and yet we are always learning more of the unfolding work of the Spirit.

Restful Work: We are eager to work hard for those things that matter most, while living in patient grace, including intentional rest.

Ministry Goals
TARGET DATE: DECEMBER 31, 2021
ONE-YEAR BENCHMARK: DECEMBER 31, 2019

OVERVIEW: The following three-year goals and one-year benchmarks provide a clear, ambitious, tangible expression of the vision and values of Young People's Ministry in the Baltimore-Washington Conference. The three-year goals have been designed as "stretch" aspirations, while the one-year benchmarks are achievable next steps in moving toward the more ambitious, longer term goals.

This document was designed collaboratively, in multiple iterations, with the input of the Interim Young People's Ministry Board, a wide circle of over 100 stakeholders throughout the conference, and our consultant team from Ministry Architects. The "preferred initial strategies" following each benchmark are not meant to be limiting or prescriptive but to provide possible next steps that the Young People's Ministry Board can draw upon as they move toward achieving each of the goals and benchmarks below.

ENGAGEMENT
Growing Local Church Youth Engagement: By December 2021, 50 churches have increased the number of youth engaged in their churches to a new level of participation (From 0 youth to 1+, from 1-4 youth to 5+, from 5-15 youth to 16+, from 16-29 youth to 30+, from 30-49 youth to 50+, 50-99,100-150, 150-200, 200-250+).
1-Year Benchmark: By December 2019, 15 churches have increased the number of youth engaged in their churches to a new level of participation (From 0 youth to 1+, from 1-4 youth to 5+, from 5-15 youth to 16+, from 16-30 youth to 30+, from 30-49 youth to 50+, 50-100,100-150, 150-200, 200-250+).
Expanding Young People's Engagement Beyond the Local Church: Between January 2019 and December 2021, an additional 2,000 youth and young adults (both from within the church and from outside the church) have participated in regional, district, conference or denomination-sponsored ministry events, including ROCK, camps, retreats, multi-cultural events, social justice programming, and other events.
1-Year Benchmark: A baseline number has been determined for how many youth and young adults participated in regional, district, conference or denomination-sponsored events in 2018.
1-Year Benchmark: A cross-cultural small group with youth and/or young adults gathered in 2019.
1-Year Benchmark: By December 2019, a listening campaign involving at least 25 youth per district has been completed, and the service or justice issue young people want to focus on for the next two years has been identified (in collaboration with the Advocacy and Action Board).

Campus Ministry: By December 2021, more than 500 college students are engaged through BWC connected ministries on at least 12 different campuses.
1-Year Benchmark: By December 2019, more than 200 college students are engaged through

BWC connected ministries on at least six different campuses.

LEADERSHIP DEVELOPMENT
Young Adult Leadership: At least five experiments in empowering young adults in leadership have been launched in the previous year (2021).
1-Year Benchmark: At least two experiments in empowering young adults in leadership have been launched in the previous year (2019).
Student Leadership: By December 2021, at least 200 middle school and high school students participated in a leadership training event sponsored or referred by the conference in the previous year.
1-Year Benchmark: By December 2019, at least 60 middle school and high school students participated in a leadership training event sponsored or referred by the conference in the previous year (2019).
1-Year Benchmark: By December 2021, at least 250 adult leaders of youth participated in at least one leadership training event sponsored or referred by the conference in the previous year (2021).

1-Year Benchmark: At least 75 adult leaders of youth participated in at least one leadership training event sponsored or referred by the conference in the previous year (2019).

INNOVATION
Innovation Systems: A comprehensive process has been established for celebrating, cultivating, learning from and maximizing innovations in young people's ministry, launching at least 10 initiatives in the past three years, with at least three of those initiatives in place for over a year.
1-Year Benchmark: At least one young adult initiative launched by December 2019 and a game plan and timeline for implementing a comprehensive process for innovations in Young People's Ministry has been created and approved.
Special Needs Ministry: All churches have been equipped to welcome families with a family member who has special needs. There is a church in every BWC district with an exemplar ministry for special needs children, youth, and young adults.
1-Year Benchmark: In collaboration with the Commission on Disability Ministry, all churches in the conference have been invited to complete a special-needs readiness assessment, and at least 75% of churches have completed it.
Mental Health Resources: All churches have knowledge about and ready access to robust mental health resources to help youth leaders at local churches address mental health issues, like anxiety, depression, and suicide, with their youth.
1- Year Benchmark: In collaboration with the Wellness and Service Board, a game plan has been drafted for supporting the mental health of youth and young adults throughout the conference and providing resources to churches to help youth leaders at local churches address mental health issues, like anxiety, depression, and suicide, with their youth.

Young People's Ministry Board Job Description
Purpose:
We nurture a culture, in and through the Young People's Ministry (YPM) Board, of loving, joyful, and hard-working teams serving together to create and sustain vibrant ministry with young people throughout the conference. The YPM Board coordinates, oversees, supports and contributes to the crafting of the vision of all young people's ministry within the conference (including, but not limited to, ROCK, campus ministry, the work of Young Adult Council, the work of the Board of Higher Education and Ministry, and camping and retreat ministry, and the work traditionally assumed by the Conference Council for Youth Ministry).).

Responsibilities:
Speak into, endorse, support, and share a three-year strategic design and execution process for

young people's ministry in the conference.

Ensure that clear communication takes place between the various areas of young people's ministry in the conference.

Coordinate and communicate a master calendar for all board-related young people's ministry programming in the conference.

Meet at least quarterly and additionally as necessary, with agendas distributed one week before each meeting, with a calm, confident, and focused approach to each meeting.

Ensure that new initiatives are aligned with the vision and strategic plan for young people's ministry in the conference.

Engage others outside the Interim Young People's Ministry Board through task forces, chaired by Board members in the following areas:

Training: Designs and implements all YPM training, with a particular focus on ensuring engagement at training events aligned with participation targets

Database: Ensures the ongoing development and maintenance of an integrated YPM database, with an initial target of 10,000 YPM stakeholders with robust information for each

Young Adult Ministry (formerly Young Adult Council): Reaches, empowers, connects, and engages young adults (18-35) in faithful expressions of ministry, aligned with the mission, goals, and values of the Interim Young People's Ministry Board. Meets quarterly.

Youth Ministry: Evaluates the effectiveness of conference-funded youth initiatives including but not limited to the Student Leadership Cohort and our flagship youth retreat, ROCK. Evaluation allows these ministries to continue to innovate and evolve so ministries remain fresh, relevant and aligned with the mission, goals, and values of the Young People's Ministry Board. Meets at least twice a year.

Campus Ministry (many functions of Board of Higher Education and Ministry): Ensures that the conference's investment in Campus Ministry is maximized for developing and multiplying world-transforming disciples with college students. This includes connecting campus ministries to the Church at all levels, equipping boards of directors or local church committees who provides for planning and implementing a program of mission and ministry, and monitoring and evaluating campus ministry.

Grants and Scholarships: Monitors, ranks and recommends persons to receive mission innovation grants and scholarships to the YPM Board for a final vote.

Student Leader Cohort (many functions of CCYM): equips today's leaders from different church sizes, cultures and locations to grow and serve their various communities as lifelong, world-transforming disciples while serving in an annual conference capacity and designing a conference-wide mission project for and by youth. Students return to their churches equipped and passionate about serving in and through their local church with an under.

Comply with all requirements of the Book of Discipline related to young people's ministry.

Assess strategic ministry needs and troubleshoot key pressure points efficiently and effectively.

Team Composition: 10 voting members (at least four of which are youth) selected by the Committee on Nominations using interest forms completed by youth and young adults and ensuring there is balanced representation from all areas (high school youth, campus ministry, Retreat and Camping ministry, and Young Adult Ministry)

Ex Officio (voice no vote): ROCK event coordinator, Retreat & Camping Ministry rep, Campus Ministry rep, two advocate advisers who hold leadership roles in the local church and have extensive experience with young people, and a Young People's Ministry staff rep

Time Commitment: Orientation meeting (seven hours), three quarterly meetings (three hours each), task force work (+/- 12 hours a year)

Retreat and Camping Ministries

The mission of Retreat and Camping Ministries (RCM) is to grow disciples of Jesus Christ through immersion in Christian community and by building relationships in the midst of God's creation. We provide unmatched opportunities to individuals and local churches for spiritual transformation through retreat and camp experiences.

In 2018, RCM saw a 6.8% increase in the total number of groups served (to 332) and a 6.2% increase in total guests served, resulting in nearly 15,000 people engaged in our ministry. Due to a decrease in the number of day camp offerings at West River, there was a slight overall decline in summer camp participation despite an increase in residential camp participation. For the sixth consecutive year, we are proud to have met our financial mandate to cover operating expenses with operating income.

Ministry Moments
2018 was a year of firsts for a unique program at West River. The Rev. Tim Warner began Camp Hope in 2005 when he wondered if the transformations he had seen in youth at camp could be used to combat systemic incarceration, which sees nearly 70% of children with an incarcerated parent also end up in incarcerated. The answer is emphatically "yes," and as the program continues to mature, the long-lasting impact it has comes more clearly into focus. While many Camp Hope alumni return to camp each summer to serve as volunteer counselors in the program, this summer saw not one, but two Camp Hope alumni serve on the West River summer staff for the first time. In addition to seeing the way camp has changed the course of former campers' lives and led them to bright futures at college and exploring God's call in their life through camp leadership positions, this summer, three campers chose to be baptized in the West River while at camp. Camp Hope is a shining example of how a community need was recognized and a camp was able to offer a unique way to share love, hope, and transformation through Jesus Christ.

While national statistics show that 1 in 5 teens has a diagnosable mental health disorder such as depression or anxiety, females are twice as likely as males to suffer these conditions and females account for 90% of eating disorders. When these frightening statistics are paired with the dipropionate lack of female leadership in politics, business, and the church, the Rev. Bonnie McCubbin wanted to make a difference. Camp had been an important part of Bonnie's life as she grew up and accepted God's call to ministry, so she wanted to create a camp program that would focus on girls to develop their self-confidence through camp activities and conversations with inspirational female leaders from our conference. LeadHer camp launched in 2018 and featured a variety of church leaders, including Bishop LaTrelle Miller Easterling. The camp had such a powerful impact on the young women who attended that a number of them have continued to meet throughout the year to encourage each other and develop as leaders.

Manidokan is a place of natural beauty and adventure. When an invasive species of beetle invaded the camp a couple years ago and killed nearly every ash tree on the property, it left a scar on the property and brought home our responsibility for creation care and the delicate balance of nature. The dead trees created a safety hazard and would need to be removed. Fortunately, a local logger was willing to work with the camp and the camp was able to make profits from the sale of the lumber. In 2018, those proceeds allowed Manidokan to install a new state-of-the-art aerial park to enhance the camp's adventure opportunities and deepen a partnership with a local outfitting company. Ropes adventures, both high and low, provide safe and hands-on experiences which strengthen community, push individuals perceived limits, and illustrate essential elements of faith formation.

We strive for our retreat and camping ministry to be available and welcoming to all people, but the reality is that some young people have more barriers preventing them from coming to camp than others. For many youth in Baltimore, some of the recognized barriers include price, parents unable to send their children away with people they didn't know, and past negative racial experiences. After a few years of running a marginally successful day camp program in Baltimore during the summer, our Baltimore City Camp Initiative was reimagined for 2018. We offered Resurrection Day Camp at John Wesley UMC in Baltimore during Holy Week in order to fill a need in the community for childcare during spring break, and to build relationships with campers and parents in a familiar setting. The week of camp was a great success and 20% of the residential camp aged campers subsequently attended a residential program at Manidokan or West River during the summer. We will continue to intentionally address barriers to camp participation so all people can experience the unmatched opportunity for spiritual transformation which camp provides.

RCM also took intentional steps this year to prepare the ministry for the future. We increased our marketing efforts, began to focus on intercultural competency training, and revised our Safe Sanctuaries policies. We also underwent a long-range planning process with a consultant to evaluate our current ministry and identify opportunities for ongoing growth and sustainability.

In 2019 RCM will:
- Implement a revised Safe Sanctuaries policy;
- Explore new technology for registration and record keeping;
- Increase our communication of the importance of giving to Camperships and how to apply for one;
- Begin to implement long-range plan recommendations that aren't dependent on major capital improvements:
- Expand West River day camp by 50%;
- Offer new adventure programming at Manidokan;
- Align staffing with growth opportunities.

It is an honor to lead our conference Retreat and Camping Ministry along with 90 year-round, part-time, and seasonal staff, and more than 250 volunteers, as we engage people in intentional community-building, spiritual formation, and personal growth through the camp and retreat experience so the world may be transformed.

Chris Schlieckert, Director of Retreat & Camping Ministries

Wellness and Missions
(formerly known as The Conference Board of Global Ministries, Para. 633)

We mobilize individuals and teams to address human need and create abundant health and wholeness for all.

The Wellness and Missions Board seeks to inspire and equip faith communities to foster spiritual, physical, and mental health for all, and to promote an understanding of the intercon- nectedness of all aspects of health, individually, locally and globally. Through intentionally building relationships, meeting needs and improving health, we will contribute to developing more disciples who grow in their love of God and all their neighbors for the flourishing of lives and communities.

Our partners in this work include: The General Board of Global Ministries; NEJ Volunteers in Mission; Maryland Voluntary Organizations Active in Disaster (VOAD); Wesley Theological

Seminary's Heal the Sick; the Board of Childcare; Maryland Council on Problem Gambling; and skilled servant workers from the Baltimore-Washington Conference.

In 2018 the BWC:
- Led mission service trips to Puerto Rico, El Salvador, Ukraine and Russia.
- Assisted more than 30 families in Frederick County after flooding.
- Clarified the most useful support and needs in local congregations seeking to create wellness within their congregations and communities.
- Identified the need for an Abundant Health Ambassador in each local congregation or cluster of congregations.
- Deepened the Integration of health, VIM, and ERT.
- Created a one-stop website that allows planners and seekers of mission trips to get the information they need: http://missiontrips.bwcumc.org/
- Gave generously through The Advance (which is "second mile giving" over and above mission shares); 984 BWC individuals and churches gave a total of $673,184.68:
- $132,330.44 for Missionary Support
- $540,854.24 Advance Projects/UMCOR/Global Health

Through the May 2019 Connectional Ministries survey that was sent to everyone with an email address in Arena (our conference database), we learned more about how 416 people are currently engaged in Abundant Health Ministries.

I've taken Volunteers in Mission Training (VIM)	29.50%
I've taken Early Response Team Training (ERT)	17.51%
I have led or attended a mission trip (MISSION)	53.96%
I or my church support(s) a UMC missionary (MISSIONARY)	45.08%
I work in construction and have volunteered or am interested in volunteering my services to rebuild homes and places of worship (CONSTRUCTION)	11.03%
I am involved in physical health advocacy or ministry (BODY)	11.99%
I am involved in mental health advocacy or ministry (MIND)	19.90%
I am involved in spiritual health advocacy or ministry (SPIRIT)	16.79%
I am a medical practitioner (MED)	3.36%
I am involved in Domestic Violence/Intimate Partner Violence prevention (DV/IPV)	6.24%
I am involved in HIV/AIDS ministry (HIV)	2.88%
My church is part of the 10,000 Church Challenge (CHALLENGE)	1.20%
I've completed Wesley Theological Seminary's "Heal the Sick" Program (WTS HTS)	1.92%
I've completed Mental Health First Aid Training (MH 1st Aid)	9.83%
I've completed the "PathWay 2 Wholeness" Program (PW2W)	0.72%
My church could serve as a resource to other congregations in one or more of these areas (AH RESOURCE)	6.95%

Our 2019 goals are:
- Ensuring that 10% of congregations have identified a Health Ambassador or equivalent;
- Increasing the number of servant leaders in the health ministry, VIM, and ERT through contacting the 589 people who have indicated they are interested in becoming engaged in Abundant Health ministries;

- Identifying at least one Wellness and Service resource congregation per district through contacting those 29 persons who have indicated that their congregation could resource other congregations;
- Launching at least 2 health & service mission trips to areas of natural or person-created disasters;
- Ensuring our ministry is fully inclusive to healthcare concerns of all and working with the BWC Advocacy and Action teams as needed to make that happen; and
- Changing our name from Abundant Health to Wellness and Service/Missions so that local congregations understand the scope of ministry.

Rev. Heath Wilson, Wellness and Missions Board, Chairperson; Rev. Joan Carter-Rimbach, Conference VIM Coordinator; Fred Sipes, Conference ERT Coordinator; and Rev. Stacey Cole Wilson, Executive Minister of Justice & Service

Conference Secretary of Global Ministries

- Interpret the programs, emphases, plans, and policies of the General Board of Global Ministries to the annual conference;
- Work with Missionary Services to promote Covenant Relationships and itineration of missionaries to share the story of God's mission and increase support for missionaries;
- Cooperate with Global Ministries in its mission program in the United States and around the globe.
- Our goal is to coordinate the itineration of missionaries visiting supporting churches. We make special efforts to have missionaries visit churches that are not currently supporting missionaries.
- Promote new Covenant Relationships;
- Maintain the list of missionaries supported throughout the annual conference;
- Mission u, a joint venture of GBGM and UMW, is the major training event for Mission Education within the BWC;
- Members of CGBGM serve on the planning committee for the annual school for adult and youth.

Missionaries are provided an opportunity every three years to visit the United States. They usually itinerate to conferences where they have four or more covenant relationships. Exceptions are made if missionaries are visiting nearby areas and visit BWC for a brief time. In December 2-5, 2018, accompanied by Heath Wilson and Katie Filano, I attended Mission Ambassadors Summit at the Impact Church in Atlanta, Ga. Some of the agenda items included Global Ministries, Mission Service and Engagement, understanding partnerships UMCOR/ UMVIM, Healthy communities and Abundant Health.

Goals 2019:
- Participate in NEJ Fall retreat for Conference Secretaries of Global Ministries;
- Promote Covenant Relationships between Missionaries and BWC churches;
- Identify CSGM relationship with the Interim Abundant Health Ministries.

Deaconess Jane Grays, Secretary of Global Ministries

Advocacy and Action

Advocacy and Action is about our faithful response to God's call for justice, mercy and hope by collaborating with individuals and organizations to transform unjust and oppressive systems.

The Interim Advocacy and Action Board inspires and develops disciples by partnering with communities to transform systems which disenfranchise, marginalize, and oppress by confronting these systems within the local church and Annual Conference; by challenging the Church be to just, and by creating a BWC presence on urgent policy matters at local, state and national levels.

In 2018, we've begun the following and named these as our ongoing priorities:
- Developing a comprehensive plan for advocacy work to identify persons, resources/ assets, needs and systems needed to affect transformational change. This is a multi-layered and multi-year priority that is being collaboratively addressed through our leadership development forms (https://www.bwcumc.org/conference-agency-leadership-nominations/), forums, conversations with leaders (i.e. local, laity, district superintendents, events/training), and intentional listening sessions.
- Deepening and strengthening our connection with our neighbors – i.e. Episcopal Diocese of Washington, Mayor's Office of Washington D.C., National Council of Churches, Interfaith Power and Light, Enterprise Maryland-DC and Baltimore, Poor People's Campaign (PPC), NAACP, Justice for Our Neighbors (JFON), Cumberland-Hagerstown and Frederick networks, Maryland Council on Problem Gambling, and SAMSHA - Opioid Addiction Resources across our districts.

Implementing and strategically addressing our NEJ Call to Action commitment through:
- Leadership Development Training - Developing Cultural Awareness and Proficiency)
  - Jan. 23, 2019 - Bishop, Cabinet, Executive Team and BWC Staff completed Intercultural Developmental Inventory (IDI) Basic Training. This training included individual and group inventory evaluations, debriefs and goal setting re: next steps.
  - Jan. 25, 2019 – BWC Debriefers Training w/Kristina Gonzalez to explore calling, cultural proficiency and readiness of persons to engage this work.
  - April 29-30, 2019 - IDI Qualified Administrator Training – to ready and develop our own pool of IDI Qualified Debriefers and Coaches. Invited persons are representative BWC lay and clergy, 1 staff person from SPACES and 4 social justice coordinators from the Episcopal Church.
  - May 8, 2019 – Board of Ordained Ministry Members Intercultural Proficiency Training
  - June 2, 2019 - Retreat and Camping Ministries Summer Staff Intercultural Proficiency Training
- Building Beloved Community: Creating courageous and safe spaces for persons to get to know one another, engage in perspective taking, individuation, justice work, and truth-telling.
  - November 2018- June 2019 - Six-month cohort in Baltimore County where persons gather across real and perceived lines of difference.
  - April 6-11, 2019 - Alabama Sojourn, 30+ Participants – Birmingham, Montgomery and Selma, Retracing the Steps of Freedom.
  - Oct. 18-19, 2019 - ReCall Summit 2019 –This year there is an emphasis on the Arts (Artivism) and how the arts (songs, art, etc.) influence justice.
  - Racial Justice Round Open Discussions and Gatherings 2018-2019 on the district and regional levels. See Racial Justice/CCORR report for more details.
- Providing at least two legislative opportunities for persons to "stand with" and address systems which disenfranchise, marginalize, and oppress, in accordance with our Social Principles and Wesleyan Heritage. We've organized the following:
  - United to Love Rally – Standing Together in Love Against All Forms of Hate
  - Legislative Advocacy Day in Annapolis
  - Hosted a Press Conference – Calling for the End of the Partial U.S. Federal Government Shutdown;

- and, have offered a faithful presence in Washington D.C. and Annapolis during Legislative Sessions.
- Developed and Implemented the Moral Courage Awards for Youth, Young Adults, and Adults.
- Awarded $8000 in Peace with Justice Awards to the following: Centennial Advocates, DC-MD JFON's New Office, Shower Ministry at Hope4All at Mt. Vernon Place UMC, Washington D.C.; and the Community Anti-Violence Program at Hughes Memorial UMC
- Awarded $10,475 for Mission Innovation Grants to local faith communities and ministries
- $5,000 to Project Transformation DC to enhance youth literacy and academic excellence in Washington, D.C. Criminal Justice and Mercy Ministries (CJAMM)
- $4,975 to Restorative Justice Ministries to foster congregations and their member's spiritual focus of mercy and compassion for all persons involved in the criminal justice system, including: families; victims; those incarcerated; returning citizens (people who have been incarcerated); and those who work within the criminal justice system, including law enforcement and court officials.
- $500 to Wesley Freedom UMC for cultural competency training.
- Organized Social Action Teams such as Creation Care, Gender Equality, Gun Violence Prevention, Immigration Reform, Racial Justice, and Wealth Equity. We are also reorganizing and reprioritizing the work of Restorative Justice in order to remove stigma and myths around our returning citizens.

Through the May 2019 Connectional Ministries survey that was sent to everyone with an email address in Arena (our conference database), we learned more about how 453 people are currently engaged in Advocacy & Action.

I am involved in racial justice advocacy	43.27%
I have read the NEJ Call to Action (CTA)	24.06%
I have committed to do my part to work toward racial justice (CTA COV)	30.46%
I have participated in a Racial Justice Gathering held at the Baltimore-Washington Conference Mission Center (CCORR)	11.70%
I or my church have used the General Commission on Religion and Race (GCORR's) Vital Conversations (VIT CONV)	15.45%
I am involved in eco-justice advocacy (ECO JUSTICE)	15.89%
I am involved in gender equality advocacy (COSROW)	20.31%
I am involved in gun violence prevention advocacy (GUN SENSE)	23.62%
I am involved in immigration rights advocacy (IMMIGRATION)	23.40%
I am involved in wealth equity (eradicating poverty) advocacy (POVERTY)	23.84%
I am involved in criminal justice advocacy (including prison ministry) (CJAMM)	18.32%
I am an advocate for LGBTQIA rights. (LGBTQIA)	48.34%
I have participated in UM Legislative Advocacy Days (ADV DAYS)	10.15%
I have participated in the BWC United to Love Rally in Washington, D.C. (UTL)	17.88%
I have participated in other marches, rallies, conferences that uplift the interrelatedness of faith in action and social justice (RALLY)	39.51%
My church could serve as a resource to other congregations in one or more of these areas (AA RESOURCE)	17.88%

By the end of 2019, we seek to:
Create a pool of trainers and partnerships who will assist congregations and leaders in developing Intercultural Proficiency.
Re-establish a strong and vital Native-American Ministry.
Re-establish a strong and vital Strengthening the Black Church for the 21st Century (SBC21)
By December 2019, collaborating with Young Peoples Ministries to host a listening campaign involving at least 25 youth per district to determine the service or justice issue young people want to focus on for the next two years.

Tom Contee, Interim Advocacy & Action Board Chair and Rev. Dr. Stacey Cole Wilson, Executive Minister of Justice and Service

Commission on Religion and Race
The purpose of the Commission on Religion and Race is to support the local churches and conference agencies with educational resources on intercultural competency, inclusiveness and equity, and help local churches reflect the context for their ministry and realities of the communities they serve.

Our 2019 goals included the following:
- Place CCoRR focus on the grassroots;
- Determine how the Vital Conversations provided by CCoRR during the 2017 Annual Conference were utilized by the local churches and their impact;
- Develop a training/workshop program based on the Vital Conversations series;
- Build the Racial Justice ministry based on the North East Jurisdiction Call to Action.

In working towards these goals, CCoRR engaged with the Conference Connectional Ministries to review covenant data collected during the Annual Conference Session and Recall Summit. Additionally, CCoRR and Connectional Ministries reviewed the NEJ Call to Action Report to determine how the report relates to the work of CCoRR and the covenant. As a result of these conversations and the conference restructuring of ministries, CCoRR became the lead on Racial Justice within Advocacy and Action. To establish the Racial Justice ministry, focus was placed on the grassroots by inviting all the individuals across the conference that had expressed desire, passion, and calling to Racial Justice to be part of designing the ministry.

The following Racial Justice gatherings were conducted with their respective objective:
- April 19, 2018: Formation of the Gatherings and Review of Call to Action;
- June 20, 2018: Identified Affinity Groups;
- September 20, 2018: Established the Racial Rapid Response Task Force;
- December 11, 2018: 2020 Racial Justice Strategic Plan.

During these gatherings, we have seen an increase in the number of faithful servants interested in the work by signing up and attending the gatherings.

The target for the end of 2019 is to achieve the following:
- Complete a protocol and design for the BWC Regional Racial Justice Rapid Response Teams;
- Completed the BWC 2020 Racial Justice Strategic Plan.

Please keep our ministry in constant prayer and if you are interested in joining this grassroots movement, contact us and we will welcome you into this vital ministry.

Moorosi Mokuena, Chair CCoRR

Deaf Ministry

Our purpose is to minister to Deaf and DeafBlind individuals and their families across the conference. Our ministry is to souls but is also to a collective effort towards confronting the lived realities of oppression for Deaf and DeafBlind individuals.

Goals:

In 2018 Christ Deaf Church (CDC) and Magothy Deaf Church (MDC) continue to offer worship that is culturally and linguistically appropriate for Deaf and DeafBlind individuals and their families. CDC now streams worship to individuals who cannot get to church. Both churches still offer food pantries, Bible Studies, and fellowship.

Deaf Shalom Zone, Inc. (DSZ) has continued to serve individuals in case management, advocacy, referral, and education, including work with literacy and immigration support. DSZ partners with Maryland agencies, such as Food Bank, Service Coordination, Community Support Services for Deaf, Towson University and Community College Baltimore County, DeafBlind Camps, Inc., Deaf Camps Inc., Maryland Consumer Rights Coalition, and Governor's Office of Deaf and Hard of Hearing.

Impact
- The Deaf and DeafBlind community are an underserved and underseen population in Baltimore. We empower them to work with the services that are available to them so that they can live their most productive and happy lives.
- 150 people each week through DZS
- 50 direct clients, each with 3-6 organizations that we assist them in working with
- Provide a culturally safe place for individuals to explore their faith questions at CDC and MDC
- Assist other churches in finding ways to serve the D/deaf people in their church in a culturally appropriate way

This Year: 2019
- MDC and CDC plan to go on retreat to collaborate on a mission project together.
- CDC and DSZ will provide an ASL class for Spanish-speaking families with Deaf children. While the parents are learning, we will provide a children's program for the Deaf children.
- MDC will host workshops on church passion and development, such as radical hospitality.
- Student ministry will re-do the youth room to make a youth-specific space.
- CDC will develop outreach to homebound people with culturally appropriate worship through live streaming and home visitation ministry.

Sandi Johnson, Lead Pastor of Deaf Ministry; Emily Hart, Associate Pastor of Deaf Ministry; Kathi Jeffra, Resource Coordinator

Commission on Archives and History/ United Methodist Historical Society and the Strawbridge Shrine Association

The past year has been one of rethinking our dual duties of preservation and propagation: working to preserve for future generations historic materials entrusted to our care, be they buildings, books or objects; and to use of these records and remnants to propagate an appreciation and enthusiasm for our United Methodist histories and traditions. Ours is truly a story of individuals and congregations of diverse background brought together over two and half centuries as "One, United to Love."

Preservation

Resources made available to the Shrine Association by the Conference Trustees in the past year made possible extensive preservation work at the Shrine, colonial homestead of Robert and Elizabeth Strawbridge, which includes the log home of John Evans, their first convert, and a scale replica in period logs of the meetinghouse, the first such structure raised by Methodists in the new world. The Shrine Association has established a Preservation Fund which will provide funding for structural conservation and preservation work. We encourage those who are able to prayerfully consider this fund.

In the coming year, attention will turn toward the Conference Archives, Library & Museum (CALM) at Lovely Lane UMC. An environment more conducive to preservation of collections is the object of proposals solicited for climate control of this space. We thank the 2018 Annual Conference for its approval of funding from the Glassman Estate for this purpose, and also Duncan Hodge, a retired engineer and Trustee at Lovely Lane, who has gotten this project underway. We expect work to begin this summer.

Propagation and Pilgrimage
The United Methodist Pilgrimage Taskforce, which began its work last year, continues to plan a program which will attract and engage visiting pilgrims, young and old, near and far, with the many and varied stories of United Methodism in this area. The Taskforce recommends a shift in focus away from detailed chronologies and descriptions, and toward engagement in the issues encountered by our forebearers in faith who, like us, with tough questions, weighed scripture, tradition, reason and their own experience in their quest to follow their Lord. The Taskforce believes the wealth of history in this conference can be used to illustrate the faith of our ancestors and the choices they made in a compelling way.

The Taskforce has begun to develop resources for use at the Strawbridge Shrine, a site associated with many momentous encounters which might illustrate decision points in their day and ours. The Shrine Association is already developing plans to enhance visitor engagement. A gift in memory of Reenactor Kenneth Steward by his family will provide wayside exhibit tablets to be erected later this year. Architect Wallace Wolf has joined the board and offered his professional services in developing a comprehensive site plan.

Upgrades at Lovely Lane will be accompanied by upgraded exhibits, a step toward implementing enhanced visitor experience there. We also hope to provide pilgrimage resources on our Conference's fifteen designated historic sites as well as learning resources for the youth of our Church in this and other conferences.

Emora Brannan, President United Methodist Historical Society; Wm. Louis Piel, Interim Co-President Strawbridge Shrine Association; Douglas Tzan, Chair United Methodist Pilgrimage Taskforce

United Methodist Women
United Methodist Women shall be a community of women whose PURPOSE is to know God and to experience freedom as whole persons through Jesus Christ; to develop a creative, supportive fellowship; and to expand concepts of mission through participation in the global ministries of the church.

VISION: Turning faith, hope, and love into action on behalf of women, children and youth around the world.

Goals for 2018
At our Conference UMW Leadership Team Planning Retreat in January, 2018, the focus was

in-depth discussion of our quadrennial (2017-2020) initiatives:
* Mass Incarceration: School-to-Prison Pipeline
* Health and Maternal Health
* Climate Justice
* Charter for Racial Justice

The goal of this Planning Retreat was to share the results of our discussion with Local Units and District Leadership Teams and to encourage the dissemination of this information within our entire membership. An emphasis was placed on educating our members regarding the relationship between zero tolerance school discipline policies and mass incarceration of persons of color. As of December, 2018, there had been over 200 local and district events which had presented the Mass Incarceration: School-to-Prison Pipeline initiative, including an original skit presented at our UMW Annual Conference Celebration. The impact was far-reaching, resulting in prayerful discussions and plans of action.

Goals for 2019
* To encourage discussion and education on how Economic Inequality plays an intertwining role within the above four initiatives.
* To rebuild our UMW District Teams within the BWC Western Region.
* To continue to celebrate and increase awareness of our 150th Anniversary and Legacy Fund through special events and information sharing.

Linda S. Yost, President, Conference United Methodist Women

Committee on Hispanic-Latino Ministries

The purpose of this committee is to "support the development, implementation, and evaluation of a Hispanic-Latino comprehensive plan of action and the strategies for working with Hispanic-Latino persons of all generations in the community (BOD 2016, ¶655)."
Goal: To identify, equip, and engage leaders to build relationships and do justice with Hispanic-Latinos in their community so that more 1st and 2nd generation Hispanic-Latinos can love God and their neighbor.

Impact:
* Hispanic-Latino Ministries (HLM) Annual Camp. More than 100 people attended this retreat. The theme was "Bridging Generations." The guest speaker was Phil Wingeier-Rayo, Professor and Dean of Wesley Theological Seminary. For the first time in the history of HLM Camp, a partnership with Pen-Del conference Hispanic-Latino Ministries happened as they participated in this event.
* The Hispanic-Latino Lay Leadership School was created in partnership with the National Plan on Hispanic-Latino Ministries. Twenty-Five people participated. Seventeen students will be receiving their missionary certification.
* The office of Hispanic-Latino Ministries offered the first Immigration Border Trip in September 2018. Ten youth and young adults participated as well as eight pastors. Out of this project, there were two outcomes:
  * Participants created an Immigration Resource for Global Migration Sunday on December 1st, 2018. This resource was published on the BWC website and shared with the United Methodist Inter-agency Immigration Task Force.
  * Participants proposed the agenda and logistics for the Immigration Town Hall.
* Hispanic-Latino Ministries lead the organization of Bishop Easterling's Immigration Town Hall. The speakers were partners from Wesley Theological Seminary, Just Neighbors, and The Norwest Annual Conference of the Methodist Church in Mexico.
* Four persons, Rev. Heather Olson (Hispanic-Latinx Committee and Pastor of Lisbon UMC), Rev. Timothy Warner (Pastor of Mill Creek Parish and Emory Grove UMC),

Rev. Stacey Cole Wilson (Executive Minister of Justice and Service), and Emma Escobar (Coordinator of Hispanic-Latino Ministries) traveled from the Baltimore-Washington Conference to El Salvador on an exploratory trip to build a relationship with the Evangelical Methodist Church in El Salvador.

Goals For 2019:
- Faithful Discipleship: Create a specialized curriculum for the second year of the Lay Leadership School on Liturgy and Music Studies so that 1) all Hispanic-Latino congregations can have worship ministries/teams 2) local worship leaders that are knowledgeable and grounded in theology. This training will start in September 2019.
- Education & Advocacy: 20 new people will experience the Immigration Border Immersion so that they can become engage in immigration policies and can inspire other to get involve in the BWC efforts on immigration.
- Connectional Commitment: 1) Support the creation of the Hispanic Youth Leadership Academy (HYLA) in DC at Wesley Theological Seminary in July 2019 so that more Hispanic-Latino youth connect to their roots and can better navigate the experiences they face. 2) Increase conference participation at MARCHA, the Hispanic-Latino Caucus of the UMC so that more leaders engage in advocacy and action at their local level on issues that affect their communities.

Read more about the El Salvador trip in January 2019: https://www.bwcumc.org/news-and-views/discovering-mission-possibilities-in-el-salvador/
Watch a series of videos on the border immersion trip: https://www.bwcumc.org/event/1317270-2019-10-11-immigration-border-immersion/

Rev. Giovanni Arroyo, Committee Chair; Emma A Escobar, Coordinator of Hispanic-Latino Ministries

In Mission Together - Eurasia Committee (Formerly: Russia Initiative)
To promote joint ministry with United Methodists in Eurasia, in particular the covenant partnership between the Baltimore-Washington Conference and the South Russia Annual Conference.

Goals in 2018:
- To continue to build an effective relationship between American and Eurasian partners in ministry, through:
  1. Relationship building and Project support. We supported, both through team participation and financially, the Youth (i.e., Young Adult) Mission Conference, a set of week-long discipling and work experiences which bring together young people from across European Eurasia and Central Asia, as well as international students. We participated in the mission at the Camp Kristall center in southern Russia, which included critical refits and accessibility upgrades. The mission also has a track record of developing and encouraging the next generation of leaders for the Eurasian churches and building relationships across the vast area served by our conferences there. The camp itself also hosts a number of strategic ministries, such as the annual "Camp Trinity" outreach to persons with physical and intellectual handicapping conditions.

     Support was also provided for the ministry work with the Roma people in the Caucasus region. This sensitive work includes educational, health and welfare, and Bible teaching support for several families belonging to an ethnic group on the fringes of society. Material helps included making available, via our church partners, sets of young girls' clothing made available through another ministry in Maryland, as an expression of love and as a small hedge against the dangers of exploitation.

We also pursued our modest efforts to make more resources available to the District leadership in the South Russia Conference, in order to help the Superintendents with efforts at training and building critical relationships between churches over a large geographical area.

2.   Leadership Development. We continued our efforts along two lines: (1) providing leadership in support of a conference for women leaders held at Camp Kristall; (2) support and encouragement for the D.Min. work of a key Russian church leader, who is to graduate in 2019.

•   To tell the story of the ministry with our Eurasian partners and encourage others to join in, through:
1.   Conference media. We have sought to communicate through print and online media, regarding God's work in Eurasia through the UMC.
2.   Interaction with local churches. We have made presentations and resourced local churches with information on the Eurasia partnership.
3.   Coordination with other conference IMTEC groups. In addition to the foregoing, we have worked to help reinforce connections between our IMTEC and those working in Russia from Virginia, Oklahoma, Ohio, Michigan, and elsewhere.
4.   Channels for further growth. We are looking for new ways to engage young people from our conference, and to provide opportunities for additional persons and congregations to be meaningfully engaged with our Eurasian partners, to the discipleship benefit of both. We continue to be challenged by limitations on prudent travel to our partners in the Crimea.

Goals for 2019:
•   Continue support of key projects, including Camp Kristall, Roma Ministry (South District), Youth Mission Conference, and Women's Conference. This is to be accomplished through direct support, mission teams, and relationship building.
•   We plan to encourage a small delegation from Baltimore-Washington to attend the Eurasia Consultation in Uzhorod, Ukraine, in August 2019. We anticipate a small team working once again with a project in southern Russia, either in connection with the Youth Mission Conference or in support of the Roma ministry.
•   We anticipate helping one leader to complete advanced training (D.Min.) in 2018-2019 through the Wesley Seminary/Cambridge program, and will be actively seeking to continue encouraging new leaders in their training. We also will be working with our Eurasian counterparts to continue developing clergy and local church leaders through continuing education and specialized leadership training.

Rev. Charles L. Harrell, Chair

Stewardship Reports

Council on Finance and Administration (CFA)

Two events define the budget report for 2018 and the proposed budget for 2020. First, we achieved a balanced budget in 2018 but the actual Collection Rate of 90.6% was a decline in mission shares (formerly apportionments) from the last three years. The budgeted rate was set at 92%. The 2020 budget reflects that change by setting the budgeted rate at 91% and keeps the Benevolence Factor at the lowered rate of 17.600%. The result is the budgeted amount for mission shares for 2020 is virtually the same as actually contributed in 2018 – a significant reduction from the budget in 2019.

Second, last year's report identified two potential risks that the CFA felt could impact both local church income and connectional giving in 2018 and 2019. We identified changes in the Federal Tax laws that may affect charitable contributions, and the February 2019 "Way Forward" vote at the Special Session of the General Conference. We have not yet seen any significant effect from the changes in the tax laws regarding charitable giving and itemized deductions in the tax laws.

The decision to approve the Traditional Plan at the Special Session in February has caused pain and turmoil throughout the Connection and within the Baltimore-Washington Conference. At the time this report is written, we are still waiting on rulings by the Judicial Council on the legality and constitutionality of some of the provisions of the Resolutions and petitions approved in St. Louis. Without regard to those rulings, the Denomination denomination will certainly revisit those issues again at General Conference in May 2020. CFA will monitor the financial effects closely through 2019 and 2020 as this process evolves.

CFA will remain vigilant in caring for the financial sustainability of our connectional ministries. There have been discussions and proposals in this and other Annual Conferences about withholding missional shares/apportionments either in support of or opposition to the Traditional Plan. I urge you not to do that and ask you to look carefully at the amounts of money devoted to BWC connectional ministries. These ministries allow our individual churches to pool their resources and reach beyond their own doors to expand our missions and help more people in need than we can do as individuals or a single church. This is the strength of our connection and I urge us to continue that outreach in the midst of our differences. Withholding our missional shares will only penalize and diminish those outreach ministries and do nothing financially to affect the implementation of or opposition to the Traditional Plan.

We understand that these events may continue to have negative effects on local churches and a ripple effect on ministries of the Baltimore-Washington Conference. CFA stresses that adverse financial effects are still only potential risks and not an absolute certainty. While these effects are currently unknown, they continue to be our principal concern. CFA is boosting its reserves and, together with other affected agencies, will follow events closely, remain flexible, and develop strategies to address their effects.

2018 Financial Results (Pre-Audit):
Income
The mission share income in 2018 was $14,045,685 with an overall collection rate of 90.6%. The collection rate budget was set at 92.0% and the mission shares received were below budget by $214,700 (1.5%). The mission share giving was $242,900 (1.7%) lower than the prior year when the Conference set a 20-year high for the collection rate.

The collection rates recorded in recent years are as follows:
2018: 90.6%   2017: 92.5%   2016: 92.1%

2015: 91.7%   2014: 90.8%   2013: 89.8%
2012: 89.1%   2011: 90.5%   2010: 90.5%
2009: 89.2%

The number of churches contributing 100% towards their mission shares remained high with 82% of our local churches meeting that standard. The number percentage of churches giving 100% of their mission shares was 82% in 2017, 84% in 2016, 83% in 2015, and 82% in 2014.

The non-mission share income in 2018 was $4.4 million, which was $223,000 (5.3%) more than budget. The primary factor in this result was the receipt of an unexpected youth grant for $159,000 for ministry within the Conference.

Expenses
The operating expenses in 2018 were $18.3 million, which was $128,200 (0.7%) less than budget. The most significant financial pressures were the legal and moving expenses that exceeded budget by $51,000 and $45,000 respectively. These were offset by under budget performance for salary and benefits of $93,000. Other expenses under budget included Discipleship Ministries - $85,000;, Unified Funding Grants - $121,000;, and partnerships - $24,000.

Overall, the resulting net income prior to audit was a positive $136,000, which is 0.7% of budget. Good expense control in 2018 ensured that the net result was positive considering mission shares that were less than budget.

BWC Apportionment Base:
The expenses of a local church as they are reported in the annual collection of statistical data, minus dollars that are spent on mission, outreach, debt service and capital projects, comprise what is known as the apportionment base for a church. The mission shares for a local church is derived by multiplying the apportionment base by the benevolence factor that is established by the Annual Conference when the budget is approved. Using this method, our current benevolence factor of 17.6% yields a mission share that is most commonly in the range of 9-12% of total local church expenses or income.

The apportionment base for the Conference is an accumulated total of the apportionment base that is calculated for each local church. The reported base decreased by 0.7% in 2018. The apportionment base trends with the year-over-year changes are as follows:

2018: $ 87,713,316 (-0.7%)
2017: $ 88,283,704 (+1.0%)
2016: $ 87,449,322 (+0.4%)
2015: $ 87,072,403 (-0.8%)
2014: $ 87,780,638 (+1.1%)
2013: $ 86,835,908 (+0.8%)
2012: $ 86,169,509 (-1.3%)
2011: $ 87,341,343 (-2.1%)
2010: $ 89,250,232

2020 Budget:
The proposed budget for 2020 builds on the strategic initiatives that were first introduced in the 2017 budget. These initiatives include:

Increase Level of CFA Reserves from 10% to 15%
With the positive fund balance from 2018, the CFA Reserves now stand at 14.7% of the

mission share budget. The 2019 budget includes $100,000 towards the increased level of CFA reserves to reach the 15% goal.

Accelerate Payment of Conference Debt
The consolidated loan for the West River Dining Hall and the Mission Center will be reduced to a balance of $1.2 million with the proposed 2020 budget that includes $550,000 towards accelerated debt payments. The loan balance stood at $5.2 million at the end of 2016 prior to starting the accelerated payments. The 2020 budget keeps the Conference on pace to pay off the loan in 2022 which will be 6 six years ahead of schedule with $1.0 million total savings in interest payments.

Fund Retiree Medical Benefits from Reserves
Retiree medical benefits will continue to be funded from the Board of Pension reserves without any additional funding coming from mission shares. The retiree medical funding in 2020 is set at $1,640,000 which is based on the current expense trends for this benefit.

The 2020 budget continues to maintain the benevolence factor at 17.6% that was reduced initially in the 2019 budget. Maintaining this level is consistent with the CFA's multi-year plan to keep making progress towards the goal that the average church's mission shares be no more than 10% of their overall income. That level is currently calculated at 11.2% based on the 2018 statistics. This is slightly higher than the 10.6% level calculated in 2017. The increase was driven by a 4.9% decline in local church income reported in the 2018 stats. The metric is down from 12.3% in 2011.

Overall, the budget proposal specifies a mission share income of $14,048,165, which is a reduction of $246,732, or 1.7% from the prior year. The budget assumes a 91.0% collection rate for the mission shares, which is consistent with the actual results in 2018 and represents a decrease from the 92.0% budget in prior years. The non-mission share income is increased by $157,982 to $4,593,349, which is driven by increases in external grants and event income.

The expense budget increases Discipleship Ministry programs by 0.5% to $11.6 million. The stewardship and administrative programs provide expense control mechanisms that enable a 2.3% reduction from $6.9 to $6.6 million. It is also noted that the General Conference apportionments are reduced to $3,401,899 which is a decrease of $79,845 (-2.3%).

Summary
The CFA continues to focus on strategic initiatives that are helping the Conference to be vital during periods of uncertainty. It is recognized that the 2020 budget lacks insight into an unknown future. However, the Conference can rest assured that the CFA will continuously monitor income and expense trends and make any necessary changes to the 2020 budget that may be appropriate.

We are encouraged in our stewardship ministry that our connection within the Conference continues to hold strong through what appears as trying times for the denomination. We are certainly blessed to have a rich, common ministry that gives us a shared purpose amidst our differences.

Phil Potter, President, Council on Finance and Administration; Paul J. Eichelberger, Conference Treasurer

Moving Committee

The purpose of the Baltimore -Washington Moving Committee is to provide comprehensive and secure relocation services for those pastors who are receiving new appointments or moving into retirement.

Our goals for 2018 were to assist all eligible pastors with the best services and in a time frame that was convenient and conducive to a smooth transition from one appointment to the next. We also strived to maximize the cost of the moves for the Conference and the taxable impact to all parties by negotiating moving rates that fought against the costs of inflation and general cost increases. The average cost to move a pastor for 2018 was $3,162.63.

The goal for 2019 is to continue to provide the best moving experience possible to the members of the Baltimore-Washington Conference and we are currently negotiating to lock in moving rates for future years and at below market rates with no or very limited increases.

It is the pleasure of eight very hard working and dedicated district coordinators to serve those in the Baltimore-Washington Conference who find themselves with moving needs due to the appointment/retirement process.

Rev. Jeff Paulson, Conference Moving Committee Chairperson

Conference Board of Pensions and Health Benefits

The Board of Pensions and Health Benefits continues to pursue its goal of enabling clergy and lay staff to accomplish their ministries without concern for their long-term financial or medical protection. We continue to position ourselves to face the challenges that lie ahead and to assist clergy and staff in their mission.

Pensions:

Pre-82 Service Funding: The 2019 Past Service Rate (PSR) is confirmed at $720. We recommend that the PSR for 2020 be set at $749. ¶1506.7 (2016 Discipline) confers authority upon the annual conference to review the annuity rate for Pre-82 service and to adjust the PSR rate as appropriate taking into consideration the changes in the economy. Such annuity rate may remain the same or be increased without restriction. Wespath Benefits and Investments actuarial valuation for Pre-82 Annuities as of January 1, 2018, showed a more than fully funded plan, requiring no monies to be paid by BWC. The pre-82 plan surplus results from increases in valuation of the securities in the account. Wespath has authorized a mechanism by which we have been able to employ some of the excess Pre-82 funds to indirectly fund our Retiree Medical Plan reserve. Pre-82 is the pension plan in place prior to 1982.

Ministerial Pension Plan (MPP) Funding: Wespath Benefits and Investments' actuarial valuation for MPP Annuities as of January 1, 2018, showed that it is also a fully funded plan, requiring no monies to be paid by BWC. Monies previously contributed to MPP continue to be held in individual participant accounts. MPP is the pension plan in place from 1982 through 2006.

Clergy Retirement Security Program (CRSP) Funding: The Baltimore-Washington Conference funds the program as follows:

CRSP Defined Contribution (DC) - BWC continues to collect 3% of participant's plan compensation (salary plus housing) to fund the Defined Contribution (DC). Two percent goes directly to the participant's DC account. The participant is now required to enroll in the United Methodist Personal Investment Plan (UMPIP) with a contribution of at least 1% of plan compensation in order to receive a match of up to 1%.

CRSP Defined Benefit (DB) – BWC continues to collect 12% of the participant's plan compensation, limited by the DAC (Denominational Average Compensation) to fund the Defined Benefit portion of CRSP.
Comprehensive Protection Plan (CPP):

BWC continues to collect 3% of a clergy participant's plan compensation (salary plus housing) for the Comprehensive Protection Plan (CPP). The CPP provides death and disability benefits for all eligible participants. As of the last General Conference, Wespath Benefits and Investments revised their policies to treat clergy mental illness in the same fashion as any other illness for CPP purposes. The Conference Board of Pensions and Health Benefits has voted to provide the necessary funds to eliminate anti-mental illness discrimination for lay employees as well.

UMLifeOptions:
Eligibility changes were approved at the 2016 General Conference to eliminate the special arrangement coverage for ordained clergy appointed to ½ or ¼ time as of 12/31/2016. Conferences were given options to purchase life and disability insurance for these clergy through UMLifeOptions.
Effective 1/1/2017, for active ordained clergy appointed to ½ or ¼ time who are now enrolled in UMLifeOptions, BWC will collect 3% of clergy participant's plan compensation (salary plus housing) to cover the premiums.

Health:
HealthFlex: Effective January 1, 2017, all eligible participants have been enrolled in the Wespath HealthFlex Exchange Plans. The HealthFlex Exchange brings more plan options; more flexibility for enrollees to select the HealthFlex plan that best fits each individual need. The HealthFlex Exchange is not a public exchange and is not associated with government agencies. It is a multiple-option group health plan designed for United Methodist Church clergy, lay employees and their families.

Retirees: Retirees who are over age 65 will continue to work with Via Benefits, formerly OneExchange, to choose policies better suited to their individual needs. Retirees are offered a stipend based on years of service. Retirees who are under age 65 or any future participants who retire before age 65 will remain on the HealthFlex Exchange plan until the month they turn 65.

Social Security: Your Board strongly recommends that all clergy of the Conference participate in Social Security, and not exercise any conscience clauses to opt out of Social Security. Eligibility for Medical benefits through Via Benefits in retirement and Disability benefits through the CPP program are both dependent on participation in Social Security and Medicare. Thus, one's irrevocable decision to opt out of Social Security is a decision to be excluded from these Conference programs as well.

Arrearage: In order to assure that nothing interferes with clergy continued medical and pension coverage, BWC first makes the necessary payments to Wespath when due and then collects the premiums from individual churches. There is a continuing problem with a small number of churches which fall behind in this pastoral compensation commitment. The Bishop's Task Force on Arrearages, comprised of two District Superintendents, the Chair of the Board of Pensions, and Conference staff, has developed approaches to more intensive management of churches which are in arrears, for medical and pension arrearages often are symptomatic of other challenges to ministry and finances the church is facing. A Church in arrears may be offered a forbearance program where collection of the arrearage is forborne for three years while the church focuses its efforts on greater effectiveness in ministry. Churches successfully completing this program may have the arrearage converted to a contingent liability, effective only in the event that the church property is sold.

During 2018, seven churches converted their arrearage into a Conditional Forbearance Mortgage as they satisfied all aspects of their forbearance agreement. This resulted in an overall arrearage reduction of $252,000. There remain five additional churches in arrears who plan to be compliant with their forbearance agreements before the end of 2019.
The objective is to make every effort to help churches return to health both in their ministry and their finances. The total arrearage at the end of 2018 for non-forbearance churches was $337,364. Arrearages for forbearance churches totaled $280,044, not including the forbearance amount of $183,000.

2019 General Conference: In response to concerns regarding proposals which may or may not be made in connection with the 2019 General Conference, the CBOPHB has reviewed its areas of responsibility to identify any possibilities that might affect the pensions and medical insurance of those for whom the CBOPHB is responsible and is confident these obligations can be met regardless of events in 2019.

Final Comments: The CBOPHB thanks Francess Tagoe, Director, Human Resources and Benefits, for her enthusiastic and professional work on behalf of our participants and the Board. She effectively communicates and administers the benefits based on Plan rules and regulations, the Book of Discipline, the Conference's policies and procedures, and all applicable state and federal laws so that there is an understanding of the benefits for our clergy and lay employees. It is her goal and the Board's goal to continue to provide the best possible benefits package for our plan participants, while maintaining the utmost care for and fiduciary responsibility to you, the Plan participants, and those in the Baltimore-Washington Conference for whom we owe the same. We wish to also give thanks to Karen Conroy, HR & Benefits Associate, Pier McPayten, Controller, and the District Superintendents who all support the work we do.

Carey James, Chair; Paul J. Eichelberger, Treasurer

Board of Trustees
The Board of Trustees holds in trust for the benefit of the Annual Conference any real or personal property, bequests, and donations conveyed to the Annual Conference, and acts to safeguard the rights and interests of the Annual Conference.

It has been the goal of the Trustees to reduce the burden to the Annual Conference of vacant properties, and to make funds available for new and resurrection ministries. Funds from Bequests and Grants have been supporting New Faith Expressions, Clergy Sabbatical, major renewal projects at the Museum & Archives, the Adullum Community Health Center at St. John's UMC (which provides screenings and health services to low income and underserved communities), the General Board of Global Ministries, Quality of Life Retreats, and Camping and Retreat Ministries. Grants and loans have been authorized for local churches to repair roofs, replace furnaces, and for repair and preservation work of the historic Strawbridge Shrine (a Heritage Landmark of the UMC).

The Trustees have made revisions to the loans and grants policies to ensure that Annual Conference funds are more available and more efficiently released. On-going work is reviewing the recording of loans, some service contracts, and other financial matters to ensure that bests interest of every member and congregation are being served by the Annual Conference.

While the Trustees would prefer never to see churches close, the board has received a few such properties in the past year. Funds from the sales or redevelopment of these properties are designated to support new ministries in their areas. The commercial tenant space in the Conference Center has been rented after a careful and detailed negotiation. This income helps to reduce the need for local churches to support the operations of the building.

John M. Strawbridge, Chair of the Board of Trustees

STEWARDSHIP RECOMMENDATIONS

STEWARDSHIP MINISTRIES
Recommendations from the Council on Finance and Administration
The proposed budget of $18,641,514 shall be adopted for 2020, including a mission share income budget of $14,048,165. This represents a decrease of 1.7% in the mission share asking compared to the 2019 budget.

The Benevolence Factor (BF) for 2020 is set at 17.60%, no change from the 2019 budget. The collection rate assumption for 2020 is set at 91.0%, which is 1% lower than the 2019 rate.

As required by The Book of Discipline, the ratio for World Service and Conference Benevolences shall be set as follows: 33% for World Services and 67% for Conference Benevolences.

The firm of Ellin & Tucker is approved as independent auditors to audit the Conference Treasurer's financial records for 2019.

The date for closing the 2019 Conference financial books shall be set at January 14, 2020, with all payments to be received by the Treasurer's office no later than January 14, 2020.

The Baltimore-Washington Conference grants authority to the Council on Finance and Administration, in consultation with the Bishop, the Cabinet, and the Discipleship Council to act on financial matters between sessions of the Annual Conference.

Phil Potter, President; Paul J. Eichelberger, Chief Financial Office and Treasurer

Narrative Summary of the 2020 Conference Budget
Budget Assumptions
Benevolence Factor – Proposed 2020: 17.600%
The benevolence factor is the percentage churches are apportioned based on their operating expenditures less exclusions. The percentage for 2020 is the same as the percentage used in 2019 (17.600%).

Mission Shares Collection Rate - Proposed 2020: 91.0%
The projected collection of the amount apportioned to churches in the 2020 Budget is 91.0%. The percentage for 2020 Is 1% less than the budgeted Collection Rate for 2019 (92%).

Revenue
Mission Shares: $14,048,165
A church's share of the local and global mission work and operating expenses of the Annual Conference as determined by the mission shares formula.

Grants: $239,100
This represents grants given directly to the conference for ministry and mission. For example, General Church grants to operate the Episcopal Office and residence.

Event Registration: $2,232,045
This includes Annual Conference registration, workshop registrations, Retreat and Camping Ministries registrations (majority of line item) and other conference events.

Publications: $4,100
This includes sales or rentals of publications, DVDs, paid UMConnection subscriptions, and other materials.

Individual Gifts:
Gifts from individuals for specific programs. These are for the conference, specifically, rather than for ministries outside of the conference. No such gifts are anticipated in 2020.

Reimbursements: $97,600
The conference receives reimbursements from denominational agencies for specific operating programs. The Mission Center tenant leases are also captured in this revenue category.

Other Income/Sources of Funds: $1,970,504
Miscellaneous income or sources of funds, such as the funding from agency reserve funds. For example, Retiree Medical expenses (majority of line item) are 100% paid from the Board of Pension Reserves. The funds from the sale of discontinued churches are used to fund a portion of the New Faith Expressions.

Interest: $50,000
An estimate of the interest the conference will earn on operating funds in investment vehicles.

TOTAL OPERATING REVENUE: $ 18,641,514

Expenses
I. DISCIPLESHIP EXPENSES
Regional Ministry Teams: $2,257,089
Funds to operate the ministries and administrative support of the Regions. The Regional Teams include:
   a.   Southern Region (Annapolis and Washington East Districts)
   b.   Baltimore Region (Baltimore Metro and Baltimore Suburban Districts)
   c.   Washington Region (Greater Washington and Central Maryland Districts)
   d.   Western Region (Frederick and Cumberland-Hagerstown Districts)

Discipleship Ministry Teams
Discipleship Ministries
Discipleship Ministries: $1,262,486
   a.   Funds to operate the ministries and administrative aspects of the Discipleship Ministries and Congregation/Leadership
   Development Teams. Funds are also allocated for Discipleship Council, Connectional Table and Board of Laity.
   b.   General and Jurisdictional Missional Shares: $3,401,899
   The funds that the General Church and Northeast Jurisdiction request for ministry and programs from each conference. The conference celebrates its track record of paying 100% of these missional shares since 1998. General Church funds include:

World Service: To help our denomination strengthen its evangelism efforts, stimulate church growth, expand Bible studies, and enrich spiritual commitment. This fund allows us to share in a worldwide ministry, including support for missionaries.
Interdenominational Cooperation: This fund allows United Methodists to have an

effective presence in the activities of ecumenical organizations.

Africa University: This fund supports the further development of the first private university for men and women in Africa.

Black College Fund: This fund represents the denomination's support of the operation and capital funding of historically black colleges and medical schools.

Ministerial Education Fund: This fund provides our church support for the recruitment and education of future pastors and bishops.

Episcopal Fund: This fund pays the salaries and benefits of active bishops in the denomination and supports retired bishops.

General Administration: This fund supports administrative areas of the church, such as the General Council on Finance and Administration, the General Conference session, and Archives and History.

Jurisdictional Administration: This fund supports mission and ministry through the Northeastern Jurisdiction.

Leadership Development and New Faith Expressions: $1,501,102
a. Grants to local churches and ministries to grow congregations and expand ministry in the community.
b. Start new churches
c. Board of Ordained Ministry
d. Certified Lay Ministry

Young People's Ministry: $2,398,845
Ministries funded by Young People's Ministry include Children, Youth, Young Adults, Campus Ministries, and Retreat and Camping ministries.
a. Youth Ministries engage and support young disciples of Jesus Christ.
b. Retreat and Camping Ministries provide opportunities for spiritual growth and formation for children and adults.
c. Campus Ministries support staffing and programs on four area college campuses.

Advocacy & Action; Abundant Health: $767,211
Social Justice Ministries such as Justice for our Neighbors, NEJ Call to Action, and Hope for the City are funded through Advocacy and Action. Funds are also devoted to Deaf Ministries. Abundant Health includes funds for our partnership ministries with other conferences, such as Zimbabwe, South Korea, Latin America, and Eurasia.

Total Discipleship Ministry Teams: $9,331,543
TOTAL DISCIPLESHIP EXPENSES: $11,588,632

II. STEWARDSHIP EXPENSES
Communications: $601,415
The publications produced by this area are tools for implementing the ministries of the Conference, such as the UMConnection newspaper, the website and e-connection.

Operations: $3,400,054
This area is responsible for overall operations of the conference facilities, and IT systems and infrastructure.

Property Ministries: The Conference Trustees oversee all property owned by the conference, to include the Conference Mission Center, three Retreat and Camping facilities, the Episcopal Residence and the leased offices in Hagerstown and on Capitol Hill.

Archives and History: The conference provides support for the preservation of our United Methodist Heritage.

Conference Chancellor: Provides legal resources to the Trustees and other conference leadership.

Annual Conference – Commission on Sessions: The commission prepares all aspects of the annual conference session including program and logistics.

Finance: $554,778
This area is responsible for maintaining and administering comprehensive fiscal and administrative policies and services. The office of the treasurer provides support and information for clergy and laity in local churches.

HR/Benefits Administration: $2,085,273
This office administers all active and retired benefit plans for clergy and laity. They also provide personnel and HR support for Conference staff.

TOTAL STEWARDSHIP EXPENSES: $6,641,520

Episcopal Leadership Ministry: $411,362
Ministries that lead our mission and develop the leadership to lead congregations, ministries and staff.

TOTAL OPERATING EXPENSES: $18,641,514

OPERATING NET: $0

SUMMARY	2018 ACTUAL (UNAUDITED)	2019 BUDGET	2020 BUDGET
Benevolence Factor	17.725%	17.600%	17.600%
Collection Rate	90.62%	92.00%	91.00%
INCOME			
MISSION SHARES***	14,045,685	14,294,897	14,048,165
NON-MISSION SHARES INCOME			
Grants	107,631	180,850	239,100
Event Income	2,151,201	2,145,359	2,232,045
Publications	1,942	4,100	4,100
Individual Gifts	7,135	0	0
Reimbursements	63,454	103,600	97,600
Other Income/Sources of Funds	2,005,958	1,971,458	1,970,504
Interest	89,399	30,000	50,000
TOTAL NON-MISSION SHARES INCOME	4,426,720	4,435,367	4,593,349
TOTAL INCOME	18,472,405	18,730,264	18,641,514
EXPENSE			
DISCIPLESHIP			
REGIONS			
Southern Region	523,400	559,484	563,246
Baltimore Region	560,864	555,534	562,296
Washington Region	522,012	558,894	562,796
Western Region	549,427	570,584	568,751
TOTAL REGIONS	2,155,703	2,244,496	2,257,089
MINISTRY TEAMS			
Discipleship Ministries	4,639,982	4,713,362	4,664,385
Note: General Church Mission Shares	*3,571,610*	*3,481,744*	*3,401,899*
Leadership Development	544,926	559,728	556,102
New Faith Expressions	584,881	945,000	945,000
Young People's Ministry	2,358,968	2,290,349	2,398,845
Advocacy and Action	455,090	553,604	631,374
Abundant Health	64,283	224,247	135,837
TOTAL MINISTRY TEAMS	8,648,130	9,286,290	9,331,543
TOTAL DISCIPLESHIP	10,803,833	11,530,786	11,588,632
STEWARDSHIP			
Operations	3,940,572	3,587,275	3,400,054
Communications	556,284	603,618	601,415
Finance	519,265	546,008	554,778
HR/Benefits	2,023,398	2,060,833	2,085,273
TOTAL STEWARDSHIP	7,039,519	6,797,734	6,641,520
EPISCOPAL OFFICE	492,579	401,744	411,362
TOTAL OPERATING EXPENSE	18,335,931	18,730,264	18,641,514
	136,474	0	0

\# - Denotes items funded from Non-Mission Share sources
   Indicates percent non-mission share if less than 100%

***Used to be Apportionments

Baltimore Region

EXPENSES	2019 BUDGET	2020 BUDGET PROPOSED
Personnel		
Total Salary	380,885	390,407
Total Benefits	111,599	114,389
Total Personnel	**492,484**	**504,796**
Travel	17,000	17,000
Continuing Education	3,200	3,200
Regional Strategy/Program		
Meetings	1,250	0
Baltimore Suburban District		
District Superintendent	2,500	900
Baltimore Suburban District	12,500	12,500
Baltimore Metropolitan District		
District Superintendent	2,500	900
Baltimore Metropolitan District	12,500	12,500
Total Regional Strategy/Program	**31,250**	**26,800**
Administration		
Copying and printing	2,400	2,200
Supplies	2,300	2,300
Postage	400	500
Telecommunications	1,500	1,500
Cell Phone	2,500	2,500
Total Administration	**9,100**	**9,000**
Property and Equipment		
Equipment	500	500
Contingency	2,000	1,000
Total Baltimore Region	**555,534**	**562,296**

Southern Region

EXPENSES	2019 BUDGET	2020 BUDGET PROPOSED
Personnel		
Total Salary	380,885	390,407
Total Benefits	111,599	114,389
Total Personnel	**492,484**	**504,796**
Travel	18,000	18,000
Continuing Education	4,800	3,200
Regional Strategy/Program		
Meetings	1,250	0
Washington East District		
District Superintendent	2,500	900
Washington East District	12,500	12,500
Annapolis District		
District Superintendent	3,050	900
Annapolis District	12,500	12,500
Total Regional Strategy/Program	**31,800**	**26,800**
Administration		
Copying and printing	2,500	2,200
Supplies	2,900	2,300
Postage	500	500
Telecommunications	1,500	1,500
Cell Phone	2,500	2,500
Total Administration	**9,900**	**9,000**
Property and Equipment		
Equipment	500	450
Contingency	2,000	1,000
Total Southern Region	**559,484**	**563,246**

Washington Region

EXPENSES	2019 BUDGET	2020 BUDGET PROPOSED
Personnel		
Total Salary	380,885	390,407
Total Benefits	111,599	114,389
Total Personnel	**492,484**	**504,796**
Travel	18,000	17,100
Continuing Education	4,000	3,600
Regional Strategy/Program		
Meetings	1,100	0
Greater Washington District		
District Superintendent	2,500	900
Greater Washington District	12,500	12,500
Central Maryland District		
District Superintendent	2,500	900
Central Maryland District	12,500	12,500
Total Regional Strategy/Program	**31,100**	**26,800**
Administration		
Copying and printing	2,700	2,200
Supplies	2,150	2,300
Postage	580	500
Telecommunications	1,830	1,500
Cell Phone	3,450	2,500
Total Administration	**10,710**	**9,000**
Property and Equipment		
Equipment	500	500
Contingency	2,100	1,000
Total Washington Region	**558,894**	**562,796**

Western Region

EXPENSES	2019 BUDGET	2020 BUDGET PROPOSED
Personnel		
Total Salary	380,885	390,407
Total Benefits	111,599	114,389
Total Personnel	**492,484**	**504,796**
Travel	25,500	22,000
Continuing Education	4,200	3,200
Regional Strategy/Program		
Meetings	1,000	0
Frederick District		
District Superintendent	2,500	900
Frederick District	12,500	12,500
Cumberland/Hagerstown District		
District Superintendent	2,500	900
Cumberland/Hagerstown District	12,500	12,500
Total Regional Strategy/Program	**31,000**	**26,800**
Administration		
Copying and printing	2,200	2,155
Supplies	2,700	2,300
Postage	500	500
Telecommunications	5,000	3,000
Cell Phone	2,500	2,500
Total Administration	**12,900**	**10,455**
Property and Equipment		
Equipment	2,500	500
Contingency	2,000	1,000
Total Western Region	**570,584**	**568,751**

Discipleship Ministries

EXPENSES	2019 BUDGET	2020 BUDGET PROPOSED
Personnel		
Total Salary	872,945	896,818
Contract Services	18,000	18,000
Total Benefits	255,773	262,768
Total Personnel	**1,146,718**	**1,177,586**
Travel	33,900	33,900
Continuing Education	13,430	13,430
Department Strategy/Program		
Discipleship Council	1,648	1,648
Connectional Table	3,832	3,832
Board of Laity	7,840	7,840
Total Department Strategy/Program	**13,320**	**13,320**
Administration		
Copying and printing	3,000	3,000
Supplies	2,500	2,500
Postage	1,250	1,250
Cell Phone	7,500	7,500
Total Administration	**14,250**	**14,250**
Contingency	10,000	10,000
Total Discipleship Ministries	**1,231,618**	**1,262,486**
GENERAL & JURISDICTIONAL MISSION SHARES		
World Services	1,844,272	1,801,332
Interdenominational Coop	48,716	47,582
African University	55,607	54,313
Black College	248,473	242,688
Ministerial Education Fund	622,910	608,407
	(155,728)	(152,102)
	467,182	456,305
Episcopal Fund	546,164	533,448
General Administration	218,992	213,893
Northeast Jurisdictional Mission Shares	52,338	52,338
Total Mission Shares	**3,481,744**	**3,401,899**
TOTAL DISCIPLESHIP MINISTRIES AND MISSION SHARES	**4,713,362**	**4,664,385**

Young People's Ministry

EXPENSES	2019 BUDGET	2020 BUDGET PROPOSED	
Children's Offering and Seminar	16,000	16,000	#
ROCK Event	230,000	230,000	#
Campus Ministry	363,440	370,000	
Camping Ministry	1,569,909	1,671,845	#
Strategy/Program			
Missional Innovation Grants	50,000	50,000	#(50%)
Young Adult Event	20,000	20,000	#(50%)
Youth Worker Retreat	20,000	20,000	
Resource Development	10,000	10,000	#(80%)
Program Support	6,000	6,000	
Administration	5,000	5,000	
Total Strategy/Program	**111,000**	**111,000**	
Total Young People's Ministry	**2,290,349**	**2,398,845**	#(82%)

Note: 2019 provides shift in Strategy/Program Funding that includes Missional Innovation Grants to Local Churches.

Leadership Development and New Faith Expressions

EXPENSES	2019 BUDGET	2020 BUDGET PROPOSED	
Leadership Development			
Strategic Growth Initiatives	178,000	178,000	
Equitable Compensation	70,000	70,000	
Congregational Leadership Development	60,000	60,000	#(25%)
Certified Lay Ministry	16,000	16,000	#
Board of Ordained Ministry	80,000	80,000	#(53%)
Ministerial Education Fund - BWC	155,728	152,102	
Total Leadership Development	**559,728**	**556,102**	
New Faith Expressions			
Grants - New Faith Ministries	385,000	385,000	
Grants - New Church Starts	300,000	300,000	
Trustee Funded Grants - New Church Starts	200,000	200,000	#
New Church Start Strategy Development	60,000	60,000	
Total New Faith Expressions	**945,000**	**945,000**	
Total Leadership Development	**1,504,728**	**1,501,102**	#(18%)

Advocacy & Action; Abundant Health

EXPENSES	2019 BUDGET	2020 BUDGET PROPOSED	
Advocacy and Action			
Peace with Justice	8,000	8,000	#
Native American Ministry	21,000	21,000	#
Latino/Hispanic Ministry	45,000	44,550	
Korean Caucus	3,120	3,120	
Deaf Ministries	243,900	251,120	
Justice for our Neighbors	77,000	77,000	
Hope for the City	26,084	26,084	
Strategy/Program			
Missional Innovation Grants	30,000	30,000	#(50%)
NEJ Call to Action	30,000	30,000	
reCALL Summit	45,000	45,000	#(89%)
Ecumenical & Interfaith Grants	0	21,000	
Grants - Advocacy, Rallies & Conferences	0	50,000	#
Contract Services	15,000	15,000	
Program Support	6,000	6,000	
Administration	3,500	3,500	
Total Strategy/Program	**129,500**	**200,500**	
Total Advocacy and Action	**553,604**	**631,374**	
Abundant Health			
Board of Global Ministries Secretary	560	560	
School of Christian Mission	3,695	3,695	
Zimbabwe Partnership	99,316	10,000	
South Korea Partnership	19,224	19,224	
Latin American Partnership	7,252	7,252	
Eurasian Partnership	16,910	16,910	
Grant - Quality of Life Retreats	0	3,696	
Grant - United Methodist Community Services	2,790	0	
Strategy/Program			
Missional Innovation Grants	50,000	50,000	#(50%)
Contract Services	15,000	15,000	
Program Support	6,000	6,000	
Administration	3,500	3,500	
Total Strategy/Program	**74,500**	**74,500**	
Total Abundant Health	**224,247**	**135,837**	
Total Advocacy & Action; Abundant Health	**777,851**	**767,211**	#(21%)

Note: 2019 provides shift in Strategy/Program Funding that includes Missional Innovation Grants to Local Churches.

518

Operations

EXPENSES	2019 BUDGET	2020 BUDGET PROPOSED	
Personnel			
Total Salary	529,457	512,951	
Total Benefits	152,730	147,833	
Total Personnel	**682,187**	**660,784**	
Travel	6,500	6,500	
Continuing Education	2,600	2,900	
Strategy/Program			
Annual Conference - Sessions	385,000	385,000	#(52%)
General/NEJ Conference	10,000	10,000	
Operations Administration			
Copying and printing	2,500	3,000	
Supplies	2,400	2,400	
Postage	750	750	
Conference Calls	600	600	
Operational Hospitality	7,200	6,700	
Cell Phone	1,600	1,600	
Contingency	5,000	5,000	
Total Operations Administration	**20,050**	**20,050**	
Conference Administration			
Conference Secretary	3,000	3,000	
Legal	123,000	123,000	
Replenish Legal Reserve	0	0	
Replenish/Increase Apportionment Reserve (15% goal)	100,000	0	
Archives	120,225	147,572	
D & O Liability Insurance	-	0	
Total Conference Administration	**346,225**	**273,572**	
Property and Equipment			
Annual Conference Property			
Conference Insurance	106,400	106,400	
Camp Debt Service	170,000	160,000	
Episcopal Residence			
Taxes/fees	10,200	10,200	
Maintenance	7,358	8,000	
Utilities	10,100	10,100	
Capital Expense	2,000	2,000	
Contingency	1,000	0	
Total Episcopal Residence	30,658	30,300	#(66%)
Total Annual Conference Property	**307,058**	**296,700**	
Regional Offices			
Lease	21,703	12,700	
Service Contracts	1,650	1,000	
Total Regional Offices	**23,353**	**13,700**	
Episcopal Office Lease	57,700	60,000	
Facilities Management and IT			
Conference Center Costs			
Office Supplies	20,000	20,000	
Postage	7,000	7,000	#
Conference Center Mortgage	574,226	535,048	#(14%)
Accelerated Mortgage Reserve	600,000	550,000	
Utilities & Service Contracts	91,990	94,750	
Maintenance/ Janitorial & Maintenance Contracts	133,746	140,000	
Improvements, furnishings	1,050	1,050	
Replacement Reserve Fund	108,500	108,500	
Information Technology Costs			
IT Services	76,320	80,000	
Software & Development	30,000	30,000	
Copiers and Machines	30,000	30,000	#(60%)
Computers and software	26,491	26,500	
Telecommunications	22,279	23,000	
Total Facilities Management and IT	**1,721,602**	**1,645,848**	
Contingency	25,000	25,000	
Total Operations	**3,587,275**	**3,400,054**	#(9%)

Operations

Page 10

BALTIMORE-WASHINGTON CONFERENCE

Finance

EXPENSES	2019 BUDGET	2020 BUDGET PROPOSED	
Personnel			
Total Salary	344,729	353,097	
Total Benefits	98,076	100,528	
Total Personnel	**442,805**	**453,625**	
Travel	1,275	1,125	
Continuing Education	3,008	2,558	
Administration			
Copying and printing	1,950	1,750	
Supplies	2,650	2,350	
Postage	1,600	1,450	
Phone	80	80	
Cell Phone	825	825	
Bank Fees	22,000	21,000	#
Document Scanning	7,500	7,000	
Financial Services Fees	19,000	19,000	
Audit	37,000	38,500	
Contract Services	1,264	1,064	
Contingency	1,550	1,450	
Total Administration	**95,419**	**94,469**	
Property and Equipment			
Equipment	700	700	
Sevice Contracts - Accounting Software	2,801	2,301	
Total Property & Equipment	**3,501**	**3,001**	
Total Finance	**546,008**	**554,778**	#(9%)

Communications

EXPENSES	2019 BUDGET	2020 BUDGET PROPOSED	
Personnel			
Total Salary	340,445	348,956	
Contract services	30,000	29,600	
Total Benefits	99,750	102,244	
Total Personnel	**470,195**	**480,800**	
Travel	15,999	14,666	
Continuing Education	3,380	2,905	
Programs and Operations			
Programs	2,500	2,500	
Fees and subscriptions	3,025	2,025	
Program supplies	10,000	10,000	
Total Regional Strategy/Program	**15,525**	**14,525**	
Administration			
Supplies	3,200	3,200	
Postage	23,000	23,000	
Copying	1,167	1,167	
Printing	62,000	52,000	#(8%)
Cell Phone	3,000	3,000	
Equipment	3,152	3,152	
Total Administration	**95,519**	**85,519**	
Contingency	3,000	3,000	
Total Communications	**603,618**	**601,415**	#(1%)

HR/Benefits

EXPENSES	2019 BUDGET	2020 BUDGET PROPOSED	
Personnel			
Total Salary	148,138	153,892	#(10%)
Total Benefits	43,404	45,090	
Total Personnel	**191,542**	**198,982**	
Travel	4,800	4,800	
Continuing Education	1,500	1,500	
Strategy and Program			
Human Resources Programs:			
Human Resources	2,500	2,500	
Staff Development	12,500	12,500	
Staff Recruitment	3,000	3,000	
Education Programs Health & Benefits	1,350	1,350	
Moving Expense	180,000	190,000	
Retiree Programs:			
Retiree Luncheon	11,000	11,000	#(18%)
Retiree Medical Premiums	1,635,000	1,640,000	#
Laity Retiree Benefits	12,000	14,000	
Total Strategy and Program	**1,857,350**	**1,874,350**	
Administration			
Copying and printing	1,977	1,977	
Supplies	1,064	1,064	
Postage	800	800	
Cell Phone	800	800	
Contingency	1,000	1,000	
Total Administration	**5,641**	**5,641**	
Total HR/Benefits	**2,060,833**	**2,085,273**	#(79%)

Episcopal Office

EXPENSES	2019 BUDGET	2020 BUDGET PROPOSED	
Personnel			
Total Salary	196,979	201,904	
Total Benefits	57,715	59,158	
Total Personnel	**254,694**	**261,062**	#(41%)
Travel	12,000	10,000	
Continuing Education	3,000	3,250	
Strategy/Program			
Episcopacy Committee	3,000	3,000	
Episcopal Discretionary	25,000	25,000	
Cabinet Budget			
Program/Retreats	30,000	35,000	
Cabinet Strategy	4,000	4,000	
Sustentation	40,000	40,000	
Contingency	2,000	2,000	
Total Strategy/Cabinet	**104,000**	**109,000**	
Bishop's Day Apart			
Clergy	10,000	10,000	
Total Bishop's Day Apart	**10,000**	**10,000**	#
Administration			
Copying and printing	1,000	1,000	
Supplies	5,000	5,000	
Postage	750	750	
Phone & Communication	3,500	3,500	
Cell Phone	4,300	4,300	
Total Administration	**14,550**	**14,550**	
Property and Equipment			
Equipment	1,500	1,500	
Total Property and Equipment	**1,500**	**1,500**	#
Contingency	2,000	2,000	
Total Episcopal Office	**401,744**	**411,362**	#(29%)

Recommendations from the Commission on Equitable Compensation

The Commission on Equitable Compensation in consultation with the cabinet is recommending that the minimum salary for 2020 be increased 2.0%, or $880, which will make the minimum salary $44,892. The Commission is also recommending no change in the minimum housing allowance of $20,263.

Kim Ayres, Chair, Commission on Equitable Compensation

Recommendations from the Conference Board of Pensions and Health Benefits

The Conference Board of Pensions and Health Benefits requests that the Annual Conference adopt the following recommendations:

1. That BWC continue to provide retiree medical to all eligible participants.
2. That in accordance with paragraph (e) of Supplement One (Pre-1982), the surviving spouse pension benefit shall continue to be 85% of the participant's formula.
3. That the special grant for Madelyn Hoffman be continued.
4. Pre-1982 Service – Past Service Rate (PSR): That the Annual Conference shall approve the following pre-1982 prior service funding plan in compliance with the Disciplinary requirement listed in ¶1506.8: The Past Service Rate (PSR) for 2019 is confirmed at $720. The PSR for 2020 will be set at $749.
5. That the Annual Conference shall approve the following funding plans based on the receipt of a favorable opinion from Wespath Benefits and Investments in compliance with the Disciplinary requirement listed in ¶1506.6.

Funded status and contributions are based on actuarial valuations as of January 1, 2018, *Pre-82 Plan*: By General Conference mandate, Pre-82 liabilities are to be fully funded by December 31, 2021. Baltimore-Washington Conference is already fully funded, with its assets with the Pre-82 Plan equal to 138% of its liabilities.

Corridor Funding: Clergy Retirement Security Program (CRSP-DB) and Ministerial Pension Plan (MPP) annuities. The funded Ratio for this funding is the same for all Conferences

Plan	Assets	Liabilities	Funded Ratio
CRSP-DB	$1.904	$1.740	109.4%
MPP Annuities	$3.885	$3.607	107.7%

Post-Retirement Medical: Based on an actuarial report received in April 2019, the Post-Retirement Medical plan is reported to have a current view funding ratio of 128.3%. The ongoing view funding ratio is 166.1%.

The funding plan as of December 31, 2018 is summarized below.

	Current View	Ongoing View
Discount Rate	4.20%	6.50%
Plan Liability	$32,734,802	$25,281,763
Plan Funding	$42,004,037	$42,004,037
Funded Status	$9,269,235	$16,722,274
Funded Ratio	128.3%	166.1%

That the following resolution, as required for IRS compliance, shall be approved:

Resolutions Relating to Rental/Housing Allowances for Retired or Disabled Clergypersons of the Baltimore-Washington Conference

The Baltimore-Washington Conference (the "Conference") adopts the following resolutions relating to rental/housing allowances for active, retired, or disabled clergypersons of the Conference:

WHEREAS, the religious denomination known as The United Methodist Church (the "Church"), of which this Conference is a part, has in the past functioned and continues to function through ministers of the gospel (within the meaning of Internal Revenue Code section 107) who were or are duly ordained, commissioned, or licensed ministers of the Church ("Clergypersons");

WHEREAS, the practice of the Church and of this Conference was and is to provide active Clergypersons with a parsonage or a rental/housing allowance as part of their gross compensation;

WHEREAS, pensions or other amounts paid to active, retired and disabled Clergypersons are considered to be deferred compensation and are paid to active, retired and disabled Clergypersons in consideration of previous active service; and

WHEREAS, the Internal Revenue Service has recognized the Conference (or its predecessors) as the appropriate organization to designate a rental/housing allowance for Clergypersons who are or were members of this Conference and are eligible to receive such deferred compensation;

NOW, THEREFORE, BE IT RESOLVED:

THAT an amount equal to 100% of the pension or disability payments received from plans authorized under The Book of Discipline of The United Methodist Church (the Discipline), which includes all such payments from the General Board of Pension and Health Benefits ("GBOPHB"), during the years 2019-2020 by each active, retired, or disabled Clergyperson who is or was a member of the Conference, or its predecessors, be and hereby is designated as a rental/housing allowance for each such Clergyperson; and

THAT the pension or disability payments to which this rental/housing allowance applies will be any
pension or disability payments from plans, annuities or funds authorized under the Discipline, including such payments from the GBOPHB and from a commercial annuity company that provides an annuity arising from benefits accrued under a GBOPHB plan, annuity or fund authorized under the Discipline, that result from any service a Clergyperson rendered to this Conference or that an active, retired or disabled Clergyperson of this Conference rendered to any local church, annual conference of the Church, general agency of the Church, other institution of the Church, former denomination that is now a part of the Church, or any other employer that employed the Clergyperson to perform services related to the ministry of the Church or its predecessors, and that elected to make contributions to, or accrue a benefit under, such a plan, annuity or fund for such active, retired, or disabled Clergyperson's pension or disability as part of his or her gross compensation.

NOTE: The rental/housing allowance that may be excluded from a Clergyperson's gross income in any year for federal income tax purposes is limited under Internal Revenue Code section 107(2) and regulations there under to the least of: (1) the amount of the rental/housing allowance designated by the Clergyperson's employer or other appropriate body of the Church (such as this Conference in the foregoing resolutions) for such year; (2) the amount actually expended by the Clergyperson to rent or provide a home in such year; or (3) the fair rental value of the home, including furnishings and appurtenances (such as a garage), plus the cost of utilities in such year.

Leadership Reports

Board of Ordained Ministry

During the 2018-19 Conference year, the Baltimore-Washington Conference Board of Ordained Ministry has served on behalf of all persons across the Conference called to representative ministries of the church as licensed, commissioned and ordained persons. The Board is comprised of 60 lay and clergy persons who serve on behalf of more than 1,200 persons under our care as either candidates for ministry, actively commissioned provisional members, Deacons and Elders in full connection, and retired members.

This year, the Board has sought to strengthen its work by engaging in several initiatives including working throughout the year to continue to clarify and affirm our values, continuing to engage in Cultural Competency training for the entire Board, and holding our second "Living Your Call" recruitment and enlistment event. We have continued to work to strengthen relationships with the seminaries with which we relate, and have worked with members of the Baltimore-Washington Conference Cabinet and staff to develop a framework and policy for Sexual Ethics and Boundaries. Additionally, the Board has developed several policies related to continuing education and the use of Ministerial Education Funds.

In accordance with paragraph 635 of the 2016 Book of Discipline, an important part of our work is serving as stewards of the process of supporting, evaluating and examining persons who have offered themselves as candidates for ordained ministry as Deacons and Elders. Our eight District Committees on Ordained Ministry and the BOOM have worked tirelessly throughout the year to ensure that processes of evaluation and examination are accomplished with integrity, fairness, and clarity for all candidates and provisional members under our care. We have continued to work to perfect several of the policies and procedures that inform our work for evaluating candidates for ministry, with the goal of discerning ways that together we can continue to engage in ministry that is faithful and fruitful toward the end of making disciples of Jesus Christ for the transformation of our communities and the world.

The Board of Ordained Ministry takes the opportunity to thank Bishop LaTrelle Easterling for her ongoing prayers, support, and guidance of our work, and the Rev. John Nupp, Executive Minister, Call and Clergy Care, for his outstanding leadership in managing and facilitating the perfecting of our practices for supporting clergy and those preparing for ordained and licensed ministry.

As we conclude this Conference year and move forward, we continue to solicit your prayers for our work on behalf of those who seek to serve Christ in the representative ministries of the church, for the Baltimore-Washington Conference, The United Methodist Church, and Christ's Church universal.

Rev. Dr. C. Anthony Hunt, Chair

Personnel Committee

The purpose of the Personnel Committee is to establish and implement policies and procedures regarding the employment and compensation of conference staff members, taking into consideration clergy who are appointed to serve on staff as it relates to the requirements of the current Book of Discipline.

The Committee's goal for 2018 was to review the BWC Staff Employee Handbook originally created March 10, 2014. After an extensive review in 2018, a draft was sent for legal review in January 2019. We are pleased to report that the BWC Staff Employee Handbook was updated and distributed to staff with a revision date of February 1, 2019.

The revised Handbook includes a "BWC Statement of Confidentiality" as an appendix. This statement was signed by employees and will be included in the new hire packet. Staff will be required to sign this statement every other year to enforce the policy. The Information Technology Policy and Procedure Manual continues to be under review by this committee and we hope to have the policy completed by the end of 2019.

The Personnel Committee will continue to ensure conference workplace standards and procedures are in compliance with Department of Labor while remaining faithful to its work on behalf of our annual conference and to the United Methodist beliefs.

I am grateful to all the committee members who faithfully serve and to the conference Office of Human Resources and Benefits for their assistance and invaluable service and look forward to their continuing support.

Laura Davis, Chair

Rules Committee
Purpose: review the rules of the session, review and update all references to the Book of Discipline, review any resolutions that propose to amend the Rules of the Session, and prepare amendments to the Rules of the Session.

Goals:
- Review the proposed changes to the structure of the Annual Conference
- Prepare for Annual Conference 2019, especially in light of the special called General Conference

Impact:
- We are still waiting for the final report to be submitted so that we can review the proposed changes
- We have been preparing changes in the rules to clarify the process for changing the Annual Conference structure in the future

We are continuing to get ready for the upcoming Annual Conference and will develop an agenda for the rest of the year in response to Annual Conference 2019.

Rev. Mark Gorman, Chair

Commission on Communications
"Your very lives are a letter that anyone can read by just looking at you. Christ himself wrote it—not with ink, but with God's living Spirit; not chiseled into stone, but carved into human lives—and we publish it." – 2 Corinthians 3:2-3 (The Message)

This year, the BWC's Communications Ministry published remarkable stories of lives shaped by the wonder and glory of God. We also did a comprehensive job of sharing information and helping people understand the significant scope and complexities of the Way Forward process, as the global church met at a called session of General Conference in February to determine its stance on same-gender marriage and the ordination of gays and lesbians.

Images played a significant role in our ministry this year. We launched our first contemplative photography retreat over a weekend in October at Camp Manidokan. Participants explored how photographs can tell stories, evoke mood and illuminate a sense of the sacred. We also worked with Good New Television to produce a live-stream townhall meeting with Bishop Easterling and Conference leaders to share and interpret the significance of the work of the Special Session of General Conference. It was viewed by more than 5,000 people.

Through our monthly UMConnection newspaper, the weekly e-connection electronic newsletter, our Website www.bwcumc.org; Facebook, Twitter, Instagram, the Conference Journal and many flyers, brochures, videos and promotional pieces, we continue to inform, equip and inspire the spiritual leaders of the Baltimore- Washington Conference. Of significant note was the gradual and steady expansion of our social media, which provides timely insights to a global audience, and the creation of LeaderPod, a podcast that highlights conversations with interesting leaders throughout the denomination.

The year ahead promises to be a significant one for The United Methodist Church, and Communications will ensure that pastors and people in the pews continue to be informed disciples who are equipped to make a difference in their communities and the world.

Institutional Reports

Africa University
Africa University thrives in ministry because of the steadfast support of the local congregations of The United Methodist Church. Thank you to the members of the Baltimore-Washington Conference for prioritizing Africa University and its ministry with an investment of 100 percent of your asking in 2018.

In giving so consistently to the Africa University Fund (AUF) apportionment, the Baltimore-Washington Conference continues to affirm the university's core mission of nurturing leaders who help communities to know Christ and to experience peace, sustainable livelihoods, food security and abundant health.

Institutional Update:
In 2018, Africa University enrolled more than 700 new students and maintained an overall enrollment of around 2,000 students. There were 25 African countries represented in the student body. Women made up 53 percent of the student population, which is almost twice the average for African higher education institutions.

Throughout 2018, Africa University weathered the challenges of Zimbabwe's depressed and uncertain socio-economic environment with creativity and prudence. The university delivered teaching, learning and community service activities of high quality without interruption, while also renewing and expanding its infrastructure. Key enhancements in 2018 included the refurbishment of three residence halls for women students and the full implementation of an ERP software system to integrate and manage all facets of the university's operations.

With conflict, poverty, and the impact of climate change persisting as the key drivers of food insecurity and the rise in internal displacement, migration, and refugeehood in Africa, the university consolidated its position as a trailblazer by offering new graduate training and research opportunities. Africa University has also continued to provide scholarships for refugee women so that their experiences, talents and ideas are integrated into the search for solutions.

Africa University delivered critical data for reducing malaria deaths in southern Africa and controlling the spread of insect-borne diseases world-wide. AU's insectary — a laboratory for rearing and studying live insects, such as mosquitos — shares its findings through the Southern Africa Centers of Excellence for Malaria Research. This data informs regional policies, practices and malaria control efforts.

For the first time in five years, and thanks to the generosity of individuals and congregations in the Baltimore-Washington Conference, there was new construction on the Africa University main campus. A second-mile gift, to honor the leadership of Bishop Marcus Matthews and to mark his retirement, enabled the university to begin work on a campus sports complex that includes a 25 by 22 meters outdoor pool.

The students, faculty, administrators and trustees of Africa University thank the members of the Baltimore-Washington Conference for their prayers and support, which continue to grow and sustain its ministry. Thank you, Baltimore-Washington United Methodists, for all that you have sown into Africa University over the past 27 years. As Africa University and the Baltimore-Washington Conference move forward together in missional engagement, we trust in God's grace for the increase.

James H. Salley, Associate Vice Chancellor for Institutional Advancement
Africa University Development Office
jsalley@gbhem.org, 615.340.7438

Board of Child Care of The United Methodist Church, Inc.
Enriching communities, one family at a time.

2018 Goals and Progress:
Expand capacity to serve more low-income families with high quality, early childhood education
- In 2018, BCC's Early Learning Program in Washington, D.C. was extensively renovated –almost doubling of capacity at the center.

Advocate for new approaches to some of the most challenging behavioral health cases within the human services sector.
- BCC successfully engaged in both state-level workgroups and meetings with leadership that resulted in new programing opportunities coming available – two of which will come online in 2019.

Impact:
- Board of Child Care of The United Methodist Church, Inc. (BCC) and The United Methodist Home for Children (UMHC) have merged as of January 1, 2019. UMHC is in Mechanicsburg, PA, and they share with BCC both a deep history rooted in faith and also a passion for serving children and families. Together, UMHC and BCC will learn best practices from one another and ultimately impact more lives across the Mid-Atlantic.
- BCC received a best practice award from the United Methodist Association for our work with Emotionally and Cognitively Developmentally Delayed (ECDD) youth.

By the end of 2019:
- Create and begin implementation of BCC's 2019-2022 strategic plan.
- Launch a new program to serve victims of sexual trafficking and grow our capacity to serve unaccompanied immigrant children.
- Continue UMHC's programmatic transformation by both introducing therapists and other roles onto the care team and also attaining CARF accreditation. Both efforts will further align UMHC's service delivery model with national best practices.
- Thank you for your support as we seek to enrich communities, one family at a time across

528

the mid-Atlantic. We are truly making an impact each and every day because of your support.

Laurie Anne Spagnola, MSW, President and CEO

Boston University School of Theology
Dear Colleagues in Ministry:

Greetings from Boston University School of Theology (BUSTH) as we live together as disciples in uncertain times!

BREAKING NEWS:
- Students: We continue to increase and celebrate diversity in our student body, creating remarkable opportunities for in-depth exchanges and fruitful collaboration.
- Faculty: We welcomed two amazing faculty this year: Shively Smith as Assistant Professor of New Testament, and Nicolette Manglos-Weber as Assistant Professor of Religion and Society.
- Online Lifelong Learning: We are launching a new Online Lifelong Learning Program at the School, offering webinars, workshops, and reading groups for professional enrichment.
- Scholarships: We continue our offer of free tuition to UMC registered candidates for ordained ministry, and we continue to build student scholarships and housing as a central campaign priority. New scholarships include the Korean Student and African Student Scholarships, and leadership fellowships for promising leaders: Raíces Latinas for Latinx leaders, Sacred Worth for leaders in the LGBTQIA+ community, Howard Thurman for African-American leadership, and Indigenous Studies Fellowships.
- Faith and Ecological Justice Program: This new student program undertakes initiatives to increase ecological awareness, education, and activism in ecological justice.
- Theology and the Arts Initiatives: Recent exhibits and events include "Moments in Time" and "Transcending Conflict."
- Grants: Henry Luce Foundation has awarded a 3-year grant to support the Educating Effective Chaplains Project. The grant supports work with other seminaries to develop models that can better prepare chaplains for effective ministry.
- Website: After several years of planning, a new School website will launch in Fall semester 2019.

PARTNERING FOR MINISTRY AND TRANSFORMATION: Preparing students for ministry means meaningful partnerships with the local spiritual community.
- Creative Callings: Our vocational project is an exciting partnership with local churches, seeking to create "a culture of call." It is sponsored through a grant from the Lilly Endowment.
- Engagement with the UMC: Many of our students are delegates, project leaders and assistants, and class participants in General Conference 2019.
- Congregational courses: The Continuing Scholar program offers current BUSTH courses to alums and local clergy as continuing education credit for a small fee per course.
- Doctor of Ministry: The DMin in Transformational Leadership is soaring with lively student cohorts that are broadly ecumenical, culturally diverse, and global. The model includes intensives, online courses, and faculty mentoring.
- Religion and Conflict Transformation Clinic: The Clinic provides internships and workshops that foster justice and peace-building.
- Travel seminars: These courses engage students with immersion journeys to the Arizona-Mexican border, Israel and Palestine, Argentina, and other sites of learning and ministry.

Attendees from the recent Serbia and Croatia Seminar presented to the 2018 Parliament of the World's Religions in Toronto, Canada.
- Ecumenical partnerships: We continue to build robust Communities of Learning with the Episcopal Church and United Church of Christ, and to develop new communities with the Unitarian Universalist and Baptist Churches.
- Partnership with Hebrew College: Together we are able to enrich interreligious learning through joint courses and public events, and also co-sponsor The Journal of Interreligious Studies and State of Formation cohort of emerging leaders.

TAKING ACTION GLOBALLY AND LOCALLY:
- Campus action: Work to improve accessibility and sustainability. BUSTH is the first certified Green School in BU, and participates actively in the Green Seminary Initiative. It has also been named as one of the "Seminaries that Change the World" for the second consecutive year.
- Internships in global service and peacemaking: We provide internships that support students who engage in ministry with churches and service organizations across the world.

COMMITMENT TO JUSTICE: Celebrating differences while joining in action.
- Faculty and students have led and participated in UMCOR; support efforts with victims of hurricanes and fires; protests on behalf of Puerto Rico, Texas, and Florida; protests of white supremacist movements; services with immigrants and DACA young people; and ecumenical and interreligious witnesses for justice in the city of Boston.
- Through student-led Town Hall meetings, the community has had deep conversations on issues that divide (including theological differences). We seek to foster respectful listening that builds community life and communal action.

OTHER NOTABLE NEWS:
- 2019 marks the 180th year of the School of Theology, originally founded as the Newbury Bible Institute in 1839.
- Our major development campaign for BUSTH will end in September 2019, and we continue working toward grand success for the future of our School and the vitality of your ministries.

As BUSTH looks to the future, we celebrate transformational leaders of the United Methodist Church, who keep the word of Jesus Christ alive. Your living legacy and faithful witness give us hope and courage for the future.

Mary Elizabeth Moore, Dean

Candler School of Theology
For more than 100 years, Candler School of Theology at Emory University has prepared real people to make a real difference in the real world. Since our founding in 1914, more than 10,000 students have graduated from Candler, where they have been shaped as thoughtful, principled, and courageous leaders dedicated to transforming the world in the name of Jesus Christ.

This is especially important to note amid the current uncertainty in our denomination. It is an honor and a privilege for Candler to be one of 13 official seminaries of The United Methodist Church. Yet true to the Methodist tradition of ecumenical openness, Candler has enthusiastically welcomed the entire Wesleyan family to our community for generations. Faculty, staff, and students from the AME Church, the AMEZ Church, the CME Church, Free Methodists, Nazarenes, and others have worked, worshiped, learned, and prayed alongside

United Methodists, and have been a vital part of shaping Candler and our mission. This diversity has been a wonderful gift and a rich blessing. As we move forward from the Special Session of General Conference, we will continue to invite and welcome wholeheartedly those from all expressions of the Wesleyan tradition. Indeed, we will continue to welcome all those who follow Jesus Christ.

Candler is also privileged to be one of seven graduate professional schools of Emory University in Atlanta. With the resources of a top-tier research institution and the reach of a global city, our students benefit from a rich academic and hands-on learning environment: The General Board of Global Ministries is in Atlanta, as are numerous public health, international development, and social service organizations. Candler's intentional involvement with our surrounding community has contributed to our inclusion on a list of "Seminaries that Change the World" for six years running. In short, there is no better place to prepare for ministry that engages our major denominational priorities: developing leaders, starting and growing churches, ministry with the poor, and improving global health.

In order to keep pace with the needs of the church and the world, Candler offers 16 degrees: six single degrees and ten dual degrees pairing theology with bioethics, business, international development, law, public health, and social work. Our Doctor of Ministry degree is 90 percent online, so students can remain in their places of ministry and immediately apply to their context what they learn in class. Our Teaching Parish program allows eligible United Methodist students to serve as pastors in local churches while they're enrolled—they earn a salary as they earn course credit and pastoral experience, plus they are mentored by an experienced United Methodist elder.

Candler's student body continues to reflect the diversity and breadth of the Christian faithful, with an enrollment of 453, reflecting 51 percent women, 39 percent people of color (U.S.), and a median age of 27 among MDivs. Students represent 44 denominations, with half coming from the Methodist family.

Candler has a deep commitment to alleviating student debt and promoting financial literacy. In 2018-2019, we awarded $5.8 million in Candler scholarships, with 100 percent of MDiv students receiving aid. Plus, our comprehensive "Faith & Finance" program teaches money management skills that serve our students now and will continue to serve them—and the churches they lead—well into the future.

Candler draws considerable strength and inspiration from its relationship with The United Methodist Church. Our ability to fulfill our mission of educating faithful and creative leaders for the church's ministries throughout the world depends upon your prayers, partnership, and support. Thank you for the countless ways you advance this vital ministry in the life of our denomination. Visit us in person or online at candler.emory.edu to see firsthand how Candler prepares real people to make a real difference in the real world.

Jan Love, Mary Lee Hardin Willard Dean and Professor of Christianity and World Politics
Candler School of Theology

United Theological Seminary
459 men and women are being equipped as faithful, fruitful pastors and Christian leaders for the Church:
- 292 Masters Students
- 167 Doctoral Students
- Third largest United Methodist seminary in the United States

Founded nearly 150 years ago by Bishop Milton Wright, father of famed aviators Wilbur and Orville Wright, United has continued that spirit of innovation through:

Online degrees:
- 98% of master's students have taken one or more course online while studying at United.
- United students live in 39 different states.
- Week-long intensives fulfill UMC residency requirements.

Live Interactive Virtual Education (LIVE):
- New grant brings the latest technology in virtual education.
- Participate in on-campus courses via webcam and enjoy live lectures and real-time discussion with faculty and peers.

Doctor of Ministry Degree:
- Become a doctor for the Church, addressing a real problem or challenge in your church or community.
- Study under a mentor who is an expert in their field and learn alongside a small group of dedicated peers.
- 3-year program that allows you to complete project as you go, leading to a 78% program graduation rate in 2017 (vs. 54% average among other seminaries)

Practical education designed to resource the Church:
- The majority of United faculty have pastored churches.
- 91% of entering United students are already serving in ministry, bringing that context to the classroom.

A focus on Church Renewal:
- 165 Course of Study students
- 42 students in the Hispanic Christian Academy (3-year Spanish online course of ministry program for Hispanic lay pastors and leaders)iv
- Certificates in Church Planting, Disability Ministry, and Supervision

Academic AND Spiritual Growth:
- 95% of students say the United community supports both their academic and spiritual growth.
- Diverse Christian Views:
- Over 30 different denominations
- 19 international students from 15 different countries
- 96% of students feel their views are respected in the classroom/seminary community and say they have been taught to respect the views of others.
- 47% of students who reported are African-American, 43% Caucasian and 10% represent other ethnicities

We thank God for the men and women coming to United because God has called them to serve the least and the lost. We pray as the Lord Jesus instructed his disciples saying, "The harvest is plentiful, but the laborers are few; therefore ask the Lord of the harvest to send out laborers into his harvest" (Luke 10:2).

Dr. Kent Millard, President, United Theological Seminary

Endnotes
1. Data represents Fall 2018 headcount enrollment, unless otherwise specified.
2. ATS 2017-2018 Annual Data Tables. Data represents Fall 2017 headcount enrollment.
3. ATS 2017-2018 Strategic Information Report for United Theological Seminary. Graduation rates represent the percentage of students who were able to complete their chosen degree within a specified period of time which approximates two times the normal length of the degree.
4. Data represents unduplicated headcount enrollment in the 2017-2018 academic year.
5. United Theological Seminary 2017-2018 Student Satisfaction Survey, in which 30% of students responded.

Wesley Theological Seminary

Fostering wisdom and courage

Wesley Theological Seminary, celebrating our 60th year in Washington, DC, has equipped Christian leadership for nearly 150 years. We prepare students to lead innovative ministries while remaining grounded in our biblical and theological traditions. President David McAllister-Wilson writes in his new book, A New Church and a New Seminary, "Leadership requires a seminary to foster both wisdom and courage."

Our faculty is chosen to prepare these kinds of leaders. In the past year, we welcomed Academic Dean Phil Wingeier-Rayo, Ph.D. plus two new faculty, the Rev. Lorena Parrish, Ph.D., Associate Professor of Urban Ministries and Director of the Community Engagement Institute, and the Rev. Anna Petrin, Ph.D., Associate Professor of Worship and Chapel Elder. Learn more about all the remarkable scholars on Wesley's faculty at wesleyseminary.edu/

Whether you are clergy or laity, an alumnus or a prospective student, looking for master's or doctoral work, or continuing education or simply deeper knowledge, Wesley stands ready to support you in your current and future call to ministry. Here are a few ways Wesley can help you grow in the wisdom of the faith and the courage to lead.

Discover exciting pathways to seminary studies

Wesley offers a 81-hour Master of Divinity, a 36-hour Master of Arts and a 60-hour Master of Theological Studies. Wesley equips all those called to serve for ordained Elder and Deacon ministries or to other ministries beyond the pulpit.

Some are able to take advantage of our modern and affordable on-campus housing and food service to be full-time residential students, living in an exciting international capital. But we understand the struggle to balance life, family, ministry, and finances. So, Wesley's Master of Divinity degree can now be completed via online, weekend, short-term intensive, and weeknight courses in 5 years, designed for those with busy ministry, work, and family lives. Check out upcoming flexible course offerings for Summer and Fall 2019 at wesleyseminary. edu/admissions/try-a-class-3/

In our 3+3 Fast Track B.A./M. Div. program, in partnership with Shenandoah University, students enter ministry with less debt after earning their degrees in six years. Learn more at www.wesleyseminary.edu/3+3degrees.

Wesley provides more than $2 million dollars annually in scholarships thanks to the consistent support of graduates, congregations and friends. Our new Generación Latinx Scholarship joins our many merit-based scholarships that enable students to afford seminary education. The Community Engagement Institute at Wesley embraces a vibrant vision to be the premier center for churches and faith-based organizations seeking new, innovative ideas and training to empower them and to engage their communities. Our Community Engagement Fellows program prepares students to engage in entrepreneurial ministry. Generous stipends are available for each Fellow while they complete their M.Div. degree. Students can focus their fellowship on Public Theology, Urban Ministry or Missional Church. Meet our current Fellows at https://www.wesleyseminary.edu/admissions/community-engagement-fellows/

Take your ministry to the next level

Wesley is a leader in Doctor of Ministry programs in specialized tracks that can include international study. Our 2020 tracks will include Church Leadership Excellence, offered in conjunction with Wesley's internationally respected Lewis Center for Church Leadership and Life Together: Spirituality for Transforming Community, and a track designed for military chaplains. Find out more or apply at www.wesleyseminary.edu/doctorofministry/.

Wesley also offers opportunities for individual study without pursuing a degree. The Certificate in Faith and Public Life explores the foundations of public theology, religious freedom, and civil discourse through graduate courses. For more information, visit www.wesleyseminary. edu/ice/programs/public-theology/public-life/

A Certificate in Wesleyan Studies is available online via the Wesley Theological Seminary Lay Academy. Topics include United Methodist identity, early church history, Christian ethics, interfaith relations, and the intersection of faith and science. The courses can also be taken for personal education and enrichment. More information can be found at www.beadisciple.com/ wesley/.

Enrich your congregational outreach and explore new dimensions of ministry
The Lewis Center continues to be on the leading edge of research for the local church. The Lewis Center's Leading Ideas e-newsletter is now the go-to source for over 20,000 people in ministry each week. From this we've launched a new podcast – Leading Ideas Talk. Sign up or listen at www.churchleadership.com/. And look for new practical online courses at lewisonlinelearning.org .

From their new location at The Methodist Building on Capitol Hill, the Center for Public Theology, under the leadership of Distinguished Professor of Public Theology Mike McCurry, equips pastors, seminarians, people of faith, and the media to create spaces for civil dialogue at the intersection of religion and politics. In its second year, the Center's Faith and Public Life Immersion for undergraduates offers a week-long experience of study and encounters with public theologians and those advocating for justice in Washington. For more information, visit http://www.wesleyseminary.edu/ice/programs/public-theology/.

The Luce Center for Arts and Religion is the only seminary-based program uniting arts and theology. The Luce Center offers regular classes and workshops with visiting artists. For information on past and upcoming opportunities visit www.luceartsandreligion.org.
The innovative online Health Minister Certificate Program prepares congregations for public health work in their parishes. Contact Tom Pruski at tpruski@wesleyseminary.edu for more information or to register for future certificate classes.

The African American Church Studies Master of Divinity specialization gives contextual preparation for the opportunities and challenges our future leaders may encounter in African American churches, while the Public Theology specialization allows master's degree students to gain community leadership and advocacy skills. Learn more at https://www.wesleyseminary. edu/admissions/african-american-church-studies/ or https://www.wesleyseminary.edu/ice/ programs/public-theology/

Through the Wesley Innovation Hub, a research project funded by the Lilly Endowment, we are working with 20 local congregations to design innovative ministries as models for ministry by and for young adults. Follow the work and connect with resources at www.wesleyseminary. edu/wesley-innovation-hub/.

Stay connected
Contact us at (202) 885-8659 or admissions@wesleyseminary.edu about how Wesley's degree programs can equip you for your next step in ministry.

Ready to join in our mission? Find out more about how you can be part of the future of Wesley at www.wesleyseminary.edu/support/. Join the Wesley Community online via Wesley's social media, www.facebook.com/wesleyseminary, on Instagram at wesleyseminary, and on Twitter at WesleyTheoSem or sign up for our electronic newsletter, eCalling, at www.wesleyseminary. edu/ecalling.

Resolutions

Common Table

As per Baltimore-Washington Conference Rule Para. 3006.2.c, this resolution was reviewed by the Conference Secretary and was found consistent with the current Book of Discipline.

Submitted by: Julie Wilson

Conference Affiliation: Interim Advocacy and Action Board, EcoJustice

Financial implications are minor. (Allergen-free bread is slightly more expensive.)

Whereas: our Communion liturgy states that "as there is one loaf, we are one in Christ;" and

Whereas: 5-10 percent of Americans suffer from some form of gluten sensitivity or worse, celiac disease [https://glutenintoleranceschool.com/gluten-intolerance-statistics/] and 2 percent of adults are allergic to milk, 1-2 percent are allergic to tree nuts or peanuts, and 0.4 percent are allergic to egg; [https://jamanetwork.com/journals/jamanetworkopen/fullarticle/2720064]

Whereas: offering gluten-free Communion at only one or two stations can feel isolating, degrading, or even shameful to people who suffer from this condition and does not address concerns over other allergens at all;

Be it resolved: that every Baltimore-Washington Annual Conference, regional, and district event that offers Communion shall offer only gluten-free, egg-free, dairy-free, nut-free bread so that all may share in a common loaf without fear of cross contamination from allergens. This shall be effective July 1, 2019.

Purchase a New Episcopal Residence

As per Baltimore-Washington Conference Rule Para. 3006.2.c, this resolution was reviewed by the Conference Secretary and was found consistent with the current Book of Discipline.

Budget Implications: The net difference between the sale and purchase transactions will require a funding plan by the Conference Trustees and the Council on Finance and Administration that may impact the Conference budget. There is no debt on the current Episcopal Residence.

Rationale: Sale and purchase of Conference property must be authorized by the Annual Conference

Submitted by: Conference Board of Trustees

Whereas: the Episcopal Residence for the Baltimore-Washington Conference was purchased by the Conference Trustees in 1996 and no debt currently exists on the property; and

Whereas: the Episcopal Residence was remediated in March and April 2019 from a black mold incident that was very disruptive to the Episcopal family; and

Whereas: the Episcopal Residence Committee and Conference Trustees approved relocating the Episcopal family to a 6-month short-term rental home on April 17, 2019; and

Whereas: upon review of the details involved with the mold remediation, the Episcopal

Residence Committee and the Conference Trustees recommend taking this opportunity to sell the existing residence and use the proceeds towards the purchase of a new residence; and

Whereas: in accordance with the ad interim procedures for selling Annual Conference property established in paragraph 2515.a of The Book of Discipline of The United Methodist Church (2016), consent has been obtained of the presiding bishop and of a majority of the district superintendents; therefore

Be it resolved: that to fulfill the procedures set forth in paragraph 2515 of The Book of Discipline of The United Methodist Church (2016), the Baltimore-Washington Conference supports the sale of the existing Episcopal Residence and the purchase of a new Episcopal Residence by the Conference Board of Trustees with support by the Episcopal Residence Committee; and

Be it further resolved: that the Council on Finance and Administration will be responsible for approving the funding plan between sessions of the Annual Conference.

Rotating Venue and Accommodation Stipends for Annual Conference

As per Baltimore-Washington Conference Rule Para. 3006.2.c, this resolution was reviewed by the Conference Secretary and was found consistent with the current Book of Discipline.

Submitted by: Rev. Dr. Rudy Bropleh, Lead Pastor, Asbury Church in Shepherdstown, W.Va.

Cosponsors: Pastor Bill Rowley, Chestnut Hill and Shenandoah Memorial Charge; Rev. Jerry Lowans, Washington Square UMC in Hagerstown; Matthew Sichel, Lay Member to Annual Conference, Wesley UMC in Hampstead; Rev. Frankie Revell, LaVale UMC

Whereas: It is in our best interest to have all representatives of our local churches in attendance at Annual Conference; to advise, consent, and share in the celebrations of past achievements and to plan for future ministry for Jesus Christ; and,

Whereas: appropriate venues, which can facilitate our gatherings, particularly in Baltimore, are located at extreme distances from our western and southern local churches; and,

Whereas: these distances can be a burden on those traveling long distances, when our plenary meetings drag into late hours to address necessary agenda items, by requiring these travelers to either put in excessively long hours of commuting or spend more than their budgets allow for accommodations; and,

Whereas, such burdens often discourage those representatives from experiencing the fullness of Annual Conference, or to forego important deliberations in plenary.

Be it resolved that: The Conference Sessions Committee will research various options for alleviating this burden on remotely located clergy and laity representatives, including, but not limited to the following:

The availability, and financial ramifications of another venue for the Annual Conference meetings that is more centrally located, geographically, which would be utilized on a rotating yearly basis with the Baltimore location; and
The cost and administrative requirements to provide free accommodations to the clergy and lay delegates who represent local churches that can demonstrate need.

Unrestricted Bequest Received by Centre Street United Methodist Church
As per Baltimore-Washington Conference Rule Para. 3006.2.c, this resolution was reviewed by the Conference Secretary and was found consistent with the current Book of Discipline.

Budget Implications: Provides funding for the long-range strategic plan adopted by the Retreat and Camping Ministries.

Rationale: Receipt of unrestricted bequests by the Conference Board of Trustees require Annual Conference approval for the designation of any expenditures.

Submitted by: Conference Board of Trustees.

Whereas: on December 17, 2018, the Centre Street United Methodist Church in Cumberland, Maryland received an unrestricted bequest from the Rice Estate in the amount of $25,000; and

Whereas: the Centre Street United Methodist Church was closed on June 30, 2018, with all real and personal, tangible and intangible property conveyed to the Baltimore-Washington Conference Board of Trustees; and

Whereas: in accordance with the procedures set forth in paragraphs 2549.6 of The Book of Discipline of The United Methodist Church (2016), the bequest to a closed church shall become the property of the annual conference board of trustees; and

Be it resolved: that through the administrative responsibilities of the Conference Board of Trustees, the Rice Bequest be designated by the Baltimore-Washington Conference to support non-urban ministries in Allegany County.

EFFECTIVE DATE: June 3, 2019

Amending the Rules: Duties of the Rules Committee
As per Baltimore-Washington Conference Rule Para. 3006.2.c, this resolution was reviewed by the Conference Secretary and was found consistent with the current Book of Discipline.

Submitted by: Mark Gorman

Conference Affiliation: Rules Committee

Whereas: The process for changing the structure of the Baltimore-Washington Annual Conference is not detailed in the current Policies and Procedures manual;

Whereas: The need for a clearer process became evident in the most recent attempt to change the Annual Conference's structure;

Whereas: In the past, the Rules Committee has played a vital role in determining the best structure for the Annual Conference;

Be it resolved: that paragraph 3002.5.e) be added to Rules of the Session as follows: The Rules Committee shall be consulted in advance and review all proposed changes to the structure of the Annual Conference and shall report its concurrence or non-concurrence to the Annual Conference as well as through available outlets such as the pre-conference publication, the Connection, and the Baltimore-Washington Annual Conference website.

Resolution to Provide Nursing and Pumping Accommodations Within the Bar at Annual Conference

As per Baltimore-Washington Conference Rule Para. 3006.2.c, this resolution was reviewed by the Conference Secretary and was found consistent with the current Book of Discipline.

Submitted by: Rev. Bonnie McCubbin, Good Shepherd UMC, Baltimore

Co-Sponsors: Rev. Lemuel Dominguez Milford Mill UMC, Pikesville; Rev. Heather Olsen, Lisbon UMC, Lisbon; Rev. Laura Norvell, Ferndale UMC, Ferndale; Rev. Julie Wilson, Calvary, UMC, Frederick; Rev. Michelle Mejia, Eastport UMC, Annapolis; Rev. Laurie Gates Ward, Good Shepherd UMC, Waldorf; Rev. Margaret Clemmons Grace UMC, Hagerstown; Rev. Leo Yates, Magothy UM Church of the Deaf/Extension Ministry-Maryland DORS

Whereas: there are no provisions for nursing or pumping mothers at Annual Conference;

Whereas: childcare at Annual Conference does not begin until 6 months of age;

Whereas: all clergy are required to attend Annual Conference in full;

Whereas: the lack of provisions for clergy and laity delegates and their very young children prohibits them from full participation to which they are elected and called to serve;

Whereas: accommodations outside the bar of Annual Conference disenfranchises the delegates and their churches;

Whereas: Annual Conference days are long and include three meals per day for adults;

Whereas: Paragraph 161(B) in the 2016 Book of Discipline states, "We believe the family to be the basic human community through which persons are nurtured and sustained in mutual love, responsibility, respect, and fidelity;" and Paragraph 162(C) affirms that children are "acknowledged to be full human beings in their own right, but beings to whom adults and society in general have special obligations…[and] children have the rights to food, shelter, clothing, healthcare, and emotional well-being…;"

Whereas: Resolution 2023 in the 2016 Book of Resolutions names the challenges and need for support in all forms for clergy families;

Whereas: the American Academy of Pediatrics states, "breastfeeding is a natural and beneficial source of nutrition and provides the healthiest start for an infant. In addition to the nutritional benefits, breastfeeding promotes a unique and emotional connection between mother and baby." The AAP acknowledges that there are many benefits to breastfeeding and health risks with not breastfeeding and reminds pediatricians that "breastfeed[ing] should be considered an investment in the short- and long-term health of the infant, rather than a lifestyle choice" and recommends that all children be fed breastmilk until at least 1 year of age (https://www.aap.org/en-us/about-the-aap/aap-press-room/Pages/AAP-Reaffirms-Breastfeeding-Guidelines.aspx);

Be it resolved: that The Baltimore-Washington Conference of The United Methodist Church will inquire on the registration form for Annual Conference each year as to the need for nursing and pumping accommodations and provide them within the bar to ensure the full inclusion of these women. We commit ourselves to work with the Arrangements Committee and other appropriate parties to:

1. Ensure this space has access to all conference proceedings, be voted to be an extension to the bar, and be within reasonable distance from the floor.
2. Specifically designate this area for nursing and pumping persons and be identified with proper signage and have adequate privacy.
3. Provide comfortable seating; access to electrical outlets from the seating; a table next to the seating; and a refrigerator for the safe storage of expressed milk. If possible and practical, access to a sink, a changing area, and trashcan will be provided. These items may be included in the rental of the facility (such as a table, chairs, or curtains) or borrowed from a local church to keep costs at a minimum.
4. Make reasonable accommodations as requested by any parent/guardian for the feeding of their young children.
5. Consult with two to three current or recent nursing or pumping women to ensure the adequacy of the designated space.

Requiring Consultations for Restructuring Proposals

As per Baltimore-Washington Conference Rule Para. 3006.2.c, this resolution was reviewed by the Conference Secretary and was found consistent with the current Book of Discipline.

Submitted by: Mark Gorman

Conference Affiliation: Rules Committee

Whereas: restructuring the Annual Conference often has broad and significant implications;

Whereas: it is advantageous to have input on restructuring proposals from experienced Annual Conference leaders;

Be it resolved: that all proposals to restructure the agencies, boards, and/or committees of the Annual Conference shall first be presented to the Discipleship Council and the Nominations Committee for consultation and votes of concurrence or non-concurrence before being considered by the Annual Conference.

Resolution Pertaining to Attendance at Meetings for General and Jurisdictional Conference Delegates

As per Baltimore-Washington Conference Rule Para. 3006.2.c, this resolution was reviewed by the Conference Secretary and was found consistent with the current Book of Discipline. (See the note at the conclusion of this resolution.)

Submitted by: Rev. Melissa Rudolph

Conference Affiliation: 2016/2019 BWC General and Jurisdictional Conference Delegation

This resolution amends the rules of the session regarding expectations of delegates as adopted by the 2014 Annual Conference.

Whereas: clergy and laity are elected to represent the Baltimore-Washington Conference the year prior to the quadrennial gatherings of United Methodists for the General and Jurisdictional Conferences and any special sessions of those bodies, according to the process adopted by the 2014 Annual Conference under the provisions of the Discipline; and

Whereas: said election is decided upon by the clergy and lay members of the Annual

Conference in order to have a diverse body, representative of the Baltimore Washington Conference; and

Whereas: members of the delegation meet monthly in preparation for their work on behalf of the annual conference, gathering to build relationships, engage in Holy Conferencing, learn about proposed legislation, and worship and pray together at meetings that are scheduled in advance for the entire year. And, that members of the delegation are in covenant with one another to fully participate in these gatherings; therefore

Be it resolved: that members of the delegation are expected to be present at all meetings prior to General and Jurisdictional Conference. Excused absences are limited to those conflicts with the calendar that are shared in writing with the Chairs and secretary of the delegation by September when the meetings commence, illness for the delegate or members of their immediate family for whom they are providing care, bereavement for the loss of a family member, and inclement weather. Absences not communicated in a timely fashion or for reasons outside of these will be considered unexcused. Additionally, delegates must attend at least half of the meeting to be counted present. A delegate is allowed two unexcused absences, after which they shall be removed from the delegation. Beginning with the 2020 delegation, the attendance record of the previous delegation will be published prior to elections.

Note: Questions have been raised by the Conference Rules Committee about the constitutionality of this resolution and about attendance policies for delegates in general. See Judicial Council Decision No. 592 (http://www.umc.org/decisions/41486).

A Resolution Calling for an Adjourned/Special Session of Annual Conference – referred to the Bishop

A Resolution for Representation of LGBTQIA+ Persons on Conference Commissions, Committees and Agencies – referred to Connectional Table

Resolution on Conservation of Conference Ministry Funding – referred to CF&A

Resolution on Doing No Harm Through the Ordination Prohibition – referred to BOOM

Resolution to Do No Harm through Marriage Prohibitions- referred to Discipleship Council

Resolution to Do No Harm Across the Northeast Jurisdiction – Share with Conference Secretaries and Bishops of each of the Annual Conference of the NEJ

Resolution to Use Conference Funds to Support LGBTQIA+ Faithful and Their Allies – Referred to CF&A

Resolution to Affiliate with the Western Jurisdiction – Referred to the Discipleship Council

Keeping Our Sacred Trust:
Sexual Ethics Policy for Ministry Leaders in the Baltimore-Washington Conference of The United Methodist Church
(Submitted by the BWC Board of Ordained Ministry and Cabinet)

I.   Purpose:
A church ministry leader is in a position of power and authority, which entails a sacred trust to maintain an environment that is safe for people to live and grow in God's love. Church ministry leaders sometimes violate the trust given them. Sexual misconduct within ministerial relationships inhibits the full and joyful participation of all in the community of God, hinders the mission of Jesus Christ, harms individuals, families, and churches, and is a betrayal of that sacred trust.

Each ministry leader has the responsibility to avoid actions and words that hurt others, and also to protect the vulnerable against actions or words that cause harm. It is both the ethical and the legal responsibility of the Annual Conference to take all reasonably available steps to protect those who participate in or may be impacted by our ministries. One way in which this Annual Conference endeavors to meet that responsibility is to ensure that there are procedures in place for making and responding to complaints of sexual misconduct. The Baltimore- Washington Conference does not condone or tolerate instances of sexual misconduct. As a conference we are committed to procedural integrity and pastoral care through a fair process of justice-making for victims and survivors, accountability for abusers, and healing for all parties.

This policy serves to provide guidelines for the prevention of incidents of sexual misconduct, and for reporting and responding to incidences of misconduct, should they occur. This policy does not supplant the formal complaint process and its attendant fair process protection as found in the *2016 Book of Discipline*. Rather, the policy stands alongside it, to ensure the deepest clarity of definitions, expectations, and processes.

II.   Theological Foundation:
Every human being is created in the image of God and therefore possesses sacred worth, which must be respected in all relationships. We are one connected body, and when one part of the body is injured physically, emotionally, or spiritually, the whole body suffers. (I Corinthians 12:12-26)

Galatians 3:26-29 reminds us that we are all God's children.
United Methodists "support equity among persons without regard to ethnicity, situation, gender," or age. (¶2044, *2016 Book of Resolutions*.) We further seek to create environments of hospitality in which persons are shown and schooled in respect, equality, and the kinship of Jesus Christ while also protected from misconduct.

Sexual misconduct is an abuse of power and authority. Such abuses are not only an act against one person, but an act against fellow ministry professionals, members in the local congregation, the church at large, and God.

III.   Definitions:
A. Ministry Leaders: Ministry leaders are defined in our context as those persons who have been entrusted with authority within a congregation or faith community and its facilities by virtue of being appointed or assigned by the Baltimore-Washington Conference, or being employed or elected by the local church or faith community (¶2044, *2016 Book of Resolutions*).
B. Sexual Misconduct: "Sexual misconduct within ministerial relationships is a betrayal of sacred trust. It is a continuum of unwanted sexual or gender-directed behaviors by either a lay or clergy person within a ministerial relationship (paid or unpaid). It can include child abuse, adult sexual abuse, harassment, rape or sexual assault, sexualized verbal comments or visuals, unwelcome touching and advances, the use of sexualized materials

including pornography, stalking, sexual abuse of youth or those without the capacity to consent, or the misuse of the pastoral or ministerial position using sexualized conduct to take advantage of the vulnerability of another" (¶2044, *2016 Book of Resolutions*).

C. Sexual Harassment: "We define sexual harassment as any unwanted sexual comment, advance, or demand, either verbal or physical, that is reasonably perceived by the recipient as demeaning, intimidating, or coercive. Sexual harassment must be understood as an exploitation of a power relationship rather than as an exclusively sexual issue" (¶161.J, *2016 Book of Discipline*). Sexual harassment "can create a hostile, offensive environment that can include unwanted sexual jokes, repeated advances, touching, or comments that insult, degrade or sexually exploit women, men, elders, children, or youth" which "alters the conditions of employment or volunteer work or unreasonably interferes with the employee or volunteer's performance" (¶2045, *2016 Book of Resolutions*).

D. Complaint: A complaint is a written, signed, and dated report claiming misconduct, as defined in ¶2702.1 (clergy) or ¶2702.3 (laity) of the *2016 Book of Discipline*, received by the Bishop (¶362).

E. Complainant: A complainant is a person who submits a written, signed, and dated complaint regarding an alleged incident of misconduct.

F. Respondent: A respondent is a person against whom a complaint is made.

G. Just Resolution: The complaint procedures in ¶362 "may include a process that seeks a just resolution." "A just resolution is one that focuses on repairing any harm to people and communities, achieving real accountability by making things right in so far as possible and bringing healing to all the parties" (¶362, *2016 Book of Discipline*).

IV. Procedures for Reporting and Responding to Complaints of Misconduct

A. Anyone who desires to discuss a concern regarding misconduct may contact their pastor, another United Methodist clergy person, a District Superintendent, or the Executive Minister of Call and Clergy Care. The contact information for District Superintendents or the Executive Minister of Call and Clergy Care may be found at www.bwcumc.org.

B. Persons may contact a confidential hotline staffed by the General Commission on the Status and Role of Women for additional information and support at: 1- 800-523-8390.

C. The two aforementioned processes are first steps toward making a formal complaint. The Report of Ministry Leader Sexual or Professional Misconduct Form is a standardized form that can be used for reporting concerns to the Bishop about misconduct in writing. The form can be obtained by contacting a District Superintendent, the Executive Minister of Call and Clergy Care, or downloaded from the conference website at bwcumc.org.

D. When an allegation of misconduct is subject to mandatory reporting requirements by the state (as can be the case with a minor or an adult incapable of self-reporting), it shall be reported to the Bishop and to the appropriate authorities and agencies. All persons serving as pastoral leaders are responsible for knowing the reporting requirements in the area where they serve.

E. The provisions of ¶361, 362, 363 and 2701-2719 of the *2016 Book of Discipline* (as well as any other relevant paragraphs) shall determine the procedure for responding to the complaint.

F. Legitimate complaints are encouraged and will be taken seriously. Retaliation against anyone who in good faith reports an act of ministerial misconduct will not be tolerated and will be handled through appropriate discipline. However, individuals who make false, frivolous, or malicious complaints will be held accountable. Immunity from prosecution of participants in administrative or judicial processes is described in ¶361.3 and ¶2701.4d of the *2016 Book of Discipline*.

G. Upon receiving a written, signed and dated complaint of sexual misconduct, immediate action will be taken in accordance with the provisions of the current *Book of Discipline* for just resolution, real accountability, and healing for all parties.

H. The Bishop or any District Superintendent may receive or initiate complaints about the performance or character of a ministry leader (¶362.a, *2016 Book of Discipline*). Confidentiality will be preserved, and general information will only be shared on a need to know basis. However, a certain degree of transparency is essential for the process of just resolution, real accountability, and healing for all parties.

V. Cyberspace and Social Media Guidelines:

Social Media is comprised of a variety of online activities and anything posted remains accessible, even if it has been deleted. Sexual and professional boundaries can be violated in cyberspace. Messages that contain threatening, obscene, offensive, vulgar, profane, pornographic, racist, sexist, hurtful, tactless, demeaning, libelous, defamatory, sexually explicit, sexual innuendo, and the like, even though no harm or hurt is intended, are inappropriate and, depending on the circumstances, may constitute sexual misconduct. Care should be taken to be wisely selective about sites visited, and messages that are posted online. Ministry leaders should know that because this type of communication can impact the ministry setting, it may be included in supervisory and disciplinary processes.

VI. Dating Between Clergy and Parishioners:

The Judicial Council asserts that dating, romantic or sexual relationships between clergy and their parishioners "are never appropriate because of the imbalance of power" (Decision 1228). Therefore, dating between clergy and their parishioners cannot be considered a situation of two consenting adults entering into a relationship, and it is an act of misconduct for a clergyperson to enter into a dating relationship with a parishioner. For the sake of maintaining healthy boundaries and preventing a betrayal of sacred trust, a clergyperson who has a genuine desire to date a parishioner must contact their District Superintendent and, in consultation with the District Superintendent, determine a reasonable course of action for discontinuing the pastor/parishioner relationship before beginning a dating relationship.

VII. Sexual and Professional Misconduct Response Teams:

Bishops or their designees shall establish and offer to all parties a response team that stands ready to be deployed and available whenever an individual or congregation experiences a trauma. Response Team ministry provides a way for judicatory leaders to enable effective assessment, intervention, training and resourcing of congregations experiencing events affecting congregational health by enlisting a group of persons with training, expertise, and resources in specific areas of ministry. A Response Team is implemented to support and facilitate the healing of all parties. The Response Team is not called to any judicial or Disciplinary processes for legal resolution of a situation.

VIII. Training Requirements for Appointed and Assigned Ministry Leaders

Per the Book of Resolutions, all United Methodist clergy are required to receive up-to-date ethics training regularly (¶2044, *2016 Book of Resolutions*). The Baltimore-Washington Conference requires all appointed ministerial professionals to complete official/approved training on professional boundaries and sexual ethics every appointive year, covering topics which may include identifying sexual misconduct, techniques for maintaining appropriate boundaries, and ways to keep one's self and congregation safe. At least one training during the quadrennium must be an in-person, on-site training event; others may be completed online. All transfers and candidates for ministry are required to complete these trainings prior to commissioning, appointment, or assignment, whichever comes first. Compliance with these trainings are a condition of employment or ministerial appointment.

This policy will be readily available for all those in ministerial positions in the Baltimore-Washington Conference at www.bwcumc.org.

CONFERENCE LEADERSHIP

"...The gifts he gave were that some would be apostles, some prophets, some evangelists, some pastors and teachers, to equip the saints for the work of ministry, for building up the body of Christ, until all of us come to the unity of the faith and of the knowledge of the Son of God, to maturity, to the measure of the full stature of Christ." Ephesians 4:2-8; 11-13 (NRSV)

In an effort to honor these gifts and our diversity, we seek to engage all in building up the body of Christ. The Conference Commission on Nominations seeks[1] to have regional, racial, gender, age and lay/clergy inclusiveness in all committees, commissions, boards and agencies (hereinafter "agencies') and chairpersons. This includes working toward having 20-30% of all agencies comprised of persons under 40.

We recommend that agencies identify their meeting dates for the year no later than September 1 of the current year. Care should be given to scheduling meetings at times when most laity are available to increase lay participation. If a member of an agency is absent from two consecutive meetings without an acceptable reason, that person shall cease to be a member.

The terms of office for a particular agency are as follows per Book of Discipline (hereinafter "BOD") and Baltimore-Washington Conference (hereinafter "BWC") policies:
1. The quadrennial system is an established part of The United Methodist structure. All members of agencies shall be elected for a quadrennial unless restricted by Discipline, charter, or some other requirement. In the event of such legal restrictions, the Tenure Limitation is still to be observed.
   a. All quadrennial terms shall commence on July 1 following the adjournment of the first Annual Conference (hereinafter "AC") session following General Conference, except the Conference Treasurer, whose term shall begin on January 1 of the following year.[3]
   b. When persons are elected quadrennially, they serve a maximum of two terms, except for the Board of Ordained Ministry members which may serve a maximum of 3 terms (BOD, ¶635.a).
2. All other terms shall commence on July 1 following the AC Session in which persons are elected or announcement of election is made.

Each agency member's name is followed by numbers in parentheses and letters:
1. Numbers indicate when a term is up and how many terms have been served on[3] that particular agency.
   a. Quadrennial terms have one number that represents how many quadrennium a person has served; e.g., (1)-elected quadrennially and in first quadrennium; (2)-elected quadrennially and in second quadrennium.
   b. Other terms have two numbers: "when the term expires"-"how many terms served"; e.g., (18-1)[3] means term expires in 2018[3] and person is serving in the first term, (18-2)[3] means term expires in 2018[3] and the person serving is in their second term.
2. Letters indicate the region in which a member's church[3] is located:
   a. BA-Baltimore Region, SO-Southern Region, WA-Washington Region, WS-Western Region
   b. Agency members are urged to immediately contact the chairperson of the agency to which they have been elected, if they are appointed to or transfer membership to a church outside the region identified, in order to allow replacement by a regional representative.
3. Chair of each Committee is designated by a * before their name.

CONFERENCE OFFICERS
President:	Bishop LaTrelle Easterling
Vice President & Lay Leader:	Delores Martin
Secretary:	Kevin Silberzahn
Treasurer/ CFO:	Paul Eichelberger
Statistician:	Rev. Daryl L. Williams
Director of Connectional Ministries:	Christie Latona
Chancellor:	Thomas Starnes

DISCIPLESHIP COUNCIL

There are 14 voting members of the Discipleship Council including the Conference Lay Leader, a youth, a young adult and 11 other persons nominated by the Conference Commission on Nominations.
Elected members of the Discipleship Council shall serve four years in two classes.
The Chairperson shall be nominated by the Commission on Nominations and elected by the Conference.
The Secretary shall be elected from the voting members of the Discipleship Council.

Class of 2021
Barbara Parrish (21-1) WS
Joe White (21-1) WS

Pam Durbin (21-2) SO
Pastor Delonta Hicks (21-2) SO

OPEN (21-2) WA
Rev. Andre Briscoe (21-1) BA

Class of 2022
Hazel Jackson (22-2) BA
Carol Travis (22-2) WA
Rev. Bob Kells (22-1) WS

*Rev. Jessica Hayden (22-2) BA
Joshua Chinagorom (22-1) SO
Rev. Jenny Cannon (22-2) WA

Lay Leader: Delores Martin

Young Adult Rep: TBD

Youth Rep: TBD

Ex officio (without vote):
Conference President: Bishop LaTrelle Easterling
Dean of the Cabinet: Rev. Rebecca Iannicelli
Director of Connectional Ministries: Christie Latona

Treasurer/CFO: Paul Eichelberger
Director of Communications: Melissa Lauber

MINISTRY RELATIONSHIP OVERSIGHT COMMITTEE

A Standing Committee of the Discipleship Council (2014 Conference Journal, p. 597)

Membership on the MROC shall include seven voting members: one representative each from the Discipleship Council on Finance and Administration, and the Board of Trustees; plus, four-at-large members recommended by the Commission on Nominations and elected by the Annual Conférence.
The committee will elect the chair.[4]

*Rev. Mary Kay Totty, WA
Rev. Jessica Hayden BA

Jamarri Bright SO
Rev. Jim Johnson WS

Daphne Hurd BA

Rev. Sheridan Allmond (Trustees)

Rick Miller (CFA)

Hazel Jackson (Discipleship Council)

Ex officio (without vote):
Director of Connectional Ministries or designee: Rev. Stacey Cole Wilson
Rebecca Iannicelli, Dean of the Cabinet

THE CONNECTIONAL TABLE

Members of the Connectional Table are identified by Annual Conference position. The full list of those positions is available on pages 566-567 of the 2014 Baltimore-Washington Conference Journal (see page 328 for the addition of Deaf Ministry representative).

Chairperson: Conference Lay Leader: Delores Martin
Conference Secretary (serves as recording secretary): Kevin Silberzahn

CONFERENCE COMMISSION ON NOMINATIONS

¶6002 Conference Policy & Procedures Manual
(2017-2020) *Selected quadrennially*

Chairperson: Sarah Ford
Secretary: Kevin Silberzahn
Conference Lay Leader: Delores Martin
Director of Connectional Ministries: Christie Latona
President UMW: Linda S. Yost
President UMM : Hampton Conway, Jr.

Young Adult Representative: TBD
Youth Representative: TBD
Lay Person Disability Concerns: Dixie Catlett (SO)
At-Large Laity: Arletta Boston (WA) & Lillian Parks (SO)

District Superintendents
Rev. Gerard Green, GW, Cabinet Representative
Rev. Ann Laprade, BS
Rev. Rebecca Iannicelli, A
Rev. Johnsie Cogman, WE

Rev. Wanda Duckett, BM
Rev. J.W. Park, CM
Rev. Edgardo Rivera, F
Rev. John Wunderlich, CH

Lay Leader from each District
Kim Carr, A
Rosalind Pinkney, WE
Richard Willson, CH
Thea Becton, BS

Rod Fry, CM
Amelia Duroska, GW
Barbara Shew, F
Ophelia Brown-Carter, BM

One appointed clergy from each District, nominated by the District Superintendent and/or the district lay leader for a quadrennium.
Rev. S. Jerry Colbert, A
Rev. Miguel Balderas, GW
Rev. LaReesa Smith-Horn, BS
Rev. Jeanne Parr, WE

Rev. Jean Lee, CM
Rev. Denise Norfleet Walker, BM
Pastor Dawn Reidy, F
Rev. Michael Bennett, CH

DISCIPLESHIP

LEADERSHIP DEVELOPMENT BOARD
Caring for the functions of ¶ 629. Board of Discipleship.

BOOM Chair (or designee)
Conference Lay Leader
Director of Lay Servant Ministries
Up to 6 people with skills and demonstrated fruitfulness in discipleship and leadership development (3 lay, 3 clergy)
Young People's Ministry leaders: one youth, one young adult
Conference Representative: Director of Leadership and Congregational Development
Ex Officio without vote: seminary reps, other staff responsible for leadership development

Class of 2021
*Pastor Nona Colbert (21-1) SO
Rev. Braulio Torres (21-1) SO
Class of 2022
Niki Ellis (22-1) BA
Rev. Phil Ayers (22-1) WA

Sherry Crockett (21-1) WS

Kevin Highfield (22-1) WA

TBD, BOOM Rep.
Delores Martin, Conference Lay Leader
Conference Rep: Rev. Rodney Smothers

Linda Flanagan, Director of Lay Servant Ministry
Nathan Jones, Youth Rep
Megan Blizzard, Young Adult Rep

Ex Officio:
Rev. John Nupp, Executive Minister of Call and Clergy Care
Rev. Chip Aldridge, Wesley Theological Seminary Representative

BOARD OF LAITY ¶631
(2017-2020) *BOD recommends members and states Lay Leader shall be Chair.* (report provided for information only)

Lay Leader and Chairperson: Delores Martin (2)
Associate Lay Leader: TBD
Director of Lay Servant Ministries: Linda Flanagan
Conference United Methodist Men: Hampton Conway, Jr. (President) and Sherman Harris (2)
Conference United Methodist Women: Linda S. Yost (1), Ann Price (1)
Certified Lay Ministry: Linda Flanagan
Youth Representative: TBD

District Lay Leaders:

Kim Carr A (1)
Rod Fry CM (1)
Richard Willson CH (1)

Rosalind Pinkney WE (1)
Amelia Duroska GW (1)

Ophelia Brown-Carter BM (2)
Barbara Shew F (2)
Thea Becton BS (2)

Ex officio: Past Conference Lay Leaders (Tom Flinn, Calvin Williams, Delores Oden)
Conference Representative: Christie Latona

NEW FAITH EXPRESSIONS BOARD

At least one person per district with experience in launching new faith expressions, in start-up enterprises, or with other capacities deemed valuable to the task of supporting new faith expressions
(no more than 12 persons in all)
Staff person(s) responsible for New Faith Expressions

Class of 2021
*Deborah Johnson (21-1) WE
Raimon Jackson (21-1) GW
Class of 2022
Rev. Stan Cardwell (22-1) AN
OPEN (22-1) CM

Kelly Crawford (21-1) BM
Rev. Kyle Durbin (21-1) CH

Rev. Dong Eun (Vivian) Lee (22-1) F
OPEN (22-1) BS

Ex Officio: Emma Escobar – Hispanic/Latino Ministries Coordinator
Conference Representative: Rev. Bill Brown

YOUNG PEOPLE'S MINISTRY BOARD

(Caring for the functions of the Board of Higher Education and Campus Ministries ¶634, and some functions of Council on Youth Ministries ¶649, and Council on Young Adult Ministries ¶650).
10 voting members at least 4 are youth, 2 campus ministry student leaders, 2 Young Adult Ministry, 2 Retreat & Camping Ministry

*Shemaiah Strickland, Young Adult SO
Michael Carrington, Young Adult BA
Maeci Curtis, Campus Ministry (FSU) WS
Margaret Brown, Campus Ministry (UMD) WA
OPEN, Youth SO

Ryan Taylor, Youth BA
OPEN, Youth WA
Jade Ruggieri, Youth WS
Miranda Tyler, RCM SO
Christie Hoffman, RCM BA

Ex officio: Matthew Surber – RCM Staff Rep; Rev. Elizabeth Jackson, Advisor; Wendy Johnson, Advisor; Becki Price – ROCK; Campus Ministry Rep. Alexis Brown
Staff Representative: Cheryl Cook

STUDENT LEADER COHORT (previously known as CCYM ¶649)—

The student cohort equips up to 30 high schoolers from different church sizes, cultures and locations to grow and serve in their various communities as lifelong disciples.
3 Youth per District plus 6 At-Large Youth

2 Youth Mentors per district (some of whom might also serve as District Youth Coordinators). These youth mentors will complete applications and will be selected by the staff rep in consultation with the District Superintendents and District Lay Leaders.

Annapolis: Kim Carr and Ben Rigsby
Cumberland-Hagerstown: TBD
Washington East: Dave Showalter
Baltimore Suburban: Susan Harry and Bill Jones

Greater Washington: Sharon Milton
Baltimore Metropolitan: Shannon Gibbs
Central Maryland: TBD
Frederick District: TBD

Conference Representative: Matthew Surber

YOUNG ADULT MINISTRY TEAM (YAC ¶650)

Book of Discipline recommends membership include one young adult selected by each district.
Members in 2 classes of 2 year terms, maximum 3 terms all members are between 18-35 years old.
(report provided for information only)

Class of 2020
*Megan Blizzard (20-2) F   Shemaiah Strickland (20-1) WE   Moses Ngaima (20-1) BS
TBD (20-1) BM

Class of 2021
Chastity Jones (21-3) AN   Cristin Cooper (21-2) CM   TBD (21-1) CH
TBD (21-1) GW
Staff Representative: Cheryl Cook

ADVOCACY & ACTION BOARD

(7 Chairs of Social Action Teams, 3 annual forum leaders, 1 Advocacy Team lead,
5 persons with gifts in grants admin, project mgmt and/or data analysis and 1 youth ambassador)

Class of 2021
*Thomas Contee (21-1) SO   Jan Taylor (21-1) BA
Rev. Shannon Sullivan WS

Class of 2022
James Wills (22-1) BA   Tracy Collins WA

Chair Criminal/Restorative Justice (CJAMM) – Rev. Sonia King (SO)
Chair Gender Equity (COSROW) – Andrea Johnson (WA)
Chair Creation Care – Mike Koob (WS)
Chair Gun Violence Prevention –William McBride (BA)
Chair Immigration Reform – Rev. Julie Wilson (WS)
Chair Racial Justice (CCORR) – Moorosi Mokuena (WA)
Chair Wealth Equity – Rev. Rudy Bropleh (WS)
Forum Leader: Ethnic Local Church Opportunities and Concerns: Rev. Stephen Tillett (SO)
Forum Leader: Christian Unity and Interfaith Relationships: Rev. Dell Hinton (BA)
Forum Leader: Small Membership Churches: Pastor Rick Oursler (SO)
Advocacy Team Lead: Katie Nash WS
Youth Ambassador - TBD

Ex officio:
UMW Representative: TBD
UMM Representative: TBD
Peace with Justice Coordinator: Rev. Diane Dixon-Proctor
Parish and Community Development: Rev. Eric King
Deaf Ministries Representative: TBD
Committee on Disability Concerns Representative: TBD
Justice for Our Neighbor Representative: TBD
Committee on Native American Ministries: Thomas Crawford
Staff Representative: Rev. Stacey Cole Wilson

WELLNESS & MISSION BOARD
(AKA BOARD OF GLOBAL MINISTRIES ¶633)

13 voting members (at least one youth/young adult, Conf. Sec. of Global Ministries, VIM Coordinator, Disaster Response Coordinator, 9 others)

*Rev. Heath Wilson WS   Rev. Nick Bufano BA   Rev. Irance Reddix BA
Sherita Gaskins-Tillett SO   Sheila Milburn SO   Rev. Twanda Prioleau BA
Kerry Revell WS   Rev. Lorraine Brown WA   Richard Gillum WA
Jackie Weavill SO Young Adult

Conf. Global Ministries Secretary: Jane Grays
UMVIM Coordinator: Rev. Joan Carter-Rimbach
Disaster Response Coordinator: Pastor Fred Sipes

Ex officio:
UMW Education & Interpretation: Barbara Terry
UMM Rep: TBD
Staff Representative: Rev. Stacey Cole Wilson

GENDER EQUITY (COSROW) ¶644
Conference rules apply – 7 members in 2 classes of 2 year terms, maximum 3 terms

Class of 2021
*Andrea Johnson (21-1) WA   Rev. Cynthia Belt (21-1) SO   OPEN (21-1) WS

Class of 2022
Rev. Martin Brooks (22-1) SO   Rev. Angela Kittrell SO (22-1)   OPEN (22-1) A
Rev. Walter Jackson (22-1) BA

Conference Representative: Rev. Stacey Cole Wilson

COMMISSION ON DISABILITY CONCERNS ¶653
Conference rules apply – 7 members in 2 classes of 2 year terms, maximum 3 terms

Class of 2020
John Harden (20-1) WA   Rev. Ella M. Lawson (20-3) BA   Darlene Koontz (20-2) WS
Rev. Lisa Wirkus (20-2) WS   Rev. Kathy Lossau (20-3) WA

Class of 2021:
*Dixie Catlett (21-1) SO   Patrick Burk (21-3) BA

Ex officio:
Deaf Ministry: Lisa Harvey
Conference Representative: Rev. Wanda Bynum Duckett

NATIVE AMERICAN MINISTRIES ¶654
Conference rules apply – 7 members in 2 classes of 2 year terms, maximum 3 terms

Class of 2021
Ronnette Cook (SO)   *Thomas Crawford (CH)   Tavonya Dyson (SO)

Class of 2022
OPEN   OPEN   OPEN
OPEN

Conference Representative: Rev. Stacey Cole Wilson

COMMISSION ON RELIGION AND RACE ¶643
Conference rules apply – 7 members in 2 classes of 2 year terms, maximum 3 terms

Class of 2020
*Moorosi Mokuena (20-2) WA   Rev. Jen Fenner (20-2) WA
Rev. Margaret Clemons (20-3) WS   Ebony Roach (20-1) BA

Class of 2021
Darrell Taylor (21-2) BA
William Carpenter (21-1) WS
Rev. Ramon McDonald (21-1) SO

Ex officio:
Rev. Giovanni Arroyo, Jen Ihlo
Conference Representative: Rev. Edgardo Rivera

DISCIPLESHIP: OTHER

UNITED METHODIST WOMEN ¶647
For information only. Elected by UMW.

President: Linda Yost
Vice President: Ruthella Lievers
Secretary: Sherie Koob
Treasurer: Sabrina White
Missions Coordinators are listed below:
Education & Interpretation: Barbara Terry
Social Action: Vacant
Membership Nurture & Outreach: Daphne Hurd

Spiritual Growth: Rita Green
Chairperson Committee on Nominations: Pamela Aulton
Communications Coordinator: Kim Marie Walker
Secretary of Program Resources: Vacant

Conference Representative: Rev. Stacey Cole Wilson

UNITED METHODIST MEN ¶648
For information only. Elected by UMM.

President: Hampton Conway, Jr.
Vice President: Ceferino Epps
Secretary: Ricardo Jefferson, Sr.
Treasurer: Garrett Henley
Prayer Advocate: Bryon Gould
Program Chairperson: Malcolm Clory, Sr.
Conference Representative: Rev. John Wunderlich

Mission Coordinator: James Williams
Scholarship Coordinator: vacant
Communications: Richard Campbell
Conf. Scouting Coordinator: Rev. Ken Lyons, Jr. & Joseph Vicek
Evangelism, Mission, & Spiritual Life: James Gainey

COMMISSION ON COMMUNICATIONS ¶646
Conference rules apply – 7 members in 2 classes of 2 year terms, maximum 3 terms

Class of 2020
*Rev. Terri Cofiell (20-2) BA
Mittie Quinn (20-2) WA

Rev. Michael Fauconnet (20-1) SO

Bresean Jenkins (20-1) GW

Class of 2021
Pastor Christine Kumar (21-2) BA
Karmalita Contee (21-1) SO

Brian Nelson (21-2) WA

Rev. Beth Hutton (21-1) WS

Conference Representative: Melissa Lauber

COMMISSION ON ARCHIVES AND HISTORY ¶641
Conference rules apply – 7 members in 2 classes of 2 year terms, maximum 3 terms

Class of 2020
Keenan Hudson (20-3) WS
Rev. Katie O'Hern (20-1) WS

Pamela Coleman (20-1) BA
Rev. Dae Sung Park (20-3) WA

Class of 2021
*Rev. Emora Brannan (21-2) BA

Rev. James Chance (21-3) SO

Rev. Stephen Ricketts (21-3) WS

Conference Historian: Rev. Emora Brannan
Conference Representative: Robert Shindle
Ex officio: representing UMC Heritage Landmarks
  - Helen Kemp, Strawbridge House (Strawbridge Shrine Assn., New Windsor, MD)
  - Daniel Fisher, Old Otterbein Church (Old Otterbein UMC, Baltimore, MD)
  - Rev. Deb Scott, Lovely Lane Meetinghouse Site (Lovely Lane UMC, Baltimore, MD)
  - Representative, Geeting Meetinghouse Site (Salem UMC, Keedysville, MD)
  - Representative, Cokesbury College Site (Cokesbury Mem. UMC, Abingdon, MD)

CONFERENCE COMMITTEE ON HISPANIC-LATINO MINISTRIES
For information only: selected by HLM

Executive Committee:

*Rev. Giovanni Arroyo	Secretary & Education and Advocacy: Rev. Heather Olson
Lucy Torres (Vice-Chair)	Faithful Discipleship: Rev. Jen Fenner
Connectional Commitment: Rev. DaeHwa Park	At-Large: Rev. Dr. Miguel Balderas and Lauren Busky

Connectional Commitment: Cory Slack, Raimon Jackson, Lucy Torres, Rev. DaeHwa Park, Rev. Edgardo Rivera

Faithful Discipleship: Lauren Busky, Henry Welcome, Rev. Jen Fenner, Rev. Miguel Balderas, and Rev. F. Douglas Powe, Jr.

Education & Advocacy: Jorge Granados-de la Rosa, Andres Arco, Mike Dean, Rev. Heather Olson, Rev. Wanda Duckett, Rev. Eliezer Valentin-Castañon, and Rebecca Cole.

Conference Representative: Emma Escobar

STEWARDSHIP MINISTRIES

COUNCIL ON FINANCE AND ADMINISTRATION ¶611-618 (2017-2020)
Per conference rules - 12 members who do not serve more than two terms and,
per BOD, individuals are elected quadrennially

*Phil Potter WA (1)	Rev. Robert Slade SO (2)	Lucinda Fisher (2) BA
Charles Myers BA (2)	Rev. Marlon Tilghman BA (2)	Gwen Morgan (2) WA
Charlie Moore SO (1)	Rev. Daryl Williams SO (1)	David Fisher (1) WS
Paul Hazen WA (2)	Rick Miller WS (2)	Betty Henderson (1) SO

Ex officio: GCFA Board Member Ken Ow
Cabinet Representative: Rev. John Wunderlich

BOARD OF TRUSTEES ¶640 and 2512
Per BOD, "shall have 12 members elected in staggered 4-year terms" and, per conference rules,
may serve a maximum of two terms

Class of 2020		
Rev. Bob Ruggieri WS (1)	Pastor Lem Dominguez BA (1)	Dick Findley SO (1)
Class of 2021		
Delila Parham SO (1)	Barbara Hutchinson SO (1)	Rev. Robert Snyder WS (2)
Class of 2022		
Sonja Brown-Jenkins WS (1)	Rev. Sherwyn Benjamin WA (1)	Rev. Diane Dixon-Proctor WA (2)
Class of 2023		
Rev. Sheridan Allmond BA (2)	*John Strawbridge BA (2)	Pastor Lucinda Kent WA (1)

Ex officio:
Bishop Easterling, Paul Eichelberger, Pier McPayten
Cabinet Representative: Rev. Johnsie Cogman

BOARD OF PENSIONS ¶639
Per BOD, "shall have 12 members elected in staggered 4-year terms" and, per conference rules may serve a maximum of
two terms. In order to stagger the classes, some members may serve fewer years than others.

Class of 2020		
*Rev. Cary James BA (1)	Alice Jackson SO (1)	Patsy Baker Blackshear SO (1)
Class of 2021		
Ed Hunt (2) BA	Donna Snyder WS (2)	Rev. Jarrett Wicklein BA (2)
Class of 2022		
Rev. Curtis Ehrgott WA (2)	Rev. Daniel Montague BA (2)	Carl Eichenwald WA (1)
Class of 2023		
Doreen Bass (WS) (1)	Rev. Chris Serufusa WS (2)	Rev. Ken Valentine SO (2)

Ex officio: Francess Tagoe
Cabinet Representative: Rev. Ann Laprade

COMMISSION ON EQUITABLE COMPENSATION ¶625.1
Conference rules apply – 7 members in 2 classes of 2 year terms, maximum 3 terms

Class of 2020
Rev. Kathy Altman WS (20-1)   Rev. MyungHa Baek (20-3) WA   JoAnne Poole (20-1) SO
*Kim Ayres (20-2) BA

Class of 2021
Scott Harper (21-1) WA   OPEN (21-1) WS   Gregory Kernan (21-2) SO

Ex officio: NEJ, Representative to National Assoc. of Equitable Compensation Committee: Deborah Tocknell
Conference Representative: Francess Tagoe

JOINT COMMITTEE ON CLERGY MEDICAL LEAVE ¶652 (2017-2020)
Per BOD, 2 persons from the Board of Ordained Ministry, 2 persons from Board of Pensions, 1 Member from the Commission on Disability Concerns and a representative from the Cabinet appointed by the Bishop

TBD (Board of Pensions)   Rev. Alicia Vanisko - (Board of Ordained Ministry)
Ray Moseley (Board of Ordained Ministry)   Rev. Kathy Lossau (Commission on Disability Concerns)
Cabinet Representative: Rev. Wanda Bynum Duckett   Patsy Blackshear – (Board of Pensions)

COMMITTEE OF PERSONNEL & POLICY
Conference rules apply – 7 members in 2 classes of 2 year terms, maximum 3 terms

Class of 2020
*Laura E. Davis (20-3) BA   Rev. Robert Hunter (20-2) WS   Rev. David Cooney (20-2) WA
Theodore Garrett, Jr. (20-2) SO   Rev. Donna Renn (20-2) WS

Class of 2021
Pastor Patricia Turnage (21-2) SO   Rosalind Pinkney (21-3) SO

Ex officio: Francess Tagoe
Conference Representative: Rev. J.W. Park

MID-ATLANTIC FOUNDATION
*The Mid Atlantic Board is an independent and self-perpetuating board.
It shall have 6 voting members from each Conference serving
4 year terms with the terms being staggered*

Paul Eichelberger WS   Clarence White BA   George Monk WA
Kristin Schol WA   Jamie Waldren WA   Rev. Karin Walker BA
Ex officio: Bishop LaTrelle Easterling

RULES COMMITTEE
*Term of office shall be four years, with one-half of the regional representatives being elected in two classes.
Chair person elected by the committee; Secretary is the Conference Secretary.*

Class of 2021
Justice Randolph (21-1) WA   Dawn Brooks (21-1) WS

Class of 2023
*Rev. Mark Gorman (23-3) BA   Kenneth Moore (23-1) SO

Bishop LaTrelle Easterling
Chair of Discipleship Council: Rev. Jessica Hayden   Conference Secretary: Kevin Silberzahn

COMMITTEE ON EPISCOPACY ¶637

Per the BOD, Lay and clergy members from the jurisdictional episcopacy committee, 2 members appointed by the Bishop and 5 members elected by the Annual Conference quadrennially for a maximum of 2 terms.
1/3 lay women, 1/3 lay men, 1/3 clergy

*Rev. James Miller (2)	Charlie Moore (1)	Rev. Ianther Mills (1)
Rev. Tim West (2)	Ella Curry (2)	Rev. Yvonne Wallace Penn (1)
	Stephanie Johnson Pettaway (2)	

Ex officio with vote: Delores Martin NEJ Rep and Rev. Terri Rae Chattin NEJ Rep

CONFERENCE MOVING COMMITTEE

The committee includes the chair plus a representative from each District. Contact information for District Representatives may be found in the Conference Journal or through the Conference Website.

*Rev. Jeff Paulson (GW)	Amanda McMurtrey (A)	Rev. Jessica Hayden (BM)
Sharon Skinner (WA)	TBD (CM)	Rev. Bob Snyder (CH)
Pastor John Lewis (F)	Deborah Johnson (WE)	

CONFERENCE SESSIONS COMMITTEE

(2017-2020) *Selected by Bishop for quadrennium*

Chairperson: Bishop LaTrelle Easterling	Worship Team Chair: Rev. Sherri Wood-Powe
Vice Chair: Delores Martin, Conference Lay Leader	Conference UMW President: Linda Yost
Secretary: Kevin Silberzahn, Conference Secretary	Conference UMM President: Hampton Conway, Jr.
Treasurer: Paul Eichelberger	Administrative Assistant to Bishop: Joyce King
Director of Connectional Ministries: Christie Latona	BOOM Chair: Rev. Anthony Hunt
Cabinet Dean: Rev. Rebecca Iannicelli	BOOM Ordination Service Coord: Rev. Scott Shumaker
Host District Superintendent: Rev. Wanda Duckett	Conference CCYM President: Karis Arnold
Director of Communications: Melissa Lauber	Host District Lay Leader: Ophelia Brown-Carter
Rules Chair: Rev. Mark Gorman	Arrangements Committee Staff Coordinator: Debbie Albrecht

BOARD OF ORDAINED MINISTRY ¶635

(Quadrennially 2017-2020)

(BOD -- BOOM Members nominated by the Bishop for 4 year term in the same year as General Conference. Members may serve maximum of 3 consecutive four year terms)

Western Region

* FR Rev. Rudolph Bropleh (1)	Rev. Jennifer Smith (1)	Rev. Eliezer Valentin-Castañon (2)
Rev. Robert Wellman (1)	Rev. Duane Jensen (2)	Don Zetterberg (1)
Rev. Malcolm Stranathan (1)		
* CH Rev. Ray Roberson (1)	Rev. Elizabeth Jackson (1)	Rev. Michael Beiber (1)
Rev. Frankie Revell (1)	Richard Willson (1)	

Washington Region

* GW Rev. Paul Johnson (1)	Rev. Stephanie Vader (2)	Rev. Yvonne Mercer-Staten (1)
Rev. Kirkland Reynolds (1)	Rev. Ginger Gaines-Cirelli (1)	Sue Conway (1)
Katie Weston (1)	Rev. Bruce Jones (1)	
*CM Rev. James Miller (1)	Rev. Mandy Sayers (2)	Rev. Andrew Cooney (1)
Geoff Kaiser (1)	Rev. Esther Holimon (2)	Rev. Tim Dowell (1)

Southern Region

* WE Rev. Pat Allen (1)	Rev. Susan Boehl (3)	Rev. Patricia Watson (1)
Kathy Rodeffer (1)	Rev. Sarah Schlieckert (2)	
* AS Rev. Carletta Allen (3)	Rev. Ron Foster (2)	Rev. Lena Marie Dennis (2)
	Rev. Jen Karsner (2)	Yolanda Perry (1)

Baltimore Region
* BM Rev. Jason Jordan Griffin (2)   Rev. Amy McCullough (2)   Rev. Sandi Johnson (1)
Rev. George Winkfield (1)   Rev. Tony Hunt (2)   Ray Moseley (2)

* BS Rev. Norman Obenshain (3)   Rev. Scott Shumaker (3)
Rev. Laurie Tingley (1)   Rev. Alicia Vanisko (1)   Merle Bayne (3)

Additional Members:
Regional Representatives of the Laity: Debby Haskins (Baltimore) (1); OPEN (Southern) (1);
Katie Weston (Washington) (1); George Pittinger (Western) (1)
Associate Member and/or Local Pastor: Rev. Frances Stewart (1)
Extension Ministers: Rev. Hi Rho Park (2)
Deacon: Rev. Lee Ferrell (3)
Chair of the Order of Elders: Rev. Melissa Rudolph (2)
Chair of the Order of Deacons: Rev. Margery Schammel (1)
Chair of the Fellowship of Local Pastors & Associate Members: Pastor S. Jerry Colbert (1)
Retired Person: Rev. Mary Jo Sims (3)
Conference Representatives: Rev. Gerard Green/Rev. John Nupp (Clergy Excellence)
*Indicates Chair of District Committee on Ordained Ministry

COMMITTEE ON ADMINISTRATIVE REVIEW ¶636 (2017-2020)
Per BOD, nominated by Bishop quadrennially

Clergy in Full Connection
Rev. Marlon Tilghman
Rev. Steve Larsen
Rev. Mary Kay Totty

Alternate Clergy in Full Connection
Rev. Clark Carr
Rev. Loretta Johnson

COMMITTEE ON CLERGY INVESTIGATION ¶2703.2 (2017-2020)
Per BOD, nominated by Bishop quadrennially

Clergy Members:
Rev. LaReesa Smith-Horn (BA)   Rev. Terri Cofiell (BA)   Rev. David Cooney (WA)
Professing members:
Maxine Jenkins (WA)   Norwood Bentley (WS)
Alternate clergy:
TBD   Rev. Alfreda Wiggins (BA)   Rev. Michael Bennett (WS)
Alternate professing members:
Griff Hall (SO)   Kirsten Gullickson (WA)   Bryon Gould (BA)

COMMITTEE ON DIACONAL MINISTRY INVESTIGATION ¶2703.3 (2017-2020)
Per BOD, nominated by Bishop quadrennially

Donnalee Sanderson (2016)

CONFERENCE DISTRICT COMMITTEES ON ORDAINED MINISTRY ¶666
Annapolis
Rev. Carletta Allen, Chair   Rev. James Bishop   Rev. Lee Ferrell
Rev. Michael Fauconnet   Rev. Ramon McDonald   Rev. Robert Walker
Rev. Phil Tocknell   Delores Oden   Rev. Clark Carr
Yolanda Perry   Rev. Meredith Wilkins-Arnold
Rev. Lena Marie Dennis   Bob Ettinger

Baltimore Metropolitan
Rev. Jason Jordan-Griffin, Chair   Rev. Sandi Johnson   Rev. Katie Grover
Rev. Twanda Prioleau   Rev. Alfreda Wiggins   Rev. George Winkfield
George Kahl   Elizabeth M. Stemley   Ophelia Brown-Carter
Rev. Bonnie McCubbin   Rev. Emora Brannan   Millie Rice
   Ray Moseley   Rev. Jay Blake

Baltimore Suburban

Rev. Norman Obenshain, Chair
Rev. Bob Clipp
Rev. Carol Pazdersky
Rev. Sheridan Allmond
Leslie McGlothlin
Rev. Melissa McDade

Rev. Melissa Rudolph
Rev. Scott Shumaker
Rev. Andrew Greenwood
Rev. Laurie Tingley
Norman Smith
Rev. Lisa Bandel

Rev. Daniel Montague
Rev. Kate Payton
Devonna Rowe
Rev. Stacey Nickerson

Central Maryland

Rev. Jim Miller, Chair
Rev. Dae Sung Park
Bettye Ames
Rev. Phil Ayers
Rod Fry
Rev. Myungha Baek

Rev. Jen Eschliman
Rev. Esther Holimon
Carolyn Taylor
Geoff Kaiser
Rev. Bonnie Scott
Joyce Shelton

Janet Fujikawa
Rev. Claire Matheny
Rev. Alice Ford
Rev. Lynn Nulton

Cumberland-Hagerstown

Rev. Ray Roberson, Chair
Kathy Kelsey
Rev. Bill Warehime
Pastor Charles Riggleman
Rev. Donna Renn

Pastor Sharon Gibson
Tom Dalton
Pastor Patricia Bittner
Rev. Barbara Suffecool
Richard Willson

Rev. Elizabeth Jackson
Rev. Doug Hoffman
Pastor Al Deal

Frederick

Rev. Rudy Bropleh, Chair
Rev. Dee Ann Dixon
Pastor Lynn Wilson
Pastor Bill Lawson

Don Zetterburg
Sherie Koob
Rev. Ken Walker
Rev. Chris Suerdieck

Rev. Bob Wellman
Rev. Eliezer Valentin-Castanon
Rev. Malcolm Stranathan
Barbara Shew

Greater Washington

Rev. Paul Johnson, Chair
Rev. Michael Armstrong
Sue Conway
Rev. Rachel Cornwell
Rev. Loretta Johnson

Judy Jones
Rev. Kathleen Kohl
Delores Martin
Les Mobray
Rev. Martha Meredith

Rev. Kirkland Reynolds
Rev. Stephanie Vader
Rev. Arthuree Wright

Washington East

Rev. Patricia Allen, Chair
Rev. George DeFord
Rev. Mark Venson
Rev. Robert Carter

Rev. Constance Smith
Hampton Conway, Jr.
Lillian Parks
Gloria Turner-Simpkins

Rev. Robert Barnes
Rev. Kenneth Moore
Pastor Kermit Moore
Rev. Linda Motter

CONFERENCE DISTRICT BOARDS OF CHURCH LOCATION AND BUILDING ¶2519

Annapolis

Rev. James Stutler, Chair
Scott Karsner

Vince Leggett
Chris Broadwell

Cynthia Clark
Bill Prehn

Baltimore Metropolitan

John (Jack) Danz, Chair
Jan Hayden
Ophelia Brown Carter

Kathy Robertson
Warren Hobbs
Jesse McCurdy

Rev. Mark Mooney

Baltimore Suburban

Rev. Sheridan Allmond, Chair
Rev. Victor Harner

Rev. Jarrett Wicklein
Ernest Gayles

Bob Frisch

Cumberland-Hagerstown

Rev. Michael Leedom, Chair

Rev. William Warehime

Rev. Robert Ruggieri

Pastor Richard Baker, Chair
Carl Haines

Dayle Walden Hall, Chair
Marc Loud
Charles Daye
Rev. Gerald Elston
Sherman Harris

Rev. Laurie Gates-Ward, Chair
Rev. Doug Hays

Frederick

Bill Wivell   Magda Morales
Pastor Ed Hall

Central Maryland & Greater Washington

Rev. Loretta Johnson   Sharon Skinner
Pastor Lucinda Kent   Rev. Jane Wood
Will McKinzie   Don Woodrow
John Nyarku
Pastor Sandi Phillips

Washington East

Pastor Irvin Beverly   Rev. Dana Jones
Guffrie Smith Jr.

LAITY SERVING
ON CONFERENCE AGENCIES

Ames, Bettye
15150 Sapling Ridge Dr, Dayton, MD 21036-1259

(410) 531-6251
bettyeames101@gmail.com

Arnold, Karis
1910 Dulany Pl, Annapolis, MD 21409-6221

(410) 268-1776
karislarnold@gmail.com

Aulton, Pamela
2310 231st St, Pasadena, MD 21122-1269

(410) 317-5394
palexana@hotmail.com

Ayres, Kimberly
501 Hampton Ln, Towson, MD 21286-1311

(410) 823-6511
kayres@towsonumc.org

Bass, Doreen
9411 Baltimore Rd, Frederick, MD 21704-6752

(301) 696-9735
Dbass39@yahoo.com

Bayne, Merle
1603 Waltham Ct, Lutherville, MD 21093-5750

(410) 321-4469
merle.bayne@comcast.net

Becton, Thea
1230 Carroll St, Baltimore, MD 21230-1809

(443) 866-7481
ryansmom0512@hotmail.com

Bentley, Norwood

(304) 279-2923
norwoodbentley@yahoo.com

Blackshear, Patsy
362 Southport Dr, Edgewater, MD 21037-2726

(410) 224-4457
pbblack@msn.com

Blizzard, Megan
1118 Jim Dot Dr, Westminster, MD 21157-7664

(410) 596-0696
megblizz@yahoo.com

Boston, Marie
16430 Batson Rd, Spencerville, MD 20868-9705

(301) 421-9638
arlejohn@verizon.net

Bright, Jamarri
1117 Gallatin Way, Pasadena, MD 21122

(410) 360-0540
jamarri@hotmail.com

Broadwell, Chris
724A Rosedale St, Annapolis, MD 21401-2300

(318) 349-7110
chris.broadwell@gmail.com

Brooks, Dawn
7113 Bradshaw Ct E, Frederick, MD 21703-7161

(301) 302-3974
dawntbrooks@gmail.com

Brown, Margaret
3044 Ascension St, Baltimore, MD 21225-1202

(410) 354-0428
mbrown60@terpmail.umd.edu

Brown-Carter, Ophelia
5785 Cedonia Ave Apt A, Baltimore, MD 21206-7623

(410) 483-6425
opheliaval@aol.com

Brown-Jenkins, Sonja
207 Shannonbrook Ln, Frederick, MD 21702-3636

(301) 676-0076
jenks@xecu.net

Burk, Patrick
4516 Warm Stone Cir, Perry Hall, MD 21128-9036
(410) 529-5416
pmlmburk@comcast.net

Busky, Lauren
8704 Fowler Ave, Baltimore, MD 21234-4231
(410) 661-3709
labusky@comcast.net

Campbell, Richard
7784 Poplar Grove Rd, Severn, MD 21144
(410) 969-9277
rcampbell@bwcumm.org

Carr, Kim
1410 Wigeon Way Apt 204, Gambrills, MD 21054-1346
(410) 451-1324
kim.p.carr@verizon.net

Chinagorom, Joshua
8012 Patuxent Landing Loop, Laurel, MD 20724
(410) 220-4596
bishopjoshua02@gmail.com

Clark, Cynthia
8008 Wingate Dr, Glenn Dale, MD 20769-2025
(301) 805-4474
cynthiaclark@gmail.com

Clory, Sr., Malcolm
3706 Walnut Ln, Suitland, MD 20746-2214
(301) 420-1906
clorystlnd@aol.com

Cole, Rebecca
908 Massachusetts Ave NW, Washington, DC 20001-4308
(401) 578-3694
rjanecole@gmail.com

Coleman, Pamela
3438 Ripple Rd, Windsor Mill, MD 21244-3603
(410) 949-5341
pcoleman1954@gmail.com

Collins, Tracy
3617 New Hampshire Ave NW, Washington, DC 20010
(202) 379-8136
tracy.collins@redhorsecorp.com

Contee, Karmalita
8111 Elora Ln, Brandywine, MD 20613-5749
(301) 502-1510
karmalita20613@verizon.net

Contee, Thomas
15101 Baden Naylor Rd, Brandywine, MD 20613-8671
(301) 412-1451
tomcontee13@gmail.com

Conway, Hampton
11835 Ellington Dr, Beltsville, MD 20705-1310
(301) 210-5091
ummhamp@yahoo.com

Conway, Sue
7304 Westwind Dr, Bowie, MD 20715-1736
(301) 464-1619
srconway@comcast.net

Cook, Ronnette
1345 Shirleyville Rd, Arnold, MD 21012
(443) 618-1118
rcook@rexelusa.com

Cooper, Cristin
4815 Tothill Dr, Olney, MD 20832-1889
(240) 432-2607
ccooper@oakdale.church

Crawford, Kelly
931 Saint Paul St Apt 2R, Baltimore, MD 21202-6502
(443) 750-8048
kellyecrawford324@gmail.com

558

Crawford, Thomas
6 South High Street, Funkstown, MD 21734-0574
(240) 217-3708
tscottcrawford.new@gmail.com

Crockett, Sherry
8358 Rocky Springs Rd, Frederick, MD 21702-2382
(301) 639-9154
Sherry@2HearGod.org

Curry, Ella
6263 Masefield Ct, Alexandria, VA 22304-3536
(703) 960-4368
ellapcurry@gmail.com

Curtis, Maeci
Simpson 123, Frostburg, MD 21532
mcurtis@frostburg.edu

Dalton, Thomas
11821 Pleasant Walk Rd, Myersville, MD 21773-9435
(301) 293-1041
tkdalton@comcast.net

Danz, John
649 Sussex Rd, Baltimore, MD 21286-7611
(410) 825-6252
john.danz123@gmail.com

Davis, Laura
1101 Dlong Rd Apt C, Catonsville, MD 21228-3707
eledavis0622@live.com

Daye, Charles
3113 Gold Mine Rd, Brookeville, MD 20833-2624
(301) 774-6883
mdaye56120@aol.com

Dean, Gerald
300 Lambson Ct, Baltimore, MD 21220-3019
(410) 335-1877
vze28zwa@verizon.net

Durbin, Pam
1703 Dryden Way, Crofton, MD 21114-1412
(410) 721-2291
pdurbin1@gmail.com

Duroska, Amelia
7304 Durbin Ter, Bethesda, MD 20817-6127
(301) 913-9491
akdduroska@gmail.com

Dyson, Tavonya
P.0 Box2021, California, MD 20619
(301) 880-6720
tngdyson@yahoo.com

Eichenwald, Carl
4406 Puller Dr, Kensington, MD 20895-4050
(301) 704-0419
ikewalden@verizon.net

Ellis, Niki
9607 Magledt Rd, Parkville, MD 21234-1816
(443) 864-1435
niki.l.ellis7@gmail.com

Epps, Ceferino
12112 Catalina Dr, Lusby, MD 20657-3420
(410) 326-0396
cefgerri@msn.com

Ettinger, Robert
1909 Main Ave, Pasadena, MD 21122-3416
(410) 360-6774
bobesue80@yahoo.com

Findley, Dick
530 Aldersgate Ct # 509, Solomons, MD 20688-3013
(410) 394-2647
findleyra@comcast.net

Fisher, Daniel
713 214th St, Pasadena, MD 21122-1301
(410) 255-7198
danielbfisher@icloud.com

Fisher, David
13816 Marsh Pike, Hagerstown, MD 21742-1657

(301) 791-0895
d.fisher@myactv.net

Fisher, Lucinda
503 Aristides Ct., Havre de Grace, MD 21078

(410) 273-6365
e-lfisher@comcast.net

Flanagan, Linda
236 Barksdale Ave, Waldorf, MD 20602-2860

(301) 645-1375
waldorfangel@gmail.com

Flinn, Tom
3250 Halter Rd, Westminster, MD 21158-1903

(410) 857-8598
TWFlinn3@aol.com

Ford, Sarah
2525 Park Heights Ter, Baltimore, MD 21215-7004

(410) 466-7605
svford1@verizon.net

Frisch, Bob
2606 Franklinville Rd, Joppa, MD 21085-2906

(410) 538-8629
cbtd@comcast.net

Fujikawa, Janet
111 Washington Grove Ln # 746, Washington Grove, MD 20880

(301) 704-3119
fujikawaj3@gmail.com

Gainey, James
9741 Starling Rd, Ellicott City, MD 21042-1776

(410) 418-5826

Garrett, Jr., Theodore
11409 Strawberry Glenn Ln, Glenn Dale, MD 20769-9123

(301) 758-5625
trgarrettjr@yahoo.com

Gaskins-Tillett, Sherita
5408 Simpkins Ct, Ellicott City, MD 21043-6579

(443) 535-8497
sdgaskins@aol.com

Gibbs, Shannon
42 Oak Grove Dr Apt B, Middle River, MD 21220-1462

(410) 218-8398
shannon_f_gibbs@yahoo.com

Gillum, Richard
1112 Nora Dr, Silver Spring, MD 20904-2136

(301) 857-1902
frank.gillum@gmail.com

Gould, Bryon
3607 W Mulberry St, Baltimore, MD 21229-2929

(443) 827-8159
bryon.gould6@gmail.com

Granados, Jorge
3455 Holmead Pl NW Apt B, Washington, DC 20010-3464

(301) 613-9496
jorge.gdlr@gmail.com

Grays, Jane
Street Address 2, Laurel, MD 20707-9457

(301) 937-6392
ladyjanegra@aol.com

Green, Rita
12410 Fellowship Ln, North Potomac, MD 20878-3409

(301) 330-9828
ritamgreen@hotmail.com

Gullickson, Kirsten
1729 Lamont St NW, Washington, DC 20010-2601

(202) 262-8419
kgullickson@prodigy.net

Haines, Carl
1780 Monarch Meadow Dr, Finksburg, MD 21048-1300

(410) 861-5913
Cha239@aol.com

Hall, Dayle
1315 Q St NW, Washington, DC 20009-4316

(202) 415-2104
daylehall@aol.com

Hall, Griff
168 Severn Way, Arnold, MD 21012

(410) 279-6639
griffhall@verizon.net

Harden, John
1930 New Hampshire Ave NW Apt 6, Washington, DC 20009-3349

(201) 375-0142
jdhbama1@icloud.com

Harper, Scott
2713 Jennings Rd, Kensington, MD 20895-2817

(301) 933-4917
sharper2525@gmail.com

Harris, Sherman
11508 Karen Dr, Potomac, MD 20854-3149

(301) 299-2984
shermanharris@comcast.net

Harry, Susan
1505 Carriage Hill Dr, Westminster, MD 21157-6501

(410) 876-2476
gwtwsue2@comcast.net

Harvey, Lisa
8597 Bay Rd, Pasadena, MD 21122-3164

(410) 437-8406
harveymart@yahoo.com

Haskins, Deborah
4400 Wentworth Rd, Baltimore, MD 21207-7477

(410) 448-1604
HaskinsD@trinitydc.edu

Hayden, Jan
142 Pleasant Valley Drive, Baltimore, MD 21228

(410) 747-7733
jhayden@cbmove.com

Hazen, Paul
1529 Q St NW Apt 3, Washington, DC 20009-3861

(202) 957-9298
phazen@ocdc.coop

Henderson, Betty
1827 Fox Hollow Run, Pasadena, MD 21122

(410) 360-0556
hayseh2001@yahoo.com

Henley, Garnett

(301) 325-8362
ghenley@howard.edu

Highfield, Kevin
Wesley House Jesus Lane, Cambridge, Cambridgeshi CB5 8BJ

(703) 231-1163
highfieldk@aol.com

Hobbs, Warren
6210 Park Heights Ave, Baltimore, MD 21215-3626

(410) 318-8232
sbblw@aol.com

Hoffmann, Christie
246 Mian Street, Reisterstown, MD 21136

(410) 526-6967
christie.l.hoffmann@gmail.com

Hudson, Keenan
7112 Virginial Ave, Sykesville, MD 21784

keenanhudson@hotmail.com

Hunt, Edward
1190 W Northern Pkwy Apt 616, Baltimore, MD 21210-1455

(410) 960-6648
Ed@edhuntjr.com

Hunter, Robert
13880 Long Rd, Thurmont, MD 21788-2261

(301) 271-4511
office@thurmontchurch.org

Hurd, Daphne
3707 Yolando Rd, Baltimore, MD 21218-2042

(410) 627-7877
daphnelhurd@icloud.com

Hutchinson, Barbara
7907 Powhatan St, New Carrollton, MD 20784-3531

(301) 577-2136
barbh2387@gmail.com

Ihlo, Jen
6263 Masefield Ct, Alexandria, VA 22304-3536

(202) 255-9192
jen.ihlo@gmail.com

Jackson, Alice
1609 Pebble Beach Dr, Bowie, MD 20721-2375

(301) 336-7595
ajac956@aol.com

Jackson, Hazel
3331 Ripple Rd, Baltimore, MD 21244-2859

(410) 496-4811
hazel.jackson@comcast.net

Jackson, Raimon
2125 Harwood Rd, District Heights, MD 20747

(301) 613-6467
emailmrjackson@gmail.com

Jenkins, Maxine
712 Downs Dr, Silver Spring, MD 20904

(301) 622-1240
mjenk83601@aol.com

Johnson, Andrea
218 S Alfred St, Alexandria, VA 22314-3639

(612) 414-2150
andrealynn.johnson@gmail.com

johnson, Deborah
1800 Palmer Rd Apt 233, Fort Washington, MD 20744-3512

(202) 309-0640
deborahj8888@gmail.
com

Johnson, Wendy
822 N Glover St, Baltimore, MD 21205-1610

(443) 278-6434
wendy_johnson@hcpss.org

Jones, Chasity
1913 Rose Pl, Upper Marlboro, MD 20774-8559

(240) 254-2498
chas.njones20@gmail.com

Jones, Joelle
1315 Rayville Rd, Parkton, MD 21120-9003

(410) 343-1690
jmj187@comcast.net

Jones, Judy
8621 Irvin Ave, Glenarden, MD 20706-1523

(301) 773-0525
Jones8621@verizon.net

Jones, William (Bill)
1315 Rayville Rd, Parkton, MD 21120-9003

(410) 343-1690
revbjones@gmail.com

Kahl, George
7903 Springway Rd, Baltimore, MD 21204-3517

(410) 337-0089
gkahl533740@comcast.net

Kaiser, Geoffrey
403 Russell Ave Apt G, Gaithersburg, MD 20877-2811

(301) 216-5580
gdkaiser10@gmail.com

Karsner, Scott
70 Church Rd, Arnold, MD 21012-2314
(410) 757-8976
scottkarsner@gmail.com

Kelsey, Katherine
1275 Lindsay Ln, Hagerstown, MD 21742-4619
(301) 964-2132
kathyke@aol.com

Kemp, Helen
2600 Strawbridge Ln, New Windsor, MD 21776-8718
(443) 536-8030
ledbug2001@yahoo.com

Kent, Lucinda
4709 Ridgeline Ter, Bowie, MD 20720-3705
(301) 385-6630
pastorcindykent@gmail.com

Kernan, Greg
7324 Woodshire Ave, Chesapeake Beach, MD 20732-3124
(301) 855-7455
gregory410@comcast.net

Koob, Michael
1400 Baker Pl W Apt 21, Frederick, MD 21702-3241
(301) 834-9332
mikekoob@hotmail.com

Koontz, Darlene
7700 Suitt Dr, Pasadena, MD 21122-3234
(410) 360-2751
darlenekoontz5@gmail.com

Lawson, Ella
7828 Spencer Rd, Glen Burnie, MD 21060-8254
(410) 437-0837
emlaw9@gmail.com

Leggett, Vincent
3436 Cohasset Ave, Annapolis, MD 21403-4822
(410) 269-7815
vincent425@comcast.net

Lievers, Ruthella
6221 Pilgrim Rd, Baltimore, MD 21214-1542
(410) 426-2781
ralievers1@comcast.net

Loud, Sr., Marc
1439 Holly Street NE, Washington, DC 20011
(202) 882-3143
mdlo1c@gmail.com

Martin, Delores
16505 Magnolia Ct, Silver Spring, MD 20905-3902
(301) 421-9441
littleone_martin@verizon.net

McBride, William
3622 Dolfield Ave, Baltimore, MD 21215-6139
suglove2002@yahoo.com

McCurdy, Jesse
104 Johnsberg Ln, Mitchellville, MD 20721-7225
1-301-249-9608
jessemccurdy@comcast.net

McGlothlin, Leslie
4 Crestmont Dr, Aberdeen, MD 21001-2401
(410) 272-4216
jlmacg@msn.com

McKinzie, Will
8126 Brookwood Farm Rd, Fulton, MD 20759-9658
(301) 442-7030
will@mckintek.com

Milburn, Shelia
shelia.milburn@navy.com

Miller, Rick
6524 Shenandoah Dr, Sykesville, MD 21784-8219
(410) 549-3523
wrmsr1953@verizon.net

Milton, Sharon   (301) 404-6626
432 Ridge Rd Apt 5, Greenbelt, MD 20770-1666   law2be@hotmail.com

Mobray, Leslie   lmobray9@gmail.com

Mokuena, Miriam   (240) 683-6480
3 Earth Star Pl, Gaithersburg, MD 20878-2778   mdmokuena@gmail.com

Mokuena, Moorosi   (240) 683-6480
3 Earth Star Pl, Gaithersburg, MD 20878-2778   moorosi_mokuena@msn.com

Monk, George   (301) 652-8700
4020 Franklin St, Kensington, MD 20895-3826   gmonk@chevychaseumc.org

Moore, Charles   (410) 757-5559
1168 River Bay Rd, Annapolis, MD 21409-4832   cmoore@telatlantic.net

Morales, Magda   (301) 620-8885
PO Box 1045, Germantown, MD 20875-1045   MagdaEMorales@aol.com

Morgan, Gwendolyn   (301) 384-0184
2109 Hidden Valley Ln, Silver Spring, MD 20904-5216   mysteny@aol.com

Moseley, Ray   (410) 922-9962
10004 Village Green Dr, Woodstock, MD 21163-1154   raymoseley@aol.com

Myers, Charles   (410) 719-8928
15 Hickory Ridge Ct, Catonsville, MD 21228-2419   chazm9@verizon.net

Nash, Katie   (301) 524-9142
859 Waterford Dr, Frederick, MD 21702-4046   katiejonash@gmail.com

Nelson, Brian   (443) 280-4935
10349 Whitewasher Way, Columbia, MD 21044-3813   briannelson88@gmail.com

Ngaima, Moses   (443) 622-2939
8340 Church Ln Apt 8, Windsor Mill, MD 21244-6106   mengaima@gmail.com

Nyarku, John   (202) 628-0009
                                                      john.nyarku@yahoo.com

Oden, Delores   (410) 647-0218
330 Baltimore Annapolis Blvd, Severna Park, MD 21146-1370   delgina@verizon.net

Ow, Ken   (301) 520-9990
13415 Rippling Brook Dr, Silver Spring, MD 20906   kenow999@gmail.com

Parham, Delila   (301) 218-0248
12010 Shadystone Ter, Mitchellville, MD 20721-2593   dparham@att.net

Parks, Lillian   (301) 283-6336
PO Box 1315, Bryans Road, MD 20616   lvparks@verizon.net

564

Parrish, Barbara
472 Arwell Ct, Frederick, MD 21703-6132

(240) 447-2285
new_creaturebp@yahoo.com

Perry, Yolanda
2435 Heath Aster Ct, Odenton, MD 21113-6015

(410) 315-9989
ybperry@yahoo.com

Pettaway, Stephanie
1514 Northgate Rd, Baltimore, Md 21218

(410) 323-7834
steppettaway@aol.com

Pinkney, Rosalind
11605 Assisi St, Upper Marlboro, MD 20772

(301) 928-1298
croomgirl@hotmail.com

Pittinger, George
1855 Monarch Meadow Ct, Finksburg, MD 21048-1342

(410) 857-2853
gpittinger@yahoo.com

Poole, JoAnne
238 Williams Rd, Glen Burnie, MD 21061-2514

(410) 913-9925
jpoole@ywgcrealty.com

Potter, Phil
4701 Berkeley Ter NW, Washington, DC 20007-1508

(202) 338-7926
phil.potter@verizon.net

Prehn, William
6395 Forest Ave, Elkridge, MD 21075-5811

(410) 796-8265
bvprehn@verizon.net

Price, Ann
11404 Dundee Dr, Mitchellville, MD 20721-2422

(301) 464-0602
pricefa@verizon.net

Price, Becki
16617 Cutlass Dr, Rockville, MD 20853-1333

(301) 774-2582
tombecki@aol.com

Quinn, Mittie
1722 Linwood Pl, McLean, VA 22101-5119

(703) 734-0724
umcmittie@gmail.com

Randolph, Justice

(202) 377-9050
justice.randolph@gmail.com

Revell, Kerry
1 N Woodlawn Ave, Lavale, MD 21502

kerry.revell@gmail.com

Rice, Millie
4629 Coleherne Rd, Baltimore, MD 21229

(410) 362-6081
blountr2002@yahoo.com

Roach, Ebony
1777 Verbena St NW, Washington, DC 20012-1048

(301) 787-4850
ebonymaria@yahoo.com

Robertson, Kathy
4109 Colonial Rd, Pikesville, MD 21208-6041

(410) 241-7119
krobertson2@msn.com

Rodeffer, Kathy
105 Warrenton Dr., Silver Spring, MD 20974-2846

(301) 937-8344
rodeffer@aol.com

Rowe, Devonna
3205 Whitefield Rd, Churchville, MD 21028-1336

(410) 734-6106
dbrce@hotmail.com

Ruggieri, Jade
10856 Wolfsville Rd, Myersville, MD 21773-8820

(443) 534-0341
jaderuggieri@gmail.com

Saunders, LaSander
6912 Blanche Rd, Baltimore, MD 21215-1306

(410) 602-1245
createinme@verizon.net

Schlieckert, Christopher
9818 Golden Russet Dr, Dunkirk, MD 20754-2603

(240) 529-8041
director@westrivercenter.org

Shelton, Joyce
4521 Mount Olney Ln, Olney, MD 20832-1011

(301) 774-4312
j_i_shelton@hotmail.com

Shew, Barbara
18 Concord Dr, Brunswick, MD 21716-1446

(301) 834-9734
bashoe99@aol.com

Silberzahn, F. Kevin
923 Slash Pine Ct, Sykesville, MD 21784-7948

(410) 549-7592
fkdennis@comcast.net

Skinner, Sharon
14220 Jib St Apt 21, Laurel, MD 20707-6178

(301) 275-6085
sharondskinner@yahoo.com

Slack, Cory
23311 Sugar Maple Ct Apt 815, California, MD 20619-4067

(301) 785-3933
nito514.ns@gmail.com

Smith, Guffrie
100 David Gray Rd, Saint Leonard, MD 20685

(410) 586-0192
guffriemsmith@hotmail.com

Smith, Norman
9540 Hickoryhurst Dr, Baltimore, MD 21236-4701

nssmithjr@verizon.net

Snyder, Donna
12477 Wolfsville Rd, Myersville, MD 21773-9303

(240) 994-0338
Donna.Snyder@insperity.com

Statesman, Jessica
920 E Belvedere Ave, Baltimore, MD 21212-3725

(410) 464-1092
jessicastatesman@gmail.com

Stemley, Elizabeth
1190 West Northern PWKY 610, Baltimore, MD 21210

(443) 850-8544
estemley1190@comcast.net

Strawbridge, John
1435 Union Ave, Baltimore, MD 21211-1906

(410) 243-5344
johnstrawbridge@hotmail.com

Strickland, Shemaiah
8731 Contee Rd Apt 202, Laurel, MD 20708-1914

(404) 771-7437
shemaiahstrickland@gmail.com

Surber, Matthew
925 Diggs Rd, Crownsville, MD 21032-1622

(443) 377-9918
MatthewLSurber@gmail.com

Taylor, Carolyn
19029 Mills Choice Rd #2, Montgomery Village, MD 20886

(301) 250-0659
taylorcarolyn53@yahoo.com

Taylor, Cynthia
4800Coyle Rd Apt 409, Owings Mills, MD 21117

(443) 394-8840
cynthiaataylor1@verizon.net

Taylor, Darrell
8801 Sonya Rd, Randallstown, MD 21133-4015

(410) 978-2399
darrellt480@gmail.com

Taylor, Jan
1414 Langford Rd, Baltimore, MD 21207-4877

(410) 245-6682
taylorjanlcpc@gmail.com

Taylor, Ryan

rdtaylor2006@gmail.com

Terry, Barbara
5304 Cecil Ave, Gwynn Oak, MD 21207-5933

(410) 977-5930
babswrightterry@gmail.com

Tocknell, Deborah
929 Generals Hwy, Millersville, MD 21108-2124

(410) 923-2642
dltocknell@gmail.com

Torres, Lucy
1631 Elkwood Ct, Annapolis, MD 21409-5477

godblessing2211@aol.com

Travis, Carol
6501 Hillwood Dr, Riverdale, MD 20737-3030

(301) 459-6303
carol6303@aol.com

Turnage, Patricia
732 Queenstown Rd, Severn, MD 21144-1220

(410) 766-6312
cottonfieldcricket@gmail.com

Turner-Simpkins, Gloria
4301 Townsley Ave, Temple Hills, MD 20748-1837

(301) 702-4870
gloriayturner@gmail.com

Tyler, Miranda
301 Rowe Boulevard, Churchton, Maryland 20733

(443) 534-5814
youthdirector@calumc.org

Vlcek, Joseph
301 Langner Ct, Ft Washington, MD 20744-6125

(301) 448-5328
jvlcek4918@aol.com

Waldren, Jamie
10490 Litle Patuxent Pkw, #280, Columbia, MD 21044

(410) 730-5055
jmwaldren@leggmason.com

Walker, Kim
1333 Farley Ct S, Arnold, MD 21012-2817

(443) 534-1619
burrwalker123@gmail.com

Weavill, Jackie
819 W Central Ave, Davidsonville, MD 21035-2318

(301) 266-8324
pastorjackie@dumc.net

Welcome, Henry

(443) 804-0417
hondu6@verizon.net

Weston, Katie
3363 Old Line Ave, Laurel, MD 20724-2235

(240) 381-2208
ktpenn@gmail.com

White, Clarence
1009 Manchester Ct, Bel Air, MD 21014-2501

(410) 638-0147
clwhite@aol.com

White, Joe
18827 Preston Rd, Hagerstown, MD 21742-2715

(240) 675-1506
rjw18827@myactv.net

White, Sabrina
2042 Knotty Pine Dr, Abingdon, MD 21009-2788

(410) 515-7629
sve2042@hotmail.com

Williams, Calvin
2035 Quill Ct, Kannapolis, NC 28083-6298

caldot53@aol.com

Williams, James
3131 Fairland Rd, Silver Spring, MD 20904-7120

(301) 890-3131
ezeqez@comcast.net

Wills, James
601 Lanoitan Rd Apt F, Baltimore, MD 21220-2729

(443) 823-9420
jameswills991@yahoo.com

Willson, Richard
1117 Fairview Rd, Hagerstown, MD 21742

(301) 739-3232
rwillson14@myactv.net

Wivell, William
16636 Toms Creek Church Rd, Emmitsburg, MD 21727-8429

(301) 447-3766
wdwrpw@gmail.com

Woodrow, Don
211 Heritage Farm Dr, Mount Airy, MD 21771-5744

(301) 829-5791

Yost, Linda
1910 Upper Forde Ln, Hampstead, MD 21074-1500

(410) 239-0429
ljyost@verizon.net

Zetterberg, Don
2189 Bellemonte Ct, Jefferson, MD 21755-9119

(301) 371-4950
DonZetterberg@comcast.net

MEMOIRS

CLERGY

REV. YUSEF JOSEPH AHMED
1943-2018

Yusef Joseph Ahmed, the son of the late Elizabeth "Judie" and Hassan Ahmed, was born Jan. 6, 1943, in Niagara Falls, New York. His mother was a cook and domestic, his father a Somali immigrant and factory worker.

Raised in Niagara Falls, NY, Greensboro, NC, and Baltimore, he graduated from Edmondson High School in 1962. He earned a Bachelor of Arts in History at Morgan State College in 1970 and a Master's in Urban Planning and Public Policy Analysis in 1972. During this period, he held a number of positions in state and regional offices. In 1978, he received a Doctor of Divinity degree.

In 1975, while sitting in Metropolitan UMC in Baltimore, God called him to preach. After much prayer and fasting, he resigned his position with the U.S. Navy and enrolled at Wesley Theological Seminary in Washington, D.C. in January 1976. He earned a Master of Divinity from the Howard University School of Religion in 1979 and in 1981 was ordained an Elder by the Baltimore-Washington Conference.

Ahmed served the people of The United Methodist Church for more than 35 years. His pastorates included: St. John UMC in Baltimore, 1976-1978; St. Matthew's UMC in Baltimore, 1978-1980; Strawbridge UMC, 1980-1984, where he increased the membership from 36 to 258 members. From 1984 to 2010, he served churches in New York, Delaware and New Jersey. He also served on district and jurisdiction boards and committees.

He taught at various community colleges and universities including Catonsville Community College, University of Maryland Baltimore County, and in Buffalo.

Ahmed believed in the benefit and importance of friendship through fraternal, civic and social organizations. He was a member since high school of the O.B.E. fraternity. He held membership in Alpha Phi Alpha Fraternity, Inc., NAACP, National Association of Black Social Workers, Free and Excepted Masons, Improved and Benevolent Protected Order of Elks of the World, and was a charter chapter member of the Optimist International.

In 1978, he was awarded the Benjamin E. Mays Scholarship at Howard University. While attending school he was given the Vernon Johns Award for Preaching. He also was awarded the Martin Luther King Jr. Award in Race Relations from Wilbur H. Waters School of Religion.

Muhammad Ahmed, his eldest son, preceded him in death.

Survivors include Towanda Stewart, Efa Ahmed-Williams, Hassan (Sheree) Ahmed, and Kareem (Amanda) Ahmed; Jeanene Goins whom he took as his daughter and she as her father; seven grandchildren; members of his extended family, a brother and friends.

The Rev. Yusef "Joseph" Ahmed, a retired Elder (no longer a member of the conference) died July 27, 2018. A funeral service was held Aug. 4, at Sharp Street Memorial UMC in Baltimore.

PASTOR WALTER "WALLY" BOSMAN
1951-2018

Walter Morris "Wally" Bosman Jr. was born Feb. 9, 1951, in Baltimore, one of eight children of the late Evelyn M. Jones and Walter Morris "Lefty" Bosman, Sr.

He served as pastor of Salem UMC in Westminster, 2005-2011, and Middleburg–Uniontown

UMC, from 2011 until he retired in November 2014.

He was a talented and accomplished musician, singer and songwriter, and an avid Civil War reenactor. In 2000, he released his studio-recorded CD, titled "He Did It All," which included nine Christian songs that he composed and performed, plus the hymn Amazing Grace written by John Newton. His family and friends enjoyed his gifted sense of humor and spontaneous wit. He was a loving and devoted husband and father.

Bosman was predeceased by his step-mother Florence Johnson Bosman and four siblings.

He is survived by his wife of 37 years, Brenda Shilling Bosman. Survivors also include his son, Corporal Alexander Patrick Bosman, USMC; three siblings; and numerous nieces and nephews.

Pastor Walter Morris "Wally" Bosman Jr., a retired Local Pastor, died Aug. 2, 2018. A Celebration of Life Service was held Aug. 8 at Deer Park UMC, which he had made his home church. The service was officiated by the Rev. John Dean.

PASTOR TONIA HEATH BROWN
1961-2019

Tonia Heath Brown was born in Baltimore July 15, 1961, the daughter of the late Frank Edward Heath Sr. and Rosetta Amanda Thornton Heath. She graduated from Baltimore City schools and received her Bachelor of Arts in religious studies from McDaniel College. She attended Lancaster Seminary.

For 38 years Brown practiced nursing as a Licensed Practical Nurse. She worked at Catholic Charities, FutureCare and Manor Care.

Before her current appointment, she was the assistant Pastor at Union Street UMC, then called to Johnsville UMC. Her ministry as pastor to Pleasant View UMC began in 2012.

Brown was preceded in death by her parents, a son Adam Nathanial Pope, and her husband Louis Carroll "Bubbles" Brown.

She is survived by her daughter Amanda Michelle Pope of Virginia; three sisters and a brother, as well as an aunt, nieces and nephews.

Pastor Tonia Heath Brown died May 7, 2019. She was the lay minister at Pleasant View UMC in Adamstown at the time of her death. A Homegoing service was held May 14 at Westminster UMC with the Rev. Leah E. White officiating. Interment followed at Western Chapel Cemetery.

PASTOR W. JACK BUSSARD
1943-2018

William Jack Bussard Jr. was born May 1, 1943, the son of the late William Jack Bussard and Ophelia Donsife Bussard.

He was an Associate Member and pastored United Methodist churches for 38 years in the Baltimore-Washington Conference. These included the Washington Village Parish in Baltimore from 1981-84; Dorguth Memorial-Union Square UMC from 1984-1990; Olive Branch-Union Square UMC from1990-91; Olive Branch UMC from 1991-93; and Cowenton UMC in White Marsh from 1993-2011. He began his service at Monkton UMC in 2011 when he retired and continued to serve throughout his retirement.

He and Annamarie Beecher married in 1989 and had six children who survive. They include his son, Kelly Bussard, and his wife Sandi; five daughters: Karen Cumber and her husband

David; Teresa Dorman and her husband Ken; Ginger Marino and her husband Kirk; Deborah Claridge and her husband Frank; and Maranda Jacob and her husband Bruce. He had 20 grandchildren and one great-granddaughter.

The Rev. William "Jack" Bussard Jr., pastor of Monkton UMC, died Nov. 20, 2018. Funeral services were held at the Lassahn Funeral Home in Kingsville, Md., Nov. 24.

WAYNE W. CHUNG
1956-2019

Wayne Wangsik Chung was born in Korea April 21, 1956. He held degrees from schools in Korea, a Master of Business Administration from the University of Wisconsin at Milwaukee, and a Master of Divinity degree from Wesley Theological Seminary in Washington, D.C. He was ordained an Elder in 2008.

He married Esther Chung in 1980. They had two children: daughter Haniee is a surgeon at Johns Hopkins; and son Jim is a federal agent.

Chung was appointed to Faith UMC in 2018. He previously served at Rockland UMC in Ellicott City, 2005-2009; Landsdowne UMC in Baltimore 2009-2015; and Friendship UMC 2015-2018.

In addition to his church appointments, Chung also served as chaplain at Asbury Methodist Village in Gaithersburg.

"The real boss of the household," says Faith UMC's announcement of his death, "is Tank, a seven-year-old Shi Tzu."

His family wrote:

"His delight is not in the strength of the horse, nor his pleasure in the legs of a man, but the Lord takes pleasure in those who fear him, in those who hope in his steadfast love. – Psalm 147:10-11."

"Wayne Chung was a man of strength. He displayed his strength of character in his quiet reserve, his refusal to partake in bickering, and instead, internalizing his pain and struggles. He displayed his physical strength in lugging around his two kids on his back, making them feel like he was invincible. But above all, he displayed strength in the conviction that he was a sinner in need of a Savior, every day. He feared the Lord and hoped in his Love, not the love or support of man. He understood that it was by grace alone, and not his own strength or righteousness, that his God delighted in him. The weaker his body became with the disease of his flesh, the stronger his conviction of God's goodness toward him. In his illness and in his death, he spoke and continues to speak loudest of his witness for his Lord, Jesus Christ."

Survivors include his wife Esther Chung, daughter Dr. Haniee Chung; son Jim Chung and his wife Tohfa.

The Rev. Wayne Chung, pastor of Faith UMC in Rockville, died at home Jan. 13. A Memorial Service was held Jan. 18 at Faith UMC. Participating in the service were Greater Washington District Superintendent the Rev. Gerard Green, and the Revs. William Louis Piel and Joye Jones.

REV. MARY WARD PINDLE CONAWAY
1943-2018

Mary Ward Pindle Conaway was born Jan. 26, 1943, in Johnson County, North Carolina, the daughter of Mary Jane Davis Ward and Albert Ward. She was educated in the public-school system.

Mary Ward accepted Christ at the age of 3 and was fully baptized at the age of 12, clearly understanding who Christ is and what He meant to her life. She sang in church and accompanied on piano many choirs from age 7-18, which greatly impacted her life. She was convicted, convinced and committed to follow Christ and conform to His Word.

Educated in the public schools of North Carolina, she pursued higher education at North Carolina College, now University, in Durham, NC. She received a BA majoring in Voice and minoring in Education. She also attended Hunter College (Fordham University) in Bronx, NY; Manhattan School of Music; and Julliard School of Music in NYC. She sang and traveled with notable groups: the Harry Belafonte singers, Leonard De Paur and The De Cormier Singers, and the Metropolitan Opera Extra Chorus.

Returning to Baltimore, she attended Coppin State College receiving an MS. Ed. and did post-graduate studies in Clinical Psychology at the University of Maryland College Park with dissertation incomplete because she was called to the Ministry. She received an MDiv. from Wesley Theological Seminary in Washington, DC and an Honorary Doctor of Humane Letters from Eastern Theological Seminary in Lynchburg, VA.

Conaway's academic credentials spanned 21 years; serving as a Preschool Teacher, Children's Program Coordinator, and a Resource Teacher for the Learning Disabled in Baltimore City until retiring in 1981.

She was ordained a Deacon under Bishop Joseph Yeakel and later an Elder under Bishop Felton Edwin May. Although she was the Register of Wills for Baltimore City (1982-2012), she successfully pastored three churches over 25 years: John Wesley UMC in Crownsville (1991-1994); Cecil Memorial UMC in Annapolis (1996-2010); and St. Luke's UMC, Baltimore (2010-2015) when she retired.

As an elected Register of Wills, she did what she thought was right: attained parity in the office, procured the services of minority contractors, and invested large sums of money with minority banking institutions. She established relationships with organizations to ease concerns regarding wills and probate to make the death of a loved-one less daunting, and she advocated for the state to donate over 100 refurbished computers.

But pastoring was her greatest love. She preached Jesus everywhere she went until her health began to fail and age requirement dictated her retirement. Joshua 14:14: "She wholly followed the Lord, the God of Israel." Receiving several honors and awards during her political and religious tenure, she paved a way in both arenas, often being the First other women could follow.

She was predeceased by her husband, Frank M. Conaway, Sr.

She leaves to cherish her memory her daughter, Monica K. Pindle of New York City; stepchildren: The Hon. Frank M. Conaway, Jr. and the Hon. Belinda Conaway Washington (Milton) of Baltimore; nine grandchildren; eight great-grandchildren; three Goddaughters and two Godsons. Also surviving are a sister, brother, sisters-in-law, brothers-in-law and nieces and nephews.

The Rev. Mary Ward Conaway, a retired Elder, went to be with her Lord Aug. 30, 2018, at Gilchrist Hospice Centers-Howard County. Few knew she'd battled cancer several times in the comfort of her home, yet many are silenced by her absence.

A Celebration of Life Homegoing Service was held Sept. 7 at Huber Memorial Life Center in Baltimore. The Rev. Marlon Tilghman officiated, and the eulogy was given by the Rev. Mamie Williams. Tributes were made by the Revs. Reginald Tarpley, Clarence Davis, Denise Norfleet-Walker and others.

REV. JAMES "JAY" DEMENT
1958-2019

James "Jay" DeMent was born June 13, 1958.

DeMent had served at the St. John's-Idlewylde Cooperative Parish from 2007 to 2012, when he was appointed to Salem UMC where he was at the time of his death. He was a trained expert in disaster preparedness and served the Baltimore Suburban District and the Conference in that capacity.

He was predeceased by his father, daughter Amie Christine DeMent, and sister.

Survivors include his wife, Mable "Chris" DeMent, daughters Amanda Heinemann and her husband Terry Heinemann, Angela Lynn DeMent, and son James Ryan DeMent; three grandchildren; he is also survived by his beloved dog Bandit.

The Rev. James "Jay" DeMent, 61, an active Elder, died March 19, 2019. He was pastor of Salem UMC in Upper Falls. A Celebration of Life Service was held March 30 at the church.

REV. HERBERT L. D. DOGGETT
1926-2018

Herbert Levi David Doggett was born June 25, 1926, in Baltimore, the youngest of three children of the late Carroll A. Doggett, Sr. and Evelyn Lee Doggett. He attended high school at Baltimore Polytechnic Institute, and Western Maryland College (now McDaniel College), before attending Union Theological Seminary in NYC for his Master of Divinity degree. He later received an Honorary Doctor of Divinity from McDaniel College, and Recognition of 50 Years of Service from the BWC Board of Ordained Ministry.

He and Joanna Mae (Hauver) Doggett married in 1946. She was a co-worker in his ministry and a schoolteacher of institutional cooking, restaurant management, and catering. She died at age 62 in 1988.

Doggett began his ministry in 1952 at Trinity in Frederick. In 1956, he moved on to Good Shepherd in Silver Spring until 1966, when he was appointed to Catonsville. In 1969, he became superintendent of the Hagerstown District, where he served until 1975 when he moved to Potomac. From 1979-1983, he pastored Hughes UMC in Wheaton. He also served six years as Director of Development at the Asbury Methodist Village in Gaithersburg, helping to raise benevolent care funds.

Doggett married Florence Lee King in 1990, with 10 of their grandchildren serving as attendants.

After retirement, Doggett, in addition to raising funds at Asbury, served as a Trustee and President of the Community Foundation of Frederick County, served interim pastorates at local churches in the conference, and guest preached. He also enjoyed photography, creative woodworking in his workshop, oil painting, and travel. For 11 years, Doggett was a volunteer Bike Patrolman for the National Park Service along the C & O Canal and worked in the Visitor Center in Williamsport.

In 1996, at age 70, he received his first computer, and quickly became proficient in its use, writing and producing greeting cards and a monthly newsletter with articles, "editorial comments" on current events, and plenty of color photographs.

Surviving, in addition to his wife, Florence Doggett, are his four sons and their wives: William, (Suzanne); Richard (Beth); Lawrence and Frederick (Tychelle); his daughters-in-law Terry Gosnell, Cynthia Doggett and Ruth Rhoderick; nine grandchildren, step-daughters Susan Heflin (Jay) and Laurie Wilson (Mike); three of Florence's grandchildren; and nine great-grandchildren.

Herbert Doggett, a retired Elder and a District Superintendent, died Sept. 3, 2018, at Homewood Frederick where he received care over the past year. A Service of Resurrection was held Sept. 16 at Middletown UMC with the Rev. Sarah Dorrance officiating.

REV. WILLIAM WARING EHLERS
1924-2019

The Rev. William Waring Ehlers, 95, died Feb. 28, 2019. A funeral service was held March 12 at the Burrier-Queen Funeral Home & Crematory in Winfield.

William Waring Ehlers was born Feb.23, 1924, in Baltimore, the son of the late William Charles Ehlers and the late Marian Crumbacker Ehlers.

He was a veteran of the U.S. Army.

Ehlers served a number of churches for nearly 40 years. These included Pipe Creek, 1952-55; Graceland Park, 1955-59; Ferndale, 1959-62; Forest Hill, 1962-68; Grace UMC at Falls Road, 1968-71; Stone Chapel-St. James in Westminster, 1971-73; Oakland in Sykesville, 1973-77; the Hereford-Mt. Carmel Charge, 1977-80; his last appointment to St. Paul UMC in Lusby, 1980-90, from which he retired.

He and Barbara Weaver Warfield, a widow, married in 1987 while he was serving St. Paul UMC. She was a registered nurse and church organist.

His hobbies included HAM Radio, traveling and photography.

He was preceded in death by his second wife Barbara Warfield Ehlers in 2011, and a daughter Dorothy Bennett.

Survivors include children: Barbara Buckley (Bill) of Woodbine, Ruth Bradley (Dave) of Bowie, David Ehlers of Ellicott City, and Carol Jackson of Ellicott City; 12 grandchildren and five great grandchildren.

REV. JAMES R. EMBREY
1933-2019

James Robert Embrey was born Sept. 15, 1933, the son of Mildred Madeline Beard and James Robert Embrey. He lived in Baltimore during his school years until he joined the Air Force. Upon discharge from the military, he was employed at the Baltimore Sun Newspapers agency for 32 years, retiring as an advertising manager.

While attending Wesley Theological Seminary, he served the congregations of Community UMC of Laurel and Gary Memorial UMC.

After returning to Berkeley County, he served the congregations of Trinity UMC where he led the Monday night "Trinity Church 6:34 Services." During the decade of the 2000s, he pastored part-time and full time the congregations of New Street UMC (2000), Middleway UMC (2001-2005), then spent three years retired. He also served at Kabletown UMC, and Darkesville Charge for six months in 2009.

He was active in Berkeley County Ministerial Association projects including vespers services at War Memorial Park. He enjoyed music and was happiest when he was leading congregational singing and participating in choir.

Survivors include his wife of 21 years, Mary Jo Embrey, and her daughter, Amy McSherry Rush; former wife and the mother of his children, Marilyn Moxley Embrey; Suzanne Ritchey and husband Tom of Knoxville, Tenn.; Michele Winberry and fiancé Dustin of Arbutus; and James Robert Embrey, Jr. and wife Sara of Nashville, Tenn.; six grandchildren and two great-grandchildren. He is also survived by sisters, a brother and sister-in-law; and nieces and nephews.

Pastor James Robert Embrey, Sr. died Jan. 16, 2019, after a 10-year struggle with Parkinson's Disease and dementia. A Celebration of Life service was held Jan 25, at the Brown Funeral Home in Martinsburg, W. Va., with the Rev. Walter Bowers officiating.

HENRY E. ERNST
1929-2019

Henry E. Ernst was born Nov. 10, 1929.

He served a number of churches from 1954 until his retirement in 2004. These included: Cedar Grove from 1954 to 1956; Camp Chapel from 1957, while attending school, to 1962; Grace in Falls Road, from 1962 to 1966; Lanham, 1966-1970; Orems UMC from 1970 to 1977; Cockeysville and Epworth UMC in Cockeysville from 1977 to 1985; Salem UMC in Upper Fall from 1985 to1992, then Pleasant Grove UMC until he retired in 1995. He continued ministry in retirement to Brandenburg UMC in Woodbine, 1996 and Floherville in Sykesville in 2004.

Ernst and his wife, Doris Ernst, attended Glyndon UMC in his retirement. Pastor Dawn Stewart commented: "He was a student of theology who loved books as much as I, a man with a passion for everything Sherlock Holmes. He was a kind, compassionate friend and encourager to this young pastor."

Survivors include his wife and daughter Kathleen Ernst of Middleton, Wisconsin.

The Rev. Henry E. Ernst, a retired Elder, died May 2, 2019. He was cremated and there was no memorial service per his wishes.

PASTOR HELEN C. FLEMING
1939-2018

Helen Fleming was born Aug. 13, 1939, to the late Cephas and Ellis Fleming in Baltimore. She had two sisters. She was educated in Baltimore City Public Schools, attended Baltimore City Junior College, Baltimore College of Commerce and Delaware University. She studied at Eastern Baptist Theological Seminary. She held a Doctor of Ministry degree from the California Graduate School of Theology.

Fleming had been in the Eastern Pennsylvania Conference and came to Baltimore-Washington Conference in 2005 in Extension Ministry in the Office of Bishop John Schol. In January 2007, she became pastor at Douglas Memorial UMC in DC and a Guide for the Washington Region. She retired in 2010, then returned to Douglas Memorial from 2011 to 2017. She filled in at St. John UMC in Pumphrey for a year, then in 2018 became pastor of Mt. Vernon Place UMC in Baltimore.

Fleming was known as a prayer warrior and a mighty woman of God. In addition to her appointments, she was director of Leadership Development under Bishop Schol, where she guided 18 churches, designed the Conference's first Discipleship Academy and the first Certified Lay Minister School. After retirement, she became a church leadership consultant. She was the founder of the Women Veterans Resource Center and received recognition for that work from First Lady Michelle Obama. She was the keynote speaker at the Africa Leadership Conference in Zimbabwe.

She assisted the United Nations and the Namibian political leaders in the transition from apartheid to independence and the election of the Namibia's first African president. The Career

Development Business School she founded and was CEO of prepared 4,000 welfare recipients for career positions. She hosted a radio and television talk show.

Fleming received many awards and citations, including as Tennessee Honorary Citizen, presented by President George W. Bush at the 2004 State of the Union address. She authored two books: "The Mind of a Preaching Woman," and "Community Partnership: Developing Community Partnership Handbook."

Survivors include her daughter, Tracye Stafford, a grandson and a granddaughter. She is also survived by a sister, many nieces and nephews.

Pastor Helen C. Fleming, a retired local pastor, died Dec. 13, 2018. She was the lead pastor at Mt. Vernon Place UMC in Baltimore. A memorial service was held Dec. 21 at Epworth Chapel UMC in Baltimore, officiated by Baltimore Metropolitan District Superintendent, the Rev. Dr. Wanda Bynam Duckett, and hosted by the Rev. Dr. C. Anthony Hunt. Bishops LaTrelle Miller Easterling and Cynthia Moore-Koikoi participated. The Rev. Dr. Rodney Smothers gave the eulogy.

REV. HAL THOMAS HENDERSON
1933-2019

Hal Thomas Henderson was born Feb. 13, 1933, in Forsyth, Ga., the son of Robert and Lucy Henderson, the oldest of three brothers. He loved to sing and sang in his school choir and Glee Club. After graduating from high school in Tennessee he moved to Detroit and started singing with the Original Five Royals, who later changed their name to The Midnighters. He sang with a Gospel Quartet and they won many awards.

In July of 1955, he and Harriette Ella Brown married three months after meeting, and were married 63 years. They had five children.

In January 1958, he received a calling that took him into a lifelong ministry serving God. He received his Local Preachers License in 1959, and Elders Orders in 1963. He served in East Tennessee and West Virginia conferences before coming to Baltimore-Washington Conference in 1970. He served Mt. Zion UMC in Baltimore from 1970 to 1973; Hamline UMC from 1973 to 1979 when he was appointed to Northwood-Appold UMC until 1982. From 1982 to 1986, he was at Hughes Memorial UMC, followed by Albright Memorial UMC 1986 to 1988. He then was appointed to Grace UMC in Fort Washington until 1993.

His final appointment, in 1993, was to the historic Ebenezer UMC in Washington, D.C., from which he retired in 1996. This was the oldest black church on Capitol Hill and the place where the first school for Black Children in Washington, D.C., was held. This is the church in which Abraham Lincoln, Frederick Douglass and many other historic figures spoke to the congregation over the years.

Henderson received countless awards across his 58 years of ministry including those coming from the President of the United States, governors, members of Congress, the President's Drug Advisory Council, and the Baltimore-Washington Conference Black Methodists for Church Renewal. He is listed in Who's Who in the Methodist Church.

In Henderson's words, "the ministry, to me, means an opportunity to show to the outside world some of the inside Christlike concerns that one should possess, if he or she is to become a good and faithful servant of God."

He was predeceased by his son, Thomas Castodaro Henderson in 1996.

Survivors include his wife of 63 years, Harriette Ella; four children: Kevin LeBron, Tjwanna Michelle, Lataska Babette and Hal Thomas Jr.; their spouses, 10 grandchildren, 10 great-grandchildren; and two brothers.

Rev. Hal Thomas Henderson Sr., died in Conyers, Ga., April 8, 2019. A Celebration of Life service was held April 17, 2019, in Stonecrest, Georgia.

PASTOR CHARLES "CHARLIE" HENRY
1938-2019

Charles William Henry was born Sept. 11, 1938, in Jefferson County, W. Va., the son of the late Abner Henry and Elizabeth Chamblin Hough.

He was an active member of Masonic Lodge # 80 AF & AM and their many associated organizations. He served as chaplain and was a life-member of FOP #83.

He retired from the Charles Town Police Department, where he was Captain. He also retired from the City of Charles Town.

Henry attended Wesley Seminary and had served with Berkeley Place/Friendship UMCs from 2000-2008, and in 2012 began serving with Inwood UMC.

He is survived by his wife of 48 years, Shirley Fritts Henry; one daughter, Sheila Owens and husband Brian of Martinsburg; one granddaughter; two brothers; and nieces, nephews and cousins.

Pastor Charles "Charlie" Henry died Feb. 3, 2019, at his home. A Celebration of Life Service was held Feb. 10 at Inwood UMC, with the Revs. John Lewis, John Yost, and Edward Grove participating. Frederick District Superintendent, the Rev. Edgardo Rivera, officiated. Private interment was in Edge Hill Cemetery.

REV BERNARD "BERNIE" F. HILLENBRAND
1925-2018

Bernard Francis Hillenbrand was born May 11, 1925, in Syracuse, N.Y., into a life of poverty. He joined the Army at 18 and fought in the European theater. He was wounded twice by German mortars in the Battle of Hurtgen Forest. After spending 1½ years recovering from his wounds, he joined the Merchant Marines. He then went on to earn a master's degree in public administration and a theology degree from Wesley Theological Seminary.

He came into ministry after a 25-year career with the National Association of Counties. He was ordained an Elder in 1989 and served primarily in extension ministries: as executive director of Community Ministries, and the Interfaith Conference Task Force on Drugs. In 1992, he pastored the Mt. Rainer Charge and in 1993 Cedar Lane UMC at Mt. Rainier, made up of two racially separated churches in Prince George's County, which merged under his leadership. He was there until retirement in 1995.

When asked in an interview why he entered the ministry so late in life, he said, "I wanted to be a priest since I was a little boy." After retiring from government service, "here was my chance to serve the church."

Hillenbrand's earlier career was as the first executive director of the National Association of Counties (NACo), where he took county government from relative obscurity to a political mainstay in Washington, D.C. He built it from one employee to 120 when he retired. In 1981, the New York Times called him "the lobbyist who put counties back on the map of politics."

After NACo, he worked as County Adviser to HUD Secretary Henry Cisneros and later Secretary Andrew Cuomo.

"He was passionate, and he was hilarious, and he was a phenomenal storyteller until the day he died" said NACo's executive director Matt Chase.

He was preceded in death by his wife, Aliceann Wohlbruck.

Survivors include his four "outstanding" children, as he told the Chevy Chase Historical Society in Oct. 2015. They are "Lisa Hillenbrand, former Director of Global Marketing for Procter & Gamble in Cincinnati; Laura Hillenbrand, author of 'Seabiscuit' and 'Unbroken'; Susan Hillenbrand Avalon, a script reviewer for Columbia Pictures in Hollywood; and John Hillenbrand, serving on matters of bankruptcy at the Washington National Judicial Center."

The Rev. Bernard "Bernie" F. Hillenbrand died Oct. 5, 2018. A memorial service was held at Foundry UMC Oct. 21, with the Rev. Ginger Gaines-Cirelli officiating. The Rev. Donald Robinson gave the meditation.

PASTOR LEWIS IRVIN KEENE
1933 – 2019

Lewis Irvin Keene was born July 5, 1933, to the late Ivey and Birdie Keene in Baltimore, the youngest of three sons. He was educated in the segregated Baltimore City Schools system, graduating from Paul Laurence Dunbar Senior H. S. in 1954. He left Morgan State Univ. after two years to work at the Old City Hospital as a supply clerk secretary. He stayed there for eight years, then transferred to Social Services of the State of Maryland where he was a dedicated caseworker until his early retirement to pursue ministry.

He and Frances Laughlin were married in 1976, after a courtship that spanned New Jersey and Baltimore. They had one son, Jamin-hill, who survives.

He heard God's call to ministry while serving at Christ UMC as the Youth Director. He graduated with honors from Morgan State University in 1979, then went to Howard University School of Divinity for his Master of Divinity. In 1980 Lewis became the pastor at Milton Ave. UMC for 10 years.

He took a leave of absence in 1990 and worked as church secretary and as a summer camp teacher at Christ UMC. In 1992, he became pastor of St. Luke UMC in the Sandtown-Winchester area of Baltimore where he pastored for 10 years until his retirement in 2002. One of his ministries was the founding of the Black Heritage Singers, now called the Lewis I. Keene Black Heritage Singers.

After retirement he continued involvement with parishioners, relatives and friends who needed attention, or serving Communion to shut ins. He was active with United Methodist Men, Secretary of the First Friday Nighters (ministers and their mates), as founder of the acapella Heritage Choir of Christ UMC, and on the staff as a minister there.

In addition to community service, Keene had many hobbies and interests from cooking and playing piano, to fishing and auto mechanics. He cooked nearly every day for his family. He was a good bowler and an avid reader. He loved travel with his family, both in the U.S. and abroad. They took several cruises. A highlight was the trip he and Frances took to Jerusalem.

"One of the things said about Lewis was that he was the People's Pastor," said the church's eulogy. "He cared about the flock, and he gave that care out to his members. Lewis had a gift for seeing God's call on certain people for the ministry and encouraged more than 12 people to enter into ministry through lay speaking, licensing, or becoming ordained ministers and pastors. Lewis was also an ENCOURAGER and a good counselor to church members and those outside of his churches. He always listened to understand and help people see themselves more clearly."

Survivors include his wife and their son, Jamin-hill Keene of California. Also surviving are a special cousin Elizabeth Carter, five nieces and nephews, two aunts, two godchildren, and many grand-nieces and -nephews, cousins and friends. His brothers Lawrence and Howard preceded him in death.

Lewis I. Keene, a retired Associate Member, died Feb. 13, 2019. The Rev. Twanda Prioleau officiated at a memorial service Feb. 23 at Christ UMC in Baltimore. Clergy from the ecumenical community participated including the Revs. Norman Horn, Bruce Foster, Regina Sewell, Arnold Anthony; and colleagues the Revs. William Butler, Herbert Watson, Bernard Keel, Clarence Davis, LaReesa Smith-Horn and Mark Groover.

REV. RAYMOND KINGSBOROUGH
1922-2018

Raymond M. Kingsborough was born Oct. 5, 1922, in Carlisle, Pa., a son of the late Leroy B. and Effie M. (Bradey) Kingsborough. He was a graduate of the Messiah Academy in Grantham. He was ordained in 1959.

Kingsborough and Pearl I. Wilhelm married in 1946 before he began his ministerial education. They had two sons and a foster daughter. His wife died in 2006, after a 60-year marriage.

Kingsborough served in the Baltimore-Washington Conference from 1957 to 1988 when he retired. His ministry was in multi-church charges. The first was in Manchester from 1957-1960, which included Miller's, Bixler's and Mt. Zion UMCs; and New Bloomfield, Pa., Charge, which included Trinity, Dellville and Snyder's UMCs from 1960-1968. He then served Deerfield and Weller's UMCs in Thurmont 1968-77; his appointment was until 1983 to Pikeside UMC in Martinsburg, W.Va.; he was then appointed to the Darlington Charge, with Darlington UMC and Rock Run UMC, from 1983 until his retirement in 1988.

Survivors include two sons: Stanford S. Kingsborough of Mechanicsburg and David L. Kingsborough (and his wife, Betty) of Duncannon; one daughter, Fay Shreve (and her husband, George) of Carlisle; two grandchildren and two great-grandchildren.

Rev. Raymond M. Kingsborough, a retired Elder, died Nov. 25, 2018, at his home in Carlisle, Pa. A funeral service was held Nov. 30 in a Carlisle Funeral Home. The Rev. Matthew D. Plant officiated. Burial is in Springville Cemetery, Boiling Springs, Pa.

REV. EDWIN HILMORE "HIL" LANGRALL
1926 - 2018

Edwin Hilmore "Hil" Langrall was born Nov. 30, 1926, in Baltimore, to the Rev. Dr. O.B. and Isabel Moore Langrall. As an active family serving in the Baltimore-Washington Conference, the family lived in various locations throughout Maryland and Washington, D.C.

He was a graduate of Western Maryland College, went to seminary at Duke University and was ordained a Deacon in 1950 and an Elder in 1952, making him among the five oldest clergy in the conference. He immediately became Director of the Wesley Foundation in Williamsburg, Va. (College of William and Mary).

Langrall served as a chaplain in the Navy with the 3rd Marine Division in Tokyo and Okinawa following the Korean War from 1955 to 1957.

In 1952, he began more than 35 years in the ministry, which, in addition to the chaplaincy, included: Shepherdstown from 1952-1955; First in Brunswick from 1957-59; St. Andrews in Hagerstown from 1959-1963; Emory in D.C., 1963-1973 from Christ UMC in Landover Hills, 1973-1980; a year at United in D.C.; then Bradbury Heights in D.C. from 1981-86; a year at Foundry UMC, then in 1987 to Eldbrooke in D.C. until his retirement in 1991.

During the 1980s, as the HIV/AIDS epidemic grew, Langrall provided pastoral counseling services in the Whitman-Walker Clinic. In retirement, he served as chairman of the board for the Quality of Life Retreats, a ministry of the Baltimore-Washington Conference dedicated to serving patients and families impacted by HIV/AIDS. In his Mt. Pleasant neighborhood, he was a member of Historic Mt. Pleasant.

In 2012, Langrall and his partner of 52 years, Richard McKenney, were officially married. Together they adopted, purchased or were found by 16 dogs, an obit in the Washington Post reported. McKenney died in 2013.

Survivors include a brother, Bob Langrall, and nephews Jim Langrall of Westminster and David Langrall of Swananoa, N.C,

The Rev. Edwin H. Langrall, a retired Elder, died Nov. 12, 2018, a couple weeks before his 92nd birthday. A private service was held at Capitol Hill UMC in early 2019.

REV. LLOYD ELMER MARCUS
1928-2018

Lloyd Elmer Marcus was born April 27, 1928, in Baltimore, the son of the late Lloyd Marcus and Gladys K Johnson. He was the first of four children.

He attended Baltimore City Public Schools and received an AA degree in psychology from Morgan State University. He then graduated from Baltimore Bible College. He continued with studies in religion and theology at Wesley Theological Seminary and Moody Bible College. While attending Ann Arundel College, he was licensed as an addiction counselor and adviser to the growing HIV/AIDS population. He considered one of his greatest accomplishments was receiving his doctoral degree, which included broadening his studies through travel to Japan, Korea, Israel and Egypt.

After he was ordained at age 26 by his Aunt Anita Bethea, he became an assistant pastor to Rev. Bethea at Holy Temple Church of Truth. In United Methodist ministry, Marcus pastored Patapsco Charge, 1988-1991, and St James UMC in Baltimore, 1997 until he retired in 2008. Following his retirement, he served for a year at Hereford Combined Charge.

Marcus was one of the first black fire fighters in Baltimore at a time when segregation was prevalent. He was the first black paramedic instructor and African American chaplain at the Baltimore City Fire Department.

He was preceded in death by his wife, Mary Marcus, three months earlier.

Survivors include Lloyd Marcus III, Gloria Marcus-Lewis, Aaron Marcus, David Marcus and Allen Marcus and their spouses; three stepchildren: Marchella Henry, Kyle Hicks and James Scrivener; 12 grandchildren and 11 great-grandchildren. Two sisters also survive.

Rev. Lloyd Marcus, a retired associate member, died June 1, 2018. Funeral services were held June 7 at St. James UMC in Baltimore, officiated by the Rev. Curtis King, with participation by the Revs. Jason Jordan-Griffith, Bruce Foster, and Baltimore Metropolitan District Superintendent, the Rev. Wanda Duckett, and others.

PASTOR THEODORE "TED" MARSH JR.
1953-2018

Theodore Daniel Marsh Jr. was born Nov. 22, 1953, in Baltimore, the son of Helen May Mayne Marsh and the late Theodore Daniel Marsh Sr. He was a 1971 graduate of Lansdowne High School and earned an Associate Degree from Catonsville Community College. He held a Bachelor of Arts degree in History from the University of Baltimore and was a graduate of Wesley Theological Seminary in Washington, DC.

Prior to the three-point charge he was serving at the time of death – Mt. Zion UMC, Grace UMC and Cherry Run UMC in Morgan County, W. Va. – he served the Rohrsville Charge from 1981-1984; Pikeside UMC from 1984-1998, when he left pastoral ministry to serve the West

Virginia Youth Advanced Plan until 2007. He then pastored Ellerslie UMC until 2014, when he was appointed to Sleepy Creek UMC in Berkeley Springs, W. Va.

Marsh served on the Cumberland-Hagerstown District Board of Church Location and Building. He was active with United Methodist Volunteers in Mission and served on the board of Camp Joy. He enjoyed hunting, fishing, cooking, teaching and was an accomplished woodworker.

Survivors include his wife, Cathy Eileen Rix Marsh; his children, Matthew Aaron Marsh of Berkeley Springs, and Sarah Beth Williams and her husband Joseph, Sr. of Dundalk, Md.; two step children, Jason Alan Shiflett of Frederick, and Charles Aaron Shiflett and his wife Mary of Abingdon; three grandchildren and one step-grandson. He is also survived by his mother and three brothers.

The Rev. Theodore "Ted" Daniel Marsh, Jr., an Associate Member, died Friday, Sept. 7, 2018, under the care of Hospice of the Panhandle. A funeral service was held Sept. 12, at Mt. Zion UMC, in Berkeley Springs, W.Va. The Rev. Michael Leedom and District Superintendent Conrad Link officiated.

REV. MAURICE S.W. MOORE
1939-2018

The Rev. Maurice S. W. Moore, 78, a retired Associate Member, died Nov. 19, 2018. He was the father of Bishop Cynthia Moore-Koikoi, who leads the Western Pennsylvania Area. His funeral service was held Nov. 28, at Sharp Street Memorial UMC in Baltimore.

Maurice Sumner Whiting Moore was born Sept. 3, 1939, the oldest son of the late Maurice Sumner Moore and Catherine Loretta Whiting. He spent his childhood in the family's four-story Harlem Avenue home in New York City. They moved to the more prestigious Ashburton neighborhood while he was growing up.

Moore was the product of Baltimore City Public Schools, graduating from Frederick Douglass High School. He attended Morgan State College as a physics major. His mother had promised God that she would give up dancing if one of her children would become a pastor. Moore fulfilled that wish by becoming Assistant Chaplain at Crownsville State Mental Hospital in 1958. In 1960, he was appointed Assistant Pastor to the five-point Mt. Airy Charge where he met his wife, Joan Simms. They married in 1962.

He received a Bachelor of Arts degree in Sociology from Loyola College of Maryland (now University) and a Master of Divinity from Lancaster Seminary, but as an act of protest for injustices he perceived during the dissolution of the US Central Conference in 1968, he chose to become an Associate Member, rather than pursue ordination as an Elder.

During his 40-year ministerial career he served in Villa Rica, Ga., and in 1963, he was appointed to the Inwood Charge in W. Va., then from 1964 to 1969 to Asbury in Shepherdstown, W. Va. From 1969-1971, he served St. Matthews UMC in Baltimore; 1971-1979, Union Memorial UMC in Aberdeen; Colesville UMC in Silver Spring, 1979-81; Sharp Street UMC in Sandy Spring, 1981-86; and Asbury UMC in Frederick for 14 years from 1986 to 2000 when he retired.

He loved The United Methodist Church and often prayed that it would be perfected in love. He was a gifted teacher and ethicist and over the years also worked as a substitute teacher, home school teacher and ethics consultant for the Veterans Administration.

Moore enjoyed playing hymns by ear on the piano and the organ he built. He wired the rooms in his parsonages for surround sound before surround sound was popular. He was a collector -- model trains, model cars, church organs and antique radios took up much space in their home. He enjoyed showing his train layouts and the coffee table that housed N scale trains. He relished his membership on the Mid-Atlantic Antique Radio Club and on the Board of

Directors for the National Capital Radio and Television Museum.

He was preceded in death by his parents and a sister.

Survivors include his wife of 56 years Joan Simms Moore, daughters Bishop Cynthia Moore-Koikoi and her husband Pastor Raphael K. Koikoi Jr., Cheryl Moore-Thomas and her husband Steve Thomas; Kyle Moore and Ronald Moore; one grandson, three sisters and four brothers.

REV. JAMES RAY "JIM" MORGAN,
1927-2018

James Ray Morgan was born March 4, 1927, in Pittsburg, Penn., to Louis Benjamin Morgan and Margaret Gene (Gibson) Morgan. He spent most of his childhood and youth in Houston, Texas.

He received a Bachelor of Arts degree from Central Bible College in 1951 and another from American University in 1958. He attended Wesley Theological Seminary and received his Master of Divinity in 1961, followed by a Doctor of Ministry in 1972. He completed post graduate studies at the Western Institute for Group and Family Therapy in California and at the C.G. Jung Institute in Zurich, Switzerland.

Morgan was called to the ministry in 1950 and served in the pastorate for more than 50 years. He started his ministry in Frankfort, Indiana, where he built an Assemblies of God church, which began in a tent. He moved to the Baltimore-Washington Conference and began his pastorates in Poolesville, from 1956-1963. He served at Oakdale Emory UMC from 1963 to 1977 and Westminster UMC, 1978-1980.

In 1980 he became the Director of Drayton Retreat Center in Worton, Md., and served there until 1988. He also pastored in Claymont, Del., from 1988 to 1992, when he retired. However, he continued serving in an interim capacity until the age of 88 and ended his career in Washington, D.C., as the pastor of a Universalist parish. His ministry focused primarily on the development and enabling of lay people to fulfill their calling. He felt that the power of the Church lay in small groups having established one at Oakdale Emory that lasted more than 30 years.

At age 65, he and his wife Beverly Morgan set sail across the Atlantic to fulfill a life-long sailing dream. They sailed the Mediterranean for two years visiting Spain, Italy and many of the Greek Islands. He was an avid athlete his entire life playing singles tennis until age 90.

He was predeceased by his wife, Beverly G. Morgan, who he met at Central Bible College. She died in 2016 after 65 years of marriage.

Survivors include three children: Daniel C. Morgan; Grayce Morgan Crockett; and Mark B. Morgan; six grandchildren and two great-grandchildren.

Morgan donated his body to George Washington University for scientific study.

The Rev. James Ray "Jim" Morgan, 91, a retired Elder, died June 2, 2018, after a brief illness. A memorial service was held at Oakdale-Emory UMC June 9.

PASTOR ZAN LEE PERRY
1951-2019

Zan Lee Perry was born Aug. 2, 1951.

A local preacher, she served churches in the 1990s, including Grace UMC in Gaithersburg from 1993-1995; and Lewin UMC in the West Baltimore District from1994-1999. She had no appointment in 1999 and discontinued a year later.

Pastor Zan Perry, a provisional member, died Feb. 2, 2019. She was a resident of Baltimore. A closed funeral service was held a few days later.

REV. RUTH CUSTER ROSS
1921-2018

Ruth Custer Ross was born May 21, 1921, in Garrett, Ind., the daughter of the late A.J. and Sadie (Grube) Custer. She had five brothers. She was a graduate of Garrett High School (1938), Purdue University (1944), and Wesley Theological Seminary (1978).

As a student she served Keen Memorial for a year. In 1978, she was appointed to Rodgers Ford UMC for three years. From 1981 to 1984, she served Westminster Parish, then was appointed to Ames UMC in Pikesville from where she retired in 1988. She also served at Timonium UMC.

She and M. Nelson Ross, who graduated from high school together, married in 1944 and had four children.

Ross had a lifelong interest in the fabric arts. She was a weaver, quilter and knitter. As a member of the Baltimore Heritage Quilters' Guild, she taught quilting. Well into her 90s, she knitted more than 500 newborn baby hats for the Dupont Hospital nursery in Fort Wayne, Ind.

She was preceded in death by her husband.

Survivors include her sons, Steven (Jean), Craig (Carol Ann), and David (Deborah), and daughter Carol Wirth; seven grandchildren; and two great-grandchildren. She is also survived by a brother, sister-in-law, several nieces and nephews.

The Rev. Ruth Custer Ross, a retired Elder, died May 8, 2018. A memorial service was celebrated at Timonium UMC May 19.

REV. JOHN THOMAS SMITH
1937-2019

John Thomas Smith was born Oct. 24, 1937, in Baltimore, the son of Charles and Matilda Smith. He was educated in the Baltimore City Public Schools. He also had an AA Degree in Business Management, a BS Degree in Business Administration from Morgan State University, and his MDiv from Wesley Theological Seminary.

His first church was Union UMC in Aberdeen, where he served from 1987 to 1992. He was appointed to St. Luke/Mt. Gregory Charge in Sykesville from 1992 to1995; then to Christ UMC in Edmondson, which he served until 1997. For the next three years he was at Howard Park UMC in Baltimore, followed by an appointment to Govans-Boundary until he retired in 2002.

He served as a chaplain with the Howard County Police Department and the Maryland State Police Department.

He and Laura Pearson Smith met in high school and married in 1957. In their 62 years together, they enjoyed travel both abroad and within the United States. They often vacationed and traveled with cousins from South Carolina. Among the Smiths' travels were Ireland, Jamaica, Cancun, the Bahamas, Canada, Alaska and the Panama Canal. They cruised the Mississippi River and the Caribbean Islands.

Survivors include his wife Laura P. Smith of Hanover, Pa.; two children, Margaret Diane Smith and Michael T. Smith and his wife Theresa; five grandchildren, 12 great-grandchildren; nieces, nephews and cousins. Also surviving is Sandy Harley, who they considered their goddaughter.

The Rev. John T. Smith, a retired Elder, died April 1, 2019. His Homegoing Service was held April 5, at Milford Mill UMC with the Rev. Lemuel Dominguez officiating.

REV. CHARLES W. STEWART
1921-2019

Charles W. Stewart was born Oct. 26, 1921. He graduated from the Lindsly School in Wheeling, W. Va., where both his parents taught. In 1943, he graduated from Mount Union College in Alliance, Ohio, and received his Bachelor of Divinity degree from Drew School of Theology in Madison, N.J. He went on for a doctorate at Union Theological Seminary in New York. He received a Ph.D. in 1955.

While at Union, he met his future wife, Alma Rowe, on a New York City street corner near the campus. They married in 1948 and had four children.

Stewart's appointments were nearly all in academia. He spent a year at Oceanside, Long Island. From 1949 to 1952, he worked with the Wesley Foundation in Columbus, Ohio, then from 1952-55, he was appointed to the Methodist Church in Mystic, Conn. His next appointment was to Denver where he taught Pastoral Care at Iliff School of Theology, 1956-62. His first book, "The Minister as a Marriage Counselor," was published in 1961.

In 1963, he spent a sabbatical year at the Menninger Foundation in Topeka, Kansas, then the family moved to Birmingham, Mich., where he was on the faculty at the new Institute of Advanced Pastoral Studies at the Cranbrook Institute from 1963 to 1966.

Their last move was to Wesley Theological Seminary in Washington, D.C., where he taught Pastoral Care and Counseling and Psychology of Religion, and, from 1966 to 1987, served as the Howard Chandler Robbins Professor of Pastoral Care. In 1985, he enjoyed a sabbatical year at Princeton Theological Seminary.

"He brought to his teaching and his students a thoughtful and kind presence as one who had one foot in pastoral ministry and the other in the emerging research in his field," said a statement from the Wesley Seminary president's office.

During his career, Stewart wrote seven books and numerous papers and articles. He served on several conference committees, advised and created counseling centers and worked with the Stephen's Ministry in the D.C. area.

During retirement, the Stewarts continued to expand on their traveling experiences with family, friends and colleagues, traveling throughout the States, Europe, Israel, Australia, New Zealand and sailing around the Caribbean. They moved to Asbury Retirement Community in 2002, when Asbury installed a pool, his one requirement.

Survivors include his wife of 70 years; his children Louise, Peter and Heather, seven grandchildren; and a great-granddaughter.

Rev. Charles Stewart, who was ordained a Deacon in 1944, was the longest serving pastor in the Baltimore-Washington Conference when he died Jan. 1, 2019. A Service of Death and Resurrection was held Jan. 19 at Asbury Village in Gaithersburg.

REV. EARL SULMONETTI
1931-2019

Earl Sulmonetti was born March 10, 1931, in Jamestown, N.Y., and grew up in New Castle, Penn. Both his father and mother were ordained Methodist ministers. He attended Baldwin Wallace College in Berea, Ohio, where he ran track and was a member of Sigma Phi Epsilon. He met his wife Juanita at school and they married in June 1955.

He then attended Wesley Theological Seminary. Upon graduation he joined the Baltimore Washington Conference and for 38 years served churches in both the Baltimore area and the Washington, D.C., area. These included: Deer Creek from 1957-58; Providence from 1958 to 1960; Chase UMC from 1960 to 1970; Patapsco UMC from 1970 to 1978; Grace UMC in Takoma Park from 1978 to 1988 and at Millian Memorial UMC until he retired in 1995..

Sulmonetti was a Maryland Master Mason. He loved most sports, but his favorite was the Baltimore Orioles. He was a season ticket holder for over 20 years. He played the violin as a young man. He loved playing cards and different games. His favorite activities were playing table tennis and bocci ball. He also enjoyed being a voice-over speaker for the Asbury TV Station. A favorite place was his little bungalow in Bethany Beach, Del.

In September 2018, - he Gaithersburg Mayor, Jud Ashman, and City Council honored Asbury's Olympians, who included Earl Sulmonetti.

As a father and grandfather, Sulmonetti was a wonderful and strong presence in his children's and grandchildren's lives. He loved coaching them on sports teams and traveling as a family.

He was predeceased by a son, Brian Sulmonetti.

Survivors include his wife of 64 years, Juanita Virginia, and his daughters Bonnie Brooks and Karen Sulmonetti, their husbands Wayne Brooks and William Short; his daughter-in-law Brenda Sulmonetti; and five grandchildren. A sister also survives.

The Rev. Earl Sulmonetti, a retired Elder, died May 5, 2019, at Asbury Methodist Village, where he and his wife lived for the past 10 years. A memorial service was held May 18, 2019, in the Guild Chapel at Asbury Methodist with the Rev. Malcom Frazier officiating.

REV. ERNEST "ERNIE" THAYIL
1931 – 2019

Ernie William Paul Thayil was born in Bombay, India, Nov. 17, 1931, to John Frederick Shem Thayil and Daisy Agnes Thyle. He attended Don Bosco High in Bombay. He graduated from Union Biblical Seminary in 1954 to pursue his dream of becoming a missionary.

He and Margaret Mary Elisha married in 1956. He became the Director of Bombay Youth for Christ just after their marriage, leaving the position for the United States in 1957 to pursue higher education. He left his wife and 8-month-old daughter for a time.

After an arduous journey on a cargo ship, he arrived in New York Dec. 5, 1957, with $14 and a bus ticket to Seattle to attend Seattle Pacific College, the path he took after a chance meeting with the college president in Bombay.

While attending college, he worked to save enough money to bring his wife and daughter to join him. Through the help of his church and many friends, he was able to bring them over just one year after he arrived.

He received a Bachelor's in Business and Economics in 1962. In 1960, while a student at SPC, he founded Operation Outreach at Seattle Pacific College, which was a short-term summer mission trip for students. That program still exists today.

The family moved to Eugene, Ore., where he attended the University of Oregon and graduated with an MBA in 1966. The Thayils returned to Seattle where he was hired by Boeing as a Systems Analyst and Sales Representative, his first career position. Their two sons were born there.

In 1970, Thayil took a position with Seattle Public Schools as a Special Assistant to the District Superintendent in charge of Planning, Research, and Evaluation. His main focus was to work on desegregating public schools in Seattle. In 1971, when his boss became the new

Superintendent of Baltimore City Public Schools, he took the Thayils with him. He was tasked with desegregating Baltimore City Public Schools and instituted a busing plan to accomplish this in a difficult transition time for the city.

He received a Masters' degree in Education from the University of Maryland in 1974, and continued there pursuing his PhD in Education, finishing all but his dissertation. Thayil served Baltimore City Public Schools for 23 years, most of the time as a principal at different levels until his retirement in 1993.

After serving as a Lay Leader for most of his life, he decided to pursue full-time ministry, and was ordained an Elder in 1999.He served several churches in the Baltimore-Washington Conference, including: Weller UMC from 1992-95; Catoctin Mountain Parish in Thurmont from 1995-96; Prospect-Marvin Charge in Mt. Airy from 1996-2002, when he retired. From 2006-2009, in retirement, he served Catoctin UMC; 2009 to January 2013; Union Bridge UMC in Johnsville; a short time at Flint Hill in Adamstown; a year at Ijamsville from 2013-14; and in 2014 to Bethesda UMC in Sykesville. He had preached his last sermon there Dec. 27, one week before his death.

He loved reading, taking walks when he was able, and an annual beach trip to Ocean City. Caring for each congregation he served was especially important to him. Spending time with his grandchildren was a special joy.

In addition to his parents, he was preceded in death by his sister, two brothers, a sister-in-law, a daughter-in-law and granddaughter.

Survivors include his wife; daughter Amy Bartholomee and her husband; sons Jonathan Thayil and Jason Thayil; seven grandchildren and a great granddaughter; four siblings and their spouses, nieces and nephews.

The Rev. Ernest "Ernie" Thayil, an ordained Elder, died Jan. 4, 2019, at Frederick Memorial Hospital after suffering a stroke a week earlier. At the time he was serving in retirement at Bethesda UMC in Sykesville. A Celebration of Life service was held in May.

REV. VERNON L. THOMPSON
1927-2018

Vernon Larue Leroy Thompson was born July 14, 1927. He was ordained an Elder in 1968.

From 1966 to his retirement in 1992, he served Keen Memorial (1966-69), Grace UMC in Cumberland (1969-71), Lodge Forest for two years, Brooklyn Heights UMC (1973-1980), and Calvary UMC in Annapolis, 1980 until he retired in 1992. Upon retirement, he continued to serve as an interim pastor in churches wherever he was needed.

Surviving is his wife Geraldine Thompson of Vero Beach, Florida.

The Rev. Vernon L. Thompson, a retired Elder, died June 1, 2018, at the Willowbrook Medical Center at Indian River Estates retirement community in Vero Beach, Florida. A memorial service was provided by the National Cremation Society in North Palm Beach July 14.

REV. JOHN C. WALKER
1927-2018

John Charles Walker was born May 6, 1927, the son of Ruth and Clay Walker. He grew up in Chevy Chase, graduated from Bethesda-Chevy Chase High School in 1945, and enlisted in the Army. He served in post-war Germany. Upon his return in 1946, he attended the University of Maryland and DePauw University in Greencastle, Ind., where he met his wife-to-be.

He and Beverly "Bobbie" Pierce were married in 1952 and moved to New Haven, Conn. for him to study for the ministry and she to work in voice and piano, skills that she used in support of his subsequent church appointments.

Walker began his ministry in 1954 as an associate at Metropolitan Memorial UMC in D.C. He was ordained in 1955. In 1960, he was appointed to Concord (later Concord-St. Andrews UMC) in Bethesda, where he remained until 1976, when he was transferred to Wesley UMC in D.C. In 1988, he was appointed to Francis Asbury UMC in Rockville and remained until he retired in 1994. He continued in ministry at St. Paul's UMC in Kensington.

Walker was a member of the Kiwanis Club of Bethesda for 62 years.

"He was an utterly non-judgmental man who lived more than nine decades of life with elegant grace and boundless optimism," said his children in remembrance.

He was preceded in death by his wife of 63 years, Beverly "Bobbie" Walker.

Survivors include his children: Betsy Walker; Jorgy Gorog and her husband Peter; and Christopher Walker and his wife Trudy; five grandchildren and one great grandchild.

The Rev. John C. Walker, a retired Elder, died Nov. 21, 2018. A Celebration of Life was held at St. Paul's UMC in Kensington Dec. 22 with the Rev. Adam Snell officiating.

REV. PAULINE V. RIDGLEY WILKINS
1932-2018

Pauline Viola Ridgley was born April 13, 1932, in Perryman, Harford County, the fourth child of George Edward and Cassie Warfield Ridgley. Following her mother's death at the age of four, she was raised by an aunt and uncle. She was a graduate of Havre de Grace High School and, with a scholarship, attended Bowie State University at the age of 16. She had degrees or certificates from Cortez Peters Business School, the University of Maryland School of Practical Nursing, George Washington College and the College of Notre Dame of Maryland where she received a BA in Business Administration. She received her M. Div. from Wesley Theological Seminary.

Prior to her call to ministry, Wilkins worked as a hospital attendant in a psychiatric ward, as a real estate agent, a technical publications editor for the Department of Defense, and a computer program analyst for C&P Telephone Company.

She began her ministry in 1991 at Christ UMC in Aquasco. This appointment was followed by Asbury UMC in D.C. from 1994-1996; and Northwood-Appold UMC in Baltimore from 1996-2002, when she retired. In retirement, she became the first female director of the Morgan State University Christian Center and, in January 2001, began pastoring the Faith Community in Baltimore for a short time.

She served at the conference level as chairperson of the Conference Board of Christian Education and as Coordinator of Pages/Tellers for Annual Conference. She was secretary/registrar of the District Committee on Ordained Ministry.

Wilkins was a great cook and hosted many family gatherings where family would gather for festive meals and games. She enjoyed theater, which she attended frequently with her daughter, Karen. She enjoyed spending time in the Caribbean with daughter Clarissa and would drive cross-country well into her eighties to visit a daughter. Her grandchildren enjoyed counting and dusting her extensive collection of turtles.

Survivors include her daughters: Valerie Lee Fraling; Cheryl Johnson; Karen Johnson Chase; and Clarissa Pritchett. She was matriarch of five generations that included eight grandchildren, 10 great-grandchildren and two great-great granddaughters.

Wilkins left a "new address" for herself: Rev. Pauline Wilkins, Heavenly Circle, Godstown, Heaven.

The Rev. Pauline V. Wilkins, a retired Elder, died Oct. 11, 2018, at home. A Celebration of Life service was held Oct. 20 at Sharp Street Memorial UMC in Baltimore. The Rev. Cary James officiated, with participation by the Revs. Raphael Koikoi, Eugene Matthews, Karen Bethea, Marlon Tilghman and Andre R. Briscoe Jr. The Rev. Antoine Love gave the eulogy.

REV. WILLIAM "CARL" ZINN
1937-2019

William "Carl" Zinn was born Aug. 24, 1937, the son of the late T.S. "Ted" Zinn and Alma "Becky" (Rechtine) Zinn Martin.

He graduated from Kingwood High School of Kingwood, W. Va. He graduated from Cumberland United Methodist College in Kentucky and received his M. Div. from Methodist Theological School in Delaware, Ohio.

Before college and seminary, he served four years in the United States Air Force.

He was also a city councilman for four years in Dunbar, W.Va.

Before coming to the Baltimore-Washington Conference, he served North Troy UCC in North Troy, Vt.; Newport Center UMC in Newport Center, Vt.; and Christ Reformed UCC in Cavetown, Md. His appointments in the Baltimore-Washington Conference were to Shiloh UMC in Hagerstown from 1992-1998; and Araby UMC in Frederick in 1998 until he retired in 2002.

He was a member of American Legion Post 28 in North Troy, Vt., and AMVETS Post 10 of Hagerstown.

In addition to his parents, he was preceded in death by his stepfather, Jay W. Martin; and one brother, Charles Deacon Zinn.

Survivors include his wife, Carolyn J. Zinn; daughter, Debra White of East Liverpool, Ohio; stepson, W. Scott Harrington of West Roxbury, Mass.; stepdaughter, Colynda J. Lucas of Ohio; seven grandchildren; and nine great-grandchildren.

The Rev. William "Carl" Zinn, an ordained Elder, died Jan. 2, 2019. A Memorial Service was held Jan. 12, 2019, at Washington Square UMC in Hagerstown, with Pastor Jerry Lowans and Hospice Chaplain Jeff Casto officiating.

CLERGY SPOUSES

ETHEL WEBBER ANKENY
1934-2018

Ethel Lucille Webber was born to the late Earl and Mary Bixler Webber Aug. 7, 1934, in Ickesburg, Penn., the only daughter with five older brothers.

She and Ed Ankeny were married in 1959 at the beginning of his ministerial career in Pennsylvania. In 1961, they moved to the Baltimore-Washington Conference where he became pastor of Cedar Grove in Parkton for four years. From 1965-68, he served Sandy Mount UMC, then the Hillsdale-Chatsworth Charge in Baltimore until 1974. From 1974-1983, his appointment was to Eastport UMC in Annapolis, and 1983-1996 to Mt. Vernon Place in Baltimore. In 1996, he was appointed superintendent of the Baltimore-North District, which he served until his retirement in 2004.

Throughout these ministries, Ethel Ankeny served along with her husband in each church. God gifted her with the ability to talk with anyone, said her family, an asset that served well in the churches. There were no strangers in her world. She was a nurse at North Arundel Hospital for a number of years and a woman of faith. Her family attests to her being a loving wife, a proud mother and a fiercely devoted grandmother.

She enjoyed finding sand dollars at Wrightsville Beach, N.C., where the family went for summer vacations.

Ankeny was preceded in death by her parents and her five older brothers.

Survivors include her husband of 60 years, the Rev. Edwin Ankeny; her children, Cherie (Ankeny) Miller and husband Chris Miller, and Jerry Ankeny and his wife Anne-Liesse Ankeny; and two grandchildren.

Ethel Lucille Ankeny, the wife of the Rev. Edwin Ankeny, a retired Elder and district superintendent, died at home Dec. 25, 2018, after a lengthy illness. A service of remembrance was held Jan. 5, 2019, at Catonsville UMC with the Rev. Mark Waddell officiating.

OZEAL S. BROWN
1924-2018

Ozeal Shyne Brown was born Feb. 16, 1924, in Homer, La., to the late Rev. Charles Howard Sr. and Lucille Harris Shyne. She was one of six children. She received a B.S. degree from Grambling State University and an M.S. from Hampton University in Virginia. She did advanced studies at Harvard and a summer course in Manchester, England. She was a devoted educational professional.

At age 21, she was a recipient of the Outstanding Service Award for her contributions to the teaching profession. She taught social studies and English. And since then, she received many awards including the Mary McLeod Bethune Award from the National Council of Negro Women; she was a lifetime member.

She married her best friend, the Rev. Arlester Brown, on Aug. 29, 1949.

They moved to Washington, D.C., in 1969 for him to attend seminary. He held a string of appointments: the Petworth Association, Brookland, Sharp Street, then from 1975 to 1983, with the CME New York-Washington Conference. In 1983, he transferred to the Baltimore-Washington Conference and pastored St. Paul UMC in Oxon Hill, 1983-1986; Hughes UMC in D.C., 1986-1988; Albright UMC in D.C., 1988-1991, at which time he retired. In 2008, he served Asbury UMC in Germantown.

Ozeal Brown was a reading program specialist for the D.C. public schools and the University of the District of Columbia in the 1970s and 1980s. She worked for the D.C. Department of Education in the Title 1 Reading Program. She was a consultant and director of the Model School Reading Program, a staff development resources and reading specialist, and worked on program for seven District of Columbia universities.

She authored several articles on education and leadership, including "Effective Change in Student Behavior."

Brown spent eight years at the White House Communications Office during the Clinton Administration. She rode on Air Force One with the President to attend the 50th graduation anniversary for her husband at Grambling State University in Louisiana.

In early 1980, Brown joined National Presbyterian Church and served as a leader in the Women's Association, as a Deacon and a member of the Business and Professional Women's Guild. She was also on the Board of Directors of IONA Senior Services.

She was preceded in death by her parents, two brothers and a sister.

Survivors include her husband of 69 years, a sister Florence Shyne Bowers and her brother Joe C. Shyne, nieces and nephews.

Ozeal S. Brown, the wife of the Rev. Arlester Brown, died Oct. 31, 2018. A memorial service was held Dec. 1 at Metropolitan Memorial UMC in Washington, D.C.

ELEANOR ROSE ENGLE EMERICK
1928-2018

Eleanor Rose Engle Emerick was born Feb. 1, 1928, at the Rose Meadow Farm in Eckhart, the daughter of William and Emma Nelson Engle. She and Louis Emerick were married in 1947 and shared 72 years of marriage before her death, 56 years of them spent in the ministry.

Those years included his appointments to the Midland Charge from 1950-56; Union Grove from 1956-1959; Trinity UMC in Cumberland from 1959-69; Berkeley Springs Charge from 1969-73; Washington Square UMC in Hagerstown from 1973-81; Glen Burnie UMC from 1981-1985; and Fallston UMC from 1985 until he retired in 1988.

Eleanor Emerick participated in each church, singing in the choirs and as a district officer in the United Methodist Women's Society.

A special ministry of hers was to give a gift from her kitchen to each shut-in church member at Christmas and Easter.

She loved to sew and made costumes for special occasions. Some of her bicentennial garments were donated to the Fort Frederick Historical Society. She was a member of several church quilting groups.

She also served as the leader of the surplus food distribution for North Arundel County.

In addition to her husband, she is survived by eight nieces and nine nephews, including three who have followed her husband into the ministry: the Revs. Craig Emerick, Steve Emerick and Mark Brooks.

Eleanor Rose Emerick, the wife of the Rev. Louis L. Emerick, died Oct. 5, 2018, at Fahrney Keedy Village. A funeral service was held Oct.10, 2018, at Emmanuel UMC in Hagerstown where she was a member. The service was officiated by the Rev. Randall Reid and nephew, the Rev. Mark Brooks.

LILLIAN FRAZIER
1920-2018

Lillian Frazier was born Aug. 7, 1920, in Marion, S.C., where she had her primary schooling and graduated from Dunbar High School in Washington, D.C. She attended Howard University, where she met her husband, who attended seminary in Boston.

The Rev. Kirklin Frazier began serving churches in the 1940s including the Hereford Charge. He started Hughes Memorial in Washington, D.C., and served at Franklin P. Nash in the late 1950s. He died in 1961.

Lillian Frazier worked for more than 30 years in the Civil Service Commission. She was active in the churches she attended, as a Sunday School teacher, with the Women's Society of Christian Service, the forerunner of the UMW, as a representative to the Board of Child Care and chairing the Council of Ministries.

In her later years she was happiest as a "great mother and great grandmother," said her son Kirklin Frazier Jr., an assistant pastor at Douglas Memorial UMC in Washington, D.C.

She is also survived by another son, Donald R. Frazier and their wives; four grandchildren; four great-grandchildren; and a niece.

Lillian Frazier, 97, the widow of the late Rev. Kirkland Frazier, died Aug. 5, 2018, two days before her 98th birthday. A funeral service was held Aug. 13 at Franklin P. Nash UMC, in Washington, D.C. The Rev. Charles Philips officiated, and the Rev. Allen Stewart gave the eulogy. Bishop Forrest Stith, a longtime family friend, participated.

DU SHUN GIM
1934-2018

Du Shun Gim was born in Seoul, Korea June 7, 1934. He graduated from high school in 1953 and studied for one year at Seoul National University before moving to the United States in 1954. He obtained a degree from Cornell University's College of Architecture in 1959 and worked for the Federal Government's U.S. Army Corps of Engineers 45 years until his retirement in 2004.

He was supportive of his wife, the Rev. Limja Huh Gim, a retired Deacon, and her career in extension ministry as a chaplain with Washington Home & Community Hospice from 2003 until she retired in 2014.

Du Shun Gim was active in the church throughout his adult life. He participated in discipleship and evangelism ministries, sang in the church choir and served as an elder. He enjoyed playing golf, meeting with friends, and watching his grandchildren's various performances and activities.

His daughter, MiYoung Wang, wrote of her father: "He was hardworking, disciplined, and always wanted us to learn as much as we could. Just as he was retiring from his career with the U.S. Army Corps of Engineers, mom wanted to go back to school and obtain a seminary education. He encouraged her and supported her in that endeavor, helping out more around the house so that she could focus on her studies and then work for 10 years doing what she enjoyed.

"My aunt would always mention that she loved the way he prayed – so humbly, with simple and sincere words – not with fancy or lofty speech – just the heartfelt words of a man who loved God and depended on Him for all things. . .

"I believe that his prayers will not expire, but that we will continue to experience blessings as a result of all the prayers he prayed while he lived here on earth."

Survivors include his wife Limja Huh Gim; daughters, MiYoung Wang, Andrea Ohnman, Grace Yakubisin; their spouses, and son Robert Gim and his wife; and eight grandchildren.

Du Shun Gim, husband of the Rev. Limja Huh Gim, died Dec. 8, 2018. A memorial service was held Dec.15, at the National Korean UMC in Rockville.

ELEANOR L. HALL
1914-2019

Eleanor L. Hall was born in Lexington, Kentucky, Oct. 21, 1914. She and Richard Hall married in 1942 and he was ordained a Methodist Elder in 1948 in the Washington Conference.

In 1949, Eleanor and Richard Hall became a strong spiritual team with his appointment to the Bowie-Lanham Charge which included Ebenezer in Lanham; Ross in Bowie and Dorsey Chapel in Glendale. In 1959, he was appointed to Simms Memorial Methodist UMC where they pastored until 1972. His last appointment was to Randall Memorial UMC, 1972 to 1975, when he retired.

She served in the churches as a pianist, usher, Sunday School and Vacation Bible School teacher, a member of the Women's Society of Christian Service, the forerunner of the UMW. She directed plays they performed. She was the Recording and Corresponding Secretary of the Washington Conference Ministers' Wives Association.

Preceding her in death in addition to her husband was a step-son, the Rev. Richard Wesley Hall III, who was an AME pastor.

Survivors include four children, all of whom have engaged in areas of leadership within The United Methodist Church. They include: Eleanor H. Hamilton and Mary Hall Gill, who serve their local churches in music and Christian Education; son Charles W. Hall Sr. as a trustee and part of the music ministry; son the Rev. Dr. R. David Hall Sr. who currently serves McKendree-Simms-Brookland UMC in Washington, D.C. Survivors also include 19 grandchildren, 44 great grandchildren and three great-great grandchildren.

Eleanor L. Hall, the wife of the late Rev. Richard W. Hall, Jr. and mother of Rev. R. David Hall, died March 14, 2019. A Memorial Service was held March 23 at McKendree-Simms-Brookland UMC where her son is pastor.

LUCY BELLE HAYNES HARRELL
1934-2018

Lucy Belle Haynes was born June 26, 1934, in High Point, N.C., the daughter of the late Colon and Mildred Swaim Hayes. She had three brothers. She graduated from Hasty High School and received her B.A. from High Point College (now University). She worked toward a master's degree at Towson University and the University of Maryland.

She and Stanley G. Harrell married in 1959. They had two children who survive.

Born to be a teacher, she taught elementary grades in Guilford County, North Carolina, and in Maryland's Washington, Carroll and Prince George's counties. She was known for helping students with learning disabilities and those with discipline problems. She made "fabulous" bulletin boards.

Harrell had a local preacher's license for more than 55 years and worked hard in the local churches her husband served, teaching Sunday school classes and as chair of different church committees. His appointments included St. Paul's in Hagerstown from 1959-1961; Central in Cumberland from 1961-1966; and Wesley UMC in Hampstead from 1966-1974. They then moved to D.C. to Mt. Vernon Place UMC from 1974-1980; Corkran Memorial from 1980-

1989; and Calvary UMC in Waldorf, from 1989 until he retired in 1997. After retirement, he served the Shiloh Charge in 2006.

In addition to being active in her husband's churches, she served on a mission team to Cuba in 1956 before Castro took over. After she retired, she set up libraries in four different churches and guided others in setting up their own.

Harrell was an avid reader, loved to cook and bake, enjoyed doing embroidery, working in the yard and cultivating house plants.

She enjoyed traveling and was a member of Wesley UMC in Hampstead, the Order of the Eastern Star, the Social Order of the Beauceant, and the Retired Teachers Association.

Survivors include her husband and their children, the Rev. Charles L. Harrell, a retired United Methodist pastor, and Patricia Harrell Daughtery and their spouses; and four grandchildren.

Lucy Belle Haynes Harrell, 84, died June 18, 2018. She was the wife of the Rev. Stanley Harrell and mother of the Rev. Charles Harrell. A funeral service was held at the Eline Funeral Home in Hampstead June 22.

CATHERINE HARTMAN
1932-2019

Catherine Neal was born April 2, 1932, in Greensboro, N.C., the daughter of the late Fred A. and Blanche W. Neal. She was a 1955 graduate of Guilford College in Greensboro, where she earned her Bachelor of Arts degree in Religious Studies. She attended graduate school at Boston University School of Theology, and at then Western Maryland College.

She and Robert H. Hartman, a retired Elder, married in 1956, early in his career in academia. They had two children. He died Feb. 11, 2007.

The family moved to Westminster in 1969 when her husband became a member of the faculty in the Philosophy and Religious Studies Department at Western Maryland College. For 20 years, he was department chairman. He remained at the school for 26 years until his retirement in 1995.

She taught special education and English at Westminster High School from 1970-1989. She became a member of Westminster UMC when they arrived in 1969, and over the years held leadership positions in the church in the areas of worship, membership, evangelism, and the Committee on the Status and Role of Women. She served on the Justice Committee, Alter Guild, Staff Parish Relations Committee, Council on Ministries, and the Administrative Board.

Hartman was a fifth-grade Sunday school teacher and was co-director of the middle school church youth program in the 1970s. She was a volunteer in the church office, at the Loaves and Fishes Soup Kitchen, and a member of the United Methodist Women for many years, and a member of the senior adult outreach program of the church.

Hartman was also active in the community, including with the Federated Woman's Club of Westminster, Inc. since 1984, a lifetime member of the American Association of University Women, a former Carroll County Branch President, a volunteer at Carroll Hospital Center from 2002-2018, and a member of the Carroll County Democratic Central Committee from 2007-2010.

She was an avid fan of the Baltimore Orioles baseball team and the Maryland Terps. She was also an animal lover.

She was predeceased by her husband and a son, David A. Hartman of Myrtle Beach, S.C.

Survivors include her daughter and son-in-law Carol and Mark Kelbaugh of Westminster, daughter-in-law Susan Hartman of Myrtle Beach, S.C., and a grandson., nieces, nephews and cousins. Two brothers and their wives also survive.

Catherine Neal Hartman, the wife of the late Rev. Robert H. Hartman, died Jan. 30, 2019. A memorial service was held at Westminster UMC Feb. 10.

ANN CONWAY SAVOY JOHNSON
1936-2018

Ann Conway Johnson was born Oct. 25, 1936, in Clara, Md., the youngest daughter of the late Rev. James A. Conway and Irene Wright Conway. She received her formal education in the public schools of Wicomico County, graduating in 1954 from the former Salisbury High School. She then studied at Atlantic Business College and Strayer Business School.

Johnson worked for the US Department of Justice for 40 years as an administrative assistant. After retirement, she was employed with the Prince George's County Board of Education and the Baltimore-Washington Conference of The United Methodist Church.

She and Charles Johnson married in 1982, a second marriage for each, at which time he served Northwood-Appold until 1986. He was then appointed to Sharp Street Memorial until he went on disability leave in 1991.

She was a member of St. Paul UMC in Oxon Hill, where she was active on various committees.

Preceding her in death were her husband, the Rev. Charles A. Johnson II, and a daughter Cara Savoy, who died a few months apart in 2011; and seven siblings.

Survivors include a son Walter B. (Kayla) Savoy Jr. of Atlanta; three step-daughters: Charlynne O. and Crystal A. Johnson, both of Baltimore, and Caron A. Johnson of Landover; four grandchildren and three step-great-grandchildren.

Ann Conway Savoy Johnson, the wife of the late Rev. Charles A. Johnson, died Dec. 30, 2018, in Upper Marlboro. A funeral service was held Jan. 11, 2019, at Jolley Memorial Chapel, P.A. in Salisbury. The Rev. Bernadette Beckett, pastor of Wesley Temple UMC in Salisbury, officiated.

PHYLLIS B. KEMP
1917-2019

Phyllis Bankert was born July 14, 1916. She and T. Ward Kemp were married in 1936 at the beginning of his ministerial career.

His student pastorates were a seven-point charge in the Martinsburg, W. Va., area. She then waited for him while he served on a Navy hospital ship during WW II. After the war, she served with him in rural churches in Alleghany, Calvert and Charles counties. Then began a period of stability as he was appointed to Bethesda Methodist Church in Hamilton, 1958-65. From there he went to Mt. Zion UMC in Howard County for three years, then to St. Luke's in Baltimore for seven years until his death in May 1975. He was 61 years old. She was a widow for more than 40 years.

Predeceasing her in addition to her husband were a son, Vincent T. Kemp and his wife, and grandson Thomas Neal Kemp, as well as siblings.

Survivors include grandchildren Dawn Lee Flanary and her husband; and Jacob Earl Selby and his wife; five great-grandchildren and one great-great-grandchild.

Phyllis B. Kemp, the wife of the late Rev. Thomas Ward Kemp, died March 9, 2019, at the age of 102, in Felton, Penn. A private service and interment were held April 22 at Oak Grove

Cemetery in Glenwood, Maryland.

GUERNEY LEON LEATHERWOOD
1934-2018

Gurney Leon Leatherwood was born Oct. 2, 1934, in Mount Airy, the son of W. Russell Leatherwood, a painter, and Anna Molesworth Leatherwood, a boarding house operator. He graduated in 1952 from Mount Airy High School and the next year took a job working in communications for the Baltimore & Ohio Railroad.

He enlisted in the Air Force in 1955 and attained the rank of master sergeant. Subsequently, he served in the Air Force Reserves and the North Dakota Air National Guard until 1963.

He and Neva Hartman married in 1962. They moved to Baltimore in 1963 and he worked as an electronics technician at Bendix Corp. in Towson for two years, then returned to the B&O and its telecommunications division. He had a long career with the B&O and its successor company CSX. He retired in 1996.

In 1979, he joined the Maryland National Guard and served as a combat engineer until being discharged in 1992.

After more than 20 years of marriage, Neva Leatherwood began her ministerial service in 1984 at Alberta Gary UMC for a year, then was appointed to Lewistown for three years. She was ordained an Elder in 1987 and from 1988-89 served Ames UMC at Pikestown and the Ames-Stone Chapel Charge until 1992, then Hughes UMC in Wheaton for two years. From 1994-1997, she was at Melville Chapel UMC in Elkridge. In 1997, she was appointed to HWR-MW Parish in Mt. Washington until she took a leave of absence in 1998. From 1999-2002, she served the Midland Charge until she retired.

An outdoorsman, Leatherwood enjoyed hunting.

He was predeceased by a son Dale Leatherwood, who died in 2000.

He is survived by his wife of 56 years, the Rev. Neva Hartman, who in retirement is a pastor at Mount Washington UMC; two sons, Glenn Leatherwood of Omaha and Dan Leatherwood of Chester Springs, Pa.; six grandchildren; and three great-grandchildren.

Gurney Leon "Woody" Leatherwood, the husband of the Rev. Neva Leatherwood, a retired pastor, died Nov. 8, 2018, from lung cancer. A memorial service was held Nov. 21 in the chapel of Bethany UMC in Ellicott City.

MARGARET ELIZABETH HUMMER LOVEJOY
1927-2018

Margaret Elizabeth Hummer was born May 20, 1927, in Baltimore, the daughter of James E. and Catherine Wrightson Hummer. She was a graduate of Bel Air High School and soon after married John Andrew Lovejoy, a World War II Navy veteran. They had three children who survive.

Lovejoy was a bookkeeper and financially helped her husband while he earned a bachelor's degree in 1950 from Asbury College in Wilmore, Kentucky. She supported him as he pursued graduate studies at the University of Kentucky and Wesley Theological Seminary, then located in Westminster. In 1954, he was ordained an Elder in the Baltimore Conference of the Methodist Church.

John Lovejoy served several churches during his ministerial career, and she was a partner in each. She sang in the choirs, taught Bible classes and was active in United Methodist Women. Those churches included Mount Vernon UMC in Hampden from 1958-61; Arlington Methodist in Pikesville from 1961-64; and Orems Methodist in Middle River, from 1964-1970. He was appointed to St. John's of Hamilton until 1978, and Pleasant Hill UMC in Reisterstown from 1978-83. His latest church before retirement was Gatch Memorial UMC in Overlea. After retirement he was assistant pastor at Grace UMC in Aberdeen. He died in 2003.

"Margaret was a great minister's wife and a full partner of any church he served in the Baltimore Conference of the Methodist Church," said the Rev. W. McCall "Mac" Roberts, retired executive director of the Maryland Bible Society and longtime friend and colleague of the Lovejoys.

In 1976, after her last child attained school age, Lovejoy became a bookkeeper-accountant at the old Maryland Bible Society office in downtown Baltimore, working in an office adjacent to Roberts. She retired in 1992.

One of her accomplishments was changing the BWC's policy on pastors moving from church to church. "The policy my mother attacked was the circumstances that the furniture and appliances at a ... parsonage in the Methodist Church, would be inherited by the incoming pastor and his family," said her son, John Steven Lovejoy.

"This created chaos and ... became a financial problem," he said. The change she effected allowed the minster's family to keep the furniture and appliances at their current residence and move them to their new parish.

Lovejoy enjoyed cooking and entertaining family, friends and parishioners. "You did not turn down a chance to have dinner at Rev. Lovejoy's home because the food would be the best, especially the desserts," her son said.

In addition to her son of Towson, she is survived by two daughters, Patricia Ann Hegberg of Hanover, Pa., and Susan Elizabeth Lovejoy of Lehighton, Pa.; six grandchildren; and four great-grandchildren.

Margaret E. Lovejoy, the wife of the late Rev. John A. Lovejoy, died Aug. 22, 2018, at the Homewood at Plum Creek Retirement Community in Hanover, Pa. Funeral services were held Sept. 1, at the First United Methodist Church there.

LARUE E. MANHART
1925-2018

LaRue E. Stout was born in Lehighton, Penn., March 31, 1925, daughter of the late Albert Stout and Minnie (Miller) Stout-Straub. She was a 1942 graduate of the former Mauch Chunk High School and was the class treasurer. She graduated from Allentown Business School in 1943 and received a bachelor's degree in business administration from Hartford Community College in 1971.

She and George Manhart were married Christmas Day in 1947. They were married 69 years until his death in 2016.

From 1966 to 1987, he served churches in the Baltimore-Washington Conference: 1966-1969 at Idlewylde; and from 1969-1971 at Fallston. In 1971 he was appointed to Wesley UMC in Baltimore and remained until 1978 when he moved to Messiah UMC in Glen Burnie. He spent a year at Fulton Seimers Memorial, then was appointed in 1982 to the Bay Brook Charge, where he remained until 1987 when he retired. He died April 1, 2016.

Manhart worked as a secretary or administrative assistant for a number of organizations including several law firms and associations from 1943 until she retired in 1987. From 1956 to 1963, she was secretary to a Methodist Church. She changed jobs fairly often because of her husband's appointments.

She was an active member of Jacob's United Church of Christ in Weissport, Penn. She was past treasurer of Jim Thorpe Alumni Association; active in women's clubs; was a volunteer for many years at the information desk at Gnaden Huetten Memorial Hospital in Lehighton, Penn. She belonged to several garden clubs.

Surviving are four nieces and their husbands; a nephew and his wife; and great-nieces, great-nephews, great-great nieces and great-great-nephews.

LaRue Eva Manhart, wife of the late Rev. George M. Manhart, died July 8, 2018. A funeral service was held July 17, at Jacob's United Church of Christ in Weissport, Penn., with Pastor Eunice Hearn officiating.

LORETTA BRYAN MILLER
1932-2019

Loretta Bryan was born June 2, 1932. She and William T. Miller were married in 1954 in Derby, Connecticut, at the beginning of his seminary and ministerial career.

She served with him in his appointments for the 38 years of his ministerial career. The appointments included: Idlewylde from 1954-56; Montgomery from 1956-58; Mt. Nebo from 1958-60; Susquehanna from 1960-65; Highland Avenue from 1965-70 during the merger which created The United Methodist Church. From then on, his appointments were for longer periods: Essex UMC from 1970-76; Ashton UMC from 1976-81; Parkside UMC from 1981-87; and Magothy UMC from1987-91, when he retired. They also made two exchange trips to England, first to Liverpool for eight weeks serving two churches, then another two churches for eight weeks to Margate on the North Sea.

She was an active member of Linden-Linthicum UMC.

She was preceded in death by her husband, William T. Miller in 2017, and a daughter, Melissa Anne Miller.

Survivors include her son, Joel B. Miller and his wife Lyn of Cheverly and two grandchildren.

Loretta Miller, the wife of the late Rev. William T. Miller, died Jan. 21, 2019. Funeral services were held Jan. 24, at Linden-Linthicum UMC in Clarksville, with the Rev. Gayle Annis-Forder officiating.

RUBY MAE PRICE
1936-2018

Ruby Mae Hanson Price was born June 26, 1936, in Clintonville, West Virginia, the daughter of the late Cecil Bernard Hanson and Anna Mary Armentrout Hanson. She graduated from Westminster High School in 1954, attended Fort Wayne Bible College and Houghton College in Houghton, New York, in 1957.

She and John Olan Price met at Houghton College. They were married for 47 years before his death May 23, 2005. His ministerial career began in 1960 at Pipe Creek Charge. From 1963 to 1977, he served St. James in West Friendship, Lonaconing and Darlington United Methodist churches before appointment to the Taylorsville Charge in 1977 where they remained until 1989. He was then appointed to Centennial Memorial UMC in Frederick until 1994. He had a short stint at Providence UMC in Kemptown, and in 1995 moved to Severn UMC where he remained until he retired in 1999.

Ruby Price worked for most of her life as a secretary and administrative assistant and retired after 18 years at the University of Maryland Cooperative Extension Service. After her husband retired and they moved to Carroll Lutheran Village she enjoyed volunteering in the chaplain's office.

Her two passions were sewing and gardening. She was particularly proud of her extensive flower gardens at her home in Seaford, Delaware. Her family was a continual source of joy. She loved spending time with her children, grandchildren, sisters and many nieces and nephews.

Survivors include four children: Timothy "Tim" David Price and wife Vanlalsiam (V.L.) of Libertytown; Loretta Ewell and husband Gary of Millsboro, DE; Linda Anne Price of Chesterfield, Virginia; Karen Price Koch and husband Jeffrey of Ashburn, Virginia; five grandchildren and three sisters.

Ruby Mae Price of Westminster, the wife of the late Rev. John Olan Price, died Oct. 24, 2018. A funeral service was held at Krug Chapel at Carroll Lutheran Village in Westminster. Interment is at Grace UMC cemetery in Hampstead.

MARILYN DYKSTRA RAKER
1938-2018

Marilyn Joyce Dykstra was born Aug. 25, 1938, to Howard and Alberta Dykstra in Dayton, Ohio. She attended several primary schools near Dayton and graduated from a public high school in the area. She had an Associate Degree from Indiana Central College, now Indianapolis University.

She and William Raker married in 1960.

She assisted her husband in the churches he served: EUB churches in Pennsylvania, the Columbia Circuit from 1960-62 and Bellefonte-Grace from 1962-65. They then moved to Olive Branch UMC in Baltimore from 1965-70; Rodgers Forge UMC from 1970-76; Fallston Charge from 1976-85; Oxon Hill UMC from 1985-92 and Arnolia UMC in Baltimore from 1992-2000, when he retired. After retirement, he served for 12 years as an associate at Towson UMC and she became an active member.

She was in the church choirs of the churches her husband served and sang in the Towson choir until illness made it impossible. She was a longtime member of the United Methodist Women. She loved small children and often kept the church nursery. One former church member wrote, "From the time that my girls were babies, she cared for them in the nursery at church."

Survivors include her husband of 58 years; two sons: Brian W. Raker and his wife Katey; and Mark D. Raker and his wife Sandra; and two grandchildren. A sister, Jean Louise Geer, also survives.

Marilyn Raker, the wife of the Rev. William "Bill" Raker, a retired Elder in the BWC, died Sept. 5, 2018, after a long illness of dementia and related ailments. A Memorial Service was held Sept. 15, at Towson UMC with the Rev. Mark Johnson officiating. Inurnment was in the Towson columbarium.

JANICE SHEESLEY
1936-2018

Janice Kemp Sheesley was born Nov. 15, 1936, the daughter of the late Evelyn Wolf, the late Joseph Kemp and the late George Wolf.

She married Dwight L. Sheesley in 1959 and they had four children. For 30 years he worked for the government, retiring in 1988, when he began seminary. He died in 2014 after 55 years together.

Janice was very involved with church activities in the churches her husband served, including Solley UMC as a student pastor in 1988, when he started at Wesley Theological Seminary, to 1991, when he graduated. He was appointed to Union Bridge/Johnsville Charge until he retired in 1999. However, he went on in retirement to serve several churches: Trinity UMC in Emmitsburg, Catoctin UMC, and returning to Johnsville part-time in 2004 where he finished his pastoral career. Janice Sheesley faithfully served along with him wherever they were.

Her favorite pastimes were crocheting, knitting and reading. She also had a love for NASCAR racing. Her sense of humor and kind heart made her a special person to a lot of people, said her daughter Cindy Hash.

She was preceded in death by her son, Dwight Sheesley Jr., and grandson, Geoffrey Ford.

Survivors include daughter Beverly Ford and husband of Severn; daughter, Cindy Hash and husband of Shrewsbury, Penn.; son Kevin Sheesley and wife of Pasadena; 12 grandchildren and five great grandchildren.

Janice Sheesley, the widow of the Rev. Dwight Sheesley, died Aug. 10, 2018, at her home in Littlestown, Penn. A service was held Aug. 16 in the chapel at Singleton & Cremation Services in Glen Burnie.

MARGARET M. THAYIL
1933-2019

Margaret Mary Elisha was born in Bombay, India, Jan. 13, 1933. She and Ernest Thayil were married in 1956 while he was director of Bombay Youth for Christ. He left to pursue higher education in 1957; his wife and baby daughter stayed behind for a time.

While attending college in Seattle, with money he'd saved and the help of church members and friends, he was able to bring his wife and child to join him a year later. They lived in Seattle through his schooling. They moved to Eugene, Oregon, where he graduated with an MBA from the University of Oregon but returned to Seattle for his employment by Boeing. Their two sons were born there.

Back to Seattle in 1970 for a position with the Seattle Public Schools as a Special Assistant to the District Superintendent, with his focus on desegregating Seattle's public schools. A year later the family moved across country to Baltimore, when his boss became Superintendent of Baltimore City Public Schools, which Ernest Thayil served for 23 years, while his family grew up.

After Ernest Thayil began pursuing full-time ordained ministry, she served with him in the churches to which he was appointed: Weller UMC from 1992-1995; Catoctin Mountain Parish in Thurmont from 1995-1996; Prospect-Marvin Charge in Mt. Airy form1996-2002, during which time he was ordained an Elder. He retired in 2002 but continued to serve: from 2006-09 at Catoctin UMC; from 2009-2013 at Union Bridge UMC in Johnsville and other short-term service, ending in Bethesda UMC in Sykesville from 2014 until his death.

In addition to her husband, she was preceded in death by a granddaughter as well as parents, brothers and sisters.

Survivors include their children: Kathleen Mary Thayil, Amy Daisy Bartholonee and husband Wayne, sons Jonathan Ernest Thayil and Jason Christopher Thayil; seven grandchildren and one great-granddaughter. Nieces and nephews also survive.

Margaret M. Thayil, the wife of the late Rev. Ernest Thayil, died March 30, 2019. He died three months earlier on Jan. 4, 2019. A Joint Celebration of Life for them was held at Jackson Chapel UMC in Frederick May 4.

ADELHEID "HEIDI" WEBER
1936-2018

Adelheid Haertwig was born in 1936, the daughter of the Superintendent of the Lutheran Free Church of Germany. She and Joe Weber met while he was studying Systematic Theology in Bonn and Berlin. They married in 1957 and had two children.

She accompanied him as he did further studies in Boston, Germany, and Switzerland and through professorships at several schools. In the late 1960s, he served at Methodist Theological School in Ohio, and the University of Geneva.

In 1973, they moved to Washington and he transferred membership into the Baltimore-Washington Conference as he began at Wesley Theological Seminary. He also pastored a German-speaking church in D.C. He died in 1986.

A June 17, 2018, obituary in the Cape Cod Times noted: "Her (Heidi Weber's) true spirit has been freed from its broken body. She endured much yet dreamed big and persevered. She showed us how to live life with strength and determination."

She is survived by her children, Robert of Golden, Colorado, and Miriam of Aptos, California, and one grandchild.

Adelheid "Heidi" Weber, the wife of the late Rev. Joseph "Joe" Weber, died May 23, 2018, at her home in Osterville, Massachusetts. A Celebration of Life and memorial service was held June 23 at St. Peter's Episcopal Church in Osterville.

ANNE WISE
1926-2019

Anne Feimster Wise is the eighth of nine children, born to the late farmer and traveling minister, Everett, and Neppie Smith Feimster, Oct. 8,1926, in Iredell County, North Carolina. Educated in the segregated public-school system, she completed her early education at Morningside High School. She first attended Bluefield College in West Virginia, to pursue an education major with a focus on early childhood learning. Then after a hiatus, she enrolled at Shaw University in Raleigh, North Carolina. She relied on campus student employment and money from relatives to augment her scholarships and limited funds.

Soon after settling into college life, she met Lewis Wise, an upperclassman, who was completing a bachelor's degree in Theology. He graduated in 1947 and they were married in 1948. She graduated in 1950 with a bachelor's degree in Early Childhood Education.

Frequent moves were part of their lives. He served small and large churches in several cities, coming into the Baltimore-Washington Conference in the early 1960s. His appointments included the Centerville Circuit from 1965-1968, and South River UMC from 1968-1974. He went on a leave of absence and retired in 1979; they made their church affiliation First UMC in Hyattsville. He died Feb. 3, 2015.

Between 1951 and 1961, the Wises had three children. Their first born died at 11 months. They settled in Washington, D.C., with two young daughters around 1963. Anne Wise was established in elementary education while her husband served United Methodist parishes and was employed at the Pentagon.

Anne Wise's unique and interactive teaching techniques were noticed and admired. She was selected to return to college and became one of the first certified physical education teachers to implement structured physical fitness programs in elementary school settings, part of an initiative that the Kennedy administration pursued to enhance children's physical fitness.

Wise became active in the Wildercroft Church of Christ in their New Carrolton neighborhood, teaching Sunday school and providing support in many ways. Her ongoing interests included maintaining a beautifully decorated, orderly home; including adding an in-ground pool and enclosed porch.

Once the grandchildren started coming, she thought her grands were the best and the brightest. She was more than adequately equipped to tutor, teach life lessons, Bible lessons and show unconditional love for her grandchildren and great grandchildren.

"The life force of Anne Feimster Wise will reverberate well beyond her earthly years due to her faith, her grounding in family and Christian values, her generosity and her ability to see the good in others," say her daughters.

Preceding her in death were her young son and eight siblings and their spouses.

Survivors include her daughters: Jewyll Davis of Laurel and Tonya Fitzgerald of New Carrolton; four grandchildren, two great grandchildren and many cousins, nieces and nephews.

Anne Wise, the wife of the late Rev. Lewis Wise, died Jan. 29, 2019. A Celebration of Life Service was held Feb. 15, at the March Life Tribute Center in Laurel. A service was held in Statesville, N.C., Feb. 22, at the First Baptist Church with the Rev. J. W. Brunson officiating.

VIII. ROLL OF THE HONORED DEAD

The list of the deceased members of the Baltimore Annual Conference prior to this year can be found in the Conference Journals of previous years. The list of deceased members of the former Washington Conference prior to 1966 will be found in the Washington Conference Journals of 1965 and previous years. The list of the deceased members of the Susquehanna Conference prior to 1970 will be found in the Susquehanna Conference journals of 1969 and previous years. The list of the deceased members of the Virginia Conference prior to 1970 will be found in the Virginia Conference Journals of 1969 and previous years.

Members of the Conference
"They rest from their labors and their works do follow them."

Name	Entered Ministry	Date of Death	Age	Years of Service
Lloyd Charles McClarren	1960	02-08-2018	91	30
Roby Harold Eastridge	1959	02-09-2018	93	30
Clifford L. Harrison	1962	02-11-2018	90	31
James W. Diggs	1996	03-07-2018	83	9
Dennis E. Dorsch	1993	03-30-2018	73	15
Ruth C. Ross	1977	05-08-2018	97	10
Vernon L. Thompson	1966	06-01-2018	92	32
Lloyd E. Marcus	1988	06-01-2018	91	27
Walter M. Bosman	2002	08-02-2018	68	12
Mary W. Conaway	1991	08-30-2018	76	24
Herbert L.D. Doggett	1951	09-03-2018	93	38
Theodore D. Marsh	1997	09-07-2018	65	21
Bernard F. Hillenbrand	1986	10-05-2018	94	9
Pauline V. Wilkins	1991	10-11-2018	87	17
Edwin H. Langrall	1950	11-12-2018	92	41
Maurice S. Moore	1960	11-19-2018	79	40
William J. Bussard	1993	11-20-2018	76	25
John C. Walker	1952	11-21-2018	92	42
Raymond M. Kingsborough	1957	11-25-2018	96	31
Helen C. Fleming	2005	12-13-2018	80	13
Charles W. Stewart	1944	01-01-2019	97	43
William Carl Zinn	1996	01-02-2019	81	4
Ernest W.P. Thayil	1996	01-04-2019	87	23
Wang (Wayne) Chung	2005	01-13-2019	63	13
James R. Embrey	2000	01-16-2019	85	6
Zan Lee Perry	1993	02-02-2019	68	7
Charles W. Henry	2000	02-03-2019	80	19
Lewis I. Keene	1984	02-13-2019	86	18
William W. Ehlers	1951	02-28-2019	95	39
James L. DeMent	2007	03-19-2019	61	12
John T. Smith	1987	04-01-2019	81	17
Hal T. Henderson, Sr.	1963	04-08-2019	86	41
Earl W. Sulmonetti	1954	05-05-2019	88	45
Henry E. Ernst	1954	05-02-2019	89	55

IX. HISTORICAL

Denominational forebears of The United Methodist Church include:

> The Methodist Church 1939-1968
> The Methodist Episcopal Church 1784-1939
> The Methodist Episcopal Church, South 1845-1939
> The Methodist Protestant Church 1830-1939
> The Associated Methodist Churches 1828-1830
> The Evangelical United Brethren Church 1946-1968
> The Church of the United Brethren in Christ 1800-1946
> The Evangelical Church 1922-1946
> The United Evangelical Church 1892-1922
> The Evangelical Association 1816-1922
> The So-Called Albright People 1809-1816
> The Newly-Formed Methodist Conference 1807-1809

Prior Conferences merged in whole or in part to form the present Baltimore-Washington Conference include:

> Baltimore M.E., M., U.M. 1784-1992
> United Brethren 1800-1830
> Eastern Ev. 1807-1839
> Maryland M.P. 1830-1939
> Virginia U.B., E.U.B., (Hagerstown) 1830-1969
> Western Pennsylvania Ev. 1839-1859
> East Baltimore M.E. 1857-1868
> Central Pennsylvania Ev., U.E., Ev., E.U.B., 1859-1964
> Baltimore M.E. (Independent) 1862-1866
> Washington M.E., M. 1864-1965
> Baltimore M.E. So. 1866-1939
> Atlantic (German) Ev., E.U.B. 1876-1964
> Maryland U.B. 1887-1901
> Pennsylvania U.B., E.U.B. 1901-1964
> Susquehanna E.U.B. 1964-1969
> Baltimore-Washington Conference 1992

NOTE: The Session number dates from the oldest uniting unit (¶724, 2004 Book of Discipline).

CONFERENCE SESSIONS

From 1784-1939, Sessions 1-155 are recorded in the Conference Journals of 1939 and previous years. 1939-1984, Sessions 156-200, are recorded in the Conference Journals of 1984 and previous years.

* = Special or Adjourned Session

Session	Place	Date	Bishop	Secretary
*	Towson, MD	Sept. 29, 1984	Joseph H. Yeakel	Walter J. Zabel
201	Westminster, MD	June 4-7, 1985	Joseph H. Yeakel	Walter J. Zabel
202	Catonsville, MD	June 17-20, 1986	Joseph H. Yeakel	Walter J. Zabel
*	Towson, MD	Nov. 22, 1986	Joseph H. Yeakel	Walter J. Zabel
203	Frostburg, MD	June 9-12, 1987	Joseph H. Yeakel	Walter J. Zabel

*Frederick, MD	Oct. 17, 1987	Joseph H. Yeakel	Walter J. Zabel
204 Westminster, MD	June 11-13, 1988	Joseph H. Yeakel	Walter J. Zabel
205 Catonsville, MD	June 10-12, 1989	Joseph H. Yeakel	Donald S. Stewart
* Frederick, MD	Oct. 21, 1989	Joseph H. Yeakel	Donald S. Stewart
206 Westminster, MD	June 8-11, 1990	Joseph H. Yeakel	Donald S. Stewart
* Frederick, MD	Sept, 29, 1990	Joseph H. Yeakel	Donald S. Stewart
207 Frostburg, MD	June 7-10, 1991	Joseph H. Yeakel	Donald S. Stewart
* Frederick, MD	Sept. 28, 1991	Joseph H. Yeakel	Donald S. Stewart
208 Westminster, MD	June 12-15, 1992	Joseph H. Yeakel	Stanley G. Harrell
* Emmitsburg, MD	Oct. 17, 1992	Joseph H. Yeakel	Stanley G. Harrell
* Baltimore, MD	March 23, 1993	Joseph H. Yeakel	Stanley G. Harrell
209 Washington, DC	June 11-14, 1993	Joseph H. Yeakel	Stanley G. Harrell
* Emmitsburg, MD	Oct. 16, 1993	Joseph H. Yeakel	Stanley G. Harrell
210 Washington, DC	June 12, 1994	Joseph H. Yeakel	Stanley G. Harrell
* Emmitsburg, MD	Oct. 15, 1994	Joseph H. Yeakel	Stanley G. Harrell
211 Washington, DC	June 9-11, 1995	Joseph H. Yeakel	Stanley G. Harrell
* Emmitsburg, MD	Oct. 14, 1995	Joseph H. Yeakel	Stanley G. Harrell
* Frederick, MD	Feb. 20, 1996	Joseph H. Yeakel	Stanley G. Harrell
212 Washington, DC	June 14-16, 1996	Joseph H. Yeakel	Stanley G. Harrell
* Emmitsburg, MD	Oct. 12, 1996	Felton Edwin May	Stanley G. Harrell
213 Washington, DC	June 19-22, 1997	Felton Edwin May	Stanley G. Harrell
* Emmitsburg, MD	Oct. 11, 1997	Felton Edwin May	Stanley G. Harrell
214 Washington, DC	June 11-14, 1998	Felton Edwin May	Stanley G. Harrell
215 Washington, DC	June 10-13, 1999	Felton Edwin May	Stanley G. Harrell
216 Washington, DC	June 15-18, 2000	Felton Edwin May	Stanley G. Harrell
217 Washington, DC	June 7-10, 2001	Felton Edwin May	Stanley G. Harrell
218 Washington, DC	June 6-9, 2002	Felton Edwin May	Stanley G. Harrell
219 Washington, DC	June 12-15, 2003	Felton Edwin May	Stanley G. Harrell
220 Washington, DC	May 27-30, 2004	Felton Edwin May	Stanley G. Harrell
221 Baltimore, MD	May 26-29, 2005	John R. Schol	Albert L. Clipp
222 Baltimore, MD	May 25-27, 2006	John R. Schol	Albert L. Clipp
223 Washington, DC	May 24-26, 2007	John R. Schol	Albert L. Clipp
224 National Harbor, MD	May 22-24, 2008	John R. Schol	Albert L. Clipp
* Washington, DC	January 17, 2009	John R. Schol	Albert L. Clipp
225 Baltimore, MD	June 4-6, 2009	John R. Schol	Albert L. Clipp
226 Baltimore, MD	June 2-4, 2010	John R. Schol	Mary Jo Sims
227 Baltimore, MD	May 26-28, 2011	John R. Schol	Mary Jo Sims
228 Baltimore, MD	May 30-June 1, 2012	John R. Schol	Mary Jo Sims
* Baltimore, MD	May 4, 2013	Marcus Matthews	Mary Jo Sims
229 Baltimore, MD	May 29-31, 2013	Marcus Matthews	Mary Jo Sims
* Towson, MD	May 15 & 17, 2014	Marcus Matthews	Mary Jo Sims
230 Baltimore, MD	May 29-31, 2014	Marcus Matthews	Mary Jo Sims
* Baltimore, MD	May 27, 2015	Marcus Matthews	Mary Jo Sims
231 Baltimore, MD	May 28-30, 2015	Marcus Matthews	Mary Jo Sims
232 Washington, DC	June 1-4, 2016	Marcus Matthews	Mary Jo Sims
233 Washington, DC	May 31-June 2, 2017	LaTrelle Easterling	Cynthia Taylor
234 Baltimore, MD	May 30-June 1, 2018	LaTrelle Easterling	Cynthia Taylor
235 Baltimore, MD	May 29-June 1, 2019	LaTrelle Easterling	Cynthia Taylor

X. MISCELLANEOUS

EXTENSION MINISTRIES

Clergy members are listed according to the categories of ¶344.1.
a. Within the connectional structures of United Methodism (¶344.1a, c)? INFORMATIONAL

Clergy	Base Salary	Housing	Total
Aldridge, Chip Dale	$58,862	$20,000	$79,862
Alsgaard, Erik	$103,130	$ -	$103,130
Anderson, Cheryl B.	$62,134	$22,000	$85,634
Arroyo, Giovanni	$73,981	$38,200	$112,181
Bentzinger, Rebecca J.	$ -	$ -	$ -
Bropleh, Laurence Konmla	$ -	$ -	$ -
Brown, Alexis F	$75,880	$ -	$75,880
Brown, William	$122,640	$ -	$122,640
Chaney, William T	$47,840	$26,999	$76,540
Cogman, Johnsie	$131,990	$ -	$131,990
Cole Wilson, Stacey	$92,910	$ -	$92,910
Duckett, Wanda Bynum	$131,990	$ -	$131,990
Green, Gerard A.	$131,990	$ -	$131,990
Heath-Mason, Joey P.	$66,310	$ -	$66,310
Hohne, Donald J	$55,000	$ -	$55,000
Iannicelli, Rebecca K.	$131,990	$ -	$131,990
Kim, Hea Sun	$71,000	$ -	$71,000
Koikoi, Raphael K.	$44,000	$20,000	$69,000
Laprade, Ann	$131,990	$ -	$131,990
Lee, KyungLim Shin	$61,000	$ -	$61,000
Ludlum, Beth	$ -	$ -	$ -
Mulenga, Maidstone	$70,000	$40,000	$110,000
Norvell, Laura	$ -	$ -	$ -
Nupp, John W	$89,310	$ -	$89,310
Park, HiRho Yoon	$63,379	$20,000	$95,379
Park, JW	$131,990	$ -	$131,990
Powe, Frederick Douglas	$105,000	$ -	$105,000
Recinos, Harold Joseph	$60,000	$ -	$60,000
Rivera, Edgardo	$131,990	$ -	$131,990
Schaefer, Mark A.	$97,800	$ -	$97,800
Smothers, Rodney	$122,640	$ -	$122,640
Teasdale, Mark R.	$51,177	$34,800	$87,477
Wunderlich, John	$131,990	$ -	$131,990
Young, Evan D.	$ -	$ -	$ -

b. To ministries endorsed by the Board of Higher Education and Ministry (¶344.1b)?
INFORMATIONAL

Clergy	Base Salary	Housing	Total
Hall, Kimberly	$66,333	$22,960	$89,293
Holmes, Christopher T.	$150,000	$ -	$150,000
Lloyd, Solomon Octavius	$59,664	$1,872	$61,536
Rector, Saundra	$52,500	$ -	$55,000
Young, Mark Condron	$ -	$ -	$ -

c. To other valid ministries under the provisions of ¶344.1d? (2/3 v)

Clergy	Base Salary	Housing	Total
Coates, Gregory A	$68,000	$ -	$68,000
Cornwell, Rachel	$ -	$ -	$ -
Frazier, Malcolm	$ -	$ -	$ -
Graves, David	$ -	$ -	$ -
Halsey, Elizabeth L.	$130,000	$ -	$130,000
Hayden, Jessica Statesman	$20,736		$20,736
Hutchinson, Whit	$ -	$ -	$ -
Johnson, Michael C.	$3,000	$ -	$3,000
King, Curtis D.	$20,000	$ -	$20,000
Lancaster, Mark Alan	$83,000	$ -	$83,000
Matheny, Claire	$ -	$ -	$ -
Pumphrey, Randy W.	$72,155	$ -	$72,155
Oskvig, Bryant Melvin	$75,300	$ -	$75,300
Reddix, Irance	$14,400	$ -	$14,400
Strong, Douglas M.	$82,000	$ -	$82,000
Tracey, Janet Deitiker	$51,000	$ -	$51,000
Thames, Theresa S.	$95,369	$ -	$95,369
Van Gilder, Kirk	$77,093	$ -	$77,093
Wood, Chris A.	$154,500	$ -	$154,500
Wright, Kevin	$150,000	$ -	$150,000
Wright, Rebecca A.	$ -	$ -	$ -
Yunger, Doratha	$ -	$ -	$ -

JOINT SCHOLARSHIP COORDINATING TASK FORCE

Fund	Student	Award	Gender	Race/ Ethnicity	Church	District
UMW	Alexis Gray	$500.00	F	African American	Metropol-itan	BM
	Amelia Baker	$500.00	F	Caucasion	Rehoboth	CH
	Aranzasu Gasca Chable	$500.00	F	Hispanic	Hughes	GW
	Brandy Smith	$500.00	F	African American	Franklin	AN
	Hayden Klemanski	$500.00	F	Caucasion	Walkers-ville	FR
	Kyah King	$500.00	F	African American	Christ	GW
	Leah Hill	$500.00	F	African American	Union	WE
	Madeline Case	$500.00	F	Caucasion	Friendship	AN
	Rebecca Denny	$500.00	F	Caucasion	Catonsville	BM
	Surreya Clark-McMillan	$500.00	F	African American	Macedonia	AN
	Swetha Thomas	$500.00	F	Asian	First India	GW
	Syncere Johnson	$500.00	F	African American	Wilson Memorial	AN
UMM	James Sayers	$400.00	M	Hispanic	La Plata	WE
	John Shaw	$400.00	M	African American	Gethse-mane	GW
	Michael Rowan	$400.00	M	Caucasion	John Wesley	CH
Trustees	David Burgess	$500.00	M	Caucasion	Liberty Grove	GW
	Kenneth Walker	$500.00	M	African American	Colesville	GW
	Natasha Teckham	$500.00	F	African American	First	GW
Francis Asbury	Annika Rudolph	$2,000.00	F	Caucasion	St Johns	BS
	Mei-Lin Vader	$2,000.00	F	Asian	Emmanuel	GW
	Natalie Deans	$2,000.00	F	Caucasion	Oakdale Emory	CM
	Jeremy Park	$750.00	M	Asian	Lanham	WE

	Robert Barnes	$750.00	M	Caucasion	Mount Oak Fellowship	WE
	Jacob Young	$600.00	M	Caucasion	Friendship	AN
	Rebekah Harner	$600.00	F	Caucasion	Perry Hall	BS
BWC Merit	Karis Arnold	$1,200.50	F	Caucasion	Calvary	A
	Rachel Cheston	$1,200.50	F	Caucasion	Brook Hill	F

AUDIT

ELLIN & TUCKER

THE BALTIMORE-WASHINGTON CONFERENCE OF THE UNITED
METHODIST CHURCH, INC., SUBSIDIARY AND AFFILIATE
COMBINED FINANCIAL STATEMENTS
DECEMBER 31, 2018 AND 2017

Baltimore-Washington Conference
The United Methodist Church

TABLE OF CONTENTS
The Baltimore-Washington Conference of the United
Methodist Church, Inc., Subsidiary and Affiliate
December 31, 2018 and 2017

INDEPENDENT AUDITORS' REPORT 1-2

COMBINED STATEMENTS OF FINANCIAL POSITION 3

COMBINED STATEMENTS OF ACTIVITIES 4-5

COMBINED STATEMENTS OF CASH FLOWS 6

NOTES TO COMBINED FINANCIAL STATEMENTS 7-22

SUPPLEMENTARY INFORMATION

    Independent Auditors' Report on Supplementary Information 23

    Combining Schedule – Statements of Financial Position 24-25

    Combining Schedule – Statements of Activities Without Donor
        Restrictions 26

    Statements of Activities – The United Methodist Church,
        Washington Area Episcopal Office 27

ELLIN & TUCKER

ELLIN & TUCKER

INDEPENDENT AUDITORS' REPORT

To the Council on Finance and Administration of
The Baltimore-Washington Conference of the United Methodist Church, Inc.

REPORT ON THE COMBINED FINANCIAL STATEMENTS

We have audited the accompanying combined financial statements of The Baltimore-Washington Conference of the United Methodist Church, Inc., Subsidiary and The United Methodist Church, Washington Area Episcopal Office (Affiliate) (collectively referred to as the Conference), which comprise the Combined Statements of Financial Position as of December 31, 2018 and 2017, and the related Combined Statements of Activities and Cash Flows for the years then ended, and the related notes to the combined financial statements.

MANAGEMENT'S RESPONSIBILITY FOR THE COMBINED FINANCIAL STATEMENTS

Management is responsible for the preparation and fair presentation of these combined financial statements in accordance with accounting principles generally accepted in the United States of America; this includes the design, implementation, and maintenance of internal control relevant to the preparation and fair presentation of combined financial statements that are free from material misstatement, whether due to fraud or error.

AUDITORS' RESPONSIBILITY

Our responsibility is to express an opinion on these combined financial statements based on our audits. We conducted our audits in accordance with auditing standards generally accepted in the United States of America. Those standards require that we plan and perform the audits to obtain reasonable assurance about whether the combined financial statements are free from material misstatement.

An audit involves performing procedures to obtain audit evidence about the amounts and disclosures in the combined financial statements. The procedures selected depend on the auditors' judgment, including the assessment of the risks of material misstatement of the combined financial statements, whether due to fraud or error. In making those risk assessments, the auditors consider internal control relevant to the entity's preparation and fair presentation of the combined financial statements in order to design audit procedures that are appropriate in the circumstances but not for the purpose of expressing an opinion on the effectiveness of the entity's internal control. Accordingly, we express no such opinion. An audit also includes evaluating the appropriateness of accounting policies used and the reasonableness of the significant accounting estimates made by management, as well as evaluating the overall presentation of the combined financial statements.

We believe the audit evidence we have obtained is sufficient and appropriate to provide a basis for our qualified audit opinion.

ELLIN & TUCKER

INDEPENDENT AUDITORS' REPORT, CONTINUED

BASIS FOR QUALIFIED OPINION

As more fully described in Note 8 to the combined financial statements, the Conference accounts for post-retirement health benefit obligations on a pay-as-you-go basis. In our opinion, accounting principles generally accepted in the United States of America require the funded status of the post-retirement health benefit obligations be recorded in the Combined Statements of Financial Position and changes in the funded status be recognized as changes in net assets in the year the change occurs. The effects on the combined financial statements of the preceding practice are not reasonably determinable.

QUALIFIED OPINION

In our opinion, except for the effects of the matter discussed in the Basis for Qualified Opinion paragraph, the combined financial statements referred to in the first paragraph present fairly, in all material respects, the financial position of the Conference as of December 31, 2018 and 2017, and the results of its operations and its cash flows for the years then ended in accordance with accounting principles generally accepted in the United States of America.

Ellin + Tucker

ELLIN & TUCKER
Certified Public Accountants

Baltimore, Maryland
May 20, 2019

612

COMBINED STATEMENTS OF FINANCIAL POSITION
The Baltimore-Washington Conference of the United
Methodist Church, Inc., Subsidiary and Affiliate
December 31, 2018 and 2017

ASSETS

	2018	2017
ASSETS		
Cash and Cash Equivalents	$ 14,652,762	$ 15,205,440
Investments, at Fair Value (Note 3)	53,133,926	51,119,888
Notes Receivable, Net (Note 4)	1,276,599	779,580
Mortgages Receivable (Note 4)	2,098,665	2,178,687
Other Receivables, Net	90,686	52,842
Prepaid Expenses	25,456	179
Property and Equipment, Net (Note 5)	10,542,743	11,085,339
Total Assets	$ 81,820,837	$ 80,421,955

LIABILITIES AND NET ASSETS

	2018	2017
LIABILITIES		
Notes Payable (Note 6)	$ 3,140,684	$ 4,054,018
Funds Due to Others (Note 1)	1,167,459	1,338,713
Accounts Payable and Accrued Expenses	1,317,203	1,272,264
Total Liabilities	5,625,346	6,664,995

COMMITMENTS AND CONTINGENCIES (Notes 7, 8 and 9)

	2018	2017
NET ASSETS		
Without Donor Restrictions:		
Operating	20,277,023	20,022,974
Episcopal Office	(67,192)	(57,227)
Net Investment in Property	2,149,884	2,809,069
Medical Benefits	5,070,593	5,070,593
Designated for Loans	3,428,265	3,428,265
Designated for Post-Retirement Health Benefits (Note 8)	42,004,037	39,086,379
	72,862,610	70,360,053
With Donor Restrictions (Note 10)	3,332,881	3,396,907
Total Net Assets	76,195,491	73,756,960
Total Liabilities and Net Assets	$ 81,820,837	$ 80,421,955

(See Independent Auditors' Report and Accompanying Notes)

ELLIN & TUCKER

COMBINED STATEMENT OF ACTIVITIES
The Baltimore-Washington Conference of the United
Methodist Church, Inc., Subsidiary and Affiliate
For the Year Ended December 31, 2018

	Without Donor Restrictions					With Donor Restrictions	Total
	Operating and Designated for Post-Retirement Health Benefits	Property	Medical Benefits	Designated for Loans	Total		
REVENUE							
Mission Shares	$ 14,045,682	$	$	$	$ 14,045,682	$ -	$ 14,045,682
Medical Payments	8,053,747				8,053,747	-	8,053,747
Investment Return, Net (Note 3)	(2,739,413)				(2,739,413)	(106,975)	(2,846,388)
Contributions and Bequests						151,643	151,643
Camping Registrations and Donations	1,580,901				1,580,901	-	1,580,901
Seminar and Event Registration	303,064				303,064	-	303,064
Annual Conference Fees	203,422				203,422	-	203,422
Funds Held for Giving						507,483	507,483
Other	10,072,773				10,072,773	56,254	10,129,027
Satisfaction of Purpose Restrictions (Note 10)	672,431				672,431	(672,431)	-
Total Revenue	32,192,607				32,192,607	(64,026)	32,128,581
EXPENSES							
Apportioned Funds:							
Discipleship	5,792,025				5,792,025	-	5,792,025
Stewardship	7,189,656				7,189,656	-	7,189,656
Leadership	2,994,461				2,994,461	-	2,994,461
General Church and Jurisdictional Mission Shares	3,571,610				3,571,610	-	3,571,610
Nonapportioned Funds:							
Program Funds	2,533,951				2,533,951	-	2,533,951
Medical (Note 8)	6,448,579				6,448,579	-	6,448,579
Funds Held for Giving	500,583				500,583	-	500,583
Depreciation		659,185			659,185	-	659,185
Total Expenses	29,030,865	659,185			29,690,050	-	29,690,050
Change in Net Assets	3,161,742	(659,185)			2,502,557	(64,026)	2,438,531
NET ASSETS - BEGINNING OF YEAR	59,052,126	2,809,069	5,070,593	3,428,265	70,360,053	3,396,907	73,756,960
NET ASSETS - END OF YEAR	$ 62,213,868	$ 2,149,884	$ 5,070,593	$ 3,428,265	$ 72,862,610	$ 3,332,881	$ 76,195,491

(See Independent Auditors' Report and Accompanying Notes)

PAGE | 4

ELLIN & TUCKER

COMBINED STATEMENT OF ACTIVITIES
The Baltimore-Washington Conference of the United Methodist Church, Inc., Subsidiary and Affiliate
For the Year Ended December 31, 2017

	Without Donor Restrictions					With Donor Restrictions	Total
	Operating and Designated for Post-Retirement Health Benefits	Property	Medical Benefits	Designated for Loans	Total		
REVENUE							
Mission Shares	$ 14,288,609	$ -	$ -	$ -	$ 14,288,609	$ -	$ 14,288,609
Medical Payments	6,056,094	-	-	-	6,056,094	-	6,056,094
Investment Return, Net (Note 3)	6,195,619	-	-	-	6,195,619	350,171	6,545,790
Contributions and Bequests	-	-	-	-	-	191,711	191,711
Camping Registrations and Donations	1,527,942	-	-	-	1,527,942	-	1,527,942
Seminar and Event Registration	296,775	-	-	-	296,775	-	296,775
Annual Conference Fees	203,210	-	-	-	203,210	-	203,210
Funds Held for Giving	-	-	-	-	-	1,041,262	1,041,262
Other	7,989,660	-	-	-	7,989,660	58,522	8,048,182
Satisfaction of Purpose Restrictions (Note 10)	1,406,480	-	-	-	1,406,480	(1,406,480)	-
Total Revenue	37,964,389	-	-	-	37,964,389	235,186	38,199,575
EXPENSES							
Apportioned Funds:							
Discipleship	4,805,622	-	-	-	4,805,622	-	4,805,622
Stewardship	5,045,862	-	-	-	5,045,862	-	5,045,862
Leadership	3,360,042	-	-	-	3,360,042	-	3,360,042
General Church and Jurisdictional Mission Shares	3,550,351	-	-	-	3,550,351	-	3,550,351
Nonapportioned Funds:							
Program Funds	2,035,190	-	-	-	2,035,190	-	2,035,190
Medical (Note 8)	6,137,239	-	-	-	6,137,239	-	6,137,239
Funds Held for Giving	1,039,213	-	-	-	1,039,213	-	1,039,213
Depreciation	-	743,880	-	-	743,880	-	743,880
Total Expenses	25,973,519	743,880	-	-	26,717,399	-	26,717,399
Change in Net Assets	11,990,870	(743,880)	-	-	11,246,990	235,186	11,482,176
NET ASSETS - BEGINNING OF YEAR	47,061,256	3,552,949	5,070,593	3,428,265	59,113,063	3,161,721	62,274,784
NET ASSETS - END OF YEAR	$ 59,052,126	$ 2,809,069	$ 5,070,593	$ 3,428,265	$ 70,360,053	$ 3,396,907	$ 73,756,960

(See Independent Auditors' Report and Accompanying Notes)

PAGE 5

BALTIMORE-WASHINGTON CONFERENCE

COMBINED STATEMENTS OF CASH FLOWS
The Baltimore-Washington Conference of the United
Methodist Church, Inc., Subsidiary and Affiliate
For the Years Ended December 31, 2018 and 2017

	2018	2017
CASH FLOWS FROM OPERATING ACTIVITIES		
Change in Net Assets	$ 2,438,531	$ 11,482,176
Adjustments to Reconcile Change in Net Assets to Net		
Cash Provided by Operating Activities:		
Depreciation	669,245	743,880
Increase in Allowance for Doubtful Accounts	162,642	261,813
Loss on Sale of Equipment	-	11,894
Realized Gain on Sale of Investments	(232,116)	(389,225)
Unrealized Depreciation (Appreciation) of Investments	3,230,363	(6,034,885)
Net Changes in:		
Other Receivables	(229,678)	(128,196)
Other Assets	(25,277)	45,213
Accounts Payable and Accrued Expenses	(126,315)	(20,482)
Net Cash Provided by Operating Activities	5,887,395	5,972,188
CASH FLOWS FROM INVESTING ACTIVITIES		
Proceeds from Sale of Investments	1,741,810	1,896,422
Purchase of Investments	(6,754,095)	(5,651,332)
Advances on Notes Receivable	(669,386)	(114,298)
Collection on Notes Receivable	201,559	219,031
Advances on Mortgage Receivable	-	(315,000)
Collection on Mortgage Receivable	80,022	68,348
Purchases of Property and Equipment	(126,649)	(100,977)
Net Cash Used in Investing Activities	(5,526,739)	(3,997,806)
CASH FLOWS FROM FINANCING ACTIVITIES		
Principal Payments on Notes Payable	(913,334)	(1,215,982)
Net Change in Cash and Cash Equivalents	(552,678)	758,400
CASH AND CASH EQUIVALENTS - BEGINNING OF YEAR	15,205,440	14,447,040
CASH AND CASH EQUIVALENTS - END OF YEAR	$ 14,652,762	$ 15,205,440
SUPPLEMENTAL DISCLOSURE OF CASH FLOW INFORMATION		
Cash Paid for Interest for the Year	$ 182,398	$ 214,243

(See Independent Auditors' Report and Accompanying Notes)

ELLIN & TUCKER

NOTE 1   SUMMARY OF SIGNIFICANT ACCOUNTING POLICIES

NATURE OF ACTIVITIES

The Baltimore-Washington Conference of the United Methodist Church, Inc. (BWC) was formed to provide for the promotion of the Christian faith, missionary, and benevolent causes.

BWC Borrower, LLC was formed to finance, manage, and maintain property and operate a management business for this purpose. BWC is the sole member of BWC Borrower, LLC.

The United Methodist Church, Washington Area Episcopal Office (Episcopal Office) was formed to manage many aspects of BWC, including presiding over sessions, overseeing fiscal and program operations, and ensuring fair process.

PRINCIPLES OF COMBINATION

The combined financial statements include the accounts of BWC, BWC Borrower, LLC and the Episcopal Office (collectively referred to as the Conference). All significant intercompany balances and transactions have been eliminated.

ACCOUNTING STANDARDS CODIFICATION

All references in the combined financial statements to the Codification refer to the Accounting Standards Codification and the Hierarchy of Generally Accepted Accounting Principles (GAAP) issued by the Financial Accounting Standards Board (FASB). The Codification is the single source of authoritative GAAP in the United States.

NEW ACCOUNTING STANDARD ADOPTED

In August 2016, the FASB issued Accounting Standards Update (ASU) 2016-14, Not-for-Profit Entities (Topic 958): Presentation of Financial Statements of Not-for-Profit Entities. The ASU amends the current reporting model for not-for-profit organizations and enhances their required disclosures. The Conference has adopted this ASU as of and for the year ended December 31, 2018 with retrospective application for the combined financial statements for the year ended December 31, 2017. As a result, the Conference changed its presentation of its net asset classes and expanded the disclosures as required by the ASU. The Conference opted not to present expenses by both their natural classification and functional classification in one location for 2018 as permitted under the ASU in the year of adoption.

(See Independent Auditors' Report)

ELLIN & TUCKER

NOTES TO COMBINED FINANCIAL STATEMENTS, CONTINUED
The Baltimore-Washington Conference of the United
Methodist Church, Inc., Subsidiary and Affiliate

BASIS OF ACCOUNTING AND PRESENTATION

The combined financial statements have been prepared on the accrual basis of accounting in accordance with GAAP. Under the accrual basis of accounting, support and revenue are recorded when earned and expenses are recorded when incurred. Net assets, revenues and expenses are classified based on the existence or absence of donor-imposed restrictions.

Net assets without donor restriction are assets that have not been restricted by donor-imposed stipulations. These resources include:

- Operating – to support operations
- Property – designated for property acquisitions
- Medical Benefits – designated by the Board to fund medical premiums
- Designated for Loans – to fund low interest loans to the United Methodist Churches
- Designated for Post-Retirement Health Benefits – to fund post-retirement health benefits

Net assets with donor restrictions consist of assets whose use is limited by donor-imposed, time or purpose restrictions.

USE OF ESTIMATES

The preparation of combined financial statements in conformity with GAAP requires management to make estimates and assumptions. These estimates and assumptions affect the reported amounts of assets and liabilities and disclosure of contingent assets and liabilities at the date of the combined financial statements and revenues and expenses during the reporting period. Actual results could differ from those estimates.

CASH AND CASH EQUIVALENTS

The Conference considers all highly liquid investments with original maturities of three months or less to be cash equivalents.

The Conference maintains its cash in financial institutions which, at times, may exceed federally insured limits. The Conference believes it is not exposed to any significant credit risk on cash and cash equivalents.

FUNDS DUE TO OTHERS

Amounts represent proceeds from the sale of a church property, which is due to the Greater Washington District.

(See Independent Auditors' Report)

INVESTMENTS

Under the Codification, investments are recorded at fair value. Investments received as gifts and bequests are recorded at fair value at the gift date. To adjust the carrying value of the investments, realized and unrealized gains and losses are reported in the Combined Statements of Activities. See Note 3 for further discussion of the valuation of investments. The Conference invests in a professionally managed portfolio that contains stocks and bonds of publicly traded companies, mutual funds, and pooled investments. Such investments are exposed to various risks, such as interest rate, market, and credit. Due to the level of risk associated with such investments and the level of uncertainty related to the changes in the value of such investments, it is at least reasonably possible that changes in risks in the near-term would materially affect investment balances and the amounts reported in the combined financial statements.

OTHER RECEIVABLES

Other receivables include amounts due from individuals and organizations related to the Conference for pension and medical costs. At December 31, 2018 and 2017, management recorded an allowance for uncollectible accounts of $1,047,553 and $966,296, respectively.

PROPERTY AND EQUIPMENT

Property and equipment greater than $2,500 are recorded at cost if purchased or fair value at the date of the donation if gifted. Lesser amounts are expensed. Depreciation is determined using the straight-line method over the estimated useful lives of the related assets.

MISSION SHARES

The Conference receives a significant portion of its revenue in the form of mission shares from local churches that are members of the Conference. Mission shares are accepted from the local churches; however, they are not a legal obligation. As such, mission shares are recognized as revenue when received, since the amount to be received is undeterminable until paid by the local churches. The Conference's mission share policy is to include mission shares received by Tuesday following the second Sunday subsequent to the date of the accompanying Combined Statements of Financial Position. Mission shares are used to fund mission and ministries of the Conference and General Church World Services.

MEDICAL PAYMENTS

The Conference receives premiums from local churches that are members of the Conference. These premiums are used to pay for medical insurance for clergy and lay employees of the Conference.

(See Independent Auditors' Report)

CONTRIBUTIONS

Contributions are recorded when the donor makes a promise to give to the Conference that is, in substance, unconditional. Contributions received and unconditional promises to give are measured at their fair values and reported as support within net assets with donor restrictions or net assets without donor restrictions depending on the existence and nature of any donor restrictions.

CAMPING REGISTRATION AND EVENTS

The Conference receives registration fees for camps owned and operated by the Conference. The Conference also hosts numerous seminars and conferences throughout the year, for which registration fees are collected by the Conference. Revenue is recognized in the year such services and events occur.

PROGRAM EXPENSE

Apportioned funds categories represent the following:

- Discipleship – All department staffing costs for the Councils on Ministries and Human Resource Development as well as the activities of the ministries, missions performed within the Conference, establishing new churches, growth of existing churches, activities and programs undertaken to develop both clergy and lay religious education, and spiritual enrichment of all clergy and lay persons within the Conference
- Stewardship – All financial and administrative components of the Conference, including the treasury function, trustees, pension and health benefits for clergy and lay employees and costs of the Conference Center offices
- Leadership – Costs for departments linked directly to the Bishop's office
- General Church and Jurisdictional Mission Shares – Funds collected by the Conference from local churches and designated by the Conference to send to General Church and World Services

RECLASSIFICATIONS

Certain prior year amounts have been reclassified to conform to the current year presentation.

NOTE 2   INCOME TAXES

The Conference is exempt from income taxes under Section 501(c)(3) of the Internal Revenue Code and is exempt from filing tax returns as a religious organization. In addition, the Internal Revenue Service has determined that the Conference is not a private foundation within the meaning of Section 509(a) of the Code.

(See Independent Auditors' Report)

620

NOTES TO COMBINED FINANCIAL STATEMENTS, CONTINUED
The Baltimore-Washington Conference of the United
Methodist Church, Inc., Subsidiary and Affiliate

The Conference follows the provisions of Accounting for Uncertainty in Income Taxes under the Income Taxes Topic of the Codification. The Codification requires the evaluation of tax positions, which include maintaining its tax-exempt status and the taxability of any unrelated business income, and does not allow recognition of tax positions which do not meet a "more-likely-than-not" threshold of being sustained by the applicable tax authority. Management does not believe it has taken any tax positions that would not meet this threshold.

NOTE 3 VALUATION OF INVESTMENTS

Investments at December 31, 2018 and 2017 consisted of the following:

	2018	2017
Common Stocks	$ 1,715,285	$ 1,804,951
Nonpublic Mutual Funds	7,484,191	7,329,630
Bond Mutual Funds	226,386	234,042
Pooled Investments	43,708,064	41,751,265
Total	$ 53,133,926	$ 51,119,888

Investment return for the years ended December 31, 2018 and 2017 consisted of the following:

	2018	2017
Interest and Dividends	$ 268,528	$ 204,884
Realized Gain on Sale of Investments	232,116	389,225
Unrealized (Loss) Gain on Investments	(3,230,363)	6,034,885
	(2,729,719)	6,628,994
Less: Investment Fees	116,669	83,204
Total	$ (2,846,388)	$ 6,545,790

The Fair Value Measurements and Disclosures Topic of the Codification establishes a hierarchal disclosure framework, which prioritizes and ranks the level of market price observability used in measuring investments and other financial instruments at fair value. The hierarchy gives the highest priority to unadjusted quoted prices in active markets for identical assets or liabilities (Level 1 measurements) and the lowest priority to unobservable inputs (Level 3 measurements). The three levels of the fair value hierarchy are described below:

(See Independent Auditors' Report)

Level 1 – Quoted prices are available in active markets for identical investments as of the reporting date. The Conference considers its investments in common stocks and mutual funds to be Level 1 investments.

Level 2 – Pricing inputs are other than quoted prices in active markets, which are either directly or indirectly observable as of the reporting date, and fair value is determined through the use of models or other valuation methodologies. The Conference considers certain nonpublic mutual funds and pooled investments to be Level 2 investments.

Level 3 – Pricing inputs are unobservable for the investment and include situations where there is little, if any, market activity for the investment. The Conference does not currently hold any Level 3 investments.

In certain cases, the inputs used to measure fair value may be categorized into different levels of the fair value hierarchy. In such cases, an investment's level within the fair value hierarchy is based on the lowest level of input that is significant to the fair value measurement. The Conference's assessment of the significance of a particular input to the fair value measurement in its entirety requires judgment and considers factors specific to the investment. There were no changes in these methodologies during the years ended December 31, 2018 and 2017.

The following are descriptions of the valuation methodologies used for assets measured at fair value:

Common Stock and Bond Mutual Funds: Valued at quoted prices in an active market

Nonpublic Mutual Funds: Valued at the net asset value per share that may be redeemed at the date of the Combined Statements of Financial Position

Pooled Investments: Investments through the General Board of Pensions and Health Benefits of the United Methodist Church (General Board), which consist of diversified nonpublic mutual funds and are valued using the net asset value per share that may be redeemed at the date of the Combined Statements of Financial Position

The methods described above may produce a fair value that may not be indicative of net realizable value or reflective of future fair values. Furthermore, while the Conference believes its valuation methods are appropriate and consistent with other market participants, the use of different methodologies or assumptions to determine the fair value of certain financial instruments could result in a different fair value measurement at the reporting date.

(See Independent Auditors' Report)

The table below presents the balances of assets and liabilities measured at fair value on a recurring basis by level within the hierarchy as of December 31, 2018:

	Level 1	Level 2	Total
Common Stocks:			
Consumer	$ 187,630	$ -	$ 187,630
Energy	21,648	-	21,648
Financial	101,804	-	101,804
Health Care	249,973	-	249,973
Industrial and Materials	445,958	-	445,958
Technology and Telecommunications	694,107	-	694,107
Utilities	14,165	-	14,165
Nonpublic Mutual Funds:			
Equity	-	1,407,298	1,407,298
Growth	-	749,784	749,784
Value	-	685,357	685,357
Bond	-	3,076,341	3,076,341
International	-	1,565,411	1,565,411
Bond Mutual Funds	226,386	-	226,386
Pooled Investments	-	43,708,064	43,708,064
Total	$ 1,941,671	$ 51,192,255	$ 53,133,926

The table below presents the balances of assets and liabilities measured at fair value on a recurring basis by level within the hierarchy as of December 31, 2017:

	Level 1	Level 2	Total
Common Stocks:			
Consumer	$ 208,454	$ -	$ 208,454
Energy	40,434	-	40,434
Financial	105,934	-	105,934
Health Care	250,578	-	250,578
Industrial and Materials	489,149	-	489,149
Technology and Telecommunications	643,423	-	643,423
Utilities	66,979	-	66,979
Nonpublic Mutual Funds:			
Equity	-	1,212,567	1,212,567
Growth	-	850,761	850,761
Value	-	780,604	780,604
Bond	-	2,818,410	2,818,410
International	-	1,667,285	1,667,285
Bond Mutual Funds	234,042	-	234,042
Pooled Investments	-	41,751,268	41,751,268
Total	$ 2,038,993	$ 49,080,895	$ 51,119,888

(See Independent Auditors' Report)

ELLIN & TUCKER

NOTE 4   NOTES AND MORTGAGES RECEIVABLE

Notes receivable of $1,276,599 and $779,580 in 2018 and 2017, respectively, represent the net amount of loans issued at interest rates ranging up to 4.5%.

Future maturities of these notes at December 31, 2018 are as follows:

Year Ending December 31,		
2019	$	267,321
2020		198,877
2021		188,676
2022		156,572
2023		128,850
Thereafter		1,016,944
		1,957,240
Less: Allowance for Doubtful Notes Receivable		680,641
	$	1,276,599

Two mortgages receivable bear interest at fixed rates of 7% and 6% and require monthly payments of principal and interest of $1,658 and $13,254 through April 2031 and January 2020, respectively. A lump-sum payment of the remaining balance is required for the mortgage receivable maturing in January 2020. A third mortgage receivable bears interest at a rate of 2% for the first year, increasing 1% annually to 6% at December 2020, through the maturity date of November 2037. Monthly payments of principal and interest of $1,594 are required in the first year, $1,740 in the second year, $1,886 in the third year, and $2,184 through maturity.

Future maturities of mortgages receivable at December 31, 2018 are as follows:

Year Ending December 31,		
2019	$	82,747
2020		1,591,671
2021		19,777
2022		21,103
2023		22,519
Thereafter		360,848
	$	2,098,665

(See Independent Auditors' Report)

NOTE 5 **PROPERTY AND EQUIPMENT**

Property and equipment as of December 31, 2018 and 2017 consisted of the following:

	2018	2017
Land	$ 1,641,316	$ 1,641,316
Building and Improvements	16,768,557	16,686,681
Furniture, Fixtures, and Equipment	2,679,157	2,598,301
Vehicles	232,142	232,143
Construction in Progress	-	14,155
	21,321,172	21,172,596
Less: Accumulated Depreciation	10,778,429	10,087,257
	$ 10,542,743	$ 11,085,339

The Conference owns approximately 570 acres of land used by the Outdoor Ministries. The land was donated to the Conference during the period 1948 through 1960 for which no value was determined and, therefore, no amount is included in the Combined Statements of Financial Position.

Depreciation expense was $669,245 and $743,880 for the years ended December 31, 2018 and 2017, respectively.

NOTE 6 **NOTES PAYABLE**

The Conference has a note payable to the Board of Childcare of the United Methodist Church. Borrowings bear interest at 3.25%, subject to adjustment at specified dates. The note requires quarterly principal and interest payments through June 30, 2029. The note is collateralized by the conference center in Maple Lawn, Maryland and the West River Methodist Center property. The balance on this note was $3,140,684 and $4,054,018 at December 31, 2018 and 2017, respectively.

Future maturities at December 31, 2018 are as follows:

Year Ending December 31,	2019	$ 413,333
	2020	413,333
	2021	413,333
	2022	413,333
	2023	413,333
	Thereafter	1,074,019
		$ 3,140,684

(See Independent Auditors' Report)

ELLIN & TUCKER

NOTE 7   PENSION EXPENSE

The Conference participates in three multi-employer pension plans, which are administered by the General Board. The Conference provides pension benefits for members of the clergy under the three plans. Services provided prior to January 1, 1982 are covered by a defined benefit plan (Pre-82 Plan). The General Board estimated the Conference's portion of the Pre-82 Plan assets exceeded accumulated benefits by approximately $28,000,000, and the total plan assets exceeded accumulated benefits by approximately $94,000,000.

Services provided subsequent to December 31, 1981 are covered by the Ministerial Pension Plan (MPP), which has components of both a defined benefit and defined contribution plan. The Conference did not contribute any funds to MPP during 2018 or 2017. The General Board estimated MPP assets exceeded accumulated benefits by approximately $177,000,000.

Services provided subsequent to December 31, 2006 are covered under the Clergy Retirement Security Program (CRSP), which has components of both a defined benefit and defined contribution plan. The Conference contributed approximately $2,510,000 and $2,520,000 to CRSP for the years ended December 31, 2018 and 2017, respectively. The General Board estimated CRSP assets exceeded accumulated benefits by approximately $108,000,000.

The risks of participating in a multi-employer plan are different from a single-employer plan in the following aspects:

a. Assets contributed to the multi-employer plan by one employer may be used to provide benefits to employees of other participating employers.

b. If a participating employer stops contributing to the plan, the unfunded obligations of the plan may be borne by the remaining participating employers.

c. If the Conference chooses to stop participating in its multi-employer plan, the Conference may be required to pay the plan an amount based on the underfunded status of the plan, referred to as a withdrawal liability.

Lay employees of the Conference are covered by a defined contribution plan (Plan). The level and funding of retirement benefits to individual participants of the Plan are determined annually by the Conference within certain guidelines established by the General Board. The Conference contributed approximately $316,000 and $312,000 to the Plan for the years ended December 31, 2018 and 2017, respectively.

(See Independent Auditors' Report)

ELLIN & TUCKER

NOTE 8 **POST-RETIREMENT HEALTH BENEFITS**

Post-retirement health benefits for all retired personnel and their spouses, widows, and widowers are provided under a discretionary plan administered by the General Board. The Conference accounts for the obligation on a pay-as-you-go basis, and the cost of post-retirement health benefits was approximately $1,355,000 and $1,292,000 for the years ended December 31, 2018 and 2017, respectively. GAAP requires the funded status of post-retirement obligations, representing the difference between plan assets and accumulated post-retirement obligations, be recorded in the Combined Statements of Financial Position and changes in the funded status be recognized as changes in net assets in the year the change occurs. At December 31, 2018, using the most recent actuarial report available, the accumulated benefit obligation for post-retirement health benefits is approximately $33,000,000, at an assumed discount rate of 4.2%. For 2018, the assumed annual rate of increase in the cost of covered health care benefits is 7%. It is assumed to decrease gradually to 5% in 2019 and remain at that level thereafter. A one percentage point increase or decrease in the assumed health care cost trend rate would have an approximate 12% to 15% effect on the accumulated benefit obligation.

NOTE 9 **COMMITMENTS AND CONTINGENCIES**

The Conference leases office space in Washington, D.C. and Hagerstown, Maryland under leases, which expire through July 2022.

At December 31, 2018, the future minimum rental commitments are as follows:

Year Ending December 31,	2019	$ 57,671
	2020	59,974
	2021	62,368
	2022	37,216
		$ 217,229

Rent expense was $71,794 and $74,995 for the years ended December 31, 2018 and 2017, respectively.

The Conference subleases space under leases which expire through July 2022. Future minimum payments expected to be received are as follows:

Year Ending December 31,	2019	$ 30,000
	2020	30,000
	2021	30,000
	2022	17,500
		$ 107,500

(See Independent Auditors' Report)

ELLIN & TUCKER

The Conference has approximately $4,000,000 of contingent receivables. These contingent receivables are conditional donations made by the Conference to churches that are members of the Conference and are required to be repaid only if the churches cease to be members.

NOTE 10   **Net Assets with Donor Restrictions**

Net assets with donor restrictions at December 31, 2018 and 2017 are restricted for the following programs:

	2018	2017
Subject to Expenditure for Specified Purpose:		
Community Grants	$ 99,757	$ -
Inner City	31,770	31,770
Disaster Relief	16,416	68,351
Kemp Horn	4,509	4,509
Sophia Dietsch Scholarship	93,520	74,995
Reinecker Health	161,925	160,017
Quality of Life	5,742	5,742
	413,639	345,384
Subject to Conference's Spending Policy and Appropriation:		
Endowment Earnings	860,566	991,567
Baldwin Memorial Earnings	1,326	-
Area of Outdoor Ministry Endowment Earnings	305,065	310,034
Trustee Restricted Fund Scholarships Earnings	14,724	12,361
Francis Asbury Capital Earnings	5,188	5,188
	1,186,869	1,319,150
Amounts Invested in Perpetuity:		
Endowment	1,253,371	1,253,371
Baldwin Memorial	152,272	152,272
Area of Outdoor Ministry Endowment	222,621	222,621
Trustee Restricted Fund Scholarships	67,786	67,786
Francis Asbury Capital	36,323	36,323
	1,732,373	1,732,373
	$ 3,332,881	$ 3,396,907

(See Independent Auditors' Report)

ELLIN & TUCKER

The net assets released from donor restrictions were used for the following purposes:

	2018	2017
Purchased Capital Additions – Capital Funds Gifts	$ -	$ 17,380
Grants and Scholarships	74,965	49,745
Funds Held for Giving	597,466	1,339,355
	$ 672,431	$ 1,406,480

NOTE 11 ENDOWMENT FUNDS

The Conference's endowment consists of various donor restricted funds established to provide a source of income for ongoing donor advised program expenses. As required by GAAP, net assets associated with endowment funds are classified and reported based on the existence or absence of donor-imposed restrictions.

INTERPRETATION OF RELEVANT LAW

The Conference is subject to the Maryland Uniform Prudent Management of Institutional Funds Act (UPMIFA) and, thus, classifies amounts in its donor-restricted endowment funds as net assets with donor restrictions because those net assets are time restricted until the Board of Directors appropriates such amounts for expenditure. Most of those net assets also are subject to purpose restrictions that must be met before reclassifying those net assets to net assets without donor restrictions. The Conference has interpreted UPMIFA as not requiring the maintenance of purchasing power of the original gift amount contributed to an endowment fund, unless a donor stipulates the contrary. As a result of this interpretation, when reviewing its donor-restricted endowment funds, the Conference considers a fund to be underwater if the fair value of the fund is less than the sum of (a) the original value of initial and subsequent gift amounts donated to the fund and (b) any accumulations to the fund that are required to be maintained in perpetuity in accordance with the direction of the applicable donor gift instrument. The Conference has interpreted UPMIFA to permit spending from underwater funds in accordance with the prudent measures required under the law. Additionally, in accordance with UPMIFA, the Conference considers the following factors in making a determination to appropriate or accumulate donor-restricted endowment funds:

(1) Duration and preservation of the fund
(2) Purposes of the Conference and the donor-restricted endowment fund
(3) General economic conditions
(4) Possible effect of inflation and deflation
(5) Expected total return from income and the appreciation of investments
(6) Other resources of the Conference
(7) Investment policies of the Conference

(See Independent Auditors' Report)

ELLIN & TUCKER

ENDOWMENT FUND COMPOSITION BY TYPE OF FUND AS OF DECEMBER 31, 2018 AND 2017

	2018	2017
Donor-Restricted Endowment Funds:		
Original Donor-Restricted Gift Amount and Amounts		
Required to be Maintained in Perpetuity by Donor	$ 1,732,373	$ 1,732,373
Accumulated Investment Gains	1,186,869	1,319,150
	$ 2,919,242	$ 3,051,523

CHANGES IN DONOR RESTRICTED ENDOWMENT FUNDS FOR THE YEARS ENDED DECEMBER 31 2018 AND 2017:

Endowment Funds, January 1, 2017	$ 2,711,494
Investment Return, Net	350,171
Appropriation of Endowment Assets for Expenditure	10,142
Endowment Funds, December 31, 2017	3,051,523
Investment Return, Net	(106,975)
Appropriation of Endowment Assets for Expenditure	25,306
Endowment Funds, December 31, 2018	$ 2,919,242

RETURN OBJECTIVES AND RISK PARAMETERS

The Conference's investment policy is to provide a common investment vehicle, which will generate a stable and continuously growing income stream to support operations. The overall investment goal is to preserve the purchasing power of the future stream of endowment payout for those funds. Other goals include maximizing return within reasonable and prudent levels of risk and maximizing the value of the endowment while maintaining liquidity needed to support spending in prolonged down markets. The Conference seeks a return on investment consistent with levels of investment risk that are prudent and reasonable given medium- to long-term capital market conditions and investment objectives.

(See Independent Auditors' Report)

ELLIN & TUCKER   PAGE | 20

ENDOWMENT SPENDING POLICY

The Conference follows the specific spending requirements of each endowment and, if there are no donor stipulations, the income is used for the purpose and mission of the Conference.

NOTE 12   LIQUIDITY AND AVAILABILITY OF FINANCIAL ASSETS

The Conference's financial assets available to meet cash needs for general expenditures within one year of the Combined Statements of Financial Position date are as follows:

	2018	2017
Cash and Cash Equivalents	$ 14,652,762	$ 15,205,440
Investments	53,133,926	51,119,888
Notes Receivable	1,276,599	779,580
Mortgage Receivables	2,098,665	2,178,687
Other Receivables	90,686	52,842
Total Financial Assets	71,252,638	69,336,437
Receivables Scheduled to be Collected in More Than One Year	(3,705,837)	(2,685,770)
Contractual or Donor-Imposed Restrictions:		
Endowment Funds	(2,919,242)	(3,051,523)
Donor Contributions Restricted to Specific Purposes	(413,639)	(345,384)
Financial Assets Available to Meet Cash Needs for General Expenditures Within One Year before Board Designations	64,213,920	63,253,760
Board-Designated Operating Reserves	(52,652,779)	(50,394,306)
Financial Assets Available to Meet Cash Needs for General Expenditures Within One Year after Board Designations	$ 11,561,141	$ 12,859,454

(See Independent Auditors' Report)

ELLIN & TUCKER

As part of the Conference's liquidity management, it has a policy to structure its financial assets to be available as its general expenditures, liabilities, and other obligations come due. Additionally, the Conference has Board-designated net assets without donor restrictions that could be made available for current operations if necessary.

NOTE 13   DONATED SERVICES

No amounts have been reflected in the combined financial statements for donated services, as no objective basis is available to measure the value of such services. However, a substantial number of volunteers donate significant amounts of time to the Conference's program services, fund-raising campaigns, and general administration.

NOTE 14   SUBSEQUENT EVENTS

The Conference has evaluated subsequent events and transactions for potential recognition or disclosure in the combined financial statements through May 20, 2019, the date the combined financial statements were available to be issued.

On February 1, 2019, the Conference entered into a lease agreement to sublease space in the Conference Center. The lease expires January 1, 2030 and requires annual payments of $62,000, subject to annual escalation of 3.25%.

(See Independent Auditors' Report)

SUPPLEMENTARY INFORMATION

ELLIN & TUCKER

ELLIN & TUCKER

INDEPENDENT AUDITORS' REPORT ON SUPPLEMENTARY INFORMATION

To the Council on Finance and Administration of
The Baltimore-Washington Conference of the United Methodist Church, Inc.

We have audited the combined financial statements of The Baltimore-Washington Conference of the United Methodist Church, Inc., Subsidiary and The United Methodist Church, Washington Area Episcopal Office as of and for the years ended December 31, 2018 and 2017, and our report thereon dated May 20, 2019, which appears on Pages 1 and 2, was qualified for accounting for post-retirement health benefit obligations. Our audits were conducted for the purpose of forming an opinion on the combined financial statements as a whole. The Combining Schedule – Statements of Financial Position, Combining Schedule – Statements of Activities Without Donor Restrictions and Statements of Activities – The United Methodist Church, Washington Area Episcopal Office are presented for purposes of additional analysis and are not a required part of the combined financial statements. Such information is the responsibility of management and was derived from and relates directly to the underlying accounting and other records used to prepare the combined financial statements. The information has been subjected to the auditing procedures applied in the audits of the combined financial statements and certain additional procedures, including comparing and reconciling such information directly to the underlying accounting and other records used to prepare the combined financial statements or to the combined financial statements themselves, and other additional procedures in accordance with auditing standards generally accepted in the United States of America. In our opinion, except for the effects on the supplementary information of the qualified opinion on the combined financial statements as described above, the information is fairly stated in all material respects in relation to the combined financial statements as a whole.

Ellin + Tucker

ELLIN & TUCKER
Certified Public Accountants

Baltimore, Maryland
May 20, 2019

COMBINING SCHEDULE – STATEMENTS OF FINANCIAL POSITION
The Baltimore-Washington Conference of the United Methodist
Church, Inc., Subsidiary and Affiliate
December 31, 2018

ASSETS

ASSETS	The Baltimore - Washington Conference of the United Methodist Church, Inc. and Subsidiary	The United Methodist Church, Washington Area Episcopal Office	Eliminations	Total
Cash and Cash Equivalents	$ 14,630,027	$ 22,735	$ -	$ 14,652,762
Investments, at Fair Value	53,133,926	-	-	53,133,926
Notes Receivable, Net	1,276,599	-	-	1,276,599
Mortgages Receivable	2,098,665	-	-	2,098,665
Other Receivables, Net	180,613	-	(89,927)	90,686
Prepaid Expenses	25,456	-	-	25,456
Property and Equipment, Net	10,542,743	-	-	10,542,743
Total Assets	$ 81,888,029	$ 22,735	$ (89,927)	$ 81,820,837

(See Independent Auditors' Report on Supplementary Information)

ELLIN & TUCKER

COMBINING SCHEDULE – STATEMENTS OF FINANCIAL POSITION, CONTINUED
The Baltimore-Washington Conference of the United Methodist
Church, Inc., Subsidiary and Affiliate
December 31, 2018

LIABILITIES AND NET ASSETS	The Baltimore - Washington Conference of the United Methodist Church, Inc. and Subsidiary	The United Methodist Church, Washington Area Episcopal Office	Eliminations	Total
LIABILITIES				
Notes Payable	$ 3,140,684	$ -	$ -	$ 3,140,684
Funds Due to Others	1,167,459	-	-	1,167,459
Accounts Payable and Accrued Expenses	1,317,203	89,927	(89,927)	1,317,203
Total Liabilities	5,625,346	89,927	(89,927)	5,625,346
NET ASSETS				
Without Donor Restrictions:				
Operating	20,277,023	-	-	20,277,023
Episcopal Office	-	(67,192)	-	(67,192)
Net Investment in Property	2,149,884	-	-	2,149,884
Medical Benefits	5,070,593	-	-	5,070,593
Designated for Loans	3,428,265	-	-	3,428,265
Designated for Post-Retirement Health Benefits	42,004,037	-	-	42,004,037
	72,929,802	(67,192)	-	72,862,610
With Donor Restrictions	3,332,881	-	-	3,332,881
Total Net Assets	76,262,683	(67,192)	-	76,195,491
Total Liabilities and Net Assets	$ 81,888,029	22,735	(89,927)	$ 81,820,837

(See Independent Auditors' Report on Supplementary Information)

ELLIN & TUCKER

PAGE | 25

636

COMBINING SCHEDULE – STATEMENTS OF ACTIVITIES WITHOUT DONOR RESTRICTIONS
The Baltimore-Washington Conference of the United Methodist
Church, Inc., Subsidiary and Affiliate
For the Year Ended December 31, 2018

	The Baltimore - Washington Conference of the United Methodist Church, Inc. and Subsidiary	The United Methodist Church, Washington Area Episcopal Office	Total
REVENUE			
Mission Shares	$ 13,760,860	$ 284,822	$ 14,045,682
Medical Payments	8,053,747	-	8,053,747
Investment Return, Net	(2,739,413)	-	(2,739,413)
Camping Registrations and Donations	1,580,901	-	1,580,901
Seminar and Event Registration	303,064	-	303,064
Annual Conference Fees	203,422	-	203,422
Other	9,959,536	113,237	10,072,773
Satisfaction of Purpose Restrictions	672,431	-	672,431
Total Revenue	31,794,548	398,059	32,192,607
EXPENSES			
Apportioned Funds:			
Discipleship	5,792,025	-	5,792,025
Stewardship	7,189,656	-	7,189,656
Leadership	2,994,461	-	2,994,461
General Church and Jurisdictional Mission Shares	3,571,610	-	3,571,610
Nonapportioned Funds:			
Program Funds	2,125,927	408,024	2,533,951
Medical	6,448,579	-	6,448,579
Funds Held for Giving	500,583	-	500,583
Depreciation	659,185	-	659,185
Total Expenses	29,282,026	408,024	29,690,050
Change in Net Assets	2,512,522	(9,965)	2,502,557
NET ASSETS WITHOUT DONOR RESTRICTIONS - BEGINNING OF YEAR	70,417,280	(57,227)	70,360,053
NET ASSETS WITHOUT DONOR RESTRICTIONS - END OF YEAR	$ 72,929,802	$ (67,192)	$ 72,862,610

(See Independent Auditors' Report on Supplementary Information)

ELLIN & TUCKER

PAGE | 26

BALTIMORE-WASHINGTON CONFERENCE

STATEMENTS OF ACTIVITIES – THE UNITED METHODIST CHURCH, WASHINGTON AREA EPISCOPAL OFFICE
The Baltimore-Washington Conference of the United Methodist
Church, Inc., Subsidiary and Affiliate
For the Years Ended December 31, 2018 and 2017

	2018	2017
REVENUE		
Mission Shares	$ 284,822	$ 314,996
Grant Income	86,252	84,560
Other	26,985	20,009
Total Revenue	398,059	419,565
EXPENSES		
Salaries and Benefits	327,314	308,514
Office Supplies	3,966	5,959
Postage	810	1,306
Printing	2,400	1,265
Equipment	-	69
Rent and Maintenance	55,457	54,551
Telecommunications	12,054	12,138
Travel	5,612	5,581
Other	411	145
Total Expenses	408,024	389,528
Change in Net Assets	(9,965)	30,037
NET ASSETS WITHOUT DONOR RESTRICTIONS - BEGINNING OF YEAR	(57,227)	(87,264)
NET ASSETS WITHOUT DONOR RESTRICTIONS - END OF YEAR	$ (67,192)	$ (57,227)

(See Independent Auditors' Report on Supplementary Information)

ELLIN & TUCKER

STATISTICAL TABLE

Align #	Church Name	Dist #	City	State	Total professing members at close of 2017 (1)	Received by PROFESSION of Faith (2a1)	Received by PROFESSION of Faith (Other Than Confirmation) (2a2)	Restored by AFFIRMATION of Faith (2b)	Transferred in from other UM churches (3)	Transferred in from non-UM churches (4)	Removed or corrected by Charge Conference action (5a)	Withdrawn from Professing Membership (5b)	Transferred out to other UM churches (6)	Transferred out to non-UM churches (7)	Removed by death (8)	Total professing members at close of 2018 (9)	Asian (9a)	African American / Black (9b)	Hispanic / Latino (9c)	Native American (9d)	Pacific Islander (9e)	White (9f)	Multi-Racial (9g)	Female (9h)	Male (9i)
1375	Adams	AN	Lothian	MD	101	4	0	1	0	0	0	0	0	0	0	102	0	100	0	0	0	2	0	67	35
1110	Asbury	AN	Annapolis	MD	332	4	2	4	0	0	6	0	0	0	0	327	0	321	2	0	0	6	0	234	93
1160	Asbury	AN	Arnold	MD	294	4	4	0	0	0	6	1	2	1	1	287	0	2	2	0	0	283	0	172	115
1360	Asbury	AN	Jessup	MD	271	4	0	0	0	0	0	0	1	0	1	272	1	262	1	0	0	2	7	219	53
1490	Asbury Town Neck	AN	Severna Park	MD	335	8	8	0	0	0	18	0	1	0	2	348	1	347	0	0	0	0	0	232	116
1115	Asbury-Broadneck	AN	Annapolis	MD	428	4	4	0	0	0	18	0	16	0	6	406	4	404	1	0	1	2	0	273	133
1420	Baldwin Memorial	AN	Millersville	MD	897	2	8	0	0	0	0	16	0	0	8	894	4	0	1	0	1	893	0	511	383
1120	Calvary	AN	Annapolis	MD	920	9	4	0	4	0	0	0	16	0	5	897	0	4	6	0	0	880	0	526	371
1125	Cape St Claire	AN	Annapolis	MD	157	1	0	1	2	2	4	0	0	0	2	153	0	4	3	0	1	147	0	94	59
1270	Carters	AN	Tracys Landing	MD	106	0	0	3	0	0	0	0	2	0	1	104	0	104	0	0	0	0	0	55	49
1130	Cecil Memorial	AN	Annapolis	MD	67	0	0	0	2	0	0	0	0	0	1	71	0	71	1	0	0	0	0	50	21
1215	Cedar Grove-Oakland	AN	Deale	MD	495	4	0	3	0	0	0	0	2	1	2	492	3	2	1	0	0	484	0	299	193
1515	Centenary	AN	Shady Side	MD	173	3	5	0	0	0	0	0	0	0	1	187	1	0	0	1	0	185	1	105	82
1438	Chews Memorial	AN	Harwood	MD	346	0	0	0	0	0	0	0	4	0	2	343	2	339	0	1	0	2	2	226	117
1180	Crofton	AN	Crofton	MD	422	8	3	0	4	0	17	0	0	0	6	422	2	4	3	0	6	407	2	238	184
1440	Community	AN	Pasadena	MD	633	3	0	0	3	2	0	0	0	2	3	977	2	3	3	0	0	974	5	650	327
7410	Community	AN	Laurel	MD	152	5	3	0	1	0	0	0	0	0	0	154	1	8	3	0	0	136	1	93	61
1190	Davidsonville	AN	Davidsonville	MD	396	0	0	0	3	6	0	0	0	0	0	404	1	1	0	0	0	402	0	238	166
1475	Delmont	AN	Severn	MD	92	0	0	0	0	0	0	0	0	0	1	91	0	3	0	0	0	88	0	49	42
1220	Dorsey Emmanuel	AN	Elkridge	MD	161	4	1	1	2	0	0	0	0	0	3	160	0	21	2	0	0	139	0	85	75
1135	Eastport	AN	Annapolis	MD	252	0	0	1	0	2	0	0	3	0	3	251	1	5	0	0	0	243	0	153	98
1235	Edgewater	AN	Edgewater	MD	55	0	0	0	0	0	2	0	2	0	1	10	0	0	0	0	0	9	0	7	3
1445	Faith	AN	Pasadena	MD	36	0	0	0	0	0	21	0	0	0	2	34	0	0	2	0	0	34	0	23	11
1268	Ferndale	AN	Glen Burnie	MD	170	10	4	0	0	0	0	0	0	0	4	155	2	0	0	0	0	153	0	98	57
7415	First	AN	Laurel	MD	468	0	4	0	0	0	0	0	0	0	0	477	0	75	24	0	0	378	0	254	223
1140	Fowler	AN	Annapolis	MD	132	5	0	0	0	0	0	0	0	0	3	131	0	131	0	0	0	0	0	80	51
1175	Franklin	AN	Churchton	MD	260	2	0	0	0	0	0	0	2	0	5	285	3	249	3	0	0	2	4	153	102
1275	Friendship	AN	Friendship	MD	499	15	7	0	5	0	0	0	1	1	4	518	0	1	0	0	0	514	0	298	220
1280	Galesville	AN	Galesville	MD	224	0	0	0	0	0	0	0	0	0	3	220	0	0	1	1	0	219	0	121	99
1320	Glen Burnie	AN	Glen Burnie	MD	463	11	3	0	3	0	0	1	3	1	12	463	3	29	2	1	0	420	7	350	113
1325	Glen Burnie	AN	Glen Burnie	MD	274	0	4	0	0	0	21	0	0	0	2	265	3	252	0	0	1	1	0	187	68
1240	Harwood Park	AN	Elkridge	MD	60	0	0	0	0	0	0	0	0	0	2	57	3	0	0	0	3	44	0	31	26
1145	Hope Memorial St Mark	AN	Edgewater	MD	175	0	0	0	4	2	8	0	0	0	0	175	0	172	0	0	0	3	0	111	64
1130	John Wesley	AN	Annapolis	MD	92	0	16	0	0	0	8	0	0	0	0	81	0	81	1	0	0	3	0	46	35
1195	John Wesley	AN	Glen Burnie	MD	253	0	0	0	2	0	25	16	0	0	4	226	0	224	2	0	1	0	0	152	74
1370	John Wesley-Waterbury	AN	Crownsville	MD	81	0	0	0	0	0	0	0	0	0	3	78	0	78	0	0	0	0	0	52	26
1425	Linthicum	AN	Linthicum	MD	842	0	0	1	0	0	0	0	2	0	14	826	2	7	3	0	7	812	0	448	378
1450	Linthicum Heights	AN	Gambrills	MD	84	0	0	0	0	0	0	0	0	0	4	81	0	1	0	0	0	1	0	57	24
1335	Macedonia	AN	Pasadena	MD	297	1	3	0	4	2	0	0	2	0	4	302	6	77	3	0	0	294	0	199	103
1148	Magothy	AN	Glen Burnie	MD	100	0	0	1	0	0	1	0	0	0	4	98	0	2	0	1	0	97	0	54	44
1265	Marley	AN	Edgewater	MD	163	2	0	2	0	7	2	0	0	1	4	165	0	4	1	0	0	164	0	108	57
1340	Mayo	AN	Edgewater	MD	222	0	3	0	0	1	0	0	0	0	1	245	0	7	0	0	0	217	0	135	87
1480	Melville Chapel	AN	Elkridge	MD	168	0	0	0	2	1	0	0	0	0	2	172	0	172	0	0	0	0	0	105	67
1165	Messiah	AN	Severn	MD	139	3	0	0	0	1	0	0	0	0	0	134	0	134	0	0	0	0	0	96	38
1460	Metropolitan	AN	Arnold	MD	599	0	0	0	0	0	32	0	0	0	0	567	1	0	1	0	0	565	0	383	184
1285	Mount Calvary	AN	Pasadena	MD	65	0	0	0	0	0	0	0	0	0	0	76	0	76	0	1	0	0	0	50	26
1150	Mount Zion	AN	Annapolis	MD	226	0	0	2	0	0	0	0	0	0	10	201	0	201	0	0	0	0	0	177	24

Column key:
- 10 — Average attendance at all weekly worship service(s)
- 10a — Persons who Worship Online
- 11a — Number of Infants and Children baptized (Age 0-12)
- 11b — Number of Teens and Adults baptized (Age 13+)
- 11T — TOTAL Number of persons baptized (all ages)
- 12 — Number of baptized members who have not become Professing
- 13 — Number of other constituents of the church
- 14 — Total enrolled in confirmation preparation classes that
- 15 — CHILDREN (0-11yrs) in all Christian groups, small groups and Sunday School
- 16 — YOUTH (12-18 yrs) in all Christian groups, small groups and Sunday School
- 17 — YOUNG ADULTS (19-30 yrs) in all Christian groups, small groups and Sunday School
- 18 — OTHER ADULTS (31+ yrs) in all Christian groups, small groups and Sunday School
- 19 — TOTAL number of persons participating in Christian formation groups (Total lines 15-18)
- 20 — Average weekly attendance, Education classes/groups that meet in Sunday Church School groups
- 22 — Number of participants in Vacation Bible School
- 23 — Number of ongoing classes (all ages) for learning in Sunday Church
- 24 — Number of ONGOING small groups, support groups, or classes
- 25 — Number of SHORT-TERM classes, support groups, or small groups offered
- 26 — Membership in United Methodist Men (UMM)
- 27 — Amount paid for projects (UMM)
- 28 — Membership in United Methodist Women (UMW)
- 29 — Amount paid for local church and community work (UMW)
- 30a — Number of UMVIM teams sent out from this church
- 30b — Number of persons sent out on UMVIM teams from this church

Align #	Church Name	10	10a	11a	11b	11T	12	13	14	15	16	17	18	19	20	22	23	24	25	26	27	28	29	30a	30b
1375	Adams	62	0	0	0	0	11	0	0	18	20	16	57	117	15	34	5	10	9	10	85	13	0	0	0
1110	Asbury	150	100	0	0	0	11	0	7	11	10	0	20	41	15	36	1	5	3	21	410	58	0	0	0
1160	Asbury	118	0	2	0	6	4	0	0	27	34	11	86	158	117	100	12	4	3	0	0	7	250	0	0
1360	Asbury	98	0	2	0	2	2	24	0	20	30	20	120	190	45	58	8	10	7	53	225	13	526	0	0
1490	Asbury Town Neck	160	0	4	0	4	0	10	0	22	8	7	75	112	15	16	4	4	1	20	3,200	30	571	1	0
1115	Asbury-Broadneck	136	0	0	0	0	0	0	0	18	10	8	16	52	45	60	5	10	7	23	138	25	136	0	0
1420	Baldwin Memorial	163	0	8	0	8	8	320	2	320	138	33	228	769	58	205	4	13	15	54	11,025	104	12,120	1	0
1120	Calvary	263	200	7	1	4	29	1,041	9	321	25	7	520	873	186	79	9	21	4	20	1,866	25	1,587	0	3
1125	Cage St Claire	84	0	3	1	4	0	52	0	20	0	0	50	74	4	0	1	1	3	10	5,300	15	20	0	0
1270	Carters	32	0	0	1	3	0	2	7	3	2	0	0	5	3	0	0	0	0	0	0	24	230	0	0
1130	Cecil Memorial	50	0	2	0	2	0	0	0	31	0	0	130	161	17	64	4	1	2	6	446	22	725	0	0
1215	Cedar Grove-Oakland	104	0	2	1	2	55	35	0	8	25	0	0	37	8	0	0	5	14	13	460	12	0	0	0
1515	Centenary	47	0	0	0	0	0	38	0	6	0	0	0	32	12	185	1	4	3	0	0	65	653	0	0
1438	Chews Memorial	65	116	1	0	3	0	1	0	42	25	2	24	263	10	80	10	5	3	0	145	10	940	1	6
1180	Community	134	0	3	0	7	78	200	3	35	14	4	192	106	30	20	0	1	4	22	3,000	0	5,800	0	0
1440	Community	190	0	7	0	0	29	176	8	0	0	0	57	0	30	5	0	6	0	25	0	15	0	0	0
7410	Community	32	9	4	0	4	0	0	0	24	35	0	5	169	21	0	4	1	7	0	0	16	6,618	0	0
1190	Davidsonville	143	0	0	0	0	0	85	0	2	2	2	110	23	12	25	0	6	1	25	3,000	15	1,026	1	15
1475	Delmont	21	3	0	0	3	11	37	0	0	0	0	23	45	4	5	4	3	2	16	0	16	1,525	0	0
1220	Dorsey Emmanuel	45	0	0	0	3	0	13	0	26	8	2	10	46	12	25	2	2	2	15	0	15	3,000	0	0
1135	Eastport	84	0	3	0	3	0	32	0	0	0	0	4	4	4	0	0	0	4	13	0	13	0	0	0
1235	Edgewater	10	63	0	0	0	0	10	0	0	0	0	20	53	22	0	0	2	0	6	0	13	4,530	0	0
1445	Faith	24	0	3	0	3	0	0	0	16	15	25	102	164	89	68	0	24	3	16	2,541	53	500	0	0
1269	Ferndale	66	100	0	0	0	55	55	0	19	19	0	20	49	40	145	12	8	2	0	0	23	1,500	1	0
7415	First	165	1	2	0	12	0	4	0	11	10	10	37	56	58	12	4	4	1	12	0	15	0	0	0
1140	Fowler	89	0	1	0	4	0	0	15	48	11	0	35	96	40	72	1	8	3	24	0	23	1,100	1	2
1175	Franklin	62	2	2	0	7	8	25	11	15	30	0	46	80	22	90	3	4	2	10	0	0	10,293	0	0
1275	Friendship	200	0	4	6	3	0	20	0	26	16	0	16	88	4	75	3	6	6	31	395	69	0	0	2
1280	Galesville	69	155	6	1	6	15	50	0	9	10	3	10	38	8	75	9	3	2	0	0	56	4,933	1	0
1320	Glen Burnie	200	200	3	1	6	55	0	0	0	0	0	50	71	20	18	20	45	0	17	0	0	2,043	1	3
1325	Hall	127	5	0	0	1	0	0	0	9	4	4	15	28	15	22	5	2	6	0	80	54	0	0	0
1295	Harwood Park	20	0	0	0	6	0	0	0	19	11	0	21	60	64	51	5	9	3	5	580	14	300	0	0
1240	Hope Memorial St Mark	65	0	0	0	0	0	0	0	3	42	23	60	27	4	20	1	12	7	0	0	47	4,735	1	10
1145	John Wesley	50	0	3	0	3	5	19	0	186	4	1	95	346	80	177	5	2	6	0	0	28	500	1	0
1330	John Wesley	92	0	0	1	6	0	0	0	15	4	0	43	67	10	26	2	9	3	15	0	0	0	1	1
1185	John Wesley-Waterbury	47	1	0	0	1	0	0	4	2	3	0	28	27	64	0	3	4	2	4	0	23	1,494	0	0
1370	Linthicum Heights	186	0	1	0	6	432	471	0	42	8	0	10	134	60	40	3	7	7	0	0	11	0	0	5
1425	Macedonia	75	0	0	0	0	5	9	0	50	4	21	21	162	10	30	1	2	1	0	0	0	1,650	0	0
1450	Magothy	93	0	0	0	2	0	20	0	14	7	0	60	17	22	0	3	7	2	13	1,865	20	0	0	0
1335	Marley	30	0	3	0	3	6	53	0	75	20	0	120	60	15	25	2	0	7	0	0	12	2,550	0	0
1148	Mayo	71	5	0	0	0	86	93	0	4	16	2	40	81	23	0	1	20	8	0	0	38	375	1	0
1265	Melville Chapel	32	0	0	0	2	0	0	0	20	6	6	40	134	10	30	3	2	4	13	0	25	250	1	0
1340	Messiah	65	0	6	0	6	0	12	1	4	2	2	28	162	13	25	6	7	1	0	0	3	2,550	0	0
1480	Metropolitan	87	0	0	0	3	0	0	0	16	16	16	40	17	8	22	6	20	4	0	0	24	375	0	0
1165	Mount Calvary	60	0	2	0	3	13	20	0	4	4	16	40	60	24	12	1	2	1	12	75	24	250	0	0
1460	Mount Carmel	83	0	3	0	3	0	0	0	7	7	0	0	0	0	0	0	0	0	0	0	0	0	0	0
1285	Mount Tabor	51	0	0	0	6	33	0	0	0	0	0	0	0	0	0	0	0	0	0	0	0	0	0	0
1150	Mount Zion	77	0	5	0	5	0	0	0	4	16	0	0	0	0	0	0	0	0	0	0	0	0	0	0

Align #	Church Name	33 TOTAL Community MINISTRIES for outreach, justice, and mercy	33a MINISTRIES focusing on global/regional health?	33b MINISTRIES focusing on engaging in ministry with the poor/socially	34 PERSONS SERVED BY community ministries for outreach, justice, and mercy	35a PERSONS SERVING (from your congregation) in mission/community ministries	36 Market value of church-owned land, buildings and equipment	36SF Overall square footage of church owned buildings	37 Market value of financial and other liquid assets	38 Debt secured by church physical assets	39 Other debt	42 General Advance Specials	43 World Service Specials	44 Annual Conference Advance Specials	45 Youth Service Fund	46 All other funds to AC Treasurer	47 Total AC Special Sunday Offerings	48a UMC CAUSES given directly	48b MISSIONS/MINISTRY COSTS
1375	Adams	95	9	68	230	68	500,000	5,940	46,656	18,083	0	40	0	0	0	0	0	550	0
1110	Asbury	6	0	2	1,500	60	4,451,433	20,361	267,303	0	0	0	0	0	0	0	0	0	4,232
1160	Asbury	11	0	2	754	182	3,100,000	18,568	72,903	0	19,068	3,681	0	156	0	0	0	0	31,794
1360	Asbury	10	1	9	30,368	137	639,400	3,500	328,000	553,657	0	25	0	0	0	0	0	0	0
1490	Asbury Town Neck	9	7	5	12,000	103	2,213,667	15,993	570,388	0	0	239	0	0	0	0	0	0	21,113
1115	Asbury-Broadneck	30	7	10	270	57	2,900,000	23,195	0	0	0	1,500	0	0	0	0	0	0	4,754
1420	Baldwin Memorial	7	2	7	1,200	40	2,159,650	435,541	1,546,681	0	0	2,145	0	1,666	0	1,000	0	10,000	26,113
1120	Calvary	14	2	14	4,310	323	11,247,809	11,857	161,933	0	0	197	0	100	0	0	0	1,309	38,316
1125	Cape St Clare	8	1	3	2,334	90	2,756,704	2,000	50,000	0	0	0	0	0	0	0	0	364	3,919
1270	Carters	0	1	5	100	18	269,000	2,608	0	0	0	20	0	0	0	0	0	0	0
1130	Cecil Memorial	1	1	1	565	5	1,202,100	19,261	361,924	297,800	0	0	0	0	0	0	0	0	164
1215	Cedar Grove-Oakland	16	2	12	4,000	163	2,619,800	9,656	124,100	0	1,356	400	0	0	0	0	0	573	3,269
1515	Centenary	20	2	6	335	70	3,260,000	6,000	284,919	0	0	400	0	0	0	0	0	7,771	1,700
1438	Chews Memorial	0	1	0	122	54	991,534	24,350	77,226	79,753	0	0	0	0	0	0	0	513	0
1180	Community	10	0	10	5,000	185	2,100,000	7,000	661,344	0	0	0	0	0	0	0	0	1,666	5,730
1440	Community	12	0	4	6,000	160	6,157,000	17,178	127,815	0	0	0	0	0	0	0	0	1,224	24,453
7410	Community	6	4	19	90,000	206	1,000,000	4,519	637,622	0	0	481	0	0	0	0	0	200	1,286
1190	Davidsonville	38	0	4	1,300	91	4,180,000	18,638	95,971	0	0	0	0	0	0	0	0	464	11,226
1475	Delmont	4	0	14	1,000	25	619,068	4,519	105,000	0	0	0	0	0	0	0	0	1,600	5,840
1220	Dorsey Emmanuel	2	0	4	700	31	1,222,000	2,500	705,866	0	0	1,600	0	0	0	0	0	135	23,319
1135	Eastport	14	0	4	35	26	2,569,064	2,640	0	0	0	0	0	0	0	0	0	0	0
1235	Edgewater	4	0	2	180	160	220,000	9,838	53,681	421,699	0	1,200	0	0	0	0	0	50	2,860
1445	Faith	6	2	4	20,700	158	550,000	17,447	349,919	0	0	2,543	0	0	0	0	0	450	15,426
1268	Ferndale	7	4	3	1,325	25	2,361,672	6,095	130,000	19,380	0	46	0	0	0	0	0	450	16,320
1415	First	10	0	3	85	56	3,150,000	7,225	516,908	272,406	0	0	0	0	0	0	0	7,287	1,242
1140	Fowler	4	0	6	440	140	783,320	21,855	106,345	0	0	0	0	300	0	900	0	77	0
1175	Franklin	6	0	6	380	15	1,000,000	8,208	256,212	0	0	0	0	0	0	0	0	0	123,890
1275	Friendship	3	0	3	400	70	4,612,400	30,000	20,000	469,830	0	0	0	0	0	0	0	0	0
1280	Galesville	2	1	3	1,000	20	1,479,466	10,172	0	0	0	0	0	0	0	0	0	0	6,262
1320	Glen Burnie	2	0	2	100	5	7,236,000	4,420	0	13,260	0	0	0	0	0	0	0	0	0
1325	Hall	0	0	0	40	15	1,500,000	0	215,000	0	0	0	0	0	0	0	0	0	0
1225	Harwood Park	4	2	4	50	2	750,000	4,407	363,000	0	0	0	0	0	0	232	0	100	0
1240	Hope Memorial St Mark	0	0	0	30	65	779,000	10,670	0	0	0	0	0	0	0	0	0	0	530
1145	John Wesley	0	0	0	0	20	600,000	1,656	0	0	0	0	0	0	0	0	0	0	0
1330	John Wesley	19	3	19	78	302	3,200,222	35,000	215,000	0	1,500	0	0	0	0	0	0	11,412	16,305
1185	John Wesley-Waterbury	12	3	2	9,706	20	831,525	19,405	363,000	0	0	0	0	0	0	0	0	450	631
1370	Linthicum Heights	2	3	2	405	24	4,445,000	7,662	75,000	0	0	0	0	0	0	0	0	300	17,681
1425	Macedonia	3	4	3	590	10	299,000	10,000	565,894	0	0	0	0	0	0	0	0	125	6,546
1450	Magothy	17	1	11	150	22	1,910,000	8,500	215,000	0	0	0	0	0	0	0	0	0	5,108
1335	Marley	1	0	1	300	25	1,300,000	8,174	76,918	0	0	25	0	0	0	0	0	0	6,143
1148	Mayo	5	0	2	2,290	3	3,415,000	5,123	468,647	0	0	45	0	0	0	0	0	0	0
1265	Melville Chapel	2	1	1	325	2	2,300,000	8,827	13,411	0	0	0	0	0	0	0	0	0	12,071
1340	Messiah	2	1	1	720	62	1,637,640	9,500	811,728	0	1,500	0	0	0	0	0	0	220	0
1400	Metropolitan	9	9	9	260	63	1,793,500	8,436	190,000	422,202	3,794	0	0	0	0	0	0	300	1,695
1165	Mount Calvary						1,782,100												
1460	Mount Carmel						1,250,000												
1285	Mount Tabor						640,000												
1150	Mount Zion						1,245,057												

Align #	Church Name	48 TOTAL — Total of UMC Causes & UMC Missions & Outreach	49 — NON-UMC CAUSES: Total amount given DIRECTLY to non-United Methodist benevolent and charitable causes (NOT sent to BWC Treasurer)	50a — Human Relations Sunday	50b — UMCOR Sunday (formerly One Great Hour of Sharing)	50c — Peace with Justice Sunday	50d — Native American Ministries Sunday	50e — World Communion Sunday	50f — U.M. Student Day	51 — Direct-billed clergy non-health benefits	52 — Direct-billed clergy health benefits	53a — Base compensation paid to/for the Senior Pastor or other person assigned or appointed in the lead pastoral role to the church	53b — Base compensation paid/for to all Associate Pastor(s) & other pastoral staff assigned or appointed to the church	53c — Base compensation paid to/for any Deacons NOT included in 53a or 53b	53a — Housing benefits paid to/for Lead Pastor or person in lead pastoral role as described in 53a	53b — Housing benefits paid to/for ALL Associate Pastor(s) & other pastoral staff assigned or appointed to the	53c — Housing benefits paid to/for any Deacons not included in 53a or 53b	56 — Paid to/for all persons included in Lines 53a-53c for accountable reimbursements	57 — Paid to/for all persons included in Lines 53a-53c for any other cash allowances (non-)
1375	Adams	550	550	0	0	0	0	0	0	13,903	14,026	15,000	0	0	15,000	0	0	1,923	0
1110	Asbury	4,232	2,523	30	0	125	35	232	309	13,765	13,652	73,050	0	0	6,727	0	0	10,000	0
1160	Asbury	31,794	10,294	0	309	75	75	75	75	6,600	0	71,212	0	0	4,956	0	0	3,376	0
1360	Asbury	0	7,655	0	0	0	0	0	0	0	0	14,700	0	0	19,866	0	0	9,823	0
1490	Asbury Town Neck	21,113	4,233	72	0	57	91	53	0	14,559	11,729	82,139	0	0	6,853	0	0	6,237	0
1115	Asbury-Broadneck	4,754	530	0	0	0	0	0	0	17,077	14,160	37,337	0	0	54,405	0	0	4,268	0
1420	Baldwin Memorial	26,113	0	0	0	0	0	0	0	14,180	61,700	74,607	0	0	0	25,000	0	12,529	0
1120	Calvary	48,316	34,629	0	0	0	0	0	0	26,863	42,503	78,271	48,410	0	0	0	0	6,403	0
1125	Cape St Claire	3,919	2,376	0	0	0	0	0	0	6,600	0	25,872	0	0	19,884	0	0	1,646	0
1270	Carters	1,289	2,519	112	0	108	136	132	99	0	0	18,671	0	0	0	0	0	0	0
1130	Cecil Memorial	528	936	140	195	167	124	83	118	0	0	20,975	0	0	0	0	0	1,442	0
1215	Cedar Grove-Oakland	3,269	9,518	5	136	55	100	125	32	14,483	12,320	62,740	0	0	19,866	0	0	1,350	0
1515	Centenary	1,700	10,290	50	136	194	100	100	0	9,708	11,729	43,149	0	0	5,500	0	0	2,495	0
1438	Chews Memorial	573	0	210	0	0	0	0	0	14,396	16,332	27,632	0	0	6,763	0	0	5,613	0
1180	Community	13,501	11,378	0	0	0	0	0	0	19,495	17,404	48,355	0	0	42,000	0	0	3,798	0
7410	Community	1,286	0	0	0	0	6	0	0	11,676	11,528	45,000	6,360	0	7,500	0	0	0	0
1190	Davidsonville	12,892	33,355	0	349	0	200	142	0	12,193	13,886	30,900	0	0	19,866	0	0	1,863	0
1475	Delmont	1,689	3,179	103	0	100	0	0	0	12,193	13,886	61,413	0	0	19,866	0	0	1,177	0
1220	Dorsey Emmanuel	6,040	6,500	0	0	295	0	0	0	0	0	15,488	0	0	9,942	0	0	3,109	0
1135	Eastport	23,319	882	62	0	107	164	89	60	11,658	13,332	19,455	0	0	9,899	0	0	132	0
1235	Edgewater	1,600	530	0	0	181	181	89	163	0	0	44,099	0	0	19,866	0	0	0	1,000
1445	Faith	2,995	225	70	145	191	40	39	75	495	0	19,999	0	0	0	0	0	132	0
1268	Ferndale	15,426	6,781	0	0	0	0	0	0	12,347	12,725	11,003	0	0	5,065	0	0	95	0
7415	First	16,320	0	0	0	0	0	0	0	0	0	27,974	0	0	961	0	0	8,639	0
1140	Fowler	1,292	360	1	0	6	6	0	0	12,347	0	69,166	0	0	19,866	0	0	0	0
1175	Franklin	450	3,048	0	0	5	0	0	0	14,143	16,408	19,335	0	0	0	0	0	5,036	0
1275	Friendship	131,177	7,178	100	140	100	125	100	100	13,834	16,892	17,168	0	0	9,933	0	0	1,129	0
1280	Galesville	0	9,573	0	0	0	0	0	0	14,419	16,164	72,127	0	0	19,755	0	0	2,475	0
1320	Glen Burnie	6,339	13,252	0	0	0	167	0	0	11,068	10,450	40,650	0	0	36,000	0	0	1,776	0
1325	Hall	0	0	0	0	0	0	0	0	14,143	47,199	68,921	0	0	0	0	0	1,200	0
1225	Harwood Park	1,292	657	0	0	0	0	0	0	6,755	16,164	16,240	0	0	20,263	0	0	4,800	0
1240	Hope Memorial St Mark	450	3,742	0	0	0	0	0	0	14,143	16,408	47,803	0	0	18,354	0	0	1,976	0
1145	John Wesley	100	100	0	0	0	0	0	60	14,616	11,466	26,500	0	0	21,855	0	0	5,253	0
1330	John Wesley	530	657	0	0	0	0	0	0	14,616	11,466	62,726	0	0	21,200	0	0	2,708	0
1185	John Wesley-Waterbury	0	0	0	0	0	0	0	0	0	0	7,000	0	0	4,656	0	0	1,705	0
1370	Linthicum Heights	11,412	30,295	70	145	191	40	39	75	14,316	24,650	91,238	0	0	31,895	0	0	1,080	0
1425	Macedonia	450	1,981	0	0	0	0	0	0	15,280	15,280	21,430	0	0	16,800	0	0	3,462	0
1450	Magothy	16,305	1,970	0	0	0	0	0	0	12,971	12,808	60,964	0	0	4,550	0	0	1,705	0
1335	Marley	931	0	0	0	0	0	0	0	6,049	6,214	54,562	0	0	16,800	12,500	0	1,080	470
1148	Mayo	17,581	1,970	0	0	0	0	0	0	13,300	12,808	10,000	0	0	4,550	0	0	3,462	0
1265	Melville Chapel	6,671	3,742	0	0	0	0	0	0	5,613	6,214	15,500	0	0	8,750	0	0	3,864	0
1340	Messiah	5,108	0	0	0	0	0	0	0	12,652	5,700	55,000	0	0	23,289	0	0	4,000	0
1400	Metropolitan	6,143	3,742	0	0	0	0	0	0	0	0	25,975	0	0	0	0	0	1,025	0
1165	Mount Calvary	0	9,437	0	0	0	167	0	0	11,570	16,104	50,590	0	0	0	0	0	3,283	391
1460	Mount Carmel	12,071	9,437	0	0	0	0	0	0	11,570	16,104	26,437	0	0	3,237	0	0	0	391
1285	Mount Tabor	220	400	0	0	0	0	0	0	0	0	52,004	0	0	7,525	0	0	1,025	0
1150	Mount Zion	2,195	200	0	0	0	0	0	0	7,285	8,605	52,004	0	0	8,108	0	0	500	0

Align #	Church Name	60	61	62	63	63a	64	65	66	67a	67b	67c	67d	67e	67f	67g
1375	Adams	10,500	9,000	1,099	0	0	4,900	64,726	69	91,430	0	0	0	0	0	0
1110	Asbury	53,277	24,233	92,624	26,941	0	0	366,675	233	0	276,441	5,179	0	0	15,935	24,084
1160	Asbury	91,909	14,630	37,673	0	0	9,512	349,381	128	221,622	70,403	6,616	0	0	35,598	0
1360	Asbury	19,475	125	11,208	0	0	8,932	104,380	147	103,904	10,206	3,613	0	0	0	18,251
1490	Asbury Town Neck	10,728	15,094	91,275	72,700	0	0	302,236	265	379,642	413,339	6,991	79	0	8,100	42,593
1115	Asbury-Broadneck	89,042	32,378	117,299	0	0	19,593	497,493	215	27,805	258,819	10,843	25	0	32,590	0
1420	Baldwin Memorial	66,619	38,567	186,606	0	0	27,709	435,181	330	424,213	615,753	808	9	0	12,270	0
1120	Calvary	271,803	4,437	63,814	0	0	60,412	951,157	105	104,335	83,598	3,196	117	0	34,060	156,686
1125	Cape St Clare	30,276	3,078	12,328	0	0	0	251,403	105	104,335	83,598	3,114	1	0	0	0
1270	Carters	15,535	4,030	23,127	29,995	0	5,170	65,455	43	75,876	710	2,100	5,013	0	0	1,098
1130	Cecil Memorial	13,000	2,006	61,177	0	0	17,850	74,728	131	0	83,329	10,630	0	0	1,560	3,066
1215	Cedar Grove-Oakland	27,078	10,771	33,716	0	0	1,000	247,324	45	101,126	240,831	10,527	0	0	600	9,120
1515	Centenary	0	12,000	17,035	0	0	4,640	195,458	79	0	143,600	3,200	0	0	119,150	12,469
1438	Chews Memorial	12,350	14,798	94,079	16,622	0	27,428	111,511	160	172,000	1,670	9,760	12	0	42,305	5,000
1180	Community	156,859	1,240	69,804	0	0	4,211	493,011	36	26,978	419,457	1,656	0	0	23,178	5,946
7410	Community	17,497	2,150	26,129	0	0	11,608	313,569	250	182,171	73,849	8,167	552	0	45,667	0
1190	Davidsonville	138,834	8,572	70,600	0	0	20,524	103,462	21	0	55,776	1,782	0	0	2,400	12,595
1475	Delmont	4,650	532	13,822	0	0	0	453,085	17	16,780	167,088	2,150	0	0	7,550	0
1220	Dorsey Emmanuel	5,600	0	55,618	0	0	0	63,872	77	110,278	46,638	2,066	0	0	46,709	0
1135	Eastport	69,740	2,497	3,788	0	0	0	77,305	13	0	40,745	1,300	0	0	0	17,047
1235	Edgewater	0	7,018	6,305	0	0	13,193	302,865	26	0	72,156	4,808	0	0	0	0
1445	Faith	3,000	550	57,004	77,224	0	19,320	33,660	70	0	38,126	7,748	204	0	4,136	0
1268	Fairdale	15,417	8,616	55,543	84,427	6,362	93,000	32,548	168	0	91,811	0	0	0	27,635	17,200
7415	First	98,873	23,081	38,200	0	272	0	156,381	54	73,463	402,121	4,436	98	0	500	0
1140	Fowler	0	6,254	27,061	0	0	0	434,352	57	219,684	70,300	10,501	0	0	1,200	20,000
1175	Franklin	19,000	15,018	98,864	15,913	0	59,326	155,328	202	120,334	171,822	2,890	0	0	822	36,544
1275	Friendship	97,027	14,577	35,497	38,420	0	12,496	105,654	72	50	26,548	11,406	416	0	175	16,375
1280	Galesville	18,278	0	82,739	0	0	0	620,387	202	0	320,793	6,103	128	0	19,642	1,264
1320	Glen Burnie	65,098	4,591	36,430	3,600	0	600	189,563	175	90,929	173,954	0	0	0	1,580	0
1325	Hall	14,470	13,617	15,000	0	0	0	417,475	27	67,640	26,000	1,788	0	0	16,500	8,110
1225	Harwood Park	0	616	26,057	0	0	50,609	192,554	22	29,053	12,364	6,398	0	0	0	200
1240	Hope Memorial St Mark	29,240	8,784	49,302	0	0	0	38,574	156	62,667	143,317	4,575	0	0	875	49,010
1145	John Wesley	38,813	5,389	7,835	0	0	8,394	137,269	64	0	0	10,866	0	0	0	17,664
1330	John Wesley	14,493	2,193	113,150	0	0	2,525	132,515	233	41,292	369,019	6,709	75	0	33,708	12,467
1185	John Wesley-Waterbury	115,317	9,509	22,960	0	0	2,350	253,086	40	0	77,075	1,000	456	0	0	0
1370	Linthicum Heights	22,857	675	26,000	0	0	10,000	59,569	95	1,300	56,091	2,516	0	30,000	500	3,890
1425	Macedonia	32,134	2,064	33,233	0	0	2,826	526,203	102	0	131,228	5,377	7,207	0	9,485	2,000
1450	Magothy	2,460	5,000	11,622	0	0	0	87,207	50	0	64,683	2,966	0	0	9,588	0
1335	Marley	39,233	1,196	21,054	0	0	0	230,756	55	0	64,853	6,167	7,207	0	8,925	14,462
1148	Mayo	8,650	6,596	28,703	0	0	18,100	76,563	121	171,155	240,882	6,176	1,247	0	39,100	2,675
1265	Melville Chapel	24,692	2,459	20,339	0	8,079	5,964	220,846	65	8,427	71,003	6,176	0	0	9,588	1,334
1340	Messiah	41,680		48,113	58,000			778,217		178,090	75,850	8,055			32,751	12,351
1480	Metropolitan	14,250		8,900				125,550				7,374				4,982
1165	Mount Calvary	32,802		19,500				196,956	129						1,500	8,300
1460	Mount Carmel	0						77,966								
1285	Mount Tabor	0						224,350								
1150	Mount Zion	7,200						175,703								

Align #	Church Name	TOTAL income for annual budget/spending plan. (67a-g) [67]	Capital campaigns [68a]	Memorials, endowments, and bequests [68b]	Other sources and projects (include UMW, UMM and "flow-through") [68c]	Special Sundays, Gen. Adv. Spec, World Srvc Spec., Conf. Adv. Spec. and other directed benevolent giving [68d]	Total income for designated causes including capital campaign and other special projects [68]	Equitable Compensation Funds received by Church or Pastor [69a]	Advance Special, apportioned, and connectional funds received by church [69b]	Other grants and financial support from institutional sources [69c]	Income from connectional / institutional sources outside the local church [69]	TOTAL CHURCH INCOME (Sum of Lines 67 + 68 + 69) [70]	Amount APPORTIONED to the local church [40a]	Amount PAID by the local church for all apportioned causes [40b]
1375	Adams	91,430	0	0	0	0	0	0	0	0	0	91,430	6,764	6,764
1110	Asbury	321,639	21,666	4,405	0	771	26,842	0	0	2,000	2,000	350,481	44,369	44,369
1160	Asbury	334,339	0	11,182	4,360	20,536	36,078	0	0	0	0	370,417	38,732	38,732
1360	Asbury	135,974	0	0	0	0	0	0	0	0	0	135,974	12,596	12,596
1490	Asbury Town Neck	437,404	0	0	0	0	0	0	0	0	0	437,404	43,408	43,408
1115	Asbury-Broadneck	484,568	0	0	0	511	511	0	0	0	0	485,079	51,063	51,063
1420	Baldwin Memorial	415,529	0	0	0	6,469	6,469	0	0	0	0	422,018	49,544	49,544
1120	Calvary	1,052,953	0	41,252	0	45,678	86,930	0	0	0	0	1,139,863	116,951	116,951
1125	Cape St Clare	226,994	0	2,250	0	7,084	9,334	0	0	0	0	236,328	25,265	25,265
1270	Carters	82,767	0	0	0	1,485	1,485	0	0	0	0	84,252	9,637	9,637
1130	Cecil Memorial	85,429	0	0	0	0	0	0	0	0	0	85,429	15,286	15,286
1215	Cedar Grove-Oakland	256,371	0	385	0	163	548	0	0	0	0	256,919	28,452	28,452
1515	Centenary	164,910	0	0	6,325	0	6,325	0	0	0	0	171,295	15,944	15,944
1438	Cheves Memorial	119,065	0	0	0	958	958	0	0	0	0	120,023	11,119	11,119
1180	Community	542,607	0	10,837	0	400	11,237	0	0	0	0	553,844	63,356	63,356
1440	Community	303,872	0	1,317	0	0	1,317	0	0	0	0	305,189	36,731	36,731
7410	Community	107,568	0	0	2,541	0	2,541	0	0	0	0	110,129	11,518	11,518
1190	Davidsonville	417,060	2,202	159	1,026	2,633	6,020	0	0	0	0	423,080	44,291	44,291
1475	Delmont	50,820	0	3,040	0	6,981	10,021	0	0	0	0	60,841	7,251	7,251
1220	Dorsey Emmanuel	67,225	0	500	0	0	500	0	0	0	0	67,725	7,843	7,843
1135	Eastport	248,258	0	9,605	0	2,354	11,959	0	0	0	0	260,217	31,346	31,346
1235	Edgewater	30,830	0	2,450	0	0	2,450	0	0	0	0	33,280	4,479	4,479
1445	Faith	39,426	0	1,508	0	0	1,508	0	0	0	0	40,934	3,955	3,955
1269	Ferndale	117,955	0	1,276	0	0	1,276	0	0	0	0	119,231	15,398	15,398
7415	First	437,788	36,257	6,650	38,564	100	81,571	0	0	0	0	519,359	43,768	43,768
1140	Fowler	90,800	0	0	0	0	0	0	0	0	0	90,000	10,100	2,000
1275	Franklin	116,528	6,350	0	0	0	6,350	0	0	0	0	122,878	19,378	19,378
1280	Friendship	418,204	96,377	0	0	51,975	148,352	0	0	0	0	566,556	49,589	49,589
1320	Galesville	151,211	23,089	7,760	0	13,978	44,827	0	0	0	0	196,038	16,991	16,991
1325	Glen Burnie	351,262	13,614	82,945	0	440	96,999	0	0	0	0	448,261	48,141	48,141
1225	Hall	199,925	0	0	4,000	0	4,000	0	0	0	0	189,925	18,164	18,164
1240	Harwood Park	42,700	0	0	0	250	250	0	0	0	0	42,950	5,534	5,534
1145	Hope Memorial St Mark	141,727	0	0	0	0	0	0	0	0	0	141,727	13,852	13,852
1390	John Wesley	97,698	0	0	0	482	482	0	0	0	0	98,150	14,860	14,860
1185	John Wesley	192,100	29,053	0	0	30,361	30,361	0	0	0	0	222,461	33,454	33,454
1370	John Wesley-Waterbury	67,242	0	0	0	1,809	1,809	0	0	0	0	69,051	7,865	7,865
1425	Linthicum Heights	413,623	0	1,206,801	0	52,548	1,259,349	0	0	0	0	1,672,971	60,868	60,868
1450	Macedonia	87,754	0	600	0	0	600	0	0	1,000	1,000	89,354	12,140	12,140
1335	Magothy	47,667	8,600	0	0	200	8,800	0	0	0	0	57,667	25,108	25,108
1140	Marley	66,248	0	26,575	0	0	26,575	0	0	0	0	94,823	8,116	8,116
1265	Mayo	189,999	4,500	3,116	0	299	7,915	0	0	0	0	197,914	29,688	29,688
1340	Melville Chapel	78,246	0	0	0	0	0	0	0	0	0	78,246	8,974	8,974
1480	Messiah	115,460	0	0	0	4,584	4,584	0	0	0	0	120,044	14,743	14,743
1165	Metropolitan	247,049	0	2,882	0	6,143	9,025	0	0	0	0	256,074	31,723	31,723
1460	Mount Calvary	89,530	0	0	0	0	0	0	0	0	0	89,530	14,800	14,800
1285	Mount Carmel	217,290	0	0	0	0	0	0	0	0	0	217,290	30,165	30,165
1150	Mount Tabor	99,951	0	0	4,342	1,053	5,395	0	0	0	0	105,346	6,090	6,090
	Mount Zion	179,590	0	0	0	300	300	0	0	0	0	179,890	15,427	6,142

Align #	Church Name	Dist #	City	State	Total professing members at the close of 2017 (1)	Received by PROFESSION of Faith (2n1)	Received by PROFESSION of Faith (Other Than Confirmation) (2n2)	Restored by AFFIRMATION of Faith (2b)	Transferred in from other UM churches (3)	Transferred in from non-UM churches (4)	Removed or corrected by Charge Conference action (5a)	Withdrawn from Professing Membership (5b)	Transferred out to other UM churches (6)	Transferred out to non-UM churches (7)	Removed by death (8)	Total professing members at the close of 2018 (9)	Asian (9a)	African American / Black (9b)	Hispanic / Latino (9c)	Native American (9d)	Pacific Islander (9e)	White (9f)	Multi-Racial (9g)	Female (9h)	Male (9i)
1410	Mount Zion	AN	Lothian	MD	451	0	2	0	0	0	0	0	0	0	5	448	2	0	2	0	0	444	0	234	214
1465	Mount Zion	AN	Pasadena	MD	153	0	0	0	0	0	0	0	0	1	2	150	0	150	0	0	0	0	0	95	55
7420	Mount Zion	AN	Laurel	MD	94	2	0	3	0	0	3	0	0	0	1	92	0	91	1	0	0	0	0	67	25
1415	Mount Zion-Ark Road	AN	Lothian	MD	89	5	1	0	0	0	3	0	0	0	3	88	0	88	0	0	0	0	0	56	32
1430	Nichols-Bethel	AN	Odenton	MD	1,639	2	1	0	7	1	41	4	3	0	12	1,631	16	43	26	0	2	1,524	20	949	682
1470	Pasadena	AN	Pasadena	MD	292	3	10	1	1	0	0	1	2	0	5	258	2	0	0	0	0	256	0	162	96
1485	Severn	AN	Severn	MD	128	0	0	0	1	0	0	0	0	0	0	129	0	11	0	0	0	118	0	75	54
1510	Severna Park	AN	Severna Park	MD	1,852	21	0	27	16	9	0	20	13	3	14	1,875	7	7	1	0	0	1,860	0	1,056	819
1380	Sollers	AN	Lothian	MD	96	0	3	0	0	0	0	0	2	0	2	95	0	95	0	0	0	0	0	62	33
1345	Solley	AN	Glen Burnie	MD	128	0	0	0	0	6	0	76	0	0	2	52	0	0	2	0	0	50	0	33	19
1255	St Andrews of Annapolis	AN	Edgewater	MD	738	5	2	0	2	0	15	0	0	2	3	741	3	0	0	0	0	738	0	443	298
1350	St Mark	AN	Hanover	MD	866	0	6	0	0	0	0	0	1	1	6	855	1	851	0	0	0	0	3	551	304
7425	St Mark's	AN	Laurel	MD	310	0	1	0	1	0	10	5	0	0	2	295	0	295	0	0	0	0	0	236	59
1520	St Matthews	AN	Shady Side	MD	166	0	0	0	0	0	5	0	0	0	3	159	0	159	0	0	0	0	0	91	68
1310	The Everlasting Love	AN	Glen Burnie	MD	48	0	1	0	0	0	0	0	0	0	0	48	48	0	0	0	0	0	0	35	13
1155	Trinity	AN	Annapolis	MD	219	0	0	0	0	0	0	0	2	0	7	210	0	5	1	0	0	204	0	135	75
1435	Trinity	AN	Odenton	MD	87	0	0	0	0	0	0	0	0	0	1	86	0	2	0	0	0	84	0	57	29
1385	Union	AN	Lothian	MD	38	0	0	0	0	0	0	0	0	0	0	38	0	38	0	0	0	0	0	21	17
1210	Union Memorial	AN	Davidsonville	MD	71	0	0	0	2	0	0	0	2	0	3	68	0	66	0	0	0	0	2	47	21
1365	Wesley Chapel	AN	Jessup	MD	112	0	0	0	0	0	2	0	0	0	0	112	0	0	0	0	0	112	0	70	42
1390	Wesley Chapel	AN	Lothian	MD	85	0	0	0	0	0	0	0	0	0	1	82	0	5	0	0	0	77	0	44	38
1355	Wesley Grove	AN	Hanover	MD	136	3	2	0	2	0	0	0	0	0	2	139	7	10	0	0	0	122	0	86	53
1290	Wilson Memorial	AN	Gambrills	MD	111	1	0	5	0	0	0	0	0	0	0	119	0	119	0	0	0	0	0	76	43
AN Total					**21,328**	**125**	**98**	**48**	**63**	**40**	**242**	**147**	**67**	**13**	**237**	**21,336**	**119**	**6,019**	**84**	**5**	**22**	**15,030**	**57**	**13,165**	**8,171**

Align #	Church Name	10	10a	11a	11b	11T	12	13	14	15	16	17	18	19	20	22	23	24	25	26	27	28	29	30a	30b
1410	Mount Zion	121	0	1	3	4	35	122	0	25	50	4	60	139	29	30	6	11	0	0	0	0	0	1	19
1465	Mount Zion	100	0	1	3	4	0	8	0	14	5	16	50	85	29	80	6	11	5	10	1,000	30	600	0	0
7420	Mount Zion	60	96	4	0	4	0	0	0	12	8	6	10	36	16	25	2	25	0	6	430	46	3,011	0	0
7415	Mount Zion-Ark Road	55	0	1	0	1	0	0	0	8	0	6	49	62	10	0	2	7	4	29	200	34	500	1	6
1430	Nichols-Bethel	291	27	0	0	0	498	265	2	156	76	23	118	373	108	57	10	17	25	21	1,252	46	4,065	0	0
1470	Pasadena	125	0	5	4	6	5	50	11	24	12	5	27	69	1	84	2	7	48	20	0	34	5,923	0	0
1485	Severn	40	0	0	0	0	46	78	0	0	3	3	51	57	1	0	1	6	0	25	0	68	7,900	3	36
1510	Severna Park	507	48	30	1	31	337	125	21	413	210	60	662	1,345	131	305	18	39	7	25	8,464	25	0	0	0
1380	Sollers	50	120	0	0	0	0	0	0	4	4	3	5	11	5	0	0	0	5	10	0	14	500	0	0
1345	Solley	36	0	3	2	5	14	10	0	5	5	3	5	10	5	73	1	1	0	0	0	25	0	0	0
1255	St Andrews of Annapolis	117	0	4	0	4	119	80	0	52	45	25	35	157	50	73	6	6	7	40	175	35	1,412	1	30
1350	St Mark	280	125	5	0	5	0	0	5	12	10	9	120	151	40	73	6	6	5	18	700	5	350	0	0
7425	St Marks	65	0	4	0	4	4	7	0	0	0	0	12	12	0	0	0	5	1	13	4,080	35	1,100	0	0
1520	St Matthews	60	30	6	0	6	4	0	0	9	13	6	15	43	20	30	0	4	6	27	0	26	0	0	0
1310	The Everlasting Love	35	0	0	0	0	0	0	0	30	3	5	31	48	0	0	0	0	0	13	0	35	4,250	0	0
1155	Trinity	113	0	2	0	2	6	26	0	40	8	11	120	169	43	68	8	10	10	25	0	37	0	0	0
1435	Trinity	29	0	1	0	1	1	10	0	2	11	0	19	70	17	45	3	2	3	3	0	0	0	0	0
1385	Union	20	0	0	0	0	0	0	0	0	3	0	15	20	0	0	0	0	0	4	0	7	0	0	0
1210	Union Memorial	43	0	0	0	0	0	7	0	0	0	0	13	13	0	0	0	2	3	12	0	20	0	0	0
1365	Wesley Chapel	17	6	2	0	2	4	0	0	5	2	0	4	4	5	12	0	0	3	0	0	2	0	0	0
1390	Wesley Chapel	30	0	0	0	0	0	0	0	94	6	6	15	22	10	30	2	2	2	0	0	0	0	0	0
1355	Wesley Grove	74	0	3	1	4	0	19	3	12	6	8	60	166	30	60	3	1	1	10	500	33	1,000	0	0
1290	Wilson Memorial	80	15	1	0	1	0	0	0		8		36	64			4								
AN Total		6,725	1,229	186	34	220	1,955	3,737	112	2,487	1,139	406	4,285	8,317	1,845	3,042	258	431	259	749	48,677	1,601	103,031	13	126

Column headers (full descriptions):
- 10: Average attendance at all weekly worship service(s)
- 10a: Persons who Worship Online
- 11a: Number of Infants and Children baptized (Age 0-12)
- 11b: Number of Teens and Adults baptized (Age 13+)
- 11T: TOTAL Number of persons baptized (all ages)
- 12: Number of baptized members who have not become Professing
- 13: Number of other constituents of the church
- 14: Total enrolled in confirmation preparation classes that
- 15: CHILDREN (0-11yrs) in all Christian groups, small groups and Sunday School
- 16: YOUTH (12-18 yrs) in all Christian groups, small groups and Sunday School
- 17: YOUNG ADULTS (19-30 yrs) in all Christian groups, small groups and Sunday School
- 18: OTHER ADULTS (31+ yrs) in all Christian groups, small groups and Sunday School
- 19: TOTAL number of persons participating in Christian formation groups (Total lines 15 – 18)
- 20: Average weekly attendance. Education classes/groups that meet in Sunday Church School groups
- 22: Number of participants in Vacation Bible School
- 23: Number of ongoing classes (all ages) for learning in Sunday Church
- 24: Number of ONGOING small groups, support groups, or classes
- 25: Number of SHORT-TERM classes, support groups, or small groups offered
- 26: Membership in United Methodist Men (UMM)
- 27: Amount paid for projects (UMM)
- 28: Membership in United Methodist Women (UMW)
- 29: Amount paid for local church and community work (UMW)
- 30a: Number of UMVIM teams sent out from this church
- 30b: Number of persons sent out on UMVIM teams from this church

Align #	Church Name	33	33a	33b	34	35a	36	36SF	37	38	39	42	43	44	45	46	47	45a	48b
1410	Mount Zion	5	3	5	724	82	4,279,820	17,895	306,600	22,510	0	150	0	0	0	0	0	0	59,731
1465	Mount Zion	3	2	3	120	110	2,192,000	14,036	0	0	0	132	0	0	0	0	0	0	5,217
7420	Mount Zion	3	1	3	2,318	16	250,000	3,980	90,000	0	0	0	0	0	0	0	0	0	6,537
1415	Mount Zion-Ark Road	1	0	1	30	20	1,146,000	7,976	50,000	0	0	0	0	0	0	0	0	0	12,522
1430	Nichols-Bethel	14	0	14	3,750	132	5,972,000	27,645	505,050	1,124,499	0	2,380	0	451	0	324	0	1,238	14,987
1470	Pasadena	6	3	3	1,608	95	3,926,320	18,245	155,796	35,364	0	390	0	0	0	0	0	0	1,825
1485	Severn	5	1	3	2,500	78	2,469,700	10,662	0	0	0	0	0	0	0	0	0	43,491	37,345
1510	Severna Park	69	6	26	33,287	1,997	9,879,000	40,059	301,950	0	0	0	0	0	0	0	0	500	200
1380	Sollers	7	2	3	60	42	785,000	48,830	211,200	0	0	0	0	0	0	0	0	513	7,741
1345	Solley	3	0	2	200	25	250,000	4,319	69,610	0	0	30	0	0	0	0	0	962	13,051
1255	St Andrews of Annapolis	7	2	5	800	150	3,151,260	64,000	359,743	1,884,917	2,785	720	0	0	0	0	0	0	23,249
1350	St Mark	10	1	4	197	15	2,600,000	12,100	410,489	0	0	0	0	0	0	0	0	0	23,955
7425	St Mark's	5	3	4	85	55	933,866	8,860	214,659	0	0	0	0	0	0	0	0	0	695
1520	St Matthews	3	3	3	121	22	2,037,420	19,388	0	513,500	0	0	0	0	0	0	0	0	1,500
1310	The Everlasting Love	3	0	3	370	215	400,000	2,563	150,045	40,000	0	0	0	0	0	0	0	0	2,873
1155	Trinity	8	2	4	850	41	4,644,000	2,934	166,310	254,784	0	0	0	0	0	0	0	0	0
1435	Trinity	0	0	0	350	15	472,443	6,300	0	0	0	0	0	0	0	0	0	838	200
1385	Union	3	0	3	1,890	24	519,100	2,538	80,000	0	0	85	0	0	0	0	0	300	2,790
1210	Union Memorial	0	1	2	1,000	18	820,763	3,600	0	0	0	0	0	0	0	0	0	150	0
1365	Wesley Chapel	3	0	0	475	4	820,000	16,988	286,606	0	0	0	0	0	0	0	0	0	0
1390	Wesley Chapel	3	1	2	640	60	631,722	1,755	297,350	0	0	0	0	0	0	0	0	0	8,420
1355	Wesley Grove	640	0	1	50	25	2,987,250		10,000	0	0	0	0	0	0	0	0	0	0
1290	Wilson Memorial	4	1	3			510,500			0	0	0	0	0	0	0	0	0	0
	AN Total	1,233	87	399	254,465	6,626	159,107,105	1,270,955	14,323,121	6,443,664	28,503	18,413	0	2,673	0	2,456	0	94,748	653,440

Column key:
- 33 — TOTAL Community MINISTRIES for outreach, justice, and mercy
- 33a — MINISTRIES focusing on global/regional health?
- 33b — MINISTRIES focusing on engaging in ministry with the poor/socially
- 34 — PERSONS SERVED BY community ministries for outreach, justice, and mercy
- 35a — PERSONS SERVING (from your congregation) in mission/community ministries
- 36 — Market value of church-owned land, buildings and equipment
- 36SF — Overall square footage of church owned buildings (furnished and unfurnished areas)
- 37 — Market value of financial and other liquid assets
- 38 — Debt secured by church physical assets
- 39 — Other debt
- 42 — General Advance Specials remitted to the Annual Conference Treasurer
- 43 — World Service Specials remitted to the Annual Conference Treasurer
- 44 — Annual Conference Advance Specials remitted to the Annual Conference Treasurer
- 45 — Youth Service Fund remitted to the
- 46 — All other funds sent to AC Treasurer for connectional mission and ministry
- 47 — Total Annual Conference Special Sunday Offerings remitted to the
- 45a — UMC CAUSES: Total amount given DIRECTLY to United Methodist causes (NOT sent to BWC Treasurer)
- 48b — MISSIONS/MINISTRY COSTS: Direct costs incurred by the local church for mission and community ministry activities

Align.#	Church Name	48 TOTAL Total of UMC Causes & UMC Missions & Outreach	49 NON-UMC CAUSES: Total amount given DIRECTLY to non-United Methodist benevolent and charitable causes (NOT sent to BWC Treasurer)	50a Human Relations Sunday	50b UMCOR Sunday (formerly One Great Hour of Sharing)	50c Peace with Justice Sunday	50d Native American Ministries Sunday	50e World Communion Sunday	50f U.M. Student Day	51 Direct-billed clergy non-health benefits	52 Direct-billed clergy health benefits	53a Base compensation paid to/for the Senior Pastor or other person assigned or appointed in the lead pastoral role to the church	53b Base compensation paid/for to all Associate Pastor(s) & other pastoral staff assigned or appointed to the church.	53c Base compensation paid to/for any Deacons NOT included in 53a or 53b	55a Housing benefits paid to/for Lead Pastor or person in lead pastoral role as described in 53a	55b Housing benefits paid to/for ALL Associate Pastor(s) & other pastoral staff assigned or appointed to the	55c Housing benefits paid to/for any Deacons not included in 53a or 53b	56 Paid to/for all persons included in Lines 53a-53c for accountable reimbursements	57 Paid to/for all persons included in Lines 53a-53c for any other cash allowances (non-)
1410	Mount Zion	59,731	1,000	0	0	0	5	0	0	13,975	11,623	74,013	0	0	4,100	0	0	3,504	0
1465	Mount Zion	5,217	800	123	0	193	0	51	0	11,343	12,089	43,203	0	0	19,866	0	0	1,526	0
7420	Mount Zion	6,537	1,205	0	0	0	0	0	0	8,587	13,804	31,465	0	0	0	0	0	1,538	0
7415	Mount Zion-Ark Road	0	200	0	1,111	0	0	0	0	15,293	14,584	29,231	0	0	9,933	0	0	1,025	0
1430	Nichols-Bethel	13,760	3,315	608	0	0	0	493	524	26,082	22,207	57,550	44,148	12,253	27,757	0	20,000	8,882	0
1470	Pasadena	14,987	900	0	0	0	0	196	0	14,184	10,320	66,000	0	0	30,000	0	0	6,356	0
1485	Severn	1,825	3,801	0	0	0	0	0	0	8,041	11,400	18,252	0	0	9,933	0	0	0	0
1510	Severna Park	80,836	86,723	0	0	0	0	0	0	42,812	78,973	119,869	53,606	69,060	19,866	19,866	19,866	17,012	0
1380	Soliers	700	300	0	0	0	0	0	0	0	0	19,240	0	0	6,622	0	0	2,050	0
1345	Solley	8,254	50	0	5	0	0	0	20	0	0	17,907	0	0	8,953	0	0	1,200	0
1255	St Andrews of Annapolis	14,013	1,650	0	0	0	0	0	0	14,574	15,235	98,998	0	0	25,584	0	0	7,520	0
1350	St Mark	23,249	1,750	0	0	0	0	0	0	14,610	16,700	71,890	0	0	31,200	0	0	1,814	0
7425	St Mark's	23,955	1,848	0	0	0	0	0	0	12,164	14,117	47,714	0	0	19,866	0	0	2,256	0
1520	St Matthews	695	2,625	400	0	100	0	137	0	12,927	11,400	36,827	0	0	13,244	0	0	2,050	0
1310	The Everlasting Love	1,500	0	0	0	0	0	0	0	4,305	0	30,728	0	0	0	0	0	0	0
1155	Trinity	2,873	58,680	0	0	0	0	0	0	12,477	15,730	69,015	0	0	0	0	0	646	0
1435	Trinity	0	500	0	0	0	0	0	0	0	0	13,109	0	0	4,554	0	0	1,025	0
1385	Union	1,038	0	0	0	0	0	0	0	0	0	12,600	0	0	0	0	0	0	0
1210	Union Memorial	300	0	0	0	0	0	0	0	0	0	26,434	0	0	10,000	0	0	450	0
1365	Wesley Chapel	2,940	4,000	0	0	0	0	50	0	0	0	0	0	0	19,065	0	0	0	0
1390	Wesley Chapel		3,607	0	0	0	0	0	0	0	0	23,250	0	0	0	0	0	2,877	0
1355	Wesley Grove		0	0	0	0	0	0	0	0	0	45,843	0	0	19,866	0	0	1,810	0
1290	Wilson Memorial	8,420	12,773	0	0	0	0	0	0	11,828	10,320	30,600	0	0	19,866	0	0	1,810	0
	AN Total	758,188	430,801	2,086	2,389	2,053	1,449	2,022	1,575	595,496	684,271	2,928,924	152,524	61,313	851,730	57,366	39,866	195,531	1,861

Column definitions:
- **60**: Paid in salary and benefits for all other church staff and diaconal ministers
- **61**: Amount spent for local church program expenses
- **62**: Amount spent for local church operating expenses
- **63**: Amount paid for principal and interest on indebtedness, loans, mortgages, etc.
- **63a**: Amount paid for capital campaign or fundraising costs
- **64**: Amount paid on capital expenditures for building, improvements, and major equipment purchases.
- **65**: Amount PAID by/for the local church on all expenditures
- **66**: Number of giving units
- **67a**: Received through pledges
- **67b**: Received from non-pledging, but identified givers
- **67c**: Received from unidentified givers
- **67d**: Amount received from interest and dividends and/or transferred from liquid assets
- **67e**: Amount received from Sale of Church Assets
- **67f**: Amount received through building use fees, contributions, and rentals
- **67g**: Amount received through fundraisers and other sources

Align #	Church Name	60	61	62	63	63a	64	65	66	67a	67b	67c	67d	67e	67f	67g
1410	Mount Zion	123,127	24,106	37,118	84,256	0	64,269	545,130	174	0	451,113	5,349	2,605	0	18,545	3,066
1465	Mount Zion	36,982	20,000	87,215	0	0	0	273,222	101	27,196	146,240	4,731	33	0	2,050	16,301
7420	Mount Zion	32,175	5,604	27,441	0	0	11,837	156,970	0	0	140,380	0	0	0	0	0
1415	Mount Zion-Ark Road	0	1,425	23,240	132,609	0	29,640	140,549	42	0	159,290	0	0	0	0	27,730
1430	Nichols-Bethel	135,808	19,564	105,010	7,854	7,658	62,631	775,513	217	0	588,746	61,927	0	0	4,760	6,919
1470	Pasadena	67,192	7,023	55,817	0	0	13,400	321,123	129	190,680	72,648	7,262	18	0	23,500	0
1485	Severn	12,380	308	48,304	0	0	30,657	139,849	29	0	84,650	5,275	6	0	400	0
1510	Severna Park	403,770	87,645	246,487	0	0	2,293	1,547,030	676	812,725	422,165	177,786	6	0	8,610	50,205
1380	Sollers	27,900	500	12,500	0	0	0	85,696	60	60,200	2,000	3,500	0	0	100	9,500
1345	Solley	7,697	993	9,671	0	0	0	61,812	22	0	35,031	9,072	27	0	700	10,705
1255	St Andrews of Annapolis	75,790	11,936	57,187	159,417	4,623	84,541	610,178	224	88,020	69,476	3,369	3,264	0	64,494	18,773
1350	St Mark	89,516	117,646	98,886	0	0	44,548	582,452	344	37,000	289,387	15,852	1,012	0	45,825	268,734
7425	St Mark's	48,411	3,187	37,997	40,688	0	3,988	219,817	68	0	147,376	8,273	26,581	0	34,000	22,233
1520	St Matthews	25,111	7,324	27,750	0	0	5,000	202,150	55	36,830	0	475	0	0	1,000	37,415
1310	The Everlasting Love	0	4,000	4,000	54,667	0	41,070	55,653	18	0	38,000	23,500	0	0	0	0
1155	Trinity	111,812	6,584	97,021	0	0	11,970	521,331	130	0	399,967	6,314	1,934	0	8,025	1,144
1435	Trinity	0	1,308	11,071	0	0	0	48,756	44	71,254	845	2,701	0	0	1,918	1,375
1385	Union	1,800	567	5,953	0	0	0	25,737	17	18,046	1,599	7,183	51	0	0	3,410
1210	Union Memorial	0	1,995	25,911	0	0	0	75,148	39	0	78,995	3,708	0	0	0	0
1365	Wesley Chapel	4,640	1,013	3,716	0	0	206	38,245	19	0	43,704	1,432	0	0	12,200	0
1390	Wesley Chapel	0	0	19,861	0	0	9,860	67,553	21	0	60,768	1,677	0	0	0	1,787
1355	Wesley Grove	19,897	2,514	26,954	0	0	0	165,954	77	0	115,253	2,991	0	0	500	4,577
1290	Wilson Memorial	0	0	10,845	0	0	0	63,580	60	87,500	0	0	0	30,000	400	0
AN Total		3,153,512	719,668	3,175,504	903,293	26,994	937,302	17,592,376	7,115	4,530,696	9,084,290	563,738	51,262	30,000	1,019,617	863,071

Align #	Church Name	67 TOTAL income for annual budget/spending plan (67a-g)	68a Capital campaigns	68b Memorials, endowments, and bequests	68c Other sources and projects (include UMW, UMM and 'flow-through')	68d Special Sundays, Gen. Adv. Spec, World Srvc Spec., Conf. Adv. Spec. and other directed benevolent giving	68 Total income for designated causes including capital campaign and other special projects	69a Equitable Compensation Funds received by Church or Pastor	69b Advance Special, apportioned, and connectional funds received by church	69c Other grants and financial support from institutional sources	69 Income from connectional / institutional sources outside the local church	70 TOTAL CHURCH INCOME (Sum of Lines 67 + 68 + 69)	40a Amount APPORTIONED to the local church	40b Amount PAID by the local church for all apportioned causes
1410	Mount Zion	480,678	82,337	1,205	0	155	83,697	0	0	0	0	564,375	44,153	44,153
1465	Mount Zion	196,551	0	0	0	499	499	0	0	0	0	197,050	34,482	34,482
7420	Mount Zion	140,380	7,640	0	0	0	7,640	0	0	0	0	148,020	16,777	16,777
1415	Mount Zion-Ark Road	159,290	0	0	0	0	0	0	0	0	0	159,290	15,988	15,988
1430	Nichols-Bethel	683,163	41,064	1,975	0	5,681	48,720	0	0	0	0	731,883	68,026	68,026
1470	Pasadena	301,027	0	0	0	1,347	1,347	0	0	0	0	302,374	39,964	39,964
1485	Severn	90,331	16,714	4,980	0	0	21,694	0	0	0	0	112,025	12,205	12,205
1510	Severna Park	1,471,497	0	11,766	0	0	11,766	0	0	0	0	1,483,263	169,982	169,982
1380	Sollers	75,300	0	0	0	250	250	0	0	0	0	75,550	13,591	13,591
1345	Solley	55,535	0	12,570	0	3,468	16,038	0	0	0	0	71,573	7,032	7,032
1255	St Andrews of Annapolis	247,396	77,871	902	24,333	720	103,826	0	0	0	0	351,222	43,013	43,013
1350	St Mark	657,810	0	0	0	2,932	2,932	0	0	0	0	660,742	70,643	70,643
7425	St Mark's	238,463	4,995	0	21,175	5,865	32,035	0	0	0	0	270,498	24,906	8,302
1520	St Matthews	75,720	0	1,200	0	537	1,737	0	0	0	0	77,457	16,884	16,884
1310	The Everlasting Love	61,500	0	0	0	0	0	0	0	0	0	61,500	9,359	6,120
1155	Trinity	416,240	0	151,800	0	0	151,800	0	0	0	0	568,040	50,756	50,756
1435	Trinity	77,862	0	325	0	0	325	0	0	0	0	78,187	5,219	5,219
1385	Union	28,254	0	10,365	5,103	0	15,468	0	0	0	0	43,722	3,779	3,779
1210	Union Memorial	86,113	0	0	0	0	0	0	0	0	0	86,113	9,973	9,973
1365	Wesley Chapel	57,336	0	2,731	0	0	2,731	0	0	0	0	60,067	2,665	2,665
1390	Wesley Chapel	64,232	0	0	1,910	338	2,248	0	0	0	0	66,480	8,048	8,048
1355	Wesley Grove	123,321	0	1,400	252,302	0	253,702	0	0	0	0	377,023	18,502	18,502
1290	Wilson Memorial	87,900	0	0	0	0	0	0	0	0	0	87,900	9,362	9,362
AN Total		16,142,674	472,329	1,630,805	366,081	247,112	2,716,327	0	0	3,000	3,000	18,862,001	1,931,024	1,890,110

Align #	Church Name	Dist #	City	State	Total professing members at the close of 2017 (1)	Received by PROFESSION of Faith (2a1)	Received by PROFESSION of Faith (Other Than Confirmation) (2a2)	Restored by AFFIRMATION of Faith (2b)	Transferred in from other UM churches (3)	Transferred in from non-UM churches (4)	Removed or corrected by Charge Conference action (5a)	Withdrawn from Professing Membership (5b)	Transferred out to other UM churches (6)	Transferred out to non-UM churches (7)	Removed by death (8)	Total professing members at the close of 2019 (9)	Asian (9a)	African American / Black (9b)	Hispanic / Latino (9c)	Native American (9d)	Pacific Islander (9e)	White (9f)	Multi-Racial (9g)	Female (9h)	Male (9i)
4110	Ames	BM	Baltimore	MD	512	7	7	0	0	0	0	0	0	0	15	518	0	500	4	0	0	6	8	356	162
3110	Arbutus	BM	Baltimore	MD	876	0	2	0	0	0	0	1	0	0	6	871	1	2	0	0	0	867	1	463	408
4115	Arlington-Lewin	BM	Baltimore	MD	123	0	2	0	0	0	0	0	3	0	0	122	0	121	0	0	0	1	0	87	35
3530	Arnolia	BM	Baltimore	MD	221	2	2	0	3	3	0	0	0	2	3	211	0	3	2	0	0	204	0	128	83
2420	Back River	BM	Essex	MD	106	2	2	1	4	1	1	0	0	0	3	113	0	4	0	0	0	109	0	71	42
3150	Beechfield	BM	Baltimore	MD	16	0	0	0	1	0	0	0	0	0	1	14	0	13	0	0	0	1	0	11	3
3145	Bethesda	BM	Baltimore	MD	64	0	1	0	0	0	0	0	0	0	1	64	2	9	0	0	0	55	0	45	19
2142	Brooklyn Community	BM	Baltimore	MD	200	0	10	1	0	3	37	0	0	1	0	162	0	4	0	0	0	156	2	98	64
4180	Catonsville	BM	Catonsville	MD	1,529	7	10	1	0	9	15	3	0	0	14	1,524	10	0	0	0	0	1,514	0	868	656
2362	Chase	BM	Baltimore	MD	193	0	1	0	0	0	0	0	0	0	0	193	0	38	0	0	0	155	0	129	64
2155	Cherry Hill	BM	Baltimore	MD	136	0	0	0	0	0	0	48	0	0	3	91	0	91	0	0	0	0	0	63	28
2160	Christ	BM	Baltimore	MD	451	1	0	0	2	0	0	0	2	0	3	449	0	441	0	0	1	6	2	295	154
3285	Christ Church of Baltimore County	BM	Baltimore	MD	204	0	1	0	0	0	2	0	1	0	1	202	4	123	0	0	0	98	5	136	66
3115	Christ Church of the Deaf	BM	White Marsh	MD	248	0	0	0	0	0	0	0	0	0	7	242	1	0	12	0	0	105	0	144	98
2570	Cowenton	BM	Baltimore	MD	82	0	1	0	0	0	0	0	0	0	1	81	0	0	0	0	0	81	0	52	29
2380	Dundalk	BM	Baltimore	MD	120	0	1	0	0	6	4	4	4	0	7	106	1	98	0	0	0	1	0	64	42
2175	Eastern	BM	Baltimore	MD	296	0	0	0	0	0	193	0	0	0	1	99	0	99	0	0	0	0	0	71	28
2180	Edan Korean	BM	Baltimore	MD	0	3	1	0	0	0	1	0	0	1	0	154	154	0	0	0	0	0	0	87	67
4120	Elderslie-St Andrews	BM	Baltimore	MD	116	0	1	0	1	0	0	0	1	0	1	116	0	114	0	0	0	52	0	92	24
4630	Emanuel	BM	Baltimore	MD	68	0	1	0	0	0	0	0	0	0	0	70	0	18	0	0	0	0	0	43	27
4610	Emmarts	BM	Catonsville	MD	59	0	3	0	2	0	22	0	2	0	0	62	1	60	2	0	0	4	0	51	11
4170	Epworth Chapel	BM	Baltimore	MD	1,192	6	24	0	2	0	0	0	1	0	8	1,194	1	1,186	1	0	0	102	3	792	402
2425	Essex	BM	Essex	MD	106	2	1	0	1	0	1	0	1	0	0	109	1	2	0	0	0	25	0	76	33
2192	Faith Community	BM	Baltimore	MD	49	0	0	0	0	0	0	0	0	0	0	47	0	21	0	0	0	70	1	25	22
3230	Good Shepherd	BM	Baltimore	MD	72	0	2	0	1	0	0	0	1	0	0	71	0	1	0	0	0	0	0	53	18
3165	Gowans-Boundary	BM	Baltimore	MD	0	0	0	0	0	0	0	0	0	1	3	102	0	100	0	0	0	2	0	72	30
3170	Grace	BM	Baltimore	MD	608	3	2	0	3	6	0	0	2	1	7	617	10	28	4	1	0	570	5	342	275
2210	Graceland	BM	Baltimore	MD	133	0	2	0	1	0	0	0	2	1	7	129	0	8	0	0	0	118	0	75	54
4130	Gwynn Oak	BM	Baltimore	MD	113	1	2	0	1	0	1	0	2	0	3	110	0	110	0	0	0	0	0	70	40
3120	Halethorpe-Relay	BM	Halethorpe	MD	186	0	2	0	6	0	0	0	2	0	3	194	0	6	0	0	0	188	0	131	63
3175	Hampden	BM	Baltimore	MD	112	0	4	1	1	2	0	2	2	0	8	112	0	0	0	0	0	112	0	73	39
3440	Hiss	BM	Baltimore	MD	727	9	4	1	9	2	10	0	2	1	12	710	4	62	1	0	3	639	1	431	279
3180	Homestead	BM	Baltimore	MD	61	0	3	0	1	1	0	4	0	0	0	54	0	54	0	0	0	0	0	38	16
4135	John Wesley	BM	Baltimore	MD	380	0	1	1	0	0	5	3	3	3	12	368	0	367	2	0	0	233	1	293	75
3125	Lansdowne	BM	Baltimore	MD	260	0	5	0	0	2	0	9	2	0	4	239	0	3	0	0	0	198	1	144	95
3540	Loch Raven	BM	Baltimore	MD	340	0	2	0	1	0	38	0	2	2	10	280	4	77	2	0	0	187	1	179	101
2410	Lodge Forest	BM	Baltimore	MD	188	0	0	0	0	1	0	0	1	0	2	187	1	0	0	0	0	179	1	99	88
3185	Lovely Lane	BM	Baltimore	MD	212	0	4	0	0	0	0	2	1	0	2	210	0	29	2	0	0	23	1	118	92
1455	Magothy Church of the Deaf	BM	Pasadena	MD	33	0	0	0	0	0	0	0	0	0	0	27	0	1	0	0	0	0	0	21	6
4145	Martin Luther King Memorial	BM	Baltimore	MD	63	1	15	0	10	4	15	15	2	0	5	71	0	70	0	0	0	0	3	60	11
2220	Metropolitan	BM	Baltimore	MD	223	8	0	1	0	1	12	12	3	0	8	214	0	213	0	0	0	50	3	146	68
3215	Mount Vernon Place	BM	Baltimore	MD	75	0	0	0	0	0	0	0	0	0	2	75	3	22	0	0	0	62	0	50	25
3220	Mount Washington-Aldersgate	BM	Baltimore	MD	132	0	0	0	0	0	14	2	0	1	0	115	42	11	0	0	0	0	0	81	34
2235	Mount Winans	BM	Baltimore	MD	49	0	4	0	0	0	0	2	1	1	2	47	0	46	0	0	0	1	0	39	8
4150	Mount Zion	BM	Baltimore	MD	237	0	0	0	1	0	0	0	1	2	5	229	0	229	0	0	0	0	0	126	103
3575	New Covenant Worship Center	BM	Baltimore	MD	165	5	6	0	0	1	0	8	0	0	5	160	0	160	0	0	0	0	0	142	18
3217	New Waverly	BM	Baltimore	MD	145	5	3	0	5	0	0	0	0	0	1	141	1	140	0	0	0	1	0	93	48
3225	Northwood-Appold	BM	Baltimore	MD	152	0	0	0	0	0	0	0	0	0	8	153	0	151	0	0	0	0	0	103	50

Align #	Church Name	1D Average attendance at all weekly worship service(s)	10a Persons who Worship Online	11a Infants/Children baptized (0-12)	11b Teens/Adults baptized (13+)	11T TOTAL baptized (all ages)	12 Baptized members not Professing	13 Other constituents	14 Confirmation prep enrolled	15 Children (0-11)	16 Youth (12-18)	17 Young Adults (19-30)	18 Other Adults (31+)	19 TOTAL participating (15-18)	20 Education class Sunday School attendance	22 VBS participants	23 Ongoing classes (all ages)	24 Ongoing small groups	25 Short-term groups	26 UMM membership	27 Amount paid projects (UMM)	28 UMW membership	29 Amount local church/community (UMW)	30a UMVIM teams sent	30b Persons sent on UMVIM teams
4110	Ames	75	150	3	7	10	0	15	7	15	5	4	11	35	12	0	3	5	3	7	200	7	0	0	0
3110	Arbutus	103	0	3	0	10	6	3	0	21	7	6	34	68	25	56	3	3	3	10	2,119	25	624	0	0
4115	Arlington-Lewin	50	0	3	0	3	6	3	0	14	10	18	13	55	15	28	2	1	0	0	0	0	0	0	0
3530	Arnolia	84	0	2	0	3	31	29	0	9	6	4	32	51	6	28	2	4	3	0	685	0	0	0	0
2420	Back River	77	0	2	0	2	72	24	2	28	3	0	62	93	4	28	2	2	0	0	0	25	2,560	0	0
3150	Beechfield	11	0	0	0	0	0	1	0	0	0	0	6	6	6	0	1	2	0	0	0	0	0	0	0
3145	Bethesda	24	0	2	0	0	8	3	0	10	0	1	23	33	8	0	1	1	0	0	0	0	0	0	0
2142	Brooklyn Community	65	0	0	0	12	0	25	5	145	80	10	98	333	70	32	15	8	5	79	2,057	85	9,740	6	145
4140	Catonsville	364	0	10	2	12	178	496	7	22	15	3	14	43	20	140	2	1	2	28	0	48	0	0	0
2362	Chase	54	0	5	0	9	11	33	0	25	10	10	7	22	30	30	2	6	0	17	300	23	211	0	0
2155	Cherry Hill	70	0	6	3	2	1	0	1	14	15	3	100	145	25	35	5	5	0	6	975	48	0	0	0
2160	Christ	110	0	6	1	1	1	0	0	25	10	10	20	38	31	10	2	1	1	6	100	6	100	0	0
3285	Christ Church of Baltimore Court	32	0	0	1	1	0	0	0	14	5	2	20	25	12	0	5	4	0	0	0	6	0	0	0
3115	Christ Church of the Deaf	57	161	0	1	1	5	12	0	9	0	0	20	25	5	0	2	2	1	6	0	0	100	0	0
2570	Cowenton	47	0	0	0	0	0	0	0	0	0	0	0	0	0	0	0	0	0	0	0	0	0	0	0
2380	Dundalk	21	0	0	0	0	0	11	0	10	6	2	53	71	51	54	3	5	3	10	0	30	175	0	0
2175	Eastern	70	0	0	0	0	4	4	0	24	25	25	74	148	60	40	4	4	3	35	600	62	1,200	0	0
2180	Eden Korean	130	0	0	0	0	0	4	3	11	12	8	38	69	16	50	5	5	0	8	0	0	0	0	0
4120	Elderslie-St Andrews	47	0	2	0	2	0	13	0	14	7	7	18	46	15	68	3	4	4	0	0	0	0	0	0
4630	Emanuel	38	0	1	0	0	2	0	0	0	0	0	18	18	0	0	2	2	2	65	26,000	0	5,000	1	3
4610	Emmarts	50	0	2	0	2	0	0	6	60	45	30	80	215	85	50	1	35	12	0	0	50	2,470	0	0
4170	Epworth Chapel	322	110	10	3	13	0	275	0	6	3	3	13	22	23	21	9	1	1	0	0	15	0	0	0
2425	Essex	80	0	2	1	3	2	5	0	2	1	4	43	50	8	0	3	0	0	0	0	0	0	0	0
2192	Faith Community	23	0	0	0	0	3	2	0	7	3	5	12	27	10	54	1	4	3	0	0	0	0	0	0
3230	Good Shepherd	34	0	2	0	2	2	26	0	8	5	5	50	131	12	54	3	0	0	0	0	0	0	0	0
3165	Govans-Boundary	30	0	0	0	2	20	41	0	10	20	5	27	60	72	40	1	6	3	0	0	0	1,484	0	0
3170	Grace	205	0	10	2	12	45	8	3	15	10	3	60	131	27	17	0	0	8	0	0	28	0	0	0
2210	Graceland	43	5	2	0	1	1	47	0	63	10	0	49	60	48	50	4	5	1	0	0	14	410	0	0
4130	Gwynn Oak	55	0	1	0	1	0	12	1	28	3	3	38	49	25	57	4	5	2	11	1,738	0	0	0	0
3120	Halethorpe-Relay	91	0	3	1	4	2	40	2	0	11	10	31	75	6	22	4	4	1	20	0	24	0	0	1
3175	Hampden	27	0	1	0	1	0	9	0	30	10	10	22	22	58	0	2	2	2	0	0	0	0	0	0
3440	Hiss	208	0	1	4	5	13	0	6	35	40	10	75	160	8	42	8	15	1	0	0	4	0	0	0
3180	Homestead	18	0	0	0	0	40	43	8	4	13	16	40	46	22	54	5	0	2	0	0	0	0	0	0
4135	John Wesley	134	0	5	0	5	26	4	0	4	15	7	17	70	11	40	3	1	1	10	100	49	1,100	0	0
3125	Lansdowne	64	0	0	0	2	3	24	0	8	7	0	27	27	7	17	4	0	5	0	0	10	0	0	0
3540	Loch Raven	99	3	2	0	2	15	28	0	8	0	0	54	65	8	50	3	0	2	0	0	10	3,800	1	5
2410	Lodge Forest	42	0	1	1	2	10	45	0	10	1	0	10	26	8	57	1	11	5	14	0	28	2,610	1	5
3185	Lovely Lane	47	0	0	0	0	16	13	0	15	0	0	4	26	8	0	1	7	0	6	0	14	0	0	0
1455	Magothy Church of the Deaf	25	0	2	0	0	1	14	0	1	0	0	6	6	6	0	0	1	0	0	0	6	0	0	0
4145	Martin Luther King Memorial	45	0	0	0	0	0	0	0	4	0	0	4	16	0	0	4	3	0	11	100	11	0	0	0
2220	Metropolitan	65	0	0	0	0	12	12	0	6	9	8	34	33	30	0	3	3	5	35	2,000	0	500	0	0
3215	Mount Vernon Place	35	0	1	0	0	20	20	0	12	9	0	15	39	8	0	0	0	9	0	0	0	4,415	0	0
3020	Mount Washington-Aldersgate	47	0	1	0	0	16	16	0	0	9	0	33	45	19	27	4	1	8	8	122	6	95	0	0
2235	Mount Winans	36	0	0	0	0	1	4	0	16	7	3	39	39	8	0	1	7	9	9	0	14	0	0	0
4150	Mount Zion	44	0	1	0	0	4	8	4	4	10	0	30	45	25	0	7	11	3	8	800	24	900	0	0
9575	New Covenant Worship Center	46	3	0	0	0	8	8	0	4	3	0	31	59	25	0	3	7	4	9	2,300	0	0	0	0
3217	New Waverly	80	0	2	3	5	8	0	5	13	4	3	20	45	45	35	3	3	3	15	0	0	0	0	0
3225	Northwood-Appold	55	0	0	0	0	0	0	4	15	4	10	20	37	43	0	4	3	3	5	100	12	0	0	0

Align #	Church Name	33 TOTAL Community MINISTRIES for outreach, justice, and mercy	33a MINISTRIES focusing on global/regional health?	33b MINISTRIES focusing on engaging in ministry with the poor/socially	34 PERSONS SERVED BY community ministries for outreach, justice, and mercy	35a PERSONS SERVING (from your congregation) in mission/community ministries	36 Market value of church-owned land, buildings and equipment	36F Overall square footage of church owned buildings (furnished and unfurnished areas)	37 Market value of financial and other liquid assets	38 Debt secured by church physical assets	39 Other debt	42 General Advance Specials remitted to the Annual Conference Treasurer	43 World Service Specials remitted to the Annual Conference Treasurer	44 Annual Conference Advance Specials remitted to the Annual Conference Treasurer	45 Youth Service Fund remitted to the	46 All other funds sent to AC Treasurer for connectional mission and ministry	47 Total Annual Conference Special Sunday Offerings remitted to the	48a UMC CAUSES: Total amount given DIRECTLY to United Methodist causes (NOT sent to BWC Treasurer)	48b MISSIONS/MINISTRY COSTS: Direct costs incurred by the local church for mission and community ministry activities
4110	Ames	7	0	7	8,000	20	3,500,000	27,000	1,000,000	0	0	0	0	0	0	0	0	0	46,039
3110	Arbutus	7	2	5	5,600	150	8,775,000	33,000	321,075	0	0	305	0	0	0	0	0	0	39,928
4115	Arlington-Lewin	1	0	6	25	7	4,949,000	16,715	653,000	0	0	0	0	0	0	0	0	0	1,575
3530	Arnolia	6	0	1	750	79	5,123,907	16,751	275,735	0	0	0	0	0	0	0	0	562	1,242
4420	Back River	4	0	4	154	110	2,700,900	8,325	0	2,555	0	0	0	0	0	0	0	75	4,003
3150	Beechfield	1	0	1	229	6	1,100,000	0	126,000	0	10,000	0	0	0	0	30	0	1,300	7,900
3145	Bethesda	15	7	11	11,500	25	3,000,000	15,084	137,790	0	0	841	0	45	0	0	0	0	2,803
2142	Brooklyn Community	12	0	12	350	60	4,312,000	16,236	0	0	0	219	0	0	0	30	0	32,961	11,761
4180	Catonsville	22	0	7	695	402	10,000,000	45,738	714,072	0	2,777	1,503	0	0	0	70	0	500	60,420
2062	Chase	6	0	5	960	32	1,590,000	7,500	209,225	0	0	0	0	0	0	0	0	463	2,588
2155	Cherry Hill	2	0	2	140	10	600,500	3,624	1,400,000	0	0	472	0	0	0	0	0	555	8,541
2160	Christ	14	0	14	4,000	75	3,000,000	14,780	0	0	5,388	0	0	0	0	0	0	18,556	10,004
2285	Christ Church of Baltimore Court	16	0	10	1,934	44	2,322,000	13,342	576,219	85,381	0	0	0	0	0	0	0	0	2,870
3115	Christ Church of the Deaf	0	0	0	2,300	56	2,037,899	13,000	56,804	0	26,779	0	0	0	0	0	0	0	8,411
2570	Cowenton	0	0	0	125	15	2,700,000	10,000	430,166	0	0	0	0	0	0	0	0	0	4,532
2380	Dundalk	0	0	0	150	0	2,755,600	21,982	84,433	0	0	34	0	0	0	0	0	0	5,928
2175	Eastern	23	3	19	2,350	32	2,000,000	0	0	0	0	0	0	0	0	0	0	0	738
2100	Eden Korean	0	0	0	275	13	1,542,200	31,058	54,622	0	19,000	0	0	271	0	0	0	0	19,400
4120	Elderslie-St Andrews	4	0	1	1,200	75	2,325,000	10,562	525,690	0	0	0	0	0	0	0	0	0	0
4630	Emanuel	0	0	0	0	7	0	0	0	0	0	0	0	0	0	0	0	0	250
4610	Emmarts	2	0	2	2	20	3,260,698	45,000	226,273	101,999	0	0	0	990	0	0	0	10,000	42,200
4170	Epworth Chapel	20	3	17	5,000	325	4,641,100	0	69,903	0	0	52	0	0	0	0	0	0	18,418
2425	Essex	6	0	4	10,328	25	4,500,000	22,355	43,159	0	0	0	0	37	0	0	0	0	8,968
2192	Faith Community	19	5	5	1,250	19	2,208,573	31,000	1,094,799	0	0	100	0	59	0	0	0	0	36,195
3230	Good Shepherd	6	1	5	2,000	60	5,000,000	21,500	2,000,000	0	0	0	0	0	0	0	0	1,000	3,000
3165	Govans-Boundary	2	0	5	175	40	13,766,170	0	9,296,780	0	19,000	8,638	0	5	0	0	0	100	20,186
3170	Grace	5	0	5	200	100	2,058,000	49,287	0	0	0	0	0	0	0	0	0	0	932
2210	Graceland	0	0	0	0	21	0	8,480	0	0	0	0	0	0	0	0	0	0	577
4130	Gwynn Oak	14	0	15	4,500	68	2,943,500	58,000	36,130	0	0	22	0	100	0	0	0	0	171
3120	Halethorpe-Relay	15	0	6	2,400	37	1,645,660	13,250	213,410	0	0	10	0	0	0	0	0	170	12,409
3445	Hampden	2	0	1	300	36	4,834,400	12,400	20,000	0	0	105	0	0	0	52	0	0	0
3440	Hiss	4	0	3	0	67	6,841,000	38,567	1,500,000	0	0	918	0	25	0	0	0	138	196
3180	Homestead	0	0	0	5,548	75	1,300,000	10,000	100,000	0	0	0	0	0	0	0	0	0	43,753
4135	John Wesley	18	2	18	3,198	45	5,000,000	27,036	0	0	0	83	0	300	0	0	0	7,939	5,087
3125	Lansdowne	7	1	3	593	66	2,500,000	16,186	212,000	0	0	1,400	0	0	0	0	0	1,000	4,108
3540	Loch Raven	6	4	2	136	7	4,112,000	26,720	562,130	0	6,257	0	0	0	0	0	0	175	4,079
2410	Lodge Forest	4	0	2	961	18	1,074,000	4,126	19,960	0	0	260	0	137	0	0	0	547	4,559
3185	Lovely Lane	2	0	7	250	23	13,411,000	25,000	2,605,637	0	0	300	0	0	0	0	0	10,488	629
1455	Magothy Church of the Deaf	14	0	35	3	100	0	0	0	0	0	0	0	0	0	0	0	0	6,900
4145	Martin Luther King Memorial	0	0	0	150	15	2,245,000	16,121	146,652	24,167	16,000	0	0	0	0	0	0	150	18,174
2220	Metropolitan	21	1	0	1,000	15	2,950,000	27,020	0	0	0	0	0	0	0	0	0	0	0
3215	Mount Vernon Place	3	1	3	430	10	13,084,360	17,280	6,475	0	0	67	0	0	0	0	0	0	3,243
3220	Mount Washington-Aldersgate	4	2	2	140	64	2,930,138	3,267	96,000	0	0	1,720	0	0	0	375	0	0	0
2235	Mount Winans	3	0	0	390	17	552,000	14,128	105,580	0	0	0	0	0	0	0	0	1,100	0
4150	Mount Zion	4	2	4	300	43	2,598,902	14,417	225,500	0	15,631	0	0	0	0	0	0	1,302	13,478
3575	New Covenant Worship Center	7	0	7	700	0	1,800,000	24,548	5,000	0	0	0	0	0	0	0	0	75	198
3217	New Waverly	5	1	3	0	5	680,025	11,876	0	0	2,300	0	0	0	0	0	0	200	3,100
2225	Northwood-Appold	5	0	5	4	0	3,000,000	28,000	3,400,000	0	45,500	0	0	0	0	0	0	360	0

Column key:
- **48 TOTAL** — Total of UMC Causes & UMC Missions & Outreach
- **49** — NON-UMC CAUSES: Total amount given DIRECTLY to non-United Methodist benevolent and charitable causes (NOT sent to BWC Treasurer)
- **50a** — Human Relations Sunday
- **50b** — UMCOR Sunday (formerly One Great Hour of Sharing)
- **50c** — Peace with Justice Sunday
- **50d** — Native American Ministries Sunday
- **50e** — World Communion Sunday
- **50f** — U.M. Student Day
- **51** — Direct-billed clergy non-health benefits
- **52** — Direct-billed clergy health benefits
- **53a** — Base compensation paid to/for the Senior Pastor or other person assigned or appointed in the lead pastoral role to the church
- **53b** — Base compensation paid/for to all Associate Pastor(s) & other pastoral staff assigned or appointed to the church
- **53c** — Base compensation paid to/for any Deacons NOT included in 53a or 53b
- **55a** — Housing benefits paid to/for Lead Pastor or person in lead pastoral role as described in 53a
- **55b** — Housing benefits paid to/for ALL Associate Pastor(s) & other pastoral staff assigned or appointed to the
- **55c** — Housing benefits paid to/for any Deacons not included in 53a or 53b
- **56** — Paid to/for all persons included in Lines 53a-53c for accountable reimbursements
- **57** — Paid to/for all persons included in Lines 53a-53c for any other cash allowances (non-

Align #	Church Name	48 TOTAL	49	50a	50b	50c	50d	50e	50f	51	52	53a	53b	53c	55a	55b	55c	56	57
4110	Amos	46,039	2,100	0	0	0	0	0	0	54,169	54,568	40,303	0	0	19,865	0	0	1,000	0
3110	Arbutus	39,928	17,207	0	0	0	0	0	0	13,729	15,120	70,730	0	0	3,842	0	0	1,966	0
4115	Arlington-Lewin	1,575	0	0	0	0	0	0	0	0	0	30,518	0	0	0	0	0	5,000	0
3530	Arnolia	1,804	16,347	0	310	0	0	0	0	12,306	12,466	48,500	0	0	19,866	0	0	2,438	0
2420	Back River	4,003	1,344	0	0	0	57	0	0	9,900	14,023	44,000	0	0	3,666	0	0	2,477	0
3150	Beechfield	7,975	100	38	0	50	37	0	0	34,140	23,130	9,000	0	0	9,000	0	0	2,000	0
3145	Bethesda	4,103	1,169	0	0	0	0	44	0	0	10,618	20,382	0	0	0	0	0	149	0
2142	Brooklyn Community	11,761	0	0	0	0	0	0	0	9,510	10,618	53,020	0	0	19,864	0	0	603	0
4180	Catonsville	93,381	91,679	0	0	0	0	0	0	13,583	19,168	57,729	0	0	28,245	0	0	8,587	0
2362	Chase	3,088	250	197	40	52	45	246	130	11,406	16,293	45,792	0	0	2,145	0	0	4,100	0
2155	Cherry Hill	8,541	0	197	40	0	0	0	0	0	0	13,196	0	0	19,000	0	0	1,600	0
2160	Christ	10,467	2,325	325	0	332	0	414	0	8,517	10,080	52,530	0	0	20,000	0	0	2,354	0
3285	Christ Church of Baltimore Court	3,425	2,376	0	0	0	0	0	0	3,867	0	22,140	0	0	9,000	0	0	0	0
3115	Christ Church of the Deaf	26,967	25	0	0	0	0	0	103	0	0	8,500	0	0	0	0	0	0	0
2570	Cowenton	4,532	308	57	0	0	7	16	0	13,660	13,660	17,500	0	0	17,500	0	0	750	0
2360	Dundalk	5,928	1,739	5	0	2	0	0	0	5,250	0	17,500	0	0	0	0	0	0	0
2175	Eastern	738	0	0	0	0	0	0	0	21,701	18,457	49,542	0	0	20,263	0	0	0	0
2180	Eden Korean	19,400	0	0	0	0	0	0	0	10,051	17,000	43,473	0	0	0	0	0	2,915	0
4120	Eldersie-St Andrews	0	0	0	0	0	0	0	0	7,131	0	32,204	0	0	10,000	0	0	842	0
4630	Emanuel	521	730	0	0	0	0	0	0	0	0	30,000	0	0	0	0	0	1,529	0
4610	Emmarts	0	0	0	0	0	0	0	0	0	0	44,887	0	0	21,641	0	0	0	0
4170	Epworth Chapel	52,200	3,000	150	150	150	150	0	250	14,684	11,400	82,698	17,000	0	19,866	0	0	5,250	0
2425	Essex	18,418	33,664	45	20	25	2	0	0	12,150	12,150	25,134	0	0	0	0	0	709	0
2192	Faith Community	8,968	150	85	0	0	0	0	0	0	11,460	12,000	0	0	0	0	0	507	0
3230	Good Shepherd	36,295	1,990	0	0	0	0	0	0	12,795	13,832	52,596	0	0	20,000	0	0	3,695	0
3165	Govans-Boundary	4,000	2,000	0	0	0	0	0	0	0	0	23,500	0	0	0	0	0	0	0
3170	Grace	20,186	45,969	10	0	10	10	10	10	23,199	34,432	79,964	27,503	0	4,504	17,683	0	7,364	0
2210	Graceland	932	0	0	0	0	0	0	0	0	0	17,500	0	0	0	0	0	0	0
4130	Gwinn Oak	577	0	58	0	0	41	132	74	0	16,557	44,533	0	0	7,039	0	0	4,823	0
3120	Halethorpe-Relay	171	1,634	36	0	0	0	0	0	10,969	11,460	46,563	0	0	7,205	0	0	1,850	0
3175	Hampden	12,579	150	0	0	48	69	198	0	0	0	15,600	0	0	0	0	0	0	0
3440	Hiss	138	28,440	25	0	0	0	0	0	12,992	12,366	50,250	0	0	19,600	0	0	744	0
3180	Homestead	196	0	16	8	21	15	94	172	0	0	51,306	1,600	0	688	0	0	0	0
4135	John Wesley	43,753	0	0	0	0	119	0	5	14,844	14,906	1,787	0	0	18,339	0	0	4,757	0
3125	Lansdowne	13,026	2,476	10	0	17	0	0	0	11,384	10,500	68,500	0	0	19,866	0	0	1,391	0
3540	Loch Raven	5,108	10,165	0	0	0	0	0	0	18,089	13,267	43,379	0	0	19,866	0	0	7,620	2,059
2410	Lodge Forest	4,254	1,856	0	0	0	0	0	0	0	0	66,586	0	0	8,940	0	0	1,845	0
3185	Lovely Lane	5,106	1,000	0	0	0	30	10	30	13,319	11,700	20,250	0	0	26,084	0	0	3,209	0
1455	Magothy Church of the Deaf	11,117	2,750	20	0	0	0	0	0	1,543	2,320	0	0	0	0	0	0	1,600	2,600
4145	Martin Luther King Memorial	7,050	440	0	0	0	0	0	0	0	0	20,300	0	0	12,000	0	0	1,600	0
2220	Metropolitan	18,174	0	0	0	0	0	0	0	28,949	26,471	24,750	0	0	24,750	0	0	2,050	0
3215	Mount Vernon Place	1,100	0	0	0	0	0	0	0	0	5,046	14,804	0	0	14,804	0	0	2,050	0
3220	Mount Washington-Aldersgate	4,545	1,900	0	0	0	0	0	150	0	0	35,220	0	0	19,866	0	0	1,729	1,963
2235	Mount Winans	75	0	0	0	0	0	0	0	0	0	16,000	0	0	4,000	0	0	1,845	0
4150	Mount Zion	13,676	900	20	32	0	30	10	30	1,543	2,320	48,658	0	0	20,263	0	0	4,100	0
3575	New Covenant Worship Center	3,300	0	0	0	0	0	0	0	0	0	21,530	0	0	19,000	0	0	200	0
3217	New Waverly	360	360	0	0	0	0	0	0	4,491	2,320	53,600	0	0	19,000	0	0	1,500	0
3225	Northwood-Appold			0	0	0	0	0	0	13,948	13,972	72,000	0	0	18,315	0	0	0	0

654

Column code key (headers read top-to-bottom in the original rotated table):

- 60 — Paid in salary and benefits for all other church staff and diaconal ministers
- 61 — Amount spent for local church program expenses
- 62 — Amount spent for local church operating expenses
- 63 — Amount paid for principal and interest on indebtedness, loans, mortgages, etc.
- 63a — Amount paid for capital campaign or fundraising costs
- 64 — Amount paid on capital expenditures for building, improvements, and major equipment purchases
- 65 — Amount PAID by/for the local church on all expenditures
- 66 — Number of giving units
- 67a — Received through pledges
- 67b — Received from non-pledging, but identified givers
- 67c — Received from unidentified givers
- 67d — Amount received from interest and dividends and/or transferred from liquid assets
- 67e — Amount received from sale of Church Assets
- 67f — Amount received through building use fees, contributions, and rentals
- 67g — Amount received through fundraisers and other sources

Algn #	Church Name	60	61	62	63	63a	64	65	66	67a	67b	67c	67d	67e	67f	67g
4110	Amos	17,783	2,600	29,697	0	0	0	276,305	0	0	95,167	8,499	0	0	4,550	21,424
3110	Arbutus	28,262	2,609	87,466	0	0	70,536	383,605	225	0	204,595	26,264	0	0	50,626	690
4115	Arlington-Lewin	24,655	2,000	21,745	0	0	0	89,260	72	112,393	0	0	13,651	0	8,500	12,700
3530	Arnolia	55,308	8,528	42,389	647	0	33,558	282,299	100	110,736	62,094	2,134	6	0	35,887	22,598
2420	Back River	14,300	800	29,629	4,990	0	4,847	129,638	80	86,733	2,196	4,393	0	0	8,502	21,747
3150	Beachfield	25,080	1,609	80,000	0	0	55,645	186,740	14	38,000	300	2,500	5,474	0	250	1,500
3145	Bethesda	43,653	296	44,492	0	0	16,390	168,349	33	0	67,239	683	6	56,981	29,040	476
2142	Brooklyn Community	286,410	40,259	39,278	0	3,571	35,641	226,315	0	575,596	91,466	0	600	0	44,400	0
4180	Catonsville	17,005	1,857	114,878	0	0	38,211	881,296	85	0	32,655	222,188	20,707	0	44,393	0
2362	Chase	15,480	1,930	36,767	0	0	0	196,494	70	0	103,681	3,845	0	0	14,475	1,198
2155	Cherry Hill	74,999	18,197	43,752	17,580	0	500	114,968	159	217,152	74,661	2,983	0	0	2,300	44,198
2160	Christ	9,600	2,490	26,706	0	0	12,900	302,606	32	24,287	70,899	2,711	30,000	0	12,200	1,519
3285	Christ Church of Baltimore County	6,000	1,572	12,203	5,012	0	0	89,374	15	42,910	9,506	1,996	44	0	5,050	1,619
3115	Christ Church of the Deaf	8,639	150	11,787	0	0	25,000	82,693	42	42,910	34,082	1,468	0	40,000	14,622	4,401
2570	Cowenton	23,539	0	35,547	0	736	0	114,694	41	128,610	22,785	2,161	0	0	14,963	0
2380	Dundalk	45,123	6,435	13,691	0	0	53,687	186,510	0	125,000	2,221	0	0	0	0	0
2175	Eastern	0	8,155	99,000	0	0	0	199,789	68	0	80,000	60,000	0	0	1,700	26,818
2180	Eden Korean	33,616	0	25,747	0	991	23,454	188,429	50	128,618	83,893	1,498	26,590	0	1,900	1,000
4120	Elderslie-St Andrews	0	0	35,077	39,454	0	40,335	67,420	30	125,000	98,496	18	18	0	0	0
4630	Emanuel	159,289	0	1	0	0	10,310	64,682	0	478,179	50,944	17,401	22	2,048	2,235	26,818
4610	Emmarts	9,394	6,435	16,302	0	0	3,538	523,877	440	0	0	1,726	569	16,500	12,180	57,017
4170	Epworth Chapel	6,220	8,155	45,175	0	0	36,000	229,220	85	38,036	62,208	6,704	223,048	0	0	5,734
2425	Essex	23,226	1,563	28,270	0	0	115,602	72,123	24	0	135,472	1,468	0	0	43,000	3,148
2192	Faith Community	12,000	2,099	45,356	0	0	2,942	245,952	43	380,930	6,586	1,200	76,312	0	45,338	0
3290	Good Shepherd	309,004	3,000	3,000	0	4,000	0	63,500	67	0	700	8,956	0	0	7,820	2,000
3165	Govans-Boundary	11,066	27,157	104,999	45,753	0	15,525	931,095	244	107,918	46,409	3,487	15,000	0	18,150	127,171
3170	Grace	55,908	2,175	15,850	0	0	6,197	182,997	43	0	135,672	2,254	131,410	0	725	0
2310	Graceland	14,983	1,667	43,986	0	0	46,054	53,939	0	54,586	61,081	13,237	0	0	3,900	23,124
4130	Gwynn Oak	1,100	6,385	13,509	0	0	34,916	153,202	41	149,524	339,425	1,867	40	0	9,445	2,465
3120	Halethorpe-Relay	98,627	2,833	18,197	0	0	43,050	65,544	48	0	18,243	11,943	1,656	0	250	45,692
3175	Hampden	300	12,379	90,942	0	0	5,578	431,340	293	99,703	328,264	1,948	0	0	5,721	3,065
3440	Hiss	62,315	424	27,985	0	0	11,651	32,259	24	0	145,861	7,110	0	0	8,657	42,280
3180	Homestead	18,363	24,994	128,431	0	0	24,032	501,893	231	54,586	229,794	6,006	0	0	17,825	4,292
4135	John Wesley	78,137	2,099	22,941	0	0	2,183	214,325	103	149,524	145,861	16,198	0	15,000	37,180	4,039
2540	Lansdowne	5,070	11,243	73,831	0	0	0	351,490	132	0	51,650	8,321	0	0	78,006	0
3125	Loch Raven	69,670	2,749	22,250	0	0	10,650	93,419	35	99,703	6,751	3,260	131,410	0	0	0
2410	Lodge Forest	0	4,787	83,514	0	0	31,591	331,241	58	0	120,896	11,175	0	0	15,599	2,000
3185	Lovely Lane	0	2,758	5,629	0	0	31,429	31,756	8	0	6,751	2,500	0	0	1,000	0
1455	Magothy Church of the Deaf	37,071	300	15,241	5,000	0	0	66,469	50	0	6,960	4,871	0	0	95,750	18,000
4145	Martin Luther King Memorial	17,460	11,634	48,199	0	5,282	10,650	204,179	136	112,207	120,896	2,500	0	0	6,750	2,590
2220	Metropolitan	6,375	5,000	136,411	0	0	31,591	265,515	175	92,540	113,805	4,675	0	0	1,000	0
3215	Mount Vernon Place	18,641	14,025	12,035	0	0	31,429	153,240	27	112,207	2,582	10,254	2,586	0	95,750	0
3220	Mount Washington-Aldersgate	35,381	100	12,300	0	200	25,000	45,662	29	9,519	93,621	2,533	0	0	5,750	617
2235	Mount Winans	6,375	34,771	58,000	0	0	0	240,196	91	0	36,793	2,357	0	0	0	0
4150	Mount Zion	18,641	3,840	28,300	0	0	25,000	124,957	42	0	119,561	5,455	0	0	7,200	21,505
3575	New Covenant Worship Center	35,381	16,000	29,000	0	0	4,000	147,253	87	119,524	104,000	1,300	0	0	8,600	10,000
3217	New Waverly	33,700	2,146	42,182	0	0	0	208,293	93	122,774	47,469	2,241	0	0	3,000	0
3225	Northwood-Appold	16,202	2,146	42,182	0	0	0	208,293	93	122,774	47,469	2,241	0	0	38,985	0

Align #	Church Name	TOTAL income for annual budget/spending plan (67a-g) [67]	Capital campaigns [66a]	Memorials, endowments, and bequests [66b]	Other sources and projects (include UMW, UMM and 'flow-through') [68c]	Special Sundays, Gen. Adv. Spec; World Srvc Spec., Conf. Adv. Spec. and other directed benevolent giving [68d]	Total income for designated causes including capital campaign and other special projects [68]	Equitable Compensation Funds received by Church or Pastor [69a]	Advance Special, apportioned, and connectional funds received by church [69b]	Other grants and financial support from institutional sources [69c]	Income from connectional / institutional sources outside the local church [69]	TOTAL CHURCH INCOME (Sum of Lines 67 + 68 + 69) [70]	Amount APPORTIONED to the local church [40a]	Amount PAID by the local church for all apportioned causes [40b]
4110	Ames	129,640	0	0	0	0	0	43,026	0	0	43,026	172,666	18,540	6,180
3110	Arbutus	282,165	0	0	0	0	0	0	0	0	0	282,165	34,834	26,125
4115	Arlington-Lewin	133,593	0	0	0	0	0	0	0	0	0	133,593	15,070	3,767
3530	Amolia	247,100	9,631	5,822	3,359	0	5,822	0	0	0	0	252,922	28,419	28,419
2420	Back River	123,577	0	710	0	601	14,301	9,000	0	0	9,000	137,878	10,835	10,835
3150	Beachfield	42,950	5,068	0	0	120	120	0	0	0	0	51,670	1,305	1,305
3145	Bethesda	104,812	0	0	0	1,382	6,450	0	0	0	0	111,262	15,217	15,217
2142	Brooklyn Community	192,849	0	0	0	0	0	0	0	0	0	192,849	20,922	20,922
4180	Catonsville	675,432	137,635	5,710	18,927	155,257	317,529	0	0	0	0	992,961	90,233	90,233
2362	Chase	143,906	4,161	400	0	3,901	8,462	0	0	0	0	152,368	17,870	17,870
2155	Cherry Hill	77,644	0	0	0	0	0	0	0	0	0	77,644	11,469	11,469
2160	Christ	269,758	17,060	0	0	5,032	22,092	0	0	0	0	291,850	40,085	16,702
3285	Christ Church of Baltimore County	86,999	0	250	0	1,706	1,956	0	0	0	0	88,954	11,760	11,760
3115	Christ Church of the Deaf	73,253	0	30,720	0	0	30,720	0	0	0	0	103,973	5,220	5,220
2570	Cowenton	63,973	150	2,120	0	144	2,414	0	0	0	0	66,387	9,754	1,200
2380	Dundalk	79,909	0	11,464	0	0	11,464	0	0	0	0	91,373	15,778	0
2175	Eastern	130,939	0	0	0	0	0	0	0	0	0	130,939	20,394	16,995
2180	Eden Korean	265,000	0	0	0	0	0	0	0	0	0	265,000	15,899	7,950
4120	Elderslie-St Andrews	113,009	3,950	0	45,165	0	49,115	0	0	0	0	163,024	18,767	18,767
4630	Emmanuel	80,342	0	3,000	0	0	3,000	0	0	0	0	83,342	11,408	11,408
4610	Emmarts	0	0	0	0	0	0	0	0	0	0	0	11,406	11,406
4170	Epworth Chapel	614,823	15,500	0	2,500	3,350	21,350	0	0	0	0	636,173	19,794	19,794
2425	Essex	148,037	1,300	908	24,132	129	26,469	0	0	11,993	11,993	186,499	53,165	53,165
2192	Faith Community	83,723	3,210	0	0	2,308	5,518	0	2,800	5,003	7,803	97,044	20,719	20,719
3230	Good Shepherd	258,598	0	430	0	36	466	0	0	0	0	259,064	14,043	4,043
3165	Govans-Boundary	46,900	0	0	0	0	0	0	5,000	0	5,000	51,900	31,101	31,101
3170	Grace	737,203	12,710	227,885	0	40	240,635	0	0	0	0	977,838	14,535	0
2210	Graceland	57,716	0	0	0	0	0	0	0	0	0	57,716	105,857	105,857
4130	Gwynn Oak	177,200	0	0	0	4,355	4,355	0	0	0	0	181,555	8,147	4,074
3120	Hallethorpe-Relay	124,385	0	49,661	0	146	49,807	0	0	0	0	174,192	27,067	8,000
3175	Hampden	71,848	0	0	0	20	20	0	0	0	0	71,868	22,802	22,802
3440	Hiss	408,163	39,040	44,695	0	6,445	90,180	0	0	0	0	498,343	51,198	6,783
3180	Homestead	23,505	0	0	0	0	0	0	0	0	0	23,505	7,122	799
4135	John Wesley	437,961	0	2,600	29,255	2,995	34,840	0	0	0	0	472,801	57,889	40,120
3125	Lansdowne	165,016	14,186	5,775	1,781	512	22,254	0	0	500	500	187,770	17,367	17,367
3540	Loch Raven	432,380	0	3,124	0	7,355	10,479	0	0	0	0	442,859	40,600	40,600
2410	Lodge Forest	97,151	0	1,800	0	0	1,800	0	0	0	0	98,951	14,417	14,417
3185	Lovely Lane	321,130	132,440	0	0	0	132,440	3,007	0	0	3,007	456,577	36,354	1,219
1455	Magothy Church of the Deaf	18,135	0	0	25,000	0	25,000	0	0	0	0	43,135	11,578	11,578
4145	Martin Luther King Memorial	156,995	0	0	0	300	300	0	0	0	0	157,295	5,162	5,162
2220	Metropolitan	234,463	12,790	0	0	2,591	15,381	0	0	0	0	249,844	20,649	20,649
3215	Mount Vernon Place	196,133	0	0	3,071	414	3,485	0	0	0	0	201,618	38,979	38,979
3220	Mount Washington-Aldersgate	110,625	0	20,750	0	3,245	23,995	0	0	0	0	134,620	10,823	10,823
2235	Mount Winans	39,943	2,376	0	96	96	2,568	0	0	0	0	42,511	6,812	6,812
4150	Mount Zion	19,076	0	0	0	189	189	0	0	0	0	19,265	33,577	12,192
3575	New Covenant Worship Center	155,121	0	0	44,000	1,200	45,200	0	0	0	0	200,321	16,706	16,706
3217	New Waverly	119,300	0	0	0	50	50	0	0	0	0	118,350	22,342	1,662
3225	Northwood-Appold	211,469	0	2,000	0	0	2,000	0	0	0	0	213,469	28,808	28,808

Align #	Church Name	Dist #	City	State	Total prof. members close of 2017 (1)	Rec'd by Profession of Faith (2a1)	Rec'd by Profession of Faith – Other Than Confirmation (2a2)	Restored by Affirmation of Faith (2b)	Transferred in from other UM (3)	Transferred in from non-UM (4)	Removed/corrected by Charge Conf. (5a)	Withdrawn from Prof. Membership (5b)	Transferred out to other UM (6)	Transferred out to non-UM (7)	Removed by death (8)	Total prof. members close of 2018 (9)	Asian (9a)	African American/Black (9b)	Hispanic/Latino (9c)	Native American (9d)	Pacific Islander (9e)	White (9f)	Multi-Racial (9g)	Female (9h)	Male (9i)
2240	Old Otterbein	BM	Baltimore	MD	75	1	0	0	1	0	12	0	0	0	1	64	0	9	0	0	0	53	2	40	24
2250	Orangeville	BM	Baltimore	MD	32	0	0	0	0	0	0	0	0	0	0	32	0	9	0	0	0	23	0	22	10
2515	Orems	BM	Baltimore	MD	331	3	1	1	2	0	2	0	1	0	2	333	1	2	2	0	0	328	0	213	120
2385	Patapsco	BM	Dundalk	MD	286	0	5	0	0	0	0	0	0	0	3	283	0	0	0	0	1	282	0	149	134
2355	Piney Grove	BM	Middle River	MD	94	0	0	0	0	0	0	0	0	0	1	97	0	3	0	0	0	93	1	63	34
4335	Salem	BM	Baltimore	MD	56	0	9	0	0	0	0	0	0	0	0	56	0	4	0	0	0	49	3	33	23
2310	Salem-Baltimore Hispanic	BM	Baltimore	MD	161	0	5	1	0	0	0	0	0	0	0	170	0	0	40	0	0	130	0	111	59
3250	Sharp Street Memorial	BM	Baltimore	MD	210	0	5	0	0	0	0	0	0	4	5	211	0	211	0	0	0	0	0	190	21
2265	St James Memorial	BM	Baltimore	MD	360	0	5	2	0	0	208	46	0	0	56	48	0	48	0	0	0	0	0	40	8
1473	St John	BM	Baltimore	MD	180	1	4	0	1	0	0	0	0	8	3	186	0	184	0	0	0	1	1	124	62
3240	St Johns	BM	Baltimore	MD	88	0	0	5	1	0	0	0	2	0	1	86	2	28	0	0	0	56	0	50	36
4155	St Luke	BM	Baltimore	MD	89	0	0	1	0	0	0	1	0	0	2	90	0	90	0	0	0	0	0	75	15
4615	St Lukes	BM	Baltimore	MD	15	0	0	0	0	0	0	0	0	0	1	14	0	12	0	0	0	2	0	12	2
2280	St Matthews	BM	Baltimore	MD	42	0	0	0	0	0	0	0	0	0	0	42	0	40	0	0	0	2	0	22	20
2390	St Matthews	BM	Baltimore	MD	214	6	0	0	0	0	0	0	1	0	5	214	0	211	0	1	0	2	0	155	59
3247	St Matthews-New Life	BM	Baltimore	MD	164	0	1	0	0	0	16	0	0	0	0	164	0	164	0	0	0	0	0	107	57
2290	St Paul Praise and Worship Cent	BM	Pikesville	MD	172	5	15	0	2	0	0	5	1	0	4	153	1	152	0	0	0	0	0	114	39
3550	Towson	BM	Towson	MD	794	0	0	0	0	0	0	0	10	4	17	780	3	6	0	0	0	768	3	465	315
4210	Trinity	BM	Catonsville	MD	101	0	2	0	5	0	1	0	1	0	2	103	0	0	0	0	0	103	0	73	30
2320	Union Memorial	BM	Baltimore	MD	296	2	5	0	0	0	0	0	2	0	12	284	0	283	0	0	0	1	0	189	95
2325	Unity	BM	Baltimore	MD	81	2	0	0	0	0	0	0	0	0	5	70	0	70	0	0	0	0	0	58	12
3260	Violetville	BM	Baltimore	MD	110	0	0	0	0	0	0	0	0	0	5	107	0	5	0	0	0	102	0	70	37
3113	Water's Edge Partnership Initiati	BM	Baltimore	MD	0	0	5	0	0	0	0	0	1	0	0	30	0	4	0	0	0	26	0	18	12
4165	West Baltimore	BM	Baltimore	MD	42	0	0	0	0	0	6	0	1	0	0	40	1	21	0	0	0	18	0	25	15
BM Total					15,646	79	162	31	49	41	620	147	38	39	312	15,086	247	6,294	72	2	5	8,420	46	9,644	5,442

Align #	Church Name	10	10a	11a	11b	11T	12	13	14	15	16	17	18	19	20	22	23	24	25	26	27	28	29	30a	30b
2240	Old Otterbein	38	0	4	1	5	5	13	1	0	1	0	12	13	8	0	0	1	1	0	0	0	0	0	0
2250	Orangeville	13	0	6	2	8	5	10	0	0	0	0	8	8	8	0	0	0	0	0	0	0	0	0	0
2515	Orems	89	0	6	2	8	20	6	0	20	3	2	32	57	16	80	2	2	2	0	0	40	2,500	0	0
2385	Patapsco	55	3	2	2	4	37	51	0	6	2	1	15	24	10	19	0	2	5	0	0	14	2,999	1	1
2355	Piney Grove	29	0	2	0	2	0	30	0	0	0	0	15	15	8	0	0	1	0	0	0	0	0	0	0
4335	Salem	32	0	0	0	0	0	0	0	10	1	1	12	12	15	0	1	0	1	0	0	15	34	0	0
2310	Salem-Baltimore Hispanic	31	0	1	0	1	0	0	0	9	3	1	24	37		32	3	3	4	9	25	23	50	0	0
3290	Sharp Street Memorial	71	0	0	0	1	0	0	0	3	9	0	25	38	39		0	5	4	0	25	14	350	0	0
2265	St James Memorial	34	0	3	0	3	43	24	0	0	0	0	0	0		0	0	0	0	15	0	22	200	0	0
1473	St John	87	0	0	1	1	0	2	1	12	5	1	14	32	17	0	2	8	2	0	0	0	0	0	0
3240	St Johns	28	75	0	1	1	0	4	1	5	1	1	17	24	6	0	2	2	3	9	0	0	0	0	0
4155	St Luke	45	0	0	0	0	0	4	0	11	11	0	9	31	10	0	1	4	4	15	0	0	0	0	0
4615	St Lukes	5	0	0	0	0	0	25	0	0	0	0	5	5		0	0	0	1	0	0	0	0	0	0
2280	St Matthews	17	0	1	0	1	0	12	0	1	0	3	7	8	10	32	2	1	6	15	2,600	24	0	0	0
2390	St Matthews	89	0	7	11	18	1	164	6	84	44	10	26	157	70	20	0	8	4	20	0	29	1,835	0	0
3247	St Matthews-New Life	120	0	0	0	0	2	29	0	20	18	4	28	76	16	175	1	10	5	0	0	17	700	0	0
2290	St. Paul Praise and Worship Cent	65	0	0	0	0	0	0	5	4	2	11	13	23	120	29	14	3	9	0	0	0	0	0	0
3550	Towson	255	0	2	0	2	210	0	0	69	40	0	225	345	5	12	2	12	3	0	0	11	432	0	0
4210	Trinity	44	4	0	0	0	0	0	0	1	0	0	12	13	22	0	5	5	3	2	407	59	500	0	0
2320	Union Memorial	90	0	1	0	1	0	0	0	0	0	10	24	24	5	40	3	3	5	16	0	57	300	0	10
2325	Unity	40	0	0	2	2	0	0	0	10	10	0	40	70	13	0	3	3	0	8	0	14	0	0	0
3260	Violetville	30	0	2	2	2	0	10	0	10	2	0	13	29		8	2	4	0	3	0	0	0	0	0
3113	Water's Edge Partnership Initiati	30	0	0	0	0	0	0	0	0	0	0	0	0		0	0	0	0	0	0	0	0	0	0
4165	West Baltimore	22	0	0	0	0	0	0	0	0	0	0	6	6		0	0	0	0	0	0	0	0	0	0
	BN Total	4,940	514	110	48	158	830	1,744	65	1,007	568	284	2,038	3,897	1,419	1,582	185	258	165	461	43,328	938	47,294	9	165

Column key:

- 10: Average attendance at all weekly worship service(s)
- 10a: Persons who Worship Online
- 11a: Number of Infants and Children baptized (Age 0-12)
- 11b: Number of Teens and Adults baptized (Age 13+)
- 11T: TOTAL Number of persons baptized (all ages)
- 12: Number of baptized members who have not become Professing
- 13: Number of other constituents of the church
- 14: Total enrolled in confirmation preparation classes that
- 15: CHILDREN (0-11yrs) in all Christian groups, small groups and Sunday School
- 16: YOUTH (12-18 yrs) in all Christian groups, small groups and Sunday School
- 17: YOUNG ADULTS (19-30 yrs) in all Christian groups, small groups and Sunday School
- 18: OTHER ADULTS (31+ yrs) in all Christian groups, small groups and Sunday School
- 19: TOTAL number of persons participating in Christian formation groups (Total lines 15-18)
- 20: Average weekly attendance, Education classes/groups that meet in Sunday Church School groups
- 22: Number of participants in Vacation Bible School
- 23: Number of ongoing classes (all ages) for learning in Sunday Church
- 24: Number of ONGOING small groups, support groups, or classes
- 25: Number of SHORT-TERM classes, support groups, or small groups offered
- 26: Membership in United Methodist Men (UMM)
- 27: Amount paid for projects (UMM)
- 28: Membership in United Methodist Women (UMW)
- 29: Amount paid for local church and community work (UMW)
- 30a: Number of UMVIM teams sent out from this church
- 30b: Number of persons sent out on UMVIM teams from this church

Align #	Church Name	33 TOTAL Community MINISTRIES for outreach, justice, and mercy	33a MINISTRIES focusing on global/regional health?	33b MINISTRIES focusing on engaging in ministry with the poor/socially	34 PERSONS SERVED BY community ministries for outreach, justice, and mercy	35a PERSONS SERVING (from your congregation) in mission/community ministries	36 Market value of church-owned land, buildings and equipment	36SF Overall square footage of church owned buildings (furnished and unfurnished areas)	37 Market value of financial and other liquid assets	38 Debt secured by church physical assets	39 Other debt	42 General Advance Specials remitted to the Annual Conference Treasurer	43 World Service Specials remitted to the Annual Conference Treasurer	44 Annual Conference Advance Specials remitted to the Annual Conference Treasurer	45 Youth Service Fund remitted to the	46 All other funds sent to AC Treasurer for connectional mission and ministry	47 Total Annual Conference Special Sunday Offerings remitted to the	48a UMC CAUSES: Total amount given DIRECTLY to United Methodist causes (NOT sent to BWC Treasurer)	48b MISSIONS/MINISTRY COSTS: Direct costs incurred by the local church for mission and community ministry activities
2240	Old Otterbein	0	0	0	0	20	19,950,000	83,300	543,000	0	0	0	0	0	0	0	0	0	805
2250	Orangeville	0	0	0	0	0	497,000	36	0	0	0	0	0	0	0	0	0	0	0
2515	Orems	16	9	14	1,596	174	1,878,200	27,200	286,607	0	0	195	0	0	0	0	0	0	0
2385	Patapsco	10	0	7	12,280	31	4,000,000	160,790	137,002	0	0	0	0	0	0	0	0	0	4,233
2355	Piney Grove	7	2	3	2,675	20	1,646,400	8,500	0	0	0	0	0	0	0	0	0	0	62
4335	Salem	0	0	0	0	0	3,376,800	17,435	3,500	0	0	0	0	0	0	0	0	0	15,870
2310	Salem-Baltimore Hispanic	3	1	1	100	10	708,310	7,310	34,000	0	0	0	0	0	0	0	0	0	0
3250	Sharp Street Memorial	5	0	5	2,150	50	1,260,460	34,905	76,000	0	30,000	0	0	0	0	0	0	1,000	13,000
2265	St James Memorial	4	0	4	1,537	9	1,250,000	2,200	0	149,836	96,000	0	0	0	0	0	0	0	2,593
1473	St John	11	1	5	425	33	1,175,000	5,094	49,731	0	0	0	0	0	0	0	0	0	845
3240	St Johns	5	5	5	2,000	67	1,750,000	11,504	44,000	0	0	350	0	0	0	0	0	340	4,631
4155	St. Luke	6	2	6	300	35	1,000,000	8,299	5,000	0	0	0	0	0	0	0	0	0	1,050
4615	St. Lukes	6	4	4	400	5	1,791,852	12,049	0	0	0	0	0	0	0	0	0	0	2,791
2280	St. Matthews	0	0	0	0	0	332,740	36	0	93,350	1,750	0	0	0	0	0	0	0	0
2390	St. Matthews	3	1	1	292	22	1,368,830	25,166	40,000	73,000	0	0	0	0	0	0	0	1,000	10,304
3247	St. Matthews-New Life	0	0	0	1,000	50	1,747,300	35,000	28,937	0	9,512	0	0	0	0	0	0	175	1,645
2290	St. Paul Praise and Worship Cent	5	1	26	6,099	625	3,005,000	12,478	2,405,000	0	0	0	0	0	0	0	0	13,324	26,909
3550	Towson	31	12	7	600	42	9,066,000	24,562	1,064,169	0	0	244	0	0	0	0	0	105	0
4210	Trinity	12	0	1	91	18	3,204,000	10,844	197,000	0	0	0	0	0	0	0	0	0	361
2320	Union Memorial	3	0	2	300	54	3,481,000	12,556	0	0	56,000	0	0	0	0	0	0	0	0
2325	Unity	2	2	2	6,000	20	2,701,000	123,240	0	0	0	0	0	0	0	0	0	0	25,000
3260	Violetville	6	0	4	250	0	723,300	11,828	0	0	0	0	0	0	0	0	0	0	0
3113	Water's Edge Partnership Initiativ	0	0	0	0	0	0	0	0	0	0	0	0	0	0	0	0	0	0
4165	West Baltimore	0	0	0	670	6	4,912,700	12,248	213,800	65,223	0	0	0	0	0	0	0	0	0
	BM Total	467	85	362	119,456	3,843	244,291,624	1,515,620	33,593,975	595,501	342,894	17,638	0	1,698	0	527	0	106,129	599,394

Align #	Church Name	48TOTAL	49	50a	50b	50c	50d	50e	50f	51	52	53a	53b	53c	55a	55b	55c	56	57
2240	Old Otterbein	805	3,000	0	0	0	0	0	0	13,979	12,759	19,833	0	0	19,866	0	0	455	0
2250	Orangeville	0	0	0	0	0	0	0	0	0	0	9,000	0	0	0	0	0	0	0
2515	Orems	0	4,475	242	0	0	59	135	90	0	0	33,420	0	0	18,483	0	0	2,382	0
2385	Patapsco	4,233	0	0	0	0	0	0	0	10,703	10,780	24,750	0	0	10,926	0	0	2,255	0
2355	Piney Grove	62	515	0	0	0	0	0	0	0	0	17,500	0	0	0	0	0	51	0
4335	Salem	15,870	0	0	0	0	0	0	0	0	0	30,000	0	0	19,200	0	0	575	0
2310	Salem-Baltimore Hispanic	0	0	0	0	0	0	0	0	0	10,728	56,267	0	0	0	4,000	0	1,431	0
3250	Sharp Street Memorial	14,000	1,846	0	0	0	0	0	0	24,016	27,612	48,742	9,080	0	20,000	0	0	5,000	0
2265	St James Memorial	2,593	0	0	0	0	0	0	0	0	0	32,000	0	0	0	0	0	0	0
1473	St John	845	0	0	0	0	0	0	0	5,671	5,700	43,199	0	0	19,866	0	0	1,303	0
3240	St Johns	4,631	0	0	0	118	0	0	0	6,318	0	23,401	0	0	11,700	0	0	2,381	0
4155	St Luke	1,390	500	0	0	0	0	0	0	0	0	15,000	0	0	15,000	0	0	4,100	0
4615	St Lukes	2,791	100	0	0	0	0	0	0	0	0	5,200	0	0	0	0	0	318	0
2280	St Matthews	0	0	0	0	0	0	0	0	0	0	13,200	0	0	0	0	0	0	0
2390	St Matthews	11,304	797	0	0	0	0	0	0	14,079	15,502	47,208	0	0	19,866	0	0	4,100	0
3247	St Matthews-New Life	175	0	0	0	0	0	0	0	1,595	4,501	40,768	0	0	0	0	0	3,800	0
2290	St. Paul Praise and Worship Cent	1,645	1,417	105	149	78	110	0	124	12,239	0	33,000	0	0	19,866	0	0	4,100	0
3550	Towson	40,233	17,691	0	0	0	0	0	0	26,003	14,906	71,886	52,530	0	32,000	10,500	0	10,544	0
4210	Trinity	466	729	0	0	38	56	76	0	0	0	32,000	0	0	0	0	0	1,741	0
2320	Union Memorial	0	0	0	0	0	0	0	0	12,784	14,400	51,245	0	0	20,886	0	0	4,114	0
2325	Unity	25,000	0	0	0	0	0	0	0	0	0	16,000	0	0	0	0	0	0	0
3260	Violetville	0	900	0	0	0	0	0	0	0	0	15,600	0	0	5,000	0	0	0	0
3113	Water's Edge Partnership Initiati	0	0	0	0	0	0	0	0	0	0	0	0	0	0	0	0	0	0
4165	West Baltimore	0	3,350	0	0	0	0	0	0	0	0	20,582	9,250	0	0	0	0	0	0
	BM Total	705,523	311,713	1,424	759	941	817	1,365	1,138	523,843	552,050	2,486,101	116,963	0	762,451	32,183	0	141,903	7,522

Column descriptions:
- 48TOTAL — Total of UMC Causes & UMC Missions & Outreach
- 49 — NON-UMC CAUSES: Total amount given DIRECTLY to non-United Methodist benevolent and charitable causes (NOT sent to BWC Treasurer)
- 50a — Human Relations Sunday
- 50b — UMCOR Sunday (formerly One Great Hour of Sharing)
- 50c — Peace with Justice Sunday
- 50d — Native American Ministries Sunday
- 50e — World Communion Sunday
- 50f — U.M. Student Day
- 51 — Direct-billed clergy non-health benefits
- 52 — Direct-billed clergy health benefits
- 53a — Base compensation paid to/for the Senior Pastor or other person assigned or appointed in the lead pastoral role to the church
- 53b — Base compensation paid/for to all Associate Pastor(s) & other pastoral staff assigned or appointed to the church
- 53c — Base compensation paid to/for any Deacons NOT included in 53a or 53b
- 55a — Housing benefits paid to/for Lead Pastor or person in lead pastoral role as described in 53a
- 55b — Housing benefits paid to/for ALL Associate Pastor(s) & other pastoral staff assigned or appointed to the
- 55c — Housing benefits paid to/for any Deacons not included in 53a or 53b.
- 56 — Paid to/for all persons included in Lines 53a–53c for accountable reimbursements
- 57 — Paid to/for all persons included in Lines 53a–53c for any other cash allowances (non-

Align #	Church Name	60	61	62	63	63a	64	65	66	67a	67b	67c	67d	67e	67f	67g
2240	Old Otterbein	16,010	9,182	28,535	0	0	0	135,108	50	59,572	0	6,184	41,000	0	5,825	8,000
2250	Orangeville	0	300	1,000	0	0	250	10,550	19	0	14,898	0	0	0	800	1,500
2515	Orems	34,220	10,024	69,801	0	0	35,337	235,449	106	0	173,737	5,741	0	0	120	28,625
2385	Patapsco	15,282	3,000	36,091	0	0	94,075	228,391	78	0	76,203	1,628	180	0	4,735	88
2355	Piney Grove	5,200	0	19,838	0	0	0	49,979	34	0	40,999	2,742	0	0	2,106	4,826
4335	Salem	4,687	0	22,079	0	0	0	113,252	28	0	69,810	4,316	0	0	39,616	501
2310	Salem-Baltimore Hispanic	5,912	80	25,245	0	0	0	102,015	30	225,531	26,112	3,928	0	0	550	529
3250	Sharp Street Memorial	16,000	0	80,250	0	0	16,450	257,251	80	79,855	7,025	821	39	0	7,200	5,250
2265	St James Memorial	20,400	175	47,390	178,840	0	7,400	306,688	42	134,462	375	6,904	0	0	4,200	25,260
1473	St John	16,364	8,662	31,106	0	0	9,950	151,255	180	50,348	23,728	6,577	0	0	0	15,247
3240	St Johns	0	2,410	41,506	0	0	0	115,294	42	59,785	6,443	2,479	0	0	30,820	0
4155	St Luke	23,200	4,600	6,900	0	0	0	74,690	47	0	2,250	1,090	0	0	0	14,025
4615	St Lukes	10,650	123	19,418	5,082	17,006	13,240	57,840	9	0	16,942	2,513	0	0	20,200	0
2280	St Matthews	0	500	400	0	0	0	14,100	27	0	9,200	0	0	0	2,000	1,600
2390	St Matthews	34,435	18,218	47,394	0	0	6,526	234,217	1,250	102,526	29,370	4,226	0	0	1,650	21,429
3247	St. Matthews-New Life	45,673	0	750	0	0	0	99,372	82	95,726	0	0	0	0	0	0
2290	St. Paul Praise and Worship Cent	29,847	1,472	12,634	3,918	0	4,450	133,295	89	584,829	3,322	584	1,306	0	34,425	18,623
3550	Towson	254,745	16,397	199,166	0	0	155,626	1,006,125	328	55,237	77,134	12,673	0	0	96,617	25,468
4210	Trinity	23,161	1,381	37,932	0	0	22,320	138,390	60	44,014	22,264	2,518	14,970	0	4,645	18,877
2320	Union Memorial	63,020	7,260	62,549	0	0	91,778	362,899	182	0	192,343	4,996	159	0	4,067	45,038
2325	Unity	0	45	18,500	3,000	0	0	62,945	53	0	0	0	0	0	0	0
3260	Violetville	6,180	1,145	20,895	0	0	3,700	61,441	35	0	46,371	1,761	0	0	1,400	1,947
3113	Water's Edge Partnership Initiati	0	0	1	0	0	0	1	23	0	0	0	7,000	0	0	0
4165	West Baltimore	27,404	1,018	42,982	10,458	0	0	119,002		0	53,883	1,475	0	0	71,950	1,928
BM Total		2,450,624	416,618	2,940,940	319,734	31,786	1,336,954	14,280,246	6,639	4,599,226	4,295,173	383,946	613,397	116,329	1,099,600	771,368

Align #	Church Name	TOTAL income for annual budget/spending plan (67a-g)	Capital campaigns	Memorials, endowments, and bequests	Other sources and projects (include UMW, UMM and "flow-through")	Special Sundays, Gen. Adv. Spec., World Srvc Spec., Conf. Adv. Spec. and other directed benevolent giving	Total income for designated causes including capital campaign and other special projects	Equitable Compensation Funds received by Church or Pastor	Advance Special, apportioned, and connectional funds received by church	Other grants and financial support from institutional sources	Income from connectional / institutional sources outside the local church	TOTAL CHURCH INCOME (Sum of Lines 67 + 68 + 69)	Amount APPORTIONED to the local church	Amount PAID by the local church for all apportioned causes
		67	66a	66b	66c	68d	68	69a	69b	69c	69	7D	40a	40b
2240	Old Otterbein	120,581	0	0	0	0	0	0	0	0	0	120,581	14,260	10,684
2250	Orangeville	17,198	0	0	0	0	0	0	0	0	0	17,198	1,826	0
2515	Orems	208,223	2,776	26,645	0	0	30,246	0	0	0	0	238,469	26,586	26,586
2385	Patapsco	82,834	0	0	209,000	825	209,000	0	0	0	0	291,834	16,296	16,296
2355	Piney Grove	50,673	0	200	0	508	708	0	0	0	0	51,381	7,328	7,328
4335	Salem	114,243	0	0	0	0	0	0	0	0	0	114,243	10,390	9,598
2310	Salem-Baltimore Hispanic	31,119	0	0	0	0	0	65,000	0	0	65,000	96,119	13,640	0
3250	Sharp Street Memorial	245,866	6,100	1,200	0	256	7,556	20,000	235	0	20,235	273,657	19,785	19,785
2265	St James Memorial	116,594	0	0	0	0	0	0	0	0	0	116,594	16,484	8,840
1473	St John	180,014	0	0	0	0	0	0	0	0	0	180,014	11,139	11,139
3240	St Johns	90,090	1,365	12,000	0	473	13,838	4,500	0	0	4,500	108,428	12,529	12,529
4155	St Luke	77,150	0	0	0	0	0	0	0	0	0	77,150	11,539	4,000
4615	St Lukes	39,655	0	0	0	0	0	0	0	0	0	39,655	8,136	6,000
2280	St Matthews	12,800	0	0	0	0	0	0	0	0	0	12,800	2,499	0
2390	St Matthews	159,201	0	0	0	1,500	1,500	24,000	0	2,500	26,500	187,201	27,768	9,706
3247	St Matthews-New Life	0	0	0	0	175	175	0	0	0	0	175	17,369	2,110
2290	St. Paul Praise and Worship Cent	153,986	0	0	0	651	651	0	0	0	0	154,637	12,196	8,131
3550	Towson	796,721	15,367	37,749	0	13,130	66,246	0	0	0	0	862,967	103,898	103,898
4210	Trinity	118,511	0	1,330	0	350	1,680	0	0	0	0	120,191	18,246	18,246
2320	Union Memorial	290,617	12,122	0	6,600	0	18,722	0	0	0	0	309,339	34,863	34,863
2325	Unity	0	0	0	500	0	500	0	0	0	0	500	7,224	400
3260	Violetville	51,479	0	10,000	0	0	10,000	0	0	0	0	61,479	8,021	8,021
3113	Water's Edge Partnership Initiati	0	0	0	0	0	0	0	0	0	0	0		0
4165	West Baltimore	136,236	0	435	5,200	545	6,180	0	0	0	0	142,416	15,832	3,958
BM Total		11,879,039	446,927	509,383	416,586	222,322	1,599,228	168,533	3,035	24,996	196,564	13,674,831	1,592,592	1,218,617

662

Align #	Church Name	Dist #	City	State	Total professing members at the close of 2017 (1)	Received by PROFESSION of Faith (2a1)	Received by PROFESSION of Faith (Other Than Confirmation) (2a2)	Restored by AFFIRMATION of Faith (2b)	Transferred in from other UM churches (3)	Transferred in from non-UM churches (4)	Removed or corrected by Charge Conference action (5a)	Withdrawn from Professing Membership (5b)	Transferred out to other UM churches (6)	Transferred out to non-UM churches (7)	Removed by death (8)	Total professing members at the close of 2018 (9)	Asian Professing Members (9a)	African American / Black Professing Members (9b)	Hispanic / Latino Professing Members (9c)	Native American Professing Members (9d)	Pacific Islander Professing Members (9e)	White Professing Members (9f)	Multi-Racial Professing Members (9g)	Female Professing Members (9h)	Male Professing Members (9i)
2335	Ames	BS	Bel Air	MD	139	3	2	0	1	0	0	0	0	0	1	142	0	139	1	0	0	2	1	88	54
2565	Asbury	BS	White Marsh	MD	28	2	2	0	0	0	0	0	0	0	0	25	0	24	0	0	0	0	0	16	9
2520	Ayres Chapel	BS	White Hall	MD	77	0	0	0	0	0	0	0	0	0	0	77	0	0	0	0	0	77	0	46	31
2340	Bel Air	BS	Bel Air	MD	1,483	17	18	4	13	8	38	4	9	8	14	1,475	6	21	7	0	0	1,437	4	829	646
3410	Bentley Springs	BS	Parkton	MD	33	0	0	0	0	0	0	0	0	0	1	32	0	0	0	0	0	32	0	21	11
4530	Buxlers	BS	Manchester	MD	73	0	0	0	0	0	0	0	0	0	3	70	0	0	0	0	0	69	1	42	28
4625	Boring	BS	Upperco	MD	26	0	0	0	0	0	0	0	0	0	0	24	0	0	0	0	0	24	0	15	9
3490	Bosley	BS	Sparks	MD	117	0	3	0	0	0	0	0	1	0	0	120	3	0	0	0	0	117	0	102	18
2530	Camp Chapel	BS	Perry Hall	MD	210	4	6	9	2	0	0	0	0	0	3	233	5	10	1	0	0	217	0	144	89
3415	Cedar Grove	BS	Parkton	MD	73	0	0	3	0	0	0	0	0	0	1	73	0	0	0	0	0	68	4	51	22
2445	Centre	BS	Forest Hill	MD	72	0	0	0	0	0	0	0	0	0	1	69	0	0	0	0	0	69	0	37	32
2545	Chesaco	BS	Baltimore	MD	49	0	0	0	0	0	0	0	0	0	1	51	0	1	0	0	0	50	0	37	14
2365	Clarks Chapel	BS	Bel Air	MD	118	2	0	0	0	0	0	12	0	0	5	119	0	0	0	0	0	3	0	75	44
3450	Cynmara	BS	Phoenix	MD	126	0	0	0	0	0	0	0	0	0	2	125	0	115	0	0	0	125	0	75	50
2125	Cokesbury	BS	Abingdon	MD	160	0	0	0	0	0	0	0	2	0	5	153	0	0	0	0	0	151	1	93	60
2540	Cranberry	BS	Perryman	MD	118	0	1	0	0	0	2	0	0	0	2	115	0	1	0	0	0	113	1	76	39
2375	Darlington	BS	Darlington	MD	106	0	0	0	0	0	0	0	0	0	3	103	0	1	0	0	0	103	0	69	34
4450	Deer Creek	BS	Forest Hill	MD	35	0	0	0	0	0	0	0	0	0	0	35	0	0	0	0	0	35	0	12	23
4415	Deer Park	BS	Reasterstown	MD	86	0	0	0	0	0	0	0	0	0	2	84	0	0	0	0	0	83	0	45	39
2550	Dublin	BS	Street	MD	168	0	0	0	0	0	0	0	2	0	4	149	0	0	0	0	1	149	0	97	52
2430	Ebenezer	BS	Fallston	MD	177	0	0	0	0	0	0	0	0	0	2	151	0	0	2	0	0	151	0	98	53
3365	Edgewood	BS	Lutherville	MD	47	3	0	0	0	0	0	0	0	0	2	48	0	48	0	0	0	0	2	29	19
2555	Emory	BS	Street	MD	477	12	2	0	0	0	0	0	0	0	4	487	0	0	0	0	0	485	2	285	202
4420	Emory	BS	Upperco	MD	260	0	0	0	0	0	0	0	0	0	2	257	0	0	0	0	0	256	1	161	96
3290	Epworth	BS	Cockeysville	MD	272	0	0	0	7	0	0	0	1	0	2	272	12	23	0	0	0	232	3	173	99
3455	Fairview	BS	Phoenix	MD	43	0	0	0	0	9	0	6	0	0	3	43	0	0	0	0	0	43	0	42	1
3510	Falls Road	BS	Sparks	MD	28	0	0	0	0	0	0	0	0	0	0	25	0	0	0	0	0	20	1	17	8
2435	Fallston	BS	Fallston	MD	1,392	8	38	0	0	0	0	0	0	0	4	1,430	3	5	2	0	0	1,416	2	790	640
3320	Fork	BS	Fork	MD	170	5	0	0	0	0	0	4	0	0	8	166	1	7	0	0	0	165	0	105	61
3460	Frames Memorial	BS	Cockeysville	MD	32	0	0	0	0	0	0	0	0	0	0	32	0	0	0	0	0	32	0	18	14
4285	Glyndon	BS	Glyndon	MD	317	5	3	0	0	0	0	0	2	0	9	315	1	1	0	0	0	312	1	187	129
3315	Gough	BS	Cockeysville	MD	40	0	0	0	0	0	0	0	0	0	0	40	0	0	0	0	0	40	0	27	13
2110	Grace	BS	Aberdeen	MD	508	4	8	2	0	2	16	0	0	0	15	505	4	40	5	0	0	475	6	298	207
4310	Grace	BS	Upperco	MD	254	0	0	0	0	0	0	0	0	0	4	253	0	0	0	0	0	253	0	142	111
4288	Greenmount	BS	Hampstead	MD	186	0	2	1	0	0	0	0	0	0	3	185	0	15	0	0	0	185	0	104	81
3290	Greenspring	BS	Owings Mills	MD	14	0	1	0	0	0	0	0	0	0	12	12	0	10	0	0	0	9	0	10	2
3455	Havre De Grace	BS	Havre de Grace	MD	740	5	10	5	1	0	0	0	1	0	2	749	2	10	0	0	0	735	0	492	257
3344	Hereford	BS	Monkton	MD	398	10	4	0	1	0	0	0	0	1	1	395	0	12	0	0	0	395	0	221	174
4460	Hopewell	BS	Havre de Grace	MD	115	0	0	0	0	0	0	0	0	0	1	113	0	0	0	0	0	112	1	73	40
3497	Hunt's Memorial	BS	Towson	MD	353	0	0	0	3	0	0	3	0	1	2	355	2	0	0	0	1	350	0	218	137
3535	Idlewylde	BS	Idlewylde	MD	40	0	0	0	0	0	0	0	0	0	0	46	0	0	0	0	0	45	1	29	17
2475	Jarrettsville	BS	Jarrettsville	MD	419	0	0	2	5	0	0	0	3	0	2	414	0	0	0	0	0	414	0	231	183
2130	John Wesley	BS	Abingdon	MD	81	2	0	0	0	0	0	0	0	0	2	84	6	84	0	0	0	0	0	52	32
3445	Linden Heights	BS	Parkville	MD	355	0	0	0	3	0	0	2	2	0	6	349	0	0	0	0	0	343	0	232	117
3380	Maryland Line	BS	Maryland Line	MD	207	2	0	2	1	4	0	0	0	0	3	105	4	1	0	0	0	104	0	60	45
3522	Mays Chapel	BS	Timonium	MD	214	3	0	0	0	0	0	0	0	0	4	217	0	0	0	0	0	207	4	136	81
4360	Mitford Mill	BS	Pikesville	MD	409	0	0	0	0	0	0	0	0	0	4	406	4	109	4	0	0	269	20	263	143
4340	Millers	BS	Manchester	MD	184	0	0	0	0	0	0	0	0	0	5	179	0	0	0	0	0	177	2	104	75

Field legend (columns, in the order printed across the top of the table):
- 20b = Number of persons sent out on UMVIM teams from this church
- 30a = Number of UMVIM teams sent out from this church
- 29 = Amount paid for local church and community work (UMW)
- 28 = Membership in United Methodist Women (UMW)
- 27 = Amount paid for projects (UMM)
- 26 = Membership in United Methodist Men (UMM)
- 25 = Number of SHORT-TERM classes, support groups, or small groups offered
- 24 = Number of ONGOING small groups, support groups, or classes
- 23 = Number of ongoing classes (all ages) for learning in Sunday Church
- 22 = Number of participants in Vacation Bible School
- 20 = Average weekly attendance, Education classes/groups that meet in Sunday Church School groups
- 19 = TOTAL number of persons participating in Christian formation groups (Total lines 15-18)
- 18 = OTHER ADULTS (31+ yrs) in all Christian groups, small groups and Sunday School
- 17 = YOUNG ADULTS (19-30 yrs) in all Christian groups, small groups and Sunday School
- 16 = YOUTH (12-18 yrs) in all Christian groups, small groups and Sunday School
- 15 = CHILDREN (0-11yrs) in all Christian groups, small groups and Sunday School
- 14 = Total enrolled in confirmation preparation classes that
- 13 = Number of other constituents of the church
- 12 = Number of baptized members who have not become Professing
- 11T = TOTAL Number of persons baptized (all ages)
- 11b = Number of Teens and Adults baptized (Age 13+)
- 11a = Number of Infants and Children baptized (Age 0-12)
- 10a = Persons who Worship Online
- 10 = Average attendance at all weekly worship service(s)

Align #	Church Name	20b	30a	29	28	27	26	25	24	23	22	20	19	18	17	16	15	14	13	12	11T	11b	11a	10a	10
2335	Ames	0	0	2,091	28	2,400	0	3	2	2	20	12	43	35	0	0	5	0	5	0	3	1	2	0	75
2565	Asbury	0	0	0	20	0	25	0	1	0	20	5	15	9	6	0	0	0	3	0	0	0	0	0	21
2520	Ayres Chapel	0	0	0	0	0	0	1	0	0	0	0	9	9	0	0	0	0	0	0	0	0	0	0	16
2340	Bel Air	25	1	200	24	0	2	24	32	18	40	117	889	290	9	104	486	17	1,898	485	20	5	15	32	486
3410	Bartley Springs	1	0	700	6	0	0	0	1	0	340	3	7	5	0	0	0	0	1	0	0	0	0	0	16
4530	Bixlers	0	0	0	0	0	0	0	1	0	0	10	13	13	0	0	0	0	0	0	0	0	0	0	20
4625	Boring	0	0	0	0	0	0	0	0	0	0	0	0	0	0	0	0	0	0	0	0	0	0	0	7
3490	Bosley	2	0	0	0	0	0	6	0	6	49	13	17	43	0	7	10	0	61	120	6	0	6	0	17
2530	Camp Chapel	7	1	0	0	0	0	0	1	3	0	57	84	15	4	14	35	5	0	0	0	0	0	0	139
3415	Cedar Grove	0	0	0	0	0	0	0	1	3	0	17	37	15	0	14	5	0	15	6	0	0	0	0	35
2445	Centre	0	0	0	0	0	0	2	2	0	0	19	23	14	0	0	0	0	0	6	1	0	1	6	41
2545	Chesaco	0	0	0	16	0	0	0	1	0	12	0	14	14	0	3	2	0	7	0	1	0	1	0	25
2665	Clarks Chapel	0	0	0	0	267	10	1	2	0	0	16	33	19	1	1	9	0	32	4	1	0	1	0	70
2125	Cokesbury	0	0	0	0	0	0	2	5	4	41	6	34	17	1	6	10	0	23	6	1	0	1	0	28
2540	Cranberry	0	0	0	7	0	0	0	1	1	0	9	9	9	0	0	0	0	16	1	1	1	0	0	42
2375	Darlington	0	0	3,116	0	0	0	2	2	0	0	2	16	14	0	0	2	0	0	0	0	0	0	0	34
2450	Deer Creek	0	0	0	11	0	0	2	5	0	0	5	10	10	0	0	0	0	0	0	1	0	1	0	23
4415	Deer Park	0	0	1,450	12	0	0	2	1	1	100	4	16	10	0	2	2	0	0	0	0	0	0	0	26
2550	Dublin	0	0	0	0	0	0	0	2	2	12	8	8	7	0	0	1	0	6	5	1	0	1	1	16
2430	Ebenezer	0	0	420	12	0	0	2	2	0	12	10	26	24	0	0	8	0	0	0	0	0	0	0	18
3265	Edgewood	0	0	3,000	2	500	0	2	4	0	80	79	8	0	0	0	30	12	0	0	3	0	3	0	30
2555	Emory	2	0	4,200	15	0	5	2	2	9	0	8	92	24	0	26	8	0	0	0	2	2	0	0	43
4420	Emory	0	0	0	22	0	19	6	7	9	0	8	8	8	0	0	0	0	7	2	2	1	1	0	125
3290	Epworth	0	0	0	14	0	0	0	3	0	0	0	8	8	0	0	38	12	132	2	17	0	17	0	42
3455	Fairview	0	0	0	0	0	0	1	1	7	0	35	97	97	0	16	0	0	0	0	0	1	0	0	120
3510	Falls Road	0	0	0	12	0	0	2	6	0	0	0	151	10	0	0	2	0	0	0	0	0	0	0	17
2435	Fallston	0	0	0	0	0	0	0	3	0	0	0	9	100	0	0	58	8	0	0	1	0	1	0	7
3320	Fork	0	0	1,400	25	0	0	24	10	9	100	54	225	100	12	55	8	8	28	34	15	3	12	75	342
3460	Frames Memorial	20	2	465	8	1,050	24	1	1	2	12	6	28	16	0	4	8	0	32	20	2	0	2	0	51
4285	Glyndon	0	0	0	0	25	5	0	6	0	62	41	199	54	15	16	114	5	59	26	4	0	4	0	9
3315	Gough	0	0	0	15	612	16	0	7	0	153	62	121	50	2	10	55	4	86	24	7	4	3	6	96
4310	Grace	22	1	7,998	66	0	0	1	1	0	120	17	50	53	10	9	16	15	18	15	0	1	0	0	15
4288	Greenmount	0	0	0	0	0	0	0	3	4	150	20	53	25	0	8	20	9	36	9	1	0	1	0	198
3390	Greenspring	0	0	2,013	2	2,463	2	3	1	6	65	27	77	46	0	14	15	0	217	171	8	3	5	0	55
2455	Havre De Grace	0	0	750	10	0	15	3	10	4	91	20	391	180	3	48	160	10	511	51	15	3	12	0	107
3344	Hereford	0	0	2,870	16	0	0	7	6	4	41	107	42	31	0	7	7	0	51	23	2	0	2	0	8
2460	Hopewell	0	0	0	23	0	9	3	4	4	52	12	107	40	1	4	30	4	23	51	0	0	0	0	186
3487	Hunt's Memorial	0	0	0	0	0	0	7	2	1	7	7	14	13	0	27	0	0	5	12	1	1	0	0	170
3535	Idlewylde	0	0	0	0	0	0	0	1	1	0	24	13	13	0	10	13	0	20	0	0	0	0	0	65
2475	Jarrettsville	0	0	1,320	25	152	23	5	1	5	50	22	33	44	5	12	21	0	35	50	2	0	2	0	120
2130	John Wesley	0	0	1,500	25	0	0	1	2	5	0	11	62	38	0	8	16	5	3	84	2	0	2	0	35
3445	Linden Heights	0	0	0	0	0	0	4	1	5	150	78	78	55	5	6	12	0	24	16	2	0	2	6	54
3380	Maryland Line	0	0	0	0	0	0	0	4	4	14	11	50	42	1	4	3	0	11	2	2	0	0	20	70
3522	Mays Chapel	0	0	0	0	0	0	1	9	9	9	12	50	42	1	4	3	0	11	36	2	0	0	0	81
4380	Milford Mill	0	0	0	0	0	0	4	4	4	14	11	50	42	1	4	3	0	11	2	2	0	0	0	30
4340	Millers	0	0	0	0	0	0	1	2	9	9	12	50	42	1	4	3	0	11	36	2	0	0	0	102

Align #	Church Name	33	33a	33b	34	35a	36	36SF	37	38	39	42	43	44	45	46	47	48a	43b
2385	Ames	4	2	2	125	40	1,600,000	10,000	0	0	0	0	0	0	0	0	0	0	918
2565	Asbury	0	0	0		0	301,000	3,600	0	0	0	0	0	0	0	0	0	0	0
2520	Ayres Chapel	2	2	2	45	25	345,700	7,100	204,813	0	0	0	0	0	0	0	0	100	371
2340	Bel Air	25	11	14	5,434	577	12,512,000	67,600	2,032,012	0	0	14,124	0	0	0	0	0	15	109,513
3410	Bentley Springs	1	1	1	300	25	2,750,000	4,580	15,750	0	0	0	0	315	0	0	0	15	2,355
4530	Bixlers	3	1	2	4,600	15	1,200,000	7,344	475,000	0	0	0	0	80	0	0	0	500	2,145
4625	Boring	1	1	1	400	8	161,000	2,367	327,660	0	0	0	0	182	0	0	0	0	0
3490	Bosley	4	0	2	100	10	2,000,000	10,200	183,000	0	0	0	0	15	0	0	0	620	0
2530	Camp Chapel	5	0	5	1,000	76	3,290,900	14,752	62,651	90,607	0	1,500	0	0	0	0	0	1,777	15,609
3415	Cedar Grove	4	0	4	750	37	455,000	4,439	582,187	0	0	0	0	0	0	0	0	0	0
2445	Centre	5	0	5	330	35	2,219,918	9,680	59,218	0	919	0	0	0	0	0	0	0	4,783
2545	Chesaco	1	1	1	0	30	759,000	4,848	0	645,954	0	0	0	0	0	0	0	0	0
2965	Clarks Chapel	5	3	5	90	90	1,095,900	8,550	85,842	0	0	150	0	0	0	0	0	0	1,510
3450	Clynmalira	6	3	2	133	7	1,778,000	6,195	684,307	0	0	544	0	0	0	0	0	165	858
2125	Cokesbury	16	6	9	607	65	2,405,000	6,200	720,000	0	0	202	0	0	0	0	0	627	10,938
2540	Cranberry	0	0	0	824	51	640,300	6,920	73,276	0	0	180	0	0	0	0	0	91	2,341
2375	Darlington	2	0	2	697	35	950,000	5,303	282,338	0	0	0	23	0	0	0	0	490	1,721
2450	Deer Creek	5	0	1	15	6	895,000	2,992	110,000	0	0	180	0	0	0	0	0	240	0
4415	Deer Park	1	0	1	0	26	943,000	3,600	240,000	0	0	0	0	0	0	0	0	0	0
2550	Dublin	5	1	5	550	15	717,100	16,200	272,950	0	0	20	0	0	0	0	0	390	0
2430	Ebenezer	0	0	0	165	6	525,000	7,500	117,629	0	0	245	0	0	0	0	0	0	0
3365	Edgewood	0	0	0	0	70	1,250,000	4,030	600,000	0	0	0	0	0	0	0	0	0	595
2555	Emory	16	6	5	430	40	1,598,500	20,440	60,155	84,194	0	274	0	0	0	0	0	1,852	12,602
4420	Emory	21	11	19	3,800	290	3,862,500	9,784	106,953	0	0	0	0	0	0	0	0	0	0
3090	Epworth	4	1	4	2,260	13	1,418,000	18,000	376,000	0	0	0	0	0	0	0	0	1,500	43,204
3455	Fairview	3	2	1	100	2	155,000	7,756	43,373	0	0	0	0	0	0	0	0	25,500	2,413
3510	Falls Road	35	6	24	75	244	6,311,285	1,000	145,000	118,801	0	5	0	0	0	0	0	828	0
2435	Fallston	9	2	2	3,100	60	571,496	39,420	906,888	0	0	0	0	0	0	0	0	0	1,841
3320	Fork	0	0	0	300	9	251,000	5,100	163,470	0	0	0	0	0	0	0	0	500	16,983
3460	Frances Memorial	4	0	2	800	140	3,174,965	2,200	200	431,000	0	5	0	0	0	0	0	3,598	632
4285	Glyndon	1	0	0	2,350	9	325,000	20,320	454,061	0	0	4,000	0	0	0	0	0	632	0
3315	Gough	4	1	4	0	91	5,230,000	0	0	558,466	0	1,000	0	0	0	0	0	0	0
2110	Grace	1	1	1	830	20	180,000	26,490	175,000	0	0	0	0	0	0	0	0	175	761
4310	Grace	0	0	0	50	28	3,048,200	13,800	85,000	0	0	2,698	0	0	0	0	0	52,084	10,210
4288	Greenmount	0	0	0	350	92	148,000	7,910	80,868	1,299,091	9,424	0	0	0	0	0	0	6,136	286,623
3090	Greenspring	19	5	16	0	47	8,397,400	500	25,000	0	0	1,576	0	0	0	0	0	1,652	0
2455	Havre De Grace	7	4	6	511	14	4,000,000	12,148	680,111	0	0	1,849	0	0	0	0	0	16,673	5,837
3344	Hereford	2	0	2	2,818	95	2,128,480	19,197	432,905	0	0	0	0	471	0	0	0	360	0
2460	Hopewell	0	0	0	800	60	2,197,380	8,500	3,693,293	0	0	0	0	0	0	0	0	0	1,792
3407	Hunt's Memorial	15	2	5	60	125	846,000	97,900	407,000	0	0	0	0	0	0	0	0	373	0
3535	Idlewylde	1	1	2	300	4	2,514,000	5,000	240,000	0	0	110	0	0	0	0	0	0	24,972
3344	Jarrettsville	2	1	1	350	100	1,065,245	13,500	100,000	0	0	0	0	0	0	0	0	0	0
2475	John Wesley	5	4	4	200	28	1,850,000	4,090	138,376	153,182	0	1,050	0	0	0	0	0	40	14,863
2130	Linden Heights	2	1	2	200	40	1,381,300	13,293	283,000	0	0	0	0	0	0	0	0	0	1,102
3445	Maryland Line	0	0	0	200		2,500,000	21,405	0	0	0	0	0	0	0	0	0	0	
3380	Mays Chapel				51		2,005,741	6,260	113,377										
5522	Milford Mill				1,250		976,538		94,036										
43340	Millers																		

		Total of UMC Causes & UMC Missions & Outreach	NON-UMC CAUSES: Total amount given DIRECTLY to non-United Methodist benevolent and charitable causes (NOT sent to BWC Treasurer)	Human Relations Sunday	UMCOR Sunday (formerly One Great Hour of Sharing)	Peace with Justice Sunday	Native American Ministries Sunday	World Communion Sunday	U.M. Student Day	Direct-billed clergy non-health benefits	Direct-billed clergy health benefits	Base compensation paid to/for the Senior Pastor or other person assigned or appointed in the lead pastoral role to the church	Base compensation paid/for to all Associate Pastor(s) & other pastoral staff assigned or appointed to the church.	Base compensation paid to/for any Deacons NOT included in 53a or 53b	Housing benefits paid to/for Lead Pastor or person in lead pastoral role as described in 53a	Housing benefits paid to/for ALL Associate Pastor(s) & other pastoral staff assigned or appointed to the	Housing benefits paid to/for any Deacons not included in 53a or 53b.	Paid to/for all persons included in Lines 53a-53c for accountable reimbursements	Paid to/for all persons included in Lines 53a-53c for any other cash allowances (non-
Align #	Church Name	48TOTAL	49	50a	50b	50c	50d	50e	50f	51	52	53a	53b	53c	55a	55b	55c	56	57
2335	Ames	918	900	81	0	0	0	0	0	13,913	13,254	46,350	0	0	20,000	0	0	5,500	0
2565	Asbury	0	200	0	0	0	0	0	0	0	0	5,720	0	0	5,720	0	0	0	0
2520	Ayres Chapel	471	0	0	0	0	0	58	0	9,934	11,400	15,652	0	0	2,349	0	0	1,750	0
2340	Bel Air	109,513	11,849	0	0	0	0	489	0	26,534	121,463	79,626	47,660	0	19,866	19,866	0	9,612	0
3410	Bentley Springs	2,370	0	0	0	0	0	0	0	0	0	6,120	0	0	0	0	0	477	0
4530	Bixlers	2,145	200	0	0	0	0	0	0	0	0	14,000	0	0	2,798	0	0	0	0
4625	Boring	500	6,604	0	0	0	0	0	0	0	0	4,000	0	0	0	0	0	0	0
3490	Bosley	0	0	0	0	0	0	0	0	0	0	7,800	0	0	12,000	0	0	0	0
2530	Camp Chapel	15,689	0	0	0	0	0	0	0	12,920	14,424	53,213	0	0	21,714	0	0	1,848	0
3415	Cedar Grove	620	150	0	0	0	0	0	0	4,399	0	17,323	0	0	0	0	0	173	0
2445	Centre	6,560	6,384	0	0	0	0	0	0	5,189	0	23,063	0	0	5,586	0	0	0	0
2545	Chesaco	0	1,073	0	0	0	0	0	0	0	0	20,000	0	0	0	0	0	341	0
2365	Clarks Chapel	1,510	0	0	0	0	0	0	0	0	5,676	13,883	0	0	0	0	0	0	550
3450	Clynmalira	858	0	0	0	0	0	0	0	0	0	35,728	0	0	10,008	0	0	1,508	0
2125	Cokesbury	11,103	36,499	0	0	0	0	0	0	10,413	11,448	45,667	0	0	5,243	0	0	3,514	0
2540	Cranberry	2,968	1,119	0	0	0	0	0	0	0	0	17,032	0	0	2,022	0	0	1,640	250
2375	Darlington	1,812	1,879	10	10	10	61	30	10	0	0	13,799	0	0	1,909	0	0	373	0
2450	Deer Creek	480	0	0	0	0	20	0	0	0	0	12,500	0	0	0	0	0	0	0
4415	Deer Park	240	384	0	0	0	0	0	0	0	0	15,000	0	0	0	0	0	783	0
2550	Dublin	0	1,374	10	0	10	9	35	20	10,354	14,117	32,211	0	0	0	0	0	841	0
2430	Ebenezer	390	1,842	380	0	78	95	90	75	12,276	16,164	23,500	0	0	5,300	0	0	2,300	0
3365	Edgewood	0	672	0	0	0	0	0	0	0	0	10,715	0	0	0	0	0	0	0
2555	Emory	0	0	0	0	0	0	0	0	12,882	15,760	54,430	0	0	0	0	0	0	0
4420	Emory	595	6,000	216	0	61	1,198	67	95	0	0	30,000	0	0	0	0	0	824	0
3290	Epworth	14,454	9,299	0	0	0	0	0	0	21,148	16,460	55,748	18,251	0	19,866	26,500	0	6,821	0
3455	Fairview	0	0	0	0	0	0	0	0	0	0	12,000	0	0	0	0	0	1,303	0
3510	Falls Road	1,500	2,500	0	0	0	0	0	0	0	0	4,944	0	0	0	0	0	1,100	0
2435	Fallston	68,704	85,773	0	0	0	0	0	0	14,499	13,491	59,246	0	0	42,000	0	0	11,000	0
3320	Fork	3,241	7,825	0	0	125	1,935	0	65	10,575	17,852	31,318	0	0	2,633	0	0	2,901	0
3460	Frames Memorial	0	0	0	0	5	10	5	5	0	0	9,895	0	0	0	0	0	0	0
4285	Glyndon	1,841	2,553	0	0	0	0	0	0	10,681	12,366	43,900	0	0	4,077	0	0	4,285	0
3315	Gough	500	0	0	0	0	0	0	0	0	0	5,043	0	0	0	0	0	0	0
2110	Grace	20,581	10,000	0	0	0	0	0	0	13,872	26,867	64,797	0	0	26,000	0	0	8,500	0
4310	Grace	632	0	0	0	0	0	0	0	0	0	16,817	14,468	0	0	0	0	0	0
4288	Greenmount	0	15,493	0	0	0	0	0	0	0	0	16,817	14,468	0	13,497	0	0	2,900	0
3390	Greenspring	175	125	0	0	0	0	0	0	0	0	11,688	0	0	0	0	0	0	0
2455	Havre De Grace	52,845	5,524	162	100	370	106	136	0	13,528	15,169	68,054	0	0	8,505	0	0	6,635	0
3344	Hereford	16,346	16,612	0	0	120	115	190	0	14,577	18,500	43,467	0	0	40,600	0	0	5,254	0
2460	Hopewell	1,652	2,436	0	0	5	71	0	0	9,984	11,627	26,407	0	0	4,500	0	0	3,780	0
3487	Hunt's Memorial	303,296	151,552	0	0	50	0	0	0	13,672	34,417	56,507	0	0	30,000	0	0	759	0
3535	Idlewylde	360	738	0	190	35	54	25	0	11,197	11,367	26,265	0	0	0	0	0	1,500	0
2475	Jarrettsville	5,837	5,837	0	0	0	0	0	0	0	0	28,697	0	0	3,993	0	0	3,315	0
2130	John Wesley	0	0	0	0	0	0	0	0	0	0	19,283	0	0	9,000	0	0	635	0
3445	Linden Heights	2,165	4,008	65	128	15	37	30	0	12,843	10,603	53,620	0	0	20,400	0	0	898	0
3380	Maryland Line	0	0	0	0	0	0	0	0	0	0	9,520	0	0	0	0	0	0	0
3522	Mays Chapel	24,972	27,932	0	0	0	210	0	0	13,044	14,460	52,000	0	0	25,000	0	0	0	0
4380	Milford Mill	14,903	200	0	0	0	0	0	0	6,890	7,047	44,897	0	0	22,361	0	0	540	0
4340	Millers	1,102	2,040	0	0	0	0	0	0	0	0	14,000	0	0	2,798	0	0	209	0

Align #	Church Name	60 Paid in salary and benefits for all other church staff and diaconal ministers	61 Amount spent for local church program expenses	62 Amount spent for local church operating expenses	63 Amount paid for principal and interest on indebtedness, loans, mortgages, etc	63a Amount paid for capital campaign or fundraising costs	64 Amount paid on capital expenditures for building, improvements, and major equipment purchases	65 Amount PAID by/for the local church on all expenditures	66 Number of giving units	67a Received through pledges	67b Received from non-pledging, but identified givers	67c Received from unidentified givers	67d Amount received from interest and dividends and/or transferred from liquid assets	67e Amount received from Sale of Church Assets	67f Amount received through building use fees, contributions, and rentals	67g Amount received through fundraisers and other sources
2335	Ames	31,568	4,255	52,672	17,670	0	29,000	260,022	80	22,000	224,593	43,280	0	0	1,470	4,852
2565	Asbury	0	7,500	5,230	0	0	0	27,830	0	35,600	3,500	650	0	0	500	350
2520	Ayres Chapel	3,400	399	16,751	0	0	4,575	72,843	16	0	34,015	3,827	0	0	4,727	13,121
2340	Bel Air	461,978	38,430	278,604	0	0	268,142	1,670,701	712	513760	705,338	36,071	859	0	0	0
3410	Bentley Springs	40	40	9,663	0	0	0	21,904	19	21,363	0	5,941	0	0	250	452
4530	Biders	2,400	60	11,473	0	0	9,167	46,622	0	0	9,110	17,345	24,398	0	250	0
4625	Boring	0	0	6,225	0	0	5,600	24,762	14	0	4,160	4,160	0	0	0	3,788
3460	Bosley	0	0	5,600	0	0	0	28,964	0	24,598	373	2,583	0	0	1,475	12,464
2530	Camp Chapel	55,726	7,044	40,232	32,628	0	102,266	389,724	179	184,380	89,516	1,000	0	0	2,575	28,353
3415	Cedar Grove	1,725	1,777	3,762	0	0	1,861	37,126	33	0	44,934	0	0	0	0	0
2445	Centre	0	2,407	16,587	0	0	8,613	89,430	36	0	84,668	2,372	0	0	5,230	6,000
2545	Chesaco	0	1,425	10,290	90,422	0	1,950	41,229	28	0	35,754	5,274	304	0	120	1,738
2365	Clarks Chapel	8,972	6,029	43,255	0	0	1,547	176,327	57	42,931	189,846	2,949	34,241	0	0	26,239
3450	Clynmaira	18,695	2,016	18,265	0	0	3,735	93,628	27	0	0	4,171	0	0	1,152	1,186
2125	Cokesbury	8,991	5,560	28,752	0	0	0	195,821	45	0	123,761	3,179	413	0	1,200	0
2540	Cranberry	0	6,704	11,999	0	0	3,613	61,446	49	0	59,776	0	1	0	300	0
2375	Darlington	0	1,990	12,342	0	0	6,530	46,763	14	0	26,471	1,261	0	0	0	0
2450	Deer Creek	0	0	2,590	0	0	35,394	54,569	22	0	34,998	0	72	0	0	0
4415	Deer Park	0	410	17,977	0	0	987	41,477	20	0	32,075	654	0	0	475	4,000
2550	Dublin	410	955	32,275	0	0	7,407	112,589	30	60,834	12,846	1,160	91	0	142	0
2430	Ebenezer	0	979	21,417	0	0	7,061	112,509	31	0	74,295	2,501	0	0	385	6,000
3365	Edgewood	9,097	310	7,450	0	0	0	37,683	0	5,500	0	4,000	0	0	300	0
2555	Emory	13,000	6,000	38,775	31,966	0	4,000	159,736	38	0	155,625	3,575	0	0	11,345	802
4420	Emory	7,543	1,434	27,434	37,475	0	6,865	142,532	165	106,810	125,029	3,556	200	0	28,133	7,320
3290	Epworth	21,245	7,696	71,710	0	0	14,330	403,575	17	0	166,791	1,884	0	0	18,872	3,772
3455	Fairview	42,739	103	31,301	0	0	5,400	57,951	8	0	32,172	822	434	0	57,087	350
3510	Falls Road	599	350	5,450	0	0	0	18,138	310	14,200	3,700	275	0	0	0	4,135
2435	Fallston	165,970	21,289	87,359	41,357	0	78,066	748,701	65	291,829	274,683	17,147	0	0	635	768
3320	Fork	13,920	4,553	26,660	0	0	0	136,061	12	0	76,453	28,753	0	0	6,902	7,320
3460	Frames Memorial	0	0	1,400	0	387	93,644	13,782	181	183,204	12,000	9,013	0	0	27,575	0
4285	Glyndon	66,008	10,996	49,778	15,254	3,081	0	346,850	190	0	61,209	7,577	980	0	323	4,135
3315	Gough	0	1,498	10,425	0	0	25,651	20,513	81	0	25,134	3,362	0	0	0	0
2110	Grace	132,089	21,686	58,485	77,822	1,282	0	535,644	500	55,009	374,853	11,147	0	0	1,880	0
4310	Grace	0	1,250	8,593	0	0	17,970	50,023	117	0	1,405	9,266	0	0	13,018	0
4288	Greenmount	16,951	1,950	17,144	0	0	0	131,137	52	0	122,565	2,241	434	0	52,547	0
3990	Greenspring	0	300	12,000	0	0	33,336	28,987	157	341,528	27,050	792	0	0	0	0
2455	Havre De Grace	93,631	8,420	68,968	0	0	3,000	387,732	34	0	313,692	8,438	77	0	1,690	7,921
3344	Hereford	53,702	5,772	70,019	110,949	0	34,998	464,618	59	189,049	0	7,007	433	0	1,800	9,783
2460	Hopewell	13,364	6,344	13,775	0	0	28,768	111,704	30	60,000	112,948	4,946	0	0	23,947	3,533
3407	Hunt's Memorial	95,892	19,586	95,266	0	0	7,322	881,431	86	0	2,000	1,236	16,570	0	2,895	517
3535	Idlewylde	0	8,200	10,500	0	0	3,000	107,998	21	0	80,453	2,533	0	0	26,080	0
2475	Jarrettsville	19,923	3,495	24,322	0	0	18,694	119,390	0	0	69,084	6,216	0	0	4,525	0
2130	John Wesley	15,342	2,071	40,125	0	0	10,211	102,410	101	0	157,401	12,408	0	0	0	11,740
3445	Linden Heights	7,356	5,338	41,302	0	0	15,739	194,818	27	167,228	51,258	1,236	257	0	0	0
3880	Maryland Line	6,000	0	6,257	18,760	0	30,313	33,353	0	0	83,614	2,533	77	0	0	0
3522	Mays Chapel	35,604	6,746	78,267	0	6,855	3,100	349,091	0	0	120,370	6,216	0	0	0	0
4380	Milford Mill	30,214	2,436	53,307	0	0	30,313	241,356	101	50,918	45,140	6,216	0	0	0	0
4340	Millers	0	1,940	15,176	0	0	3,100	49,351	27	0	0	12,408	0	0	4,525	0

Align #	Church Name	TOTAL income for annual budget/spending plan (67a-g) — 67	Capital campaigns — 68a	Memorials, endowments, and bequests — 68b	Other sources and projects (include UMW, UMM and "flow-through") — 68c	Special Sundays, Gen. Adv. Spec., World Srvc Spec., Conf. Adv. Spec. and other directed benevolent giving — 68d	Total income for designated causes including capital campaign and other special projects — 68	Equitable Compensation Funds received by Church or Pastor — 69a	Advance Special, apportioned, and connectional funds received by church — 69b	Other grants and financial support from institutional sources — 69c	Income from connectional / institutional sources outside the local church — 69	TOTAL CHURCH INCOME (Sum of Lines 67 + 68 + 69) — 70	Amount APPORTIONED to the local church — 40a	Amount PAID by the local church for all apportioned causes — 40b
2335	Ames	296,095	25,000	0	0	1,144	26,144	0	0	0	0	322,339	23,941	23,941
2565	Asbury	40,600	0	0	5,230	0	5,230	0	0	0	0	45,830	3,460	3,460
2520	Ayres Chapel	50,963	0	0	0	114	114	0	0	0	0	51,077	6,104	6,104
2340	Bel Air	1,260,755	113,270	87,083	0	83,449	263,802	0	0	15,000	15,000	1,559,557	162,945	162,945
3410	Bentley Springs	26,704	0	400	0	0	400	0	0	0	0	27,104	3,234	3,234
4530	Bixlers	51,565	0	625	0	0	625	0	0	0	0	52,190	4,379	4,379
4605	Boring	6,743	0	0	0	0	0	0	0	0	0	6,743	1,833	1,833
3490	Bosley	39,756	0	5,155	0	0	5,155	0	0	0	0	44,911	3,564	3,564
2530	Camp Chapel	304,824	52,403	15,905	0	0	68,308	0	0	0	0	373,132	30,520	30,520
3415	Cedar Grove	44,934	0	0	0	0	0	0	0	0	0	44,934	5,336	5,336
2445	Centre	98,270	740	930	1,600	1,500	4,770	0	0	0	0	103,040	15,041	15,041
2545	Chesaco	42,886	0	2,020	0	0	2,020	0	0	0	0	44,906	6,150	6,150
2365	Clarks Chapel	219,339	0	0	0	0	0	0	0	0	0	219,339	13,455	13,455
3450	Clynmalira	83,681	0	575	4,611	0	5,186	0	0	0	0	88,867	12,538	12,538
2125	Cokesbury	128,220	0	2,780	0	0	2,780	0	0	0	0	131,000	10,462	10,462
2540	Cranberry	63,977	25	0	0	142	167	5,000	0	0	5,000	69,144	5,614	5,614
2375	Darlington	40,517	0	11,921	0	0	11,921	0	110	0	110	52,548	5,614	5,614
2450	Deer Creek	35,070	0	0	0	0	0	0	0	0	0	35,070	3,390	3,390
4415	Deer Park	37,204	0	2,277	0	0	2,277	0	0	0	0	39,481	5,696	5,696
2550	Dublin	74,931	0	670	0	127	797	0	0	0	0	75,728	11,837	11,837
2430	Ebenezer	76,938	4,887	1,845	0	863	7,595	0	0	0	0	84,533	10,400	10,400
3365	Edgewood	15,085	0	0	0	0	0	0	0	0	0	15,085	5,536	5,536
2555	Emory	159,500	0	3,025	0	0	3,025	0	0	0	0	162,525	19,348	19,348
4420	Emory	140,130	0	11,010	0	0	11,010	0	0	0	0	151,140	14,258	14,258
3290	Epworth	303,618	36,262	175	0	0	36,437	0	0	0	0	340,055	41,078	41,078
3455	Fairview	52,668	0	300	0	0	300	0	0	0	0	52,968	7,245	7,245
3510	Falls Road	18,175	0	0	0	0	0	0	0	0	0	18,175	2,294	2,294
2435	Fallston	718,066	45,110	1,590	0	0	46,700	0	0	0	0	764,766	58,947	58,947
3320	Fork	108,978	0	625	22,000	6,718	29,343	0	0	0	0	138,321	12,458	12,458
3460	Frames Memorial	12,350	0	0	0	0	0	0	0	0	0	12,350	2,457	2,457
4285	Glyndon	259,176	141,434	6,250	0	0	147,684	0	0	0	0	406,860	30,667	30,667
3315	Gough	25,134	0	0	0	0	0	0	0	0	0	25,134	3,047	3,047
2110	Grace	389,254	89,071	8,985	0	5,039	103,095	0	0	0	0	492,349	45,294	45,294
4310	Grace	88,119	0	0	210	423	633	0	0	0	0	88,752	8,263	8,263
4288	Greenmount	134,469	12,686	2,280	0	2,478	17,444	0	0	0	0	151,913	12,947	12,947
3390	Greenspring	27,050	0	0	0	0	0	0	0	0	0	27,050	4,690	4,690
2455	Havre De Grace	343,485	2,093	5,390	8,591	62,910	78,984	0	0	0	0	422,469	42,881	42,881
3244	Hereford	336,409	28,310	0	0	775	29,085	0	0	0	0	365,494	35,059	35,059
2467	Hopewell	0	0	0	0	0	0	0	0	0	0	0	13,183	13,183
3487	Hunt's Memorial	381,276	2,477	6,505	450	24,646	36,078	0	0	0	0	417,354	46,506	46,506
3535	Idlewylde	64,482	0	250	0	803	1,053	0	0	0	0	65,535	5,469	5,469
2475	Jarrettsville	88,691	0	470	0	200	670	0	0	0	0	89,561	16,619	16,619
2130	John Wesley	87,674	0	100	1,258	0	1,358	0	0	0	0	89,032	12,954	12,954
3445	Linden Heights	189,727	580	3,600	0	385	4,565	0	0	0	0	194,292	20,242	17,206
3380	Maryland Line	53,011	0	429	0	0	429	0	0	0	0	53,440	1,365	1,365
3522	Mays Chapel	256,527	17,000	945	0	0	17,945	0	0	0	0	274,472	34,307	34,307
4380	Milford Mill	215,401	17,662	430	60	560	18,712	0	0	0	0	234,113	28,248	28,248
4340	Millers	61,073	0	5,355	0	0	5,355	0	0	0	0	66,428	8,986	8,986

Aligq #	Church Name	Dist #	City	State	Total professing members at the close of 2017 (1)	Received by PROFESSION of Faith (2a1)	Received by PROFESSION of Faith (Other Than Confirmation) (2a2)	Restored by AFFIRMATION of Faith (2b)	Transferred in from other UM churches (3)	Transferred in from non-UM churches (4)	Removed or corrected by ChargeConference action (5a)	Withdrawn from Professing Membership (5b)	Transferred out to other UM churches (6)	Transferred out to non-UM churches (7)	Removed by death (8)	Total professing members at the close of 2018 (9)	Asian Professing Members (9a)	African American / Black Professing Members (9b)	Hispanic / Latino Professing Members (9c)	Native American Professing Members (9d)	Pacific Islander Professing Members (9e)	White Professing Members (9f)	Multi-Racial Professing Members (9g)	Female Professing Members (9h)	Male Professing Members (9i)
3385	Morkton	BS	Morkton	MD	68	0	0	0	0	0	0	0	0	0	5	100	0	0	0	0	0	100	0	64	36
3425	Mount Carmel	BS	Parkton	MD	181	0	0	0	0	0	0	0	0	0	4	177	0	0	0	0	0	177	0	97	80
4425	Mount Gilead	BS	Reisterstown	MD	63	4	2	0	0	0	0	0	0	0	2	61	2	0	0	0	0	61	0	36	25
4390	Mount Olive	BS	Randallstown	MD	365	4	0	0	0	0	0	0	1	0	2	370	2	179	2	0	0	184	3	220	150
2345	Mount Tabor	BS	Bel Air	MD	46	0	0	0	0	0	0	0	0	0	4	42	0	0	0	0	0	42	0	31	11
2580	Mount Vernon	BS	Whiteford	MD	30	0	0	0	0	0	0	0	0	0	0	30	0	1	0	0	0	29	0	15	15
2350	Mount Zion	BS	Bel Air	MD	848	14	13	0	8	0	26	0	0	0	6	869	14	17	15	0	0	823	5	478	391
3325	Mount Zion	BS	Mechanicsburg	PA	57	0	0	0	0	0	0	0	0	0	0	50	0	0	0	0	0	50	0	25	25
4525	Mount Zion	BS	Upperco	MD	110	0	0	0	0	0	0	0	0	0	6	115	0	0	0	0	0	115	0	65	50
4265	Mount Zion-Finksburg	BS	Finksburg	MD	145	0	6	0	0	0	0	5	0	0	5	145	0	0	0	0	0	145	5	106	39
3500	New Beginnings Fellowship	BS	Jarrettsville	MD	15	0	0	0	0	0	0	0	0	0	0	15	0	13	0	0	0	2	0	9	6
2412	New Hope Christian Fellowship	BS	Edgewood	MD	0	0	2	0	0	0	0	0	0	0	0	45	0	33	0	0	0	12	0	25	20
2525	Norrisville	BS	White Hall	MD	182	0	0	0	0	0	0	0	2	0	0	177	0	0	0	0	0	177	0	97	80
3430	Parke Memorial	BS	Parkton	MD	116	0	0	0	0	0	0	0	0	0	1	115	0	0	0	0	0	115	0	62	53
4430	Patapsco	BS	Finksburg	MD	118	0	0	0	0	0	0	0	0	0	5	113	0	1	0	0	0	112	0	67	46
2535	Perry Hall	BS	Baltimore	MD	369	2	1	0	2	0	0	1	0	0	1	376	2	3	0	0	0	366	5	279	97
3475	Pine Grove	BS	Parkton	MD	154	7	0	0	0	0	0	0	0	0	7	136	0	3	0	0	0	132	0	58	78
3570	Pine Grove	BS	White Hall	MD	16	0	0	0	0	0	0	0	0	0	0	16	0	14	0	0	0	2	0	11	5
4175	Piney Grove	BS	Reisterstown	MD	10	0	0	0	0	0	0	0	0	0	0	10	0	10	0	0	0	0	0	6	4
4520	Pleasant Grove	BS	Reisterstown	MD	80	0	0	0	0	0	0	0	0	0	0	82	0	0	0	0	0	82	0	50	32
4370	Pleasant Hill	BS	Owings Mills	MD	153	0	0	0	0	0	0	0	2	0	1	163	6	58	0	0	0	99	5	107	56
3465	Poplar Grove	BS	Cockeysville	MD	63	0	0	0	0	0	0	0	0	0	0	63	0	0	0	0	0	63	0	38	25
2415	Presbury	BS	Edgewood	MD	119	0	0	0	0	0	3	0	1	0	4	111	3	6	0	0	0	102	0	73	38
3370	Providence	BS	Towson	MD	57	0	0	0	0	0	0	0	0	0	0	57	3	0	0	0	0	54	0	37	20
4435	Reisterstown	BS	Reisterstown	MD	688	0	2	0	8	0	94	19	0	0	6	570	0	26	1	0	2	535	3	338	232
2378	Rock Run	BS	Havre de Grace	MD	78	0	0	0	0	0	0	0	0	0	0	78	0	0	0	0	0	78	0	48	30
2560	Salem	BS	Upper Falls	MD	439	0	0	0	0	0	0	0	0	0	0	439	0	3	0	0	0	436	5	244	195
3340	Salem	BS	Hampstead	MD	148	0	0	0	0	0	0	0	0	0	0	145	0	0	0	0	0	145	0	81	64
4325	Shiloh	BS	Hampstead	MD	231	0	0	0	2	0	0	0	0	0	1	228	1	2	0	0	0	225	0	132	96
2370	Smiths Chapel	BS	Churchville	MD	184	2	0	0	0	0	0	0	0	0	0	188	0	0	0	0	0	188	0	132	56
3375	St Johns	BS	Lutherville	MD	51	0	0	0	0	0	0	0	1	0	1	49	4	6	0	0	0	43	0	39	10
4320	St Johns	BS	Hampstead	MD	692	0	0	0	0	1	0	0	4	0	1	690	0	0	0	0	0	690	0	410	280
3345	St Luke	BS	Morkton	MD	12	0	0	0	0	0	0	1	0	0	3	6	0	6	0	0	0	6	0	4	2
4440	St Luke	BS	Reisterstown	MD	52	4	0	0	0	0	0	11	0	0	3	44	2	44	0	0	0	26	0	36	8
2595	St Paul	BS	White Hall	MD	86	7	0	0	0	0	0	0	2	0	1	85	0	0	0	0	0	85	0	50	35
3435	Stablers	BS	Parkton	MD	48	0	0	0	0	0	0	0	0	0	0	48	0	0	0	0	0	48	0	42	6
3310	Texas	BS	Cockeysville	MD	72	15	4	2	0	0	0	0	0	0	0	72	1	4	0	0	2	62	0	53	19
3525	Timonium	BS	Timonium	MD	437	15	4	0	3	0	0	0	0	0	7	454	3	33	3	0	0	415	3	279	175
2115	Union	BS	Aberdeen	MD	239	2	0	0	2	0	0	0	0	0	2	239	0	235	0	0	0	0	0	163	76
3135	Union	BS	Baldwin	MD	105	0	0	0	0	0	0	0	1	0	2	107	0	2	0	0	0	105	0	63	44
2510	Union Chapel	BS	Joppa	MD	172	0	0	0	0	0	0	0	0	0	4	172	0	0	2	0	0	172	0	121	51
3350	Union Chapel	BS	Morkton	MD	15	0	0	0	0	0	0	0	0	0	0	10	0	8	0	0	0	2	0	5	5
3555	Vernon	BS	White Hall	MD	26	0	0	0	0	0	0	0	0	0	0	26	2	0	0	0	0	26	0	17	9
4410	Wards Chapel	BS	Randallstown	MD	412	7	0	0	0	0	0	0	2	0	6	411	2	9	0	1	0	399	0	247	164
3335	Waugh	BS	Glen Arm	MD	141	0	0	2	0	0	4	0	0	0	0	142	0	1	0	0	0	141	0	89	53
4330	Wesley	BS	Hampstead	MD	430	0	0	0	0	0	0	53	1	0	5	368	0	0	0	1	0	365	0	190	178
2470	Wesleyan Chapel	BS	Aberdeen	MD	112	0	0	0	0	0	0	0	0	0	2	109	0	1	1	0	0	108	0	71	38
3560	West Liberty	BS	White Hall	MD	100	0	0	0	0	0	0	0	0	2	2	98	2	3	0	0	0	93	0	66	32

Align #	Church Name	10	10a	11a	11b	11T	12	13	14	15	16	17	18	19	20	22	23	24	25	26	27	28	29	30a	30b
3885	Monkton	18	0	2	0	2	0	6	0	30	8	0	11	11	9	0	1	1	8	0	0	13	5,573	0	0
3425	Mount Carmel	48	30	1	0	1	0	6	0	30	0	2	25	65	10	18	3	2	2	4	0	0	0	0	0
4425	Mount Gilead	17	0	0	0	0	0	5	0	0	0	0	2	2	0	0	0	2	1	0	0	0	0	0	0
4390	Mount Olive	95	0	3	0	3	0	8	5	21	14	5	18	58	30	0	4	2	1	5	100	51	1,070	0	0
2345	Mount Tabor	20	0	0	0	0	0	8	0	0	0	0	0	0	5	0	0	4	0	4	0	4	370	0	0
2580	Mount Vernon	20	0	0	0	0	0	0	0	0	0	0	0	0	5	0	1	0	0	1	0	2	0	0	0
2350	Mount Zion	639	0	9	19	28	12	0	22	184	107	49	254	594	171	389	28	36	17	1	0	0	0	5	36
3325	Mount Zion	25	0	0	0	0	81	0	0	7	0	0	0	7	7	0	1	1	0	0	0	0	50	0	0
4525	Mount Zion	28	0	0	0	0	11	0	0	0	0	0	0	0	7	0	1	1	3	0	0	0	1,555	5	36
4265	Mount Zion-Finksburg	74	0	5	0	5	0	3	3	6	3	2	26	37	4	0	0	1	12	0	0	0	0	0	0
3500	New Beginnings Fellowship	11	0	0	0	0	0	0	0	0	0	0	0	0	0	0	0	0	0	0	0	0	0	0	0
2412	New Hope Christian Fellowship	35	0	4	1	5	18	3	0	36	0	5	10	15	15	14	1	0	0	0	0	10	265	1	1
2555	Norrisville	75	0	0	0	0	8	0	0	0	0	0	12	12	20	60	4	0	1	1	0	0	0	0	0
3430	Parke Memorial	16	0	0	0	0	14	10	0	0	0	0	7	7	6	0	0	0	0	0	0	0	0	0	0
2535	Patapsco	37	0	3	0	3	0	83	0	6	1	1	22	22	15	30	2	2	3	1	0	25	4,027	0	0
3475	Perry Hall	158	0	0	0	0	55	40	2	45	20	0	55	120	70	50	6	5	2	0	0	20	1,140	3	0
3570	Pine Grove	58	0	1	0	1	11	40	0	51	20	10	20	101	39	38	3	2	2	0	500	0	0	0	0
4175	Pine Grove	13	0	0	0	0	0	0	0	0	0	0	3	4	0	0	0	0	0	0	0	0	0	0	0
4520	Piney Grove	6	0	1	0	1	0	0	0	6	0	0	4	4	4	0	1	2	0	0	0	9	800	0	0
4370	Pleasant Grove	31	0	0	2	3	4	57	0	0	3	2	8	10	8	30	6	2	3	0	0	0	0	0	0
3465	Pleasant Hill	82	35	1	0	1	18	36	0	9	0	0	34	57	26	10	0	4	0	0	0	0	0	0	0
2415	Presbury	12	0	0	0	0	8	10	0	0	14	1	10	11	10	0	4	1	1	0	0	0	0	0	0
3370	Providence	43	0	0	0	0	14	49	0	4	0	1	6	11	10	19	0	1	0	1	0	0	0	0	0
4435	Reisterstown	24	0	0	0	0	4	4	0	20	22	4	10	10	30	60	0	1	0	0	0	9	2,448	0	0
2378	Rock Run	147	100	0	0	0	55	151	15	30	5	24	38	84	10	3	7	9	10	0	0	76	11,569	1	12
2560	Salem	47	0	1	0	1	2	25	0	11	5	0	10	27	47	0	1	6	27	0	0	0	0	0	0
3340	Salem	35	0	1	3	0	0	37	0	30	0	0	13	18	9	12	7	4	2	0	0	20	500	0	15
4325	Shiloh	30	0	0	1	1	0	10	0	5	1	0	8	18	6	0	1	2	1	0	0	10	820	0	0
2370	Smiths Chapel	46	0	1	0	1	1	6	0	0	6	0	7	7	2	35	2	1	2	0	0	10	800	0	0
4320	St Johns	99	0	2	1	3	4	12	0	28	1	3	6	31	16	0	4	2	1	0	0	54	3,197	2	0
3375	St Johns	35	0	1	0	1	4	6	0	5	14	0	1	1	22	200	1	2	1	0	0	0	0	0	0
3345	St Luke	4	0	1	1	1	4	40	0	6	0	0	15	28	0	0	4	7	0	0	0	0	0	0	0
4440	St Luke	30	0	1	0	1	0	0	0	0	2	3	7	7	7	58	1	4	2	0	0	0	0	0	0
2585	St Paul	46	0	1	0	1	0	0	0	0	1	0	5	7	0	0	1	2	0	0	0	0	0	0	0
3435	Stablers	18	0	0	0	0	18	0	0	0	2	0	5	7	0	0	1	3	0	0	0	0	0	2	0
3310	Texas	25	0	1	0	1	12	3	15	38	0	0	12	12	14	12	3	5	1	0	0	46	3,283	0	0
3325	Timonium	155	0	12	1	13	102	107	15	11	22	4	52	124	31	12	3	8	0	2	0	19	435	0	0
2115	Union	57	0	1	12	1	7	42	2	0	5	0	39	59	12	0	2	4	0	0	0	4	0	0	0
2510	Union	19	0	1	0	4	9	5	0	0	1	2	4	7	8	0	2	1	1	0	0	45	3,966	1	15
2910	Union Chapel	83	0	1	0	0	0	10	0	0	4	0	30	34	20	0	5	2	2	0	0	0	0	0	0
3950	Union Chapel	10	0	3	0	0	0	15	0	0	0	0	4	4	3	0	2	2	2	0	0	10	820	0	0
3555	Vernon	12	0	0	0	0	0	32	0	4	1	0	18	73	45	0	4	1	1	0	0	10	800	0	0
4410	Wards Chapel	86	0	3	0	1	19	15	12	12	27	16	18	11	7	0	2	2	2	0	0	10	3,197	0	2
3395	Waugh	18	0	1	0	1	0	32	7	24	1	4	83	132	45	12	4	5	1	0	0	54	1,954	2	2
4330	Wesley	92	0	3	0	3	55	42	12	3	21	1	9	15	7	78	10	6	0	14	1,000	20	2,825	0	10
2470	Wesleyan Chapel	31	0	0	0	0	35	40	0	6	3	4	9	15	11	41	2	9	0	1	0	9	260	0	0
3560	West Liberty	20	0	1	0	1	11	20	0	6	3	2	17	28	5	0	3	3	0	1	0	0	0	0	0

Column key:
- 10 — Average attendance at all weekly worship service(s)
- 10a — Persons who Worship Online
- 11a — Number of Infants and Children baptized (Age 0-12)
- 11b — Number of Teens and Adults baptized (Age 13+)
- 11T — TOTAL Number of persons baptized (all ages)
- 12 — Number of baptized members who have not become Professing
- 13 — Number of other constituents of the church
- 14 — Total enrolled in confirmation preparation classes that
- 15 — CHILDREN (0-11yrs) in all Christian groups, small groups and Sunday School
- 16 — YOUTH (12-18 yrs) in all Christian groups, small groups and Sunday School
- 17 — YOUNG ADULTS (19-30 yrs) in all Christian groups, small groups and Sunday School
- 18 — OTHER ADULTS (31+ yrs) in all Christian groups, small groups and Sunday School
- 19 — TOTAL number of persons participating in Christian formation groups (Total lines 15 - 18)
- 20 — Average weekly attendance Education classes/groups that meet in Sunday Church School groups
- 22 — Number of participants in Vacation Bible School
- 23 — Number of ongoing classes (all ages) for learning in Sunday Church
- 24 — Number of ONGOING small groups, support groups, or classes
- 25 — Number of SHORT-TERM classes, support groups, or small groups offered
- 26 — Membership in United Methodist Men (UMM)
- 27 — Amount paid for projects (UMM)
- 28 — Membership in United Methodist Women (UMW)
- 29 — Amount paid for local church and community work (UMW)
- 30a — Number of UMVIM teams sent out from this church
- 30b — Number of persons sent out on UMVIM teams from this church

Align #	Church Name	33 TOTAL Community MINISTRIES for outreach, justice, and mercy	33a MINISTRIES focusing on global/regional health?	33b MINISTRIES focusing on engaging in ministry with the poor/socially	24 PERSONS SERVED BY community ministries for outreach, justice, and mercy	35a PERSONS SERVING (from your congregation) in mission/community ministries	36 Market value of church-owned land, buildings and equipment	36SF Overall square footage of church owned buildings (furnished and unfurnished areas)	37 Market value of financial and other liquid assets	38 Debt secured by church physical assets	39 Other debt	42 General Advance Specials remitted to the Annual Conference Treasurer	43 World Service Specials remitted to the Annual Conference Treasurer	44 Annual Conference Advance Specials remitted to the Annual Conference Treasurer	45 Youth Service Fund remitted to the	46 All other funds sent to AC Treasurer for connectional mission and ministry	47 Local Annual Conference Special Sunday Offerings remitted to the	48a UMC CAUSES: Total amount given DIRECTLY to United Methodist causes (NOT sent to BWC Treasurer)	48b MISSIONS/MINISTRY COSTS: Direct costs incurred by the local church for mission and community ministry activities
3385	Monkton	2	0	2	500	25	875,000	6,637	287,000	0	0	0	0	0	0	0	0	25	75
3425	Mount Carmel	4	2	2	75	25	2,100,122	6,919	300,000	0	0	0	0	207	0	0	0	1,500	990
4425	Mount Gilead	0	0	0	35	20	934,100	4,636	275,955	0	0	0	0	0	0	0	0	184	0
4390	Mount Olive	6	2	4	720	60	4,440,115	201,000	218,272	0	0	308	0	0	0	0	0	144	24,053
2345	Mount Tabor	2	0	2	30	4	698,000	5,160	59,089	0	0	0	0	0	0	0	0	0	1,874
2580	Mount Vernon	0	0	0	0	386	1,017,400	6,104	72,020	0	0	0	0	0	0	0	0	0	0
2350	Mount Zion	16	8	12	903	4	5,851,584	33,205	1,159,616	0	0	0	0	0	0	0	0	1,217	321,240
3325	Mount Zion	1	1	1	25	0	800,000	4,000	167,805	0	0	0	0	0	0	0	0	4,200	418
4525	Mount Zion	0	0	0	60	0	760,000	7,800	3,500	0	0	0	0	0	0	0	0	0	0
4265	Mount Zion-Finksburg	2	0	2	320	12	965,000	8,450	45,000	0	0	880	0	0	0	0	0	0	3,715
3500	New Beginnings Fellowship	0	0	0	0	0	545,000	1,344	0	0	0	0	0	0	0	0	0	284	0
2412	New Hope Christian Fellowship	0	0	0	35	7	0	0	0	0	0	0	0	0	0	0	0	381	0
2625	Norrisville	2	0	2	200	75	1,513,000	7,362	157,683	0	0	1,353	0	0	0	0	0	73	0
3430	Parke Memorial	2	0	2	150	5	1,489,330	8,000	375,108	0	0	0	0	0	0	0	0	252	0
4430	Patapsco	4	0	4	100	20	1,195,600	5,736	60,193	0	0	0	0	94	0	0	0	146	11,620
2535	Perry Hall	4	1	4	7,500	125	3,362,300	273,500	700,000	0	0	0	0	0	0	0	0	0	0
3475	Pine Grove	2	0	3	200	61	3,241,626	9,650	750,384	0	0	0	0	0	0	0	0	0	0
3570	Pine Grove	0	0	0	20	5	90,000	2,471	0	0	0	0	0	0	0	0	0	0	0
4175	Piney Grove	5	3	5	35	5	390,000	2,000	0	0	0	0	0	0	0	0	0	0	1,133
4520	Pleasant Grove	14	3	7	494	29	1,723,402	7,116	1,334,843	0	0	0	0	0	0	0	0	0	2,563
4370	Pleasant Hill	3	0	3	400	56	1,918,521	10,000	426,047	0	0	0	0	0	0	0	0	0	6,800
3465	Poplar Grove	0	0	0	1,500	10	440,800	3,600	218,400	0	0	0	0	0	0	0	0	0	3,386
2415	Presbury	12	3	9	750	25	1,200,000	9,859	22,500	0	0	0	0	0	0	0	0	400	0
3370	Providence	4	3	4	200	2	1,507,818	13,602	237,857	0	0	7,662	0	0	0	0	0	477	42,270
4435	Reisterstown	24	9	11	2,432	192	5,644,000	37,853	1,078,039	0	0	0	0	0	0	0	0	0	0
2378	Rock Run	0	0	0	0	12	500,000	5,762	7,459	0	0	3,010	0	2,013	0	0	0	0	18,000
2550	Salem	8	5	7	300	400	2,700,000	14,456	104,135	0	0	955	0	200	0	0	0	2,500	0
3340	Salem	1	1	1	1,000	6	1,081,000	4,000	50,000	0	0	200	0	0	0	0	0	0	0
4325	Shiloh	5	2	5	120	25	1,827,800	9,890	0	0	0	200	0	0	0	0	0	240	0
2370	Smiths Chapel	1	0	4	4,270	8	1,327,100	9,484	552,790	0	0	0	0	0	0	0	0	0	0
3275	St Johns	3	0	3	260	8	1,364,000	138,540	504,100	0	0	123	0	0	0	0	0	50	0
4320	St Johns	1	0	0	600	1	4,100,000	0	16,135	0	0	0	0	0	0	0	0	458	0
3345	St Luke	2	1	2	30	8	175,000	2,349	0	0	0	0	0	0	0	0	0	100	0
4440	St Luke	4	2	3	8	8	1,391,300	3,080	50,000	0	0	2,906	0	58	0	0	0	0	0
2585	St Paul	4	0	4	100	75	734,805	1,765	77,270	0	0	35	0	50	0	0	0	952	0
3435	Stablers	0	0	0	275	7	388,600	4,450	45,941	0	0	0	0	0	0	0	0	200	0
3310	Texas	1	0	1	3,000	15	830,460	32,988	11,804	0	0	5,545	0	0	0	0	0	847	300
3525	Timonium	6	5	4	175	100	5,629,500	5,000	571,775	0	138,301	461	0	0	0	0	0	0	2,450
2115	Union	0	0	0	367	71	470,000	3,686	121,866	0	0	630	0	0	0	0	0	300	705
3135	Union	3	0	3	0	26	625,179	0	123,937	0	0	0	0	0	0	0	0	260	0
2510	Union Chapel	2	0	2	65	75	850,000	850	0	0	0	0	0	0	0	0	0	2,279	0
3350	Union Chapel	6	3	6	125	50	85,000	2,500	1,442,098	0	0	2,500	0	0	0	0	0	0	400
3555	Vernon	3	0	2	35	4	650,000	17,660	119,564	0	0	40	0	0	0	0	0	640	11,139
4410	Wards Chapel	3	2	2	79	77	3,000,000	3,195	94,899	0	0	1,246	0	205	0	0	0	0	2,469
3335	Waugh	5	0	1	237	25	856,500	21,300	109,109	0	0	125	0	51	0	0	0	300	16,626
4330	Wesley	5	3	2	70	87	4,960,100	2,300	24,543	0	0	0	0	0	0	0	0	0	0
2470	Wesleyan Chapel	5	0	2	255	30	1,187,420	13,334	0	0	0	0	0	0	0	0	0	0	0
3560	West Liberty	10	3	4	350	100	2,550,000	13,334	24,543	0	0	0	0	0	0	0	0	300	20,411

Align #	Church Name	48 Total of UMC Causes & UMC Missions & Outreach	49 NON-UMC CAUSES	50a Human Relations Sunday	50b UMCOR Sunday	50c Peace with Justice Sunday	50d Native American Ministries Sunday	50e World Communion Sunday	50f U.M. Student Day	51 Direct-billed clergy non-health benefits	52 Direct-billed clergy health benefits	53a Base compensation — lead pastoral role	53b Base compensation — Associate Pastor(s) & other pastoral staff	53c Base compensation — Deacons	55a Housing benefits — Lead Pastor	55b Housing benefits — Associate Pastor(s) & staff	55c Housing benefits — Deacons	56 Accountable reimbursements	57 Other cash allowances (non-accountable)
3385	Morkton	100	300	0	0	0	0	0	0	0	0	23,091	0	0	0	0	0	3,000	0
3425	Mount Carmel	2,490	900	0	0	0	0	0	0	11,443	11,400	37,000	0	0	0	0	0	4,000	0
4425	Mount Gilead		1,200	0	0	0	0	0	0			4,000	0	0	0	0	0	4,000	0
4390	Mount Olive	24,237	0	0	0	0	10	0	0	11,518	12,474	50,000	0	0	19,866	0	0	2,132	0
2345	Mount Tabor	2,018	0	0	0	0	25	35	0			12,500	0	0	0	0	0		0
2580	Mount Vernon	321,240	313,496	0	0	0	0	0	0	14,803	80,428	16,000	0	0	0	0	0	1,804	0
2350	Mount Zion	418	418	0	0	0	0	0	0			98,468	0	0	0	0	0	0	0
3325	Mount Zion	1,217	581	0	0	0	0	0	0			10,540	0	0	0	0	0	1,400	0
4525	Mount Zion	4,200	2,250	0	0	0	0	0	0			20,750	0	0	0	0	0	4,250	0
4265	Mount Zion-Finksburg	3,715		0	0	0	0	0	0			14,600	0	0	0	0	0	0	0
3500	New Beginnings Fellowship	0	12,239	0	0	0	0	0	0			15,650	0	0	0	0	0	0	0
2412	New Hope Christian Fellowship	284	710	0	0	0	0	0	0	12,421	10,498	0	0	2,650	11,920	0	0	3,418	0
2525	Norrisville	381	1,943	0	151	0	0	0	0			29,489	0	0	0	0	0	1,325	0
3430	Parke Memorial	73	1,037	0	0	0	153	119	0	13,002	18,814	6,879	0	0	25,000	0	0	974	0
4430	Patapsco	11,872	201	0	0	0	0	0	0	11,566	14,533	12,904	0	0	0	0	0	5,600	0
2535	Perry Hall	146		0	0	0	0	0	0			51,291	0	0	0	0	0	3,054	0
3475	Pine Grove	0	1,500	0	0	0	0	0	0			51,406	0	0	0	0	0	0	0
3570	Pine Grove	1,133	734	0	0	0	0	0	0			5,000	0	0	0	0	0	550	0
4175	Piney Grove	2,563	3,000	0	0	0	0	0	0	13,222	15,129	4,000	0	0	24,000	0	0	1,664	0
4520	Pleasant Grove	6,800	900	0	0	0	0	0	0			12,000	0	0	25,000	0	0	7,000	0
4370	Pleasant Hill	3,386	200	0	0	0	0	0	0	10,350	12,560	75,000	0	0	0	0	0	1,000	0
3465	Poplar Grove	400	100	0	0	0	0	0	0			13,000	0	0	3,196	0	0	1,952	0
2415	Presbury	42,770	1,358	0	0	0	0	0	0	13,884	17,339	27,600	0	0	19,000	0	0	2,443	0
3370	Providence	477	1,225	0	0	0	0	0	0			3,780	0	0	0	0	0	0	0
4435	Reisterstown	18,000		0	0	0	0	0	0	13,448	17,720	48,713	0	0	0	0	0	0	0
2276	Rock Run	0	5,148	0	134	0	0	0	0			9,600	0	0	25,000	0	0	3,000	0
2560	Salem	2,600	3,720	91	965	595	91	91	91			58,724	0	0	0	0	0	7,474	0
3340	Salem	0	7,162	0	0	200	0	510	0			27,000	0	0	0	0	0	981	0
4325	Shiloh	240	1,819	200	0	200	200	200	200			12,688	0	0	4,637	0	0	237	0
2370	Smiths Chapel	0	900	0	0	75	20	45	40	24,328	32,502	15,000	0	0	3,500	0	0	1,500	0
3375	St Johns	50	60	0	0	0	0	0	0			26,545	0	0	7,800	0	0	3,900	0
4320	St Johns	458	3,304	0	0	0	0	0	0			22,615	19,456	0	0	0	0	64	0
3345	St Luke	100		0	600	0	0	0	0			5,000	0	0	0	0	0	0	0
4440	St Luke	300	2,500	0	0	0	0	0	0			12,000	0	0	7,946	0	0	2,279	0
2585	St Paul	3,402	30,931	15	0	25	0	30	25			19,866	0	0	0	0	0	526	0
3435	Stablers	905	2,592	0	0	0	0	0	0			6,120	0	0	0	0	0	1,000	0
3310	Texas	847	2,008	0	0	0	0	0	0	4,153	4,724	16,000	0	0	19,700	0	0	4,185	0
3525	Timonium	0	2,780	0	0	0	0	0	0	13,538	21,196	63,550	0	0	0	0	0	379	0
2115	Union	700	300	0	0	0	0	5	0	480	11,875	13,750	0	0	12,000	0	0	582	0
3135	Union	260		0	0	0	0	0	0	12,075		5,000	0	0	6,095	0	0	3,425	0
2510	Union Chapel	13,418	1,246	0	0	0	0	0	0			53,655	0	0	0	0	0	0	0
3350	Union Chapel	2,469	1,432	0	150	0	0	0	0			5,040	0	0	0	0	0	0	0
3555	Vernon	17,266	4,939	0	0	25	34	30	0			3,740	0	0	0	0	0	3,811	0
4410	Wards Chapel	0		0	81	0	71	25	0	13,320	14,050	42,704	0	0	38,961	0	0	1,500	0
3335	Waugh	20,711	100	21	0	25	25	89	25			20,300	0	0	1,310	0	0	4,100	0
4330	Wesley			10	0	75	0	0	0	12,600	14,460	56,000	0	0	12,000	0	0	2,520	0
2470	Wesleyan Chapel			0	0	45	10	0	11			20,840	0	0	3,000	0	0	130	0
3560	West Liberty		100	0	0	0	0	0	0			6,660	0	0	7,200	0	0		0

672

Align #	Church Name	60	61	62	63	63a	64	65	66	67a	67b	67c	67d	67e	67f	67g
3385	Munkton	0	598	8,306	0	0	0	41,044	24	0	29,855	1,849	0	0	9,000	4,602
3425	Mount Carmel	11,368	250	13,307	0	0	0	98,721	35	78,850	7,400	8,500	0	0	0	0
3425	Mount Gilead	0	1,250	8,215	0	0	7,171	24,202	32	0	14,656	3,694	1,489	0	63,861	818
4390	Mount Olive	61,023	11,196	87,040	0	0	20,800	334,219	124	95,524	33,700	9,250	83,299	0	0	3,660
2345	Mount Tabor	1,500	340	4,001	0	0	5,819	30,926	19	0	20,672	6,951	0	0	5,000	0
2580	Mount Vernon	0	0	8,000	0	0	250	26,165	20	0	25,000	1,800	0	0	500	0
2350	Mount Zion	559,059	70,056	136,712	0	0	0	1,754,545	20	0	1,393,998	18,196	53	0	0	0
3325	Mount Zion	0	0	4,990	0	0	15,550	32,819	28	0	14,648	0	0	0	3,500	1,423
4525	Mount Zion	5,200	1,662	3,434	0	0	0	37,227	68	0	3,000	0	0	0	4,500	0
4265	Mount Zion-Finksburg	7,020	5,225	12,050	0	0	0	60,026	0	0	88,500	10,025	3,800	0	0	14,750
3500	New Beginnings Fellowship	6,775	3,715	5,953	0	0	0	40,603	0	0	20,079	1,336	0	0	0	22,651
2412	New Hope Christian Fellowship				0	0	0	1	0	0	0	0	0	0	0	0
2525	Norrisville	12,347	3,496	19,853	0	0	12,676	142,715	70	0	81,237	15,784	112	0	1,150	42,076
3430	Parke Memorial	0	457	15,951	0	0	18,110	54,204	26	0	41,761	569	0	0	25,418	0
4430	Patapsco	0	2,776	8,699	0	0	0	31,713	42	0	28,536	4,042	206	0	0	1,974
2535	Perry Hall	59,970	5,532	24,432	0	1,952	63,639	316,946	180	212,336	16,835	5,190	426	0	40,739	5,647
3475	Pine Grove	8,713	3,429	24,770	0	0	39,240	173,992	0	7,247	81,754	9,116	0	0	0	189
3570	Pine Grove	0	800	4,370	0	0	0	10,770	24	0	3,400	420	0	0	0	6,600
4175	Piney Grove	0	2,000	4,000	0	0	0	13,428	11	8,100	3,000	0	0	0	0	5,880
4520	Pleasant Grove	14,817	2,413	32,729	0	0	5,458	107,043	53	0	56,936	2,215	24,375	0	630	0
4370	Pleasant Hill	26,378	4,915	53,569	0	0	0	255,179	100	81,593	5,080	4,241	105,000	0	14,000	1,423
3465	Poplar Grove	0	0	6,200	0	0	1,200	33,361	28	0	18,500	0	10	0	0	14,750
2415	Presbury	6,495	1,009	11,100	0	7,697	2,450	90,950	43	0	79,889	2,241	15	0	3,090	22,651
3370	Providence	16,980	1,658	18,081	0	0	9,613	79,386	211	356,329	44,816	1,409	132	0	17,050	3,434
4435	Reisterstown	178,715	24,822	134,230	0	0	0	595,494	23	0	185,521	21,233	0	0	25,063	4,702
2378	Rock Run	1,590	1,613	11,665	59,400	0	10,304	44,665	150	0	40,605	5,413	1,900	0	0	27,700
2560	Salem	56,000	9,500	46,500	0	0	56,000	338,663	43	0	214,500	2,600	44	0	2,650	27,200
3340	Salem	10,320	4,072	15,245	0	0	11,563	54,633	30	0	45,166	6,959	46	0	13,830	0
2370	Shiloh	7,100	4,134	10,773	0	0	5,083	103,328	66	0	50,203	10,984	45	0	630	5,880
4325	Smiths Chapel	0	786	27,989	0	0	39,050	133,834	28	0	60,386	5,682	8	0	14,000	49,251
3375	St Johns	24,715	3,798	39,998	0	0	44,002	176,959	36	0	68,310	7,106	310	0	59,329	49,251
4320	St Johns	0	1,570	20,355	0	0	0	11,121	6	0	4,175	805	71	0	2,686	0
3345	St Luke	0	0	4,484	0	0	0	27,442	28	0	44,345	7,106	0	0	752	7,563
2585	St Luke	6,731	933	9,966	0	0	1,619	64,410	36	0	68,310	6,580	310	50,000	0	12,693
3435	St Paul	0	300	5,477	0	0	0	14,458	18	0	7,830	5,140	0	0	12,800	0
3310	Stablers	3,000	175	5,800	0	0	500	43,355	28	0	36,000	7,106	0	0	31,505	11,160
3525	Texas	164,992	13,745	22,953	0	0	10,027	366,374	158	190,895	100,156	8,403	10,931	0	0	0
2115	Timonium	12,490	265	20,382	0	0	37,000	101,623	24	80,613	12,037	2,375	0	0	0	0
3135	Union	0	3,278	22,250	0	0	7,928	55,681	87	0	22,171	998	0	0	920	920
2510	Union	36,850	1,100	3,100	0	0	0	176,472	7	0	165,879	5,908	25	0	0	0
3850	Union Chapel	0		4,730	0	0	0	11,840	9	0	4,000	400	0	0	0	0
3555	Union Chapel	3,375			0	0	0	14,587		0	25,360		0	0	7,200	6,083
4410	Vernon				0	0								0		
3335	Wards Chapel	56,560	13,362	61,933	0	0	50,424	346,164	90	217,973	33,946	3,313	32,995	0	7,200	6,083
4330	Waugh	8,071	390	14,722	0	0	5,725	63,384	26	0	32,716	520	6,800	0	0	5,711
2470	Wesley	57,251	7,718	70,849	0	0	7,661	301,644	120	0	263,824	3,436	25	0	815	24,781
3560	Wesleyan Chapel	4,500	1,184	6,396	0	0	0	49,208	26	54,747	4,451	1,415	343	0	815	24,781
	West Liberty	13,617	512	18,144	0	0	21,556	95,376	25	0	43,212	1,415	0	0	45,597	24,765

Align #	Church Name	67 TOTAL income for annual budget/spending plan. (67a-g)	68a Capital campaigns	68b Memorials, endowments, and bequests	68c Other sources and projects (include UMW, UMM and 'flow-through')	68d Special Sundays, Gen. Adv. Spec, World Srvc Spec., Conf. Adv. Spec. and other directed benevolent giving	68 Total income for designated causes including capital campaign and other special projects	69a Equitable Compensation Funds received by Church or Pastor	69b Advance Special, apportioned, and connectional funds received by church	69c Other grants and financial support from institutional sources	69 Income from connectional / institutional sources outside the local church	70 TOTAL CHURCH INCOME (Sum of Lines 67 + 68 + 69)	40a Amount APPORTIONED to the local church	40b Amount PAID by the local church for all apportioned causes
3335	Monkton	45,306	0	950	0	0	950	0	0	0	0	46,256	5,649	5,649
3425	Mount Carmel	94,550	0	0	1,200	0	1,200	0	0	0	0	94,550	12,732	6,346
4425	Mount Gilead	20,657	0	0	1,200	0	1,200	0	0	0	0	21,857	2,366	2,366
4390	Mount Olive	289,302	0	59,000	0	184	59,184	0	0	1,900	1,900	350,366	33,933	33,933
2345	Mount Tabor	32,623	0	1,950	0	309	2,259	0	0	0	0	34,882	4,720	4,720
2580	Mount Vernon	26,800	0	0	0	0	0	0	0	0	0	26,800	5,464	1,575
2350	Mount Zion	1,394,498	24,724	0	12,000	50,715	137,439	0	0	45,000	45,000	1,576,937	158,469	158,469
3325	Mount Zion	32,897	0	725	0	0	725	0	0	0	0	33,622	1,321	1,321
4525	Mount Zion	3,500	0	0	0	0	0	0	0	0	0	3,500	5,966	2,983
4265	Mount Zion-Finksburg	106,925	0	1,720	0	1,590	3,300	0	0	0	0	110,225	9,551	9,551
3500	New Beginnings Fellowship	21,415	0	0	0	0	0	0	0	0	0	21,415	4,795	4,795
2412	New Hope Christian Fellowship		0	0	0	0	0	0	0	0	0	0	0	0
2525	Norrisville	140,359	0	3,285	0	0	3,285	0	0	0	0	143,644	12,721	12,721
3430	Parke Memorial	67,748	0	25	0	331	356	0	0	0	0	68,104	5,590	5,590
4430	Pascasco	34,758	151	2,786	0	1,534	4,471	0	0	0	0	39,229	4,250	4,250
2535	Perry Hall	280,747	13,473	1,135	0	500	15,108	0	0	0	0	295,855	36,757	36,757
3475	Pine Grove	98,732	0	0	0	0	0	0	0	0	0	98,732	16,652	16,652
3570	Pine Grove	10,420	0	0	0	0	0	0	0	0	0	10,420	1,843	600
4175	Piney Grove	16,900	0	0	0	0	0	0	0	0	0	16,900	1,378	1,378
4520	Pleasant Grove	84,156	0	300	0	0	300	0	0	0	0	84,456	12,095	12,095
4370	Pleasant Hill	211,337	0	11,006	0	0	11,006	30,000	0	0	30,000	252,343	29,403	29,403
3465	Poplar Grove	33,250	5,000	0	0	0	5,000	0	0	0	0	38,250	4,361	4,361
2415	Presbury	107,871	0	0	0	0	0	5,000	0	0	5,000	112,871	8,652	8,652
3370	Providence	63,290	0	2,000	0	1,239	3,239	0	0	0	0	66,529	8,331	8,331
4435	Reisterstown	50,720	0	5,838	0	0	5,838	0	0	0	0	56,558	66,601	66,601
2378	Rock Run	591,712	0	249,274	33,220	0	282,494	0	0	0	0	874,206	8,191	8,191
2560	Salem	249,950	35,000	9,000	0	4,000	48,000	0	0	0	0	297,350	31,172	31,172
3340	Salem	89,380	0	1,550	0	12,058	13,608	0	0	0	0	102,988	12,660	12,660
4325	Shiloh	56,196	0	0	0	0	0	0	0	0	0	56,196	6,154	6,154
2370	Smiths Chapel	55,930	35	23,422	0	0	23,457	0	0	0	0	79,387	8,467	8,467
3375	St. Johns	131,684	0	550	0	952	1,502	0	0	10,000	10,000	143,186	12,412	12,412
4320	St. Johns	178,529	0	1,050	1,000	0	2,050	0	0	0	0	180,579	18,695	18,695
3345	St. Luke	4,980	0	0	0	0	0	0	0	0	0	4,990	1,596	1,463
4440	St. Luke	101,908	0	563	0	0	563	0	0	0	0	101,908	7,480	3,092
2585	St. Paul	14,481	0	0	0	1,287	2,155	0	0	0	0	16,636	7,744	7,744
3435	Stablers	48,600	0	2,155	500	0	300	0	0	0	0	48,900	1,935	1,935
3310	Texas	362,050	4,900	6,604	0	630	12,714	0	0	0	0	364,764	5,093	5,093
3525	Timonium	95,025	0	0	0	0	0	0	0	0	0	95,025	53,903	10,267
2115	Union	23,169	0	0	0	0	0	0	0	0	0	23,169	11,554	11,554
3135	Union	172,732	0	2,735	0	0	2,735	0	0	0	0	176,913	5,723	5,723
2510	Union Chapel	4,400	0	0	25,801	0	0	0	0	0	0	4,400	23,559	23,559
3550	Union Chapel	25,360	0	8,195	0	3,735	49,584	0	0	1,446	1,446	25,360	1,753	1,000
3595	Vernon	301,510	0	0	0	0	0	0	0	0	0	351,094	2,482	2,482
4410	Wards Chapel	45,747	11,853	10,935	0	0	49,584	0	0	0	0	55,947	33,747	33,747
4395	Waugh	292,081	16,642	2,990	999	1,520	29,496	0	0	10,200	10,200	322,377	7,111	7,111
4330	Wesley	59,541	0	0	0	0	2,990	0	0	0	0	62,531	31,229	31,229
2470	Wesleyan Chapel	114,989	0	0	300	0	300	0	0	0	0	115,289	7,563	7,563
3560	West Liberty		0	0	0	0		0	0	0	0		6,746	6,746

Table 1

	Code	William Watters Memorial (2485)	Wiseburg (3565)	BS Total
Male Professing Members	9i	73	32	7,665
Female Professing Members	9h	94	47	11,704
Multi-Racial Professing Members	9g	2	0	74
White Professing Members	9f	163	79	17,747
Pacific Islander Professing Members	9e	0	0	8
Native American Professing Members	9d	0	0	2
Hispanic / Latino Professing Members	9c	2	0	46
African American / Black Professing Members	9b	0	0	1,393
Asian Professing Members	9a	0	0	99
Total professing members at the close of 2018	9	167	79	19,369
Removed by death	8	7	2	261
Transferred out to non-UM churches	7	0	0	1B
Transferred out to other UM churches	6	0	0	36
Withdrawn from Professing Membership	5b	3	0	130
Removed or corrected by ChargeConference action	5a	0	0	163
Transferred in from non-UM churches	4	0	0	23
Transferred in from other UM churches	3	0	0	62
Restored by AFFIRMATION of Faith	2b	0	0	30
Received by PROFESSION of Faith (Other Than Confirmation)	2a2	0	0	147
Received by PROFESSION of Faith	2a1	1	0	138
Total professing members at the close of 2017	1	176	81	19,649
State		MD	MD	
Dist #		8S	8S	
City		Jarrettsville	White Hall	
Church Name		William Watters Memorial	Wiseburg	
Align #		2485	3565	BS Total

Table 2

	Code	William Watters Memorial (2485)	Wiseburg (3565)	BS Total
Number of persons sent out on UMVIM teams from this church	30b	2	0	158
Number of UMVIM teams sent out from this church	30a	0	0	16
Amount paid for local church and community work (UMW)	29	4,053	0	84,573
Membership in United Methodist Women (UMW)	28	18	2	885
Amount paid for projects (UMM)	27	0	2,115	11,184
Membership in United Methodist Men (UMM)	26	0	10	198
Number of SHORT-TERM classes, support groups, or small groups offered	25	10	0	246
Number of ONGOING small groups, support groups, or classes	24	0	0	277
Number of ongoing classes (all ages) for learning in Sunday Church	23	0	0	239
Number of participants in Vacation Bible School	22	8	25	2,925
Average weekly attendance: Education classes/groups that meet in Sunday Church School groups	20	11	0	1,597
TOTAL number of persons participating in Christian formation groups (Total lines 15 - 18)	19	18	8	5,305
OTHER ADULTS (31+ yrs) in all Christian groups, small groups and Sunday School	18	11	8	2,492
YOUNG ADULTS (19-30 yrs) in all Christian groups, small groups and Sunday School	17	3	0	236
YOUTH (12-18 yrs) in all Christian groups, small groups and Sunday School	16	1	0	768
CHILDREN (0-11yrs) in all Christian groups, small groups and Sunday School	15	3	0	1,809
Total enrolled in confirmation preparation classes that	14	1	0	144
Number of other constituents of the church	13	0	37	3,823
Number of baptized members who have not become Professing	12	1	0	1,666
TOTAL Number of persons baptized (all ages)	11T	2	0	204
Number of Teens and Adults baptized (Age 13+)	11b	0	0	55
Number of Infants and Children baptized (Age 0-12)	11a	2	0	149
Persons who Worship Online	10a	0	0	440
Average attendance at all weekly worship service(s)	10	49	16	6,375
Align #		2485 William Watters Memorial	3565 Wiseburg	BS Total

Table 3

	Code	William Watters Memorial (2485)	Wiseburg (3565)	BS Total
MISSIONS/MINISTRY COSTS: Direct costs incurred by the local church for mission and community ministry activities	48b	0	0	1,070,709
UMC CAUSES: Total amount given DIRECTLY to United Methodist causes (NOT sent to BWC Treasurer)	48a	0	243	135,028
Total Annual Conference Special Sunday Offerings remitted to the	47	0	0	0
All other funds sent to AC Treasurer for connectional mission and ministry	46	0	0	0
Youth Service Fund remitted to the	45	0	0	0
Annual Conference Advance Specials remitted to the Annual Conference Treasurer	44	0	207	4,148
World Service Specials remitted to the Annual Conference Treasurer	43	0	0	23
General Advance Specials remitted to the Annual Conference Treasurer	42	0	81	57,567
Other debt	39	0	0	148,644
Debt secured by church physical assets	38	0	0	3,381,305
Market value of financial and other liquid assets	37	266,337	154,882	28,402,654
Overall square footage of church owned buildings (furnished and unfurnished areas)	36SF	20,000	3,350	1,600,616
Market value of church-owned land, buildings and equipment	36	1,041,300	1,500,000	181,562,830
PERSONS SERVING (from your congregation) in mission/community ministries	35a	38	12	5,509
PERSONS SERVED BY community ministries for outreach, justice, and mercy	34	165	600	67,730
MINISTRIES focusing on engaging in ministry with the poor/socially	33b	0	0	304
MINISTRIES focusing on global/regional health?	33a	0	0	115
TOTAL Community MINISTRIES for outreach, justice, and mercy	33	1	0	463
Align #		2485 William Watters Memorial	3565 Wiseburg	BS Total

Table 1 (Lines 49–57, ABTOTAL)

Line description	Code	William Watters Memorial (2485)	Wiseburg (3565)	BS Total
Paid to/for all persons included in Lines 53a-53c for any other cash allowances (non-	57	0	0	800
Paid to/for all persons included in Lines 53a-53c for accountable reimbursements	56	2,414		183,402
Housing benefits paid to/for any Deacons not included in 53a or 53b	55c	0	0	0
Housing benefits paid to/for ALL Associate Pastor(s) & other pastoral staff assigned or appointed to the	55b	0	0	46,366
Housing benefits paid to/for Lead Pastor or person in lead pastoral role as described in 53a	55a	10,600	0	676,416
Base compensation paid to/for any Deacons NOT included in 53a or 53b	53c	0	0	2,650
Base compensation paid/for to all Associate Pastor(s) & other pastoral staff assigned or appointed to the church.	53b	0	0	114,303
Base compensation paid to/for the Senior Pastor or other person assigned or appointed in the lead pastoral role to the church	53a	23,500	11,180	2,577,000
Direct-billed clergy health benefits	52	0	0	743,634
Direct-billed clergy non-health benefits	51	0	0	491,475
U.M. Student Day	50f	130		767
World Communion Sunday	50e	37		2,341
Native American Ministries Sunday	50d	0		4,550
Peace with Justice Sunday	50c	125		2,066
UMCOR Sunday (formerly One Great Hour of Sharing)	50b	0		2,109
Human Relations Sunday	50a	60		1,321
NON-UMC CAUSES: Total amount given DIRECTLY to non-United Methodist benevolent and charitable causes (NOT sent to BWC Treasurer)	49	11,562		853,853
Total of UMC Causes & UMC Missions & Outreach	ABTOTAL	243		1,205,737

Table 2 (Lines 60–67g)

Line description	Code	William Watters Memorial (2485)	Wiseburg (3565)	BS Total
Amount received through fundraisers and other sources	67g	0	6,135	535,672
Amount received through building use fees, contributions, and rentals	67f	1,425	450	693,084
Amount received from Sale of Church Assets	67e	0	0	50,000
Amount received from interest and dividends and/or transferred from liquid assets	67d	0	212	352,102
Received from unidentified givers	67c	2,306	6,120	498,236
Received from non-pledging, but identified givers	67b	97,371	46,322	8,200,384
Received through pledges	67a	0		3,753,748
Number of giving units	66	40		5,886
Amount PAID by/for the local church on all expenditures	65	104,705	44,605	16,712,434
Amount paid on capital expenditures for building, improvements, and major equipment purchases	64	0	13,107	1,455,410
Amount paid for capital campaign or fundraising costs	63a	0		22,054
Amount paid for principal and interest on indebtedness, loans, mortgages, etc.	63	0		533,703
Amount spent for local church operating expenses	62	28,934	14,361	2,773,559
Amount spent for local church program expenses	61	13,600	926	467,305
Paid in salary and benefits for all other church staff and diaconal ministers	60	1,707	0	2,911,511

Table 3 (Lines 40a–70)

Line description	Code	William Watters Memorial (2485)	Wiseburg (3565)	BS Total
Amount PAID by the local church for all apportioned causes	40b	11,505	5,031	1,600,398
Amount APPORTIONED to the local church	40a	11,505	5,031	1,666,845
TOTAL CHURCH INCOME (Sum of Lines 67 + 68 + 69)	70	115,658	71,687	15,977,677
Income from connectional/institutional sources outside the local church	69	0	0	123,656
Other grants and financial support from institutional sources	69c	0	0	83,546
Advance Special, apportioned, and connectional funds received by church	69b	0	0	110
Equitable Compensation Funds received by Church or Pastor	69a	0		40,000
Total income for designated causes including capital campaign and other special projects	68	14,556	12,448	1,770,795
Special Sundays, Gen. Adv. Spec, World Srvc Spec., Conf. Adv. Spec. and other directed benevolent giving	66d	12,265		285,115
Other sources and projects (include UMW, UMM and 'flow-through')	68c	0		116,430
Memorials, endowments, and bequests	68b	2,291	3,260	607,274
Capital campaigns	66a	0	9,188	759,976
TOTAL income for annual budget/spending plan. (67a-g)	67	101,102	59,239	14,083,226

Align. #	Church Name	Dist. #	City	State	Total professing members at the close of 2017 (1)	Received by PROFESSION of Faith (2a1)	Received by PROFESSION of Faith (Other Than Confirmation) (2a2)	Restored by AFFIRMATION of Faith (2b)	Transferred in from other UM churches (3)	Transferred in from non-UM churches (4)	Removed or corrected by Charge Conference action (5a)	Withdrawn from Professing Membership (5b)	Transferred out to other UM churches (6)	Transferred out to non-UM churches (7)	Removed by death (8)	Total professing members at the close of 2018 (9)	Asian (9a)	African American / Black (9b)	Hispanic / Latino (9c)	Native American (9d)	Pacific Islander (9e)	White (9f)	Multi-Racial (9g)	Female (9h)	Male (9i)
5290	Allegany	CH	Frostburg	MD	81	0	0	0	0	0	0	0	0	0	0	81	0	0	0	0	0	81	0	52	29
5510	Alpine	CH	Berkeley Springs	WV	39	4	0	0	0	0	0	0	0	0	0	43	0	0	0	0	0	43	0	26	17
5315	Asbury	CH	Hagerstown	MD	68	0	9	0	0	0	1	0	0	0	0	55	0	44	0	0	0	8	3	34	21
5110	Barton	CH	Barton	MD	119	0	0	0	0	0	0	0	0	0	6	115	0	0	0	0	0	114	0	77	38
6115	Benevola	CH	Boonsboro	MD	448	4	0	0	0	0	0	0	0	2	11	479	0	8	0	0	0	470	1	265	214
6135	Bethel	CH	Smithsburg	MD	490	0	1	0	0	0	4	0	1	0	9	521	1	0	0	0	0	517	3	286	235
6345	Bethel	CH	Rohrersville	MD	133	0	0	0	0	0	0	0	0	0	3	148	0	0	0	0	0	148	0	112	36
5580	Calvary	CH	Great Cacapon	WV	173	0	0	0	3	0	0	0	1	0	3	117	0	0	0	0	0	117	0	60	57
5620	Calvary	CH	Ridgeley	WV	49	0	1	0	0	0	0	0	0	0	0	173	1	0	0	0	0	169	0	99	74
5130	Carlos	CH	Frostburg	MD	56	0	0	0	0	0	0	0	0	0	2	48	0	0	0	0	0	47	0	27	21
5380	Catalpa	CH	Hancock	MD	9	0	0	0	0	0	0	0	0	0	0	56	0	1	0	0	0	56	0	31	25
5185	Centenary	CH	Cumberland	MD	83	0	0	0	0	0	0	0	0	0	1	9	0	0	0	0	0	9	0	5	4
5150	Central	CH	Cumberland	MD	64	0	0	0	0	0	0	0	0	0	0	82	2	0	0	0	0	81	0	38	44
5155	Centre Street	CH	Cumberland	MD	287	0	0	0	0	0	0	0	287	0	0	64	0	0	0	0	0	62	0	40	24
5630	Cherry Run	CH	Hedgesville	WV	58	0	0	0	0	0	0	0	0	0	0	58	0	0	0	0	0	58	0	29	29
5160	Christ	CH	Cumberland	MD	507	0	0	0	0	0	0	0	0	0	9	503	0	0	0	0	0	503	0	312	191
5140	Crescaptown	CH	Crescaptown	MD	532	4	0	0	0	0	0	0	0	0	3	521	1	3	0	0	0	517	0	286	235
5165	Davis Memorial	CH	Cumberland	MD	144	5	0	0	0	0	0	0	1	0	0	148	0	0	0	0	0	148	0	112	36
5440	Dawson	CH	Rawlings	MD	125	0	0	0	0	0	0	0	0	0	3	117	0	0	0	0	0	117	0	68	49
5295	Eckhart	CH	Frostburg	MD	171	0	0	0	3	0	4	0	3	1	2	169	0	0	0	0	0	169	0	88	81
5265	Ellerslie	CH	Ellerslie	MD	183	1	0	0	0	0	0	0	0	0	2	178	0	0	0	0	0	178	0	108	70
5177	Emmanuel	CH	Cumberland	MD	144	0	0	0	3	0	0	0	4	0	2	141	0	0	0	0	0	141	0	83	58
5320	Emmanuel	CH	Hagerstown	MD	454	0	3	0	2	0	0	0	0	0	4	455	0	1	1	0	0	454	0	278	127
5180	Fairview Avenue	CH	Cumberland	MD	47	0	0	0	0	0	0	0	0	0	0	47	0	0	0	0	0	47	0	30	17
5390	First	CH	Lonaconing	MD	302	2	0	0	1	0	0	0	2	1	3	299	0	0	0	0	0	299	0	151	148
5515	First	CH	Berkeley Springs	WV	490	1	3	0	0	0	0	0	0	1	4	497	0	0	0	0	0	497	0	293	194
5270	Flintstone	CH	Flintstone	MD	14	0	2	0	0	0	0	0	0	0	0	17	0	0	0	0	0	17	0	14	3
5310	Frostburg	CH	Frostburg	MD	583	7	11	0	2	2	0	0	0	0	4	584	0	1	1	1	0	559	1	349	235
6425	Garfield	CH	Smithsburg	MD	264	3	0	0	3	0	0	0	0	0	2	284	2	20	0	0	0	280	2	160	124
5325	Grace	CH	Hagerstown	MD	742	0	4	0	2	11	0	0	0	0	22	720	1	0	5	0	0	713	0	466	254
5410	Grace	CH	Midland	MD	226	0	10	0	0	0	0	0	0	1	1	225	1	0	0	0	0	224	0	115	110
5635	Grace	CH	Berkeley Springs	WV	80	0	0	0	0	0	0	0	80	0	0	0	0	0	0	0	0	0	0	0	0
5525	Greenwood	CH	Berkeley Springs	WV	126	0	2	0	2	0	0	0	0	0	2	131	0	1	0	1	0	128	1	78	53
5365	Hancock	CH	Hancock	MD	265	7	11	4	3	0	0	0	0	0	5	286	0	0	0	0	0	286	0	157	129
5530	Highland	CH	Berkeley Springs	WV	105	3	4	2	2	0	0	0	0	2	3	108	0	0	0	0	0	108	0	58	50
5625	Holy Cross	CH	Ridgeley	WV	143	0	0	0	6	0	0	0	1	0	0	149	0	0	0	0	0	149	0	87	62
5330	John Wesley	CH	Hagerstown	MD	580	0	2	0	2	0	0	0	0	0	6	575	1	0	0	0	0	573	1	360	215
5370	Lavale	CH	Lavale	MD	518	0	0	0	7	11	0	0	0	1	11	534	0	0	0	0	0	534	0	340	194
5242	McKendree of Potomac Park	CH	Cumberland	MD	86	0	0	0	0	0	0	0	0	0	0	67	0	34	0	0	0	33	0	42	25
5295	Melvin	CH	Cumberland	MD	277	0	0	0	0	0	0	0	0	2	3	275	2	0	0	0	0	273	2	171	104
5540	Michaels	CH	Hedgesville	WV	8	1	0	0	0	0	0	0	0	0	2	13	0	0	0	0	0	13	0	7	6
5450	Mount Bethel	CH	Smithsburg	MD	249	0	0	0	0	0	15	0	0	0	0	249	0	0	0	0	0	249	0	147	102
5115	Mount Carmel	CH	Big Pool	MD	38	1	4	0	2	0	0	1	0	0	4	24	0	0	0	0	0	24	0	18	6
6120	Mount Carmel	CH	Rohrersville	MD	21	0	0	0	0	0	0	0	0	0	6	21	0	0	0	0	0	21	0	13	8
5275	Mount Hermon	CH	Cumberland	MD	69	0	0	0	3	0	0	0	0	0	0	75	0	0	0	0	0	75	0	47	28
6130	Mount Lena	CH	Boonsboro	MD	154	0	4	0	4	2	0	0	4	2	6	161	2	1	0	0	0	158	0	94	67
6125	Mount Nebo	CH	Boonsboro	MD	385	1	0	0	0	0	0	0	1	0	6	314	1	0	0	0	0	313	0	184	130
5545	Mount Olivet	CH	Berkeley Springs	WV	92	2	2	0	0	0	0	0	0	0	4	89	0	0	0	0	0	89	0	47	42

Align #	Church Name	10	10a	11a	11b	11T	12	13	14	15	16	17	18	19	20	22	23	24	25	26	27	28	29	30a	30b
5290	Allegany	22	0	0	1	1	5	0	0	0	0	0	10	10	0	0	0	0	0	0	0	0	0	0	0
5510	Alpine	32	0	0	0	0	5	15	0	4	0	0	14	19	15	0	2	0	1	0	0	0	0	0	0
5315	Asbury	26	0	1	7	8	0	4	0	2	3	0	30	35	8	0	1	2	1	9	638	9	1,000	0	0
5110	Barton	26	0	4	0	4	50	8	0	25	22	0	55	102	3	35	8	12	2	0	0	0	0	0	2
6115	Benevola	94	0	4	5	9	20	0	0	100	25	10	98	233	37	42	11	8	5	0	0	0	0	0	0
5135	Bethel	157	0	0	5	5	0	0	0	0	0	0	4	4	67	0	3	3	0	0	0	0	0	0	0
6345	Bethel	32	0	1	0	1	2	0	0	3	8	0	15	28	3	0	1	3	0	0	0	6	1,150	0	0
5580	Calvary	35	0	3	2	5	3	10	0	5	2	2	25	32	15	0	3	3	3	0	0	0	0	0	0
5620	Calvary	36	0	0	0	0	0	0	0	0	2	0	0	0	18	0	0	0	0	0	0	0	0	0	0
5130	Carlos	7	0	0	0	0	0	10	0	0	0	0	0	0	0	0	0	0	0	0	0	0	0	0	0
5380	Catalpa	12	0	1	1	2	0	15	0	0	0	3	12	12	11	0	2	1	0	0	0	0	0	0	0
5185	Centenary	25	0	3	0	3	0	0	0	0	5	0	5	10	8	10	5	1	0	0	0	6	0	0	0
5150	Centre	20	0	0	0	0	2	12	0	0	0	0	3	6	6	16	1	2	2	0	0	0	0	0	0
5155	Centre Street	18	0	0	0	0	40	55	0	0	0	0	31	42	17	20	0	0	1	0	0	0	0	0	0
5630	Cherry Run	50	15	2	0	2	0	0	0	6	2	4	50	62	35	32	5	3	2	14	0	14	1,006	0	0
5160	Christ	91	0	1	3	4	6	0	0	10	2	0	3	18	18	70	1	0	0	0	7,607	0	3,490	0	0
5140	Cresaptown	65	0	0	1	1	13	0	0	19	5	1	16	27	10	0	3	5	2	0	1,200	0	9,000	0	0
5105	Davis Memorial	26	0	1	0	1	0	0	0	8	0	17	19	34	23	32	3	1	1	0	0	16	719	0	0
5440	Dawson	70	0	0	0	0	29	13	0	12	0	0	22	52	30	70	7	2	0	0	0	16	956	0	0
5255	Eckhart	42	0	0	0	0	0	25	0	60	4	16	51	74	0	0	4	0	1	0	0	0	0	0	0
5265	Ellerslie	71	0	4	0	4	1	0	0	0	9	0	110	198	66	0	6	16	0	0	0	6	100	0	0
5177	Emmanuel	165	35	1	1	2	0	13	5	0	12	0	30	35	20	0	3	6	3	14	0	17	1,802	0	1
5320	Emmanuel	13	0	1	0	1	0	25	0	0	0	0	80	170	46	99	0	4	2	25	0	0	0	0	0
5180	Fairview Avenue	46	0	1	3	4	0	58	0	0	1	7	0	0	20	17	4	6	11	0	0	0	0	0	0
5390	First	109	0	3	0	3	2	26	2	5	3	0	40	248	15	25	6	1	0	0	0	0	900	0	0
5515	First	12	35	3	0	3	1	0	0	2	0	0	19	22	18	30	3	2	0	0	0	8	0	0	0
5270	Flintstone	149	0	1	0	1	0	8	0	7	0	2	75	87	66	35	2	5	1	0	0	13	860	0	0
5310	Frostburg	47	0	14	14	14	12	9	0	8	10	0	16	29	10	43	10	16	0	0	0	0	0	0	0
6425	Garfield	88	0	0	0	0	5	0	0	12	0	0	0	0	0	0	2	6	1	0	0	8	0	0	0
5325	Grace	50	0	1	0	1	15	0	0	7	0	4	33	70	24	17	4	2	0	0	0	13	6,763	0	0
5410	Grace	0	0	0	0	0	1	20	0	8	0	0	57	86	40	25	6	1	1	0	0	0	0	0	0
5635	Grace	50	0	1	0	1	0	0	0	12	0	0	40	48	24	30	2	5	0	0	0	32	0	0	0
5525	Greenwood	108	0	2	2	2	0	50	0	7	15	10	33	70	112	35	7	2	1	25	0	0	0	0	0
5365	Hancock	24	0	7	7	14	151	167	7	71	20	2	57	86	40	43	4	1	1	10	0	0	0	0	0
5530	Highland	80	0	1	1	3	3	20	0	8	6	0	40	48	33	0	2	5	0	0	0	0	0	0	0
5625	Holy Cross	79	0	3	0	3	16	28	0	71	6	0	61	138	47	0	7	2	0	0	0	0	3,500	0	0
5930	John Wesley	208	0	14	0	14	14	40	0	8	11	0	28	42	5	0	4	1	1	0	0	30	500	0	0
5370	Lavale	29	1,700	0	0	0	5	10	0	10	0	0	32	55	12	0	1	0	0	0	0	38	2,217	0	0
5242	Mckendree of Potomac-Park	69	0	1	0	1	0	0	0	5	0	0	12	14	6	43	0	0	0	0	0	13	0	0	0
5595	Melvin	11	0	0	0	0	0	2	0	4	0	0	6	6	30	0	1	1	0	0	0	0	0	0	0
5540	Michaels	56	0	1	2	3	15	20	0	10	5	4	55	55	7	0	1	0	1	0	0	9	0	0	0
5450	Mount Bethel	19	0	0	1	1	1	0	0	5	0	0	9	9	9	0	4	0	0	0	0	0	0	0	0
5115	Mount Carmel	10	0	1	0	1	0	0	0	4	0	0	9	9	0	0	1	2	1	0	0	8	0	0	0
6120	Mount Carmel	30	0	1	2	2	12	0	0	0	12	0	12	20	7	18	1	1	0	0	0	12	0	0	0
5275	Mount Hermon	95	0	0	0	0	14	0	1	5	3	0	11	20	16	9	1	5	0	0	0	13	618	0	2
6125	Mount Lena	57	0	1	2	3	0	0	1	4	4	1	21	19	13	85	4	2	2	15	4,252	7	2,190	1	7
6130	Mount Nebo	27	0	0	2	2	0	20	1	0	6	0	30	30	20	0	2	0	0	0	0	25	0	2	0

Column legend:

- **23** — TOTAL Community MINISTRIES for outreach, justice, and mercy
- **33a** — MINISTRIES focusing on global/regional health?
- **33b** — MINISTRIES focusing on engaging in ministry with the poor/socially
- **34** — PERSONS SERVED BY community ministries for outreach, justice, and mercy
- **35a** — PERSONS SERVING (from your congregation) in mission/community ministries
- **36** — Market value of church-owned land, buildings and equipment
- **36SF** — Overall square footage of church owned buildings (furnished and unfurnished areas)
- **37** — Market value of financial and other liquid assets
- **38** — Debt secured by church physical assets
- **39** — Other debt
- **42** — General Advance Specials remitted to the Annual Conference Treasurer
- **43** — World Service Specials remitted to the Annual Conference Treasurer
- **44** — Annual Conference Advance Specials remitted to the Annual Conference Treasurer
- **45** — Youth Service Fund remitted to the...
- **46** — All other funds sent to AC Treasurer for connectional mission and ministry
- **47** — Total Annual Conference Special Sunday Offerings remitted to the...
- **45a** — UMC CAUSES: Total amount given DIRECTLY to United Methodist causes (NOT sent to BWC Treasurer)
- **48b** — MISSIONS/MINISTRY COSTS: Direct costs incurred by the local church for mission and community ministry activities

Align #	Church Name	23	33a	33b	34	35a	36	36SF	37	38	39	42	43	44	45	46	47	45a	48b
5290	Allegany	2	0	2	18	8	659,000	2,419	25,773	0	0	0	0	0	0	0	0	0	0
5510	Alpine	2	1	2	205	12	279,000	2,600	97,364	0	0	0	0	0	0	0	0	0	0
5315	Asbury	3	1	1	5	2	750,000	1,355	115,000	0	0	0	0	0	0	0	0	0	0
5110	Barton				0	0	1,447,000	11,412	160,857	0	0	0	0	0	0	0	0	0	0
6115	Benevola	10	1	9	800	55	2,100,000	0	266,748	0	0	4,599	0	100	0	0	0	0	9,338
5135	Bethel	15	4	10	800	200	2,500,000	24,034	220,036	0	0	1,827	0	1,201	0	0	0	0	16,570
6345	Bethel	0	0	0	0	0	0	4,558	147,000	0	0	0	0	0	0	0	0	0	5,720
5580	Calvary	0	0	0	0	1	3,000,000	10,360	51,994	0	0	0	0	0	0	0	0	0	4,312
5620	Calvary	6	0	6	60	14	1,475,000	1,890	82,000	0	0	0	0	0	0	0	0	0	3,891
5130	Carlos	3	0	0	105	4	350,000	1,064	23,242	0	0	0	0	0	0	0	0	0	0
5380	Catalpa	0	0	0	0	10	275,000	5,122	0	0	0	0	0	0	0	0	0	200	0
5185	Centenary	3	0	3	0	0	140,000	8,529	137,334	0	0	0	0	0	0	0	0	425	0
5150	Central	0	0	0	0	0	556,000	0	0	0	0	0	0	0	0	0	0	0	0
5155	Centre Street	0	0	0	0	0	1,215,000	5,900	14,520	0	0	0	0	0	0	0	0	0	0
5630	Cherry Run	0	0	0	0	11	0	14,832		0	0	0	0	0	0	0	0	0	0
5160	Christ	25	2	16	1,786	100	365,500	6,901	267,314	0	0	0	0	0	0	0	0	0	0
5140	Cresaptown	0	0	0	0	2	632,000	6,866	87,266	0	0	791	0	0	0	0	0	607	0
5165	Davis Memorial	0	0	0	160	40	2,744,000	14,586	269,000	0	0	273	0	0	0	0	0	0	0
5440	Dawson	0	0	0	250	27	1,074,500	8,799	105,676	0	0	956	0	0	0	0	0	0	161
5265	Eckhart	0	0	0	10	2	316,000	27,195	194,379	0	0	0	600	0	0	0	0	210	0
5285	Ellerslie	6	1	6	800	29	1,106,000	14,870	418,807	0	0	0	0	0	0	0	0	0	0
5177	Emmanuel	0	0	0	10	120	559,000	7,730	11,379	0	0	1,995	0	0	0	0	0	0	1,300
5320	Emmanuel	0	0	1	900	0	1,587,000	13,000	60,000	0	0	222	0	0	0	0	0	0	1,498
5180	Fairview Avenue	10	8	10	431	46	2,300,000	204,000	0	0	0	5,000	0	60	0	0	0	1,200	0
5390	First	0	0	0	100	90	125,000	6,640	161,450	0	0	0	0	0	0	0	0	0	0
5515	First	0	0	0	0	7	1,867,140	21,477	160,697	0	128,197	0	0	175	0	0	0	175	150
5270	Flintstone	10	1	10	1,600	75	2,913,000	3,117	11,060	0	0	0	0	0	0	0	0	0	3,229
5310	Frostburg	3	1	1	775	62	761,000	0	1,500	0	0	0	0	0	0	0	0	0	0
6425	Garfield	1	0	1	1,620	30	3,500,000	16,145	293,018	0	0	0	0	43	0	0	0	43	5,991
5325	Grace	0	0	0	0	0	1,329,000	9,874	22,000	0	0	25	0	0	0	0	0	0	0
6410	Grace	0	0	0	0	0	4,675,340	0	900,000	0	0	0	0	0	0	0	0	0	0
5635	Grace	0	3	5	1,685	57	375,000	11,794	150,363	0	0	0	0	0	0	0	0	0	0
5525	Greenwood	9	3	5	2,074	90	0		0	0	0	113	0	0	0	0	0	968	979
5365	Hancock	13	6	6	40	20	1,157,000		1,775,010	0	0	0	0	0	0	0	0	0	856
5530	Highland	6	1	2	600	27	1,780,605		16,949	0	0	0	0	0	0	0	0	0	0
5625	Holy Cross	3	2	2	230	70	255,000		114,770	0	0	0	0	0	0	0	0	0	7,000
5330	John Wesley	8	0	5	2,422	76	10,323,000		0	0	0	7,352	0	340	0	0	0	0	0
5370	LaVale	7	1	5	500	10	4,641,246	48,080	497,494	0	0	1,070	0	0	0	0	0	0	37,647
5242	McKendree of Potomac Park	0	0	0	0	40	622,000	26,426	870,110	0	0	0	0	0	0	0	0	254	0
5095	Melvin	4	0	1	3,500	13	280,000	5,164	185,000	0	0	0	0	0	0	0	0	0	755
5540	Michaels	3	1	2	130	48	194,000	4,000	0	0	0	0	0	0	0	0	0	100	562
5450	Mount Bethel	1	0	0	200	0	796,000	3,326	419,394	0	0	0	0	0	0	0	0	0	0
5115	Mount Carmel	0	0	0	0	5	226,000	3,400	133,000	0	0	0	0	0	0	0	0	0	2,870
6120	Mount Carmel	8	2	6	15	45	370,000	3,500	0	0	0	0	0	0	0	0	0	0	2,964
5275	Mount Hermon	4	1	3	180	30	350,000	2,804	33,385	0	0	0	0	0	0	0	0	350	999
6125	Mount Lena	7	2	5	330	112	644,000	6,272	153,669	0	0	408	0	0	0	0	0	408	3,291
6130	Mount Nebo	6	5	6	501	80	5,156,000	27,501	264,464	1,228,953	0	0	0	0	0	0	0	626	644
5545	Mount Olivet						487,500	1,700	88,453	0	0	113	0	0	0	0	0	0	

Align #	Church Name	48TOTAL Total of UMC Causes & UMC Missions & Outreach	49 NON-UMC CAUSES: Total amount given DIRECTLY to non-United Methodist benevolent and charitable causes (NOT sent to BWC Treasurer)	50a Human Relations Sunday	50b UMCOR Sunday (formerly One Great Hour of Sharing)	50c Peace with Justice Sunday	50d Native American Ministries Sunday	50e World Communion Sunday	50f U.M. Student Day	51 Direct-billed clergy non-health benefits	52 Direct-billed clergy health benefits	53a Base compensation paid to/for the Senior Pastor or other person in lead pastoral role	53b Base compensation paid to/for all Associate Pastor(s) & other pastoral staff	53c Base compensation paid to/for any Deacons NOT included in 53a or 53b	55a Housing benefits paid to/for Lead Pastor or person in lead pastoral role	55b Housing benefits paid to/for ALL Associate Pastor(s) & other pastoral staff	55c Housing benefits paid to/for any Deacons not included in 53a or 53b	56 Paid to/for all persons included in Lines 53a-53c for accountable reimbursements	57 Paid to/for all persons included in Lines 53a-53c for any other cash allowances (non-
5290	Allegany	0	340	0	0	0	0	0	0	0	0	1,382	0	0	2,310	0	0	840	0
5510	Alpine	0	1,329	0	0	0	0	0	0	0	0	7,500	0	0	0	0	0	900	0
5515	Asbury	0	0	0	0	0	0	0	0	0	0	18,500	0	0	10,900	0	0	2,100	0
5110	Barton	0	2,090	0	0	0	0	0	0	0	0	14,300	0	0	0	0	0	14,300	0
6115	Benevola	9,338	9,860	0	0	200	200	100	0	11,616	16,164	44,899	0	0	19,866	0	0	4,740	0
5135	Bethel	16,570	4,115	0	0	0	0	310	63	11,366	16,102	50,514	0	0	5,343	0	0	4,157	0
6345	Bethel	5,720	5,720	0	0	0	0	0	0	0	0	13,200	0	0	0	0	0	804	3,000
5580	Calvary	4,312	100	0	0	0	0	0	0	0	0	6,720	0	0	6,174	0	0	0	0
5620	Calvary	8,891	90	0	0	0	0	0	0	0	0	13,000	0	0	6,000	0	0	1,500	0
5130	Carlos	0	200	0	0	0	0	0	0	0	0	1,382	0	0	2,310	0	0	840	0
5380	Catalpa	200	200	0	0	0	0	0	0	0	0	3,000	0	0	0	0	0	0	0
5185	Centenary	425	10,925	0	0	0	0	0	0	0	0	12,500	0	0	0	0	0	0	0
5150	Central	0	0	0	0	0	0	0	0	0	0	8,000	0	0	7,600	0	0	0	0
5155	Centre Street	607	0	0	0	0	0	0	0	6,389	10,007	8,604	0	0	2,667	0	0	1,260	0
5630	Cherry Run	0	0	0	182	0	0	17	65	5,154	9,621	11,330	0	0	4,319	0	0	0	0
5160	Christ	0	1,706	0	0	167	167	0	0	10,267	13,800	45,431	0	0	10,300	0	0	3,124	0
5140	Cresaptown	161	4,038	0	0	0	0	0	0	8,900	10,500	21,575	0	0	4,304	0	0	804	0
5165	Davis Memorial	0	0	0	0	0	0	0	0	0	0	8,902	0	0	2,250	0	0	1,034	0
5440	Dawson	210	635	0	0	0	0	0	0	0	0	3,964	0	0	4,304	0	0	4,460	0
5255	Ekhart	1,300	1,550	0	0	0	0	0	13	0	0	21,500	0	0	9,768	0	0	3,000	0
5265	Ellerslie	1,498	905	95	24	0	0	22	0	0	0	24,575	0	0	9,000	0	0	1,179	0
5177	Emmanuel	1,200	3,708	0	0	0	0	0	0	11,201	13,633	56,829	0	0	3,168	0	0	3,457	0
5320	Emmanuel	150	1	0	0	0	0	0	0	809	15,299	6,484	0	0	6,000	0	0	0	0
5180	Fairview Avenue	8,404	1,350	25	0	0	0	0	0	12,686	20,422	15,134	0	0	2,400	0	0	1,818	0
5890	First	0	175	0	0	0	0	0	0	12,924	47,000	47,000	0	0	28,000	0	0	4,602	0
5515	First	5,991	100	80	98	116	108	71	42	11,531	16,164	7,875	0	0	0	0	0	5,117	0
5270	Flintstone	0	4,243	0	0	0	0	10	0	0	11,132	45,657	0	0	0	0	0	1,915	0
5310	Frostburg	0	0	0	0	0	0	0	0	8,690	15,975	26,063	0	0	22,000	0	0	2,931	0
6425	Garfield	0	3,490	0	0	0	0	0	0	13,122	18,014	48,000	0	0	2,881	0	0	2,187	0
5325	Grace	0	775	0	0	0	0	0	0	8,869	13,594	15,050	0	0	0	0	0	0	0
5410	Grace	979	856	0	0	0	0	0	0	0	0	0	0	0	3,844	0	0	1,810	147
5635	Grace	856	4,790	0	0	0	0	0	0	10,238	11,032	10,987	0	0	6,554	0	0	4,663	0
5525	Greenwood	0	75	0	0	0	0	0	0	0	0	45,250	0	0	0	0	0	1,200	0
5865	Hancock	7,968	1,990	0	0	115	661	97	76	10,908	16,828	10,000	0	0	5,525	0	0	1,500	0
5530	Highland	0	100	0	0	0	0	0	0	0	0	24,744	0	0	5,693	0	0	1,744	293
5625	Holy Cross	37,647	9,550	260	618	0	0	0	0	12,661	11,032	49,480	0	0	11,845	0	0	4,500	3,441
5330	John Wesley	254	655	0	0	0	0	0	0	12,661	16,828	53,045	0	0	0	0	0	3,000	0
5370	LaVale	0	4,390	0	0	0	0	0	0	0	0	7,500	0	0	15,400	0	0	0	500
5242	McKendree of Potomac Park	855	1,345	0	0	0	0	0	0	0	0	10,320	0	0	0	0	0	0	0
5295	Melvin	662	1,124	0	0	0	0	0	0	0	0	4,008	0	0	18,600	0	0	2,400	0
5540	Michaels	7	600	0	0	0	0	0	0	0	0	26,400	0	0	985	0	0	884	0
5450	Mount Bethel	2,870	5,831	0	0	0	0	0	0	0	0	14,821	0	0	0	0	0	403	0
5115	Mount Carmel	3,314	857	0	0	0	0	0	0	0	0	6,600	0	0	1,300	0	0	2,400	0
6120	Mount Carmel	1,407		0	0	0	0	0	0	0	0	10,500	0	0	25,000	0	0	3,333	0
5275	Mount Hermon	3,917		0	0	0	0	0	0	0	0	23,600	0	0	3,844	0	0	1,810	146
6125	Mount Lena			0	0	0	0	0	0	12,424	14,365	46,866	0	0		0	0		
6130	Mount Nebo			0	230	0	30	0	0	12,424	14,365	10,987	0	0		0	0		
5545	Mount Olivet	644		0	0	0	0	0	0	0	0	3,844	0	0		0	0		

Altgn #	Church Name	60	61	62	63	63a	64	65	66	67a	67b	67c	67d	67e	67f	67g
5290	Allegany	0	365	4,467	0	0	900	12,170	11	0	2,700	9,550	1	0	0	0
5510	Alpine	1,510	558	6,602	0	0	1,389	24,012	24	0	22,844	0	349	0	0	0
5315	Asbury	2,400	560	2,855	0	750	2,699	46,601	30	49,216	3,761	1,200	0	0	0	1,318
5110	Barton	9,030	0	10,291	0	0	40,736	97,336	32	0	37,956	1,505	22,557	0	3,300	0
6115	Benevola	26,673	9,835	54,602	0	0	40,023	263,145	79	0	179,066	8,877	513	0	3,625	4,811
5135	Bethel	37,242	12,311	45,834	0	0	1,481	238,860	134	0	197,596	9,233	201	0	2,290	0
6345	Bethel	4,500	0	15,000	0	0	0	54,520	27	0	63,537	550	0	0	100	3,090
5580	Calvary	5,907	415	3,781	0	0	0	31,650	33	0	26,536	5,537	0	0	0	0
5620	Calvary	5,079	10,534	17,441	0	3,500	3,500	73,731	18	61,679	5,686	0	0	0	0	0
5130	Carlos	0	0	2,157	0	0	0	8,502	7	0	0	5,520	100	0	0	0
5380	Catalpa	0	300	1,200	0	0	0	5,558	9	0	6,000	1,000	0	0	0	0
5195	Centenary	5,970	788	10,748	0	0	15,600	62,258	22	0	27,785	0	0	0	0	0
5150	Central	3,100	908	13,659	0	0	0	33,177	5	27,875	2,500	4,234	0	0	0	0
5155	Centre Street	0	0	1	0	0	0	16,397	0	0	0	0	0	0	0	0
5630	Cherry Run	1,200	0	217	0	0	0	31,456	0	0	0	25,582	0	0	6,500	0
5160	Christ	16,382	2,412	13,733	0	0	12,988	78,604	31	52,046	2,700	10,271	0	0	0	5,779
5140	Chesaptown	23,932	4,334	29,948	0	0	0	160,321	68	0	125,536	12,453	7,522	0	1,270	16,500
5165	Davis Memorial	11,800	0	7,152	0	0	0	70,952	2	21,300	42,900	22,700	9,055	0	0	0
5440	Dawson	6,303	876	12,485	0	0	0	39,275	69	0	11,420	350	20	0	303	820
5255	Eckhart	0	2,867	8,029	0	0	6,864	36,072	50	0	34,774	10,218	0	0	0	0
5265	Ellerslie	1,800	3,902	13,989	0	0	30,220	120,475	75	0	71,405	5,324	3,317	0	8,572	0
5177	Emmanuel	10,722	100	17,105	0	0	26,446	99,725	0	87,521	3,349	5,188	0	0	0	100
5320	Emmanuel	58,161	11,041	57,210	0	0	17,048	275,937	7	0	256,159	10,000	0	0	1,715	0
5180	Fairview Avenue	0	0	5,665	0	0	0	22,675	0	0	8,410	1,780	0	0	0	4,514
5390	First	5,712	3,619	23,747	0	0	1,873	66,168	49	0	51,469	2,823	2,017	0	5,026	12,599
5515	First	40,152	10,460	55,791	0	0	25,788	277,261	120	131,163	233,190	12,986	12,606	0	1,565	4,105
5270	Flintstone	0	0	3,398	0	0	0	13,169	0	0	10,118	0	0	0	150	0
5310	Frostburg	57,598	10	58,712	43,000	2,808	19,098	271,247	119	0	56,213	7,457	9	0	40,607	13,150
6425	Garfield	0	0	29,520	0	0	0	109,562	37	0	62,552	7,991	0	0	0	5,000
5325	Grace	42,764	2,767	49,076	0	0	11,272	208,667	98	0	150,157	0	0	0	460	1,179
5410	Grace	3,900	1,227	12,110	0	150	800	75,934	19	0	42,295	27,225	0	0	0	0
5635	Grace	0	0	1	0	0	0	1	0	0	0	0	0	0	0	0
5525	Greenwood	0	1,901	17,542	0	0	0	54,945	42	0	58,505	7,400	58	0	250	2,000
5365	Hancock	19,788	11,003	26,103	0	0	0	160,774	55	0	99,012	34,657	11,094	0	0	0
5530	Highland	3,770	4,557	6,720	0	0	6,800	34,522	0	79,510	25,049	2,137	147	0	795	9,508
5625	Holy Cross	24,096	6,985	19,302	0	0	0	104,527	63	11,484	10,810	4,344	0	0	50	301
5380	John Wesley	56,298	6,985	89,579	0	0	48,999	331,748	123	0	195,595	2,733	0	0	960	80
5370	LaVale	97,862	24,460	45,284	0	0	195,320	546,039	177	0	330,415	15,713	10,468	0	0	2,800
5242	Mckendree of Potomac Park	4,065	0	17,820	0	1,148	1,269	36,379	22	9,721	21,100	0	0	0	0	3,403
5295	Melvin	9,692	6,829	23,026	0	0	0	85,414	50	0	42,716	11,993	134	0	0	0
5540	Michaels	0	142	4,798	0	0	0	12,667	13	0	0	17,588	11	0	0	7,977
5450	Mount Bethel	2,952	1,927	8,240	0	0	0	71,227	37	0	61,462	2,021	2,996	0	0	0
5115	Mount Carmel	0	666	3,589	0	0	0	29,679	18	38,103	2,910	0	0	0	5,100	1,400
6120	Mount Carmel	0	0	8,855	0	0	0	22,405	15	0	10,946	3,107	29	0	0	200
5275	Mount Hermon	0	1,312	2,154	0	0	2,188	19,187	17	0	27,407	9,441	0	0	0	4,646
6125	Mount Lena	6,291	7,602	11,766	0	0	4,166	64,444	44	0	59,650	10,456	338	0	0	0
6130	Mount Nebo	48,905	4,036	25,852	93,600	0	14,279	299,996	118	0	204,120	4,355	0	0	4,365	0
5645	Mount Olivet	4,036	0	7,528	0	0	0	49,252	24	0	0	39,261	326	0	50	13,467

Align #	Church Name	TOTAL income for annual budget/spending plan. (67a-g) 67	Capital campaigns 68a	Memorials, endowments, and bequests 68b	Other sources and projects (include UMW, UMM and 'flow-through') 68c	Special Sundays, Gen. Adv. Spec, World Srvc Spec., Conf. Adv. Spec. and other directed benevolent giving 68d	Total income for designated causes including capital campaign and other special projects 68	Equitable Compensation Funds received by Church or Pastor 69a	Advance Special, apportioned, and connectional funds received by church 69b	Other grants and financial support from institutional sources 69c	Income from connectional / institutional sources outside the local church 69	TOTAL CHURCH INCOME (Sum of Lines 67 + 68 + 69) 70	Amount APPORTIONED to the local church 40a	Amount PAID by the local church for all apportioned causes 40b
5290	Allegany	12,251	0	1,022	0	0	1,022	0	0	0	0	13,273	1,565	1,565
5510	Alpine	23,193	0	1,170	0	0	1,170	0	0	0	0	24,363	4,224	4,224
5315	Asbury	55,495	0	0	0	0	0	0	0	0	0	55,495	6,588	6,588
5110	Barton	65,318	0	5,500	0	0	5,500	0	0	0	0	70,818	6,591	6,591
6115	Benevola	196,892	0	925	0	1,700	2,625	0	0	0	0	199,517	24,313	10,130
5135	Bethel	209,320	0	2,005	11,853	1,542	15,400	0	0	0	0	224,720	30,424	30,424
6345	Bethel	67,277	0	0	0	0	0	0	0	0	0	67,277	6,576	6,576
5580	Calvary	32,073	0	0	0	0	0	0	0	0	0	32,073	4,241	4,241
5620	Calvary	67,365	0	0	0	90	90	0	0	0	0	67,455	7,696	7,696
5130	Carlos	5,620	0	0	0	0	0	0	0	0	0	5,620	1,313	1,313
5380	Catalpa	7,000	0	0	0	0	0	0	0	0	0	7,000	958	958
5185	Centenary	27,785	0	0	0	0	0	0	0	0	0	27,785	5,312	5,312
5150	Central	34,609	0	115	250	0	365	0	0	0	0	34,974	6,076	0
5155	Centre Street	0	0	0	0	0	0	0	0	0	0	0	0	0
5630	Cherry Run	25,582	0	0	0	0	0	0	0	0	0	25,582	2,713	2,713
5160	Christ	71,519	1,700	1,655	0	1,786	5,141	0	0	155	155	76,815	8,173	8,173
5140	Cresaptown	152,560	0	2,935	0	784	3,719	0	0	0	0	156,279	20,144	20,144
5165	Davis Memorial	91,155	0	0	0	0	0	0	0	0	0	91,155	9,265	9,265
5440	Dawson	34,213	0	2,675	0	0	2,675	0	0	0	0	36,888	6,629	6,629
5255	Eckhart	44,992	0	2,474	0	0	2,474	0	0	0	0	47,466	3,515	3,515
5265	Ellerslie	88,619	0	2,730	0	1,000	3,730	0	0	0	0	92,349	8,291	8,291
5177	Emmanuel	96,058	26,446	955	0	322	27,723	0	0	0	0	123,781	11,267	11,267
5320	Emmanuel	267,974	0	1,530	0	0	1,530	0	0	0	0	269,504	30,902	30,902
5180	Fairview Avenue	10,190	0	0	0	100	100	0	0	0	0	10,290	3,240	3,240
5390	First	63,832	517	1,533	767	0	2,817	0	0	0	0	66,649	10,365	10,365
5515	First	262,357	0	0	0	0	0	0	0	0	0	262,357	47,030	23,515
5270	Flintstone	14,483	0	0	0	0	0	0	0	0	0	14,483	3,079	1,796
5310	Frostburg	248,056	46,882	0	0	0	46,882	0	0	0	0	294,938	25,710	25,710
6425	Garfield	83,702	7,900	2,395	0	0	10,295	0	0	0	0	93,997	8,706	8,706
5325	Grace	155,617	0	52,207	0	0	52,207	0	0	0	0	207,824	38,421	12,007
5410	Grace	70,699	0	1,068	0	2,168	3,236	0	0	0	0	73,935	8,163	8,163
5635	Grace	0	0	0	0	0	0	0	0	0	0	0	0	0
5525	Greenwood	65,963	2,552	11,500	7,984	0	22,036	0	0	0	0	87,999	5,575	5,575
5365	Hancock	147,013	2,225	2,200	450	0	4,875	0	0	0	0	151,888	21,069	21,069
5530	Highland	27,332	0	350	0	169	519	0	0	0	0	27,851	3,485	3,485
5625	Holy Cross	104,997	0	3,963	0	1,434	5,397	0	0	0	0	110,394	10,749	10,749
5330	John Wesley	220,631	18,710	56,110	0	3,005	77,825	0	0	0	0	298,456	40,521	40,521
5370	LaVale	347,168	15,346	3,692	68,733	0	87,771	0	0	0	0	434,939	40,056	40,056
5242	McKendree of Potomac Park	33,755	0	1,151	0	55	1,206	0	0	0	0	34,961	5,640	5,640
5295	Melvin	58,112	0	0	0	0	0	0	0	0	0	58,112	8,828	8,828
5540	Michaels	17,599	0	0	0	0	0	0	0	0	0	17,599	2,209	2,209
5450	Mount Bethel	76,624	0	50	0	0	50	0	0	0	0	76,674	8,608	8,608
5115	Mount Carmel	43,034	0	1,125	0	50	1,175	4,580	0	0	4,580	48,789	4,431	4,431
6120	Mount Carmel	20,553	0	0	0	0	0	0	0	0	0	20,553	2,553	2,553
5275	Mount Hermon	37,077	0	0	0	0	0	0	0	0	0	37,077	2,619	2,619
6125	Mount Lena	74,090	0	1,025	0	0	1,025	0	0	0	0	75,115	7,946	7,946
6130	Mount Nebo	212,840	55,731	800	0	386	56,917	0	0	0	0	269,757	27,412	13,706
5545	Mount Olivet	52,104	0	100	1,228	0	1,328	0	0	0	0	53,432	5,008	5,008

Align #	Church Name	Dist #	City	State	Total professing members at the close of 2017 (1)	Received by PROFESSION of Faith (2a1)	Received by PROFESSION of Faith (Other Than Confirmation) (2a2)	Restored by AFFIRMATION of Faith (2b)	Transferred in from other UM churches (3)	Transferred in from non-UM churches (4)	Removed or corrected by ChargeConference action (5a)	Withdrawn from Professing Membership (5b)	Transferred out to other UM churches (6)	Transferred out to non-UM churches (7)	Removed by death (8)	Total professing members at the close of 2018 (9)	Asian (9a)	African American / Black (9b)	Hispanic / Latino (9c)	Native American (9d)	Pacific Islander (9e)	White (9f)	Multi-Racial (9g)	Female (9h)	Male (9i)
5550	Mount Pleasant	CH	Berkeley Springs	WV	44	0	0	1	0	0	0	1	0	0	2	42	0	0	0	0	0	42	0	25	17
5425	Mount Savage	CH	Mount Savage	MD	172	2	15	1	0	0	0	0	1	0	8	180	0	0	0	0	0	178	0	114	66
5460	Mount Tabor	CH	Oldtown	MD	126	2	0	0	0	0	0	0	0	0	5	123	0	0	0	0	0	122	1	64	59
5555	Mount Zion	CH	Berkeley Springs	WV	65	0	2	1	8	0	0	0	0	0	1	75	0	0	0	0	0	75	0	40	35
5585	Mount Zion	CH	Great Cacapon	WV	66	0	0	0	0	0	0	0	0	0	0	67	0	0	0	0	0	67	0	40	27
6325	Mount Zion	CH	Myersville	MD	169	0	0	0	0	0	0	0	0	0	3	165	0	0	0	0	0	165	0	78	87
6350	Mount Zion	CH	Sabillasville	MD	85	0	0	0	0	0	0	0	0	0	0	85	0	0	0	0	0	85	0	57	28
5280	Murleys Branch	CH	Flintstone	MD	18	0	9	0	1	0	0	0	1	0	3	24	0	0	0	0	0	24	0	15	9
5210	New Covenant	CH	Cumberland	MD	647	0	0	0	0	0	0	0	0	0	4	643	0	3	1	1	1	637	0	364	279
5430	Oldtown	CH	Oldtown	MD	108	2	0	0	0	0	0	0	0	0	0	110	0	0	0	0	0	110	0	70	40
5435	Oliver's Grove	CH	Oldtown	MD	52	9	0	0	0	0	0	0	0	0	0	61	0	0	0	0	0	61	0	41	20
5340	Otterbein	CH	Hagerstown	MD	984	0	0	1	3	6	277	0	4	0	16	696	2	15	0	0	1	676	0	399	297
5375	Park Place	CH	Lavale	MD	114	0	0	0	2	2	15	0	0	0	3	116	2	1	0	1	0	115	0	65	51
5120	Parkhead	CH	Big Pool	MD	50	0	0	2	2	2	4	0	0	0	2	37	0	0	0	0	0	37	0	21	16
5610	Paw Paw	CH	Paw Paw	WV	54	0	0	0	0	0	0	0	0	0	2	50	0	0	0	0	0	44	0	33	17
5385	Piney Plains	CH	Little Orleans	MD	129	0	3	4	2	0	0	1	0	0	0	138	0	2	4	0	0	138	0	80	58
6430	Pleasant Walk	CH	Myersville	MD	113	0	0	0	0	0	0	0	0	0	1	112	0	0	0	0	0	111	0	65	47
5285	Prosperity	CH	Flintstone	MD	133	1	1	0	4	0	0	0	0	0	2	137	0	1	0	0	0	137	0	78	59
5445	Rawlings	CH	Rawlings	MD	169	0	11	0	11	2	10	4	2	1	12	77	2	0	0	0	0	75	0	42	35
5470	Rehoboth	CH	Williamsport	MD	593	7	11	1	0	3	0	0	0	0	2	595	2	4	0	0	0	579	10	350	245
6250	Salem	CH	Keedysville	MD	103	5	0	0	0	3	0	2	2	0	2	107	0	1	1	0	0	106	0	60	47
6435	Salem	CH	Myersville	MD	243	1	3	0	2	3	0	2	0	2	6	239	2	0	4	0	0	233	0	131	108
5415	Shaft	CH	Frostburg	MD	71	0	0	0	0	0	0	0	0	0	0	71	0	0	0	0	0	71	0	46	25
5355	Shiloh	CH	Hagerstown	MD	171	0	3	1	1	1	0	0	0	0	6	165	1	1	0	0	0	163	0	95	70
5345	St Andrews	CH	Hagerstown	MD	162	0	0	0	0	0	0	0	0	0	8	159	1	1	0	0	0	157	0	101	58
5125	St Paul	CH	Big Pool	MD	42	0	0	0	1	1	0	0	42	0	2	0	0	0	0	0	0	0	0	0	0
5455	St Paul's	CH	Smithsburg	MD	118	0	0	0	0	0	0	0	1	0	2	115	0	0	0	0	0	115	0	66	49
5615	Sulphur Springs	CH	Oldtown	MD	57	0	0	0	0	0	0	0	0	0	0	57	0	0	0	0	0	57	0	39	18
5245	Trinity	CH	Cumberland	MD	32	0	0	0	0	0	0	0	0	0	0	32	0	0	0	0	0	32	0	24	8
5640	Trinity-Asbury	CH	Berkeley Springs	WV	117	0	0	0	0	0	0	0	0	0	3	121	2	0	0	0	0	119	0	69	52
5570	Union Chapel	CH	Berkeley Springs	WV	296	0	0	0	0	10	0	0	0	0	3	305	0	0	0	0	0	304	0	177	128
5463	Vale Summit	CH	Frostburg	MD	108	0	0	0	0	0	0	0	0	0	3	105	0	0	0	0	0	105	0	61	44
5360	Washington Square	CH	Hagerstown	MD	331	0	0	0	0	0	0	0	0	0	5	326	0	0	0	0	0	325	1	242	84
5575	Wesley Chapel	CH	Berkeley Springs	WV	112	0	0	0	0	0	0	0	0	0	2	110	0	0	0	0	0	110	0	67	43
5465	Westernport	CH	Westernport	MD	88	0	0	0	0	0	0	0	0	0	0	88	0	0	0	0	0	88	0	57	31
5475	Williamsport	CH	Williamsport	MD	295	0	0	0	3	0	0	1	0	0	4	294	0	0	1	0	0	293	0	202	92
5250	Zion	CH	Cumberland	MD	112	0	0	0	0	0	0	0	0	0	0	110	0	0	0	0	0	110	0	59	51
CH Total					16,650	56	112	27	77	52	326	12	437	17	237	15,739	22	144	19	4	2	15,520	28	9,354	6,385

BALTIMORE-WASHINGTON CONFERENCE

		Average attendance at all weekly worship service(s)	Eersons who Worship Online	Number of Infants and Children baptized (Age 0-12)	Number of Tenns and Adults baptized (Age 13+)	TOTAL Number of persons baptized (all ages)	Number of baptized members who have not become Professing	Number of other constituents of the church	Total enrolled in confirmation preparation classes that	CHILDREN (0-11yrs) in all Christian groups, small groups and Sunday School.	YOUTH (12-18 yrs) in all Christian groups, small groups and Sunday School.	YOUNG ADULTS (19-30 yrs) in all Christian groups, small groups and Sunday School.	OTHER ADULTS (31+ yrs) in all Christian groups, small groups and Sunday School.	TOTAL number of persons participating in Christian formation groups (Total lines 15 - 18).	Average weekly attendance: Education classes/groups that meet in Sunday Church School groups.	Number of participants in Vacation Bible School	Number of ongoing classes (all ages) for learning in Sunday Church	Number of ONGOING small groups, support groups, or classes	Number of SHORT-TERM classes, support groups, or small groups offered	Membership in United Methodist Men (UMM)	Amount paid for projects (UMM)	Membership in United Methodist Women (UMW)	Amount paid for local church and community work (UMW)	Number of UMVIM teams sent out from this church	Number of persons sent out on UMVIM teams from this church
Align #	**Church Name**	**10**	**10a**	**11a**	**11b**	**11T**	**12**	**13**	**14**	**15**	**16**	**17**	**18**	**19**	**20**	**22**	**23**	**24**	**25**	**26**	**27**	**28**	**29**	**30a**	**30b**
5550	Mount Pleasant	12	0	0	0	0	0	4	1	0	0	0	0	0	7	0	1	1	1	0	0	0	0	0	0
5425	Mount Savage	55	0	2	0	2	0	0	0	17	18	5	27	67	27	59	5	2	0	0	0	4	0	0	0
5460	Mount Tabor	23	0	1	0	1	0	16	6	14	10	9	17	50	25	25	6	3	1	0	0	15	8,350	0	0
5555	Mount Zion	28	0	0	0	0	1	6	0	0	2	0	28	30	28	0	2	1	0	0	0	0	0	0	0
5585	Mount Zion	17	0	2	1	3	0	0	0	2	0	0	11	13	13	0	2	0	0	0	0	6	194	0	0
6325	Mount Zion	58	0	0	0	0	0	56	0	0	40	3	28	71	23	35	5	7	6	5	0	8	755	0	0
6350	Mount Zion	18	0	0	0	0	0	3	0	0	0	0	25	25	0	0	0	0	2	0	0	0	0	0	0
5280	Murleys Branch	24	0	1	0	1	0	0	0	3	0	0	0	3	3	0	0	0	1	0	0	12	405	0	0
5210	New Covenant	111	0	3	1	4	51	61	0	26	16	2	46	90	33	25	6	4	2	0	0	14	500	0	0
5430	Oldtown	59	0	0	3	3	0	15	6	10	5	10	14	39	14	35	7	3	3	0	0	0	0	0	0
5435	Oliver's Grove	41	0	0	0	0	0	32	6	3	14	9	20	46	25	35	3	3	3	0	0	0	0	0	0
5340	Otterbein	244	0	0	0	0	107	257	0	98	65	92	287	542	125	86	11	9	8	0	0	90	5,154	3	34
5375	Park Place	49	0	1	0	1	10	11	0	1	0	0	16	17	9	0	2	4	4	17	0	17	2,650	0	0
5120	Parkhead	30	1	0	0	0	4	17	0	8	0	4	15	27	20	25	2	1	0	0	0	0	0	0	0
5610	Paw Paw	18	2	0	0	0	0	5	0	5	0	0	12	17	5	0	1	1	0	0	0	13	264	0	0
5385	Piney Plains	55	0	0	0	0	1	0	0	8	2	0	20	30	10	10	1	1	0	0	0	13	3,500	0	0
6430	Pleasant Walk	9	0	0	0	0	18	1	0	0	0	0	4	4	4	0	1	0	0	0	0	0	0	0	0
5285	Prosperity	52	0	4	0	4	0	0	0	12	4	3	10	29	47	100	2	0	2	0	0	8	4,200	0	0
5445	Rawlings	40	0	0	0	0	0	10	0	3	5	1	12	21	4	25	4	0	0	0	0	0	0	0	0
5470	Rehoboth	267	11	2	3	5	101	275	7	25	30	30	225	310	50	59	5	6	2	0	0	15	0	0	0
6250	Salem	49	0	0	2	2	0	33	5	6	18	13	23	60	14	0	14	20	10	0	0	0	0	0	0
6435	Salem	84	0	0	0	0	16	10	1	38	14	4	60	116	52	17	7	5	4	0	0	13	6,000	0	0
5415	Shaft	28	0	0	0	0	0	12	0	0	0	0	9	9	9	0	1	0	0	0	0	8	194	0	0
5355	Shiloh	67	10	1	0	1	0	2	4	8	15	10	20	53	31	30	9	3	2	0	0	0	0	0	0
5345	St Andrews	60	4	2	2	4	0	25	0	12	0	4	35	51	24	30	5	2	5	3	249	0	0	0	0
5125	St Paul	0	0	0	0	0	0	0	0	0	0	0	0	0	0	0	0	0	0	0	0	0	0	0	0
5455	St Paul's	30	0	0	0	0	0	0	0	0	0	0	2	2	0	0	0	0	1	0	0	0	0	0	0
5615	Sulphur Springs	15	0	0	0	0	0	0	0	1	1	0	16	18	13	0	1	0	0	0	0	0	0	0	0
5245	Trinity	18	0	0	0	0	0	0	0	0	0	0	8	8	0	0	0	2	0	0	0	0	0	0	0
5640	Trinity-Asbury	45	0	3	2	5	5	23	0	21	0	14	12	47	25	125	2	1	1	0	0	0	0	0	0
5570	Union Chapel	152	0	2	2	4	8	8	0	14	11	2	84	111	35	4	6	4	2	6	1,100	0	0	0	0
5463	Vale Summit	62	0	0	0	0	22	0	0	5	4	0	16	25	7	0	0	3	0	0	0	0	0	0	0
5360	Washington Square	73	110	1	0	1	0	0	0	11	1	0	22	34	33	0	8	1	1	4	190	0	0	0	0
5575	Wesley Chapel	36	0	0	0	0	0	0	0	2	0	0	27	29	10	20	2	1	1	0	0	0	0	0	0
5465	Westernport	28	0	0	0	0	0	0	0	3	0	0	16	19	0	0	0	0	0	0	0	0	0	0	0
5475	Williamsport	88	0	2	0	2	25	58	0	3	4	1	14	22	11	13	3	2	3	11	0	0	0	0	0
5250	Zion	17	0	0	0	0	0	0	0	0	0	0	5	5	5	0	0	0	0	0	0	0	0	0	0
CH Total		**4,610**	**1,925**	**83**	**61**	**144**	**779**	**1,588**	**56**	**1,043**	**519**	**300**	**2,401**	**4,263**	**1,704**	**1,465**	**256**	**189**	**118**	**119**	**15,226**	**559**	**69,637**	**6**	**46**

Align #	Church Name	TOTAL Community MINISTRIES for outreach, justice, and mercy (33)	MINISTRIES focusing on global/regional health? (33a)	MINISTRIES focusing on engaging in ministry with the poor/socially (33b)	PERSONS SERVED BY community ministries for outreach, justice, and mercy (34)	PERSONS SERVING (from your congregation) in mission/community ministries (35a)	Market value of church-owned land, buildings and equipment (36)	Overall square footage of church owned buildings (furnished and unfurnished areas) (36SF)	Market value of financial and other liquid assets (37)	Debt secured by church physical assets (38)	Other debt (39)	General Advance Specials remitted to the Annual Conference Treasurer (42)	World Service Specials remitted to the Annual Conference Treasurer (43)	Annual Conference Advance Specials remitted to the Annual Conference Treasurer (44)	Youth Service Fund remitted to the (45)	All other funds sent to AC Treasurer for connectional mission and ministry (46)	Total Annual Conference Special Sunday Offerings remitted to the (47)	UMC CAUSES: Total amount given DIRECTLY to United Methodist causes (NOT sent to BWC Treasurer) (48b)	MISSIONS/MINISTRY COSTS: Direct costs incurred by the local church for mission and community ministry activities (48b)
5550	Mount Pleasant	5	4	1	191	12	207,500	0	108,319	0	0	0	0	0	0	0	0	0	0
5425	Mount Savage	5	0	0	1,300	0	100,000	0	83,000	39,419	0	0	0	0	0	0	0	400	0
5460	Mount Tabor	0	0	0	495	50	175,000	2,640	36,000	0	0	0	0	0	0	0	0	0	350
5555	Mount Zion	0	0	0	0	0	530,000	6,100	26,523	0	0	0	0	0	0	0	0	0	0
5585	Mount Zion	3	2	3	600	18	119,000	0	109,972	0	0	197	0	469	0	0	0	698	6,675
6325	Mount Zion	8	6	6	318	40	3,179,000	14,347	9,500	0	0	0	0	0	0	0	0	0	8,859
6350	Mount Zion	0	0	0	400	18	311,167	2,260	3,200	0	0	0	0	0	0	0	0	900	0
5280	Murleys Branch	0	3	0	50	21	72,000	2,325	296,281	0	0	0	0	0	0	0	0	0	2,555
5210	New Covenant	8	3	6	400	65	2,300,000	16,338	36,000	0	0	0	0	0	0	0	0	500	0
5430	Oldtown	0	0	0	850	75	384,000	3,280	36,000	0	0	600	0	0	0	0	0	0	484
5435	Oliver's Grove	0	0	0	650	45	292,000	3,302	0	0	0	0	0	0	0	0	0	0	600
5340	Otterbein	37	19	26	3,003	526	10,123,600	40,000	1,982,777	0	0	750	0	0	0	0	0	421	5,505
5375	Park Place	0	0	7	150	31	1,515,400	0	116,140	0	0	0	0	0	0	0	0	0	0
5120	Parkhead	2	0	0	150	20	466,000	2,336	0	0	0	0	0	0	0	0	0	8	0
5610	Paw Paw	3	0	0	37	13	913,600	8,800	0	0	0	0	0	0	0	0	0	150	234
5385	Piney Plains	7	0	3	56	30	555,000	4,800	51,000	0	0	0	0	50	0	0	0	506	0
6430	Pleasant Walk	5	3	3	70	9	499,000	2,951	0	0	0	0	0	0	0	0	0	0	0
5285	Prosperity	0	0	0	0	0	438,800	0	126,895	0	0	0	0	0	0	0	0	0	4,481
5445	Rawlings	6	1	3	700	100	1,400,000	10,250	548,210	0	0	1,000	0	0	0	0	0	735	4,500
5470	Rehoboth	5	0	4	825	80	2,292,000	9,000	72,077	0	0	0	0	0	0	0	0	0	15,702
6250	Salem	9	2	2	0	35	1,800,000	8,750	1,296,496	0	0	0	0	50	0	0	0	0	0
6435	Salem	0	0	5	331	60	1,056,000	6,645	54,973	0	0	600	0	792	0	0	0	36	0
5415	Shaft	16	5	3	30	0	300,000	6,806	618,378	0	0	0	0	0	0	0	0	610	0
5355	Shiloh	13	5	12	575	45	526,800	10,056	221,500	0	0	2,041	0	15	0	0	0	70	0
5345	St Andrews	3	1	12	0	0	1,200,000	6,152	0	0	0	0	0	0	0	0	0	1,508	0
5125	St Paul	0	0	1	1,000	11	0	0	210,194	0	0	0	0	0	0	0	0	0	4,179
5455	St Paul's	1,000	0	2	102	20	1,537,000	8,064	23,398	0	0	0	0	0	0	0	0	100	0
5615	Sulphur Springs	4	0	0	600	6	78,100	6,790	11,000	0	0	0	0	0	0	0	0	0	0
5245	Trinity	6	1	2	10,526	45	1,250,000	2,547	380,746	0	0	0	0	0	0	0	0	0	4,118
5640	Trinity-Asbury	10	0	5	260	156	1,330,500	25,319	117,373	0	0	0	0	0	0	0	0	0	16,092
5570	Union Chapel	7	0	6	490	30	1,210,000	5,100	254,032	0	0	0	0	0	0	0	0	100	0
5463	Vale Summit	5	0	2	400	40	423,000	400	0	0	0	0	0	0	0	0	0	0	0
5360	Washington Square	12	0	10	2	35	2,646,000	23,950	37,749	0	0	0	0	0	0	0	0	0	0
5575	Wesley Chapel	11	0	7	7,460	0	831,600	0	80	0	0	0	0	0	0	0	0	0	1,724
5465	Westernport	0	0	0	0	0	400,000	0	592,220	0	0	0	0	0	0	0	0	0	0
5475	Williamsport	0	0	0	0	72	4,410,400	0	91,000	0	0	3,230	0	0	0	0	0	364	5,473
5250	Zion	0	0	0	0	0	1,100,000	0	0	0	0	0	0	0	0	0	0	0	0
CH Total		1,367	97	274	54,263	3,366	114,720,298	958,185	16,564,996	1,269,372	128,197	33,462	600	3,539	0	0	0	12,536	202,358

Align #	Church Name	48TOTAL Total of UMC Causes & UMC Missions & Outreach	49 NON-UMC CAUSES: Total amount given DIRECTLY to non-United Methodist benevolent and charitable causes (NOT sent to BWC Treasurer)	50a Human Relations Sunday	50b UMCOR Sunday (formerly One Great Hour of Sharing)	50c Peace with Justice Sunday	50d Native American Ministries Sunday	50e World Communion Sunday	50f U.M. Student Day	51 Direct-billed clergy non-health benefits	52 Direct-billed clergy health benefits	53a Base compensation paid to/for the Senior Pastor or other person assigned or appointed in the lead pastoral role to the church	53b Base compensation paid/for to all Associate Pastor(s) & other pastoral staff assigned or appointed to the church	53c Base compensation paid to/for any Deacons NOT included in 53a or 53b	55a Housing benefits paid to/for Lead Pastor or person in lead pastoral role as described in 53a	55b Housing benefits paid to/for ALL Associate Pastor(s) & other pastoral staff assigned or appointed to the	55c Housing benefits paid to/for any Deacons not included in 53a or 53b.	56 Paid to/for all persons included in Lines 53a-53c for accountable reimbursements	57 Paid to/for all persons included in Lines 53a-53c for any other cash allowances (non-
5550	Mount Pleasant	0	5,500	0	0	0	0	0	0	0	0	7,500	0	0	0	0	0	900	0
5425	Mount Savage	400	3,329	0	0	0	0	0	0	0	0	21,375	0	0	9,768	0	0	3,862	0
5460	Mount Tabor	350	2,100	0	0	0	0	0	0	0	0	15,635	0	0	1,167	0	0	1,500	0
5555	Mount Zion	0	295	0	0	0	0	0	0	0	0	8,604	0	0	2,667	0	0	800	0
5585	Mount Zion	7,373	1,500	0	0	0	0	0	0	0	0	7,300	0	0	3,500	0	2,113	0	0
6325	Mount Zion	8,859	2,043	0	0	46	0	0	0	10,851	19,810	48,228	0	0	6,854	0	0	0	0
6350	Mount Zion	900	1,767	0	0	0	0	0	0	0	0	6,125	0	0	7,000	0	0	300	0
5280	Murleys Branch	2,555	100	0	0	0	0	0	0	12,032	15,480	52,075	0	0	0	0	0	875	0
5210	New Covenant	500	3,370	0	0	0	0	0	0	9,673	12,259	15,635	0	0	3,692	0	0	5,000	0
5430	Oldtown	484	1,000	0	0	0	0	0	0	13,809	13,027	68,340	0	0	1,167	0	0	1,500	0
5435	Oliver's Grove	600	700	0	0	0	0	0	0	0	0	13,600	0	0	1,167	0	0	1,500	0
5340	Otterbein	5,505	24,555	266	0	0	0	0	0	0	0	14,821	0	0	20,000	0	0	6,000	0
5375	Park Place	421	0	0	750	750	500	0	0	0	0	4,489	0	0	10,000	0	0	2,500	600
5120	Parkhead	8	4,350	0	0	0	0	0	0	0	0	6,500	0	0	985	0	0	884	0
5610	Paw Paw	384	75	26	0	0	25	24	0	0	0	5,000	0	0	3,600	0	4,214	1,511	500
5385	Piney Plains	506	1,000	0	0	0	0	0	0	0	0	9,800	0	0	2,913	0	0	0	780
6430	Pleasant Walk	0	2,216	0	0	0	0	0	0	720	0	13,500	0	0	7,000	0	0	557	0
5285	Prosperity	5,216	325	0	0	0	0	0	0	0	0	76,200	0	0	0	0	0	1,400	0
5445	Rawlings	4,500	500	0	0	0	0	0	0	0	0	50,262	0	0	1,500	0	0	1,415	0
5470	Rehoboth	15,702	25,353	0	0	0	0	0	0	14,887	15,384	12,900	0	0	24,850	0	0	6,136	0
6250	Salem	36	623	0	0	0	0	0	0	0	0	23,000	0	0	10,500	0	0	2,778	0
6435	Salem	610	21,874	0	0	0	0	0	0	11,333	11,983	47,450	0	0	5,903	0	0	3,416	0
5415	Shaft	70	8,677	0	0	0	0	0	0	0	0	21,400	0	0	1,922	0	0	1,875	0
5355	Shiloh	0	625	0	0	0	0	0	0	0	0	5,200	0	0	19,000	0	0	2,000	0
5345	St Andrews	1,508	491	150	0	105	100	20	120	0	0	5,200	0	0	4,521	0	0	1,389	0
5125	St Paul	0	1,151	0	0	0	0	0	0	10,676	15,426	25,250	0	0	0	0	0	0	0
5455	St Paul's	100	0	0	0	0	0	99	0	10,788	15,626	50,529	0	0	0	0	0	2,122	0
5615	Sulphur Springs	4,179	200	0	0	0	0	0	0	0	0	2,310	0	0	0	0	0	1,200	0
5245	Trinity	0	227	0	0	0	0	0	0	0	0	5,200	0	0	0	0	0	2,763	0
5640	Trinity-Asbury	4,118	33,412	0	0	0	0	0	0	0	0	25,250	0	0	8,853	0	0	7,554	0
5570	Union Chapel	16,092	6,147	0	0	0	0	0	0	12,255	19,415	50,529	0	0	0	0	0	3,360	1,300
5463	Vale Summit	0	275	0	0	0	0	0	0	0	0	2,310	0	0	2,310	0	0	7,554	0
5360	Washington Square	1,724	1,018	0	0	0	0	0	0	0	0	40,278	0	0	16,000	0	0	3,360	0
5575	Wesley Chapel	0	2,300	0	0	0	0	0	0	10,685	14,569	21,445	0	0	7,147	0	0	1,667	0
5465	Westerport	5,473	0	0	0	0	0	0	0	0	0	11,700	0	0	11,700	0	0	1,843	0
5475	Williamsport	364	0	175	144	25	160	160	100	12,745	15,643	43,412	0	0	43,412	0	0	5,000	0
5250	Zion			0	0	0	0	0	0	0	0	12,500	0	0	28,600	0	0		0
CH Total		214,894	246,906	1,077	2,046	1,524	1,951	930	481	310,409	413,204	1,758,776	0	0	478,736	0	6,327	170,363	10,707

Align #	Church Name	60	61	62	63	63a	64	65	66	67a	67b	67c	67d	67e	67f	67g
		Paid in salary and benefits for all other church staff and diaconal ministers	Amount spent for local church program expenses	Amount spent for local church operating expenses	Amount paid for principal and interest on indebtedness, loans, mortgages, etc.	Amount paid for capital campaign or fundraising costs	Amount paid on capital expenditures for building, improvements, and major equipment purchases.	Amount PAID by/for the local church on all expenditures	Number of giving units	Received through pledges	Received from non-pledging, but identified givers	Received from unidentified givers	Amount received from interest and dividends and/or transferred from liquid assets	Amount received from Sale of Church Assets	Amount received through building use fees, contributions, and rentals	Amount received through fundraisers and other sources
5550	Mount Pleasant	1,300	153	5,526	0	0	37,941	60,426	12	0	27,161	6,128	1,608	0	0	0
5425	Mount Savage	10,536	4,516	16,810	0	0	0	81,270	12	0	66,189	5,438	0	0	0	46,947
5460	Mount Tabor	0	1,078	5,037	13,638	0	1,170	32,449	25	0	0	35,423	1,800	0	0	1,200
5555	Mount Zion	1,384	514	5,870	0	4,539	17,407	37,425	11	0	34,945	2,915	0	0	1,473	6,820
5585	Mount Zion	850	1,405	4,121	0	0	15,026	46,745	70	0	0	30,962	4	0	18,742	6,910
6325	Mount Zion	29,040	1,945	29,274	0	0	0	185,751	17	0	122,661	6,795	56	0	0	0
6350	Mount Zion	0	742	4,847	0	0	0	23,316	15	0	13,520	3,281	0	0	0	0
5280	Murleys Branch	0	0	1,651	0	0	0	13,324	0	7,529	0	20,123	0	0	0	2,970
5210	New Covenant	31,827	7,917	27,039	0	0	14,849	196,754	117	0	139,578	19,982	16,001	0	50	19,804
5430	Oldtown	600	652	4,711	0	0	0	52,518	43	0	26,401	13,760	30	0	0	1,688
5435	Oliver's Grove	0	667	5,041	0	360	0	29,380	35	0	25,985	11,159	22	0	6,150	1,000
5340	Ottobein	226,920	45,427	53,110	0	0	78,493	627,494	256	0	458,435	5,119	591	0	800	0
5375	Park Place	10,217	2,208	19,230	0	0	1,608	70,280	60	0	64,857	4,561	10	0	0	0
5120	Parkhead	8,756	1,886	6,522	0	0	0	43,432	13	0	44,768	4,190	0	0	0	0
5610	Paw Paw	0	487	11,292	0	0	0	25,345	14	0	18,735	20,223	11	0	0	0
5385	Piney Plains	0	467	6,930	0	0	0	26,007	50	0	12,177	2,944	1,756	0	150	766
6430	Pleasant Walk	0	0	6,382	0	0	1,075	26,422	35	0	63,139	1,850	45	0	20	2,972
5285	Prosperity	0	1,800	10,290	0	0	5,375	38,699	45	0	19,246	0	95	0	1,220	0
5445	Rawlings	6,800	4,200	19,590	7,682	0	0	59,882	73	31,313	0	29,743	339	0	821	2,429
5470	Rehoboth	109,758	16,587	37,754	0	0	5,589	411,671	210	0	403,280	15,328	0	0	0	7,507
6250	Salem	13,457	2,303	21,850	0	0	5,837	77,703	45	0	72,466	6,704	8,198	0	0	0
6435	Salem	117,771	13,439	16,461	0	0	23,032	187,231	73	0	121,965	7,080	83	0	0	0
5415	Shaft	0	650	10,072	0	0	0	45,278	25	0	27,965	3,896	0	0	0	0
5955	Shiloh	7,067	2,625	17,965	0	0	8,651	93,131	60	0	64,290	1,276	2,000	0	500	5,928
5345	St Andrews	21,450	4,399	19,537	0	0	29,513	176,934	78	0	124,360	17,158	7,080	0	0	6,500
5125	St Paul	0	0	1	0	0	0	26,415	0	0	38,209	0	0	0	0	0
5455	St Paul's	2,400	391	17,100	0	0	250	52,020	31	0	0	43,356	3	0	12,973	0
5615	Sulphur Springs	0	586	5,020	0	0	0	18,183	35	0	21,700	5,549	0	0	0	500
5245	Trinity	1,425	25	13,900	0	0	1,600	26,812	125	0	0	0	7,733	0	2,790	0
5640	Trinity-Asbury	11,817	1,919	12,211	0	0	66,665	76,557	45	0	40,139	7,148	0	0	10,120	2,012
5570	Union Chapel	35,471	11,273	25,836	0	0	6,836	296,914	65	0	199,980	8,290	109	0	300	0
5463	Vale Summit	0	619	6,233	0	0	0	30,562	26	0	29,628	0	5,197	0	0	0
5360	Washington Square	21,017	4,502	38,134	0	0	1,346	166,567	15	0	128,104	11,270	0	0	1,683	2,299
5575	Wesley Chapel	943	463	6,544	0	0	0	49,211	108	0	36,676	4,150	355	0	0	0
5465	Westernport	0	0	7,250	0	0	0	24,866	18	10,250	4,300	4,598	61,600	0	1,070	0
5475	Williamsport	79,695	10,176	47,357	0	0	5,123	293,511	108	0	218,961	0	0	0	0	0
5290	Zion	4,065	0	8,462	0	0	0	29,827	18	0	12,891	2,986	0	0	0	0
	CH Total	1,304,142	302,286	1,459,652	157,920	13,255	859,131	8,610,952	3,731	618,712	5,570,042	749,942	191,564	0	145,915	237,089

Align #	Church Name	67 TOTAL income for annual budget/spending plan (67a-g)	68a Capital campaigns	68b Memorials, endowments, and bequests	68c Other sources and projects (include UMW, UMM and 'flow-through')	68d Special Sundays, Gen. Adv. Spec., World Srvc Spec., Conf. Adv. Spec. and other directed benevolent giving	68 Total income for designated causes including capital campaign and other special projects	69a Equitable Compensation Funds received by Church or Pastor	69b Advance Special, apportioned, and connectional funds received by church	69c Other grants and financial support from institutional sources	69 Income from connectional / institutional sources outside the local church	70 TOTAL CHURCH INCOME (Sum of Lines 67 + 68 + 69)	40a Amount APPORTIONED to the local church	40b Amount PAID by the local church for all apportioned causes
5550	Mount Pleasant	34,897	0	0	0	0	0	0	0	0	0	34,897	1,606	1,606
5425	Mount Savage	118,574	0	0	0	0	0	0	0	0	0	118,574	10,674	10,674
5460	Mount Tabor	38,423	0	0	0	0	0	0	0	0	0	38,423	4,412	4,412
5555	Mount Zion	46,153	0	6,207	0	0	6,207	0	0	0	0	52,360	3,653	3,653
5585	Mount Zion	37,876	0	0	0	610	610	0	0	0	0	38,486	3,289	3,289
6325	Mount Zion	148,254	0	16,210	0	515	16,725	0	0	0	0	164,979	19,841	10,996
6350	Mount Zion	24,330	0	0	0	0	0	0	0	0	0	24,330	2,760	2,760
5280	Murleys Branch	23,093	0	0	0	0	0	0	0	0	0	23,093	2,018	2,018
5210	New Covenant	195,415	0	18,539	0	6,047	24,586	0	0	7,500	7,500	227,501	22,973	22,973
5430	Oldtown	36,707	2,010	85	0	0	2,095	0	0	0	0	38,802	4,237	4,237
5435	Oliver's Grove	37,174	0	0	0	0	0	0	0	0	0	37,174	4,070	4,070
5340	Otterbein	479,367	0	173,964	0	4,475	178,439	0	0	300	300	658,106	69,292	69,292
5375	Park Place	71,367	0	485	0	0	485	0	0	0	0	71,852	9,896	9,896
5120	Parkhead	49,339	0	0	0	0	0	4,586	0	0	4,586	53,925	4,720	4,720
5610	Paw Paw	22,925	0	0	0	166	166	0	0	2,360	2,360	25,451	3,432	3,432
5385	Piney Plains	21,150	0	0	0	0	0	0	0	0	0	21,150	2,647	2,647
6430	Pleasant Walk	19,869	0	285	0	2,410	2,695	0	0	0	0	22,564	3,278	3,278
5295	Prosperity	64,404	0	0	0	0	0	0	0	0	0	64,404	4,493	4,493
5445	Rawlings	55,754	0	525	0	0	525	0	0	0	0	56,279	7,877	7,877
5470	Rehoboth	433,362	271,514	2,750	25,488	1,665	301,417	0	0	0	0	734,779	54,789	54,789
6250	Salem	79,973	0	2,500	0	0	2,500	0	0	0	0	82,473	9,819	9,819
6435	Salem	145,491	0	16,780	25,849	0	42,629	0	0	0	0	188,120	15,755	15,755
5415	Shaft	34,752	0	1,230	0	292	1,522	0	0	0	0	36,274	7,137	7,137
5355	Shiloh	79,798	0	5,511	0	582	6,093	0	0	0	0	85,891	14,138	14,138
5345	St Andrews	134,756	0	1,995	0	3,281	5,276	0	0	0	0	140,032	17,959	17,959
5125	St Paul	0	0	0	0	0	0	0	0	0	0	0	0	0
5455	St Paul's	52,458	0	0	0	0	0	0	0	0	0	52,458	7,106	7,106
5615	Sulphur Springs	17,161	0	918	0	0	918	0	0	0	0	18,079	1,698	1,698
5245	Trinity	24,990	0	760	0	0	760	0	0	0	0	25,750	3,235	3,235
5640	Trinity-Asbury	103,360	0	660	2,154	0	2,814	0	0	1,500	1,500	107,674	9,626	9,626
5570	Union Chapel	205,829	0	3,690	0	0	3,690	0	0	0	0	209,519	18,412	18,412
5463	Vale Summit	36,885	0	350	0	0	350	0	0	0	0	37,235	2,647	2,647
5360	Washington Square	141,591	11,316	664	0	0	11,980	0	0	0	0	153,571	19,440	19,440
5575	Wesley Chapel	52,283	0	635	0	0	635	0	0	0	0	52,918	6,738	6,738
5465	Westernport	18,700	0	0	0	0	0	0	0	0	0	18,700	3,616	3,616
5475	Williamsport	286,229	0	2,850	0	1,727	4,577	0	0	0	0	290,806	36,293	36,293
5250	Zion	15,877	0	0	0	0	0	0	0	0	0	15,877	4,436	4,436
CH Total		7,513,264	462,849	422,553	144,756	36,361	1,066,519	9,166	0	11,815	20,981	8,600,764	966,211	672,169

Align #	Church Name	Dist #	City	State	Total professing members at the close of 2017 (1)	Received by PROFESSION of Faith (2a1)	Received by PROFESSION of Faith (Other Than Confirmation) (2a2)	Restored by AFFIRMATION of Faith (2b)	Transferred in from other UM churches (3)	Transferred in from non-UM churches (4)	Removed or corrected by Charge Conference action (5a)	Withdrawn from Professing Membership (5b)	Transferred out to other UM churches (6)	Transferred out to non-UM churches (7)	Removed by death (8)	Total professing members at the close of 2018 (9)	Asian Professing Members (9a)	African American / Black Professing Members (9b)	Hispanic / Latino Professing Members (9c)	Native American Professing Members (9d)	Pacific Islander Professing Members (9e)	White Professing Members (9f)	Multi-Racial Professing Members (9g)	Female Professing Members (9h)	Male Professing Members (9i)
7245	Alberta Gary Memorial	CM	Columbia	MD	82	0	2	0	0	0	9	0	0	0	1	74	0	0	0	0	0	74	0	37	37
6110	Arcady	CM	Frederick	MD	186	0	1	0	0	0	0	0	0	0	2	185	0	1	1	0	0	184	0	126	59
9265	Asbury	CM	Germantown	MD	47	0	0	0	0	0	0	0	0	0	0	47	0	47	0	0	0	0	0	37	10
9110	Ashton	CM	Ashton	MD	241	17	2	0	12	2	18	2	1	4	6	213	17	40	1	2	0	212	0	121	92
4235	Bethany	CM	Ellicott City	MD	1,124		2	4	0	5	12	2	1	5	3	1,132			3	1	0	1,072	3	639	493
9185	Bethesda	CM	Damascus	MD	304	8	5	1	5	5	11	3	2	1	3	327	4	1	2	2	1	312	0	160	167
6285	Calvary	CM	Mount Airy	MD	704	3	3	1	0	0	0	4	1	4	0	695	1	13	6	7	0	684	7	389	306
7350	Christ	CM	Columbia	MD	90	3	1	1	0	0	3	3	0	0	0	89	1	5	2	0	0	66	0	50	39
9175	Clarksburg	CM	Clarksburg	MD	129	1	0	1	1	0	0	0	0	0	0	129	1	5	0	0	0	123	0	72	57
9270	Community of Faith	CM	Clarksburg	MD	584	6	2	1	9	3	0	1	4	0	4	587	12	45	17	5	2	495	11	348	239
6235	Covenant	CM	Montgomery Village	MD	59	0	2	1	1	0	0	0	0	0	0	19	15	19	12	0	0	0	0	14	5
9490	Daisy	CM	Lisbon	MD	15	0	0	0	0	0	0	1	0	0	0	19	0	0	0	0	0	19	0	14	5
9190	Damascus	CM	Damascus	MD	1,382	15	5	2	9	3	0	0	2	4	8	1,399	2	27	0	0	3	1,341	1	813	586
9225	Dickerson	CM	Dickerson	MD	76	0	0	1	0	0	0	0	1	0	1	74	2	0	0	1	0	74	0	43	31
4575	Ebenezer	CM	Sykesville	MD	355	9	0	0	0	0	11	0	0	0	2	329	2	0	0	2	0	327	0	178	151
6230	Ellicott City Korean Mission	CM	Ellicott City	MD	67	0	0	0	0	0	6	0	0	0	1	62	120	62	0	0	0	0	0	54	8
4236	Emory	CM	Ellicott City	MD	123	0	11	0	2	3	6	0	0	0	2	123	0	2	0	0	0	3	0	64	59
4245	Emory Grove	CM	Gaithersburg	MD	97	5	3	1	0	0	1	0	0	0	1	94	0	2	0	0	0	92	0	53	41
9240	Epworth	CM	Gaithersburg	MD	194	5	3	1	2	0	1	0	0	1	3	204	1	202	0	2	0	0	1	154	50
9250	Epworth	CM	Gaithersburg	MD	778	0	6	0	0	0	5	1	0	0	3	761	36	201	72	2	0	469	0	481	300
4345	Fairview	CM	Gaithersburg	MD	389	0	0	0	9	0	0	0	1	0	5	388	5	173	10	0	0	200	0	228	160
6382	Faithpoint	CM	New Windsor	MD	61	0	9	1	2	1	0	0	0	0	1	65	2	65	2	0	0	130	5	49	16
6380	Flint Hill	CM	Monrovia	MD	135	4	0	0	0	0	0	0	0	0	2	146	3	6	0	5	1	41	0	74	72
4230	Flohrville	CM	Adamstown	MD	44	0	0	0	1	0	0	0	0	0	0	42	1	1	0	0	0	28	5	29	13
9230	Forest Grove	CM	Germantown	MD	29	0	0	0	2	0	0	0	0	0	0	32	0	0	2	0	0	38	0	19	13
9210	Friendship	CM	Dickerson	MD	28	0	0	0	0	0	0	0	0	0	0	38	0	35	0	0	0	1	0	22	16
4240	Gather	CM	Damascus	MD	109	0	0	0	0	0	0	0	0	0	0	36	0	3	0	0	0	107	0	24	12
7365	Gary Memorial	CM	Sykesville	MD	125	1	0	0	1	1	6	2	4	1	2	107	28	26	0	0	0	108	1	62	45
9285	Glen Mar	CM	Ellicott City	MD	1,394	24	0	8	3	4	17	2	2	0	4	1,401	2	5	7	1	0	1,339	1	769	632
9255	Glenelg	CM	Ellicott City	MD	392	14	1	2	0	4	0	0	2	0	4	395	5	523	0	6	0	388	0	215	181
9260	Goshen	CM	Gaithersburg	MD	519	18	0	0	0	0	9	0	0	0	18	530	21	120	8	9	4	3	0	323	207
9355	Grace	CM	Gaithersburg	MD	890	5	0	0	1	5	3	0	3	0	4	887	1	164	1	0	0	721	4	482	405
9315	Hopkins	CM	Highland	MD	173	0	1	3	0	0	0	0	0	0	3	170	0	0	0	0	0	4	0	110	60
9510	Howard Chapel-Ridgeville	CM	Mount Airy	MD	194	4	5	0	0	0	0	4	6	0	6	191	0	1	1	1	0	189	0	107	84
6235	Hyattstown	CM	Clarksburg	MD	71	0	0	0	0	0	0	0	0	0	3	72	0	0	0	0	0	22	0	41	31
9180	Ijamsville	CM	Ijamsville	MD	75	0	1	0	0	0	0	0	0	0	1	77	0	0	0	4	0	71	4	47	30
7355	Jennings Chapel	CM	Woodbine	MD	186	5	0	2	2	1	0	10	2	0	2	181	19	47	0	6	0	181	0	114	67
6310	Linden-Linthicum	CM	Clarksville	MD	1,045	5	6	0	0	0	0	13	12	0	3	1,023	0	1	8	6	0	942	0	552	471
6310	Lisbon	CM	Lisbon	MD	306	0	1	0	0	1	0	2	2	0	6	303	0	179	0	0	4	302	0	162	141
9385	Locust	CM	Columbia	MD	195	6	18	3	0	0	0	0	0	0	3	185	0	0	0	8	0	2	0	145	40
9425	Marvin Chapel	CM	Mount Airy	MD	101	4	5	1	1	1	3	0	0	0	3	99	0	2	4	2	0	99	1	66	33
9215	Memorial	CM	Poolesville	MD	307	6	3	3	1	1	0	0	6	6	3	306	11	4	4	4	0	299	0	171	135
4585	Mill Creek Parish	CM	Derwood	MD	334	6	6	0	0	5	0	22	8	8	3	305	7	2	5	2	0	285	0	175	130
9335	Montgomery	CM	Damascus	MD	690	0	5	1	7	1	0	0	1	1	6	700	1	0	0	0	0	681	0	979	321
4455	Morgan Chapel	CM	Woodbine	MD	105	6	0	0	0	0	0	0	0	0	3	41	0	0	0	0	0	41	0	22	19
	Mount Carmel	CM	Brookeville	MD	76	0	0	0	0	0	0	0	0	0	2	62	0	0	0	0	0	62	0	39	23
	Mount Gregory	CM	Glenwood	MD	57	0	2	1	0	0	3	0	0	0	4	53	0	53	0	0	0	0	0	32	21

Align #	Church Name	10	10a	11a	11b	11T	12	13	14	15	16	17	18	19	20	22	23	24	25	26	27	28	29	30a	30b
7345	Alberta Gary Memorial	28	6	1	0	1	1	3	0	7	0	0	4		4	0	0	0	2	0	0	0	0	0	0
6110	Araby	47	0	1	0	1	4	0	0	0	0	0	4	14	8	14	3	1	1	0	0	13	2,413	0	0
9265	Asbury	35	0	0	0	0	0	0	0	0	5	0	0	10	0	0	5	0	1	10	0	0	0	0	0
9110	Ashton	86	0	2	0	2	23	121	0	23	46	0	39	108	25	102	5	4	3	0	0	50	6,123	0	0
4235	Bethany	404	4	2	0	2	271	266	17	130	104	14	323	564	120	175	14	31	4	0	0	0	0	0	0
9185	Bethesda	136	4	4	1	5	0	16	0	34	25	0	98	171	100	45	8	20	5	20	2,000	17	635	1	0
6085	Calvary	244	0	7	1	8	172	199	8	25	40	0	52	117	33	0	4	2	3	0	0	0	0	0	5
7350	Christ	59	0	4	1	5	0	16	4	10	11	0	20	41	10	55	4	2	0	0	0	0	0	0	0
9175	Clarksburg	28	0	0	0	0	12	18	0	7	4	0	7	18	8	0	8	2	1	0	0	17	50	0	0
9270	Community of Faith	10	0	0	0	0	0	7	0	0	0	0	10	10	10	0	0	2	2	0	0	0	0	0	0
9235	Covenant	169	0	0	0	0	155	0	6	15	15	0	66	96	90	105	5	2	1	0	0	31	1,147	0	0
9490	Daisy	10	0	0	0	0	0	0	0	15	0	0	0	0	30	0	0	5	2	0	0	0	0	0	0
9190	Damascus	206	26	4	15	19	79	234	15	64	66	50	201	381	216	168	15	5	1	18	700	40	6,000	1	8
9225	Dickerson	11	0	1	1	2	1	1	9	13	15	18	60	6	72	78	8	7	7	0	0	0	0	0	0
4575	Ebenezer	139	0	2	1	3	23	11	0	38	15	1	12	13	14	0	9	9	4	42	0	0	1,300	0	0
6230	Ebenezer	36	0	0	0	0	0	4	0	0	0	0	0	6	0	0	0	3	0	0	0	0	0	0	0
4236	Ellicott City Korean Mission	100	30	0	0	0	0	0	0	7	15	15	50	87	48	0	8	4	4	0	0	50	0	0	0
4245	Emory	53	0	0	0	0	7	5	0	5	6	4	19	24	5	5	3	3	3	0	0	6	0	0	0
9240	Emory Grove	123	0	5	0	5	30	8	5	7	43	25	80	97	90	119	3	36	35	22	4,560	9	1,300	0	0
9245	Epworth	266	0	1	0	1	12	329	0	96	6	6	120	284	90	145	3	11	3	15	100	6	0	0	0
9250	Fairhaven	83	0	2	1	3	0	22	0	13	0	0	32	61	18	77	2	2	2	0	0	31	1,147	0	0
4945	Fairview	35	0	3	0	3	1	0	0	0	0	12	2	14	12	0	1	2	2	0	0	0	0	0	0
6382	FaithPoint	110	45	0	0	0	15	140	0	35	115	27	103	280	0	79	10	10	4	0	0	0	500	0	0
6380	Flint Hill	12	0	0	0	0	0	0	0	0	0	0	0	0	0	0	0	1	0	0	0	0	0	0	0
4230	Florisville	12	0	0	0	0	4	1	0	5	0	0	0	0	0	0	0	0	0	0	0	0	0	0	0
9230	Forest Grove	9	0	0	0	0	0	7	0	7	0	0	9	19	18	24	2	2	0	0	0	4	0	0	0
9210	Friendship	30	0	0	0	0	0	0	1	6	5	3	15	29	0	0	0	2	12	2	0	0	0	0	0
4280	Gaither	28	0	0	0	0	0	0	0	0	0	0	0	0	18	0	0	0	0	0	0	0	0	0	0
4240	Gary Memorial	36	0	0	0	0	0	0	0	0	0	0	9	0	0	0	0	2	0	0	0	0	0	0	0
7365	Glen Mar	630	78	18	4	22	594	2,313	24	265	131	43	880	1,319	186	413	21	48	49	30	0	12	0	0	0
9295	Glenelg	168	0	2	1	1	50	53	0	49	50	2	24	125	35	109	11	7	11	24	0	24	2,399	0	0
9255	Goshen	195	241	5	1	6	5	0	14	64	18	5	56	143	37	75	6	2	2	17	2,765	50	3,400	0	0
9260	Grace	279	125	5	0	5	111	240	14	40	25	14	54	133	50	96	10	4	4	45	842	22	0	0	0
9290	Hopkins	67	0	0	0	0	0	10	4	15	14	3	35	67	22	25	3	4	1	22	0	12	1,360	0	0
9355	Howard Chapel-Ridgeville	20	0	0	0	0	43	43	0	10	25	0	33	33	16	0	4	4	1	0	0	11	2,740	0	0
9315	Hyattstown	24	0	0	0	0	0	12	0	0	0	0	8	8	3	0	1	1	1	0	0	12	0	0	0
6235	Ijamsville	38	0	0	0	0	0	0	0	5	0	0	20	20	6	0	5	8	0	0	0	0	0	0	0
9510	Jennings Chapel	151	0	2	1	3	0	121	7	12	43	0	16	18	16	54	5	11	6	20	4,000	0	0	0	0
9180	Linden-Linthicum	62	0	2	0	2	0	5	5	22	10	0	130	211	41	0	12	11	2	15	1,500	0	0	0	0
9350	Lisbon	93	0	0	0	0	0	0	0	8	0	0	12	30	7	12	3	4	0	15	7,298	22	0	0	0
7355	Locust	28	0	2	0	2	13	1	1	7	12	0	30	50	26	0	2	13	3	0	0	0	900	0	0
6310	Marvin Chapel	101	23	2	0	0	82	125	0	17	30	1	43	91	16	59	3	4	2	30	0	22	7,226	0	0
9385	Memorial	143	14	3	3	0	5	76	0	46	45	25	100	201	73	134	6	10	1	29	0	0	0	0	0
9425	Mill Creek Parish	221	24	6	4	10	37	200	6	141	45	0	136	322	92	227	14	13	7	0	0	0	573	0	0
9215	Montgomery	21	0	1	0	0	0	0	0	0	0	0	6	6	4	0	3	1	4	0	0	0	0	0	0
4585	Morgan Chapel	15	0	1	0	1	0	15	0	0	0	0	3	3	0	0	1	1	1	0	0	10	0	0	0
9335	Mount Carmel	21	0	0	0	0	0	0	0	0	0	0	7	7	0	0	5	1	8	0	0	0	0	0	0
4455	Mount Gregory	39	0	0	0	0	0	0	0	0	0	0	7	3	0	0	5	1	8	9	240	23	361	0	0

Align #	Church Name	TOTAL Community MINISTRIES for outreach, justice, and mercy (33)	MINISTRIES focusing on global/regional health? (33a)	MINISTRIES focusing on engaging in ministry with the poor/socially (33b)	PERSONS SERVED BY community ministries for outreach, justice, and mercy (34)	PERSONS SERVING (from your congregation) in mission/community ministries (35a)	Market value of church-owned land, buildings and equipment (36)	Overall square footage of church owned buildings (furnished and unfurnished areas) (36SF)	Market value of financial and other liquid assets (37)	Debt secured by church physical assets (38)	Other debt (39)	General Advance Specials remitted to the Annual Conference Treasurer (42)	World Service Specials remitted to the Annual Conference Treasurer (43)	Annual Conference Advance Specials remitted to the Annual Conference Treasurer (44)	Youth Service Fund remitted to the (45)	All other funds sent to AC Treasurer for connectional mission and ministry (46)	Total Annual Conference Special Sunday Offerings remitted to the (47)	UMC CAUSES: Total amount given DIRECTLY to United Methodist causes (NOT sent to BWC Treasurer) (48a)	MISSIONS/MINISTRY COSTS: Direct costs incurred by the local church for mission and community ministry activities (48b)
7345	Alberta Gary Memorial	0	0	0	0	0	918,000	4,100	45,446	0	0	0	0	0	0	0	0	0	8,221
6110	Araby	0	0	0	0	20	1,227,000	41,270	167,364	0	0	0	0	0	0	0	0	0	7,749
9265	Asbury	0	0	20	20	0	910,200	910	10,000	1,139,512	0	0	0	0	0	0	0	0	0
9110	Ashton	11	3	18	1,200	125	4,500,000	269,310	379,677	1,015,746	7,299	3,975	0	0	0	0	0	0	10,172
4235	Bethany	20	1	2	24,740	645	5,328,728	43,190	736,782	0	0	847	0	0	0	0	0	8,030	45,820
9185	Bethesda	7	3	6	450	10	3,900,000	19,600	279,115	75,000	0	0	0	0	0	0	0	250	5,822
6285	Calvary	4	1	2	23,784	130	9,750,000	50,900	760,143	0	0	0	0	0	0	0	0	225	20,468
7350	Christ	4	0	2	27	20	625,000	17,444	918,099	0	0	0	0	0	0	0	0	0	225
9175	Clarksburg	5	2	2	30	8	1,393,626	5,154	676,800	0	0	0	0	0	0	0	0	681	0
9270	Community of Faith	24	2	4	500	30	676,800	35,600	281,258	374,374	0	255	0	0	0	0	0	150	90,825
9235	Covenant	3	0	0	3	37	2,164,094	16,629	500	0	0	0	0	0	0	0	0	15,384	275
9490	Daisy	5	3	5	7,260	5	445,200	1,408	512,562	1,368,473	0	2,800	0	0	0	0	0	610	8,712
9190	Damascus	11	1	5	115	632	4,910,000	43,900	3,361,866	14,240	0	0	0	0	0	0	0	350	600
9225	Dickerson	2	5	18	710	14	620,000	7,000	0	0	0	0	0	0	0	0	0	0	31,948
4575	Ebenezer	14	1	1	22	325	1,374,800	9,930	437,198	0	0	0	0	0	0	0	0	500	635
6230	Ebenezer	4	3	6	50	12	825,000	0	80,359	0	0	1,010	0	0	0	0	0	450	7,500
4236	Ellicott City Korean Mission	5	3	9	4,439	31	0	8,440	780,997	184,621	232,605	380	0	0	0	0	0	0	1,129
4245	Emory	11	1	1	150	37	2,500,000	25,895	320,000	0	0	0	0	0	0	0	0	7,000	22,224
9240	Emory Grove	22	0	0	1,918	180	1,871,300	30,000	101,000	0	0	562	0	0	0	0	0	0	37,929
9245	Epworth	14	7	9	4,250	65	6,758,800	10,403	39,281	0	0	0	0	0	0	0	0	0	6,289
9250	Fairhaven	2	0	1	25	5	2,450,000	3,400	9,428	0	0	0	0	0	0	19	0	1,128	0
4345	Fairview	15	7	7	2,400	240	300,000	4,054	0	0	0	0	0	0	0	0	0	0	7,784
6382	FaithPoint	4	0	0	50	7	30,765	0	0	0	0	0	0	0	0	0	0	0	0
6380	Flint Hill	0	0	0	80	0	873,000	2,254	104,771	0	0	0	0	0	0	0	0	200	0
4030	Flohrville	0	0	0	0	8	439,400	24,670	345,140	0	0	0	0	0	0	0	0	576	100
9230	Forest Grove	10	3	2	130	8	320,634	8,000	1,416,653	6,459,650	0	57	0	401	0	0	0	6,500	336
9210	Friendship	8	0	0	300	32	450,000	10,000	182,979	109,204	0	0	0	0	0	0	0	1,707	800
4980	Gaither	20	0	23	31,561	40	763,000	53,000	34,018	1,208,286	0	30,196	0	0	0	0	0	27,874	0
4040	Gary Memorial	49	3	6	1,307	3,444	1,750,000	7,052	2,935,244	0	0	0	0	0	0	0	0	0	61,186
7365	Glen Mar	16	1	7	1,048	215	17,000,000	9,945	130,000	0	0	7,692	0	0	0	0	0	0	34,271
9285	Glenelg	11	1	1	100	199	2,365,567	259,000	594,745	0	0	0	0	0	0	0	0	1,559	70,556
9255	Goshen	2	0	2	50	100	2,450,000	2,315	459,976	47,433	0	20,000	0	0	0	0	0	0	0
9260	Grace	2	2	2	150	30	4,300,000	6,200	36,800	0	0	714	0	0	0	0	0	470	0
9290	Hopkins	13	2	13	500	40	3,555,000	4,494	132,802	0	0	0	0	0	0	0	0	647	0
9355	Howard Chapel-Ridgeville	8	4	2	2	10	600,000	3,641	638,776	566,451	0	1,316	0	20	0	0	0	0	0
9315	Hyattstown	20	5	15	300	10	800,000	6,800	290,600	0	0	0	0	0	0	0	0	2,333	200
6235	Ijamsville	0	0	0	1,000	33	547,153	11,786	1,071,506	0	0	0	0	0	0	0	0	0	576
9510	Jennings Chapel	0	0	0	6,782	110	738,500	51,987	130,000	0	0	89	0	0	0	0	0	470	0
9190	Linden-Linthicum	11	11	10	1,000	60	1,487,600	7,880	236,807	0	0	5,692	0	0	0	0	0	647	6,500
9350	Lisbon	3	0	2	330	43	5,316,040	6,101	268,468	47,433	0	0	0	0	0	0	0	0	1,707
7355	Locust	16	5	5	1,500	41	1,847,000	19,948	419,362	75,634	0	99	0	0	0	0	0	27,874	8,040
6310	Marvin Chapel	3	2	7	1,211	75	1,093,600	23,680	36,650	0	0	0	0	0	0	0	0	0	94,441
9385	Memorial	0	0	0	0	317	419,951	36,612	52,816	0	0	5,692	0	0	0	0	0	2,333	683
9425	Mill Creek Parish	0	0	0	0	16	3,660,000	4,028	47,300	0	0	1,769	0	0	0	0	0	0	8,040
9215	Montgomery	0	0	0	0	0	5,646,000	6,000	419,362	0	0	0	0	0	0	0	0	0	94,441
4585	Morgan Chapel	0	0	0	0	0	4,237,000	7,425	36,650	0	0	0	0	0	0	0	0	2,333	0
9335	Mount Carmel	0	0	0	0	0	1,200,000	4,028	52,816	0	0	0	0	0	0	0	0	0	12,850
4455	Mount Gregory	0	0	0	0	0	578,000	6,000	47,300	0	0	0	0	0	0	0	0	397	683

Align #	Church Name	Total of UMC Causes & UMC Missions & Outreach (48TOTAL)	NON-UMC CAUSES: Total amount given DIRECTLY to non-UMC causes (49)	Human Relations Sunday (50a)	UMCOR Sunday (50b)	Peace with Justice Sunday (50c)	Native American Ministries Sunday (50d)	World Communion Sunday (50e)	U.M. Student Day (50f)	Direct-billed clergy non-health benefits (51)	Direct-billed clergy health benefits (52)	Base comp. Senior Pastor (53a)	Base comp. Associate Pastor(s) (53b)	Base comp. Deacons (53c)	Housing benefits Lead Pastor (55a)	Housing benefits ALL Associate Pastor(s) (55b)	Housing benefits Deacons (55c)	Accountable reimbursements (56)	Non-accountable cash allowances (57)
7345	Alberta Gary Memorial	8,221	1,400	0	0	0	0	0	0	0	0	11,231	0	0	11,231	0	0	290	0
6110	Araby	7,748	6,061	0	0	0	0	0	0	0	0	3,000	0	0	40,000	0	0	0	0
9265	Asbury	0	0	0	0	0	0	0	0	0	0	0	0	0	0	0	0	0	0
9110	Ashton	10,172	4,500	0	0	0	0	0	0	0	0	0	24,000	0	0	0	0	0	0
4235	Bethany	45,800	25,706	0	0	0	0	0	0	12,962	11,827	51,626	0	0	24,000	0	0	1,299	0
9185	Bethesda	5,822	42,837	0	0	0	0	0	0	42,380	71,540	89,462	73,909	0	19,866	39,732	0	4,734	0
6285	Calvary	28,498	21,577	0	0	0	0	0	0	0	0	68,500	62,360	0	8,661	0	0	4,415	0
7350	Christ	475	0	0	0	0	0	50	0	13,509	32,838	58,819	0	0	25,933	0	0	2,653	0
9175	Clarksburg	0	295	20	0	0	25	58	0	0	0	25,626	0	0	0	0	0	1,855	0
9270	Community of Faith	91,706	14,253	0	0	0	0	0	0	23,942	23,984	15,135	0	0	11,720	0	0	0	0
9235	Covenant	425	300	25	0	0	0	0	0	9,223	7,677	20,000	0	0	0	0	0	1,051	0
9490	Daisy	24,096	30,871	0	0	0	1,379	0	0	0	0	38,575	0	0	45,625	0	0	500	0
9190	Damascus	1,210	3,891	0	0	0	0	25	0	26,187	55,277	6,000	0	0	0	0	0	0	0
9225	Dickerson	32,298	0	0	0	0	0	0	0	5,499	0	49,133	39,580	0	49,000	26,900	0	7,445	0
4575	Ebenezer	635	0	0	0	0	0	0	0	13,221	12,875	13,330	0	0	1,990	0	0	0	0
6230	Ebenezer	8,000	3,000	0	0	0	0	0	0	5,700	0	60,077	0	0	19,866	0	0	5,967	20,800
4236	Ellicott City Korean Mission	1,579	0	0	0	0	0	0	0	0	0	20,800	0	0	1,320	0	1,320	20,800	0
4245	Emory	22,224	7,617	263	0	55	45	76	45	2,738	0	29,149	0	0	0	0	0	4,100	0
9240	Emory Grove	37,929	7,534	225	0	232	0	0	449	0	0	29,348	0	0	14,652	0	0	0	1,968
9245	Epworth	13,289	2,490	0	0	0	0	0	0	11,071	19,000	0	0	0	35,398	0	0	3,564	0
9250	Fairhaven	0	0	0	0	235	285	279	280	13,602	13,441	64,815	0	0	5,562	0	0	10,551	0
4345	Fairview	8,912	3,642	0	0	0	0	0	0	600	0	49,308	0	0	36,991	0	0	4,615	300
6382	FaithPoint	0	0	0	0	0	0	0	0	0	11,400	16,000	0	0	2,000	0	0	0	0
6380	Flint Hill	0	100	0	0	0	0	0	0	12,173	0	58,719	0	0	8,909	0	0	859	0
4230	Flohrville	100	0	0	0	0	0	0	0	0	0	9,177	0	0	0	0	0	0	0
9230	Forest Grove	536	1,300	50	30	0	0	0	0	0	0	15,000	0	0	0	0	0	0	0
9210	Friendship	1,376	350	0	150	100	170	0	0	0	0	13,332	0	0	0	0	0	0	0
4200	Gaither	67,686	1,780	0	0	0	0	20	0	0	0	8,183	0	0	16,916	0	0	310	0
4240	Gary Memorial	35,978	2,003	10	0	278	162	182	157	24,669	0	15,957	10,918	0	0	0	0	0	945
7365	Glen Mar	67,686	125,387	0	0	0	0	0	0	13,371	31,694	25,000	0	0	20,000	0	0	300	0
9285	Glenelg	98,430	9,963	0	0	0	0	0	0	13,050	11,676	84,245	54,117	0	40,833	55,630	0	9,640	0
9255	Goshen	0	14,036	804	0	0	0	0	0	14,701	17,589	61,983	0	0	20,462	0	0	4,565	0
9260	Grace	0	84,500	0	0	225	494	215	125	11,194	64,064	80,610	0	0	16,349	0	0	5,145	0
4290	Hopkins	1,559	75	0	0	0	0	0	75	12,719	15,894	31,855	0	0	24,000	0	0	8,115	1,082
9355	Howard Chapel-Ridgeville	0	4,500	0	0	0	170	0	0	8,862	10,500	51,718	0	0	15,710	0	0	1,350	0
9315	Hyattstown	0	16,357	0	0	0	0	0	0	0	0	15,135	0	0	19,866	0	0	4,067	0
6235	Ijamsville	470	21,983	0	0	0	0	0	0	0	0	19,263	0	0	11,720	0	0	0	0
9510	Jennings Chapel	1,330	681	0	0	0	0	0	0	0	0	24,879	0	0	3,632	0	0	0	0
9180	Linden-Linthicum	8,040	918	0	0	0	0	882	0	14,400	17,999	69,579	0	0	30,015	0	0	1,568	0
9350	Lisbon	94,441	3,070	173	0	72	137	0	0	9,518	11,340	41,594	0	0	0	0	0	3,892	0
7355	Locust	0	40,001	45	0	-10	150	529	277	13,453	11,623	62,029	0	0	21,784	0	0	1,537	0
6310	Marvin Chapel	2,333	100	0	0	170	0	0	0	5,007	6,274	13,304	0	0	19,866	0	0	2,504	0
9385	Memorial	12,850	3,070	0	0	0	0	0	0	13,700	12,366	69,380	0	0	15,710	0	0	2,148	0
9425	Mill Creek Parish	94,441	40,001	0	0	0	0	0	0	25,892	17,900	84,872	43,973	0	0	25,740	0	5,327	0
9215	Montgomery	2,333	100	0	0	0	0	0	0	14,672	17,999	73,763	0	0	25,000	0	0	2,590	0
4585	Morgan Chapel	12,850	264	0	0	0	0	0	0	546	0	0	0	0	16,362	0	0	310	0
9335	Mount Carmel	397	0	0	0	0	0	0	0	0	0	17,818	0	0	21,933	0	0	0	3,000
4455	Mount Gregory	397	264	0	0	0	0	0	0	9,433	10,028	22,288	0	0	21,933	0	0	3,001	0

		Paid in salary and benefits for all other church staff and diaconal ministers	Amount spent for local church program expenses	Amount spent for local church operating expenses	Amount paid for principal and interest on indebtedness, loans, mortgages, etc.	Amount paid for capital campaign or fundraising costs	Amount paid on capital expenditures for building, improvements, and major equipment purchases.	Amount PAID by/for the local church on all expenditures	Number of giving units	Received through pledges	Received from non-pledging, but identified givers	Received from unidentified givers	Amount received from interest and dividends and/or transferred from liquid assets	Amount received from Sale of Church Assets	Amount received through building use fees, contributions, and rentals	Amount received through fundraisers and other sources
Align #	Church Name	60	61	62	63	63a	64	65	66	67a	67b	67c	67d	67e	67f	67g
7345	Alberta Gary Memorial	7,280	477	18,520	0	0	9,508	76,594	32	0	53,055	5,276	49	0	17,200	531
6110	Araby	5,539	6,023	14,801	0	0	13,027	105,274	64	0	54,635	1,637	0	0	1,100	1,013
9265	Asbury	11,175	0	9,800	0	0	0	53,012	23	0	42,556	2,451	0	0	0	8,874
9110	Ashton	101,793	3,994	87,511	144,599	0	33,432	540,457	100	165,217	94,825	9,113	0	0	29,410	61,982
4235	Bethany	291,318	67,150	103,979	106,960	0	142,056	1,251,014	430	606,778	510,040	25,695	1,133	0	18,476	19,544
9185	Bethesda	42,913	15,051	38,127	0	0	66,853	398,588	70	0	296,330	4,751	0	0	0	0
6285	Calvary	260,894	21,421	97,992	167,126	1,715	30,583	768,596	319	357,930	231,288	13,403	1,469	0	23,042	2,483
7350	Christ	0	1,581	12,166	0	0	1,306	52,442	31	72,503	15,261	1,500	0	0	0	0
9175	Clarksburg	7,018	1,515	27,751	0	0	0	72,390	37	23,200	12,684	2,923	35,458	0	100	0
9270	Community of Faith	34,000	0	23,548	0	0	0	138,607	40	56,315	36,740	1,249	0	0	10,250	2,490
9235	Covenant	72,441	43,857	97,372	112,897	0	68,806	655,807	230	435,216	63,006	0	328	0	26,652	0
9490	Daisy	0	400	2,500	0	0	0	14,327	11	0	0	0	0	0	0	1,500
9190	Damascus	332,707	37,160	173,727	9,381	0	0	983,861	472	0	883,382	11,805	910	0	44,961	243
9225	Dickerson	0	0	16,950	3,767	0	0	48,198	20	0	31,860	690	0	0	0	0
4575	Ebenezer	38,283	15,421	38,628	0	0	6,715	279,973	107	0	215,560	7,240	952	0	9,900	8,161
6230	Ebenezer	0	0	11,220	0	0	0	86,689	63	0	44,267	3,520	3	0	0	0
4236	Ellicott City Korean Mission	13,600	18,000	16,900	0	0	0	92,749	62	0	232,248	0	0	0	0	0
4245	Emory	21,705	1,762	15,412	0	0	5,587	108,611	41	0	78,497	2,125	20,000	0	3,700	3,170
9240	Emory Grove	116,611	21,214	42,758	38,277	0	22,219	352,549	144	227,191	19,037	5,965	0	0	35,919	51,752
9245	Epworth	110,723	53,253	195,826	0	0	73,199	654,753	239	404,210	92,497	8,509	4,561	0	54,925	0
9250	Fairhaven	36,329	5,520	79,653	0	0	46,521	341,156	59	273,436	4,592	3,175	3,862	0	14,120	0
4345	Fairview	0	0	1	0	0	1,500	23,114	65	0	0	250	0	0	0	2,800
6382	FaithPoint	31,248	479	9,440	0	0	1,409	168,321	53	0	135,255	3,566	31	0	0	0
6380	Flint Hill	0	0	9,831	0	2,800	0	23,970	10	0	17,015	2,169	4	0	0	10,954
4230	Flohrville	0	195	4,165	0	0	0	24,092	0	24,803	0	0	93	0	0	4,370
9230	Forest Grove	0	20	3,700	0	0	300	21,089	13	0	17,500	0	70	0	0	7,000
9210	Friendship	7,250	1,309	21,734	0	0	0	70,299	0	0	0	0	0	0	0	0
4280	Gaither	0	0	39,045	0	0	0	81,500	28	0	69,478	1,730	808	0	0	2,840
4240	Gary Memorial	7,125	400	40,900	0	0	0	104,651	31	0	70,783	3,488	50	0	0	2,021
7365	Glen Mar	720,821	72,880	136,975	926,667	20,669	72,980	2,667,417	1,146	1,178,803	385,928	30,293	403	0	31,661	60,630
9285	Glenelg	110,185	16,643	64,043	22,834	0	212,866	630,160	163	253,726	78,092	42,530	0	0	40,003	3,318
9255	Goshen	61,562	25,208	111,035	209,207	0	4,550	607,550	336	0	478,319	30,586	0	0	33,781	35,847
9260	Grace	256,119	54,062	298,891	0	0	42,580	1,066,827	3,890	488,455	155,518	13,761	57,698	0	39,542	0
9290	Hopkins	16,225	4,548	27,022	0	0	7,218	143,561	71	0	103,194	3,035	0	0	475	21,508
9355	Howard Chapel-Ridgeville	0	1,122	30,142	0	0	79,019	328,543	49	0	75,339	811	669	0	0	0
9315	Hyattstown	5,598	2,258	21,810	0	0	0	75,406	18	0	36,055	1,387	8,767	0	0	0
6235	Ijamsville	0	500	4,358	0	0	0	35,258	27	0	30,155	3,052	120	0	16,000	0
9510	Jennings Chapel	6,222	2,009	16,138	0	0	5,838	87,609	0	0	59,466	1,773	0	0	13,386	2,255
9180	Linden-Linthicum	187,281	16,761	149,047	194,923	0	35,476	816,445	232	337,051	261,610	9,734	16	0	49,080	5,903
9350	Lisbon	12,250	0	49,790	0	0	16,016	155,938	58	0	127,332	4,742	0	0	0	30,440
7355	Locust	21,863	3,956	39,665	0	0	85,630	288,265	136	0	198,193	5,189	0	0	24,817	0
6310	Marvin Chapel	1,478	341	11,327	0	0	0	54,613	25	0	32,492	2,165	0	0	0	0
9385	Memorial	48,755	27,841	57,901	30,272	0	84,038	415,099	120	263,757	12,672	3,150	5,215	0	20,365	3,761
9425	Mill Creek Parish	104,938	25,459	70,933	71,928	0	4,259	640,785	111	388,406	52,527	9,214	0	0	79,855	3,246
9215	Montgomery	106,610	31,645	145,913	0	0	0	503,225	187	0	431,619	17,654	7,380	0	800	8,769
4585	Morgan Chapel	0	339	7,617	0	0	0	42,324	21	0	23,975	3,789	30	0	1,865	3,945
9335	Mount Carmel	0	0	11,172	0	0	0	32,990	0	0	16,143	2,973	7,000	0	300	2,805
4455	Mount Gregory	10,045	4,239	14,439	0	0	21,465	122,700	30	50,672	3,457	3,237	0	0	275	14,444

Align #	Church Name	TOTAL income for annual budget/spending plan (67a-g) [67]	Capital campaigns [68a]	Memorials, endowments, and bequests [68b]	Other sources and projects (include UMW, UMM and 'flow-through') [68c]	Special Sundays, Gen. Adv. Spec., World Srvc Spec., Conf. Adv Spec. and other directed benevolent giving [68d]	Total income for designated causes incl. capital campaign and other special projects [68]	Equitable Compensation Funds received by Church or Pastor [69a]	Advance Special, apportioned, and connectional funds received by church [69b]	Other grants and financial support from institutional sources [69c]	Income from connectional/institutional sources outside the local church [69]	TOTAL CHURCH INCOME (Sum of Lines 67 + 68 + 69) [7D]	Amount APPORTIONED to the local church [40a]	Amount PAID by the local church for all apportioned causes [40b]
7345	Alberta Gary Memorial	76,111	0	0	0	0	0	0	0	0	0	76,111	8,436	8,436
6110	Araby	58,385	0	0	0	0	0	0	0	0	0	58,385	9,075	9,075
9265	Asbury	53,891	0	0	0	0	0	0	0	0	0	53,891	8,037	8,037
9110	Ashton	360,547	0	3,334	174,531	0	177,865	0	0	0	0	538,412	48,767	48,767
4235	Bethany	1,181,666	0	29,617	78,782	137,742	246,141	0	0	0	0	1,427,807	126,322	126,322
9185	Bethesda	301,081	623	800	0	44,199	45,622	0	0	0	0	346,703	42,202	42,202
6285	Calvary	629,615	0	20,515	182,402	46,566	249,483	0	0	0	0	879,098	81,032	81,032
7350	Christ	89,264	0	0	0	170	170	0	0	0	0	89,434	6,753	6,753
9175	Clarksburg	74,365	0	0	0	551	551	0	0	0	0	74,916	9,388	9,388
9270	Community of Faith	107,044	0	0	10,500	0	10,500	0	0	0	0	117,544	8,906	8,906
9235	Covenant	525,202	0	0	0	0	0	0	0	0	0	525,202	50,945	50,945
9490	Daisy	1,500	0	0	0	0	0	0	0	0	0	1,500	4,152	4,152
9190	Damascus	941,301	20,168	3,540	33,700	4,502	61,910	0	0	0	0	1,003,211	122,397	122,397
9225	Dickerson	32,550	0	0	0	0	0	0	0	0	0	32,550	5,452	5,452
4575	Ebenezer	241,813	142,606	17,048	0	17,403	177,057	0	0	0	0	418,870	29,931	29,931
6230	Ebenezer	47,790	0	0	0	0	0	0	0	0	0	47,790	4,094	4,094
4236	Elliott City Korean Mission	232,248	0	0	0	0	0	15,000	0	0	15,000	247,248	0	0
4245	Emory	107,492	229	595	300	2,924	4,048	0	0	0	0	111,540	14,597	14,597
9240	Emory Grove	339,864	0	0	11,727	1,244	12,971	0	0	14,500	14,500	367,335	39,375	39,375
9245	Epworth	564,702	68,297	250	0	0	68,547	0	65,000	0	65,000	698,249	65,290	65,290
9250	Fairhaven	299,185	0	8,299	0	0	8,299	0	0	0	0	307,484	36,802	36,802
4345	Fairview	3,050	0	0	0	0	0	0	0	0	0	3,050	3,013	3,013
6362	FaithPoint	138,852	0	986	0	0	986	0	0	0	0	139,838	15,504	12,920
6380	Flint Hill	30,142	0	986	0	0	986	0	0	0	0	31,128	4,862	4,862
4230	Flohrville	29,266	0	0	0	0	0	0	0	0	0	29,266	3,432	3,432
9230	Forest Grove	24,570	0	0	0	0	0	0	0	0	0	24,570	3,287	3,287
9210	Friendship	0	0	0	0	0	0	0	0	0	0	0	0	0
4280	Gaither	74,856	0	0	0	87	87	0	0	0	0	74,943	11,335	11,335
4240	Gary Memorial	76,342	0	5,900	0	0	5,900	0	0	0	0	82,242	11,713	11,713
7365	Glen Mar	1,687,718	796,880	11,257	1,961	829	810,927	0	0	2,270	2,270	2,500,915	212,208	212,208
9285	Glenelg	417,669	6,475	700	34,725	707	42,607	0	0	0	0	460,276	45,591	45,591
9255	Goshen	578,533	0	0	0	0	0	0	0	0	0	578,533	52,714	52,714
9260	Grace	754,974	0	1,071,490	0	45,136	1,116,626	0	0	0	0	1,871,600	101,384	101,384
9290	Hopkins	127,212	0	7,890	0	0	7,890	0	0	0	0	135,102	16,164	12,470
9355	Howard Chapel-Ridgeville	76,819	0	301,188	0	0	301,188	0	0	0	0	378,007	14,990	14,990
9315	Hyattstown	46,209	0	0	0	1,084	1,084	0	0	0	0	47,293	8,864	8,864
6235	Ijamsville	49,327	0	0	0	56	56	0	0	0	0	49,383	6,637	6,637
9510	Jennings Chapel	76,880	0	100	9,466	910	10,476	0	0	0	0	87,356	9,407	9,407
9180	Linden-Linthicum	663,394	98,355	690	32,053	19,223	150,321	0	0	0	0	813,715	72,087	72,087
9350	Lisbon	162,514	0	0	0	0	0	0	0	0	0	162,514	12,023	12,023
7355	Locust	228,199	30,744	0	0	347	31,091	0	0	0	0	259,290	23,747	23,747
6310	Marvin Chapel	34,657	0	0	0	334	334	0	0	0	0	34,991	10,926	10,926
9385	Memorial	308,920	0	52,135	78,596	0	130,731	0	0	0	0	439,651	40,060	40,060
9425	Mill Creek Parish	533,248	0	325	0	31,021	31,346	0	0	0	0	564,594	61,905	61,905
9215	Montgomery	466,222	0	4,742	0	0	4,742	0	0	0	0	470,964	63,663	42,654
4585	Morgan Chapel	33,604	0	0	8,024	0	8,024	0	0	0	0	41,628	2,704	2,704
9385	Mount Carmel	29,221	0	0	0	0	0	0	0	0	0	29,221	5,403	1,200
4455	Mount Gregory	72,085	2,422	0	0	0	2,422	0	0	0	0	74,507	5,168	5,168

Column codes:
- **1** – Total professing members at the close of 2017
- **2a1** – Received by PROFESSION of Faith
- **2a2** – Received by PROFESSION of Faith (Other Than Confirmation)
- **2b** – Restored by AFFIRMATION of Faith
- **3** – Transferred in from other UM churches
- **4** – Transferred in from non-UM churches
- **5a** – Removed or corrected by Charge Conference action
- **5b** – Withdrawn from Professing Membership
- **6** – Transferred out to other UM churches
- **7** – Transferred out to non-UM churches
- **8** – Removed by death
- **9** – Total professing members at the close of 2018
- **9a** – Asian Professing Members
- **9b** – African American / Black Professing Members
- **9c** – Hispanic / Latino Professing Members
- **9d** – Native American Professing Members
- **9e** – Pacific Islander Professing Members
- **9f** – White Professing Members
- **9g** – Multi-Racial Professing Members
- **9h** – Female Professing Members
- **9i** – Male Professing Members

Align #	Church Name	Dist #	City	State	1	2a1	2a2	2b	3	4	5a	5b	6	7	8	9	9a	9b	9c	9d	9e	9f	9g	9h	9i
4590	Mount Olive	CM	Mount Airy	MD	68	6	0	0	0	0	0	0	0	0	1	73	0	0	0	0	0	73	0	42	31
4190	Mount Olivet	CM	Catonsville	MD	75	0	0	0	0	0	7	0	0	0	5	63	0	63	0	0	0	0	0	49	14
9340	Mount Tabor	CM	Laytonsville	MD	84	0	0	0	0	0	0	0	0	0	0	84	0	0	0	0	0	84	0	40	44
4250	Mount Zion	CM	Ellicott City	MD	46	0	1	0	0	0	0	0	46	0	0	0	0	0	0	0	0	0	0	0	0
9310	Mount Zion	CM	Highland	MD	582	0	0	0	8	1	5	0	1	0	8	582	3	10	2	0	0	563	4	309	273
9370	Mount Zion	CM	Olney	MD	89	0	3	0	3	4	1	0	4	1	1	89	0	84	0	0	0	5	0	73	16
9220	Mountain View	CM	Damascus	MD	99	0	0	3	0	0	56	13	8	3	2	97	0	0	0	0	0	97	0	53	44
9375	Oakdale Emory	CM	Olney	MD	864	0	1	0	3	1	0	0	0	0	4	787	6	23	6	1	1	746	4	477	310
9320	Pleasant Grove	CM	Ijamsville	MD	98	0	0	0	0	0	0	0	0	0	1	97	0	0	0	0	0	97	0	59	38
9360	Poplar Springs	CM	Mount Airy	MD	92	0	0	0	1	1	0	0	0	0	1	91	0	0	0	0	0	91	0	55	36
6315	Prospect	CM	Mount Airy	MD	134	0	0	0	0	0	0	0	0	0	0	134	0	0	0	0	0	133	1	80	54
9325	Providence	CM	Monrovia	MD	192	0	0	0	0	0	0	0	0	0	3	189	1	0	1	0	0	186	1	101	88
9255	Rockland	CM	Ellicott City	MD	65	0	0	0	0	0	0	0	0	0	0	65	0	0	0	0	0	0	0	0	0
9150	Salem	CM	Brookeville	MD	160	5	1	0	0	0	0	0	0	0	1	157	3	1	1	0	0	149	3	90	67
9275	Salem	CM	Germantown	MD	142	4	0	0	0	0	3	0	0	3	2	141	0	1	0	0	0	139	1	87	54
9445	Sharp Street	CM	Sandy Spring	MD	180	0	0	1	0	0	0	0	0	0	1	104	0	99	0	0	0	4	1	74	30
9365	Simpson	CM	Mount Airy	MD	37	2	0	0	0	0	0	0	1	0	1	36	0	36	0	0	0	0	0	29	7
4565	St James	CM	Marriottsville	MD	221	0	0	0	0	0	0	0	1	0	2	207	2	0	0	0	0	203	2	111	96
7360	St John United Church	CM	Columbia	MD	72	1	2	0	0	0	4	10	0	0	2	74	2	31	0	0	0	41	0	45	29
4460	St Luke	CM	Sykesville	MD	50	0	0	0	5	0	0	0	0	0	1	65	0	0	0	0	0	63	2	37	28
9145	St Marks	CM	Boyds	MD	31	3	3	0	2	4	5	1	5	0	1	29	0	29	0	0	0	0	0	23	6
9345	St Paul	CM	Laytonsville	MD	142	0	0	0	0	0	0	0	0	0	7	129	0	3	0	0	0	126	0	73	56
4465	St Paul's	CM	Sykesville	MD	493	41	0	0	18	0	0	0	0	0	3	490	0	8	0	0	0	482	0	245	245
9280	Trinity	CM	Germantown	MD	264	0	1	0	1	0	0	2	0	0	0	256	15	49	3	0	0	189	0	141	115
9470	Washington Grove	CM	Washington Grove	MD	94	0	0	1	0	0	0	0	0	0	5	91	0	0	0	1	0	90	1	50	41
6385	Wesley Chapel	CM	Frederick	MD	171	0	0	0	0	0	0	0	0	5	7	166	0	0	0	0	0	165	1	99	67
4225	Wesley Freedom	CM	Eldersburg	MD	1,767	15	0	0	0	0	0	0	0	0	3	1,857	12	7	0	0	0	1,836	2	1,032	825
9515	Wesley Grove	CM	Gaithersburg	MD	256	0	1	0	0	0	2	2	0	0	1	122	1	3	2	0	0	112	4	58	64
4343	West Liberty	CM	Marriottsville	MD	98	0	0	0	0	0	0	0	0	0	0	97	0	87	0	0	0	4	6	54	43
9580	West Montgomery	CM	Dickerson	MD	150	0	0	0	0	0	0	0	0	0	0	150	0	149	0	0	0	1	0	114	36
CM Total					**21,552**	**201**	**141**	**36**	**100**	**50**	**242**	**103**	**179**	**61**	**204**	**21,018**	**366**	**2,862**	**190**	**31**	**14**	**17,475**	**80**	**12,099**	**6,919**

Align.#	Church Name	10	10a	11a	11b	11T	12	13	14	15	16	17	18	19	20	22	23	24	25	26	27	28	29	30a	30b
4590	Mount Olive	25	0	3	0	3	0	15	6	28	8	0	10	46	10	0	0	1	0	0	0	12	1,231	0	0
4190	Mount Olivet	21	0	0	0	0	0	0	0	0	0	0	7	7	5	20	2	2	1	5	8,160	22	580	0	0
9340	Mount Tabor	13	0	0	0	0	4	0	0	0	0	0	6	6	5	20	0	2	1	5	0	14	1,400	0	0
4250	Mount Zion	0	0	4	1	5	3	0	0	0	0	0	6	6	0	0	0	1	0	0	0	14	0	0	0
9310	Mount Zion	236	0	0	0	0	110	110	0	173	33	8	146	360	62	165	14	12	10	10	250	100	2,458	3	23
9370	Mount Zion	30	0	0	0	0	0	2	0	2	6	0	9	17	14	0	0	2	5	0	0	14	400	0	0
9220	Mountain View	24	33	13	5	18	0	2	0	5	2	0	5	7	4	0	0	2	0	0	0	0	0	0	0
9375	Oakdale Emory	630	0	0	0	0	2	197	0	663	156	62	437	1,318	91	330	11	51	32	35	27,792	38	3,330	1	6
9320	Pleasant Grove	28	0	0	0	0	567	0	0	2	4	0	20	22	7	10	3	2	1	0	0	21	600	0	0
9360	Poplar Springs	25	0	0	0	0	0	0	0	4	0	0	27	35	24	0	0	0	0	0	0	0	0	0	0
6315	Prospect	26	0	1	0	1	0	7	0	6	0	0	6	6	0	0	2	2	1	0	0	9	1,000	0	0
9325	Providence	68	0	0	1	2	5	18	2	5	6	0	6	12	10	38	0	0	3	0	0	12	2,000	0	0
4255	Rockland	0	0	0	0	0	2	40	0	2	2	0	49	62	10	0	2	0	0	7	1,080	0	0	0	0
9150	Salem	53	0	2	0	2	0	0	5	8	9	2	6	62	10	0	0	3	4	12	500	30	1,360	0	0
9275	Salem	10	0	0	5	7	191	0	0	0	0	0	8	8	2	0	0	1	0	6	0	9	0	0	0
9445	Sharp Street	65	0	2	0	0	10	0	0	24	19	0	27	27	25	0	0	0	15	12	0	0	0	0	0
9365	Simpson	20	0	0	0	0	0	0	0	14	6	0	8	8	6	42	0	0	1	6	0	9	0	0	0
4565	St James	80	0	1	0	1	0	47	4	6	6	8	44	95	28	0	1	5	1	0	0	15	1,698	1	6
7360	St John United Church	97	0	0	3	3	0	0	1	14	6	0	13	33	10	0	2	3	0	0	0	0	0	0	0
4460	St Luke	35	0	3	0	3	0	47	0	6	6	0	5	10	0	0	1	2	0	0	0	0	0	0	0
9145	St Marks	17	0	0	1	1	44	3	2	7	0	0	5	5	3	1	0	1	1	0	0	8	3,525	0	0
9345	St Paul	37	4	1	0	4	40	59	3	39	85	14	50	188	34	10	8	1	2	24	0	8	8,600	0	0
4465	St Paul's	150	5	4	2	0	40	101	0	56	49	6	40	151	20	122	7	5	6	0	0	30	0	0	0
9280	Trinity	120	0	1	2	0	4	1	0	4	0	0	18	46	20	60	0	5	6	0	0	2	0	0	0
9470	Washington Grove	19	0	0	0	0	5	41	0	15	12	1	18	28	20	8	2	3	2	0	0	4	1,200	0	0
6385	Wesley Chapel	58	30	0	0	0	9	900	41	561	193	20	357	1,131	263	726	25	18	7	0	200	12	1,450	0	0
4225	Wesley Freedom	555	0	36	6	42	900	47	41	561	193	20	357	1,131	263	726	25	18	7	0	200	12	1,450	0	0
9515	Wesley Grove	43	0	0	0	0	47	47	0	6	6	0	16	28	10	78	2	2	2	0	0	18	3,600	0	0
4343	West Liberty	35	0	0	0	0	14	14	0	6	6	0	13	13	5	19	0	4	4	12	0	9	0	0	0
9580	West Montgomery	35	0	0	0	0	0	0	0	7	0	0	15	15	12	30	3	4	0	10	0	15	0	0	0
CM Total		**7,496**	**688**	**150**	**55**	**205**	**2,703**	**6,207**	**205**	**2,880**	**1,524**	**402**	**4,227**	**9,033**	**2,165**	**4,054**	**295**	**423**	**299**	**441**	**61,987**	**639**	**71,558**	**6**	**42**

Column headers:
- 10: Average attendance at all weekly worship service(s)
- 10a: Persons who Worship Online
- 11a: Number of Infants and Children baptized (Age 0-12)
- 11b: Number of Teens and Adults baptized (Age 13+)
- 11T: TOTAL Number of persons baptized (all ages)
- 12: Number of baptized members who have not become Professing
- 13: Number of other constituents of the church
- 14: Total enrolled in confirmation preparation classes that
- 15: CHILDREN (0-11yrs) in all Christian groups, small groups and Sunday School.
- 16: YOUTH (12-18 yrs) in all Christian groups, small groups and Sunday School.
- 17: YOUNG ADULTS (19-30 yrs) in all Christian groups, small groups and Sunday School.
- 18: OTHER ADULTS (31+ yrs) in all Christian groups, small groups and Sunday School.
- 19: TOTAL number of persons participating in Christian formation groups (Total lines 15 - 18).
- 20: Average weekly attendance, Education classes/groups that meet in Sunday Church School groups.
- 22: Number of participants in Vacation Bible School
- 23: Number of ongoing classes (all ages) for learning in Sunday Church
- 24: Number of ONGOING small groups, support groups, or classes
- 25: Number of SHORT-TERM classes, support groups, or small groups offered
- 26: Membership in United Methodist Men (UMM)
- 27: Amount paid for projects (UMM)
- 28: Membership in United Methodist Women (UMW)
- 29: Amount paid for local church and community work (UMW)
- 30a: Number of UMVIM teams sent out from this church
- 30b: Number of persons sent out on UMVIM teams from this church

Align #	Church Name	33 Total Community Ministries (outreach, justice, mercy)	33a Ministries focusing on global/regional health	33b Ministries focusing on engaging in ministry with the poor/socially	34 Persons served by community ministries	35a Persons serving in mission/community ministries	36 Market value of church-owned land, buildings and equipment	36.5F Overall square footage of church-owned buildings	37 Market value of financial and other liquid assets	38 Debt secured by church physical assets	39 Other debt	42 General Advance Specials	43 World Service Specials	44 Annual Conference Advance Specials	45 Youth Service Fund	46 All other funds sent to AC Treasurer	47 Total AC Special Sunday Offerings	48b UMC Causes (given directly)	48b Missions/Ministry costs (direct costs)
4590	Mount Olive	7	0	5	450	40	860,000	6,400	125,000	0	0	0	0	0	0	0	0	2,000	1,096
4190	Mount Olivet	0	0	3	45	3	375,000	300	2,570	0	0	35	0	0	0	0	0	0	545
9340	Mount Tabor	4	0	3	110	15	770,000	4,500	260,000	0	0	0	0	0	0	200	0	100	0
4250	Mount Zion	0	0	0	0	0	0	0	0	0	0	0	0	0	0	0	0	0	0
9310	Mount Zion	6	0	3	18,100	1,000	6,897,000	26,600	424,739	16,893	1,500	9,925	0	0	0	0	0	38,112	908
9370	Mount Zion	3	1	2	278	33	431,500	3,210	75,000	19,954	0	251	0	0	0	0	0	251	2,312
9220	Mountain View	31	6	31	100	20	741,144	67,600	560,519	0	0	0	0	0	0	0	0	43,907	1,317
9375	Oakdale Emory	3	0	1	99,999	1,000	11,636,838	5,288	0	2,440,041	0	211	0	164	0	0	0	100	0
9320	Pleasant Grove	3	2	1	800	25	682,200	5,587	134,424	0	0	600	0	238	0	0	0	0	420
9360	Poplar Springs	12	10	10	5,552	38	952,750	8,370	35,000	0	0	0	0	0	0	0	0	216	1,994
6315	Prospect	0	0	0	0	26	510,300	67,000	187,850	0	0	0	0	0	0	0	0	4,206	9,838
9325	Providence	0	0	0	0	100	1,540,350	0	0	0	0	0	0	0	0	0	0	0	0
4255	Rockland	4	0	4	263	162	0	7,600	315,730	0	0	0	0	0	0	0	0	0	0
9150	Salem	0	0	0	100	5	2,000,000	4,878	281,000	0	0	0	0	0	0	0	0	0	0
9275	Salem	4	1	3	250	60	1,000,000	3,000	60,000	0	0	0	0	0	0	0	0	0	0
9445	Sharp Street	0	0	0	0	0	1,212,000	1,500	0	0	0	2,950	0	0	0	0	0	3,150	1,876
9365	Simpson	6	2	6	1,500	110	150,000	15,600	593,969	0	0	75	75	476	0	0	0	461	43
4565	St James	4	0	0	300	93	4,601,200	1,344	501,487	0	0	0	0	0	0	-9	0	94	0
7360	St John United Church	0	0	0	0	2	0	87,120	0	0	1,592	0	0	0	0	0	0	0	0
4460	St Luke	0	0	0	0	0	583,500	14,000	0	0	0	0	0	0	0	0	0	0	46
9145	St Marks	18	0	10	0	52	479,000	20,100	112,336	0	1,277	2,500	0	70	0	0	0	0	0
9345	St Paul	6	11	0	1,175	210	2,297,500	13,740	400,000	0	0	2,544	0	588	0	0	0	0	33,312
4465	St Paul's	2	0	2	0	55	3,554,000	4,200	0	406,345	0	1,097	0	0	0	0	0	0	916
9280	Trinity	3	0	3	75	15	1,980,967	4,785	16,530	0	0	50	0	435	0	0	0	0	1,147
9470	Washington Grove	23	0	3	200	45	900,000	36,867	212,156	0	0	0	0	0	0	0	0	0	1,147
6385	Wesley Chapel	25	0	23	60,000	715	1,771,300	6,200	829,932	2,149,173	0	7,035	0	0	0	0	0	250	50,352
4225	Wesley Freedom	5	11	15	1,425	42	3,578,555	6,800	550,000	0	0	0	0	0	0	0	0	346	3,824
9515	Wesley Grove	0	0	4	601	61	700,000	6,629	253,000	0	0	0	0	0	0	0	0	0	4,799
4343	West Liberty	0	0	0	0	0	517,100	0	400,000	0	0	0	0	0	0	0	0	0	0
9580	West Montgomery	0	0	0	0	0	1,451,600	0	0	0	0	0	0	0	0	0	0	0	0
	CM Total	502	119	344	311,473	11,301	165,416,562	1,646,573	25,669,530	17,671,230	244,273	104,627	75	2,392	0	210	0	171,336	712,334

Column key:
- **48TOTAL** — Total of UMC Causes & UMC Missions & Outreach
- **49** — NON-UMC CAUSES: Total amount given DIRECTLY to non-United Methodist benevolent and charitable causes (NOT sent to BWC Treasurer)
- **50a** — Human Relations Sunday
- **50b** — UMCOR Sunday (formerly One Great Hour of Sharing)
- **50c** — Peace with Justice Sunday
- **50d** — Native American Ministries Sunday
- **50e** — World Communion Sunday
- **50f** — U.M. Student Day
- **51** — Direct-billed clergy non-health benefits
- **52** — Direct-billed clergy health benefits
- **53a** — Base compensation paid to/for the Senior Pastor or other person assigned or appointed in the lead pastoral role to the church
- **53b** — Base compensation paid/for to all Associate Pastor(s) & other pastoral staff assigned or appointed to the church
- **53c** — Base compensation paid to/for any Deacons NOT included in 53a or 53b
- **55a** — Housing benefits paid to/for Lead Pastor or person in lead pastoral role as described in 53a
- **55b** — Housing benefits paid to/for ALL Associate Pastor(s) & other pastoral staff assigned or appointed to the church
- **55c** — Housing benefits paid to/for any Deacons not included in 53a or 53b
- **56** — Paid to/for all persons included in Lines 53a-53c for accountable reimbursements
- **57** — Paid to/for all persons included in Lines 53a-53c for any other cash allowances (non-)

Align #	Church Name	48TOTAL	49	50a	50b	50c	50d	50e	50f	51	52	53a	53b	53c	55a	55b	55c	56	57
4590	Mount Olive	3,096	0	0	0	0	0	0	0	0	0	8,644	0	0	14,956	0	0	4,725	0
4190	Mount Olivet	545	0	25	0	0	0	0	0	0	0	11,725	0	0	5,237	0	0	963	0
9340	Mount Tabor	100	0	0	0	0	0	0	0	0	0	17,125	4,732	0	17,125	0	0	0	1,367
4250	Mount Zion	0	12,625	0	0	0	0	0	0	13,818	17,818	69,825	0	0	20,065	0	0	1,673	0
9310	Mount Zion	39,020	0	200	0	0	0	0	0	0	0	15,318	0	0	12,000	0	0	221	0
9370	Mount Zion	251	108,607	0	0	79	860	0	0	0	0	22,075	0	0	9,933	0	0	2,050	500
9220	Mountain View	2,312	0	0	0	0	0	0	0	11,523	11,400	104,387	60,438	0	24,183	9,561	0	24,883	0
9375	Oakdale Emory	45,224	244	0	0	0	0	0	0	32,603	44,890	22,075	0	0	9,933	0	0	2,050	0
9320	Pleasant Grove	100	783	0	0	0	0	0	0	0	0	23,913	0	0	3,632	0	0	1,841	0
9360	Poplar Springs	420	8,673	0	0	10	92	10	0	11,196	11,400	13,304	0	0	0	0	0	0	516
6315	Prospect	2,210	0	0	725	0	0	0	0	10,832	10,320	47,642	0	0	4,885	0	0	622	500
9325	Providence	4,206	3,880	0	0	0	0	0	0	0	0	0	0	0	0	0	0	0	0
4255	Rockland	0	0	0	0	0	0	0	0	12,704	15,760	80,085	4,632	0	5,761	0	0	363	0
9150	Salem	9,838	0	0	0	0	0	0	0	0	0	17,000	0	0	2,861	0	0	500	0
9275	Salem	0	2,350	0	0	0	0	0	0	4,001	4,170	40,000	0	0	0	0	0	0	0
9445	Sharp Street	0	2,869	0	0	0	0	0	0	0	0	13,780	0	0	0	0	0	0	0
9365	Simpson	5,026	0	0	0	0	0	0	0	9,937	11,467	44,166	0	0	0	0	0	1,314	0
4565	St. James	504	3,655	0	0	0	0	0	0	13,239	11,760	17,692	0	0	18,798	0	0	3,929	0
7360	St. John United Church	94	5,766	59	788	0	0	75	100	0	0	22,000	0	0	0	0	0	941	0
4460	St. Luke	0	2,709	96	0	0	0	0	0	5,422	16,164	10,655	0	0	1,822	0	0	661	0
9145	St. Marks	46	303	0	0	0	0	0	0	26,395	39,501	12,525	0	0	5,206	0	0	10,524	0
9345	St. Paul	33,312	400	0	0	20	0	170	0	15,909	21,811	63,827	42,636	0	19,866	9,746	0	1,109	0
4465	St. Paul's	916	0	25	170	45	0	0	0	10,705	21,492	56,939	0	0	21,288	0	0	1,453	0
9280	Trinity	0	19,169	0	0	0	0	0	0	10,746	12,377	34,000	0	0	19,450	0	0	4,222	0
9470	Washington Grove	2,294	2,789	0	0	0	0	0	63	26,355	30,200	52,100	0	0	7,592	0	0	9,117	0
6385	Wesley Chapel	50,602		0	0	0	0	0	0	11,475	11,400	65,839	45,573	0	30,000	0	0	363	0
4225	Wesley Freedom	4,170		0	0	0	0	0	0	0	0	17,000	4,632	0	2,861	20,008	0	0	0
9515	Wesley Grove	4,799		0	0	0	0	0	0	6,256	5,700	16,824	0	0	0	0	0	2,500	0
4343	West Liberty			0	0	0	0	0	0	0	0	42,060	0	0	22,944	0	0	0	0
9580	West Montgomery			0	0	0	0	0	0									2,500	
	CM Total	883,670	681,040	2,020	1,863	1,531	3,809	2,571	1,571	631,110	814,335	2,743,291	471,500	0	950,445	187,317	1,320	207,091	31,495

Align #	Church Name	60 Paid in salary and benefits for all other church staff and diaconal ministers	61 Amount spent for local church program expenses	62 Amount spent for local church operating expenses	63 Amount paid for principal and interest on indebtedness, loans, mortgages, etc.	63a Amount paid for capital campaign or fundraising costs	64 Amount paid on capital expenditures for building, improvements, and major equipment purchases.	65 Amount PAID by/for the local church on all expenditures	66 Number of giving units	67a Received through pledges	67b Received from non-pledging, but identified givers	67c Received from unidentified givers	67d Amount received from interest and dividends and/or transferred from liquid assets	67e Amount received from Sale of Church Assets	67f Amount received through building use fees, contributions, and rentals	67g Amount received through fundraisers and other sources
4590	Mount Olive	0	760	10,588	0	0	9,770	58,332	30	0	46,866	1,899	9,500	0	4,642	1,753
4190	Mount Olivet	8,320	3,595	11,917	0	0	28,401	78,375	40	0	49,815	1,689	2	0	525	4,732
9340	Mount Tabor	0	107	17,545	0	12,447	8,592	58,181	13	0	32,820	899	899	0	19,953	22,940
4250	Mount Zion	0	0	0	0	0	0	659		0	0	0	0	0	0	0
9310	Mount Zion	241,006	30,911	86,080	74,527	0	65,858	768,278	248	452,555	201,000	5,365	899	0	59,743	7,847
9370	Mount Zion	0	3,078	30,247	10,135	0	3,912	82,929	28	31,816	14,027	0	0	0	510	0
9220	Mountain View	2,400	0	9,300	192,011	0	0	76,087	33	0	43,209	100	0	0	1,000	4,000
9375	Oakdale Emory	788,491	117,114	89,949	0	0	0	1,828,156	587	0	1,869,390	85,095	4,443	0	45,431	0
9320	Pleasant Grove	2,808	0	11,131	0	0	0	56,386	26	0	54,917	0	71	0	0	14,442
9360	Poplar Springs	2,948	1,290	17,874	0	0	2,543	81,978	25	0	46,305	3,905	0	0	8,609	6,777
6315	Prospect	14,302	0	19,875	0	0	0	64,382	64	0	49,063	6,187	681	0	1,596	16,349
9325	Providence	16,712	2,572	38,477	0	0	16,760	181,405	71	0	188,309	2,883	0	0	634	0
4255	Rockland	0	0	1	0	0	0	1	0	0	0	0	0	0	0	0
9150	Salem	36,603	3,983	23,973	0	0	3,805	222,876	69	119,018	69,237	3,312	0	220,000	5,190	50
9275	Salem	0	200	16,000	0	0	2,000	50,586	12	0	9,256	700	0	0	6,220	10,300
9445	Sharp Street	12,680	3,000	34,000	0	1,500	4,000	125,110	55	97,000	90,000	2,700	1,000	0	0	2,684
9365	Simpson	1,620	0	9,108	0	0	0	27,778	28	0	720	2,640	40	0	0	0
4565	St James	38,510	2,948	50,351	0	0	0	174,597	92	150,674	27,855	2,066	67	0	13,931	685
7360	St John United Church	37,185	4,589	37,860	133,673	7,364	9,750	175,343	85	139,881	2,531	3,171	0	0	0	3,646
4460	St Luke	9,221	594	12,685	0	0	2,465	61,269	64	0	52,306	1,850	0	0	0	3,595
9145	St Marks	2,400	1,585	12,043	3,973	232	1,032	35,181	22	0	37,229	1,568	0	0	0	7,096
9345	St Paul	25,860	2,527	34,368	0	0	29,877	124,235	64	75,589	39,132	8,452	0	0	975	0
4465	St Paul's	80,362	36,123	62,100	49,792	3,025	13,646	516,065	196	0	427,344	7,369	0	0	505	17,379
9280	Trinity	79,380	11,585	92,497	0	0	0	405,920	157	177,992	79,787	1,358	1,240	0	136,395	7,080
9470	Washington Grove	0	0	14,044	0	0	15,415	108,823	24	0	35,758	2,821	584	0	68,858	11,510
6385	Wesley Chapel	0	9,669	19,572	0	1,060	39,265	147,680	65	0	103,491	48,404	0	0	520	27,470
4225	Wesley Freedom	299,558	62,810	176,274	0	0	18,589	1,129,171	705	173,998	766,433	1,922	0	0	87,116	49,390
9515	Wesley Grove	20,084	2,199	37,807	0	0	1,852	147,826	52	0	69,099	0	0	0	12,520	120
4343	West Liberty	7,092	2,061	4,250	0	0	0	42,135		33,724	0	0	0	0	120	36,312
9580	West Montgomery	0	0	22,604	0	0	0	106,462	58	0	78,822	0	0	0	57,490	15,027
CM Total		4,947,446	909,313	3,524,596	2,502,949	50,812	1,472,488	23,243,604	12,327	7,059,916	10,369,198	507,660	175,698	220,000	1,174,443	659,763

Align #	Church Name	TOTAL income for annual budget/spending plan. (67a-g) 67	Capital campaigns 68a	Memorials, endowments, and bequests 68b	Other sources and projects (include UMW, UMM and 'flow-through') 68c	Special Sundays, Gen. Adv. Spec, World Srvc Spec., Conf. Adv. Spec. and other directed benevolent giving 68d	Total income for designated causes including capital campaign and other special projects 68	Equitable Compensation Funds received by Church or Pastor 69a	Advance Special, apportioned, and connectional funds received by church 69b	Other grants and financial support from institutional sources 69c	Income from connectional / institutional sources outside the local church 69	TOTAL CHURCH INCOME (Sum of Lines 67 + 68 + 69) 70	Amount APPORTIONED to the local church 40a	Amount PAID by the local church for all apportioned causes 40b
4590	Mount Olive	64,660	0	2,270	0	0	2,270	0	0	0	0	66,930	5,793	5,793
4190	Mount Olivet	56,763	27,901	0	2,572	379	30,852	0	0	0	0	87,615	7,412	7,412
9340	Mount Tabor	76,612	0	100	0	0	100	0	0	0	0	76,712	8,613	8,613
4250	Mount Zion	0	0	0	0	0	0	0	0	0	0	0	5,077	658
9310	Mount Zion	719,562	17,078	5,365	0	37,091	59,534	0	0	0	0	779,096	83,263	83,263
9370	Mount Zion	54,200	0	0	0	251	251	828	5,000	0	5,828	60,279	7,016	7,016
9220	Mountain View	48,309	0	2,300	0	0	2,300	0	0	0	0	50,609	7,832	5,094
9375	Oakdale Emory	2,004,359	40,412	15,207	0	0	55,619	0	0	700	700	2,060,678	185,815	185,815
9320	Pleasant Grove	54,917	0	0	0	0	0	0	0	0	0	54,917	7,914	7,914
9360	Poplar Springs	73,332	0	0	0	0	0	0	0	0	0	73,332	7,220	7,220
6315	Prospect	63,623	0	0	0	0	0	0	0	0	0	63,623	9,899	9,899
9325	Providence	208,856	0	2,311	0	6,385	8,696	0	0	0	0	217,552	19,204	19,204
4255	Rockland	0	0	0	0	0	0	0	0	0	0	0	0	0
9150	Salem	196,757	0	0	0	0	0	0	0	0	0	196,757	26,484	26,484
9275	Salem	236,226	0	0	0	0	0	0	0	0	0	236,226	7,530	7,530
9445	Sharp Street	201,000	0	0	0	2,600	2,600	0	0	0	0	203,600	22,759	22,759
9365	Simpson	3,404	0	0	0	0	0	0	0	0	0	3,404	3,279	3,279
4565	St James	195,140	0	6,118	34,095	899	41,112	0	0	0	0	236,252	21,052	6,316
7360	St John United Church	145,230	0	0	0	1,930	1,930	0	0	0	0	147,160	18,770	18,770
4460	St Luke	59,123	3,560	0	0	59	3,619	0	0	0	0	62,742	9,238	9,238
9145	St Marks	42,674	0	0	0	0	0	0	0	0	0	42,674	4,998	1,666
9345	St Paul	124,360	100	250	0	6,115	6,465	0	0	0	0	130,825	14,009	14,009
4465	St Paul's	436,301	1,471	68,015	0	13,210	82,696	0	0	0	0	518,997	52,658	52,658
9280	Trinity	418,922	204,369	0	0	600	204,969	0	0	0	0	623,891	47,451	37,242
9470	Washington Grove	113,056	650	2,295	0	566	3,511	0	0	0	0	116,567	11,477	6,820
6385	Wesley Chapel	119,682	0	7,194	0	0	7,194	0	0	0	0	126,876	13,293	13,293
4225	Wesley Freedom	1,104,005	95,530	510	0	75,091	171,131	0	0	0	0	1,275,136	113,693	113,693
9515	Wesley Grove	132,931	0	4,425	3,600	346	8,371	0	0	0	0	141,302	14,457	14,457
4343	West Liberty	70,156	0	0	0	0	0	0	0	0	0	70,156	5,257	5,257
9580	West Montgomery	151,339	0	0	0	0	0	0	0	0	0	151,339	10,555	4,398
CM Total		20,156,588	1,557,870	1,656,761	698,034	499,557	4,412,232	15,828	70,000	17,470	103,298	24,662,108	2,314,150	2,163,429

Align #	Church Name		Dist #	City	State	1	2a1	2a2	2b	3	4	5a	5b	6	7	8	9	9a	9b	9c	9d	9e	9f	9g	9h	9i
6510	Arden		FR	Martinsburg	WV	430	11	2	0	0	0	0	3	2	1	2	435	0	0	0	0	0	435	0	255	180
6180	Asbury		FR	Frederick	MD	251	1	2	0	1	1	25	3	2	1	10	215	0	212	0	0	0	3	0	149	65
6590	Asbury		FR	Charles Town	WV	1,196	5	5	0	1	1	0	0	0	0	6	1,203	1	7	1	0	0	1,194	0	735	468
6700	Asbury		FR	Shepherdstown	WV	755	11	10	4	8	0	0	3	0	0	3	774	0	593	3	0	0	127	50	410	364
6520	Bedington		FR	Martinsburg	WV	459	4	0	0	0	0	0	0	0	0	3	458	0	0	0	0	0	458	0	243	215
6645	Berkeley Plaza		FR	Martinsburg	WV	36	0	0	0	0	0	0	0	0	0	1	35	0	0	0	0	0	35	0	27	8
6515	Bethel		FR	Bakerton	WV	68	0	0	0	0	0	0	0	0	0	1	67	0	0	0	0	0	67	0	43	24
6445	Bethesda		FR	Sykesville	MD	93	0	0	0	0	0	0	0	3	0	2	88	0	0	0	0	0	88	0	54	34
6720	Bethesda		FR	Shepherdstown	WV	73	0	0	0	0	0	0	0	0	0	0	73	0	0	0	0	0	73	0	42	31
6650	Blairton		FR	Martinsburg	WV	121	0	0	0	1	1	0	0	0	0	2	119	0	0	0	0	0	119	0	79	40
6560	Bolivar		FR	Harpers Ferry	WV	42	0	0	0	0	0	0	1	0	0	0	41	0	0	0	0	0	41	0	36	5
4580	Brandenburg		FR	Sykesville	MD	41	11	6	0	1	0	0	0	0	0	0	41	0	0	2	1	0	41	0	29	12
6185	Brook Hill		FR	Frederick	MD	800	0	0	0	0	0	0	0	0	0	6	812	0	0	0	0	0	800	0	449	363
6150	Buckeystown Rt 85		FR	Buckeystown	MD	133	0	8	0	0	0	0	0	1	0	0	133	0	0	0	0	0	133	0	75	58
6145	Buckeystown Rt 80		FR	Buckeystown	MD	0	0	1	0	0	0	0	0	0	0	0	0	0	0	0	0	0	0	0	0	0
6525	Bunker Hill		FR	Bunker Hill	WV	147	4	0	0	0	1	0	0	0	0	4	150	0	0	0	0	0	150	0	86	64
6590	Butlers Chapel		FR	Martinsburg	WV	56	7	0	0	0	0	8	0	1	0	0	50	0	0	0	0	0	50	0	24	26
4260	Calvary		FR	Finksburg	MD	432	7	0	0	7	0	0	3	5	0	3	426	0	3	0	3	0	420	0	219	207
6190	Calvary		FR	Frederick	MD	829	0	0	0	0	1	0	11	0	0	12	807	4	3	5	0	0	471	0	458	349
6655	Calvary		FR	Martinsburg	WV	485	0	0	0	1	0	0	1	0	2	9	476	0	0	0	0	0	471	0	240	236
6565	Camp Hill-Wesley		FR	Harpers Ferry	WV	57	0	1	0	0	0	0	0	2	0	2	62	0	2	3	0	0	60	0	32	30
6355	Catoctin		FR	Thurmont	MD	70	2	0	1	0	0	0	0	0	0	0	70	0	2	0	0	0	70	0	43	27
6210	Centennial Memorial		FR	Frederick	MD	270	0	1	0	0	0	48	0	0	0	1	269	0	15	3	0	0	251	0	150	119
6570	Chestnut Hill		FR	Harpers Ferry	WV	169	0	0	0	0	0	0	0	0	0	0	121	0	15	0	0	0	121	0	78	43
6545	Clarksville		FR	Inwood	WV	132	2	12	0	0	0	4	0	2	0	2	127	0	0	0	0	0	127	0	65	62
4535	Deer Park		FR	Westminster	MD	366	0	0	0	5	0	0	3	0	0	3	369	0	1	0	0	0	368	0	221	148
6260	Deerfield		FR	Sabillasville	MD	80	0	1	0	3	0	0	0	0	1	0	77	0	1	0	0	0	77	0	48	29
6160	Doubs-Epworth		FR	Adamstown	MD	32	0	0	0	0	0	0	0	1	0	1	31	0	0	0	0	0	31	0	19	12
6575	Engle		FR	Harpers Ferry	WV	67	0	0	0	1	0	0	3	1	2	3	58	0	0	0	0	0	58	0	36	22
6660	Friendship		FR	Hedgesville	WV	49	0	0	0	0	0	0	0	0	1	1	48	0	0	0	0	0	48	0	37	11
6550	Gerardstown		FR	Gerardstown	WV	38	0	0	0	0	0	0	0	0	0	3	38	0	0	0	0	0	38	0	22	16
6555	Greensburg		FR	Martinsburg	WV	194	0	0	0	0	0	0	0	0	2	3	191	0	3	0	0	0	188	0	124	67
6640	Harmony		FR	Falling Waters	WV	102	1	4	0	0	0	0	0	0	0	1	101	0	1	0	0	0	100	0	71	30
6610	Hedgesville		FR	Hedgesville	WV	447	0	5	0	5	0	0	0	0	0	5	446	0	4	2	0	0	441	0	217	229
6155	Hopehill		FR	Frederick	MD	257	1	0	0	0	0	0	1	6	1	2	266	0	0	0	0	0	259	0	147	119
6615	Inwood		FR	Inwood	WV	123	0	0	0	0	0	0	0	0	0	4	118	6	0	0	0	0	112	0	78	40
6330	Jackson Chapel		FR	Frederick	MD	170	4	4	0	0	0	0	0	0	0	0	173	0	104	1	0	0	69	0	94	79
6240	Jefferson		FR	Jefferson	MD	310	0	0	0	2	0	0	0	0	0	4	293	0	252	1	0	0	41	0	194	99
4450	Johnsville		FR	Sykesville	MD	46	2	2	0	0	0	0	0	0	0	1	88	0	0	0	0	0	88	0	52	36
4523	Johnsville		FR	Union Bridge	MD	45	2	2	0	0	0	0	0	0	0	1	47	0	34	0	0	0	13	0	29	18
6630	Leetown		FR	Leetown	WV	182	0	0	0	0	0	0	0	0	0	3	161	0	0	0	0	0	181	0	84	77
6265	Lewistown		FR	Lewistown	MD	111	0	0	0	0	0	0	0	0	0	1	111	0	0	0	0	0	111	0	84	27
6800	Liberty Central		FR	Libertytown	MD	156	0	0	0	0	0	0	0	0	0	0	156	0	1	1	0	0	155	0	95	61
6375	Lingamore		FR	Union Bridge	MD	163	0	0	0	0	0	0	0	0	0	3	160	0	0	0	0	0	159	0	101	59
6670	Marvin Chapel		FR	Union Bridge	MD	294	0	0	0	2	0	0	0	0	0	2	293	0	0	0	0	0	293	0	176	117
6755	Memorial		FR	Inwood	WV	77	0	0	0	0	0	0	0	0	0	1	77	0	0	0	0	0	77	0	45	32
6760	Mt. Zion		FR	Summit Point	WV	137	0	0	0	0	0	0	0	0	0	1	137	0	0	0	0	0	137	0	70	67
4475	Messiah		FR	Taneytown	MD	268	0	0	0	0	0	78	0	0	0	2	89	0	1	0	0	0	88	0	60	29

Column legend:
- 10 — Average attendance at all weekly worship service(s)
- 10a — Persons who Worship Online
- 11a — Number of Infants and Children baptized (Age 0-12)
- 11b — Number of Teens and Adults baptized (Age 13+)
- 11T — TOTAL Number of persons baptized (all ages)
- 12 — Number of baptized members who have not become Professing
- 13 — Number of other constituents of the church
- 14 — Total enrolled in confirmation preparation classes that
- 15 — CHILDREN (0-11yrs) in all Christian groups, small groups and Sunday School
- 16 — YOUTH (12-18 yrs) in all Christian groups, small groups and Sunday School
- 17 — YOUNG ADULTS (19-30 yrs) in all Christian groups, small groups and Sunday School
- 18 — OTHER ADULTS (31+ yrs) in all Christian groups, small groups and Sunday School
- 19 — TOTAL number of persons participating in Christian formation groups (Total lines 15-19)
- 20 — Average weekly attendance: Education classes/groups that meet in Sunday Church School groups
- 22 — Number of participants in Vacation Bible School
- 23 — Number of ongoing classes (all ages) for learning in Sunday Church
- 24 — Number of ONGOING small groups, support groups, or classes
- 25 — Number of SHORT-TERM classes, support groups, or small groups offered
- 26 — Membership in United Methodist Men (UMM)
- 27 — Amount paid for projects (UMM)
- 28 — Membership in United Methodist Women (UMW)
- 29 — Amount paid for local church and community work (UMW)
- 30a — Number of UMVIM teams sent out from this church
- 30b — Number of persons sent out on UMVIM teams from this church

Align #	Church Name	10	10a	11a	11b	11T	12	13	14	15	16	17	18	19	20	22	23	24	25	26	27	28	29	30a	30b
6510	Arden	115	0	3	5	8	0	0	0	47	25	23	65	160	51	68	8	6	1	10	4,000	23	2,095	1	9
6180	Asbury	80	165	0	0	4	4	0	0	7	1	2	106	116	4	25	2	3	0	0	0	12	500	0	0
6530	Asbury	271	15	0	0	0	0	0	0	110	40	0	82	232	96	81	11	20	5	39	2,000	50	5,000	2	20
6700	Asbury	335	0	4	1	5	0	1	0	33	25	35	295	388	60	53	7	20	2	0	0	0	19,500	0	0
6520	Bedington	161	0	0	1	8	0	120	0	29	19	12	115	175	19	95	9	1	0	11	6,680	17	0	1	12
6645	Berkeley Place	22	0	0	0	0	0	4	0	3	0	0	5	8	3	0	1	3	0	0	0	0	0	0	0
6515	Bethel	7	0	0	0	0	0	4	0	0	0	0	0	0	0	0	0	1	0	0	0	0	0	0	0
4445	Bethesda	14	0	0	0	0	121	0	0	0	0	0	6	6	0	0	0	0	0	0	0	10	200	0	0
6720	Bethesda	32	0	1	2	3	0	27	3	5	2	3	13	23	18	42	3	2	1	0	679	0	0	0	0
6650	Blairton	63	0	1	0	1	0	0	0	4	1	0	12	10	10	45	0	1	0	0	1,565	0	0	0	0
6560	Bolivar	16	0	0	0	0	0	26	4	4	0	0	8	10	10	45	0	0	0	0	1,580	0	0	0	0
4580	Brandenburg	34	7	2	1	3	30	10	11	4	0	0	10	14	8	98	3	29	10	4	0	20	2,580	0	0
6185	Brook Hill	431	0	10	3	13	143	11	11	32	103	10	195	340	78	40	8	2	0	15	2,500	20	1,563	2	35
6150	Buckeystown Rt 85	70	0	1	0	1	20	0	0	10	3	0	26	41	15	15	7	0	0	15	0	20	6,771	0	0
6145	Buckeystown Rt 80	0	0	0	0	0	0	0	0	0	0	0	0	0	0	0	0	0	0	0	0	26	7,306	0	0
6525	Bunker Hill	62	8	0	2	2	6	35	0	5	4	2	43	54	33	45	5	4	4	21	0	71	0	0	0
6590	Butlers Chapel	34	0	0	0	0	0	0	0	0	0	0	0	0	15	170	0	4	0	0	0	12	0	0	0
4260	Calvary	82	0	0	0	0	7	16	4	16	32	9	40	97	32	52	7	12	1	0	150	12	0	2	1
6190	Calvary	272	0	6	0	6	94	165	7	51	40	31	157	279	116	0	13	1	6	21	900	12	500	2	19
6655	Calvary	92	0	4	1	4	35	341	0	19	4	4	33	60	28	0	7	1	6	0	0	0	0	0	0
6505	Camp Hill-Wesley	32	0	0	0	0	0	42	0	8	0	0	10	18	4	0	1	3	0	2	0	0	1,667	0	0
6355	Catoctin	29	0	0	0	0	0	32	0	0	1	0	18	19	10	21	3	8	0	10	0	0	0	0	0
6210	Centennial Memorial	142	0	0	1	1	15	32	0	2	0	2	26	30	9	60	7	0	1	0	0	0	0	0	2
6570	Chestnut Hill	48	0	1	0	1	0	0	0	0	0	0	22	22	15	54	6	7	3	0	0	0	0	0	0
6545	Darkesville	95	0	0	0	0	0	0	0	0	0	0	28	28	45	17	6	9	0	0	0	0	2,000	0	0
4535	Deer Park	91	0	3	0	3	0	45	2	20	5	26	56	107	31	0	2	3	3	2	0	29	1,400	0	20
6260	Deerfield	59	0	0	0	0	0	19	0	12	2	0	5	19	17	0	2	2	2	9	0	24	1,354	0	0
6160	Dolds-Epworth	33	0	0	0	0	3	28	0	0	0	0	5	5	17	0	2	2	6	5	1,757	6	1,500	0	0
6575	Engle	16	0	1	0	1	0	0	0	0	0	2	4	6	16	0	5	2	0	10	1,500	11	300	0	0
6660	Friendship	27	0	0	5	5	0	0	1	0	1	0	4	5	17	0	1	5	1	18	4,132	25	388	0	0
6550	Gandtown	11	0	0	1	1	0	0	0	5	2	0	16	23	36	27	2	0	8	0	0	7	0	0	0
6555	Gerrardstown	15	0	7	0	7	7	45	0	14	0	0	18	41	10	56	2	5	0	0	0	19	3,007	1	20
6665	Greensburg	35	0	3	6	3	5	56	0	0	27	0	73	7	5	28	5	3	3	0	0	8	0	0	0
6640	Harmony	38	0	0	2	2	5	0	0	22	8	0	15	88	5	25	1	7	4	0	0	8	0	0	0
6610	Hedgesville	149	0	5	0	5	4	14	18	6	5	0	32	19	23	121	6	4	0	0	0	14	3,332	1	20
6155	Hopehll	33	0	0	0	0	0	0	0	0	3	0	7	16	5	0	3	1	0	0	0	0	4,760	0	0
6615	Inwood	38	0	2	0	2	5	26	10	18	10	32	56	17	30	0	1	2	0	0	0	0	885	0	0
6330	Jackson Chapel	220	0	0	0	0	0	0	0	0	0	0	6	28	18	0	2	2	0	0	0	0	2,199	0	0
6240	Jefferson	49	0	1	0	1	4	20	0	10	7	0	19	17	19	34	2	2	2	0	0	0	3,600	0	0
4450	Johnsville	31	0	0	0	0	0	0	1	0	6	0	16	14	15	0	1	0	0	0	0	0	1,875	0	0
4523	Johnsville	24	0	0	0	0	0	4	0	12	2	0	17	38	23	24	2	2	0	0	0	0	0	0	0
6630	Leetown	39	0	0	0	0	11	0	0	0	0	0	28	18	5	0	2	2	2	0	0	0	0	0	0
6265	Lewistown	53	0	2	2	0	0	10	0	5	2	0	17	19	30	21	1	2	0	0	0	11	0	0	0
6800	Liberty Central	52	0	1	1	2	0	0	0	0	0	0	14	18	18	12	1	1	0	0	0	0	0	0	0
6375	Langamore	57	0	2	0	2	0	0	0	7	1	0	38	39	19	0	2	2	2	0	0	0	885	0	0
6670	Marvin Chapel	25	0	1	0	1	0	0	0	0	4	0	18	18	18	10	1	2	2	0	0	0	2,199	0	0
6755	Memorial	46	0	1	1	1	0	0	0	7	0	0	19	19	19	0	2	2	0	0	0	11	3,600	0	0
4475	Messiah	45	0	1	0	3	3	10	0	15	0	0	15	22	15	25	2	1	27	10	1,000	20	1,875	0	0

Align #	Church Name	33	33a	33b	34	35a	36	36SF	37	38	39	42	43	44	45	46	47	46a	48b
6510	Arden	0	0	2	2,150	160	1,200,000	13,230	120,798	73,289	0	0	0	1,943	0	0	0	3,663	12,130
6180	Asbury	4	0	2	2,000	120	1,500,000	26,469	24,300	196,802	0	0	0	0	0	0	0	0	4,631
6530	Asbury	1	1	2	50	40	6,005,100	45,846	1,654,554	672,000	0	2,730	0	0	0	0	0	45,516	0
6700	Asbury	13	1	1	676	152	5,590,982	28,989	526,068	1,911,495	2,762	0	0	0	0	0	0	0	32,949
6520	Bedington	0	0	3	150	30	1,300,000	18,298	248,007	0	0	0	0	0	0	0	0	9,534	19,125
6645	Berkeley Place	1	0	0	400	0	161,000	2,544	0	0	0	0	0	0	0	0	0	100	0
6515	Bethel	0	3	1	50	6	387,674	1,800	42,121	0	0	100	0	0	0	0	0	0	0
4445	Bethesda	6	3	3	656	10	1,311,400	4,721	433,093	0	0	300	0	219	0	0	0	1,393	0
6720	Bethesda	0	0	3	300	10	85,333	1,400	46,016	0	0	0	0	50	0	0	0	305	0
6650	Blairton	12	0	8	5,200	28	1,350,000	4,064	12,000	0	0	0	0	0	0	0	0	0	0
6560	Bolivar	3	0	1	5	3	1,300,000	4,591	0	0	0	0	0	500	0	0	0	500	0
4580	Brandenburg	1	0	1	50	20	489,000	2,910	82,027	0	0	6,660	0	0	0	0	0	0	500
6185	Brook Hill	0	4	4	200	50	4,695,000	35,687	702,860	0	0	4,522	0	0	0	0	0	1,905	94,840
6150	Buckeystown Rt 85	0	0	0	2,500	30	4,000,000	10,772	275,000	0	0	0	0	452	0	0	0	30,948	3,077
6145	Buckeystown Rt 80	0	0	0	0	0	0	0	0	0	0	0	0	0	0	0	0	1	0
6525	Bunker Hill	0	0	0	5,550	0	3,518,064	9,390	50,509	108,521	0	0	0	0	0	0	0	0	900
6590	Butlers Chapel	0	0	7	0	0	190,000	4,000	70,000	0	0	0	0	0	0	0	0	0	0
4260	Calvary	10	7	11	765	39	2,356,000	10,692	179,188	0	0	0	0	0	0	0	0	0	20,354
6190	Calvary	11	5	6	3,100	160	13,883,000	57,665	2,717,724	0	8,160	7,068	0	0	0	0	0	22,987	31,955
6655	Calvary	0	5	9	361	2	2,787,044	27,739	424,179	0	0	0	0	274	0	0	0	1,191	3,808
6565	Camp Hill-Wesley	1	0	6	25	47	1,043,131	14,802	90,439	0	0	0	0	0	0	0	0	0	0
6355	Catoctin	26	15	6	625	34	375,000	2,064	16,488	0	0	0	0	0	0	0	0	0	0
6210	Centennial Memorial	2	0	2	5,500	4	5,500,000	20,000	1,452,856	30,577	0	0	0	0	0	0	0	0	14,696
6570	Chestnut Hill	0	1	1	3	4	957,000	1,200	205,000	0	0	0	0	0	0	0	0	500	6,355
6545	Darkesville	6	1	1	0	44	1,767,500	4,526	148,744	0	0	0	0	0	0	0	0	0	0
4535	Deer Park	0	0	1	0	0	1,900,000	16,009	290,837	0	0	0	0	0	0	0	0	0	2,143
6260	Deerfield	0	0	0	0	16	440,000	4,536	166,377	0	0	1,862	0	0	0	0	0	0	0
6160	Doubs-Epworth	7	3	3	560	4	485,000	3,132	78,330	0	0	0	0	0	0	0	0	0	568
5575	Engle	1	1	1	0	3	436,000	1,680	12,000	0	0	0	0	0	0	0	0	200	0
6660	Friendship	5	5	4	400	50	300,000	3,900	3,000	0	0	500	0	0	0	0	0	200	0
6550	Gardtown	18	3	2	0	172	100,000	1,600	75,000	0	0	0	0	0	0	0	0	50	0
6555	Gerrardstown	3	0	3	1,100	35	900,000	8,602	239,876	0	0	0	0	33	0	0	0	400	0
6665	Greensburg	9	5	9	320	30	575,000	15,745	32,000	0	0	0	0	0	0	0	0	0	0
6640	Harmony	8	0	9	3,577	150	2,082,500	11,958	125,221	0	0	0	0	0	0	0	0	11,604	4,036
6610	Hedgesville	4	0	0	1,000	41	1,972,000	4,140	24,000	0	0	0	0	0	0	0	0	0	1,505
6195	Hopehill	5	1	1	300	0	1,089,300	8,200	33,000	377,862	0	0	0	0	0	0	0	200	200
6615	Inwood	3	0	3	1,500	30	1,400,000	5,742	150,000	0	0	200	0	0	0	0	0	0	0
6330	Jackson Chapel	3	0	1	500	15	2,200,000	4,291	0	1,060,000	0	0	0	0	0	0	0	1,140	10,142
6240	Jefferson	1	3	3	1,000	35	420,000	1,500	26,000	0	0	0	0	200	0	0	0	510	3,320
4450	Johnsville	0	0	0	0	41	250,000	5,454	20,000	0	0	0	0	2,162	0	100	0	0	500
4523	Johnsville	7	0	1	35	30	650,000	6,600	365,581	0	0	0	0	0	0	56	0	0	0
6630	Leetown	5	0	3	1,000	15	439,900	9,132	32,744	0	0	467	0	0	0	0	0	0	76
6265	Lewistown	1	0	1	71	35	1,260,000	10,605	0	0	0	0	0	0	0	0	0	350	0
6800	Liberty Central	0	0	0	4,500	68	1,159,400	4,000	300,000	0	0	0	0	0	0	0	0	1,350	3,995
6375	Linganore	7	7	7	115	1	2,299,578	3,684	5,315	0	0	0	0	0	0	0	0	0	0
6670	Marvin Chapel	0	0	0	0	0	893,000		20,000	0	0	0	0	0	0	0	0	0	0
6755	Memorial	3,270	0	0	55	55	587,500		0	0	0	0	0	0	0	0	0	0	0
4475	Messiah	16	3	5	95	25	1,240,000	3,100	349,100	0	0	3,155	0	529	0	0	0	1,610	0

Column key:
- 33: TOTAL Community MINISTRIES for outreach, justice, and mercy
- 33a: MINISTRIES focusing on global/regional health?
- 33b: MINISTRIES focusing on engaging in ministry with the poor/socially
- 34: PERSONS SERVED BY community ministries for outreach, justice, and mercy
- 35a: PERSONS SERVING (from your congregation) in mission/community ministries
- 36: Market value of church-owned land, buildings and equipment
- 36SF: Overall square footage of church owned buildings (furnished and unfurnished areas)
- 37: Market value of financial and other liquid assets
- 38: Debt secured by church physical assets
- 39: Other debt
- 42: General Advance Specials remitted to the Annual Conference Treasurer
- 43: World Service Specials remitted to the Annual Conference Treasurer
- 44: Annual Conference Advance Specials remitted to the Annual Conference Treasurer
- 45: Youth Service Fund remitted to the
- 46: All other funds sent to AC Treasurer for connectional mission and ministry
- 47: Total Annual Conference Special Sunday Offerings remitted to the
- 46a: UMC CAUSES: Total amount given DIRECTLY to United Methodist causes (NOT sent to BWC Treasurer)
- 48b: MISSIONS/MINISTRY COSTS: Direct costs incurred by the local church for mission and community ministry activities

Column legend (line numbers and descriptions):

- **57** — Paid to/for all persons included in Lines 53a-53c for any other cash allowances (non-
- **56** — Paid to/for all persons included in Lines 53a-53c for accountable reimbursements
- **55c** — Housing benefits paid to/for any Deacons not included in 53a or 53b.
- **53b(H)** — Housing benefits paid to/for ALL Associate Pastor(s) & other pastoral staff assigned or appointed to the
- **55a** — Housing benefits paid to/for Lead Pastor or person in lead pastoral role as described in 53a
- **53c** — Base compensation paid to/for any Deacons NOT included in 53a or 53b
- **53b(B)** — Base compensation paid/for to all Associate Pastor(s) & other pastoral staff assigned or appointed to the church.
- **53a** — Base compensation paid to/for the Senior Pastor or other person assigned or appointed in the lead pastoral role to the church
- **52** — Direct-billed clergy health benefits
- **51** — Direct-billed clergy non-health benefits
- **50f** — U.M. Student Day
- **50e** — World Communion Sunday
- **50d** — Native American Ministries Sunday
- **50c** — Peace with Justice Sunday
- **50b** — UMCOR Sunday (formerly One Great Hour of Sharing)
- **50a** — Human Relations Sunday
- **49** — NON-UMC CAUSES: Total amount given DIRECTLY to non-United Methodist benevolent and charitable causes (NOT sent to BWC Treasurer)
- **48TOTAL** — Total of UMC Causes & UMC Missions & Outreach

57	56	55c	53b(H)	55a	53c	53b(B)	53a	52	51	50f	50e	50d	50c	50b	50a	49	48TOTAL	Align #	Church Name
0	508	0	0	17,797	0	0	38,601	5,037	4,778	0	0	0	0	0	0	7,718	15,793	6510	Arden
0	424	0	0	20,000	46,512	0	46,512	10,749	10,954	0	0	0	0	0	0	3,874	4,631	6180	Asbury
0	5,534	0	0	30,000	0	0	44,843	10,430	11,817	0	0	0	0	0	0	10,943	45,516	6530	Asbury
5,600	0	0	0	24,000	0	0	76,607	11,370	14,429	0	0	0	0	0	0	0	32,949	6700	Asbury
0	5,227	0	0	3,904	0	14,646	51,500	15,229	11,598	0	0	0	0	0	0	21,212	28,659	6520	Berdington
0	0	0	0	9,900	0	0	2,100	0	0	0	0	0	0	0	0	1,452	100	6645	Berkeley Place
0	31	0	0	0	0	0	6,600	0	0	0	0	0	0	0	0	375	0	6515	Bethel
0	0	0	0	0	0	0	21,900	0	0	65	144	152	98	85	82	200	1,393	4445	Bethesda
0	2,066	0	0	3,700	0	0	11,667	0	0	0	0	0	0	0	0	949	305	6720	Bethesda
0	0	0	0	10,000	0	0	24,319	0	0	0	0	0	0	0	0	18,000	500	6650	Blarton
163	0	0	0	0	0	0	12,000	0	0	168	0	0	0	0	341	395	500	6560	Bolivar
0	3,547	0	0	5,000	0	0	19,084	0	0	0	320	220	269	0	0	9,850	2,405	4580	Brandenburg
0	6,690	0	5,517	23,400	0	46,118	72,649	31,649	25,690	0	225	0	0	0	0	57,580	125,788	6185	Brook Hill
0	4,028	0	0	6,776	0	0	23,190	0	0	0	0	0	0	0	0	2,050	3,078	6150	Buckeystown Rt 85
0	0	0	0	0	0	0	0	0	0	0	0	0	0	0	0	0	0	6145	Buckeystown Rt 80
0	3,141	0	0	0	0	0	44,435	9,168	8,332	0	0	0	0	0	0	5,081	500	6525	Bunker Hill
0	2,400	0	0	6,000	0	0	10,894	0	0	0	0	0	0	0	0	250	0	6590	Butlers Chapel
0	360	0	0	35,933	0	0	32,344	12,826	12,290	0	0	0	0	0	0	4,213	20,354	4260	Calvary
0	4,367	0	19,866	22,000	8,500	44,399	72,215	39,880	28,705	0	0	0	0	0	0	12,479	54,942	6190	Calvary
0	1,036	0	0	19,866	0	0	44,253	11,160	11,388	0	0	0	0	0	0	813	4,989	6655	Calvary
0	0	0	0	20,556	0	0	688	0	0	0	0	0	0	0	0	2,759	0	6565	Camp Hill-Wesley
2,000	0	0	4,980	17,704	0	0	0	0	0	0	0	0	0	0	0	4,976	0	6355	Catoctin
3,196	4,100	0	0	19,866	0	26,000	43,572	14,988	15,086	0	0	0	0	0	0	5,000	15,196	6210	Centennial Memorial
0	2,117	0	0	4,769	0	0	21,600	12,150	12,290	0	0	0	0	0	0	1,200	6,355	6570	Chestnut Hill
19,000	0	0	0	19,000	0	0	36,000	14,215	0	0	0	0	0	0	0	14,600	0	6545	Clarksville
0	383	0	0	19,866	0	0	43,150	11,370	11,318	45	35	0	0	180	0	3,897	2,143	4635	Deer Park
0	0	0	0	13,000	0	0	9,000	0	0	0	50	0	0	0	0	1,500	0	6260	Deerfield
0	710	0	4,980	7,500	0	4,443	1,200	0	0	0	0	0	0	0	0	200	788	6160	Douds-Epworth
0	709	0	0	9,900	0	0	1,000	0	0	0	0	200	200	200	200	1,288	200	6575	Engle
0	0	0	0	12,000	0	0	2,100	0	0	0	0	0	0	0	0	175	50	6660	Friendship
0	1,129	0	0	3,659	0	0	19,290	0	0	0	0	0	0	0	0	0	400	6550	Gandztown
0	3,200	0	0	12,500	0	0	15,187	0	0	0	0	0	0	0	0	578	0	6555	Gerrardstown
0	1,601	0	0	22,000	0	0	55,550	11,400	13,044	0	50	0	0	0	0	3,600	0	6665	Greensburg
0	2,390	0	0	9,883	0	0	46,899	12,727	9,688	0	0	0	120	0	40	11,464	15,640	6640	Harmony
0	0	0	0	0	0	0	0	0	0	70	0	0	0	0	0	15	1,505	6610	Hedgesville
0	3,000	0	0	21,000	0	0	15,000	10,450	11,236	0	0	0	0	0	0	0	400	6155	Hopewill
0	0	0	0	0	0	0	0	0	0	0	0	0	0	0	0	0	0	6615	Inwood
0	909	0	4,980	0	0	15,344	51,939	0	0	0	0	0	0	0	200	1,500	11,262	6330	Jackson Chapel
0	846	0	0	0	0	0	5,759	0	0	0	0	0	0	0	0	2,075	3,830	6240	Jefferson
0	0	0	0	0	0	0	9,000	0	0	0	0	0	0	0	0	0	500	4450	Johnsville
0	0	0	0	13,975	0	0	26,525	0	0	0	0	0	0	0	0	0	0	4523	Johnsville
0	0	0	0	12,900	0	0	22,900	0	0	0	0	0	120	0	0	1,062	76	6630	Leetown
0	1,312	0	0	5,092	0	0	20,207	16,266	11,474	0	0	0	0	0	0	805	4,345	6265	Lewistown
0	3,582	0	0	1,923	0	0	45,802	12,651	9,912	0	0	50	0	0	0	7,300	1,350	6900	Liberty Central
0	482	0	0	6,900	0	0	43,189	0	0	0	0	0	0	0	0	7,414	0	6375	Linganore
0	2,800	0	0	0	0	0	10,310	0	0	0	0	0	0	0	0	1,932	0	6670	Marvin Chapel
0	216	0	0	19,500	0	0	10,500	0	0	0	0	0	0	0	0	0	0	6755	Memorial
0	800	0	0	5,483	0	0	20,714	0	0	100	100	100	100	500	100	2,099	1,610	4475	Messiah

Align #	Church Name	60 Paid in salary and benefits for all other church staff and diaconal ministers	61 Amount spent for local church program expenses	62 Amount spent for local church operating expenses	63 Amount paid for principal and interest on indebtedness, loans, mortgages, etc.	63a Amount paid for capital campaign or fundraising costs	64 Amount paid on capital expenditures for building, improvements, and major equipment purchases	65 Amount PAID by/for the local church on all expenditures	66 Number of giving units	67a Received through pledges	67b Received from non-pledging, but identified givers	67c Received from unidentified givers	67d Amount received from interest and dividends and/or transferred from liquid assets	67e Amount received from Sale of Church Assets	67f Amount received through building use fees, contributions, and rentals	67g Amount received through fundraisers and other sources
6510	Arden	19,786	12,031	48,397	44,422	0	24,787	263,817	93	0	183,107	15,078	0	0	1,967	0
6180	Asbury	47,150	10,984	13,565	33,648	0	0	273,603	0	0	204,160	9,657	6	0	675	5,720
6530	Asbury	107,354	5,773	34,378	190,674	0	0	546,469	262	0	318,566	32,781	714	0	2,525	46
6700	Asbury	48,602	30,172	77,944	169,194	0	15,675	554,922	386	0	545,921	11,097	2,794	0	39,097	18,924
6520	Bedington	36,479	12,094	35,487	0	0	0	286,161	0	0	271,088	4,590	0	0	980	0
6645	Berkeley Place	3,225	1,652	4,094	0	0	0	25,758	15	0	0	18,837	0	0	0	0
6515	Bethel	0	364	5,636	0	0	1,799	19,558	8	0	14,418	946	66	0	35	0
4445	Bethesda	9,126	291	11,629	0	0	0	53,380	10	0	15,385	3,838	14,161	0	17,980	0
6720	Bethesda	1,333	87	7,325	0	0	0	32,523	26	0	41,585	3,890	45	0	200	0
6650	Blanton	0	1,232	9,420	0	0	0	70,910	52	17,537	80,578	7,582	0	0	0	0
6560	Bolivar	5,740	478	11,914	0	0	0	31,401	13	0	15,139	2,873	19	0	550	2,679
6580	Brandenburg	0	1,052	11,443	0	0	62,046	73,442	40	0	76,898	21,045	328	0	9,600	1,453
6185	Brook Hill	296,992	19,899	128,234	0	0	4,265	965,437	328	0	748,083	107,524	3,709	0	430	116,196
6150	Buckeystown Rt 85	20,735	4,403	24,274	0	0	0	108,565	43	0	107,524	2,743	0	0	0	4,227
6145	Buckeystown Rt 80	0	0	0	0	0	0	1,560	0	0	0	0	0	0	0	0
6525	Bunker Hill	19,212	4,476	33,002	41,415	0	4,835	184,983	60	0	154,271	30,231	324	0	2,780	0
6590	Butlers Chapel	36,200	8,101	8,151	0	7,213	0	36,708	29	0	74,492	5,160	17	1,500	1,660	51,958
4260	Calvary	234,639	31,646	48,372	0	13,000	49,939	271,854	120	0	121,666	9,596	13,254	0	89,270	21,125
6190	Calvary	55,670	9,748	162,006	0	0	198,526	1,030,928	343	499,990	161,376	12,903	63,000	0	1,126	2,766
6655	Calvary	5,896	2,116	49,023	0	0	95,487	336,037	101	42,506	200,456	3,386	3,000	0	10,500	576
6565	Camp Hill-Wesley	25,201	250	14,429	0	0	13,556	65,703	30	0	685	3,234	7	0	0	0
6355	Catoctin	0	2,294	8,837	0	0	0	45,447	19	0	38,226	27,553	103,000	0	4,260	1,849
6210	Centennial Memorial	8,400	0	30,779	0	0	83,857	306,218	70	56,134	43,880	0	5	0	13,730	0
6570	Chestnut Hill	35,541	3,689	14,277	4,170	0	0	132,748	33	0	0	5,191	250	0	10,646	8,989
6545	Darkesville	0	0	6,700	0	0	0	132,748	20	0	152,888	14,273	0	0	0	27,000
4535	Deer Park	0	1,969	46,009	0	0	14,826	217,989	101	225,126	8,400	4,000	223	0	0	0
6260	Deerfield	0	0	2,532	0	0	2,679	32,276	47	0	20,285	2,698	0	0	0	0
6160	Doubs-Epworth	2,500	1,111	3,951	0	0	13,563	37,829	21	0	20,902	25,997	0	0	0	0
6575	Engle	5,643	2,423	7,674	0	0	4,464	27,059	7	6,000	0	0	223	0	0	0
6660	Friendship	0	225	4,380	0	0	9,395	16,874	16	0	0	46,803	3,224	0	100	10,303
6550	Garretown	29,988	559	3,800	0	0	0	73,819	17	29,360	24,390	45,462	80	460	910	3,437
6555	Gerrardstown	7,603	0	24,669	0	0	6,107	51,033	22	0	167,688	6,883	0	0	900	1,823
6665	Greensburg	0	10,611	14,800	0	0	0	238,592	52	0	116,000	0	0	0	900	7,823
6640	Harmony	0	2,796	36,936	0	0	10,030	193,967	70	0	60,883	37,953	0	0	500	1,500
6610	Hedgesville	16,556	1,085	33,651	0	0	0	76,754	44	0	0	20,000	5	0	116,663	10,224
6195	Hopehill	0	950	6,631	39,710	0	0	291,125	182	0	71,219	0	743	0	396	0
6615	Inwood	0	1,000	0	0	0	85,000	339,557	65	0	0	0	57	0	0	0
6330	Jackson Chapel	0	808	68,447	0	0	17,435	85,694	28	0	54,678	3,255	83	0	275	4,729
6240	Jefferson	50,010	0	6,906	0	0	0	13,852	30	0	53,692	11,380	2,218	0	0	0
4450	Johnsville	24,386	2,287	2,757	0	0	24,303	84,027	34	0	108,890	2,416	163	0	200	3,175
4523	Johnsville	14,565	0	31,035	0	0	15,000	79,316	40	0	69,361	2,755	0	0	200	12,639
6630	Leetown	0	4,177	8,623	0	0	1,377	106,869	60	0	94,900	4,769	38	0	406	2,748
6265	Lewistown	5,010	1,142	18,993	0	0	12,074	115,690	22	0	34,463	8,410	13	0	0	0
6800	Liberty Central	1,375	3,629	13,841	0	0	2,649	146,203	23	0	44,645	5,003	1	0	0	0
6375	Linganore	10,400	0	22,055	0	0	409	37,169	57	0	103,698	0	0	0	0	0
6670	Marvin Chapel	13,554	1,465	6,403	0	0	9,452	51,623	0	0	0	0	0	0	0	0
6755	Memorial	0	0	8,398	0	0	0	92,534	0	0	0	0	0	0	0	0
4475	Messiah	0	0	19,610	0	0	0	0	0	0	0	0	0	0	0	0

Algn.#	Church Name	TOTAL income for annual budget/spending plan (67a-g) [67]	Capital campaigns [68a]	Memorials, endowments, and bequests [68b]	Other sources and projects (include UMW, UMM and 'flow-through') [68c]	Special Sundays, Gen. Adv. Spec., World Srvc Spec., Conf. Adv Spec. and other directed benevolent giving [68d]	Total income for designated causes including capital campaign and other special projects [68]	Equitable Compensation Funds received by Church or Pastor [69a]	Advance Special, apportioned, and connectional funds received by church [69b]	Other grants and financial support from institutional sources [69c]	Income from connectional/institutional sources outside the local church [69]	TOTAL CHURCH INCOME (Sum of Lines 67 + 68 + 69) [70]	Amount APPORTIONED to the local church [40a]	Amount PAID by the local church for all apportioned causes [40b]
6510	Arden	200,152	0	0	0	0	0	0	0	0	0	200,152	22,219	22,219
6190	Asbury	220,218	0	0	0	0	0	0	0	0	0	220,218	24,600	24,600
6530	Asbury	354,632	0	30,735	2,000	0	32,735	0	0	0	0	387,367	46,477	46,477
6700	Asbury	598,909	0	3,087	0	10,029	13,116	0	0	0	0	612,025	55,655	55,655
6520	Bedington	295,582	0	500	0	0	500	0	0	0	0	296,082	32,461	32,461
6645	Berkeley Place	18,837	0	0	0	0	0	0	0	0	0	18,837	2,935	2,935
6515	Bethel	15,465	0	0	0	0	0	0	0	0	0	15,465	3,429	3,429
4445	Bethesda	51,334	150	0	773	572	1,495	0	0	0	0	52,829	7,855	7,855
0720	Bethesda	45,720	0	4,985	0	0	4,985	0	0	0	0	50,705	5,091	5,091
6650	Blairton	105,697	0	0	0	0	0	0	0	0	0	105,697	7,439	7,439
6560	Bolivar	17,824	0	0	0	0	0	0	0	0	0	17,824	5,951	5,951
4580	Brandenburg	81,782	0	3,300	0	1,707	5,007	0	0	0	0	86,789	7,343	7,343
6185	Brook Hill	895,452	21,147	27,544	0	2,395	51,087	0	0	0	0	946,539	98,438	98,438
6150	Buckeystown Rt 85	118,633	0	17,120	4,726	0	21,846	0	0	0	0	140,479	15,766	15,766
6145	Buckeystown Rt 80	0	0	0	0	0	0	0	0	0	0	1,560	1,560	1,560
6525	Bunker Hill	187,606	6,260	5,065	0	3,145	15,270	0	0	0	0	202,876	15,769	15,769
6590	Butlers Chapel	74,492	0	0	0	0	0	0	0	0	0	74,492	4,178	4,178
4260	Calvary	181,861	21,112	0	0	4,581	25,693	0	0	0	0	207,554	26,213	10,922
5190	Calvary	763,476	8,415	0	0	0	8,415	0	0	0	0	771,891	89,690	89,690
6555	Calvary	298,610	53,585	1,290	1,784	0	56,659	0	0	0	0	355,269	32,604	32,604
6565	Camp Hill-Wesley	62,843	6,254	0	0	0	6,254	0	0	0	0	69,097	5,504	5,504
6355	Caboctin	42,043	1,305	0	0	214	1,519	0	0	0	0	43,562	4,679	4,679
6210	Centennial Memorial	258,693	0	645	0	0	645	0	0	0	0	259,338	19,127	19,127
6570	Chestnut Hill	71,718	0	350	0	0	350	0	0	0	0	72,068	8,832	8,832
6545	Clarksville	0	0	0	0	0	0	0	0	0	0	0	12,833	12,833
4535	Deer Park	177,964	0	9,731	0	4,101	13,932	0	0	0	0	191,796	23,675	23,675
6260	Deerfield	49,673	0	0	0	0	0	0	0	0	0	49,673	3,776	3,776
6160	Doubs-Epworth	24,285	0	0	0	0	0	0	0	0	0	24,285	2,721	2,721
6575	Engle	23,823	0	250	0	118	368	0	0	0	0	24,191	3,472	3,472
6660	Friendship	25,997	0	0	0	0	0	0	0	0	0	25,997	3,265	3,265
6550	Gandtown	0	0	0	0	0	0	0	0	0	0	0	674	674
6655	Gerrardstown	60,430	0	0	0	0	0	0	0	0	0	60,430	8,864	8,864
6665	Greensburg	53,740	0	0	0	2,850	2,850	0	0	0	0	56,590	6,984	1,746
6640	Harmony	219,037	4,568	0	0	37,153	30,218	0	2,500	0	2,500	256,255	25,251	25,251
6610	Hedgesville	125,606	0	1,065	0	100	9,268	0	0	0	0	134,874	6,240	6,240
6155	Hopehill	69,606	0	0	0	0	100	0	0	0	0	69,706	3,848	3,848
6615	Inwood	39,953	0	0	0	0	0	0	0	0	0	39,953	3,873	3,873
6330	Jackson Chapel	372,013	0	0	0	0	0	0	0	0	0	372,013	19,979	19,979
5240	Jefferson	72,358	0	6,732	0	0	13,228	0	0	0	0	85,586	8,803	8,803
4523	Johnsville	57	0	0	0	0	0	0	0	0	0	57	1,595	1,595
4450	Johnsville	63,020	0	29,030	0	0	29,030	0	0	0	0	92,050	9,359	9,359
6630	Leetown	73,490	8,372	13,741	0	924	14,665	0	0	0	0	88,155	7,072	7,072
6265	Lewistown	114,844	0	700	0	0	9,072	0	0	0	0	123,916	12,466	12,466
6600	Liberty Central	84,754	0	745	0	0	745	0	0	0	0	85,499	10,761	10,761
6375	Linganore	102,861	0	203	0	1,787	1,990	0	0	0	0	104,851	16,759	16,759
6670	Marvin Chapel	34,476	0	0	0	0	0	0	0	0	0	34,476	4,800	4,800
6755	Memorial	53,056	0	0	0	0	0	0	0	0	0	53,056	8,214	8,214
4475	Messiah	108,701	0	100	0	435	535	0	0	0	0	109,236	13,263	13,263

Align #	Church Name	Dist #	City	State	Total professing members at the close of 2017 (1)	Received by PROFESSION of Faith (2a1)	Received by PROFESSION of Faith (Other Than Confirmation) (2a2)	Restored by AFFIRMATION of Faith (2b)	Transferred in from other UM churches (3)	Transferred in from non-UM churches (4)	Removed or corrected by Charge Conference action (5a)	Withdrawn from Professing Membership (5b)	Transferred out to other UM churches (6)	Transferred out to non-UM churches (7)	Removed by death (8)	Total professing members at the close of 2018 (9)	Asian (9a)	African American / Black (9b)	Hispanic / Latino (9c)	Native American (9d)	Pacific Islander (9e)	White (9f)	Multi-Racial (9g)	Female (9h)	Male (9i)
4490	Middleburg	FR	Westminster	MD	34	0	0	0	0	0	0	0	0	0	0	34	0	1	0	0	0	33	0	20	14
6280	Middletown	FR	Middletown	MD	1,092	21	13	0	6	3	30	4	4	0	2	1,089	11	1	7	0	2	1,068	0	597	492
6635	Middleway	FR	Kearneysville	WV	135	0	12	0	1	0	0	0	4	0	2	132	9	1	0	0	1	130	10	74	58
6335	Mount Carmel	FR	Frederick	MD	435	0	2	0	0	0	0	0	4	0	6	445	9	5	0	0	1	406	10	237	208
6390	Mount Pleasant	FR	Frederick	MD	94	0	2	0	0	0	0	0	2	0	2	90	3	6	0	0	0	84	0	52	38
6735	Mount Wesley	FR	Shepherdstown	WV	105	0	0	0	0	0	0	0	0	0	0	107	0	0	14	0	0	104	0	66	41
6410	Mount Zion	FR	Frederick	MD	15	1	0	0	0	0	0	0	0	0	0	15	1	0	0	0	0	15	4	8	7
6675	Mount Zion	FR	Martinsburg	WV	136	0	0	0	0	0	0	0	1	0	1	130	0	115	0	0	0	9	0	63	67
6580	Murrill Hill	FR	Harpers Ferry	WV	23	0	0	0	0	0	0	0	0	0	0	23	0	0	0	0	0	23	7	14	9
6137	New Hope of Greater Brunswick	FR	Brunswick	MD	381	0	10	0	0	0	6	0	0	0	6	385	0	0	0	0	0	378	7	218	167
6640	New Hope of New Windsor	FR	New Market	MD	68	0	0	0	0	0	0	0	0	0	0	68	0	1	1	0	0	67	0	33	35
6340	New Market	FR	New Market	MD	229	0	3	0	0	2	0	0	2	0	3	233	4	0	0	0	0	233	0	124	109
6750	New Street	FR	Shepherdstown	WV	351	0	0	0	1	0	0	0	0	1	3	345	2	1	0	0	0	336	4	182	163
4275	Oakland	FR	Sykesville	MD	257	0	0	6	0	0	0	0	0	0	0	253	3	0	0	0	0	253	2	152	101
5535	Oakland	FR	Charles Town	WV	141	0	0	0	0	0	0	0	0	107	0	43	0	1	1	0	0	38	2	28	15
6680	Otterbein	FR	Martinsburg	WV	460	0	0	0	2	0	0	0	1	0	11	450	0	0	1	0	0	446	0	307	143
6730	Paynes Chapel	FR	Bunker Hill	WV	86	9	0	2	0	0	0	0	0	0	6	97	0	4	0	0	0	97	0	49	48
6725	Pikeside	FR	Martinsburg	WV	360	0	0	0	3	8	0	0	0	1	6	365	1	17	0	0	0	361	0	205	160
6165	Pleasant View	FR	Adamstown	MD	20	0	4	0	0	0	0	0	0	0	1	17	0	0	0	0	0	8	0	13	4
6685	Salem	FR	Martinsburg	WV	8	0	0	0	0	0	0	0	0	0	0	8	3	0	0	0	0	8	0	5	3
6255	Sandy Hook	FR	Knoxville	MD	14	0	0	0	0	0	0	0	1	0	7	18	4	0	0	0	0	18	1	11	7
4443	Sandy Mount	FR	Finksburg	MD	394	0	0	0	0	0	0	2	0	0	0	385	0	0	0	0	0	385	0	213	172
6715	Shenandoah Memorial	FR	Harpers Ferry	WV	22	0	0	0	0	0	0	2	0	0	0	22	1	0	0	0	0	21	1	14	8
6585	Silver Grove	FR	Harpers Ferry	WV	88	0	0	0	0	0	0	0	0	0	5	88	0	2	0	0	0	88	0	51	37
6690	St Lukes	FR	Martinsburg	WV	611	5	4	0	5	4	25	5	4	1	0	610	0	1	2	0	0	605	0	361	249
4620	St Paul	FR	New Windsor	MD	173	0	0	0	1	4	0	0	0	0	1	156	1	0	1	0	0	155	0	94	62
4540	St. James	FR	Westminster	MD	218	0	0	0	0	0	0	0	0	0	0	217	1	0	0	0	0	217	0	130	87
4545	Stone Chapel	FR	New Windsor	MD	70	0	0	0	0	0	0	0	0	0	1	71	1	138	0	0	0	70	15	45	26
4365	Strawbridge	FR	New Windsor	MD	161	0	0	0	2	2	0	0	0	0	7	164	1	1	0	0	0	11	0	97	67
4485	Taylorsville	FR	Mount Airy	MD	255	0	0	0	3	0	0	0	0	0	1	251	0	0	2	2	0	247	0	141	110
6360	Thurmont	FR	Thurmont	MD	162	0	3	1	0	3	0	0	3	3	1	149	3	0	0	0	0	147	3	86	63
6170	Tom's Creek	FR	Emmitsburg	MD	370	0	0	0	1	0	9	0	0	0	2	372	4	2	0	1	0	365	8	217	155
6175	Trinity	FR	Emmitsburg	MD	169	1	0	1	4	0	0	0	0	0	0	169	0	0	0	0	0	169	0	99	70
6225	Trinity	FR	Frederick	MD	764	3	1	0	0	0	0	0	1	3	6	761	4	17	0	0	0	729	0	457	304
6710	Trinity	FR	Martinsburg	WV	527	3	0	8	0	0	0	2	0	0	8	522	0	0	3	0	0	522	0	296	226
4550	Union Street	FR	Westminster	MD	125	0	0	0	3	0	0	0	1	0	0	113	1	111	0	0	0	2	0	79	34
4510	Uniontown	FR	Westminster	MD	41	0	0	0	0	0	0	0	0	0	1	40	0	0	0	0	0	34	0	24	16
6760	Uvilla	FR	Shepherdstown	WV	72	3	0	0	0	0	0	0	0	0	0	82	8	0	0	0	0	82	0	46	36
6420	Walkersville	FR	Walkersville	MD	725	13	2	0	1	0	6	3	5	0	4	726	1	0	0	0	0	717	1	446	280
6365	Weller	FR	Thurmont	MD	302	0	2	1	0	0	22	0	0	0	4	295	1	1	0	0	0	294	0	181	114
4555	Westminster	FR	Westminster	MD	592	0	0	0	3	0	0	0	0	1	15	586	0	0	0	0	0	584	0	347	239
6740	Williams Memorial	FR	Shepherdstown	WV	152	0	0	0	0	0	0	0	0	1	0	151	0	1	0	1	0	151	0	91	60
4560	Zion	FR	Westminster	MD	191	0	0	0	0	0	0	0	0	0	0	191	0	0	0	0	0	190	0	112	79
FR Total					**21,531**	**124**	**137**	**23**	**67**	**25**	**267**	**49**	**48**	**125**	**236**	**21,066**	**61**	**1,670**	**59**	**8**	**9**	**19,132**	**129**	**12,130**	**8,836**

Align #	Church Name	10 Avg attendance at all weekly worship service(s)	10a Persons who Worship Online	11a Infants/Children baptized (0-12)	11b Teens/Adults baptized (13+)	11T TOTAL persons baptized (all ages)	12 Baptized members not professing	13 Other constituents	14 Enrolled in confirmation prep	15 Children (0-11)	16 Youth (12-18)	17 Young Adults (19-30)	18 Other Adults (31+)	19 TOTAL Christian formation	20 Avg weekly attendance education	22 VBS participants	23 Ongoing classes (all ages)	24 Ongoing small groups	25 Short-term groups	26 UMM membership	27 Amount paid projects (UMM)	28 UMW membership	29 Amount paid local church/community (UMW)	30a UMVIM teams sent	30b Persons sent on UMVIM teams
4490	Middleburg	17	0	0	0	0	0	2	0	0	0	0	6	8	8	0	1	0	0	0	0	0	0	0	0
6280	Middletown	350	14	2	4	13	192	191	21	197	140	59	180	576	138	190	17	15	12	11	0	12	0	1	0
6635	Middleway	76	0	9	4	13	17	17	0	12	2	2	42	56	40	60	6	4	2	4	1,100	16	865	1	5
6335	Mount Carmel	181	15	9	1	11	28	302	0	36	54	10	100	200	60	100	9	4	2	5	0	16	0	0	0
6390	Mount Pleasant	26	0	1	2	3	0	10	0	4	6	0	12	16	9	0	9	4	2	5	0	5	0	1	0
6735	Mount Wesley	54	0	0	0	0	0	5	0	15	6	0	41	62	34	72	1	1	3	4	0	4	3,200	0	10
6410	Mount Zion	8	0	0	0	0	3	0	1	0	0	7	22	57	26	41	3	1	0	19	0	36	2,990	0	0
6675	Mount Zion	68	0	1	6	7	0	45	0	9	19	0	7	7	7	0	6	3	0	0	3,200	19	1,463	0	0
6580	Murrill Hill	18	0	0	1	3	5	0	0	0	15	10	100	200	47	82	1	14	10	0	0	10	0	0	0
6137	New Hope of Greater Brunswick	149	87	2	0	2	14	190	0	75	15	8	6	9	3	8	6	1	6	0	0	0	0	2	43
4640	New Hope of New Windsor	16	0	0	0	0	0	0	0	0	2	12	55	93	40	70	1	1	2	17	0	46	0	0	0
6340	New Market	86	15	0	0	0	0	76	0	28	28	5	56	117	26	35	11	7	4	0	0	0	0	0	1
6750	New Street	63	0	2	0	2	0	55	0	21	4	3	20	47	40	25	4	2	3	12	0	15	0	0	0
4275	Oakland	62	0	0	0	0	25	10	0	18	5	5	22	31	19	0	2	2	0	0	0	0	0	0	0
6535	Oakland	39	0	1	0	2	10	1	0	4	2	3	22	90	65	50	5	5	3	12	0	12	0	0	0
6680	Otterbein	101	0	2	4	4	0	10	0	10	6	5	75	37	15	0	3	3	2	3	0	0	0	0	0
6730	Paynes Chapel	35	0	1	4	4	0	0	11	15	6	2	15	90	32	0	5	3	2	12	1,500	12	0	0	0
6725	Pikeside	97	86	0	1	1	0	29	0	13	6	5	40	64	12	50	5	5	4	3	0	13	0	0	0
6165	Pleasant View	20	0	1	0	1	0	0	0	0	6	5	12	12	12	0	4	3	0	4	0	4	0	0	0
6685	Salem	8	0	0	0	0	0	0	0	0	0	0	0	0	0	0	0	1	0	0	0	0	0	0	0
6255	Sandy Hook	14	0	0	0	0	3	0	0	14	4	0	11	29	29	45	0	4	1	0	0	0	0	0	0
4443	Sandy Mount	131	23	2	4	4	26	0	0	10	0	1	1	2	2	0	3	4	3	0	0	0	0	0	0
6715	Shenandoah Memorial	18	150	0	0	0	17	41	13	10	0	0	12	22	24	0	7	6	0	0	0	0	0	0	0
6595	Silver Grove	50	0	1	8	9	0	0	0	60	33	25	120	238	83	77	6	5	1	0	0	0	0	0	0
6690	St Lukes	195	0	1	0	3	0	25	5	8	7	5	27	48	10	27	6	2	9	0	0	0	0	0	0
6620	St Paul	59	0	0	1	1	2	14	0	12	2	4	5	5	5	17	3	4	4	0	0	22	4,209	1	0
4540	St. James	15	0	0	0	0	2	13	0	8	4	5	24	28	45	25	2	1	2	0	0	0	0	0	0
4545	Stone Chapel	24	0	1	0	1	6	6	0	22	0	4	88	142	25	35	3	4	1	26	635	40	868	0	0
4365	Strawbridge	90	0	1	2	3	8	6	0	32	17	15	88	21	13	5	3	6	2	0	0	27	3,349	0	0
4485	Taylorsville	57	0	1	1	2	2	41	0	12	2	0	15	21	17	35	7	6	1	0	0	0	0	0	0
63160	Thurmont	105	0	3	0	3	0	180	8	32	33	0	28	93	43	5	6	6	3	0	0	10	500	0	0
6170	Tom's Creek	138	0	2	1	3	2	45	8	12	7	4	65	88	47	24	7	5	2	0	0	0	0	0	0
6175	Trinity	35	0	0	0	0	0	10	3	8	12	0	15	130	5	0	6	2	1	0	0	23	1,315	0	0
6225	Trinity	210	0	10	1	11	26	80	13	30	48	15	65	169	45	65	7	1	9	0	0	0	0	1	20
67310	Trinity	80	0	1	3	0	17	25	0	71	18	32	32	25	7	70	6	3	2	0	0	0	0	0	0
4550	Union Street	45	0	0	0	0	0	10	0	2	2	0	6	10	12	24	3	1	0	0	0	0	0	0	0
4510	Uniontown	25	0	1	0	1	0	12	8	1	0	2	12	16	12	0	2	5	2	0	0	0	0	0	0
6760	Uvilla	35	0	0	3	6	2	190	0	25	7	5	80	122	12	60	4	2	1	0	0	23	1,350	0	0
6420	Walkersville	120	0	2	3	3	2	17	0	13	12	6	33	59	38	200	7	15	20	0	0	0	0	0	0
6365	Weller	99	10	0	2	2	232	494	13	353	131	10	343	837	104	250	13	2	9	0	750	9	11,590	1	0
4555	Westminster	244	3	3	1	5	0	17	0	13	7	0	5	21	5	25	1	15	4	12	0	109	1,990	0	17
6740	Williams Memorial	17	0	0	0	0	0	19	0	10	5	0	6	48	12	0	0	0	0	0	750	16	0	1	17
4560	Zion	45	0	0	0	0	13	19	0	10	5	0	12	21	12	25	0	3	0	8	2,079	16	1,990	0	0
	FR Total	7,030	591	134	61	195	1,062	3,256	104	1,729	1,011	424	3,490	6,654	2,230	2,920	310	278	219	318	37,707	926	108,571	16	216

Align #	Church Name	33	33a	33b	24	35a	36	36f	37	38	39	42	43	44	45	46	47	46a	48b
4490	Middleburg	1	0	1	400	3	250,000	2,580	40,000	0	0	0	0	0	0	0	0	770	268
6280	Middletown	21	0	21	2,820	263	4,834,000	24,477	762,000	996,036	0	0	0	0	0	0	0	18,533	35,608
6635	Middleway	6	0	0	400	30	1,007,700	0	389,816	20,219	0	0	0	0	0	0	0	300	0
6335	Mount Carmel	6	0	0	450	70	3,998,806	9,500	142,485	1,838,892	2,010	0	0	0	0	0	0	0	15,536
6390	Mount Pleasant	4	0	4	750	16	646,000	3,515	20,000	0	0	0	0	0	0	0	0	0	2,870
6735	Mount Wesley	4	0	4	325	22	510,000	2,437	0	0	0	0	0	0	0	0	0	0	0
6410	Mount Zion	4	2	2	25	7	279,000	2,940	4,000	0	0	20	0	0	0	0	0	0	915
6675	Mount Zion	3	0	2	260	52	1,600,000	5,500	87,000	108,666	504	0	0	600	0	0	0	667	714
6580	Murrill Hill	0	0	14	1	0	300,000	1,800	10,000	0	0	0	0	0	0	0	0	240	7,676
6137	New Hope of Greater Brunswick	16	2	0	2,500	400	1,274,400	15,240	139,000	0	0	0	0	0	0	0	0	3,376	32,943
4640	New Hope of New Windsor	3	0	0	8	11	453,700	4,400	149,394	0	0	0	0	0	0	0	0	0	561
6340	New Market	4	2	14	130	160	1,840,000	13,283	73,120	99,938	0	0	0	0	0	0	0	1,800	15,955
6760	New Street	8	0	8	1,400	50	2,272,426	20,000	60,000	3,000	0	0	0	0	0	0	0	150	1,316
4275	Oakland	12	2	10	500	45	1,500,000	14,000	77,867	227,500	23,000	1,415	0	0	0	0	0	0	10,463
6535	Oakland	11	2	9	1,238	38	2,260,000	11,152	37,293	0	0	0	0	0	0	0	0	0	16,240
6680	Otterbein	5	0	3	556	100	793,000	13,204	475,940	0	0	0	0	0	0	0	0	1,480	1,200
6730	Paynes Chapel	0	0	0	100	0	1,290,000	0	58,199	0	0	0	0	0	0	0	0	0	0
6725	Pikeside	0	0	0	150	175	177,000	1,800	11,696	0	0	0	0	0	0	0	0	0	0
6165	Pleasant View	0	0	0	0	0	79,200	3,000	0	0	0	257	0	0	0	0	0	0	0
6605	Salem	0	0	0	0	0	250,000	20,810	0	0	0	0	0	0	0	0	0	1	0
6255	Sandy Hook	15	7	11	1,500	35	3,673,027	5,684	167,072	0	0	14,902	0	0	0	0	0	878	15,472
4443	Sandy Mount	0	0	0	0	0	3,000	0	18,800	0	0	0	0	0	0	0	0	100	0
6715	Shenandoah Memorial	34	21	25	5,310	220	225,000	24,368	0	0	0	0	0	0	0	0	0	3,858	709
6585	Silver Grove	11	4	4	2,050	40	4,357,000	20,181	352,722	0	0	0	0	0	0	0	0	4,530	18,442
6690	St. Lukes	1	0	0	10	8	800,000	4,780	197,309	0	0	0	0	0	0	0	0	0	0
4620	St. Paul	2	1	2	583	17	940,000	7,314	92,308	0	0	2,170	0	0	0	0	0	368	880
4540	St. James	2	3	5	140	27	1,149,600	2,060	285,709	0	0	0	0	0	0	0	0	100	5,120
4545	Stone Chapel	11	1	1	3,100	116	596,000	4,917	64,602	0	0	0	0	0	0	0	0	50	0
4365	Strawbridge	24	24	24	1,100	110	1,000,000	11,850	350,360	0	0	0	0	0	0	0	0	644	0
4485	Taylorsville	20	4	8	1,950	85	1,900,000	15,083	247,802	0	542,856	329	0	348	0	0	0	0	18,039
6360	Thurmont	1	0	1	400	25	3,200,000	4,200	110,977	0	0	287	0	0	0	0	0	2,529	35,759
6170	Tom's Creek	10	2	8	4,000	450	1,160,000	22,336	981,777	0	1,633	1,317	0	0	0	0	0	3,500	3,380
6175	Trinity	5	1	2	446	111	5,584,000	22,757	78,410	25,000	0	0	0	0	0	0	0	0	70
6225	Trinity	0	0	0	0	7	6,750,000	6,250	6,567,458	0	0	0	0	0	0	0	0	50	341
6710	Trinity	5	1	4	400	12	542,012	2,600	200,000	0	0	0	0	0	0	0	0	341	0
4550	Union Street	0	0	1	142	2	350,000	4,500	0	0	0	0	0	0	0	0	0	700	3,285
4510	Uniontown	5	1	0	1,000	30	700,000	12,032	385,196	0	58,722	250	0	0	0	0	0	1,000	1
6760	Uvilla	0	0	0	335	90	3,200,000	26,902	23,609	0	0	50	0	0	0	0	0	335	9,038
6420	Walkersville	2	2	2	3,744	679	2,371,000	43,681	857,745	0	0	11,270	0	0	0	0	0	5,395	627
6365	Weller	19	10	13	3,369	0	7,246,300	5,000	0	36,000	0	0	0	0	0	0	0		
4555	Westminster	23	6	10	17	0	635,000	8,800	75,000	0	0	0	0	251	0	0	0		
6740	Williams Memorial	0	0	0	116	70	812,000									156			
4560	Zion	0	0	2															
FR Total		3,761	127	311	87,855	5,468	159,878,577	927,016	25,475,007	7,785,797	639,347	59,331	0	8,061	0	156	0	187,501	526,348

Align #	Church Name	48 TOTAL – Total of UMC Causes & UMC Missions & Outreach	49 – NON-UMC CAUSES: Total given DIRECTLY to non-UMC causes	50a – Human Relations Sunday	50b – UMCOR Sunday	50c – Peace with Justice Sunday	50d – Native American Ministries Sunday	50e – World Communion Sunday	50f – U.M. Student Day	51 – Direct-billed clergy non-health benefits	52 – Direct-billed clergy health benefits	53a – Base comp. Senior Pastor	53b – Base comp. Associate Pastor(s)/staff	53c – Base comp. Deacons NOT in 53a/53b	55a – Housing benefits Lead Pastor	55b – Housing benefits Associate Pastor(s)/staff	55c – Housing benefits Deacons not in 53a/53b	56 – Accountable reimbursements	57 – Other cash allowances
4490	Middleburg	1,038	260	0	0	0	0	0	0	0	0	10,359	0	0	1,440	0	0	780	200
6280	Middletown	54,141	85,475	0	0	0	0	0	0	23,842	56,988	76,257	43,293	0	19,863	2,371	0	9,230	0
6635	Middleway	300	6,799	0	0	0	0	0	0	24,619	23,392	36,800	0	0	0	0	0	2,104	0
6335	Mount Carmel	15,536	4,066	0	0	0	0	0	0	0	0	51,898	0	0	19,866	0	0	4,646	2,750
6390	Mount Pleasant	2,870	3,500	0	0	0	0	0	0	0	0	7,000	0	0	2,500	0	0	3,200	0
6735	Mount Wesley	0	12,000	0	0	0	0	0	0	0	0	15,187	3,750	0	12,500	0	0	0	0
6410	Mount Zion	915	915	0	0	0	0	0	0	0	0	3,438	0	0	0	0	0	0	0
6575	Mount Zion	1,381	1,200	0	0	0	0	0	0	0	0	27,517	0	0	19,866	0	0	7,981	0
6580	Murrill Hill	7,916	7,436	0	0	0	0	0	0	0	0	14,800	0	0	0	0	0	0	0
6137	New Hope of Greater Brunswick	36,319	650	0	0	0	0	0	0	11,618	16,301	45,485	10,760	0	3,932	0	0	4,100	0
4640	New Hope of New Windsor	661	0	0	0	0	0	0	0	0	0	10,500	0	0	4,600	19,866	0	1,070	0
6340	New Market	17,755	6,324	0	0	0	0	0	0	0	0	0	45,821	0	0	0	0	1,198	0
6790	New Street	1,466	5,000	0	0	0	0	0	0	11,502	20,150	45,000	0	0	16,500	0	0	0	0
4275	Oakland	0	1,100	0	0	0	0	0	0	6,009	7,660	35,175	0	0	14,909	0	0	2,014	0
6535	Oakland	10,463	4,770	12	280	0	15	84	125	0	2,656	51,170	0	0	7,950	0	0	0	0
6680	Ottabein	16,240	9,051	0	0	0	0	0	0	12,827	11,400	12,810	0	0	19,933	0	0	5,503	0
6730	Paynes Chapel	1,200	4,350	0	0	0	0	0	0	0	0	36,343	0	0	12,810	0	0	0	0
6725	Pikeside	1,480	16,096	0	0	0	0	0	0	7,744	7,150	7,351	0	0	14,500	0	0	0	0
6165	Pleasant View	0	0	0	0	0	0	0	0	0	0	1,200	0	0	0	0	0	261	0
6605	Salem	1	1,045	0	0	0	0	0	0	0	0	9,150	3,000	0	0	0	0	4,867	0
6255	Sandy Hook	16,350	3,720	0	0	0	0	0	0	11,703	11,180	57,903	0	0	4,814	0	0	1,000	0
4443	Sandy Mount	100	0	0	0	0	0	0	0	0	0	11,000	0	0	0	0	0	0	780
6715	Shenandoah Memorial	3,858	29,131	0	0	0	0	0	0	0	0	18,000	0	0	0	0	0	5,500	0
6985	Silver Grove	5,239	8,000	0	0	0	0	0	0	12,736	11,933	57,500	20,000	0	19,866	0	0	2,400	0
6690	St. Lukes	18,442	397	0	0	0	0	0	0	0	0	22,699	0	0	10,000	0	0	0	0
4620	St. Paul	368	2,764	0	0	0	0	0	0	10,240	13,452	14,200	0	0	4,800	0	0	3,481	0
4540	St. James	980	150	0	0	0	0	0	0	0	0	8,658	0	0	6,424	0	0	3,840	0
4545	Stone Chapel	5,170	4,610	0	0	0	0	0	222	10,968	11,400	29,417	0	0	0	0	0	514	0
4365	Strawbridge	644	2,082	0	0	60	0	0	504	15,237	19,719	41,070	0	0	19,866	0	0	3,480	780
4485	Taylorsville	0	25,164	0	0	145	879	2,218	0	10,277	19,348	76,092	0	0	0	0	0	4,100	0
6360	Thurmont	18,039	0	106	419	0	66	0	0	9,586	16,164	45,675	0	0	5,128	419	0	2,889	0
6170	Tom's Creek	5,924	0	0	0	0	0	64	29	8,230	0	17,462	0	0	19,967	0	0	6,500	0
6175	Trinity	39,259	17,704	0	0	30	0	0	0	16,320	29,478	61,739	0	0	20,263	0	0	5,465	0
6225	Trinity	3,380	15,500	0	0	0	0	0	0	13,378	0	62,295	0	0	19,866	0	0	3,660	0
6710	Trinity	120	5,922	0	0	0	0	0	0	700	0	22,000	0	0	0	0	0	759	0
4550	Union Street	341	50	0	0	0	0	0	0	0	0	12,000	0	0	0	0	0	1,259	0
4510	Uniontown	700	0	0	0	0	0	0	0	0	0	8,750	0	0	2,700	0	0	2,119	0
6760	Uvilla	4,285	21,987	0	0	0	0	0	0	12,560	15,574	72,849	0	0	0	0	0	12,800	1,500
6420	Walkersville	336	6,341	144	0	0	0	0	222	9,106	10,703	43,647	0	0	19,866	0	0	0	0
6365	Weller	14,433	28,645	356	0	0	0	0	504	26,022	30,067	56,100	0	0	7,310	0	0	1,500	0
4555	Westminster	627	0	0	0	0	0	0	0	0	0	11,667	0	0	0	0	0	0	0
6740	Williams Memorial	0	1,000	0	0	0	0	0	0	0	0	35,000	22,711	0	31,520	15,000	0	0	2,400
4560	Zion	0	0	0	0	0	0	0	0	0	0	0	0	0	0	0	0	0	3,000
	FR Total	715,849	576,066	1,281	1,664	1,022	1,692	3,240	1,228	478,723	616,660	2,516,211	300,285	55,012	881,011	72,580	0	176,365	40,569

Align #	Church Name	50 Paid in salary and benefits for all other church staff and diaconal ministers	61 Amount spent for local church program expenses	62 Amount spent for local church operating expenses	63 Amount paid for principal and interest on indebtedness, loans, mortgages, etc.	63a Amount paid for capital campaign or fundraising costs	64 Amount paid on capital expenditures for building, improvements, and major equipment purchases	65 Amount PAID by/for the local church on all expenditures	66 Number of giving units	67a Received through pledges	67b Received from non-pledging, but identified givers	67c Received from unidentified givers	67d Amount received from interest and dividends and/or transferred from liquid assets	67e Amount received from Sale of Church Assets	67f Amount received through building use fees, contributions, and rentals	67g Amount received through fundraisers and other sources
4490	Middleburg	0	26,861	2,492	172,993	0	0	18,916	12	0	18,290	1,750	0	0	0	0
6080	Middletown	113,591	2,552	91,733	8,760	0	69,972	913,522	198	658,169	54,193	8,918	3	0	14,918	70,309
6635	Middleway	0	9,442	40,449	130,835	193	1,150	109,633	48	0	89,670	12,576	803	0	8,400	6,832
6335	Mount Carmel	110,702	2,310	22,142	0	0	7,533	454,461	217	175,700	188,894	6,680	144	0	54,000	8,399
6390	Mount Pleasant	7,500	1,460	5,275	0	0	0	38,248	16	0	53,667	4,595	0	0	600	1,686
6735	Mount Wesley	0	102	15,480	12,635	0	12,500	79,899	24	27,025	61,500	10,000	0	0	0	0
6410	Mount Zion	16,800	4,948	7,000	0	0	0	19,164	6	6,890	0	0	0	0	0	0
6675	Mount Zion	0	0	10,487	0	0	8,479	115,994	78	23,795	98,277	8,586	0	0	925	8,928
6580	Murrill Hill	35,255	2,529	2,024	0	0	340	35,666	169	0	0	6,313	228	0	0	0
6137	New Hope of Greater Brunswick	0	1,067	17,765	0	0	28,111	238,934	11	0	168,431	6,859	15	0	1,015	3,558
4640	New Hope of New Windsor	27,633	4,125	8,972	42,047	0	1,285	31,490	102	0	10,886	6,625	400	0	11,187	1,764
6340	New Market	26,000	2,600	30,360	0	0	12,185	231,636	29	0	163,580	3,774	0	0	38,988	6,621
6750	New Street	19,414	9,631	43,000	0	0	8,000	190,246	0	124,000	6,400	0	242	0	400	6,200
4275	Oakland	0	1,700	20,600	968	0	12,375	149,658	18	0	112,745	3,070	0	0	15,750	24,000
6535	Oakland	0	0	15,077	0	0	5,500	45,414	109	0	48,368	4,000	0	0	0	6,359
6680	Otterbein	53,473	10,198	21,268	0	0	0	241,772	35	0	217,997	23,159	1,227	0	410	0
6730	Paynes Chapel	3,549	3,648	4,038	0	0	500	59,667	66	2,045	48,872	8,393	0	0	0	4,136
6725	Pikeside	25,543	2,300	20,961	0	0	0	157,245	20	158,510	4,257	0	0	0	0	0
6165	Pleasant View	0	3,973	3,000	0	0	5,576	26,308	3	40,531	0	0	0	0	0	0
6685	Salem	0	261	7,101	0	0	0	5,330	12	5,500	0	0	0	1,653	0	0
6255	Sandy Hook	969	5,034	51,474	0	0	15,512	24,232	105	0	20,655	5,150	0	0	0	13,350
4443	Sandy Mount	74,213	450	6,265	0	0	0	301,786	22	0	246,311	4,908	0	0	42,164	790
6715	Shenandoah Memorial	0	21,487	3,968	0	0	0	20,531	16	1,020	16,800	0	0	0	0	0
6585	Silver Grove	0	5,876	39,292	0	0	8,880	29,813	154	0	35,793	0	0	320	90	31,810
6690	St Lukes	103,947	2,275	7,499	121,100	0	52,700	381,462	65	0	359,199	27,323	676	143,000	0	4,809
4620	St Paul	24,628	4,476	21,905	0	0	450	186,459	15	0	115,714	2,000	482	0	1,520	3,879
4540	St James	2,998	2,486	16,946	0	0	38,478	38,182	19	0	26,287	463	115	0	380	10,712
4545	Stone Chapel	14,336	1,871	27,458	0	1,934	1,331	139,161	60	75,750	39,351	3,180	66	550	0	10,085
4365	Strawbridge	10,040	3,889	65,077	0	0	0	82,142	93	0	4,178	7,618	20,000	0	0	0
4485	Taylorsville	25,331	13,166	45,685	0	0	49,134	168,014	151	0	129,914	3,649	0	0	90	41,155
6360	Thurmont	10,719	32,000	25,523	0	0	6,248	291,888	126	46,437	237,101	21,425	162	0	0	86,500
6170	Tom's Creek	9,969	43,029	82,000	0	0	16,521	310,585	28	0	187,370	12,002	0	0	2,713	0
6175	Trinity	13,053		103,404	0	0	35,000	164,177	312	0	48,662	5,678	500	0	476	0
6225	Trinity	139,656		5,160	0	0	65,048	544,317	90	307,905	230,997	1,000	224,473	0	5,614	2,014
6710	Trinity	181,739		16,486	0	0	0	600,442	23	0	96,308	5,697	0	0	170	0
4550	Union Street	5,880		6,841	0	0	0	37,841	22	0	0	0	133	0	0	823
4510	Uniontown	7,220		68,403	0	0	98,120	46,406	133	46,153	23,200	1,873	750	0	8,600	8,974
6760	Uvilla	0		29,587	0	0	36,513	20,865	77	0	2,500	3,345	46	0	320	4,618
6420	Walkersville	113,234		100,045	21,588	0	30,234	498,985	357	0	317,991	12,070	4	0	17,063	0
6365	Weller	30,337		2,098	0	162	0	203,708	35	443,257	150,045	2,505	608	0	949	0
4555	Westminster	179,401		21,234	0	0	0	664,060		0	132,653	7,975	0	0	2,185	2,190
6740	Williams Memorial	0			5,156	0	0	25,632		0	36,412	9,117	0	0		0
4560	Zion	0	2,000			0	0	72,835		0	37,765	7,910	375	0	375	
	FR Total	2,500,421	482,335	2,375,107	1,116,139	22,502	1,412,210	15,920,980	6,165	3,009,330	8,465,669	734,444	542,824	147,483	558,573	712,301

Align #	Church Name	TOTAL income for annual budget/spending plan (67a-g) [67]	Capital campaigns [68a]	Memorials, endowments, and bequests [65b]	Other sources and projects (include UMW, UMM and 'flow-through') [65c]	Special Sundays, Gen. Adv. Spec, World Srvc Spec., Conf. Adv Spec. and other directed benevolent giving [68d]	Total income for designated causes including capital campaign and other special projects [68]	Equitable Compensation Funds received by Church or Pastor [69a]	Advance Special, apportioned, and connectional funds received by church [69b]	Other grants and financial support from institutional sources [69c]	Income from connectional/institutional sources outside the local church [69]	TOTAL CHURCH INCOME (Sum of Lines 67 + 68 + 69) [70]	Amount APPORTIONED to the local church [40a]	Amount PAID by the local church for all apportioned causes [40b]
4490	Middleburg	20,040	0	0	0	300	300	0	0	0	0	20,340	2,347	2,347
6280	Middletown	806,510	82,092	4,910	0	6,193	93,195	0	0	0	0	899,705	67,512	67,512
6635	Middleway	118,281	0	0	0	6,240	6,240	0	0	0	0	124,521	10,719	10,719
6335	Mount Carmel	433,817	10,200	3,436	0	14,042	27,678	0	0	12,500	12,500	473,995	29,784	29,784
6390	Mount Pleasant	60,538	0	0	0	0	0	0	0	0	0	60,538	4,543	4,543
6735	Mount Wesley	98,525	0	0	0	12,000	12,000	0	0	0	0	110,525	7,552	7,552
6410	Mount Zion	0	0	0	0	0	0	0	0	0	0	0	3,044	3,044
6675	Mount Zion	123,606	750	3,332	0	0	4,082	0	0	0	0	127,688	12,081	12,081
6580	Murrill Hill	30,108	0	0	0	0	0	0	0	0	0	30,108	3,150	3,150
6137	New Hope of Greater Brunswick	180,091	21,746	5,747	0	21,192	48,685	0	12,500	3,000	15,500	244,276	22,228	22,228
6640	New Hope of New Windsor	30,462	0	0	167,402	0	167,402	0	0	0	0	197,864	4,205	4,205
6340	New Market	212,878	6,375	4,540	23,775	3,779	38,469	0	0	0	0	251,347	21,420	21,420
6750	New Street	137,400	0	275	0	0	275	0	0	0	0	137,675	19,915	19,958
4275	Oakland	155,565	0	0	0	501	501	0	0	0	0	156,066	17,416	17,416
6535	Oakland	58,727	0	0	0	0	0	0	45,372	0	45,372	104,099	35,953	0
6680	Otterbein	241,808	0	0	6,000	7,423	13,423	0	0	0	0	255,231	37,809	32,768
6730	Paynes Chapel	63,446	0	0	0	150	150	0	0	0	0	63,596	6,762	6,762
6725	Pikeside	158,510	0	0	0	0	0	0	0	0	0	158,510	19,625	19,625
6165	Pleasant View	46,015	0	0	0	0	0	0	0	0	0	46,015	2,763	2,763
6685	Salem	5,500	0	0	0	0	0	0	0	0	0	5,500	1,130	1,130
6255	Sandy Hook	27,458	0	0	0	0	0	0	0	0	0	27,458	2,187	2,187
4443	Sandy Mount	306,733	0	1,980	0	3,042	5,022	0	0	0	0	311,755	45,016	45,016
6715	Shenandoah Memorial	18,930	0	500	0	0	500	0	0	0	0	19,430	2,166	2,166
6585	Silver Grove	35,793	0	0	0	0	0	0	0	0	0	35,793	3,859	3,537
6690	St Lukes	386,522	0	15,149	0	9,153	24,302	0	0	0	0	410,824	51,049	51,049
4620	St Paul	294,720	0	8,000	0	190	8,190	0	0	0	0	302,910	14,215	14,215
4540	St. James	32,421	300	2,140	0	765	3,205	0	0	0	0	35,626	6,305	5,780
4545	Stone Chapel	46,525	0	719	0	2,338	3,057	0	0	0	0	49,582	16,148	16,148
4365	Strawbridge	98,874	505	340	0	1,085	1,930	0	0	0	0	100,804	9,992	9,992
4485	Taylorsville	163,738	535	7,030	0	0	7,565	0	0	0	0	171,303	21,497	21,497
6360	Tharmont	258,526	0	302,012	0	0	302,012	0	0	0	0	560,538	25,395	25,395
6170	Tom's Creek	289,839	0	6,086	0	677	6,763	0	0	0	0	296,602	18,368	18,368
6175	Trinity	141,316	0	3,915	0	4,746	8,661	0	0	0	0	149,977	13,570	13,570
6225	Trinity	546,016	0	211,798	0	0	211,798	0	0	0	0	757,814	58,599	58,599
6710	Trinity	328,662	0	4,058	0	2,599	6,657	0	0	0	0	335,319	67,438	67,438
4550	Union Street	0	0	0	0	0	0	0	0	0	0	0	7,021	270
4510	Uniontown	34,629	0	0	0	540	540	0	0	0	0	35,169	4,675	4,675
6760	Uvilla	62,042	0	0	0	0	0	0	0	0	0	62,042	3,074	3,074
6420	Walkersville	351,788	11,026	2,505	0	20,673	34,204	0	0	0	0	385,092	41,895	41,895
6365	Weller	153,503	41,599	2,990	0	0	44,479	0	0	0	0	197,982	20,340	20,340
4555	Westminster	586,678	0	176,970	0	3,132	180,102	0	0	0	0	766,780	73,651	73,651
6740	Williams Memorial	47,719	0	1,475	0	2,826	4,301	0	0	0	0	52,020	3,684	3,684
4560	Zion	66,042	0	655	0	0	655	0	0	0	0	66,697	10,350	10,350
	FR Total	14,170,624	312,782	930,380	206,460	193,698	1,643,320	0	60,372	15,500	75,872	15,889,816	1,625,294	1,527,722

Align #	Church Name	Dist #	City	State	Total professing members at the close of 2017 (1)	Received by PROFESSION of Faith (2a1)	Received by PROFESSION of Faith (Other Than Confirmation) (2a2)	Restored by AFFIRMATION of Faith (2b)	Transferred in from other UM churches (3)	Transferred in from non-UM churches (4)	Removed or corrected by Charge Conference action (5a)	Withdrawn from Professing Membership (5b)	Transferred out to other UM churches (6)	Transferred out to non-UM churches (7)	Removed by death (8)	Total professing members at the close of 2018 (9)	Asian (9a)	African American / Black (9b)	Hispanic / Latino (9c)	Native American (9d)	Pacific Islander (9e)	White (9f)	Multi-Racial (9g)	Female (9h)	Male (9i)
7380	Ager Road	GW	Hyattsville	MD	181	0	0	0	0	0	0	0	0	0	0	181	24	111	0	0	0	46	0	122	59
7110	Albright Memorial	GW	Washington	DC	48	0	0	0	0	0	0	0	0	0	3	45	3	45	0	0	0	0	0	35	10
7115	Asbury	GW	Washington	DC	980	0	1	0	1	0	14	0	0	0	22	946	3	939	0	0	0	4	0	596	350
8145	Bells	GW	Camp Springs	MD	63	19	0	7	8	1	4	0	1	0	3	57	0	39	4	0	1	18	5	33	24
9122	Bethesda	GW	Bethesda	MD	945	0	0	0	0	0	0	0	0	0	0	972	22	39	0	0	0	928	0	516	456
7120	Bradbury Heights	GW	Washington	DC	45	2	0	0	0	5	60	0	0	0	0	45	0	45	4	0	0	1	0	32	13
7625	Brighter Day	GW	Washington	DC	391	3	3	0	0	0	13	0	0	1	2	325	0	323	1	0	0	1	0	231	95
7125	Brightwood Park	GW	Washington	DC	206	4	7	2	0	0	0	0	0	0	6	198	0	193	2	1	0	4	0	131	67
9160	Cabin John	GW	Cabin John	MD	112	0	0	2	6	0	0	0	2	0	0	115	1	1	0	0	0	93	0	68	47
7135	Capitol Hill	GW	Washington	DC	207	3	7	5	0	3	1	0	0	0	3	226	2	15	3	0	3	202	4	135	91
7615	Centenary	GW	Flatts FL	BX	36	0	0	0	0	0	0	0	2	0	0	36	0	12	0	1	0	20	0	22	14
7325	Cheverly	GW	Cheverly	MD	143	3	1	4	0	0	5	0	2	0	6	144	0	48	0	0	4	93	2	99	45
9165	Chevy Chase	GW	Chevy Chase	MD	451	0	14	4	3	0	0	0	0	0	0	445	8	5	1	0	1	424	0	274	171
7140	Christ	GW	Washington	DC	100	0	0	1	0	0	4	0	1	0	0	114	2	105	0	0	1	5	1	73	41
7475	Church of The Redeemer	GW	Temple Hills	MD	214	8	1	8	5	0	0	0	0	1	0	219	0	218	0	0	0	1	0	120	99
9450	Colesville	GW	Silver Spring	MD	375	0	0	1	3	0	8	0	0	0	8	375	6	267	4	0	1	92	5	248	127
7335	College Park	GW	College Park	MD	139	0	0	0	0	0	0	0	2	0	2	137	3	30	7	0	0	95	0	90	47
7396	College Park Hispanic Initiative	GW	College Park	MD		0	0	0	0	0	0	0	0	0	2	25	0	1	25	0	0	0	0	15	10
7145	Community	GW	Washington	DC	72	0	0	0	0	0	0	0	0	0	4	66	0	66	0	0	0	0	0	41	25
9130	Concord-St. Andrews	GW	Bethesda	MD	405	0	1	0	0	1	2	0	1	0	12	392	62	38	6	0	0	280	6	285	107
7155	Douglas Memorial	GW	Washington	DC	142	0	0	0	0	0	0	0	0	5	0	137	0	137	0	0	0	0	0	117	20
7160	Dumbarton	GW	Washington	DC	305	0	4	1	1	0	0	1	5	0	4	305	11	7	19	0	0	266	2	161	144
7165	Ebenezer	GW	Washington	DC	119	0	0	0	1	0	0	0	0	0	0	119	0	118	0	1	0	0	0	88	31
7440	Emmanuel	GW	Laurel	MD	618	8	3	4	5	2	3	10	0	4	3	631	14	21	5	0	0	575	14	372	259
7175	Emory	GW	Washington	DC	669	7	7	1	1	6	7	4	2	4	4	661	0	650	0	0	0	10	1	384	290
9410	Faith	GW	Rockville	MD	437	0	29	1	2	0	5	0	1	1	11	410	3	7	4	0	5	391	0	231	179
7385	First	GW	Hyattsville	MD	1,016	5	3	1	2	0	0	3	4	1	11	1,036	3	657	12	0	2	357	5	664	372
8190	Forest Memorial	GW	Forestville	MD	240	6	3	1	2	2	71	3	5	4	3	239	0	63	0	0	0	176	0	130	109
7180	Foundry	GW	Washington	DC	920	1	10	7	10	28	29	15	6	5	9	870	31	77	14	0	2	619	127	446	424
7427	Francis Asbury National Korean	GW	Rockville	MD	234	0	0	0	7	1	0	0	1	6	3	212	211	0	0	0	0	1	0	117	95
7185	Franklin P Nash	GW	Washington	DC	58	0	2	0	0	1	0	0	1	1	1	59	0	567	0	0	0	0	0	32	32
7320	Gethsemane	GW	Capitol Heights	MD	573	6	0	0	4	0	0	1	2	1	11	567	10	104	1	0	10	75	0	356	211
9475	Glenmont	GW	Silver Spring	MD	201	0	0	1	1	0	1	5	0	1	5	200	0	104	0	0	0	80	10	120	80
9455	Good Hope Union	GW	Silver Spring	MD	386	6	16	0	0	3	1	0	0	0	0	386	0	385	0	0	0	1	0	252	134
7445	Good Shepherd	GW	Silver Spring	MD	371	0	0	0	0	0	4	0	0	0	0	384	4	273	13	0	4	88	2	226	158
7370	Grace	GW	Farmount Heights	MD	77	0	0	0	0	0	0	0	0	77	0	0	0	0	0	0	0	0	0	0	0
7465	Grace	GW	Takoma Park	MD	164	0	0	0	0	0	0	0	0	0	3	164	0	164	0	0	0	147	0	101	63
9480	Hughes	GW	Wheaton	MD	227	0	7	0	3	0	3	4	0	0	5	220	8	39	18	0	0	147	0	133	87
7190	Hughes Memorial	GW	Washington	DC	210	0	0	1	1	0	18	0	0	1	0	190	0	190	0	0	0	85	0	146	44
7183	InspireDC	GW	Washington	DC	0	0	0	0	0	0	0	0	0	0	0	100	0	15	0	0	0	85	0	70	30
0420	Jerusalem-Mt. Pleasant	GW	Rockville	MD	151	0	7	0	3	0	0	0	0	0	5	149	0	148	1	0	0	0	0	123	26
7210	Jones Memorial	GW	Washington	DC	201	0	0	0	0	4	0	0	1	0	9	187	4	187	0	0	6	0	0	118	69
9155	Liberty Grove	GW	Burtonsville	MD	443	12	1	1	8	1	0	6	1	7	6	449	4	74	19	0	6	344	2	285	164
7215	Lincoln Park	GW	Washington	DC	239	0	0	0	0	0	33	0	0	0	4	205	0	204	1	0	0	0	0	109	96
7610	Marsden First	GW	Smith's	HS01	116	0	0	0	0	0	0	0	0	0	0	117	0	113	0	0	0	4	0	79	38
7620	McKendree-Simms-Brookland	GW	Washington	DC	362	0	0	0	0	0	0	0	0	0	7	362	0	362	0	0	0	0	0	240	122
7462	Memorial First India	GW	Silver Spring	MD	243	11	0	0	0	0	9	0	0	0	3	248	212	8	2	0	0	20	6	129	119
7630	Metropolitan Memorial	GW	Washington	DC	1,199	0	11	0	0	0	0	0	0	0	9	1,199	22	92	6	1	0	1,078	0	709	490

Align #	Church Name	10	10a	11a	11b	11T	12	13	14	15	16	17	18	19	20	22	23	24	25	26	27	28	29	30a	30b
7380	Ager Road	55	0	0	0	0	0	0	0	0	0	0	0	0	0	0	0	1	2	0	0	0	0	0	0
7110	Albright Memorial	23	0	0	0	1	0	0	0	11	9	3	0	11	3	0	1	3	0	0	0	5	0	0	0
7115	Asbury	252	130	1	0	5	44	50	0	43	9	28	162	242	30	14	3	6	28	21	15,073	100	6,400	0	0
8145	Bells	21	0	0	0	0	0	15	1	5	3	3	0	23	3	30	0	3	0	0	0	0	0	0	0
9122	Bethesda	342	0	11	4	15	0	12	0	73	39	21	122	255	90	245	3	7	13	0	0	0	0	1	6
7120	Bradbury Heights	23	101	0	0	0	0	41	0	5	1	3	0	17	2	0	7	1	1	0	0	0	0	0	0
7625	Brighter Day	145	0	7	4	11	152	433	19	30	15	1	89	138	50	50	0	4	1	10	0	37	995	0	6
7125	Brightwood Park	50	0	2	0	2	24	9	2	6	7	5	15	29	6	30	1	4	1	10	0	16	0	0	0
9160	Cabin John	76	0	1	0	11	0	0	0	12	11	28	22	50	35	0	1	9	3	0	0	0	0	0	0
7135	Capitol Hill	175	60	9	2	0	66	200	4	99	9	0	232	368	67	35	5	0	24	0	0	0	0	0	0
7615	Centenary	25	0	0	0	0	0	0	0	11	0	7	11	11	11	0	0	12	0	0	0	0	0	0	0
7925	Cheverly	71	0	5	1	6	7	68	3	53	4	7	40	112	33	20	1	8	6	10	790	30	600	0	0
9165	Chevy Chase	152	10	2	0	2	92	400	0	39	35	2	167	167	25	64	6	2	6	12	2,081	0	10,000	0	0
7140	Christ	45	0	0	0	0	2	26	0	7	7	15	44	60	20	0	2	12	5	25	600	25	400	0	11
7475	Church of The Redeemer	75	0	5	0	5	0	70	8	5	2	5	50	75	15	15	3	1	1	15	2,205	25	2,075	2	0
9450	Colesville	130	0	2	0	3	0	45	0	19	17	4	11	62	12	0	0	0	3	0	600	15	2,202	0	0
7335	College Park	80	0	0	1	0	0	0	0	20	20	8	19	48	25	38	0	12	0	17	0	0	0	0	0
7396	College Park-Hispanic Initiative	25	0	1	1	0	45	0	0	0	5	0	48	50	15	25	0	2	4	0	0	0	0	0	0
7145	Community	53	0	0	0	0	0	0	0	5	5	0	0	19	0	0	0	6	1	0	0	0	0	0	0
9130	Concord-St. Andrews	40	0	0	0	2	20	25	0	2	10	2	32	50	5	0	0	2	0	17	0	0	0	0	0
7155	Douglas Memorial	25	0	0	0	0	0	0	0	0	0	19	7	19	17	0	2	6	4	0	0	0	310	0	0
7160	Dumbarton	86	5	0	1	1	25	82	0	19	13	2	17	136	60	0	6	0	1	10	0	24	0	0	0
7165	Ebenezer	64	0	1	0	7	2	0	0	9	9	11	17	41	14	21	7	14	24	12	0	0	310	0	34
7440	Emmanuel	167	24	6	6	7	0	110	9	210	60	50	96	470	50	140	15	0	7	18	0	16	500	2	16
9410	Emory	378	315	11	4	3	8	18	0	66	36	38	150	409	85	72	0	7	24	10	0	44	1,000	2	0
7175	Faith	127	0	4	0	4	46	197	5	31	23	5	246	132	43	0	6	4	6	20	0	10	970	0	0
8190	First	269	0	0	3	3	5	144	0	15	8	0	73	88	20	40	4	4	4	3	0	38	0	0	0
7365	Forest Memorial	30	0	5	0	12	0	0	0	17	6	105	65	43	15	0	2	19	0	40	0	10	0	0	0
7180	Foundry	511	1,006	9	1	11	105	823	12	185	55	23	470	815	191	0	9	17	10	20	6,990	60	0	0	0
9427	Francis Asbury National Korean	170	0	0	3	0	0	0	0	13	15	0	90	141	23	25	5	20	2	16	2,144	91	1,480	0	8
7185	Franklin P Nash	90	0	3	1	4	0	0	0	0	0	10	14	27	7	0	0	0	8	20	2,443	12	1,939	0	0
7320	Gethsemane	141	0	1	0	1	1	20	0	30	10	0	110	160	0	50	20	12	12	27	1,908	48	1,242	0	0
9475	Glenmont	90	10	0	0	0	0	28	0	6	0	0	55	68	20	30	4	6	0	17	1,300	59	2,150	0	0
9455	Good Hope Union	140	0	4	5	12	28	37	6	35	15	12	85	107	15	82	12	0	8	15	0	31	0	0	0
7445	Good Shepherd	130	0	7	0	4	47	17	0	0	10	8	35	92	30	0	6	2	11	0	0	0	0	0	0
7370	Grace	0	0	0	0	0	0	0	0	0	0	6	0	0	0	0	0	2	0	15	0	0	0	0	0
7465	Grace	80	0	0	0	0	0	0	0	15	0	0	20	58	15	35	2	2	0	0	0	23	1,835	0	0
9480	Hughes	99	10	0	1	1	24	15	0	11	3	3	86	106	6	0	3	9	11	13	0	0	0	0	0
7190	Hughes Memorial	70	0	0	0	0	0	35	0	10	8	3	50	68	15	80	0	0	5	5	300	30	1,425	0	0
7183	InspireDC	100	0	0	0	0	0	0	0	0	1	0	0	0	0	0	0	0	0	0	0	39	425	1	0
9420	Jerusalem-Mt. Pleasant	46	0	0	0	0	0	0	0	16	286	8	67	69	28	24	3	5	13	0	0	0	0	0	0
7210	Jones Memorial	69	0	0	1	0	52	52	12	87	7	10	42	619	60	53	11	6	0	10	1,000	20	4,000	0	0
9155	Liberty Grove	153	5	10	1	11	0	10	0	10	4	8	245	62	12	20	2	6	0	14	0	12	0	0	0
7215	Lincoln Park	100	0	1	0	1	17	17	0	12	10	22	35	47	22	50	5	6	8	0	0	61	0	1	0
7610	Marsden First	56	0	0	4	4	0	0	0	0	8	10	25	120	28	0	6	7	0	14	0	26	0	0	2
7620	McKendree-Simms-Brookland	141	0	2	1	3	16	21	0	21	14	8	43	99	33	50	7	6	5	12	0	122	0	2	0
7462	Memorial First India	127	0	7	3	10	0	0	0	21	13	22	173	361	55	43	11	7	8	20	0	122	4,000	0	0
7630	Metropolitan Memorial	270	0	9	1	9	9	732	14	143	35	10	361	361	55	32	11	7	8	20	0	122	40,000	0	0

Align #	Church Name	33 TOTAL Community MINISTRIES for outreach, justice, and mercy	33a MINISTRIES focusing on global/regional health?	33b MINISTRIES focusing on engaging in ministry with the poor/socially	34 PERSONS SERVED BY community ministries	35a PERSONS SERVING (from your congregation)	36 Market value of church-owned land, buildings and equipment	36SF Overall square footage of church owned buildings	37 Market value of financial and other liquid assets	38 Debt secured by church physical assets	39 Other debt	42 General Advance Specials	43 World Service Specials	44 Annual Conf. Advance Specials	45 Youth Service Fund	46 All other funds to AC Treasurer	47 Total AC Special Sunday Offerings	48a UMC CAUSES given DIRECTLY	48b MISSIONS/MINISTRY COSTS (local church)
7380	Ager Road	1	0	1	1	0	3,245,000	25,750	20,000	0	0	0	0	0	0	0	0	0	3,100
7110	Albright Memorial	4	0	2	251	17	7,841,370	23,095	1,479,082	152,810	0	0	0	0	0	0	0	0	175
7115	Asbury	12	2	12	12,638	146	17,534,874	46,378	724,000	0	437,046	0	0	0	0	0	0	0	46,054
8145	Bells	2	1	1	75	15	3,798,000	39,329	105,000	210,830	0	250	0	0	0	0	0	2,870	28,154
9122	Bethesda	5	1	4	345	198	6,837,000	39,612	7,143	0	0	0	0	0	0	0	0	0	145
7120	Bradbury Heights	4	0	4	381	25	1,420,900	0	80,830	462,401	0	0	0	0	0	0	0	3,294	2,552
7625	Brighter Day	3	1	3	6,673	120	6,970,390	47,800	21,743	0	325	0	0	0	0	0	0	800	0
7125	Brightwood Park	9	0	3	50	7	2,100,000	23,266	160,000	0	0	0	0	0	0	0	0	12,055	0
9160	Cabin John	0	0	0	0	0	1,480,000	0	999,346	0	0	0	0	0	0	2,948	0	0	61,537
7135	Capitol Hill	19	2	17	2,741	160	5,465,930	22,474	50,331	0	0	0	0	0	0	0	0	0	0
7615	Centenary	0	0	0	0	0	2,300,000	5,150	1,482	0	0	200	0	0	0	0	0	16,411	180
7325	Cheverly	9	2	4	2,400	130	6,500,000	22,005	1,297,000	84,379	0	5,151	0	0	0	0	0	0	27,354
9165	Chevy Chase	12	5	7	2,300	10	10,267,712	39,050	204,000	0	0	1,022	0	0	0	0	0	500	3,625
7140	Christ	2	0	2	150	40	4,909,220	10,428	81,081	0	0	100	0	0	0	0	0	3,394	16,857
7475	Church of The Redeemer	5	5	5	100	120	1,630,000	19,254	280,314	264,034	0	81	0	0	0	0	0	0	11,700
9450	Colesville	7	1	4	1,500	36	5,968,856	9,236	80,000	0	0	0	0	20	0	100	0	0	37,532
7395	College Park	5	0	2	325	3	3,626,000	0	0	0	0	120	0	84	0	0	0	0	0
7396	College Park-Hispanic Initiative	0	0	0	0	0	0	0	0	0	0	0	0	0	0	0	0	0	7,345
7145	Community	2	2	2	3,040	12	1,965,940	17,238	5,000	0	0	0	0	0	0	0	0	0	37,678
9130	Concord-St. Andrews	2	0	2	2,000	15	4,700,000	25,870	750,000	0	4,000	0	0	0	0	0	0	0	0
7155	Douglas Memorial	5	3	3	2,381	25	2,590,480	15,000	80,000	0	0	0	0	0	0	0	0	1,597	10,755
7160	Dumbarton	13	0	8	114,495	93	5,316,000	11,118	301,516	436,814	1,169,580	0	0	0	0	0	0	0	0
7165	Ebenezer	3	0	3	0	3	5,196,550	16,021	2,318,410	0	0	0	0	0	0	0	0	230	0
7440	Emmanuel	55	8	29	6,000	8,500	2,984,500	12,933	755,765	200,000	0	0	0	0	0	0	0	10,320	0
7175	Emory	7	1	6	9,445	382	6,709,900	26,684	375,000	0	0	11,500	0	0	0	0	0	82,150	33,439
9410	Faith	2	0	9	1,700	150	13,408,200	21,500	292,000	0	0	7,097	0	117	0	250	0	17,357	122,227
7385	First	4	2	2	10,500	250	4,304,000	240,620	525,382	2,853,411	24,811	0	0	0	0	0	0	7,950	5,646
8190	Forest Memorial	13	4	12	5,126	390	31,520,000	26,379	0	0	0	0	0	0	0	0	0	0	15,287
9427	Francis Asbury National Korean	0	0	0	0	0	4,000,000	60,000	1,568,658	200,000	6,662	0	0	0	0	125	0	14,003	0
7180	Foundry	10	0	10	1,000	150	2,479,000	0	594,861	614,770	0	0	0	592	0	0	0	7,193	230,595
7185	Franklin P Nash	10	4	10	4,000	260	2,789,020	0	277,099	266,316	0	0	0	0	0	0	0	0	0
7320	Gethsemane	5	1	10	1,188	102	4,200,000	30,687	56,706	0	0	1,361	0	0	0	0	0	155	40,498
9475	Glenmont	32	4	10	2,950	210	3,499,367	21,600	10,814	250,000	0	0	0	0	0	0	0	0	2,773
9455	Good Hope Union	6	1	26	0	0	4,316,527	20,456	0	0	0	1,412	0	0	0	0	0	0	281
7445	Good Shepherd	16	6	8	1,000	74	0	0	200,000	250,000	0	0	0	0	0	0	0	10,200	10,200
7370	Grace	6	0	6	2,077	32	2,500,000	40,200	632,784	0	0	4,067	0	0	0	0	0	0	0
7465	Grace	6	4	9	2,442	44	10,822,200	40,923	16,350	0	0	21	0	0	0	0	0	0	1,800
9480	Hughes	3	0	8	650	17	3,307,000	10,368	0	0	0	0	0	0	0	0	0	2,121	4,264
7190	Hughes Memorial	15	6	6	2	20	1,081,600	4,164	8,940	0	0	0	0	0	0	0	0	0	4,799
7183	InspireDC	6	0	3	7,930	345	6,200,105	8,700	0	0	0	0	0	0	0	0	0	0	0
9420	Jerusalem-Mt Pleasant	2	0	3	365	5	6,568,320	25,203	132,385	0	0	0	0	0	0	0	0	0	5,959
7210	Jones Memorial	15	5	15	0	28	3,400,000	20,167	50,000	673,224	0	0	0	50	0	0	0	700	1,550
9155	Liberty Grove	6	1	5	15,323	60	2,739,178	0	279,181	2,130,705	0	0	0	0	0	0	0	811	64,276
7215	Lincoln Park	6	0	0	200	50	10,007,400	23,350	750,600	393,424	0	0	0	0	0	0	0	2,000	7,000
7010	Marsden First	0	0	0	500		10,200,000	21,992	605,000	200,000	0	0	0	0	0	0	0	0	0
7020	McKendree-Simms-Brookland	1	1	0			25,000,000	76,000	0	0	6,796	0	0	0	0	0	0	8,549	55,088
7462	Memorial First India	0	1	0					0	0	0	0	0	0	0	0	0	350	0
7030	Metropolitan Memorial	0	0	0					21,187,380	0	0	0	0	0	0	0	0	2,703	967,631

Align #	Church Name	48TOTAL (Total of UMC Causes & UMC Missions & Outreach)	49 (NON-UMC CAUSES: Total amount given DIRECTLY to non-United Methodist benevolent and charitable causes (NOT sent to BWC Treasurer))	50a (Human Relations Sunday)	50b (UMCOR Sunday formerly One Great Hour of Sharing)	50c (Peace with Justice Sunday)	50d (Native American Ministries Sunday)	50e (World Communion Sunday)	50f (U.M. Student Day)	51 (Direct-billed clergy non-health benefits)	52 (Direct-billed clergy health benefits)	53a (Base compensation paid to/for the Senior Pastor or other person assigned or appointed in the lead pastoral role in the church)	53b (Base compensation paid/for to all Associate Pastor(s) & other pastoral staff assigned or appointed to the church)	53c (Base compensation paid to/for any Deacons NOT included in 53a or 53b)	55a (Housing benefits paid to/for Lead Pastor or person in lead pastoral role as described in 53a)	55b (Housing benefits paid to/for ALL Associate Pastor(s) & other pastoral staff assigned or appointed to the church)	55c (Housing benefits paid to/for any Deacons not included in 53a or 53b)	56 (Paid to/for all persons included in Lines 53a-53c for accountable reimbursements)	57 (Paid to/for all persons included in Lines 53a-53c for any other cash allowances (non-...))
7380	Agar Road	3,100	0	0	0	0	0	0	0	0	0	22,500	0	0	0	0	0	2,100	0
7110	Albright Memorial	175	0	0	0	0	0	0	0	0	0	23,688	0	0	0	0	0	0	0
7115	Asbury	48,054	1,300	0	0	0	0	0	0	17,785	13,821	77,458	45,000	0	36,602	0	0	3,413	0
8145	Bells	0	0	0	0	0	0	0	0	0	0	20,295	0	0	20,295	0	0	0	0
9122	Bethesda	31,024	45,544	0	0	0	0	0	0	26,568	33,971	77,250	0	0	25,000	0	0	1,367	0
7120	Bradbury Heights	145	145	0	0	0	0	0	0	0	12,676	0	0	0	0	0	0	4,510	0
7625	Brighter Day	5,036	600	0	0	0	0	0	0	13,914	11,400	48,867	0	0	25,000	0	0	295	0
7125	Brightwood Park	800	0	0	0	0	0	0	0	6,463	11,400	47,000	0	0	0	0	0	0	0
9160	Cabin John	73,592	36,346	0	0	0	0	0	0	10,736	14,624	44,400	0	47,130	3,600	0	15,300	5,999	600
7135	Capitol Hill	0	0	0	0	0	0	0	0	25,146	11,400	61,497	0	0	30,000	0	0	0	0
7615	Centenary	180	2,336	315	200	587	615	456	558	0	11,827	41,162	0	0	0	0	0	4,100	1,000
7325	Cheverly	43,765	6,186	0	0	0	0	0	0	12,654	6,380	50,500	0	0	20,000	0	0	3,597	0
9165	Chevy Chase	3,625	1,106	40	0	45	212	55	20	13,727	13,121	68,850	0	0	19,886	0	0	1,601	996
7140	Christ	17,357	4,401	0	0	0	30	155	100	9,721	10,452	43,203	0	0	2,295	0	0	3,752	0
7475	Church of The Redeemer	15,094	9,511	630	0	0	0	39	0	5,671	0	32,824	0	0	17,213	0	0	5,539	4,286
9450	Colesville	37,532	310	0	0	0	0	294	0	13,433	90	53,235	35,896	0	30,240	24,400	0	387	200
7335	College Park	0	0	0	0	0	0	0	0	11,157	15,534	25,795	22,097	0	4,945	6,622	0	0	0
7396	College Park Hispanic Initiative	7,345	200	0	0	0	0	0	0	0	11,400	0	0	0	0	0	0	0	0
7145	Community	37,678	0	30	0	0	0	0	0	0	0	33,935	0	0	9,555	0	0	415	0
9130	Concord-St. Andrews	10,755	0	162	0	0	0	0	0	12,452	15,710	47,473	0	0	6,068	0	0	0	0
7155	Douglas Memorial	1,597	7,652	84	0	0	0	0	0	0	11,400	21,000	5,200	0	0	0	0	11,329	0
7160	Dumbarton	230	195	0	0	0	0	0	0	13,389	0	66,203	0	0	5,438	0	0	0	0
7165	Ebenezer	43,259	27,670	0	0	0	0	0	0	0	0	21,509	0	0	21,509	0	0	1,500	0
7440	Emmanuel	204,427	14,560	0	250	268	0	0	0	14,392	61,953	59,106	30,000	0	23,720	0	0	0	2,550
7175	Emory	23,003	20,921	0	0	536	179	170	95	20,628	34,744	88,400	0	0	30,000	0	0	2,228	4,350
9410	Faith	23,247	0	0	90	5	2	0	364	14,192	12,029	95,637	0	0	25,000	0	0	6,000	0
7385	Forest Memorial	0	0	0	0	0	0	0	0	14,523	14,460	77,162	0	0	24,480	0	0	0	0
8190	Foundry	244,618	46,982	0	0	0	0	0	0	60,412	97,136	21,982	164,890	5,179	10,300	78,508	3,167	26,904	13,000
9427	Francis Asbury National Korean	7,193	0	0	0	0	0	0	0	12,871	12,504	86,664	0	0	52,800	5,000	0	0	0
7195	Franklin P Nash	0	0	0	0	0	0	0	0	0	0	49,455	0	0	0	0	0	0	0
7320	Gethsemane	40,498	844	0	0	0	0	617	293	13,390	13,560	24,408	0	0	21,616	0	0	8,144	500
9475	Glenmont	2,928	10,535	0	50	0	166	55	0	12,953	6,620	59,698	0	0	20,860	0	0	0	0
9455	Good Hope Union	281	400	0	0	0	0	0	45	12,232	27,617	46,320	0	0	21,084	0	0	5,000	0
7445	Good Shepherd	10,200	3,537	0	423	0	158	226	0	13,381	15,202	60,915	0	0	31,000	0	0	0	0
7370	Grace	0	0	0	0	0	0	0	0	0	5,253	46,254	0	0	0	0	0	0	0
9480	Hughes	1,800	800	0	0	0	0	0	0	6,955	10,450	22,500	0	0	32,000	0	0	2,100	0
7190	Hughes Memorial	6,385	5,623	85	0	45	105	1	40	22,852	14,631	54,275	46,397	0	7,356	0	0	5,825	0
7183	InspiratiOC	4,799	0	0	0	54	33	133	0	12,888	6,020	56,736	0	0	0	0	0	5,250	0
9420	Jerusalem - Mt. Pleasant	0	0	0	0	0	0	0	0	0	5,500	55,306	0	0	21,566	0	0	0	0
7210	Jones Memorial	5,059	0	0	0	115	0	0	0	5,407	0	46,587	0	0	28,701	0	0	6,247	0
9155	Liberty Grove	2,250	1,351	0	0	0	0	0	0	11,206	0	71,741	0	0	19,866	0	0	5,200	0
7215	Lincoln Park	65,087	3,000	0	0	0	0	0	0	13,400	0	52,000	0	0	20,630	0	0	2,015	0
7610	Marsden First	9,000	2,269	0	0	0	0	0	0	8,500	0	56,816	0	0	0	0	5,000	4,500	0
7620	McKendree-Simms-Brookland	63,637	19,525	0	0	0	0	0	0	28,678	29,004	58,607	0	0	6,709	0	0	8,000	0
7462	Memorial First India	350	0	0	0	0	0	0	0	12,576	15,120	51,932	0	0	5,758	0	0	2,000	0
7630	Metropolitan Memorial	970,334	9,264	0	0	0	0	0	0	25,733	150,036	90,928	113,894	0	29,613	25,433	0	15,853	0

Column definitions:

- **60** — Paid in salary and benefits for all other church staff and diaconal ministers
- **61** — Amount spent for local church program expenses
- **62** — Amount spent for local church operating expenses
- **63** — Amount paid for principal and interest on indebtedness, loans, mortgages, etc.
- **63a** — Amount paid for capital campaign or fundraising costs
- **64** — Amount paid on capital expenditures for building, improvements, and major equipment purchases.
- **65** — Amount PAID by/for the local church on all expenditures
- **66** — Number of giving units
- **67a** — Received through pledges
- **67b** — Received from non-pledging, but identified givers
- **67c** — Received from unidentified givers
- **67d** — Amount received from interest and dividends and/or transferred from liquid assets
- **67e** — Amount received from Sale of Church Assets
- **67f** — Amount received through building use fees, contributions, and rentals
- **67g** — Amount received through fundraisers and other sources

Align #	Church Name	60	61	62	63	63a	64	65	66	67a	67b	67c	67d	67e	67f	67g
7380	Ager Road	27,502	1,500	18,000	0	0	5,000	87,240	30	60,000	1,000	500	60	0	15,000	0
7110	Albright Memorial	13,860	1,269	46,009	22,000	0	4,900	112,901	35	0	79,033	1,531	0	0	17,700	12,317
7115	Asbury	243,095	92,849	406,560	62,378	0	67,277	1,272,098	344	916,619	39,513	21,309	2,832	0	127,055	17,769
8145	Bells	3,690	1,043	49,240	0	1,768	0	86,631		0	60,466	2,189	0	0	65,773	3,857
9122	Bethesda	225,950	37,275	177,277	39,456	0	11,954	896,388	342	682,469	107,258	10,727	2,108	0	87,034	0
7120	Bradbury Heights	14,726	891	14,726	0	0	17,945	84,919	26	500	60,035	2,067	419	0	16,874	0
7625	Brighter Day	25,027	10,566	70,336	112,840	1,158	16,180	365,200	341	0	313,158	5,216	18	0	117,540	0
7125	Brightwood Park	37,750	2,147	12,263	0	0	21,284	141,450		0	132,766	0	400	0	12,922	8,600
9160	Cabin John	0	9,788	22,820	0	0	2,500	120,164	82	0	130,323	7,069	0	0	3,680	0
7135	Capitol Hill	167,949	9,563	89,449	0	0	50,144	697,954	126	364,935	31,637	9,812	0	0	74,467	29,195
7615	Centenary	0	1	39,462	0	0	8,000	100,477	130	0	33,251	0	13	0	15,935	0
7325	Cheverly	68,711	6,300	100,652	0	0	103,515	339,315		117,198	71,064	8,718	0	0	98,050	4,947
9165	Chevy Chase	144,679	19,820	121,654	16,505	3,699	0	664,344	60	328,861	0	0	0	0	0	0
7140	Christ	48,950	1,987	63,257	0	0	0	217,836	101	66,637	78,740	0	193	0	15,441	2,385
7475	Church of The Redeemer	26,400	5,350	20,244	0	0	0	156,528	232	144,799	15,351	4,403	0	0	39,267	5,339
9450	Colesville	144,281	16,242	106,693	26,018	0	70,500	566,091	36	313,113	134,619	6,024	526	0	48,744	447
7395	College Park	9,031	7,399	25,524	0	0	0	140,769		97,966	5,984	128	129	0	56,600	0
7396	College Park Hispanic Initiative	0	0	1	0	0	0	1	42	0	0	0	0	0	0	0
7145	Community	0	500	15,391	0	0	0	98,830	125	61,856	5,268	2,685	0	0	4,868	3,985
9130	Concord-St. Andrews	36,712	16,129	84,725	0	0	50,000	348,579		169,942	25,723	1,716	0	0	98,013	0
7155	Douglas Memorial	0	1,905	17,880	0	0	2,175	60,415	81	0	75,848	4,000	25	0	18,070	2,352
7160	Dumbarton	107,465	5,159	32,314	0	0	14,461	315,126	116	287,699	8,818	3,169	19	0	30,855	3,600
7165	Ebenezer	30,148	17,650	42,640	32,839	0	3,660	197,606	195	101,375	14,153	3,853	234	0	79,544	48,295
7440	Emmanuel	200,050	6,200	102,101	55,520	0	192,971	611,049	367	326,579	114,628	9,215	1,803	0	109,000	0
7175	Emory	91,869	0	213,161	0	0	7,061	976,096	193	0	110,842	15,612	113	0	0	72,069
7410	Faith	256,028	31,284	176,694	0	0	78,205	820,740	461	464,794	110,826	3,232	0	0	119,230	19,985
7385	First	248,441	31,405	187,279	0	0	0	826,448		454,781	0	0	31,545	0	162,507	26,203
8190	Forest Memorial	29,346	449	71,649	0	0	0	143,130	29	0	78,180	2,979	0	0	3,570	4,159
7180	Foundry	575,182	140,540	749,257	211,936	48,419	120,883	2,938,721		387,677	66,711	44,153	0	0	0	0
9427	Francis Asbury National Korean	38,000	4,000	67,000	172,718	5,000	10,371	394,066	99	0	37,270	0	0	0	0	27,634
7185	Franklin P Nash	82,606	1,300	9,208	5,981	0	0	40,423	233	85,000	265,184	6,009	296	716,137	14,550	26,082
9475	Glenmont	83,764	35,799	136,707	0	0	6,000	472,360	46	214,009	0	5,990	0	0	95,282	24,729
9455	Good Hope Union	60,310	7,816	214,744	0	0	0	470,761		0	296,144	5,866	137	0	45,996	12,642
7445	Good Shepherd	73,909	8,230	65,251	0	0	7,826	373,600	55	139,814	77,359	7,358	0	0	53,003	0
7370	Grace	0	6,459	73,909	0	0	0	341,194		0	0	0	0	0	0	0
7465	Grace	30,000	0	4,500	0	0	0	75,675	150	63,000	5,000	7,000	500,000	0	50,000	0
9480	Hughes	115,158	400	133,965	0	0	41,260	596,665	150	213,534	79,987	13,216	33	0	169,789	3,416
7190	Hughes Memorial	89,210	20,494	70,954	4,446	0	10,438	329,966	123	251,843	3,115	2,338	0	0	56,693	23,761
7193	ImpariDC	0	10,075	1	0	0	0	1	68	0	0	0	0	0	0	0
9420	Jerusalem-Mt. Pleasant	37,389	0	38,175	0	0	42,754	234,115	47	151,651	129,000	2,069	0	0	21,420	11,087
7210	Jones Memorial	19,332	5,959	15,800	0	0	0	149,076	257	0	183,045	2,000	0	0	47,104	0
9155	Liberty Grove	190,072	1,500	103,059	112,046	0	12,510	702,028	279	307,259	273,436	7,008	0	0	6,725	14,000
7215	Lincoln Park	52,624	27,989	66,621	0	0	90,000	343,598	32	0	1,692,926	9,528	0	290,000	0	725
7610	Marsian First	66,600	2,000	39,265	71,048	0	0	253,407	233	500	207,003	23,189	6	0	29,656	5,803
7620	McKendree-Simms-Brookland	80,015	1,200	177,069	4,824	0	150,364	673,702	60	114,515	92,085	3,118	0	0	3,288	30,032
7462	Memorial First India	47,167	14,519	62,598	0	0	53,266	316,895		159,030		13,509	2,309	0	46,000	5,235
7630	Metropolitan Memorial	1,054,865	121,000	314,946	0	0	93,474	3,330,280	487	658,670	319,193	10,640	617,832	0	289,397	62,834

Aligg #	Church Name	TOTAL income for annual budget/spending plan (67a-g) [67]	Capital campaigns [68a]	Memorials, endowments, and bequests [68b]	Other sources and projects (include UMW, UMM and 'flow-through') [68c]	Special Sundays, Gen. Adv. Spec., World Srvc Spec., Conf. Adv. Spec. and other directed benevolent giving [68d]	Total income for designated causes including capital campaign and other special projects [68]	Equitable Compensation Funds received by Church or Pastor [69a]	Advance Special, apportioned, and connectional funds received by church [69b]	Other grants and financial support from institutional sources [69c]	Income from connectional / institutional sources outside the local church [69]	TOTAL CHURCH INCOME (Sum of Lines 67 + 68 + 69) [70]	Amount APPORTIONED to the local church [40a]	Amount PAID by the local church for all apportioned causes [40b]
7380	Ager Road	76,560	0	0	8,900	0	0	0	0	0	0	76,560	16,242	7,458
7110	Albright Memorial	110,581	0	0	3,840	0	8,900	0	0	0	0	119,481	14,757	1,000
7115	Asbury	1,125,005	42,955	67,422	14,545	6,250	120,467	0	45,000	0	45,000	1,290,562	156,506	156,506
8145	Bells	132,285	7,371	1,100	0	670	23,686	0	0	0	0	155,971	12,363	12,363
9122	Bethesda	889,596	4,144	6,770	0	525	11,439	0	0	0	0	901,035	104,831	104,831
7120	Bradbury Heights	79,476	0	0	0	0	0	0	0	0	0	79,476	6,400	6,400
7625	Brighter Day	436,333	0	0	0	0	0	0	0	0	0	436,333	18,848	18,848
7125	Brightwood Park	154,306	0	0	0	0	0	0	0	0	0	154,306	13,648	13,648
9160	Cabin John	141,472	0	2,500	0	0	2,500	0	0	0	0	143,972	14,120	14,120
9150	Capitol Hill	510,046	209,167	1,545	0	14,166	270,712	0	0	700	700	781,458	64,531	64,531
7615	Centenary	449,186	0	0	0	0	0	0	0	0	0	449,186	16,116	16,116
7325	Cheverly	299,990	0	1,635	8,000	0	23,801	0	0	0	0	323,791	36,778	36,778
9165	Chevy Chase	328,861	0	0	0	0	0	0	0	0	0	328,861	69,957	69,957
7140	Christ	163,396	21,580	15,112	0	0	36,692	0	0	0	0	200,088	25,508	25,508
7475	Church of The Redeemer	200,159	0	0	0	81	81	5,750	0	0	5,750	205,990	16,596	16,596
9450	Colesville	503,473	25,867	3,595	23,874	0	64,268	0	0	0	0	567,741	61,260	61,260
7335	College Park	160,678	0	0	0	969	969	0	0	0	0	161,647	15,933	15,933
7996	College Park Hispanic Initiative	0	0	0	0	0	0	0	0	0	0	0	0	0
7145	Community	78,662	0	0	0	0	0	0	0	0	0	78,662	10,865	1,614
9130	Concord-St. Andrews	295,394	0	0	0	0	0	367	0	0	367	295,761	41,393	41,393
7155	Douglas Memorial	100,270	0	0	0	0	0	0	0	0	0	100,270	15,042	15,042
7160	Dumbarton	334,166	0	2,590	0	0	8,160	0	0	0	0	342,326	38,720	38,720
7165	Ebenezer	247,240	0	0	0	405	405	0	0	0	0	247,645	24,706	24,706
7440	Emmanuel	559,656	0	147,698	0	5,570	154,060	0	0	700	700	714,416	61,521	61,521
7175	Emory	800,325	67,968	0	0	405	82,480	0	0	0	0	882,805	74,330	74,330
9410	Faith	718,180	0	4,065	0	6,362	12,801	0	0	0	0	730,981	94,139	94,139
7385	First	679,491	0	48,905	0	14,512	50,396	0	0	0	0	729,887	92,624	92,624
8190	Forest Memorial	120,433	0	0	0	0	0	0	0	0	0	120,433	21,770	1,623
7180	Foundry	528,175	84,748	0	34,550	1,591	119,298	10,000	0	0	10,000	657,473	273,663	273,663
9427	Francis Asbury National Korean	37,270	0	0	0	0	0	0	0	0	0	37,270	32,052	5,000
7185	Franklin P Nash	1,113,258	7,355	0	78,517	0	86,927	0	20,000	0	20,000	1,220,185	37,270	5,372
7320	Gethsemane	340,010	8,965	885	0	1,055	11,306	0	0	0	0	351,316	47,463	47,463
9475	Glenmont	360,745	4,461	0	0	1,456	5,657	0	0	0	0	366,402	48,163	48,163
9455	Good Hope Union	277,534	0	0	0	1,196	7,679	0	0	400	400	285,613	32,589	32,589
7445	Good Shepherd	0	0	0	0	7,679	0	0	0	0	0	0	42,978	35,815
7370	Grace	125,300	0	0	0	0	2,000	0	0	0	0	127,300	18,928	0
7465	Grace	529,942	0	0	2,599	2,000	16,652	0	32,500	0	32,500	579,094	74,471	74,471
9480	Hughes	337,803	9,831	0	1,900	495	9,316	0	0	2,000	2,000	349,119	39,971	39,971
7190	Hughes Memorial	0	0	0	0	0	0	0	0	0	0	0	0	0
7183	Inspire/DC	186,227	0	0	0	0	0	0	0	0	0	186,227	21,894	10,000
0420	Jerusalem-Mt. Pleasant	175,534	0	1,570	0	0	1,570	0	0	0	0	177,104	18,879	9,050
7210	Jones Memorial	518,037	89,153	0	0	0	103,322	0	0	1,500	1,500	622,659	67,711	67,711
9155	Liberty Grove	573,691	0	0	0	1,597	1,900	0	0	55,000	55,000	630,591	28,695	28,695
7215	Lincoln Park	1,752,090	0	0	0	1,597	1,597	0	0	0	0	1,753,677	25,637	2,000
7610	Marsden First	357,956	0	0	0	5,384	5,384	0	0	0	0	363,340	60,272	60,272
7620	McKendree-Simms-Brookland	318,162	0	0	0	0	0	0	0	0	0	318,162	32,084	32,084
7462	Memorial First India	0	0	0	0	0	0	0	0	0	0	0	0	0
7630	Metropolitan Memorial	2,166,566	0	0	0	0	0	0	0	700	700	2,167,266	314,907	314,907

Align #	Church Name	Dist #	City	State	1 Total professing members at the close of 2017	2a1 Received by PROFESSION of Faith	2a2 Received by PROFESSION of Faith (Other Than Confirmation)	2b Restored by AFFIRMATION of Faith	3 Transferred in from other UM churches	4 Transferred in from non-UM churches	5a Removed or corrected by ChargeConference action	5b Withdrawn from Professing Membership	6 Transferred out to other UM churches	7 Transferred out to non-UM churches	8 Removed by death	9 Total professing members at the close of 2018	9a Asian Professing Members	9b African American / Black Professing Members	9c Hispanic / Latino Professing Members	9d Native American Professing Members	9e Pacific Islander Professing Members	9f White Professing Members	9g Multi-Racial Professing Members	9h Female Professing Members	9i Male Professing Members
9430	Milian Memorial	GW	Rockville	MD	350	0	2	0	2	0	16	8	2	0	0	321	11	28	28	1	0	253	0	211	110
7485	Mizo	GW	Rockville	MD	145	0	2	0	0	3	3	0	0	9	0	137	137	0	0	0	0	0	0	68	69
7230	Mount Vernon	GW	Washington	DC	93	0	0	0	0	3	3	0	0	0	2	89	0	89	0	0	0	0	0	55	34
7235	Mount Vernon Place	GW	Washington	DC	183	0	1	0	6	4	3	0	0	0	0	188	9	25	5	1	4	143	1	111	77
7240	Mount Zion	GW	Washington	DC	141	4	0	1	1	0	6	0	0	0	2	139	0	138	0	0	0	1	0	84	55
7375	Mowatt Memorial	GW	Greenbelt	MD	73	0	0	0	0	0	3	0	0	0	0	70	1	16	0	0	0	53	0	51	19
9140	North Bethesda	GW	Bethesda	MD	340	3	2	3	1	1	34	0	5	6	8	303	16	59	6	1	2	209	10	189	114
9460	Oak Chapel	GW	Silver Spring	MD	144	3	0	0	3	0	3	0	0	0	1	137	13	42	4	0	0	78	0	80	57
7245	Petworth	GW	Washington	DC	18	0	0	0	0	0	0	0	0	0	0	18	0	18	0	0	0	0	0	12	6
9390	Potomac	GW	Potomac	MD	815	8	10	0	4	0	0	0	2	2	7	828	24	16	9	0	0	775	4	428	400
9250	Randall Memorial	GW	Washington	DC	187	5	1	0	0	0	0	0	0	0	2	189	0	189	0	0	0	0	0	108	81
9440	Rockville	GW	Rockville	MD	459	0	1	0	2	2	100	0	0	0	19	344	11	24	0	0	0	309	0	195	149
7255	Ryland-Epworth	GW	Washington	DC	15	8	1	1	5	1	15	3	0	1	0	19	1	16	6	0	0	2	8	15	4
9466	Silver Spring	GW	Silver Spring	MD	992	8	1	5	5	1	1	3	1	1	8	984	18	349	0	0	0	603	8	660	324
7265	Simpson-Hamline	GW	Washington	DC	125	1	0	0	0	0	5	0	0	0	2	122	3	121	0	0	0	1	0	96	26
7330	St Paul	GW	Chevy Chase	MD	54	0	0	0	0	0	0	0	6	3	1	54	19	47	0	0	0	3	1	41	13
9330	St Paul's	GW	Kensington	MD	784	11	6	4	8	2	38	5	6	0	4	792	4	19	10	3	6	723	12	454	338
7275	United	GW	Washington	DC	147	0	0	0	0	0	0	0	4	3	1	147	4	2	0	0	0	139	0	76	71
7340	University	GW	College Park	MD	163	0	0	0	0	0	38	7	4	3	4	82	13	14	8	0	5	42	0	50	32
7280	Van Buren	GW	Washington	DC	61	0	0	0	0	0	0	0	0	0	1	60	0	57	0	0	0	3	0	56	4
GW Total					20,323	137	157	61	102	79	535	62	52	130	268	19,913	1,065	8,502	254	111	54	9,789	238	12,143	7,770

Align #	Church Name	10 Average attendance at all weekly worship service(s)	10a Persons who Worship Online	11a Number of Infants and Children baptized (Age 0-12)	11b Number of Teens and Adults baptized (Age 13+)	11T TOTAL Number of persons baptized (all ages)	12 Number of baptized members who have not become Professing	13 Number of other constituents of the church	14 Total enrolled in confirmation preparation classes that	15 CHILDREN (0-11yrs)	16 YOUTH (12-18 yrs)	17 YOUNG ADULTS (19-30 yrs)	18 OTHER ADULTS (31+ yrs)	19 TOTAL number of persons participating in Christian formation groups	20 Average weekly attendance: Education classes/groups	22 Number of participants in Vacation Bible School	23 Number of ongoing classes (all ages)	24 Number of ONGOING small groups	25 Number of SHORT-TERM classes	26 Membership in United Methodist Men (UMM)	27 Amount paid for projects (UMM)	28 Membership in United Methodist Women (UMW)	29 Amount paid for local church and community work (UMW)	30a Number of UMVIM teams sent out	30b Number of persons sent out on UMVIM teams
9430	Millian Memorial	82	0	2	0	2	0	41	0	31	10	0	57	98	22	76	6	2	0	75	1,400	15	1,050	0	0
7485	Mizo	80	0	6	0	6	59	28	0	40	5	34	98	177	100	0	0	0	0	0	0	53	0	0	0
7230	Mount Vernon	30	0	3	0	3	0	0	0	0	0	0	20	20	4	0	0	2	3	9	0	0	0	0	0
7235	Mount Vernon Place	140	0	7	2	9	24	17	0	65	0	35	42	142	46	0	1	7	9	0	2,500	20	100	0	0
7240	Mount Zion	55	0	2	0	2	2	23	0	2	4	12	45	63	12	0	7	5	2	20	0	6	150	0	0
7375	Mowatt Memorial	30	0	2	0	2	2	35	0	0	5	2	17	24	14	0	2	2	2	0	0	0	0	0	0
9140	North Bethesda	106	0	0	1	1	0	0	3	15	4	10	36	65	43	0	1	3	3	0	0	0	0	0	0
9460	Oak Chapel	41	0	1	0	1	0	30	0	8	10	0	20	38	10	0	3	3	3	0	0	10	0	0	0
7245	Petworth	20	0	0	0	1	4	0	0	0	0	0	4	4	4	17	0	2	1	0	0	0	342	0	0
9390	Potomac	91	10	3	2	5	3	83	8	24	34	8	50	116	40	5	5	4	3	150	8,790	150	0	0	0
7250	Randall Memorial	85	20	4	1	2	0	65	8	0	15	2	56	73	15	0	1	5	2	8	1,000	15	0	0	0
9440	Rockville	108	0	0	1	2	0	65	0	0	1	0	16	17	25	28	5	2	0	26	0	26	0	0	0
7255	Ryland-Epworth	24	0	9	0	0	0	10	0	105	39	10	180	334	0	0	0	1	12	0	0	0	0	0	0
9466	Silver Spring	236	5	0	0	9	0	0	8	6	4	6	77	93	118	83	8	16	0	0	0	12	1,109	0	0
7265	Simpson-Hamline	58	0	0	0	0	20	2	0	5	6	1	47	59	10	0	2	13	4	0	0	13	3,400	0	0
7330	St Paul	29	0	12	4	16	114	9	0	226	115	17	159	517	20	24	6	1	27	0	0	0	5,066	0	0
9330	St Paul's	344	60	0	0	0	0	161	11	16	2	40	18	76	58	126	11	13	5	0	0	0	70	0	0
7275	United	50	50	1	0	1	0	0	0	0	0	17	25	42	25	0	1	5	0	65	25,000	95	0	0	0
7340	University	51	50	0	0	0	3	37	0	3	2	0	5	10	15	0	2	4	11	0	0	0	0	0	0
7280	Van Buren	19	22	0	0	0	0	2	0	3	2	0	5	10	5	0	1	4	0	0	0	0	0	0	0
	GW Total	7,201	1,843	176	55	231	937	4,367	123	2,041	1,107	705	4,374	8,227	1,894	1,697	244	341	401	744	75,624	1,443	91,295	9	78

Align #	Church Name	33 TOTAL Community MINISTRIES for outreach, justice, and mercy	33a MINISTRIES focusing on global/regional health?	33b MINISTRIES focusing on engaging in ministry with the poor/socially	34 PERSONS SERVED BY community ministries for outreach, justice, and mercy	35a PERSONS SERVING (from your congregation) in mission/community ministries	36 Market value of church-owned land, buildings and equipment	36SF Overall square footage of church owned buildings (furnished and unfurnished areas)	37 Market value of financial and other liquid assets	38 Debt secured by church physical assets	39 Other debt	42 General Advance Specials remitted to the Annual Conference Treasurer	43 World Service Specials remitted to the Annual Conference Treasurer	44 Annual Conference Advance Specials remitted to the Annual Conference Treasurer	45 Youth Service Fund remitted to the	46 All other funds sent to AC Treasurer for connectional mission and ministry	47 Total Annual Conference Special Sunday Offerings remitted to the	48a UMC CAUSES: Total amount given DIRECTLY to United Methodist causes (NOT sent to BWC Treasurer)	48b MISSIONS/MINISTRY COSTS: Direct costs incurred by the local church for mission and community ministry activities
9430	Milian Memorial	6	0	6	3,067	40	5,573,000	34,897	81,038	0	0	470	0	0	0	0	0	1,000	10,733
7485	Mizo	0	0	0	0	0	226,067	1,332	0	0	0	0	0	0	0	0	0	802	60,847
7230	Mount Vernon	5	0	5	5,112	30	2,105,300	10,446	0	132,741	0	0	0	0	0	0	0	0	5,879
7235	Mount Vernon Place	23	0	12	504	75	47,800,000	51,583	4,576,314	0	0	1,237	0	0	0	0	0	5,075	66,242
7240	Mount Zion	4	0	4	5,010	150	12,496,380	7,836	73,334	0	0	0	0	0	0	0	0	360	5,040
7375	Mowatt Memorial	2	1	1	1,000	10	1,038,000	9,057	0	0	0	464	0	0	0	0	0	464	1,441
9140	North Bethesda	5	2	3	56	50	7,083,600	24,560	974,003	0	0	3,318	0	0	0	0	0	4,428	0
9460	Oak Chapel	2	0	2	30	8	3,000,000	19,228	27,096	101,000	30,162	0	0	0	0	0	0	0	1,736
7245	Petworth	7	2	5	1,610	17	4,133,000	16,108	0	0	2,090	0	0	0	0	0	0	0	2,082
9390	Potomac	9	0	7	500	100	10,852,802	40,192	565,869	542,579	0	216	0	0	0	0	0	525	192,299
7250	Randall Memorial	9	0	9	5,500	70	2,500,000	8,364	0	474,361	0	0	0	0	0	0	0	0	4,398
9440	Rockville	1	0	1	500	85	17,107,800	57,750	317,954	0	0	151	0	0	0	0	0	922	3,386
7255	Ryland-Epworth	4	0	3	70	4	5,531,581	0	11,991	0	5,100	0	0	0	0	0	0	0	27,013
9466	Silver Spring	21	9	16	4,779	845	21,088,802	110,310	751,723	0	0	0	0	0	0	0	0	27,000	34,659
7265	Simpson-Hamline	8	1	7	5,955	25	18,000,000	22,979	47,394	0	0	0	0	0	0	0	0	0	18,252
7330	St Paul	0	0	0	54,000	0	1,919,590	15,832	1,927,218	0	0	0	0	0	0	0	0	0	12,280
9330	St Paul's	4	0	2	2,606	450	7,545,000	24,396	1,765,864	0	0	3,000	0	0	0	0	0	45,154	44,456
7275	United	0	0	4	7,000	29	23,643,430	36,000	1,528,736	0	0	0	0	0	0	0	0	1,565	17,472
7340	University	11	0	0	10,160	59	7,500,000	34,483	0	0	0	110	0	0	0	100	0	1,250	6,480
7280	Van Buren	4	2	3	15	12	1,803,660	0	0	0	6,443	0	0	0	0	0	0	0	18,952
	GW Total	444	85	323	330,713	14,312	478,215,851	1,717,553	50,021,717	10,843,801	1,693,015	41,348	0	863	0	3,523	0	286,078	2,405,753

Align #	Church Name	48TOTAL Total of UMC Causes & UMC Missions & Outreach	49 NON-UMC CAUSES: Total amount given DIRECTLY to non-United Methodist benevolent and charitable causes (NOT sent to BWC Treasurer)	50a Human Relations Sunday	50b UMCOR Sunday (formerly One Great Hour of Sharing)	50c Peace with Justice Sunday	50d Native American Ministries Sunday	50e World Communion Sunday	50f U.M. Student Day	51 Direct-billed clergy non-health benefits	52 Direct-billed clergy health benefits	53a Base compensation paid to/for the Senior Pastor or other person assigned or appointed in the lead pastoral role to the church	53b Base compensation paid/for to all Associate Pastor(s) & other pastoral staff assigned or appointed to the church	53c Base compensation paid to/for any Deacons NOT included in 53a or 53b	55a Housing benefits paid to/for Lead Pastor or person in lead pastoral role as described in 53a	55b Housing benefits paid to/for ALL Associate Pastor(s) & other pastoral staff assigned or appointed to the	55c Housing benefits paid to/for any Deacons not included in 53a or 53b	56 Paid to/for all persons included in Lines 53a-53c for accountable reimbursements	57 Paid to/for all persons included in Lines 53a-53c for any other cash allowances (non-accountable)
9430	Millian Memorial	11,733	0	0	0	0	0	0	0	15,573	20,126	48,912	0	0	27,500	0	0	3,031	5,604
7485	Mizo	61,649	11,120	0	0	0	0	0	0	9,950	0	32,500	24,000	0	15,000	0	0	5,450	0
7230	Mount Vernon	5,879	0	0	0	0	0	0	0	0	13,380	33,576	0	0	10,967	0	0	341	0
7235	Mount Vernon Place	73,317	27,152	274	0	45	134	170	40	14,724	17,471	71,650	0	0	32,350	0	0	5,177	0
7240	Mount Zion	5,400	244	0	0	0	0	0	0	14,604	14,569	62,574	0	0	22,140	0	0	0	0
7375	Mowatt Memorial	1,905	2,328	0	0	0	0	0	0	0	0	21,105	0	0	4,199	0	0	377	0
9140	North Bethesda	4,428	11,692	0	0	0	0	0	0	14,233	9,776	48,816	0	0	49,000	0	0	5,896	0
9460	Oak Chapel	1,736	0	0	0	0	0	0	0	9,575	6,885	43,996	0	0	19,866	0	0	1,500	0
7245	Petworth	2,082	0	0	0	0	0	0	0	0		21,500	0	0	3,308	0	0	0	0
9390	Potomac	192,824	0	0	0	0	0	0	0	16,224	16,135	76,500	0	0	48,654	0	0	4,930	0
7250	Randall Memorial	4,398	3,750	122	0	0	0	37	0	13,064	11,400	57,325	0	0	20,000	0	0	5,942	0
9440	Rockville	3,386	2,933	0	0	0	0	0	0	11,550	11,760	44,303	0	0	19,866	0	0	698	0
7255	Ryland-Epworth	27,935	0	100	0	108	95	108	160	0	0	16,097	0	0		0	6,622	1,367	0
9466	Silver Spring	61,659		0	2,671	150	0	150	0	10,582	12,945	56,987	0	0	32,493	0	0	4,100	0
7265	Simpson-Hamline	18,252		0	1,054	321	501	519	100	14,116	12,089	62,358	0	0	28,500	11,000	0	8,110	0
7330	St. Paul	12,280	4,948	150	0	0	0	0	0	10,370	16,250	49,399	45,191	0	19,866	0	0	1,100	0
9330	St. Paul's	89,610	75,681	406	0	0	0	0	0	27,583	26,158	80,946	0	0	35,000	0	0	7,721	0
7275	United	19,037	47,155	0	0	0	0	0	0	0	0	56,543	0	0	27,306	22,598	0	727	0
7340	University	7,730	250	0	0	0	0	0	0	13,161	13,441	45,611	0	0	33,330	0	0	0	3,600
7280	Van Buren	18,952		0	0	0	55	0	0	0	0	25,008	0	0		0	0	169	0
	GW Total	2,691,831	494,905	2,398	4,738	2,299	2,285	3,327	1,815	731,302	944,738	3,202,294	532,525	52,309	1,181,472	173,561	25,089	212,805	36,686

Align #	Church Name	50	61	62	63	63a	64	65	66	67a	67b	67c	67d	67e	67f	67g
9430	Millian Memorial	93,127	19,045	121,871	0	0	0	371,961	117	154,179	52,003	2,956	274	16,000	66,652	0
7485	Mizo	0	11,112	13,121	0	0	2,235	197,394	90	0	216,013	10,311	0	0	0	0
7230	Mount Vernon	0	4,312	28,697	0	0	232	85,388	138	553	80,444	779	0	0	100	17,572
7235	Mount Vernon Place	291,213	15,109	295,145	0	0	53,669	1,017,791	265	244,529	121,930	8,405	225,000	0	253,462	0
7240	Mount Zion	10,200	3,534	49,313	0	0	6,617	219,467	229	0	0	4,747	0	0	75,000	21,788
7375	Mowatt Memorial	6,270	3,074	13,315	0	0	11,608	73,546	40	0	39,521	5,249	0	0	38,235	333
9140	North Bethesda	91,514	11,000	125,304	0	0	0	431,813	67	158,591	101,490	4,233	10	0	138,846	8,734
9460	Oak Chapel	26,834	7,151	80,043	4,197	0	45,000	250,077	16	60,860	19,104	1,525	33,273	0	128,507	88
7245	Petworth	31,650	1,900	61,131	50,265	0	34,532	183,602	251	43,037	1,691	7,251	0	0	102,000	0
9390	Potomac	159,606	39,614	183,787	0	0	29,885	903,156	75	287,073	203,172	3,193	7,207	0	285,633	0
7250	Randall Memorial	37,440	400	29,402	202,199	62,282	0	201,099	36	0	57,301	5,680	0	0	0	0
9440	Rockville	89,136	13,019	120,331	0	0	37,257	616,405	307	215,732	0	863	19,866	0	136,270	14,859
7255	Ryland-Epworth	15,756	2,565	56,645	0	0	0	147,912		34,399	2,923	10,000	23,000	0	55,945	5,238
9466	Silver Spring	352,546	75,638	205,929	0	0	17,474	868,998	57	270,113	248,698	2,400	4,100	0	510,000	9,100
7265	Simpson-Hamline	0	44,352	98,281	0	0	14,729	336,073		121,000	25,000	3,420	0	0	136,000	0
7330	St. Paul	0	4,200	42,300	0	0	6,355	190,933	34	54,331	3,500	17,139	0	0	98,000	0
9330	St. Paul's	268,204	82,922	274,840	0	0	29,946	1,209,348	393	524,110	421,195	4,859	8,667	0	117,560	0
7275	United	133,133	19,229	86,210	0	0	19,764	441,267	72	50,616	13,322	5,354	49,006	0	271,515	4,402
7340	University	86,428	14,493	99,148	0	0	0	359,782	52	0	164,185	0	0	0	85,830	30,014
7280	Van Buren	4,612	605	3,936	2,436	0	0	63,468	19	0	57,813	0	0	0	23,400	0
	GW Total	6,600,252	1,124,457	6,059,870	1,328,060	122,326	1,666,181	30,632,171	8,101	9,925,748	8,197,846	395,508	1,281,618	#####	4,880,557	661,631

Align #	Church Name	TOTAL income for annual budget/spending plan (67a-g) [67]	Capital campaigns [68a]	Memorials, endowments, and bequests [68b]	Other sources and projects (include UMW, UMM and 'flow-through') [68c]	Special Sundays, Gen. Adv. Spec, World Srvc Spec., Conf. Adv. Spec. and other directed benevolent giving [68d]	Total income for designated causes including capital campaign and other special projects [68]	Equitable Compensation Funds received by Church or Pastor [69a]	Advance Special, apportioned, and connectional funds received by church [69b]	Other grants and financial support from institutional sources [69c]	Income from connectional / institutional sources outside the local church [69]	TOTAL CHURCH INCOME (Sum of Lines 67 + 68 + 69) [70]	Amount APPORTIONED to the local church [40a]	Amount PAID by the local church for all apportioned causes [40b]
9430	Millian Memorial	292,064	0	1,545	0	470	2,015	0	0	0	0	294,079	61,758	4,969
7485	Mizo	226,324	11,265	0	0	16,925	28,190	0	0	0	0	254,514	11,257	11,257
7230	Mount Vernon	99,448	0	5,024	0	0	5,024	0	0	0	0	104,472	12,690	1,384
7235	Mount Vernon Place	853,326	0	79,870	0	2,575	82,445	0	0	0	0	935,771	123,005	123,005
7240	Mount Zion	101,535	0	0	0	175	175	0	0	0	0	101,710	27,370	27,370
7375	Mowatt Memorial	78,089	5,600	235	0	3,270	9,105	0	0	0	0	87,194	8,901	8,901
9140	North Bethesda	412,920	0	10,000	0	1,119	11,119	0	0	0	0	424,039	53,043	53,043
9460	Oak Chapel	245,065	0	0	0	0	0	0	0	0	0	245,065	33,277	4,600
7245	Petworth	148,253	3,457	0	32,282	1,119	35,739	0	0	0	0	186,992	16,417	16,417
9390	Potomac	790,336	6,675	250	20,000	27,052	53,977	0	0	3,000	3,000	844,313	84,732	84,732
7250	Randall Memorial	205,790	0	0	0	0	0	0	0	0	0	205,790	25,906	21,353
9440	Rockville	449,708	0	9,143	0	0	9,143	0	0	0	0	458,851	59,150	59,150
7255	Ryland-Epworth	94,130	0	0	0	0	0	0	0	0	0	94,130	10,648	10,648
9466	Silver Spring	1,067,049	270,113	0	0	0	270,113	0	0	0	0	1,337,162	110,581	35,286
7265	Simpson-Hamline	297,600	0	0	0	0	0	0	0	0	0	297,600	35,286	35,286
7230	St Paul	159,251	0	475	0	0	475	0	0	0	0	159,726	23,315	23,315
9330	St Paul's	1,088,671	219,155	8,940	0	4,418	232,513	0	0	0	0	1,321,184	135,530	135,530
7275	United	344,714	0	0	0	0	0	0	0	5,712	5,712	350,426	27,509	27,509
7340	University	334,389	0	720	0	3,463	4,183	0	0	0	0	338,572	45,925	45,925
7280	Van Buren	81,213	480	0	0	0	480	0	0	1,900	1,900	83,593	7,750	7,750
GW Total		26,365,045	1,159,310	421,494	229,007	177,740	1,987,551	16,117	77,500	91,612	185,229	28,537,825	3,239,303	2,891,238

Align #	Church Name	Dist #	City	State	1	2a1	2a2	2b	3	4	5a	5b	6	7	8	9	9a	9b	9c	9d	9e	9f	9g	9h	9i
8390	Alexandra Chapel	WE	Indian Head	MD	115	4	0	0	0	0	0	0	0	0	3	112	0	110	0	0	0	2	0	81	31
8130	Asbury	WE	Brandywine	MD	260	0	0	3	0	0	0	0	0	0	3	260	0	253	0	0	0	4	3	162	98
8480	Bethel	WE	Upper Marlboro	MD	44	5	2	0	0	1	1	2	2	1	3	35	0	8	0	0	0	27	0	28	7
8515	Bethesda	WE	Valley Lee	MD	85	0	0	2	2	0	0	0	0	0	3	85	0	2	0	0	0	83	0	55	30
8120	Bowie	WE	Bowie	MD	94	0	0	2	0	0	0	0	0	0	1	94	2	28	1	0	0	63	0	37	57
8370	Brookfield	WE	Brandywine	MD	141	2	2	0	2	2	0	0	3	0	1	137	0	3	0	0	0	132	2	80	57
8460	Brooks	WE	Saint Leonard	MD	395	0	0	0	0	0	31	0	0	0	2	362	3	362	0	0	0	0	0	224	138
8520	Calvary	WE	Waldorf	MD	419	3	0	0	0	1	0	0	0	0	7	412	0	6	0	1	0	399	4	240	172
8425	Carroll-Western	WE	Prince Frederick	MD	193	0	0	0	0	0	0	0	0	0	4	192	0	2	0	1	0	188	0	117	75
8155	Cheltenham	WE	Cheltenham	MD	298	8	0	1	0	0	0	3	0	0	4	294	0	294	0	0	0	0	0	176	118
8260	Chicamuxen	WE	La Plata	MD	57	0	4	0	0	0	0	0	2	0	4	55	0	0	0	0	0	55	0	34	21
8115	Christ	WE	Aquasco	MD	202	7	0	2	0	0	0	0	0	0	4	204	0	204	0	0	0	0	0	131	73
8170	Clinton	WE	Clinton	MD	180	0	10	0	1	0	0	0	0	0	0	198	0	176	0	0	0	20	1	118	80
8295	Community With A Cause	WE	Lexington Park	MD	38	0	0	1	0	0	0	0	0	0	0	48	0	37	0	0	0	11	0	28	20
8175	Coopers	WE	Dunkirk	MD	38	0	0	0	0	1	2	0	0	0	1	38	0	0	0	0	0	37	0	26	12
7480	Corkran Memorial	WE	Temple Hills	MD	124	0	0	0	0	0	0	0	0	0	3	121	1	45	1	0	0	70	4	72	49
8330	Eastern	WE	Lusby	MD	104	0	0	0	1	0	0	0	0	1	0	100	1	0	0	0	0	97	0	64	36
8285	Ebenezer	WE	Lanham	MD	434	4	4	1	0	0	0	6	0	0	3	432	3	432	1	1	0	0	0	269	163
7310	Emmanuel	WE	Beltsville	MD	508	0	0	0	0	0	6	0	1	2	1	490	7	62	0	0	0	389	23	323	167
8240	Emmanuel	WE	Huntingtown	MD	215	0	1	0	1	0	0	0	0	0	1	212	1	2	0	1	0	211	0	119	93
8110	Faith	WE	Accokeek	MD	77	0	4	0	0	0	0	3	0	0	7	136	0	5	3	0	0	98	0	44	92
6540	First Saints Community Church	WE	Leonardtown	MD	746	7	0	5	6	0	0	0	2	0	7	747	1	16	0	1	0	716	14	436	311
8225	Glenn Dale	WE	Glenn Dale	MD	89	0	10	1	0	1	67	0	0	0	2	87	3	0	3	1	0	64	0	56	31
8525	Good Shepherd	WE	Waldorf	MD	488	8	2	1	3	0	0	0	6	0	2	429	12	21	8	0	0	359	4	244	185
8215	Grace	WE	Fort Washington	MD	511	4	2	0	1	0	0	13	6	6	6	521	1	519	0	0	0	0	0	270	251
8230	Hollywood	WE	Hollywood	MD	310	0	0	1	0	0	0	0	0	0	6	290	1	0	0	0	0	289	0	173	117
8245	Huntingtown	WE	Huntingtown	MD	474	7	1	1	0	0	0	0	1	5	2	487	0	6	1	0	0	485	0	307	180
8235	Immanuel	WE	Brandywine	MD	165	0	0	0	0	0	0	1	0	0	1	163	0	0	0	0	0	162	0	100	63
8265	Indian Head	WE	Indian Head	MD	36	0	13	5	6	0	0	0	0	1	0	36	1	0	0	0	0	30	0	24	12
8950	Journey of Faith Church, The	WE	Waldorf	MD	163	0	0	0	1	1	0	0	2	0	0	172	0	166	0	0	0	6	0	109	63
8275	La Plata	WE	La Plata	MD	1188	3	0	0	1	1	2	0	0	0	5	1190	3	7	1	1	0	1174	3	722	468
8290	Lanham	WE	Lanham	MD	186	2	1	1	0	0	10	7	0	2	5	188	3	72	1	0	0	98	13	115	73
8320	Lexington Park	WE	Lexington Park	MD	234	6	11	5	1	0	10	0	0	0	2	239	0	5	0	0	0	231	1	136	103
8420	Metropolitan	WE	Indian Head	MD	298	0	11	1	0	0	0	0	3	0	7	294	0	292	0	0	0	1	1	166	128
6150	Mount Calvary	WE	Charlotte Hall	MD	40	0	0	0	0	0	5	0	0	0	0	41	4	1	0	0	0	36	0	25	16
8365	Mount Harmony-Lower Marlboro	WE	Owings	MD	422	9	6	1	4	4	0	0	0	0	5	428	1	1	1	0	0	423	0	259	169
8475	Mount Hope	WE	Sunderland	MD	127	1	0	0	0	0	1	0	3	0	5	78	1	23	3	0	0	49	6	49	29
8355	Mount Oak	WE	Mitchellville	MD	223	0	5	0	2	5	0	0	0	0	5	221	4	126	3	0	0	88	0	100	121
8430	Mount Olive	WE	Prince Frederick	MD	124	9	0	3	0	0	24	4	4	0	0	128	0	1	3	0	0	93	2	93	35
8350	Mount Zion	WE	Mechanicsville	MD	609	3	2	0	3	1	0	0	4	0	5	585	0	1	0	0	0	574	2	349	236
8450	Mount Zion	WE	Saint Inigoes	MD	82	0	1	0	1	0	6	0	0	0	1	82	0	82	0	0	0	0	1	45	37
8485	Nottingham-Myers	WE	Upper Marlboro	MD	154	3	13	0	0	0	2	0	1	2	9	148	0	146	1	0	0	2	1	87	61
8335	Olivet	WE	Lusby	MD	212	0	0	4	7	0	1	0	1	1	5	224	0	6	0	1	0	215	3	146	78
8380	Oxon Hill	WE	Oxon Hill	MD	184	0	0	1	3	3	0	0	0	0	5	180	43	79	0	1	0	53	4	120	60
8250	Patuxent	WE	Huntingtown	MD	247	3	3	0	0	0	0	0	1	0	5	245	0	245	0	0	0	0	0	162	162
8180	Peters	WE	Dunkirk	MD	85	0	0	0	0	0	0	0	0	0	0	87	0	86	0	1	0	1	0	52	83
8270	Pisgah	WE	Marbury	MD	95	0	0	1	0	1	0	0	0	0	3	96	0	1	0	1	0	93	0	61	35
8255	Plum Point	WE	Huntingtown	MD	193	3	0	0	0	0	0	0	0	3	3	193	0	184	0	0	0	2	7	112	81

Column legend (line numbers):

- 10 — Average attendance at all weekly worship service(s)
- 10a — Persons who Worship Online
- 11a — Number of Infants and Children baptized (Age 0-12)
- 11b — Number of Teens and Adults baptized (Age 13+)
- 11T — TOTAL Number of persons baptized (all ages)
- 12 — Number of baptized members who have not become Professing
- 13 — Number of other constituents of the church
- 14 — Total enrolled in confirmation preparation classes that
- 15 — CHILDREN (0-11yrs) in all Christian groups, small groups and Sunday School
- 16 — YOUTH (12-18 yrs) in all Christian groups, small groups and Sunday School
- 17 — YOUNG ADULTS (19-30 yrs) in all Christian groups, small groups and Sunday School
- 18 — OTHER ADULTS (31+ yrs) in all Christian groups, small groups and Sunday School
- 19 — TOTAL number of persons participating in Christian formation groups (Total lines 15 - 19)
- 20 — Average weekly attendance Education classes/groups that meet in Sunday Church School groups
- 22 — Number of participants in Vacation Bible School
- 23 — Number of ongoing classes (all ages) for learning in Sunday Church
- 24 — Number of ONGOING small groups, support groups, or classes
- 25 — Number of SHORT-TERM classes, support groups, or small groups offered
- 26 — Membership in United Methodist Men (UMM)
- 27 — Amount paid for projects (UMM)
- 28 — Membership in United Methodist Women (UMW)
- 29 — Amount paid for local church and community work (UMW)
- 30a — Number of UMVIM teams sent out from this church
- 30b — Number of persons sent out on UMVIM teams from this church

Align #	Church Name	10	10a	11a	11b	11T	12	13	14	15	16	17	18	19	20	22	23	24	25	26	27	28	29	30a	30b
8390	Alexandria Chapel	19	0	0	0	0	0	7	0	7	1	0	0	8	0	10	0	0	0	9	584	15	0	4	12
8130	Asbury	50	0	0	0	0	0	0	0	10	2	0	12	24	15	30	1	2	0	13	0	16	800	1	6
8480	Bethel	23	0	1	0	1	0	9	0	0	2	0	18	19	0	0	1	2	1	0	0	0	0	0	0
8515	Bethesda	50	0	2	0	1	0	9	0	0	6	3	19	39	20	0	6	3	2	12	500	0	0	0	0
8120	Bowie	34	21	1	0	0	19	112	0	3	6	0	7	16	11	0	6	4	1	0	0	0	0	0	0
8370	Brookfield	18	0	0	0	0	0	3	0	0	6	0	12	12	4	4	1	2	2	0	0	0	0	0	0
8460	Brooks	162	0	10	8	18	0	41	0	12	5	6	50	84	20	36	6	3	0	22	3,600	72	2,486	0	0
8520	Calvary	68	0	0	0	0	18	0	0	10	5	0	60	76	25	0	4	2	0	21	2,037	21	2,685	0	0
8425	Carroll-Western	95	33	5	3	8	0	41	0	25	13	20	18	76	25	0	7	5	1	10	0	25	0	0	0
8155	Cheltenham	40	0	0	0	0	0	0	0	3	0	0	14	12	12	0	3	2	0	0	0	0	0	0	0
8260	Chicamuxen	25	0	0	0	0	0	0	0	3	6	5	14	28	11	0	2	5	1	16	0	0	230	0	0
8115	Christ	60	20	2	0	2	23	12	0	24	10	7	65	119	5	10	3	21	3	25	2,220	41	3,000	3	0
8170	Clinton	126	0	4	4	4	0	106	0	2	1	20	49	53	25	0	0	1	0	0	0	0	0	0	0
8995	Community With A Cause	60	0	0	0	0	0	5	0	2	1	2	21	25	4	0	0	4	0	9	0	0	0	0	0
8175	Coopers	25	0	0	0	0	0	0	0	4	0	3	13	16	6	0	1	0	0	0	0	0	0	0	0
7480	Corkran Memorial	30	0	0	0	1	19	14	0	26	3	3	26	36	6	8	4	5	0	11	1,456	30	1,373	0	0
8930	Eastern	38	0	0	0	3	18	35	0	10	10	6	42	84	12	45	2	3	0	0	0	41	3,200	0	0
8285	Ebenezer	128	0	0	0	0	3	54	0	8	9	0	18	35	28	24	2	2	0	2	45	13	3,366	0	0
7310	Emmanuel	106	0	3	0	11	5	34	0	10	9	0	20	39	8	227	15	30	30	5	350	28	0	0	0
8240	Emmanuel	70	0	0	2	3	160	1	9	203	95	30	266	594	9	205	7	1	2	7	549	63	2,929	0	7
8110	Faith	35	0	0	0	0	0	446	0	0	0	0	12	12	130	0	7	15	2	29	1,099	68	10,450	0	0
8640	First Saints Community Church	428	0	11	8	11	68	78	8	28	38	13	151	230	6	205	9	5	2	95	0	29	3,300	2	27
8225	Glenn Dale	39	25	0	0	1	13	5	7	0	0	0	12	12	56	105	7	15	1	0	0	31	853	0	0
8525	Good Shepherd	212	0	4	8	1	0	78	2	28	25	15	205	315	90	65	9	5	4	0	0	16	9,012	0	0
8215	Grace	285	0	8	12	12	24	13	12	70	35	3	56	101	50	203	7	5	3	0	450	70	0	0	0
8230	Hollywood	127	0	0	0	24	180	54	2	12	0	0	122	214	74	23	3	11	8	0	0	27	5,797	1	5
8245	Huntingtown	221	0	2	2	219	3	34	2	6	4	0	9	19	5	30	3	2	0	19	0	16	150	0	0
8235	Immanuel	49	0	0	0	3	0	1	2	4	5	4	15	23	5	112	7	8	1	0	0	70	2,900	0	0
8265	Indian Head	31	0	0	0	3	56	0	14	10	66	6	48	59	35	35	10	28	0	0	0	15	1,750	0	0
8550	Journey of Faith Church; The	110	25	4	4	3	0	0	0	275	0	48	350	739	120	112	3	4	2	29	3,128	29	0	0	0
8275	La Plata	330	0	2	2	11	0	16	6	15	10	1	4	30	15	35	7	5	1	0	2,854	24	1,390	0	0
8290	Lanham	52	0	5	5	114	0	51	43	20	20	11	105	181	52	28	2	9	3	13	13,688	49	0	0	0
8320	Lexington Park	222	16	1	0	0	0	1	0	8	15	0	83	117	41	0	8	0	0	0	5,514	16	550	0	0
8420	Metropolitan	101	0	11	0	12	49	51	9	2	5	1	23	33	0	90	10	10	10	32	140	47	9,047	0	0
8150	Mount Calvary	35	4	4	0	6	0	106	5	60	3	6	40	157	26	0	4	11	1	20	0	35	900	0	0
8365	Mount Harmony-Lower Marlboro	160	0	11	5	6	6	0	3	5	13	1	15	24	65	61	8	6	0	5	0	14	500	0	0
8475	Mount Hope	42	3	1	0	1	0	0	0	31	13	1	86	131	20	52	7	11	3	78	0	15	0	0	0
8355	Mount Oak	159	0	4	0	5	49	106	19	5	42	18	32	41	45	30	4	6	0	1	0	18	800	0	0
8430	Mount Olive	79	4	0	0	1	0	0	8	83	4	0	66	209	4	108	8	11	10	11	0	13	0	0	0
8350	Mount Zion	165	0	3	0	5	68	170	4	6	8	6	8	24	5	16	3	3	2	28	3,178	12	800	0	0
8450	Mount Zion	25	0	1	0	1	0	0	0	2	10	11	40	42	28	0	3	8	6	0	0	—	—	—	—
8495	Nottingham-Myers	109	0	1	0	1	0	0	3	5	3	0	40	77	15	26	3	6	2	—	—	—	—	—	—
8335	Olivet	127	0	1	0	1	11	0	0	15	8	0	80	110	—	50	3	6	—	—	—	—	—	—	—
8380	Oxon Hill	72																							
8250	Patuxent	58																							
8180	Peters	46																							
8270	Pisgah	65																							
8255	Plum Point	65																							

Align #	Church Name	33	33a	33b	34	35a	36	36SF	37	38	39	42	43	44	45	46	47	48a	48b
8390	Alexandria Chapel	0	0	0	14,000	32	277,900	2,480	5,388	0	0	0	0	0	0	0	0	0	0
8130	Asbury	2	3	1	130	30	1,158,310	5,066	336,000	0	0	0	0	0	0	0	0	3,276	500
8460	Bethel	5	3	2	880	22	528,530	3,990	0	0	0	0	0	0	0	800	0	0	13,135
8515	Bethesda	6	5	5	250	60	600,000	3,366	1,063	0	0	0	0	0	0	0	0	0	0
8120	Bowie	1	1	1	43	11	1,362,655	3,264	65,573	0	0	0	0	0	0	0	0	0	1,402
8370	Brookfield	2	0	0	350	0	673,400	3,116	159,600	0	0	300	0	0	0	0	0	0	954
8460	Brooks	0	3	7	0	60	2,755,167	21,691	0	1,921,032	0	0	0	0	0	0	0	794	8,006
8520	Calvary	10	0	0	3,876	0	1,362,300	16,162	525,000	247,065	0	1,014	0	0	0	0	0	2,056	0
8425	Carroll-Western	0	0	0	0	0	631,999	3,955	0	0	0	0	0	0	0	0	0	500	966
8155	Cheltenham	3	3	3	250	40	1,597,000	6,849	129,370	0	0	1,666	0	0	0	0	0	0	0
8260	Chicamuxen	0	3	3	15	20	608,400	0	0	0	0	0	0	0	0	100	0	500	0
8115	Christ	4	10	10	570	34	650,000	6,767	131,796	0	0	0	0	0	0	0	0	418	1,340
8170	Clinton	20	10	10	485	110	1,689,091	9,688	114,500	0	0	0	0	0	0	0	0	1,775	14,092
8295	Community With A Cause	3	0	0	500	12	20,000	1,759	103,550	10,317	0	0	0	0	0	0	0	250	1,775
8175	Coopers	4	4	4	355	5	252,000	23,150	8,200	272,168	0	0	0	0	0	0	0	0	31,299
7480	Corkran Memorial	6	3	3	450	45	3,879,000	3,461	1,046,138	423,678	13,139	0	0	0	0	0	0	1,596	6,895
8330	Eastern	4	1	2	47	15	428,964	10,037	118,526	0	0	360	0	0	0	0	0	0	12,117
8285	Ebenezer	5	2	5	325	38	2,698,981	22,162	10,300	0	0	45	0	0	0	128	0	3,900	0
7310	Emmanuel	11	3	3	4,139	165	1,572,400	44,000	10,000	0	0	996	0	0	0	0	0	0	0
8240	Emmanuel	6	2	3	2,500	75	2,066,000	10,261	1,208,678	0	0	0	0	0	0	0	0	0	4,112
8110	Faith	3	3	3	250	20	1,758,200	26,535	251,000	0	0	7,491	0	0	0	0	0	600	50,631
8540	First Saints Community Church	14	2	11	5,143	18	1,663,000	4,300	103,119	0	0	0	0	381	0	0	0	0	0
8925	Glenn Dale	2	5	0	5	150	4,676,657	25,000	1,325,072	0	0	2,445	0	0	0	0	0	3,000	36,798
8525	Good Shepherd	3	3	4	3,168	150	3,887,934	9,072	629,206	0	0	2,398	0	0	0	0	0	0	909
8235	Grace	13	5	2	1,300	200	3,852,713	11,546	331,941	0	0	9,862	0	55	0	0	0	4,506	38,326
8230	Hollywood	7	5	6	600	288	3,148,975	15,504	59,425	0	0	225	0	0	0	100	0	930	0
8245	Huntingtown	1	2	1	809	30	1,936,248	9,221	57,000	0	0	0	0	0	0	0	0	0	6,258
8235	Immanuel	8	5	8	400	44	693,000	4,300	63,000	0	0	0	0	0	0	0	0	0	9,532
8265	Indian Head	7	1	5	1,780	50	2,192,000	15,000	169,534	1,016,194	0	0	0	0	0	0	0	0	36,241
8650	Journey of Faith Church,The	14	2	12	2,359	250	1,220,000	23,400	692,484	1,076,262	0	3,745	0	0	0	0	0	2,498	1,639
8275	La Plata	3	0	0	14,500	10	2,161,380	12,200	196,388	0	0	0	0	0	0	0	0	6,096	19,212
8290	Latham	7	0	4	50	115	2,100,000	14,865	0	230,900	0	0	0	0	0	0	0	100	1,306
8320	Lexington Park	18	0	11	3,500	98	3,043,000	9,398	23,000	0	0	0	0	0	0	0	0	0	3,523
8420	Metropolitan	2	2	0	623	20	2,678,200	3,240	16,632	410,618	0	0	0	0	0	0	0	10,309	70,743
8150	Mount Calvary	14	10	10	150	140	438,600	20,978	62,000	0	88,000	55	0	0	0	0	0	0	0
8365	Mount Harmony-Lower Marlboro	7	0	2	195	78	3,051,000	4,496	194,298	0	0	0	0	0	0	0	0	0	10,985
8475	Mount Hope	6	0	5	165	135	1,170,000	25,343	125,793	4,912	0	0	0	0	0	0	0	55	0
8355	Mount Oak	6	0	5	600	69	6,909,000	15,881	213,984	988,003	0	0	0	0	0	0	0	0	0
8430	Mount Olive	25	6	19	3,647	735	2,670,000	16,984	0	0	0	2,185	0	0	0	0	0	10,655	27,046
8350	Mount Zion	0	0	0	50	10	3,140,000	0	129,810	0	0	0	0	0	0	0	0	0	0
8450	Mount Zion	0	0	0	19,000	127	400,000	13,808	204,032	0	0	0	0	0	0	0	0	0	13,529
8465	Nottingham-Myers	12	6	18	1,156	110	2,563,000	4,905	43,380	1,158,375	34,036	494	0	0	0	0	0	3,818	7,188
8335	Olivet	32	26	0	178	80	1,102,400	25,609	33,295	0	33,436	0	0	0	0	0	0	2,706	2,818
8380	Oxon Hill	4	0	2	80	33	1,503,900	4,310	4,200	0	6,156	0	0	0	0	0	0	0	4,922
8250	Patuxent	2	0	0	300	19	820,000	3,500	0	0	0	0	0	0	0	0	0	1,360	4,185
8180	Peters	0	0	4	19	0	1,157,700	0	0	0	0	0	0	0	0	0	0	0	463
8270	Pisgah	40	0	40	367	65	293,730	0	0	173,802	14,000	0	0	0	0	0	0	0	2,180
8255	Plum Point	2	0	1	1,200	170	1,345,000	5,743	136,117	0	0	0	0	0	0	0	0	690	2,180

Column key:
- 33 — TOTAL Community MINISTRIES for outreach, justice, and mercy
- 33a — MINISTRIES focusing on global/regional health?
- 33b — MINISTRIES focusing on engaging in ministry with the poor/socially
- 34 — PERSONS SERVED BY community ministries for outreach, justice, and mercy
- 35a — PERSONS SERVING (from your congregation) in mission/community ministries
- 36 — Market value of church-owned land, buildings and equipment
- 36SF — Overall square footage of church owned buildings (furnished and unfurnished areas)
- 37 — Market value of financial and other liquid assets
- 38 — Debt secured by church physical assets
- 39 — Other debt
- 42 — General Advance Specials remitted to the Annual Conference Treasurer
- 43 — World Service Specials remitted to the Annual Conference Treasurer
- 44 — Annual Conference Advance Specials remitted to the Annual Conference Treasurer
- 45 — Youth Service Fund remitted to the
- 46 — All other funds sent to AC Treasurer for connectional mission and ministry
- 47 — Total Annual Conference Special Sunday Offerings remitted to the
- 48a — UMC CAUSES: Total amount given DIRECTLY to United Methodist causes (NOT sent to BWC Treasurer)
- 48b — MISSIONS/MINISTRY COSTS: Direct costs incurred by the local church for mission and community ministry activities

Align #	Church Name	48TOTAL — Total of UMC Causes & UMC Missions & Outreach	49 — NON-UMC CAUSES: Total amount given DIRECTLY to non-United Methodist benevolent and charitable causes (NOT sent to BWC Treasurer)	50a — Human Relations Sunday	50b — UMCOR Sunday (formerly One Great Hour of Sharing)	50c — Peace with Justice Sunday	50d — Native American Ministries Sunday	50e — World Communion Sunday	50f — U.M. Student Day	51 — Direct-billed clergy non-health benefits	52 — Direct-billed clergy health benefits	53a — Base compensation paid to/for the Senior Pastor or other person assigned or appointed in the lead pastoral role to the church	53b — Base compensation paid/for to all Associate Pastor(s) & other pastoral staff assigned or appointed to the church	53c — Base compensation paid to/for any Deacons NOT included in 53a or 53b	55a — Housing benefits paid to/for Lead Pastor or person in lead pastoral role as described in 53a	55b — Housing benefits paid to/for ALL Associate Pastor(s) & other pastoral staff assigned or appointed to the	55c — Housing benefits paid to/for any Deacons not included in 53a or 53b	56 — Paid to/for all persons included in Lines 53a-53c for accountable reimbursements	57 — Paid to/for all persons included in Lines 53a-53c for any other cash allowances (non-)
8390	Alexandria Chapel	3,776	0	0	0	0	0	0	0	0	0	27,089	0	0	0	0	0	0	0
8130	Asbury	13,135	1,910	97	0	0	0	0	0	3,359	5,263	10,775	0	0	15,467	0	0	300	0
8480	Bethel	0	13,135	0	0	0	30	0	0	6,659	6,970	43,750	0	0	11,667	0	0	2,320	0
8515	Bethesda	0	300	0	33	10	0	0	0	0	0	27,000	0	0	0	0	0	0	0
8120	Bowie	1,402	2,271	0	0	0	47	144	0	8,127	7,671	39,748	0	0	3,714	0	0	1,130	0
8370	Brookfield	954	9,788	0	0	0	0	0	0	10,071	11,690	38,686	0	0	0	0	0	0	0
8460	Brooks	8,800	1,500	0	0	0	0	0	0	15,461	19,096	80,438	0	0	36,840	0	0	15,971	0
8520	Calvary	2,056	0	0	0	155	0	156	0	14,561	0	37,470	0	0	37,079	0	0	1,064	19,200
8425	Carroll-Western	966	2,930	0	0	0	0	0	0	5,778	0	38,520	0	0	0	0	0	0	0
8195	Cheltenham	500	1,000	0	0	0	0	0	0	9,900	11,323	44,000	0	0	0	0	0	0	0
8260	Chicamuxen	0	1,615	0	0	0	0	0	0	0	0	17,400	0	0	0	0	0	500	0
8115	Christ	1,798	17,069	98	323	164	381	0	0	13,464	11,400	33,298	0	0	3,795	0	0	417	2,050
8170	Clinton	14,092	0	0	0	0	0	0	0	0	0	61,000	0	0	0	0	0	5,167	0
8295	Community With A Cause	3,550	750	0	0	0	0	0	89	0	0	13,000	0	0	0	0	0	1,618	900
8175	Coopers	31,549	661	0	0	0	0	0	55	0	0	19,594	0	0	0	0	0	2,350	0
7480	Corkran Memorial	0	230	55	0	0	80	0	89	0	0	23,493	0	0	0	0	0	2,000	0
8330	Eastern	8,491	2,193	0	0	0	0	0	55	0	0	14,383	0	0	0	0	0	0	0
8205	Ebenezer	12,117	250	172	0	175	0	62	0	10,625	9,470	81,239	0	0	19,866	0	0	7,667	0
7310	Emmanuel	3,900	4,078	100	0	25	731	20	190	10,777	12,424	47,899	0	0	0	0	0	4,100	0
8240	Emmanuel	4,112	0	15	216	153	0	23	0	10,467	14,817	43,572	0	0	19,866	0	0	929	0
8110	Faith	50,631	0	0	0	56	230	50	54	2,156	0	26,349	0	0	0	0	0	0	0
8540	First Saints Community Church	600	798	39	0	0	0	50	0	38,945	40,525	77,366	95,092	0	30,568	39,732	0	13,237	0
8925	Glenn Dale	39,798	74,964	0	40	150	45	305	0	11,970	13,448	30,000	0	0	36,500	0	0	3,289	0
8525	Good Shepherd	0	0	125	0	0	0	0	0	13,535	13,515	62,400	0	0	22,148	0	0	2,429	0
8215	Grace	5,415	15,786	196	0	289	976	380	357	14,453	11,400	80,730	0	0	20,000	0	0	8,300	0
8230	Holly wood	29,256	25,715	0	0	0	0	226	0	14,020	26,534	56,210	0	0	19,866	0	0	3,090	0
8245	Huntingtown	0	4,359	0	0	0	0	0	0	13,176	15,960	67,494	0	0	10,260	0	0	5,244	0
8235	Immanuel	6,258	2,620	0	0	130	85	0	18	0	0	26,537	0	0	0	0	0	2,460	0
8265	Indian Head	9,532	0	210	0	0	0	0	0	0	0	9,634	0	0	19,866	0	0	2,820	0
8550	Journey of Faith Church, The	38,739	4,817	0	0	50	90	261	0	18,995	16,540	51,000	0	0	19,866	0	0	3,994	0
8275	La Plata	1,639	525	0	0	50	0	0	225	14,806	27,258	66,494	0	0	39,866	0	0	6,747	0
8290	Larham	25,308	0	0	0	0	0	0	0	0	0	28,720	0	0	12,000	0	0	902	0
8320	Lexington Park	1,406	20,603	0	50	146	50	50	0	21,505	28,920	62,250	28,810	0	29,000	12,070	0	4,233	1,300
8420	Metropolitan	3,523	15,540	0	50	0	0	0	50	12,558	11,316	46,350	0	0	23,417	0	0	0	0
8150	Mount Calvary	61,052	500	47	0	0	0	0	0	0	0	26,500	0	0	0	0	0	1,050	0
8365	Mount Harmony-Lower Marlboro	0	20,340	0	0	0	0	0	0	13,337	10,345	65,500	0	0	0	0	0	9,073	0
8475	Mount Hope	10,985	0	0	0	243	412	0	0	0	0	24,500	0	0	36,000	0	0	1,796	0
8355	Mount Oak	0	37,725	140	0	0	0	0	0	13,544	19,336	49,330	0	0	19,866	0	0	0	0
8430	Mount Olive	37,901	1,800	0	0	0	0	0	0	1,577	0	27,294	0	0	5,197	0	0	1,421	0
8350	Mount Zion	0	12,853	0	0	0	0	0	270	14,467	12,709	21,430	0	0	0	0	0	0	0
8450	Mount Zion	13,509	150	0	0	0	0	0	0	0	0	32,328	0	0	0	0	0	0	0
8485	Nottingham-Myers	11,005	900	65	0	0	0	0	0	13,468	11,370	37,311	0	0	2,462	0	0	376	5,400
8335	Olivet	5,524	10,920	0	0	60	0	0	0	11,658	11,400	51,052	0	0	30,035	0	0	3,734	0
8380	Oxon Hill	4,922	2,383	0	0	0	0	0	0	11,699	11,351	40,969	0	0	0	0	0	5,100	960
8250	Patuxent	5,545	735	0	0	0	0	0	0	0	0	23,450	0	0	2,820	0	0	0	0
8180	Peters	463	1,849	0	0	0	0	0	0	0	0	10,335	0	0	1,600	0	0	0	0
8270	Pisgah	2,870	4,268	160	75	60	40	50	50	13,074	13,133	40,968	0	0	14,665	0	0	2,500	200
8255	Plum Point		1,000	0	0	0	0	0	0				0	0	2,820	0	0	600	0

		Paid in salary and benefits for all other church staff and diaconal ministers	Amount spent for local church program expenses	Amount spent for local church operating expenses	Amount paid for principal and interest on indebtedness, loans, mortgages, etc.	Amount paid for capital campaign or fundraising costs	Amount paid on capital expenditures for building, improvements, and major equipment purchases.	Amount PAID by/for the local church on all expenditures	Number of giving units	Received through pledges	Received from non-pledging, but identified givers	Received from unidentified givers	Amount received from interest and dividends and/or transferred from liquid assets	Amount received from Sale of Church Assets	Amount received through building use fees, contributions, and rentals	Amount received through fundraisers and other sources
Align #	**Church Name**	**60**	**61**	**62**	**63**	**63a**	**64**	**65**	**66**	**67a**	**67b**	**67c**	**67d**	**67e**	**67f**	**67g**
8390	Alexandria Chapel	0	1	5,495	0	0	0	37,849	36	41,120	558	199	0	0	0	6,705
8130	Asbury	30,364	5,977	29,060	0	0	11,528	134,231	125	0	103,852	9,040	0	0	0	16,296
8480	Bethel	1,706	700	13,846	0	0	11,083	140,516	35	62,600	30,000	32,318	324	0	996	1,149
8515	Bethesda	0	2,600	10,020	0	0	1,164	48,309	59	0	63,699	1,739	0	1,000	0	7,091
8120	Bowie	2,470	3,135	20,790	0	0	0	103,276	62	0	71,447	3,064	1	0	95	5,838
8370	Brookfield	0	1,217	15,374	0	0	0	95,747	40	0	47,998	1,623	12,374	0	0	5,778
8460	Brooks	103,491	17,564	84,348	133,400	0	0	581,129	0	0	572,283	15,118	0	0	3,750	0
8520	Calvary	28,967	2,391	35,646	21,292	0	2,725	235,236	91	84,968	94,374	3,965	0	0	25,305	0
8425	Carroll-Western	21,471	1,500	6,061	0	0	0	91,947	0	0	123,299	1,346	0	0	0	5,500
8155	Cheltenham	18,189	750	26,268	0	0	6,973	138,257	0	0	116,707	3,199	311	0	375	11,297
8260	Chicamuxen	0	139	12,563	0	0	0	39,452	26	44,565	0	0	0	0	0	0
8115	Christ	35,836	8,985	26,271	0	0	0	128,387	85	0	145,691	2,475	0	0	0	28,836
8170	Clinton	50,535	6,157	55,294	0	0	0	253,249	240	249,915	0	3,066	0	0	9,232	19,606
8295	Community With A Cause	0	9,023	32,863	0	0	0	75,456	53	0	88,471	7,003	93	0	0	0
8175	Coopers	14,989	600	8,315	0	0	739	56,445	27	0	51,761	4,170	0	0	0	0
7480	Corkran Memorial	10,370	13,029	40,081	0	0	0	121,183	30	0	84,465	1,500	0	0	25,000	0
8330	Eastern	6,757	1,236	19,029	0	0	911	53,044	49	48,829	0	0	0	0	0	5,630
8285	Ebenezer	79,559	10,951	72,253	53,692	0	53,435	450,695	145	372,397	12,801	5,553	1,267	0	43,561	1,949
7310	Emmanuel	82,787	3,819	52,082	0	0	0	229,433	163	156,078	42,647	3,782	113	0	875	11,237
8240	Emmanuel	21,639	4,064	17,503	0	0	0	156,440	62	0	157,090	2,238	39	0	1,350	0
8110	Faith	17,516	2,198	36,338	4,834	0	0	109,923	41	0	87,720	2,942	0	0	12,815	24,953
8540	First Saints Community Church	183,686	42,707	155,421	41,832	0	66,528	1,000,211	389	0	883,480	21,699	3,209	1,000	0	0
8225	Glenn Dale	26,353	228	38,175	0	0	34,995	217,182	0	125,785	601	4,413	20	0	30,526	4,544
8525	Good Shepherd	119,822	22,512	75,453	0	0	24,000	501,326	199	253,519	126,760	3,345	0	0	46,195	1,297
8215	Grace	56,353	2,922	89,815	0	0	0	329,414	338	0	624,646	8,491	2,523	0	810	1,307
8230	Hollywood	87,286	15,641	109,170	0	0	9,096	408,601	193	0	249,519	4,773	176	0	8,735	145
8245	Huntingtown	154,473	36,451	82,330	0	0	35,183	543,737	185	0	510,831	13,938	0	0	620	0
8235	Immanuel	0	3,218	27,235	0	0	7,034	83,222	33	72,667	15,259	3,505	4	0	835	10,746
8265	Indian Head	1,350	5,547	4,811	0	500	5,231	62,536	0	34,748	7,271	1,739	0	0	0	5,646
8550	Journey of Faith Church;The	38,768	2,000	29,488	79,929	0	64,000	344,694	163	0	234,775	100,201	0	0	600	0
8275	La Plata	156,296	10,967	149,656	74,569	0	113,570	801,387	400	0	593,190	11,023	212	0	3,125	21,857
8290	Lanham	32,214	17,694	47,032	0	0	14,712	177,778	15	51,862	19,431	8,188	73,700	0	21,200	3,558
8320	Lexington Park	129,217	19,736	75,245	55,908	0	6,000	581,696	198	372,966	212,208	9,335	0	0	3,194	0
8420	Metropolitan	49,685	18,437	65,893	0	0	5,856	288,945	0	0	249,378	3,043	28	0	3,300	32,421
8150	Mount Calvary	15,283	5,490	11,198	0	0	0	76,068	35	3,600	82,000	4,500	2	0	0	0
8365	Mount Harmony-Lower Marlboro	33,560	13,883	64,041	68,505	5,167	38,100	450,091	180	130,697	132,566	8,079	0	0	1,220	39,186
8475	Mount Hope	11,760	300	13,853	4,300	0	11,531	77,812	44	0	66,400	2,510	0	0	0	0
8355	Mount Oak	190,012	14,958	133,939	11,846	0	74,287	636,289	0	0	526,231	0	0	0	14,675	0
8430	Mount Olive	38,023	3,610	53,081	78,189	0	22,215	268,962	141	21,060	163,591	2,041	777	0	26,300	46,354
8350	Mount Zion	105,357	7,050	53,370	0	0	44,962	407,472	183	204,768	103,156	6,236	900	0	7,649	6,130
8450	Mount Zion	0	400	700	0	0	0	26,553	36	0	0	500	0	0	0	0
8485	Nottingham-Myers	33,320	7,498	49,930	100,747	250	592	272,349	37	0	178,625	4,418	0	0	3,173	14,380
8335	Olivet	15,212	10,060	39,693	0	0	26,759	225,579	114	174,888	0	4,503	14	0	4,180	1,131
8380	Oxon Hill	38,993	4,996	46,308	0	0	5,601	215,761	57	0	204,654	2,264	1	0	22,940	3,711
8250	Patuxent	35,072	1,837	16,432	0	0	0	119,460	97	0	155,086	1,451	0	0	0	0
8180	Peters	23,872	2,470	7,240	1,002	0	0	80,844	62	0	78,161	340	0	0	0	0
8270	Pisgah	0	0	21,126	0	0	0	58,217	2	43,690	0	6,098	0	0	0	0
8255	Plum Point	21,289	3,200	28,340	33,623	0	0	178,829	84	124,046	0	2,809	68	0	0	44,122

Align #	Church Name	TOTAL income for annual budget/spending plan (67a-g) [67]	Capital campaigns [68a]	Memorials, endowments, and bequests [68b]	Other sources and projects (include UMW, UMM and 'flow-through') [68c]	Special Sundays, Gen. Adv. Spec., World Srvc Spec., Conf. Adv. Spec. and other directed benevolent giving [68d]	Total income for designated causes including capital campaign and other special projects [68]	Equitable Compensation Funds received by Church or Pastor [69a]	Advance Special, apportioned, and connectional funds received by church [69b]	Other grants and financial support from institutional sources [69c]	Income from connectional / institutional sources outside the local church [69]	TOTAL CHURCH INCOME (Sum of Lines 67 + 68 + 69) [70]	Amount APPORTIONED to the local church [40a]	Amount PAID by the local church for all apportioned causes [40b]
8390	Alexandria Chapel	48,582	0	0	0	0	0	0	0	0	0	48,582	7,019	5,264
8130	Asbury	129,188	0	0	5,861	2,678	8,539	0	0	0	0	137,727	16,355	16,355
8480	Bethel	127,387	0	675	0	0	675	0	0	0	0	128,062	14,715	14,715
8515	Bethesda	73,529	0	0	0	0	0	0	0	0	0	73,529	7,225	7,225
8120	Bowie	80,445	0	0	0	311	311	0	0	0	0	80,756	13,686	13,686
8370	Brookfield	67,773	0	1,775	0	0	1,775	0	0	0	0	69,548	7,519	7,519
8460	Brooks	591,151	0	0	0	0	0	0	0	0	0	591,151	54,802	54,802
8520	Calvary	208,612	0	5,915	0	864	6,779	0	0	0	0	215,391	25,010	25,010
8425	Carroll-Western	130,145	0	0	0	0	0	0	0	0	0	130,145	16,361	16,361
8155	Cheltenham	133,889	0	6,250	0	582	6,832	0	0	0	0	140,721	14,682	14,682
8260	Chicamuxen	44,565	0	0	0	0	0	0	0	0	0	44,565	5,300	5,300
8115	Christ	177,002	0	0	0	0	0	0	0	0	0	177,002	18,170	18,170
8170	Clinton	281,819	0	0	0	1,870	1,870	0	0	0	0	283,689	29,439	29,439
8295	Community With A Cause	95,567	0	0	0	0	0	0	0	0	0	95,567	4,860	4,860
8175	Coopers	55,931	0	0	0	89	89	0	0	0	0	56,020	5,469	5,469
7480	Corkran Memorial	110,965	42,953	0	0	580	43,533	0	0	0	0	154,498	14,651	0
8330	Eastern	54,459	0	0	0	0	0	0	0	0	0	54,459	10,308	10,308
8285	Ebenezer	437,528	0	2,022	0	1,818	3,840	0	0	0	0	441,368	41,054	41,054
7310	Emmanuel	214,732	0	0	0	1,300	1,300	0	0	0	0	216,032	39,940	1,360
8240	Emmanuel	160,717	0	0	0	665	665	0	0	0	0	161,382	15,415	15,415
8110	Faith	128,430	0	17,600	0	665	18,265	0	0	0	0	146,695	14,733	14,733
8540	First Saints Community Church	909,388	6,815	3,283	59,290	350	69,738	0	0	0	0	979,126	116,410	116,410
8225	Glenn Dale	165,889	3,417	0	0	1,150	4,567	0	0	0	0	170,456	20,115	20,115
8525	Good Shepherd	431,116	60,579	600	23,099	0	84,278	0	0	0	0	515,394	41,792	30,000
8215	Grace	637,777	55,961	0	0	2,630	58,591	0	0	0	0	696,368	41,792	41,792
8230	Hollywood	263,348	0	1,045	7,350	23,094	31,489	0	0	0	0	294,837	35,122	35,122
8245	Huntingtown	525,389	0	27,820	0	35,036	62,856	0	0	0	0	588,245	57,970	57,970
8235	Immanuel	103,016	0	230	0	0	230	0	0	0	0	103,246	12,379	12,379
8265	Indian Head	49,404	0	1,470	0	4,670	6,140	0	0	0	0	55,544	4,399	4,399
8550	Journey of Faith Church,The	335,576	0	72,568	0	0	72,568	0	0	0	0	408,144	42,366	10,592
8275	La Plata	629,407	0	4,920	0	0	4,920	0	0	0	0	634,327	92,941	92,941
8290	Lanham	177,839	1,142	2,250	5,892	25	9,309	0	0	31,996	31,996	219,144	21,140	21,140
8320	Lexington Park	597,703	1,650	0	0	0	1,650	0	0	0	0	599,353	62,811	62,811
8420	Metropolitan	289,170	0	0	0	95	95	0	0	0	0	289,265	38,187	38,187
8150	Mount Calvary	90,102	0	0	0	300	300	0	0	0	0	90,402	12,524	12,524
8365	Mount Harmony-Lower Marlboro	311,748	86,137	8,225	0	44,553	138,915	0	0	0	0	450,663	31,555	31,555
8475	Mount Hope	68,910	0	0	0	1,118	1,118	0	0	0	0	70,028	10,313	10,313
8355	Mount Oak	540,906	13,453	7,300	0	0	20,753	0	0	0	0	561,659	43,531	43,531
8430	Mount Olive	260,123	0	2,230	0	3,070	5,300	0	0	0	0	265,423	17,907	17,907
8350	Mount Zion	329,899	21,571	0	16,611	100	42,422	0	0	0	0	372,321	43,822	43,822
8450	Mount Zion	500	0	0	0	100	100	0	0	0	0	600	3,873	3,873
8485	Nottingham-Myers	200,596	0	1,430	0	7,426	21,045	0	0	18,501	18,501	240,142	19,475	4,869
8335	Olivet	184,716	16,732	0	0	3,415	25,788	0	0	0	0	210,504	17,891	17,891
8380	Oxon Hill	233,570	0	5,003	200	3,215	8,418	0	0	0	0	241,988	30,375	30,375
8250	Patuxent	156,537	0	0	0	0	0	0	0	0	0	156,537	16,673	16,673
8100	Peters	78,501	8,810	0	0	87	8,897	0	0	0	0	87,398	11,116	11,116
8270	Pisgah	49,788	0	0	0	0	0	0	0	0	0	49,788	6,760	6,760
8255	Plum Point	171,045	0	375	0	425	800	0	0	0	0	171,845	18,077	18,077

Align #	Church Name	Dist #	City	State	1. Total professing members at close of 2017	2a1. Received by Profession of Faith	2a2. Received by Profession of Faith (Other Than Confirmation)	2b. Restored by Affirmation of Faith	3. Transferred in from other UM churches	4. Transferred in from non-UM churches	5a. Removed or corrected by Charge Conference action	5b. Withdrawn from Professing Membership	6. Transferred out to other UM churches	7. Transferred out to non-UM churches	8. Removed by death	9. Total professing members at close of 2018	9a. Asian	9b. African American/Black	9c. Hispanic/Latino	9d. Native American	9e. Pacific Islander	9f. White	9g. Multi-Racial	9h. Female	9i. Male
8205	Providence-Fort Washington	WE	Ft Washington	MD	120	0	0	2	0	0	1	2	2	0	1	113	0	8	1	0	10	94	0	70	43
7315	Queens Chapel	WE	Beltsville	MD	768	0	0	0	0	0	0	2	2	0	8	758	0	751	3	0	0	4	0	482	276
7495	Savage	WE	Savage	MD	272	0	0	0	2	0	0	0	1	0	0	274	1	3	5	0	0	265	0	157	117
8140	Shiloh	WE	Bryans Road	MD	24	1	0	0	1	0	1	0	0	0	0	24	0	3	0	0	0	21	0	19	5
8375	Shiloh Community	WE	Newburg	MD	182	1	1	1	0	1	0	0	0	0	8	176	0	176	0	0	0	0	0	138	38
8415	Smith Chapel	WE	La Plata	MD	99	1	0	0	0	0	5	0	11	0	1	82	0	81	0	0	0	0	1	50	32
8185	Smithville	WE	Dunkirk	MD	158	4	0	0	0	0	29	0	0	0	1	132	0	0	0	0	0	131	1	79	53
8470	Solomons	WE	Solomons	MD	266	0	1	0	0	0	10	0	0	0	3	254	0	0	0	1	1	251	1	132	122
8440	St. John	WE	Lusby	MD	114	0	0	0	0	0	0	0	3	0	0	111	0	111	0	0	0	0	0	66	45
8445	St Luke	WE	Ridge	MD	82	5	2	0	2	5	0	0	4	0	7	83	0	82	0	0	0	1	0	55	28
8125	St. Matthews	WE	Bowie	MD	543	0	9	2	0	0	0	2	2	0	1	545	5	50	8	0	0	479	3	354	191
8280	St Matthews	WE	La Plata	MD	27	9	4	13	3	0	0	2	7	0	6	30	0	30	0	0	0	0	0	16	14
8345	St Paul	WE	Lusby	MD	564	5	0	2	0	0	0	4	0	0	7	563	2	4	0	0	0	557	0	325	238
8385	St Paul	WE	Oxon Hill	MD	605	5	0	8	2	8	0	0	4	0	4	617	0	608	6	0	0	0	3	421	196
8160	St. Edmonds	WE	Chesapeake Beach	MD	179	0	0	0	7	0	0	0	4	1	10	180	0	180	0	0	0	0	0	137	43
8435	Trinity	WE	Prince Frederick	MD	937	9	3	31	0	0	137	0	0	0	1	802	2	2	0	0	0	798	0	443	359
8490	Union	WE	Upper Marlboro	MD	313	4	0	2	5	0	0	0	0	0	0	332	0	329	0	0	0	3	0	199	133
8165	Wards Memorial	WE	Owings	MD	61	0	0	0	2	0	0	0	0	0	2	61	0	61	0	0	0	0	0	48	13
8465	Waters Memorial	WE	Saint Leonard	MD	256	0	3	0	5	0	0	0	0	0	3	259	0	0	0	0	0	254	5	147	112
8510	Westphalia	WE	Upper Marlboro	MD	850	0	0	0	2	0	0	0	0	0	3	880	0	877	0	0	0	0	3	552	328
8325	Zion	WE	Lexington Park	MD	244	0	0	0	0	0	0	0	3	1	3	246	0	239	0	0	0	2	5	158	88
8535	Zion Wesley	WE	Waldorf	MD	233	0	3	2	0	0	0	0	3	0	0	229	0	223	4	0	0	0	2	136	93
	WE Total				18,602	114	132	88	63	35	349	47	59	36	211	18,287	107	8,125	72	6	41	9,610	126	11,130	7,157
	BWC Total				155,281	971	1,066	344	583	345	2,764	697	916	439	1,968	151,816	2,086	35,009	796	69	155	112,923	778	91,469	60,147

		Average attendance at all weekly worship service(s)	Persons who Worship Online	Number of Infants and Children baptized (Age 0-12)	Number of Tenns and Adults baptized (Age 13+)	TOTAL Number of persons baptized (all ages)	Number of baptized members who have not become Professing	Number of other constituents of the church	Total enrolled in confirmation preparation classes that	CHILDREN (0-11yrs) in all Christian groups, small groups and Sunday School.	YOUTH (12-18 yrs) in all Christian groups, small groups and Sunday School.	YOUNG ADULTS (19-30 yrs) in all Christian groups, small groups and Sunday School.	OTHER ADULTS (31+ yrs) in all Christian groups, small groups and Sunday School.	TOTAL number of persons participating in Christian formation groups (Total lines 15 - 18).	Average weekly attendance: Education classes/groups that meet in Sunday Church School groups.	Number of participants in Vacation Bible School	Number of ongoing classes (all ages) for learning in Sunday Church	Number of ONGOING small groups, support groups, or classes	Number of SHORT-TERM classes, support groups, or small groups offered	Membership in United Methodist Men (UMM)	Amount paid for projects (UMM)	Membership in United Methodist Women (UMW)	Amount paid for local church and community work (UMW)	Number of UMVIM teams sent out from this church	Number of persons sent out on UMVIM teams from this church
Align #	**Church Name**	**10**	**10a**	**11a**	**11b**	**11T**	**12**	**13**	**14**	**15**	**16**	**17**	**18**	**19**	**20**	**22**	**23**	**24**	**25**	**26**	**27**	**28**	**29**	**30a**	**30b**
8205	Providence-Fort Washington	68	0	1	0	1	0	52	0	8	2	1	17	28	8	12	3	3	0	12	0	32	10,398	0	0
7315	Queens Chapel	227	0	5	0	5	0	0	0	15	18	19	92	144	30	78	5	4	1	59	30,743	72	5,184	3	32
7435	Savage	46	0	0	0	0	22	15	0	10	7	3	9	29	6	0	2	2	1	4	0	5	3,727	0	0
8140	Shiloh	20	0	0	0	0	2	12	0	4	2	5	6	17	6	0	1	2	1	0	0	0	0	0	0
8375	Shiloh Community	38	0	0	0	0	0	0	0	0	0	0	0	0	0	0	0	0	1	13	0	18	0	0	0
8415	Smith Chapel	46	38	0	0	0	3	8	0	3	6	0	8	17	16	15	2	5	1	12	85	19	970	0	0
8185	Smithville	59	0	2	0	2	32	32	4	8	4	0	33	45	12	13	3	2	8	0	0	23	1,660	0	1
8470	Solomons	40	0	0	0	0	0	0	0	9	2	2	10	23	6	0	1	1	1	0	0	0	0	0	0
8340	St John	59	0	1	0	1	0	17	0	12	14	4	38	68	65	35	2	8	4	0	0	0	0	0	0
8445	St Luke	66	0	1	0	1	0	0	0	21	17	0	26	64	64	44	0	64	0	0	0	18	1,024	0	0
8125	St Matthews	206	0	4	0	4	4	200	5	45	30	12	75	162	50	98	7	18	3	18	250	118	5,732	2	8
8280	St Matthews	25	0	0	0	0	0	0	0	0	0	0	27	27	0	0	0	2	0	0	0	0	0	0	0
8345	St Paul	149	6	0	2	2	0	250	9	81	25	6	99	211	98	117	7	8	0	0	0	0	0	0	0
8385	St Paul	257	0	3	0	3	3	0	0	36	20	10	205	271	60	100	5	3	8	21	2,051	45	7,640	0	0
8160	St. Edmonds	85	0	1	0	1	0	0	0	3	7	0	45	55	11	25	2	6	0	0	0	26	2,000	0	0
8435	Trinity	227	0	4	0	4	0	287	0	29	40	10	85	164	85	90	8	25	0	0	0	0	0	0	0
8490	Union	138	40	1	4	5	1	47	0	40	10	15	85	150	20	40	3	6	2	36	7,200	30	6,725	0	0
8165	Wards Memorial	36	0	0	0	0	0	1	0	10	3	4	40	57	25	12	9	4	3	0	0	0	0	0	0
8465	Waters Memorial	45	0	1	1	2	1	3	0	4	10	0	10	24	8	35	3	2	1	15	0	10	0	0	0
8510	Westphalia	373	175	6	0	6	0	65	20	79	9	22	488	598	60	45	5	4	4	88	1,000	80	4,516	0	0
8325	Zion	72	0	2	1	3	7	6,000	0	5	11	10	73	99	16	11	2	2	3	79	500	1	200	0	0
8535	Zion Wesley	50	7	1	0	1	0	0	0	15	10	2	20	47	10	62	2	2	3	15	0	34	0	1	12
WE Total		**7,006**	**389**	**109**	**52**	**161**	**903**	**8,788**	**135**	**1,670**	**858**	**424**	**4,048**	**7,000**	**1,918**	**2,516**	**230**	**454**	**192**	**932**	**83,213**	**1,412**	**118,133**	**17**	**110**
BWC Total		**51,383**	**7,619**	**1,097**	**421**	**1,518**	**####**	**33,510**	**944**	**14,666**	**7,494**	**3,181**	**27,355**	**52,696**	**14,772**	**20,211**	**###**	**2,656**	**1,899**	**3,962**	**376,946**	**8,613**	**694,092**	**92**	**951**

Align #	Church Name	33	33a	33b	34	35a	36	36SF	37	38	39	42	43	44	45	46	47	48a	48b
		TOTAL Community MINISTRIES for outreach, justice, and mercy	MINISTRIES focusing on global/regional health?	MINISTRIES focusing on engaging in ministry with the poor/socially	PERSONS SERVED BY community ministries for outreach, justice, and mercy	PERSONS SERVING (from your congregation) in mission/community ministries	Market value of church-owned land, buildings and equipment	Overall square footage of church owned buildings (furnished and unfurnished areas)	Market value of financial and other liquid assets	Debt secured by church physical assets	Other debt	General Advance Specials remitted to the Annual Conference Treasurer	World Service Specials remitted to the Annual Conference Treasurer	Annual Conference Advance Specials remitted to the Annual Conference Treasurer	Youth Service Fund remitted to the	All other funds sent to AC Treasurer for connectional mission and ministry	Total Annual Conference Special Sunday Offerings remitted to the	UMC CAUSES: Total amount given DIRECTLY to United Methodist causes (NOT sent to BWC Treasurer)	MISSIONS/MINISTRY COSTS: Direct costs incurred by the local church for mission and community ministry activities
8205	Providence-Fort Washington	0	0	0	0	0	6,200,000	13,607	602,782	0	1,179	3,948	0	0	0	0	0	0	0
7315	Queens Chapel	5	2	2	750	97	5,478,600	27,250	53,375	2,802,133	0	647	0	0	0	0	0	0	12,363
7435	Savage	6	6	6	365	120	2,260,000	11,629	0	0	0	0	0	0	0	0	0	0	261
8140	Shiloh	6	1	3	4,850	18	1,814,400	6,917	35,280	82,684	4,000	30	0	0	0	0	0	52	5,256
8375	Shiloh Community	1	0	0	1	0	1,147,500	0	95,000	0	0	0	0	0	0	0	0	0	0
8415	Smith Chapel	6	0	5	410	6	329,000	3,661	154,000	0	0	0	0	0	0	0	0	0	2,368
8185	Smithville	13	1	12	1,000	72	2,204,000	5,899	205,106	0	0	0	0	0	0	0	0	0	4,916
8470	Solomons	5	1	5	2,500	20	1,100,000	5,771	194,144	0	0	402	0	2,033	0	0	0	400	9,619
8340	St John	3	0	1	87	53	817,912	7,718	14,012	0	0	0	0	30	0	0	0	0	0
8445	St Luke	18	5	8	4,000	150	260,280	2,768	722,615	0	3,811	0	0	0	0	394	0	36,000	15,100
8125	St Matthews	2	2	2	55	27	4,722,370	36,878	14,700	1,204,000	0	0	0	0	0	0	0	8,528	5,818
8280	St Matthews	16	16	16	4,500	160	224,600	1,480	278,683	448,687	1,175	160	0	0	0	0	0	0	23,101
8345	St Paul	16	16	0	6,000	280	2,000,000	19,271	202,156	0	0	715	0	0	0	0	0	437	900
8385	St Paul	3	0	0	75	40	3,961,673	17,961	0	0	0	0	0	0	0	0	0	0	33,749
8160	St Edmonds	0	0	25	935	125	591,000	5,680	430,534	55,477	0	1,425	0	0	0	0	0	3,250	4,148
8435	Trinity	0	0	0	3,300	112	6,639,500	40,325	130,000	0	0	500	0	0	0	0	0	1,000	200
8490	Union	6	0	0	206	12	1,181,700	27,300	2,500	0	3,789	0	0	0	0	0	0	0	1,806
8165	Wards Memorial	136	0	136	136	190	1,054,600	14,389	95,291	175,756	0	145	0	0	0	0	0	0	30,200
8465	Waters Memorial	8	3	5	2,000	121	3,000,000	23,431	205,601	3,585,156	3,508	0	0	0	0	0	0	0	0
8510	Westphalia	10	0	10	0	15	6,482,100	5,467	163,300	0	0	0	0	0	0	0	0	0	
8325	Zion	3	1	2	125		1,023,700	8,096	157,318	0	0	0	0	0	0	0	0	0	
8535	Zion Wesley						534,000			0	0	0	0	0	0	0	0	0	
	WE Total	624	127	492	125,455	6,926	139,682,469	810,470	12,794,494	16,287,239	206,229	41,253	0	2,504	0	1,522	0	111,700	594,832
	BWC Total	8,861	842	2,809	1,351,410	57,291	########	########	207,045,496	64,276,909	3,431,102	373,559	698	25,878	0	8,394	0	1,105,056	6,777,168

Column descriptions:

- **48TOTAL** — Total of UMC Causes & UMC Missions & Outreach
- **49** — NON-UMC CAUSES: Total amount given DIRECTLY to non-United Methodist benevolent and charitable causes (NOT sent to BWC Treasurer)
- **50a** — Human Relations Sunday
- **50b** — UMCOR Sunday (formerly One Great Hour of Sharing)
- **50c** — Peace with Justice Sunday
- **50d** — Native American Ministries Sunday
- **50e** — World Communion Sunday
- **50f** — U.M. Student Day
- **51** — Direct-billed clergy non-health benefits
- **52** — Direct-billed clergy health benefits
- **53a** — Base compensation paid to/for the Senior Pastor or other person assigned or appointed in the lead pastoral role to the church
- **53b** — Base compensation paid/for to all Associate Pastor(s) & other pastoral staff assigned or appointed to the church
- **53c** — Base compensation paid to/for any Deacons NOT included in 53a or 53b
- **55a** — Housing benefits paid to/for Lead Pastor or person in lead pastoral role as described in 53a
- **55b** — Housing benefits paid to/for ALL Associate Pastor(s) & other pastoral staff assigned or appointed to the
- **55c** — Housing benefits paid to/for any Deacons not included in 53a or 53b
- **56** — Paid to/for all persons included in Lines 53a-53c for accountable reimbursements
- **57** — Paid to/for all persons included in Lines 53a-53c for any other cash allowances (non-)

Align #	Church Name	48TOTAL	49	50a	50b	50c	50d	50e	50f	51	52	53a	53b	53c	55a	55b	55c	56	57
8205	Providence-Fort Washington	0	215	243	0	0	0	0	0	5,850	0	27,000	0	0	12,000	0	0	2,395	0
7315	Queens Chapel	12,363	0	0	0	0	0	0	0	13,972	11,400	77,565	0	0	17,640	0	0	6,475	0
7435	Savage	261	1,505	0	0	0	0	0	0	12,201	11,400	19,060	0	0	8,000	0	0	709	0
8140	Shiloh	5,256	1,878	10	0	0	10	65	0	0	0	0	0	0	11,000	0	0	500	1,696
8375	Shiloh Community	52	0	0	0	0	0	0	50	0	0	20,800	0	0	0	0	0	0	0
8415	Smith Chapel	0	0	50	0	0	60	30	0	13,024	13,508	24,000	0	0	7,000	0	0	1,825	0
8185	Smithville	2,368	23,786	68	0	0	0	141	0	5,417	5,243	61,318	0	0	4,914	0	0	3,340	0
8470	Solomons	5,316	1,000	82	0	0	0	0	0	9,708	11,491	42,714	0	0	3,311	0	0	3,472	0
6340	St John	9,619	9,619	418	0	0	333	0	250	15,143	12,320	28,766	0	0	3,614	0	0	0	0
8445	St. Luke	0	0	5	0	0	0	0	0	23,124	14,569	15,000	0	0	41,516	0	0	3,716	0
8125	St Matthews	51,100	128,376	0	560	430	640	650	30	14,713	22,800	51,409	0	0	3,616	0	0	5,207	0
8280	St Matthews	0	0	0	0	0	0	0	0	6,287	10,397	7,350	0	0	0	0	0	3,000	0
8345	St Paul	14,346	36,390	0	0	42	115	47	0	15,344	40,489	68,206	0	0	48,562	0	0	6,226	0
8385	St Paul	23,101	4,217	5	0	0	0	532	0	13,939	11,760	56,255	53,891	0	14,650	20,808	0	8,374	0
8160	St. Edmonds	1,337	1,317	0	0	0	0	0	0	0	0	31,076	0	0	43,000	0	0	2,000	0
8435	Trinity	36,999	17,484	0	0	0	0	0	0	0	0	52,910	0	0	19,866	0	0	9,064	0
8490	Union	5,148	306	500	0	500	500	500	500	0	0	72,000	0	0	14,137	0	0	7,186	0
8165	Wards Memorial	200	0	0	0	0	0	0	0	0	0	26,262	0	0	9,933	0	0	1,000	0
8465	Waters Memorial	1,806	3,496	0	0	0	0	25	0	2,752	2,752	22,438	0	0	54,984	0	0	0	0
8510	Westphalia	30,200	2,000	300	0	0	0	0	0	17,166	16,164	93,000	0	0	23,056	0	9,953	6,857	0
8325	Zion	0	6,168	75	75	75	150	150	150	13,539	14,379	62,196	0	0	4,966	0	0	9,353	0
8535	Zion Wesley	0	0	0	0	0	75	275	75	0	0	18,869	0	0	0	0	0	1,538	2,649
	WE Total	706,532	558,567	3,320	1,372	2,853	5,306	3,768	2,413	570,561	615,774	2,829,849	177,783	0	892,681	72,610	9,953	211,905	34,355
	BWC Total	7,882,224	4,153,671	14,927	16,940	14,289	21,859	19,564	10,988	4,332,919	5,384,666	21,042,446	1,665,883	191,284	6,675,142	641,983	82,555	1,499,365	164,015

Align #	Church Name	60 Paid in salary and benefits for all other church staff and diaconal ministers	61 Amount spent for local church program expenses	62 Amount spent for local church operating expenses	63 Amount paid for principal and interest on indebtedness, loans, mortgages, etc.	63a Amount paid for capital campaign or fundraising costs	64 Amount paid on capital expenditures for building, improvements, and major equipment purchases	65 Amount PAID by/for the local church on all expenditures	66 Number of giving units	67a Received through pledges	67b Received from non-pledging, but identified givers	67c Received from unidentified givers	67d Amount received from interest and dividends and/or transferred from liquid assets	67e Amount received from Sale of Church Assets	67f Amount received through building use fees, contributions, and rentals	67g Amount received through fundraisers and other sources
8205	Providence-Fort Washington	18,325	10,200	59,224	125,324	0	28,262	322,051	71	103,013	33,032	1,596	4,308	0	33,939	0
7315	Queens Chapel	79,473	13,831	147,929	230,400	0		676,784	262	0	623,419	9,228	0	0	19,500	11,711
7435	Savage	33,881	2,925	35,403	0	0	4,053	135,335	67	12,579	78,961	2,644	0	0	3,065	12,518
8140	Shiloh	4,200	1,250	18,045	6,902	1,550	800	50,797	18	0	33,250	4,587	0	0	0	6,409
8375	Shiloh Community	20,187	600	23,923	15,020	0	0	75,622	60	40,000	20,000	1,265	0	0	0	1,200
8415	Smith Chapel	24,769	2,360	31,990	0	0	0	101,078	82	82,621	0	593	0	0	0	0
8185	Smithville	44,413	4,441	48,231	0	0	19,743	243,920	67	0	182,289	1,926	125	0	7,810	3,849
8470	Solomons	9,545	6,589	25,044	0	0	15,119	181,694	26	0	109,278	27,026	60,000	0	825	0
8340	St John	0	2,544	19,411	0	0	0	123,900		104,088	0	3,997	0	0	0	0
8445	St Luke	600	700	13,046	145,573	0	19,051	38,098	288	35,120	2,643	23,820	26,005	0	25,812	10,211
8125	St Matthews	19,848	19,848	203,260	2,407	0	772	1,019,942	19	455,978	138,767	514	191	0	37,717	4,120
8280	St Matthews	600	600	12,676	31,947	0	20,471	34,360	197	0	0	7,517	154	0	2,875	13,178
8345	St Paul	122,734	7,042	55,249	0	0	34,612	534,604	367	217,885	181,798	35,099	0	0	0	0
8385	St Paul	177,808	38,603	133,210	57,926	0	7,573	635,109	79	0	595,713		0	0	2,500	7,229
8160	St Edmonds	17,549	3,574	16,212	26,193	0	21,531	126,651	188	105,294	22,761	10,012	302	0	3,500	19,051
8435	Trinity	189,350	28,395	92,438	0	0	9,871	687,456	31	539,089	432,566	3,231	32	0	300	5,463
8490	Union	77,207	15,324	104,938	0	0	0	406,569	0	0	130		0	0	0	0
8165	Wards Memorial	17,025	2,828	16,354	23,640	1,754	5,000	91,254	898	67,692	69,708	3,512	22	0	50	5,205
8465	Waters Memorial	12,465	0	26,917	288,000	2,000	0	129,370	188	0	60,097	9,344	0	0	12,448	0
8510	Westphalia	141,000	25,000	75,000	0	0	0	816,459	75	1,086,989	229,582	4,136	22	0	12,100	7,752
8325	Zion	46,920	14,287	24,672	0	0	0	245,240		0	63,834	1,793	0	0	0	16,377
8535	Zion Wesley	0	0	16,940	0	9,394		55,721		0	0		0	0	0	
	WE Total	3,396,838	570,189	3,308,587	1,717,000	20,615	885,668	18,447,233	7,537	5,525,116	10,190,510	495,622	187,397	2,000	485,072	511,673
	BWC Total	27,294,746	4,992,171	26,217,915	8,576,798	310,344	########	145,539,996	57,501	39,022,492	64,373,112	4,329,096	3,395,772	########	########	4,952,565

Align #	Church Name	67 TOTAL income for annual budget/spending plan. (67a-g)	68a Capital campaigns	68b Memorials, endowments, and bequests	68c Other sources and projects (include UMW, UMM and 'flow-through')	68d Special Sundays, Gen. Adv. Spec, World Srvc Spec., Conf. Adv. Spec. and other directed benevolent giving	68 Total income for designated causes including capital campaign and other special projects	69a Equitable Compensation Funds received by Church or Pastor	69b Advance Special, apportioned, and connectional funds received by church	69c Other grants and financial support from institutional sources	69 Income from connectional / institutional sources outside the local church	70 TOTAL CHURCH INCOME (Sum of Lines 67 + 68 + 69)	40a Amount APPORTIONED to the local church	40b Amount PAID by the local church for all apportioned causes
8205	Providence-Fort Washington	175,968	20,213	102,220	9,382	739	132,554	0	0	0	0	308,522	29,065	29,065
7315	Queens Chapel	663,858	0	0	0	2,540	2,540	0	0	0	0	666,398	65,089	65,089
7435	Savage	109,767	4,804	50	423	215	5,492	4,735	0	0	4,735	119,994	16,964	4,241
8140	Shiloh	44,246	0	0	0	115	115	0	0	0	0	44,361	5,104	851
8375	Shiloh Community	62,465	0	700	0	0	700	0	0	0	0	63,165	15,227	15,227
8415	Smith Chapel	83,214	0	0	0	301	301	0	0	0	0	83,515	13,556	13,556
8185	Smithville	195,999	0	3,495	0	20,348	23,843	0	0	0	0	219,842	24,348	24,348
8470	Solomons	197,129	0	8,000	9,895	140	18,035	0	0	0	0	215,164	26,149	21,553
8340	St John	108,085	0	0	0	0	0	0	0	0	0	108,085	18,085	18,085
8445	St Luke	37,763	0	0	0	0	0	0	0	0	0	37,763	5,636	5,636
8125	St Matthews	680,593	0	21,189	0	15,676	36,865	0	0	0	0	717,458	87,932	87,932
8280	St Matthews	4,634	0	0	0	0	0	0	0	0	0	4,634	3,939	3,939
8345	St Paul	458,286	21,312	1,480	18,369	20,183	61,344	0	0	0	0	519,630	59,232	59,232
8385	St Paul	633,841	0	0	0	0	0	0	0	0	0	633,841	71,607	71,607
8160	St. Edmonds	112,523	0	0	0	0	0	0	0	0	0	112,523	14,679	14,679
8435	Trinity	592,715	0	3,331	9,860	19,009	32,200	0	0	0	0	624,915	81,101	81,101
8490	Union	444,792	0	500	500	0	1,000	0	0	0	0	445,792	39,831	39,831
8165	Wards Memorial	68,122	0	0	0	0	0	0	0	0	0	68,122	13,448	13,448
8465	Waters Memorial	78,497	13,120	14,405	0	85	27,610	0	0	0	0	106,107	10,800	10,800
8510	Westphalia	1,168,878	34,902	5,825	0	0	40,727	0	0	0	0	1,209,605	67,088	67,088
8325	Zion	253,592	41,013	0	0	0	41,013	0	0	0	0	294,605	30,520	30,520
8535	Zion Wesley	82,004	0	0	0	0	0	0	0	0	0	82,004	10,309	10,309
	W/E Total	17,397,390	454,594	336,116	165,732	238,750	1,195,194	4,735	0	50,397	55,132	18,647,716	1,968,842	1,823,870
	BWC Total	127,717,850	5,628,647	6,514,768	########	1,900,655	########	254,379	211,017	298,336	763,732	144,872,736	15,324,261	13,987,573

XII. INDEX

Other Helpful Contacts

WESTERN REGIONAL OFFICE..410-309-34808
  703 W. Patrick St, Frederick, MD 21701
MANIDOKAN OUTDOOR MINISTRY CENTER..301-834-7244, manidokan@gmail.com
WEST RIVER RETREAT & CAMP CENTER...800-922-6795
  5100 Chalk Point Rd,West River, MD 20778
  Chris Schlieckert, Director, director@westrivercenter.org
  Amy Marshall, Administrative Assistant, admin@bwccampsandretreats.com
CAMP HARMISON...410-867-0991
  9 miles East along Rt. 9, Berkeley Springs, WV; Keith Puffenberger, Caretaker
LOVELY LANE MUSEUM... 410-889-4458
  2200 St. Paul St, Baltimore, MD 21218; Robert Shindle, Director, rshindle@bwcumc.org
MID-ATLANTIC UNITED METHODIST FOUNDATION
  Headquarters: PO. Box 820 Valley Forge, PA 19482, 800-828-9093 x211
  BWC Office: Frank Robert, 11711 East Market Place, Fulton, MD 20759, 410-309-3475
COKESBURY BOOK STORE......................877-758-7134, www.cokesbury.com
INFOSERV: General Church Information.....................................infoserv@umcom.org

General Church Agencies

GENERAL BOARD OF CHURCH AND SOCIETY.......................................202-488-5600
  100 Maryland Ave., NE, Washington, DC 20002-5664
GENERAL BOARD OF DISCIPLESHIP...877-899-2780
  P.O. Box 340003, Nashville, TN 37203-0003........................E-mail: gbod@gbod.org
GENERAL BOARD OF GLOBAL MINISTRIES...800-862-4246
  458 Ponce De Leon Ave NE, Atlanta, GA 30308.............E-mail: info@umcmission.org
GENERAL BOARD OF HIGHER EDUCATION AND MINISTRY................615-340-7400
  P.O. Box 340007, Nashville, TN 37203-0007
WESPATH/GENERAL BOARD OF PENSION & HEALTH BENEFITS.......800-851-2201
  1901 Chestnut Ave, Glenview, IL 60025-1604....................................Fax: 847-475-5061
GENERAL COMMISSION ON ARCHIVES AND HISTORY........................973-408-3189
  36 Madison Ave., P.O. Box 127, Madison, NJ 07940..........E-mail: research@gcah.org
GC CHRISTIAN UNITY & INTER-RELIGIOUS CONCERNS .212-749-3553
  Room 1300, 475 Riverside Dr., New York, NY 10115......E-mail: info@gccuic-umc.org
GENERAL COMMISSION ON RELIGION AND RACE.............................202-547-2271
  100 Maryland Ave., NE, Suite 400, Washington, DC 20002-5680
GENERAL COMMISSION ON THE STATUS AND ROLE OF WOMEN......800-523-8390
  1200 Davis St., Evanston, IL, 60201
GENERAL COUNCIL ON FINANCE AND ADMINISTRATION................ 866-367-4232
  P.O. Box 340029, Nashville, TN 37203-0029....................................Fax: 615-329-3394
UNITED METHODIST COMMUNICATIONS
  810 12th Ave., P.O. Box 320, Nashville, TN 37202-0320..........................615-742-5400
....E-mail: umcom@umcom.org

Other Related Institutions

ASBURY VILLAGE...301-216-4103
  201 Russell Avenue, Gaithersburg, MD 20877-2801
ASBURY-SOLOMONS...410-394-3000
  1100 Asbury Circle, Solomons, MD 20688
BOARD OF CHILD CARE...410-922-2100
  3300 Gaither Road, Baltimore, MD 21244
N.M. CARROLL HOME (MANOR)...410-669-4270
  701 N. Arlington Avenue, Baltimore, MD 21217

CORRECTION FORM, 2019 JOURNAL

Much of the information in this Journal, including addresses and phone numbers are pulled from Arena, the online database of the Baltimore-Washington Conference. If you find your personal or church contact information is incorrect, please follow the instructions below. Each person is responsible for keeping their own information up to date.

Logging into Arena:
1. In your browser, go to www.bwcumc.org and click on "Sign In" at the top of the page.
2. If you know your username and password, type them in the fields provided.
3. If you've forgotten your username or password, click on "Forgot your Password" in the body of that page. Follow the instructions to request your username and password. This information will be sent to the e-mail address linked to your record.
4. We highly recommend you change your user name and password to something that's easy to remember. You may do so by clicking on "My Contact Info" on the left navigation and following the instructions below.

Changing your contact information:
1. Follow the instructions above to log in.
2. Once logged in, on the left navigation, click on "My Contact Info."
3. Click the "Edit" box at the top of the page.
4. Type changed information into the appropriate fields.

Errors in appointment history or church relationships may be reported to Office of Communications AND your Regional Administrator by June 30, 2020.
Office of Communications
11711 East Market Place
Fulton, MD 20759

PLEASE PRINT OR TYPE:
Name of Submitter_____

Correction/Change of Status
Old:_____
New:_____

Correction Notation
Page_____of the 2019 Journal, line_____which reads:
_____
_____

Should be corrected to read:
_____
_____
_____
_____

If you have further questions, please contact your Regional Administrator, listed on the inside back cover of this book.